Last Words

of

Notable People

Last Words

of

Notable People

Final Words of More Than 3500
Noteworthy People Throughout History

Compiled by
William B. Brahms

Reference Desk Press, Inc.
Haddonfield, New Jersey

www.referencedeskpress.com

To
Matthew and Giovanna

Copyright © 2010 by William Bernard Brahms

Publisher Cataloging-in-Publication Data
Brahms, William B. (1966 -)
    Last Words of Notable People – Final Words of More Than
    3500 Noteworthy People Throughout History/ by William B. Brahms.
        p. cm.
    Includes bibliographic references and index
    ISBN 978-09765325-2-1
    1. Last Words.   2. Death--Quotations, maxims, etc.
    3. Quotations Dictionaries.   I. Title
    PN6328.L3 B7 2010
    808.8—dc22   2010906738

Manufactured in the United States of America
Printed on acid-free, recycled paper
(90% recycled, 30% post consumer waste, 100% processed chlorine-free)
Reference Desk Press, Inc. supports the Green Press Initiative (GPI).

SAN: 256-4300

Reference Desk Press, Inc.
305 Briarwood Avenue
Haddonfield, NJ 08033-2907

info@referencedeskpress.com

www.referencedeskpress.com

Introduction

I became interested in Last Words while researching another book: *Notable Last Facts* (2005). The quotes appeared with such frequency that I began to collect them. When I started to track down information on them, I found that although many books have been written about Last Words, very few authors told readers where the quotes came from. And invariably, among the few books that provided Sources, the quotes were in one place while the Sources were in another. Moreover, quotes presented as Last Words often turned out not to be final utterances, although they may have dealt with death and dying.

Sometimes Last Words compilers constructed direct quotations from indirect ones. Also, some books gave such sparse information about the speaker or the Source that it was difficult to tell who made the quote or where it came from. A few books grouped the names by categories; others listed them chronologically. If the book had no index or table of contents, finding a name was often a challenge.

In *Last Words of Notable People*, the emphasis is not on how famous, witty, amusing, tragic or profound the quote is but where it originated, how accurate it is, and what made the person notable who said it. Each entry includes a brief biography with enough information to identify the individual and his or her claim to notability. And it tells the reader where the quote came from. All entries are listed alphabetically and are indexed.

You will notice the term "doubtful" next to some Last Words entries. This label indicates the quotation is probably bogus as the person's final words. See, for example, Rabelais. Books of quotations, apothegms, maxims and anecdotes offer several versions of his Last Words. But if you check his listing in this book, you will find historians do not even know when the great man died let alone what he said! Chaplin, Defoe and Montaigne all spoke the words attributed to them as Last Words, but they said them in different contexts. In each instance, the quote appeared in his works long before he died but somehow over the years evolved into his final utterance. Some of these bogus quotes have been circulating for centuries.

Today, thanks to powerful Internet search engines, it is possible to track down information in a way that earlier writers could never have imagined. But there is a downside to Internet material: Some websites apparently have taken dubious quotes from other websites. The result is a proliferation of suspect Last Words.

Many of the names in *Last Words of Notable People* have two, three, or more Last Words attributed to the same person. When the quotes are different, they are prefixed with the tag "Different Last Words" and are enumerated. If they are similar to other quotes presented for the same individual, they are identified as "Variations." I do not mean to imply that these are the *only* Last Words for that individual. It just means that among the materials examined, these are the dissimilarities I found.

Tracking down Last Words can be an exercise in frustration for the purist or the researcher who wants to know the exact words the speaker uttered or wrote before dying. It is difficult, or even impossible, to check the authenticity of someone's Last Words after the person has died. The passage of time can make verification difficult. Sources can be corrupted. Written notes can be changed, erroneously transcribed, or reported incorrectly. Even videotapes and photographs can be tampered with. Many Last Words were initially oral tradition or hearsay and are often dependent on the vested interests of a single witness or other person close to the speaker.

The last recorded words a person said might be misconstrued. Sometimes the quote was made while the person was dying, but it was not necessarily his or her final words. Family members may have distorted the Last Words because they could not understand the speaker. Or perhaps they felt the speaker's Last Words were not dignified enough to become part of history, especially if the person was a prominent clergyman, politician or other public figure.

Sometimes the people who were dying could not speak for themselves. Perhaps their speech was impaired by a stroke or their teeth were gone, or their voice was weak from prolonged ill health. Their Last Words may be interpreted for them by family or friends. See, for example, the Last Words of Princess Victoria Ka'iulani of Hawaii. She uttered one word, but bystanders were not sure whether she said "Mama," "Papa" or "Koa" (nickname for her cousin). We may never know for sure whether English statesman William Pitt the Younger said "How I *love* my country" or "How I *leave* my country" or neither and instead expressed a desire for "Bellamy's veal pies."

If you have ever had experience working with documents translated from one language to another, you know meanings can get lost in translation. French Revolutionary casualty Madame Roland's Last Words have been translated from French to English as: "O Liberty how you are mocked" and "Oh Liberty, what crimes are committed in thy name." Subtle transformations in translation changed composer Franz Joseph Haydn's "Children, be comforted. I am well" to the more prosaic "Cheer up children, I'm all right."

About the "Notable People" in this book: Some professions are better represented than others. Politicians, military people and clergy are high on the list. Sports figures, writers, artists, martyrs and musicians are also well documented. So are criminals. Among these groups, Last Words are often carefully recorded. Sometimes media people are eager to hang onto the Last Words of a celebrity for the sake of newsworthiness.

The brief biographies that accompany each entry aim to tie the Last Words uniquely to that person. The state of the individual's health or the things he or she held important acquire special importance when put together with his or her final pronouncements. Russian-born novelist Vladimir Nabokov's Last Words were about butterflies. They take on more significance if the reader knows that the author of *Lolita* was also a world-class lepidopterist and mentioned butterflies in his writings. Many Notable People experienced physical pain or mental torment. Knowing a person suffered from an illness or had a disability can also give insights into his or her Last Words. Mendelssohn's "Weary, very weary" makes sense when you know death came at the end of a series of strokes that sapped the energy from the 38-year-old composer.

Many books, compilations and other materials were consulted in putting together this collection of sourced Last Words. *Last Words of Notable People* is unique among them in that it offers all the following features:

- All the information is in an easy-to-find dictionary format.
- Brief biographies for more than 3,500 names identify the individuals and their claims to fame.
- Every listing is labeled with "Last Words" and "Source."
- If an individual has two or more Last Words quotations that are dissimilar, they are labeled "Different Last Words." If the quotes are similar they are labeled "Variations."
- Last Words that appear to be bogus are identified as "Doubtful." An explanation is given as well as the Source for that information.
- Information about each Source is provided; for example, author, date and city of publication, and relationship or connection of the notable person to the author of the Source, if known.
- Full titles of books, magazines and other periodicals used as Sources are given to facilitate finding them in the library or on the Internet.
- An annotated bibliography and name index are included.

The goal of *Last Words of Notable People* is to aid the librarian, researcher, historian, author, news writer or merely the curious. Regardless of what drew you to it, you will find this truly original core reference is fascinating, interesting, and informative.

William B. Brahms

Abbey, Edward Paul

(1927-1989) American writer. Advocate of protecting the environment. Known as Thoreau of the American West. Notable works: *The Brave Cowboy; Desert Solitaire; The Monkey Wrench Gang; A Voice Crying in the Wilderness*. Died at age 62 at his home near Tucson, Arizona.
Last Words: "I did what I could."
Source: *Epitaph for a Desert Anarchist: The Life and Legacy of Edward Abbey* by James Bishop (New York, 1994).

Abbot, Robert

(1560-1617) English prelate, educator, writer, theologian. Anglican Bishop of Salisbury. Older brother of George Abbot, Master of Balliol College, Oxford. Archbishop of Canterbury. Notable work: *De Antichristo*. Died at age 57.
Last Words: "Come Lord Jesu, come quickly, finish in me the work that Thou has begun; into Thy hands, O Lord, I commend my spirit, for Thou has redeemed me. O God of truth, save me Thy servant, who hopes and confides in Thee alone; let Thy mercy, O Lord, be shewn unto me; in Thee have I trusted, O Lord, let me not be confounded for ever."
Source: *Life of Abbot* by Arthur Onslow (Guildford, England, 1777).

Abbott, Burton W.

(1928-1957) American murderer. Found guilty of killing a teenage girl. He claimed he was framed. Executed at age 29 in the gas chamber at San Quentin Prison, California.
Different Last Words:
(1) "I can't admit it, Doc. Think of what that would do to my mother. She could not take it." Spoken to Dr. David Schmidt at San Quentin. His Last Words were revealed as his "confession" after his execution.
Source: *Bloodletters and Badmen: A Narrative Encyclopedia of American Criminals from the Pilgrims to the Present* by Jay Robert Nash (New York, 1995).
(2) "Thank you." Spoken to Warden Harley O. Teets after the warden shook his hand and said, "God bless you."
Source: "California: Race in the Death House" (*Time* magazine, March 25, 1957).

Abbott, Charles, 1st Baron Tenterden

(1762-1832) British jurist, lawyer, educator. Fellow at Oxford. Lord chief justice. Knighted in 1818. Raised to peerage in 1827. Died at age 70. Buried at Foundling Hospital, London, of which he was governor.
Last Words: "Gentlemen, you are all dismissed." He died with these words on his lips as he addressed an imaginary jury.
Source: *Memoir of Thomas, First Lord Denman, Formerly Lord Chief Justice of England* by Sir Joseph Arnould (London, 1873).
Variation: "Gentlemen of the jury, you may retire."
Source: *The Lives of Twelve Eminent Judges of the Last and of the Present Century* by William C. Townsend (London, 1846).
Variation: "Gentlemen of the jury, you will now consider of your verdict."
Source: *The Last Words (Real and Traditional) of Distinguished Men and Women Collected from Various Sources* by Frederic Rowland Marvin (New York, 1901).

Abbott, Emma

(1850-1891) American singer. Opera soprano. Notable performances: *Romeo and Juliette; La Traviata; H.M.S. Pinafore; Martha; La Sonnambula*. Organized Abbott English Opera Company and toured extensively in U.S. Became ill on tour. Died at age 40 in Salt Lake City, Utah.
Last Words: "I am not afraid to die."
Source: *The Life and Professional Career of Emma Abbott* by Sadie E. Martin (Minneapolis, MN, 1891).

Abd-Ar-Rahman III, Umayyad ruler of Cordoba

(891-961) Muslim Emir and caliph of Cordoba, Spain. Eighth Umayyad ruler of Cordoba. Surnamed An-Nâsir-Lideen Illah or Lidinillah, meaning the defender of the religion of God. Brought Islamic Spain under control of a central government. Made Cordoba a key center of learning in Europe. Died in Cordoba. The following message was found in a closet in his room after he died:
Last Words (written, doubtful): "I have now reigned above fifty years in victory or peace; beloved by my subjects, dreaded by my enemies, and respected by my allies. Riches, honor, power and pleasure have waited on my call, nor does any earthy blessing appear to have been wanting for my felicity. In this

situation I have diligently numbered the days of pure and genuine happiness which have fallen to my lot and they amount to FOURTEEN—O man! Place not thy confidence in this present world!"

Source: *The History of the Decline and Fall of the Roman Empire,* Vol. V, by Edward Gibbon (London, 1788).

Writer and historian Frederic Rowland Marvin noted that "Though these sad words correctly express the spirit of the man who is reported to have spoken them, they are purely traditional."

Source: *The Last Words (Real and Traditional) of Distinguished Men and Women Collected From Various Sources* by Frederic Rowland Marvin (New York, 1901).

Abdullah ibn al-Zubair

(624-692) Arab leader. Grandson of Abu Bakr, father-in-law of prophet Muhammad. Son of Zubair, the brother-in-law of Muhammad's wife Aisha. Proclaimed himself caliph of Islam. Killed at Mecca when Umayyad caliph Abd al-Malik attacked his forces.

Last Words: "No one need ask where Abdullah is; whoever wants him will meet him in the first ranks. O my Lord, the troops of Syria are assailing me in great numbers, and have already torn aside a part of the veils that cover thy sanctuary. O my Lord, I am weak and oppressed on all sides. Send thy phalanxes to my aid."

Source: "Mèmoire historique sur la vie d'Abd Allah ben Zobair" by Véase Etienne-Marc Quatrèmere in *Nouveau Journal Asiatique* (Paris, 1832).

Abdur Rahman Khan, Emir of Afghanistan

(1844?-1901) Afghan ruler. Grandson of Dost Mahommed Khan who established the Barakzai dynasty in Afghanistan. Emir of Afghanistan 1880 to 1901. Strong leader who brought order back to the Afghan government after the Second Anglo-Afghan War. Regarded by western scholars as the founder of modern Afghanistan.

Last Words: "My last words to you, my son and successor, are: Never trust the Russians." Spoken to his son Habibullah, who succeeded him when he died in 1901.

Source: *Afghan's Two-Party Communism: Parcham and Khalq* by Anthony Arnold (Stanford, CA, 1983).

Abelard, Peter

(1079-1142) French philosopher, educator, theologian, writer. Major figure in Scholasticism. Notable work: *Sic et Non* (tr. *Yes and No.*) Had ill-fated love affair with Heloise. Father of her son Astrolabe. Their story is known through their letters. Abelard died at age 63 in the priory of St. Marcel at Chalon-sur-Saône. His body was moved to the Paraclete at the request of Heloise. Later, her body was placed in his coffin. In 1817, the bodies were moved to Paris.

Last Words: "Je ne sais." (tr. "I don't know.")

Sources: *The Art of Dying: An Anthology,* ed. by Francis Birrell and F. L. Lucas (London, 1930); *Last Words: Variations on a Theme in Cultural History* by Karl S. Guthke (Princeton, NJ, 1992).

Abercromby, Sir Ralph

(1734-1801) Scottish-born military officer. Lieutenant general in British Army during Napoleonic Wars. Died at age 66 of injuries at the Battle of Aboukir Bay.

Last Words: "Only a soldier's blanket! Make haste and return it to him at once." His response while being carried to the beach. He asked what had been placed under his head. His aide-de-camp said: "Only a soldier's blanket."

Source: *Battles of the Nineteenth Century* by Archibald Forbes, Arthur Griffiths and George Alfred Henty (London, 1896-1897).

Abernethy, John

(1764-1831) British surgeon. On staff of St. Bartholomew Hospital 1787 to 1827. Specialized in aneurysm surgery. Believed most local diseases were caused by digestive disorders. Wrote many medical books. Abernethy biscuit (cookie) created by and named for him. He enjoyed celebrity for his eccentricities and blunt manner. Mentioned in Edgar Allan Poe's story, *The Purloined Letter*. Died at age 67 at his home in Enfield, England.

Last Words: "Is there anybody in the room?"

Source: *Memoirs of John Abernethy* by George Macilwain (New York, 1853).

Abimelech, King of Shechem

(fl. 12th century B.C.) Biblical figure. Son of Gideon. Because he was of lowly birth (his mother was a concubine), he had to use force to gain power to rule. Members of his mother's family helped him kill all of his 71 half-brothers except one. He made himself king of Shechem. Ruled for three years after the death of his father. Injured by a millstone thrown by a woman from a wall above him. Believing he would die from a wound inflicted by a woman, he asked his armor bearer to kill him. He died at Thebes.

Last Words: "Evagina gladium tuum, et percute me, ne forte dicatur quod a femina interfectus sim."
Source: Judges 9:54 (Latin Vulgate Bible).
Variation: "Draw thy sword, and slay me, that men say not of me, a women slew him."
Sources: Judges 9:54 (King James Version; 21st Century King James Version).
Variation: "Draw your sword and kill me, so that it will not be said of me, 'A woman slew him.'"
Source: Judges 9:54 (New American Standard Version).
Variation: "Draw your sword and kill me, lest they say of me, 'A woman killed him.'"
Source: Judges 9:54 (English Standard Version).
Variation: "Draw your sword and kill me, so that they can't say, 'A woman killed him.'"
Source: Judges 9:54 (New International Version).
Variation: "Draw your sword and kill me, lest men say of me, 'A woman killed him.'"
Sources: Judges 9:54 (New King James Version; Darby Translation).
Variation: "Draw thy sword, and kill me: lest it should be said that I was slain by a woman."
Source: Judges 9:54 (Douay-Rheims Translation).
Variation: "Draw thy sword, and thou hast put me to death, lest they say of me, 'A woman slew him.'"
Source: Judges 9:54 (Young's Literal Translation).

Accoramboni, Vittoria

(1557-1585) Italian noblewoman. Famed for her beauty. Had her first husband murdered so she could marry Paolo Giordano Orsini, the Duke of Bracciano. After the duke died, one of his relatives had her murdered. Died at age 28 in Salo, Italy. She was later portrayed in John Webster's tragic play *White Devil, or Vittoria Corombona* and the novel *Vittoria Accoramboni* by Ludwig Tieck.
Last Words: "Jesus! I pardon you." Uttered as she knelt before a crucifix.
Source: *Vittoria Accoramboni* by Domenico Gnoli (Florence, Italy, 1870).

Ace, Johnny

(1929-1954) American musician. Birth name John Marshall Alexander Jr. Had eight R&B Top Ten records, including three No. 1 hits. Killed at age 25 while playing Russian roulette at City Auditorium in Houston, Texas, where he was performing.
Last Words: "I'll show you that it won't shoot." His cause of death was ruled "playing Russian roulette—self inflicted."
Source: "Death and the Rhythm-and-Bluesman: The Life and Recordings of Johnny Ace" by James M. Salem (*American Music*, Fall 1993).

Achard de Saint-Victor

(1100?-1172) French prelate. Abbot of St.-Victor (Paris). Bishop of Avranches. Friend of Thomas à Becket.
Last Words: "Tis enough, my brothers: till now I have struggled against my illness; I have forced myself to conceal from you the pain tearing at my bowels; now that the malady has reached my vital parts I can no longer dissimulate. What I enjoin above all, the one thing needful, is to take care lest the author of evil sow hatred among you and break the peace of the brethren. You are not unaware that hatred cleaves man from God and closes heaven to him. No suffering can expiate hate; it is not redeemed by martyrdom; it is a stain that all the blood in us would fail to wash. So I go to join my fathers. Place my body in the midst of the sepulchres of our brethren."
Source: *Vie de Saint Achard, abbè de Jumièges: extraite des Annales de Hainaut* by Jacques de Guyse (Paris, 1830).

Achterberg, Gerrit

(1905-1962) Dutch poet. Much of his earlier work centered on a desire to be united with a beloved one in death. He spent six years in a psychiatric hospital after he shot and killed a woman. Notable work: *Ballade van de gasfitter* (sonnets). Died at age 56 in Oud-Luesden, The Netherlands.
Last Words: "Ja, maar niet te veel." (tr. "Yes, but not too many.") His response to his companion's question as to whether she

should bake some potatoes. They had just parked their car. He answered then suffered a fatal heart attack.

Source: *Het refrein is hein: Leven en sterven in een verpleeghuis* by B. Keizer (Amsterdam, The Netherlands, 2003).

Adam, Alexander

(1741-1809) Scottish educator, writer. Sir Walter Scott's schoolmaster. Rector of Edinburgh High School from 1769 to 1809. Notable work: *Roman Antiquities*. Died at age 68 after a brief illness during which he occasionally thought he was still teaching in a classroom.

Last Words: "That Horace was very well said; you did not do it so well. But it grows dark, very dark—the boys may dismiss."

Source: *Memoirs of the Life of Sir Walter Scott* by John G. Lockhart (Boston, 1901).

Variation: "It grows dark; boys you may go."

Source: "Dying Words of Noted Persons" in *Miscellaneous Notes and Queries with Answers in All Departments of Literature*, Vol. II (Manchester, NH, 1885).

Adams, Abigail Smith

(1744-1818) American First Lady. Wife of John Adams, 2nd President of the U.S. Mother of U.S. President John Quincy Adams. Known for her witty and insightful letters. Two volumes were first published in 1840 by her grandson Charles Francis Adams. Died at age 73 of typhoid fever at her home in Braintree, Massachusetts.

Different Last Words:

(1) "Do not grieve, my friend, my dearest friend. I am ready to go. And John, it will not be long." Spoken to her husband.

Source: *Abigail Adams* by Dorothie Bobbé (New York, 1966).

(2) "If I cannot be useful, I do not wish to live."

Source: The *Adams Women: Abigail and Louisa, Their Sisters and Daughters* by Paul C. Nagel (New York, 1987).

Adams, Alice/Alicia

(1756-1843) American matron. Full name Alicia Adams Ripley Lawrence. One-time sweetheart of Nathan Hale. Also sought after by Nathan's brother Ethan.

Last Words: "Where is Nathan?"

Source: *Nathan Hale, 1776. Biography and Memorials* by Henry Phelps Johnston (New York, 1901).

Adams, Charles Francis, Sr.

(1807-1886) American lawyer, politician, writer, diplomat. Son of U.S. President John Quincy Adams, grandson of U.S. President John Adams. Member U.S. House of Representatives from Massachusetts. U.S. minister to Great Britain in U.S. Civil War. Built first Presidential library in U.S. for his father. Died at age 79 in Boston.

Last Words (doubtful): "I am now perfectly willing to go myself. My mission is ended and I may rest."

Source: *A Conspectus of American Biography: Being an Analytical Summary of American History and Biography, Containing also the Complete Indexes of the National Cyclopedia of American Biography* by George Derby (New York, 1906).

Adams spoke these words in August 1877, when he saw the printed copy of his father's *Memoirs* that he had compiled. He died nine years later.

Source: *Charles Francis Adams* by Charles Francis Adams (Boston, 1900).

Adams, Edwin

(1834-1877) American actor. Began his theatrical career in 1853 in Boston in *The Hunchback*. By the 1860s, he was one of America's major actors. Joined Edwin Booth's acting company in 1869. Notable performances: *Hamlet; Romeo and Juliet; Enoch Arden*. Made his final appearance in San Francisco in 1876. Died at age 43 of tuberculosis in Philadelphia.

Last Words: "Good-bye Mary, good-bye forever." Spoken to his wife.

Source: *Dying Testimonies of Saved and Unsaved: Gathered from Authentic Sources* by Solomon Benjamin Shaw (Chicago, 1898).

Adams, Frederick W.

(1786-1858) American physician, theologian, writer. Notable work: *Theological Criticism: or, Hints of the Philosophy of Man and Nature*. Died at age 72 in Montpelier, Vermont.

Last Words: "If there is a Christian's God, I am not afraid to trust myself in his hands."

Source: "Medical Men of Montpelier" by Sumner Putnam in *The History of the Town of Montpelier, Including that of the Town of East Montpelier, for the First One Hundred and Two Years* (Montpelier, VT, 1882).

Adams, Henry Brooks

(1838-1918) American historian, educator.

Grandson of President John Quincy Adams. Son of Charles Francis Adams. Assistant professor of history at Harvard. Notable works: *History of the United States during the Administrations of Jefferson and Madison* (9 vol.); *The Education of Henry Adams; Mont-Saint-Michel and Chartres*. Died at age 80 in Washington, D.C.

Different Last Words:

(1) "Dear child, keep me alive." Spoken to his secretary companion. He died the following day.

Source: *Henry Adams and His Friends* by Harold Dean Cater (Boston, 1947).

(2) "Goodnight, my dear." Spoken to his housekeeper as she left his room. He died in his sleep.

Source: *Henry Adams, Selected Letters* by Henry Adams and Ernest Samuels (Cambridge, MA, 1992).

Adams, John

(1735-1826) 2nd President of the U.S. American lawyer, statesman, diplomat, politician, writer. Father of John Quincy Adams. Delegate to First Continental Congress. Helped frame Declaration of Independence. Ambassador to England. Vice President of the U.S. under Washington, before becoming President. Retired after he ran unsuccessfully for re-election in 1800 and lost to Thomas Jefferson. Wrote books on freedom, government and constitutions. Died at age 90 in Quincy, Massachusetts, on July 4, 1826, on the 50th anniversary of the Declaration of Independence and on the same day Thomas Jefferson died.

Different Last Words:

(1) (doubtful): "Jefferson survives."

Source: Various Last Words compilations and Internet websites.

(2) "Jefferson..." or "Thomas Jefferson..." Only Jefferson's name was clearly understood among the final words Adams spoke. His son John Quincy Adams noted in his diary that his father's Last Words were "indistinctly uttered," however, the younger Adams was traveling from Washington to Massachusetts when his father died and had to rely on others for that information. The only family member present at John Adams's death was Louisa Smith, the adopted daughter of Abigail Adams. She told Eliza Quincy, the wife of Boston's mayor, that the final words John Adams distinctly spoke were Jefferson's name. The rest of his words were so inarticulate she could not catch their meaning. The word "survives" apparently was supplied by later writers and historians, many of whom pointed out the irony of the two American Presidents dying on the same day.

Sources: *Mortal Remains: Death in Early America,* ed. by Nancy Isenberg and Andrew Burstein (Philadelphia, 2003); "Jefferson Still Survives" by Andrew Burstein (George Mason University's History News Network, March 2002).

(3) (doubtful): "Independence forever!"

Source: "Brief Biographies of the Signers" by the Editors (*The Ladies' Repository,* Vol. 24, January 1864).

Adams, John

(1772-1863) American educator. Principal of Phillips Academy at Andover, Massachusetts. Principal of school for girls in Jacksonville, Illinois. Organized many Sunday Schools for American Sunday School Union while living there. Died at age 90 in Jacksonville during the U.S. Civil War.

Last Words (written): "This day I enter my ninety-first year. The year just closed has been one of trial and deep solicitude. My country! Oh my country! I do not expect to see peace restored during the short remainder of my stay, but I am earnestly looking forward to that everlasting rest which remaineth to the people of God. God reigns. He will accomplish His purposes. Amen and Amen." Last entry in his journal.

Source: *The Story of John Adams, a New England Schoolmaster* by Mary Elizabeth Brown and Helen Gilman Brown (New York, 1900).

Adams, John Quincy

(1767-1848) 6th President of the U.S. American politician, diplomat, lawyer, diarist. Son of John Adams. Present at signing of Treaty of Paris in 1783 ending American Revolution. Sent to Europe in 1814 to sign Treaty of Ghent ending War of 1812. Minster to England 1817 to 1823. Member U.S. House of Representatives from Massachusetts. Kept a detailed diary for 60 years. Had a stroke as he was about to make a speech in Congress in February 1848. Collapsed on the floor of the House in Washington, D.C. Remained semiconscious until he died two days later at age 80.

Last Words: "This is the last of earth! I am content."

Sources: *The Truly Great: A Discourse Appropriate to the Life and Character of John Quincy Adams* by Edwin Hubbell Chapin (Boston, 1848); "Illness and Death of John Quincy Adams" (*Little's Living Age*, No. 201, March 18, 1848), citing an account published in *The New York Courier and Enquirer*, February 25, 1848; *Life and Public Services of John Quincy Adams* by William H. Stewart (Auburn, NY, 1849). This source quotes Adams's "Last Words" on the title page.

Adams, Maude

(1872-1953) American actress. Birth name Maude Ewing Adams Kiskadden. Used mother's maiden name Adams on stage. Notable performances: *Peter Pan; What Every Woman Knows; The Little Minister; The Merchant of Venice.* Headed drama department at Stephens College in Missouri. Died at age 80 at her summer home in Tannersville, New York.

Last Words: "Life is still full of joy. Thumbs up for joy and adventure." Spoken a few hours before she died.

Source: "Maude Adams Funeral Set For Monday" (*Oakland* [California] *Tribune*, July 18, 1953).

Adams, Samuel

(1722-1803) American politician, writer. Member Committees of Correspondence. Delegate to Continental Congresses. Signed Declaration of Independence. Lieutenant governor and governor of Massachusetts. Died at age 81 in Boston.

Last Words (doubtful): "From the rising to the setting of the sun, may his kingdom come."

Source: *A Conspectus of American Biography: Being an Analytical Summary of American History and Biography, Containing also the Complete Indexes of the National Cyclopedia of American Biography* by George Derby (New York, 1906).

Adams did speak these words, but they were not the last ones he said. They were part of a speech he delivered to the Continental Congress in Philadelphia on August 11, 1776. Julia Ward Howe reprinted the speech in her book and entitled it "American Independence."

Sources: *Masterpieces of American Eloquence: Christian Herald Selection* by Julia Ward Howe (New York, 1900); *Builders of the Republic: Some Great Americans Who Have Aided in the Making of the Nation* by Margherita Arlina Hamm (New York, 1902).

Adams, Sylvester Louis

(1955-1995) American murderer. Convicted and executed at age 39 for kidnapping and strangling a teenage boy. First person executed by lethal injection in South Carolina. He had a low IQ and was mentally impaired. Neither fact was mentioned by his attorney. Later, a juror said she would not have voted for the death penalty if she has known Adams was mentally disabled. Her dissenting vote would have spared his life. One of the most famous cases of the nearly 50 mentally disabled people executed since 1985.

Last Words: "I'm the happiest man in the world! I'm not afraid to die! I'm not crazy! I'm going to be reaching that white house tonight!"

Source: "South Carolina Executes Man for Killing Neighbor" (*New York Times,* August 19, 1995).

Adams, Walter Frederick

(1871-1952) British clergyman. Roman Catholic priest. Member of Cowley Fathers Mission House. Spiritual adviser of C.S. Lewis for many years. Adams died at an altar in Oxford after a sharp attack of pain.

Last Words: "I come, Lord Jesus."

Source: *The Collected Letters of C. S. Lewis, Volume 1: Family Letters, 1905-1931* by Clive Staples Lewis (San Francisco, CA, 2004).

Adcock, Michael Clinton

(1969-1992) American soldier. U.S. Army reservist called up to serve in Operation Desert Storm. Two days after arriving in the Middle East, his unit was chemically attacked near Al-Jubayl. He was sent back to the United States. Died at age 22 in Gainesville, Florida, from metastatic lymphoma and multiple cancers. His is considered the first death widely attributed to "Gulf War Syndrome." Adcock argued that his cancer was the result of exposure in the Gulf. His mother's subsequent testimony in Congressional hearings widely influenced the media.

Last Words: "Mama, fight for me. Don't let this happen to another soldier." She repeated in the Congressional hearings the final words her son spoke to her.

Source: "A Normative Construction of Gulf War Syndrome" by David B. Mahoney (*Perspectives in Biology and Medicine,* 44.4, Autumn 2001).

Addams, Jane

(1860-1935) American social reformer, peace activist. Founded Hull House in Chicago slums. Notable work: *Twenty Years at Hull House* (autobiography). Shared Nobel Peace Prize with Nicholas Murray Butler in 1931. Died at age 74 in Chicago.

Last Words: "Always, always. Water for me." Her response to her physician who asked if she would like a little water.

Source: *Jane Addams: A Biography* by James H. Linn (New York, 1935). The author was the son of her older sister Mary and knew his aunt for nearly 60 years.

Addison, Joseph

(1672-1719) English writer, poet, politician, essayist. Contributed to *The Tatler*. Co-founded *The Spectator*. Notable work: *Cato* (tragedy). Friend of Swift. Secretary to Earl of Sunderland as Lord Lieutenant of Ireland. Married Charlotte, Countess of Warwick. Suffered from asthma and later from dropsy. Had to resign for failing health. Died at age 47 in London.

Last Words: "See in what peace a Christian can die."

Source: *Conjectures on Original Composition: In a Letter to the Author of Sir Charles Grandison* by Edward Young and Samuel Richardson (London, 1759).

Variation: "I have sent for you to see how a Christian can die." Spoken to his stepson, the Earl of Warwick.

Source: *A New Biographical Dictionary: Containing a Brief Account of the Lives and Writings of the Most Eminent Persons and Remarkable Characters in Every Age and Nation* by Stephen Jones (London, 1805).

Adenauer, Konrad Hermann Josef

(1876-1967) German statesman, lawyer, politician. Known as Der Alte. First chancellor of West Germany. Chairman of Christian Democratic Union. *Time* magazine's Man of the Year in 1953. Died at age 91 in Rhöndorf, Germany.

Different Last Words:

(1) "Do jitt et nix zo kriesche." (tr. "No reason to weep.") Spoken in Rhineland dialect.

Source: *Konrad Adenauer: A German Politician and Statesman in a Period of War* by Hans-Peter Schwarz (Providence, RI, 1997).

Variation: "Kein Grund zum Weinen." (tr. "No reason to cry.")

Source: *Lexikon der letzten Worte: letzte Botschaften berühmter Männer und Frauen von Konrad Adenauer bis Emiliano Zapata* by Werner Fuld (Munich, Germany, 2002).

(2) "Stick together. See as much as possible of one another."

Source: *Last Words: A Dictionary of Deathbed Quotations* by C. Bernard Ruffin (Jefferson, NC, 1995). Indicated the quote is "indirect." Cited as a source *Konrad Adenauer* by Terrence Prittie (Chicago, 1971), who wrote that the last coherent thought Adenauer put into words was that members of his family should stick together and see as much as possible of one another.

Adkins, Janet Elaine

(1935-1990) American assisted suicide advocate. Alzheimer's patient. Died at age 54 in Portland, Oregon. First suicide assisted by Dr. Jack Kevorkian, controversial pathologist, champion of the right to die by assisted suicide. He served seven years in prison for the death of another assisted suicide patient.

Last Words: "I love you." Spoken to her son Neil Adkins.

Source: "As Memory and Music Faded Oregon Woman Chose Death" by Timothy Egan (*New York Times*, June 7, 1990).

Adler, Alfred

(1870-1937) Austrian psychologist, psychiatrist. Originally a Freudian, he turned away from Freud's emphasis on sex to inferiority complex as cause of psychopathic problems. Founded individual psychology. Died at age 67 of heart attack in Aberdeen, Scotland, while presenting a series of lectures at the university.

Last Words: "Kurt." His son's name.

Source: *Alfred Adler, A Biography* by Phyllis Bottome (New York, 1939).

Agassiz, Jean Louis Rodolphe (Louis)

(1807-1873) Swiss-born American naturalist, zoologist, geologist, paleontologist, glaciologist, educator, lecturer. Authority on fossil forms and ice ages. Gave series of lectures in U.S. in 1846. Liked America so much he remained permanently. He became a U.S. citizen in 1861. Professor of natural history at Harvard. Founded Museum of Comparative Zoology at Harvard. Notable work: *Études sur les glaciers*. Died at age 66 in Cambridge, Massachusetts.

Last Words: "Le jeu est fini." (tr. "The play is finished.")

Source: *Life, Letters and Works of Louis Agassiz,* Vol. 2, by Jules Marcou (New York, 1896). Marcou was a geologist who worked with Agassiz.

Agatha, Saint

(231?-251) Sicilian noblewoman, holy woman, martyr. When she repelled the advances of a Roman prefect, she was sentenced to be burned at the stake but was saved by an earthquake. She died a martyr in prison.

Different Last Words:

(1) "Lord Jesus, Who hast created me and preserved me from my infancy, Who hast shielded my body from stain and my soul from the love of the world, Who hast enabled me to triumph over all my sufferings, receive my soul now, in Thy mercy!"

Source: *The Golden Legend or Lives of the Saints.* Compiled by Jacobus de Voragine, Archbishop of Genoa, 1275, 1st ed., 1470. English ed. by William Caxton, 1483, ed. by F.S. Ellis (Edinburgh, 1900).

Variation: "Lord, you who created me, and protected me from my infancy, and made me act with courage in my youth; you who took away from me love of the world, kept my body free from pollution; who made me overcome the hangman's tortures, the sword, fire, and chains; who gave me the virtue of patience in the midst of tortures; I beg you to receive my soul now: for it is time that you order me to leave this world here, and to come to your mercy."

Source: *Acta Sanctorum,* ed. by John Bollandus and Godfrey Henschenius, Vol.1 (Paris/Rome, 1863-1870).

(2) (doubtful): "The service of Jesus Christ is the highest nobility and the truest freedom." She spoke these words four days before she died.

Source: "St. Agatha, Virgin and Martyr, 5th Feb." (*Scottish Magazine and Churchman's Review,* Vol. I, 1849).

Agatho or Agathon, Saint

(577?-681) Sicilian-born Greek prelate, holy man. Believed to have been 100 years old when he was elevated to the papacy. Served as pope of the Roman Catholic Church from 678 to 681. During his pontificate, an ecumenical council put an end to the Monothelite heresy of previous papacies. At the council, a letter from him was read, explaining the traditional belief that Christ was of two wills, divine and human. This helped heal a schism. Agatho is venerated as a saint by both Roman Catholics and Eastern Orthodox. Saint-Agathon is the name of a commune in the Côtes-d'Armor department in Bretagne in northwestern France.

Last Words: "I presume it not, until I have come before Him; for otherwise are the judgments of God, and otherwise the judgments of man…Show me your charity, and speak not to me, for I am wholly occupied." His response when asked: "Art thou not confident that thy works have been according to God's will?"

Source: *The Golden Legend or Lives of the Saints.* Compiled by Jacobus de Voragine, Archbishop of Genoa, 1275, 1st ed., 1470. English ed. by William Caxton, 1483, ed. by F.S. Ellis (Edinburgh, 1900).

Agesilaus II, King of Sparta

(444-c. 360 B.C.) Spartan ruler. Son of Archidamus II and his second wife Eupolia. Brother of Cynisca (the only woman in ancient history to achieve an Olympic victory). Younger half-brother of Agis II. Died in Egypt while commanding Spartan mercenaries.

Last Words: "If I have done any honorable exploit, that is my monument; but if I have done none at all, your statues will signify nothing." Spoken when he was asked if he wanted a memorial erected in his honor.

Source: "Historical Illustrations" (*The Expositor and Current Anecdotes,* Vol. XII, No. 1, October 1909).

Agesistrata

(d. 241 B.C.) Spartan noblewoman. Mother of Agis IV, King of Sparta.

Last Words: "I pray that it may redound to the good of Sparta." Spoken as she was about to be hanged.

Source: "Agis" in *Lives of the Noble Grecians and Romans* by Plutarch, tr. by John Dryden (Chicago, 1952).

Agis IV, King of Sparta

(265?-241 B.C.) Spartan ruler. Proposed reforms that would bring about redistribution of land and property. Opposed by Leonidias II. Sentenced to die by the Spartan Ephori. Executed. His mother and grandmother were executed at the same time.

Last Words: "Weep not, friend, for me, who dies innocent, by the lawless act of wicked men. My condition is much better than theirs." Spoken when he was sentenced to death.

Source: "Agis" in *Lives of the Noble Grecians and Romans* by Plutarch, tr. by John Dryden (Chicago, 1952).

Agnew, Andrew, 7th Baron of Lochnaw

(1793-1849) Scottish nobleman, politician. Member of Parliament. Scottish Sabbatarian promoter. Proposed bill to force people to observe Sabbath more closely. The public attacked his plan by singing the humorous ballad *St. Andrew Agnew's Agony Bill.* Died at age 56 of scarlet fever in Edinburgh.

Last Words: "Did the doctors really say I was not to get up?—If they said so, then I won't get up; but I feel well.—No, I will keep them (the pillows) as the doctors left them."

Source: *Memoirs of Sir Andrew Agnew* by Thomas M'Crie (Edinburgh, 1852).

Agrestis, Julius

(d. 69) Roman centurion. Committed suicide when his information about the size of the enemy's army was doubted by Emperor Vitellius. Tacitus mentioned that some of his contemporaries said Agrestis was slain by Vitellius, but either way, it shows his courage and loyalty.

Last Words: "Since you require some decisive proof, and I can no longer serve you in any other way either by my life or death, I will give you a proof which you can believe."

Source: *The Annals and the Histories* by Publius Cornelius Tacitus, tr. by Alfred John Church and William Jackson Brodribb (Chicago, 1952).

Agrippa, Heinrich Cornelius

(1486-1535) German philosopher, physician, occultist. Known as Agrippa von Nettesheim. Lectured on theology in Cologne, Pisa, Turin and elsewhere. Practiced medicine in France. Skilled in alchemy and occult sciences. Notable work: *De occulta philosophia.* Died at age 48 in Grenoble, France.

Last Words: "Abi perdita bestia, que me perdidisti." (tr. "Begone thou wretched beast, which hast utterly undone me.") A curious story circulated that Agrippa was always accompanied by a devil in the form of a black dog. When he felt death was near, he repented his sins and removed the collar from the dog's neck as he spoke these Last Words. The dog is said to have jumped into a river when Agrippa died and was never

seen again.

Source: *Cornelius Agrippa: The Life of Henry Cornelius Agrippa von Nettesheim, Doctor and Knight, Commonly Known as a Magician* by Henry Morley (London, 1856).

Agrippina

(15?-59) Roman noblewoman. Known as Agrippina Minor and Colonia Agrippina. Sister of Caligula. Mother of Emperor Nero. Poisoned her uncle Emperor Claudius and her second and third husbands to secure the crown for her son who eventually killed her. Contemporary accounts of her Last Words appear in the writings of Publius Cornelius Tacitus and Cassius Dio. The version by Tacitus is shorter: "Ventrem feri!" (tr. "Smite my womb!" or "Strike here!"). It indicates that Agrippina pointed to her womb (which bore Nero). Dio's version is longer and typically is translated with additional words including addressing Anicetus and speaking of Nero, or in and after Goldsmith's 1799 translation, as "the monster," to which Tacitus only refers.

Variations (Tacitus):

(1) "Smite my womb!"

Sources: *The Annals and the Histories* by Publius Cornelius Tacitus, tr. by Alfred John Church and William Jackson Brodribb (Chicago, 1952); "Tacitus" in Classic Latin Course in English by William Cleaver Wilkinson (Meadville, PA, 1893).

(2) "Strike here!"

Sources: *The Annals of Imperial Rome* by Publius Cornelius Tacitus, tr. by Michael Grant (New York, 1973); *A History of the Roman Emperors* by Charles Abraham Elton (London, 1825); *History of the Roman Empire, from the Accession of Augustus to the End of the Empire of the West* by Thomas Keightley and Joshua Toulmin Smith (Boston, 1841).

Variations (Dio):

(1) "Strike here, Anicetus, strike here, for this bore Nero."

Sources: *Dio's Rome,* Vol. V, by Cassius Dio Cocceianus, tr. and ed. by Herbert Baldwin Foster and Joannes Zonaras (Troy, New York, 1906); *Representing Agrippina* by Judith Ginsburg (Oxford, England, 2006).

(2) "Strike here, Anicetus, for it was here that Nero was born."

Source: *The Empresses of Rome* by Joseph McCabe (New York, 1911).

(3) "Strike here! This is the womb that gave birth to Nero."

Sources: *Woman and Her Master,* Vol. II, by Lady Sydney Owenson Morgan (Philadelphia, 1840);

Representative Women by Edwin Paxton Hood (London, 1853).

(4) "Strike here where Nero's head once rested!"

Source: *The Story of the Romans* by Hélène Adeline Guerber (New York, 1896).

(5) "Strike here! Strike the womb that conceived Nero."

Source: *Blood and Splendor* by Daniel Myerson (New York, 2001).

Variations (Dio, after Goldsmith):

(1) "Strike here, for this place gave birth to a monster."

Sources: *The Roman History*, Vol. II, by Oliver Goldsmith (Dublin, Ireland, 1799); *A Gazetteer of the Old and New Testaments* by William Fleming (Edinburgh, 1838); *Anecdotes from Roman, English, and French History* Selected by A.H. (London, 1853); *Ancient History*, 4 vol. [in 1] by John Robinson and Francis Young (London, 1873).

(2) "Strike here, strike the womb which bore a monster!"

Source: *A History of the Romans Under the Emperors* by Dawson Massy (London, 1863).

(3) "Strike here, for this womb has given a monster birth."

Source: *A New Universal Biography* by John Platts (London, 1825).

(4) "Strike here! Level your rage against the womb which gave birth to such a monster."

Source: *Last Words of Remarkable Persons* compiled by J. M. H. (London, 1877).

Aguilar, Grace

(1816-1847) English writer, novelist. Notable works: *Home Influence; A Mother's Recompense* (novels). Also wrote on Jewish history and religion, including *The Spirit of Judaism; The Jewish Faith* and *The Women of Israel*. Her works were popular in the U.S. She was in frail health much of her life. Died at age 31 while visiting Frankfurt, Germany.

Last Words: "Though He slay me, yet will I trust in Him."

Source: "Grace Aguilar" in *The Jewish Encyclopedia*, ed. by Isidore Singer, Cyrus Adler, et al. (New York, 1901-1906).

Agustín I, see Iturbide, Agustín de.

Aikau, Edward Ryan ("Eddie")

(1946-1978) American surfer, lifeguard, waterman. Died at age 31 while tracing an ancient Polynesian migration route between Hawaii and Tahiti, 2,400 miles south of Honolulu on *Hokule'a,* a canoe-like boat. When his boat sprang a leak and capsized, Aikau decided to use his surfboard to paddle for help to Lana'i, Hawaii, 12 miles away. He made a leash from nylon rope and attached it to his board.

Last Words: "Don't worry, I can do it. I can get to land." The crew was found the next day and made it safely back to Honolulu. Aikau was never found.

Source: *Honolulu Advertiser,* March 5, 2000.

Variation: "I'll be okay. Everything will be okay." Spoken as he stroked away on his surfboard toward Lana'i.

Source: *Eddie Would Go: The Story of Eddie Aikau, Hawaiian Hero and Pioneer of Big Wave Surfing* by Stuart Holmes Coleman (New York, 2004).

Ainsworth, William Harrison

(1805-1882) British writer, novelist, publisher, editor. First success was as a writer of historical romances with *Rookwood*. Wrote 39 novels. Edited *Bentley's Magazine; The New Monthly Magazine; Ainsworth's Magazine*. Died at age 76 in Reigate, Surrey, England.

Last Words (written): "Dr. Holman thought me much wasted since I last saw him and so I am in no doubt. Your Affectionate Cousin —W. Harrison Ainsworth." Written five days before he died.

Source: *William Harrison Ainsworth and His Friends,* Vol. II, by S. M. Ellis (London, 1911).

Aitken, William Maxwell, see Beaverbrook, 1st Baron.

Akbar, the Great, Emperor of Hindustan

(1542-1605) Mogul ruler of India. Son of Humayun. Grandson of Babur. Emperor of Hindustan. Birth name Jalal ud-Din Mohammed. Wise and tolerant ruler who excelled at diplomacy and organization. Expanded boundaries of his empire in India. Died at age 62 in Agra, India. Succeeded by his son Jahangir.

Last Words: "I cannot bear that any misunderstanding should subsist between you and those who have for so many years shared in my toils and been the companions of my glory." Spoken on his deathbed to his nobles and his last surviving son. He asked their forgiveness if he had wronged them, then died.

Source: *Akbar and the Rise of the Mughal Empire* by G. B. Malleson (London, 1890).

Akiba ben Joseph

(50?-132) Jewish rabbi, educator, martyr. One of the first Jewish scholars to compile Hebrew oral laws. Joined in revolt of Bar Cocheba against Hadrian in 132 A.D. Taken prisoner. Tortured. Died in Palestine. One of the martyrs mentioned in Jewish penitential prayer.

Last Words: "Shema Yisrael Adonai Eloheinu Adonai Echad." (tr. "Hear, O Israel! Adonai is our God! Adonai is One!").

Source: "Akiba ben Joseph" in *The Jewish Encyclopedia,* ed. by Isidore Singer, Cyrus Adler, et al. (New York, 1901-1906).

Akutagawa, Ryūnosuke

(1892-1927) Japanese writer. Known as Father of the Japanese short story. His short stories "Rashōmon" and "In the Grove" were combined into the 1950 Akira Kurosawa-directed film *Rashōmon*. Akutagawa committed suicide at age 35 by taking an overdose of a barbiturate, fearing he had inherited his mother's mental illness. His friend Masao Kume read his suicide note aloud at a press conference the day after his death. Part of his suicide note is shown here.

Last Words (written): "Probably no one who attempts suicide—is fully aware of all his motives, which are usually too complex. At least in my case it is prompted by a vague sense of anxiety—about my own future. — As for my vague sense of anxiety about my own future, I think I analyzed it all in 'A Fool's Life,' except for a social factor, namely the shadow of feudalism cast over my life. This I omitted purposely, not at all certain that I could really clarify the social context in which I lived. — P.S. Reading a life of Empedocles, I felt how old is this desire to make a god of oneself. This letter, so far as I am conscious, never attempts this. On the contrary, I consider myself one of the most common humans. You may recall those days of twenty years ago when we discussed 'Empedocles on Etna'—under the linden trees. In those days I was one who wished to make a god of myself."

Source: *Akutagawa: An Introduction* by Beongcheon Yu (Detroit, 1972).

Alacoque, Saint Margaret Mary

(1647-1690) French holy woman. Roman Catholic nun, mystic. Also known as Marguerite Marie Alacoque. Entered Visitation Convent in 1671. Had visions of Jesus Christ. Died at age 43 in Burgundy, France. Canonized in 1920.

Last Words: "I need nothing but God, and to lose myself in the heart of Jesus." Spoken as she received the Last Rites just before she died.

Source: *The Encyclopedia of Catholic Saints: October* (Philadelphia, 1966).

Albert, Prince Consort of Queen Victoria

(1819-1861) German-born English royalty. Full name Albert Francis Charles Augustus Emmanuel of Saxe-Coburg-Gotha. Married Queen Victoria in 1840. Created Prince Consort in 1857. Played a key role in staging England's Great Exhibition in 1851. Died at age 42 at Windsor Castle. His physicians diagnosed his illness as typhoid, but some believe he died of cancer. Queen Victoria described his final moments in her journal. His Last Words were spoken in German.

Different Last Words:

(1) "Gutes Weibchen." (tr. "Good little wife.")

Source: *King Without a Crown* by Daphne Bennett (Philadelphia, 1977).

Variation: Just before he lost consciousness, Victoria whispered in his ear: "Es ist dein kleines Frauchen." (tr. "It is your little woman.") She asked him for "ein kuss" (tr. "a kiss"), which he gave before dying.

Source: *Albert and Victoria: The Rise and Fall of the House of Saxe-Coburg-Gotha* by E. J. Feuchtwanger (London, 2006).

Variation: "You have not forgotten the important communication to Nemours?... Gutes Frauchen." (tr. "Good little woman.")

Source: *The Life of His Royal Highness, the Prince Consort* by Theodore Martin. Authorized by Queen Victoria (London, 1875-1880).

(2) "I have had wealth, rank and power, but if this were all I had, how wretched I should be." A few minutes later he said: "Rock of Ages cleft for me. Let me hide myself in thee."

Source: *New Testament Illustrations: One Thousand Selected Passages from the New Testament* by William Jones (Hartford, CT, 1975).

Albert I, King of the Belgians

(1875-1934) Belgian monarch. Succeeded uncle Leopold II in 1909. Refused to yield to German ultimatum in World War I. Took personal command of Belgian armed forces during war. Died at age 58 at Marche-les-Dames, near Namur. Fell to his death while rock climbing in Belgium.

Last Words: "Follow the path for another fifty yards. I am going back to the foot of the rocks to make another climb. If I feel in good form I shall take the difficult way up; if I do not I shall take the easy one. I shall join you in an hour." Spoken to his rock-climbing companions.

Source: *Albert of Belgium, Defender of Right* by Emile Cammaerts (New York, 1935).

Albert II, Margrave of Brandenburg-Kulmbach ("Alcibiades")

(1522-1557) German nobleman. Son of Margrave Casimir of Brandenburg-Kulmbach. Known as Alcibiades because of his combative disposition. Supported Holy Roman Emperor Charles then turned against him. He later rejoined the emperor but was defeated by the Duke of Brunswick-Wolfenbüttel. He fled to France where he supported French King Henry II. Died at age 34 in Pforzheim, Germany.

Last Words: "Lord Jesu!"

Source: *Markgraf Albrecht Alcibiades* by Johannes Voight (Berlin, Germany, 1852).

Albert Victor, Duke of Clarence and Avondale ("Prince Eddy")

(1864-1892) British royalty. Full name Albert Victor Christian Edward. Known as Prince Eddy. Son of King Edward VII and Alexandra of Denmark. Grandson of Queen Victoria. Betrothed to Princess Mary of Teck. Died at age 28 of pneumonia and flu in Sandringham House, Norfolk.

Last Words: "Who is that?" Repeated over and over as he was dying.

Source: *Clarence: The Life of H.R.H. the Duke of Clarence and Avondale (1864-1892)* by Michael Harrison (London, 1972).

Albertoni, Blessed Ludovica or Louisa

(1473-1533) Italian widow. Christian. Spent her fortune on the underprivileged. Baked bread for the poor with gold and silver coins in it. Died at around age 59. Beatified in 1671. Bernini did a sculpture of her.

Last Words: "Father, into Thy hands I commend my spirit."

Source: *Butler's Lives of the Saints* by Alban Butler, Herbert J. Thurston and Donald Attwater (New York, 1956).

Alcott, Amos Bronson

(1799-1888) American writer, educator. Father of writer Louisa Mae Alcott. Prominent member of Transcendentalists. Friend of Ralph Waldo Emerson. Founded Concord Summer School of Philosophy in 1879. Had stroke in 1882. Died six years later at age 89 in Concord, Massachusetts.

Last Words: "I am going up. Come with me." Spoken to his daughter Louisa. She died two days later.

Source: "Artists and Daughters in Louisa May Alcott's Diana and Persis" by Natania Rosenfeld (*New England Quarterly,* Vol. 64, No. 1, March 1991).

Alcott, Louisa May

(1832-1888) American writer. Daughter of Amos Bronson Alcott. Influenced by family friends Ralph Waldo Emerson and Henry David Thoreau. Nurse in Union Hospital in U.S. Civil War. Her novel *Little Women,* published in 1868 and 1869, became a classic. Died at age 56 in Boston two days after her father.

Last Words: "Is it not meningitis?" She had been in ill health for many years and took a turn for the worse after she visited her father. She did not have meningitis. She may have died of mercury poisoning, the after-effect of an earlier treatment for typhoid fever.

Source: *Louisa May Alcott: Her Life, Letters and Journals* by Ednah D. Cheney (Boston, 1889).

Alderson, Sir Edward Hall

(1787-1857) British jurist. Justice of Common Pleas. Knighted in 1830. Baron of Exchequer. Died at age 69 in London.

Last Words: "The worse, the better for me." His response when asked how he felt.

Source: *Selections From the Charges and Other Detached Papers of Baron Alderson with an Introductory Notice of His Life* by Sir Edward Hall Alderson, ed. by Charles Alderson (London, 1858).

Aldrich, Thomas Bailey

(1836-1907) American writer, poet, editor,

journalist, war correspondent. Notable works: *The Story of a Bad Boy* (novel based on his childhood); *Marjorie Daw* (short story). Editor of *Atlantic Monthly*. Was part of an illustrious New England literary group that included Holmes, Longfellow, Lowell and Whittier. Died at age 71 in Boston, a few days after he was taken ill.

Last Words: "In spite of all, I am going to sleep; put out the lights."

Source: *The Life of Thomas Bailey Aldrich* by Ferris Greenslet (Boston, 1908).

Alem, Leandro Nicéforo

(1841-1896) Argentine politician, political reformer. Uncle and political teacher of Hipólito Yrigoyen. Organized Youth Civic Union, which led to Radical Civic Union (UCR). Was one of the leaders of the revolution that forced Juárez Celman to resign. Failed in an uprising in 1893 and lost supporters. Disappointed and feeling betrayed, he committed suicide at age 55 by shooting himself inside his carriage. Two cities, a town and a park were named in his honor.

Last Words (written): "¡Sí, que se rompa, pero que no se doble!" (tr. "Yes, that is broken, but does not bend!") It was originally spoken more than a century earlier and was published in a 1789 history of Latin America. Sometimes quoted as: "¡Se quiebra pero no se dobla!" (tr. "It breaks but it does not bend!") Suicide note.

Source: *Alem: su vida, su obra, tragedia de su muerte, las doctrinas democráticas del fundador de la Unión Cívica Radical a través de documentos, discursos y escritos* by Leandro Nicéforo Alem (Buenos Aires, Argentina, 1928).

Alexander I, King of Yugoslavia

(1888-1934) Montenegrin-born Yugoslavian monarch. King of Serbs, Croats and Slovenes from 1921 to 1929. First King of Kingdom of Yugoslavia from 1929 to 1934. Assassinated at age 45 in Marseilles while on state visit to France. Gunman was member of Macedonian revolutionary group. Assassination was caught on film. French foreign minister Jean-Louis Barthou was accidentally killed by French police.

Last Words (doubtful): "Save Yugoslavia. Take good care of the queen."

Source: *The Turning Point: The Assassination of Louis Barthou and King Alexander I of Yugoslavia* by Allen Roberts (New York, 1970).

Variation (doubtful): "Safeguard Yugoslavia."

These Last Words were probably intended to imbue Alexander's memory with a heroic mystique. But most observers doubt that he was able to say anything after he was shot.

Source: *The First Yugoslavia: Search for a Viable Political System* by Alex N. Dragnich (Stanford, CA, 1983).

Alexander I, Emperor and Tsar of Russia

(1777-1825) Russian ruler. Son of Paul I. Placed on the throne after a palace revolt removed his father and ended with Paul's murder. Alexander ruled Russia during Napoleon's march on Moscow. He was disillusioned during the final years of his reign, especially after the death of his only daughter. Died at age 47 of typhus while visiting Taganrog. Left no heirs. Succeeded by his brother Nicholas I. Legend sprang up that Alexander had not died but had abandoned the throne and assumed the identity of a wandering holy man.

Different Last Words:

(1) "What a beautiful day." Spoken when the window blinds in his room were opened.

Source: *Historical Memoirs of Emperor Alexander I and the Court of Russia* by Madame la Comtesse de Choiseul-Gouffier (London, 1904).

(2) "Give me the remedies that you judge necessary." Spoken when told his physician proposed to apply leeches.

Source: *Alexander of Russia: Napoleon's Conqueror* by Henri Troyat (New York, 1983).

Alexander II, Emperor and Tsar of Russia

(1818-1881) Russian ruler. Son of Nicholas I. Ruled Russia from 1855 to 1881. Serfs were emancipated in 1861, during his reign. Injured by explosion of grenade thrown at his carriage near palace by terrorist organization. Died at age 62 in St. Petersburg a few hours later.

Last Words: "More quickly—inside—carry me to the palace—there—to die."

Source: *Alexander II, Détails inédits sur sa vie intime et sa mort* by Victor Laferté (Paris, 1882). Victor Laferté was the pseudonym of Princess Katharina Dolgoruky, second wife of Alexander II, whom he married in 1880. After his death, she moved to Geneva and published this book.

Variation: "Quick—home—take me to the palace—there—to die." Spoken haltingly. His final words were reported by his guards.

Source: *Studies in* Russia by Augustus John Cuthbert Hare (New York, 1902). This quote is very similar to his wife's version published in 1882 and may simply be a difference in translation.

Variation: "Home to die—It's cold."

Source: *Alexander III of Russia* by Charles Lowe (New York, 1895).

Alexander III, Emperor and Tsar of Russia

(1845-1894) Russian ruler. Son of Alexander II. Ruled Russia from 1881 to 1894. Died at age 49 of nephritis at the summer palace in the Crimea. Succeeded by his son Nicholas II.

Different Last Words:

(1) "I feel the end approaching. Be calm. I am quite calm." He then sent for a priest and received Holy Communion. A half hour later, Ivan Szergijeff, the priest, administered the Last Rites and stayed with him until he died. Alexander said "How good!" as the priest placed his hands on his head after he received the Last Rites.

Sources: *Alexander III of Russia* by Charles Lowe (New York, 1895); *The Last Grand Duchess: Her Imperial Highness Grand Duchess Olga Alexandrovna* by Ian Vorres (New York, 1965).

(2) (doubtful): "This box was presented to me by the Emperor of Prussia."

Source: "Dying Words of Noted Persons" in *Miscellaneous Notes and Queries with Answers in All Departments of Literature*, Vol. II, No. 31 (Manchester, NH, 1885). The quote also appears in several Last Words compilations and Internet websites.

The quotation was published in 1885, nine years before Alexander III died.

Alexander III, King of Macedon ("Alexander the Great")

(356-323 B.C.) Macedonian ruler, military leader. Known as Alexander the Great. Son of Philip II of Macedon. One of the greatest generals of the ancient world. Conquered Syria and Egypt. Founded Alexandria. Invaded Persia. Attempted to conquer India but got only as far as Ganges before retreating. Died at age 33 of fever in the palace of Nebuchadnezzar II in Babylon.

Different Last Words:

Alexander was asked on his deathbed to name his successor. Some of those present say his final utterance was:

(1) "Kratistos!" (tr. "To the strongest!")

Sources: "Alexander" in *Lives of the Noble Grecians and Romans* by Plutarch, tr. by John Dryden (Chicago, 1952); *Anabasis of Alexander* by Arrian (London, 1893).

Others say he murmured:

(2) "Krateros." The name of a Macedonian general who was favored as one of his successors. Alexander's voice may have been indistinct because of the fever that eventually killed him.

Source: *The Mask of Jove: A History of Graeco-Roman Civilization from the Death of Alexander to the Death of Constantine* by Stringfellow Barr (Philadelphia, 1966).

Alexander VI, Pope

(1431-1503) Spanish prelate. Took name Rodrigo Borgia when he became ward of his uncle Cardinal Alfonso Borgia. Father of Cesare and Lucretia Borgia. Reigned as pope from 1492 to 1503. Generous patron of the arts. Died at age 72 in Rome.

Last Words: "Va bene, va bene, arrivo. Aspettate un momento." (tr. "I come. I come. It is right. Wait a moment.")

Source: *Lucretia Borgia* by Ferdinand Gregorovius (New York, 1903).

Alexis I, Tsar of Russia

(1629-1676) Russian ruler. Second tsar of the Romanoffs. Son of Mikhail I. Father of Peter the Great. Greatly expanded Russian territory through war. Died at age 46 in Moscow.

Last Words: "I would never have married had I known that my time would be so brief. If I had known that, I would not have taken upon myself double tears."

Source: *Tsar Alexis: His Reign and His Russia* by Joseph T. Fuhrmann (Gulf Breeze, FL, 1981).

Alfieri, Count Vittorio

(1749-1803) Italian poet, playwright. Often considered founder of Italian tragedy. Notable works: *Cleopatra; Orestes; Antigone; Philip the Second* (dramas). Died at age 54 in Florence, Italy.

Last Words: "Stringetemi la mano, mi cara, mi sento morire." (tr. "Press my hand, dear friend, I am dying.") Spoken to Countess Stolberg (Countess of Albany) who lived with him. They may have been secretly married.

Source: "Lives of Literary and Scientific Men of Italy, Spain and Portugal" in *Lardner's Cabinet Cyclopedia* Vol. II (London, 1835), excerpted from "Lives of Literary Men" by Charles William Wason (*The Monthly Review,* Vol. III, September-December 1835).

Variation: "Clasp my hand, dear friend; I die."

Source: "Dying Words of Noted Persons" in *Miscellaneous Notes and Queries with Answers in All Departments of Literature*, Vol. II (Manchester, NH, 1885).

Alfonso of Spain, Prince of Asturias

(1907-1938) Spanish royalty. Eldest son of Alfonso XIII of Spain. Count of Covadonga. Had hemophilia. Died at age 31 after a car crash in Miami, Florida.

Last Words: "¡Mi madre! ¡Mi madre! Where is my mother? I'm all alone in this country. Don't leave me, Jack."

Sources: *Miami Herald,* September 7, 1938; *The Spanish Bourbons* by John D. Bergamini (New York, 1974).

Alfonso XII, King of Spain

(1857-1885) Spanish ruler. Only son of Queen Isabella II, who was driven from throne in 1868 revolt. Full name Francisco de Asís Fernando Pío Juan María Gregorio Pelayo. Ruled Spain after First Spanish Republic ended and monarchy was restored. Died at age 27 of tuberculosis in Madrid.

Last Words: "I don't deserve to be cared for as you have cared for me. I know that when I have gone you will care for Spain as I have myself."

Source: *Royal Vendetta, The Crown of Spain 1829-1965* by Theo Aronson (London, 1966).

Alfonso XIII, King of Spain

(1886-1941) Spanish ruler. Posthumous son of Alfonso XII. Became king at birth. Mother was regent until he succeeded to the throne in 1902. Married a granddaughter of Queen Victoria. Attempt was made to assassinate them on their wedding day. Went into exile in 1931 during Spanish Civil War. Settled in Rome, Italy. Abdicated in 1941 in favor of son Don Juan shortly before he died. Died at age 54 in Rome.

Last Words: "Spain, My God!" Spoken while kissing a crucifix.

Source: *King Alfonso* by Robert Sencourt (London, 1942).

Alford, Henry

(1810-1871) English clergyman, editor, educator, hymnist. First editor of *Contemporary Review*. Dean of Canterbury. Notable work: 4 vol. edition of New Testament in Greek. Died at age 60 in Canterbury, England.

Last Words: "Will you move a vote of thanks for his kindness in performing the ceremony?" He wanted the archdeacon thanked for his funeral service.

Source: *Life Journals and Letters of Henry Alford, DD,* ed. by his Widow (London, 1874).

Alfred, King of the West Saxons ("Alfred the Great")

(849-899) Saxon ruler. King of the West Saxons in England. Known as Alfred the Great. Succeeded his brother Ethelred in 871. Spent several years repelling Danish invaders and saving English from conquest by Denmark.

Different Last Words:

(1) "I desire to leave to the men that come after me a remembrance of me in good works."

Source: *The Conquest of England* by John Richard Green (New York, 1884).

(2) "Thou my dear son, set thee now beside me, and I will deliver thee true instructions. My son, I feel that my hour is coming. My countenance is wan. My days are almost done. We must now part. I shall to another world, and thou shalt be left alone in all my wealth. I pray thee (for thou art my dear child) strive to be a father, and a lord to thy people. Be thou the children's father, and the widow's friend. Comfort thou the poor, and shelter the weak; and, with all thy might, right that which is wrong. And, son, govern thyself, by law; then shall the Lord love thee, and God above all things shall be thy reward. Call thou upon him to advise thee in all thy need, and so shall he help thee, the better to compass that which thou wouldest."

Source: *The History of the Anglo-Saxons* by Sharon Turner (London, 1852). Turner drew on what is called the conclusion of the "Cotton MSS" upon which a commentary was made by Sir John Spelman. He pointed out that the writing was not that of the king, per se, as it was not in the Saxon tongue, but appeared to be a collection of some later author "in a broken English." Humfrey Wanley, another scholar, said the fragment is in Norman Saxon from the time of about Kings Henry II or Richard I, and there is a copy–the "Galba MS"–in the Bodleian Library at Oxford.

Alger, Horatio, Jr.

(1832-1899) American writer, clergyman. Unitarian. Wrote more than 100 books about boys who struggled to escape poverty and adversity. Their goodness was predictably rewarded with wealth and success. Notable series: *Ragged Dick; Luck and Pluck; Tattered Tom.* Died at age 57 of heart disease in Natick, Massachusetts.

Last Words: "Splendid! I'll sleep now. I shall have a nap. Later I can pack and leave on the evening train. But I'm tired. Let me rest."

Source: *Horatio Alger, or the American Hero Era* by Ralph D. Gardner (New York, 1978).

Ali ibn Abi Talib

(600?-661) Muslim caliph. Cousin/son-in-law of the Prophet Muhammad. The fourth "rightfully guided" Caliph of (Shiite sect) Islam. Ali's right to succeed to the caliphate is an article of faith that divided the Muslim world into two great sects, Sunni and Shia, but he is highly respected by both. He had children by Muhammad's daughter Fatima Zahra, as well as children by other wives. His descendants are revered today as imams, sharifs and sayyids/syeds.

Last Words: "Fuzto wa Rabbil Ka'bah." (tr. "By the Lord of the Ka'bah. I have succeeded.") Spoken as he was assassinated by Jabbar ibn Sulma with a poison sword.

Source: *The Seerah of Muhammad (The Last Prophet: A Model of All Time)* by Abul Ḥasan Ali Nadwi (Lucknow, India, 2004).

Ali Pasha of Tepalen

(1741-1822) Albanian soldier in the service of Turkey. Birth name Ali Arslan. Known as Lion of Janina and the Mohammedan Bonaparte. Made Pasha of Janina. Deposed by Sultan Mahmoud in 1820. Shot and killed by soldiers of Hassan Pasha in 1822. Dumas gave a fictionalized version of Ali Pasha's downfall in *The Count of Monte Cristo.*

Last Words: "Go my friend, dispatch poor Vasiliky, that these dogs may not profane her beauteous form." Kyra Vasiliky was his wife.

Source: *Life of Ali Pacha.* Anonymous (London, 1822).

Alice Maud Mary, Princess

(1843-1878) British royalty. Daughter of Queen Victoria and Prince Albert. Grand Duchess of Hesse. Great-grandmother of Prince Phillip, Duke of Edinburgh. Died at age 35 of diphtheria in Darmstadt, Germany.

Last Words: "I will sleep quietly now."

Source: "Princess Alice Maud Mary" (*Harper's Bazaar,* February 16, 1884).

Alison, Archibald

(1656-1680) Scottish Covenanter. Tried, sentenced, executed in Edinburgh. Wrote a lengthy testimony that was read at his execution. It detailed his reasons for being a Covenanter and the events that led to his arrest. Last few lines are given here:

Last Words: "Return, my soul, unto thy quiet rest. Farewell all created comforts in time, and welcome Father, Son and Holy Ghost, into Thy hands I commit my spirit."

Source: *A Cloud of Witnesses for the Royal Prerogatives of Jesus Christ; Being the Last Speeches and Testimonies of Those Who Have Suffered for the Truth in Scotland Since the Year 1680* by John Henderson Thomson (Edinburgh, 1714).

Allen, Clarence Ray

(1930-2006) American murderer. At age 76, he was the oldest man executed on California's Death Row. Put to death for the 1980 murders of three workers at a Fresno market. Defense lawyers were unable to convince the U.S. Supreme Court that Allen was too old and feeble to be executed and had already suffered enough after spending 23 years on Death Row.

Last Words (written): "My last words will be Hoka hey, it's a good day to die. Thank you very much. I love you all. Goodbye." His Last Words were a written statement in which he referred to his Native American heritage and the war cry attributed to Crazy Horse at the Battle of the Little Big Horn.

Source: "Allen, 76, Becomes Oldest Man Executed on California Death Row" by Ray Huard (*San Diego Union-Tribune,* January 18, 2006).

Allen, Ethan

(1738-1789) American military officer. Served in French and Indian War. Revolutionary War general. Vermont folk hero. Leader of Green Mountain Boys. Seized Fort Ticonderoga. Captured at Montreal, held prisoner 1775 to 1778. Died at age 51 of a stroke in Burlington, Vermont.

Last Words: "Waiting, are they? Waiting, are they? Well, God damn 'em, let 'em wait!" His response to his parson (some accounts say physician) who tried to comfort him by saying "General Allen, the angels are waiting for you."
Source: *Ethan Allen* by Stewart H. Holbrook (New York, 1940).

Allen, Gracie

(1895-1964) American comedian, actress. Comedy partner of husband George Burns. *Burns and Allen Show* ran 17 years on radio, 8 years on television. Appeared in several movies. Heart problems caused her to retire in 1958. Died at age 69 of a heart attack in Los Angeles.
Last Words: "I'm sorry, boys, I'm all wet."
Source: *Gracie: A Love Story* by George Burns (New York, 1988).

Allen, Jonathan Macomber

(1823-1892) American educator, abolitionist. Member of first graduating class of Alfred's Select School. Founder and second president of Alfred University. Received degree from Oberlin and returned to Alfred as teacher of mathematics. While at Oberlin, he worked with the Underground Railroad. Died at age 69 of heart failure.
Last Words: "I am happy, why cannot you be so." Spoken to his family physician Dr. E.C. Greene, who advised him not to go to chapel to begin the year's work.
Source: *Allegany County and Its People: A Centennial Memorial History of Allegany County, New York* by Robert Morris (Alfred, NY, 1896).

Allen, Loraine

(1763-1783) American woman. Daughter of American Revolution hero Ethan Allen by Allen's first wife, Mary Brownson. Loraine's mother was a pious Christian; one of Loraine sisters became a nun. Ethan Allen, on the other hand, was a Deist. Loraine died at age 19 in Arlington, Vermont.
Last Words: "I am about to die; shall I believe in the principles you have taught me, or shall I believe what my mother has taught me?" Ethan Allen's response was: "Believe what your mother has taught you."
Source: "Ethan Allen" in *An American Biographical and Historical Dictionary* by William Allen (Boston, 1832).

Allen, William O'Mera,
see Manchester Martyrs.

Allende y Gossens, Salvador

(1908-1973) Chilean politician. President of Chile. Tried to redistribute his nation's wealth and land. Overthrown by a military coup. Died at age 65 in fighting at the presidential palace in Santiago. Cause of death is uncertain. It was officially ruled suicide by machine gun.
Last Words: "Long live Chile! Long live the people! Long live the workers! These are my last words, and I am certain that my sacrifice will not be in vain. I am certain that, at the very least, it will be a moral lesson that will punish felony, cowardice and treason." Farewell speech, broadcast at 9:10 a.m., September 11, 1973, Santiago, Chile.
Source: *Salvador Allende Reader: Chile's Voice of Democracy* by Salvador Allende Gossens, James D. Cockcroft and Jane Canning (Melbourne, Australia, 2000).

Allingham, William

(1824-1889) Irish poet, editor. Wife was watercolorist Helen Paterson. Friend of Dante Gabriel Rossetti who illustrated some of his work. Notable works: *Day and Night Songs; Irish Songs and Poems*. Editor of *Fraser's Magazine*. Died at age 65 in London.
Last Words: "I see such things as you can not dream of." Spoken when he emerged briefly from a semicoma.
Source: *Alfred Lord Tennyson: A Memoir* by Hallam Tennyson (New York, 1898).
Variation: "I am seeing things that you know nothing of."
Source: *The Diaries,* ed. by H. Allingham and D. Radford (London, 1907). H. Allingham was his wife Helen Paterson Allingham, noted watercolorist and illustrator.

Alphege, Alfege, Ælfheah or Elphege, Saint

(954-1012) English prelate, holy man, martyr. Bishop of Winchester, Archbishop of Canterbury. Captured by Vikings in 1011. Refused to be ransomed. Murdered in Greenwich, Kent. An account of his death appears in the *Anglo-Saxon Chronicle*. He was canonized in 1078. Just before Thomas à Becket was killed, he prayed to Saint Alphege.

Last Words: "Christianorum carnes paganis dentibus conterendas dare. Ego equidem id faciam, si quod paupertas ad vitam paraverat, vestries hoc morsibus abutendum tradam." (tr. "You urge me in vain. I am not the man to provide Christian flesh for pagan teeth to devour, and it would be so acting if I delivered unto you that which the poor have laid by for their subsistence.")

Source: *Histoire de la Conquète de l'Angleterre par les Normands* by Augustin Thierry (Paris, 1867), citing *Osberni Vita S. Elphegi; Anglia sacrct*, t. II, p. 138. — *Eadmeri Hist. nov, lib*. I, p. 4, ed. Selden.

Variation: "You urge me in vain; I am not the man to provide Christian flesh for pagan teeth, by robbing my flocks to enrich their enemies."

Source: "Dying Words of Distinguished Persons" in *The Encyclopedia of Death and Life in the Spirit-World,* Vol. I, by J.R. Francis (Chicago, 1895).

Altgeld, John Peter

(1847-1902) German-born American politician, businessman. Governor of Illinois. Died at age 55 of a cerebral hemorrhage suffered after delivering a speech in Joliet, Illinois, on behalf of the Boers. Altgeld Hall, University of Illinois, Urbana, was named for him.

Last Words: "How do you do, Cushing? I am glad to see you." Spoken to his last visitor.

Source: *Altgeld of Illinois: A Record of His Life and Work* by Waldo R. Browne (New York, 1924).

Alva or Alba, 3rd Duke of
Alvarez de Toledo, Ferdinand

(1508-1582) Spanish nobleman, statesman, military officer. General and governor of Spanish Netherlands. Established Council of Troubles (Bloody Council) that condemned to death thousands of dissidents who were not given a chance to appeal. Died at age 74 in Lisbon, Portugal.

Last Words: "Too late." Spoken when he heard the king sent notice he would visit him.

Source: *Landmarks of History III. Modern History: from the Reformation to the Fall of Napoleon* by Charlotte Mary Yonge (London, 1857).

Amboise, Georges d'

(1460-1510) French prelate. Bishop of Montauban. Archbishop of Narbonne. Arch-

bishop of Rouen. Cardinal and prime minister under Louis XII. Tried to create schism between French church and Rome to secure his election to pope. Failed but was named papal legate in France for life. Gained great wealth. Died at age 50 of gout attack in Lyons, France.

Last Words: "I believe."

Source: *Vie du Cardinal d'Amboise* by Louis Le Gendre (Rouen, France, 1724).

Ambrose, Saint

(340?-397) German-born prelate, holy man, hymnist. Studied in Rome. Bishop of Milan. Reorganized singing and tonality in Christian church. Ambrosian music named for him. Introduced Ambrosian chant (plainsong). Father of Roman Catholic Church.

Different Last Words:

(1) "Old though he be, he is the best of all." His reply when Simplicianus was mentioned as his possible successor as bishop.

Source: *The Golden Legend or Lives of the Saints.* Compiled by Jacobus de Voragine, Archbishop of Genoa, 1275, 1st ed., 1470. English ed. by William Caxton, 1483, ed. by F.S. Ellis (Edinburgh, 1900).

Variation: "I have not so behaved myself among you, that I should be ashamed to live longer: nor am I afraid to die, because we have a good master." A short time later he shouted "He is old but good!" three times upon hearing the name "Simplician."

Source: *The Lives of the Primitive Fathers, Martyrs, and Other Principal Saints: Compiled from Original Monuments and Other Authentic Records,* Vol. XII, by Alban Butler and Charles Butler (Edinburgh, 1798-1800).

(2) "I see the Lord Jesus at my bedside, smiling at me." Spoken while the Bishop of Lodi was praying with him.

Source: *Last Words: Final Thoughts of Catholic Saints and Sinners* by Paul Thigpen (Cincinnati, OH, 2006).

Amelia, Princess

(1783-1810) English royalty. Youngest of six daughters of George III, King of England, and Queen Charlotte. Died at age 27 of tuberculosis and erysipelas at Augusta Lodge, Windsor, Berkshire, England.

Last Words (doubtful): "Remember me." She did say these words but she lingered a few days after she spoke them. Amelia had a mourning ring made for her father—a lock of her hair under crystal, set with diamonds.

As she placed it on his finger, she said, "Remember me." Her death caused him such grief that he never fully recovered from her loss.

Sources: *The Every-Day Book or Everlasting Calendar* by William Hone (London, 1827); *Dictionary of National Biography: From The Earliest Times to 1900,* Vol. I, ed. by Sir Leslie Stephen, George Smith and Sir Sidney Lee (London, 1921-1922).

Amery, John

(1912-1945) British fascist. His father Leopold Amery was British secretary of state for India during World War II. John made propaganda broadcasts and recruited for Nazi Germany. Suggested forming British volunteer force (British Free Corps) for Hitler. Convicted of treason at the end of World War II. Only person to plead "guilty" to treason in a British court. Executed at age 33 in London.

Last Words: "Oh Pierrepont." Spoken to British executioner Albert Pierrepont who took Amery's hand and placed it behind his back.

Source: "How Britain Made Its Executioners" by Dominic Casciani (BBC *News,* June 1, 2006).

Ames, Fisher

(1758-1808) American statesman, politician. Member U.S. House of Representatives from Massachusetts during the first four sessions of Congress. Named president of Harvard in 1803 but had to decline because of failing health. Died at age 50 in Dedham, Massachusetts.

Last Words: "I have peace of mind. It may arise from stupidity, but I think it is founded on a belief of the Gospel. My hope is in the mercy of God through Jesus Christ."

Source: *Travels in New England and New York,* Vol. IV, by Timothy Dwight (London, 1823).

Amis, Sir Kingsley William

(1922-1995) English novelist, poet, biographer, critic, educator. Father of writer Martin Amis. Notable works: *Lucky Jim; The Green Man; You Can't Do Both* (novels). Knighted in 1990. Died at age 73 of injuries sustained in a fall in London.

Last Words: "Oh, come on."

Source: "Amis Gives His Last Words" by Michael Saunders and Jim Sullivan (*Boston Globe,* October 10, 2000).

Anastasia, Albert

(1902-1957) American gangster. Executioner for Murder, Inc. Killed at age 55 in a gangland-style execution while sitting in a chair at the Park Sheraton Hotel barbershop in New York City.

Last Words: "A quick haircut."

Source: *Bloodletters and Badmen: A Narrative Encyclopedia of American Criminals from the Pilgrims to the Present* by Jay Robert Nash (New York, 1995).

Anaxagoras

(500?-428 B.C.) Greek philosopher. Taught Pericles, Euripides and possibly Socrates in Athens. Banished from Athens for life for impiety, c. 432 B.C. Died in Ionia.

Last Words: "Give the boys a holiday." His reply when asked if he wanted anything.

Source: *Lives and Opinions of the Eminent Philosophers,* Book II, by Diogenes Laertius, tr. by C.D. Yonge (London, 1896).

Anaxarchus

(fl. c. 350 B.C.) Greek philosopher. Disciple of Democritus. Forced to land in Cyprus. Was captured and placed in mortar and ordered to be pounded to death by iron pestles.

Last Words: "Pound, pound the pouch containing Anaxarchus; ye pound not Anaxarchus."

Source: *Lives and Opinions of the Eminent Philosophers,* Book II, by Diogenes Laertius, tr. by C.D. Yonge (London, 1896).

Anaxibius

(d. 389 B.C.) Spartan military officer. Commander who was ambushed by Athenians and killed during the Corinthian War.

Last Words: "Men, it is good for me to die on this spot, where honor bids me; but for you, yonder your path lies. Hurry and save yourselves before the enemy can close with us." Twelve men remained and fell with him. The rest fled, but dropped one by one.

Source: *The Works of Xenophon* by H.G. Dakyns (New York, 1897).

Andersen, Hans Christian

(1805-1875) Danish writer. Famed for fairy tales. Notable tales: *The Emperor's New Clothes; The Little Mermaid; The Ugly Duckling; The Snow Queen; The Princess and the Pea.* Developed chronic bronchitis and liver cancer. Spent his final years living with the Melchior family who cared for him. Died at age 70 in Copenhagen, Denmark. His stories have inspired ballets, plays, movies, songs and other art forms.

Last Words: "Don't ask me how I am! I understand nothing more." His response when spoken to. He was very drowsy during his last two days and wanted only to be left alone.

Source: *Hans Christian Andersen: A Biography* by Robert Nisbet Bain (New York, 1895).

Anderson, Violette Neatley

(1882-1937) English-born American lawyer, activist, businesswoman. First black woman assistant city prosecutor in Chicago. First black woman admitted to practice before the U.S. Supreme Court. As national president of her college sorority Zeta Phi Beta she lobbied and eventually got Congress to pass the Bankhead-Jones Bill designed to help poor black tenant farmers and sharecroppers. Died at age 54 of cancer in Chicago while preparing to preside at her sorority's annual boule.

Last Words: "Tell the girls to keep on going ahead. Put over the boule with a bang. Don't let my passing throw the slightest shadow of gloom. The organization has a grand mission before it." Spoken to Claude Barnett.

Source: "Violette Neatley Anderson" in *Notable Black American Women*, Book II (Farmington Hills, MI, 1996).

André, John

(1751?-1780) British military officer, spy. Major in American Revolution. Sent by the British to negotiate with Benedict Arnold to betray the fortress on the Hudson River. Captured in New York trying to escape with information. Hanged as a spy at about age 29 in Tappan, New York. He wanted to die a soldier's death by firing squad rather than by hanging but his request was denied.

Different Last Words:

(1) "Must I die in this manner?"

Source: *The Literary Magazine and British Review,* Vol. 2, 1789.

(2) "It will be but a momentary pang." At the moment he was to die, he was asked if he wished to say more. He replied: "Nothing, but to request that you will witness to the world that I die like a brave man."

Source: *Pictorial History of America From the Earliest Times to the Close of the Mexican War, Embracing the Most Remarkable Events Which have Transpired Since the Discovery of America* by John Frost (Philadelphia, 1853).

Variation: "I pray you to bear me witness that I meet my fate like a brave man."

Source: *American History Stories,* Vol. II, by Mara L. Pratt (Chapel Hill, NC, 2007).

Variation: "All I request of you, gentleman, is that you will bear witness to the world that I die like a brave man." A moment later he said in a near whisper: "It will be but a momentary pang."

Source: "The execution of Major Andre." Letter dated March 20, 1834, from Benjamin Russell to Dr. James Thacker (*The New-England Magazine*, Vol. 6, 1834).

Variation (doubtful): "Remember that I die as becomes a British officer, while the manner of my death must reflect disgrace on your commander."

Source: *London General Evening Post,* November 14, 1780.

In *The Pictorial Field-book of the Revolution*, Lossing described the *London General Evening Post* article as a "pretended account" that was "abusive to Washington." He denied that André uttered any such sentiment.

Source: *The Pictorial Field-book of the Revolution; Or, Illustrations, by Pen and Pencil, of the History, Biography, Scenery, Relics, and Traditions of the War for Independence*, Vol. II, by Benson John Lossing (New York, 1852).

Andrew the Apostle, Saint

(d. 70?) Biblical figure, holy man. First Disciple of Jesus; brother of St. Peter. Said to have been crucified while preaching in Greece.

Different Last Words:

(1) "O cross, most welcome and long looked for; with a willing mind joyfully and desirously I come to thee, being the scholar of Him which did hang on thee; because I have been always thy lover, and have coveted to embrace thee."

Source: *Book of Martyrs and the Acts and Monuments of the Church* by John Fox (or Foxe). First published 1563, ed. by John Cumming (London, 1851).

(2) "Do thou, Jesu Christ, whom I have seen, whom I hold, whom I love, in whom I am and shall be, receive me in peace into thine everlasting tabernacles, that by my going out there may be an entering in unto

thee of many that are akin to me and that they may rest in thy majesty."
Source: "Acts of Andrew" in *An Introduction to the New Testament Apocrypha* by F. Lapham (London, 2003).

Andrew, James Osgood

(1794-1871) American prelate. One of the first bishops of the Methodist Episcopal Church, South. Served many years as minister in Georgia and the Carolinas. Died at age 76 in Mobile, Alabama. Andrew College in Cuthbert, Georgia, named for him.
Last Words: "God bless you all!"
Source: *The Life and Letters of James Osgood Andrew, with Glances at His Contemporaries and at Events in Church History* by Rev. George G. Smith (Nashville, TN, 1883).

Andrews, Eusebius

(d. 1650) English royalist, lawyer. Arraigned on charge of conspiring to destroy the government. Condemned to die. Executed at Tower Hill, London.
Last Words: "Lord Jesus, receive me!" Spoken on the scaffold before being beheaded
Source: *Dictionary of National Biography, from the Earliest Times to 1900* by Sir Leslie Stephen, George Smith and Sir Sidney Lee (London, 1921-1922).

Andrews, Roy Chapman

(1884-1960) American explorer, zoologist, writer. Director of American Museum of Natural History. Led expeditions in Southeast Asia, China, Burma, Mongolia, Alaska. World authority on whales. Notable books: *On the Trail of Ancient Man; Meet Your Ancestors; Beyond Adventure; The Amazing Planet.* His books helped popularize natural science. Died at age 76 of a heart attack in Carmel, California.
Last Words: "There's that pain again! I can feel it in my arm and in my head."
Source: *Washington Post,* March 12, 1960.

Andronicus I Comnenus, Eastern Roman Emperor

(1110?-1185) Byzantine ruler. Grandson of Alexius I. Captured Constantinople from Emperor Alexius II. Married widow of Alexius II. Had short reign, 1183-1185. Later overthrown and killed.
Last Words: "Oh, Lord, have mercy! Wherefore wilt thou break a bruised reed?"
Source: *Cambridge Medieval History,* Vol. IV; *The Byzantine Empire* by J.M. Hussey (Cambridge, England, 1966-1967).
Variation: "Lord, have mercy upon me. Wilt thou break a bruised reed?"
Source: *The Last Words (Real and Traditional) of Distinguished Men and Women Collected From Various Sources* by Frederic Rowland Marvin (New York, 1901).

Angélique, Mere, see **Arnauld, Jacqueline Marie.**

Anne of Austria, Queen and Regent of France

(1601-1666) European noblewoman. Daughter of Philip III of Spain. Queen consort of Louis XIII of France. Estranged from husband. Influenced by Cardinal Richelieu. When Louis XIII died, she acted as regent for her son Louis XIV. Retired to a convent where she died at age 64. She was a central character the novel *The Three Musketeers by* Dumas.
Last Words: "Monsieur de Montaigu, consider what I owe to God, the favor He has shown me, and the great indulgence for which I am beholden to Him." She looked at her hands once known for their beauty and said: "Observe how they are swelled; time to depart."
Source: *Anne d'Autriche* by Jean de La Varende (Paris, 1938).

Anne, Queen of Great Britain and Ireland

(1665-1714) British monarch. Second daughter of James II. Succeeded to throne in 1702, after the death of William III. Last Stuart sovereign. Had borne 17 children but only one survived infancy: William, Duke of Gloucester, who died at age 11. Act of Union with Scotland was enacted in 1707 during her reign, making her the first monarch of Great Britain and Ireland. Died at age 49 in Saint James Palace, London.
Different Last Words:
(1) "Use it for the good of my people." Spoken as she handed a symbolic staff of the Treasury to Lord Shrewsbury.
Source: *Anne of England. The Biography of a Great Queen* by M.R. Hopkinson (New York, 1934).
(2) (doubtful): "Oh my brother! Oh my poor brother!" Spoken repeatedly as she was dying. She was referring to her half-brother,

the Old Pretender, who was excluded from succession to the British throne because he was a Roman Catholic.

Source: *Agnes Strickland's Queens of England,* Vol. II, ed. by Rosalie Kaufman (Boston, 1894).

Justin McCarthy wrote that it was the sort of story that touched many hearts "but the whole statement rests on no clear and direct evidence claiming any serious consideration from the writer of history."

Source: *The Reign of Queen Anne*, Vol. II, by Justin McCarthy (London, 1902).

Annenberg, Moses ("Moe")

(1877-1942) American newspaper publisher. Imprisoned for tax evasion. In failing health, he died at age 65, a month after his release from prison.

Last Words: "Walter, who knows what is the scheme of things? My suffering has all been for the purpose of making you a man." He whispered his Last Words to his son.

Source: *Legacy: A Biography of Moses and Walter Annenberg* by Christopher Ogden (Boston, 1999).

Anselm, Saint

(1033-1109) English prelate, philosopher, writer, holy man. Archbishop of Canterbury. One of the earliest scholastic authors. Notable works: *Cur Deus Homo; De Veritate, Proslogion.* Died in Canterbury, England. Canonized in 1494. Declared Doctor of the Roman Catholic Church in 1720.

Last Words: "Yes, if it be His will, I shall obey it willingly. But were He to let me stay with you a little longer till I have resolved a problem about the origin of the soul, I would gladly accept the boon; for I do not know whether anyone will work it out when I am gone. If I could but eat, I think I should pick up a little strength. I feel no pain in any part of my body; only I cannot retain nourishment, and that exhausts me."

Source: *Life and Times of St. Anselm* by Martin Rule (London, 1883).

Variation: "And, indeed, if it be His will, I shall gladly obey it; but should He rather will that I remain with you yet so long a time as that I may solve a problem which I am turning over in my mind, as to the origin of the soul, I should welcome the delay, because I know not whether, when I am gone, there will be anyone left to solve it."

Spoken to one of the clergy who noticed his extreme weakness and commented that he was about to leave this world.

Source: *St. Anselm of Canterbury,* Vol. II, by James Macmullen Rigg (London, 1896).

Variation: "I shall gladly obey His call; yet I should also feel grateful if He would grant me a little longer time with you, and if I could be permitted to solve a question—the origin of the soul."

Source: *The Last Words (Real and Traditional) of Distinguished Men and Women Collected From Various Sources* by Frederic Rowland Marvin (New York, 1901).

Anselmi, Albert

(1883-1929) Italian-born American gangster. Organized crime murderer. Part of duo with John Scalise. Brought to America the Sicilian custom of rubbing a bullet with garlic assuming that if the bullet did not kill person, the garlic would cause gangrene. Also introduced "handshake hit"–shaking hand of the hit before killing him. Part of team that took out Dion O'Bannion. Questioned about St. Valentine's Day Massacre. Died at age 44. Killed along with Scalise and Joseph Giunta, by Al Capone with a baseball bat at a party before his trial.

Last Words: "Not me, Al. Honest to God. Jonnie. It was his idea. His and Joe's. Believe me, Al, I wouldn't—." Some Mafia historians note that the exact details may have been embellished to make Capone sound more fearsome. The story is widely reported and typically says Anselmi begged Capone for mercy and indicted his already beaten partners.

Source: *The Mafia Encyclopedia: From Accardo to Zwillman* by Carl Sifakis (New York, 1987).

Anthony, Susan Brownell

(1820-1906) American suffragist, social reformer. Active in temperance, women's suffrage, and anti-slavery movements. Founder and president of National Woman Suffrage Association. Died at age 86 of heart disease and pneumonia in Rochester, New York.

Last Words: "Make them." Spoken on her deathbed to a young woman she wanted to be her successor. The woman had expressed concern that she would not be allowed to take Anthony's place.

Source: *Susan B. Anthony: A Biography of a Singular Feminist* by Kathleen Barry (New York, 1988).

Anthony's Last Words are sometimes given as "Failure is impossible." She did speak these words, but they were not her last. She said them at a public gathering celebrating her 86th birthday in Washington, D.C., in 1906.

Source: *Life and Work of Susan B. Anthony* by Ida Husted Harper (Indianapolis, IN, 1908). The author was a close friend and collaborator of Anthony.

Anthony of Padua, Saint

(1195-1231) Portuguese-born Augustine monk, holy man. Became a Franciscan monk. Teacher of theology. Preached in southern France, northern Italy. Died at age 36 at Poor Clare convent on way to Padua. Canonized in 1232, one year after he died.

Last Words: "I see my God. He calls me to Him."

Source: "The Last Words of Great Men" by Rev. Thomas P. Hughes (*The Homiletic Review*, Vol. XLIV, December 1902).

Antonia, Mother

(1825-1872) American nun. Birth name Teresa Dreer. Second Superior of Convent and Academy of Sisters of St. Francis in Oldenburg, Indiana, Diocese of Vincennes. Sisters of St. Francis of the Third Order Regular oversaw 76 parochial schools and 10 academies. Later they founded Marian College. Mother Antonia died at age 46 in Oldenburg.

Last Words: "Pray! Trust in God, and do your duty!" Spoken to the weeping sisters gathered around her deathbed as she raised her eyes to a crucifix.

Sources: *History of the Catholic Church in the Diocese of Vincennes* by Herman Joseph Alerding (Indianapolis, IN, 1883); *Historical Sketch of the Convent and Academy of the Sisters of St. Francis in Oldenburg, Indiana* (Oldenburg, IN, 1901).

Antoninus Pius, Emperor of Rome

(86-161) Roman emperor. Succeeded Hadrian in 138. Full name Titus Aurelius Fulvus Boionius Arrius Antoninus. Adopted by Hadrian. Encouraged arts, sciences, social reform, political moderation during a peaceful reign. One of his daughters married Marcus Aurelius, his adopted son who became his successor.

Last Words: "Æquanimitas." (tr. "Tranquility.") His reply when asked the password.

Source: *Real-Encyclopädie der Classischen Altertumswissenschaft* by August Friedrich von Pauly and Georg Wissowa (Stuttgart, Germany, 1893).

Antony, Mark

(83?-30 B.C.) Roman triumvir, military officer. General under Julius Caesar. Grandson of Roman orator Marcus Antonius. Related to Julius Caesar on mother's side. One of Second Triumvirate. Cleopatra's lover. He was defeated by Octavian at Actium in 31 B.C. Killed himself rather than be captured and killed by his enemy. His romance with Cleopatra has been written about by several authors including Shakespeare, Plutarch and Dryden. Major movies such as *Antony and Cleopatra* (1973) and *Cleopatra* (1934 and 1963) also have told their story.

Different Last Words:

(1) "You must not pity me in this last turn of fate. You should rather be happy in the remembrance of our love, and in the recollection that of all men I was once the most famous and the most powerful, and now, at the end, have fallen not dishonorably, a Roman by a Roman vanquished." Spoken to Cleopatra.

Source: *The Life and Times of Marc Antony* by Arthur Weigall (New York, 1931).

(2) "It is well done, Eros, you show your master how to do what you had not the heart to do yourself." He took out his sword and committed suicide. Eros, his servant, had drawn his sword and stabbed himself.

Source: "Mark Antony" in *Lives of the Noble Grecians and Romans* by Plutarch, tr. by John Dryden (Chicago, 1952).

Antony, Saint

(250?-356) Egyptian monk, holy man. Founder of Christian monasticism. Spent 20 years living in solitude in the desert. Founded monastery in 305. As a very old man, he went to Alexandria to preach against the Arians. He then went home to the desert where he died at age 105.

Last Words: "I indeed go the way of the Fathers, as it is written—for I perceive that I am called by the Lord." And he asked them to give one of his sheepskins to Athanasius, and also the cloak which was under him, which had been a present from the bishop, even though it had grown old, he desired to return it to him. "And for the rest, children, farewell, for Antony is going, and is with you no more." Saying this, when they had embraced him, he stretched out his feet, and, as if he saw friends coming to him, grew joyful on their account (for, as he lay, his countenance was bright), he departed, and was gathered to his fathers.

Source: *The Life & Labours of S. Thomas of Aquin*, Vol. 2 by Roger Bede Vaughan (London, 1872), citing *Vita et Conversio S. P. N. Antonii*, n. 91 and *Pratolog Graec., Vol. XXVI.*

Variation: "And let my word be kept secret by you, so that no one knows the place but you alone. For in the resurrection of the dead I shall receive my body incorruptible once again from the Savior. Distribute my clothing. To Bishop Athanasius give the one sheepskin and the cloak on which I lie, which he gave to me new, but I have by now worn out. And to Bishop Serapion give the other sheepskin, and you keep the hair garment. And now God preserve you, children, for Antony is leaving and is with you no longer."

Source: *The Life of Antony and the Letter to Marcellinus* by Athanasius, tr. with introduction by Robert C. Gregg (Mahwah, NJ, 1980).

Apollonia, Saint

(d. 249) Egyptian deaconess, holy woman, martyr. Lived in Alexandria and was known for her holiness. Tortured by pulling her teeth out. Patron saint of dentistry. Executed when Roman Emperor Decius decreed the death of all Christians. She was given a choice: renounce her faith or be burned. She chose martyrdom.

Last Words (doubtful): "Take your hands off me and give me a little time to think it over." Spoken immediately before jumping into the fire.

Source: *Last Words: A Dictionary of Deathbed Quotations* by C. Bernard Ruffin (Jefferson, NC, 1995).

The story of Apollonia was first told in Eusebius's *Ecclesiastical History,* written in the early 300s, with no quotations. In the late 1200s, it was extended and retold in the *Golden Legend* by Jacobus de Voragine. It is from this version that later accounts filled in the dialog.

Sources: *The Ecclesiastical History of Eusebius Pamphilus, Bishop of Cesarea, in Palestine: in Ten Books*, tr. by Christian Frederic Cruse (Philadelphia, 1833); *The Golden Legend or Lives of the Saints.* Compiled by Jacobus de Voragine, Archbishop of Genoa, 1275, 1st ed., 1470. English ed. by William Caxton, 1483, ed. by F.S. Ellis (Edinburgh, 1900).

Appel, George

(1886-1928) American murderer. Killed in electric chair by executioner Robert G. Elliott, who also executed Sacco, Vanzetti, Bruno Hauptman and Ruth Snyder. Elliot kept a diary and detailed log of everyone he executed that was later turned into a book. Of Appel's execution on August 9, 1928, Elliot wrote: "He was one of the toughest men I ever saw to sit in the chair."

Last Words: "Well folks, you'll soon see a baked apple." (Sometimes quoted as "Well, folks, you are about to see a baked Appel.")

Source: *Agent of Death, Memoirs of an Executioner* by Robert Greene Elliott with Albert R. Beatty (New York, 1940).

Appleton, Jesse

(1772-1819) American clergyman, educator. President of Bowdoin College. Died at age 47 of a pulmonary infection in Brunswick, Maine.

Last Words: "Glory to God in the highest. The whole earth shall be filled with his glory." During his final hours, he prayed a great deal. He mingled these praises with his petitions.

Source: *Lectures Delivered at Bowdoin College and Occasional Sermons by Jesse Appleton, Late President of Bowdoin College* (Brunswick, ME, 1822).

Appleton, Samuel

(1766-1853) American businessman, philanthropist. Established cotton mills at Waltham and Lowell, Massachusetts. Funded Appleton Cabinet at Amherst College, Hitchcock Ichnological Cabinet and Appleton Chapel at Harvard University. Died at age 87 in Boston. Appleton, Wisconsin, named for him.

Last Words: "I will now try to sleep." Spoken to his wife.

Source: "Notice of Samuel Appleton, Esq." (*The New England Historical and Genealogical Register,* Vol. VIII, No. 1, January 1854).

Appleton, Thomas Gold

(1812-1884) American writer, poet, art

collector. Patron of arts who supported Boston Public Library and Museum of Fine Arts. Studied art in Florence. Lived in Rome, Paris. Known for his wit. Oscar Wilde used one of his remarks in his play *A Woman of No Importance*: "Good Americans when they die, go to Paris." Became a Unitarian. Died at age 72 of pneumonia in New York City.

Last Words: "How interesting this all is!"

Source: *Cambridge Sketches* by Frank Preston Stearns (Philadelphia, 1905).

Aquinas, Saint Thomas

(1225?-1274) Italian clergyman, philosopher, hymnist, holy man. Dominican theologian. One of the greatest scholastic thinkers and writers. Lectured in Rome, Paris, Cologne. Had great influence on Roman Catholic Church. Notable work: *Summa theologica*. Thomistic philosophy was named for him. Wrote eucharistic hymns, including "Pange lingua." Pope Gregory summoned him to defend the papacy at Lyons while he was suffering from a fever. Died at about age 49 at an abbey on the way. Canonized in 1323. Made Doctor of Church in 1567.

Last Words: "I receive Thee, redeeming the price of my soul. Out of love for Thee have I studied, watched through many nights, and exerted myself. Thee did I preach and teach. I have never said aught against Thee. Nor do I persist stubbornly in my views. If I have ever expressed myself erroneously on this Sacrament, I submit to the judgment of the holy Roman Church, in the obedience of which I now part from this world." Spoken while receiving the Eucharist.

Source: *The Life & Labours of S. Thomas of Aquin*, Vol. 2 by Roger Bede Vaughan (London, 1872) citing Tocco, *Boll.*, Cap. X., n. 59.—[*Ystoria Sancti Thome de Aquino* de Guillaume de Tocco (1323)].

Arago, Dominique François Jean

(1786-1853) French physicist, statesman. Worked in astronomy, optics, electromagnetism. Member of French Academy of Sciences. Active in 1830 July Revolution. Died at age 67 in Paris.

Last Words: "I intend to resign my situation of perpetual secretary to the Academy, since I can no longer discharge its duties." Spoken to Jean-Baptiste Biot, an associate of Arago at the Academy.

Source: *Ouvres complétes de François Arago,* ed. by J.A. Barral (Paris, 1854-1862).

Aram, Eugene

(1704-1759) English schoolmaster, murderer. Conducted own defense claiming evidence against him was circumstantial. Confessed after his conviction. Executed at about age 55 in York, England. His story inspired *Eugene Aram* (novel) by Bulwer Lytton and *The Dream of Eugene Aram* (ballad) by Thomas Hood.

Last Word: "No." His reply on the scaffold when asked if he had anything to say.

Source: *The Trial and Life of Eugene Aram; Several of His Letters and Poems; and His Plan and Specimens of an Anglo-Celtic Lexicon; with Copious Notes and Illustrations, and an Engraved Facsimile of the Handwriting of This Very Ingenious but Ill-fated Scholar* (Richmond, VA, 1832).

Aratus

(271-213 B.C.) Greek military officer. General. Son of Clinias. Slowly poisoned by Taurion with toxin that was not strong and violent. It caused fever, dull cough and gradually death. Died at Aegium, Greece.

Last Words: "These, O Cephalon, are the wages of a king's love." Spoken when a friend saw him spitting blood.

Source: "Aratus" in *Lives of the Noble Grecians and Romans* by Plutarch, tr. by John Dryden (Chicago, 1952).

Archer, Thomas

(1653-1685) Scottish clergyman, Covenanter, martyr. Made a final statement on the scaffold at his execution in Edinburgh.

Last Words: "Fear of death does not fright or trouble me: I bless the Lord for my lot." Following this he sung the 73rd Psalm from the 24th verse to the end.

Source: *The Scots Worthies: Containing a Brief Historical Account of the Most Eminent Noblemen, Gentlemen, Ministers, and Others, Who Testified or Suffered for the Cause of Reformation in Scotland: From the Beginning of The Sixteenth Century to the Year 1688* by John Howie (Glasgow, Scotland, 1829).

Archimedes of Syracuse

(287?-212 B.C.) Greek mathematician, philosopher, inventor. Originated Archimedes Principle in physics. Was in the marketplace studying some figures he made in the sand.

Killed at age 75 in Syracuse by a Roman soldier who did not know who he was.

Different Last Words:

(1) "Noli turbare circulos meos." (tr. "Do not disturb my circles.") A common translation of what Archimedes supposedly said.

Source: *The German Classics of the Nineteenth and Twentieth Centuries: Masterpieces of German Literature* by Kuno Francke, William Howard Guild and Isidore Singer (New York, 1913).

Variation: "Noli, obsecro, istum disturbare." (tr. "Please do not disturb this.") Latin phrase came from Valerius Maximus. A slightly different wording is given by Porfirius.

Source: *Brewer's Famous Quotations: 5000 Quotations and the Stories Behind Them* by Nigel Rees (London, 2006).

Variation: "Stand away, fellow, from my diagram." Spoken to the Roman soldier who then killed him.

Source: *The Works of Archimedes* tr. by Sir Thomas Heath (London, 1920).

Variation: "Wait until I have finished my problem." Spoken to a Roman soldier who had ordered him to follow him.

Source: *Last Words of Saints and Sinners: 700 Final Quotes from the Famous, the Infamous, and the Inspiring Figures in History* by Herbert Lockyer (Grand Rapids, MI, 1969).

Aretino, Pietro

(1492-1556) Italian writer, poet. satirist, playwright. Known as the Scourge of Princes for the power of his writing. His six volumes of letters offer lively descriptions of his 16th-century world. Patrons were Francis I of France and Emperor Charles V. His portrait was painted by Titian. Died at age 64 in Venice.

Last Words: "Keep the rats away now that I am all greased up." Believed to have been spoken after he received the Last Rites.

Source: *Aretino: Scourge of Princes* by Thomas C. Chubb (New York, 1940).

Ariosto, Ludovico

(1474-1533) Italian poet, playwright. Notable works: *Orlando Furioso* (epic poem); *La Cassaria; La Lena* (plays). Died at age 58 of tuberculosis in Ferrara. Named by Longfellow as one of the Immortal Four of Italy (along with Dante, Petrarch and Tasso).

Last Words: "This is not my home."

Source: *The Last Words (Real and Traditional) of Distinguished Men and Women Collected from Various Sources* by Frederic Rowland Marvin (New York, 1901).

Armistead, Lewis Addison

(1817-1863) American military officer. Confederate brigadier general who fought in Pickett's division at the Battle of Gettysburg in the U.S. Civil War. As his men reached the Union position on Cemetery Ridge, he placed his hat on his sword and held it high for his men to see and follow. Died at age 46 at Gettysburg.

Different Last Words:

(1) "Say to General Hancock for me that I have done him and you all a grievous injury which I shall always regret." His words were intended for his close friend, General Winfield Scott Hancock.

Sources: "Armistead, Lewis A." by Amy J. Kinsel in *Encyclopedia of American History: Civil War and Reconstruction, 1856 to 1869,* ed. by Joan Waugh and Gary B. Nash (New York, 2003); *Winfield Scott Hancock* by David M. Jordan (Bloomington, IN, 1988).

(2) "Give them the cold steel, boys."

Source: *The United States* by Karl Baedeker (Leipzig, Germany, 1909).

Variation: "Come on boys. Give them the cold steel!"

Source: *None Died in Vain* by Robert Leckie (New York, 1990).

Armour, Philip Danforth

(1832-1901) American businessman, philanthropist. Meat-packing innovator, organizer. Formed Armour & Co. Donated money to found Armour Institute of Technology. Died at age 68 of pneumonia in Chicago. Armour, South Dakota, was named for him.

Last Words: "I am not afraid to die."

Source: *Philip Danforth Armour* by Harper Leech and John C. Carroll (New York, 1938).

Armstrong, Herbert Rowse

(1870-1922) British lawyer, military officer. Major in Royal Engineers. Solicitor of Hay. Arrested when a guest in his house was poisoned with arsenic. Arsenic was found in Armstrong's possession. His wife's body was exhumed and found to contain arsenic. He claimed she was a suicide. He made no confession and denied his guilt. Executed at age 53 by hanging for the murder of his wife. When he was hanged, he had the dubious distinction of being the only solicitor so executed in modern times.

Last Words: "I am coming, Katie!" Called out to his dead wife.

Source: *A History of Capital Punishment* by John Laurence (New York, 1960).

Arnauld, Jacqueline Marie (Mere Angélique)

(1591-1661) French nun. One of 20 children of French lawyer Antoine Arnauld. Marie Angélique de Sainte Madeleine. Abbess of Port Royal, Paris, where she died.

Different Last Words:

(1) "Jesus, oh Jesus, you are my God, my justice, my strength, my all."

Source: *Angelique Arnauld, Abbess of Port-Royal* by Frances Martin (London, 1873).

(2) "How human you are still!" Spoken to the weeping nuns who were with her when she died.

Source: *The Nuns of Port Royal* by Mary E. Lowndes (London, 1909).

Arnaz, Desi

(1917-1986) Cuban-born American musician, actor, television producer. Star of stage, screen and television. Birth name Desiderio Alberto Arnaz y de Acha III. Creator of *I Love Lucy* situation comedy. Died at age 69 of lung cancer in Del Mar, California.

Last Words: "I love you too, honey. Good luck with your show." Spoken on the phone to his former wife Lucille Ball. His daughter Lucie held the phone while he said his Last Words to her mother.

Source: *Desilu: The Story of Lucille Ball and Desi Arnaz* by Coyne Steven Sanders and Thomas Gilbert (New York, 1993).

Arndt, Johann

(1555-1621) German clergyman, theologian. Lutheran. Notable devotional book: *Vom wahren Christentum (True Christianity)*. His works influenced the Protestant world and were among the most widely used in Mennonite communities in Germany, Switzerland and Canada.

Last Words: "Now I have overcome." Spoken to his wife just before he died.

Source: *Pious Memorials, Or, The Power of Religion Upon the Mind in Sickness and at Death* by Richard Burnham and James Hervey (London, 1754).

Arnold, Benedict

(1741-1801) American military officer, trai-

tor. When he was passed over for promotion during the American Revolution, he negotiated with British Major John André to surrender to the British West Point, an American fort on the Hudson River. Eventually he joined the British. Died at age 60 in disgrace in London.

Last Words: "Let me die in the old uniform in which I fought my battles for freedom. May God forgive me for putting on any other." He wanted to wear his old Continental Army uniform.

Source: *Benedict Arnold: Military Racketeer* by Edward Dean Sullivan (New York, 1932).

Arnold, Thomas

(1795-1842) English educator, historian. Father of poet Matthew Arnold. Headmaster of Rugby School. Influenced development of modern public school system in England. Professor of modern history at Oxford. Died suddenly at age 46 of angina pectoris at Rugby, Warwickshire.

Last Words: "Ah, very well."

Source: *The Life and Correspondence of Thomas Arnold* by Arthur Penrhyn Stanley (New York, 1910). The author was one of his pupils.

Arnould, Madeleine Sophie

(1744-1802) French operatic singer, actress. Made her debut at Paris Opera when she was 17. First singer to perform the title role in Gluck's *Iphigénie*. Known for her wit as well as her singing. Her witty remarks were published in the book *Arnouldiana*. Died at age 58 in Paris.

Last Words: "Ah! c'etait le bon temps! J'etait si malheureuse." (tr. "Ah! The times were good! It was I who was so unhappy.") Her response to her priest who asked her how much she had suffered.

Source: *History of the Opera: from Monteverdi to Donizetti* by Henry Sutherland Edwards (London, 1862).

Arouet, François-Marie, see **Voltaire.**

Arsentiev, Francys

(1958-1998) American mountain climber. She and her husband Sergui were attempting to reach Everest's summit from its dangerous North Face without breathing equipment. No woman had ever successfully completed that challenge, and about one in six climbers who attempt it die. Both

Francys and Sergui reached the summit but died in their descent. Before she died at age 40, Francys was spotted by British climber Ian Woodhall and his wife Cathy O'Dowd, who abandoned their own ascent in an attempt to rescue her.

Last Words: "I'm an American. Please don't leave me." Spoken to Woodhall, who was having difficulty moving her. Woodhall was forced to abandon his rescue mission and leave her to die on Mount Everest. His own climbing partner was suffering and on the verge of freezing to death. Sergui's body was found in 1999. Woodhall recovered Francys's body in June 2007.

Source: "I Left a Woman to Die on Everest. I Had to Go Back to Bury Her; Brit Climber Haunted by Failed Rescue Bid" by Samantha Wostear (*The* [London] *Sun*, June 18, 2007).

Artagerses

(d. 402 B.C.) Cadusian leader. Follower of Artaxerxes II. Galloped up to Cyrus and tossed his javelin at him but Cyrus's armor repelled it. Cyrus then threw his weapon at Artagerses, hit his neck and killed him.

Last Words: "O most unjust and senseless of men, who are the disgrace of the honored name of Cyrus, are you come here leading the wicked Greeks on a wicked journey, to plunder the good things of the Persians, and this with the intent of slaying your lord and brother, the master of ten thousand times ten thousand servants that are better men than you? As you shall see this instant; for you shall lose your head here, before you look upon the face of the king."

Source: "Artaxerxes" in *Lives of the Noble Grecians and Romans* by Plutarch, tr. by John Dryden (Chicago, 1952).

Arvers, Alexis-Félix

(1806-1850) French writer, poet, playwright. Known for one poem, "Un secret" written when he was 25. Died at age 44 in Paris.

Last Words: "Ah! Coquereau, I forgot to mention one of the greatest faults of my life. I have spoken badly of Charles X!" Spoken to his confessor.

Source: *Poésies. mes heures perdues,* ed. by Abel d'Avrecourt (Paris, 1900).

Asano, Naganori (Takumi no Kami)

(1667-1701) Japanese ruler. Daimyo of Akō.

Attempted to assassinate protocol officer Kira Yoshinaka while on bad terms with him. Asano was forced to commit suicide after he failed to kill Kira. His 47 loyal retainers sought revenge for his death. After they killed Kira, they committed hara-kiri (ritual suicide). Asano's story is a popular theme of kabuki and bunraku plays and Japanese movies and literature. His Last Words were a death poem he composed for his seppuku (hara-kiri) at age 33.

Last Words:
"I wish I could enjoy /
the rest of Spring /
as the cherry blossoms are yet in bloom /
in spite of the spring breeze /
which is attempting to blow off all their petals."

Source: *Jisei no kotoba* by Susumu Nakanishi (Tokyo, 1986).

Ascham, Roger

(1516?-1568) English classical scholar, writer, humanist. Notable work: *The Scholemaster* (1563; treatise on classical education written in the vernacular). Tutor and later secretary to Elizabeth I.

Last Words: "I desire to die and be with Christ."

Source: *Disertissimi viri Rogeri Aschami…familiarum epistolarum* (London, 1576).

Ashby, Turner

(1828-1862) American military officer. Confederate brigadier general in U.S. Civil War. Thomas J. ("Stonewall") Jackson's cavalry commander in Shenandoah Valley. Killed at age 33 at Harrisonburg, Virginia, early in the war. Turner Ashby High School in Bridgewater, Virginia, was named for him.

Different Last Words:

(1) "Charge Men! For God's sake charge!" After he spoke these words, he waved his sword then was hit in the chest with a musket bullet and killed.

Source: *Life and Campaigns of Lieut.-Gen. Thomas J. Jackson (Stonewall Jackson)* by Robert Lewis Dabney (New York, 1866).

(2) "Forward my brave men!" When his horse was shot and fell, Ashby rushed forward on foot, shouting these words. He took about six steps then fell over dead, shot in

the heart with a musket ball.

Source: *Life of Turner Ashby* by Thomas Almond Ashby (New York, 1914). The author was Turner's cousin.

Askew, Anne

(1521?-1546) English poet, martyr. Refused to renounce her Protestant faith. Forced into marriage. Religious differences drove them apart. Tried to divorce her husband. Left home and lived with her brother. Husband had her put in Newgate Prison on suspicion of heresy. Transferred to Tower of London. Tortured so much she could not walk to her execution. Woodcut in Foxe shows her being burned at the stake. First-hand account of her ordeal and beliefs were published as *Examinations.* She gained fame after death for her tenacity in holding onto her beliefs.

Last Words: "I come not here to deny my Lord and Master."

Source: *Book of Martyrs and the Acts and Monuments of the Church* by John Fox (or Foxe). First published 1563, ed. by John Cumming (London, 1851).

Asplund, Carl Oscar Vilhelm Gustafsson

(1871-1912) Swedish-born American farmer. Victim of the *Titanic* disaster. The Asplund family was traveling from Sweden to Worcester, Massachusetts. Selma Asplund and her youngest children Lillian and Edvin were lowered into a lifeboat. Carl Asplund and three of his sons went down with the ship. Lillian was the last living American survivor when she died at age 99 in 2006. For most of her life she shunned media attention and would not discuss that night. Her mother thought it was not right to talk about the tragedy. However, Selma Asplund did give one interview in 1912 to the *Worcester Telegram & Gazette* in which she explained her escape from the ship and her husband's Last Words to the family. The family's separation led to incorrect early reports that other family members survived, but they proved false.

Last Words: "Go ahead, we will get into one of the other boats."

Source: "Final American survivor of Titanic disaster dies" (*USA Today*, May 7, 2006).

Assad, Hafez (Al-Assad)

(1930-2000) Syrian leader. President of Syrian Arabic Republic. Credited with stabilizing rule and consolidation of power of Syria's central government after decades of coups and counter-coups. Died at age 69 of heart attack in Damascus.

Last Words: "Our destiny is to build a better future for our countries, a safe future for our children. We have to give them something better than we inherited." Spoken to Emile Lahoud, Lebanon's president.

Source: "Our Destiny Is to Build a Better Future for Our Countries, a Safe Future for Our Children" by Don Mills (*National* [Ontario] *Post*, June 12, 2000).

Aste, Marcello

(1657-1709) Italian nobleman, prelate. Apostolic nuncio to Switzerland, Germany. Archbishop of Ancona. Created cardinal priest in 1699. When he was taken ill, doctors sent him to a Dominican convent in Bologna where he died at about age 51.

Last Words: "I wish to die sitting, in tribute to the most worshipful will of my good and precious Jesus."

Source: *Ristretto della vita di Marcello Cardinal d'Aste Romano Vescovo d'Ancona* by Lodovico Maria Pandolfini (Rome, 1711).

Astor, John Jacob, I

(1763-1848) German-born American businessman, financer, fur trader. Established Astoria, Oregon, as a trading post. Invested in New York real estate. Richest man in U.S. with fortune of $20 million when he died at age 84 in New York City.

Last Words: "There, I told you that she would pay it if you went the right way to work with her." Spoken when Astor received an overdue rent payment. During his final days, he was concerned that a tenant owed him rent and that he must get it from her. The tenant was broke, so Astor's son paid the woman's rent and said the money came from her.

Source: *Life of John Jacob Astor* by James Parton (New York, 1865).

Astor, John Jacob, IV

(1864-1912) American businessman. Great-grandson of John Jacob Astor I. Served in the Spanish-American War. Victim of *Titanic* disaster. His pregnant wife Madeline survived. Eyewitness reported that Astor grabbed onto the sides of a raft. When his feet and hands froze he let go and drowned at age 47.

Different Last Words:

(1) "The ladies have to go first—Get into the lifeboat to please me—Good-bye, dearie. I'll see you later." Spoken to his wife Madeline.

Source: *They Went That-a-Way. How the Famous, the Infamous and the Great Died* by Malcolm Forbes with Jeff Bloch (New York, 1988).

(2) "With pleasure." Spoken to K. Whiteman, ship's barber, last survivor to speak to Astor. Whiteman was standing beside Astor on the passenger deck, helping women into the boats. He told Astor he was going to jump overboard and take a chance by swimming out and being picked up by one of the boats. He warned Astor that he "better come along." Astor replied: "No, thank you, I think I'll have to stick." Whiteman asked Astor if he would mind shaking hands with him. Astor said "With pleasure" then gave him a hearty handshake before Whiteman jumped into the water. Whiteman was picked up four hours later by a lifeboat. Astor eventually slipped into the water and died of the cold.

Source: *Sinking of the Titanic and Great Sea Disasters* by Logan Marshall (Philadelphia, 1912).

Astor, Nancy Witcher Langhorne

(1879-1964) American-born English socialite, politician. Known for quick wit. Married William Waldorf, 2nd Viscount Astor. Succeeded him as member of Parliament when he succeeded to the peerage in 1919. First woman to sit in the House of Commons. Surrendered her seat in 1945 at age 65. Died at age 84 at daughter's home Grimsthorpe, Lincolnshire. During a final illness, she woke briefly and found all her family around her bedside.

Last Words: "Jakie, is it my birthday or am I dying?" Spoken to her son.

Source: *Nancy Astor: A Lady Unashamed* by John Grigg (Boston, 1980).

Astor, William Backhouse

(1792-1875) American businessman. Son of John Jacob Astor. Richest man in America in 1848 when his father died. Managed and greatly enlarged family's real estate holdings. Built Astor Library. Known as the Landlord of New York. Died at age 83 in New York City.

Last Words: "I might have lived another year if I had not caught this cold, but I am satisfied to go now. I am eighty-four years old—long past the allotted time of man—and at my age, life becomes a burden."

Source: *The Astors* by Harvey O'Connor (New York, 1941).

Astros, Paul-Thérèse-David d'

(1772-1851) French prelate, writer. Assisted with formulation of Concordat of 1801. Imprisoned after being accused of excommunicating Napoleon. Appointed Roman Catholic archbishop of Toulouse. Elevated to cardinal in 1850 but died at age 78 in Toulouse before receiving his title.

Last Words: "Neither life nor death, nor any being can separate us from Him."

Source: *Vie du Cardinal d'Astros* by R.P. Caussette (Paris, 1853).

Atahualpa or Atabalipa

(1500?-1533) Inca emperor of Peru. Last ruler of the Incas. Accused of plotting against Spanish conquistador Pizarro and his men. Tried and executed. Burned at the stake at about age 33 by Pizarro.

Last Words: "What have I done, or my children, that I should meet such a fate? And from your hands, too, you who have met with friendship and kindness from my people who have received nothing but benefits from my hands."

Source: *The Power of Gold: The History of an Obsession* by Peter L. Bernstein (New York, 2000).

Atatürk, Mustafa Kemal

(1881-1938) Turkish statesman, military officer. Founder and first president of Republic of Turkey. Notable military career before and during World War I. After the war, he became active in the national resistance movement beginning as general inspector to oversee demobilization of Ottoman military units and Nationalist organizations. Became increasingly involved in independence movement—the Turkish War of Independence that ended with the Treaty of Lausanne and recognized the new nation's independence in 1923. He succeeded in abolishing the Caliphate and separating church and state as well as bringing about cultural changes. Died at age 57 in Istanbul.

Last Words: "What time is it?" Spoken to his doctors.

Source: *Ghost on Horseback: The Incredible Ataturk* by Ray Brock (New York, 1954).

Atcheson, George C., Jr.

(1896-1947) American diplomat, government official. Diplomatic aide to General Douglas MacArthur. Army plane he and 12 others were on en route from Tokyo to Washington, D.C., sank after making an emergency landing in rough seas west of Honolulu.

Last Words: "Well, it can't be helped." One of the survivors said that as the plane fell, Atcheson shrugged his shoulders, shook his head sadly and spoke these words.

Source: "Religion: Exit Lines" (*Time* magazine, January 17, 1955).

Athanasios Diakos or
Athanasios the Deacon

(1788-1821) Greek military officer, martyr. Commander during Greek War of Independence. Birth name Athanasios Nikolaos Massavetas. Became monk. Ordained Greek Orthodox deacon. Altercation with Ottoman pasha forced him to flee to nearby mountains where he became a klepht (guerrilla). He assumed the pseudonym Diakos (Deacon). Served as a mercenary. Formed his own band of klephts. Fought at the Battle of Alamana. Captured by Turks. Killed when he refused to join Ottoman army. His barbaric death at age 33 by impalement and burning made him a martyr to the cause of Greek freedom.

Last Words: "I was born a Greek, I shall die a Greek."

Source: *The Flame of Freedom. The Greek War of Independence 1821-1833* by David Brewer (Stamford, CT, 2001).

Atticus, Titus Pomponius

(109-32 B.C.) Roman philosopher, writer. Epicurean. Born in Rome. Educated with Cicero. Original name Titus Pomponius. Added Atticus when he moved to Athens to escape the civil war. When he became ill in 32 B.C., he believed his condition was incurable and starved himself to death. Died at age 77 in Athens. Although none of his writings remain, biographical material about him survives, including a work by Cornelius

Nepos and Cicero's *Letters to Atticus.*

Last Words: "How much care and diligence I have employed to restore my health on this occasion, there is no necessity for me to state at length, since I have yourselves as witnesses; and since I have, as I hope, satisfied you, that I have left nothing undone that seemed likely to cure me, it remains that I consult for myself. Of this feeling on my part I have no wish that you should be ignorant; for I have determined on ceasing to feed the disease; as, by the food and drink that I have taken during the last few days, I have prolonged life only so as to increase my pains, without hope of recovery. I therefore entreat you, in the first place to give your approbation of my resolution, and in the next, not to labor in vain by endeavoring to dissuade me from executing it."

Source: *Justin, Cornelius Nepos, and Eutropius* by John Selby Watson, Marcus Junianus Justinus, Cornelius Nepos and Eutropius (London, 1876).

Attlee, Clement Richard, 1st Earl Attlee and Viscount Prestwood

(1883-1967) British lawyer, politician, statesman, writer. Leader of the British Labour party. Served as prime minister after World War II. Notable works: *The Social Worker; The Labour Party in Perspective; A Prime Minister Remembers; As It Happened.* Created 1st Earl Attlee and Viscount Prestwood. Died at age 84 in London.

Last Words: "Hullo, Griff. How are you getting on?" Spoken to his aide Charlie Griffiths.

Source: *Attlee* by Kenneth Harris (New York, 1982).

Aubigné, Théodore Agrippa d'

(1552-1630) French Huguenot commander, writer, poet. Notable work: *Les Tragiques.* Served under Condé and Henry of Navarre. Went into exile in Switzerland when Henry was assassinated. Died at age 78 in Geneva.

Last Words: "It comes at last, the happy day: Let thanks be given to God in heaven, while we learn pleasure in His way."

Source: *Agrippa d'Aubigné* by S. Rocheblave (Paris, 1910).

Aubry (or Aubrey or Auberry), François (or Francis) Xavier ("F.X.")

(1824-1854) French Canadian-born American rider, trader, frontiersman. Set a series of horse and mule riding records in 1848 that made him a national hero. Made fastest trip ever (136 hours) from Independence, Missouri, to Santa Fe over the Santa Fe Trail by foot and horseback and won $1,000. He met his end in a saloon fight when Aubry misfired his gun and Richard H. Weightman stabbed him with a Bowie knife. He died at age 29 on the floor of the saloon. A cutoff on the Santa Fe Trail, an Army fort and a Kansas town were named for him.

Last Words: "Let me bleed."

Source: "A Forgotten Man Endowed with True Grit Set a Land Speed Record in 1848" by Bill Gilbert (*Sports Illustrated*, December 10, 1979).

Audebert, Ann

(1502?-1549) French matron, martyr. Burned at the stake in Paris at about age 47. When the rope was fastened around her waist, she called it her wedding girdle as she would be married to Christ.

Last Words: "I was once married to a man on Saturday, and now I shall be married to God on the same day of the week." Spoken as she suffered a gruesome death.

Source: *Book of Martyrs and the Acts and Monuments of the Church* by John Fox (or Foxe). First published 1563, ed. by John Cumming (London, 1851).

Audubon, John James

(1785-1851) Haitian-born American ornithologist, artist. Emigrated to U.S. in 1803. Notable work: *Birds of America*, which gained for him acclaim as a leading naturalist. Eyesight began to fail when he was 60. Mental facilities also faded. Died at age 66 at his home Minnie's Land in New York. Sons and a friend helped finish his work. Mount in Colorado, mountain in Alaska, county in Iowa and towns in Iowa, New Jersey and Pennsylvania named for him.

Last Words: "Yes, yes, Billy! You go down that side on Long Pond, and I'll go this side, and we'll get the ducks." His response to his friend William Bakewell. He never spoke again.

Source: *John James Audubon* by Alice Ford (Norman, OK, 1964).

Augustine, Saint

(354-430) Numidian-born theologian, philosopher, holy man, writer. Son of Patricius,

a Roman official, and Monica, a Christian. Converted to Christianity in 386. Lived in Carthage, Rome, Milan. Bishop of Hippo. Doctor of the Church. Notable works: *The City of God; Confessions* (description of his conversion). Fell ill with fever, in Hippo during attack by Vandals. Died at age 76.

Last Words: "O Lord, shall I die at all? Shall I die at all? Yes. Why, then, oh Lord, if ever, why not now? O! why not now? But thy will be done. Come, Lord Jesus."

Source: *The Last Witness, or The Dying Sayings of Eminent Christians and Noted Infidels* by Osmond Cleander Baker (New York, 1869).

Augustus, Gaius Julius Caesar Octavianus, Emperor of Rome

(63 B.C.-14 A.D.) Roman ruler. First emperor of Roman Empire. Born Gaius Octavius. Gained name Gaius Julius Caesar Octavianus when he was adopted by Caesar. "Augustus" was added later to recognize his position and service. Greatly expanded Roman Empire in central and northern Europe. Beautified city of Rome. Died at age 77 in Nola, Italy.

Different Last Words:

(1) "Acta est fabula plaudite." (tr. "The drama is over." Attributed. Phrase traditionally spoken at the end of Roman plays.

Source: *Chambers Biographical Dictionary* (Edinburgh, 1997).

Variation: "Vos plaudite." (tr. "You applaud.") Spoken after being commended on how he played his part in life."

Source: "Dying Words of Noted Persons" in *Miscellaneous Notes and Queries with Answers in All Departments of Literature*, Vol. II (Manchester, NH, 1885).

(2) "Livia! live mindful of our union; and now farewell." Spoken to his wife.

Source: "The Emperor Augustus" in *The Lives of the Twelve Caesars* by C. Suetonius Tranquillus, tr. by Alexander Thomson, revised by Thomas Forester (London, 1901).

Aurangzeb or Aurungzebe, Emperor of Hindustan

(1618-1707) Mogul ruler. Son of Shah Jahan. Emperor of Hindustan. Under his reign Mogul empire reached its greatest power. Known as the Great Mogul. Assumed title Alamgir (Conqueror of the World). Died at age 88 in Ahmednagar, India.

Last Words (written): "The agonies of death

come fast upon me. I am going. Whatever good or evil I have done, it was for you. No one has seen the departure of his own soul; but I know that mine is departing." Written in a letter to his favorite son.
Source: *The Art of Dying: An Anthology*, ed. by Francis Birrell and F. L. Lucas (London, 1930).
Variation (written): "Wherever I look I see nothing but the Divinity.—I have committed numerous crimes and I know not with what punishments I may be seized.—The agonies of death come upon me fast.—I am going. Whatever good or evil I have done, it was for you." Letter to his youngest and favorite son.
Source: *The History of India: The Hindu and Mahometan Periods* by Hon. Mountstuart Elphinstone, Edward Byles Cowell (London, 1866).
Variation (written): "Soul of my soul.—Now I am going alone. I grieve for your helplessness. But what is the use? Every torment I have inflicted, every sin I have committed, every wrong I have done, I carry the consequence with me. Strange that I came with nothing into the world, and now go away with this stupendous caravan of sin! Wherever I look I see only God.—I have greatly sinned, and I know not what torment awaits me. Let not Muslims be slain and the reproach fall upon my useless head. I commit you and your sons to God's care, and bid you farewell. I am sorely troubled. Your sick mother Udaipuri would fain die with me.—Peace!" Letter written to his favorite son, Kam Bakhsh.
Source: *History of India*, Vol. IV, ed. by A.V. Williams Jackson (London, 1907).

Aurelius, Quintus
(fl. c. 1st century B.C.) Roman citizen. Wealthy farmer who discovered he was on Sulla's proscribed list when he checked it in the Forum.
Last Words: "Woe is me, my Alban farm has informed against me!"
Source: "Sulla" in *Lives of the Noble Grecians and Romans* by Plutarch, tr. by John Dryden (Chicago, 1952).

Aurthur, Jonathan B.
(1948-2004) American writer. His son Charley Aurthur committed suicide in 1996 by leaping onto the Santa Monica Freeway. After his son's death, Jonathan quit his job

and wrote *The Angel and the Dragon: A Father's Search for Answers to His Son's Mental Illness and Suicide* to help other parents of troubled teens. Two years later, Jonathan Aurthur committed suicide at age 56 in Angeles National Forest by jumping to his death. A suicide note was found inside his automobile.
Last Words (written): "I jumped near the entrance to the dam."
Source: "Jonathan Aurthur, 56, Wrote Book on Son's Suicide, Later Took Own Life" (*Los Angeles Times*, December 11, 2004).

Austen, Jane
(1775-1817) English writer, novelist. Notable works: *Emma; Mansfield Park; Northanger Abbey; Persuasion; Pride and Prejudice; Sense and Sensibility.* Ill for several months. In final days, was totally incapacitated with condition later diagnosed as Addison's disease. Died at age 41 in Winchester, England.
Last Words: "I want nothing but death." Spoken to her sister Cassandra who asked if there was anything she wanted. Some of her other final words were: "God grant me patience, pray for me, oh, pray for me!"
Source: Letter from Cassandra Austen to her niece Fannie Knight after the death of her sister Jane, July 18, 1817. *Letters of Jane Austen* by Jane Austen (London, 1884).

Austin, Samuel
(1760-1830) American clergyman, educator. "New-Light" Congregational disciple of Jonathan Edwards. President of University of Vermont. Died at age 70 in Glastonbury, Connecticut.
Last Words: "Blessed Jesus, sanctify me wholly." After speaking these words, he said he was drowsy, then fell asleep and died.
Source: "Samuel Austin, D.D. 1784-1830" by William Buell Sprague in *Annals of the American Pulpit: Or, Commemorative Notices of Distinguished American Clergymen of Various Denominations from the Early Settlement of this Country to the Close of the Year Eighteen Fifty-five with Historical Introductions*, Vol. II (New York, 1857).

Austin, Stephen Fuller
(1793-1836) American frontiersman, statesman. Established colony in Texas in 1821. Founder of Republic of Texas. Secretary of state of Republic of Texas. Died at

age 43 of pneumonia in Columbia, Texas. City of Austin and Austin County, Texas, were named for him.

Last Words: "Texas recognized! Archer told me so. Did you see it in the papers?"

Source: *The Life of Stephen F. Austin* by Eugene C. Barker (Nashville, TN, 1925).

Austin, Tom

(d. 1694) British murderer, thief. Brutally killed his wife, aunt and his five (some accounts say seven) children before being stopped by his uncle. When he was executed in 1694, notes reprinted in *The Newgate Calendar* listed him as "Highwayman, guilty of unparalleled butchery."

Last Words: "Nothing, only there's a woman yonder with some curds and whey, and I wish I could have a penny-worth of them before I am hanged, because I don't know when I shall see any again." His response when asked if he had anything he wished to say before he died.

Source: "A Most Extraordinary and Diabolical Murderer" in *The Terrific Register: Or, Record of Crimes, Judgments, Providences, and Calamities*, Vol. 1 (London, 1825).

Avaroa or Abaroa, Eduardo

(1838-1879) Bolivian military officer, engineer. Colonel and hero of War of the Pacific that pitted Chile against Bolivia and Peru. A leader of civilian resistance to Chilean invasion that was the first armed conflict of the war. Part of badly outnumbered Bolivian force defending bridge over Topáter River. He refused to surrender and was killed at age 40. Statue of him stands in Plaza Abaroa (Abaroa Square) in La Paz. Eduardo Avaroa Province and the Eduardo Avaroa Andean Fauna National Reserve were named in his honor. The anniversary of his death is a national holiday in Bolivia.

Last Words: "¿Rendirme? ¡Que se rinda su abuela, carajo!" (tr. "Surrender? Your grandmother should surrender, you bastard!") Spoken to Chilean forces that surrounded him and asked him to surrender. His Last Words are part of Bolivian folklore and have even been reproduced on a series of postage stamps.

Source: "The Politics and Semiotics of the Smallest Icons of Popular Culture: Latin American Postage Stamps" by Jack Child (*Latin American Research Review*, Vol. 40, No. 1, February 2005).

Averill, James ("Jim")

(1851-1889) American businessman, cattle thief. Operated a brothel with Ella ("Cattle Kate") Watson in Rawlins, Wyoming. Both were lynched by a vigilante group of cattlemen. Averill died in a canyon near the Sweetwater River. The lynching party was arrested but never faced trial.

Last Words: "Stop your fooling, fellows." Spoken to the cattlemen as they prepared to lynch him. One of the vigilantes later told a reporter: "We didn't mean to hang 'em, only scare 'em a little."

Source: *Bloodletters and Badmen: A Narrative Encyclopedia of American Criminals from the Pilgrims to the Present* by Jay Robert Nash (New York, 1995).

Avery, Isaac Erwin

(1928-1863) American military officer. Confederate colonel in U.S. Civil War. Leader of 6th Regiment North Carolina Troops. Killed at age 34 at Gettysburg.

Last Words (written): "Tell father that I died with my face to the enemy." On a scrap of paper.

Source: *The Civil War in North Carolina: Letters and Civilians' Letters and Diaries, 1861-1865,* ed. by Christopher M. Warford (Jefferson, NC, 2003).

Azeglio, Marchese Massimo Taparelli d'

(1798-1866) Italian writer, statesman. Marchese. Son-in-law of Manzoni. Leader of risorgimento. Helped incite revolution with his writings. Premier of Sardinia. Notable work: *Degli ultimi casi di Romagna* (attack on the secular power of the pope). Died at age 67 in Florence.

Last Words: "Ah, Luisa, you always arrive just as I'm leaving." Spoken to his separated wife, Luisa Blondel, who had come to see him after hearing he was ill.

Source: *Manzoni and His Times: A Biography* by Archibald Colquhoun (London, 1954).

Babar, Baber or Babur

(1483-1530) Mogul ruler. Founder of Mogul Empire in India. Nickname of Zahir ud-Din Muhammad. Descendant of Tamerlane and Genghis Khan. Died at age 48 in Agra.

Different Last Words:

(1) (doubtful): "Oh God! If a life may be exchanged for a life, I who am Babar give

my life and my being for Humayan." Spoken at the sick bed of his son Humayan. Babar lived for three more months.

Source: *A History of India* by Sir George Dunbar (London, 1926).

(2) "I give your brothers to your keeping. Be faithful to them and all the people."

Source: *Babur, The Tiger: First of the Great Moguls* by Harold Lamb (Karachi, Pakistan, 1989).

Babcock, Maltbie Davenport

(1858-1901) American clergyman, writer, poet, hymnist. Presbyterian minister known for hymn "This is My Father's World." Committed suicide at age 42 while at the International Hospital in Naples, Italy. A large window by Louis Comfort Tiffany, titled *The Holy City*, was installed at Brown Memorial Presbyterian Church in Baltimore in Babcock's memory. He served as pastor there from 1886 to 1900.

Last Words: "I have swallowed corrosive sublimate." Spoken to the superintendent and nurse in his hospital room.

Source: "Dr. Babcock's People Plunged in Grief; The Pastor's Body to be Brought Here for Burial. More Details on his Death. Criticism of the Naples Hospital Management—Dr. Babcock's Poem 'Emancipation'— Eulogies of Clergymen" (*New York Times*, May 21, 1901).

Babel, Isaac Emmanuelovich

(1894-1941) Russian writer, playwright. Arrested during the Stalin purges of the 1930s. Died at age 45 in a Moscow prison. Notable works: *Odessa Tales; Red Cavalry* (his experiences with a cavalry detachment in Poland).

Last Words: "I am only asking for one thing—let me finish my work."

Source: *The Complete Works of Isaac Babel,* ed. by Nathalie Babel, tr. by Peter Constantine (New York, 2001). Nathalie Babel was his daughter.

Babington, Anthony

(1561-1586) English conspirator. Roman Catholic leader of unsuccessful Babington Plot to assassinate Queen Elizabeth I and install on throne Elizabeth's prisoner, Roman Catholic Mary Stuart, Queen of Scots. Imprisoned in Tower of London and tried by special commission. Executed at age 24.

Different Last Words:

(1) "Spare me, Lord Jesus." Spoken several times in Latin. He was still alive when taken down from the gallows.

Source: *Dictionary of National Biography*, *from the Earliest Times to 1900,* by Sir Leslie Stephen, George Smith and Sir Sidney Lee (London, 1921-1922).

(2) "The murder of the Queen had been represented to me as a deed lawful and meritorious. I die a firm Catholic." Spoken on the scaffold.

Source: *The Last Words (Real and Traditional) of Distinguished Men and Women Collected From Various Sources* by Frederic Rowland Marvin (New York, 1901).

Variation: "A deed lawful and meritorious."

Source: *History of England* by James Anthony Froude (London, 1870). Froude paraphrased all but these five words.

Bachaumont, Louis Petit de

(1690-1771) French nobleman, writer, journalist, critic. Born of a noble family, brought up at court of Versailles. In Paris, he kept a journal of news that dealt largely with scandals and accounts of books suppressed by the censor. His journal was published anonymously as *Mémoires secrets pour servir à l'histoire de la République des Lettres*. After his death, it was continued under other authors until 1779. An incomplete edition was undertaken in 1830. Extracts were published in 1859.

Last Words (spoken): "Le prêtre ne put jamais tirer autre chose du mourant que: 'Monsieur, vous avez bien de la bonté.'" (tr. "The priest could never draw another thing from dying but 'Dear Sir, you are so kind.'")

Source: *The Art of Dying: An Anthology,* ed. by Francis Birrell and F. L. Lucas (London, 1930).

Last Words (written): He copied a scandalous song about the adulterous and pregnant Duchess of Durford that ended with these lines:

"Lovely Mary/
Were I the archangel for you/
Destined that work to do/
How I would worship you/
Lovely Mary."

Source: *Mémoires secrets pour servir à l'histoire de la République des Lettres* by Louis Petit de Bachaumont (London, 1784).

Bachman, John

(1790-1874) American clergyman, naturalist, educator. Lutheran. Colleague of John James Audubon. Co-authored *The Viviparous Quadrupeds of North America* with

Audubon. Two of Audubon's sons married two of Bachman's daughters. Bachman's warbler, and Bachman's sparrow were named for him. Died at age 84 of paralysis in Charleston, South Carolina.

Last Words: "I love her—I love you all." Spoken about a relative.

Source: *John Bachman, The Pastor of St. John's Lutheran Church, Charleston* by C.L. Bachman (Charleston, SC, 1888). The author was his daughter Catherine.

Bacon, Francis, 1st Baron Verulam and Viscount St. Albans

(1561-1626) English philosopher, statesman, writer. Member of Parliament. Attorney general. Lord keeper of the Great Seal. Lord chancellor in court of James I. Notable work: *Novum Organum* in which he presented his scientific method. Became ill while doing an experiment on preserving meat with snow. Died at age 65 in London.

Last Words (written): "My very good Lord, I was likely to have had the fortune of Caius Plinius the elder, who lost his life by trying an experiment about the burning of the mountain Vesuvius. For I was also desirous to try an experiment or two, touching the conservation and induration of bodies. As for the experiment itself, it succeeded excellently well; but in the journey (between London and Highgate) I was taken with such a fit of casting, as I know not whether it were the stone, or some surfeit, or cold, or indeed a touch of them all three. But when I came to your Lordship's house, I was not able to go back, and therefore was forced to take up my lodging here, where your housekeeper is very careful and diligent about me; which I assure myself your Lordship will not only pardon towards him, but think the better of him for it. For indeed your Lordship's house was happy to me, and I kiss your noble hands for the welcome which I am sure you gave me to it, etc. I know how unfit it is for me to write to your Lordship with any other hand than mine own; but in troth my fingers are so disjointed with this fit of sickness, that I cannot steadily hold a pen." Last lines of letter to the Earl of Arundel and Surrey.

Source: *The Letters and the Life of Francis Bacon Including All His Occasional Works* by Sir Francis

Bacon and James Spedding (London, 1868-1890).

Last Words (written, doubtful): "My name and memory I leave to men's charitable speeches, to foreign nations, and the next ages." Although these are given as his last written words, they are actually the last line of his will.

Source: *The Last Words (Real and Traditional) of Distinguished Men and Women Compiled from Various Sources* by Frederic Rowland Marvin (New York, 1901). Cited as "From the Will of Lord Bacon."

Last Words (spoken): "Thy creatures, O Lord, have been my books, but Thy Holy Scriptures much more. I have sought Thee in the fields and gardens, but I have found Thee, O God, in Thy Sanctuary–Thy Temple."

Source: *Death-bed Scenes or Dying With and Without Religion* by D.W. Clark (New York, 1851).

Baedeker, Frederick William

(1823-1906) German clergyman. Pioneer evangelist in Russian Empire and Near East. Member of Plymouth Brethren Movement. Brother of Karl Baedeker, publisher of world-famous travel handbooks. Frederick spent many years in Russia. Was allowed to visit prisons. Died at age 83.

Last Words: "I am going in to see the King in His beauty!"

Source: *Dr. Baedeker and His Apostolic Work in Russia. With Introductory Notes by Princess Nathalie Lieven and Lord Radstock* by Robert Sloan Latimer (London, 1907).

Baer, Maximilian Adelbert ("Max")

(1909-1959) American professional athlete, boxer, actor. One-time Heavyweight Champion of the World. Acted in more than 20 films. Checked into a Hollywood hotel after refereeing a boxing match. Had heart attack while shaving. Desk clerk told him house doctor would come to his room. He jokingly replied: "No dummy, I need a people doctor." A physician arrived. A rescue squad administered oxygen. Baer had a second attack, slumped over and died at age 50.

Last Words: "Oh, God, here I go!"

Source: *The Literary Life and Other Curiosities* by Robert Hendrickson (Middlesex, England, 1982). Also appears on maxbaer.org and numerous other Internet websites.

Baesell, Norman F.

(d. 1944) American military officer. U.S.

Army Air Force lieutenant colonel. Fellow passenger with musician Glenn Miller in plane from England to France during World War II. Miller looked over the nine-passenger Norseman as takeoff time approached and was concerned that the plane had only one engine. He took his seat, looked around, then and asked: "Hey where the hell are the parachutes?"

Last Words: "What's the matter Miller, do you want to live forever?" Baesell's response to Miller. The plane vanished over the English Channel.

Source: *Glenn Miller & the Age of Swing* by George Snow and Jonathon Green (London, 1976).

Bagehot, Walter

(1826-1877) British economist, political theorist, writer, journalist, editor. Married Eliza Wilson, whose father was founder and editor of *The Economist.* Bagehot worked for *The Economist* and succeeded Wilson as editor. Notable works: *The English Constitution; Lombard Street; Physics and Politics; Economic Studies.* Died at age 51 in Langport, England.

Last Words: "Let me have my own fidgets." Spoken as he refused his sister's help with his pillows.

Source: *The Collected Works of Walter Bagehot,* ed. by Emily I. Barrington (London, 1915). The editor was Bagehot's sister-in-law.

Bailey, Chauncey Wendell, Jr.

(1949-2007) American journalist, editor, television and radio personality. Known for addressing issues that affected the African-American community. Worked for *Detroit News; Hartford Courant; Oakland Tribune;* United Press International as well as radio station KDIA and television station KNTV and KSBT in a career that spanned 37 years. When he died at age 57, he was editor-in-chief of the five San Francisco Bay Area Post newspapers. Murdered for a story he was investigating involving Your Black Muslim Bakery. On his routine walk to work he was stalked and shot to death by Devaughndre Broussard, a 19-year-old handyman who worked at the bakery.

Last Words: "Don't kill me." Reported by an anonymous witness.

Source: "Cops: Killer 'Stalked' Editor Prior to Am-bush" by Harry Harris and Martin G. Reynolds (*Oakland Tribune*, August 8, 2007).

Bailli or Baillie, Roche le

(d. 1605) French physician, astrologer. Known as La Riviere. Before he died, he distributed all his money and property among his servants on the condition that they leave his house immediately. They did. When the physician arrived, he found nothing left but the bed he was lying on.

Last Words: When the physician remarked this circumstance to him, he replied that he must now go likewise, "as his baggage was sent off before him." He died immediately after speaking these words.

Source: *The Book of Death* by Samuel Dobree (London, 1819).

Bailly, Jean-Sylvain

(1736-1793) French astronomer, orator, politician. President of States-General. First mayor of Paris following French Revolution. Convicted of contriving July massacre. Guillotined at age 57 in Paris.

Last Words: "Je tremble, mais c'est de froid." (tr. "I tremble but it is from the cold.") His response when someone at his execution noticed he was trembling.

Source: *Paris, ou, Le livre des cent-et-un*, Vol. 2 (Paris, 1832).

Variation: "My friend, I am cold."

Source: *Jean-Sylvain Bailly* by Fernand-Laurent (Paris, 1927).

Bainham, James

(d. 1532) English martyr. Protestant son of Sir Alexander Bainham, sheriff of Gloucestershire. Burned at the stake for heresy. A woodblock illustration of his burning is in Foxe's *Book of Martyrs.*

Last Words. "O ye papists: behold, ye look for miracles, and here now ye may see a miracle, for in this fire I feel no more pain than if I were in a bed of down, but it is to me as sweet as a bed of roses." Spoken in the midst of the flames, when his legs and arms were half consumed by fire.

Source: *Book of Martyrs and the Acts and Monuments of the Church* by John Fox (or Foxe). First published 1563, ed. by John Cumming (London, 1851).

Baker, Edward Dickinson

(1811-1861) British-born American military officer, lawyer, politician. U.S. Army colonel in Mexican War and Union Army in U.S. Civil War. Member of U.S. House of Representatives from Illinois and later the U.S. Senate from Oregon. He was a long-time close friend of President Abraham Lincoln, who named one of his sons for him. Baker was shot and died at age 50 at the Battle of Ball's Bluff, Virginia. Earlier that day, he replied to a fellow soldier who told him to lie down to avoid enemy fire: "No, my son, and when you get to be a United States Senator, you will not lie down either." Baker was the only sitting U.S. Senator killed in the Civil War. His death led to formation of the Congressional Joint Committee on the Conduct of the War. Baker City, Baker County in Oregon, three Fort Bakers and Baker Street in San Francisco were named in his honor.

Last Words: "See, he falls." Spoken when he saw that a Confederate horseman across the field had been hit. At that moment, Baker was shot four times and killed by a Confederate soldier.

Sources: *The War of the Rebellion: A Compilation of the Official Records of the Union and Confederate Armies*, Series 1, Vol. 5, by U.S. War Dept. (Washington, D.C., 1881); *Harvard's Civil War* by Richard F. Miller (Lebanon, NH, 2005).

Baker, James

(1823-1862) American military officer. Colonel in Union Army in U.S. Civil War. Leader of 2nd Iowa Infantry, First Brigade, Second Division, Army of West Tennessee. Shot and killed at age 38 in Corinth, Mississippi, while head of his regiment.

Last Words: "I die content. I have seen my regiment victoriously charging the enemy."

Source: *The War of the Rebellion: A Compilation of the Official Records of the Union and Confederate Armies*, Series 1, Vol. 17, by U.S. War Dept. (Washington, D.C., 1886).

Variation: "Thank God, I fell while my regiment was victoriously charging!"

Source: *Iowa Colonels and Regiments: Being a History of Iowa Regiments in the War of the Rebellion; and Containing a Description of the Battles in Which They Have Fought* by Addison A. Stuart (Des Moines, IA, 1865).

Variation: "Thank God, when I fell, my regiment was victoriously charging!"

Sources: "Report of Major Weaver" in *The Rebellion Record,* Vol. 5, by Frank Moore (New York, 1863);

Roster and Record of Iowa Soldiers in the War of the Rebellion, Together With Historical Sketches of Volunteer Organizations, 1861-1866. Vol. II, 9th-16th Regiments-Infantry by William H. Thrift (Des Moines, IA, 1908).

Baker, Josephine

(1906-1975) American-born French singer, dancer, actress. Popular entertainer in Paris. Became French citizen. Worked with French Resistance against Nazis during World War II. Adopted 12 children she called her Rainbow Tribe. Died at age 68 of a massive cerebral hemorrhage in Paris.

Last Words: "Oh, you young people act like old men. You are no fun." Spoken as she left a party in her honor.

Source: *Josephine: The Hungry Heart* by Jean-Claude Baker and Chris Chase (Boston, 1995). Jean-Claude was her son.

Baker, Lena

(1901-1945) American execution victim. Executed at age 43. Only American woman executed in an electric chair in the 20th century. Baker's case is controversial. While locked in a gristmill, she pulled a gun away from Ernest B. Knight, a white man who was also wielding a metal pipe. She shot him in self-defense. An all-white male jury convicted her of murder in a one-day trial. She should not have been tried for more than manslaughter. In 2006, the Georgia Board of Pardons and Paroles issued a formal pardon for only the third time in its history and acknowledged that "a grievous error" had been made. Baker's picture and her Last Words were put on display with the retired electric chair in the museum at Georgia State Prison in Reidsville.

Last Words: "I am ready to meet my God."

Source: "Post Execution Pardon. One-Day Trial in 1944 Sent Georgia Woman to Electric Chair" by Carlos Campos and Bill Torpy (*Atlanta Journal-Constitution,* August 16, 2005).

Baker, Theodore

(d. 1887) American murderer. Has unusual distinction in the history of American jurisprudence of having been hanged twice. In 1885, Baker was accused of killing Frank S. Unruh, the husband of his lover, and was lynched from a telegraph pole in an act of vigilante justice. He was left for dead. When the sheriff arrived, he was cut down. He later gave a description of the hanging to a newspaper reporter. He said he had no consciousness or memory until late the next day. Baker was formally tried and found guilty of Unruh's murder. The case later went through a famous appeal. Baker publicly spoke out against the death penalty. A year and a half after the crime, he uttered his Last Words. On the gallows the day he was hanged a second time, he joked about the attendant shifting the knot: "That's right; I have been in the habit of having it a little higher up." Baker was executed May 6, 1887, in Springer, New Mexico.

Last Words: "Gentleman, I am sorry it ends this way. Let her go."

Sources: "Twice Hanged. How it Feels to be Swung From the Gallows" (*Te Aroha News*, July 9, 1887); "The Man Who Was Hanged Twice" by Robert J. Torrez (*True West*, December 1989); "A Lynching Party Foiled" (*New York Times*, December 25, 1885); "Hanged in New-Mexico" (*New York Times*, May 7, 1887).

Balboa, Vasco Núñez de

(1475-1519) Spanish explorer. First European to see the Pacific Ocean. Served under the new governor of Panama. Accused of sedition. Convicted and executed by beheading at age 44, in Acla, Panama.

Last Words: "That is false. I always have served my king loyally and sought to add to his domains." His response to the herald who called out: "Such is the punishment imposed on this traitor, this usurper of the rights of the Crown" as he was led to his execution.

Source: *Nuñez de Balboa* by Paul Gaffarel (Paris, 1882).

Variation: "That is a great falsehood! As sure as my last moments are at hand; I never had a thought except of the most loyal and faithful devotion to my king nor had any other desire than to increase his dominions with power and ability."

Source: *Penny Cyclopaedia of the Society for the Diffusion of Useful Knowledge,* Vol. III, by Society for the Diffusion of Useful Knowledge (London, 1835).

Baldwin, Elias Jackson ("Lucky")

(1828-1909) American businessman, investor, gambler. He acquired great wealth through mining, landholding investments and horseracing. He founded the original Santa Anita Park horseracing track on his California estate and bred and raced some of finest race horses of his time. Baldwin Hills district in Los Angeles, the city of Baldwin Park and the Baldwin Stakes at Santa Anita are among the many things named in his honor. He died at age 80.

Last Words: "By gad, I'm not licked yet." He used this phrase throughout his life and on his deathbed.

Source: *San Francisco's Golden Era: A Picture Story of San Francisco Before the Fire* by Lucius Morris Beebe and Charles Clegg (San Francisco, CA, 1960).

Baldwin, James Arthur

(1924-1987) American-born writer, playwright. Notable works: *Go Tell It on the Mountain; Nobody Knows My Name; The Fire Next Time; Blues for Mister Charlie.* Moved to France in 1940s to escape American racial bigotry. Died at age 63 of stomach cancer at his home in Saint Paul, France.

Last Words: "I'm bored."

Source: *James Baldwin: Artist on Fire* by William J. Weatherly (New York, 1989).

Ball, Lucille

(1911-1989) American actress, comedian. Starred on radio sitcom *My Favorite Husband* with first husband Desi Arnaz, 1948 to 1951. Television version *I Love Lucy* aired 1951 to 1956, *Lucille Ball-Desi Arnaz Show* aired 1957 to 1958. Died at age 77 of heart failure in Los Angeles, California.

Last Words: "My Florida water." Her response when asked if she wanted anything.

Source: *Desilu: The Story of Lucille Ball and Desi Arnaz* by Coyne Steven Sanders and Tom Gilbert (New York, 1993).

Balzac, Honoré de

(1799-1850) French writer, novelist. Family name Balssa. Friend of Hugo, Lamartine, George Sand. Credited as founder of realistic novel. Spent 20 years writing his masterpiece: *La Comédie humaine,* a work that covered all views of Paris life. He never finished it. Notable novels in the series: *Le Pere Goriot; Eugene Grandet.* Died at age 51 of heart disease in Paris.

Different Last Words:

(1) "I can no longer read or write. De Balzac." Written across the bottom of a letter

his wife wrote.

Source: *Honore de Balzac* by Katherine P. Wormeley (Boston, 1892).

(2) (doubtful): "Only Bianchon can save me." Bianchon was the fictional physician in *La Comédie humaine.*

Source: *Prometheus: The Life of Balzac* by André Maurois (New York, 1966).

Variation (doubtful): "Ah oui! Je sais. Il me faudrait Bianchon—Bianchon me sauverait lui!" (tr. "Ah yes! I know. I need Bianchon— Bianchon would save me! ")

Source: *Balzac, Sa vie prodigieuse, son mariage, ses derniers moments* by Octave Mirbeau (Paris, 1918).

Variation (doubtful): "Allez chercher Bianchon!" (tr. "Go look for Bianchon.") Balzac supposedly mustered up enough strength to make this one final request of his old friend Dr. Nacquart.

Source: *En Marge de "La Comédie humaine" la Vie de Docteur Horace Bianchon, Grande Consultant de la Monarchie de Juliette* by Fernand Lotte (Cairo, Egypt, 1947).

Michael D. Garval wrote that Balzac's appeal to Dr. Nacquart sounded too good to be true. He mentioned the supposed Last Words of Balzac as an example of the many deathbed stories circulating that may be apocryphal, the product of posthumous mythmaking.

Source: *"A Dream of Stone": Fame, Vision, and Monumentality in Nineteenth-Century French Literary Culture* by Michael D. Garval (Newark, DE, 2004).

Bancroft, George

(1800-1891) American historian, statesman, diplomat, writer. Notable work: *History of the United States* (10 vol.). U.S. secretary of the navy. Established U.S. Naval Academy at Annapolis. Wrote Andrew Johnson's first annual message as President. U.S. minister to Great Britain. Died at age 90 in Washington, D.C.

Last Words (doubtful): "I cannot remember your first name." Spoken to a guest, George Frisbie Hoar, who replied: "It is George like yours." Then Bancroft said what are often quoted as his Last Words: "What is your last name?" This conversation with Hoar took place more than a month before Bancroft died and was told to Bancroft's son the day after Bancroft died.

Source: *Autobiography of Seventy Years*, Vol. II, by George Frisbie Hoar (New York, 1905).

Bankhead, Tallulah Brockman

(1902-1968) American actress. Stage, screen, radio, television star. Daughter of William Brockman Bankhead, member and speaker of house in U.S. House of Representatives. Granddaughter of Senator John Hollis Bankhead. Notable TV shows: *The Big Show; All-Star Revue; Batman* (as Black Widow). Died at age 66 in a New York hospital of influenza complicated by emphysema.

Last Words: "Codeine…bourbon."

Source: *Tallulah, Darling: A Biography of Tallulah Bankhead* by Denis Brian (New York, 1980).

Bannister, John

(1760-1836) English comedian, artist, theatrical manager. Son of Charles Bannister, English actor and singer. Started as a painter but switched to the stage. Famed as one of the best comics of his day. Retired in 1815. Later was manager of Drury Lane Theater. Friend of Gainsborough. Died at age 76.

Last Words: "My hope is in Christ."

Source: *Memoirs of John Bannister, Comedian* by John Adolphus (London, 1838).

Barbellian, W. N. P., see Cummings, Bruce Frederick.

Barber, Thomas Washington

(1820?-1855) American abolitionist, farmer. Free-state citizen who joined the anti-slavery movement in Kansas. A few miles outside Lawrence, unarmed and on their way home to their families, Barber, his brother Robert and brother-in-law Thomas M. Pierson were approached by a large group of pro-slavery men and ordered to return to the city. Barber refused. He and his horse were shot. After riding a few feet, he slipped from his horse and fell to the ground dead. His horse died that night. Barber became one of the "free-state martyrs" and is the subject of Whittier's poem "The Burial of Barber." Barber County, Kansas, was named for him.

Last Words: "That fellow hit me." Spoken in a faint voice before falling from his horse.

Source: *Personal Recollections of Pardee Butler* by Pardee Butler and Rosetta Butler Hastings (Cincinnati, OH, 1889).

Barbirolli, Sir John

(1899-1970) English musician, cellist, conductor. Birth name Giovanni Battista Barbirolli. Knighted in 1949. Conducted major symphony orchestras throughout the world. Died at age 70 of a heart attack in London a few hours after rehearsing the Philharmonia Orchestra.

Last Words: "Anyway, I can get a good rest in the morning. There's no rehearsal till three." Spoken to his wife when he woke during the night.

Source: *Barbirolli, Conductor Laureate* by Michael Kennedy (London, 1971). His biography was written a year after he died at his request and with the cooperation of his wife.

Barbusse, Henri

(1873-1935) French writer, essayist, novelist, poet, editor. Notable work: *Under Fire* (novel based on his experiences; depicted powerful realistic view of World War I.) Became Communist after the Russian Revolution. Went to Russia. Died at age 62 in Moscow.

Last Words: "Telephone and say that they must still enlarge it—Always larger, broader, more universal—It's the only means of saving the world." He was speaking about the war in Ethiopia. He wanted forces sent there to intensify the military action.

Source: *Henri Barbusse* by Jacques Duclos and Jean Fréville (Paris, 1946).

Barfield, Margie Velma

(1932-1984) American murderer. Executed at age 52 in Central Prison, Raleigh, North Carolina, for the murder of her boyfriend. First woman executed in U.S. since 1962 moratorium on capital punishment was lifted. First woman put to death by lethal injection.

Last Words: "I want to say that I am very sorry for all the hurt that I have caused. I know that everybody has gone through a lot of pain, all the families connected, and I am sorry and I want to thank everybody who has been supporting me all these six years. I want to thank my family for standing with me through this, and my attorneys and all the support to me, everybody, the people with the prison department. I appreciate their kindness and everything they have shown me during these six years."

Source: "1ˢᵗ Woman Executed in U.S. Since 1962" (*Chicago Tribune*, November 2, 1984).

Baring, Maurice

(1874-1945) English writer, journalist, war correspondent, novelist, poet, playwright, critic. Wrote poems, plays, novels. Russian scholar, translator. Reported on Russo-Japanese war in Manchuria. Member of Royal Air Force reserve. Friend of Chesterton, Belloc, Waugh, Beerbohm. Died at age 71 in Beauly, Scotland.

Last Words: "Whatever you would like me to have." His response when asked what he would like for lunch.

Source: *Maurice Baring: A Postscript* by Laura Lovat (London, 1947). The author was a friend of Baring.

Barker, Arthur R. ("Dock" or "Doc")

(1899-1939) American murderer, robber. Member of the Karpis-Barker gang. Son of Kate ("Ma") Barker. Died at age 39 attempting to escape from Alcatraz in California with Henri Young and Rufus McCain. Barker was killed. Young and McCain were recaptured and sent to solitary confinement.

Last Words: "I'm all shot to hell!"

Source: *Haunting Sunshine* by Jack Powell (Sarasota, FL, 2001).

Barker, Kate ("Ma")

(1873-1935) American crime family matriarch. Known as Ma Barker. Birth name Arizona Donnie Clark. In 1935, she and Freddie, youngest of her four sons, were found in a hideout in Florida. Although never charged with a crime, she was killed at age 61 in a shootout with the FBI.

Last Words: "All right! Go ahead!" Spoken to her son.

Source: "The Kidnapping of Edward George Bremer, St. Paul, Minnesota: History and Early Association with the Karpis-Barker Gang Prior to the Abduction of Mr. Bremer," FBI File 7-576 Sec. 241, November 19, 1936.

Barkley, Alben William

(1877-1956) American politician. Member U.S. House of Representatives and U.S. Senate from Kentucky. 35ᵗʰ Vice President of the U.S. Died at age 79 of heart failure in Lexington, Virginia, while serving in the U.S. Senate.

Last Words: "I am willing to be a junior. I am glad to sit in the back row, for I had

rather be a servant in the house of the Lord than to sit in the seats of the mighty." Spoken while he was addressing a mock Democratic Convention at Washington and Lee University.
Source: "Barkley Dies Giving Talk! Senator has Heart Attack in Virginia" (*Chicago Tribune*, May 1, 1956).

Barksdale, William
(1821-1863) American military officer, politician, lawyer, newspaper editor. Member U.S. House of Representatives from Mississippi. Editor of *Columbus* [Mississippi] *Democrat*, a pro-slavery newspaper. Captain in Mexican War. Brigadier general in Confederate Army in U.S. Civil War. Leader of 13th Mississippi Regiment. Shot attempting a charge into the Peach Orchard at Gettysburg, Pennsylvania. Left for dead by his own troops. Died at age 41 in Gettysburg.
Last Words: "Tell my wife I am shot, but we fought like hell." Spoken to the Federal surgeon attending to him. His Last Words to his own troops were similar. He told his aide W.R. Boyd "I am killed! Tell my wife and children that I died fighting at my post."
Source: *Confederate Military History; A Library of Confederate States History,* ed. by Clement A. Evans (Atlanta, GA, 1899).

Barnardo, Thomas John
(1845-1905) Irish-born English physician, philanthropist, social reformer. Did pioneering work in care of impoverished children. Instrumental in securing passage of major parliamentary child welfare legislation. First of Dr. Barnardo's Homes for destitute and orphaned children opened 1870. Died at age 60 of angina pectoris in London.
Last Words: "Syrie, my head is so heavy. Let me rest it on your face." Spoken to his wife.
Source: "The Death of Dr. Barnardo" by Richard Cavendish (*History Today;* Vol. 55, No. 9, September 2005).
Variation: "Oh, Syrie! My head feels so heavy!" He laid his head on her breast, gasped for air and died.
Source: *Doctor Barnardo: Physician, Pioneer, Prophet: Child Life Yesterday and To-day* by John Wesley Bready (London, 1930).

Barnato, Barney
(1852-1897) British speculator. Birth name Barnett Isaacs. Traveled to South Africa and became a millionaire in Kimberley diamond trade. Engineered Kaffir boom in mining stocks in 1895. Committed suicide at age 44 at sea.
Last Words: "What's the time?" Spoken on the voyage back to London with his family. His nephew replied: "Thirteen minutes past three." Barnato then jumped overboard. Attempts to save him failed.
Source: *Barney Barnato: from Whitechapel Clown to Diamond King* by Richard Lewinsohn (New York, 1938).

Barnave, Antoine Pierre Joseph Marie
(1761-1793) French political leader, orator. Active in the group that came to be known as Jacobins. He later deserted their cause and became a constitutional monarchist. Impeached for treason. Guillotined at age 32 in Paris.
Last Words: "This then is my reward?" Spoken as he was being executed.
Source: *The French Revolution: A History* by Thomas Carlyle (London, 1837).

Barnes, Robert
(1495-1540) English clergyman, martyr. Was among first English Roman Catholics who converted to Lutheranism. Condemned without trial for religious views. Executed at about age 45 by burning at Smithfield.
Last Words: "I trust in no good works that ever I did, but only in the death of Christ. I do not doubt but through Him to inherit the kingdom of Heaven. But imagine not that I speak against good works, for they are to be done, and verily they that do them not shall never enter into the kingdom of God." Spoken to onlookers as he was committed to the flames.
Source: *Book of Martyrs and the Acts and Monuments of the Church* by John Fox (or Foxe). First published 1563, ed. by John Cumming (London, 1851).

Barneveld or
Barneveldt, Jan van Olden
(1547-1619) Dutch statesman, lawyer. Helped William the Silent in struggle for Dutch independence from Spain. Negotiated truce with Spain. Also helped to concentrate military power in the hands of Maurice of Nassau. Illegally arrested, condemned as traitor and executed at age 71. One of his

sons escaped. The other was executed.

Different Last Words:

(1) "Oh, God, what then is man?" Spoken as he bent his head for the executioner.

Source: *A Wanderer in Holland* by E.V. Lucas (New York, 1915).

(2) "Maak het kort, maak het kort." (tr. "Make it short. Make it short.")

Source: *Juliana/druk 1: de jonge jaren van de Prinses der Nederlanden* by M. Crispijn, Geert van Dormaal (Kampen, The Netherlands, 2006).

Variation: "Be quick, man, be quick."

Source: "Dying Words of Noted Persons" in *Miscellaneous Notes and Queries with Answers in All Departments of Literature*, Vol. II (Manchester, NH, 1885).

Variation: "Be quick about it. Be quick." Spoken to the executioner.

Source: *The Life and Death of John of Barneveld* by John L. Motley (New York, 1904).

Barnum, Phineas Taylor ("P.T.")

(1810-1891) American showman, entrepreneur, writer, politician. Known for hoaxes, exaggerations, ballyhoo and for the entertainment spectacle that became Ringling Brothers Barnum and Bailey Circus. Opened American Museum (of curiosities) in 1842. Brought Swedish singer Jenny Lind to U.S. for concert tour. Imported Jumbo the elephant from England. Exhibited Tom Thumb. Wrote several books including *The Art of Money-Getting*. Served in Connecticut legislature. Mayor of Bridgeport, Connecticut. Ran unsuccessfully for U.S. Congress (1867). Died at age 81 in Bridgeport.

Different Last Words:

(1) "Yes." Spoken around 4 a.m. when asked if he wished a drink of water. He spent the day in a semiconscious state at his home in Bridgeport, surrounded by family and friends and died at 6:22 p.m. Earlier, he asked his physician to administer sedatives when all hope was gone.

Source: "The Great Showman Dead. Last Hours of the Life of Phineas T. Barnum, The Veteran Manager Sinks Into a Peaceful Sleep that Knows No Waking—The Funeral To Be Private at His Express Desire" (*New York Times,* April 8, 1891).

(2) "Nancy, I want you to know that my last thoughts are of you." Spoken to his wife before falling into a deep sleep. The following morning he roused himself from his lethargy to speak a few words of farewell to his friends and family. As the day pro-

gressed, he slipped into unconsciousness and died.

Source: *P.T. Barnum Legend and the Man* by A.H. Saxton (New York, 1995).

(3) (doubtful): "How were the circus receipts tonight at Madison Square Garden?"

Source: Various Last Words compilations and Internet websites.

It is unlikely that these were his Last Words. See (1) and (2) above.

Barrie, Sir James Matthew, 1st Baronet

(1860-1937) Scottish playwright, novelist. Gained fame with play *Peter Pan, the Boy Who Wouldn't Grow Up.* Also wrote autobiographical novels, including *The Little Minister.* Stopped writing for 14 years then produced two final works, both Biblical plays. Created a baronet in 1913. Died at age 77 of pneumonia in London.

Last Words: "I can't sleep."

Source: *The Story of J.M.B. (Sir James M. Barrie): A Biography* by Dennis Mackail (New York, 1941).

Barron, Clarence Walker

(1855-1928) American editor, publisher, writer. Established Boston, Philadelphia News Bureaus. Founded *Barron's Financial Weekly* (1921). President of Dow Jones & Co. Publisher of *Wall Street Journal.* Died at age 73 in Battle Creek, Michigan.

Last Words: "What is the news?"

Source: *They Told Barron,* ed. by Arthur Pound and Samuel T. Moore (New York, 1930).

Barrow, Isaac

(1630-1677) English theologian, mathematician, educator. First Lucasian professor of mathematics at Cambridge. Notable work: *Methods of Tangents.* Isaac Newton attended his lectures on tangents. Barrow gave up mathematics in 1669 and devoted all his efforts to religion. Appointed vice chancellor of Cambridge in 1675. Died at age 47 in London.

Last Words: "I have seen the glories of the world."

Source: *The English Church From the Accession of Charles I to the Death of Anne (1625-1714)* by William Holden Hutton (London, 1903).

Barrymore, Ethel

(1879-1959) American actress. Star of stage and screen. Birth name Ethel Blythe. Daughter of Maurice and Georgiana Barrymore.

Sister of Lionel and John Barrymore. Nominated for four Academy Awards; won Best Supporting Actress Oscar in 1944 for *None But the Lonely Heart*. Died at age 79 in Beverly Hills, California.

Last Words: "Are you happy? I'm happy." Spoken to her maid Anna when she woke up during the night. She then fell back asleep and died several hours later. Her Last Words have also been reported as "Is everybody happy? I want everybody to be happy. I know I'm happy."

Source: *Great Times, Good Times. The Odyssey of Maurice Barrymore* by James Kotsilibas-Davies (New York, 1977).

Barrymore, Georgianna Emma Drew

(1854-1893) American actress. Daughter of actor John Drew. Wife of Maurice Barrymore. Mother of Ethel, John and Lionel Barrymore. Died at age 38 in Santa Barbara, California.

Last Words: "Oh, my poor kids. What will ever become of them?"

Source: *Confessions of an Actor* by John Barrymore (Indianapolis, IN, 1926).

Barrymore, John

(1882-1942) American actor. Star of stage, screen and radio. Birth name John Sidney Blythe. Known as The Great Profile. Son of Maurice and Georgianna Barrymore. Brother of Lionel and Ethel Barrymore. Famed as Shakespearean stage actor in early years. Left stage for motion pictures in 1923. Popular radio actor during final years. Died at age 60 in Los Angeles, California.

Different Last Words:

(1) "You heard me, Mike." His response to his brother Lionel who asked him to repeat something he did not understand.

Source: *Good Night, Sweet Prince* by Gene Fowler (New York, 1944).

(2) "Tell me Gene, is it true that you are the illegitimate son of Buffalo Bill?" Spoken to close friend and future biographer Gene Fowler, who reported a different set of last words for Barrymore. The "Buffalo Bill" version was reported in a subsequent book by Will Fowler, Gene's son. This version is also reported in several biographical sources including those about Barrymore and Gene Fowler.

Source: *The Young Man from Denver* by Will Fowler (New York, 1962).

(3) "This is wonderful! What a wonderful place!" Spoken to his brother Lionel.

Source: "Barrymore Makes Last Exit Smiling" (*Kingsport* [Tennessee] *Times*, May 31, 1942).

Barrymore, Maurice

(1849-1905) India-born English and American actor, playwright. Spent half his life in America. Birth name Herbert Blythe. His marriage to Georgianna Drew united two great acting families. Father of Lionel, John and Ethel Barrymore. Maurice suffered a mental breakdown and spent his last four years in a sanitarium in Amityville, New York. Died there at age 55.

Last Words: "Our trade falls heavily upon these feeble folk." The words were a line from his play *Nadjeska.*

Source: *Great Times, Good Times. The Odyssey of Maurice Barrymore* by James Kotsilibas-Davies (New York, 1977).

Barth, Karl

(1886-1968) Swiss theologian, educator. Protestant Reformed. Professor at Göttingen, Munster, and Basel. Pope Pius XII called him the most important theologian since Thomas Aquinas. Barth was featured on the cover of *Time* magazine in 1962. He died at age 82 in Basel.

Last Words: "God sits in the regiments! That is why I am not afraid. Stay confident in also the darkest moments! Let us hope not fall, the hope for all people, for all the peoples of the world. God let us not fall, not a single one of us and all of us together. It is governed." Spoken in a telephone conversation with friend Eduard Thurneysen the evening before he died.

Source: *Theodizee und Geschichtstheologie: ein Versuch der Überwindung der Problematik des Deutschen Idealismus bei Karl Barth* by Tsutomu Haga (Göttingen, Germany, 1991).

Variation: "Keep your chin up! Never mind! He [God, Christ] will reign!" Another translation of the conclusion of his telephone conversation with Thurneysen.

Sources: *Christian Anarchy: Jesus' Primacy Over the Powers* by Vernard Eller (Grand Rapids, MI, 1987); *Karl Barth: His Life from Letters and Autobiographical Texts* by Eberhard Busch, tr. by John Bowden (Philadelphia, 1976).

Variation: "We shall not be downhearted!

Never! For 'He reigns.'" Barth was quoting the Last Words of J. C. Blumhardt.

Source: *The Great Passion* by Eberhard Busch, Darrell L. Guder, Geoffrey W. Bromiley and Judith J. Guder (Grand Rapids, MI, 2004).

Barthou, Jean-Louis

(1862-1934) French politician, lawyer, statesman. Minister of foreign affairs. Prime minister of France. Primary figure behind the 1935 Franco-Soviet Treaty of Mutual Assistance. Member of the French Academy. Killed at age 72 in Marseille when he tried to prevent the assassination of King Alexander I of Yugoslavia.

Last Words: "I suffer terribly. I am thirsty." Whispered just before he died.

Source: *The Turning Point: The Assassination of Louis Barthou and King Alexander I of Yugoslavia* by Allen Roberts (New York, 1970).

Bartók, Béla Viktor János

(1881-1945) Hungarian-born American musician, composer, pianist, ethnomusicologist, educator. Left Europe in 1940, during World War II. Settled in U.S. Became American citizen in 1945. Notable works: *Miraculous Mandarin* (opera, orchestra); *Kossuth Symphony;* concertos; sonatas; string quartets; orchestral suites. Published many Hungarian, Romanian and Middle Eastern folksongs. Died at age 64 of leukemia in New York City. Body returned to Hungary in 1988 when the Cold War ended.

Last Words: "I am only sad that I have to leave with a full trunk."

Source: *The Naked Face of Genius: Béla Bartók's American Years* by Agatha Fassett (Boston, 1958). Book focuses on the last years of Bartók's life. The author was a friend of Bartók and his wife.

Barton, Clarissa Harlow ("Clara")

(1821-1912) American nurse, humanitarian, teacher. Aided battlefield casualties in U.S. Civil War. After the war, she helped identify many victims of Andersonville Prison. Founder and first president of the American Red Cross. Died at age 90 in Glen Echo, Maryland.

Last Words: "Let me go! Let me go!"

Source: *Clara Barton: Daughter of Destiny* by Blanche Colton Williams (Philadelphia, 1941).

Bartow, Francis Stebbins

(1816-1861) American lawyer, politician, military officer. Representative to Georgia's Secession Convention and to Confederate Congress. Confederate brigadier general in U.S. Civil War. Killed at age 44 in Manassas, Virginia at the First Battle of Bull Run; one of first high-ranking Confederate casualties. Monument inscribed with his Last Words erected where he died. Plaque replaced it in 1936, without his Last Words, but claiming he was the "first Confederate officer to give his life on the field." Bartow County, Georgia; Bartow, Georgia; Bartow, Florida; Bartow Elementary School in Savannah; and *Francis S. Bartow* (Liberty ship) named for him. Several slightly different versions of his Last Words exist.

Last Words: "Boys, they've killed me, but never give it up!"

Source: "The Rebels of the Potomac—Correspondence of the *Louisville Courier*" (*New York Times*, September 22, 1861).

Variation: "My God, boys, they have got me, but never give up the field."

Source: "Joel S. Yarborough, Co. F, 8th Georgia Volunteer Infantry, Autobiography" on file in Georgia Department of Archives (unpublished, 1861).

Variation: "Boys, they have killed me, but never give up the field."

Source: *The History of Bartow County; Formerly Cass* by Lucy Josephine Cunyus (Cartersville, GA, 1933).

Variation: "They have killed me boys! Never give up the field."

Source: "Biographical Portrait of Francis S. Bartow, and Bartow Monument and Battle of First Manassas" by Robert E.L. Krick, courtesy of Manassas National Park.

Variation: "They have killed me, but boys, never give it up!"

Source: *First Blood: Fort Sumter to Bull Run* by William C. David, et al. (New York, 1983).

Basedow, Johann Bernhard

(1723-1790) German educator, educational reformer, writer. Designed complete system of elementary education intended to develop intelligence of students in contact with realities, not only with mere words. Established a model school for children in Dessau. Notable work: *Elementarwerk.* Died at age 66 in Magdeburg, Germany.

Last Words: "Rich will seciret sein zum Besten meiner Mitmenschen." (tr. "I desire to be dissected for the benefit of my fellow men.")

Sources: *Essays von Max Müller: Basedow* (Leipzig, 1876); "Johann Bernhard Basedow and the Philanthropinum," ed. by Henry Barnard, tr. by Karl von Raumer (*American Journal of Education,* No. XIV, September 1858).

Bashkirtseff, Marie

(1859-1884) Russian-born noblewoman. writer, diarist, artist, painter. Birth name Mariya Konstantinovna Bashkirtseva. Friend of Guy de Maupassant. Known for her autobiographical *Journal,* published posthumously. Died at age 25 of tuberculosis in Paris.

Last Words: "We shall go out together." Spoken as she watched a candle burn down on a table by her bedside.

Source: *Fountains of Youth, The Life of Marie Bashkirtseff* by Dormer Creston, ed. by Dorothy Julia Baynes (New York, 1937).

Basilone, John ("Manila John")

(1916-1945) American military soldier. Known as Manila John. First U.S. Marine to win Congressional Medal of Honor in World War II. Only marine also to win Navy Cross. Killed at age 28 at Iwo Jima when a mortar shell exploded near him. USS *Basilone* was named in his honor.

Last Words: "C'mon you guys! Let's get these guns off the beach."

Source: *Forgotten Heroes–Inspiring American Portraits from Our Leading Historians,* ed. by Susan Ware (New York, 1998).

Bass, Sam

(1851-1878) American train robber, western frontiersman. His gang robbed the Union Pacific train of $60,000. Texas Rangers caught him during a string of Texas train and stagecoach robberies. Bass was shot several times. Doctor told him he didn't have long to live. Died at age 27 in Texas. Portrayed in several movies and television dramas.

Last Words: "Let me go," and a few minutes later, "The world is bobbing around me."

Source: "Sam Bass and the Myth Machine" by Helena Huntington Smith (*The American West,* January 1970).

Bastiat, Claude Frédéric

(1801-1850) French economist, politician, social philosopher, writer. Advocated free trade and opposed socialism. Notable works: *Harmonies of Political Economy; Economic*

Sophisms. He contended that if economic conditions were left alone, they would work for the common good. Died at age 49 of tuberculosis in Rome.

Last Words: "I am not able to explain myself."

Source: *Frédéric Bastiat* by Georges de Nouvion (Paris, 1905).

Battie, William

(1704-1776) English physiologist, educator, writer. President of College of Physicians. Physician at St. Luke's Hospital. Proprietor of private asylum for insane in Clerkenwell. Published first book on treating mental illness in 1758. Known for his eccentricities in dress and behavior. Died at age 72 in London after a paralytic stroke. The term "batty" (meaning crazy) is derived from his name.

Different Last Words:

(1) "Young man, you have heard, no doubt, how great are the terrors of death. This night will probably afford you some experience; but you may learn, and may you profit by the example, that a conscientious endeavor to perform his duty though life will ever close a Christian's eyes with comfort and tranquility!" Spoken to the young man who had been entrusted with his care.

Source: *Memoirs of Celebrated Etonians* by John Heneage Jesse (London, 1875).

(2) "Your highness has made me too great for my house."

Source: *Famous Sayings and Their Authors: A Collection of Historical Sayings in English, French, German, Greek, Italian, and Latin* by Edward Latham (London, 1906).

Baudelaire, Charles Pierre

(1821-1867) French writer, poet, critic, translator. Influential poet and critic. Associate of Daumier, Liszt, Hugo, Flaubert, Balzac, among others. Translated works of Poe. Notable work: *Les fleurs du mal* (*Flowers of Evil,* his sole collection). Spent his last two years semi-paralyzed following a stroke. Also suffered from aphasia. Died at age 46 in Paris.

Last Words: "Cré nom!" (tr. "Holy name!") He could express only this one phrase.

Source: "Baudelaire's Aphasia: From Poetry to Cursing" by S. Dieguez and J. Bogousslavsky ["Neurological Disorders in Famous Artists," Part 2] (*Frontiers of Neurology and Neuroscience,* Vol. 22, 2007).

Baum, Lyman Frank (L. Frank)

(1856-1919) American writer, journalist, playwright. Pen names Edith Van Dyne, Schuyler Stanton, Floyd Akers. *Father Goose: His Book*, one of his earliest works, was a best seller. Published first Oz book in 1900: *The Wonderful World of Oz.* Died at age 63 of a stroke in Hollywood, California.

Last Words: "Now we can cross the shifting sands together." Spoken to his wife before he slipped into unconsciousness. The "shifting sands" refer to the impassible desert that surrounds the Land of Oz.

Source: "Baum, L. Frank" by Elizabeth H. Oakes in *American Writers, American Biographies* (New York, 2004).

Baxter, Charles

(1814-1847) American military officer. Lieutenant colonel of 1st New York Volunteers, Company B during the Mexican War. Command of New York Volunteers was given to him after the injury of Colonel Burnett. Baxter was killed during the taking of Chapultepec in Mexico City. Orange Street in New York City was renamed Baxter Street in his honor.

Last Words: "Then say to him that the New York Regiment was there and that I fell where I should have fallen, at the head of it." Spoken to a doctor who was sitting at his bedside writing a letter to Baxter's father.

Source: *Documents of the Board of Alderman of the City of New York,* Vol. XV, Part I (New York, 1849).

Baxter, John Clifford

(1958-2002) American businessman. Former Enron Corporation executive who resigned in 2001. Found dead at age 43 in his car in Sugar Land, Texas, from a self-inflicted gunshot. Left a suicide note.

Last Words (written): "Carol, I am so sorry for this. I feel I just can't go on. I have always tried to do the right thing but where there was once great pride now it's gone. I love you and the children so much. I just can't be any good to you or myself. The pain is overwhelming. Please try to forgive me. Cliff —J. Clifford Baxter." Suicide note to his wife.

Source: "Baxter's Suicide Note Cites Emotional Burden" by Eric Hanson (*Houston Chronicle*, April 12, 2002).

Baxter, Richard

(1615-1691) English clergyman, theologian, writer. Puritan and Nonconformist. Notable work: *The Saints' Everlasting Rest.* Persecuted for moderate position toward dissenters. Forced out of Church of England in 1662. Later, imprisoned 18 months for libeling the church. Died at age 76 in London.

Different Last Words:

(1) "Death, death. O I thank Him, I thank Him. The Lord teach you to die."

Source: *The Reverend Richard Baxter Under the Cross (1662-1691)* by Frederick J. Powicke (London, 1927).

(2) "I have pain—there is no arguing against sense—but I have peace, I have peace. I am almost well."

Source: *The Last Words (Real and Traditional) of Distinguished Men and Women Collected From Various Sources* by Frederic Rowland Marvin (New York, 1901).

Bayard, George Dashiell

(1835-1862) American military officer. Union brigadier general under General Ambrose E. Burnside in U.S. Civil War. One of the youngest generals in the Army. Killed at age 26 at Fredericksburg, Virginia.

Last Words (written): "My black mare and sorrel horse I give to you, father. There are about sixty dollars in my pocket-book. There are papers in my trunk to be turned over to the [Quartermaster's] Department, to settle. Once more, good bye, beloved father, mother, sisters, all. Ever yours, George D. Bayard." Letter to his family.

Source: *The Life of George Dashiell Bayard* by Samuel J. Bayard (New York, 1874). The author was his father.

Last Words (spoken): "Tell McClellan that my last regret as a military man is that I did not die serving under him."

Source: *A Conspectus of American Biography: Being an Analytical Summary of American History and Biography, Containing also the Complete Indexes of the National Cyclopedia of American Biography* by George Derby (New York, 1906).

Bayard, Pierre Terrail de

(1473?-1524) French military officer. Known as the Knight Without Fear and Without Reproach. Killed in battle in Italy.

Different Last Words:

(1) "At least I may die facing the enemy." After being shot, he was helped back on his horse and placed next to a tree. He died a

few moments after he spoke these words.

Source: *The Last Words (Real and Traditional) of Distinguished Men and Women Collected From Various Sources* by Frederic Rowland Marvin (New York, 1901).

(2) "It is not I who am to be commiserated, but you, far more, who fight against your king and your country." His response to the Constable of Bourbon when he heard words of pity directed toward him as he lay mortally wounded.

Source: *Biographie universelle,* Book III, by J. Fr. Michaud and Louis Gabriel Michaud (Paris, 1811-1862).

Variation: "I am not to be pitied who died a true man, serving my king; but you are to be pitied who carry arms against your prince, your country, and your oath."

Source: *Last Words of Saints and Sinners: 700 Final Quotes from the Famous, the Infamous, and the Inspiring Figures in History* by Herbert Lockyer (Grand Rapids, MI, 1969).

Variation: "Sir, thank you; one does not pity me who dies as a man of good, serving my king; but one needs pity you, who carries the weapons against your prince, your fatherland, your oath."

Source: *The Art of Dying: An Anthology,* ed. by Francis Birrell and F. L. Lucas (London, 1930).

Variation: "Pity me not: I die as a man of honor ought, in the discharge of my duty: they indeed are objects of pity who fight against their king, their country and their oath....God and my country!"

Source: *Famous Last Words & Tombstone Humor* by Gyles Brandreth (New York, 1989).

Beaconsfield, 1st Earl of, see Disraeli, Benjamin.

Beall, John Yates

(1835-1865) American military soldier, spy. Confederate in U.S. Civil War who attempted to seize a Federal warship on Lake Erie and free Confederate prisoners. Tried by court martial for violating laws of war and acting as a spy. Sentenced to be hanged. President Lincoln refused to grant him clemency. Executed at age 30 on Governors Island, New York. A legend soon began circulating that John Wilkes Booth killed Lincoln in retaliation for Beall's execution. The story claimed Booth was a close school friend of Beall and had sought Lincoln's pardon for him. Supposedly, at first the President said yes, but because of public outrage, he changed his mind and allowed the execution to go forward. Booth was traumatized by Beall's death and the assassination followed. The legend has since been debunked.

Last Words: "I protest against this execution. It is absolute murder—brutal murder. I die in the service and defense of my country."

Source: "Military Execution, Execution of John Y. Beall, the Lake Erie Pirate and Rebel Spy" (*New York Times,* February 25, 1865).

Beamer, Todd Morgan

(1968-2001) American victim of September 11, 2001, terrorism attack. Was passenger aboard United Airlines Flight 93. After his plane was hijacked, Beamer and other passengers learned via cell phone that the World Trade Center had been attacked using airplanes. Realizing their plane was to be used by the terrorists, Beamer told GTE phone operator Lisa Jefferson some of the plane's passengers were planning to "jump on" the hijackers. Jefferson heard Beamer's last audible words before he and several fellow passengers took the plane down and crashed it in a field in Somerset, Pennsylvania. He died at age 32. A post office in Cranbury, New Jersey, Todd Beamer High School in Federal Way, Washington, and the Todd M. Beamer Student Center at Wheaton College have been named for him.

Last Words: "Are you guys ready? Let's roll." The phone line from Flight 93 was still open when the GTE operator heard Todd Beamer speak these words. Beamer's phrase "Let's roll" became a battle cry for those fighting the 9/11 terrorists.

Source: "The phone line from Flight 93 was still open when a GTE operator heard Todd Beamer say: 'Are you guys ready? Let's roll'" by Jim McKinnon (*Pittsburgh Post-Gazette,* September 16, 2001).

Beard, George Miller

(1839-1883) American physician, neurologist. Noted for research in neurasthenia and mental disease. Coined term neurasthenia. Leading electrotherapist of his era. Notable works: *Electricity as a Tonic; Our Home Physician*. Described some symptoms of Tourette syndrome in 1880. Died at age 43 in New York.

Last Words: "Tell the doctors it is impossible for me to record the thoughts of a dying man. It would be interesting to do so, but I cannot. My time has come. I hope others will carry on my work." Described as "almost" his Last Words spoken to bystanders at his deathbed.

Source: *Dictionary of American Biography,* Vol. III (New York, 1959).

Variation: "I should like to record the thoughts of a dying man for the benefits of science, but it is impossible."

Source: *The Last Words (Real and Traditional) of Distinguished Men and Women Collected From Various Sources* by Frederic Rowland Marvin (New York, 1901). Marvin cited Beard's obituary as his source.

Beard, James Andrew

(1903-1985) American chef, writer. Author of many cook books that have become classics. Established cooking school in 1955. Died at age 81 in New York City.

Last Words: "I can't anymore." He was no longer able to talk.

Source: *James Beard: A Biography* by Robert Clark (New York, 1993).

Beardsley, Aubrey Vincent

(1872-1898) English artist, illustrator. Most of his work was in black and white. Leading exponent of Art Nouveau. Died at age 25 of tuberculosis in Menton, France.

Last Words (written, doubtful): "I implore you to destroy all copies of Lysistrata—by all that is holy—all obscene drawings." Letter to his London publisher with the heading "Jesus is our Lord & Judge."

Source: Various Last Words compilations and Internet websites.

Although this quote is frequently cited as Beardsley's Last Words, he wrote the letter nine days before he died.

Source: "Final Days. Aubrey Beardsley, English illustrator," *The People's Almanac 3* by David Wallechinsky & Irving Wallace (New York, 1981).

Variation: "Burn all my bawdy pictures."

Source: "Lionel Johnson, Ernest Dowson, Aubrey Beardsley" in *The Circus and Other Essays and Fugitive Pieces* by Joyce Kilmer and Robert Cortes Holliday (New York, 1921).

Beaton or Bethune, David

(1494-1546) Scottish prelate, statesman. Roman Catholic Archbishop of St. Andrews. Appointed cardinal in 1538. Appointed chancellor of Scotland in 1543. Persecuted Protestants. Arranged arrest, trial and execution of Reformation preacher George Wishart. Wishart's sympathizers murdered Beaton in revenge at his castle two months later.

Last Words: "I am a priest; I am a priest! Fie! Fie! All is gone." Spoken as his assassins prepared to kill him.

Source: *History of England* by James Anthony Froude (London, 1898).

Beatrix, Grand Duchess of Bavaria

(1403?-1447) Bavarian royalty. Daughter of Duke Ernst of Bavaria. Sister of Duke Albert III of Bavaria.

Last Words (written): "To the Duke of Bavaria: Our warm devotion and all love and goodness in our power. Noble prince, dear brother, it is proper that you should know that we fell ill last Monday and though we had hope of getting the better of our infirmity, we notice that the weakness and sickness is going from bad to worse. Therefore we beg you in all friendliness to send promptly one or two of your councilors here to Neumarket, so that if God the Almighty calls us, your brotherly affection may know what sort of departure we made." Letter sent to her brother Albert III, Duke of Bavaria, on March 11, 1447, the day before she died.

Source: *Abschiedsbriefe* by Wilhelm Treichlinger (Berlin, Germany, 1934).

Beauchamp, Jeroboam Orville

(1802-1826) American lawyer, murderer. Killed Colonel Solomon P. Sharp, who seduced then made slanderous accusations against his wife. Beauchamp was convicted and sentenced to die by hanging. He and his wife attempted double suicide twice, by taking laudanum and by stabbing. He survived both attempts; she stayed with him until he went to the gallows then died of knife wounds. Beauchamp was hanged at age 23 in Frankfort, Kentucky. Their tragic story inspired several books and stories, including Edgar Allan Poe's *Politian: A Tragedy*, Mary E. MacMichael's *The Kentucky Tragedy* and Robert Penn Warren's *World Enough and Time*.

Last Words: "Farewell child of sorrow—Farewell child of misfortune and persecution—you are now secure from the tongue of slander—for you I have lived; for you I die." Spoken to his wife Ann.

Sources: *Lexington Kentucky Reporter*, July 7, 1826; "Poe's Politian and the Beauchamp-Sharp Tragedy" by William J. Kimball (*Poe Studies*, 4:2, December 1971).

Beaufort, Henry

(1377?-1447) French-born English prelate, statesman, nobleman. Son of John of Gaunt. Bishop of Lincoln and Winchester. Chancellor of Oxford 1397. Became cardinal in 1417. Chancellor of England 1403-1405, 1413-1417 and 1424-1426. Crowned Henry VI King of France and England in 1431. Died at Winchester.

Different Last Words:

(1) "Away! Away! Why thus do ye look at me?" Cried out with his hands raised seeming to behold some horrible sight.

Source: *Historia Anglicana Ecclesiastica* by Nicholas Harpsfield (1622).

(2) "I pray you all pray for me."

Source: "Dying Words of Noted Persons" in *Miscellaneous Notes and Queries with Answers in All Departments of Literature*, Vol. II (Manchester, NH, 1885).

(3) "Why should I die having so much riches? If the whole realm could save my life, I am able by policy to get it, or by riches to buy it. Fie, will not death be hired, nor will money buy anything?" Spoken to his chaplain on his deathbed.

Source: *The Popular History of England* by Charles Knight (New York, 1881).

Variation: "And must I then die? Will not my riches save me? I could purchase the kingdom, if that would prolong my life. Alas! there is no bribing death."

Source: *Dying Testimonies of Saved and Unsaved: Gathered from Authentic Sources* by Solomon Benjamin Shaw (Chicago, 1898).

Variation: "And must I then die? Will not my riches save me? What is there no bribing death?"

Source: "Dying Words of Distinguished Persons" in *The Encyclopedia of Death and Life in the Spirit-World*, Vol. I, by J.R. Francis (Chicago, 1895).

Beaufort, Henry, 3rd Duke of Somerset

(1436-1464) English nobleman, military officer. Lancastrian commander in the War of the Roses. Defeated at the Battle of Hexham. Beheaded soon afterward at age 27.

Last Words: "Lord Jesus, save me."

Source: *History of England* by James Anthony Froude (New York, 1898).

Beaumont, Joseph

(1794-1855) English clergyman, physician. Prominent Wesleyan Methodist minister. Known as a strong advocate of overseas missions and as an outspoken political liberal. While conducting a service at the Waltham Street Chapel in Hull, England, he announced a hymn then collapsed and died at age 60.

Last Words: "Thee, while the first Archangel sings, He hides his face behind his wings."

Source: *The Life of the Rev. Joseph Beaumont, M.D.* by Joseph Beaumont (London, 1856). The author was his son.

Beaverbrook, 1st Baron, William Maxwell Aiken ("Lord Beaverbrook")

(1879-1964) Canadian-born British politician, statesman, newspaper publisher. Published *Daily Express* and *Evening Standard*. Active in British government during World War II. Minister of aircraft production, minister of supply, minister of state. Raised to peerage in 1917. Died at age 85 at his home near Leatherhead, Surrey.

Last Words: "But maybe I wouldn't wake up." Spoken to his physician who recommended he get some rest.

Source: *Lord Beaverbrook: A Life* by Anne Chisholm and Michael Davie (New York, 1993).

Beck, Ludwig August Theodor

(1880-1944) German military officer. General, chief of staff. Executed for involvement in Stauffenberg plot to assassinate Adolf Hitler in 1944, during World War II. Ordered to commit suicide at age 64 in Berlin.

Last Words: "If it doesn't work this time, then please help me." Spoken the same day as the failed plot after two attempts to shoot himself. He succeeded on his third attempt.

Source: *The Rise and Fall of the Third Reich* by William L. Shirer (New York, 1960).

Beck, Martha

(1921-1951) American murderer. She and lover Raymond Fernandez were known as the Lonely Hearts killers. Found victims through Lonely Hearts ads in newspapers. Electrocuted at Ossining (Sing Sing) prison,

New York. The movie *Lonely Hearts* (2007) is based on their late-1940s crime spree. Beck's Last Words were her final statement to the press.

Last Words: "What does it matter who is to blame? My story is a love story, but only those tortured with love can understand what I mean. I was pictured as a fat unfeeling woman. I am not unfeeling, stupid or moronic. The prison and the death house have only strengthened my feeling for Raymond and in the history of the world how many crimes have been attributed to love?" As she was being placed in the electric chair, she whispered "So long" but made no other sound.

Source: *Women Who Died In The Chair—The Dramatic True Stories of Six Women Who Committed the Deadliest Sin* by Wenzell Brown (New York, 1963).

Variation: "My story is a love story, but only those who are tortured by love can understand what I mean. I was pictured as a fat, unfeeling woman. True, I am fat, but if that is a crime, how many of my sex are guilty. I am not unfeeling, stupid or moronic. My last words and my last thoughts are: Let him who is without sin cast the first stone."

Source: *The 1950s' Most Wanted: The Top 10 Book of Rock & Roll Rebels, Cold War Crises and All-American Oddities* by Robert Rodriguez (Dulles, VA, 2006).

Becket, Saint Thomas à

(1118?-1170) English prelate, holy man, statesman. Archbishop of Canterbury. Chancellor of England. Murdered at about age 52 in Canterbury Cathedral by knights in the court of King Henry II for challenging his authority. Canonized in 1172. Henry VIII had his grave plundered in 1538. *Murder in the Cathedral* by T.S. Eliot is a poetic dramatization of Becket's assassination.

Last Words: "I do commend my cause to God, the Virgin, St. Denis of France and St. Alphege of England, and all the tutelar saints of Canterbury." Spoken as he covered his eyes with his hands.

Source: *St. Thomas of Canterbury* by Edwin Abbott Abbott (London, 1898).

Variation: "I confide my soul and the cause of the Church of God, to the Virgin Mary, to the patron saints of this church and St.

Dennis."

Source: "Dying Words of Noted Persons" in *Miscellaneous Notes and Queries with Answers in All Departments of Literature*, Vol. II (Manchester, NH, 1885).

Variation: "I confide my soul and the cause of the Church to God.—I charge you in the name of the Almighty not to hurt any other person here."

Source: *Last Words of Saints and Sinners: 700 Final Quotes from the Famous, the Infamous, and the Inspiring Figures in History* by Herbert Lockyer (Grand Rapids, MI, 1969).

Variation: "I accept death for the name Jesus and the Church."

Source: *Saints and Feast Days: Lives of the Saints* by Sister of Notre Dame of Chardon, Ohio (Chicago, 1985).

Variation: "For the name of Jesus and the defense of the Church, I am willing to die."

Source: *Book of Catholic Quotations Compiled from Approved Sources Ancient, Medieval and Modern*, ed. by John Chapin (New York, 1956).

Variation: "For the name of Jesus and the protection of the church I am ready to embrace death."

Source: *Materials for the History of Thomas Becket, archbishop of Canterbury* by James Robertson and J.B. Shepperd (London, 1875-85).

Variation: "I am prepared to die for Christ and for His Church. I charge you in the name of the Almighty not to hurt any other person here, for none of them have been concerned in the late transactions." Spoken as he approached the altar in Canterbury Cathedral, where he was assassinated.

Source: *Famous Last Words & Tombstone Humor* by Gyles Brandreth (New York, 1989).

Beckford, William Thomas

(1760-1844) English novelist, art collector. Notable work: *Vathek, An Arabian Tale* (Gothic novel). Inherited a fortune when he was young. Was once one of the richest men in England. Lived in seclusion in Fonthill Abbey, an English Gothic Revival building with a 260-foot tower built in 1796. The tower fell in 1800. He rebuilt it even taller. It collapsed again in 1825. The rest of the abbey later was demolished. Beckford died at age 83 in Bath, England.

Last Words (written): "Come quick! Quick!" Message to his daughter.

Source: *The Life and Letters of William Beckford of Fonthill (Author of "Vathek")* by Lewis Melville (New York, 1910).

Bécquer, Gustavo Adolfo

(1836-1870) Spanish writer, poet. Birth name Gustavo Adolfo Domínguez Bastida. Changed name to Bécquer as his brother Valeriano Bécquer, a painter, had done. Died at age 34 in Madrid. Although moderately well known during his life, he gained the greatest notoriety after his death when most of his works were published. He is considered one of the great Spanish writers of his era.

Last Words: "¡Todo Mortal!" (tr. "All mortal!") Spoken while delirious from fever.

Source: *Gustavo Adolfo Bécquer* by Gabriel Celaya (Madrid, Spain, 1972).

Beddoes, Thomas Lovell

(1803-1849) English dramatist, writer, poet. Notable work: *Death's Jest-Book, or, The Fool's Tragedy* (dramatic poem published posthumously in 1850. He kept revising it throughout his life.). He was melancholy and eccentric. Had an obsession with death that pervaded his work and his life. He made repeated attempts at self-destruction. Committed suicide at age 45 by poisoning in Basel, Switzerland. Left a suicide note.

Last Words (written): "I am food for what I am good for—worms. I ought to have been among other things a good poet. Life was too great a bore on one peg & that a bad one.—Buy for Dr. Ecklin above mentioned Reade's best stomach pump." Written at the end of his suicide note.

Source: *The Works of Thomas Lovell Beddoes,* ed. by H.W. Donner (London, 1935).

Bede, Beda or Baeda, Saint ("The Venerable")

(673-735) Anglo-Saxon scholar, historian, theologian. Spent his life reading, teaching and writing at a monastery in Jarrow (northern England, near Newcastle. Only ruins remain). Notable work: *Historia ecclesiastica gentis Anglorum (Ecclesiastical History of the English People),* using local chronicles, biographies, public documents, letters. Died at age 62 in Jarrow. Made Doctor of the Church by Pope Leo XIII.

Last Words: "It is finished. Take mine head between thy hands and raise me. Full fain would I sit with my face to my holy oratory,

where I was ever wont to pray, that sitting so I may call on my Father. Glory be to the Father and to the Son and to the Holy Ghost." He died as he breathed the words "Holy Ghost."

Source: *The Venerable Bede* by G.F. Browne (New York, 1919).

Variation: "Hold my head that I may have the pleasure of looking towards my little oratory, where I used to pray, and that I may once more call upon the Heavenly Father. Glory be to the Father and to the Son and to the Holy Ghost."

Source: *Last Words of Saints and Sinners: 700 Final Quotes from the Famous, the Infamous, and the Inspiring Figures in History* by Herbert Lockyer (Grand Rapids, MI, 1969).

Variation: "Write quickly… Well, thou hast spoken truly 'It is finished'—Glory to the Father, and to the Son, and to the Holy Ghost." Spoken to a scribe who was writing down his translation of the Gospel of St. John.

Source: *Dictionary of National Biography, from the Earliest Times to 1900,* by Sir Leslie Stephen, George Smith and Sir Sidney Lee (London, 1921-1922).

Variation: "Well you have spoken truly: 'It is finished'" Spoken to his scribe, but addressing Christ. "Glory be to the Father and to the Son and to the Holy Spirit!"

Source: *Last Words: Final Thoughts of Catholic Saints and Sinners* by Paul Thigpen (Cincinnati, OH, 2006).

Variation: "Thou hast said truly, 'consummatum est.'" (tr. "It is finished.") Spoken to his scribe.

Sources: *The Last Words (Real and Traditional) of Distinguished Men and Women Collected From Various Sources* by Frederic Rowland Marvin (New York, 1901). Marvin cited *Lippincott* (unknown). Similar versions appear in *Disputatio historico-theologica de Bedae Venerabilis, presbyteri Anglo-Saxonis, vita et scriptis* by Henricus Gehle (Leiden, The Netherlands, 1838); *Historical Works of Venerable Bede* by J.A. Giles (London, 1843-1844).

Variation: "Glory be to the Father and to the Son, and to the —."

Source: "Dying Words of Noted Persons" in *Miscellaneous Notes and Queries with Answers in All Departments of Literature*, Vol. II (Manchester, NH, 1885).

Bedell, William

(1571-1642) English-born prelate, educator, translator. Anglican Bishop of Kilmore and Ardagh, Ireland. Provost of Trinity College. Translated Old Testament into Irish. Seized by rebels and imprisoned in a ruined castle for several weeks. Died from exposure.

Different Last Words:

(1) "I have kept the faith once given to the saints; for the which cause I have also suffered these things; but I am not ashamed, for I know whom I have believed, and I am persuaded that He is able to keep that which I have committed to Him against that day."
Source: *The Life of William Bedell, D.D. Bishop of Kilmore in Ireland* by Gilbert Burnet (London, 1685).

(2) "Be of good cheer. Be of good cheer. Whether we live or die we are the Lord's."
Source: *A True Relation of the Life and Death of the Right Reverend Father in God William Bedell, Lord Bishop of Kilmore in Ireland* by Thomas Wharton Jones (London, 1872).

Bee, Barnard Elliott, Jr.

(1824-1861) American military officer. Son of Barnard Elliott Bee, Cabinet member in Republic of Texas. Grandson of Thomas Bee, member of Continental Congress. Confederate general in U.S. Civil War. Wounded at Manassas. He died at age 37 the following day. Made a statement shortly before he died that gave rise to nickname "Stonewall" for General Thomas J. Jackson.

Last Words: "There is Jackson standing like a stone wall! Rally behind the Virginians. Let us determine to die here and we will conquer. Follow me."
Source: *Life of Lieut.-Gen. Thomas J. Jackson (Stonewall Jackson),* Vol. I, by R.L. Dabney (London, 1864).

Variation: "There is Jackson standing like a stone wall. Let us determine to die here, and we will conquer. Follow me." (It is the same quote without "Rally behind the Virginians.")
Source: *Stonewall Jackson: A Military Biography* by John Esten Cooke (New York, 1866).

Beebe, Roderick

(1933-1978) American airline pilot. Victim of airline disaster. Pilot on DC-8 that ran out of fuel. Died at age 45. The accident led to training that is now part of Crew Resource Management (CRM).

Last Words: "Portland Tower, United 173, Mayday! We're—the engines are flaming out—we're going down. We're not going to be able to make the airport." Spoken just before plane crashed on December 28, 1978.

Source: *The Air Up There: More Great Quotations on Flight* by Dave English (New York, 2003), citing the NTSB, 13:50 EST October 31, 1999.

Beecher, Catharine Esther

(1800-1878) American educator, feminist, writer. Daughter of Lyman Beecher. Sister of Harriet Beecher Stowe and Henry Ward Beecher. Promoted suffrage and equal educational opportunities for women. Died at age 77 in Elmira, New York.

Last Words (written): "I hope to be in Phil. in about ten days. I am stronger than for yrs. but take no new responsibilities."
Source: *Saints, Sinners, and Beechers* by Lyman Beecher Stowe (Indianapolis, IN, 1934). The author was the grandson of Catharine's sister Harriet Beecher Stowe.

Beecher, Frederick H.

(1841-1868) American military officer. Army lieutenant. Nephew of Henry Ward Beecher and Harriet Beecher Stowe. Fought in the Indian Wars. Died at age 27 in a battle where the Cheyenne fought to defend their land. The engagement became known as the Battle of Beecher Island. Military station at mouth of Little Arkansas River was later renamed Camp Beecher in his honor.

Last Words: "I have my death wound, General. I am shot and dying." The general responded in disbelief. Beecher continued: "Yes, Good night." A few minutes later, Beecher murmured: "My poor mother." He then drifted into semiconsciousness and made incoherent comments about the fight before he died.
Source: *The Battle of Beecher Island and the Indian War of 1867-1869* by John H. Monnett (Boulder, CO, 1992).

Beecher, Henry Ward

(1813-1887) American clergyman, newspaper editor. Son of Lyman Beecher. Congregationalist. Noted for abolitionist orations. Died at age 73 in Brooklyn, New York.

Different Last Words:

(1) "Well high enough to hit you, doctor." His response to his physician who asked how high he could raise his arm.
Source: *Life and Work of Henry Ward Beecher* by Thomas W. Knox (Hartford, CT, 1887).

(2) "Now comes the mystery."
Source: *A Conspectus of American Biography: Being*

an Analytical Summary of American History and Biography, Containing also the Complete Indexes of the National Cyclopedia of American Biography by George Derby (New York, 1906).

(3) "Going out into life—that is dying."

Source: *Last Words of Saints and Sinners: 700 Final Quotes from the Famous, the Infamous, and the Inspiring Figures in History* by Herbert Lockyer (Grand Rapids, MI, 1969).

(4) "You were saying that I could not recover."

Source: *The Most Famous Man in America* by Debby Applegate (New York, 2006).

Beecher, Lyman

(1775-1863) American clergyman, theologian, educator. Presbyterian. First president of Lane Theological Seminary in Cincinnati. His moderate approach to Calvinism was criticized by old school Presbyterians, causing him to be charged with heresy in 1835. The case lasted three years then was withdrawn. Beecher was a temperance movement leader. His temperance sermons were published and distributed widely in the United States and Great Britain. Father of 13 children, including Catharine, Harriet and Henry Ward. Died at age 87 in Brooklyn, New York.

Last Words: "I have fought a good fight, I have finished my course, I have kept the faith; henceforth there is laid up for me a crown, which God, the righteous Judge, will give me at that day. That is my testimony— write it down.—That is my testimony." Words of St. Paul.

Source: *Saints, Sinners, and Beechers* by Lyman Beecher Stowe (Indianapolis, IN, 1934). The author was his great-grandson.

Beerbohm, Sir Henry Maximilian ("Max")

(1872-1956) British writer, caricaturist, satirist, humorist, critic. Half brother of actor-producer Herbert Beerbohm Tree. Drama critic for *Saturday Review*. Noted caricaturist. Several books of his drawings have been published. Knighted in 1939. Spent his last 45 years in Rapallo, Italy, where he died at age 83.

Last Words: "Thank you for everything." His response to his secretary-companion when asked if he slept well. He had married her secretly shortly before he died.

Source: *Time* magazine, May 28, 1956.

Beesley or Bisley, Blessed George

(d. 1591) English clergyman, martyr. Ordained a Roman Catholic priest in 1587. Captured in 1590 and tortured until he was reduced to a skeleton. He would not betray his fellow Catholics. He was one of the 85 Martyrs of England and Wales beatified by Pope John Paul II in 1987.

Last Words: "Absit mihi gloriari nisi in Cruce Domini Nostri Jesu Christi" and after a pause, "Good people, I beseech God to send all felicity."

Source: "Ven. George Beesley" by B. Camm in *The Catholic Encyclopedia* (New York, 1907).

Beethoven, Ludwig van

(1770-1827) German musician, composer, pianist, conductor. Moved to Vienna in 1792. Spent the rest of his life there. Notable works: symphonies, concertos, sonatas, chamber, choral and orchestral music. Hearing loss began in his 20s. He did not tell others about his increasing deafness until in his 30s when he could no longer conceal it. Also had a debilitating disease for many years. Died at age 57 in Vienna.

Different Last Words:

(1) "Schade! Schade! Zu spaet!" (tr. "Too bad! Too bad! It's too late!" Sometimes translated as "It's a pity, a pity. Too late!") He was referring to two bottles of wine from Mainz that were brought to his bedside by a servant. Beethoven felt he was too ill to drink it. This occurred at about 12:45 p.m. and was recorded by Anton Schindler who said Beethoven became delirious almost immediately afterward and fell into a coma. Beethoven died the next day during a thunderstorm which may account for some reports that he shook his fist at the sky as his final words.

Sources: *Life of Beethoven* by Louis Nohl, tr. John J. Lalor (Chicago, 1881); *Beethoven* by Soloman Maynard (London, 1977) and other major biographies.

(2) (doubtful): "Plaudite amici, comedia finita est!" (tr. "Applaud my friends. The comedy is ended.") Lines traditionally spoken at the end of commedia dell'arte performances. Beethoven said this to his friends Anton Schindler and Stephen von Breuning. However, these were not his Last Words.

Beethoven subsequently discussed business matters with Schindler: He wanted Schindler to write to the Philharmonic Society and thank them for the wine they had sent him. The letter was written as Beethoven had requested and it provides detailed information about Beethoven's last days. It identifies "Schade! Schade! Zu spaet!" as his Last Words.

Sources: *Beethoven's Letters: A Critical Edition with Explanatory Notes,* Vol. II by Dr. A. C. Kalischer, tr. with preface by J. S. Shedlock (London, 1909); *Grove's Dictionary of Music and Musicians,* ed. by J.A Fuller Maitland (Philadelphia, 1925).

(3) (doubtful): "I shall hear" or variation "I shall hear in heaven." This quote was reported in a 19th-century source and has been reprinted in later quotation books. According to witnesses present at his death, there is no record of Beethoven saying this.

Source: *The Last Words (Real and Traditional) of Distinguished Men and Women Collected from Various Sources* by Frederic Rowland Marvin (New York, 1901).

(4) (doubtful): "Do you hear the bell? The scene is being shifted." This was a reference to the practice employed between scenes in Viennese theatre. The quote was reported by the celebrated singer Luigi Lablache, who claimed he was present at Beethoven's death. There is no record to indicate Lablache was a witness to his death. However, he was one of the torch bearers at Beethoven's funeral.

Source: "Beethoven—An Art Study" by Wilhelm von Lenz tr. J.B. Bridgeman (*The Musical World,* August 9, 1856).

(5) (doubtful): "Is it not true, Hummel, that I have some talent after all?" Spoken to fellow composer Johann Nepomuk Hummel. Although Hummel had visited Beethoven not long before his death, he was not present when he died. Hummel was one of Beethoven's pallbearers.

Source: "Last Moments of Beethoven" (*The Guardian –A Monthly Magazine for Young Men and Ladies,* Vol. XXVIII, ed. by Rev. B. Bausman, D.D., 1877). Reprint of a story that appeared *Harper's New Monthly Magazine* in 1854. This version is repeated in several sources.

Béhaine, Pierre Joseph-Georges Pigneau de

(1741-1799) French prelate, educator. Bishop. Left France in 1765 to establish a seminary in Vietnam (Cochinchina). Appointed bishop 1771. Created vicar apostolic of Cochin 1799. Died at age 57 in Vietnam.

Last Words: "Here I am finally. Here I am at the end of the tumultuous career that, whatever my repugnance, I have kept to for so long. My troubles will soon be over and my true happiness is coming, since I have all confidence in the mercy of my God. I willingly leave this world where I have been thought happy in that I have had public admiration, been respected by great, esteemed kings. I can't say that I regret all these honors—it's just that they add up to vanity and trouble."

Source: *Notice sur Mgr Pierre-Joseph-Georges Pigneau de Béhaine, évêque d'Adran et prince de Cochinchine, ministre plénipotentiaire du roi Louis XVI, général en chef des armées annamites, négociateur et signataire du traité de 1787 entre la France et la Cochinchine* by M. l'abbé J. Jardinier Vervins (Paris, 1866).

Behan, Brendan Francis

(1923-1964) Irish writer, playwright, journalist, song writer. Member of the Irish Republican Army. Wrote books and songs in Gaelic and English. Gained fame with *Borstal Boy* (1958), his account of three years in Borstal Prison after his arrest by the British while on a sabotage mission. Died at age 41 at Meath Hospital, Dublin, Ireland.

Different Last Words:

(1) "Bless you, Sister. May all your sons be bishops." Spoken to the nurse who was near his hospital bed taking his pulse.

Source: "A Dying Art: The Classy Exit Line" (*Time* magazine, January 16, 1984).

(2) "You made one mistake. You married me." Spoken to his wife.

Source: *Brendan* by Ulick O'Conner (Englewood Cliffs, NJ, 1970).

Belasco, David

(1853-1931) American playwright, impresario, director, theatrical producer. Wrote, directed, or produced more than 100 Broadway plays. Notable plays: *Hearts of Oak, The Heart of Maryland; Du Barry*. During his professional career, he was known as the most powerful person in the New York theater. Died at age 77 in New York City. The

Belasco Theatre was named in his honor.
Last Words: "Doctor, I'm fighting for my life!"
Source: "Exit a Character" (*Time* magazine, May 25, 1931).

Belgrano, Manuel

(1770-1820) Argentine politician, economist, lawyer, military officer. Full name Manuel José Joaquín del Corazón de Jesús Belgrano. Founder of la Bandera Argentina. Created the national flag of Argentina. Leader of Jujuy Exodus (Éxodo Jujeño), which prepared the groundwork for victories of the War of Independence in the northwest of Argentina. Leader of Argentine Declaration of Independence in 1816. He believed Argentina should be a constitutional monarchy led by an Inca descendant, but his idea did not gain support. Died of dropsy at age 50 in Buenos Aires. A monument complex (Monumento Nacional a la Bandera, National Flag Memorial) in Rosario and the ship ARA *General Belgrano* (sank during the Falklands War), among others, were named in his honor.
Last Words: "¡Ay, patria mía!" (tr. "Oh, my homeland!")
Source: *Monumento nacional a la bandera* (National monument in Rosario, Argentina).

Bell, Acton, Currer and Ellis, see Brontë, Anne, Charlotte and Emily.

Bell, Alexander Graham

(1847-1922) Scottish-born American inventor. Worked in U.S. most of his life. Teacher, consultant, researcher for Clarke School for the Deaf in Massachusetts for 51 years. Gained fame and wealth with invention of telephone, photophone. Founding member National Geographic Society. Died at age 75 in Nova Scotia.
Different Last Words:
(1) "But I have to. So little done. So much to do." Response to his wife Mabel, to whom he was dictating, after she said: "Please don't hurry."
Source: *Life Stories of the Great Inventors* by Henry and Dana Lee Thomas (New York, 1948).
(2) "No," expressed in sign language to his wife who whispered to him "Don't leave me."

Source: *The Telephone Book: Technology, Schizophrenia, Electric Speech* by Avital Ronell (Lincoln, NE, 1989).

Bell, Sir Charles

(1774-1842) Scottish anatomist, surgeon, educator. Professor of surgery at Edinburgh. Noted for his research on the nervous system. Knighted in 1831. Died at age 68 of angina pectoris at North Hallow, Worcestershire. Bell's palsy, Bell's phenomenon, Bell's spasm and Bell's nerve named for him. Distantly related to Dr. Joseph Bell, Arthur Conan Doyle's inspiration for Sherlock Holmes.
Last Words: "Hold me in your arms." Spoken to his wife.
Source: *The Life and Labours of Sir Charles Bell* by Amédée Pichot (Paris, 1858).

Bell, John Any

(1817?-1831) English murderer. Killed a 13-year-old boy for nine shillings. Put to death at age 14. Youngest person executed at Maidstone; 5,000 people watched the execution. He was the last person under 16 to be executed in Great Britain.
Last Words: "Lord have mercy on us. All people be warned by me."
Source: *The Hanging Tree. Execution and the English People 1770-1868* by V.A.C. Gatrell (Oxford, England, 1994).

Bellamy, Edward

(1850-1898) American writer, novelist, futurist. Socialist. Notable work: *Looking Backward,* 1888 utopian novel set in the year 2000, which predicted radio, movies and television. The novel was Bellamy's platform for tackling problems of social and political inequality in America. It was one of the best sellers of the 19th century. "Bellamy Clubs" were established where members discussed the impact Bellamy's ideas could have on society. In 1891, he founded *New Nation,* a magazine that served as a forum for his views. His success with his first novel prompted him to write *Equality.* Died at age 48 in Chicopee Falls, Massachusetts.
Last Words: "What can happen to me? I can only die."
Source: *The Blindman's World and Other Stories* by Edward Bellamy, with prefatory sketch by W.D. Howells (Boston, 1898).

Bellamy, Joseph

(1719-1790) American clergyman, writer, educator, theologian. Great-grandfather of writer/futurist Edward Bellamy. Received theological training from Jonathan Edwards. Life-long pastor of Congregational Church, Bethlehem, Connecticut. Revivalist during Great Awakening. Died at age 71 in Bethlehem.

Last Words: "I will tell them for ever that Jesus is precious." Reply to a friend who asked: "If God should send you to hell, what would you do there?"

Source: *Illustrative Gatherings, or Preachers and Teachers, a Manual of Figures, Proverbs, Quotations, etc. Adapted for Christian Teaching* by George Seaton Bowes (London, 1860).

Bellarmine, Saint Robert Francis Roundus

(1542-1621) Italian prelate, theologian, holy man, writer. Archbishop of Capua. Jesuit. Made cardinal in 1598. Defender of the Roman Catholic Church. Active in the Vatican. Director of the Roman College. Notable work: *Disputations on the Controversies of the Christian Faith.* Informed Galileo about papal ban on his teaching heliocentric system. Died at age 78 in Rome. Canonized in 1930. Made Doctor of the Church in 1931.

Different Last Words:

(1) "And in life everlasting, Amen." The end of the Nicene Creed. He then whispered in his final instant of life: "Jesus, Jesus, Jesus."

Source: *The Life and Work of Blessed Robert Francis Cardinal Bellarmine* by James Brodrick (London, 1928).

(2) "It is safest to trust in Jesus." His response when asked whether it is safer to trust in the Virgin Mary than Jesus.

Source: *English Hearts and English Hands; or, The Railway and the Trenches* by Catherine Marsh (New York, 1862).

Bellingham, John

(1771-1812) English merchant, assassin. Imprisoned in Russia for leaving the country in a clandestine manner. British government declined his request to be compensated for his imprisonment. He murdered prime minister Spencer Perceval in the House of Commons on May 11, 1812. Bellingham surrendered immediately and was brought to trial on May 13. He was hanged on May 18.

Last Words: "I thank God for having enabled me to meet my fate with so much fortitude and resignation."

Source: *The Chronicles of Crime: Or the New Newgate Calendar: Being a Series of Memoirs and Anecdotes of Notorious Characters Who Have Outraged the Laws of Great Britain from the Earliest Period to 1841* by Camden Pelham (London, 1886).

Bellini, Vincenzo

(1801-1835) Italian-born musician, composer. Notable operas: *I Puritani; Norma; La Sonnambula.* Also composed songs and instrumental works. Died at age 33 of dysentery near Puteaux, France.

Last Words: "Perhaps some day they will hear my music without even saying 'Poor Bellini'."

Source: *Vincenzo Bellini* by William C. Lloyd (London, 1908).

Belmont, Alva Erskine Smith Vanderbilt

(1853-1933) American socialite, suffragette. Married and divorced William K. Vanderbilt. Married Oliver H.P. Belmont. Daughter married 9th Duke of Marlborough. Died at age 80.

Last Words: "The important thing is knowing how to live. Learn a lesson from my mistakes. I had too much power before I knew how to use it and it defeated me in the end. It drove all sweetness out of my life except the affection of my children. My trouble was I was born too late for the last generation and too early for this one. If you want to be happy, live in your own time." Spoken to a friend as she commiserated about growing old.

Source: *Fortune's Children: The Fall of the House of Vanderbilt* by Arthur T. Vanderbilt II (New York, 1989).

Belushi, John Adam

(1949-1982) American comedian, actor. Member of cast of *Saturday Night Live.* Notable movies: *Animal House; 1941; The Blues Brothers; Neighbors; Continental Divide.* Died at age 33 of cocaine and heroin overdose at Sunset Strip hotel in Los Angeles, California.

Last Words: "Just don't leave me alone."

Source: "Feeling so good you could DIE" ([Montreal] *Gazette,* April 29, 1990).

Bender, Tony

(1899-1962) American gangster. Birth name Anthony C. Strollo. Reputed to have set up more hits than anyone. Notorious for switching allegiance among New York crime families: Salvatore Maranzano then Lucky Luciano, Genovese, Frank Costello and Albert Anastasia then back to Genovese then to Luciano, Meyer Lansky, Carlo Gambino and Frank Costello. Finally swore allegiance as Genovese lieutenant. Died at age 62 in New York City.

Last Words: "I'm only going out for a few minutes. Besides, I'm wearing thermal underwear." Spoken to his wife who asked him to put on his top coat before he went out because it was chilly. He never returned.

Source: *The Mafia Encyclopedia: From Accardo to Zwillman* by Carl Sifakis (New York, 1987).

Benedek, Ludwig August von

(1804-1881) Hungarian-born Austrian military officer, politician. General who served in Galicia, Italy, Hungary, Solferino. Governor of Hungary. Court-martialed for disastrous defeat by Prussians in 1866; halted by imperial order. He was allowed to retire to Graz, where he died at age 76.

Last Words (written): "Relieved to hear that you feel better. I had a very bad night—am now stronger. Your poor Louis." Letter to his wife.

Source: *Benedeks Nachgelassene Papiere,* ed. by Heinrich Friedjung (Dresden, Germany, 1904).

Benedict, Lewis

(1817-1864) American lawyer, politician, military officer. New York state assemblyman. Union brevet brigadier general in U.S. Civil War. Commander of 162nd New York Volunteer Infantry. Captured at Williamsburg. Spent several months in Confederate prison. Killed at age 46 while in command of brigade at the Battle of Pleasant Hill, Louisiana.

Last Words: "Colonel, rally your men and advance as soon as possible."

Source: *A Memorial of Brevet Brigadier-General Lewis Benedict, Colonel of the 162d New York* (Albany, NY, 1866).

Benedict XIV, Pope

(1675-1758) Italian scholar, prelate. Birth name Prospero Lorenzo Lambertini. Ruled as pope from 1740 to 1758. Patron of the arts. Worked to improve city of Rome. Died at age 83 in Rome.

Last Words: "Sic transit gloria mundi." (tr. "Thus passes the glory of the world.")

Source: *The Chair of Peter; a History of the Papacy* by Friedrich Gontard, tr. by A.J. and E.F Peeler (New York, 1964).

Benedict of Nursia, Saint

(480-547?) Italian holy man. Founder of Western Christian monastic communities. Rule giver for cenobitic monks. Died about age 67 in Monte Cassino. Canonized in 1220. In 1964, Pope Paul VI named St. Benedict Patron Saint of Europe.

Last Words: "Don't grieve. I won't leave you alone." Whispered to his family before he received his last Holy Communion.

Source: *St. Benedict, Hero of the Hills* by Mary Fabyan Windeatt (New York, 1943).

Benezet, Anthony

(1713-1784) French-born American educator, philanthropist, social reformer. Concerned about educating slaves and Indians. Exposed injustices against early Americans, especially those affecting African Americans, Native Americans and women. Died at age 71 in Philadelphia.

Last Words: "We have lived long, in love and peace." Spoken to his wife.

Source: *Memoirs of the Life of Anthony Benezet* by Roberts Vaux (Philadelphia, 1817).

Benjamin, Judah Philip

(1811-1884) American lawyer, statesman, politician. Member U.S. Senate from Louisiana. Attorney general in Confederate cabinet during U.S. Civil War. Escaped to England in 1865 when war ended. Established successful law practice in London. Retired in 1883. Died at age 72 in Paris.

Last Words (written): "What I require is warmth—will it never come?" Written in a letter.

Source: *Judah P. Benjamin* by Pierce Butler (Philadelphia, 1907).

Benjamin, Park

(1809-1864) American writer, journalist, poet, lecturer. Born in British Guiana. Died at age 55 in New York.

Last Words: "Why should I not know you, Mary?" His response to his wife who asked if he knew her.

Source: *A Conspectus of American Biography: Being an Analytical Summary of American History and Biography, Containing also the Complete Indexes of the National Cyclopedia of American Biography* by George Derby (New York, 1906).

Bennett, Enoch Arnold (Arnold)

(1867-1931) English writer, journalist, novelist, playwright. Notable novels: *The Old Wives' Tale; Clayhanger; Anna of the Five Towns; Buried Alive.* Died at age 63 of typhoid fever in London.

Last Words "Everything is going wrong, my girl." Spoken to Dorothy Cheston Bennett, his second wife.

Source: *Arnold Bennett, A Biography* by Reginald Pound (New York, 1953).

Benson, Robert Hugh

(1871-1914) English clergyman, writer. Wrote semimystical historical and modern novels with highly religious tone. Notable works: *Come Rack! Come Rope!; The Lord of the World.* Brother of English authors A.C. (Arthur Christopher) Benson and Edward Frederick Benson. Father was Archbishop of Canterbury. Ordained priest of Church of England by his father. Converted to Roman Catholicism. Ordained priest in 1904 and named monsignor in 1911. Died three years later at age 42.

Last Words: "Arthur, don't look at me! Nurse stand between my brother and me.... Jesus, Mary and Joseph, I give you my heart and my soul."

Source: *The Life of Monsignor Robert Hugh Benson* by C.C. Martindale, S.J. (London, 1916).

Bentham, Jeremy

(1748-1832) English political theorist, economist, jurist, reformer, writer. Founder of utilitarianism. Helped found *Westminster Review* (utilitarian journal). Notable works: *The Rationale of Judicial Evidence; Constitutional Code.* Died at age 84 in London. His mummified body, dressed in his clothes, is kept in a wooden cabinet at University College, London, which he helped found.

Last Words: "I now feel that I am dying. Our care must be to minimize pain. Do not let the servants come into the room, and keep away the youths; it will be distressing to them, and they can be of no service."

Source: *Jeremy Bentham, His Life and Work* by Charles M. Atkinson (London, 1905).

Benton, Thomas Hart

(1782-1858) American politician, lawyer. Granduncle of American artist of same name. Member Tennessee State Senate. Member U.S. Senate, U.S. House of Representatives from Missouri. First senator to serve 30 consecutive years. Ran unsuccessfully for senator in 1850 and for governor in 1856. Wrote several books in his later years, including a criticism of the Supreme Court's decision in the Dred Scott case. Died at age 76 in Washington, D.C.

Different Last Words:

(1) "I am comfortable and content." His last audible words.

Source: *Life of Thomas Hart Benton* by William Montgomery Meigs (Philadelphia, 1904).

(2) "Do you hear that? Kitty, that is the death rattle." Spoken to his nurse who had put her head on his chest to listen.

Source: *Magnificent Missourian: The Life of Thomas Hart Benton* by Elbert B. Smith (Philadelphia, 1958).

Béranger, Pierre Jean de

(1780-1857) French poet. Known for liberal, humanitarian views. Wrote witty, lively, lyric, sometimes ribald poems. Some of his political poems (such as "Chansons inedites") sent him to prison in 1821 and 1828. But the public loved them. His song "Le Roi d'Yvetot" mocked Napoleon and echoed the public's desire for peace after the long Napoleonic wars. Died at age 76 in Paris.

Last Words: "My God, my God! Enlighten us. Inspire in a united mankind the love of the good, the love of well being.—To do good, to live for others—that's happiness. Charity, charity, for all the world to be happy. —Widows, small boys—help them."

Source: *Béranger la chanson, la politique, la société* by J. Lucas-Dubreton (Paris, 1934).

Berenger of Tours

(998-1088) French clergyman, theologian. Heretic. Attacked church dogma. Condemned for heresy. Recanted and spent final years atoning in solitude on an island near Tours, France. Died at age 90.

Last Words: "Today, on the day of His Epiphany, my Lord Jesus Christ will appear to me, either for Glory, as I in my repentance should like, and as I hope, or for Condemnation, as others would like, and as I fear."

Source: *Berenger von Tours* by Joseph Schnitzer (Stuttgart, Germany, 1892).

Variation: "I shall not long hesitate between conscience and the Pope, for I shall soon appear in the presence of God, to be acquitted, I hope; to be condemned, I fear."

Source: *The Last Words (Real and Traditional) of Distinguished Men and Women Collected From Various Sources* by Frederic Rowland Marvin (New York, 1901).

Bérenger, Madame De

(1767-1794) French noblewoman. Birth name [Marquise de] Charlotte Henriette Tardieu-Malessy. Became a political prisoner. Executed at about age 27 with her family during the French Revolution.

Last Words: "Be composed, my dearest parent, nor let an emotion of regret accompany you to the tomb. You have all your family with you; to you they look up for consolation; since your virtues are about to receive the recompense they merit in the mansions of innocence and peace." Spoken to her mother, who was executed along with her brother, sister and her father.

Source: *The Percy Anecdotes: Original and Select* Vol. XX by Sholto and Reuben Percy (London, 1826).

Variation: "Dearest madam, be consoled: why are you not happy? You die innocent, and in the same innocence all your family follow you to the tomb, and will partake with you, in a better state, the recompense of virtue."

Source: *Noble Deeds of Woman; or, Examples of Female Courage and Virtue* by Elizabeth Starling (Boston, 1850).

Variation: "Be of good cheer; we shall all die together. You need have no regret: your family accompanies you, and your virtues will soon be rewarded in the sojourn of innocence and peace."

Source: *Woman in France During the Eighteenth Century*, Vol. 2, by Julia Kavanagh (London, 1864).

Berg, Alban Maria Johannes

(1885-1935) Austrian musician, composer. Known for his 12-note or dodecaphonic works. Also composed art songs, instrumental music. Notable works: *Wozzeck; Lulu* (operas); *Concerto for Violin and Orchestra.*

Died at age 50 in Vienna. May have died from blood poisoning caused by an insect bite.

Last Words: "Auftakt. Auftakt." (tr. "An upbeat. An upbeat.") Moaned in a delirious fever.

Source: *Encyclopedia of the Great Composers and Their Music* by Milton Cross and David Ewen (Garden City, NY, 1962).

Berg, Morris ("Moe")

(1902-1972) American athlete, spy. Professional baseball player. Catcher for Boston Red Sox. Spied for U.S. during World War II. Died at age 70 of injuries sustained in a fall at his home.

Last Words: "How did the Mets do today?" Spoken to his nurse.

Source: *Moe Berg: Athlete, Scholar, Spy* by Louis Kaufman, Barbara Fitzgerald and Tom Sewell (Boston, 1975).

Berg, Nicholas Evan

(1978-2004) American businessman. Victim of terrorism. Executed at age 26 by a militant Islamic group in retaliation for abuses committed at Abu Ghraib prison in Iraq. His execution by beheading by Abu Musa'b al Zarqawi was videotaped.

Last Words: "My name is Nick Berg. My father's name is Michael. My mother's name is Susan. I have a brother and sister, David and Sarah. I live in . . . Philadelphia." Berg did not live or work in Philadelphia. He lived and worked about 35 miles away. Some observers theorize that he may have been sending a message by saying "Philadelphia."

Source: "Militants Behead American Hostage in Iraq" (*FoxNews*, May 11, 2004). The video was originally posted on a website run by the militant Islamist group Muntada al-Ansar.

Bergman, Ingrid

(1915-1982) Swedish actress. Star of stage and screen. Nominated for seven Academy Awards; won three: *Gaslight; Anastasia; Murder on the Orient Express.* Won two Emmy Awards: *The Turn of the Screw; A Woman Called Golda.* Died at age 67 in London, England, following breast cancer surgery.

Last Words: "Do I look all right? Give me my brush and my makeup." Her response when she learned she had a visitor.

Source: *As Time Goes By, The Life of Ingrid Bergman* by Laurence Leamer (New York, 1986).

Berlioz, Louis Hector (Hector)

(1803-1869) French musician, composer, critic. Pioneer of modern orchestration. Notable works: *Symphonie Fantastique; Harold in Italy; Damnation of Faust; Beatrice and Benedict; Les Troyens*. Died at age 65 at his home in Paris.

Different Last Words:

(1) "Enfin, on va joue ma musique." (tr. "They are finally going to play my music.")

Source: *Berlioz: Volume Two: Servitude and Greatness, 1832-1869* (Berkeley, CA, 2003).

(2) "Ça m'est égal." (tr. "It doesn't matter to me.") Spoken after reciting Shakespeare: "Life's but a walking shadow, a poor player, fthat struts and frets his hour upon the stage, and then is heard no more; it is a tale told by an idiot, full of sound and fury, signifying nothing."

Source: *The Art of Dying: An Anthology,* ed. by Francis Birrell and F. L. Lucas (London, 1930).

Variation: "That is my signal." Spoken after reciting Shakespeare: "Life's but a walking shadow, a poor player, that struts and frets his hour upon the stage, and then is heard no more; it is a tale told by an idiot, full of sound and fury, signifying nothing."

Source: *Last Words of Saints and Sinners: 700 Final Quotes from the Famous, the Infamous, and the Inspiring Figures in History* by Herbert Lockyer (Grand Rapids, MI, 1969).

(3) "Oh, Mere Recio, it is finished!" Spoken to his wife.

Source: *Berlioz* by D. Kern Holoman (Cambridge, MA, 1989).

Bernadette of Lourdes, Saint, see Soubirous, Saint Bernadette.

Bernadotte, Count Folke

(1895-1948) Swedish nobleman, diplomat. Count. Negotiated release of 15,000 prisoners from German concentration camps during World War II. United Nations mediator in Palestine. Assassinated at age 53 when his motorcade was ambushed in downtown Jerusalem.

Last Words: "I'll need it." His response as he drove away after he inspected a bullet in his vehicle's wheel and a newspaper man

shouted "Good luck."

Source: *Count Folke Bernadotte* by Ralph Hewins (Minneapolis, MN, 1950).

Bernard, Claude

(1813-1878) French physiologist, writer. Investigated digestion, liver, sympathetic nervous system. Researched effect of carbon monoxide on the body. Wrote text that became a standard: *Introduction to the Study of Experimental Medicine*. Elected Chevalier of the Legion of Honor and Commander. Died at age 65 in Paris. First French scientist to be given a state funeral.

Last Words: "This time it will serve me for the voyage from which there is no return, the voyage of eternity." Spoken when he began to feel cold and a cover was placed on his feet.

Source: *Claude Bernard, Physiologist* by J.M.D. Olmsted (New York, 1938).

Bernard, Sir Francis

(1712-1779) English-born, American colonial statesman, architect, writer, nobleman. Governor of New Jersey and Massachusetts. Designer of Harvard Hall at Harvard University. Published several series of *Letters from America*. Died at age 76 in Buckinghamshire, England. Bernards Township and Bernardsville, New Jersey, and Bernardston, Massachusetts, were named for him.

Last Words: "Never fear; if you will but have patience I don't doubt we shall get through; but take care how you ever get in such a scrape again." Spoken a few minutes before he died.

Source: *The Bernards of Abington and Nether Winchendon: A Family History* by Mrs. Napier Higgins (London, 1903).

Bernard of Clairvaux, Saint

(1090?-1153) French clergyman, hymnist, writer, holy man. Founder and first abbot of Cistercian Monastery of Clairvaux. Promoter of Crusade in 1146. Wrote many hymns. Died at age 63 at Clairvaux. Canonized in 1173. Declared Doctor of the Church in 1830.

Different Last Words:

(1) "I know not to which I ought to yield—to the love of my children, which urges me to stay here, or to the love of God, which

draws me to Him." Spoken to his monks.

Source: *Life and Times of St. Bernard* by M. l'Abbé Ratisbonne (New York, 1855).

Variation: Not given as a direct quote. Bernard said he was in a strait between two desires, to tarry with them or to depart, but he would submit to the divine will. He then closed his eyes and opened them no more.

Source: *Saint Bernard Abbot of Clairvaux, Selections from his Writings,* tr. by Horatio Grimley (Cambridge, England, 1910).

(2) "May God's will be done." Spoken when told his last hour was at hand.

Source: *The Last Words (Real and Traditional) of Distinguished Men and Women Collected from Various Sources* by Frederic Rowland Marvin (New York, 1901).

Bernhardt, Sarah

(1844-1923) French actress. Birth name Henriette Rosine Bernard. Known as The Divine Sarah for her speaking voice, beauty, graceful movements. Notable roles: *La dame aux camellias; Froufrou; Fedora; La Tosca.* An accident led to the amputation of her leg in 1915. She continued to perform until 1922. Died at age 79 in Paris. Had a huge funeral.

Last Words: "All my life reporters have tormented me enough. I can tease them now a little by making them cool their heels." Spoken as she lay dying when she learned reporters were waiting outside. Later, she said: "How slow my death agony is." She died a short time later.

Source: *Madame Sarah* by Cornelia Otis Skinner (New York, 1967).

Bernstein, Leonard

(1918-1990) American musician, composer, pianist, conductor. Musical director of New York Philharmonic. Winner of many Emmy, Grammy and Tony awards. Notable compositions: *On the Town; Fancy Free; Wonderful Town; West Side Story; Candide.* His appearances on television shows such as *Omnibus* and *Young People's Concerts* drew many new fans to classical music. Died at age 72 of a heart attack and lung failure in New York City.

Last Words: "What is this?" He asked his doctor and his assistant about a shot.

Source: *Leonard Bernstein: A Life* by Meryle Secrest (New York, 1994).

Berrigan, Philip

(1923-2002) American clergyman, peace activist. Roman Catholic priest who along with his brother Daniel was listed on the FBI's "Ten Most Wanted List" as well as nominated for a Nobel Peace Prize. Began antiwar campaign after serving in U.S. Army during World War II. Was appalled at violence of war and racism in the southern U.S. Became a civil rights activist. Took part in Montgomery Bus boycotts and sit-ins. Became more radical during Vietnam War. Was the first American priest arrested and jailed for civil disobedience, serving six years. In 1980 he and Daniel created the Plowshares Movement. Died at age 79 from cancer in Baltimore, Maryland.

Last Words: "I die with the conviction, held since 1968 and Catonsville, that nuclear weapons are the scourge of the earth, to mine for them, manufacture them, deploy them, use them, is a curse against God, the human family and the earth itself." Dictated to his wife Liz.

Source: *A Persistent Peace: One Man's Struggle for a Nonviolent World* by John Dear (Chicago, 2008).

Berry, Caroline Ferdinande Louise, Duchesse de

(1798-1870) French-born royalty. Daughter of Francis I of the Two Sicilies. Wife of French prince Charles Ferdinand, duc de Berry. After father-in-law King Charles X was overthrown, she went into exile. She was imprisoned after she returned to France in 1832 and organized an unsuccessful uprising that attempted to gain the throne for her son, Henri, Comte de Chambord. She secretly married a second time. When it was discovered that she was pregnant, she was released from prison. Died at age 71 in Brunsee, Austria.

Last Words: "Is not this dying with true courage and true greatness?"

Sources: "Dying Words of Noted Persons" in *Miscellaneous Notes and Queries with Answers in All Departments of Literature,* Vol. II (Manchester, NH, 1885); "Dying Words of Distinguished Persons" in *The Encyclopedia of Death and Life in the Spirit-World,* Vol. I, by J.R. Francis (Chicago, 1895).

Berry, Charles Ferdinand, Duc de

(1778-1820) French-born nobleman. Born

Charles Ferdinand de Bourbon. Son of King Charles X of France. Shot by a political fanatic as he was leaving the Paris Opera House with his wife. Died the next day at age 42.
Different Last Words:
(1) "Blessed Virgin, have mercy."
Source: *Mémoires sur la vie et la mort du duc de Berry* by François-Rene de Chateaubriand (Paris, 1820).
(2) "Sire grâce, grâce pour la vie de l'homme!" (tr. "Sir, pardon, pardon the life of the man!") Spoken to King Louis XVIII about the man who shot him.
Source: *The Art of Dying: An Anthology,* ed. by Francis Birrell and F. L. Lucas (London, 1930).

Berry, Hiram Gregory

(1824-1863) American military officer. Union major general in U.S. Civil War. Commanded brigade in Army of the Potomac during Peninsular Campaign and Battle of Fredericksburg. Commanded 2nd Division 3rd Corps at the Battle of Chancellorsville in Virginia. Shot and killed at age 38 in Chancellorsville.
Last Words: "I am dying, carry me to the rear." Spoken to an attendant.
Source: *Chancellorsville* by Stephen W. Sears (Boston, 1996).

Bérulle, Pierre de

(1575-1629) French prelate, statesman, writer. Cardinal. Founded French Congregation of the Oratory that established seminaries and improved education. Died at age 54 while saying Mass in Paris.
Last Words: "I do bless.—May Jesus and Mary bless, rule and govern." Spoken as he blessed his congregation.
Source: *Le cardinal de Bérulle* by l'Abbé M. Houssaye (Paris, 1875).

Bessarion, Johannes

(1395?-1472) Byzantine prelate, translator. Birth name Basilius Bessarion. Archbishop of Nicaea. Humanist. Worked to unite Greek and Roman churches. Translated Aristotle, Xenophon. Died in Ravenna, Italy.
Last Words: "Thou art just, O Lord, and just are Thy decrees; but Thou art good and merciful, and Thou wilt not recall our failings."
Source: *Le Cardinal Bessarion* by Henri Vast (Paris, 1878).

Bessette, Blessed Alfred (Brother André/Frère André)

(1845-1937) French-Canadian clergyman. Born Alfred Bessette. Also known as Brother André (Frère André). Holy Cross Brother credited with many miraculous healings. Died at age 92 in Ville Saint-Laurent, Quebec. A million people honored him when he died. Beatified in 1982.
Last Words: "My God, how it hurts! Oh I suffer!"
Source: *The Life of Brother André: The Miracle Worker of St. Joseph* by C. Bernard Ruffin (Huntington, IN, 1988).

Bestuzhev-Ryumin, Mikhail Pavlovich

(1801-1826) Russian military officer. Helped organize Decembrist revolt. Involved in staging an uprising. Caught, sentenced and executed by hanging in St. Petersburg along with four others. At age 25, he was the youngest of those hanged.
Last Words: "Nothing succeeds with me. Even here, I meet with disappointment." Spoken when the rope broke.
Source: *European Republicans* by William James Linton (London, 1892).

Bethune, Mary McLeod

(1875-1955) American educator, civil rights activist. Adviser to U.S. President Franklin D. Roosevelt. Oversaw merger that created Bethune-Cookman College. Died at age 79 in Daytona Beach, Florida.
Last Words: "Life is wonderful. I am wonderful." Spoken to her family before she died of a heart attack.
Source: *Mary McLeod Bethune: A Biography* by Rackham Holt (Garden City, NY, 1964).

Bevan, Aneurin

(1897-1960) Welsh-born British statesman, politician. Minister of health. Minister of labor. Deputy leader of the British Labour party. Died at age 62 of cancer at Chesham, Buckinghamshire, England.
Different Last Words:
(1) "I will not become a surgeon's plaything."
Source: *Aneurin Bevan: A Biography* by Michael Foot (New York, 1974).
(2) (doubtful): "I want to live because there are one or two things I want to do."

Source: Various Last Words compilations and Internet websites.

Bevan made the comment to his friend Archie Rush in March 1960, four months before he died.

Source: *Bevan* by Francis and Clare Beckett (London, 2004).

Béze, Théodore de or Beza, Theodorus

(1519-1605) French theologian, educator. Leader of Protestant Reformation in France. Professor of Greek at Lausanne, Switzerland. Theological professor and university president in Geneva, Switzerland. Died at age 86 in Geneva.

Last Words: "Is the city in full safety and quiet?" Asked visitors about the city of Geneva. When he was assured that all was well, he collapsed and died.

Source: *Theodore Beza: The Counselor of the French Reformation 1519-1605* by Henry M. Baird (New York, 1899).

Bhutto, Benazir

(1953-2007) Pakistani politician. Chair of the Pakistan Peoples Party. She was the eldest child of former prime minister Zulfikar Ali Bhutto, and the first woman elected to lead a Muslim state, serving twice as prime minister of Pakistan. She was assassinated at age 54 after a rally in Rawalpindi, two weeks before the 2008 Pakistani general elections, where she was a leading opposition candidate.

Last Words: "Long live Bhutto!"

Source: "Bhutto's Last Words: 'Long Live Bhutto!'" (*Pakistan Times*, December 30, 2007).

Bhutto, Zulfikar Ali

(1928-1979) Pakistani politician. President, prime minister of Pakistan. Father of Benazir Bhutto. Tried on charges of conspiracy to murder a political opponent. Hanged at age 51 in Rawalpindi.

Different Last Words:

(1) (doubtful): "A poet and a revolutionary, that is what I have been all these years. And that is how I shall remain until the last breath is gone from my body."

Source: *"If I am assassinated…"* by Zulfikar Ali Bhutto (New Delhi, India, 1979).

This quote is often cited as his Last Words, but it was spoken much earlier. The quote comes from a document Bhutto wrote in prison in 1978 and refers to a story from his youth that he mentioned in the document.

(2) "These—" Spoken on the scaffold just before he was hanged. Colonel Rafi-ud-Din, who was nearby, conjectured that Bhutto may have wanted to say "These are hurting me," referring to the way the tight handcuffs were twisting his arms. But the colonel could not hear his final words.

Source: *The Last 323 Days of Mr. Bhutto* by Col. Rafi-ud-Din (London, 1997). The author was security battalion commander at the Rawalpindi Jail.

(3) "Oh Lord, help me for I am innocent." Spoken at the foot of the gallows.

Source: *Portrait of a Political Murder* by Harbans Singh Bhatia (New Delhi, India, 1979). Book cites Nawa-i-Waqt, an Urdu daily newspaper account. Variations in other Indian sources include: "God help me I am innocent" or "Help me God, I am innocent."

Bickerstaff, Isaac, see Swift, Jonathan.

Bickersteth, Edward

(1786-1850) English clergyman. Evangelist. Rector of Walton, Hertfordshire. Compiled more than 700 hymns in *Christian Psalmody*. Brother of Henry, Baron Langdale. Father of Edward Henry Bickersteth, who became Bishop of Exeter. Grandson became Bishop of South Tokyo, Japan. Died at age 63 in Walton.

Last Words: "The Lord bless thee, my child, with overflowing grace, now and for ever." Spoken to one of his children.

Source: *Memoir of the Rev. Edward Bickersteth* by T.R. Birks (New York, 1851).

Biddle, Nicholas

(1750-1778) American military officer. One of first five captains of the Continental Navy. In 1778, the *Randolph,* 32-gun frigate ship he captained, encountered the British 64-gun ship-of-the-line HMS *Yarmouth*. After Biddle was wounded in the leg, he was propped in a chair and continued fighting. He spoke his Last Words just before *Randolph's* magazine blew up, killing 310 men on board. Only four crew members survived. They were rescued at sea after four days in the water. Two of them provided an account of what happened to the ship. One was on the quarterdeck near Biddle and the surgeon who was attending him. Biddle died at age 27, off the coast of Barbados. Four ships of the U.S. Navy have been named for him. American poet Philip Freneau wrote "On the Death of Captain Nicholas Biddle" to commemorate the disaster.

Last Words: "I am only slightly wounded."

Source: *A Conspectus of American Biography: Being an Analytical Summary of American History and Biography, Containing also the Complete Indexes of the National Cyclopedia of American Biography* by George Derby (New York, 1906).

Bidwell, Daniel Davidson

(1819-1864) American military officer. Brigadier general in Union Army in U.S. Civil War. Killed at age 45 at the Battle of Cedar Creek, Virginia.

Last Words: "Oh, my poor wife. Doctor, see that my record is right at home. Tell them I died at my post doing my duty."

Source: *Three Years in Six Corps* by George T. Stevens (Albany, NY, 1866).

Bierce, Ambrose Gwinnett

(1842-1914?) American satirist, writer, journalist. Friend of Bret Harte, Mark Twain, Joaquin Miller. Notable works: *The Devil's Dictionary; An Occurrence at Owl Creek Bridge.* Had long career with *San Francisco Examiner* as columnist and contributor. Disappeared in Mexico. Last heard from in late December 1913 at age 71. One report claimed he was killed in the war between Pancho Villa and Carranza. He may have been killed in January 1914 in the siege of Ojinaga.

Last Words (written): "If you hear about my being stood up against a Mexican stone wall and shot to rags please know that I think it's a pretty good way to depart this life." Letter sent from Chihuahua.

Source: "Bierce, Ambrose Gwinnett" by Robert A. Wiggins in *Encyclopedia Americana* (Danbury, CT, 1985).

Biffle, Ira Oris

(1886-1934) American aviator, military officer. Taught Charles Lindbergh to fly. Member Army Air Corps. 1st Lieutenant, U.S. Army. Died at age 47 of a heart ailment in a Chicago hospital.

Last Words: "I'm afraid I can't make it." Spoken to his wife from his hospital bed as he reached for her hands.

Source: "Biffle, Flier, Dies; Lindbergh Mentor. Began as Pilot in the Army in 1914 and was Teacher of Many Prominent Aviators. A Pioneer of the Air Mail. Got Half of $400 Check which Lindbergh's Mother Gave Him for His First Lessons" (*New York Times*, April 8, 1934).

Bilac, Olavo Brás Martins dos Guimarães

(1865-1918) Brazilian writer, poet, political activist. Famed as one of the most important poets of his era in Brazil; founding member of Brazilian Academy of Literature. Awarded title Prince of Brazilian Poets. Patron of Brazilian Military Service. Wrote lyrics for the "Brazilian Flag Anthem." Died at age 53 in Rio de Janeiro.

Last Words: "Dêem-me café, vou escrever!" (tr. "Give me coffee, I'm going to write!") His Last Words were reported in newspapers when he died.

Source: *Vida e Poesia de Olavo Bilac* by Fernando Jorge (São Paulo, Brazil, 1963).

Bilbo, Theodore Gilmore

(1877-1947) American politician, white supremacist. Twice governor of Mississippi, Member U.S. Senate from Mississippi from 1935 to 1947. Known for derisive "anti-Negro" views on voting and segregation. Terms as governor and senator marred by extreme racist remarks and corruption. Barred from taking seat in U.S. Senate in January 1947, pending dismissal of charges that he intimidated African-American voters and accepted favors from war contractors. Later in 1947, a large part of his jaw was removed during cancer surgery. On his deathbed, he attempted to rectify some of his disrespect for African Americans in what would become his final news interview.

Last Words: "I am honestly against the social intermingling of Negroes and whites but I hold nothing personal against the Negroes as a race. They should be proud of their God-given heritage just as I am proud of mine. I believe Negroes should have the right [to indiscriminate use of the ballot], and in Mississippi too—when their main purpose is not to put me out of office and when they won't try to besmirch the reputation of my state." Spoken to Leon Lewis, editor of *Negro South*, an African-American newspaper in June 1947. Died at age 69 in New Orleans, Louisiana.

Source: "He Died a Martyr" (*Time* magazine, September 1, 1947). *Time* described these Last Words as his "final say on the matter."

Billings, Josh, see Shaw, Henry Wheeler (Josh Billings).

Billy the Kid, see Bonney, William H.

Bingham, Sybil Moseley

(1792-1848) American missionary to Hawaii. Her husband and her son were noted missionaries Hiram Bingham and Hiram Bingham II. Her grandson, explorer Hiram Bingham III, found Machu Picchu. and later was U.S. senator and governor of Connecticut. Died in Massachusetts at about age 56.

Last Words: "The Lord be praised! The Lord cares for me! Stop, stop, I live! Hiram! Almost overcome.—Break the bands!" Spoken to her husband.

Source: *Yankees in Paradise: The New England Impact on Hawaii* by Bradford Smith (Philadelphia, 1956).

Birney, David Bell

(1825-1864) American lawyer, military officer. Son of James G. Birney, 1844 Antislavery party Presidential candidate. David Birney was lieutenant colonel of a Pennsylvania militia regiment that became part of the 23rd Regiment of Pennsylvania Volunteers in the U.S. Civil War. Fought with Army of the Potomac. Promoted to major general for leadership at Chancellorsville. Wounded at Gettysburg. After Grant selected him to command 10th Army Corps, Birney became seriously ill with malaria and was ordered home to Philadelphia where he died at age 39.

Last Words: "Boys! Keep your eyes on that flag." Spoken while delirious.

Sources: *Life of David Bell Birney* by Oliver W. Davis, published anonymously 1867; Official Records (*Army and Navy Journal,* Oct. 22, 29, Nov. 19, 1864).

Biron, Armand-Louis de Gontaut, Duc de

(1747-1793) French military officer. Commander with French forces in American Revolution. Also known as Duc de Lauzon. Guillotined in French Revolution during Reign of Terror. Was eating oysters and drinking wine when executioner arrived. Guillotined at age 46.

Last Words: "It's finished gentlemen. I leave for the great voyage." Spoken to other prisoners. Earlier, he said to the executioner: "Take this wine. You must need some in your profession."

Source: *Le Duc de Lauzon* by Gaston Maugras (Paris, 1895).

Bishop, Bernice Pauahi

(1831-1884) Hawaiian royalty, philanthropist. Great-granddaughter of Kamehameha I. Last surviving descendant of Kamehameha dynasty. Refused to accept the throne. Married businessman Charles Reed Bishop. Concerned about the decline of traditional Hawaiian life and culture. Donated her entire estate to establish schools for Hawaiian boys and girls. Died at age 52 of cancer in Honolulu. The Bishop Museum was founded in her honor by her husband.

Last Words: "Happiness is not money. Having so much I feel responsible and accountable. Pray, and bid all my friends pray, for I need help from on high." After speaking these words, she fell into a coma and died a week later.

Source: *Princess Pauahi and Her Legacy* by Cobey Black and Kathleen Mellen (Honolulu, HI, 1965).

Bishop, Isabella Lucy Bird

(1832-1904) English writer, lecturer, humanitarian. First woman fellow of Royal Geographical Society. Notable works: *The Englishwoman in America; The Hawaiian Archipelago; A Lady's Life in the Rocky Mountains; Unbeaten Tracks in Japan; Journeys in Persia and Kurdistan.* She founded several hospitals in Korea and China. Died at age 72 in Edinburgh.

Last Words: "Oh what shouting there will be."

Source: *The Life of Isabella Bird (Mrs. Bishop): Hon. Member of the Oriental Society* by Anna M. Stoddart (London, 1908).

Bishop, Jesse Walter

(1933-1979) American murderer. First person executed in Nevada following the reinstatement of capital punishment in 1976. Executed at age 46 for killing newlywed man in Las Vegas hotel casino during robbery attempt. Took 10 minutes to die in gas chamber at Nevada State Prison. Last person

executed in Nevada with lethal gas. Method of execution was changed to lethal injection. Last Words: "This is just one more step down the road of life that I've been heading all my life. Let's go." Refused to authorize an appeal when given chance just before he entered gas chamber.
Source: "'Let's Go' Death Comes to a Bishop" (*Time* magazine, November 5, 1979).

Bismarck, Otto Eduard Leopold von, Prince of Bismarck-Schönhausen, Duke of Lauenberg

(1815-1898) Prussian nobleman, statesman, military leader. Known as the Iron Chancellor. Given title Count of Bismarck-Schönhausen in 1865. Created prince in 1871. First chancellor of German Empire. Instituted many economic and social reforms, including universal suffrage; reformed coinage and protective tariff. Nationalized Prussia's trains and made Germany a colonizer. Died at age 83 at Friedrichsruh. Bismarck, North Dakota, Bismarck Archipelago and Sea, many schools and a battleship were named for him.
Different Last Words:
(1) "I do not want a lying official epitaph. Write on my tomb that I was the faithful servant of my master, the Emperor William, King of Prussia."
Source: *Bismarck* by C. Grant Robertson (New York, 1919).
(2) "Ich danke, Dir, mein Kind." (tr. "I thank you, my dear child.") Spoken to his daughter as she wiped dampness from his forehead.
Source: *Blood and Iron: Origin of the German Empire as Revealed by the Character of Its Founder, Bismarck* by John Hubert Greusel (New York, 1915).

Bixby, Bill

(1934-1993) American actor, director. Birth name Wilfred Bailey Bixby. Starred in television series: *My Favorite Martian; The Courtship of Eddie's Father; The Incredible Hulk*. Appeared on numerous other programs and in movies. Died at age 59 in Century City, California. Bixby's wife and longtime friend Dick Martin were at his bedside.
Last Words: "Thanks for the laughter."
Source: *Last Words: A Dictionary of Deathbed Quotations* by C. Bernard Ruffin (Jefferson, NC, 2005). Ruffin noted "according to a tabloid" and gave as his

source *National Enquirer*, December 7, 1993.

Bizet, Georges

(1838-1875) French musician, composer, pianist. Birth name Alexandre Césare Léopold Bizet. Wrote operas and for orchestra, chorus and piano. Notable works: *Carmen; L'Arlésienne; The Pearl Fishers; Symphony in C Major*. Died at age 36 at Bougival near Paris of heart disease complicated by a throat inflammation.
Last Words: "My arms, Maria, I have a cold sweat, a sweat of death. How are you going to tell my father?" Spoken to Maria Reiter, a young woman who lived with the Bizets.
Source: *Diseases of Famous Composers: Twenty-two Pathographies from Bach to Bartok* by Franz Hermann Franken (Rockville, MD, 1996).

Black, Hugo LaFayette

(1886-1971) American lawyer, jurist, politician. Member U.S. Senate from Alabama. Associate justice of U.S. Supreme Court 1937 to 1971. Died at age 85 of a stroke at National Naval Medical Center, Bethesda, Maryland.
Last Words: "It doesn't matter." Spoken to his wife who asked if he wanted to watch television coverage of his retirement.
Source: *Mr. Justice and Mrs. Black: The Memoirs of Hugo L. Black and Elizabeth Black* (New York, 1986).

Black Elk, Nicholas (Hehaka Sapa)

(1863-1950) Native American holy man. Oglala Lakota. Survived Battle of Little Big Horn and 1890 Wounded Knee massacre. Toured with Buffalo Bill's Wild West Show. Converted to Roman Catholicism in 1904. Autobiography printed in 1932. In later years he was a spokesperson on Lakota life. Died at age 87.
Last Words: "It seems like I will go any time now, so if your car is all right, go after your younger brother. I want to see him." Spoken a few minutes before he died.
Source: *Black Elk: Holy Man of the Oglalas* by Michael F. Steltenkamp (Norman, OK, 1993).

Blackburn, Gideon

(1772-1838) American clergyman, missionary, educator. Presbyterian. Preached in western states and territories and was missionary to Cherokee. President of Center College in Kentucky. Blackburn Theological

Seminary, now Blackburn College, in Carlinville, Illinois, was named for him. Died at age 65 in Carlinville.

Last Words (doubtful): "Darkness will soon be here, and I shall probably not see this world any more; but if I do not, I shall open my eyes on a world wonderfully different from this....Hall, get ready to preach as soon as you can, and then preach Christ! Preach Christ and Him crucified! Preach with all your power and nothing else."

Source: *A Conspectus of American Biography: Being an Analytical Summary of American History and Biography, Containing also the Complete Indexes of the National Cyclopedia of American Biography* by George Derby (New York, 1906).

Blackburn spoke these words to J.W. Hall around 1823. In 1848, Hall recounted the incident and noted that Blackburn recovered and lived for 15 more years.

Source: *Annals of the American Pulpit: Or, Commemorative Notices of Distinguished American Clergymen of Various Denominations,* Vol. IV, by William B. Sprague (New York, 1859).

Blackie, John Stuart

(1809-1895) Scottish educator, translator. Notable works: translations of Aeschylus and Iliad. Professor of Greek at Edinburgh University 1852 to 1882. Died at age 85 in Edinburgh.

Last Words: "The Psalms of David and the songs of Burns, but the Psalmist first... Psalms, poetry."

Source: *John Stuart Blackie* by Anna M. Stoddart (Edinburgh, 1895).

Blackwell, Alexander

(1700?-1747) English physician, writer, adventurer. Notable work: *A Curious Herbal* (published with his wife Elizabeth; known for its beautiful herbal plant illustrations). Went to Sweden to drain marshes. Appointed royal physician after curing the king. Accused of trying to overthrow the kingdom by altering the line of succession. Charged with treason and beheaded. Protested his innocence to the end.

Last Words: "I am sorry for the mistake but this is the first time I've been beheaded." Spoken after he laid his head on the wrong side of the block and was corrected by the executioner.

Source: *London Walks* by Anton Powell (London, 1996).

Blaine, James Gillespie

(1830-1893) American statesman, politician, editor, journalist. Known as the Plumed Knight. Newspaper editor in Portland and Kennebec, Maine. Member U.S. Senate from Maine; speaker of the house. U.S. secretary of state. Unsuccessful nominee for U.S. President. First president Pan American Congress. Died at age 62 in Washington, D.C.

Last Words: "No, I didn't." His reply to his daughter who asked: "You had a hard night, didn't you?"

Source: *Biography of James G. Blaine* by Gail Hamilton (Norwich CT, 1895). "Gail Hamilton" was the pen name of Abigail Dodge, a cousin by marriage of Blaine. She was a member of his household for many years.

Blair, Eric Arthur, see Orwell, George.

Blair, John Durburrow

(1759-1823) American clergyman. Presbyterian. Grandson of Samuel Blair. Assigned to Virginia, where he preached many years. George Wythe Munford used Blair and Rev. John Buchanan as the subjects of his book *The Two Parsons,* about the early days of Richmond, Virginia. Blair died at age 63 in Richmond.

Last Words: "Lord Jesus, into thy hands I commend my spirit! I should like once more to speak to this congregation, but shall not be able to do that."

Source: *The Christian World Magazine and Foreign Christian Union,* Vol. XIV (New York, 1863).

Blair, Samuel

(1712-1751) Irish-born American clergyman, educator. Grandfather of John Durburrow Blair. Assigned to church in New Londonderry (Fagg's Manor), Pennsylvania. Established school where many noted Presbyterian leaders were educated. Toured New England and played a major role in splitting Presbyterian Church. He became ill when he was to meet Trustees of New Jersey College (now Princeton University). Died at age 39.

Last Words: "The Bridegroom has come and we shall now have all things." Spoken a minute or two before he died.

Source: *The Christian World Magazine and Foreign*

Christian Union, Vol. XIV (New York, 1863).

Variation: "The Bridegroom is coming and we shall now have all things."

Source: *A Conspectus of American Biography: Being an Analytical Summary of American History and Biography, Containing also the Complete Indexes of the National Cyclopedia of American Biography* by George Derby (New York, 1906).

Blair, William

(1766-1822) British physician, surgeon, writer. Wrote pamphlets on vaccination, the management of penitentiaries, and a book on venereal disease. Inventor of a cipher. Died at age 56 in London.

Last Words: "Reach me that blessed Book, that I may lay my hands on it once more. I rest in Christ." After he placed his hand on the Bible, he reclined his head and died peacefully.

Source: "Obituary of William Blair, Esq." in *The Missionary Herald for the Year 1823* by American Board of Commissioners for Foreign Missions (Boston, 1823).

Blake, Daniel

(1740?-1763) English burglar, murderer. Menial laborer in the household of Lord Dacre. Blake, who lived beyond his means, murdered a co-worker after a burglary. Hanged for the murder of John Murcott, Dacre's butler.

Last Words: "Be careful to attend divine worship; profane not the Sabbath; repent of your sins, and make a timely peace with God. Behold the consequence of my iniquities! Fear God, and honor your parents, for neglecting which I must suffer a disgraceful death." Spoken to the crowd at his place of execution.

Source: *The Newgate Calendar: Comprising Interesting Memoirs of the Most Notorious Characters who have been Convicted of Outrages on the Laws of England Since the Commencement of the Eighteenth Century; with Occasional Anecdotes and Observations, Speeches, Confessions, and Last Exclamations of Sufferers*, Vol. II, by Andrew Knapp and William Baldwin (London, 1825).

Blake, William

(1757-1827) English writer, artist, poet, novelist, mystic. Worked closely with his wife, whom he taught to paint and draw. Notable works: *Songs of Innocence* (first book of poems, illustrated and printed by himself); *Songs of Experience; The Little Child Lost; Jerusalem*. Wrote a series of prophetic books he claimed were dictated by angels. Died at age 69 in London.

Different Last Words:

(1) "My beloved, they are not mine—no—they are not mine." Spoken to his wife about songs he was singing.

Source: *The Life of William Blake* by Mona Wilson (New York, 1949).

(2) He told his wife they would not be parted and he would always be with her to take care of her. Another account says just before he died he began singing about the things he saw in Heaven.

Source: *The Poems of William Blake* by William Blake, ed. by William Butler Yeats (London, 1893).

Blanc, Mel

(1908-1989) American actor. Voice of Porky Pig, Bugs Bunny, Daffy Duck, Barney Rubble, Dino the Dinosaur and more than 400 other characters and 1,500 voices that were used in more than 3,000 cartoons. Died at age 81 in Los Angeles, California.

Last Words (doubtful): "That's all Folks!" Spoken while filming a commercial for Buick automobiles. These were the last words he recorded. Although he died very soon after recording them, most likely they were not the last ones he spoke.

Sources: "Mel Blanc, Wizard of Cartoon Voices Dies at 81" (*Orange County Register*, July 11, 1989); "That's All Folks" (*Pittsburgh Post-Gazette*, July 10, 1990).

Blanchard, Sophie

(1778-1819) French balloonist. Birth name Marie Madeleine Sophie Armant. Wife of Jean-Pierre Blanchard, world's first professional balloonist. She was the first woman to work as a professional balloonist. After her husband died in 1809, she continued ballooning and made more than 60 ascents. She died at age 41 in a ballooning accident over Tivoli Gardens in Paris. Her hydrogen-filled balloon caught fire and became tangled before she hit a roof and fell to her death.

Last Words: "À moi!" (tr. "My!" or "Help me!")

Source: *Les ballons: Histoire de la locomotion aérienne depuis son origine jusqu'a nos jours* by Julien Turgan (Paris, 1851).

Blanche of Castile,
Queen Consort of Louis VIII of France

(1188?-1252) Spanish-born French royalty.

Wife of Louis VIII of France. Third daughter of Alfonso VIII, King of Castile, and Eleanor of England, a daughter of Henry II. Mother of Louis IX. Acted as regent twice.

Last Words: "Help, ye saints of God! Fly hither, ye angels of the Lord and receive my soul and bear it before the All High!"

Source: *Blanche of Castile* by Regine Pernoud (London, 1975).

Blandick, Clara

(1880-1962) American actress. Star of stage and screen. Birth name Clara Dickey. Appeared in more than 150 movies. Best known for her portrayal of Auntie Em in the 1939 film classic *The Wizard of Oz*. Also known for her theater work. In failing health and agonizing pain, she committed suicide at age 82.

Last Words (written): "I am now about to make the great adventure. I cannot endure this agonizing pain any longer. It is all over my body. Neither can I face the impending blindness. I pray the Lord my soul to take. Amen." Suicide note.

Source: "Actress Clara Blandick Plays Farewell Scene" (*Los Angeles Times*, April 16, 1962).

Blandy, Mary

(1720-1752) English spinster, murderer. Executed by hanging for killing her father, attorney Francis Blandy, with arsenic at the request of her lover, Captain William Henry Cranstoun. Hanged at age 31 in Oxford, England, before a crowd of 5,000 people.

Last Words: "Gentlemen, don't hang me high for the sake of decency. I am afraid I shall fall."

Source: *The Newgate Calendar: Comprising Interesting Memoirs of the Most Notorious Characters who have been Convicted of Outrages on the Laws of England Since the Commencement of the Eighteenth Century; with Occasional Anecdotes and Observations, Speeches, Confessions, and Last Exclamations of Sufferers,* Vol. III, by Andrew Knapp and William Baldwin (London, 1825).

Blasco Ibáñez, Vicente

(1867-1928) Spanish writer, novelist, politician. Founded *El Pueblo* (journal). Famous for his novels about World War I. Imprisoned many times for political activism. Notable works: *The Four Horsemen of the Apocalypse; La Barraca (The Cabin); Blood*

and Sand. Died at age 60, a political exile in Menton, France.

Last Words: "My garden—my garden!"

Source: *Blasco Ibáñez. Su Vida, su Obra, su Muerte, sus Mejores Páginas* by Ramon Martinez de la Riva (Madrid, Spain, 1929).

Blatchford, Samuel

(1767-1828) English-born American clergyman, educator. Grandfather of U.S. Supreme Court justice of the same name. First president of Rensselaer Polytechnic Institute. Died at age 61 in Lansingburgh, New York.

Last Words (doubtful): "I feel like a passenger waiting to be carried over Jordan."

Source: *A Conspectus of American Biography: Being an Analytical Summary of American History and Biography, Containing also the Complete Indexes of the National Cyclopedia of American Biography* by George Derby (New York, 1906).

While Blatchford did say these words during his final days, they were not his Last Words. He made many equally quotable statements during that time. Rev. Ravaud K. Rodgers was with him during much of this time and he wrote down a number of Blatchford's comments. He included them in a letter he wrote in June 1857 in response to a request for reminiscences he could provide about Blatchford's character. The letter was printed in Sprague's *Annals of the American Pulpit*.

Source: *Annals of the American Pulpit: Or, Commemorative Notices of Distinguished American Clergymen of Various Denominations,* Vol. IV, by William B. Sprague (New York, 1859).

Blaurer or Blarer, Ambrosius

(1492-1564) Swabian religious reformer in Germany and Switzerland. Influenced by Luther and Zwingli. Fled into exile when Roman Catholics gained control. Died at age 71 in Winterthur, Switzerland.

Last Words: "O my Lord Jesus Christ, this made you in your great thirst desire nothing, but you were given gall and vinegar."

Source: *Ambrosius Blaurer's des Schwäbischen Reformators Leben und Schriften* by Theodor Pressel (Stuttgart, Germany, 1861).

Blavatsky, Helena Petrovna ("Madame Blavatsky")

(1831-1891) Russian-born American theologist. Birth name Helena von Hahn. Founder of Theosophy and American Theosophical Society. Early pioneer in New Age thinking. Died at age 59 in London.

Different Last Words:

(1) "I do my best, doctor." Spoken in a whisper to her doctor shortly before she died.

Source: *H.P.B.: In Memory of Helena Petrovna Blavatsky* by Some of Her Pupils (London, 1891).

(2) (doubtful): "Keep the link unbroken! Do not let my last incarnation be a failure." This was the last statement made public about her work by the society; however, she said it two days before she died. The quote is frequently cited as her Last Words with regard to her work.

Source: *The Life of Helena Blavatsky* by Ian Wilson from a video and transcript published by the Blavatsky Trust (London, 1994).

Bledsoe, William M.

(1821?-1863) American soldier. U.S. Civil War Confederate guerrilla who rode with Quantrill, a pro-Confederate raider. Killed at Baxter Springs while retreating from Lawrence, Kansas. Buried along the Arkansas River in Oklahoma Territory.

Last Words: "Fletch, that outfit has shot and killed me. Take my two pistols and kill all of them." Spoken to fellow guerrilla Fletch Taylor. The guerrillas shot everyone on the wagon from which Bledsoe was killed.

Sources: *Three Years with Quantrill* by O.S. Barton (Norman, OK, 1992); *Quantrill of Missouri* by Paul R. Petersen (Nashville, TN, 2003).

Blevins, Andy (a.k.a. Andy Cooper)

(c.1860s-1887) American horse thief, gunfighter. Involved in Pleasant Valley War and numerous gunfights. After refusing to be arrested, he was gunned down in his doorway by lawman Commodore Perry Owens. He died in Holbrook, Arizona.

Last Words: "Oh, Commodore, don't do that!"

Source: *A Little War of Our Own* by Don Dedera (Flagstaff, AZ, 1988). ·

Blewett, Charles

(1855?-1877) U.S. Army scout. Indian fighter. Killed during Nez Perce outbreak of 1877. Ambushed after he failed to heed the warning of his partner William Foster that they must escape. Blewett was killed by Red Spy (Seeyakoon Ilppilp), a Nez Perce.

Last Words: "Not until I get me an Indian." Spoken to Foster, who had shouted to Blewett that they must escape capture.

Sources: *Last Words: Dying in the Old West* by Garry Radison (Austin, TX, 2002); *Tales the Western Tombstones Tell* by Lambert Florin (Seattle, WA, 1967). Florin said Blewett called back to Foster words that sounded something like "Not until I get me an Indian."

Bloch, Marc Leopold

(1886-1944) French historian, educator. Professor of history at University of Strasbourg and at the Sorbonne. Resistance fighter during World War II. Captured, interrogated, tortured and killed by the Nazis. Died at age 57 near Lyons, France.

Last Words: "Long live France!" Spoken as he went before a German firing squad .

Source: *Memoirs of War, 1914-1915* by Marc Bloch, ed. by Carole Fink (New York, 1988).

Blomfield, Charles James

(1786-1857) English prelate, editor. Anglican Bishop of London. Father of English architect Sir Arthur William Blomfield. Edited plays of Aeschylus, Euripides, Callimachus and others. Died at age 71 at his residence in Fulham, England.

Last Words: "I am dying."

Source: *Memoirs of Charles James Blomfield, D.D., Bishop of London, with Selections from his Correspondence,* ed. by Alfred Blomfield (London, 1863). Alfred was his son.

Blood, Thomas

(1628-1680) Irish thief, soldier. Served in Cromwell's army. Tried to steal Crown Jewels of England from Tower of London. Attempted to capture Dublin Castle and the Duke of Ormond. Blood escaped arrest and was later pardoned and given land in Ireland. Died at age 52 at his home in Westminster.

Last Words: "I do not fear death."

Source: *The Last Words (Real and Traditional) of Distinguished Men and Women Collected from Various Sources* by Frederic Rowland Marvin (New York, 1901).

Blücher, Gebhard Leberecht von, Prince of Wahlstatt

(1742-1819) Prussian military officer. Field marshal. Played key role in fight against

Napoleon at Waterloo. When Napoleon retreated from Paris, his troops moved in. Named Prince Blücher of Wahlstatt by his king for his role in defeating Napoleon. Retired to his estate in Krieblowitz, Silesia (now Poland), in 1815. Died at age 76.

Last Words: "Sie haben manches von mir gelernt; jetzt sollen Sie auch noch lernen, wie man In Ruhe stirbt." (tr. "You've learned many a thing from me. Now you are to learn how peacefully a man can die.") Spoken to Count Nostitz, Blücher's former aide-de-camp.

Source: *Der Feldmarschall Fürst Blücher von Wahlstatt und seine Umgebungen* by Friedrich Förster (Leipzig, Germany, 1820).

Blum, Léon

(1872-1950) French politician, statesman, writer. Leader of Socialist party, Popular Front. Edited *Le Populaire*. First Socialist and first Jewish premier of France. Prisoner of Germans during World War II. Rescued from a concentration camp in 1945. Provisional president of France 1946-1947. Notable work: "For All Mankind" (wartime essay). Died at age 77 near Paris.

Last Words: "It's nothing. Don't worry about me." Spoken as he suffered a heart attack.

Source: *Léon Blum* by Jean Lacouture (New York, 1982).

Blum, Robert

(1807-1848) German rebel, writer, orator. Liberal leader. Active in 1848 revolutionary movement. Caught carrying a message to Viennese insurgents. Arrested and shot at age 40 in Vienna, Austria.

Last Words: "I want to look death in the eye....I die for freedom. May my country remember me!" Spoken as he was being executed. He tried to decline the blindfold.

Source: *Robert Blum und Seine Zeit* by Wilhelm Liebknecht (Nuremberg, Germany, 1896).

Bluntschli, Johann Kaspar

(1808-1881) Swiss jurist, educator, legal scholar, statesman. Professor in Zurich, Munich, Heidelberg. Pioneer in codifying international law. Notable work: *Modern Law of Nations*. Died at age 73 in Karlsruhe, Germany.

Last Words: "Glory be to God in the highest, peace on earth, good will towards men."

Source: *Notice sur M Bluntschli* by Alphonse Rivier (Brussels, Belgium, 1882).

Blythe, James

(1765-1842) American clergyman, educator. Presbyterian. First president of Hanover College. Also held presidency of Transylvania College. Clergyman and later chemistry professor at Transylvania. Member of faculty of Lexington Medical School. Died at age 76 in Hanover, Indiana.

Different Last Words:

(1) "I am in a strait betwixt two; having a desire to depart and be with Christ, which is far better."

Source: *Annals of the American Pulpit: Or, Commemorative Notices of Distinguished American Clergymen of Various Denominations,* Vol. IV, by William B. Sprague (New York, 1859).

(2) "I shall be satisfied when I awake with thy likeness; that is the word of God, and it comforts me."

Source: *A Conspectus of American Biography: Being an Analytical Summary of American History and Biography, Containing also the Complete Indexes of the National Cyclopedia of American Biography* by George Derby (New York, 1906).

Boas, Franz

(1858-1942) German-born American anthropologist, ethnologist, writer, educator. Authority on Native American languages. Taught anthropology at Columbia University 41 years. Curator of anthropology at American Museum of Natural History. Actively campaigned against Nazi racial theories. Died at age 84 in New York City.

Last Words: "It isn't necessary to wear oneself out repeating that racism is either a monstrous error or a shameless lie. The Nazis themselves have recently had to appreciate the accuracy of the facts that I have brought together on the European emigrants to America."

Source: *Renaissance 1* by Paul Rivet (Paris, 1943).

Bocarmé, Count Hippolyte, Visart de

(1790-1851) Belgian nobleman, murderer. Had financial problems. The death of his wealthy brother-in-law Gustave Fougnies would solve them, but not if Fougnies married and a wife could claim his estate. When the count learned Fougnies was planning to marry, he poisoned him with nicotine. But when he poured vinegar down Fougnies' throat to kill the smell of the nicotine, he created burns on his victim's mouth that made police suspicious. He was arrested, tried and executed by guillotine in Mons, before a crowd of thousands. The case is a classic in forensic detection.

Last Words: "I trust the blade is sharp."

Sources: *Crime on the Continent* by Horace Wyndham (London, 1928); *Written in Blood: A History of Forensic Detection* by Colin Wilson and Damon Wilson (New York, 2003).

Bodwell, Joseph Robinson

(1818-1887) American businessman, politician. Opened quarries and organized granite company. Served twice in Maine legislature. Elected governor 1886. Died at age 69 at his home in Hallowell, Maine, while in office.

Last Words: "Get me there quickly." Spoken when he asked to be returned to his chair.

Source: *In Memoriam Hon. Joseph R. Bodwell, Governor of Maine, Published by Order of the Governor and Council* (Augusta, ME, 1888).

Böhme, Boehme, Bohm, Boehm, Behme or Behmen, Jakob

(1575-1624) German cobbler, mystic, metaphysician, writer. Had mystical experiences and visions throughout his youth. He believed a vision revealed to him the spiritual structure of the world and explained the relationship between God and man, as well as good and evil. He was controversial for his visions as well as his reformist views. Notable works: *Aurora (The Rising of the Dawn); The Way to Christ*. Had a following throughout Europe known as Behmenists. Died at age 49 in Silesia.

Last Words: "Nun fahre ich hin ins Paradies!" (tr. "Now I go hence into paradise!")

Source: *Zeit, Tod und Ewigkeit* by Horst Gädtke (Norderstedt, Germany, 2006).

Variation: "Hört ihr die Musik? Dorthin gehe ich jetzt." (tr. "Do you hear the music? Now I go hence.")

Sources: *Lexikon der letzten Worte: letzte Botschaften berühmter Männer und Frauen von Konrad Adenauer bis Emiliano Zapata* by Werner Fuld (Munich, Germany, 2002); *The Last Words (Real and Traditional) of Distinguished Men and Women Collected From Various Sources* by Frederic Rowland Marvin (New York, 1901).

Boerhaave, Hermann

(1668-1738) Dutch physician, scientist, philosopher, educator. Held chairs of botany and chemistry at University of Leiden. Elected to French Academy of Sciences. and Royal Society of London. Identified Boerhaave's Syndrome. Notable works: *Institutiones medicae; Elementa chemiae*. Died at age 69 in Leiden.

Last Words: "He that loves God ought to think nothing desirable but what is pleasing to the Supreme Goodness." Spoken to his friend the Rev. Mr. Schultens who tried to console him that even the best men, including Job himself, would become impatient.

Source. "Hermann Boerhaave" in *The Works of Samuel Johnson* (Troy, NY, 1903).

Bogart, Humphrey DeForest

(1899-1957) American actor. Appeared in more than 75 films. Nominated for three Academy Awards; won best actor Oscar for *The African Queen* (1952). Died at age 58 of throat cancer in Los Angeles, California.

Different Last Words:

(1) "Goodbye, Kid. Hurry back." Spoken to his wife Lauren Bacall as she left the hospital to pick up their children. She told him she would be back soon then kissed him. He was comatose when she returned. He died in his sleep the next day.

Source: *Lauren Bacall: By Myself* by Lauren Bacall (New York, 1978).

(2) (doubtful): "I should never have switched from Scotch to Martinis."

Source: Various Last Words compilations and Internet websites.

This quote appeared in the 1975 novel *What Are the Bugles Blowing For?* by Nicolas Freeling when a patient was informed he had throat cancer. By 1982 it was "attributed" to Bogart as his "Last Words" in a book of quotations. Eventually, some later Last Words collections dropped the word "attributed" and simply claimed these were Bogart's Last Words.

Source: *What Are the Bugles Blowing For?* by Nicolas Freeling (New York, 1975).

Bogue, David

(1750-1825) Scottish clergyman, writer, historian. Presbyterian and Independent Congregationalist. A founder of London

Missionary Society. Also helped found British and Foreign Bible Society and the Religious Tract Society. Notable work: *History of Dissenters from the Revolution to 1808*. Died at age 75 in Brighton, England, while preaching for a missionary society.

Last Words: "Is he?" Spoken in response to news that a certain doctor was coming.

Source: *Memoirs of the Life of Rev. David Bogue* by James Bennett (London, 1827). Bennett collaborated with Bogue on *History of Dissenters.*

Boig, James

(d. 1681) Scottish Covenanter. Friend of Donald Cargill. Executed for his role in the Bothwell uprising and Sanquhar Declaration (which disowned King's authority).

Last Words (written): "I am once fairly on the way, and within the view of Immanuel's land, and in hopes to be received an inhabitant there within the space of twenty-six hours at most. Farewell all earthly comforts, farewell all worldly vanities, farewell all carnal desires; welcome cross, welcome gallows, welcome Christ, welcome heaven and everlasting happiness. I have no more spare time. Grace, mercy and peace be with you. Amen!" Letter to his brother from Edinburgh written the day he was executed.

Source: *A Cloud of Witnesses for the Royal Prerogatives of Jesus Christ: Being the Last Speeches and Testimonies of Those Who Have Suffered for the Truth in Scotland Since the Year 1680* by John Henderson Thomson (Edinburgh, 1714).

Boileau-Despréaux, Nicolas

(1636-1711) French critic, writer, poet. Studied law and theology, then turned to literature. Notable works: *Satires; L'Art poétique; Le Lutrin.* Credited with establishing principles on which French classical literature was based. Died at age 74 in Paris.

Last Words: "It is a great consolation to a poet on the point of death that he has never written a line injurious to good morals."

Source: "Dying Words of Noted Persons" in *Miscellaneous Notes and Queries with Answers in All Departments of Literature*, Vol. II (Manchester, NH, 1885).

Variation: "It is a great consolation for a dying poet to have never written a word against morality."

Source: *The Last Words (Real and Traditional) of Distinguished Men and Women Collected from Various Sources* by Frederic Rowland Marvin (New York, 1901).

Boleyn, Anne, Queen Consort of England

(1507?-1536) English noblewoman. Daughter of Sir Thomas Boleyn, Earl of Wiltshire. Second wife of King Henry VIII. Mother of Elizabeth I. Charged with adultery with several lovers. Condemned to death by unanimous vote of a group of her peers. Beheaded at Tower Green.

Different Last Words:

(1) "Friends and good Christian people, I am here in your presence to suffer death, whereto I acknowledge myself adjudged by the law, how justly I will not say; I intend not an accusation of any one. I beseech the Almighty to preserve His majesty long to reign over you: a more gentle or mild Prince never swayed sceptre. His bounty towards me hath been special. If any one intend an inquisitive survey of my actions, I entreat them to judge favorably of me, and not rashly to admit any censorious conceit; and so I bid the world farewell beseeching you to commend me in your prayers to God." After she was blindfolded and knelt at the block, she repeated several times: "To Jesus Christ I commend my soul; Lord Jesu receive my soul." Spoken from the scaffold at her execution.

Source: *Memoirs of the Life of Anne Boleyn* by Elizabeth Ogilvy Benger (Philadelphia, 1822). This account of Anne Boleyn's speech at her execution was made by the Tudor chronicler Edward Hall.

(2) "It is small, very small indeed." Spoken as she clasped her neck with her hands while she knelt on the scaffold.

Source: *Gleanings for the Curious from the Harvest-fields of History* by C.C. Bombaugh (Hartford, CT, 1875).

Variation: "The executioner is, I believe, very expert; and my neck is very slender." Later, on the scaffold, she repeated: "O God have pity on my soul. O God, have pity on my soul."

Source: *Famous Last Words* by Barnaby Conrad (New York, 1961).

Variation: "O Lord God, have pity on my soul, have pity on my soul."

Source: *A Crown for Elizabeth* by Mary M. Luke (London, 1970).

Bolingbroke, Henry Saint John, 1st Viscount

(1678-1751) English nobleman, statesman,

political philosopher. Birth name Henry St. John. Created viscount in 1712. Friend of Voltaire, Swift, Pope. Tory member of Parliament. Secretary of war. Favored Jacobite restoration. Dismissed by King George I. Later pardoned. Died at age 73 in London.

Last Words: "God who placed me here will do what He pleases with me hereafter, and He knows best what to do."

Source: *Bolingbroke and His Times* by Walter Sichel (New York, 1902).

Bolívar, Simón

(1783-1830) South American soldier, statesman. Revolutionary leader. Full name Simon Jose Antonio de la Santisima Trinidad Bolivar y Palacios. Known as El Libertador (The Liberator). Helped end Spanish domination of South America. Helped Peru gain independence. Resigned as supreme chief, 1830. Died at age 47 near Santa Marta, Colombia, possibly from tuberculosis. Upper Peru was named Bolivar (later Bolivia) in his honor.

Different Last Words:

(1) "Let us go. They have no use for us here! José! Bring the luggage. They do not want us here!" Spoken as he was dying.

Source: *Man of Glory, Simon Bolivar* by Thomas Rourke (New York, 1939).

Variation: "Let us go—let us go—these people don't want us in this land! Let us go boys. My baggage, take my luggage on board the frigate."

Source: *Bolivar* by Salvador de Madariaga (London, 1952).

(2) "The people sent me to the tomb, but I forgive them."

Source: *A History of the Nineteenth Century Year by Year* by Edwin Emerson Jr. (New York, 1902).

(3) (doubtful): "There have been three great fools in history: Jesus, Don Quixote and I." Bolivar did say this, but these were not his Last Words. He said this a few days before he died.

Source: *Venezuela* by Krzysztof Dydynski and Charlotte Beech (Oakland, CA, 2004).

Böll, Heinrich Theodor

(1917-1985) German writer, novelist, playwright, essayist. One of Germany's major post-World War II writers. Awarded Georg Büchner Prize in 1967 and Nobel Prize for Literature in 1972. When Aleksandr Solzhenitsyn was expelled from the Soviet Union, he first took refuge in Heinrich Böll's cottage. Böll was popular in the Soviet Union for his dark depiction of capitalism. Died at age 67 in Bornheim-Merten, near Cologne. Heinrich Böll Foundation and a special Heinrich Böll Archive in the Cologne Library are named in his honor.

Last Words: "Wie autoritär man wird wenn man keine Zeit mehr hat, höflich zu sein." (tr. "How authoritarian one is when one has no time to be polite.")

Source: *Lexikon der letzten Worte; letzte Botschaften berühmter Männer und Frauen von Konrad Adenauer bis Emiliano Zapata* by Werner Fuld (Munich, Germany, 2002).

Bolles, Donald F.

(1928-1976) American, writer, journalist. Brother of writer Richard Nelson Bolles. Nominated for Pulitzer Prize in 1965 for stories about bribery and kickbacks in Arizona commissions. Named Reporter of the Year by Arizona Press Club, 1974, for stories about a conflict-of-interest scandal in the Arizona legislature. Mortally injured when a car bomb exploded. Died at age 47 in Phoenix, Arizona, eleven days later. His wrecked car is the centerpiece of an exhibit at the Newseum in Washington, D.C.

Last Words: "Mafia—Emprise—They finally got me—John Adamson—find him." Spoken to the people who rushed to his aid. Bolles' Last Words led to the arrest of John Adamson. who was sentenced to death for his murder. In 1988, Adamson's death penalty was overturned. Emprise was Emprise Corp., sports enterprise that controlled Arizona horse and dog racing tracks.

Source: "Donald F. Bolles" in *Contemporary Authors* (Farmington Hills, MI, 2002).

Bolton, Robert

(1572-1631) English clergyman, writer. Puritan preacher. Notable work: *Four Last Things: Death, Judgment, Hell and Heaven.* Had severe illness in final years. Died at age 59. Many of his works were published posthumously.

Last Words: "Truly no. The greatest I feel is your cold hand." Spoken to a dear friend who took him by the hand when he was dying and asked him if he felt much pain. The following day, he prayed for his wife and children and died that afternoon.

Source: "Life of Robert Bolton" in *Abel Redevivus: Or, The Dead Yet Speaking. The Lives and Deaths of the Modern Divines* by Thomas Fuller (London, 1867).

Bolton, Samuel

(1606-1654) English clergyman, theologian. Puritan. Minister at St. Martin's Ludgate. Celebrated interpreter of Scripture. Died at age 48. He gave instructions in his last will and testament that he was to be buried as a private Christian without the outward pomp of a Master of Cambridge. He was buried as he wished.

Last Words: "I hope to rise in the day of judgment and appear before God not as a doctor but as a humble Christian."

Source: *The Lives of the Puritans: Containing a Biographical Account of Those Divines Who Distinguished Themselves in the Cause of Religious Liberty from the Reformation under Queen Elizabeth to the Act of Uniformity in 1662* by Benjamin Brook (London, 1813).

Bonaparte, Elizabeth Patterson

(1785-1879) American wife of Jerome Bonaparte, youngest brother of Napoleon I. Met Bonaparte in Baltimore in 1803, when he was in the French navy. Married in Baltimore. Had son Jerome Bonaparte-Patterson in 1805. The marriage was not recognized by Napoleon and was annulled soon afterward. Elizabeth died at age 94 in Baltimore.

Last Words: "Except taxes." Her response to a comment that nothing was certain apart from death.

Source: *The Life and Letters of Madame Bonaparte* by Eugene Lemoine Didier (New York, 1879).

Bonaparte, Joséphine de Beauharnais, see Josephine, Empress of the French.

Bonaparte, Napoleon (I), see Napoleon I.

Bonaparte, Maria Paulina, Duchess of Guastalla

(1780-1825) Corsican-born noblewoman. Sister of Napoleon I. First name originally Carlotta. Famed for her beauty, extravagance and promiscuity. First husband Victor Leclerc died 1802. Married Prince Camillio Borghese in 1803. Made Duchess of Guastalla by Napoleon. Died at age 44 of cancer in Florence. Only child died at age 8.

Italian sculptor Antonio Canova's marble semi-nude reclining sculpture of her: *Pauline Bonaparte Borghese as Venus Victrix* (1808), is one of his most famous works.

Last Words: "I always was beautiful." Spoken as she looked at herself in a mirror.

Source: *The Sisters of Napoleon, Elisa, Pauline, and Caroline Bonaparte After the Testimony of Their Contemporaries* by Joseph Turquan (London, 1908).

Bonaparte, Mathilde Laetitia Wilhelmine

(1820-1904) Italian-born noblewoman. Niece of Napoleon I. Daughter of Napoleon's brother Jerome Bonaparte and second wife, Catherine of Württemberg. Married Prince Anatole Demidoff. Famed hostess. Died at age 83 in Paris.

Last Words: "It is the sun of Austerlitz!"

Source: *The Princess Mathilde Bonaparte* by Philip W. Sergeant (London, 1915).

Bonchamps, Charles-Melchior Artus, Marquis de

(1760-1793) French politician, military officer, nobleman. Captain of grenadiers in French royal army. Fought in American Revolution. Leader of Vendéan insurrection of Royalists against the Republic during the French Revolution. Originally a staunch defender of the French monarchy but resigned his command at the outbreak of the Revolution. Later chosen as general by insurgents of Vendée. Died at age 33 after being wounded at the Battle of Cholet.

Last Words: "I command that their lives should be spared." Spoken to his aide during his final moments. He had learned several thousand prisoners were to be killed. The peasants heard his command and called out for mercy. The prisoners were saved.

Source: *Dames of High Estate* by Madame De Witt, tr. by Charlotte M. Yonge (London, 1872).

Variation: "Grâce aux prisoniers, Bonchamps l'ordonne!" (tr. "Pardon for the prisoners, Bonchamps commands it!")

Source: *Famous Sayings and Their Authors: A Collection of Historical Sayings in English, French, German, Greek, Italian, and Latin* by Edward Latham (London, 1906).

Bonhoeffer, Dietrich

(1906-1945) German clergyman, theologian. Lutheran. Involved in an assassination attempt against Hitler in 1944, during World

War II. Executed at age 39 by hanging at Schoenberg Prison by one of Hitler's men.

Last Words: "This is the end for me, the beginning of life." Reported by witnesses. His final act was to celebrate Communion with fellow prisoners.

Source: "Theologian Struggled with Courage vs. Conscience" by G. Jeffrey MacDonald (*USA Today*, January 31, 2006).

Boniface, Saint

(680?-754) English reformer, missionary, prelate, holy man. Birth name Winfrid or Wynfrid. Benedictine monk. Bishop, archbishop and primate of Germany. Known as the Apostle of Germany. Killed along with companions near Dokkum by Frisians angry that Boniface and the others had destroyed their shrines.

Last Words: "I thank Thee Lord Jesus, Son of the Living God." Spoken as hot lead was poured into his mouth.

Source: *The Golden Legend or Lives of the Saints.* Compiled by Jacobus de Voragine, Archbishop of Genoa, 1275, 1st ed., 1470. English ed. by William Caxton, 1483, ed. by F.S. Ellis (Edinburgh, 1900).

Bonnet, Charles

(1720-1793) Swiss naturalist, philosopher. Credited with discovering parthenogenesis. Charles Bonnet syndrome named for him. Failing eyesight forced him to abandon his research. Died at age 73 at his home in Genthod, near Geneva, Switzerland, after a long, painful illness.

Last Words: "So he repents? Let him come and all will be overlooked." Spoken to his wife. He believed a servant had stolen important papers. His wife promised to bring in the servant and have him admit his guilt.

Source: *Charles Bonnet, Philosophe et Naturaliste* by Le duc de Caraman (Paris, 1859).

Bonney, William H. ("Billy the Kid")

(1859?-1881) American murderer. Birth name Henry McCarty. Known as Billy the Kid. Born in New York City. Family moved to Kansas when he was young. Claimed to have killed 21 people. Killed by Sheriff Pat Garrett at ranch near Fort Sumter New Mexico. His age is not known. Probably around 21.

Last Words: "¿Quien es? Quien es?" (tr. "Who is there? Who is there?")

Source: *The Saga of Billy the Kid* by Walter Noble Burns (New York, 1926).

Bonnot, Jules Joseph

(1876-1912) French anarchist, murderer, thief. Member of the Bonnot Gang. Committed a robbery in 1911 using a limousine as his get-away car. The group split up in 1912. When police tried to arrest Bonnot, he shot and killed one officer and wounded another. He was apprehended and killed after police used dynamite on the building in a Paris suburb where he fled.

Last Words (written): "I am a famous man. My name has been trumpeted to the four corners of the globe." Written when cornered in building.

Source: *The Bonnot Gang* by Richard Parry (London, 1987).

Boone, Daniel

(1734-1820) American military officer, frontiersman, hunter. Explored and settled the American frontier. Blazed the Wilderness Road. Guided settlers into Kentucky. Died at age 85 at the home of his son Nathan in Missouri. Many American places named for him, including counties in eight states.

Last Words: "Do not grieve. I have lived to a good old age and am going to a world of happiness. I am going. My time has come."

Source: *Daniel Boone: The Life and Legend of an American Pioneer* by John Mack Faragher (New York, 1992).

Booth, Catherine Mumford

(1829-1890) English social worker, preacher. Co-founded Salvation Army with husband William in 1878. Designed the Army's flag and the famous poke bonnet. Died at age 61 of breast cancer at her home in Clacton-on-Sea, England.

Different Last Words:

(1) "Pa." Spoken as she died in her husband's arms.

Source: *The Life of Catherine Booth the Mother of the Salvation Army* by Frederick St. George de Latour Booth-Tucker (New York, 1892). He was the husband of William and Catherine's daughter Emma Moss Booth-Tucker.

(2) "The waters are rising, but so am I. I am not going under but over. Do not be concerned about dying; go on living well, the dying will be right."

Source: *Last Words of Saints and Sinners: 700 Final*

Quotes from the Famous, the Infamous, and the Inspiring Figures in History by Herbert Lockyer (Grand Rapids, MI, 1969).

Booth, Edwin Thomas

(1833-1893) American actor. Son of Junius Brutus Booth. Brother of John Wilkes Booth. Notable roles: Hamlet, Othello, Iago, Lear. Founded Players Club in Gramercy Park, New York City. Died at age 59 at the Players Club.

Last Words: "How are you yourself, old fellow?" His response to his young grandson who asked: "How are you, dear Grandpa?"

Source: *Prince of Players* by Eleanor Ruggles (New York, 1953).

Booth, John Wilkes

(1838-1865) American actor, murderer. Lincoln's assassin. Brother of Edwin Booth. Son of Junius Brutus Booth. After the assassination, he was trapped by soldiers while hiding in a barn at the Richard Garrett farm near Bowling Green, Virginia. Soldiers set fire to the barn to drive Booth from it. Booth was struck in neck when shots were fired into barn. He was dragged from the fire onto porch of the Garrett house where he spoke his Last Words. Died at age 26.

Last Words: "Tell my mother—I died—for my country. I thought I did for the best. Useless! Useless!"

Source: *Harper's Weekly*, May 13, 1865.

Variation: "Tell my mother I died for my country. I did what I thought was for the best—kill me—kill me—My hands, useless useless."

Source: "Booth's Fate, Particulars of His Capture and Death. Account of his Last Moments—His Sufferings and His Last Words" (*New York Times*, April 29, 1865).

Booth, Junius Brutus

(1796-1852) English-born American actor, theatrical manager. Father of John Wilkes Booth, Edwin Booth and Junius Brutus Booth. Notable roles: Richard III, Shylock, Othello, Iago. Went to the United States in 1821 and spent the next 30 years performing throughout the country. Became ill on a steamboat en route from New Orleans to Cincinnati for an engagement. Died at age 56 aboard the steamboat.

Last Words: "Pray, pray, pray."

Source: *Passages, Incidents, and Anecdotes in the Life of Junius Brutus Booth (The Elder)* by Asia Booth Clarke (New York, 1866). Clarke was one of the ten children of Junius Brutus Booth.

Booth, William ("General Booth")

(1829-1912) English clergyman, evangelist, social worker. Methodist minister. Formed East London Revival Society in 1865 that later became the Christian Mission. In 1878 it was renamed the Salvation Army. Booth died at age 83 in London.

Last Words: "I'm leaving you a bonnie handful. Railton will be with you." Spoken to his son William Bramwell Booth who became General when his father died. George Scott Railton was William Booth's assistant and had worked with him almost 40 years.

Source: *God's Soldier: General William Booth* by St. John Ervine (New York, 1935).

Boothby, Sir Robert John Graham, 1st Baron Boothby of Buchan and Rattray Head

(1900-1986) British politician, statesman, broadcaster, writer. Vice-chairman of Committee on Economic Affairs. Parliamentary secretary to Winston Churchill. Advocated entry into the European Community (now the European Union). British delegate to Consultative Assembly of the Council of Europe. Rector of St. Andrew's University. Chairman of Royal Philharmonic Orchestra. President of Anglo-Israel Association. Appeared often on BBC radio program, *Any Questions?* Raised to the peerage in 1958. Died at age 86 in Westminster, England.

Last Words: "I love you so much; look after the dogs." Spoken to his wife Wanda.

Source: *Robert Boothby: A Portrait of Churchill's Ally* by Robert Rhodes James (New York, 1991).

Borah, William Edgar

(1865-1940) American lawyer, statesman, politician. Member U.S. Senate from Idaho. Known for his oratory and isolationism. Unsuccessful Republican candidate for U.S. President in 1936. Died at age 74 of a cerebral hemorrhage in Washington, D.C., while serving as senator. Funeral services were held in the U.S. Senate Chamber.

Last Words: "Mary." He spoke his wife's name.

Source: *Washington Post,* January 20, 1940.

Borghese, Maria Paulina, see Bonaparte, Maria Paulina.

Borgia, Cesare

(1475/76-1507) Italian nobleman, politician, prelate. Illegitimate son of Rodrigo Borgia (later Pope Alexander VI). Brother of Lucretia Borgia. Archbishop and cardinal of Valencia. Relinquished cardinal's office. Tried to rid self of papal control. His cruelty and treachery led the pope to take away his castles. He was imprisoned for two years in Spain. Escaped to Navarre where he was killed at age 31 at siege of Castle of Viana. He was the political hero portrayed by Machiavelli in *The Prince.*

Last Words: "I had provided in the course of my life, for everything except death. And now, alas, I am to die, though entirely unprepared." Spoken a short time before his death.

Sources: *Landmarks of History II. Middle Ages: From the Reign of Charlemagne to that of Charles* by Charlotte Mary Yonge (London, 1853); *Death-bed Scenes; Dying With and Without Religion Designed to Illustrate the Truth and Power of Christianity* by Davis W. Clark (New York, 1852).

Variation: "I die unprepared." Spoken as he lay dying.

Source: *Book of Catholic Quotations Compiled from Approved Sources Ancient, Medieval and Modern,* ed. by John Chapin (New York, 1956).

Borgia, Lucretia, Duchess of Ferrara

(1480-1519) Italian noblewoman. Illegitimate daughter of Rodrigo Borgia (later Pope Alexander VI). Sister of Cesare Borgia. Generous patron of arts. Divorced from Giovanni Sforza. Married Alphonso of Aragon who was murdered (probably by her brother Cesare). Married Alfonso d'Este. Contracted puerperal fever after birth of her fifth child. Died at age 38.

Last Words (written): "Most Holy Father and Honored Master: With all respect I kiss your Holiness's feet and commend myself in all humility to your holy mercy. Having suffered for more than two months, early in the morning of the 14th of the present, as it pleased God, I gave birth to a daughter, and hoped then to find relief from my sufferings, but I did not, and shall be compelled to pay my debt to nature. So great is the favor which our merciful Creator has shown me that I approach the end of my life with pleasure, knowing that in a few hours, after receiving for the last time all the holy sacraments of the Church, I shall be released. Having arrived at this moment, I desire as a Christian, although I am a sinner, to ask your Holiness, in your mercy, to give me all possible spiritual consolation, and your Holiness's blessing for my soul. Therefore, I offer myself to you in all humility and commend my husband and my children, all of whom are your servants, to your Holiness's mercy. In Ferrara, June 22, 1519, at the fourteenth hour. Your Holiness's humble servant. Lucretia d'Este." Letter to Pope Leo X.

Source: *Lucretia Borgia* by Ferdinand Gregorovius (New York, 1903).

Börne, Ludwig

(1786-1837) German writer, political activist. Satirist. Political writer. Birth name Löb Baruch. Changed his name when he converted from Judaism to Christianity (Lutheranism) in 1818. Was a leader of the post-Romantic Young Germany movement. Sought social reforms and political freedom. Was critical of Germany's politics and stage. Settled in Paris 1830. Died at age 50 of tuberculosis.

Last Words: "Pull back the drapes! I'd gladly see the sun .—Flowers—Music."

Source: *Ludwig Börne, sein Leben und sein Wirken* by Michael Holzmann (Berlin, Germany, 1888).

Borodin, Aleksandr

(1833-1887) Russian musician, composer, chemist. Illegitimate son of a Georgian prince. Trained in medicine and chemistry. Lectured on chemistry at Saint Petersburg School of Medicine for Women. Bellaire encouraged him to spend his leisure time on music. He became identified as part of a Russian musical group known as The Five or the Mighty Handful (along with Balakirev, Cesar Cui, Mussorgsky and Rimsky-Korsakov). Notable works: *Polovtsian Dances* from *Prince Igor; In the Steppes of Central Asia.* Died suddenly at age 53 at a party in St. Petersburg. His opera *Prince Igor,* incomplete at his death, was finished by Rimsky-Korsakov and Glazunov. Borodin received a Tony Award posthumously in 1954 for the Broadway musical *Kismet,* which included several of his compositions.

Last Words (written): "I shall say no more about it and leave the description of the festivity to the more expert pen of your other correspondents." Letter to his wife who was in Moscow. He was referring to the musical party he planned to attend the next day.

Source: *Masters of Russian Music* by M.D. Calvocoressi and Gerald Abraham (New York, 1936).

Last Words (spoken): "If you are really so fond of evening dress, I will in the future always wear my frock coat whenever I come to see you, so that you should never have any cause for displeasure." Spoken to another guest. After he said these words, he suffered a ruptured aneurysm, collapsed and died.

Source: *Last Words: A Dictionary of Deathbed Quotations* by C. Bernard Ruffin (Jefferson, NC, 2005).

Borromeo, Saint Charles

(1538-1584) Italian prelate, holy man. Archbishop of Milan. Cardinal. Founded Helvetic College in Milan. Founded order of Oblate of Saint Ambrose. Helped implement reforms of the Council of Trent. Died at age 46 in Milan. Canonized in 1610.

Different Last Words:

(1) "Ecce venio." (tr. "Behold I come.") Spoken on his deathbed.

Source: "St. Charles Borromeo" in *Catholic Encyclopedia* (New York, 1908).

(2) "At once." His response when asked if he wished Viaticum (Eucharist given at time of death).

Source: *Reformer: St. Charles Borromeo* by Margaret Yeo (Milwaukee, WI, 1938).

Bosco, Saint John (Don Bosco)

(1815-1888) Italian clergyman, holy man. Known as Don Bosco. Roman Catholic priest who founded the order of Salesian Fathers. Died at age 72 in Turin. Canonized in 1934.

Different Last Words:

(1) "Thy will be done."

Source: *St. John Bosco* by Augustine Auffray (London, 1930).

(2) "Jesus, Mary and Joseph I give you my heart and soul!" Prayed on his deathbed after he made a request of a fellow priest: "When I can no longer speak and someone comes to ask my blessing, lift up my hands and make it with the sign of the cross. I will make the intention."

Source: *Last Words: A Dictionary of Deathbed Quotations* by C. Bernard Ruffin (Jefferson, NC, 1995).

Bossuet, Jacques Bénigne

(1627-1704) French prelate, orator, writer. Famed for funeral orations. Tutor to the Dauphin. Roman Catholic Bishop of Meaux. Died at age 76 in Paris.

Last Words: "Lord, I suffer grievously, but I am not confounded. For I know in Whom to trust. Thy will be done."

Source: *Bossuet and His Contemporaries* by Henrietta Farrer Lear (London, 1874).

Variation: "I suffer the violence of pain and death, I but I know whom I have believed."

Source: *The Last Words (Real and Traditional) of Distinguished Men and Women Collected From Various Sources* by Frederic Rowland Marvin (New York, 1901).

Bottomley, Horatio William

(1860-1933) English journalist, editor, politician, swindler. Member of Parliament. Gained reputation for sensational, ultra national patriotic and political activities. Created patriotic magazine called *John Bull.* Charged and convicted for fraud. Sentenced to seven years in prison and expelled from Parliament. Died at age 73 in a London hospital, with one of his loyal followers, Peggy Primrose, at his bedside. *Time* magazine wrote a lengthy obituary on him entitled "Death of John Bull."

Last Words: "Nurse, I want some milk. I must have milk. I will have milk."

Sources: *Horatio Bottomley: A Biography* by Julian Symons (London, 1955); "Death of John Bull" (*Time* magazine, June 5, 1933).

Boufflers, Stanislas Jean, Chevalier de

(1738-1815) French statesman, military officer, nobleman, clergyman, librarian, writer. Began his career as a priest. Became a Knight of Malta. Served as governor of Senegal. Member of states-general. During the French Revolution he took refuge with Prince Henry of Prussia. After the war, he focused on being a librarian and writer. Notable work: *Aline, reine de Golconde (Aline, Queen of Golconde)*. His *Œuvres completes* (complete works) were published in 1803. Died at age 76.

Last Words: "My friends believe that I am sleeping."

Source: *The Chevalier de Boufflers: A Romance of the French Revolution* by Nesta H. Webster (New York, 1924).

Bouhours, Dominique

(1628-1702) French grammarian, critic. Jesuit. Endeavored to promote accuracy and authenticity in the French language. Died in Paris.

Last Words: "Je vais ou je vas mourir, l'un et l'autre se dit ou se disent." (tr. "I am about to—or I am going to—die: either expression is correct.")

Source: *Nouvelle Biographie Générale depuis les Temps les plus Reculés jusqu'à nos jours. Avec les Renseignements Bibliographiques,* ed. by Firmin Didot Frères (Paris, 1853).

Bouldin, Thomas Tyler

(1781-1834) American politician, lawyer. Member U.S. House of Representatives from Virginia. Brother of James Wood Bouldin, also a representative from Virginia. Selected to fill the uncompleted term of John Randolph of Roanoke, Virginia, when Randolph died. Bouldin died while addressing the House of Representatives about Randolph's death.

Last Words: "Mr. Randolph's death was not here announced. But I cannot tell the reason why his death was not announced without telling what I told a friend I should say in case—." He then collapsed and died.

Source: *Abridgment of the Debates of Congress from 1789 to 1856.* Vol. XII (New York, 1860).

Bourbon, Henri I de, Prince de Condé, see **Condé, Henri I de Bourbon, Prince de.**

Bourbon, Louis de

(1437-1482) French prelate. Son of Charles I de Bourbon. Roman Catholic Bishop of Liege. Murdered at age 45 at Werz, near Liege by Comte Guillaume de la Marck.

Last Words: "Mercy, mercy, my lord of Aremberg. I am your prisoner." Spoken to his assailant.

Source: *Louis de Bourbon, Evéque-Prince de Liège* by Ed. Garnier (Paris, 1860).

Bourbon, Louis I de, Prince de Condé, see **Condé, Louis I de Bourbon, Prince de.**

Bourbon, Louis II de, Prince de Condé, see **Condé, Louis II de Bourbon, Prince de.**

Bourbon-Contè, Louis Antoine Henri de, see **Enghien, Duc d'.**

Bourg, Anne du

(1521-1559) French magistrate, educator. Protestant. Attacked royal policy of repression against Calvinists. Falsely accused of murder. Executed at age 38 in Paris.

Different Last Words:

(1) "My friends, I am not here as a thief or murderer, but on account of the Gospel. My God, forsake me not, that I forsake Thee not." Spoken on the gallows at his execution.

Sources: "Dissertation sur le procès d'Anne du Bourge" in *Collections des meilleurs dissertations...relatifs à l'histoire de France,* XVIII (Paris, 1838); *La France protestante* by Eugène Haag (Paris, 1886).

(2) "Six feet of earth for my body, and the infinite heavens for my soul is what I shall soon have." Shouted at the sight of the scaffold.

Sources: *The Life of Mary, Queen of Scots* by Alphonse de Lamartine (New York, 1887); *The Lovers of the World* by Edgar Saltus (New York, 1898).

Bourmont, Louis-Auguste-Victor de, Count de Ghaisnes

(1773-1846) French military officer, politician, royalist. Served under Napoleon. Deserted four days before Waterloo to serve Louis XVIII. Minister of war. Marshal of France. Died at age 73 on family estate in Anjou.

Last Words: "Je veux voir Alexandre, César, Charlemagne...Jesus Christ le Sauveur des—." (tr. "I want to see Alexander, Caesar, Charlemagne and Jesus Christ the Savior of—").

Source: *Un gentilhomme de grand chemin, le maréchal de Bourmont (1773-1846) d'apres ses papiers inédits* by Gustav Gautherot (Paris, 1926).

Bouvier, Auguste

(1826-1893) Swiss educator, theologian.

Protestant. Professor of theology in Geneva. Asserted that for salvation, sin must be condemned as odious. Also, humanity must accept suffering and death as just, and freely submit to them. Died at age 67 in Geneva.
Last Words: "My God!…My God!"
Source: *Auguste Bouvier, Théologien Protestant* by J. Emile Roberty (Paris, 1901).

Bow, Clara Gordon

(1905-1965) American actress. Silent screen star. Known as the It Girl. Retired while in her 20s. Diagnosed with schizophrenia. Died at age 60 of a heart attack in Los Angeles.
Last Words (doubtful): "I've been working hard for years and I need a rest. So I'm figuring on going to Europe for a year or more when my contract expires."
Source: Various Last Words compilations and Internet websites.
Bow had been out of films and away from contracts for more than 30 years when she died. Her last film was in 1933. She had retired from films after a second nervous breakdown for which she was institutionalized for a time. In her later years she became a recluse. She died alone except for a live-in nurse. She was watching an old Gary Cooper western when her heart stopped.
Source: "The Silencing of Clara Bow" by Christina Ball (*Gadfly*, March/April 2001).

Bowditch, Henry Ingersoll

(1808-1892) American physician, medical writer, health reformer, abolitionist. Son of Nathaniel Bowditch. Advanced public health movement in U.S. Notable works: *Public Hygiene in America; Soil Moisture as a Cause of Consumption*. President of American Medical Association. Antislavery crusader. Friend of Frederick Douglass. Died at age 83 in Boston, Massachusetts.
Last Words: "No dear—wish that the end would come." His response when asked if he was suffering.
Source: *Life and Correspondence of Henry Ingersoll Bowditch* by Vincent Y. Bowditch (Boston, 1902). The author was his son.

Bowditch, Nathaniel

(1773-1838) American mathematician, astronomer, actuary. Father of Henry Ingersoll Bowditch. Translated Laplace's *Celestial Mechanics*. Published *The New American*

Practical Navigator (manual for sailors). President Essex Fire and Marine Insurance Co.; Massachusetts Hospital Life Insurance Co. Died at age 64 of stomach cancer in Boston.
Different Last Words:
(1) "How delicious. I have swallowed a drop from 'Siloa's brook that flow'd fast by the oracle of God'" ("Siloa's brook that flow'd…" is from Milton's *Paradise Lost*.)
Source: *Memoir of Nathaniel Bowditch* by Nathaniel Ingersoll Bowditch (Boston, 1841). The author was his son.
(2) "Good-bye, my son; my work is done; and if I knew I were to be gone when the sun sets in the West, I would say, 'Thy will, O God, be done. So live that, sinking in thy last long sleep, Calm thou mayst smile, while all around thee weep.'"
Source: *A Conspectus of American Biography: Being an Analytical Summary of American History and Biography, Containing also the Complete Indexes of the National Cyclopedia of American Biography* by George Derby (New York, 1906).

Bowdre, Charlie

(d. 1880) American outlaw, murderer, thief. Member of Billy the Kid's gang. Trapped by Sheriff Pat Garrett in a deserted farmhouse in Stinking Springs, New Mexico. Bowdre was hit several times. The Kid urged him to go outside and seek revenge by killing some of the posse before he died. Bowdre tried to take a few steps but fell and died.
Last Words: "I wish, I wish, I wish. I'm dying."
Source: *Billy the Kid: A Short and Violent Life* by Robert M. Utley (Lincoln, NE, 2000).

Bowen, Joshua Robert

(1849-1878) American murderer, gunfighter. Found guilty of murdering Thomas Holderman/Halderman while he slept. Bowen's case is noteworthy because he claimed the murder was committed by his brother-in-law, the notorious John Wesley Hardin. Bowen proclaimed his innocence even on the gallows where he spoke his Last Words confronted by the brother of the murder victim. Bowen asked the man if he believed he [Bowen] had killed his brother. The man responded that he did. Bowen was hanged at age 28 in Gonzales, Texas, in front of 4,000 people.

Different Last Words:
(1) "You believe a doggone lie! I didn't do it. It was my blasted brother-in-law John Wesley Hardin! Spoken to the murder victim's father. The executioner ignored his plea and hanged him.
Source: *Get Along, Little Dogies: The Chisholm Trail Diary of Hallie Lou Wells: South Texas, 1878* by Lisa Waller Rogers (Lubbock, TX, 2001).
(2) "O Lord receive my spirit."
Source: *Gonzales Daily Inquirer,* May 18, 1878.

Bowles, Samuel
(1826-1878) American journalist, publisher, editor-in-chief. His father founded the *Springfield Republican* (Massachusetts newspaper). Bowles took control of the paper after his father died. When he died at age 51 he also was succeeded by his son.
Last Words: "You may be sure that in another world there will always be one soul praying for you." Spoken to his nurse.
Source: *The Life and Times of Samuel Bowles* by George S. Merriam (New York, 1885).

Boyd, Jerry ("F.X. Toole")
(1930-2002) American athlete. Boxer, trainer, writer. Pen name F.X. Toole. Two of his short stories in the collection *Rope Burns: Stories from the Corner* were later adapted into the 2004 Oscar-winning movie, *Million Dollar Baby.* Boyd was finishing his first novel *Pound for Pound* when he died. It was published posthumously in 2006 to excellent reviews.
Last Words: "Doc, get me a little more time, I gotta finish my book." Reported by his children.
Source: "Pound for Pound Punches Above Its Weight" by Bob Minzesheimer (*USA Today,* August 15, 2006).

Boyd, Kenneth Lee
(1948-2005) American murderer. Killed his wife and her father. Executed at age 57 by lethal injection in North Carolina. Became the 1,000[th] person executed in the U.S. since the judicially sanctioned execution moratorium ended 28 years earlier. Boyd did not want to be the 1,000[th] prisoner to be executed: "I'd hate to be remembered like that. I don't like the idea of being picked by a number."
Last Words: "Look after my son and grandchildren. God bless everybody in here." Spoken to daughter-in-law Kathy Smith just before he was executed.
Source: "U.S. Carries Out 1,000[th] Execution" (BBC News, December 2, 2005).

Boyd, William
(1758-1807) American clergyman. Presbyterian. Trustee of College of New Jersey (now Princeton University). Pastor of Presbyterian Church at Lamington, New Jersey, from 1784 until he died.
Last Words: "I am not afraid to die."
Source: *The Christian World Magazine and Foreign Christian Union,* Vol. XIV (New York, 1863).

Boyer, John
(1845-1871) French-Canadian (by some accounts part Native American) murderer. Killed two men who had raped his sister and mother. Boyer was the first person legally executed in the Wyoming Territory. He was also tried by the first jury on which a woman served. Hanged at age 26 in Cheyenne (or Laramie), Wyoming.
Last Words: "Look at me! I no cry. I no woman. I man! I die brave!"
Source: "Look at Me...I Die Brave" by Larry K. Brown (*True West,* December 1995).

Boyle, Robert
(1627-1691) Irish-born English physicist, chemist, philosopher. Repeatedly refused peerage. Member of a group that was later chartered as the Royal Society. Made major contributions in the fields of chemistry, pneumatics, and theory of matter. Separated chemistry from alchemistry. Credited with coining the term "chemical analysis." Notable works: *New Experiments Physical-Mechanical Touching the Spring and Weight of the Air; The Sceptical Chemist.* Died at age 65 in London. Boyle's Law was named for him.
Last Words (doubtful): "We shall there desire nothing that we have not, except more tongues to sing more praises to him or at least a capacity to pay him greater thanks for what we have." Boyle wrote these words many years before he died. The quotation was taken from a letter he wrote in 1648. It was published in 1660 in *Seraphic Love: Some Motives and Incentives to the Love of*

God, a book of his writing.
Source: *Seraphic Love: Some Motives and Incentives to the Love of God* by Robert Boyle (Edinburgh, 1825).

Boz, see Dickens, Charles John Huffam.

Bozzaris or Botsaris, Marco or Markos

(1788?-1823) Greek soldier. Fought in Greek war of independence. Shot and killed during attack on Turkish camp at Karpenisi. Commemorated in poem *Marco Bozzaris* by American poet Fitz-Greene Halleck.
Last Words: "To die for liberty is a pleasure, not a pain."
Source: *Polyglot Reader and Guide for Translation, Consisting of a Series of English Extracts, with Their Translation into French, German, Spanish and Italian* by Jean Roemer (New York, 1857).

Brace, Charles Loring

(1826-1890) American clergyman, social reformer. Methodist minister. Social service advocate. Helped establish Children's Aid Society of New York. Founder of Orphan Trains that ran for almost 75 years, placing as many as 200,000 children from poor, crowded urban homes onto Midwestern farms and other rural locations. Died at age 64 of Bright's disease.
Last Words: "I wish you would send this to Mr. Potter." He was commenting on a newspaper story about the success of a sanitarium on Long Island.
Source: *The Life and Letters of Charles Loring Brace,* ed. by his daughter Emma Brace (New York, 1894).

Braddock, Edward

(1695-1755) British military officer. Commander in America during French and Indian Wars. Used poor judgment when he marched to Fort Duquesne, where more than half of his men were killed in a surprise attack on July 9, 1755. He died of wounds four days later.
Different Last Words:
(1) "We shall know better how to deal with them next time."
Source: "Braddock, Edward" by Harrison K. Bird, *Encyclopedia Americana*, Vol. 4 (Danbury, CT, 1985).
(2) "Who would have thought it?"
Source: *A Conspectus of American Biography: Being an Analytical Summary of American History and Biography, Containing also the Complete Indexes of the National Cyclopedia of American Biography* by George Derby (New York, 1906).
(3) "Is it possible? All is over." Described as

the only words anyone heard Braddock utter.
Sources: *History of the Early Settlement and Indian Wars of Western Virginia* by William De Hass (Philadelphia, 1851); *History of Ohio,* Vol. I, by Emilius Oviatt Randall (New York, 1912).

Bradford, Alden

(1765-1843) American clergyman, journalist, historian, biographer, statesman. Congregational pastor and later clerk of Supreme Court of Boston. Secretary of state for Massachusetts. Notable works: *History of Massachusetts; Memoir of the Life and Writings of Rev. Jonathan Mayhew, D.D.* Died in Boston at age 77.
Last Word: "Peace."
Source: *A Conspectus of American Biography: Being an Analytical Summary of American History and Biography, Containing also the Complete Indexes of the National Cyclopedia of American Biography* by George Derby (New York, 1906).

Bradford, Andrew

(1686-1742) American publisher, printer. Published *American Weekly Mercury*, first Pennsylvania newspaper. Began *American Magazine*, first colonial magazine. Died at age 56 in Philadelphia.
Last Words (doubtful): "O Lord, forgive the errata!"
Source: Various Last Words compilations and Internet websites.
Frederic Rowland Marvin said the quote rests on the doubtful authority of an old letter signed by George E. Clarkson but did not identify him.
Source: *Last Words (Real and Traditional) of Distinguished Men and Women Collected From Various Sources* by Frederic Rowland Marvin (New York, 1901).

Bradford, John

(1510?-1555) English clergyman, martyr. Protestant chaplain to Bishop Ridley and King Edward VI. Arrested and accused of sedition on accession of Queen Mary. Tried, condemned as heretic. Burned at the stake at age 45. Many spectators witnessed his execution.
Last Words: "Be of good comfort, brother; for we shall have a merry supper with the Lord this night.— Straight is the way, and narrow is the gate, that leadeth to eternal salvation, and few there be that find it."

Spoken to John Leaf, another young martyr condemned to burn at the stake with him.

Source: *Book of Martyrs and the Acts and Monuments of the Church* by John Fox (or Foxe). First published 1563, ed. by John Cumming (London, 1851).

Variation: "Be of good comfort, brother, for we shall have a merry supper with the Lord this night: if there be any way to heaven on horseback or in fiery chariots, this is it." Spoken to a fellow martyr.

Source: *The Last Words (Real and Traditional) of Distinguished Men and Women Collected From Various Sources* by Frederic Rowland Marvin (New York, 1901).

Bradford, William

(1590-1657) English-born American politician, Pilgrim, writer. Primary architect and second signer of Mayflower Compact. Principal leader of Plymouth Colony. Governor of Plymouth Colony for 30 years. Notable work: *History of Plymouth Plantation*. His journal provides insights into the Plymouth Plantation and is considered one of the most important historical documents written by a 17th-century American. Bradford is credited with proclaiming what is now viewed as the first Thanksgiving. Died at age 67 in Plymouth.

Last Words: "The Spirit of God has given me a pledge of my happiness in another world, and the first fruits of my eternal glory."

Source: *A Conspectus of American Biography: Being an Analytical Summary of American History and Biography, Containing also the Complete Indexes of the National Cyclopedia of American Biography* by George Derby (New York, 1906).

Brady, Hugh

(1764-1851) American military officer. Fought in the Battle of Chippewa in the War of 1812. U.S. Army brevetted brigadier general, major general. Removed Native Americans from Michigan. Local militia unit, the Brady Guards, was named for him. Died at age 86 in Detroit, Michigan, from injuries sustained when thrown from a carriage.

Last Words: "Let the drum beat; my knapsack is slung; I am ready to die." Spoken to his physician when told he would not recover from his injuries.

Source: "General Hugh Brady" by George C. Bates in

Michigan Pioneer Historical Collections 2 (1877-1878).

Brady, James Buchanan ("Diamond Jim")

(1856-1917) American financier. Sold railroad supplies. Known as Diamond Jim for the large collection of diamonds and other gems he wore with different outfits. Enjoyed eating. Weighed more than 300 pounds. Died at age 60 of urinary problems in Atlantic City, New Jersey. Endowed foundation at Johns Hopkins to study urology. Movie *Diamond Jim* (1935) was based on his life.

Last Words: "Someday, doctor, you'll understand how much I appreciate your interest in me."

Source: *Diamond Jim: The Life and Times of James Buchanan Brady* by Parker Morell (New York, 1934).

Brahe, Tycho

(1546-1601) Danish astronomer. Compiled table of refractions. Discovered new star in Cassiopeia. Found errors in astronomy tables. Fixed the positions of more than 700 stars. Moved to Prague when he received an appointment from Emperor Rudolf II. Notable works: *Astronomiae instauratae progymnasmata; Astronomiae instauratae-mechanica* (descriptions of his theories and instruments). Worked with Kepler. Gave his astronomical observations to Kepler. Became ill at a banquet. Died at age 55 in Prague, 11 days later.

Last Words: "Ne frustra vixisse videar." (tr. "Let me not seem to have lived in vain!")

Sources: Account by Johann Kepler, quoted in *Tycho Brahe* by J.L.E Dreyer (1890); *The Life and Times of Tyco Brahe* by J.A. Gode (1947).

Brahms, Johannes

(1833-1897) German-born musician, composer, pianist. Moved to Vienna, Austria, in 1863. Wrote in all classical musical forms except opera. Notable works: *A German Requiem;* four concertos; four symphonies; *Academic Festival Overture* (written to acknowledge his honorary doctorate from the University of Breslau); children's nursery tune (known popularly as the "Brahms Lullaby"). Devoted friend of Clara Weick Schumann. Died at age 63 in Vienna.

Last Words: "Ja, das ist schön!" (tr. "Yes, that tastes nice!") Spoken after he sat up in his deathbed and sipped a glass of wine.

Source: *The Unknown Brahms* by Robert Haven Schauffler (New York, 1936).

Variation: "O, das schmeckt gut. Danke." (tr. "Oh, that tastes good. Thanks.")

Source: *Lexikon der letzten Worte: letzte Botschaften berühmter Männer und Frauen von Konrad Adenauer bis Emiliano Zapata* by Werner Fuld (Munich, Germany, 2002)

Brainerd, David

(1718-1747) American clergyman. Missionary to Native Americans of New York, New Jersey and eastern Pennsylvania. Active in Great Awakening religious revival. Died at age 29, probably of tuberculosis at the home of Jonathan Edwards in Northampton, Massachusetts. Edwards preached his funeral sermon and published his journal. It was widely read and influenced others to become missionaries. Despite being expelled from Yale; the university later named Brainerd Hall at Yale Divinity School for him. David Brainerd Christian School in Chattanooga, Tennessee, was also named for him.

Different Last Words:

(1) "It is another thing to die than people have imagined."

Source: *An Account of the Life of the Late Rev. David Brainerd* (with *Journal* and Brainerd's letters) by Jonathan Edwards (New Haven, CT, 1822).

(2) "My soul was this day, at turns, sweetly set on God; I longed to be with him, that I might behold his glory. I felt sweetly disposed to commit all to him, even my dearest friends, my dearest flock, my absent brother, and all my concerns for time and eternity. O that his kingdom might come in the world; that they might all love and glorify him, for what he is in himself; and that the blessed Redeemer might see of the travail of his soul, and be satisfied! Oh, come Lord Jesus, come quickly. Amen."

Source: *Memoirs of the Rev. David Brainerd: Missionary to the Indians on the Borders of New York, New Jersey and Pennsylvania. Chiefly Taken From His Own Diary by Rev. Jonathan Edwards of Northampton Including His Journal, Now for the First Time Incorporated with the Rest of His Dairy in Regular Chronological Series* by Sereno Edwards Dwight (New Haven, CT, 1822).

(3) "My work is done. Oh, to be in heaven, to praise and glorify God with His holy angels!"

Source: "David Brainerd" in *American Biographical and Historical Dictionary, Containing an Account of the Lives, Characters and Writings* (Boston, 1832).

Variation: "I am almost in eternity. I long to be there. My work is done. I have done with my friends; all the world is nothing to me. Oh, to be in heaven to praise and glorify God with His holy angels."

Source: *Dying Testimonies of Saved and Unsaved: Gathered from Authentic Sources* by Solomon Benjamin Shaw (Chicago, 1898).

Variation: "I am almost in eternity. I long to be there. My work is done. The watcher is with me; why tarry the wheels of his chariot?"

Source: *The Last Words (Real and Traditional) of Distinguished Men and Women Collected from Various Sources* by Frederic Rowland Marvin (New York, 1901).

Branch, Mary

(1716?-1740) English murderer. Executed at age 24 in Ivelchester, Somersetshire, for murdering a teenage girl. Her daughter Elizabeth was also executed for the crime.

Last Words: "Good people, pity my unhappy case, who, while young, was trained up in the paths of cruelty and barbarity; and let all present take warning by my unhappy end, so as to avoid the like crimes. You see I am cut off in the prime of life, in the midst of my days—Good people, pray for me!"

Source: "Elizabeth and Mary Branch, Executed for Murder" in *The Newgate Calendar: Comprising Interesting Memoirs of the Most Notorious Characters Who Have Been Convicted of Outrages on the Laws of England Since the Commencement of the Eighteenth Century: With Occasional Anecdotes and Observations Speeches, Confessions and the Last Exclamations of Sufferers* by Andrew Knapp and William Baldwin (London, 1828). Collated and ed. with some appendices by J.L. Rayner and G.T. Crook (London, 1926).

Brandsma, Titus

(1881-1942) Dutch clergyman, writer, journalist, educator. Carmelite priest who was appointed National Spiritual Adviser to Dutch Catholic journalists. He opposed printing of any Nazi propaganda. Was seized and sent to Dachau concentration camp. He gave his rosary to the nurse who administered the injection that would kill him. The nurse, although raised Catholic, had forgotten the prayers.

Last Words: "Well if you can't say the first

part, surely you can still say 'Pray for us sinners.'" Spoken to the nurse who killed him by lethal injection

Source: *Young Faces of Holiness: Modern Saints in Photos and Words* by Ann Ball (Huntington, IN, 2004).

Brandt, Karl

(1904-1948) German physician, military officer, politician. Nazi general. Senior medical official of German government during World War II. Hitler's personal physician. Tried as a war criminal at Nuremberg. His was the first Nuremberg war crimes trial. Executed at age 44 in Landsberg Prison.

Last Words: "It is no shame to stand on this scaffold. I served my fatherland as others before me."

Source: *The Nazi Doctors and the Nuremberg Code: Human Rights and Human Experimentation* by George J. Annas and Michael A. Grodin (New York, 1992).

Brant, Joseph (Thayendanegea)

(1742-1807) Native American leader. Mohawk chief, activist. Aided British during American Revolution. Terrorized New York frontier. Became perhaps the best-known Native American of his generation. After the war, he went to England where he met King George III. Later he promoted a Native American confederacy to help his people hold onto their land. Translated New Testament into Mohawk. Died at age 65 at his Burlington Bay home.

Last Words: "Have pity on the poor Indians. If you can get any influence with the great, endeavor to do them all the good you can." Spoken to his adopted nephew John Norton.

Source: *Life of Joseph Brant (Thayendanegea): Including the Border Wars of the American Revolution, and Sketches of the Indian Campaigns of Generals Harmar, St. Clair and Wayne,* Vol. II, by William L. Stone (Albany, NY, 1865).

Brasidas

(d. 422 B.C.) Spartan military officer. General in Peloponnesian War. Saved Megara and Methone from Athenian attack. Defeated Athenian general Cleon at Amphipolis. Died in the battle that also killed Cleon.

Last Words: "These men do not mean to face us; we have their spears and their heads are shaking; such behavior always shows

that an army is going to run away. Open me the gates as I ordered, and let us boldly attack them at once."

Source: *Thucydides, tr. into English, to which is Prefixed an Essay on Inscriptions and a Note on the Geography of Thucydides* by Benjamin Jowett (Oxford, England, 1900).

Brecht, Bertolt

(1898-1956) German writer, poet, playwright, stage director. Birth name Eugen Berthold Friedrich Brecht. Made significant innovative contributions to dramatic staging. Lived in Scandinavia and United States 1933 to 1947. Returned to Germany after World War II. Operated an internationally known theater company with his wife and collaborator actress Helene Weigel. Notable works and productions include collaborations with composer Kurt Weill: *The Threepenny Opera; He Who Says Yes; Rise and Fall of the City of Mahoganny.* Died at age 58 in East Berlin.

Last Words: "Laßt mich in Ruhe!" (tr. "Leave me alone!")

Source: *Brecht Chronik 1898-1956* by Werner Hecht (Frankfurt, Germany, 1997).

Breitinger, Johann Jakob

(1701-1776) Swiss scholar, critic, writer. Influenced Schiller, Goethe and Klopstock. Notable work: *Kritische Dichtkunst.* Collaborated with Johann Bodner, another Swiss scholar. Died at age 75 in Zurich.

Last Words: "Living or dying, we are the Lord's."

Source: *Breitinger und Zürich* by J.G. Mörikofer (Leipzig, Germany, 1874).

Bremer, Fredrika

(1801-1865) Finnish-born Swedish writer, novelist, social reformer. First novel *The H Family* was about everyday life in Sweden. Lived briefly in U.S. (1849 to 1851). Wrote of her experiences in *Homes of the New World: Impressions of America.* Championed emancipation and education of women. Died at age 64 in Sweden.

Last Words: "Ah! my child, let us speak of Christ's love—the best, the highest love!" Spoken to a nurse.

Source: *Life, Letters and Posthumous Works of Fredrika Bremer,* ed. by Charlotte Bremer, tr. by Fred. Milow (New York, 1880). Charlotte was her sister.

Brennan, Mollie (or Molly)

(c.1850s-1876) American dancer, folk figure. Dance hall girl. Died at Lady Gay Saloon in Sweetwater, Texas, trying to protect Bat Masterson. Shot and killed when she jumped in front of a gun fired by former boyfriend Corporal Melvin King. Masterson responded by killing King.

Last Words: "Don't shoot! You're drunk!"

Source: *The Lawmen: The Authentic Wild West* by James D. Horan (New York, 1980).

Brereton, Sir William

(d. 1536) English royal servant. Involved in adultery accusations against Anne Boleyn. Executed on trumped up charges. Beheaded with Anne Boleyn on Tower Hill, London.

Last Words: "I have deserved to die, if it were a thousand deaths. But the cause wherefore I die, judge ye not. But if you judge, judge the best!" Spoken as he faced the executioner's axe.

Source: *Life of Anne Boleyn* by Philip W. Sergeant (New York, 1924).

Brewster, Sir David

(1781-1868) Scottish physicist, writer, editor, inventor. Edited *Edinburgh Encyclopedia*. Distinguished in science of optics. Improved the stereoscope. Invented kaleidoscope. Designed lenses for lighthouses. A founder of the British Association. Knighted for his achievements in science. Died at age 88 in Allerly near Melrose, Scotland. Brewster's angle was named for him.

Last Words: "I shall see Jesus who created all things, Jesus who made the worlds. I shall see Jesus and that will be grand. I feel so safe, so satisfied."

Source: *The Home Life of Sir David Brewster* by Margaret Maria Gordon (Edinburgh, 1869). The author was his daughter.

Variation: "I shall see Jesus, who created all things; Jesus, who made the worlds; I shall see Him as He is. Yes; I have had the Light for many years, and oh, how bright it is I feel so safe, so satisfied!"

Source: "Short Arrows—Notes on Christian Life and Work in All Fields—The Experience of a Natural Philosopher" (*The Quiver*, Ser. 3, Vol. 28, 1893).

Bridget of Sweden, Saint
(Birgitta Birgersdottir)

(1303?-1373) Swedish nun, holy woman, mystic. Founder of Bridgettine (or Brigettine) Order. The only saint in the last thousand years who was also the mother of a saint, Saint Catherine of Vadstena of Sweden. Bridget died in Rome. Canonized in 1391. Brigitta Chapel (built in 1651) and district known as Brigittenau were named for her.

Last Words: "In manus tuas, Domine, commendo spiritum meum." (tr. "Into Thy hands, O Lord I commend my spirit.") She was reciting Psalm 30:6.

Sources: *The Divine Office—a Study of Roman Breviary* by Rev. E. J. Quigley (Rockcorry, Ireland, 1920); *Book of Catholic Quotations Compiled from Approved Sources Ancient, Medieval and Modern*, ed. by John Chapin (New York, 1956).

Bridgman, Laura Dewey

(1829-1889) American educator. Sensory handicapped. Lost voice, vision and hearing when she contracted scarlet fever at age two. First blind deaf-mute American to receive significant education in the English language, some 50 years before Helen Keller. Charles Dickens wrote an account of her school that was read by Helen's mother and inspired her to hire Anne Sullivan, teacher and former pupil of the school. Sullivan learned the manual alphabet from Bridgman that she took back to Helen, along with a doll Bridgman had made for her. Bridgman died at age 59 in Boston. A Liberty ship was named for her.

Last Word (written): "M-O-T-H-E-R." Spelled on the hands of Mrs. Smith, a school staff member. On the second effort Mrs. Smith guessed the word and Bridgman nodded. It was her last effort to communicate.

Sources: *Fifty-Eighth Annual Report of the Trustees of the Perkins Institute and Massachusetts School for the Blind for the Year Ending September 30, 1889* (Boston, 1890); *Laura Bridgman, Dr. Howe's Famous Pupil and What He Taught Her* by Maud Howe Elliott and Florence Howe Hall (Boston, 1903).

Briggs, George Nixon

(1796-1861) American politician, reformer. Lifelong advocate of temperance. Baptist layman. Member U.S. House of Representatives from Massachusetts. Governor of Massachusetts. Accidentally killed at age 65 in Pittsfield, Massachusetts, when a gun discharged unexpectedly.

Last Words: "You won't leave me again, will you?" Spoken to his son.

Source: *Great in Goodness: A Memoir of George N. Briggs, Governor of the Commonwealth of Massachusetts, from 1844-1851* by William Carey Richards (Boston, 1867).

Bright, John

(1811-1889) British statesman, politician, orator. Radical and liberal Quaker. Member of Parliament. Associated with Richard Cobden and formation of Anti-Corn Law League. Strong critic of British foreign policy. Advocated free trade. Attacked the landlord class and appealed for laws that would benefit the middle class. One of England's strongest supporters of the North in U.S. Civil War. Died at age 77 in Rochdale, Lancashire.

Last Words (doubtful): "There is nothing that gives me as much pleasure as poetry, except little children." May not be his Last Words. Bright is known to have used this expression often.

Sources: *The Review of Reviews* by William Thomas Stead (London, 1895); *The North American Review* by Making of America Project (Boston, 1892).

Brindley, James

(1716-1772) English engineer. Built England's first major canal. Also built bridges, locks and tunnels. Supervised construction of Worsley & Manchester, Bridgewater, Grand Trunk, Birmingham canals and others. Died at age 56 in Turnhurst while talking with visiting canal builders who were having difficulty making their canal hold water.

Last Words: "Then puddle it, puddle it, and puddle it again." (Puddling = trampling clay to make it smooth and waterproof.) Some sources say these were "almost his last words."

Source: *Lives of the Engineers* by Samuel Smiles (London, 1904).

Brisbane, Albert

(1809-1890) American sociologist, writer. Father of Arthur Brisbane. Proposed that society be organized into small self-sustaining communal groups. American advocate of Fourierism. Studied under Fourier for two years. Contributed columns on Fourierism to the *New York Tribune*. Died at age

80 in Richmond, Virginia.

Last Words: "My love, turn me over—towards you." Spoken to his wife.

Source: *Albert Brisbane: A Mental Biography* by Redelia Brisbane (Boston, 1893). The author was his wife. She edited and wrote an introduction to his autobiography that was published posthumously.

Brisbane, Arthur

(1864-1936) American editor, writer. Son of Albert Brisbane. Influential editor of Hearst's *New York Evening Journal* from 1897 to 1921. Involved in late 19th-century yellow journalism war. Donated land in New Jersey that is now Allaire State Park. Died of heart attack at age 72 in New York City. Stone memorial honoring him stands in New York City's Central Park.

Last Words: "This is the best of all possible worlds."

Source: *Brisbane, A Candid Biography* by Oliver Carlson (New York, 1937).

Briscoe, Joe

(d. 1876) Irish-born American buffalo hunter. Killed near Fort Griffin, Texas, in an argument with fellow buffalo hunter/ gunfighter Sheriff Pat Garrett. Briscoe was wielding an axe when he was shot by Garrett.

Last Words: "Won't you come over here and forgive me?" Spoken to Garrett after Briscoe said to him: "I'm dying, Pat." Garrett was reportedly moved to tears by the apology.

Sources: *Billy the Kid, a Bio-bibliography* by Jon Tuska (Westport, CT, 1983); *Encyclopedia of Western Gunfighters* by Bill O'Neal (Norman, OK, 1991).

Britten, Edward Benjamin, Lord Britten of Aldeburgh

(1913-1976) British musician, composer, conductor, pianist. Notable works: *Young Person's Guide to the Orchestra; Peter Grimes* (opera); *A Ceremony of Carols*. Composed incidental music for radio, stage and movies. Died at age 63 of heart failure at home in Aldeburgh, Suffolk, soon after becoming first composer to be made life peer as Lord Britten of Aldeburgh.

Last Words: "Good night, Mike." Spoken to a friend.

Source: *Benjamin Britten A Biography* by Humphrey Carpenter (New York, 1992).

Brock, Sir Isaac

(1769-1812) British military officer. Major general who commanded an army in Upper Canada in the beginning months of the War of 1812. Invaded Michigan, captured Detroit. Knighted for his action. Killed at age 43 during the Battle of Queenston Heights. Brock University, Brockville, Ontario, and Brock, Saskatchewan, named for him.

Last Words: "Push on, the York volunteers." He lived long enough to request that his fall might not be noticed or prevent the advance of his brave troops. He added a wish that was not distinctly understood, that some token of remembrance be transmitted to his sister.

Source: *The Life and Correspondence of Major-General Sir Isaac Brock, K. B.,* ed. by Ferdinand Brock Tupper (London, 1845). The editor was the son of Isaac's sister.

Brocklesby, Richard

(1722-1797) English physician, publisher, writer. Surgeon general of British army. Fellow of the Royal Society and the College of Physicians. Published several medical books. Friend of Dr. Samuel Johnson. Attended him on his deathbed. Died at age 75.

Last Words: "What an idle piece of ceremony this buttoning and unbuttoning is to me now." Spoken to servants who had undressed him before putting him in bed.

Source: *The General Biographical Dictionary: Containing an Historical and Critical Account of the Lives and Writings of the Most Eminent Persons in Every Nation, Particularly the British and Irish from the Earliest Accounts to the Present Time,* Vol. VII, by Alexander Chalmers (London, 1813).

Broderick, David Colbreth

(1820-1859) American politician. Member U.S. Senate from California. Killed in a duel with David S. Terry after the 1859 election. Terry—California state supreme court chief justice—lost the election and blamed it on Broderick, who died three days after the duel. Terry was tried and acquitted. Broderick's death at age 39 created so much hostility toward Terry he was forced to leave San Francisco. He retired to Stockton, California.

Different Last Words:

(1) "I die. Protect my honor."

Source: *The Life of David C. Broderick, a Senator of the Fifties* by Jeremiah Lynch (New York, 1911).

(2) "Baker, when I was struck, I tried to stand firm, but the blow blinded me and I could not." Spoken to Colonel E. D. Baker.

Source: "David C. Broderick" in *Representative and Leading Men of The Pacific: Being Original Sketches of the Lives and Characters of the Principal Men, Living and Deceased, of the Pacific States and Territories—Pioneers, Politicians, Lawyers, Doctors, Merchants, Orators, and Divines—To which are Added Their Speeches, Addresses, Orations, Eulogies, Lectures, and Poems, Upon a Variety of Subjects, Including the Happiest Forensic Efforts of Baker, Randolph, McDougall, T. Starr King and Other Popular Orators* by Oskar T. Shuck (San Francisco, CA, 1870).

Brodie, Sir Benjamin Collins, 1st Baronet

(1783-1862) British physician, educator, writer. Surgeon to King George IV. Professor of anatomy, physiology, surgery. President of Royal Society. Awarded baronage in 1834. Notable work: *Diseases of the Joints* (reduced number of unnecessary amputations). Died at age 79 of rheumatic fever at Torquay, Devon, England.

Last Words: "After all, God is very good." Heard by his physician Dr. Thompson.

Source: *Sir Benjamin Brodie* by Timothy Holmes (New York, 1896).

Brontë, Anne

(1820-1849) English novelist, poet. Pen names Currer Ellis and Acton Bell. Wrote only two novels: *Agnes Grey* and *The Tenant of Wildfell Hall.* Died at age 29 of tuberculosis in Scarborough where she asked to be taken so that she could have a final view of the sea. She was the second Brontë sister to die of tuberculosis within a year.

Last Words: "Take courage, Charlotte. Take courage." Spoken to her sister.

Source: *The Brontë Story* by Margaret Lane (New York, 1953).

Brontë, Charlotte

(1816-1855) English novelist. Pen name Currer Bell. Married Arthur Bell Nicholls in 1854. Notable works: *Jane Eyre; Villette.* Died at age 39 while pregnant in Haworth, Yorkshire, England.

Last Words: "Oh, I am not going to die, am I? He will not separate us, we have been so happy." Spoken to her husband.

Source: *The Life of Charlotte Brontë* by Elizabeth C. Gaskell (New York, 1960).

Brontë, Emily Jane

(1818-1848) English poet, novelist. Pen name Ellis Bell. *Wuthering Heights* was her only novel. Went to her brother Branwell's funeral and caught a chill. Became ill. Died soon afterward at age 30 of tuberculosis in Haworth, Yorkshire, England.

Different Last Words:

(1) "If you will send for a doctor, I will see him now." Spoken to her sister Charlotte.

Source: *The Life of Charlotte Brontë* by Elizabeth C. Gaskell (New York, 1960).

(2) "No, no!" Her response to attempts to get her to bed. She died on a sofa.

Source: *Notes and Queries a Medium of Inter-Communication for Literary Men, Artists, Antiquaries, Genealogists, etc.* Ser. 3, Vol. 10 (Oxford, England, 1905).

Brontë, Patrick

(1777-1861) Irish-born English clergyman. Curate at Haworth. Father of one son, Patrick Branwell, and five daughters, Maria, Elizabeth, Charlotte, Emily and Anne. Five of his children died of tuberculosis while young. Patrick outlived all his children and left no direct descendants. He died at age 84 in Haworth, Yorkshire, England.

Last Words: "While there is life, there is will."

Source: "Dying Words of Noted Persons" in *Miscellaneous Notes and Queries with Answers in All Departments of Literature*, Vol. II (Manchester, NH, 1885).

Brontë, Patrick Branwell

(1817-1848) English writer, artist. Brother of Anne, Charlotte, Emily, Elizabeth and Maria Brontë. Studied portrait painting. The group picture he painted of Anne, Charlotte and Emily around 1835 is in the National Portrait Gallery in London. He was an alcoholic and addicted to opium. While working as a tutor, he was seduced by a woman known as Mrs. Robinson. Branwell's experiences with her were part of the inspiration for the character Benjamin Braddock in the 1967 movie *The Graduate*. Died at age 31 of tuberculosis in Haworth, Yorkshire, England.

Last Words: "Amen." Spoken at the end of a prayer.

Source: *The Brontës* by Clement Shorter (New York, 1908).

Brooke, Gustavus Vaughan

(1818-1866) Irish actor. Specialized in playing dramatic characters. Notable roles: Richard III, Romeo, Macbeth, Virginius, Hamlet, Othello, Iago, Brutus. Died at age 47 when his ship went down in a storm en route to Australia.

Last Words: "No! no! Good-bye. Should you survive, give my last farewell to the people of Melbourne." His response as the only remaining lifeboat pulled away.

Source: *The Life of Gustavus Vaughan Brooke, Tragedian* by W.L. Lawrence (Belfast, Ireland, 1892).

Brooke, Sir James

(1803-1868) British statesman, adventurer. Born in Benares, India. First white Raja of Sarawak. Knighted in 1848. Ruled until he died at age 65 at his estate in Devonshire, England. His heirs continued to rule until 1946. Brook was the model for Lord Jim in Joseph Conrad's novel *Lord Jim*.

Last Words (written): "My dear Arthur—." He had started to write a letter then he had a stroke and died.

Source: *The Raja of Sarawak* by Gertrude L. Jacob (London, 1876).

Brooke, Rupert

(1887-1915) English poet. Known for wartime poems especially *1914 and Other Poems* published after he died. Works were popular after World War I. Died at age 27 of septicemia from a mosquito bite (or from food poisoning) on a hospital ship in the Aegean Sea off Scyros on the way to Gallipoli during World War I.

Last Word: "Hallo." Spoken as a friend helped lift him into a small boat that would take him to the hospital ship.

Source: *Red Wine of Youth* by Arthur Stringer (Indianapolis, IN, 1948).

Brooke, Stopford Augustus

(1832-1916) Irish clergyman, writer, biographer. Author of books on Tennyson, Browning, Shakespeare, Milton. Chaplain to Queen Victoria. Left Church of England and preached as a Unitarian minister. Died at age 84 in Surrey, England.

Last Words: "It will be a pity to leave all that." Spoken as the news was being read to him.

Source: *Life & Letters of Stopford Brooke* by Lawrence P. Jacks (London, 1917).

Brookings, Robert Somers

(1850-1932) American businessman, philanthropist. Created three organizations that merged into Brookings Institution, a leading U.S. think tank. Died at age 82 in Washington, D.C.

Last Words: "I have done everything I wanted to do. This is the end." Spoken to a nurse at his bedside.

Source: *Brookings: A Biography* by Hermann Hagedorn (New York, 1936).

Brooks, Charles

(1829-1892) American murderer. First man hanged in Spokane, Washington. He had shot his wife on a downtown Spokane street. Executed at age 63 in Spokane.

Last Words: "I am going to Heaven. I'm completely ready to go, for I know I've been forgiven all my sins."

Source: "Hanging in Old Spokane" by Gary Williams (*Western Frontier*, November, 1982).

Brooks, Elbridge Gerry

(1816-1878) American clergyman. Minister of First Universalist Church of Lynn, Massachusetts. Renowned for his sermons. Died at age 62 in Philadelphia.

Last Words: "My head is pillowed upon the bosom of the dear God." His response when he was asked how he felt.

Source: *Lifework of Elbridge Gerry Brooks: Minister in the Universalist Church* by Elbridge Streeter Brooks (Boston, 1881). The author was his son.

Brooks, Gordon Barrett

(d. 1979) New Zealand airline pilot. Victim of airline disaster. Flight engineer of ill-fated Air New Zealand DC-10 Flight 901. Shortly after take-off, the DC-10 crashed into the side of Mount Erebus, Antarctica. Brooks was in another well-known air incident. He was second officer on New Zealand Flight 103 that went to the aid of a Cessna plane that was lost in the Pacific in 1978. The rescue was depicted in the television movie *Mercy Mission: The Rescue of Flight 771.*

Last Words: "Four hundred feet."

Source: *Mayday: Accident Reports and Voice Transcripts from Airline Crash Investigations* by Marion F. Sturkey (Plum Branch, SC, 2005).

Brooks, John

(1752-1825) American statesman, military officer, politician. Served in the Continental Army. Member Massachusetts state senate. Governor of Massachusetts. Adjutant general of Massachusetts. Died at age 72 in Medford, Massachusetts.

Last Words (written): "I see nothing terrible in death. In looking to the future; I have no fear. I know in whom I have believed.—I look back upon my past life with humility. I am sensible of many imperfections that cleave to me.—I now rest my soul on the mercy of my adorable Creator, through the only mediation of His son, our Lord. Oh, what a ground of hope there is in that saying of an apostle that God is in Christ reconciling a guilty world to Himself, not imputing their trespasses unto them. In God I have placed my eternal all; and into his hands I commend my spirit." Written testimony.

Source: *Life and Letters of Phillips Brooks* by Alexander Viets Griswold Allen (New York, 1900).

Brooks, Phillips

(1835-1893) American prelate, writer. Episcopal Bishop of Massachusetts. Wrote the words for the popular carol "O Little Town of Bethlehem.*"* Notable work: *Lectures on Preaching* (delivered at Yale Divinity School, 1877). Died at age 57 in Boston after serving as bishop for only 15 months. Phillips Brooks House at Harvard Yard was named for him.

Different Last Words:

(1) "There is no other life but the eternal."

Source: *A Conspectus of American Biography: Being an Analytical Summary of American History and Biography, Containing also the Complete Indexes of the National Cyclopedia of American Biography* by George Derby (New York, 1906).

(2) "Take me home. I must go home."

Source: *Life and Letters of Phillips Brooks* by Alexander Viets Griswold Allen (New York, 1900).

Variation: "Katie, you may go. I shall not need you anymore. I am going home."

Source: *Best Thoughts of Best Thinkers: Amplified, Classified, Exemplified and Arranged as a Key to Unlock the Literature of All Ages* by Hialmer Day Gould and Edward Louis Hessenmueller (Cleveland, OH, 1904).

Brooks, Willis B.

(1854-1902) American rancher, gunfighter.

Participant in McFarland-Brooks feud that took place in and around Spokogee, Indian Territory, during the late 1890s and early 1900s. Died at age 48.

Last Words: "I will kill you." Spoken to George Riddle moments before he shot him and in turn was shot by Lon Riddle and Jim McFarland.

Source: "1902 Gunfight at Spokogee" by Edward Herring (*Wild West*, April 1997).

Broughton, William Grant

(1788-1853) English-born Australian prelate. Anglican Bishop of New South Wales. Died at age 64 in London. First post-Reformation bishop to be buried at Canterbury Cathedral. Broughton River and Port Broughton were named for him.

Last Words: "Let the earth be filled with His glory."

Source: *Notes and Queries*: *A Medium of Intercommunication for Literary Men, Artists, Antiquaries, Genealogists, etc.*, Series 2, No. 36 (Oxford, England, 1856).

Broun, Heywood

(1888-1939) American writer, journalist, newspaper editor. Full name Matthew Heywood Campbell Broun. Founded American Newspaper Guild (The Newspaper Guild). Worked as sportswriter, columnist and editor. Started popular column "It Seems to Me" while at the *New York World.* Known for his writing on social issues and championing of the underdog. He believed journalists could help right social ills. Left the *World* in 1929 when some of his columns defending Sacco and Vanzetti were withheld from publication. Died at age 51 in New York.

Last Words: "I've been pretty sick, Connie, but now I'm going to be all right." Spoken to his wife. He was suffering from pneumonia.

Source: *Heywood Broun: A Biographical Portrait* by Dale Kramer (New York, 1949).

Brown, Abel

(1810-1844) American clergyman. Abolitionist. Baptist. Active helping fugitive slaves in Albany, Troy and Sand Lake area of New York. Published *Tocsin of Liberty*, weekly abolition newspaper that reported activities of fugitive slaves being helped by the Underground Railroad. Died at age 34 in Troy, New York.

Last Words: "Must I be sacrificed? Let me alone, every one of you!" Spoken when he imagined he was being mobbed.

Source: *Memoir of Rev. Abel Brown By His Companion C.S. Brown* (Worcester, MA, 1849). C.S. Brown was Abel Brown's second wife, Catherine.

Brown, E.P.

(d. 1856) American abolitionist. Member of Free State group trying to drive pro-slavery activists out of Leavenworth County, Kansas. Killed in January 1856 during violent fighting about whether Kansas, still a territory, should be admitted to the Union as a free or slave state. The decision was left to residents by provisions of the Kansas-Nebraska Act of 1854. Brown was one of many victims of this fighting.

Last Words: "They murdered me like cowards." Spoken to his wife. She tried to find the cause of his death, but he had strength only to say these few words.

Source: "Important from Kansas. Full Particulars of the Trouble at Leavenworth. Attack on the Ballot Boxes...Foul and Cowardly Murder of Brown of Leavenworth" (*New York Daily Times*, February 4, 1856).

Brown, Francis

(1784-1820) American educator, clergyman. President of Dartmouth College. Removed from his presidency as part of actions that resulted in the "Dartmouth College Case." He was reinstated following the 1819 decision in favor of the college: the U.S. Supreme Court ruled that private charters were contracts and thus immune to interference from state legislatures. Brown's health deteriorated during the four-year legal battle. He died at age 35, a short time after the court's decision was announced.

Last Words: "Glorious Redeemer, take my spirit!"

Source: *The History of Dartmouth College* by Perry Smith (Boston, 1878).

Brown, James Joseph, Jr.

(1933-2006) American singer, songwriter, record producer, actor. Known as the Godfather of Soul. His music played an important role in the evolution of gospel and rhythm and blues into modern soul, funk, rock and hip hop. Won two Grammy Awards. Inaugural member of Rock and Roll Hall of Fame. Died at age 73 of congestive heart failure in Atlanta, Georgia.

Last Words: "I'm going away tonight." Spoken to Charles Bobbit, his personal manager.

Sources: "James Brown, the 'Godfather of Soul,' Dies at 73" (CNN and CNN.com, December 25, 2006); *Body Bag Religion* by Greg Williams (Bloomington, IN, 2008).

Brown, John (abolitionist)

(1800-1859) American abolitionist. Head of the Kansas anti-slavery movement. Attacked the Army arsenal at Harper's Ferry and stole weapons to be used in his revolt. Overcome by local militia and regular troops led by Robert E. Lee. Arrested, convicted of treason and hanged at age 59. He is commemorated in the folk song "John Brown's body lies a-mouldering in the grave, but his soul is marching on."

Different Last Words:

(1) (written): "I, John Brown, am now quite certain that the crimes of this guilty land will never be purged away but with blood. I had as I now think vainly flattered myself that without very much bloodshed it might be done." Scribbled on a note on the gallows and handed to the guard just prior to being hanged. A photographic copy of John Brown's Last Words was displayed at the 1892-93 Columbian Exposition (Chicago World's Fair).

Source: *The Soul of John Brown* by Stephen Graham (New York, 1920).

(2) (spoken): "No, but don't keep me waiting longer than necessary." Spoken on the gallows in response to the sheriff who asked if Brown wanted a handkerchief to throw as a signal to cut the drop.

Source: "The Hanging of John Brown: Charlestown, Virginia, December 2, 1859" (*American History,* Vol. 40, No. 4, October 2005).

Variation: "I am ready at any time — do not keep me waiting."

Source: *A Conspectus of American Biography: Being an Analytical Summary of American History and Biography, Containing also the Complete Indexes of the National Cyclopedia of American Biography* by George Derby (New York, 1906).

Variation: "No, I do not want it—but do not detain me any longer than is absolutely necessary." Spoken to Sheriff Campbell who asked Brown if he wanted to take a handkerchief in his hand to drop as a signal when he was ready.

Source: *The Life, Trial and Execution of Captain John Brown, Known as "Old Brown of Ossawatomie" with a Full Account of the Attempted Insurrection at Harper's Ferry Compiled from Official and Authentic Sources* (New York, 1859).

Brown, John (clergyman)

(1722-1787) Scottish clergyman, theologian. Biblical commentator. Notable work: *Self-Interpreting Bible and Dictionary of the Bible.* Went to Haddington in 1751 and remained there the rest of his life.

Last Words: "My Christ!"

Source: *Life and Remains* [Anonymous] (Aberdeen, Scotland, 1845).

Brown, John Ashley, Jr.

(1961?-1997) American murderer, thief. Executed by lethal injection in Louisiana for the 1984 murder of a man during a robbery outside a New Orleans restaurant.

Last Words: "Wow."

Source: *Last Suppers: Famous Final Meals from Death Row* by Ty Treadwell and Michael Vernon (Port Townsend, WA, 2001).

Brown, Karla Faye Tucker

(1959-1998) American murderer. Convicted for killing two people. She was the first woman executed in Texas since the Civil War. Became a born-again Christian on death row. Married prison chaplain Dana Lane Brown by proxy. Executed by lethal injection at age 38 in Huntsville, Texas.

Last Words: "Yes sir. I would like to say to all of you, the Thornton family and Jerry Dean's family that I am so sorry. I hope God will give you peace with this. Baby, I love you. Ron, give Peggy a hug for me. Everybody has been so good to me. I love all of you very much. I'm going to be face to face with Jesus now. Warden Baggett, thank all of you so much. You have been so good to me. I love all of you very much. I will see you all when you get there. I will wait for you." Spoken when asked if she had a final statement.

Source: *Killing Women: The Visual Culture of Gender and Violence* by Susan Lord and Annette Burfoot (Waterloo, ON, 2006).

Brown, Moses

(1742-1804) American military officer. Naval captain who commanded some of the largest privateers of New England during the American Revolution. Engaged in several battles. When the U.S. Navy was formed, Newburyport, Massachusetts, merchants built the *Merrimack* for the government and placed Brown in command. He was part of a squadron commanded by Barry and Decatur. Brown captured the French vessels *Le Phenix; Le Magicien; Le Bonaparte* and *Le Brillante* during 1799 and 1801. He was serving in the merchant marines when he died at age 62 in Newburyport.

Last Words: "I have seen enough. Carry me below."

Source: *Moses Brown, Captain U.S.N.* by Edgar Stanton Maclay (New York, 1904).

Brown, Owen

(1824-1889) American abolitionist, activist. Son of John Brown. Last surviving participant in Brown's 1859 Raid at Harpers Ferry, Virginia. Owen and six other protestors escaped through swamps and forests pursued by armed soldiers, citizens and tracking dogs. Two of the protestors were eventually caught, but Owen made it to the safety of his brother's home on an island in Lake Erie. He later moved to Pasadena, California, and was involved in other movements, particularly temperance. Died at age 64 at the home of his brother-in-law in Pasadena.

Last Words: "It is better to be in a place and suffer wrong than to do wrong." These were the last words that could be distinguished.

Source: "Funeral of Owen Brown—The Last Survivor of John Brown's Históric Raid on Harpers Ferry, Va., in 1859" (*Pasadena Standard*, January 12, 1889).

Brown, William B.

(1828-1861) American military officer. Confederate Army colonel in U.S. Civil War. Commander of First Calvary Regiment (known as "Brown's Cavalry"), 6th Division, Missouri State Guard. He blew an old hunting horn when charging the enemy. Died at the second battle of Boonville while leading about 800 men into combat.

Last Words: "Rear my children for Christ. Teach them that religion is a pearl above price."

Source: *Portrait and Biographical Record of Lafayette and Saline Counties, Missouri, Containing Biographical Sketches of Prominent and Representative Citizens, Together with Biographies and Portraits of All the Presidents of the United States* (Chicago, 1893).

Browne, Maximilian Ulysses von, Baron de Camus and Mountany

(1705-1757) Austrian nobleman, military officer. Son of one of the Irish "Wild Geese." Reichgraf (Count of the Empire). During Seven Years War, volunteered to serve under Prince Charles of Lorraine. Killed at age 51 while leading a bayonet charge at the Battle of Prague. From 1888 to 1918, the 36th Austrian infantry was named in his honor.

Last Words: "Tell Prince Charles of Lorraine to march out instantly and attack Marshall Keith or all is lost."

Source: *The Roll of the House of Lacy: Pedigrees, Military Memoirs and Synoptical History of the Ancient and Illustrious Family of De Lacy, from the Earliest Times, in All Its Branches, to the Present Day: Full Notices on Allied Families and a Memoir of the Brownes (Camas)* by Edward de Lacy Harnett de Lacy-Bellingari (Baltimore, MD, 1928).

Browning, Elizabeth Barrett

(1806-1861) English poet. Wife of Robert Browning. Notable works: *Aurora Leigh; Sonnets from the Portuguese*. Serious injury to her spine as a child left her frail and an invalid. Traumatized when her brother and friends drowned in 1838. Spent many years confined to her room. Met Robert Browning in 1844. Married and moved to Italy, where she spent the rest of her life. Son Pen Browning was born in 1849. She died at age 55 in Florence. Her romance with Robert Browning was the inspiration for Rudolf Besier's play and movie *The Barretts of Wimpole Street*.

Last Words: "Beautiful." Her response to her husband who had asked how she felt.

Source: *The Brownings: A Victorian Idyll* by David Loth (New York, 1929).

Browning, Robert

(1812-1889) English poet. Admired the work of poet Elizabeth Barrett. Wrote and met her. Married her and took her to Italy. Son Pen born in 1849. Notable poems: "The Ring and the Book"; "My Last Duchess"; "Fra Lippo Lippi"; "The Pied Piper of

Hamelin"; "Pippa Passes." Died at age 77 in Venice.

Different Last Words:

(1) "How gratifying!" His response to a telegram his son Pen had just read to him. His new poetry collection *Asolando*, which had been released in London, received a positive review and the book was nearly sold out.

Source: *Robert Browning A Portrait* by Betty Miller (New York, 1952).

(2) "I'm dying. My dear boy. My dear boy." Spoken to his son who had just brought him news that *Asolando* have been very well received.

Source: *Robert Browning: The Major Works* by Robert Browning, Adam Roberts and Daniel Karlin (Oxford, England, 2005).

Brownson, Nathan

(1742-1796) American statesman, politician. Delegate to Continental Congress. Member of Provincial Congress, Georgia State House of Representatives and delegate to Georgia state convention to ratify federal Constitution in 1788. Member and president of Georgia State Senate. Died at age 54 in Riceboro, Georgia.

Last Words: "The scene is now closing; the business of life is nearly over. I have like the rest of my fellow-creatures, been guilty of foibles, but I trust to the mercy of my God to pardon them and to his justice to reward my good deeds."

Source: *Historical Collections of Georgia: Containing the Most Interesting Facts, Traditions, Biographical Sketches, Anecdotes, Etc., Relating to Its History and Antiquities* by George White (New York, 1854).

Bruce, Sir David

(1855-1931) Australian-born British physician, microbiologist, pathologist. Military officer. Major general. Specialist in tropical diseases. Discovered bacteria that caused undulant (or Malta) fever in humans and brucellosis in animals. Found that the tsetse fly caused sleeping sickness. Knighted in 1908. Died at age 77 of cancer in London.

Last Words: "If any notice is taken of my scientific work when I am gone, I should like it to be known that Mary is entitled to as much credit as I am." Mary was his wife, Mary Elizabeth Steele Bruce, whom he mar-

ried in 1883. She was awarded the Order of the British Empire for her scientific work.

Source: *Annals of Internal Medicine*, 115:351, 1965. Cited in *Familiar Medical Quotations*, ed. by Maurice B. Strauss, M.D. (Boston, 1968).

Bruce, Robert (clergyman)

(1554-1631) Scottish clergyman, theologian. Descendant of James I of Scotland. Moderator of the General Assembly of the Church of Scotland. Had a ministry at the Church of Edinburgh. Named Privy Councilor by James VI. Died at age 76.

Last Words: "Now God be with you, my dear children; I have breakfasted with you, and shall sup to-night with the Lord Jesus Christ." He died soon after speaking these words.

Source: *The Scottish Nation: Or the Surnames, Families, Literature, Honours, and Biographical History of the People of Scotland* by William Anderson (Edinburgh, 1862).

Bruce, Robert, King of Scotland, see Robert I, King of the Scots (The Bruce).

Bruch, Max Christian Friedrich

(1838-1920) German musician, composer, conductor. Notable works: *Kol Nidrei* (based on Hebrew themes); *Scottish Fantasy* (violin and orchestra); *Violin concertos, Nos. 1, 2, 3*. Composition teacher of Respighi, Oscar Straus, Vaughan Williams. Died at age 82 in Friedenau, Germany.

Last Words: "Can I not go to my home once again by flying there in a zeppelin?" Spoken to his daughter.

Source: *Max Bruch: His Life and Works* by Christopher Fifield (New York, 1988).

Brueys d'Aigalliers, François-Paul, Comte de

(1753-1798) French naval officer. Vice-admiral. Commanded fleet from his ship *L'Orient* in the Battle of the Nile where the French Revolutionary Navy was defeated by Admiral Horatio Nelson and the Royal Navy. Killed when a cannon shot almost cut him in half.

Last Words: "Un admiral français doit mourir sur son banc de quart." (tr. "A French admiral must die on the bench of the watch.") He insisted on remaining at his post after he spoke these Last Words. The ship exploded an hour later after being under heavy fire.

Source: *Armana Prouvençau pèr lou bèl an de Diéu 1862* (Avignon, France, 1862).

Variation: "An admiral ought to die giving orders."

Source: "Dying Words of Noted Persons" in *Miscellaneous Notes and Queries with Answers in All Departments of Literature*, Vol. II (Manchester, NH, 1885).

Brummell, George Bryan ("Beau")

(1778-1840) English fashion arbiter, trend setter, dandy, gambler. Credited with popularizing men's trouser suits and ties. Close friend of Prince of Wales (later King George IV). British consul at Caen, France. Died at age 62 in a mental asylum in Caen in debt and suffering from syphilis-induced dementia.

Last Words: "I do try." Reply to an English clergyman after repeated entreaties that he should try to pray.

Source: *Beau Brummell* by William Jesse (London, 1844).

Bruno, Giordano

(1548-1600) Italian philosopher. Trained as a Dominican. Denounced to the Inquisition by a nobleman. Imprisoned in Rome seven years. Refused to recant. Burned at the stake at age 52 for heresy in Rome.

Different Last Words:

(1) "Maiori forsan cum timore sententiam in me fertis, quam ego accipiam." (tr. "You feel more fear yourselves in convicting me than I do in receiving your sentence.") Spoken after the death sentence was announced.

Source: *Eros and Magic in the Renaissance* by Ioan P. Culianu, tr. by Margaret Cook (Chicago, 1987).

(2) "I die a martyr and willingly. My soul shall mount up with the smoke to paradise."

Source: *Vita di Giordano Bruno* by V. Spampanato (Messina, Italy, 1921).

Variation: "I die a martyr's death and I die willingly, knowing that with the smoke my soul will ascend to Paradise."

Source: *Giordano Bruno In Memoriam of the 17ᵗʰ February 1600* by Alois Riehl, tr. by Agnes Fry (London, 1905).

Variation: "I die a martyr and willingly."

After his execution, his ashes were thrown into the Tiber River and his name was placed among the accursed on the rolls of the Church.

Source: *Giordano Bruno: Philosopher and Martyr* by

Daniel Garrison Brinton and Thomas Davidson (Philadelphia, 1890).

Brunt, John Thomas

(1790?-1820) English shoemaker, conspirator. Member of the Cato Street Conspiracy, a failed attempt to assassinate members of the British Cabinet at a London dinner party. Conspiracy was thwarted by police. Eleven men were arrested. Brunt was one of five found guilty of high treason and executed.

Last Words: He is the only one of the Cato conspirators for whom no direct Last Words quotes are given. He said very little. He asked a bystander to get him some snuff from his waistcoat pocket as his hands were tied. He faced his execution with great coolness and said he wondered where the jailer would put him. He supposed it would be somewhere where he should sleep well. He made a present of his body to King George IV.

Source: *Old and New London: A Narrative of Its History, Its People and Its Places* by Walter Thornbury and Edward Walford (London, 1881).

Brutus, Marcus Junius

(85?-42 B.C.) Roman politician, conspirator. Sided with Pompey against Caesar and was later pardoned. Led assassination plot against Caesar. Raised an army in Macedonia. Defeated at Philippi by Octavius and Antony. Committed suicide.

Different Last Words:

(1) "O wretched Valour, thou wert but a name, and yet I worshipped thee as real indeed. But now, it seems, thou wert but Fortune's slave." Spoken before calling on one of the bystanders to kill him.

Source: *Roman History* by Cassius Dio, Vol. XLVII, tr. by Earnest Cary (Cambridge, MA, 1927).

(2) "We must flee; yet not with our feet, but with our hands." Strato, a friend, held a sword upon which Brutus threw himself.

Sources: *True Stories from Ancient History: Chronologically Arranged, from the Creation of the World to the Death of Charlemagne* by a Mother [Maria E Halsey Budden] (London, 1837); A similar translation appears in *Horace: A Biography* by Henry Dwight Sedgwick (Cambridge, MA, 1947) and in *The Portable Rabelais: Selected by François Rabelais* (New York, 1946). Each quote varies by only a few words

Bryan, William Jennings

(1860-1925) American politician, lawyer,

statesman. Known as The Great Commoner. Member of U.S. House of Representatives from Illinois. Candidate for U.S. President 1896, 1900, 1908. Made his famous "Cross of Gold" speech (supporting free coinage of silver) at the 1896 convention. U.S. secretary of state under Wilson; resigned, fearing U.S. reaction to *Lusitania* sinking might drag U.S. into war. Prosecutor in Scopes trial. Died suddenly at age 65 in Dayton, Tennessee, five days after the trial ended.

Last Words (written): "With hearts full of gratitude to God."
Source: *The Peerless Leader, William Jennings Bryan* by Paxton Hibben (New York, 1929).

Last Words (spoken): "Seems there's hardly time enough for resting, none at all for dying." Spoken to his son just before going upstairs, where he died.
Source: *The Commoner: William Jennings Bryan* by Charles Morrow Wilson (New York, 1970).

Bryant, Charles ("Black-Faced Charlie")
(d. 1891) American murderer, train robber. Member of the Dalton Gang. His nickname came from powder burns on his face. He was shot by Deputy Marshal Ed Short while trying to escape custody aboard a train that was transporting him from Hennessey, Oklahoma, to Wichita, Kansas. Died near Waukomis, Oklahoma. Short was also killed in the gunfight.

Last Words: "Please pull my boots off, and don't tell the folks back home."
Source: *West of Hell's Fringe: Crime, Criminals, and the Federal Peace Officer in Oklahoma Territory, 1889-1907* by Glenn Shirley (Norman, OK, 1990).

Bryant, William Cullen
(1794-1878) American poet, editor, lawyer. One of the five Fireside Poets. (the others: Longfellow, Whittier, Oliver Wendell Holmes Sr., James Russell Lowell.) Notable works: "Thanatopsis"; "To a Waterfowl." Editor of *New York Evening Post* 50 years; part owner most of that time. Died at age 84 in New York City after a fall. Bryant Park in New York City was named for him.

Last Words: "Whose house is this? What street is this? Would you like to see Miss Fairchild?" (His niece.) Spoken after he fell and hit his head on the sidewalk.
Source: *William Cullen Bryant* by Parke Godwin (New York, 1883). Godwin worked with Bryant at the *New York Evening Post*. He married Bryant's daughter. In addition to the biography, he edited four volumes of Bryant's work.

Variation: "Whose house is this? What street are we in? Why did you bring me here?"
Source: *A Conspectus of American Biography: Being an Analytical Summary of American History and Biography, Containing also the Complete Indexes of the National Cyclopedia of American Biography* by George Derby (New York, 1906).

Brynner, Yul
(1920-1985) Russian-born American actor. Birth name Yuliy Borisovich Brynner. Star of stage and movies. Notable performances: Siamese king in Rodgers and Hammerstein musical *The King and I* (stage and screen); Ramses II in Cecil B. DeMille's *The Ten Commandments;* Chris Adams in *The Magnificent Seven.* Died at age 65 of cancer in New York.

Last Words: "About time!" Spoken to his son at Brynner's deathbed, prior to losing consciousness for the last time. He had announced he had given up smoking.
Sources: *Yul Brynner: The Inscrutable King* by Jhan Robbins (New York, 1987); *Yul: The Man who Would be King* by Rock Brynner (New York, 1989). Rock was Yul's son.

Buber, Martin
(1878-1965) Austrian-Israeli Jewish philosopher, writer, editor, educator, theologian. His work centered on ideals of religious consciousness, community and interpersonal relations through retelling Hasidic tales, Biblical commentary, and philosophical dialogue. Taught at University of Frankfurt in Germany and Hebrew University in Jerusalem. Edited *Der Jude* magazine. Notable work: *Ich und Du* (tr. *I and Thou*). Died at age 87 in Jerusalem.

Last Words: "I am not afraid of death, but of dying." Spoken to Ernst Simon. He was repeating a statement made by Dr. Conyers in 1832.
Source: *Martin Buber's Life and Work: The Later Years, 1945-1965* by Maurice S. Friedman (New York, 1983).

Bucer or Butzer, Martin
(1491-1551) German clergyman, educator, reformer. Dominican who converted to Lutheranism. Tried unsuccessfully to unite

Roman Catholics and Protestants. Went to England at invitation of Archbishop Thomas Cranmer. Appointed professor of theology at Cambridge. Died at age 59 at Cambridge. In 1557, Queen Mary had his body exhumed and burned and his tomb demolished. His honor was later restored in the reign of Elizabeth I.

Different Last Words:

(1) "He governs and disposes all." Spoken as he pointed three fingers upward.

Source: *Martin Butzer der Elsässiche Reformator* by Alfred Erichson (Strasbourg, France, 1891).

(2) "Cast me not off, O Lord, now in my old age, when my strength faileth me. He hath afflicted me sore; but he will never, never cast me off. I am wholly Christ's, and the devil has nothing to do with me; and God forbid that I should not now have experience of the sweet consolation in Christ." Spoken to John Bradford who had come to visit him.

Sources: *Christian Records or, A Short and Plain History of the Church of Christ* by Thomas Sims (London, 1828); *Anecdotes, Illustrative of a Select Passage in Each Chapter of the Old Testament* by John Whitecross (Philadelphia, 1835).

Buchanan, George

(1506-1582) Scottish humanist, historian. Played important role in prosecution of Mary, Queen of Scots. Tutored James VI. Keeper of the Privy Seal. Died at age 76 in Edinburgh.

Different Last Words:

(1) "Tell the people who sent you that I am summoned to a higher tribunal." His response when he was summoned to explain something objectionable in his writings.

Source: *George Buchanan: A Biography* by Donald Macmillan (Edinburgh, 1906).

(2) "It matters little to me; for if I am but once dead they may bury me or not bury me as they please. They may leave my corpse to rot where I die if they wish."

Source: *The Last Words (Real and Traditional) of Distinguished Men and Women Collected From Various Sources* by Frederic Rowland Marvin (New York, 1901).

Buchanan, James

(1791-1868) 15th President of the U.S. American lawyer, politician, statesman, diplomat, U.S. secretary of state. Member U. S. House of Representatives and U.S. Senate from Pennsylvania. Minister to Russia, Great Britain. Only President (so far) who was never married. Held office just prior to the start of the Civil War. His administration was torn by issues of slavery and secession. Died at age 77 at Wheatland, his home in Lancaster, Pennsylvania.

Last Words: "Whatever the result may be, I shall carry to my grave the consciousness that at least I meant well for my country. O Lord God Almighty, as Thou wilt!"

Source: *The Life of James Buchanan* by George Ticknor Curtis (New York, 1883).

Buchanan, Robert Williams

(1841-1901) English poet, theater producer, publisher, novelist. Notable work: *London Poems*. Attacked the literary merit of the Pre-Raphaelites in *The Fleshly School of Poetry* in 1871. The quarrel engendered by the article lasted several years. He had a paralytic seizure in 1900 from which he never recovered. Died at age 59 in London.

Last Words: "I should like to have a good spin down Regent Street."

Source: *Robert Buchanan. Some Account of His Life, His Life's Work and His Literary Friendships* by Harriett Jay (London, 1903). The author was the sister of Buchanan's wife Mary, who died in 1881 after a long illness.

Büchner, Georg

(1813-1837) German writer, poet, playwright, educator. Brother of philosopher-physician Ludwig Büchner. Lecturer at the University of Zurich. Notable works: *Dantons Tod* (tr. *Danton's Death*); *Wozzeck* (basis for Alban Berg's opera). Died at age 24 of typhus in Zurich, Switzerland. Most of his works were not published until after he died.

Last Words: "We do not suffer too much, we suffer too little, for it is through suffering that we attain God. We are death, dust, ashes—how are we to complain?"

Source: "Georg Büchner" in *Werke und Briefe*, ed. by Werner R. Lehmann (Munich, Germany, 1988).

Buck, Rufus

(d. 1896) Native American outlaw. Euchee (Yuchi or Uchee) leader of a gang in Indian Territory of Arkansas-Oklahoma. Gang members were captured, tried—by Hanging Judge Parker—for murder, robbery and rape. They were hanged in 1896. After Buck was executed, a poem he wrote just before he was hanged was found in back of a picture of his mother that was hanging on his cell wall.

Last Words (written):
"I dreamt I was in Heaven
Among the angels fair;
I'd never seen none so handsome
That twine in golden hair.
They looked so neat and sang so sweet
And play'd the Golden Harp.
I was about to pick an angel out
And take her to my heart:
But the moment I began to plea,
I thought of you, my love.
There was none I'd ever seen so beautiful
On earth or Heaven above,
Goodbye my dear wife and Mother.
Also my sister.
Rufus Buck, Yours truly."
Source: *Law West of Fort Smith: A History of Frontier Justice in Indian Territory 1834-1896* by Glenn Shirley (Lincoln, NE, 1969).

Buckingham, Dukes of, see Villiers.

Buckland, Francis Trevelyan
(1826-1880) English surgeon, zoologist, naturalist. Inspector of salmon fisheries. Known for his research on fish culture. Son of Rev. William Buckland, Dean of Westminster, who was also an eminent scientist and geologist. Died at age 64 in London.
Different Last Words:
(1) "God is so good, so good to the little fishes, I do not believe He would let their inspector suffer shipwreck at last."
Source: *Life of Frank Buckland* by George C. Bompas (London, 1885). George C. Bompas was Buckland's brother-in-law.
(2) "I am going on a strange journey and I shall see many strange animals by the way."
Source: *Best Thoughts of Best Thinkers: Amplified, Classified, Exemplified and Arranged as a Key to Unlock the Literature of All Ages* by Hialmer Day Gould and Edward Louis Hessenmueller (Cleveland, OH, 1904).

Buckle, Henry Thomas
(1821-1862) English historian, writer. Adopted scientific approach to writing history. Notable work: *History of Civilization* (unfinished). Died at age 40 of typhoid fever

in Damascus, Syria.
Last Words: "Poor little boys!" He was referring to the traveling companions in his care.
Source: *The Life and Writings of Henry Thomas Buckle* by Alfred Henry Huth (New York, 1880).

Buckminster, Joseph Stevens
(1784-1812) American clergyman, writer. Noted lecturer and scholar. Taught Daniel Webster. His hymns, sermons and memoir have been published. Notable work: *The Dangers and Duties of Men of Letters* (address before Phi Beta Kappa society at Harvard). Had an epileptic attack and died few days later at age 28.
Last Words: "I desire to be still, and await the will of God."
Source: *Memoirs of Rev. Joseph Buckminster, D.D., and of His Son, Rev. Joseph Stevens Buckminster* by Eliza Buckminster Lee (Boston, 1849). The author was the sister of Joseph Stevens Buckminster.
Variation: "I am in the hands of God."
Source: *A Conspectus of American Biography: Being an Analytical Summary of American History and Biography, Containing also the Complete Indexes of the National Cyclopedia of American Biography* by George Derby (New York, 1906).

Buddha
(563?-483? B.C.) Indian philosopher. Family name Gautama; personal name Siddhartha. Founder of Buddhism. Left family at age 29 to devote self to study of religion. Many years later, he attained Nirvana and became Buddha, the Enlightened One. Began to preach doctrines of Buddhism. Died at age 80.
Last Words: "I exhort you: All compounded things are subject to vanish. Strive with earnestness!"
Source: *Last Days of the Buddha*, tr. from the Pali by Sister Vajira & Francis Story (Kandy, Sri Lanka, 1998).
Variation: "Now, then, monks, I exhort you: All fabrications are subject to decay. Bring about completion by being heedful."
Source: "The Great Discourse on the Total Unbinding," tr. from the Pali by Thanissaro Bhikkhu in *Noble Strategy: Essays on the Buddhist Path* (Valley Center, CA, 1999).
Variation: "Now then monks, I address you; subject to decay are compound things; strive with earnestness." Spoken to assembled monks. He asked if any had doubts. All were silent. He spoke these words then went into

a series of trances. At the fourth stage, he reached Nirvana.

Source: *The Life of Buddha as Legend and History* by Edward J. Thompson (London, 1969).

Variation: "Beloved, that which causes life, causes also decay and death. Never forget this; let your minds be filled with this truth. I called you to make it known to you."

Source: *Encyclopedia Britannica,* 9th ed. (New York, 1875-1889).

Budgell, Eustace

(1686-1737) English writer, poet, pamphleteer. Works appeared in *The Tatler, Guardian, Spectator.* Cousin of Joseph Addison. Lost a fortune in the South Sea Bubble. Suspected of theft. Committed suicide at age 50 by jumping from a boat into the River Thames at London Bridge.

Last Words (written): "What Cato did, and Addison approved, cannot be wrong." Written on a piece of paper.

Source: *General Biography; Or, Lives, Critical and Historical, of the Most Eminent Persons of All Ages, Countries, Conditions, and Professions: Arranged According to Alphabetical Order* by John Aikin, William Enfield, Mr. Nicholson, Thomas Morgan and William Johnston (London, 1799-1815).

Budgett, Samuel

(1794-1851) English grocer, philanthropist. Used his wealth to help his community, Kingswood Hill, Bristol, England. Died at age 56.

Different Last Words:

(1) "O dear!"

Source: *The Successful Merchant: Sketches of the life of Mr. Samuel Budgett, late of Kingswood Hill* by William Arthur (New York, 1853).

(2) "With glorious clouds encompassed round,

Whom angels dimly see,

Will the unsearchable be found,

or God appear to me?"

These were the words of a hymn by Charles Wesley. Budgett died suddenly after speaking them.

Source: *The Model Merchant, or Memoirs of Samuel Budgett,* abridged by Mrs. Myers from the work of William Arthur (Philadelphia, 1858).

Buffalo Bill, see
Cody, William Frederick.

Buffon, Georges-Louis Leclerc, Comte de

(1707-1788) French naturalist, biologist, mathematician. Co-authored 44-vol. *Histoire Naturelle.* Member French Academy. Notable work: *Les Époques de la Nature* (challenged the idea that the earth was only 6,000 years old as taught by the Church. His ideas influenced future naturalists, including Lamarck and Darwin.) Given title Comte de Buffon in 1773. Died at age 81 in Paris.

Different Last Words:

(1) "Citoyens, je me nomme Buffon" (tr. "Citizens, I am Buffon.").

Source: *One Thousand Sayings of History* by Walter Fogg (New York 1929).

(2) "Mais donne donc! Mais donne donc!" (tr. "Then give it to me! Give it to me!")

Source: "Derniers moments et agonie de M. le comte de Buffon" in *Correspondance inédite de Buffon* by Henri Nadault de Buffon (Paris, 1860). The author was Buffon's great-grandnephew.

Bugeaud, Thomas Robert, Marquis de la Picconerie, Duc d'Isly

(1784-1849) French military officer. Governor-general of Algeria. Marshal of France. Earned the title Duc d'Isly after winning a decisive battle along the Isly River. Died at age 64 in Paris during a cholera epidemic.

Last Words: "It is all over with me."

Source: *Le Maréchal Bugeaud: d'après sa correspondance intime et des documents inédits, 1784-1849* by Count Henri Amédée Le Lorgne Ideville (London, 1884).

Bull, George

(1634-1710) English prelate, theologian, writer. Anglican bishop of St. David's, Pembrokeshire, Wales. Notable works: *Defensio Fidei Nicenae; Treatise on Corruption of the Church in Rome.* Died at age 75.

Last Word: "Amen."

Source: *The Life of Dr. George Bull, Late Lord Bishop of St. David's* by Robert Nelson (London, 1714).

Bull, Ole Bornemann

(1810-1880) Norwegian musician, virtuoso violinist, composer. Toured widely. Often referred to as Norway's first international celebrity. He was greatly influenced by the violin playing of Paganini. In 1853, Bull purchased 120,000 acres of land in Pennsylvania. Ole Bull State Park—part of Susquehannock State Forest—was the original site of a Norwegian colony he tried unsuccessfully to create there. The remains of the unfinished Ole Bull Castle are in the park. He died at age 70 in Lysø, Norway. The village of Oleona (spelled Oleana on some maps) in Potter County, Pennsylvania, was named for him.

Last Words: "Please play Mozart's *Requiem.*"

Sources: "Dying Words of Noted Persons" in *Miscellaneous Notes and Queries with Answers in All Departments of Literature,* Vol. II, (Manchester, NH, 1885); "Dying Words of Distinguished Persons" in *The Encyclopedia of Death and Life in the Spirit-World,* Vol. I, by J.R. Francis (Chicago, 1895).

Bullard, Eugene Jacques

(1894-1961) American military officer. First African-American combat pilot. Known as The Black Swallow of Death. Joined French Foreign Legion during World War I. Transferred to the Lafayette Escadrille. Lived in Paris after the war. Returned to U.S. in 1930. Died at age 67 of stomach cancer in New York City. Posthumously commissioned 2nd lieutenant in the U.S. Air Force in 1994.

Last Words: "Don't fret honey, it's easy." He died a short time later.

Source: *The Black Swallow of Death: The Incredible Story of Eugene Jacques Bullard, the World's First Black Combat Aviator* by P.J. Carisella and James W. Ryan (New York, 1972).

Buller, Sir Redvers Henry

(1839-1908) British military officer. General. Served in China, Egypt, South Africa. Awarded Victoria Cross in 1879 for heroism during the Anglo Zulu War. Served in the Boer War. Knighted in 1886. Criticized because of success of Boers in early stages of the war. Retired after the speech he made in response to criticisms of his actions in South Africa was viewed as a breach of discipline. Died at age 68 in Downes, Devon, England.

Last Words: "Well, I think it is about time to go to bed now."

Source: *The Life of General The Right Honourable Sir Redvers Buller* by C.H. Melville (London, 1923).

Bullinger, Heinrich

(1504-1575) Swiss clergyman, theologian, reformer. Successor to Zwingli as head of Zurich Church and pastor at Grossmünster. Author of many treatises, commentaries and letters. Known for his lucid and scholarly

mind. Influential theologian of the Protestant Reformation. Died at age 71 in Zurich.

Last Words: "If the Lord will make any further use of me, and my ministry, I will willingly obey him; but if he pleases (as I much desire) to take me out of this miserable life, I shall exceedingly rejoice to be taken from this corrupt age, to go to my Savior Christ. Socrates was glad when his death approached, because he thought he should go to Hesiod, Homer, and other learned men deceased, whom he expected to meet in the other world: how much more do I rejoice, who am sure that I shall see my Savior Christ, the saints, patriarchs, prophets, apostles, and all holy men who have lived from the beginning of the world! Since I am sure to partake of their felicity, why should not I be willing to die, to enjoy their perpetual society in glory?" Spoken shortly before he died.

Sources: *The Afflicted Man's Companion: Or, A Directory for Families and Persons Afflicted with Sickness or Any Other Disease* by John Willison (Glasgow, Scotland, 1821); *The Pleasing Expositor; Or, Anecdotes Illustrative of Select Passages of the New Testament* by John Whitecross (New York, 1831).

Bülow, Hans Guido von

(1830-1894) German musician, pianist, conductor, composer. Directed first performances of Richard Wagner's *Die Meistersinger* and *Tristan.* Studied under Wagner, Liszt. Married and divorced from Liszt's daughter Cosima, who later married Wagner. Died at age 64 in Cairo, Egypt, where he had gone for his health

Last Words: "Schlecht." (tr. "Bad.") His response when asked how he was feeling.

Source: *Leben* by Marie von Bülow (Leipzig, Germany, 1921). Marie von Bülow, his second wife, was actress Marie Schanzer whom he married in 1882.

Bumby, John Hewgill

(1808-1840) English clergyman. Methodist missionary to the Maori. Died at age 31 by drowning in a river just six weeks after he arrived in New Zealand.

Last Words: "O dear, dear, dear me! We are dead." Spoken as he clung to a canoe.

Source: *The Life of the Rev. John Hewgill Bumby: With a Brief History of the Commencement and Progress of the Wesleyan Mission in New Zealand* by Rev. Alfred Barrett (London, 1852).

Bunche, Ralph Johnson

(1904-1971) American diplomat, mediator, educator, writer, social theorist, politician. Faculty member, Howard University. Helped write United Nations charter. Won 1950 Nobel Peace Prize for arranging armistice agreements that ended 1948 Arab-Israeli war. Oversaw peacekeeping missions in Congo, Cyprus and Suez Canal. Highest ranking U.S. member of U.N. as undersecretary general for special political affairs. Winner of U.S. Medal of Freedom in 1963. Died at age 67 in New York City.

Last Words: "No." His response to a physician who asked if he was in pain.

Source: *Ralph Bunche: UN Peacemaker* by Peggy Mann (New York, 1975).

Bundy, Theodore Robert ("Ted")

(1946-1989) American murderer. Serial killer. Confessed to killing more than 30 young women across the U.S. between 1974 and 1978. Actual number of victims is unknown. Executed at age 42 in Florida.

Last Words: "Jim and Fred, I'd like you to give my love to my family and friends." Jim was attorney James Coleman; Fred was Rev. Fred Lawrence.

Source: "Tears and Prayers: Killer Ted Bundy Executed in Florida" (*San Francisco Chronicle,* January 25, 1989).

Bunker, Chang and Eng

(1811-1874) Brothers Chang and Eng, the original Siamese twins, were born conjoined in Thailand (then known as Siam). Brought to U.S. in 1829 at age 18. Earned fame touring as freaks. Retired and married sisters Sarah Ann and Adelaide Yeats. Had 21 children. Made their home in Mt. Airy, North Carolina. Adopted the surname Bunker. Died at age 63 in Mt. Airy. Both bodies were sent to a medical college in Philadelphia to determine how they were conjoined and the causes of their deaths. Chang may have died of a cerebral clot; Eng, very soon after, of fright.

Chang's Last Words: "[My] breathing was so bad that it would kill me to lie down." Spoken to Eng who wanted to retire. Chang died later that night.

Eng's Last Words: "May the Lord have mercy on my soul." Spoken to his wife.

Source: "Never Alone at Last: World-Famous as Medical Curiosities, the Original Siamese Twins Married, Brought up Families, and as American Citizens, Became Prosperous Planters in the Old South" by Jonathan Daniels (*American Heritage,* Vol. 13, No. 5, August, 1982).

Bunsen, Christian Karl Josias, Baron von

(1791-1860) Prussian diplomat, theologian, scholar. Created Baron von Bunsen in 1857. Supported German constitutional movement. Ambassador to the Court of St. James (England); resigned when his advice was rejected. Died at age 69 in Bonn.

Last Words: "Very kind, very glad!" Spoken as he took a visitor's hand.

Source: *Memoirs of Baron Bunsen* by Frances Baroness Bunsen (London, 1868). The author was his wife. One of his last requests was that she write his memoirs.

Bunsen, Frances Baroness

(1791-1876) Welsh-born painter, writer. Watercolorist. Birth name Frances Waddington. Married Prussian scholar and diplomat Baron Christian Karl Josias von Bunsen, who later became Prussian ambassador to Great Britain. At his request she wrote and published a memoir of his life. Died at age 85 in Karlsruhe, Germany.

Last Words: "Amen."

Source: *The Life and Letters of Frances, Baroness Bunsen,* Vol. II, by Augustus John C. Hare (New York, 1879).

Buñuel, Luis

(1900-1983) Spanish-born film writer, director. Worked in Spain, France, Mexico and the United States. One of cinema's most important directors and writers. Notable works: *That Obscure Object of Desire; Diary of a Chambermaid; Nazarin; The Discreet Charm of the Bourgeoisie.* Died at age 83 in Mexico City.

Last Words: "Ahora, me muero." (tr. "Now, I'm dying.")

Source: "Luis Buñuel" by Unión de Escritores y Artistas de Cuba (*Unión,* Issues 38-39, 2000).

Bunyan, John

(1628-1688) English clergyman, writer. Imprisoned from 1660 to 1672 for preaching without a license; imprisoned again briefly in 1675. Wrote most of his books in jail. Served as Baptist pastor in Bedford many years. First part of *The Pilgrim's Progress,* published in 1678, was an immediate success. He became ill while traveling in the rain from Reading to London. Died at age 59 at a friend's house in Holborn.

Last Words: "Weep not for me but yourselves. I go to the Father of our Lord Jesus Christ, Who will, no doubt, through the mediation of His Blessed Son, receive me, though a sinner, where I hope that we ere long shall meet to sing the new song and remain for everlastingly happy, world without end. Amen."

Source: *Tinker and Thinker: John Bunyan, 1628-1688* by William Hamilton Nelson (Chicago, 1928).

Burbank, Luther

(1849-1926) American horticulturist, botanist. Pioneer of plant breeding science. Developed hundreds of new fruit, vegetable and flower varieties. Died at age 77 of a heart attack in Santa Rosa, California.

Last Words: "Oh, Doctor, I am very sick." Spoken to Dr. Joseph. H. Shaw.

Source: "Santa Rosa Mourns Passing of Burbank. Will Hold Memorial Service and Close Schools in Honor of Genius in Floriculture. Burial in Garden Likely. Wizard of Plant Breeding Passed Away, Still Skeptical as to Hereafter" (*New York Times*, April 11, 1926).

Burckhardt, Jacob

(1818-1897) Swiss historian, historiographer. Primarily a historian of art and culture, he became influential as a historian of civilization. Defined the Age of the Renaissance as something to be studied as a period in its entirety not just art and architecture, but for the social institutions and its daily life as well. Notable works: *The Civilization of the Renaissance in Italy; Force and Freedom: Reflections in History.* Died at age 78 in Basel, Switzerland.

Last Words: "Adie liebs Katzedischli." (tr. "Farewell my dear little cat's table.") Spoken in a Basel dialect. Meaning is cryptic.

Source: "Jacob Burckhardt: Historian of Civilization" by Olivier Burckhardt (*Contemporary Review*, 271:1582, November 1997).

Burdett-Coutts, 1st Baroness Angela Georgina

(1814-1906) English noblewoman, philanthropist. Daughter of Sir Francis Burdett, parliamentary reformer. Inherited large for-

tune from her grandfather when she was 23. Devoted time and money to philanthropy. Played important role in Victorian English society. Close friend of Chares Dickens who carried on a correspondence with her and dedicated one of his books to her. The title 1st Baroness Burdett-Coutts was conferred on her in 1871. Died at age 92 in London.

Last Words: "They were true and good friends to me." She was referring to the vicar and Mrs. Twining.

Source: *Lady Unknown: The Life of Angela Burdett-Coutts* by Edna Healy (New York, 1978).

Burgess, George

(1809-1866). American prelate, writer, poet. Protestant Episcopal bishop of Maine. Notable works: *The Book of Psalms, Translated into English Verse; Sermon on the Christian Life.* Sent to Haiti in the interest of the church. Died suddenly at age 57 while resting on the deck of a ship near Port au Prince, West Indies. A book of his *Poems* was published after he died.

Last Words: "I will lie down now."

Source: *Memoir of George Burgess, D.D.* by Alexander Burgess (Philadelphia, 1869). The author was his brother. He was also a bishop.

Burghley or Burleigh, Lord, see Cecil, William.

Burke, Edmund

(1729-1797) Irish-born British philosopher, politician, writer, statesman, orator. Known for his oratory in the House of Commons. Notable speeches: *Speech on American Taxation; Speech for Conciliation with America* (expressed his sympathy toward American colonies). Leading conservative within the Whig party. Was opposed to the French Revolution. He attacked it in what has been described as his greatest writing: *Reflections on the Revolution in France* (1790). It sparked a major controversy and caused Thomas Paine to write *Rights of Man.* Burke died at age 68 at Beaconsfield, Buckinghamshire,

Last Words: "God bless you."

Source: *Wisdom and Genius of the Right Hon. Edmund Burke* by Peter Burke (London, 1845).

Burke, Robert O'Hara

(1821-1861) Irish explorer, policeman,

adventurer. Led first expedition of white men across Australia from the south to the north coast. Left Melbourne in August 1860. Burke and three men reached the coast in February 1861. On the return trip he died of starvation when his group was abandoned.
Last Words (written): "I hope that we shall be done justice to. We have fulfilled our task, but we have been aban—. We have not been followed up as we expected and the depot party abandoned their post. King has behaved nobly —. He has stayed with us to the last and placed the pistol in my hand, leaving me lying on the surface as I wished." (June 28, 1861). Final entries in his journal.
Source: *The History of Australian Exploration from 1788 to 1888* by Ernest Favenc (Sydney, Australia, 1888).

Burkitt, William
(1650-1703) English theologian, clergyman. Biblical scholar. Vicar in Dedham, Essex. Notable works: *Expository Notes with Practical Observations on the New Testament* (Biblical commentary; Matthew through John); *Acts through Revelation*. Died at age 53 in Essex, England, after a week-long struggle with a fever.
Last Words: "Come, Lord Jesus."
Source: *Last Hours of Eminent Christians from the Commencement of the Christian Era to the Death of George III: Compiled from the Best Authorities, and Chronologically Arranged* by Henry Clissold (London, 1829).

Burn, Andrew R.
(1742-1814) English military officer. Major general in Royal Marines. Died at age 72.
Last Words: "Nobody, nobody but Jesus Christ: Christ crucified is the stay of my poor soul." Spoken when he was asked if he wished to see anyone in particular.
Source: *Memoirs of the Life of the Late Major-General Andrew Burn of the Royal Marines* by Andrew Burn, John Allen and Olinthus Gregory (London, 1815). Information in his memoirs came from his journals.

Burnett, Frances Eliza Hodgson
(1849-1924) English-born American writer. Family emigrated to Tennessee in 1865. She married S.M. Burnett in 1873. Divorced him and married Stephen Townsend in 1900. Second marriage also ended in divorce. Notable works: *Little Lord Fauntleroy*; *The Secret Garden*. Died at age 74 of heart failure at her home on Long Island, New York.
Last Words: "With the best that was in me I have tried to write more happiness into the world."
Source: *The Romantick Lady* by Vivian Burnett (New York, 1927). The author was the son of Frances and Dr. Swann Moses Burnett. He was her model for Little Lord Fauntleroy.

Burney, Charles
(1726-1814) English musician, organist, composer, musicologist. Earned doctor of music at Oxford. Notable work: *A General History of Music* (4 vol. published between 1776 and 1789). He was among the first music historians. Father of English writer Fannie Burney. He had a very wide circle of friends, including King George III, Dr. Johnson, Boswell, Rousseau, Pitt the Younger and Diderot. Died at age 88 at Chelsea Hospital, London, where he was organist and had lived since 1783.
Last Words: "All this will soon pass away as a dream."
Source: *The Great Dr. Burney: His Life, His Travels, His Works, His Family and His Friends*, Vol. II, by Percy A. Scholes (London, 1948).

Burns, Sir George, 1st Baronet
(1795-1890) Scottish ship owner. One of the founders of Cunard Line. Awarded baronage in 1889. Died at age 94 at his home in Castle Wemyss, Renfrewshire, Scotland.
Last Words: "Lord Jesus, come, come. I am waiting. I am ready. Home, home. Give me patience to wait Thy time, but Thou knowest what I suffer."
Source: *Life of Sir George Burns* by Edwin Hodder (London, 1890).

Burns, Kyle W.
(1984-2004) American military solder. Lance corporal in U. S. Marines. Died at age 20 in Al Anbar Province, Iraq. Killed in Operation Iraqi Freedom. One of the soldiers profiled in Jim Sheeler's book *Final Salute* that describes how the families of dead soldiers are notified. The book is based on Sheeler's 2006 Pulitzer Prize-winning coverage.
Last Words: "I'm hit." He spoke these words while ensuring that other marines survived.

Source: *Final Salute: A Story of Unfinished Lives* by Jim Sheeler (New York, 2008).

Burns, Robert

(1759-1796) Scottish poet, military officer. National poet of Scotland. Surname originally spelled Burnes. Wrote poems and songs in Scottish vernacular. Wrote more than 360 songs, including: "Auld Lang Syne"; "John Anderson, My Jo"; "Sweet Afton"; "Ye Banks and Braes o' Bonnie Doon"; "A Red, Red Rose." Fell ill with rheumatic fever. Died at age 37 of heart disease in Dumfries. Buried with full military honors as a member of the Dumfriesshire Volunteers.

Different Last Words:

(1) "That damned rascal, Matthew Penn." Penn was a solicitor in Dumfries who wrote Burns a letter pressuring him for payment for a uniform he ordered for the Dumfriesshire Volunteers.

Source: *The Complete Works of Robert Burns*, ed. by Alexander Smith (London, 1868).

Variation: "That damned scoundrel Matthew Penn." This version originated with Robert Green Ingersoll and seems to have sprung from a lecture given by him. The "rascal" version is more likely accurate.

Source: *The Works of Robert G. Ingersoll*, Vol. III, by Robert Green Ingersoll (New York, 1915).

(2) (doubtful): "John, don't let the awkward squad fire over me!" Spoken to John Gibson, one of his fellow volunteers. Although this quote is often mentioned as his Last Words, he said it a few days before he died.

Source: *The Works of Robert Burns* by Allan Cunningham (London, 1840).

Variation: (doubtful) "Don't let that awkward squad fire over my grave."

Source: *The New Monthly Belle Assemblée* by Joseph Rogerson (London, 1838). See (2).

Burr, Aaron

(1756-1836) American lawyer, politician, adventurer, military officer. Served in the American Revolution. Fought at the Battle of Monmouth. New York state attorney general. Member U.S. Senate from New York. 3rd Vice President of the U.S. Challenged and killed Alexander Hamilton in a duel. Tried for treason for attempting to set up a republic in Texas. Died at age 80 in Port

Richmond, Staten Island, New York.

Different Last Words:

(1) "Madame." Burr and Madame Elizabeth Jumel were married in 1833 and divorced a short time later.

Source: *Aaron Burr: A Biography Compiled from Rare, and in Many Cases Unpublished, Sources* by Samuel H. Wandell and Meade Minnigerode (New York, 1925).

(2) (doubtful): "On that subject I am coy." Spoken in response to the efforts of his friend, Reverend P.J. Van Pelt, to get him to acknowledge existence of God. Burr was a known atheist. This quote is sometimes given as his Last Words and used as an example of an atheist resisting conversion, even at the end of his life. Some accounts say he did show signs of embracing faith in his last moments. One source indicates this was near the last statement he made. But his definitive last statement was: "Madame."

Source: *The Life and Times of Aaron Burr*, Vol. II by James Parton (Boston, 1892).

Burr, Raymond William Stacey

(1917-1993) Canadian-born American actor, vintner. Notable television drama roles: *Perry Mason* and *Ironside*. Won two Emmy awards for *Perry Mason*. Operated Raymond Burr Vineyards in California. Died at age 76 in Healdsburg, California.

Last Words: "I think the worst is over. One day we'll be together again." Spoken to his companion, Robert Benevides.

Source: *Last Words: A Dictionary of Deathbed Quotations* by C. Bernard Ruffin (Jefferson, NC, 2005). Ruffin gave as his source *National Enquirer*, September 28, 1993.

Burris, Gary

(1956-1997) American murderer. Shot and killed a cab driver in Indianapolis in 1980. Executed at age 40 by lethal injection in Indiana.

Last Words: "Beam me up!" His Last Words were a reference to the television show *Star Trek*.

Source: *Last Suppers: Famous Final Meals from Death Row* by Ty Treadwell and Michael Vernon (Port Townsend, WA, 2001).

Burroughs, John

(1837-1921) American naturalist, ornithologist, poet, essayist, writer. Became a close friend of Walt Whitman while working in

Washington, D.C. Wrote Whitman's first biography: *Notes on Walt Whitman as Poet and Person* (1867). Moved to Catskills of New York. Gained fame with his essays on nature and rural themes. Notable books: *Ways of Nature; Birds and Poets; Wake-Robin.* Died at age 83 of a heart attack while traveling on a train from California to his home in New York.

Last Words: "How far are we from home?"

Source: *The Life and Letters of John Burroughs* by Clara Barrus (Boston, 1925). Barrus was a devoted follower and frequent companion. She was named his official biographer after his death.

Burroughs, William Seward

(1914-1997) American essayist, social critic. Major counterculture figure. Died of heart failure at age 83 in Lawrence, Kansas.

Last Words (written): "Love? What is it? Most natural painkiller. What there is— LOVE." Entry written in his journal. He had a heart attack the day he wrote it and died the next day.

Source: "Final Words" by William S. Burroughs (*New Yorker,* August 18, 1997).

Burrows, William Ward

(1785-1813) American military officer. Naval lieutenant during First Barbary War and War of 1812. Son of William Ward Burrows, second commandant of U.S. Marine Corps. The younger Burrows distinguished himself at Tripoli on board the *Constitution.* Died at age 27 while in command of the brig *Enterprise* from injuries sustained in an engagement with the British brig HMS *Boxer.* Awarded Congressional Gold Medal. Three U.S. Navy ships were named for him.

Last Words: "I am satisfied. I die content." Spoken when the sword of his enemy was presented to him. He clasped his hands, exclaimed these words then died a few minutes after the victory.

Source: *The Pictorial History of the American Navy: Comprising Lives of Its Distinguished Commanders* by John Frost (New York, 1854).

Burton, Lady Isabel Arundell

(1831-1896) English writer. Her husband was explorer and writer Sir Richard Francis Burton. She worked on translations of *The Arabian Nights* and *Baital Pachisi* with her husband. She is remembered for burning

some of his papers and manuscripts after his death, including his revised translation of *The Perfumed Garden* (*The Scented Garden*), which consisted of Burton's extensive notes on pedophilia. She feared that few people would read it for the "scientific spirit in which it was written," but rather for "filth's sake." Died at age 65 in London from cancer. She was portrayed in the movie *Mountains of the Moon.* The Lady Isabel Burton Award is infamously named in her honor.

Last Words: "Thank God." Spoken after receiving the last sacrament.

Source: *The Romance of Isabel Lady Burton: The Story of Her Life* by William Henry Wilkins (New York, 1908).

Burton, Richard

(1925-1984) Welsh actor. Stage and screen star. Birth name Richard Walter Jenkins Jr. Nominated for seven Academy Awards. Nominated for seven Golden Globes; won two. Died at age 59 of a cerebral hemorrhage in Geneva, Switzerland, before he was to begin filming *Wild Geese II.*

Last Words (written): "Our revels now are ended." Written in a note found on his nightstand. He had jotted down a line from Shakespeare's *The Tempest.*

Source: *Biography* magazine, January 2002.

Burton, Sir Richard Francis

(1821-1890) British explorer, traveler, translator. Married Isabel Arundell in 1861. Spent life in the army and consular service. Fluent in many languages. Notable work: translation of *Arabian Nights (The Thousand and One Nights).* Published more than 40 books on his travels and explorations. Knighted in 1886. Risked prosecution and imprisonment when he secretly translated and published *Kama Sutra, The Perfumed Garden* and other banned works. Died at age 71 of a heart attack in Trieste where he was a consul.

Last Words: "Quick, Puss, chloroform— ether—or I am a dead man!" Spoken to his wife.

Source: *The Arabian Knight: A Study of Sir Richard Burton* by Seton Dearden (New York, 1937).

Variation: "Oh, Puss, chloroform—ether— quick. I am dying, I am dead."

Source: *The Life of Richard Burton* by Thomas Wright (London, 1906).

Burton, Robert

(1577-1640) English clergyman, scholar, writer. Pen name Democritus Junior. Rector of Segrave, Leicestershire. Vicar at Oxford University. Notable work: *The Anatomy of Melancholy*. The one book that gave him fame was written as treatment for his depression. In its preface he wrote: "I write of melancholy, by being busy to avoid melancholy. There is no greater cause of melancholy than idleness, no better cure than business." Died at age 62 at Oxford. Because he died at or near the date he calculated to die, some students thought he had committed suicide. There is no evidence to support this supposition. He was buried with solemnity at the Cathedral in Oxford.

Last Words (doubtful): "Be not solitary, be not idle."

Source: Various Last Words compilations and Internet websites.

Burton did use this expression, but these were not his Last Words. They were used in *The Anatomy of Melancholy* almost 20 years before he died. In the book, he admonished his readers to observe a short precept: "Give not away to solitariness and idleness." He then concluded with the quote "Be not solitary, be not idle."

Source: *The Anatomy of Melancholy* by Robert Burton, ed. by Rev. A.R. Shilleto, Vol. I (London, 1893).

Bushemi, John A.

(1917-1944) American photographer, filmmaker. Assigned to the staff of *Yank Magazine: The Army Weekly* during World War II. After he was transferred to Hawaii to open *Yank's* Pacific bureau, he learned filmmaking techniques from Colonel Frank Capra, famed Hollywood director. Bushemi was fatally wounded at age 26 by an enemy mortar shell on Eniwetok while filming an American landing.

Last Words: "Be sure to get those pictures back to the office."

Source: *One Shot: The World War II Photography of John Bushemi* by Ray E. Boomhower (Indianapolis, IN, 2004).

Bushnell, Horace

(1802-1876) American clergyman, writer. Congregational pastor in Hartford, Connecticut. Retired in 1859 because of poor health. Died at age 73 in Hartford. City park in Hartford was named for him.

Last Words: "Well, now, we are all going home together; and I say, the Lord be with you, and in grace and peace and love, and that is the way I have come along home." His words were a Benediction to his family.

Source: *Horace Bushnell: Preacher and Theologian* by Theodore T. Munger (Boston, 1899).

Busoni, Ferruccio Benvenuto

(1866-1924) Italian musician, pianist, composer, conductor, teacher. Composed operas, symphonic poem, concertos, works for piano, orchestra, chamber music. Notable works: *Doktor Faust* (unfinished opera); Piano transcriptions of organ works of Bach. Taught and concertized in the U.S. from 1891 to 1894. Died at age 58 of kidney failure in Berlin.

Last Words: "Dear Gerda, I thank you for every day we have been together." Spoken to his wife Gerda Sjöstrand whom he married in 1890.

Source: *Ferruccio Busoni: A Biography* by Edward J. Dent (London, 1933).

Butler, Arthur John

(1844-1910) English translator, scholar. Translated Dante's *The Divine Comedy*. Fellow of Trinity College, Cambridge. Died at age 65 in Chertsey, England. Buried in Wantage.

Last Words: "...where the larks sing." He wanted to be buried at Wantage, his birthplace.

Source: *Memoir of Arthur John Butler* by Sir Arthur Thomas Quiller-Couch (London, 1917).

Butler, Benjamin Franklin (lawyer)

(1795-1858) American lawyer, statesman, educator. Law partner of Martin Van Buren. Attorney general of U.S. under Andrew Jackson. Served briefly as U.S. secretary of war. Helped found New York University. Professor at New York University. Died at age 72 in Paris while on his first visit to Europe. Fort Butler, North Carolina, was named for him (now gone).

Different Last Words:

(1) "I die a happy man. I die a happy man. Rock of Ages, cleft for me."

Source: *Proceedings and Addresses on the Occasion of the Death of Benjamin F. Butler of New York* (New York, 1859).

(2) "I have peace, perfect peace. 'Thou wilt keep him in perfect peace whose mind is stayed on Thee.'" He was quoting Isaiah 26:3.

Source: *A Conspectus of American Biography: Being an Analytical Summary of American History and Biography, Containing also the Complete Indexes of the National Cyclopedia of American Biography* by George Derby (New York, 1906).

Butler, Benjamin Franklin (politician)

(1818-1893) American politician, lawyer, military officer. Union general in U.S. Civil War. Member U.S. House of Representatives from Massachusetts. Governor of Massachusetts. Died at age 74 in Washington, D.C.

Last Words: "That's all, West. You need not do anything more." Spoken to his valet.

Source: *Ben Butler, the South Called Him Beast!* by Hans Louis Trefousse (New York, 1957).

Butler, Joseph

(1692-1752) English prelate, theologian, philosopher. Bishop of Durham. Bishop of Bristol. Dean of St. Paul's. Notable works: *Sermons on Human Nature; The Analogy of Religion, Natural and Revealed, to the Constitution and Course of Nature* (putting forth his theory of ethics). Died at age 60 in Bath, England.

Last Words: "True, and I am surprised that though I have read that Scripture a thousand times over, I never felt its virtue till this moment; and now I die happy." His final response during a deathbed conversation with his chaplain. The chaplain had called his attention to Scripture (John 6:37).

Source: *Memoirs of the Life, Character and Writings of Joseph Butler* by Thomas Bartlett (London, 1839).

Butler, Richard

(1743-1791) American military leader. General. George Washington conferred the honor on him of receiving Cornwallis' sword of surrender at Yorktown. Butler gave the honor to his second in command Ebenezer Denny. After the war, Butler was killed at age 48 in Saint Clair's defeat, a battle against Native Americans led by Chief Little Turtle. Some 600 men were killed in one of the greatest single losses the U.S.

Army ever sustained against Native Americans.

Last Words: "Edward, I am mortally wounded; leave me to my fate, and save my brother Thomas (Major Thomas Butler)." Spoken to his nephew, Colonel Edward Washington Butler. The account of his final words came from a letter written by Edward to General Robert Patterson

Source: *Major-General Anthony Wayne and the Pennsylvania Line in the Continental Army* by Charles Janeway Stillé (Philadelphia, 1893).

Butler, Samuel

(1835-1902) English novelist, satirist. Notable works: *Erewhon* (satirical novel published anonymously, popular in his lifetime); *The Way of All Flesh* (largely autobiographical novel that satirized family life in Victorian England). Died at age 66 in London.

Last Words: "Have you brought the check book, Alfred?"

Source: *Samuel Butler, Author of Erewhon, A Memoir* by Henry Festing Jones (London, 1919).

Butt, Archibald Willingham

(1865-1912) American military officer. Victim of *Titanic* disaster. Major. Military aide to U.S. Presidents Theodore Roosevelt and William Howard Taft. Served in Spanish-American War, Philippines and Cuba. While in Europe in 1912, he met Pope Pius X who gave him a message to take to President Taft. Butt sailed home on the *Titanic*. During the trip, he was joined by Francis David Millet, who painted his portrait. Butt and Millet were both lost when the *Titanic* sank. Butt has a grave marker in Arlington National Cemetery, although his body was never recovered. Taft spoke at a memorial service at Butt's home, attended by 1,500 mourners. Millet-Butt Memorial Fountain in Washington, D.C., was constructed in the Ellipse near the White House and was dedicated in 1914 by Taft.

Last Words: "Good-bye, Miss Young. Good luck to you, and don't forget to remember me to the folks back home." Spoken as he helped Marie Young into a lifeboat. Young was a music instructor to President Roosevelt's children and had known Major Butt while Roosevelt occupied the White House.

She was the source of this quote.

Source: *Sinking of the Titanic and Great Sea Disasters* by Logan Marshall (Philadelphia, 1912).

Buxton, Sir Thomas Fowell, 1ˢᵗ Baronet

(1786-1844) British philanthropist, social reformer, abolitionist, politician, brewer. Member of Parliament. Helped revise the penal code and improve prison conditions. Opposed to capital punishment. Helped reduce the number of crimes punishable by death down to eight from more than 200. One of the founders of the Society for the Mitigation and Gradual Abolition of Slavery (later known as the Anti-Slavery Society). Notable works: *An Inquiry, Whether Crime and Misery are Produced or Prevented, by Our Present System of Prison Discipline; The African Slave Trade and Its Remedy.* Died at age 57 in Norfolk, England.

Last Words: "Christ is most merciful—most merciful to me—I do put my trust in Him."

Source: *Memoirs of Sir Thomas Fowell Buxton Baronet with Selections from His Correspondence* by Charles Buxton (London, 1848). The author was his son.

Byles, Mather

(1707-1788) American poet, clergyman, essayist. Tory. Grandson of Increase Mather. Nephew of Cotton Mather. Pastor of Hollis Street Congregational Church, Boston, more than 40 years. One of New England's earliest humorists. Notable works: *Poems on Several Occasions; The Conflagration.* Suffered from painful sciatica during his last five years. Died at age 81.

Last Words: "I have almost got to that land where there are no bishops." Spoken to his friend Rev. Samuel Parker in an almost inaudible voice.

Source: *The Famous Mather Byles, the Noted Boston Tory Preacher, Poet, and Wit, 1707-1788* by Arthur Wentworth Hamilton Eaton (Boston, 1914).

Variation: "I feel as if I had about got to that land where there are no bishops."

Source: *A Conspectus of American Biography: Being an Analytical Summary of American History and Biography, Containing also the Complete Indexes of the National Cyclopedia of American Biography* by George Derby (New York, 1906).

**Byng, Julian Hedworth George,
1ˢᵗ Viscount of Vimy**

(1862-1935) British military officer. Known as Bungo. Served in World War I in France

and Gallipoli. Commander of British Third Army. Governor general of Canada. Commissioner of metropolitan police. Held the rank of field marshal. Died at age 73 in Essex, England.

Last Words: "My Pog." Spoken to his wife. Pog was her pet name.

Source: *Byng of Vimy: General and Governor General* by Jeffrey Williams (London, 1983).

Byrne, Donn, see
Donn-Byrne, Brian Oswald Patrick.

**Byron, George Gordon,
6ᵗʰ Baron Byron ("Lord Byron")**

(1788-1824) English poet. Lame from birth with a club foot. Became famous with "Childe Harold's Pilgrimage." "Don Juan," his masterpiece, was started in 1819 but not finished. He joined the Greek war for independence. Became ill with fever and chills. Lapsed into unconsciousness. Died of malaria at age 36 in Missolonghi, Greece.

Different Last Words:

(1) "Let not my body be sent to England. Here let my bones molder. Lay me in the first corner without pomp or nonsense." Instructions given to chief physician Dr. Julius Millingen who was at his bedside during Byron's last few days.

Source: *Famous Last Words: Apt Observations, Pleas, Curses, Benedictions, Sour Notes, Bon Mots, and Insights from People on the Brink of Departure* by Alan Bisbort (San Francisco, CA, 2001).

(2) "I want to go to sleep now." Spoken when he briefly regained consciousness. He died within 24 hours.

Source: *Byron, the Last Journey* by Harold Nicolson (London, 1924).

Variation: "Now I must sleep." Spoken in Greek.

Source: *Last Words of Saints and Sinners: 700 Final Quotes from the Famous, the Infamous, and the Inspiring Figures in History* by Herbert Lockyer (Grand Rapids, MI, 1969).

Variation: "I must sleep now."

Source: *The Last Words (Real and Traditional) of Distinguished Men and Women Collected from Various Sources* by Frederic Rowland Marvin (New York, 1901).

**Cabrini, Saint Frances Xavier
("Mother Cabrini")**

(1850-1917) Italian-born American holy woman. Roman Catholic nun. Established orphanages, nurseries, hospitals, schools.

Founded Missionary Sisters of the Sacred Heart. Died at age 67 in Chicago. First American citizen to be canonized (1946). Cabrini Green housing project in Chicago and Cabrini College in Radnor, Pennsylvania, were named for her.

Last Words: "Bring me anything you like. If I don't take it, I may take something else." Spoken when she was asked what she would like for lunch.

Source: *Too Small a World: The Life of Mother Cabrini* by Theodore Maynard (Milwaukee, WI, 1945).

Cadogan, William Bromley

(1751-1797) English clergyman. Son of Earl of Cadogan. Methodist minister. Assigned to St. Giles, Reading and St. Luke's Chelsea. Died at age 45 in Reading.

Last Words: "I thank you for all your faithful services; God bless you." Spoken to his servant of many years. Then he continued repeating the prayer "Not my will, but thine be done."

Source: *The Works of the Rev. Richard Cecil: With a Memoir of His Life,* Vol. III, by Richard Cecil (New York, 1825).

Cadoudal, Georges

(1771-1804) French royalist politician, conspirator. Fought against the Revolution in France. Endeavored to restore Bourbons. Led Chouannerie royalist uprising. Involved in failed attempt to kidnap Napoleon. Captured and executed by guillotine at age 33 in Paris. *Execution of Georges Cadoudal and his Accomplices* is depicted in a print by Armand de Polignac.

Last Words: "For what? Isn't this the hour of my death?" His response on the scaffold when he was told to keep saying "Hail Mary, full of grace" until the hour of his death.

Source: *Georges Cadoudal et la Chouannerie* by Georges de Cadoudal (Paris, 1887).

Caesar, Gaius Julius, Emperor of Rome

(100-44 B.C.) Roman ruler, general, statesman. Assassinated on the Ides of March in the Roman Senate by a group of nobles that included Brutus and Cassius.

Last Words: Highly debated and not known with certainty. Often shown in Latin as "Et tu, Brute!," spoken when he spotted his close friend Brutus among his attackers.

Some authorities translate Caesar's Last Words as: "What, art thou, too, one of them? Thou, my son!" The words "my son" are included to show the difference in age between Caesar and Brutus and not as an indication that Brutus was Caesar's son. Suetonius gave a Greek translation: "Kai su teknon?" ("You too my child?"). But many historians theorize that Caesar would not speak his final words in Greek, especially at such a time of astonishment. He would have uttered them in his familiar tongue: Latin. The probability, therefore, is that Caesar's Last Words were as often shown: "Et tu, brute."

Source: "Gaius Julius Caesar" in *The Lives of the Twelve Caesars* by C. Suetonius Tranquillus, tr. by Alexander Thomson, rev. by Thomas Forester (London, 1901).

Caesar Augustus, see Augustus, Gaius Julius Caesar Octavianus.

Cagney, James Francis

(1899-1986) American actor. Screen star. Known for fast-talking streetwise gangster roles. Nominated for three Academy Awards; won Oscar for song-and-dance role as George M. Cohan in *Yankee Doodle Dandy.* Died at age 86 of a heart attack in Stanfordville, New York.

Last Words: "Give my love to Ron and Nancy." He was referring to President and Mrs. Reagan. In 1984, President Reagan presented Cagney with the U.S. government's highest civilian honor, the Presidential Medal of Freedom. Reagan delivered the eulogy at Cagney's funeral.

Source: "Personalities" by Chuck Conconi (*Washington Post*, September 21, 1988).

Cajetan, Saint

(1480-1547) Italian scholar, clergyman, holy man. Religious reformer, lawyer. Birth name Cajetan or Gaetamo dei Conti di Tiene. Helped the sick and poor. Founder of the Order of Clerics Regular, or Theatines. Died at age 66 in Naples. Canonized in 1671.

Last Words: "My Savior died on a cross. Allow me at least to die on wood." His response to a person who encouraged him to lie on a mattress when he was dying.

Source: *Butler's Lives of the Saints* by Herbert J.

Thurston and Donald Attwater (Westminster, MD, 1956).

Calamity Jane, see Canary, Martha Jane.

Caldclough, James

(1715?-1739) English highwayman. Executed for robbery at Tyburn by hanging.

Last Words: "I humbly beg that all you young men who I leave behind me would take warning in time, and avoid bad houses as well as bad company. Remember my dying words, lest some of you come to the same end, which I pray God, you never may. What I am now going to suffer is the just punishment for my crimes; for, although I did not commit murder, yet I look upon myself equally guilty, as the poor gentleman must have died had he not met with assistance. Were I able to make satisfaction to those whom I have wronged, I would do it; but alas! I cannot, and therefore I pray that they will forgive me. I hope my life will be at least some satisfaction, as I have nothing besides to give; and, as I die in charity with all mankind, may the Lord Jesus receive my soul!"

Source: *The Newgate Calendar: Comprising Interesting Memoirs of the Most Notorious Characters Memoirs of the Most Notorious Characters who have been Convicted of Outrages on the Laws of England Since the Commencement of the Eighteenth Century with Occasional Anecdotes and Observations, Speeches, Confessions and Last Exclamation of Sufferers*, Vol. IV, by Andrew Knapp and William Baldwin (London, 1828).

Calderón, Rodrigo, Count of Oliva

(1570-1621) Spanish adventurer. Marquis de las Siete Iglesias. Had position of power and influence during the reign of Philip III. Accused of murders. Also accused of using witchcraft against Queen Margarita when she died in childbirth. He was arrested, brutally tortured and executed. Wore Franciscan robe at his execution. Reviled at first, but then public sentiment turned in his favor. He became a folk hero to his countrymen.

Last Words: "All my life I have carried myself gracefully." Spoken to his confessor who criticized him for being concerned about his appearance when he was about to be executed on the scaffold. His attitude and composure prompted the expression among Spanish-speaking people: "Con más orgullo que Don Rodrigo en la horca." (tr. "With more pride than Don Rodrigo on the scaffold").

Sources: *Soul of Spain* by Havelock Ellis (Boston, 1909); *Select Prose of Robert Southey,* ed. by Jacob Zeitlin (New York, 1916).

Caldwell, Merritt

(1806-1848) American educator, writer. Principal of Maine Wesleyan Academy. Professor of mathematics, political economy and metaphysics at Dickinson College. Introduced first natural science (biology) classes. Advocate of total abstinence. Delegate to World's Temperance Conference. Had to resign from Dickinson in 1848 due to failing health. Died at age 41 of tuberculosis a few months later in Portland, Maine.

Last Words: "Glory to Jesus! He is my trust; He is my strength! Jesus lives; I shall live also!" Spoken to his wife.

Source: *Dying Testimonies of Saved and Unsaved: Gathered from Authentic Sources* by Solomon Benjamin Shaw (Chicago, 1898).

Calhoun, John Caldwell

(1782-1850) American lawyer, politician, statesman, political philosopher. Member U.S. Senate and House of Representatives from South Carolina. 7th Vice President of the U.S., secretary of war, secretary of state. Strong proponent of slavery and states' rights. Too ill to speak during his last days in the Senate. Died at age 68 of tuberculosis in Washington, D.C.

Last Words: "The South! The poor South!"

Source: *Biographical Dictionary of the United States Executive Branch, 1774-1989* by Robert Sober (New York, 1990).

Calhoun, Simeon Howard

(1804-1876) American missionary, linguist, scholar. Missionary to Holy Land 1837 to 1875. Arabic, Turkish language scholar. Helped translate first Bible into Turkish. Awarded honorary degree from alma mater Williams College. Died at age 72 in Buffalo, New York.

Last Words: "Were the Church of Christ what she ought to be, twenty years would not pass away without the story of the cross being uttered in the ears of every living man."

Source: "A Missionary Revival" (*The Free Church of Scotland Monthly Record*, July 1, 1878).

Caligula, Gaius

(12?-41) Roman emperor. Caligula is a nickname. Full name Gaius Julius Caesar Augustus Germanicus. Squandered empire's wealth. His savagery, wickedness and brutality caused many to conspire against him. Killed at age 29 by a member of the Praetorian Guard whom he had insulted.

Last Words: He cried out that he was still alive as he was being stabbed by the guard. He received 30 wounds. Suetonius did not give a direct quote for Caligula's last word.

Source: "Gaius Caesar Caligula" in *The Lives of the Twelve Caesars* by C. Suetonius Tranquillus, tr. by Alexander Thomson, revised by Thomas Forester (London, 1901).

Callicrates

(500?–476 B.C.) Spartan soldier. Described by Herodotus as "the most beautiful man, not among the Spartans only, but in the whole Greek camp." He was struck by an arrow on his side as he waited for his general to consult the victims of the battle against Persians at Plataea.

Last Words: "I grieve, not because I have to die for my country, but because I have not lifted my arm against the enemy, or done any deed worthy of me, much as I have desired to achieve something." Spoken to Arimnestus, one of the Plataeans.

Source: "Calliopé," Book IX, *The History of Herodotus*, tr. by George Rawlinson (Chicago, 1955).

Calvin, John

(1509-1564) French theologian, reformer. Roman Catholic who abandoned his religion for Protestantism. Left France for Switzerland, where he established the foundations of his beliefs known as Calvinism. Died at age 55 in Geneva.

Last Words: "Thou bruisest me, O Lord, but it is enough for me that it is Thy hand."

Source: *History of the Christian Church* by Philip Schaff (New York, 1910).

Variation: "Thou, Lord, bruisest me; but I am abundantly satisfied, since it is from Thy hands."

Source: *Best Thoughts of Best Thinkers: Amplified, Classified, Exemplified and Arranged as a Key to Unlock the Literature of All Ages* by Hialmer Day Gould

and Edward Louis Hessenmueller (Cleveland, OH, 1904).

Cambronne, Comte Pierre Jacques Etienne

(1770-1842) French military officer. General. Accompanied Napoleon to Elba. Commanded division of Imperial Guard at Waterloo. Retired to his birthplace near Nantes in 1823. Died at age 71 in Nantes. Place Cambronne in Paris named for him.

Last Words: "Ah! mademoiselle, man is thought to be something, but he is nothing:"

Source: *Cambronne, sa vie civile, politique et militaire, écrite d'aprés les documents, inédite des Archives nationale et des Archives du Ministère de la guerre. Ouvrage orné de deux portraits et d'un dessin en trois couleurs* by Leon Brunschvigg (Nantes, France, 1894).

Cambyses, King of Persia

(d. 522 B.C.) Persian ruler. Son of Cyrus the Great. Succeeded him as king of Persia in 529 B.C. Conquered Egypt, 525 B.C. Died of gangrene in Syria after being stabbed in his thigh. He had reigned seven years and five months. His exploits are described in Herodotus's *History*.

Last Words: "I charge ye all, and especially such of you as are Achaemenids, that you do not tamely allow the kingdom to go back to the Medes. Recover it one way or another, by force or fraud, by fraud, if it is by fraud that they have seized on it; by force, if force has helped them in their enterprise. Do this, and then may your land bring you forth fruit abundantly, and your wives bear children, and your herds increase, and freedom be your portion for ever: but do it not—make no brave struggle to regain the kingdom— and then my curse be on you, and may the opposite of all these things happen to you— and not only so, but may you, one and all, perish at the last by such a fate as mine!" Spoken to the Persians when he knew he was doomed to die.

Source: "Thalia," Book III, *The History of Herodotus*, tr. by George Rawlinson (Chicago, 1955).

Cameron, Archibald

(1707-1753) Scottish physician. Joined Charles Edward Stuart (Bonnie Prince Charlie) in an armed revolt. Tried and found guilty of high treason. Wrote several letters in Tower of London supporting his actions.

Died at age 46. Last Jacobite to be executed for treason.

Last Words: "I have now done with this world, and am ready to leave it." Spoken to a clergyman in the cart on his way to be executed. As the clergyman was leaving the cart, he nearly missed the steps. Cameron called to him in a cheerful voice and said: "Take care how you go; I think you don't know this way as well as I do." He then gave the signal and the cart moved away from under him.

Source: *The Newgate Calendar: Comprising Interesting Memoirs of the Most Notorious Characters Memoirs of the Most Notorious Characters who have been Convicted of Outrages on the Laws of England Since the Commencement of the Eighteenth Century with Occasional Anecdotes and Observations, Speeches, Confessions and Last Exclamation of Sufferers*, Vol. IV, by Andrew Knapp and William Baldwin (London, 1828).

Cameron, James

(1801-1861) American military officer. Brother of Simon Cameron, secretary of war for Abraham Lincoln. Union colonel in U.S. Civil War. Led 79th New York Volunteer Infantry, a regiment that dressed in full Scottish regalia and called itself the Cameron Highlanders. Killed at age 60 at the Battle of Bull Run. A statue of him was unveiled in Sunbury, Pennsylvania, in 1879.

Different Last Words:

(1) "Scots! Follow me!" His words were the war cry he shouted as he went into battle.

Source: *Harper's Weekly*, August 10, 1861.

(2) "Come on, boys! The rebels are in full retreat!"

Source: *Nurse and Spy in the Union Army* by S. Emma E. Edmonds (Hartford, CT, 1865).

Cameron, Julia Margaret Pattle

(1815-1879) English photographer. Born in Calcutta, India. Renowned for her celebrity portraits and innovative way of cropping pictures. Married Charles Hay Cameron, son of Lady Margaret Hay. Lived many years in England. Friend and neighbor of Tennysons. Died at age 61 in Kalutara, Ceylon (now Sri Lanka).

Last Words: "Beautiful."

Source: *From Life: The Story of Julia Margaret Cameron and Victorian Photography* by Victoria C. Olsen (New York, 2003). Olsen notes Cameron's Last Word "beautiful" is "reputed." "Beautiful" was the Last Word of another famous Victorian-era British woman: Elizabeth Barrett Browning.

Camoëns or Camões, Luis Vas de

(1524?-1580) Portuguese writer, poet. Notable work: *Lusiads,* epic about the voyages of Vasco da Gama. Also wrote sonnets, odes, satires, comedies. Led an adventurous life. Participated in a campaign against Morocco; lost right eye. Lived in India from 1553 to 1569. Died of plague in Lisbon. Many of his poems were not published until after he died.

Last Words (written): "Who ever heard tell that on such a tiny bed so great a calamity would have its fulfillment? And I—as if this had not been enough—align myself on its side; for the effort to withstand so many sorrows would appear as a kind of impudence. And so I shall conclude my life, and all will see how I was so attached to my country that I was not satisfied to die *in* it, but to die *with* it."

Source: *Luis de Camoens Leben* by Wilhelm Storck (Paderborn, Germany, 1890).

Camp, Henry Ward

(1839-1864) American military officer, educator, attorney. Major with 10th Connecticut Infantry in Union Army in U.S. Civil War. Killed at age 25 in action near Richmond, Virginia.

Last Words: "Come on, boys! Come on!" Shouted to his men as he waved his sword.

Source: *The Knightly Soldier* by H. Clay Trumbull (Boston, 1865).

Campan, Jeanne Louise Henriette Genet

(1752-1822) French educator, writer. Friend of Marie Antoinette and Napoleon. Notable work: *Memoir of the Private Life of Marie Antoinette*. Appointed head of a school for daughters of officers of the Legion of Honor in 1803. Died at age 69 in Mantes, France.

Last Words: "How imperious one is when one no longer has time to be polite!"

Source: *Mme. Campan à Ecouen* by Louis Bonneville de Marsangy (Paris, 1879).

Campbell, Archibald, 1st Marquess of Argyll

(1607-1661) Scottish nobleman. Covenanter. 8th Earl of Argyll. Created 1st Marquess of Argyll in 1641. Opposed Charles I's religious policy in Scotland. Defended

Scottish liberties. Executed for complicity with Cromwell's government during Restoration.

Different Last Words:

(1) "Yes, and not only a Protestant, but with a heart hatred of Popery, of Prelacy, and of all superstition." His response to a clergyman who called out to him at his execution: "My Lord dies a Protestant."

Source: *History of England* by Thomas B. Macaulay (London, 1849).

(2) "I am not afraid to be surprised with fear." Spoken to George Hutchinson, a preacher, just before Campbell laid his head on the block. He proclaimed his innocence, knelt down and prayed in silence then gave the signal, the lifting of his hand, for the blade to descend.

Source: *Men of the Covenant: The Story of the Scottish Church in the Years of the Persecution* by Alexander Smellie (London, 1904).

Campbell, Archibald, 9th Earl of Argyll

(1629-1685) Scottish nobleman, Covenanter. Son of 1st Marquis and 8th Earl of Argyll. Inherited father's title and estate. Attempted to assist Duke of Monmouth by raising Scotland against James VII. Arrested. Beheaded at Edinburgh.

Last Words: "Lord Jesus, receive me into Thy glory." Repeated three times at his execution.

Source: *A Scots Earl in Covenanting Times: Being the Life and Times of Archibald, 9th Earl of Argyll (1629-1685)* by John Willcock (Edinburgh, 1907).

Campbell, Donald

(1921-1967) British automobile and motorboat racer. Son of Sir Malcolm Campbell. Broke many speed records. Killed at age 46 when his boat *Bluebird K7* flipped and disintegrated at speed in excess of 300 mph.

Last Words: "The water's dark green and I can't see a bloody thing. Hallo the bow is up. I'm going. I'm on my back. I'm gone." Paul Evans, in charge of radio communications, was the last person to hear Campbell.

Source: BBC News On this Day, January 4, 1967.

Variation: "The water is dark green and I can't see anything...It's tramping badly! I'm on my back! She's going."

Source: "Campbell Dies as Jet Hydro Flips, Explodes" (*Utica* [New York] *Daily Press*, January 6, 1967).

Variation: "The water is dark green, and I can't see anything...She's tramping! She's tramping! I'm on my back! She's going!"

Source: "Scorecard" (*Sports Illustrated*, January 16, 1967).

Campbell, George

(1850-1881) American lawman. One-time marshal of El Paso, Texas, who was replaced by Dallas Stoudenmire. Campbell was shot and killed by Stoudenmire at the Battle of Keating's Saloon in El Paso.

Last Words: "You big son-of-a-bitch, you murdered me!" Moaned to Stoudenmire as he rolled Campbell over on his back.

Source: *Dallas Stoudenmire: El Paso Marshal* by Leon Claire Metz (Norman, OK, 1993).

Campbell, Richard

(1746?-1781) American military officer. Fought in American Revolution. Lieutenant-colonel of Virginia Regiment at Guilford Courthouse, Hobkirk's Hill Ninety-six. Died at the Battle of Eutaw Springs, South Carolina, in 1781 during a British charge. Some writers confuse him with Virginia Brigadier-General William Campbell (1745-1781), even to the extent of having Richard's Last Words misattributed to William.

Last Words: "I die contented." Spoken when he heard the British were retreating.

Source: "Richard Campbell" in *Encyclopedia of Virginia Biography,* ed. by Lyon Gardiner Tyler (New York, 1915).

Campbell, Thomas

(1777-1844) Scottish-born British poet, writer. Edited *New Monthly Magazine*. Lord rector of Glasgow. Notable patriotic lyrics: "Ye Mariners of England"; "The Soldier's Dream." Died at age 66 in Boulogne, France. Buried in Westminster Abbey.

Last Words: "Thank you—much obliged." Spoken after he had been given something to drink.

Source: *Life and Letters of Thomas Campbell,* ed. by William Beattie, M.D. (London, 1855).

Campbell, Timothy John ("Tim")

(1840-1904) Irish-born American politician. Family emigrated to U.S. when he was five. Member New York Assembly. Member U.S. House of Representatives from New York. Died at age 64 in New York City.

Last Words: "See here, little girl, you've been up all night, tending to me like an angel. I'll know them when I see the real kind. Don't you worry. I'm real comfortable, and I want you to go and get a little rest. Don't you bother about old Tim." Spoken to his nurse who had been caring for him.
Source: "East Side's Friend, Tim Campbell is Dead: Last Wish Was for Comfort of His Nurse" (*New York Times*, April 8, 1904).

Campbell, Willielma Maxwell, Lady Glenorchy

(1741-1786) Scottish philanthropist. Known as Lady Glenorchy. Wife of John Campbell, Viscount Glenorchy, eldest son of John Campbell, 3rd Earl of Breadalbane and Holland, one of Scotland's greatest landowners. She became a patroness of evangelical missionary work after coming under the influence of the sister of Rowland Hill (evangelical Anglican preacher). She devoted her wealth to furthering evangelical causes. John Wesley attempted to persuade her to join his Methodists without success. She established a number of chapels in Scotland and England and influenced many to enter the ministry. Known for Lady Glenorchy's Chapel in Edinburgh, the subject of a drawing by John Ruskin.
Last Words: "If this is dying, it is the easiest thing imaginable."
Source: "Dying Words and Thoughts" (*New York Daily Times*, October 13, 1852).

Campion, Saint Edmund

(1540-1581) English clergyman, martyr. Anglican deacon who was suspected of papist leanings. Joined Jesuits. Professor of rhetoric at Prague. Indicted for conspiracy to dethrone the queen. Executed as a traitor at age 41 at Tyburn. Canonized in 1970.
Last Words: "Yes, for Elizabeth, your Queen and my Queen, unto whom I wish a long quiet reign with all prosperity." His response when he was asked what queen he prayed for.
Source: *Edmund Campion* by Evelyn Waugh (Boston, 1946).

Canaris, Wilhelm Franz

(1887-1945) German military officer. Admiral. Head of Abwehr (German military intelligence service) during World War II. Canaris intervened to save many victims of Nazi persecution, including hundreds of Jews. Heinrich Himmler suspected him of treason. Hitler dismissed Canaris from the Abwehr and had him placed under house arrest. He was court-martialed, sentenced to death and executed in April 1945, a few weeks before the end of the war. The 1954 movie *Canaris* is based on his life. He is depicted in the 1976 film *The Eagle Has Landed*.
Last Words: "Ich sterbe für mein Vaterland, ich habe ein reines Gewissen." (tr. "I die for my country. I have a clear conscience.")
Source: *Canaris: Patriot und Weltbürger* by Karl Heinz Abshagen (London, 1989).

Canary, Martha Jane ("Calamity Jane")

(1856-1903) American frontierswoman, scout. Married Clinton Burke in 1885. Earned nickname Calamity Jane around 1872. Known as White Devil of the Yellowstone. Helped nurse sick during smallpox epidemic in Deadwood area in 1876. Friend of Wild Bill Hickok. Toured with Wild West shows. Died of complications of pneumonia in South Dakota. Fame in popular culture began when she was first mentioned in dime novels in 1877. Musical *Calamity Jane* based on her adventures. Central character in HBO *Deadwood*. Mentioned in many movies, books, songs, television series.
Last Words: "It's the twenty-seventh anniversary of Bill's [Hickok's] death." Her response when asked: "What's the date?" She then said "Bury me next to Bill." A short time later she was dead. Her friends arranged for her to be buried near him. Newspaper reporters changed the date of her death to August 3, to match his (the 27th anniversary of his murder).
Source: "Calamity Jane: Frontierswoman" by James D. Horan in *Heroic and Outrageous Women,* ed. by Gemma Alexander (Edison, NJ, 2002).

Candy, John Franklin

(1950-1994) Canadian comedian, actor. Screen and television star. Performed with *Second City TV*. Notable movies: *Stripes; Only the Lonely; Uncle Buck; Planes, Trains and Automobiles; National Lam-*

poon's Vacation. Was staying in a hotel in Durango, Mexico, while filming *Wagons East*. His bodyguard found him dead. He had suffered a fatal massive heart attack at age 43.

Last Words: "I'm so tired, all I want to do is go home and be with my family." Spoken to a night watchman at the hotel.

Source: *The Hollywood Book of Death: The Bizarre, Often Sordid, Passing of More Than 125 American Movie and TV Idols* by James Robert Parish (New York, 2001).

Candy Darling

(1944-1974) Actor, female impersonator. Birth name James ("Jimmy") Lawrence Slattery. Was part of Andy Warhol's factory. Appeared in some of Warhol's movies. Gained fame in Lou Reed songs "Candy Says" and "Walk on the Wild Side." Committed suicide at age 29.

Last Words (written): "To whom it may concern, By the time you read this I will be gone. Unfortunately before my death I had no desire left for life. Even with all my friends and my career on the upswing I felt too empty to go on in this unreal existence. I am just so bored by everything. You might say bored to death. It may sound ridiculous but is true. I have arranged my own funeral arrangements with a guest list and it is paid for.—Goodbye for Now. Love Always, Candy Darling. Tinkerbell Hi!" Suicide note. "Tinkerbell" was a writer for *Interview* magazine who committed suicide by jumping from a window.

Source: "They All Want a Piece of Andy. Celebrity Knows Untold Story Behind 'Warhol Diaries'" by Lloyd Sachs (*Chicago Sun-Times*, May 28, 1989).

Canitz, Freiherr Friedrich Rudolf Ludwig von

(1654-1699) German writer, poet, diplomat. Wrote odes, elegies and satires that set standards for style in German literature. Notable work: *Nebenstunden unterschiedener Gedichte.* Worked at various embassies during 1680s and 1690s. Made privy councilor by the elector Frederick III. Created Freiherr (Baron) by Emperor Leopold I. Died at age 44 in Berlin.

Last Words: "Oh if the appearance of this earthly and created thing is so beautiful and quickening, how much more will I be enraptured at the sight of the unspeakable glory of the Creator Himself!" Spoken as he looked out the window shortly before he died.

Source: *Christian Life, Its Course, Its Hindrances, and Its Helps. Sermons, Preached Mostly in the Chapel of Rugby School* by Thomas Arnold (London, 1841).

Canning, Charles Fox

(1782-1815) British military officer. Lieutenant colonel of 3rd Regiment of Foot Guards. Aide de camp to Duke of Wellington in battles in Portugal, Spain and France. Killed in action at age 32 at Waterloo.

Last Words: "Thank heaven! My Leader lives." Spoken just before he was shot and killed. His Last Words are part of a long inscription on a monument to him at Waterloo that tells his story. He was buried where he fell.

Source: *Seven Weeks in Belgium, Switzerland, Lombardy, Piedmont, Savoy,* Vol. 1, by John Roby (London, 1838).

Canning, George

(1770-1827) British statesman, politician. While he was foreign minister, South American colonies gained British recognition. Held post of prime minister just three months. Died at age 57 at Chiswick House, Middlesex, England.

Last Words: "Spain and Portugal." Murmured while delirious.

Source: *Historical Characters: Mackintosh, Talleyrand, Canning, Corbett, Peel* by Sir Henry Bulwer-Lytton (London, 1870).

Cano, Alonzo

(1601-1667) Spanish painter, architect, sculptor. Known as the Michelangelo of Spain. Notable works: Granada Cathedral (architecture); *Seven Joys of the Virgin* (series of paintings); *St. Peter; St. Paul; Virgin and Child* (sculptures). Died at age 66 in Granada.

Last Words: "Vex me not with this thing, but give me a simple cross, that I may adore it, both as it is in itself and as I can figure it to my mind." His response when he declined accepting an elaborate but poorly carved crucifix and was asked: "Was it not the image of his Lord?"

Source: *Annals of the Artists of Spain* by William Stirling-Maxwell (London, 1891).

Canonchet (Nanuntenoo)

(d. 1676) Native American leader. Narragansett chief. Last great Narragansett sachem. Refused to allow submission of his people. Was killed by a colonial firing squad during King Philip's War. Several locations in Rhode Island were named for him.

Last Words: "I like it well. I shall die before my heart is soft or I have said anything unworthy of myself."

Source: *Lives of Famous Indian Chiefs, from Cofachiqui, the Indian Princess, and Powhatan; Down to and Including Chief Joseph and Geronimo* by Norman Barton Wood (Aurora, IL, 1906).

Canova, Antonio

(1757-1822) Italian sculptor, painter. Works are in Louvre and Vatican. Exponent of neoclassic movement. Did portrait statues of Napoleon and his family. Notable work: *Pauline Bonaparte Borghese as Venus Victrix* (sculpture). Died at age 65 in Venice.

Last Words: "Pure and amiable spirit." Spoken three times.

Source: *Memoirs of Antonio Canova, with a Critical Analysis of His Works and an Historical Overview of Modern Sculpture* by J.S. Memes (Edinburgh, 1825).

Capel, Arthur, Lord Capel of Hadham

(1604-1649) English nobleman, royalist leader, military officer. General. Created Lord Capel of Hadham by Charles I in 1641. Fought for the king in England's Civil War. Captured at Colchester in 1648. Condemned to death for his loyalty to Charles I. Executed at Westminster Hall.

Last Words: "God Almighty stanch this blood, God Almighty stanch, stanch this issue of blood; this will not do the business. God Almighty find out another way to do it." Spoken at his execution.

Source: *The Dying Speeches and Behaviour of the Several State Prisoners that Have Been Executed the Last 300 Years. With Their Several Characters, from Cambden, Spotswood, Clarendon, Sprat, Burner, &c. and a Table Shewing How the Respective Sentences were Executed, and Which of Them Were Mitigated, or Pardon'd. Being a Proper Supplement to the State-Trials* (London, 1720).

Capote, Truman

(1924-1984) American writer. Novelist, screenwriter. Birth name Truman Streckfus Persons. Notable works: *In Cold Blood; Breakfast at Tiffany's*, both of which were made into successful films. More than 20 movies and TV dramas have been produced from Capote's stories, novels and screenplays. Died at age 59 in Los Angeles, California.

Last Words: "Mama—Mama—Mama."

Source: *Truman Capote: In Which Various Friends, Enemies, Acquaintances and Detractors Recall His Turbulent Career* by George Plimpton (New York, 1997).

Captain Jack (Kintpuash)

(1837?-1873) Native American leader. Modoc leader of group that killed Klamath medicine man. Resisted arrest. Sought refuge on California lava beds. Killed U.S. Army General Edward Canby at peace commission meeting. Fled. Captured. Hanged at Fort Klamath, Oregon, for Canby's murder. His head was sent to the Army Medical Museum in Washington, D.C. It was later transferred to the Smithsonian Institution. In 1984, his remains were returned to his descendants.

Last Words: "Well preacher, I tell you what I'll do with you. I will give you twenty-five head of ponies if you will take my place today, as you said it is such a nice place, because I do not like to go right now."

Source: *Border Outlaws of Montana, North Dakota & Canada* by Barbara Hegne (Eagle Point, OR, 1993).

Carême, Marie-Antoine or Antonin

(1784?-1833) French chef. Founder of French haute cuisine. First celebrity chef. Died at about age 48, possibly of low-level carbon monoxide from cooking in a small, underventilated kitchen.

Last Words: "Tomorrow, bring me some fish. Yesterday, the quenelles of sole were very good, but your fish was not right. You hadn't seasoned it well."

Source: *Cooking for Kings: The Life of Antonin Carême, the First Celebrity Chef* by Ian Kelly (London, 2003).

Carew, Sir George

(1504?-1545) English military officer. Vice admiral in navy. Knighted in the 1530s. Commanded *Mary Rose*, flagship of fleet that tried to halt French armada. *Mary Rose* sank off the coast of Portsmouth, England. Carew and many crew members were lost. Four centuries later the *Mary Rose* was raised and restored.

Last Words: "I have a sort of knaves whom I cannot rule." Spoken to his uncle Sir Gawen Carew, who hailed him from another ship.

Source: *The Life and Times of Sir Peter Carew, Kt.,* ed. by John Maclean (London, 1857).

Carey, William

(1761-1834) English clergyman, Baptist missionary. First missionary to India. Sent there by Baptist Missionary Society. Known as the Father and Founder of Modern Missions. Spent 41 years in India. Died at age 72 in India.

Last Words: "Mr. Duff, you have been speaking about Dr. Carey. When I am gone, say nothing about Dr. Carey—speak about Dr. Carey's Saviour." Spoken to Alexander Duff, missionary who was one of his last visitors.

Source: *Baptist Mission Portraits* by John Allen Moore (Macon, GA, 1994).

Caritativo, Bart Luis

(1906-1958) Filipino murderer. House boy who ingratiated himself with a wealthy family then killed for money and land and attempted to make it look like murder-suicide. Executed at age 52 in the gas chamber at San Quentin, California.

Last Words: "God bless you all.—God bless you all."

Source: *Murderers Sane & Mad; Case Histories in the Motivation and Rationale of Murder* by Miriam Allen De Ford (London, 1965).

Carlos, Prince of Spain (Don Carlos)

(1545-1568) Spanish royalty. Son of King Philip II of Spain. Mentally deranged. Imprisoned by order of his father. Died mysteriously at age 23. May have been murdered. Schiller's play *Don Carlos* was based on his life; the play became the basis of Verdi's opera *Don Carlos*.

Last Words: "God be propitious to me, a sinner."

Source: *Don Carlos, Leben, Verhaftung und Tod dieses Prinzen* by Leopold A. Warnkönig (Stuttgart, Germany, 1864).

Carlyle, Jane Welsh Baille

(1801-1866) Scottish matron. Wife of Scottish writer and historian Thomas Carlyle. In failing health the last 18 months of her life. Was found dead at age 64 in her carriage in Hyde Park, London.

Last Words: "Good night and thank ye!"

Source: *Letters and Memorials of Jane Welsh Carlyle,* Vol. II, by Jane Welsh Carlyle, Thomas Carlyle and James Anthony Froude (London, 1883).

Carlyle, Thomas

(1795-1881) Scottish-born writer, satirist, social critic, historian. Notable work: *The French Revolution* (3-vol. history that established his reputation as a historian). Did very little publishing after his wife died in 1866. Died at age 85 in London.

Last Words: "So this is death! Well." Overheard by his niece. He died the next morning.

Source: *Carlyle in Old Age* by David Alec Wilson and David Wilson MacArthur (New York, 1934).

Carmichael, John

(1728-1785) Scottish-born American clergyman. Presbyterian. Pastor of Church of the Forks of the Brandywine in Pennsylvania. Published articles that encouraged independence during the American Revolution.

Last Words: "Oh that I had a thousand tongues that I might employ them all in inviting sinners to Christ."

Source: *Encyclopedia of the Presbyterian Church in the United States of America: Including the Northern and Southern Assemblies,* ed. by Alfred Nevin (Philadelphia, 1884).

Carnegie, Andrew

(1835-1919) Scottish-born American industrialist, philanthropist. Founded Carnegie Steel Company that later merged with United States Steel Corporation. Endowed multimillions of dollars on public libraries, public education, international peace. Provided most of the funding for Carnegie Hall, New York City. Carnegie Institute was his gift to the people of Pittsburgh. Died at age 83 in Lenox, Massachusetts.

Last Words: "I hope so, Lou." His response when his wife said: "I hope you will rest well, Andrew." His wife was Louise Whitfield Carnegie, who died in 1946 at age 89.

Source: *The Life of Andrew Carnegie* by Burton J. Hendrick (New York, 1932).

Carnot, Marie François Sadi

(1837-1894) French engineer, politician. 4th president of French Republic. Stabbed by Italian anarchist Sante Jeronimo Caserio.

Had just delivered a speech at a public banquet at Lyons Exposition. Died of injuries at age 56 in Lyons.

Last Words: "I am very touched by your presence and I thank you for what you are doing for me." Spoken to the people who gathered around him when he was wounded.

Source: *L'Assassinat du Président Carnot* by A. Lacassagne (Lyons, France, 1894).

Carolan, Turlough or Torlogh, see O'Carolan, Turlough or Torlogh.

Caroline of Anspach, Queen of Great Britain and Ireland

(1683-1737) German-born British royalty. Daughter of Marquis of Brandenburg-Anspach. Wife and consort of George II. Queen of Great Britain and Ireland. Princess of Wales. Died at age 54 in London.

Different Last Words:

(1) "I have now got an asthma. Open the window. Pray."

Source: *The Wits and Beaux of Society* by Grace and Philip Wharton (New York, 1890).

(2) "Pray louder that I may hear."

Source: *Lives of the Hanoverian Queens of England* by Alice Drayton Greenwood (London, 1909).

Carpenter, Louis

(1829-1863) American jurist, military officer. Colonel in the U.S. Civil War, before returning to his hometown of Lawrence. Victim of Lawrence, Kansas, massacre led by William Clarke Quantrill during the war. Carpenter was a judge and reporter for the state supreme court and candidate for state attorney general. Died at age 33.

Last Words: "New York." His response to the guerrillas who came upon the judge. They questioned where he was from then shot him. When he tried to escape, they shot him again in the head.

Source: *The Lawrence Massacre by a Band of Missouri Ruffians Under Quantrill* by Richard Cordley (Lawrence, KS, 1865).

Carpio, Lope Felix de Vega, see Vega, Lope de.

Carroll, Charles

(1737-1832) American politician. Known as Charles Carroll of Carrollton. Member of Continental Congress. Member U.S. Senate from Maryland. A founder of the Baltimore and Ohio Railroad. Last surviving signer of the Declaration of Independence. Died at age 95 in Baltimore. Many U.S. counties and towns are named for him.

Last Words: "Thank you, Doctor."

Source: *Charles Carroll of Carrollton* by Ellen Hart Smith (Cambridge, MA, 1942).

Carroll, John

(1735-1815) American prelate, educator. First Roman Catholic bishop and archbishop in U.S. Served Archdiocese of Baltimore. Established Georgetown, St. Mary's College for Boys (now Loyola), Mt. St. Mary's, Emmitsburg. Died at age 80 in Baltimore. John Carroll University and several high schools are named in his honor.

Last Words: "Sir, my hopes have always been fixed on the cross of Christ." Spoken to a Protestant minister who noted that his hopes must now be fixed on another world.

Source: *Book of Catholic Quotations Compiled from Approved Sources Ancient, Medieval and Modern*, ed. by John Chapin (New York, 1956).

Carroll, Lewis, see Dodgson, Charles Lutwidge.

Carson, Christopher Houston ("Kit")

(1809-1868) American military officer, trapper, guide, Indian agent for U.S. government. Was also mountain man, rancher, farmer, explorer. Brevetted brigadier-general for his service in Mexican War, Indian Wars and U.S. Civil War. Became legend through dime novels and movies.

Different Last Words:

(1) "Adios, compadre. Adios!" (tr. "Farewell comrade. Farewell!") Spoken as he held the hand of his friend Aloys Scheurich. He died at age 58 of an aneurysm at the home of General William Henry Penrose in Fort Lyon, Colorado.

Source: *History of the Penrose Family* by Josiah Leach (Philadelphia, 1903).

(2) (doubtful): "Wish I had time for just one more bowl of chili."

Source: Various Last Words compilations and Internet websites. Some of these sources describe the quote as "alleged."

Carstares or Carstairs, John

(1623-1685?) Scottish clergyman, Covenanter, martyr. Minister in Glasgow. Father of William Carstares. Several ministers, including Carstares, James Nasmyth and James Veitch were accused of using seditious language in their sermons. Carstares' Last Words were written down by William Creighton, a minister, and preserved in the Advocates Library, Edinburgh.

Last Words: "If it were possible that Christ and his interest in this world could ruin I would much rather fall with him than stand with any and all powers of the world; but, as I am persuaded that these cannot perish, I am confident in the Lord, these shall revive in all of the churches of Christ."

Source: *The Scots Worthies: Containing a Brief Historical Account of the Most Eminent Noblemen, Gentlemen, Ministers, and Others, Who Testified or Suffered for the Cause of Reformation in Scotland: From the Beginning of the Sixteenth Century to the Year 1688* by John Howie (Glasgow, Scotland, 1829).

Carstares or Carstairs, William

(1649-1715) Scottish clergyman. Known as Cardinal Carstares. Imprisoned five years without trial as suspected adherent of William of Orange. Endured thumbscrew torture without divulging secrets. When William III was crowned, Carstares was his main adviser on Scottish matters. Royal chaplain to Queen Anne. Died at age 66 in Edinburgh.

Last Words: "I have peace with God through our Lord Jesus Christ."

Source: *William Carstares: A Character and Career of the Revolutionary Epoch (1649-1715)* by Robert Herbert Story (London, 1874).

Carter, Richard

(d. 1692) English naval officer. Rear admiral. Killed in the naval Battle of Barfleur between French and Anglo-Dutch ships. After he was struck and fatally injured by one of his yardarms, he would not allow his men to carry him below, nor would he give up his sword.

Last Words: "Fight the ship; fight the ship as long as she can swim."

Source: *The History of England From the Accession of James II* by Thomas Babington Macaulay (London, 1849).

Carteret, John, Earl Granville,

(1690-1763) English statesman, orator, diplomat. Second Baron Carteret. Chief minister of George II. Served as lord lieutenant of Ireland, secretary of state, lord president of the council. Succeeded to title of Earl

Granville in 1744. Died at age 72 in Bath, England.

Last Words: "It has been the most glorious war and it is now the most honorable peace this nation ever saw." While on his deathbed, he listened to a reading of the preliminaries of the 1763 Treaty of Paris that would end the French and Indian War/Seven Years' War.

Source: *Carteret, the Brilliant Failure of the Eighteenth Century* by W. Baring Pemberton (London, 1936).

Cartwright, Thomas

(1535-1603) English clergyman. Influential head of Puritans. His attacks on the church caused him to lose his professorship at Cambridge. Fled abroad in 1573. Returned to England in 1585. On his deathbed, he deeply lamented the unnecessary troubles he caused in the church by the schism he had fomented. Helped Puritans draft a petition to King James to express their grievances.

Last Words: "I wish I could begin life again so as to testify to the world the dislike I have of my former ways."

Source: "Cartwright, Thomas" in *A New General Biographical Dictionary*, Vol. VI, by Hugh James Rose (London, 1857).

Caruso, Enrico

(1873-1921) Italian singer. One of the world's great operatic tenors. World's first recording star. Appeared at the Metropolitan Opera more than 600 times in 37 different productions. Notable performances: *La Boheme; Rigoletto; Pagliacci; Otello.* Became ill with bronchial pneumonia that developed into pleurisy. Died at age 48 in Naples, his hometown.

Last Words: "Doro, I can't get my breath." Spoken to his wife.

Source: *Enrico Caruso, His Life and Death* by Dorothy Caruso (New York, 1945). Dorothy Park Benjamin married Caruso in 1918.

Carver, George Washington

(1864-1943) American botanist, agricultural researcher, educator. Son of African-American slaves. Earned BS and MS degrees at Iowa State University. Worked in agricultural extension service in the South. Taught former slaves farming self-sufficiency. Suggested many commercial uses for peanuts, sweet potatoes and other plants. His research produced more than 300 byproducts and helped revolutionize the economy of the South. Faculty member at Tuskegee Institute (now Tuskegee University), Alabama. Carver Research Foundation was established at Tuskegee in 1940. Winner of many honors, including Spingarn and Roosevelt. Died at age 79 in Tuskegee.

Last Words: "I think I'll sleep now."

Source: "The Quiet Saint—George Washington Carver" by John Lenti (*Clarity—A Magazine of Spiritual Teachings & Practices for Everyday Living*, Spring 2005).

Cary, Alice

(1820-1871) American poet. Had very little formal education. Sister of Phoebe Cary, also a poet. Their poems attracted the attention of Poe, Greeley and Whittier, among others. Contributor to *Harper's* and *Atlantic Monthly* and other periodicals. Died at age 50 at her home in New York City after a long illness.

Last Words: "I want to go away."

Source: *A Memorial of Alice and Phoebe Cary* by Mary Clemmer (Boston, 1885).

Cary, Phoebe

(1824-1871) American poet. Had very little formal education. Sister of Alice Cary, also a poet. Their poems attracted the attention of Poe, Greeley and Whittier, among others. Contributor to *Harper's* and *Atlantic Monthly* and other periodicals. Died at age 46 in Newport, Rhode Island, five months after her sister.

Last Words: "O God, have mercy on my soul!"

Source: *A Memorial of Alice and Phoebe Cary* by Mary Clemmer (Boston, 1885).

Casals, Pablo

(1876-1973) Spanish musician, cellist, conductor, composer, pianist. Catalonian. Birth name Pau Carlos Salvador Defilló de Casals. Left Spain in 1939 during the Spanish Civil War. Had a brilliant career as one of world's greatest cellists. Settled in Puerto Rico, his mother's birthplace, in 1956. Died at age 96 in San Juan.

Last Words: "The driver's a maniac. He'll kill us all." Spoken in an ambulance while on his way to a hospital.

Source: *Pablo Casals* by Robert Baldock (Boston, 1992).

Casanova or Casanova de Seingalt, Giacomo or Giovanni Jacopo

(1725-1798) Italian adventurer, librarian, writer. Known for his libertine lifestyle. In 1785, after he tired of his nomadic life, he settled down in Bohemia, where he served as librarian to Count von Waldstein until he died. Wrote his *Memoirs*, a 12-vol. account of his travels and amours, that provide a vivid description of 18th-century European life. Died at age 73 in Dux, Bohemia (now Czech Republic).

Last Words: "I have lived as a philosopher and die as a Christian."

Source: *Giacomo Casanova: Chevalier de Seingalt* by Bonamy Dobrée (New York, 1933).

Casaubon, Isaac

(1559-1614) Swiss theologian, scholar, librarian. Part of influential triumvirate of 16th-century classical scholars (with Scaliger, Lipsius). Held a library position in France, where he earned a reputation as a scholar. Moved to England in 1610. Remained there the rest of his life. Spent his last years defending the Anglican church against attack. Died at age 55 in London. Buried in Westminster Abbey.

Last Words: "Then you think, my lord that I have been all along a dissembler in a matter of the greatest moment!" His response to the French ambassador who had sent someone to ask in what religion he professed to die.

Source: "Isaac Casaubon, the Scholar" (*The Unitarian Review and Religious Magazine*, Vol. 4, September 1875).

Casement, Sir Roger David

(1864-1916) Irish patriot, poet, revolutionary, nationalist. Knighted 1911. Negotiated declaration that stated Germany would not invade Ireland during World War I. Tried to recruit Irish prisoners-of-war in Germany who would fight against Britain. Captured and tried upon returning to Ireland. His conviction was based upon a medieval document that defined treason; its interpretation came down to a comma. His activities were on German soil not British, which was the traditional definition of treason. But the court decided a comma should be read in the text, crucially widening the designation "in the realm or elsewhere" to mean where acts were done, and not just where the king's enemies may be. Casement was sentenced to die and was hanged at age 51 at Pentonville Prison in London. He is remembered as a traitor in England but revered in Ireland as a martyr to the cause of Irish nationalism and as a founding father of the Irish State. He is also known in history as the man whose fate hung on a comma.

Last Words: "I die for my country!"

Source: "Casement Brave at Execution, 'I Die for My Country!' His Last Utterance After a Prayer. Crowd Jeered as He Died. But a Small Group of Irish Men and Women Knelt in Prayer. Body Refused to Family. Government Says He Agreed to Raise Brigade for Germany to Fight in Egypt. Casement Brave at Execution" (*New York Times*, April 4, 1916).

Variation: "I die for my country, into Thy hands, O Lord, I commend my spirit. Jesus, receive my soul." At that point the gallows trap was sprung.

Source: *History of the Sinn Fein Movement and the Irish Rebellion of 1916* by Francis P. Jones (New York, 1917).

Variation: "Lord Jesus, receive my soul" and as the noose was being attached, he added: "For God and Kathleen ni Houlihane."

Source: *Roger Casement: The Black Diaries, With a Study of His Background, Sexuality, and Irish Political Life* by Jeffrey Dudgeon (Belfast, Ireland, 2002).

Caserio, Sante Geronimo

(1873-1894) Italian anarchist, assassin. Killed Marie François Sadi Carnot, president of French Third Republic, at the Lyons Exposition. Executed by guillotine at age 21.

Last Words: "Courage, comrades, anarchy lives!" Spoken as he stood in front of the guillotine.

Source: *L'Assassinat du Président Carnot* by Alexandre Lacassagne (Paris, 1894).

Cassel, Karl Gustav

(1866-1945) Swedish economist, educator, writer. University professor in Stockholm. One of the founders of modern economics in Sweden. Developed theory of purchasing power parity. Notable works: *The Downfall of the Gold Standard; Fundamental Thoughts in Economics*. Died at age 78 in Stockholm.

Last Words: "A world currency." Spoken on his deathbed.

Source: "Biography of Gustav Cassel" in *The New*

Palgrave: A Dictionary of Economics, ed. by John Eatwell, Murray Milgate and Peter Newman (Basingstoke, England, 1998).

Castlereagh, Viscount, see Stewart, Robert.

Castrillón, Manuel Fernández

(1780s-1836) Cuban-born Mexican military officer. Major general in Mexican Army. Friend of general and Mexican president Antonio López de Santa Anna. Castrillón fought in Mexico's War of Independence, and later against the Texans in their battle for independence. He was a commander at the Alamo. He refused to abandon his ground as his troops fled. Texas General and Secretary of War Thomas J. Rusk tried to have his life spared but he was shot and killed on the battlefield by forces led by Sam Houston at the Battle of San Jacinto.

Last Words: "I've been in 40 battles and never showed my back. I'm too old to do it now!"

Sources: *The Day of San Jacinto* by Frank X. Tolbert (New York, 1959); *Towering Texan: A Biography of Thomas J. Rusk* by Cleburne Huston (Waco, TX, 1971).

Castro Tartas, Isaac de

(1623?-1647) French-born Portuguese Marano Jewish martyr. Persecuted by the Inquisition. Refused to convert to Christianity. He and five others were executed by being burned at the stake. He spoke his Last Words as he was consumed by flame.

Last Words: "Hear, O Israel! The Lord our God is One!" He then spoke his Last Word: "Echad" (tr. "One") It was reported that the martyrdom of Castro Tartas so affected some of the Inquisitors that they determined to stop burning heretics at the stake.

Source: "Isaac de Castro Tartas" by Gotthard Deutsch and Meyer Kayserling in *The Jewish Encyclopedia* (New York, 1901-1906).

Catesby, Robert

(1573-1605) English conspirator. Accomplice in Rye Plot (attempt to kidnap James I in 1603). Chief instigator in Gunpowder Plot (attempt to blow up Houses of Parliament in 1605). Betrayed. Fled to the Midlands. Found and killed in a shootout at Holbeach House when officers tried to arrest him.

Last Words: "Stand by me, Tom, and we

will die together." Tom was Thomas Wintour (or Winter), one of the Gunpowder Plot conspirators. Wintour was hit in the right arm. Catesby was shot and killed when he went outside.

Source: *Monthly Packet of Evening Reading for Members of the English Church,* ed. by Charlotte M. Yonge, Christabel R. Coleridge and Arthur Innes (London, 1883).

Cathcart, George

(1794-1854) British military officer, statesman, politician. Army general. Diplomat who represented England at the Court of Russia and during the Congress of Vienna. Governor of Cape of Good Hope. Granted first constitution to the colony. Ended eighth Kaffir War and crushed Basutos. Died at age 60 at the Battle of Inkerman during the Crimean War.

Last Words: "I fear we are in a mess."

Source: *The Victorians at War, 1815–1914, An Encyclopedia of British Military History* by Harold E. Raugh Jr. (Santa Barbara, CA, 2004).

Catherine of Alexandria, Saint

(d. c. 307) Christian holy woman, martyr. Beheaded after an attempt to torture her failed.

Last Words: "Oh hope and salvation of them that believe, Oh honor and glory of virgins! Jesus, good King, I implore thee that whosoever shall celebrate the memory of my passion, or shall call upon me at the moment of death or in any necessity, may obtain the benefit of Thy mercy!"

Source: *The Golden Legend or Lives of the Saints.* Compiled by Jacobus de Voragine, Archbishop of Genoa, 1275, 1st ed., 1470. English ed. by William Caxton, 1483, ed. by F.S. Ellis (Edinburgh, 1900).

Catherine of Aragon

(1485-1536) Spanish and English royalty. Daughter of Ferdinand and Isabella of Spain. First queen of Henry VIII of England. Mother of Queen Mary I. Bore six children; all but Mary were stillborn or died in infancy. Marriage to Henry VIII was annulled in 1533. Died at age 51 at Kimbolton Castle, Cambridgeshire.

Last Words: "Lord, into Thy hands I commend my spirit."

Source: *Catherine of Aragon* by Francesca Claremont (London, 1939).

Catherine of Siena, Saint

(1347-1380) Italian holy woman, mystic, writer. Roman Catholic. Doctor of the Church. Known for visions and revelations. Author of letters, devotional works. Died at age 33 in Rome. Canonized in 1461.

Last Words: "No, I have not sought vainglory, but only the glory and praise of God!"

Source: *Lives of the Saints* by S. Baring-Gould (Edinburgh, 1914).

Catlin, George

(1796-1872) American artist, traveler, writer. Devoted his career to documenting way of life of Native Americans on their own lands. Created more than 2,000 portraits, drawings and sketches of them. Notable work: *My Life Among the Indians.* Died at age 76 in Jersey City, New Jersey.

Last Words: "What will happen to my Gallery?" Catlin was concerned about works that had been taken from him in 1852.

Source: *Letters and Notes on the Manners, Customs, and Conditions of the North American Indians, Written During Eight Years' Travel (1832-1839) Amongst the Wildest Tribes of Indians in North America* by George Catlin (New York, 1973). Source describes the quote as "almost his last words."

Cato, Marcus Porius (the Younger)

(95-46 B.C.) Roman philosopher, military officer, statesman. Stoic. Great-grandson of Cato the Elder. Committed suicide to avoid capture when he learned of Caesar's victory at Thapsus. His nephew and son-in-law Brutus was one of the assassins who killed Caesar in 44 B.C.

Different Last Words:

(1) "Shut the door." Spoken to his servant before he stabbed himself.

Source: "Cato the Younger" in *Lives of the Noble Grecians and Romans* by Plutarch, tr. by John Dryden (Chicago, 1952).

(2) "Now I am master of myself." Spoken after his second attempt to stab himself. His friends rushed to his aid after his first attempt and dressed his wound while he was unconscious. He gained consciousness and succeeded in taking his life on his second try.

Source: *Brewer's Dictionary of Phrase and Fable* by Ebenezer Brewer, rev. by Ivor H. Evans (New York, 1970).

(3) "Have my friends yet embarked? Does

anything yet remain that could be done to serve them?"

Source: *Last Words of Saints and Sinners: 700 Final Quotes from the Famous, the Infamous, and the Inspiring Figures in History* by Herbert Lockyer (Grand Rapids, MI, 1969).

Cauchy, Baron Augustin Louis

(1789-1857) French mathematician, physicist, astronomer, educator. Professor of astronomy at Sorbonne. Developed wave theory in optics. Worked on theory of elasticity. Wrote many papers on hydrodynamics, planetary motions, numbers theory and differential equations. Pioneer in formulating and proving calculus theorems. Died at age 68 at Sceaux, France. Cauchy Integral Theorem is named for him.

Different Last Words:

(1) "No, I do not suffer much—Jesus, Mary, Joseph."

Source: *La Vie et Les Travaux du Baron Cauchy* by C.A. Valson (Paris, 1868).

(2) "Men pass away, but their deeds abide."

Source: *Mathematical Circles Revisited: A Second Collection of Mathematical Stories and Anecdotes* by Howard W. Eves (Boston, 1971).

Cavell, Edith Louise

(1865-1915) English nurse. Helped about 200 English, French, Belgian soldiers escape to the Dutch border during World War I. Captured by Germans, condemned to death by court-martial and shot. Died at age 50.

Different Last Words:

(1) "They have all been very kind to me here. But this I would say, standing, as I do, in view of God and eternity, I realize that patriotism is not enough; I must have no hatred or bitterness toward anyone." Spoken in prison, the night before her execution.

Sources: *Edith Cavell* by Helen Judson (New York, 1941); *The* [London] *Times,* October 23, 1915.

(2) "Ask Mr. Gahan to tell my loved ones that my soul, I believe, is safe, and that I am glad to die for my country." Spoken to the chaplain as she neared the place where she would be executed by firing squad.

Source: *Nightingale Man* by Jane Toombs (Leicester, England, 2002).

Cavendish, Henry

(1731-1810) French-born English physicist, chemist. Son of Lord Charles Cavendish. Discovered hydrogen, which he called inflammable air. Calculated density of the Earth. He formed no close personal relationships during his entire lifetime. Was so solitary and reclusive that some modern experts on behavior theorize he may have had Asperger's syndrome (a form of autism). Died at age 78 in London. Much of his work was not published until after he died.

Last Words: "Mind what I say, I am going to die. When I am dead, but not till then, go to Lord George Cavendish and tell him of the event. Go!" Spoken to his valet. When the valet returned, he was dead.

Source: *The Life of the Honourable Henry Cavendish* by George Wilson (London, 1851).

Cavendish, Spencer Compton 8th Duke of Devonshire

(1833-1908) British statesman, nobleman. Member of House of Commons. Declined office of prime minister three times. Died at age 74 at Cannes, France, while returning from a trip to Egypt. A statue of him is on the east side of Whitehall, London. Another is in the Carpet Gardens at Eastbourne.

Last Words: "The game is over and I am not sorry."

Source: *Life of Spencer Compton, Eighth Duke of Devonshire* by Bernard Holland (London, 1911).

Cavour, Camillo Benso, Conte di

(1810-1861) Italian statesman, Led movement to unify Italy and free it from Austria. First prime minister of Kingdom of Italy. Fell ill in 1860, possibly of malaria. Died at age 50 in Turin.

Different Last Words:

(1) "Libera chiesa in libero stato." (tr. "A free church in a free state!")

Sources: *Cavour* by Maurice Paléologue (London, 1927); *Dublin Review,* Vol. VXIII, ed. by Nicholas Patrick Wiseman, January-June, 1872.

Variation: "Friar, friar, a free church in a free state." An hour later he said: "Italy is made—all is safe."

Source: *Famous Last Words* by Barnaby Conrad (Garden City, NY, 1961).

(2) "No, your Majesty, tomorrow you will not see me here." Spoken to Victor Emmanuel, who as he turned away in tears had said to Cavour: "I shall come to see you again tomorrow."

Source: *The Last Words (Real and Traditional) of Distinguished Men and Women Collected from Various Sources* by Frederic Rowland Marvin (New York, 1901). Marvin gave "Lippincott" as his source.

Caxton, William

(1422?-1491) English printer, translator. Learned printing in Cologne, Germany. The first printing in England was done on Caxton's press. He printed the first books in the English language. Died in London.

Last Words (written): "God then give us His grace and find in us such a house that it may please Him to lodge therein, to the end that in this world He keeps us from adversity spiritual. And in the end of our days He brings us with Him into His realm of heaven for to be partners of the glory eternal, which grant to us the Holy Trinity. Amen." His Last Words were printed.

Source: *William Caxton* by Henry R. Plomer (London, 1925).

Cayce, Edgar

(1877-1945) American psychic, prophet. Known as the Sleeping Prophet. Claimed that while in self-induced sleep he could channel information on many subjects, including Atlantis, reincarnation and astrology. Last reading September 17, 1944, was for himself. The reading told him the time had come for him to stop working and rest. On January 1, 1945, he announced he would be buried on January 5. Cayce died at age 67 on January 3 and was buried two days later in Virginia Beach, Virginia.

Last Words: "Oh, I don't know. I don't know much about music." Spoken to his wife who had asked him about music he heard.

Sources: "Edgar Cayce, Clairvoyant (1877-1945)" in *Armageddon: Doomsday in Our Lifetime?* by Bob Leaman and Michael Coyne (Richmond, Victoria, Australia, 1986); *My Years with Edgar Cayce* by Mary Ellen Carter (New York, 1972).

Cazotte, Jacques

(1719-1792) French writer, royalist, poet. Notable work: *Diable amoureux* (fantasy). Guillotined at age 72 in Paris as a royalist during the French Revolution.

Different Last Words:

(1) "I die as I have lived, faithful to God and my King."

Source: *Biographie universelle,* Book VII, by J. Fr. Michaud and Louis Gabriel Michaud (Paris, 1811-1862).

(2) "My dear wife, my dear children, do not weep: do not forget me, but above all, remember never to offend God."

Source: "M. Cazotte's Prophecies" in *The Mirror of Literature, Amusement, and Instruction,* Vol. 37, by Reuben Percy, John Timbs and John Limbird (London, 1841).

Ceauşescu, Elena

(1916-1989) Romanian matron. Wife of Nicolae Ceauşescu, general secretary of Romanian Communist Party; vice-prime minister of Romania. Leader of Romania from 1965 to 1989, when coup and revolution removed him from power. Elena and Nicolae were arrested and sentenced to death by a military court on charges of genocide and other crimes in December 1989. They were executed in Târgovişte soon afterward.

Last Words: "Stop it, Nicu. Look, they're going to shoot us like dogs. I can't believe this. Is the death penalty still in force in Romania?" Spoken just prior to her execution as her husband hummed "Internationale" and then commented that he would be judged by history.

Source: "The Bear Slayer: During His Quarter Century of Dictatorial Rule Nicolae Ceausescu Treated the Brown Bears of Romania Almost as Badly as He Treated the People. Only His Gamekeepers Saw the Grisly Reality" by David Quammen (*The Atlantic Monthly*, July-August 2003).

Cecil, Robert, 1st Earl of Salisbury

(1563-1612) English nobleman, statesman. Born with a deformed spine. Known as Crooked-backed Earl or Robin Crookback. Secretary of state, chief minister to James I. Created Baron Cecil in 1603, Viscount Cranborne in 1604 and Baron of Salisbury in 1605. Died at age 48 at St. Margaret's Priory in Marlborough en route to Bath.

Last Words: "Ease and pleasure quake to hear of death; but my life full of care and miseries, desireth to be dissolved." Spoken to his friend Sir William Cope.

Source: *The Zurich Letters: Comprising the Correspondence of Several English Bishops and Others with Some of the Helvetian reformers, During the Early Part of the Reign of Queen Elizabeth* by John Hunter and Hastings Robinson (Cambridge, England, 1842).

Cecil, William, 1st Baron Burghley (or Burleigh)

(1520-1598) English statesman, educator. Baron Burghley (or Burleigh). One of Queen Elizabeth I's most powerful advisers. Lord high treasurer. Father of Robert Cecil. Died at age 77 at his London home.

Last Words: "I have ever found thee true to me and I now trust thee with all." Spoken as he gave his will to his steward.

Source: *Memoirs of the Life and Administration of the Right Honourable William Cecil, Lord Burghley* by Rev. Edward Nares (London, 1831).

Cecilia, Saint

(d.c. 200) Roman holy woman. Christian martyr. An attempt to kill her in her bath failed. She was then decapitated but lived for three days after being struck. Patron saint of music and of the blind.

Different Last Words:

(1) "I obtained three days' delay, that I might commend myself and all these to thy beatitude, and that thou mightest consecrate this my house as a church." Spoken to Bishop Urban.

Source: *The Golden Legend or Lives of the Saints.* Compiled by Jacobus de Voragine, Archbishop of Genoa, 1275, 1st ed., 1470. English ed. by William Caxton, 1483, ed. by F.S. Ellis (Edinburgh, 1900).

(2) "Are these the gods that you worship, or are they blocks of wood and pieces of stone?" Her response when ordered to be sacrificed to the gods of Rome

Source: *The Church of Apostles and Martyrs* by Henri Daniel-Rops (London, 1960).

Cenci or Cenzi, Beatrice

(1577-1599) Italian noblewoman. Imprisoned with stepmother Lucrezia in the castle where she said her father raped her. She conspired with her stepmother and brother to have her father killed. The family was arrested and confessed to the murder. Beatrice, Lucrezia and brother Giacomo were beheaded for the crime. Their story has provided the plot of several works in the arts including *The Cenci,* tragedy by Shelley; *Les Cenci,* novel by Stendhal; and *Beatrix Cenci*, opera by Alberto Ginastera.

Last Words: "Jesus, Mary." Spoken at her execution.

Source: *Storia di Beatrice Cenci* by Carlo Tito Dalbono (Naples, Italy, 1864).

Cenci or Cenzi, Lucrezia Petroni

(d. 1599) Italian noblewoman. Wife of Francesco Cenci. Stepmother of Beatrice Cenci (or Cenzi). Imprisoned with Beatrice in the castle where Beatrice said her father raped her. Lucrezia conspired with her family to have her father killed. The family was arrested and confessed to the murder. Lucrezia, Beatrice and her brother Giacomo were executed for the crime. Their story has been the plot of several works in the arts including *The Cenci,* tragedy by Shelley; *Les Cenci,* novel by Stendhal; and *Beatrix Cenci*, opera by Alberto Ginastera.

Last Words: "Jesu Mary. O let thine ears consider well the voice of my complaint."

Sources: *Notes and Queries: a Medium for Inter-Communication for Literary Men, General Readers, etc.* by William Henry Thomas, (John) Doran, Henry Frederick Turle, Joseph Knight, Vernon Horace Rendall and Florence Hayllar (London, 1878); *Storia di Beatrice Cenci* by Carlo Tito Dalbono (Naples, Italy, 1864).

Cermak, Anton Joseph

(1873-1933) Czech-born American politician. Mayor of Chicago, Illinois. Killed when struck by bullets intended for President-elect Franklin D. Roosevelt, by assassin Giuseppe Zangara. Cermak died at age 59 in Chicago.

Different Last Words:

(1) (doubtful): "I'm glad it was me instead of you." This quote was much publicized as the words spoken by Cermak to Roosevelt as they sped to the hospital. But people who knew Cermak noted they were out of character. John Dienhart, a Chicago reporter traveling with Cermak, admitted later that he made up the quote.

Source: *American Pharaoh: Mayor Richard J. Daley: His Battle for Chicago and the Nation* by Adam Seth Cohen and Elizabeth Taylor (Boston, 2000).

(2) "Kiss me." Spoken to his wife in the hospital.

Source: *Last Words: A Dictionary of Deathbed Quotations* by C. Bernard Ruffin (Jefferson, NC, 1995).

Cerretti, Bonaventura

(1872-1933) Italian prelate. Had apostolic assignments in Mexico, the U.S., Australia and New Zealand as well as Italy. Created cardinal of Roman Catholic Church in 1925. Died two months after taking appointment as cardinal-bishop of Velleeri.

Last Words: "Pray for us." Spoken after hearing that the Pope was praying for him.

Source: *Il Cardinale Bonaventura Cerretti* by Giuseppe de Luc (Rome, 1939).

Cervantes, Miguel de

(1547-1616) Spanish writer, poet, playwright. Birth name Miguel de Cervantes Saavedra. Saw military service in the naval battle at Lepanto in 1571. Seriously wounded aboard a galley. Permanently injured his left arm. Captured by Moors in 1775 and held prisoner as a slave for five years. His major works were published toward the end of his life. Despite his fame, he struggled against poverty. Notable work: *Don Quixote de la Mancha* (novel; viewed by many to be the greatest work in Spanish literature). Died at age 68 in Madrid.

Different Last Words:

(1) (written): "Already my foot is in the stirrup. Already, great lord and master, the agonies of death are upon me, as I send you these lines. Yesterday they administered to me the Last Rites. Today I am writing this. Time is short, agony grows, hope lessens. Only the will to live keeps me alive. Would that life might last until I might kiss the feet of your Excellency. Seeing your Excellency back in Spain, hale and hearty, might restore me to life. But, if it be decreed that I must die, Heaven's will be done! May your Excellency know, at least, what my wish was, and know also that he had in me, a servant so faithful as to have wished to serve your Excellency even after death!"

Source: *Cervantes* by T.R. Ybarra (New York, 1931).

(2) (written): "Adieu to gaiety, adieu to humor, adieu, my pleasant friends! I must now die, and I wish for nothing better than speedily to see you well contented in another world." Written shortly before he died for the preface of a book he was working on but did not finish.

Source: *Historical View of the Literature of the South of Europe* by J. C. L. Simonde de Sismondi, tr. by Thomas Roscoe (London, 1853).

Cézanne, Paul

(1839-1906) French painter. Grew up in Aix-en-Provence, France, with close friend Émile Zola. Both moved to Paris in 1863.

Early paintings show Romantic and Impressionist influences. Later works are post-Impressionistic. Notable works: *Still Life with a Curtain; Les Grandes Baigneuses* (The Bathers); *The Card Players*. Cézanne had a disagreement with Zola in 1886 after Zola used him as the model for a failed artist in his novel *L'Ouevre*. Cezanne returned to Aix in 1895. Had very little recognition until a 1904 exhibition. Became ill after getting caught in rainstorm. Died at age 67 of pneumonia a short time later.

Different Last Words:

(1) "Pontier. Pontier." Spoken while delirious. He repeated the surname of sculptor Auguste-Henri Pontier, curator of Aix museum, who refused to display his paintings.

Source: "Letter from Paris," by Genet (*The New Yorker*, July 24, 1954).

(2) "Paul." Spoke the name of his son.

Source: *Last Words: A Dictionary of Deathbed Quotations* by C. Bernard Ruffin (Jefferson, NC, 1995).

Chadwick, John White

(1840-1904) American clergyman, writer, poet. Leading Unitarian preacher. Minister of Second Unitarian Church in Brooklyn, New York. Prolific writer. Notable works: *Cap'n Chadwick, Marblehead Skipper and Shoemaker; Theodore Parker: Preacher, Reformer*. Died at age 64 in Brooklyn.

Last Words: "Good-bye." Spoken to his wife.

Source: *A Conspectus of American Biography: Being an Analytical Summary of American History and Biography, Containing also the Complete Indexes of the National Cyclopedia of American Biography* by George Derby (New York, 1906).

Chaffee, Roger B.

(1935-1967) American astronaut, pilot. Victim of spacecraft disaster. Killed at age 31 with astronauts Virgil I. ("Gus") Grissom and Edward H. White during training exercise for *Apollo I*, atop a Saturn IB rocket. Chaffee crater on the far side of the Moon and Chaffee Hill on Mars were named for him. Star Gamma Velorum was named "Regor" ("Roger" spelled backward) in his honor. Also named for him: Roger B. Chaffee Elementary School, Huntsville, Alabama; an artificial island in San Pedro Bay off southern California; Roger B. Chaffee

Planetarium in Grand Rapids, Michigan; Roger B. Chaffee Park in Fullerton, California, among many others.

Last Words: "We've got a bad fire—let's get out—we're burning up!—I'm reporting a bad fire, I'm getting out—Oh, Oh (scream)."

Source: *Report of Apollo 204 Review Board to the Administrator, National Aeronautics and Space Administration,* Apollo 204 Review Board (National Aeronautics and Space Administration, 1967).

Chaikin, Joseph

(1935-2003) American theater director, actor, playwright. Founder of The Open Theater, an experimental theater co-operative. Notable work: *The Presence of the Actor.* Winner of six Obie Awards: three for acting, two for directing and one for Lifetime Achievement. Died at age 67 in New York City.

Last Words: "I don't know." His response to his sister who asked him what was wrong when he seemed distressed. He died a short time later.

Source: "Joseph Chaikin 67; Actor and Innovative Director" (*New York Times,* June 24, 2003).

Chaliapin, Feodor Ivanovich

(1873-1938) Russian singer. Operatic basso. Left Russia in 1921; eventually settled in Paris. Notable performances: *Boris Godunov; Mefistofele; Prince Igor; Don Carlo; Khovanshchina; Don Quichotte.* Made many concert appearances. Died at age 65 in Paris.

Last Words: "Masha, why is it so dark in this theater? Tell them to turn on the lights!" Spoken to his wife as he was dying.

Source: "Feodor Chaliapin" liner notes by Victor Borovsky for recording, *Chaliapin: Prima Voce.* Afterword by Maria Hudson Davies (nee Chaliapin) (Nimbus Records).

Chalmers, Thomas

(1780-1847) Scottish theologian, mathematician, clergyman, educator. Professor of moral philosophy at St. Andrews. Leader of the Free Church of Scotland. Died at age 67 in Edinburgh.

Last Words: "A general good-night."

Source: *Memoirs of the Life and Writings of Thomas Chalmers, D.D., LL.D* by Rev. William Hanna (New York, 1851). The author was married to Chalmers' daughter Anne.

Chamberlain, Arthur Neville

(1869-1940) British statesman. Prime minister. Attacked for failing to proceed aggressively after Britain failed to liberate Norway from Nazis in World War II. Failed to get vote of confidence. Resigned as prime minister in March 1940. Died at age 71 of cancer in November.

Last Words: "Approaching dissolution brings relief."

Source: *Facts About the British Prime Ministers: A Compilation of Biographical and Historical Information* by Dermot Englefield, Janet Seaton and Isobel White (New York, 1995).

Chambers, Robert

(1802-1871) Scottish publisher, writer. Founder of Edinburgh publishing firm W & R Chambers. Specialized in reference works such as *Chambers Encyclopedia, Chambers Cyclopedia of Literature.* Also wrote *Book of Days* (two volumes of calendar-related curiosities and anecdotes). Awarded doctor of laws degree from St. Andrews, Scotland, in 1869. Died at age 68 in St. Andrews.

Last Words: "Quite comfortable. Quite happy—nothing more!"

Source: *Memoir of Robert Chambers: With Autobiographic Reminiscences of William Chambers* by William Chambers (Edinburgh, 1872). The author was Robert's brother and associate in the family's publishing business.

Chamfort, Sébastien Roch Nicolas

(1741-1794) French writer, wit. Notable work: *Maximes,* published posthumously. Took part in storming of Bastille. Killed himself at age 53 in Paris during Reign of Terror when he was about to be arrested by order of the Convention.

Last Words: "Ah! mon ami je m'en vais enfin de ce monde, où il faut que le coeur se brise ou se bronze." (tr. "My friend, I'm finally taking leave of this earth, a place where one's heart must either break or be hard as bronze.") Spoken to Abbe Emmanuel Sieyès.

Source: *Encyclopedia Britannica,* 11th ed. (New York, 1910-1911).

Championnet, Jean Étienne Vachier

(1762-1800) French military officer. General in Napoleon's armies. Captured Naples and formed Parthenopean Republic. Died of plague in Antibes.

Last Words: "My friends, take care to console my mother. Would that I had been able to die like Joubert!" Joubert was a French soldier who served with distinction and was killed in action.

Source: *Championnet, général des armées de la République Française* by A.R.C. de Saint-Albin (Paris, 1861).

Chanel, Gabrielle Bonheur ("Coco")

(1883-1971) French fashion designer. Known as Coco. Founded House of Chanel. Revolutionized industry by creating comfortable, casually elegant clothing for women. Fashion leader for more than five decades, beginning in the 1920s. Died at age 88 in Paris.

Last Words: "You see, this is how you die."

Source: *Chanel* by Axel Madsen (New York, 1999).

Variation: "So this is how they let you die."

Source: *Coco Chanel: Her Life, Her Secrets* by Marcel Haedrich (Boston, 1972).

Channing, William Ellery

(1780-1842) American clergyman. Unitarian. Known as Apostle of Unitarianism. Pastor of Federal Street Church, Boston, for many years. Died at age 62 in Bennington, Vermont.

Different Last Words:

(1) "I have received many messages from the Spirit."

Source: *William Ellery Channing: Minister of Religion* by John White Chadwick (Boston, 1903).

(2) "You need not be anxious concerning tonight. It will be very peaceful and quiet with me."

Sources: "Dr. Channing" in *The Christian Teacher; A Theological and Literary Journal,* Vol. 5 (London, 1843); *William Ellery Channing: A Centennial Memory* by Charles T. Brooks (Boston, 1880).

Chaplin, Sir Charles Spencer ("Charlie")

(1889-1977) British-born actor. Hollywood silent film star. Founded United Artists with Mary Pickford, Douglas Fairbanks Sr. and W.D. Griffith. While vacationing abroad, he was denied reentry to U.S in 1952. Settled in Switzerland with wife Oona O'Neil and their children. Received Honorary Oscar in 1972. Knighted in 1975. Died at age 88 at his home in Switzerland.

Last Words (doubtful): "Why not? After all, it belongs to him." His response to a priest who said: "May the Lord have mercy on your soul."

Source: Various Last Words compilations and Internet websites.

The quote is from *Monsieur Verdoux* (1947), a movie Chaplin made 30 years before he died.

Source: *Monsieur Verdoux* (movie) (Charles Chaplin Productions, 1947).

Chapman, Annie

(1841-1888) English murder victim. Birth name Eliza Ann Smith. Killed by Jack the Ripper.

Last Words: "I haven't enough now, but keep my bed for me, I shan't be long." Remarked as she left her regular pub. She needed eight pence to pay for a bed in her lodging house in Whitechapel, so she went out on the street to earn it.

Source: *City of Dreadful Delight: Narratives of Sexual Danger in Late Victorian London* by Judith R. Waikowitz (Chicago, 1992).

Chapman, Gerald

(1891-1926) American murderer, robber. Killed a police officer in New Britain, Connecticut. Was first to be named Public Enemy No. 1 by the press. Caught, tried and convicted. Executed by hanging at age 36 in Connecticut.

Last Words: "Death itself isn't dreadful, but hanging seems an awkward way of entering the adventure."

Source: *Gentleman Gerald: The Crimes and Times of Gerald Chapman America's First Public Enemy No. 1* by H. Paul Jeffers (New York, 1995).

Chapman, Graham

(1941-1989) English physician, comedian, actor, writer. Founding member of British comedy team Monty Python's Flying Circus. Notable movies: *Monty Python and the Holy Grail; Life of Brian.* Had spinal and throat cancer. Died at age 48 of pneumonia in Maidstone, England.

Last Words: "The events of this last year have renewed my faith in human nature." Spoken to Reverend Tony Porter at the hospital where he died.

Source: "Python Pals Send Chapman a Flower Foot" (*San Jose Mercury News*, October 14, 1989).

Chapman, John Jay

(1862-1933) American writer, essayist,

playwright, lawyer. Switched to writing after ten years of law. Known for his essays. Critic of American public education. Died at age 71 in Poughkeepsie, New York.

Last Words: "No, the mute, the mute. I want to play on the open strings." His response to his wife. He had told her he wanted something taken away. She asked if he meant the pillow.

Source: *The Triple Thinkers: Twelve Essays on Literary Subjects* by Edmund Wilson (New York, 1938).

Chapman, Raymond Johnson ("Ray")

(1891-1920) American athlete. Professional baseball player. Shortstop for Cleveland Indians who was hit by a pitch thrown in a game between Cleveland and New York Yankees. Died in New York City hospital 12 hours later at age 29. To date, he is the only modern major league player to die as a direct result of being hit by a pitch.

Last Words: "Don't call Kate. I don't want her to worry. But if you do, tell her I'm all right." Spoken in the hospital.

Source: "Tragedy and Triumph Ray Chapman's Death in 1920 Slowed But Did Not Stop the Indians' Quest for First Pennant" by Bob Dolgan (The [Cleveland] *Plain Dealer*, August 4, 1995).

Chapman, Robert Hett

(1771-1833) American clergyman. Presbyterian missionary, educator. President of University of North Carolina during War of 1812. Resigned in 1816 after school term was marked with conflict caused by his Federalist views. Organized Presbyterian church in Chapel Hill. Died at age 62 while at home of son-in-law in Winchester.

Last Words: "And now my friends, leave me alone that I may commune with my God and die."

Source: *The Chapman Family: or The Descendants of Robert Chapman, one of the First Settlers of Saybrook, Conn., with Genealogical Notes of William Chapman, Who Settled in New London, Conn.; Edward Chapman, Who Settled at Windsor, Conn.; John Chapman, of Stonington, Conn.; and Rev. Benjamin Chapman, of Southington, Conn.* by Frederick William Chapman (Hartford, CT, 1854).

Charlemagne, Holy Roman Emperor

(742-814) Ruler of the Franks. Son of Pepin III, the Short. Name means Charles the Great. Charles I. King of the Franks. Emperor of the West. Died of pleurisy (or fe-

ver) at age 71 in Aachen (Aix-la-Chapelle; now in Germany). The end of his conquests marked the beginning of the Holy Roman Empire.

Last Words: "Lord, into Thy hands I commend my spirit."

Source: *A History of Charles the Great (Charlemagne)* by J.I. Mombert (London, 1888).

Charles I, Emperor of Austria-Hungary

(1887-1922) Austro-Hungarian ruler. Full name Karl Franz Josef Ludwig Hubert George Maria von Habsburg-Lothringen. Ruled as Charles I, Emperor of Austria and as Charles IV (or Karoly IV), King of Hungary. Last reigning ruler of House of Hapsburg. Nephew of Francis Ferdinand, grandnephew of Emperor Francis Joseph. Forced to abdicate in 1918. Died at age 34 of pneumonia in Madeira, Portugal. Beatified in 2004. Known as Blessed Karl.

Last Words: "I can't go on much longer—Thy will be done.—As you will it, Jesus!" He died holding a crucifix in his hands.

Sources: *A Heart for Europe: The Lives of Emperor Charles and Empress Zita of Austria-Hungary* by James and Joanna Bogle (Leominster, MA, 1990); *Stalking the Holy: The Pursuit of Saint-Making* by Michael W. Higgins (Toronto, ON, 2006).

Charles V, Holy Roman Emperor

(1500-1558) Spanish ruler. Son of Philip I of Spain. Grandson of Ferdinand and Isabella. Ruled Spain as Charles (Carlos) I. Resigned control of Naples, Netherlands, Spain and Indies. Gave crown to his brother Ferdinand. Retired to a monastery. Formally abdicated in 1558. Died soon afterward at age 58.

Last Words: "It is time.—Ay, Jesus."

Source: *Emperor of the West: A Study of Charles the Fifth* by D.B. Wyndham Lewis (London, 1932).

Charles I, King of England, Scotland and Ireland

(1600-1649) English ruler. Son of James VI of Scotland. Grandson of Mary Queen of Scots. Reigned from 1625 to 1649. Lost the throne during English Civil War. Tried and condemned as a tyrant and enemy of the nation. Beheaded at age 48.

Different Last Words:

(1) (doubtful): "Remember." Spoken to William Juxon, Archbishop of Canterbury, while Charles was on the execution block.

(Some versions say "Remember me.") Charles did say "Remember" to the archbishop. But it was not his final statement. He then spoke to his executioner.

Source: *King Charles I, His Execution. King Charles His Speech Made upon the Scaffold at Whitehall-Gate Immediately Before His Execution on Tuesday the 30 of Jan . 1649 with a Relation of the Manner of His Going to Execution. Published by Special Authority* (London, 1649).

(2) "Stay for the sign." When Charles placed his head on the block, the executioner bent down to make sure his hair was not in the way. Charles thought the executioner was preparing to strike. His Last Words were spoken to him. The executioner replied that he would wait for a sign. When Charles stretched out his hands, the executioner instantly severed his head with one blow.

Source: *The Oxford Book of Royal Anecdotes,* ed. by Elizabeth Longford (Oxford, England, 1991).

Charles II, King of England, Scotland and Ireland

(1630-1685) English ruler. Son of Charles I. Known as the Merry Monarch for his pleasant disposition. Patron of theater. Encouraged science. Personally helped extinguish Great Fire of London in 1666. Had no legitimate children but many illegitimate ones, most of whom he acknowledged and ennobled. Had a stroke but lingered several days. Died at age 54.

Different Last Words:

(1) "Open the curtains that I may once more see day." After his doctors bled him, he lost his power of speech and lay almost insensible until he died around noon.

Sources: *History of England,* Vol. 1, by Thomas Babington Macaulay (London, 1849); *Charles II: The Man and the Statesman* by Maurice Ashley (New York, 1971); *Merry Monarch: The Life and Likeness of Charles II* by Hesketh Pearson (New York, 1960).

(2) "Let not poor Nell starve." Nell was actress Eleanor ("Nell") Gwynn, mistress of the king. Other sources give this quote but spell her nickname Nelly or Nellie and her surname Gwyn or Gwynne.

Source: *History of My Own Times* by Gilbert Burnet (London, 1724).

(3) "That clock must be wound tomorrow."

Source: *The Tragedy of Charles II in the Years 1630 to 1660* by Hester W. Chapman (London, 1964).

(4) "You must pardon me, gentlemen, for being a most unconscionable time a-dying."

Source: "Wit of Charles II" (*Literary World: A Journal of Science Literature and Art*, Vol. VIII, January-June 1851). This source states these words were spoken "near his last moments."

Variation: "I have been a most unconscionable time a-dying, but I beg you to excuse it." Spoken to the attendants and notables gathered around his deathbed.

Source: *Bartlett's Book of Anecdotes* by Clifton Fadiman and André Bernard (Boston, 2000).

Charles V, King of France

(1337-1380) French ruler. Son of John II. Known as Charles the Wise for his intelligence and effectiveness as leader. First prince to use the title Dauphin (eldest son of the King of France). Ascended to the throne in 1364. Died at age 43 in Vincennes, France. Succeeded by his 12-year-old son Charles VI.

Last Words: "Withdraw, my friends, withdraw and go away a little, so I can rest from the bother and labor I did not shirk."

Source: *Histoire de Charles V* by R. Delachenal (Paris, 1931).

Charles VI, King of France

(1368-1422) French ruler. Son of Charles V. Member of the Valois dynasty. Crowned king at age 12. Known as Charles the Well Loved, Charles the Mad. Began showing psychotic behavior in his 20s. (Now believed to be schizophrenia.) During his reign, France was invaded by King Henry V of England. Charles died in Paris. Succeeded by his son Charles VII.

Last Words: "Odette! Odette!" He was calling his mistress, Odette de Champdivers.

Source: *Les Mots de la fin* by Claude Aveline (Paris, 1957).

Charles VIII, King of France

(1470-1498) French ruler. Son of Louis XI. Known as Charles the Affable. Assumed the throne in 1483 when he was 13. Died at age 27 in Amboise, France, after he struck his head while passing through a doorway. All four of his children died before him. The throne passed to a cousin who ruled as Louis XII.

Different Last Words:

(1) "I hope never again to commit a mortal sin, nor even a venial one, if I can help it."

Source: *Dictionary of Phrase and Fable* by E. Cobham Brewer (Philadelphia, 1898). Brewer's source was Philippe de Comines (or Comynes), a French chronicler who wrote an extensive memoir of the reign of Charles VIII.

(2) "Mon Dieu et la glorieuse Vièrge Marie, Monseigneur Saint Claude et Monseigneur Saint Blaise me soient en aide!" (tr. "My God and the blessed Virgin Mary, my lord Saint Claude, and my lord Saint Blaise, help me!")

Source: *Anne of Brittany* by Helen Josephine Sanborn (Boston, 1917).

Charles IX, King of France

(1550-1574) French ruler. Son of Henry II and Catherine de Médici. Assumed the throne in 1560 at age 10. In frail health. Let his mother rule. His reign was marked by brutal civil wars and fighting, including the St. Bartholomew's Day massacre (murder of thousands of Protestant Huguenots in and around Paris in 1572). Charles was haunted by the massacre. He lost his desire to rule. Died at age 24 of tuberculosis in Vincennes.

Different Last Words:

(1) "Ah, my nurse, my dearest nurse, what blood and murders! Ah, I have had but wicked counsel! O my God, forgive me all that, and, so it please Thee, have mercy on me!" Spoken to his Huguenot nurse.

Source: *Charles IX: La France et le controle de l'Espagne* by Pierre Champion (Paris, 1939).

Variation: "Nurse, nurse, what murder! What blood! Oh! I have done wrong. God pardon me!" He was referring to the St. Bartholomew Massacre that he did nothing to halt. It lasted 7 days and killed more than 5,000 people in Paris and 50,000 country-wide.

Source: *The Last Words (Real and Traditional) of Distinguished Men and Women Collected from Various Sources* by Frederic Rowland Marvin (New York, 1901). In a footnote, Marvin mentioned *Winslow's Anatomy of Suicide* as his source.

Variation: "Oh, my nurse, my nurse! What blood, what murders, what evil counsels have I followed! Oh, my God, pardon me and have mercy upon me if Thou canst. I know not what I am! What shall I do? I am lost. I see it well."

Source: *Dying Testimonies of Saved and Unsaved: Gathered from Authentic Sources* by Solomon Benjamin Shaw (Chicago, 1898).

(2) "Sleeping or waking, the murdered Huguenots seem ever present to my eyes with ghastly faces and weltering in blood. I wish the innocent and helpless have been spared."

Source: *The Huguenots: Their Settlements, Churches and Industries in England and Ireland* by Samuel Smiles (London, 1867).

(3) "If Jesus my Saviour should number me among His redeemed!" Spoken after he bid farewell to his mother. He repeated these words three times then spoke no more.

Source: *The Massacre of St. Bartholomew* by Henry White (New York, 1868).

Charles X, King of France

(1757-1836) French ruler. Charles Philippe, Count d'Artois. Son of Louis, Dauphin of France. Grandson of Louis XV. Last Bourbon King of France. Became king when his brother died. Ruled from 1824 to 1830, then abdicated during the July Revolution. Died at age 79 of cholera in Gorizia (in present-day Italy) after six years in exile.

Different Last Words:

(1) "I forgive, from my heart, those who have made themselves my enemies, and, more particularly, those who have been led away by the advice of others. I have forgiven them for a long time before God. To my grandson will devolve the happiness and glory of pardoning them before men."

Source: *The Rise and Fall of Louis Philippe, Ex-king of the French: Giving a History of the French Revolution, from Its Commencement, in 1789* by Benjamin Perley Poore (Boston, 1848).

(2) "May God protect you, my children. Walk in the paths of justice. Do not forget me. Pray for me sometimes."

Source: *Les Mots de la fin* by Claude Aveline (Paris, 1957).

Charles II, King of Spain, Naples and Sicily

(1661-1700) Spanish ruler. Son of Philip IV of Spain. Last Hapsburg king of Spain Reigned from 1665 to 1700. Died childless. His death began the War of the Spanish Succession. Caroline Islands named for him.

Last Words (doubtful): "Now I am as one of the dead." Charles spoke these words on October 2, 1700, when he bequeathed his kingdom to Philip of Anjou. He died on November 1st.

Source: *The Popular History of England: An Illustrated*

History of Society and Government from the Earliest Period to Our Own Times, Vol. VI, by Charles Knight (New York, 1880).

Charles III, King of Spain

(1716-1788) Spanish ruler. Son of Philip V. Duke of Parma. King of the Two Sicilies. Ruled Spain from 1759 to 1788. Had a reputation for fairness, philanthropy. Known as an enlightened despot. Died at age 72.

Last Words: "I do not need this extremity to forgive them. They were forgiven the moment of doing me injury." His response when asked if he forgave his enemies.

Source: *The Spanish Bourbons: The History of a Tenacious Dynasty* by John D. Bergamini (New York, 1974).

Charles IX, King of Sweden

(1550-1611) Swedish ruler. Youngest son of Gustavus I, King of Sweden. Brother of John III. Duke of Södermanland. Swedish nationalist. Defender of Protestantism. Died at age 61 in Nyköping.

Last Words: "I am the King of Sweden who seal the religion and liberty of the German nation in my blood."

Source: *War and Policy: Essays* by Spenser Wilkinson (New York, 1900).

Variation: "I am the King of Sweden who *do* seal the religion and liberty of the German nation in my blood."

Source: *Four Princes: Or, The Growth of a Kingdom; a Story of the Christian Church Centered Around Four Types* by James Augustin Brown Scherer (Philadelphia, 1902). Both versions appear with near equal frequency.

Charles XII, King of Sweden

(1682-1718) Swedish ruler. Military genius. Known as "Alexander of the North" and "The Madman of the North." Assumed the throne when he was 15. Killed at age 36 by a cannon shot at the siege of Fredrikshald in Danish-controlled Norway. The Swedish Empire collapsed with his death.

Last Words: "Don't be afraid."

Source: *Charles XII and the Collapse of the Swedish Empire, 1682-1719* by Robert Nisbet Bain (New York, 1895).

Charles, Thomas

(1755-1814) Welsh clergyman. Compiled four-volume Biblical dictionary in Welsh. Organized Welsh Calvinistic Methodists. Established system of circulating Sunday Schools. Died at age 59 in Bala, Wales. Statue of him stands outside the Methodist chapel in Bala.

Last Words: "Yes, if the Lord pleases." His response when he was offered some wine, hoping it might help him.

Source: *Thomas Charles' Spiritual Counsels* by Rev. Edward Morgan (London, 1831).

Charlotte Augusta, Princess of Wales

(1796-1817) British royalty. Only child of George IV and Caroline of Brunswick. Married Leopold of Saxe-Coburg. Died at age of 21 at Claremont House, London, after 50 hours of labor. Cause of death: possibly postpartum hemorrhage. Her child was stillborn.

Different Last Words:

(1) "You make me drunk. Pray leave me quiet. I feel it affects my head."

Source: *Wordsworth Dictionary of Phrase and Fable* by E. Cobham Brewer (Hertfordshire, England, 2006).

Variation: "They have made me tipsy." Spoken after she was given hot wine and brandy by her doctor. When he left the room, he heard her call: "Stocky. Stocky." He ran back to her room and she was dead. "Stocky" was her German physician Christian Friedrich Stockmar.

Source: *Daughter of England* by Dorothy M. Stuart (London, 1952).

(2) "Is there any danger?" Spoken to her medical attendants. They replied that they required her to compose herself. She breathed a gentle sigh then died.

Source: "Death of the Princess Charlotte and Her Infant Son" (*Blackwood's Magazine,* Vol. II, October 1817-March 1818).

Charlotte Sophia, Queen of Great Britain

(1744-1818) British royalty. Niece of Duke of Mecklenburg-Strelitz. Married George III in 1761. Mother of 15 children. Grandmother of Queen Victoria. Interested in botany. Helped establish what is today Kew Gardens. Died at age 74 sitting in an armchair, holding the hand of her eldest son (George IV) at the family retreat in Surrey (now Kew Palace). Charlotte County and Charlottesville, Virginia; Charlotte, North Carolina, are among several places in North America named for her.

Last Words: "Very true." Spoken after she

heard the comment: "This is a life of toil and trouble; but there is another life beyond it, in which none shall know trouble."

Source: *Memoir of Her Majesty Sophia Charlotte of Mecklenburg-Strelitz, Queen of Great Britain* by William Marshall Craig (Liverpool, England, 1818).

Charmion

(d. 30 B.C.) Servant of Cleopatra. Committed suicide with her mistress. She was portrayed in movies about Cleopatra in 1917, 1934, 1953 and 1963. Shakespeare based Charmion's last words in *Antony and Cleopatra* on Plutarch's account.

Last Words: "Extremely well, and as became the descendant of so many kings." Spoken as she adjusted Cleopatra's crown. A messenger had asked: "Was this well done of your lady, Charmion?" She then fell dead by the bedside.

Source: "Antony" in *Lives of the Noble Grecians and Romans* by Plutarch, tr. by John Dryden (Chicago, 1952).

Chase, Salmon Portland

(1808-1873) American statesman, jurist, lawyer, politician, abolitionist. Defended many fugitive slaves. Unsuccessfully sought presidency of U.S. Member U.S. Senate from Ohio. Governor of Ohio. While secretary of the U.S. treasury, he was responsible for having "In God We Trust" placed on U.S. money. He introduced the modern system of banknotes. Chief justice of the U.S. Died at age 65 in New York City while in office. His face appeared on the $10,000 bills printed between 1928 and 1946.

Different Last Words:

(1) "Goodnight." Spoken to friends who were present. He retired around 10 p.m. and died the next morning following a paralytic stroke.

Source: *An Account of the Private Life and Public Services of Salmon Portland Chase* by Robert Bruce Warden (Cincinnati, OH. 1874). Warden could give no satisfactory account of Chase's last hours. There was little warning that death was imminent. He had to depend on borrowed information that left something to be desired.

(2) "Fire!" Spoken to a servant at his daughter's house while pointing to the fireplace. Shortly afterward he went into convulsions and died three hours later.

Source: *The Washington Evening Star*, May 8, 1873.

Chastelard, Pierre de Boscosel de

(1540-1563) French poet, musician. Pursued Mary Queen of Scots. Executed by beheading for twice hiding in her bed-chamber. She forgave him after the first time, but not after the second. Died at age 23 in St. Andrews, Scotland.

Last Words: "Adieu, toi si belle et si cruelle, qui me tues et que je ne puis cesser d'aimer!" (tr. "Goodbye you who are so beautiful and so cruel who would kill me but I would never cease loving.") Spoken as he was about to be executed. His Last Words were from "Hymn of Death" by the French poet Pierre Ronsard.

Source: *Nouvelle Biographie Générale depuis les temps les plus reculés jusqu'à nos jours, avec les renseignements bibliographiques et l'Indication des sources à consulter* by Jean Chrétien Ferdinand Hoefer (Paris, 1854).

Chateaubriand, Vicomte François August René de

(1768-1848) French nobleman, writer, traveler, statesman. Famed for antirevolutionary views, mysticism, poetical prose style. Opposed Napoleon. Lived in England. Traveled in North America. Wrote three novels dealing with North America and North American Indians: *Atala; René; and Les Natchez.* Also wrote *Voyage in Amerique,* a very descriptive account of his travels in America. Died at age 79 in Paris during the 1848 revolution. Chateaubriand sauce was named for him.

Last Words: "I want to go there." His response on hearing about fighting in Paris.

Source: *Chateaubriand* by André Maurois, tr. by V. Fraser (New York, 1938).

Chavez, Georges

(1887-1910) French-born Peruvian pilot. Aviation pioneer. Birth name Jorge Chavez Dartnell. Killed in a plane crash near Domodossoia after he became the first pilot to fly across the Alps from Switzerland to Italy. Died at age 23, a few days after the crash of his Bleriot monoplane.

Last Words: "Arriba. Siempre arriba." (tr. "Higher. Always higher.") The phrase was later adopted as the motto of the Peruvian Air Force.

Source: *First Aviators* by Curtis Prendergast (Alexandria, VA, 1980).

Chayefsky, Sidney Aaron ("Paddy")

(1923-1981) American writer, playwright. Worked as screenwriter in early years of live television and later in movies. Academy-Award winning works: *Marty; The Hospital; Network.* Tony award-nominated works: *Middle of the Night; The Tenth Man; Gideon.* Also wrote the novel *Altered States.* Occasionally appeared as lyricist *(Marty)* or in cameo acting/voice parts *(Marty; The Hospital).* Died at age 58 in New York City.
Last Words (written): "I tried. I really tried." Note to his wife Susan, written on a pad of paper.
Source: "Sidney Aaron Chayefsky" in *The Scribner Encyclopedia of American Lives, Volume 1: 1981-1985* (New York, 1998).

Chekhov, Anton Pavlovich

(1860-1904) Russian playwright, short-story writer. His writing influenced authors in Europe and America. Notable works: *The Seagull; The Cherry Orchard; Uncle Vanya; The Three Sisters.* Had pulmonary tuberculosis. As his health deteriorated, he sought help at a health resort in Badenweiler, Germany. Died there at age 44.
Last Words: "I haven't drunk champagne for a long time." He told his physician he was dying. Then he spoke these words as he accepted a glass of champagne that was offered to him. He died a short time later.
Source: *Life of Chekhov* by Irene Nemirovsky (London, 1950).

Chénier, André Marie de

(1762-1794) French poet, politician, activist, journalist. Protested against excesses of the Reign of Terror during the French Revolution. Guillotined at age 32 in Paris. Most of his poetry was published posthumously. His life inspired the opera *Andrea Chénier* by Giordano.
Different Last Words:
(1) "Yes. Since I find a friend so true; My fortune has an aspect new." Spoken when he saw Jean-Antoine Roucher, another French poet, in the cart with him as he approached the guillotine.
Source: *Vie intime d'André Chénier* by Jeanne Galzy (Paris, 1947).

(2) (doubtful): "And yet, I did have something here." Spoken with his hand on his heart, just before being guillotined. The quote came from the Alexandre Dumas novel *The First Republic* (1894), written a century after Chenier died. In the novel, Chénier put his hand to his head and spoke the words, only to be corrected by a friend who said "No, it was there!" while touching his heart.
Source: *André Chénier* by Francis Scarfe (Oxford, England, 1965).

Chenoweth (Welawa)

(d. 1856) Native American leader. Cascades chief. One of nine Native American warriors found guilty of taking part in the Yakima Uprising (Cascades Massacre). Each man was placed on a barrel with a rope around his neck. As the barrel was kicked from under him, his neck broke. When the barrel was kicked from under Chenoweth he did not die immediately. A soldier shot him to prevent a lingering death by strangulation.
Last Words: "I am not afraid to die." He gave a war whoop and shouted these words as he was dying.
Source: "Yakima Uprising" by Richard G. Killbane (*True West,* November 1998).

Cherokee Bill, see Goldsby, Crawford.

Chesterfield, 4th Earl of, Philip Dormer Stanhope

(1694-1773) British statesman, writer, diplomat. Lord lieutenant of Ireland. His *Letters to His Son* became a classic. Published by his widow in 1774, they described the ideal 18th-century gentleman. Chesterfield was deaf and blind during his final year. Died at age 78 at his home in London. Counties and towns in Virginia and South Carolina were named for him.
Last Words: "Give Dayrolles a chair." Spoken when his valet ushered Solomon Dayrolles, a life-long friend, into his sickroom.
Source: *Life of Lord Chesterfield; an Account of the Ancestry, Personal Character & Public Services of the Fourth Earl of Chesterfield* by W.H. Craig (London, 1907).

Chesterton, Gilbert Keith ("G.K.")

(1874-1936) English journalist, writer, artist. Author of priest-detective Father Brown

mystery books. Friend and collaborator of Hilaire Belloc (illustrated his books). Convert and advocate of Roman Catholicism. Had weekly radio program on BBC during his final years. Died at age 62 at Beaconsfield, Buckinghamshire, England.
Different Last Words:
(1) "The issue is now clear. It is between light and darkness and everyone must choose his side."
Source: *Gilbert Keith Chesterton* by Maisie Ward (New York, 1944).
(2) "Hello, my darling! Hello, my dear!" Spoken in his sickroom to his wife Frances and friend Dorothy Collins when he recognized them.
Source: *Wisdom and Innocence: A Life of G.K. Chesterton* by Joseph Pearce (San Francisco, CA, 2004).

Cheung, Leslie

(1956-2003) Hong Kong-born actor, musician. Birth name Leslie Cheung Kwok-Wing. One of the creators of Cantopop. Named Asian Biggest Superstar by China Central Television in 2000 and Most Favorite Actor in 100 Years of Chinese Cinema in 2005. Notable songs: "Who Can Be with Me"; "Monica." His movie *Farewell My Concubine* was the first Chinese film to win the Golden Palm Award at Cannes Film Festival. It also won a Golden Globe for Best Foreign Film and Oscar nominations for Best Foreign Film and Best Cinematography. Cheung was named one of 10 Chinese Cultural Idols of the 20th Century. He suffered from depression. Committed suicide at age 46 in Hong Kong.
Last Words (written): "Depression! Many thanks to all my friends. Many thanks to Professor Felice Lieh-Mak This year has been so tough. I can't stand it anymore. Many thanks to Mr. Tong. Many thanks to my family. Many thanks to Fei-Fei (Lydia Shum Din-ha). In my life I did nothing bad. Why does it have to be like this?" Professor Felice Lieh-Mak was Cheung's last psychiatrist. Suicide note.
Source: *Time of Leslie Cheung* by Chitose Shima (Tokyo, 2004).

Chevalier, Maurice

(1888-1972) French actor, singer, entertainer. Star of stage and screen. Popular in U.S. and Europe. Nominated for Academy Award in 1930. Awarded honorary Academy Award 1959 for contributions to the world of entertainment for more than a half century. Nominated for two Golden Globes 1958, 1959. Died at age 83 in Paris.
Last Words: "Y'a d'la joie." (tr. "There's fun in the air.") Spoken just before he slipped into a coma.
Source: *Fade to Black: A Book of Movie Obituaries* by Paul Donnelley (New York, 2003).

Chickering, Hannah Balch

(1817-1879) American prison reformer. One of the founders of Dedham Temporary Asylum for Discharged Female Prisoners in Massachusetts in 1864.
Last Words: "Say only that I was at peace. More than this, if repeated, might indicate a deeper spiritual experience than I ever had."
Source: *Recollections of Hannah B. Chickering* by Sarah E. Dexter (Cambridge, MA, 1881).

Childers, Robert Erskine

(1870-1922) Irish writer, nationalist. Notable work: *The Riddle of the Sands* (novel). Arrested by Irish Free State forces and court-martialed for possessing an automatic pistol. One of the first to be sentenced to death under the Free State's Emergency Powers legislation. Executed at age 52 by firing squad in Dublin.
Last Words: "Take a step forward, lads. It will be easier that way."
Source: *The Riddle of Erskine Childers* by Andrew Boyle (London, 1977).

Chin, Vincent Jen

(1955-1982) Asian-American murder victim. Killed by two laid-off white autoworkers who were motivated by racial hatred toward Asians, whom they blamed for the decline in Detroit's auto industry. Ironically, their racial hatred was directed toward Japan, however, Chin was Chinese-American. His murder became a rallying point for Asian-Americans and a key point in the beginning of a pan-ethnic Asian-American movement.
Last Words: "It's not fair."
Source: "A Slaying in 1982 Maintains Its Grip on Asian-Americans" by Lynette Clemetson (*New York Times*, June 18, 2002).

Choate, Joseph Hodges

(1832-1917) American lawyer, diplomat. Headed U.S. delegation at International Peace Conference at The Hague. U.S. ambassador to Great Britain. Second cousin of Rufus Choate. Died at age 85 in New York City.

Last Words: "I am feeling very ill. I think this is the end."

Source: *The Life of Joseph Hodges Choate* by Edward Sanford Martin (New York, 1920).

Choate, Rufus

(1799-1859) American lawyer, politician. Member U.S. House of Representatives, U.S. Senate from Massachusetts. Died at age 59 in Halifax, Nova Scotia, en route to Europe.

Last Words: "I don't feel well. I feel faint."

Source: *Rufus Choate: The Wizard of the Law* by Claude M. Fuess (New York, 1928).

Chou En-lai, see Zhou Enlai.

Chopin, Frèdèric François

(1810-1849) Polish-born musician, composer, pianist. Moved to Paris in 1831. Composed mostly for piano. Notable works: mazurkas, polonaises, etudes, preludes, nocturnes, ballades, scherzos, sonatas, concertos. Intimate friend of Madame George Sand from 1836 to 1847, then became estranged. Revolution of 1848 ended his patronage when the Orleanist monarchy ended. Died at age 39 of tuberculosis.

Different Last Words:

(1) "Plus" (tr. "No more"). His response to his physician who asked if he was in pain.

Source: *The Life and Death of Chopin* by Casimir Wierzynski, tr. by Norbert Guterman (London, 1951).

(2) "Now I am at the source of Blessedness!" Spoken as he pressed a crucifix to his heart.

Source: *Chopin: The Man and His Music* by James Huneker (New York, 1900).

(3) "The Earth is suffocating.—Swear to make them cut me open, so that I won't be buried alive."

Source: *The Corpse: A History* by Christine Quigley (Jefferson, NC, 2005).

(4) "Who is near me?" He was told it was Gutman, his favorite pupil.

Sources: *Life of Chopin* by Franz Liszt, tr. by Martha Walker Cook (1866); *Frederic Chopin* by Maurycy

Karasowski, tr. by Emily Hill (London, 1879); *Great Composers Through the Eyes of Their Contemporaries* by Otto Zoff (New York, 1951).

Christian III, King of Denmark and Norway

(1503-1559) Danish and Norwegian monarch. Son of Frederick I. Known as Father of the People. Allied with Protestant Germans against Hapsburgs. Died at age 55 in Kolding, Denmark.

Last Words: "Now I will sing, and you must sing with me, that it may be said that the king sang himself to the grave."

Source: *One Thousand Sayings of History* by Walter Fogg (New York 1929).

Christian IV, King of Denmark and Norway

(1577-1648) Danish and Norwegian monarch. His reign was a time of economic and cultural growth for his kingdom. He decreed that Oslo should be rebuilt after the 1624 fire destroyed the city. Other major public buildings were constructed during his reign. Died at age 70 at Rosenborg Castle in Copenhagen.

Last Words: "Now comes the fight." Spoken while holding the hand of his pastor.

Source: *Christian IV, King of Denmark and Norway* by John Allyne Gade (London, 1928).

Christian IX, King of Denmark

(1818-1906) Danish ruler. Son of Fredrich Wilhelm, Duke of Schleswig-Holstein-Sanderburg-Glucksburg. Father of Princess Alexandra of Denmark who married Edward VII of Britain. Ruled from 1863 to 1906. Grandsons included four monarchs: Nicholas II of Russia; Constantine of Greece; George V of Great Britain; Christian X of Denmark. Died at age 87.

Last Words: "I think I can sleep a little."

Source: *Christian IX* by Hans Roger Madol (London, 1936).

Christian X, King of Denmark

(1870-1947) Danish monarch. Son of King Frederick VIII and Louise of Sweden and Norway. Became king of Denmark when he was 42. Last king of Iceland; reigned 1918 to 1944. Known for fairness and kindness to his subjects. Ruled during World War II, when Danish people saved lives of 7,500

Danish Jews by refusing to let them be captured by the Nazis. Died at age 76 after a heart attack in Copenhagen.

Last Words: "My task on this earth is over. I am at peace with my God and myself. I am so tired."

Source: "King Christian Dies in Denmark at 76. Hero to His People for Stand as Ruler Toward Germans—Frederik IX Succeeds Him" (*New York Times,* April 21, 1947).

Christian, Fletcher

(1764-1793) English sailor, mutineer. Master's mate on HMS *Bounty* who seized command of ship from Captain William Bligh in 1789. Christian married Maimiti, daughter of a local Tahitian chief, and settled on Pitcairn Island. In 1808, An American seal-hunting boat visited Pitcairn and found John Adams was the sole survivor of the mutineers. Adams and Maimiti claimed Christian had been murdered in 1793 during a conflict between Tahitian men and the mutineers. In 1817, a Pitcairnian woman named Jenny, who left the island, said Christian was shot while working by a pond next to the home of his pregnant wife. Christian has been portrayed in movies by Errol Flynn, Clark Gable, Marlon Brando and Mel Gibson.

Last Words: "God forgive me! I have been a great sinner. Pray for me, Adams. I feel so very cold —I shiver, and I can hardly see the large tree, which I know is not a fathom from me. Good-night, Adams—good-night! Ha!—it was another shot, and some one else is—." Christian died after speaking these words to Adams.

Source: *Jack Adams, the Mutineer* by Frederick Chamier (New York, 1853).

Christina, Queen of Sweden

(1626-1689) Swedish monarch. Daughter of Gustavus Adolphus. Full name Maria Christina Alexandra. Abdicated then tried twice to regain throne. Died in Rome. Buried in St. Peter's Basilica. *Queen Christina,* a Hollywood version of her life, starring Greta Garbo, appeared in 1933.

Last Words (written): "Christina lived LXIII years." Her Last Words were the simple inscription she requested for her grave.

Source: *Memoirs of Christina, Queen of Sweden* by

Henry Woodhead (London, 1863).

Christman or Chrismond, John A.

(1840?-1864) American military soldier. Private in Union Army in U.S. Civil War. Served in Company A, 12th Regiment, West Virginia Volunteers. Killed at New Market, Virginia. His Last Words are ironic. He had commented jokingly, moments before being shot, about being killed that day.

Last Words: "Hickory, I hope I will be killed today." When told he shouldn't talk that way, he replied: "Well, I don't care."

Sources: *History of the Twelfth West Virginia Volunteer Infantry: The Part It Took in the War of the Rebellion 1861-1865* by William Hewitt (Steubenville, OH, 1892); *The Battle of New Market* by William C. Davis (New York, 1975).

Christodule or Christodoulos, Saint

(1025?-1093) Christian monk, holy man. Born in Nicaea, Bithynia. Started construction on the monastery of Saint-Jean-le-Théologian at Patmos in 1088. Had to stop construction in 1091 and go into exile to avoid attacks from the Seljuk Turks who were attacking the region. Sought refuge on island of Euripos (Euboea), where he died. His body was later taken to Patmos.

Last Words: "My children, do not be ungrateful toward the desert isle of Patmos, where we have labored so hard." His Last Words were about where he wanted to be buried.

Source: *Saint Christodule et la réforme des Convents grecs au Xie siècle* by Édouard Le Barbier (Paris, 1863).

Christophe, Henry, King of Haiti

(1767-1820) Haitian monarch, military leader. Leader in Haitian Revolution. Established kingdom in North Haiti. Declared himself King Henry I of Haiti. Created many architectural marvels, including the Citadelle at La Ferriére, but he was an unpopular tyrannical and autocratic ruler. Faced with a coup, he shot and killed himself with a silver bullet at age 53 in Haiti.

Last Words: "Since the people of Haiti no longer have faith in me, I know what to do."

Source: *Christophe, King of Haiti* by Hubert Cole (New York, 1967).

Chrysippus

(280?-206? B.C.) Greek philosopher. Leader

of Stoics. Born in Cilicia. Went to Athens 260 B.C. where he became a disciple of Cleanthes.

Last Words: "Now give the ass a drink of pure wine to wash down the figs." Spoken after a donkey had eaten his figs. He died soon afterward, apparently from a heart attack.

Source: *Lives and Opinions of the Eminent Philosophers,* Book VII, by Diogenes Laertius, tr. by C.D. Yonge (London, 1896).

Chrysogonus, Saint

(d. c. 304) Christian holy man. Teacher of Anastasia, daughter of a Roman nobleman. Imprisoned during the persecutions of Diocletian. Beheaded. His body was thrown into the sea. It was washed ashore and buried.

Last Words: "I adore the one God in heaven, and I spurn thy proffered dignities as clay!" Spoken to Diocletian.

Source: *The Golden Legend or Lives of the Saints.* Compiled by Jacobus de Voragine, Archbishop of Genoa, 1275, 1st ed., 1470. English ed. by William Caxton, 1483, ed. by F.S. Ellis (Edinburgh, 1900).

Chrysostom, Saint John

(347-407) Syrian-Greek prelate, holy man. Patriarch of Constantinople. Important for his preaching as well as his opposition to abuse by ecclesiastical and political leaders. Orthodox Church and Eastern Catholic Churches honor him as a saint and count him among the Three Holy Hierarchs. He is also recognized by the Roman Catholic Church as a saint and a Doctor of the Church. Other churches of the Western tradition, including the Anglican Communion and some Lutheran churches, commemorate him as well. Died in Comana on his way to his place of exile. His relic was looted in the 1200s and returned by Pope John Paul II in 2007.

Last Words: "Glory be to God for all things."

Source: *Dialogue cum Theodoro, Ecclesioe Romanoe Diacono, de vit et conversatione b. Joh. Chrysostomi* by Plaudius (written c. 408), ed. Bigot (Paris, 1680).

Chuang-Tzu or Zhuang-Tze

(369?-286? B.C.) Chinese philosopher, teacher, writer. Taoist. Exponent of doctrines of Lao-Tzu. Little is known about his life.

Last Words: "Above ground, I shall be food for kites; below I shall be food for mole-crickets and ants. Why rob one to feed the other?" His Last Words were to calm the fears of his followers who worried that the carrion kite—a species of hawk—would eat the body of their Master.

Source: *Musings of a Chinese Mystic,* ed. by Lionel Giles (London, 1906).

Chubbuck, Christine

(1944-1974) American television news reporter. Committed suicide by shooting herself in the head during a live telecast. Died 14 hours later at age 29 in a Sarasota, Florida, hospital.

Last Words: "In keeping with Channel 40's policy of bringing you the latest in blood and guts, and in living color, we bring you another first, an attempted suicide." Statement she read to viewers just before shooting herself.

Source: "Christine Chubbuck: 29, Good-Looking, Educated. A Television Personality. Dead. Live and in Color" by Sally Quinn (*Washington Post,* August 4, 1974).

Chudleigh or Pierrepont, Elizabeth, Duchess of Kingston-upon-Hull

(1720-1788) English noblewoman, adventuress. Countess of Bristol. Known for her beauty and wild, undisciplined lifestyle. Maid of honor to Princess of Wales. Married a commoner then married the Duke of Kingston-upon-Hull. Found guilty of bigamy by the House of Lords. Died at age 68 in Paris.

Last Words: "I will lie down on the couch; I can sleep, and after that I shall be entirely recovered." Spoken to her attendants after drinking a second glass of Madeira and walking around her room.

Source: *Anecdotes of the Aristocracy, and Episodes in Ancestral Story* by Sir Bernard Burke (London, 1849).

Church, Frank Forrester

(1924-1984) American politician. Member U.S. Senate from Idaho. Died at age 59 of cancer in Bethesda, Maryland.

Last Words: "John, it is very, very interesting." Spoken to a relative who asked him how he was doing spiritually.

Source: *Father and Son: A Personal Biography of Senator Frank Church of Idaho* by F. Forrester Church (New York, 1985). F. Forrester Church, his son, was minister of All Souls Unitarian Church in New York City when the book was published.

Churchill, Charles

(1731-1764) English clergyman, poet, satirist. Ordained Anglican priest who left his church. Notable works: *Roscaid; Apology; The Ghost; The Candidate*. Ally of John Wilkes, English political reformer who accused King George III of lying then was prosecuted for libel and expelled from the House of Commons. Churchill died at age 33 of typhoid fever en route to meet John Wilkes in exile in France.

Different Last Words:

(1) "What a fool I have been!"

Source: *Poetical Works of Charles Churchill,* ed. by Rev. George Gilfillan (Edinburgh, 1855).

(2) "Thank God! I die in England." Spoken a few minutes after he landed at Dover.

Source: "Notes and Queries" (*Oxford Journals,* Vol. 6 May 22, 1842).

Churchill, Jennie Jerome

(1854-1921) American-born English wife of Randolph Churchill. Mother of British prime minister Winston S. Churchill. Broke her ankle in 1921. Gangrene set in and her leg was amputated. When an artery burst, she went into a coma and died soon afterward at age 67. Her life was the subject of *Jennie,* television miniseries. She was also portrayed in the film *Young Winston*.

Last Words: "Nurse! Nurse! I'm pouring blood." Spoken to a nurse when her leg began to hemorrhage.

Source: *Jennie: The Life of Lady Randolph Churchill* by Ralph G. Martin (Englewood Cliffs, NJ, 1971).

Churchill, John, 1st Duke of Marlborough

(1650-1722) British military officer. Commander. Led British and allied armies to major victories over Louis XIV of France at Blenheim, Ramillies, Oudenarde. Dismissed in 1711 in a misunderstanding over his use of public money. Called back in 1715 to organize defense of the kingdom against the Jacobites. Died at age 72.

Different Last Words:

(1) "Yes." His response when asked if he would like to go to bed.

Source: *Marlborough: His Life and Times* by Winston S. Churchill (London, 1938).

(2) "Yes, and I joined in them." His re-

sponse when asked by the Duchess if he heard the prayers as usual on the night of June 15th. He died the next day.

Source: "Marlborough's Dispatches" (*Blackwood's Edinburgh Magazine,* Vol. 60, July-December 1846).

Churchill, Randolph Frederick Edward Spencer

(1911-1968) British politician, military officer, writer, journalist. Only son of Winston Churchill. Died of a heart attack at age 57. Had completed two volumes of his father's biography. He was mentioned in the H.G. Wells novel *The Shape of Things to Come,* published in 1934. He was one of those who predicted World War II.

Last Words: "No, I don't think I do. But I believe that when you die all the goodness in you comes together as a force." His response when asked if he believed in God.

Source: *Randolph, A Study of Churchill's Son* by Brian Roberts (London, 1984).

Churchill, Sir Winston Leonard Spencer

(1874-1965) British statesman, soldier, politician, writer. Became prime minister in 1940 after Chamberlain left office. Resigned in 1945 at end of World War II. Held post again 1951-1955. Notable works: *The Second World War* (6 vol.); *The World Crisis* (4 vol.); *Marlborough, His Life and Times* (6 vol.); *While England Slept.* Won Nobel Prize for Literature in 1953. Died at age 90 in London.

Last Words: "I'm bored with it all." Spoken just before he slipped into a coma.

Sources: *Simpson's Contemporary Quotations: The Most Notable Quotations: 1950-1988,* compiled by James B. Simpson (Boston, 1988); *The Facts of Death* by Tony McCarthy (Cork, Ireland, 2006).

Chyträus, David

(1531-1600) German theologian, historian, reformer. Lutheran. Birth name David Kochhaff. Notable books: *On Sacrifice; Baptism and the Lord's Supper.*

Last Words: "I have concluded the history of this century and put the finishing touches to it, and not another word will I write."

Source: *David Chyträus als Historiker* by Peter Paulsen (Rostock, Germany, 1897).

Variation: "Mehr schreibe ich nicht." (tr. "I write no more.")

Source: *Lexikon der letzten Worte: letzte Botschaften*

berühmter Männer und Frauen von Konrad Adenauer bis Emiliano Zapata by Werner Fuld (Munich, Germany, 2002)

Cicero, Marcus Tullius

(106-43 B.C.) Roman lawyer, statesman, orator, writer, politician. Famed as a brilliant lawyer and orator. Notable treatises: *On the Orator; On the State; On Laws.* Became an enemy of Caesar's adopted son Octavian. Killed in his villa by supporters of Octavian. Many of Cicero's letters and speeches survived.

Last Words: "Here, veteran! If you think it is right, strike." Spoken to the soldier who killed him.

Source: *Life of Marcus Tullius Cicero* by William Forsyth (London, 1950).

Cilley, Jonathan

(1802-1838) American politician. Member U.S. House of Representatives from Maine. Served in Maine legislature. His brother Joseph Cilley served as U.S. senator from New Hampshire. His son, Jonathan Prince Cilley, was a brevetted brigadier general in the Union Army. Cilley was killed in a duel with Kentucky Congressman William J. Graves after serving part of one term in Congress. Cilley had claimed a Virginian was responsible for a newspaper article that charged another congressman with immorality. Nathaniel Hawthorne, a personal friend, published two biographical sketches about Cilley.

Last Words: "I am shot."

Sources: "Report of the Committee on the Late Duel" by U.S. Congress House. Committee appointed to investigate the causes which led to the death of the Hon. Jonathan Cilley (Washington, D.C., 1838); "Dying Words of Distinguished Persons" in *The Encyclopedia of Death and Life in the Spirit-World,* Vol. I, by J.R. Francis (Chicago, 1895); *Nathaniel Hawthorne, the American Years* by Robert Cantwell (New York, 1948).

Clanton, Joseph Isaac ("Ike")

(1847-1887) American cattleman, rancher, outlaw. Some sources erroneously report that Ike Clanton was shot and killed by the Earp brothers at the OK Corral gunfight in Tombstone, Arizona, in 1881. He died in northern Arizona six years after the OK Corral fight. He was cornered and killed by a cattlemen's association agent as he resisted arrest on a charge of cattle rustling.

Last Words (doubtful): "God, God, won't somebody give me some more cartridges for a last shot." Clanton kept repeating these words as he lay dying. Wyatt Earp was standing over him as he tried to lift his gun to shoot.

Source: Various Last Words compilations and Internet websites.

Ike Clanton was alone on horseback when he was shot and killed. His Last Words are unknown.

Source: "Detailed Statements of the Killing of Ike Clanton, By Detective Brighton, and the Breaking Up of a Well Known Gang of Desperadoes" (*Apache County* [Arizona] *Critic*, June 18, 1887).

Clanton, William Harrison ("Billy")

(1862-1881) American outlaw. The only Clanton to die in the O.K. Corral gunfight in Tombstone, Arizona. He shot Virgil Earp in the leg then fell dead on the ground, a victim of the Earps and Doc Holliday.

Last Words: "Get a doctor and put me to sleep—Pull off my boots. I always told my mother I'd never die with my boots on. [Later] They murdered me! Clear the crowd away from the door and give me air. I've been murdered—[Later] Drive the crowd away."

Source: *Encyclopedia of Western Gunfighters* by Bill O'Neal (Norman OK, 1979).

Clare, John

(1793-1864) English poet. Known as the Northamptonshire Ploughboy Poet or Northamptonshire Peasant Poet. His poems were especially concerned with nature. Suffered from melancholy. In 1837 he was declared insane and confined to a mental institution. While there, he wrote more than 500 poems. Died of a stroke at age 70 at Northampton General Lunatic Asylum.

Last Words: "I have lived too long.—I want to go home."

Source: *Life and Remains of John Clare, the Northamptonshire Peasant Poet,* ed. by J.L. Cherry (London, 1873).

Clare of Assisi, Saint

(1193-1253) Italian nun, holy woman. Cofounder of Poor Clares religious order. Influenced by Francis of Assisi. Served as abbess from 1215 until her death in 1253. In frail health during the last 30 years of her life. Died at the monastery of San Damiano, near Assisi. Canonized in 1255.

Last Words: "Go peacefully, because you will have good guidance on the way. Go because He who created you and blessed you always watching over you as a mother watches over her child, has also loved you tenderly." Her Last Words were recorded by one of the sisters.

Source: *The Life of St. Clare Virgin* by Fra Tommaso da Celano, tr. by Catherine Bolton Magrini (Assisi, Italy, 2004).

Clark, George Rogers

(1752-1818) American military officer. General in the American Revolution. Brother of William Clark (of Lewis and Clark). As leader of Kentucky militia, he was the highest-ranking American military officer on the northwestern frontier during the war. Captured Kaskaskia and Vincennes. Known as Conqueror of the Northwest. Died at age 66 in Louisville, Kentucky.

Last Words (doubtful): "Everybody can die but me."

Although he said this not long before he died, there is no known indication that these were his Last Words. He made this remark when he learned of a friend's death.

Sources: *Background to Glory: The Life of George Rogers Clark* by John Edwin Bakeless (Philadelphia, 1957); "Clark, George Rogers" in *The McGraw-Hill Encyclopedia of World Biography* (New York, 1973); "Clark, George Rogers" in *Encyclopedia of World Biography* by Paula K. Byers (Detroit, MI, 1998).

Clarke, Adam

(1762-1832) Irish-born English clergyman, theologian. Bible commentator. Methodist. Notable work: *Commentary on the Bible* (8 vol.) Active in Wesleyan Missionary Society. Victim of 1832 cholera epidemic. Died at age 70 in London.

Last Words: "I do! I do!" His response when told he must put his soul into the hands of his God and his trust in the merits of his Saviour.

Source: *The Life of the Rev. Adam Clarke* by John Wesley Etheridge (New York, 1859).

Claude, Jean

(1619-1687) French clergyman, theologian. One of the Protestant leaders driven out of France by King Louis XI. He had been involved in a controversy over maintaining the Edict of Nantes and was expelled when it was revoked.

Last Words: "I am so oppressed that I can attend only to two of the great truths of religion—the mercy of God, and the gracious aids of the Holy Spirit.—My whole resource is to the mercy of God. I expect a better life than this; Our Lord Jesus Christ is my only righteousness."

Source: *The English Presbyterian Messenger*, Vol. 1, May 1845-December 1847.

Variation: "Son, our Lord Jesus Christ is my only righteousness; I need no other; he is all-sufficient."

Source: *Miscellaneous Works of Robert Robinson: to Which Are Prefixed Brief Memoirs of His Life and Writing,* Vol. I, by Robert Robinson (Harlow, England, 1807).

Claudius, Matthias

(1740-1815) German poet, lyricist, novelist. Pen name Asmus. Wrote in low-German dialect. Some of his poems have become folk songs. Died at age 74 in Hamburg.

Last Words: "Lead me not into temptation and deliver me from evil. Good night!"

Source: *Matthias Claudius* by Urban Roedl (Berlin, Germany, 1934).

Variation: "Nun ist's aus! Gute Nacht, gute Nacht." (tr. "Now it's out! Good night, good night.") Whispered as he looked at his wife.

Source: *Lexikon der letzten Worte: letzte Botschaften berühmter Männer und Frauen von Konrad Adenauer bis Emiliano Zapata* by Werner Fuld (Munich, Germany, 2002).

Clay, Henry

(1777-1852) American lawyer, statesman, politician. Founder and leader of Whig party. U.S. secretary of state. Member U.S. Senate and U.S. House of Representatives from Kentucky. Candidate for U.S. President twice; defeated both times. Drafted and worked for enactment of the Compromise of 1850, series of resolutions he hoped would avoid civil war. Suffered from tuberculosis. Died at age 75 in Washington, D.C. Fifteen U.S. counties were named for him.

Last Words: "I believe, my son, I am going."

Source: *Henry Clay* by Thomas Hart Clay (Philadelphia, 1910). The author was a grandson of Henry Clay.

Cleburne, Patrick Ronayne

(1828-1864) Irish-born American military

officer, pharmacist, lawyer. Confederate major general in U.S. Civil War. Popular division commander. Known as Stonewall of the West. Killed at the Battle of Franklin in Tennessee. Counties in Alabama and Arkansas were named for him. City and lake in Texas were also named for him.

Last Words: "General, I have my division in two lines and am ready. General, I am more hopeful of the success of our cause than I have ever been since the war commenced." Spoken to General Hood. Cleburne died a short time later. Hood repeated these Last Words in a speech in 1867.

Source: "Personal Items" (*New York Times,* January 24, 1867).

Clemenceau, Georges Eugene Benjamin

(1841-1929) French politician, statesman, physician, journalist. War correspondent with Grant's Army in U.S. Civil War. Founded and edited *L'Aurore.* Known as the Tiger. Leader of radical left. Member Chamber of Deputies, senator, prime minister of France. Headed delegation at peace conference after World War I. Survived assassination attempt in 1919. Had strong distrust of Germany and predicted trouble. Died at age 88 in Paris.

Last Words: "This time it will be a long one." Spoken to a friend about a heart attack he just had. He died the following day.

Source: "Clemenceau, 'Father of Victory,' Dies; Passes Away at 88 After Hours in a Coma" by P.J. Philip (*New York Times,* November 24, 1929).

Clemens, Olivia Langdon

(1845-1904) American matron. Wife of Samuel L. Clemens (Mark Twain). Died at age 58 in Florence, Italy, where they had moved for her health.

Last Words: "He is singing a good-night carol to me." Spoken to her maid Katy about her husband who was playing the piano.

Source: *Mark and Livy: The Love Story of Mark Twain and the Woman Who Almost Tamed Him* by Resa Willis (New York, 2003).

Clemens, Samuel Langhorne ("Mark Twain")

(1835-1910) American humorist, writer. Pen name Mark Twain. Notable works: *Tom Sawyer; Huckleberry Finn; The Prince and the Pauper; A Connecticut Yankee in King Arthur's Court.* Except for his autobiography, he did little writing after his wife Olivia died in 1904. His health began to fail and he found himself more alone when his daughter Clara married and daughter Jean died in 1909. He died the following year at age 75 at his home in Redding, Connecticut.

Last Words: "Good bye. If we meet—." Spoken to his daughter Clara.

Source: *My Father Mark Twain* by Clara Clemens (New York, 1931).

Clément, Jacques

(1567-1589) French clergyman, assassin. Fanatical Dominican friar who murdered King Henry III of France. Clément's body was quartered and burned.

Last Words: "Yes, yes, yes, and kill him, too." His response when asked if he dared to look an angry king in the face.

Source: *The Annales, or, General Chronicle of England* by John Stow and Edmund Howes (London, 1615).

Clement XI, Pope

(1649-1721) Italian prelate. Birth name Giovanni Francesco Albani. Ruled as pope 21 years. Died at age 71 in Rome. Succeeded by Innocent XIII.

Last Words: "See how all the honors of the world come to an end. Only that is great which is great in God's sight. Make it your endeavor to be a saint."

Source: *A History of the Popes* by Ludwig Pastor (St. Louis, MO, 1941).

Clement XII, Pope

(1652-1740) Italian prelate. Birth name Lorenzo Corsini. Archbishop of Nicomedia. Nuncio to Vienna. Cardinal Bishop of Frascati. Elected pope at age 78. Died at age 87. Was almost totally blind during the last eight years of his papacy.

Last Words: "No, neither on that point do we feel any remorse of conscience." His response to Father Barberini who said to him: "A pontiff may have some omissions to repent of."

Source: *The Lives and Times of the Roman Popes* by The Chevalier Artaud De Montor (New York, 1911).

Clement XIV, Pope

(1703-1774) Italian prelate. Birth name Giovanni Vincenzo Antonio Ganganelli. Founded Clementine Museum in Vatican.

Died at age 68 in Rome, a year after issuing an apostolic brief suppressing the Jesuits.

Last Words: "I am dying and I know why." The Last Words he uttered were said to have supported the claim that ex-Jesuits had poisoned him for having suppressed their order. *The Gentleman's Magazine* wrote about Clement's Last Words in 1842 and concluded they could be interpreted in other ways that do not necessarily imply poisoning.

Source: "Cases of Alleged Assassination—Don Carlos" (*The Gentleman's Magazine*, April 1842).

Clemente, Roberto Walker

(1934-1972) Puerto Rican athlete. Professional baseball player. National hero. Played for the Pittsburgh Pirates from 1955 to 1972. Led them to two World Series (1960, 1971). Killed at age 38 in a plane crash en route to Nicaragua. The plane was loaded with relief supplies for earthquake victims. Clemente was inducted into the Baseball Hall of Fame in 1973.

Last Words: "Si vas a morir, morirás." (tr. "If you're going to die, you're going to die.") Spoken at the airport in Puerto Rico when asked about the safety of the trip.

Source: "Clemente No Muere" by Manuel Genet (*El Nuevo Diario*, December 28, 2007).

Clemmer, Mary

(1831-1884) American writer, journalist, poet. Full name Mary Clemmer Ames Hudson. Notable works: *Memorial of Alice and Phoebe Cary; Ten Years in Washington.* Seriously injured when thrown from a carriage in 1878. Died at age 53 of a cerebral hemorrhage in Washington, D.C.

Last Words: "Thank you." Spoken to the person who had just given her water.

Source: *An American Woman's Life and Work. A Memorial of Mary Clemmer* by Edmund Hudson (Boston, 1886). The author was her second husband. They married in 1883, a year before she died. He published a complete edition of her works in 1885.

Cleopatra

(69-30 B.C.) Egyptian queen. Daughter of Ptolemy XII Auletes. Had two children by Mark Antony. Killed herself when she learned Octavianus was going to exhibit her in Rome as a trophy of war.

Last Words (doubtful): "So here it is." Spoken when she saw an asp among some figs. Plutarch said what really happened to Cleopatra is unknown. He recited several accounts. She may have died from poison. It was known that she carried poison in a hollow bodkin she wore in her hair. However, some scholars claim an asp was brought to her in a bunch of figs.

Source: "Antony" in *Lives of the Noble Grecians and Romans* by Plutarch, tr. by John Dryden (Chicago, 1952).

Variation: "Here thou art, then!"

Source: *History of the Roman Republic* by Jules Michelet, tr. by William Hazlitt (London, 1847).

Cleveland, Stephen Grover

(1837-1908) 22nd President of the U.S. (1885-1889) and 24th President of the U.S. (1893-1897). American statesman, politician, lawyer, sheriff. Mayor of Buffalo. Governor of New York. Defeated for presidency by Benjamin Harrison in 1888. A few months after he took office for his second term, Cleveland was afflicted with mouth cancer. His upper jaw was removed and he was fitted with an artificial one. The surgeries were secret. That same year, 1893, his daughter Esther was the first child of a U.S. President to be born in the White House. Cleveland died at age 71 of a heart attack at his home in Princeton, New Jersey.

Last Words: "I have tried so hard to do right."

Source: *Grover Cleveland, the Man and the Statesman* by Robert McElroy (New York, 1923).

Clifford, Thomas, 1st Baron Clifford of Chudleigh

(1630-1673) English statesman, politician. Raised to Baron Clifford of Chudleigh in 1672. Comptroller of the household. Served briefly as lord high treasurer. Suffered from a painful condition known as "the stone" before he died. In his diary, John Evelyn reported that Lord Clifford's servant found him locked in his room strangled with his cravats on the bed tester. The servant reached Clifford before he was dead. He was heard to utter these Last Words.

Last Words (doubtful): "Well, let men say what they will, there is a God, above." Evelyn's story of Clifford's suicide was later discounted as rumor.

Source: *Report and Transactions by Devonshire Association for the Advancement of Science, Literature and Art* (Plymouth, England, 1884).

Clift, Montgomery

(1920-1966) American actor. Star of stage and screen. Nominated for four Academy Awards and one Golden Globe. Died at age 45 in New York City.

Last Words: "Absolutely not." His response to his caregiver Lorenzo James who asked him if he wanted to see the movie *The Misfits* on television.

Source: *Montgomery Clift, a Biography* by Patricia Bosworth (New York, 1978).

Clifton, John Talbot

(1868-1928) British adventurer, explorer, world traveler. Squire of Lytham Hall and Lord of Manor of Anstey and Kildalton Castle on the Isle of Islay, Scotland. Fell ill in Africa. Was too ill to be taken home.

Last Words: "Oh, I offer it." Spoken to his wife.

Source: *The Book of Talbot* by Violet Clifton (New York, 1933). Violet Mary Beauclerk Clifton was his wife.

Clive, Robert, 1ˢᵗ Baron Clive of Plassey

(1725-1774) British military officer, statesman. General. Given Irish peerage as Baron Clive of Plassey in 1762. Knighted in 1764. Administrator in India. Known as Clive of India. Helped establish British India. Charged with abuse of office but acquitted by Parliamentary committee of enquiry after a long investigation. Suffered from mental illness now believed to be manic depression. Acute abdominal pains caused him to become addicted to opium. Committed suicide at age 49 at his home in London.

Last Words: "To be sure." His response as he took out the penknife he used to kill himself.

Source: *The Life of Robert, First Lord Clive* by the Rev. G.R. Gleig (London, 1869).

Cloots, Jean Baptiste, Baron de ("Anacharsis")

(1755-1794) Prussian-born French revolutionary. Full name Jean Baptiste du Val-de-Grâce Baron de Cloots. Known as Anacharsis Cloots. Guillotined during the French Revolution with followers of Jacques Hébert by order of Robespierre. Hébert had led a movement to dechristianize France.

Last Words: "In the name of the earth, in the name of humanity, do not confuse me in your memory with those common fellows! No patched up peace!"

Source: *Anacharsis Cloots, L'Orateur du Genre Humain* by Georges Avenel (Paris, 1865).

Cobain, Kurt Donald

(1967-1994) American musician. Leader of grunge rock group Nirvana, created in 1986. Married Courtney Love 1992. Had daughter Frances. Committed suicide at age 27 in Seattle, Washington. Left suicide note.

Last Words (written): "Frances and Courtney, I'll be at your altar. Please keep going Courtney, for Frances for her life will be so much happier without me. I LOVE YOU. I LOVE YOU." Last lines in a suicide note.

Source: *Nirvana: The Day-to-day Illustrated Journals* by Carrie Borzillo-Vrenna (New York, 2003).

Cobbe, Frances Power

(1822-1904) Irish-born English feminist, journalist, social reformer. Influential defender of women's rights. Pioneer animal rights activist. Worked to abolish vivisection. Helped establish Ragged Schools in Bristol. Worked to reform workhouses. Died at age 81 in Hengwrt, Wales

Last Words (written): "I am touched by your affectionate words, dear Blanche, but nobody must be sorry when that time comes, least of all those who love me." Part of a letter.

Source: *Life of Frances Power Cobbe, As Told By Herself*, ed. by Blanche Atkinson (London, 1904).

Cobden-Sanderson, Thomas James

(1840-1922) English lawyer, bookbinder, printer, artist. Withdrew from law to work in handicrafts. Friend of William Morris. Involved in Arts and Crafts movement. Co-founder of Doves Bindery and Press in Hammersmith, London. Designed font known as Doves Type that was used exclusively by the bindery to print an English Bible and other books. When the press closed in 1916, Cobden tossed the type into the Thames at Hammersmith Bridge to prevent further use of it. Died at age 81 in London.

Last Words (written): "Every day, every day, my Guide says to me, Are you ready! And I say to my Guide, I am ready. And my Guide says, March. And to the end, one day more, I march. Oh, every day, every day, am I ever on the ever-diminishing way, to the end, the end." Last entry in his journal.

Source: *The Journals of Thomas James Cobden-Sanderson, 1879-1922* (London, 1926).

Cochin, Pierre-Suzanne-Augustin

(1823-1872) French politician, writer. Studied economic, political and social issues. Vice mayor, mayor of 10th district in Paris. Died at age 48 in Versailles.

Last Words (written): "It would be more manly to found the Republic because its name quiets the passions of the multitude, and we can present a braver front to Europe under that name than that of the Monarchy. But you cannot raise the dead to life. The Republic has been killed by her own children, the odious 1790s, the foolish 1848. 1870 has carried her to the grave. She was killed by Robespierre and Marat, then by all the word-mongers, who have dealt in plots, in debts, and foolish actions, who have three times ascended this chariot of the people." Written in an unfinished letter.

Source: *Memoirs of the Count de Falloux,* ed. by C.B. Pitman (London, 1888).

Cochise

(1812?-1874) Native American leader. Chiricahua Apache chief who fought to defend his homeland from invaders. U.S. government signed a treaty with him but broke it within a few years. He died while visiting friend Thomas Jeffords. Dramatized versions of Cochise's war years were told in the movie *Broken Arrow* in 1950 and in the TV series of the same name in 1956. The town of Cochise and Cochise County, Arizona, were named for him.

Last Words: "I believe good friends will meet somewhere." Spoken to Jeffords when asked if they would meet again.

Source: *The Great Chiefs* by Benjamin Copps (Alexandria, VA, 1972).

Variation: "I think I will die about ten o'clock tomorrow morning. Do you think we will see each other again?" Spoken after

his friend Indian agent Tom Jeffords replied that he did not know. Cochise added: "I don't know. It is not clear to my mind, but I think we will somewhere up there."

Source: *Pioneer Days in Arizona* by Frank Cummins Lockwood (New York, 1932).

Cocteau, Jean Maurice Eugène Clément

(1889-1963) French writer, poet, designer, boxing manager, filmmaker. Surrealist. Notable films: *Beauty and the Beast; Orpheus.* Notable plays: *Le Bel Indifferent; Les Parents terribles.* Died at age 74 at his home in Milly-la-Forêt, shortly after he heard of the death of his friend French singer Edith Piaf.

Different Last Words:

(1) "The boat is going down."

Source: *What a Way to Go: Fabulous Funerals of the Famous and Infamous* by Adele Q. Brown (San Francisco, CA, 2002).

(2) (doubtful): "The day of my birth, my death began its walk. It is walking toward me, without hurrying."

Source: Various Last Words compilations and Internet websites.

These reputed Last Words of Cocteau were written by him 24 years before he died. This quote is so fitting as Cocteau's Last Words that people accept it as such.

Source: "Postambule" in *La Fin du Potomac* (1939); later published in *Collected Works,* Vol. 2 (1947).

Cody, William Frederick ("Buffalo Bill")

(1846-1917) American scout, hunter, frontiersman. Pony Express rider. Showman. His Wild West Shows were popular attractions for many years in U.S. and Europe. Retired to his ranch in Wyoming. Cody earned the nickname Buffalo Bill after he killed many buffalo to feed railroad workers in 1867-68. Died at age 70 of kidney failure while visiting his sister in Denver. Cody, Wyoming, which he helped found, is named for him.

Last Words: "I wish Johnny would come!" Johnny was his foster son.

Source: *Memories of Buffalo Bill* by Louisa Frederici Cody in collaboration with Courtney Ryley Cooper (New York, 1920). Louisa Frederici married Buffalo Bill in 1866. She died in 1921.

Coffin, Charles Carleton

(1823-1896) American historian, writer, journalist. *Boston Journal* correspondent in U.S. Civil War. Among the first to report many war events, including the Battle of Bull Run, capture of Fort Henry, attack on Sumter by *Monitor,* attacks on Fort McAllister and Gettysburg. After the war, he reported from Asia and Europe. Notable works: *Old Times in the Colonies; The Boys of '76; Building the Nation.* Died suddenly of apoplexy at age 72 in Brookline, Massachusetts.

Last Words: "If it were not for this pain, I should get up and write."

Source: *Charles Carleton Coffin, War Correspondent, Traveler, Author and Statesman* by William Elliot Griffis (Boston, 1898).

Coghill, George Ellett

(1872-1941) American anatomist, researcher, educator. Professor of comparative anatomy at Wistar Institute in Philadelphia. Known for research on nervous system of Amphibia. Died at age 69 in Gainesville, Florida.

Last Words: "Why, that's what we used to give the babies." Spoken to a nurse who gave him a spoonful of peppermint water.

Source: *George Ellett Coghill: Naturalist and Philosopher* by C. Judson Herrick (Chicago, 1949).

Cohan, George Michael

(1878-1942) American composer, playwright, producer, actor. Notable plays he wrote, produced and directed: *The Song and Dance Man; Forty-five Minutes from Broadway; The Merry Malones.* Notable songs: "You're a Grand Old Flag"; "I'm a Yankee Doodle Dandy." Awarded Congressional Gold Medal in 1936. The movie *Yankee Doodle Dandy* is a fictionalized story of his life. Died at age 64 of cancer in New York City.

Last Words: "Look after Agnes." Agnes Mary Nolan was his second wife, whom he married in 1907.

Source: *George M. Cohan, Prince of the American Theater* by Ward Morehouse (Philadelphia, 1943). The author was his friend.

Cohn, Harry

(1891-1958) American film producer. Cofounder, president and production director of Columbia Pictures. Died at age 66 of a heart attack in Phoenix, Arizona.

Last Words: "It's no use. It's too tough. It's just too tough." Spoken in the ambulance just before he died.

Source: *King Cohn: The Life and Times of Harry Cohn* by Bob Thomas (London, 1967).

Coke, Sir Edward

(1552-1634) English jurist, legal scholar, politician. Member of Parliament. Known as Lord Coke or Lord Cooke. Lord chief justice of England. Prosecuted Gunpowder Plot conspirators. Disgraced for defending Parliament against James I. Discharged and imprisoned. Notable works: *Institutes* (especially Vol. 1 known as *Coke Upon Littleton*). His legal work laid the groundwork for fundamental English documents created with the Restoration, including Petition of Right, Habeas Corpus Act, and Act of Settlement. Died at age 82 at Stoke Poges, Buckinghamshire, England.

Last Words: "Thy kingdom come, Thy will be done."

Source: *The Life of Sir Edward Coke, Lord Chief Justice of England in the Reign of James I with Memoirs of His Contemporaries* by Cuthbert W. Johnson (London, 1837).

Colbatch, John

(1664-1748) English clergyman, educator, perfectionist. Professor of moral philosophy. Last Words: "Arrogat, my lord." In his delirium as he was dying, he remembered a comment he made ten years earlier to an English judge who misquoted Horace and said "abrogating" The comment was made during the prosecution of a libel lawsuit he brought against Richard Bentley.

Source: *Portraits in Miniature* by Lytton Strachey (New York, 1931).

Colbert, Auguste-François-Marie

(1777-1809) French military officer. Fought with Napoleon Bonaparte's army in Egypt. Killed at Cacabelos, Spain, by a British sharpshooter with a single shot. Lingered 15 minutes. The French claimed there was a wager among the British to see who could shoot Colbert. British rifleman Thomas Plunkett won by shooting him through the head. With their leader killed, the French withdrew. The British later denied any financial reward had been offered for shooting Colbert.

Last Words: "You are then very much afraid today of dying!" Spoken in response to a warning to keep out of the line of fire.

Source: *Traditions et Souvenirs Touchant le Temps et la Vie du Général Auguste Colbert (1793-1809)* by Auguste Napoléon Joseph Colbert-Chabanais (Paris, 1882). The author was his son.

Cole, Thomas

(1801-1848) English-born American artist. Landscape painter. Family moved to America in 1819. Founder of Hudson River School. Gained popularity with landscapes of Hudson River Valley and Catskill Mountains. Settled in Catskills in 1832. Notable works: *The Course of Empire; The Voyage of Life.* Died at age 47 of pneumonia at his home in Catskill, New York.

Last Words: "I want to be quiet."

Source: *The Life and Works of Thomas Cole, N.A* by Rev. Louis L. Noble (New York, 1853). Cole designed a building for Saint Luke's Church and for the rector, the Reverend Louis L. Noble, who was his friend and eventual biographer.

Coleridge, Samuel Taylor

(1772-1834) English writer, poet, critic. Notable works: *Christabel; Kubla Khan*, both published unfinished, and *The Rime of the Ancient Mariner.* Friend of Wordsworth. Began using opium as a painkiller. Became an addict. Had no financial security. Left his family dependent on friends. From 1816 until he died, he lived at the home of physician Dr. James Gilman in Highgate near London. Died at age 61 at Highgate. When he died, he left only books and manuscripts.

Last Words (written): "I beg, expect, and would fain hope of [his relatives] according to their means such a contribution as may suffice collectively for a handsome Legacy for that most faithful, affectionate and disinterested servant, Harriet Macklin [his nurse]. Henry can explain. I have never asked for myself. S.T. Coleridge." Letter asking for financial help for his servant.

Source: *The Letters of Samuel Taylor Coleridge,* ed. by Kathleen Raine (London, 1950).

Coleridge-Taylor, Samuel

(1875-1912) English musician, composer. Son of Sierra Leone physician and English woman. Notable works: *Hiawatha* trilogy; *Symphonic Variations on an African Air;*
African Dances; Negro Melodies. Died at age 37 of pneumonia in Croydon, England.

Last Words: "All the papers will call me a Creole."

Source: *Samuel Coleridge-Taylor, Musician: His Life and Letters* by W.C. Berwick Sayers (London, 1927).

Colette, Sidonie Gabrielle Claudine

(1873-1954) French writer, novelist. Gained fame with series of autobiographical stories about a character named Claudine. Notable work: *Gigi* (written when she was 72; became a successful movie). Died at age 81 in her apartment in the Palais-Royal, Paris.

Last Words: "Look, Maurice, look!" Spoken to her husband. She made an arc gesture with her arm, pointing out the swallows flying by outside, her mounted butterflies and other things she found to be beautiful. She spoke no more and died the following day.

Source: "Foreword" by Clifton Fadiman in *Famous Last Words* by Barnaby Conrad (Garden City, NY, 1961). Recollections of Colette's husband Maurice Goudeket.

Coligny, Gaspard de Châtillon, Comte de

(1519-1572) French military officer, nobleman. Admiral of France. Leader of Huguenots. Died at age 53 in slaughter of Huguenots at St. Bartholomew's Day massacre in Paris. Killed by a servant of the Duke of Guise and thrown from a window.

Different Last Words:

(1) "Honor these gray hairs, young man." Spoken to his assassin.

Source: *Dictionary of Phrase and Fable* by E. Cobham Brewer (Philadelphia, 1898).

Variation: "Young man, you ought to consider my age and my infirmity. But you will not make my life shorter."

Source: *Gaspard de Coligny* by Walter Besant (London, 1879).

Variation: "Young man thou sightest to respect my years, and my infirmity of the body; but it is not thou that canst shorten my days." Spoken to Besine just before being stabbed through the chest.

Source: *Last Words of Saints and Sinners: 700 Final Quotes from the Famous, the Infamous, and the Inspiring Figures in History* by Herbert Lockyer (Grand Rapids, MI, 1969).

(2) "O my brother, I now perceive that I am beloved of my God, seeing that for His most holy name's sake I suffer these wounds."

Spoken to Maure, preacher to the Queen of Navarre.

Source: *Book of Martyrs or, a History of the Lives, Sufferings, and Triumphant Deaths of the Primitive as well as the Protestant Martyrs* originally by John Fox[e] with alterations and additions by Charles A. Goodrich (Hartford, CT, 1830).

Colley, Thomas

(d. 1751) English chimney sweep, murderer. Hanged for murder of an old woman he believed was a witch. Became penitent during his final days. Before he died, he signed a lengthy declaration he wanted distributed among townspeople. Part of it is given here:

Last Words (written): "Good People, I beseech you all to take warning by an unhappy man's suffering that you be not deluded into so absurd and wicked a conceit as to believe there are any such things as witches.—I pray God that none of you—may hereafter be induced to think that you have a right in any shape to prosecute, much less endanger the life of a fellow creature. I beg of you all to pray to God to forgive me, and to wash clean my polluted soul in the blood of Jesus Christ, my Saviour and Redeemer. So exhorteth you all, the dying THOMAS COLLEY."

Source: *The Criminal Recorder: Or, Biographical Sketches of Notorious Public Characters, Including Murderers, Traitors, Pirates, Mutineers, Incendiaries...and Other Noted Persons Who Have Suffered the Sentence of the Law, &c* (Nottingham, England, 1815-1819).

Collingbourne or Colyngbourne, William

(d. 1484) English conspirator. Tudor agent. Schemed against Richard III. Arrested and executed for treason. He made up a rhyme about Richard III:

"The Cat, the Rat, and Lovell our Dog,
    Rule all England under a Hog."

The Cat was Sir William Catesby, Speaker of the House of Commons. The Rat was Sir Richard Ratcliffe. The Dog was Viscount Francis Lovell. The Hog was King Richard III. Collingbourne was hanged, cut down alive and disemboweled.

Last Words: "Lord Jesus, yet more trouble." Spoken to the executioner as he pulled Collingbourne's bowels from his body.

Sources: *Elizabeth of York: The Mother of Henry VIII* by Nancy Lenz Harvey (New York, 1973); *The Last*

Words (Real and Traditional) of Distinguished Men and Women Collected from Various Sources by Frederic Rowland Marvin (New York, 1901). Marvin gave as his source *Fab. Chron.*

Collins, Anthony

(1676-1728) English deist, writer. Disciple of John Locke. Notable works: *Use of Reason; Discourse of Free Thinking.*

Last Words: "I have always endeavored to the best of my ability to serve God, my King and my country. I go to the place God has designed for those who love Him."

Source: *Biographies of Ancient and Modern Celebrated Freethinkers: Reprinted from an English Work Entitled "Half-hours with the Freethinkers"* by Charles Bradlaugh, Anthony Collins and John Watts (Boston, 1858).

Collins, James ("Jim")

(1937-1979) New Zealand pilot, disaster victim. Captain of Air New Zealand DC-10 Flight 901, a scheduled Antarctic sightseeing flight from Auckland International Airport in New Zealand.

Last Words: "Go-around power please." Spoken in response to Flight Engineer Gordon Brooks' comment: "Don't like this" spoken just before the Ground Proximity Warning System alerted the crew that there was trouble. Within 30 seconds, the plane crashed into the side of Mt. Erebus, killing 257 aboard in what was New Zealand's deadliest disaster ever. *Erebus: The Aftermath,* a television miniseries, focusing on the investigation and the Royal Commission of Inquiry, was televised in New Zealand and Australia in 1988.

Source: *Mayday: Accident Reports and Voice Transcripts from Airline Crash Investigations* by Marion F. Sturkey (Plum Branch, SC, 2005).

Collins, Joel

(c. 1850s-1877) American bartender, outlaw. Member of the Sam Bass gang. Suspected of robbing a train. Shot to death by soldiers in an ambush at Buffalo Station, Kansas.

Last Words: "Pard, if we are going to die, we might as well die game."

Source: *The Authentic Wild West: The Outlaws* by James D. Horan (New York, 1977).

Collinson, Harry

(1945-1991) British city official. Chief planning officer of Derwentside District

Council. His death was the first murder recorded live in Great Britain by dozens of journalists and TV crew members. He was shot by Albert Dryden, a landowner in Butsfield, County Durham. Collinson was supervising the demolition of a bungalow Dryden had built illegally without permits. Dryden, who also hit a BBC reporter and a policeman, was sentenced to life in prison. The footage shocked the nation, created a media frenzy and spurred a debate about whether the killing was murder or an act of insanity.

Last Words: "Can you get a shot of the gun?" Spoken to a BBC camera crew when Dryden pulled out a gun.

Source: *Death on a Summer's Day* by David Blackie (London, 2006). Blackie was present the day of the incident and was serving as a police sergeant. He was the only writer Dryden would agree to speak to about the events after his conviction.

Colombini, Giovanni (Blessed John)

(1300?-1367) Italian clergyman, holy man. Founded Apostolic Clerks of St. Jerome, a society of lay brothers, who cared for the sick. Their nickname was Jesuati (Jesuates), not to be confused with the Jesuits. The group was suppressed in 1668. Colombini was beatified by Pope Gregory XIII.

Last Words: "Father, into Thy hands I commend my spirit."

Source: *Vita del Beato Giovanni Colombini* by Feo Belcari (Verona, Italy, 1817).

Colquhoun, Lady Janet Sinclair

(1781-1846) Scottish noblewoman, writer. Wife of Sir James Colquhoun. Known for her piety and benevolence and for her religious writing. Notable work: *Hope and Despair, a Narrative.*

Last Words: "Where is he? I cannot see him." Spoken when her grandson was brought to see her.

Source: *Life of Lady Colquhoun* by Rev. James Hamilton (New York, 1851).

Colt, Samuel

(1814-1862) American inventor, manufacturer, gun maker. Inventor of the first practical revolving firearm. Cylinder automatically revolved when gun was cocked. Colt suffered from malaria. Died at age 47 in Hartford, Connecticut.

Last Words: "It is all over now."

Source: *The Home, the Arm, and the Armory of Samuel Colt: A Memorial* (New York, 1866).

Columba, Saint

(521-597) Irish clergyman, missionary, holy man. Missionary to North Britain. Built several monasteries including the one at Iona. Known as the Dove of the Church. Columba is one of the patron saints of Ireland. Died at Iona.

Last Words: "Dear children, this is what I commend with my Last Words—let peace and charity, that is mutual and sincere, reign always among you! If you act thus, following the example of the saints, God who strengthens the just will help you, and I, who shall be near Him, will intercede on your behalf, and you shall obtain of Him not only all the necessities of the present life in sufficient quantity, but still more the rewards of eternal life, reserved for those who keep His law."

Source: *The Monks of the West from St. Benedict to St. Bernard. Vol. III. Authorised Translation* by Charles Forbes Montalembert, Francis Aidan Gasquet and Aurlien Courson (Edinburgh, 1861-1867).

Columbus, Christopher

(1451-1506) Italian navigator, explorer. Made four voyages of discovery to the Western Hemisphere for Spain between 1492 and 1504. Was sent home in chains after his third voyage because of complaints of trouble among colonists. Stripped of his honors. Died at age 55 in Valladolid, Spain, before honors could be reinstated. His body was moved to Seville and then to the Caribbean island of Santo Domingo where it was moved again to Havana. Several locations, including Santo Domingo and Seville, have graves claiming to be that of Columbus.

Last Words: "Into Thy hands, O Lord, I commend my spirit," quoting Luke 23:46.

Source: *The Life and Voyages of Christopher Columbus* by Washington Irving (New York, 1868).

Combe, Andrew

(1797-1847) Scottish physiologist, phrenologist, writer. Younger brother of George Combe. Influenced by the work of German physician Johann Gaspar Spurzheim who co-founded phrenology. Notable work: *Physiology of Digestion.* Died at age 49 of tuberculosis in Edinburgh.

Last Words: "Happy, happy."

Source: *The Life and Correspondence of Andrew Combe M.D.* by George Combe (Edinburgh, 1850). The author was his brother.

Combe, George

(1788-1858). Scottish lawyer, phrenologist, writer. Brother of Andrew Combe. Early follower of phrenology. Became a disciple after visiting German physician Johann Gaspar Spurzheim. Co-founded Edinburgh Phrenological Society in 1820. Notable work: *The Constitution of Man* (sold about 350,000 copies). Died at age 69 in Moor Park, Surrey, England.

Last Words: "From my present sensations, I should say I was dying—and I am glad of it."

Source: *The Life of George Combe, Author of "The Constitution of Man"* by Charles Gibbon (London, 1878).

Comte, Isidore Auguste Marie François Xavier

(1798-1857) French philosopher. Developed scientific method for studying social structures that formed the basis of modern sociology. Created positivism—the belief that focuses on humanity instead of the supernatural. Helped establish sociology as a science. Notable work: *The Course of Positive Philosophy.* Died at age 59 of cancer in Paris.

Last Words: "C'est une perte irreparable." (tr. "What an irreparable loss!")

Source: "Notes Taken During Discussions at the Grote Club Meetings, February-November 1867" by A. Marshall (*Marshall Studies Bulletin* No. 6, 1996).

Condé, Henri I de Bourbon, Prince de

(1552-1588) French royalty. Son of Louis I de Bourbon. Joined Huguenots but renounced them at St. Bartholomew's Day massacre. Went to Germany. Died at age 35 of wounds received while fighting against Holy League at Coutras. His son Henri II was born posthumously.

Last Words: "Hand me my chair; I feel extremely weak."

Source: *History of the Princes de Condé, in the XVIth and XVIIth Centuries* by Le Duc d'Aumale (London, 1872).

Condé, Louis I de Bourbon, Prince de

(1530-1569) French royalty, military officer, religious reformer. Son of Charles de Vêndome, Duke Charles IV of Bourbon. Protestant leader, general. Involved in Conspiracy of Amboise. Commanded Huguenots in religious war. Captured, released. Went to war again. Murdered at the Battle of Jarnac by order of the Duke of Anjou.

Last Words: "Ah, D'Argence, D'Argence! You will not be able to save me." Spoken to D'Argence, who told him to hide his face.

Source: *History of the Princes de Condé in the XVIth and XVIIth Centuries* by Le Duc d'Aumale (London, 1872).

Condé, Louis II de Bourbon, Prince de

(1621-1686) French royalty, military officer. Duc d'Enghien. General with many victories. Known as the Great Condé. Elder son of Henri II of Bourbon. Friend of Racine, Moliere, Boileau, La Bruyère. Spent his last 10 years in retirement at Chantilly. Died at age 65 at Fontainebleau.

Last Words: "In Thy justice free me."

Source: *The Great Condé* by Eveline Godley (London, 1915).

Conder, Josiah

(1789-1859) London bookseller, editor, hymnist. Blinded in his right eye as a child. Notable work: *Congregational Hymn Book* (sold 90,000 copies). Edited 30-vol. *Modern Traveller*. Died at age 66 in Hampstead, Middlesex, England.

Last Word: "Amen."

Source: *Josiah Conder: A Memoir* by Eustace R. Conder (London, 1857). The author was his son.

Confucius or K'ung-fu-tzü or Kung-fu-tse

(551?-479 B.C.) Chinese philosopher. Founder of Confucianism. Spent last years in city of Ch'üfu where he was buried. Died at about age 72.

Different Last Words:

(1) "No intelligent monarch arises. There is not one in the kingdom that will make me his master. My time has come to die."

Source: *The Story of Confucius, His Life and Sayings,* ed. by Brian Brown (Philadelphia, 1927).

(2) "I have taught men how to live."

Source: *The Last Words (Real and Traditional) of Distinguished Men and Women Collected from Various Sources* by Frederic Rowland Marvin (New York, 1901).

Connelly, Cornelia

(1809-1879) American-born English religious leader, nun. Birth name Cornelia Augusta Peacock. Married Episcopalian minister Pierce Connelly. Both converted to Roman Catholicism. Her husband became a priest then later left the order. Cornelia became a nun. Founded Society of the Holy Child Jesus. Died at age 70 at St. Leonards-on-Sea, Sussex, England.

Last Words: "In this flesh I shall see my God!"

Source: *Life of Cornelia Connelly* by a member of the Society (London, 1922).

Conolly or Connolly, Arthur

(1807-1842) British military officer, explorer, writer. Intelligence officer. Member Sixth Bengal Light Cavalry. Worked for British East India Company. Coined name "The Great Game" to describe the conflict between the British and Russian empires. Beheaded by order of Amir of Bokhara.

Different Last Words:

(1) "Stoddard, we shall see each other in Paradise, near Jesus." Spoken to Charles Stoddard, a fellow prisoner.

(2) "Stoddard became a Mussulman, and yet you have killed him. I am prepared to die." His response when told his life would be spared if he denounced Christianity and adopted the religion of Muhammad.

Source: *Lives of Indian Officers* by John William Kaye (London, 1895). The execution of Conolly is clouded by uncertainty. It has been described differently by eyewitnesses to the beheading. These quotes were provided by the executioners.

Conrad, Joseph

(1857-1924) Ukrainian-born British writer, seaman. Novelist. Birth name Józef Teodor Konrad Korzeniowski. Worked 20 years in French and English merchant marine service. Left the service to concentrate on writing. Notable works: *Heart of Darkness* (reflected his despair at the human depravity he witnessed in the Belgian Congo); *Lord Jim; Typhoon*. Many of his stories have the sea as background. Married an English woman and spent the rest of his life in England. Died at age 66 at Oswalds, Bishopbourne, Kent.

Last Words: "Here—."

Source: *The Last Twelve Years of Joseph Conrad* by Richard Curle (New York, 1928). British writer and traveler Richard Curle was a friend of Conrad.

Conradin, Duke of Swabia

(1252-1268) Swabian nobleman. Known as Conrad the Younger. Last descendant of the House of Hohenstaufen. Involved in a struggle with Charles of Anjou. Defeated, captured, tried as a traitor and condemned to death. Beheaded at age 16 in Naples.

Last Words: "O my mother! How deep will be thy sorrow at the news of this day!" Uttered as he awaited execution.

Source: *The See of Rome in the Middle Ages* by Oswald J. Reichel (London, 1870).

Dante included this quote in *The Divine Comedy* as Conradin's last words. It appears in the version translated by Longfellow.

Source: *The Divine Comedy* by Dante Alighieri, tr. by Henry Wadsworth Longfellow (Boston, 1886-91). Dante's work dates from 1308-1321.

Consalvi, Ercole

(1757-1824) Italian prelate, statesman, ecclesiastical diplomat. Chamberlain to Pope Pius VI. Appointed cardinal and secretary of state by Pope Pius VII. Helped restore Papal States at 1815 Congress of Vienna. Died at age 66 in Rome.

Last Words: "My mind is at rest."

Source: *The Chair of Peter: A History of the Papacy* by Friedrich Gontard (New York, 1964).

Constant de Rebecque, Henri-Benjamin

(1767-1830) Swiss-born French writer, politician. Settled in Paris at beginning of the French Revolution. Opposed Napoleon. Banished along with friend Madame de Staël for denouncing his military ascendancy. Returned to France 1814. Became member of Chamber of Deputies. Notable work: *Adolphe* (semi-autographical novel). His correspondence and journals have also been published. Died at age 63 in Paris.

Last Words: "The rest tomorrow." He was unable to finish making corrections to proofs for the final volume of his *History of Religions*.

Source: *Constant, His Private Life and his Contribution to the Cause of Liberal Government in France 1767-1830* by Elizabeth W. Schermerhorn (London, 1924).

Constantine XI (Constantine Palaeologus), Emperor of Byzantium

(1404-1453) Byzantine ruler. Last Christian

emperor of Byzantium. Killed at age 49 defending Constantinople from the Turks.

Last Words (doubtful): "So there is no Christian who wishes to free me from this life?" He was then killed by two soldiers.

Source: *Les Mots de la fin* by Claude Aveline (Paris, 1957).

Stories about Constantine's Last Words abound, but the chroniclers may have used more fantasy than fact when describing his last moments. What really happened to him is unclear.

Source: "The Death of the Emperor," *Byzantium: Constantine XI and the Fall of Constantinople* (BBC—January 26, 2007).

Conti, Princesse de

(1637-1672) Italian royalty. Niece of Mazarin. Birth name Anne Marie Martinozzi. Married Armand of Bourbon. Became Princesse de Conti.

Last Words: "Mon Dieu!" (tr. "My God!") Cried out her Last Words after she called out the name of her servant: "Céphise." The princess was struck down with apoplexy. Her last minutes were described by Madame de Sevigne.

Source: *La princesse de Conti d'apres Correspondance Inedite* by Édouard de Barthelemy (Paris, 1875).

Cook, Arthur Bernard

(1868-1952) British classicist, archaeologist, perfectionist. Notable work: *Zeus: A Study in Ancient Religion.* Died at age 83.

Last Words: "That is a mistranslation." Spoken to the dean who was reading the opening words of the 121st Psalm to him: "I will lift up mine eyes unto the hills, from whence cometh my help."

Source: "Arthur Bernard Cook" in *The Proceedings of the British Academy* (London, 1982).

Cook, James

(1728-1779) English mariner, navigator, explorer. Last voyage was a search for a northwest passage between the Atlantic and Pacific oceans in North America. Charted the Pacific coast of North America. Went to Hawaii. When one of Cook's boats was stolen, a fight followed. A Hawaiian chief was killed by a member of Cook's party. Warriors attacked and killed Cook at Kealakekua Bay. He was 50.

Last Words (written): "We could not but be struck with the singularity of the scene; and perhaps there were few on board who ever lamented our having failed in our endeavors to find a northern passage homeward last summer. To this disappointment we owed our having it in our power to revisit the Sandwich Islands, and to enrich our voyage with a discovery which, although the last, seemed in many respects to be the most important that had hitherto been made by Europeans throughout the extent of the Pacific Ocean." His description of his encounter with Hawaiian natives.

Source: *Captain Cook* by Walter Besant (London, 1890).

Cooke, Jay

(1821-1905) American banker, financier. Helped finance U.S. Civil War for the North. His bank, Jay Cooke & Company, financed construction of the Northern Pacific Railroad. Forced into bankruptcy in the Panic of 1873. Regained his wealth by investing in a Utah silver mine. Died at age 83 in Ogontz, Pennsylvania.

Last Words: "That was the right prayer." Spoken after he overheard a prayer for the dead.

Source: *Jay Cooke, Financier of the Civil War* by Ellis P. Oberholtzer (Philadelphia, 1907).

Cooke, Sam

(1931-1964) American singer, songwriter. Born Samuel Cook; added "e" to name. Performed rhythm and blues, soul, gospel, pop Notable hits: "You Send Me"; "Chain Gang"; "Wonderful World." Had 29 Top Forty hits between 1957 and 1965. Died at age 33 in a Los Angeles motel after he got into a fight with the motel manager. Given Grammy Lifetime Achievement Award posthumously in 1999.

Last Words: "Lady, you shot me." Spoken just before he died.

Source: *Dream Boogie: The Triumph of Sam Cooke* by Peter Guralnick (New York, 2005).

Cooke, Terence

(1921-1983) American prelate. Roman Catholic archbishop and cardinal of New York. Died at age 62 of leukemia.

Last Words: "Maura, you were always so good and kind to me. You've got to be very

brave, just like my sister." Spoken to house-keeper Maura O'Kelly, who worked in the Madison Avenue residence of the archbishop.
Source: *Thy Will Be Done: A Spiritual Portrait of Terence Cardinal Cooke* by Benedict J. Groeschel and Terrence L. Weber (New York, 1990).

Cooke, William Winer

(1846-1876) American military officer. Union officer in U.S. Civil War. Appointed 2nd lieutenant U.S. 7th Cavalry in 1866. Promoted a year later. Regimental adjutant for General George Custer. Killed at age 30 with Custer at Little Big Horn.
Last Words (written): "Benteen, Come on. Big village. Be quick. Bring packs. P.S. Bring packs. W.W. Cooke." Message to Captain F.W. Benteen at the direction of Custer.
Source: *The Story of the Little Big Horn* by Col. W.A. Graham (Harrisburg, PA, 1945).

Cookman, Alfred

(1828-1871) American clergyman. Methodist. Began preaching at age 16. Had pastorates in Philadelphia, Harrisburg, Wilmington, New York and other cities. Died at age 43 in Newark, New Jersey.
Last Words: "My son, your pa has been all day long sweeping close by the gates of death.—How sweet and quiet everything seems; I feel like resting now."
Source: *Life of Alfred Cookman* by Henry B. Ridgway (New York, 1873).

Coolbaugh, Michael Robert

(1972-2007) American athlete. Professional baseball player, coach. Brother of former Major League player Scott Coolbaugh. Played briefly with Milwaukee Brewers and St. Louis Cardinals. After an injury cut short his playing career Michael served as first-base coach for the Double A Tulsa Drillers (Colorado Rockies affiliate). Killed at age 35 when he was struck on the head by a line drive. After the 2007 season, Major League Baseball officials decided base coaches would wear helmets starting with the 2008 season.
Last Words: "If you're going first to third, you've got to be sure." Spoken to the runner on first base.
Source: "A Death in the Baseball Family" by S. L.

Price (*Sports Illustrated*, September 24, 2007).

Coolidge, John Calvin

(1872-1933) 30th President of the U.S. American politician, lawyer. Mayor of Northampton, Massachusetts. Member Massachusetts Senate. Lieutenant governor, governor of Massachusetts. Vice President of the U.S. Succeeded to presidency on the death of Warren G. Harding in 1923. Elected President in 1924. Died at age 60 at his home in Northampton.
Last Words: "Good morning, Robert." Spoken to a handyman as he passed him on the stairway at his home in Northampton. A short time later, his wife found him dead on the bedroom floor.
Source: *Great Stories from Great Lives,* ed. by Herbert Victor Prochnow (New York, 1944).

Cooper, Anthony Ashley, 7th Earl of Shaftesbury

(1801-1885) English philanthropist. Known as Lord Ashley. Worked to improve working conditions and end child labor in mines. Urged 10-hour work days. Banned boys as chimney sweeps. Encouraged model tenements. Endeavored to improve lunacy laws. Died at age 84 in Folkestone, Kent.
Last Words: "Thank you." Spoken to his valet who handed something to him.
Source: *The Life and Work of the Seventh Earl of Shaftesbury* by Edwin Hodder (London, 1887). The author was a friend.

Cooper, Sir Astley Paston, 1st Baronet

(1768-1841) British physician, surgeon, researcher. Received baronetcy in 1821. Conducted research on hernia. Published works on fractures, breast diseases. Surgeon at Guy's Hospital. Attended King George IV. Cooper's ligament, Cooper's hernia, Cooper's disease, and more, were named for him. Died at age 72 in London.
Last Words: "Good-bye. God bless you!"
Source: *The Life of Sir A. Cooper* by Bransby Blake Cooper (London, 1843). Bransby Blake Cooper was Sir Ashley Paston Cooper's nephew. He was a surgeon at Guy's Hospital, London.

Cooper, Gary

(1901-1961) American actor. Screen star. Nominated for five Academy Awards. Won for *High Noon, Sergeant York*. Received honorary award from the Academy in 1961.

Won several other awards including Golden Globe and Laurel. Died at age 60 in Beverly Hills, California.

Last Words: "We'll pray for a miracle; but if not, and that's God's will, that's all right too." Spoken when he learned his prostate and colon cancer had metastasized to his lungs and bones.

Source: *Gary Cooper Off Camera: A Daughter Remembers* by Maria Cooper Janis (New York, 1999).

Cooper, Dame Gladys Constance

(1888-1971) English actress. Star of stage, screen and television. Nominated for three Academy Awards and two Tony awards. Named Dame Commander of the Order of the British Empire in 1967. Died at age 82 of pneumonia at Henley-on-Thames, Oxfordshire.

Last Words: "If this is what viral pneumonia does to one, I really don't think I shall bother to have it again." Spoken to her nurse as she looked into a mirror while she brushed her hair. She died in her sleep a short time later.

Source: *Robert Morley's Book of Bricks* by Robert Morley (New York, 1979). Morley was her son-in-law.

Copeland, John Anthony

(1836-1859) American abolitionist, protestor. One of two free African Americans from North Carolina who took part in John Brown's raid on the federal arsenal at Harpers Ferry, Virginia. Captured, tried, convicted of treason, sentenced to death by court in Charlestown, Virginia. Executed by hanging at age 25.

Last Words: "If I am dying for freedom, I could not die for a better cause—I had rather die than be a slave." Spoken on his way to the gallows.

Source: *Judgment Day, Part 4 (1831-1865)* "People & Events: John Brown's Black Raiders, 1859" (Oberlin College Archives).

Copernicus, Nicolaus

(1473-1543) Polish astronomer. Founder of modern astronomy. Established theory that that the Earth rotates on its axis and planets revolve in orbits around Sun. He finished his masterpiece *The Revolutions of Heavenly Bodies* in 1530 but withheld publication because of political and religious prejudices against his heliocentric theory. His friends encouraged him to print it when he was on his deathbed. Died at age 70 in Frombork, Poland.

(1) (doubtful): "Non parem Pauli gratiam requiro Veniam Petri neque posco: sed quam in crucis ligno dederas latroni Sedulus oro." (tr. "I ask not the grace accorded to Paul; not that given to Peter; give me only the favor which thou didst show to the thief on the cross.")

Source: Various Last Words compilations and Internet websites.

Copernicus wanted these words inscribed on his tomb. This inscription is taken from a poem by Aeneas Sylvius Piccolomini who later became Pope Pius II. It was put upon the monument of Copernicus at Thorn by Dr. Melchior Pyrnesius about 1589.

Sources: *History of the Christian Church,* Vol. 7, by Philip Schaff and David Schley Schaff (New York, 1910); *Poland* by William Richard Morfill (London, 1893).

(2) "Now, O Lord, set thy servant free." (Luke 2:29).

Source: "Dying Words of Distinguished Persons" in *The Encyclopedia of Death and Life in the Spirit World,* Vol. I, by J.R. Francis (Chicago, 1895). This quote appears in many Last Words compilations.

Copleston, Edward

(1776-1849) British prelate, writer, educator. Dean of St. Paul's. Professor of poetry at Oxford, Provost of Oriel, Dean of Chester. Bishop of Llandaff in Cardiff, Wales. Died at age 73 in Llandaff.

Last Words: "I expect soon to die, and I die in the firm faith of the redemption wrought by God in man through Christ Jesus, assured that all who believe in Him will be saved."

Source: *Memoir of Edward Copleston, Bishop of Llandaff, with Selections from His Diary and Correspondence* by William James Copleston (London, 1851). The author was his nephew.

Copley, John Singleton

(1738-1815) American artist. Born and raised in Boston. Leading artist in colonial America. Renowned portrait painter. Settled in London in 1775, where he painted historical subjects. Member Royal Academy of Art. Notable works: *The Death of Major Pierson; The Siege of Gibraltar.* Died at age 77 in London. His son John Singleton Copley became 1st Baron Lyndhurst and served three times as lord chancellor of England.

Last Words: "Happy, happy, supremely happy!" His response when asked how he felt.

Source: *The Domestic and Artistic Life of John Singleton Copley, R.A.* by Martha Babcock Amory (Boston, 1882). The author was Copley's granddaughter.

Coppin or Copping, John

(d. 1583) English martyr. Follower of Robert Browne. Hanged along with Elias Thacker at Bury St. Edmunds for distributing Browne's treatises.

Last Words: "My lord, your face we fear not, and for your threats we dare not, and to come to your service we dare not." These Last Words, addressed to the judge, have been ascribed to both Coppin and Thacker.

Source: "Coppin or Copping, John" in *Dictionary of National Biography* by Leslie Stephen (New York, 1887).

Coppola, Anna Augustine ("Ann")

(1921-1962) American wife of gangster Michael (Trigger Mike) Coppola. Committed suicide in Rome, Italy.

Last Words (written): "Mike Coppola— Someday, somehow, a person, or God, or the law shall catch up with you, you yellow-bellied bastard. You are the lowest and biggest coward I have ever had the misfortune to meet." Suicide note.

Source: *Bloodletters and Badmen: A Narrative Encyclopedia of American Criminals from the Pilgrims to the Present* by Jay Robert Nash (New York, 1995).

Coppola, Frank James

(1944-1982) American murderer, thief. Former policeman. Executed for beating a woman to death during a robbery. First person executed in Virginia after reinstatement of the death penalty. For his last meal, he had a cheese and egg sandwich and asked for a wine recommendation. He appeared unfazed by his impending execution, commenting: "What the hell? We all have to die. At least I can say when."

Last Words: "Fire it up!"

Source: *Last Suppers: Famous Final Meals from Death Row* by Ty Treadwell and Michael Vernon (Port Townsend, WA, 2001).

Corbet, Miles

(1595-1662) English politician, lawyer, regicide. Son of Sir Thomas Corbet, Oliver Cromwell's attorney. Served on the parliamentary committee that arranged the trial of King Charles I. Was the last of 59 signatories on the death certificate for Charles I. After the Restoration, he fled to the Netherlands but was arrested and returned to England. He was tried, found guilty then hanged, drawn and quartered at Tyburn gallows.

Last Words: "For this for which we are to die I was no contriver of it; when the business was motioned I spoke against it. But being passed in Parliament I thought it was my duty to obey. I never did sit in that which was called the high court of justice but once."

Source: "Corbet, Miles" in *Dictionary of National Biography* by Leslie Stephen (New York, 1887).

Corbet or Corbett, Richard

(1582-1635) English prelate, poet. Bishop of Oxford. Bishop of Norwich. Friend of Ben Jonson and John Donne. Died in Norwich. His poems were not published until after he died.

Last Words. "Good night, Lushington." Spoken as his friends gathered around his deathbed. Thomas Lushington was his chaplain at Norwich Cathedral.

Source: *Brief Lives* by John Aubrey, ed. by Oliver Lawson Dick (London, 1950).

Corbulo, Gnaeus Domitius

(d. c. 67) Roman military officer. General. Half sister married Caligula. Constructed a canal between the Rhine River and the Meuse estuary while assigned to Germania. Suspected of conspiracy and recalled by Nero. Ordered to commit suicide.

Last Word: "Axios." (tr. "Well deserved!") Spoken as he threw himself on his sword.

Source: *A New Classical Dictionary of Greek and Roman Biography, Mythology, and Geography*, partly based upon the *Dictionary of Greek and Roman Biography and Mythology* by William Smith, ed. by Sir Charles Anthon (New York, 1851).

Corday, Charlotte

(1768-1793) French revolutionist, murderer. Full name Marie Anne Charlotte Corday d'Armont. Horrified at the excesses of the Reign of Terror. Gained entrance to the room of Terrorist leader Marat. Stabbed him to death in his bath. Arrested, tried and convicted by a revolutionary tribunal. Guillotined at age 24, four days after Marat was killed.

Different Last Words:

(1) "Monsieur, I don't know how to thank you for your kindness. I have only this to offer you. Keep it as a remembrance of me." Spoken just before her execution. She cut off a lock of her hair for the artist who painted her portrait. The painting, by Jean-Jacques Hauer, is now in the museum at Versailles.

Source: "Les femmes de la Revolution" by Jules Michelet in *Great Short Biographies of the World*, ed. by Barrett H. Clark (New York, 1937).

(2) "I have reason to be curious, I have never seen one before." Spoken to her executioner who tried to shield her from the sight of the guillotine.

Source: *Last Words of Saints and Sinners: 700 Final Quotes from the Famous, the Infamous, and the Inspiring Figures in History* by Herbert Lockyer (Grand Rapids, MI, 1969).

Corder, William

(1803-1828) English murderer. Tried, convicted and executed at about age 25 for the 1827 murder of his lover Maria Marten at the Red Barn in Polstead, Suffolk, England. The crime was known as The Red Barn Murder. The two had arranged to meet at the barn before eloping. Corder murdered her and fled to London where he married and started a new life. He sent letters claiming Maria was fine, but her body was later found buried in the barn after her stepmother dreamed about the murder. After the execution, suspicion fell on the stepmother who was rumored to be having an affair with Corder. Her dream occurred just days after he married someone else. The Red Barn Murder story became a media sensation. An 1828 broadside about the crime is reputed to have sold a million copies. The murder also inspired books, songs, plays and several movies.

Last Words: "I am guilty. My sentence is just: I deserve my fate. And may God have mercy on my soul." Spoken moments before he was hanged.

Source: *Advocacy and the Making of the Adversarial Criminal Trial 1800–1865* by David Cairns (Wotton-under-Edge, England, 1999).

Corey, Giles

(1612?-1692) American execution victim. Massachusetts farmer accused of being a warlock. Pressed to death by stones for not entering a plea of guilty or not guilty at his witchcraft trial in Salem. Rocks were piled on him for two days. He refused to speak except for his Last Words. His wife Martha was one of 19 people hanged for witchcraft. He testified against her. Giles Corey is a character in Arthur Miller's *The Crucible.*

Last Words: "More weight!"

Source: *Salem Possessed: The Social Origins of Witchcraft* by Paul Boyer and Stephen Nissenbaum (Cambridge, MA, 1974).

Corneille, Pierre

(1606-1684) French playwright, lawyer, poet. Abandoned law to write for the theater. Creator of French tragedy. Famed as one of the great French tragic poets. Notable works: *Le Cid; Médée; Horace; Cinna.* Died at age 78 in Paris.

Last Words: "Je n'en suis pas moins Pierre Corneille" (tr. "I am none the less Pierre Corneille.")

Source: *One Thousand Sayings of History* by Walter Fogg (New York, 1929).

Cornificia the Younger or
Annia Aurelia Cornificia Faustina or
Annia Cornificia Faustina Minor

(160-212) Roman noblewoman. Daughter of Roman Emperor Marcus Aurelius and Faustina the Younger. Sister of Roman Empress Lucilla and Roman Emperor Commodus. Named for her aunt Annia Cornificia Faustina. During the reign of Pertinax in 193, she became involved in an affair with the emperor. In 212, Roman Emperor Caracalla ordered her death.

Last Words: "Poor, unhappy soul of mine, imprisoned in a vile body, fare forth, be freed, show them that you are Marcus' daughter, whether they will or no." After she spoke these words, she removed her ornaments, opened her veins, and died.

Source: *Roman History* by Cassius Dio, Vol. IX, tr. by Earnest Cary (Cambridge, MA, 1927).

Cornstalk (Hokoleskwa)

(1720?-1777) Native American leader. Shawnee chief. Played key role in Dunmore's War (1774). Negotiated the first Native American treaties with the newly founded United States, in which he tried to keep his people neutral in the American Revolution.

Last Words: "My son, the Great Spirit has seen fit that we should die together, and has sent you here to that end; it is his will. Let us submit." Spoken after hearing of a murderous plot against him. After he spoke, he turned and was shot several times and killed. Cornstalk's son Redhawk was also killed.

Source: *History of the Indian Tribes of Hudson's River: Their Origin, Manners and Customs, Tribal and Subtribal Organizations, Wars, Treaties, etc., etc.* by Edward Manning Ruttenberger (Albany, NY, 1872).

Corot, Jean Baptiste Camille

(1796-1875) French artist. Landscape painter associated with Barbizon School (naturalist artists from Paris area who painted in fields). Notable works: *Woman with the Pearl; Woman in the Studio; View of the Colosseum; Spring*. Died at age 78 in Paris.

Different Last Words:

(1) "Look how beautiful it is! I have never seen such admirable landscapes." Spoken just before he died. He moved his right hand to the wall as though he were painting.

Source: *Six Portraits: Della Robbia, Correggio, Blake, Corot, George Fuller, Winslow Homer* by Schuyler Van Rensselaer (Boston, 1889).

(2) (doubtful): "I hope with all my heart there will be painting in heaven." Corot did speak these words, but they were not his last ones. He said them when he laid down his brush for the last time.

Sources: *Life as Service: Some Chapters on Being Christianly Useful* by Henry Lewis (London, 1909); *Living Biographies of Great Painters* by Henry Thomas and Dana Lee Thomas (New York, 1940).

Coryat or Coryate, Thomas

(1577?-1617) English traveler, writer, eccentric. Traveled in Europe and Asia, mostly by foot. Published a narrative of his journeys: *Coryat's Crudities*. Introduced forks to England from Italy and promoted their use. Was ridiculed for his efforts. Died of a dysentery-related disease while traveling in Surat, India.

Last Words: "Sack! Sack—is there any such thing as sack? I pray you give me some sack!" Sack was a wine popular in the 16th and 17th centuries.

Source: *Coryat's Crudities* (London, 1776).

Cosin, John

(1594-1672) English prelate. Anglican Bishop of Durham. Chaplain to exiled members of the English royal household in Paris (1642-1660). Returned to England with the Restoration. One of the revisers of the *Book of Common Prayer*. Died at age 77 in London.

Last Word: "Lord."

Source: *A Life of John Cosin, Bishop of Durham, 1660-1672* by Percy H. Osmond (London, 1913).

Costello, Lou

(1906-1959) American comedian, actor. Screen star. Birth name Louis Francis Cristillo. Half of Abbott and Costello comedy team. Made many films with Bud Abbott. Appeared in 38 episodes of the *Abbott and Costello Show* on television in 1952-53. Died of a heart attack at age 52 in Los Angeles, California.

Different Last Words:

(1) "I think I'll be more comfortable." Spoken to a nurse who was the only person in his hospital room. Costello said this after expressing the desire to turn on his side. The nurse reported this to Costello's manager Eddie Sherman, and it is this version that appeared in the following day's newspapers.

Sources: "Heart Attack Fatal to Famed Comedian at 52 in Hospital" by Walter Ames (*Los Angeles Times*, March 4, 1959); "Comic Costello is Dead at 52" (*The Los Angeles Evening Mirror News*, March 4, 1959).

(2) "That was the best ice cream soda I ever tasted." Spoken to his longtime manager Eddie Sherman who had gotten the strawberry soda for him at his request. Costello then had another heart attack and died.

Source: *The Hollywood Book of Death: The Bizarre, Often Sordid, Passing of More Than 125 American Movie and TV Idols* by James Robert Parish (New York, 2001).

Cotton, John

(1584-1652) English-born American clergyman, writer. Puritan. His writings include numerous sermons. Notable work: *Milk for Babes* (1646 catechism considered the first American children's book). It was incorporated into *The New England Primer* around

1701. Pastor of First Church of Boston. Died at age 67 in Boston.

Different Last Words:

(1) "The God that made you and bought you with a great price, redeem your bodies and souls unto Himself." Spoken to his children whom he had called to his side.

Source: *A Conspectus of American Biography: Being an Analytical Summary of American History and Biography, Containing also the Complete Indexes of the National Cyclopedia of American Biography* by George Derby (New York, 1906).

(2) "God hath done it already, brother." His response to Wilson, his colleague, who promised to pray that God would grant him the light of His countenance.

Source: *Sketches of New England Divines* by David Sherman (New York, 1860).

Cotton, Joshua

(d. 1835) American abolitionist, protestor, lynching victim. Member of the Mystic Clan, a slave revolt group. Implicated in a plot to instigate a slave uprising. Lynched by a vigilante Committee of Safety along with six others in Livingston, Mississippi.

Last Words: "Take care of yourselves tonight and tomorrow night!" Spoken to the crowd that lynched him, inferring to them that the Mystic Clan would seek revenge for the lynching.

Source: "Gunfighters & Lawmen" by George Gardiner (*Wild West*, June 1988).

Courmourgi or Cumurgi, Ali

(d. 1716) Ottoman Turkish military leader, sultan. Grand Vizier to Achmet III. Killed in a battle at Peterwaradin after recovering Peloponnesus from the Venetians for which he gained notability. He is mentioned in Lord Byron's poem "The Siege of Corinth."

Last Words: "Oh that I could thus serve all the Christian dogs!" Spoken after he carried out his last order: the decapitation of a German general and some prisoners.

Sources: "Dying Words of Distinguished Persons" in *The Encyclopedia of Death and Life in the Spirit-World*, Vol. I, by J.R. Francis (Chicago, 1895); *Byron: Selected Poems* by Lord George Gordon Byron, ed. by Susan J. Wolfson (New York, 1996).

Courtright, Timothy Isaiah ("Jim")

(1848-1887) American gunfighter. Known as Longhaired Jim. Got into an argument with Luke Short inside a saloon. When they went outside to settle it, both men went for their guns. Short shot Courtright five times before Courtright could return a single shot.

Last Words: "Ful, they've got me." Spoken to police officer John Fulford who found Courtright gasping for breath.

Source: "The Gunfight at White Elephant Saloon" by Jerry Adams (*Trade Token Tales*, 1997).

Couzens, James Joseph

(1872-1936) American politician, industrialist. Pioneer in mass production of automobiles. Worked for Henry Ford. Mayor of Detroit. Republican member of U.S. Senate from Michigan. Enthusiastic supporter of the New Deal of President Franklin Delano Roosevelt. Died at age 64 in Detroit.

Last Words: "Don't worry. They can't kill an old dog like me. I'll see you later, Mother. Don't worry." Spoken to his wife and son prior to surgery from which he never regained consciousness.

Source: *Independent Man: The Life of Senator James Couzens* by Harry Barnard (Detroit, 2002).

Coveney, Joseph

(1805?-1897) American atheist. Self-proclaimed as "one of the most noted infidels in the United States." On his deathbed, his children asked him to renounce his belief and ask God for forgiveness. He refused. Residents of Buchanan, Michigan, were outraged in 1874 when his anti-Christianity monument was unveiled.

Last Words: "Die as I lived. I disbelieve in God, the Bible, and the Christian Religion."

Source: "Death of an Infidel: Last Words of Joseph Coveney of Michigan Were 'Die As I Lived.'" (*American Heritage*, Vol. 26, No. 5, August 1975).

Cowan, Frederick W.

(1944-1977) American murderer. Disgruntled ex-employee of Neptune Moving Company of New Rochelle, New York. Showed up at work armed with guns and grenades. Killed four coworkers and a policeman; injured five others before killing himself.

Last Words: "Tell the mayor that I'm sorry to be causing the city so much trouble."

Source: *Bloodletters and Badmen: A Narrative Encyclopedia of American Criminals from the Pilgrims to the Present* by Jay Robert Nash (New York, 1995).

Coward, Sir Noel

(1899-1973) English actor, playwright,

composer. Knighted 1970 for service to the theater. Notable works: *Blithe Spirit; Brief Encounter; Private Lives* (plays); "Mad Dogs and Englishmen" (song).

Last Words: "Goodnight, my darlings. See you tomorrow." Spoken to friends Graham Payne and Cole Lesley as Coward headed off to bed at his hilltop retreat in Jamaica. Died at age 73 of a heart attack later that evening.

Source: *International Gossip: A History of High Society, 1970-1980* by Andrew Barrow (London, 1983).

Cowles, Anna Roosevelt

(1855-1931) American social activist. Politically informed sister of Theodore Roosevelt, 26th President of the U.S. Advised her brother and mentored her nieces, one of whom was future First Lady Eleanor Roosevelt. Known as Bamie and Aunt Bye. Died at age 76 at her home in Farmington, Connecticut.

Last Words: "Never mind. It's all right." Spoken to Sara Roosevelt, mother of Franklin Delano Roosevelt.

Source: *Bamie, Theodore Roosevelt's Remarkable Sister* by Lilian Rixey (New York, 1963).

Cowper, William

(1731-1800) English lawyer, poet, hymnist, translator. Collaborated on *Olney Hymns*. Notable works: *Poems; The Task*. Episodes of depression caused him to abandon his law career. Institutionalized for melancholia. Mary Unwin, widow of Rev. Morley Unwin, nursed him through many bouts of depression and encouraged him with his writing. He died at age 68 in East Dereham, Norfolk, England.

Last Words: "What does it signify?"

Source: *The Stricken Deer* by David Cecil (Indianapolis, IN, 1930). "I Was a Stricken Deer" is the title of one of Cowper's poems.

Variation: "What can it signify?" Spoken to one of his attendants who had just offered him some refreshments.

Source: *The Last Words (Real and Traditional) of Distinguished Men and Women Collected From Various Sources* by Frederic Rowland Marvin (New York, 1901).

Cox, David

(1783-1859) English artist. Landscape painter, watercolorist. Earned very little from painting in early years. Made living by teaching drawing. Wrote several books on art techniques. Had stroke in 1853. His eyesight began to deteriorate in 1857. Died at age 76 at his home in Harborne, Birmingham, England. Paintings sold in his final years and after he died commanded large sums.

Last Words: "God bless you."

Source: *David Cox* by F. Gordon Roe (New York, 1924).

Coy, Bernard

(1900-1946) American murderer, convicted criminal. Discovered by guards when he and five other men tried to escape from Alcatraz in California. Three men were returned to their cells. Coy and two others refused and were shot and killed.

Last Words: "It doesn't matter. I figure I licked the Rock anyway."

Source: *Bloodletters and Badmen: A Narrative Encyclopedia of American Criminals from the Pilgrims to the Present* by Jay Robert Nash (New York, 1995).

Crabbe, George

(1754-1832) English writer, poet, physician, clergyman. Stories depicted realistic portrayal of life. Notable works: *The Village; The Borough; Tales of the Hall*. Unable to make a living with his writing, he turned to the clergy. Ordained 1782. Served as curate, chaplain. Became vicar of Trowbridge, Wiltshire, in 1813. Collected and kept records of beetles. Addicted to opium many years. Died in Trowbridge at age 77. Benjamin Britten's opera *Peter Grimes* was based on Crabbe's *The Borough* (story about a fisherman haunted by ghosts of his murdered apprentices).

Last Words: "All is well at last! You must make an entertainment. God bless you! God bless you!"

Source: *Life of George Crabbe* by His Son (Oxford, England, 1834).

Craddock, Ida C.

(1857-1902) American social activist. Free speech and women's rights advocate. Opened an office in Chicago offering sexual counseling to married couples. Craddock's serious instructional manuals on human sexuality were viewed as obscene. Their distribution led to morality charges, detention in jail and a stay in a hospital for the insane. Distribution of "Right Marital Living" and "The Wedding Night" led to obscenity charges and a guilty plea. She refused to plead insanity as a condition to avoid prison time. Instead she committed suicide at age 45, the day before she was to report to federal prison. Her Last Words were a lengthy public suicide note condemning Anthony Comstock, a politician dedicated to morality. Her battle with Comstock was depicted in the 2006 play *Smut*. The last paragraph of her public suicide note is given here.

Last Words (written): "I have still other teachings to follow this, upon the marriage relation, later on. I have written a book of between 450 and 500 pages upon "Marriage" in which my teachings are set forth more fully. This book, in manuscript form, is at present stored in a safe place, in friendly hands. It will not be given to the public until such time as the public shows itself ready for it, and prepared to protect this fuller and franker book from prosecution. Meanwhile, however, 'Right Marital Living' remains unindicted; it sets forth a gospel of marriage which is being preached by no other teacher in America. Its teachings will make your married lives healthier, happier, holier. Will you publicly voice your demand for this little book, 'Right Marital Living,' and protect it from Anthony Comstock? — Ida C. Craddock." She also wrote a final letter to her mother.

Source: *Speaking of Sex: the Rhetorical Strategies of Frances Willard, Victoria Woodhull and Ida Craddock* by Inez Schaechterle, Ph.D. Dissertation, Bowling Green State University, Bowling Green, OH, August 2005; Craddock's papers are in the Special Collections, Morris Library, University of Southern Illinois, Carbondale, IL.

Craigie, Pearl Mary Teresa Richards

(1867-1906) American-born English writer, novelist, playwright. Pen name John Oliver Hobbes. Notable works: *Some Emotions and a Moral* (novel); *The Ambassador* (play). Died of heart failure in her sleep at age 38 in London.

Last Words (written): "Excellent journey—crowded train, reached here by nine—

fondest love—Pearl." Sent in a telegram.

Source: *Life of John Oliver Hobbes Told in Her Correspondence with Numerous Friends, with a Biographical Sketch by her Father, John Morgan Richards* (London, 1911).

Craik, Dinah Maria Mulock

(1826-1887) English writer, novelist, poet. Birth name Dinah Maria Mulock. Known as Miss Mulock. Wrote more than 40 books of children's stories, women's novels, poetry and travel. Much of her writing is characterized by piety and sentimentality. Notable work: *John Halifax, Gentleman* (novel). Died of heart failure at age 61.

Last Words: "Oh, if I could live four weeks longer! But no matter, no matter." Spoken as she was helping to prepare her daughter Dorothy's wedding.

Source: "Mrs. Craik" by Martin Frances (*Athenaeum*, October 22, 1887).

Crane, Harold Hart (Hart)

(1899-1932) American writer, novelist, poet. Notable works: *The Bridge; White Buildings*. Won Guggenheim fellowship in 1931. Went to Mexico to get background for a poem. Committed suicide at age 32 en route from Mexico to U.S by jumping from the steamship *Orizaba*.

Last Words: "Good-bye, everybody!" Spoken to other passengers as he jumped overboard.

Source: *Voyager: A Life of Hart Crane* by John Unterecker (New York, 1969).

Crane, Stephen Townley

(1871-1900) American novelist, short-story writer, poet, war correspondent. First novel *Maggie, Girl of the Streets* was rejected by publishers. He published it himself. Eventually other writers, including William Dean Howells and Hamlin Garland, recognized its value. *Red Badge of Courage* brought him fame but very little money. Worked as reporter for *New York World* and *New York Journal* during Spanish-American War. Spent a year in England where he became a friend of Joseph Conrad. Went to Germany to seek medical help for tuberculosis. Died at age 28 at a health resort in Badenweiler.

Last Words: "Robert, when you come to the hedge that we all must go over, it isn't so

bad. You feel sleepy, and you don't care. Just a little dreamy anxiety, which world you're really in, that's all."
Source: *Stephen Crane* by John Berryman (New York, 1950).

Cranmer, Thomas

(1489-1556) English prelate. Religious reformer. Archbishop of Canterbury. Churchman during reign of Henry VIII. Condemned to death for high treason and heresy. Excommunicated. Recanted then withdrew his retraction at his execution. When he was ordered to read it publicly, he refused to do so. Burned at the stake at age 66.
Last Words: "This hand having sinned in signing the writing must be the first to suffer punishment! This hand—hath offended!" Spoken at the stake as he placed his right hand—the hand that wrote the retraction—in the fire to be burned first.
Source: *The Three Pelicans: Archbishop Cranmer and the Tudor Juggernaut* by Arthur Styron (New York, 1932).
Variation: "This unworthy right hand."
Source: *The Last Words (Real and Traditional) of Distinguished Men and Women Collected from Various Sources* by Frederic Rowland Marvin (New York, 1901). Marvin gave *Bakers Chron.* as his source.

Crantor

(fl. late 4th century B.C.) Greek philosopher. Born in Soli, Cilicia. Was the first commentator on Plato.
Last Words: "Sweet in some corner of native soil to rest." His reply when asked where he wished to be buried.
Source: *Lives and Opinions of the Eminent Philosophers,* Book IV, by Diogenes Laertius, tr. by C.D. Yonge (London, 1896).

Crates of Thebes

(fl. 4th century B.C.) Greek philosopher. Cynic. Disciple of Diogenes. Gave up fortune to devote himself to attaining self-control and virtue. One of his pupils was Zeno of Citium.
Last Words: "You're going, noble hunchback, you are going to Pluto's realms, bent double by old age." Laertius said he was "humpbacked from age."
Source: *Lives and Opinions of the Eminent Philosophers,* Book VI, by Diogenes Laertius, tr. by C.D. Yonge (London, 1896).
Variation: "Ah! poor humpback! Thy many

long years are at last conveying thee to the tomb: thou shalt soon visit the palace of Pluto."
Source: *The Last Words (Real and Traditional) of Distinguished Men and Women Collected from Various Sources* by Frederic Rowland Marvin (New York, 1901).

Cratesicleia

(fl. 3rd century B.C.) Spartan heroic woman. Mother of King Cleomenes. Ordered to be put to death by Ptolemy. She begged to be killed before her children but her wish was not granted. She was forced to watch their death.
Last Word: "O, children, whither are ye gone!"
Source: "Life of Cleomenes" in *The Parallel Lives,* Vol. X, by Plutarch, tr. by Bernadotte Perrin (Cambridge, MA, 1954-1962).

Craven, Tunis Augustus Macdonough

(1813-1864) American military officer. Naval lieutenant commander of the *Mohawk* that intercepted illegal slave traders. During U.S. Civil War, he commanded the *Tecumseh* that sank in Mobile Bay killing him and 104 others. He was the subject of a patriotic poem titled with his Last Words.
Last Words: "You first, sir." Spoken to his pilot as he stepped back to let him pass as the *Tecumseh* was sinking
Source: *"You First, Sir": A Poem in Memory of Commander Craven (United States Navy), a Christian Gentleman and Hero* by George Fitzhugh Worthington (Philadelphia, 1865).

Crawford, Francis Marion

(1854-1909) Italian-born American writer, novelist. Son of sculptor Thomas Crawford. Spent entire life in Italy. Traveled in Far East and studied Asian languages. Wrote historical romances. First novel, *Mr. Isaacs,* was very successful. Died at age 55 in Sorrento, Italy.
Last Words: "I love to see the reflection of the sun on the bookcase."
Source: *My Cousin F. Marion Crawford* by Maud Howe Elliott (New York, 1934).

Crawford, Joan

(1904-1977) American actress. Screen star. Birth name Lucille Fay LeSueur. Made more than 70 movies. Nominated twice for Academy Award; won for *Mildred Pierce.*

Died at age 72 of cancer in New York City. *Mommie Dearest*, book and movie about her life, was written by Christina, one of her four adopted children.

Last Words: "Damn it! Don't you dare ask God to help me!" Shouted at her housekeeper who had begun to pray aloud.

Source: *The Big Book of Death* by Bronwyn Carlton (New York, 1995).

Crazy Horse (Tashunca-Uitco)

(1842?-1877) Native American leader. Oglala Sioux chief who was at the Battle of Little Big Horn. Surrendered at Fort Robinson, Nebraska, after the battle but was killed by the bayonet of a guardhouse sentry who was attempting to imprison him. Crazy Horse Memorial, begun in 1948, is in the Black Hills of South Dakota near Mount Rushmore.

Different Last Words:

(1) "Cousin, you killed me! You are with the white people."

Source: *To Kill an Eagle: Indian Views of the Death of Crazy Horse* by Edward and Mabel Kadlecek (Boulder, CO, 1981).

(2) "Let me go; you've got me hurt now!" These were his last words of which there is any account. Spoken after he was pierced by a bayonet.

Source: *The Death of Crazy Horse: A Tragic Episode in Lakota History* by Richard Hardorff (Lincoln, NE, 2001).

(3) At some time in his dying moments, he is believed to have told his father: "Ah, my father, I am hurt bad. Tell the people it is no use to depend on me any more."

Source: "The Last Stand of Crazy Horse" by Kenneth W. Hayden (*Wild West*, December 2002).

Cream, Thomas Neil

(1850-1892) Scottish physician. Murderer. Hanged at age 42 at Newgate Prison for the murder of four London prostitutes but he may have murdered more.

Last Words: "I'm Jack—" [the Ripper?]. Screamed at his execution as the trap was sprung just before he died.

Source: *A History of Capital Punishment* by John Laurence (New York, 1960).

Creighton, Mandell

(1843-1901) English prelate. Anglican historian, educator, scholar. Notable work: *History of the Papacy*. Professor of ecclesiastical history at Cambridge. Edited *English Historical Review*. Bishop of Peterborough. Bishop of London. Became very ill in 1900. Died the following year at age 57.

Last Word: "God."

Source: *Life and Letters of Mandell Creighton* by Louise Creighton (London, 1904). Louise von Glehn Creighton, his wife, was also a scholar.

Crippen, Hawley Harvey

(1862-1910) American-born English physician. Convicted wrongly of murder. After his wife Cora disappeared, parts of a body were found in his cellar. They were identified as her remains. Crippen was tried, convicted and executed at age 48 for her murder. DNA tests on the body parts in 2007 indicated the remains were not those of Cora and that Crippen was innocent of the crime for which he had been put to death.

Last Words (written): "I feel sure my worries and troubles here will soon be ended, as I shall be to-morrow in God's hands and have perfect faith that he will let my spirit be with you always, and that after this earthly separation is finished he will join our souls forever. The rest of this letter shall be sacred to you and me. There will be no time for letters Wednesday morning." Portion of the letter written to Ethel le Neve the day before he died was described by *Lloyd's Weekly* as Crippen's "last words." He had been intimately involved with le Neve, a typist who worked for him several years.

Sources: "Crippen's Farewell to Miss Leneve. No Admission of Guilt in Letter Pouring Out His Love and Anguish" (*New York Times,* November 27, 1910); "CSI East Lansing—science shows innocent man hanged in famous British murder case" (Michigan State University: MSU Newsroom Special Reports, 2007).

Crittenden, John Jordan

(1787-1863) American statesman, politician, lawyer. Member U.S. Senate from Kentucky. Attorney general of U.S. Governor of Kentucky. Opposed the Mexican War and annexation of Texas. Crittenden Compromise, named for him, was an attempt to avert Civil War. Died at age 75 in Frankfort, Kentucky.

Last Words: "Tom, come and raise me up, and arrange my pillow. That's right, Tom."

Source: *The Life of John J. Crittenden with Selections From His Correspondence and Speeches* by Mrs. Chapman Coleman (Philadelphia, 1873). The author was his daughter Anna Mary.

Crittenden, William Logan

(1823-1851) American mercenary soldier. Nephew of American statesman John J. Crittenden. Fought in Mexican War but resigned U.S. Army. He joined Spanish general Narciso Lopez in an attempt to liberate Cuba from Spanish rule. Crittenden's capture caused a notorious international incident. Shortly before he was executed with 50 others in Havana, Crittenden was told to kneel. He refused and replied with his Last Words. His words inspired a poem by Mrs. Morgan L. Betts.

Last Words: "A Kentuckian never turns his back on an enemy and kneels only to God."

Source: "A Kentuckian Kneels to None but God," poem by Mrs. Morgan L. Betts in *Library of Southern Literature* by Edwin Anderson Alderman, Joel Chandler Harris and Charles William Kent (New Orleans, LA, 1908).

Variation: "An American kneels only to his God and always faces his enemy."

Source: *Cuba in 1851: A Survey of the Island* by Alexander Jones (New York, 1851).

Variation: "A Kentuckian kneels to none except his God, and always dies facing the enemy."

Source: *A Soldier's Reminiscences in Peace and War* by Brig.-Gen. Richard W. Johnson (Ret.) (Philadelphia, 1886).

Variation: "I will kneel only to my God."

Source: "Dying Words of Noted Persons" in *Miscellaneous Notes and Queries with Answers in All Departments of Literature*, Vol. II (Manchester, NH, 1885).

Crockett, David ("Davy")

(1786-1836) American frontiersman, politician, military officer. Member U.S. House of Representatives from Tennessee. As colonel, led band of Tennessee volunteers to Texas to help Americans gain independence from Mexico. They joined other Americans at the Alamo in San Antonio. An assault by the Mexican army killed all 180 American defenders, including Crockett. His actions at the Alamo made him a national hero. A city, county and forest were named for him.

Last Words (doubtful): "I'm warning you boys, I'm a screamer."

Source: Various Last Words compilations and Internet websites.

According to biographies of Crockett, he lunged at Santa Anna when he saw Mexican soldiers stabbing defenseless American prisoners at the Alamo. Before he could reach the Mexican leader, he was attacked by several of Santa Anna's men. Crockett fell and died without uttering a word.

Sources: *Life of Col. David Crockett* by Davy Crockett (Philadelphia, 1860); *David Crockett: His Life and Adventures* by John Stevens Cabot (New York, 1875).

Croker, John Wilson

(1780-1857) Irish-born British politician, writer, essayist, literary critic. Tory leader. Secretary to Admiralty. Contributed many articles to *Quarterly Review*. Said to have been the first to apply the word "conservative" to politics (1830). Died at age 76 in St. Albans Bank, Hampton, England.

Last Words: "Oh, Wade!" Spoken to his servant who was putting him to bed.

Source: *The Croker Papers: Correspondence and Diaries of John Wilson Croker*, ed. by Louis J. Jennings (New York, 1884).

Croll, James

(1821-1890) Scottish geologist, climatologist. Mostly self-educated. Pioneer in field of geological studies of climate change. Notable works: *Climate and Time; Philosophic Basis of Evolution*. Worked for Geological Survey of Scotland. Elected fellow of Royal Society; honorary degree from University of St. Andrews. Retired in ill health in 1880. Died at age 69 in Perth, Scotland.

Last Words: "I'll take a wee drop o' that. I don't think there's much fear o' me learning to drink now!" He was asking for a teaspoon of whiskey.

Source: *Autobiographical Sketch of James Croll, with Memoir of His Life and Work* by James Croll, ed. by James Campbell Irons (London, 1896).

Crome, John

(1768-1821) English artist. Landscape painter. Founder of Norwich School of Painting. (Norwich painters took their inspiration from rural scenery around the city of Norwich, England.) Known as Old Crome (or John Crome the Elder) to distinguish him from his son, landscape painter John Bernay Crome (Young Crome). Died at age 52 in Norwich.

Last Words: "Hobbema, my dear Hobbema. How I have loved you!" Hobbema was a 17th-century Dutch master who influenced Crome.

Source: *Dictionary of Painters and Engravers, Biographical and Critical* by Michael Bryan, Robert Edmund Graves, and Sir Walter Armstrong (London, 1886-1889).

Cromer, Robert

(1957-2007) American murderer, rapist. Convicted and executed at age 50 for killing a camper and raping a woman at a campsite on the same night in 1987. His death by lethal injection was the first execution in Arizona since 2000.

Last Words: "Yes. Go Raiders." His response when asked if he had any Last Words. He was referring to the Oakland Raiders professional football team.

Source: "Killer Fan Loyal to the End" (*The* [London] *Sun*, June 18, 2007).

Cromwell, Oliver

(1599-1658) English military officer, politician. General in English Civil War. Ruled England as Lord Protector of the Commonwealth. Parliament petitioned him to become king in 1657 but he refused. Died at age 59 at Whitehall, London, at the height of his power. Buried at Westminster Abby. In 1661, his body was exhumed, hanged and decapitated.

Different Last Words:

(1) "It is not my design to drink or sleep; but my design is to make what haste I can to be gone."

Source: *The Letters and Speeches of Oliver Cromwell with Elucidations by Thomas Carlyle*, ed. by S.C. Lomas (London, 1904).

(2) "My own faith is all in God." Spoken just before he slipped into a coma.

Source: *Cromwell, The Lord Protector* by Antonia Fraser (New York, 1973).

(3) "Then I am safe." Spoken in response to his chaplain who assured him that "once in grace is always in grace."

Source: *The Last Words (Real and Traditional) of Distinguished Men and Women Collected from Various Sources* by Frederic Rowland Marvin (New York, 1901).

Cromwell, Thomas, 1st Earl of Essex

(1485?-1540) English statesman, administrator. Adviser to Henry VIII. Negotiated Henry's marriage to Anne of Cleves. Named 1st Earl of Essex. Two months later, he was charged with treason and executed by beheading. Hundreds of spectators were on hand for the execution.

Different Last Words:

(1) "The devil is ready to seduce us, and I have been seduced: but bear me witness that I die in the Catholic faith of the holy church, and I heartily desire you to pray for the King's grace that he may long live with you in health and prosperity, and after him that his son prince Edward, that goodly imp, may long reign over you. And once again I desire you to pray for me, that so long as life remaineth in this flesh, I waver nothing in my faith." Spoken on the scaffold.

Source: *The Annales, or, Generall Chronicle of England* by John Stow and Edmund Howes (London, 1615).

(2) A Spanish witness said Cromwell beseeched people to pray for him. When he noticed his friend Thomas Wyatt weeping, he said "Oh, Wyatt, good-by and pray to God for me." Wyatt could not answer. Cromwell then said these Last Words: "Oh, Wyatt, do not weep, for if I were not more guilty than thou wert, when they took thee, I should not be in this pass." The Spaniard reported that the executioner then took Cromwell's head off his body with a single stroke of the ax.

Source: *Henry the Eighth* by Francis Hackett (New York, 1929).

(3) "Oh, God, I prostrate myself to my deserved punishment; Lord be merciful to Thy prostrate servant."

Source: *Last Words of Saints and Sinners: 700 Final Quotes from the Famous, the Infamous, and the Inspiring Figures in History* by Herbert Lockyer (Grand Rapids, MI, 1969).

Crosby, Harold Lillis ("Bing")

(1903-1977) American singer, actor, entertainer. Recording artist. Star of stage, screen, radio, television. Nominated for three Academy Awards; won for *Going My Way*. Awarded many other awards including Grammy Lifetime Achievement. Member *Radio Hall of Fame*. Appeared on *Kraft Music Hall; Philco Radio Time; Bing Crosby Show*. Earned 23 gold records and two platinum. *White Christmas* was the largest selling record in the world. Died at age 74 of a heart attack on a golf course near Madrid, Spain, after completing a tour of England.

Last Words: "That was a great game of golf, fellers."

Source: "The Bing Dynasty: On the 100th Anniversary of Crosby's Birth, We Celebrate the Granddaddy of Celebrity Golf—Profile—Remembering the Crosby Golf Tournament, as well as the Friendship between Bing Crosby and Bob Hope—Biography" by Tom Callahan (*Golf Digest*, May 2003).

Crosby, Howard

(1826-1891) American clergyman, educator, writer. Founder of the Society for the Prevention of Crime. Professor of Greek, Rutgers. Pastor of Presbyterian Church. Chancellor of University of City of New York. Pastor of Broadway of Presbyterian Church from 1864 to 1891. Died at age 65 of pneumonia in New York City.

Last Words: "I place my hand in the hand of Jesus."

Source: *Memorial Papers and Reminiscences of Howard Crosby, D.D. LL.D.*, ed. by Mary Crosby (New York, 1892). The author was his sister.

Cross, Edward Ephraim

(1832-1863) American newspaper editor, military officer. Established the first newspaper in the Arizona Territory. Union colonel in U.S. Civil War. Shot in the stomach at the Battle of Wheatfield during the Gettysburg campaign. Died the next day in a field hospital.

Last Words: "I think the boys will miss me."

Source: *The Generals of Gettysburg: The Leaders of America's Greatest Battles* by Larry Tagg (Cambridge, MA, 2003).

Crowfoot (Isapo-Muxika)

(1830?-1890) Native American leader. Chief of Blackfoot Nation of Canada. Spokesman for Blackfoot Confederacy. Peace advocate. Helped negotiate construction of Canadian-Pacific Railway through Blackfoot territory. Ill during his last decade of life. Spoke Last Words when he was near death. Died of tuberculosis at Blackfoot Crossing, Alberta, Canada.

Last Words: "A little while and I will be gone from among you, whither I cannot tell. From nowhere we come, into nowhere we go. What is life? It is the flash of a firefly in the night, it is the breath of a buffalo in the winter time. It is the little shadow which runs across the grass and loses itself in the sunset."

Source: *The North-West Mounted Police, 1873-1893* by John Peter Turner (Ottawa, ON, 1950).

Crowley, Edward Aleister (Aleister)

(1875-1947) English writer, occultist, mystic, artist, astrologer, social critic. Heroin addict who influenced popular culture. Died at age 72 in Hastings, England.

Last Words (doubtful): "I am perplexed." He died alone, so this is debatable.

Source: *Do What Thou Wilt: A Life of Aleister Crowley* by Lawrence Sutin (New York, 2000).

Crowley, Francis ("Two Gun")

(1911-1931) American bank robber, murderer. Went on robbery spree that ended in a siege. Held off hundreds of police in a gun battle witnessed by thousands of onlookers. Killed a Long Island, New York, policeman. Arrested, brought to trial and convicted. Electrocuted at age 19.

Last Words: "My last wish is to send my love to my mother." Spoken just before he was electrocuted at Ossining (Sing Sing) prison in New York.

Source: *Twenty Thousand Years in Sing Sing* by Warden Lewis Edward Lawes (New York, 1932).

Crumpton, Boudinot ("Bood Burris")

(1872?-1891) American murderer. Executed by hanging at age 19 at Fort Smith, Indian Territory (Arkansas), for murdering his traveling companion. He claimed he was innocent.

Last Words: "To all you who are present, especially you young men, the next time you are about to take a drink of whiskey, look closely into the bottom of the glass and see if you cannot observe in there a hangman's noose." Spoken on the gallows.

Source: *Law West of Fort Smith: A History of Frontier Justice in the Indian Territory 1834-1896* by Glenn Shirley (Lincoln, NE, 1957).

Crutchfield, Stapleton

(1835-1865) American military officer. Colonel in Confederate Army in U.S. Civil War. Served with Stonewall Jackson's Corps Reserve Artillery. Wounded at Chancellorsville in 1863. Was in ambulance with General Stonewall Jackson who had been shot. Crutchfield was killed at age 29 at Sailor's Creek, Virginia. His portrait hangs at Virginia Military Academy, where he graduated as a member of the class of 1855 with first honors.

Last Words: "Take my watch and letters to my wife. Tell her I died at the front."

Source: *To Appomattox* by Burke Davis (New York, 1959).

Cullen, William

(1710-1790) Scottish physician, chemist, educator, inventor. Known for innovative teaching methods. Invented method of refrigeration (cooling air by evaporation of liquids in a vacuum). Noted for writing on mental illness. Died at age 89 in Edinburgh. Cullen Prize awarded by Edinburgh Royal College of Physicians to recognize his lifetime of clinical research and academic excellence.

Last Words: "I wish I had the power of writing or speaking, for then I would describe to you how pleasant a thing it is to die." (Some variations leave out the words "or speaking.")

Source: *Famous Sayings and Their Authors: A Collection of Historical Sayings in English, French, German, Greek, Italian, and Latin* by Edward Latham (London, 1906).

Cummings, Bruce Frederick

(1889-1919) English diarist, biologist. Pen name W.N.P. Barbellion (Wilhelm Nero Pilate Barbellion) Assistant entomologist, British Museum of Natural History, London. Had multiple sclerosis. Published extracts from his diaries as *Journal of a Disappointed Man* that recorded the slow progress of his disease. Died at age 30 in Buckinghamshire, England.

Last Words: "The kindness almost everybody has shown the *Journal*, and the fact that so many have understood its meaning have entirely changed my outlook. My horizon is cleared, my thoughts are tinged with sweetness, and I am content."

Source: *A Last Diary* by W.N.P. Barbellion (New York, 1920).

Cummings, Edward Estlin ("e.e.")

(1894-1962) American writer, poet. Known for innovations such using lowercase instead of capital letters. Notable work: *Tulips and*

Chimneys. Died at age 67 in North Conway, New Hampshire.

Last Words: "I'm going to stop now, but I'm going to just sharpen the ax before I put it up, dear." Spoken to his wife who told him to stop chopping wood on such a hot day.

Source: *Home Before Dark: A Personal Memoir of John Cheever by His Daughter* by Susan Cheever (New York, 2001). Cheever was a friend of Cummings.

Cummins, George David

(1822-1876) American prelate. Bishop. Withdrew from Protestant Episcopal ministry. Organized Reformed Episcopal Church. Died suddenly at age 53.

Last Words: "Jesus! Precious Savior!"

Source: *Memoirs of George David Cummins, D.D.* by Alexandrine Cummins (New York, 1878). The author was his widow.

Cunard, Maud Alice ("Emerald")

(1872-1948) American-born British society hostess known for her parties. Birth name Maud Burke. Married into the famous Cunard shipping family. Close friend of Edward VIII and Wallis Simpson, Duchess of Windsor. Died at age 75 of pleurisy and cancer London.

Last Words: "No. Open a bottle for the nurse and yourself." Her response when offered a sip of champagne.

Source: *Those Remarkable Cunards: Emerald and Nancy* by Daphne Vivian Fielding (New York, 1968).

Curie, Marja Sklodowska (Madame Curie)

(1867-1934) Polish-born physicist, chemist. Her work on radioactivity with husband Pierre earned them and A.H. Becquerel the Nobel Prize for Physics (1903). She won the Nobel Prize for Chemistry (1911) for her work on radium and its compounds. The term *curie,* a unit of radium emanation, was named for her. Died at age 67 of leukemia in Savoy, France.

Last Words: "I don't want it. I want to be alone." Spoken to her doctor who offered her an injection to ease her pain.

Source: *Madame Curie* by Eve Curie (New York, 1937). The author was her daughter. The book was made into the movie *Madame Curie* in 1943 and garnered seven Academy Award nominations.

Curley, James Michael

(1874-1958) American politician. Mayor of

Boston. Member U.S. House of Representatives from Massachusetts. Governor of Massachusetts. Died at age 83 in Boston.

Last Words: "I wish to announce the first plank in my campaign for reelection—we're going to have the floors in this goddamned hospital smoothed out." Spoken to his son on his way back to his hospital room after surgery for stomach cancer.

Source: *The Rascal King: The Life and Times of James Michael Curley (1874-1958)* by Jack Beatty (Reading, MA, 1992).

Curran, John Philpot

(1750-1817) Irish statesman, lawyer, writer, orator, wit. Defended leaders of United Irishmen after the 1798 rebellion. Member of Irish Parliament. Died at age 67 in Brompton, England.

Last Words: "This is surprising since I have been practicing all night." Spoken to his physician who told him he was coughing with more difficulty.

Source: *The Complete Book of Death and Dying* by Clarence Jones (New York, 1997).

Curtis, George William

(1824-1892) American writer, editor, public speaker, political activist, reformer. President of National Civil Service Reform League and New York Civil Service Reform Association. Wrote for *New York Tribune* and *Harper's Weekly* among other periodical. Died at age 68 on Staten Island, New York. Curtis High School, Staten Island, was named for him.

Last Words: "Nothing, but to continue to love me." Spoken in response to his younger brother who asked if anything could be done for him.

Source: *George William Curtis* by Edward Cary (Boston, 1894).

Cushing, Harvey William

(1869-1939) American surgeon, writer, educator. Professor of surgery. Eminent specialist in brain surgery. Author of medical books. Won Pulitzer Prize for *The Life of Sir William Osler*. Died at age 70 in New Haven, Connecticut. Cushing's disease and Cushing's syndrome are named for him. Harvey Cushing/John Hay Whitney Medical Library at Yale University was named for him.

Last Words: "Pat, you have the 'touch'— you're a good doctor." Spoken to his nephew who had rearranged his pillows.

Source: *Harvey Cushing, a Biography* by John F. Fulton (Springfield, IL, 1946).

Cushman, Charlotte Saunders

(1816-1876) American actress. First great U.S. dramatic performer. Notable roles: Lady Macbeth; Nancy Sykes *(Oliver Twist);* Romeo (to her sister's Juliet). Toured with George Macready in 1844. Appeared in London. Died at age 59 of breast cancer and pneumonia.

Last Words: "Punch, brothers! Punch with care!" Spoken to her nephew Ned who offered her a sip of punch. Her response was a line from a jingle she had read recently in a magazine article that amused her.

Source: *Bright Particular Star: The Live & Times of Charlotte Cushman* by Joseph Leach (New Haven, CT, 1970).

Cuspinian, Johannes

(1473-1529) German-born Viennese humanist, diplomat, writer, historian, librarian. Birth name Johannes Spieshammer or Spiesheimer. Curator and chief librarian at University of Vienna. Prefect of city of Vienna. Notable work: *History of the Roman Emperors.* Died at age 55 in Vienna.

Last Words (written): "That you have not visited me in my grievous and deadly sickness—what even strangers do—will be noted at the appointed time. Through my manservant I informed myself of your situation and sent you wine and other good things. By your behavior you have marked yourself out as a sneak and intriguer, and I shall see that our posterity knows about it What is another man to you! In order that you may be aware of my intention, even when my hand is a corpse's, I am putting it in writing. Let it be goodbye, then. It goes badly with me, but I am what I always was." Written to Johann Brassican, another humanist.

Source: *Abschiedsbriefe* by Wilhelm Treichlinger (Berlin, Germany, 1934).

Custer, George Armstrong

(1839-1876) American military officer. U.S Army lieutenant colonel. Cavalry commander in Civil and Indian wars. Defeated and killed by Native Americans led by Sioux chiefs Sitting Bull and Crazy Horse at the Battle of the Little Big Horn in Montana. Died at age 36. The battle is also known as Custer's Last Stand. Several U.S. counties, a town, mountain, peak, forest and national park were among the places named for Custer.

Last Words (written): "My Darling—I have but a few moments to write as we start at twelve, and I have my hands full of preparations for the scout. Do not be anxious about me. I hope to have a good report sent to you by the next mail, Your devoted boy, Autie." Letter to his wife.

Sources: *Son of the Morning Star* by Evan S. Connell (San Francisco, CA, 1984); "The Unforgettable Custers" by Stephanie Cooper Shulsinger (*Real West,* September, 1975).

Cut Nose (Neesh-ne-park-ke-ook)

(fl. late 1700s-mid-1800s) Native American leader. Nez Percé chief. Spent time with Lewis and Clark and provided guides for their trip over the Lolo Trail.

Last Words: "My children, I leave you. Love that which is good. Be always at the side that is right and you will prosper." Recorded by Nez Percé leader Richard.

Source: *History of Oregon* by Charles Henry Carey (Chicago, 1922).

Cuthbert, Saint

(635?-687) English prelate, holy man. Monk who lived as a hermit on Farne Island ten years, then left the island. Appointed Bishop of Lindesfarne. Preferred life of a hermit; returned to Farne, where he died.

Last Words: "And know and remember, that if of two evils you are compelled to choose one, I would rather that you should take my bones, and leave these places, to reside wherever God may send you, than consent in any way to the wickedness of schismatics, and so place a yoke upon your necks. Study diligently, and carefully observe the Catholic rules of the Fathers, and practice with zeal those institutes of the monastic life which it has pleased God to deliver to you through my ministry. For I know that although during my life some have despised me, yet after my death you will see what sort of man I was, and that my doctrine was by

no means worthy of contempt."

Source: *Life by Bede with Ecclesiastical History of the English Nation* (London, 1990).

Cutler, Benjamin Clarke

(1798-1863) American clergyman. In charge of first city mission of Episcopal church in New York. Received honorary doctorate from Columbia University. Episcopal rector of St. Ann's Church, Brooklyn, New York, for 30 years. Died at age 65 in Brooklyn.

Last Words: "Lift me up, lift me right up!"

Source: *Memoirs of Rev. Benjamin C. Cutler, D. D., Late Rector of St. Ann's Church, Brooklyn, N.Y.* by Rev. Horatio Gray (New York, 1865).

Cutter, Charles

(1846-1864) American military soldier. Private in Union Army in U.S. Civil War. Served in the 1st Massachusetts Heavy Artillery. Died at age 17 in a military hospital from mortal wounds to the abdomen. His Last Words were heard and recorded by American poet Walt Whitman.

Last Words: "Oh, nothing. I was only looking around to see who was with me." Spoken to Whitman who asked him if anything was wrong. The poet was attending Cutter while serving as a volunteer at a Washington, D.C., hospital.

Source: *The Wounded Dresser* by Walt Whitman (Boston, 1898).

Cuvier, Clementine

(1805-1827) French female. Daughter of French naturalist Georges Cuvier. She and her sisters are credited with making direct contributions to their father's work.

Last Words: "You know we are sisters for eternity.—There is life, it is only there that there is life." Spoken to a friend.

Source: *The Flower Faded. A Short Memoir of Clementine Cuvier, with Reflections by the Author* by Rev. John Angell James (New York, 1835).

Cuvier, Baron Georges

(1769-1832) German-born French naturalist, zoologist, nobleman. Birth name: Georges Léopold Chrétien Frédéric Dagobert Cuvier. Professor of animal anatomy at French National Museum of Natural History. Pioneer in field of comparative anatomy and of paleontology. Showed the significance of fossil records. Named peer for life in 1819. Died at age 62 of cholera in Paris after an illness of just a few days. Several living and extinct animals were named for him.

Different Last Words:

(1) "Nurse, it was I who discovered that leeches have red blood." Spoken to his nurse as leeches were applied to his body.

Source: *Dictionary of Phrase and Fable* by E. Cobham Brewer (Philadelphia, 1898).

(2) "It is very delightful to see those I love still able to swallow." Spoken to his daughter-in-law as she took a glass of lemonade.

Source: *Memoirs of Baron Cuvier* by Mrs. R. Lee (New York, 1833).

Cyprian, Saint

(d. 258) Christian holy man, prelate, martyr. Bishop of Carthage. Beheaded. Left letters and other writings as valuable sources of Church history.

Last Words: "God be thanked." Spoken to the judge who condemned him.

Source: *Lives of the Saints* by S. Baring-Gould (Edinburgh, 1914).

Variation: "Thanks be to God."

Source: *The Last Words (Real and Traditional) of Distinguished Men and Women Collected from Various Sources* by Frederic Rowland Marvin (New York, 1901).

Cyrus the Elder, King of Persia

(600?-529 B.C). Persian ruler. Son of Cambyses I. Father of Cambyses II. King of Persia. Founder of the Persian Empire under the Achaemenid Dynasty. Known as The Great or The Elder. Killed fighting the Massagetae, a tribe from the southern deserts of Kharesm and Kizilhoum, after ignoring his adviser, Croesus, who warned him not to continue forward.

Last Words: "Show kindness to your friends, and then shall you have it in your power to chastise your enemies. Good-bye, my dear sons, bid your mother good-bye for me. And all my friends, who are here or far away, good-bye."

Source: *Education of Cyrus* by Xenophon, Book 8 (London, 1914).

Variation: "Farewell dear children, and say farewell to your mother as from me; farewell, all my friends, present and absent." Closing sentences of his last speech.

Source: *The Last Words (Real and Traditional) of Distinguished Men and Women Collected from Various Sources* by Frederic Rowland Marvin (New York, 1901).

Cyrus the Younger

(424?-401 B.C.) Persian prince. Conspired against his brother Artaxerxes, the king. Led an army to Babylonia, was defeated and killed.

Last Words: "Clear the way, villains, clear the way."

Source: "Artaxerxes" in *Lives of the Noble Grecians and Romans* by Plutarch, tr. by John Dryden (Chicago, 1952).

Czolgosz, Leon

(1873-1901) American anarchist, assassin. Shot and killed President William McKinley at the Pan-American Exposition in Buffalo, New York. Convicted of murder and executed at age 28 by electrocution at Auburn Prison, New York.

Last Words: "I killed the President because he was the enemy of the good people, the good working people. I am not sorry for my crime." As the prison guards strapped him into the chair, he spoke through clenched teeth, "I am sorry I could not see my father."

Source: "I Am Not Sorry" by Jeremy W. Kilar (*Michigan History*, Vol. 79, No. 6, 1995).

da Costa, Uriel

(1585-1640) Portuguese-born Jewish philosopher. Rationalist. His Jewish ancestors were forced to become Christians. Birth name Gabriel da Costa. Became a Jew and changed his name to Uriel da Costa (or Acosta). Persecuted and tormented many years for his religion. Committed suicide at about age 55 in Amsterdam after writing his autobiography. German writer Karl Gutzkow wrote a play about his life: *Der Sadduzäer von Amsterdam* (1834).

Last Words (written): "There, you have the true story of my life. I have shown what role I played in this vain world-theater and in my unimportant and restless life. Now, fellow men, make your just and dispassionate judgment, speaking freely according to the truth, as becomes men who are really men. If you find something which arouses your sympathy, then realize and mourn the sad lot of Man which you share. And let there be no confusion about this: The name that I bore as a Christian in Portugal was Gabriel de Costa; among the Jews—would that I had never got involved with them!—I was known, by a small change, as Uriel." From his autobiography: *Example of a Human Life.*

Source: *Uriel da Costa, oder die Tragodie der Gesinnung* by Josef Kastein (Berlin, Germany, 1932).

Daggett, Shoshone Mike

(1845?-1911) Native American family head. Died near Winnemucca, Nevada, in what may have been the last Native American massacre in the United States. Daggett's family was falsely accused of killing a white man. They were pursued relentlessly. To avoid starvation, they killed a few cattle. When a stockman and three sheepherders came to investigate, the desperate Indians killed them to save themselves. A posse killed Daggett and his band.

Last Words: "Me Shoshone! Me Shoshone! Me heap good Injun!"

Source: *The Last Free Man: The True Story of Shoshone Mike and His Band of Indians in 1911* by Dayton O. Hyde (New York, 1973).

Dahlgren, John Adolphus Bernard

(1809-1870) American military officer. Rear admiral. Headed Union Ordnance Department during U.S. Civil War. Designed Dahlgren gun that was used extensively in the war. Died at age 60 while Commander of Washington Navy Yard. Several ships were named for him.

Last Words: "Madeleine, I will take nothing more until you go to your breakfast, which you must require." Spoken to his wife.

Source: *Memoirs of Admiral Dahlgren* by Madeleine Vinton Dahlgren (Boston, 1882). The author was his wife. In addition to his *Memoirs,* she published his *Notes of Maritime and International Law* (Boston, 1872).

Dahlgren, Ulric

(1842-1863) American military officer. Union Army colonel in U.S. Civil War. While attempting to sweep into Richmond, Virginia, and assassinate Jefferson Davis and his cabinet, Dahlgren was led into an ambush by an informer. Died at age 21 after being shot four times by General Fitz Lee's soldiers.

Last Words: "Surrender, you damned rebels, or I'll shoot you."

Source: *The Civil War: A Book of Quotations,* ed. by Bob Blaisdell (Minneola, NY, 2004).

Dalberg, Karl Theodor Anton Maria von

(1744-1817) German prelate, nobleman. Grand Duke of Frankfurt. Archbishop-elector of Mainz. Arch chancellor of Holy Roman Empire. Primate of Confederation of the Rhine. Friend of Goethe and Schiller. Died at age 73 while Archbishop of Regensburg.

Last Words: "Love! Life!—God's will!" Spoken as he proposed a toast.

Source: *Karl von Dalberg und seine Zeit: Zur Biographie und Charakteristik des Fürsten Primas* by Karl Olivier Beaulieu-Marconnay (Weimar, Germany, 1879).

d'Albret, Jeanne (Jean III or Joan III), Queen of Navarre

(1528-1572) Navarrese monarch. French royalty. Known as Jeanne III or Joan III. Daughter of Henry II. Wife of Duke of Vendome. Mother of King Henry IV of France. Devout Huguenot who made Calvinism the state religion. During her reign, Roman Catholic churches were destroyed and Catholic services were banned. The conflict led to a religious war in 1562. When she died at age 44 in Paris, unfounded rumors circulated that she had been poisoned by Catherine de Medici, her son's prospective mother-in-law.

Different Last Words:

(1) "Weep not for me, I pray you; for God, by this sickness, calls me hence to enjoy a better life; and now I shall enter into the desired haven, toward which this frail vessel of mine has been a long time steering."

Source: *The Silent Pastor: or Consolations for the Sick* by Thomas Sadler (London, 1847).

(2) "Yes, more willing than to linger here in this world of vanity." Her response to one of her attendants who whispered: "Are you willing to go?"

Source: *Great and Good Women: Biographies for Girls* by Lydia Howard Sigourney (Edinburgh, 1871).

d'Alleray, Legrand

(c. early 1700s-1793) Elderly French statesman. He and his wife were taken to a revolutionary tribunal during the French Revolution. Accused of corresponding with their son who was in exile. Executed.

Last Words: "I thank you for the efforts you made to save me; but it would be necessary to purchase our lives by a lie. My wife and myself prefer rather to die. We have grown old together without ever having lied; we will not do so now to save a remnant of life. Do your duty. We will not accuse you of our death, we will accuse the law only." The juries wept from emotion but sent him to the scaffold.

Source: *History of the Girondists: Or, Personal Memoirs of the Patriots of the French Revolution from Unpublished Sources* by Alphonse de Lamartine (London, 1856).

Dalton, Frank

(1859-1887) American lawman. Deputy U.S. marshal. One of the infamous Dalton brothers. Killed at age 28 in Oklahoma while trying to arrest horse thief Dave Smith. Smith shot him and Will Towerly finished him off. Frank Dalton was portrayed in the NBC television series *The Outlaws* in a two-part episode "The Daltons Must Die" in 1961.

Last Words: "Please don't fire. I'm preparing to die."

Source: "The Tragic Death of Deputy U.S. Marshal Frank Dalton" by Phillip Steele (*NOLA Quarterly*, Vol. XVI, No. 4, October-December 1992).

Dalton, Robert ("Bob")

(1867-1892) American train robber, bank robber. Member of Dalton Brothers gang. Killed, along with brother Gratton ("Grat") Dalton during the Battle of Coffeyville, a botched bank robbery.

Last Words: "Don't mind me, boy. I'm done for. Don't surrender! Die game." Spoken to his brother Emmett after Bob was shot, and moments before a volley of bullets was shot at both of them. Bob died instantly. Emmett survived, despite being hit 20 times.

Source: *Pictorial History of the Wild West; A True Account of the Bad Men, Desperadoes, Rustlers, and Outlaws of the Old West—and the Men Who Fought Them to Establish Law and Order* by James David Horan and Paul Sann (London, 1954).

Variation: "It's no use."

Source: *The Outlaws: The Authentic Wild West* by James David Horan (New York, 1977).

Damien of Molokai, Saint

(1840-1889) Belgian clergyman, missionary. Birth name Joseph de Veuster. Known as Father Damien. Member of Congregation of the Sacred Hearts of Jesus and Mary. Devoted his life to the lepers of Hawaii. Moved to the island of Molokai in 1872. Died at age of 48 of leprosy on Molokai. Canonized in 2009.

Last Words: "Well! God's will be done, He knows best. My work with all its faults and failures, is in His hands, and before Easter I shall see my Savior."

Source: *Father Damien, a Journey from Cashmere to His Home in Hawaii* by Edward Clifford (London, 1889). Clifford visited Damien on Molokai in 1888.

Damiens, Robert-François

(1715-1757) French assassin. Tried to assassinate King Louis XV at Versailles in 1757. Tortured and executed in Paris. Last person to be executed in France with gruesome torture form of death penalty used for regicides.

Last Words: "My God, have pity on me! Jesus, deliver me."

Source: *Lettres inédites adressées par la poète Robbé de Beauveset au dessinateur Aignan Desfriches pendant le procès de Rob. Fr. Damiens* (1757) by Pierre-Honoré Robbé de Beauveset, ed. by Georges d' Heylli (Paris, 1885).

Damrosch, Walter Johannes

(1862-1950) German-born American musician, conductor, composer, educator. Son of conductor/composer/violinist Leopold Damrosch. Brother of conductor Frank Damrosch. Reorganized New York Symphonic Society as a permanent orchestra. He conducted it for many years. Died at age 88 in New York City.

Last Words: "Just back from Japan. They loved us in Tokyo. Rave reviews everywhere. Marvelous! Marvelous!"

Source: *The Damrosch Dynasty: America's First Family of Music* by George Whitney Martin (Boston, 1983).

Dancourt, Florent Carton

(1661-1725) French writer, actor, playwright. Notable work: *Le Chevalier à la mode*. Notable role: Alceste in the *Misanthrope* by Molière. Died at age 64. His daughters Manon and Marie Anne (Mimi) gained success on the stage of the Theatre François.

Last Words: "God's will be done! My grave is dug. My last bed is made; as we make our bed so we must lie." His response when his daughter told him: "Father, a man who dies

well is half saved. "
Source: *Men and Women of France, During the Last Century* by Arsène Houssaye (London, 1852).

Dandridge, Dorothy Jean

(1922-1965) American actress, singer. Star of stage, television and screen. Notable movies: *Bright Road; Carmen Jones; Porgy and Bess.* Nominated for Academy Award for *Carmen Jones.* First African-American to receive an Oscar nomination for Best Actress. Died at age 42. The television movie *Introducing Dorothy Dandridge* is based on her career. Her autobiography *Everything and Nothing* was published posthumously in 1970.
Last Words (written): "In case of my death, don't remove anything I have on—scarf, gown or underwear. Cremate me right away. If I have anything—money, furniture, get it to my mother Ruby Dandridge. She will know what to do. Dorothy Dandridge." The note, found in her apartment, was addressed to "Whomever discovers me." An autopsy revealed she died of an embolism, but medical findings showed she had overdosed on an antidepressant. A psychiatric team ruled that the cause of her death remained unresolved.
Source: *The Hollywood Book of Death: The Bizarre, Often Sordid, Passings of More Than 125 American Movie and TV Idols* by James Robert Parish (Chicago, 2002).

Danks, Hart Pease

(1834-1903) American musician, composer. Known for songs and hymns. Member of Songwriters Hall of Fame. Notable song: "Silver Threads Among the Gold." Although the song sold more than 3 million copies, Danks made nothing from it. He had sold all rights to it for very little money. Died in poverty at age 69.
Last Words (written): "It's hard to die alone and—." Written in a note.
Source: *A History of Popular Music in America* by Sigmund Spaeth (New York, 1948).

D'Annunzio, Gabriele

(1863-1938) Italian writer, playwright, military officer, eccentric, fascist. World War I pilot with a reputation for sensational exploits. In 1919, he declared Fiume an independent state as the Italian Regency of Carnaro, with himself as "Duce." His constitution and actions foreshadowed and influenced much of the later Italian fascist system. The city surrendered in 1920. Died of stroke at age 74 at Lake Garda, Italy.
Different Last Words:
(1) "Stop!—Turn home!—I'm bored—I'm bored!" Spoken to his chauffeur.
Source: *D'Annunzio Aneddotico* by Tommaso Antongini (Milan, Italy, 1939).
(2) "I want to see again in springtime the city that I love. I have been thinking about this trip with joy and with trembling." He then went to rest and was found dead in bed a short time later.
Source: *Last Words: A Dictionary of Deathbed Quotations* by C. Bernard Ruffin (Jefferson, NC, 1995).

Danton, Georges Jacques

(1759-1794) French lawyer, revolutionary leader. Voted for the death of King Louis XVI. Seized, imprisoned, condemned and guillotined at age 34 with 14 others, including Camille Desmoulins.
Different Last Words:
(1) "Samson, you will show my head to the people. It is worth seeing." Samson was his executioner.
Source: *Danton* by Hermann Wendel (New Haven, CT, 1935).
Variation: "You will show my head to the people, after my death; it is worth the pains." Spoken to his executioner.
Source: *History of Europe: from the Commencement of the French Revolution to the Restoration of the Bourbons in 1815* by Archibald Alison Sr. (Edinburgh, 1849-50).
(2) (doubtful): "My name is Danton; my dwelling will soon be in annihilation; but my name will live in the Pantheon of history!" Spoken to the judges who asked him his name, residence, etc.
Source: *The Last Words (Real and Traditional) of Distinguished Men and Women Collected from Various Sources* by Frederic Rowland Marvin (New York, 1901). Marvin gave as his source *Lamartine*.
Several sources state that Danton did say this to the judge after he was arrested in March 1794. But none indicate that these were his Last Words or were even spoken immediately before he died. He was not executed until April 1794.
Sources: *Progress: a Monthly Magazine of Advanced Thought* (London, 1883-1887); *A Biographical*

Dictionary of Freethinkers of All Ages and Nations by J. M. Wheeler (London, 1889).

Darden, Willie Jasper

(1923-1988) American accused murderer, thief. Arrested and convicted in 1974 for shooting and killing a man in a furniture store robbery in Lakeland, Florida. Darden was steadfast in his insistence that he was innocent. The case was appealed to the U.S Supreme Court in 1985. The Court upheld his conviction 5-4. When he was executed in 1988, many thought he did not commit the crime. He became a poster boy for banning capital punishment.

Last Words: "I tell you, I am not guilty of the charge for which I am about to be electrocuted."

Source: *"Who Was Willie Darden?" Executing Justice: The Moral Meaning of the Death Penalty* by Lloyd Steffen (Cleveland, OH, 1998).

Darius III, King of Persia

(380-330 B.C.) Persian ruler. Great-grandson of Darius II. Last king of Achaemenid dynasty. Spent his reign in a struggle with Alexander the Great who defeated him and brought the Persian Empire to an end. Darius was assassinated by order of Bessus, his satrap.

Last Words: "But Alexander, whose kindness to my mother, my wife, and my children I hope the gods will recompense, will doubtless thank you for your humanity to me. Tell him, therefore, in token of my acknowledgment, I give him this right hand."

Source: "Alexander" in *Lives of the Noble Grecians and Romans* by Plutarch, tr. by John Dryden (New York, 1932).

Darnell, Linda

(1923-1965) American actress. Screen star. Real name Monetta Eloyse Darnell. Notable movies: *Forever Amber; The Mark of Zorro; Blood and Sand; Hangover Square.* Burned seriously in a house fire in Glenview, Illinois; died at age 41 the next day.

Last Words: "I love you, baby, I love you." Spoken to her daughter at the Cook County Hospital Burn Treatment Center.

Source: *The Hollywood Book of Death: The Bizarre, Often Sordid, Passings of More Than 125 American Movie and TV Idols* by James Robert Parish (Chicago, 2002).

Darwin, Charles Robert

(1809-1882) English scientist, naturalist, writer, traveler. Demonstrated evidence and support for theory that species originated through evolutionary change by mechanism of natural selection. Notable works: *On the Origin of Species; The Descent of Man.* Died at age 73 in Downe, Kent, England.

Last Words: "I am not the least afraid to die."

Source: *The Life and Letters of Charles Darwin,* ed. by Sir Francis Darwin (New York, 1899). The editor was his son.

Darwin, Erasmus

(1731-1802) English scientist, writer, poet, philosopher, inventor, physician. Grandfather of Charles Darwin. Conducted experiments in galvanism. Produced several inventions but patented none of them. Member of Lunar Society. Notable works: *The Botanic Garden; Zoönomia.* Died at age 70.

Last Words: "There is no time to be lost." Spoken to his wife when he felt his condition was worsening. He asked her to bleed him instantly. She declined. After he spoke these words, she asked him to direct her. He then sank into a chair and died.

Source: *Evolution, Old and New; or, The Theories of Buffon, Dr. Erasmus Darwin, and Lamarck, as Compared with That of Mr. Charles Darwin* by Samuel Butler (London, 1882).

Davenant or D'Avenant, William

(1606-1668) English writer, poet, playwright, theater manager. Poet laureate of England in 1638. Supported Charles I in a civil war. Sentenced to death by Cromwellians. Imprisoned in Cowes Castle and later the Tower of London. Released by the intercession of John Milton. During the Restoration, Davenant was given a patent to operate a theater. Died at age 62 in London.

Last Words (doubtful): "I shall ask leave to desist, when I am interrupted by so great an experiment as dying."

Source: Various Last Words compilations and Internet websites.

These were Davenant's words, but they were not his Last Words. He wrote them 18 years earlier, in 1650, as a postscript to a poem while in prison at Cowes Castle.

Source: *Essays on Shakespeare* by Karl Elze (New York, 1874).

David, Jacques-Louis (Louis)

(1748-1825) French artist, painter. Founder of French classical school of painting. Court painter to Louis XVI and Napoleon. Notable works: *Napoleon Crossing the Alps; The Coronation of Napoleon; Napoleon in his Imperial Robes*. Went into exile in Brussels, Belgium, in 1816. Died at age 77 in Brussels.

Last Words: "Too dark. Too light. The dimming of the light is not well enough indicated. This place is blurred. However, I must admit that's a unique head of Leonidas." Spoken when a print of his *Leonidas at Thermopylae* was brought to him to examine. He used his cane to point to places where corrections were needed. He died a short time later.

Source: *Louis David, son école et son temps: souvenirs* by E.J. Delécluze (Paris, 1855).

Davidson, Lucretia Maria

(1808-1825) American writer, poet. Wrote 278 poems that gained her a creative reputation after her death. Died at age 16 in Plattsburgh, New York. Her cause of death was either consumption (tuberculosis) or an eating disorder (anorexia nervosa). Edgar Allen Poe wrote about her and her sister, also a writer who died in her teens. Poe was critical of earlier romanticized treatments of her life, particularly by English biographer Robert Southey, who wrote about her in 1827 and laid the groundwork for much of what was later said about her.

Last Words: "Death, which once looked so dreadful to me, is now divested of all its terrors." Her final words were provided by her mother, who said Lucretia spoke often and calmly of her approaching death.

Sources: *Lives of Sir William Phips, Israel Putnam, Lucretia Maria Davidson* (Boston, 1837); *Poetic Remains* by Lucretia Maria Davidson (New York, 1852).

Davidson, William

(1781-1820) Jamaican-born English cabinetmaker, conspirator. Member of Cato Street Conspiracy, a failed attempt to assassinate British government officials at a London dinner party. The conspiracy was thwarted by the police. Eleven men were arrested. Five were found guilty of high treason and executed. Davidson was the only one of the five who prayed and showed remorse before he was executed.

Last Words: "God bless you all. Good-bye. God save the king!" He prayed with great fervency and expressed penitence for his crimes before he was hanged.

Source: *Old and New London: A Narrative of Its History, Its People and Its Places* by Walter Thornbury and Edward Walford (London, 1881).

Daviess, Joseph Hamilton

(1774-1811) American lawyer, military officer. Major and commander of the Dragoons of Indiana Militia at the Battle of Tippecanoe. Married sister of Chief Justice John Marshall. Daviess was the first attorney west of the Appalachians to argue a case before the U.S. Supreme Court. He brought treason charges against Aaron Burr that were dismissed with the assistance of Burr's attorney Henry Clay. Daviess was killed fighting with Governor Harrison's troops against Tecumseh's village at Prophetstown. Counties in Illinois, Indiana, Kentucky and Missouri were named for him.

Last Words: "Under no circumstances let me fall into the hands of savages."

Source: *A Conspectus of American Biography: Being an Analytical Summary of American History and Biography, Containing also the Complete Indexes of the National Cyclopedia of American Biography* by George Derby (New York, 1906).

Davis, Cushman Kellogg

(1838-1900) American lawyer, military officer, politician. Union Army first lieutenant in U.S. Civil War. Member of U.S. Senate from Minnesota. Member of commission that met in Paris in September 1898 to arrange peace terms after Spanish-American war. Also served in Minnesota house of representatives and briefly as governor of Minnesota. Died at age 62 in St. Paul, Minnesota.

Last Words: "Oh that I might live five more years for my country's sake."

Source: "Cushman K. Davis of Minnesota Dead; Senator's End Came After Hours of Unconsciousness. Was Delirious for a Week. Unable in His Weakened Condition to Withstand the Poisons Due to Kidney Disease" (*New York Times*, November 28, 1900).

Davis, Jefferson Finis

(1808-1889) American politician, military officer, statesman. Member U.S. House of

Representatives, U.S. Senate from Mississippi. Secretary of war in cabinet of U.S. President Franklin Pierce. Colonel of volunteer regiment in Mexican War. Served in Mississippi legislature before U.S. Civil War. President of Confederate States of America. Spent final years in retirement at his estate near Biloxi, Mississippi. Died at age 81 in New Orleans.

Last Words: "Pray excuse me. I cannot take it." Spoken when he was urged to take some medicine.

Source: *Jefferson Davis, His Life and Personality* by Morris Schaff (Boston, 1922).

Davis, Jerome Dean

(1838-1910) American missionary, educator, theologian, military officer. Served as lieutenant colonel in military. First foreign teacher in a Japanese college. Encouraged education of women with establishment of Kobe Women's College and Doshisha Girls' School. Died at age 72 in Oberlin, Ohio.

Last Words: "I have no other message than my life; my life is my message to my children." Spoken to his loved ones the day before his death.

Source: *Davis: Soldier, Missionary; a Biography of Rev. Jerome D. Davis, D.D., Lieut-Colonel of Volunteers and for Thirty-nine Years a Missionary of the American Board of Commissioners for Foreign Missions in Japan* by J. Merle Davis (Boston, 1916).

Davis, Richard Harding

(1864-1916) American journalist, war correspondent, novelist, playwright, editor. Managing editor of *Harper's Weekly*. Gained fame for his coverage of the Spanish-American War, Second Boer War and World War I. Model for Charles Dana Gibson's dashing "Gibson man." Mentioned in Sinclair Lewis's book, *Dodsworth* as an example of the exciting, adventure-seeking hero. Died at age 52 of a heart attack in Mount Kisco, New York.

Last Words (written): "That France and her Allies succeed should be the hope and prayer of every American. The fight they are waging is for the things the real unhyphenated American is supposed to hold most high and most dear. Incidentally, they are fighting his fight, for their success will later save him, unprepared as he is to defend him-self, from a humiliating and terrible thrashing. And every word and act of his now that helps the Allies is a blow against frightfulness, against despotism, and in behalf of a broader civilization, a nobler freedom, and a much more pleasant world in which to live."

Source: *Richard Harding Davis and His Day* by Fairfax Davis Downey (New York, 1933).

Davis, Ruth Elizabeth ("Bette")

(1908-1989) American actress. Stage and screen star. First actress to receive 10 Academy Award nominations. Won for *Jezebel* and *Dangerous*. First woman to receive Lifetime Achievement Award from American Film Institute. Davis was placed second, behind Katharine Hepburn, on the American Film Institute's list of the greatest female stars of all time. Davis was the co-founder of the Hollywood Canteen and was the first female president of the Academy of Motion Picture Arts and Sciences. Died at age 81 at the American Hospital in Neuilly-sur-Seine, France.

Last Words: "Tell B.D. I'm sorry. I loved her. I really did love her." She was speaking about her daughter Barbara who had become estranged from her mother in later years.

Source: *Last Words: A Dictionary of Deathbed Quotations* by C. Bernard Ruffin (Jefferson, NC, 2005). Ruffin gave as his source *National Enquirer*, October 16, 1989.

Davis, Sammy, Jr.

(1925-1990) American entertainer, singer, dancer, actor. Star of stage, screen and television. He began as a child performer in vaudeville. Broke many performance color barriers. Was a member of the "Rat Pack," along with Frank Sinatra, Dean Martin, Joey Bishop and Peter Lawford. His television shows include *Sammy and Company* and *The Sammy Davis Jr. Show*. Died at age 64 of throat cancer in Los Angeles, California.

Last Words (doubtful): "Don't cry for me. I'll be dancing in heaven."

Source: Various Last Words compilations and Internet websites.

It is unlikely that he spoke these Last Words. Davis's larynx was removed a few weeks before he died from throat cancer, leaving him unable to talk. His wife indicated that the cancer had taken his voice but "he could still talk with his feet."

Sources: "The Cancer That Silenced Mr. Wonderful's Song" by Sue Rochman (*Cancer Research Magazine* 2:3, 2007); *In Black and White: The Life of Sammy Davis, Jr.* by Wil Haygood (New York, 2003).

Davis, Samuel ("Sam")

(1842-1863) American soldier, scout, spy. Private in Confederate First Tennessee Volunteer Infantry in U.S. Civil War. Known as the Boy Hero of the Confederacy. Captured near Minor Hill, Tennessee, in possession of Union battle plans. Arrested as spy and sentenced to die unless he divulged the name of his contact. He refused and was hanged at age 21 by the Union Army.

Last Words: "Do you suppose were I your friend that I would betray you? Sir, if you think I am that kind of man, you have missed your mark. You may hang me a thousand times and I would not betray my friends." His response when asked whether he would save himself by identifying his contact. After saying a prayer with a chaplain, he stepped upon the trap and said: "I am ready."

Sources: *Southern by the Grace of God* by Michael Andrew Grissom (Gretna, LA, 1989); *Valor in Gray: The Recipients of the Confederate Medal of Honor* by Gregg S. Clemmer (Staunton, VA, 1996).

Davis, Thomas Osborne

(1814-1845) Irish politician, writer, poet. Part of the Young Ireland movement. Established newspaper, *The Nation*. Notable work: "A Nation Once Again" (song). Died at age 30 of tuberculosis.

Last Words (written): "I had a bad attack of scarletina, with a horrid sore throat.—In four days I hope to be able to look at light business for a short time." Letter to Charles Cavan Duffy, co-founder of *The Nation*.

Source: *Short Life of Thomas Davis, 1840-1846* by Sir Charles Gavan Duffy (London, 1896)

Davis, Varina Anne Banks Howell

(1826-1906) American matron, journalist. First Lady of the Confederacy. Wife of Jefferson Davis. Moved to New York City after her husband died in 1889. Wrote column for *New York World*. Died at age 80 in New York after a bout of pneumonia.

Last Words: "My darling child, I am going to die this time but I'll try to be brave about it. Don't you wear black. It is bad for your health and will depress your husband." Spoken to her daughter. She then repeated a prayer: "Oh Lord, in Thee have I trusted, let me now be confounded."

Sources: *First Lady of the South: The Life of Mrs. Jefferson Davis* by Isabel Ross (New York, 1973); *Varina Howell, Wife of Jefferson Davis* by Mrs. Dunbar Rowland. Preface by Eron Rowland (New York, 1931).

Davy, Sir Humphry, 1st Baronet

(1778-1829) English chemist, philosopher, educator, inventor. Professor of chemistry. President of the Royal Society. Experimented with nitrogen, hydrogen, other gases. First to prepare sodium, calcium, potassium. Invented miner's safety lamp. Discovered properties of nitrous oxide. Knighted in 1812. Created baronet in 1818. Died at age 50 in Geneva, Switzerland.

Last Words: "I am dying; and when it is all over, I desire that no disturbance of any kind may be made in the house; lock the door, and let everyone retire to his *own* apartment." Spoken to his brother as death approached.

Source: "Sir Humphry Davy" in *The Parent's Cabinet of Amusement and Instruction* (London, 1858). Footnote states Davy's memoir was taken from biographies by Dr. Paris and by Humphry Davy's brother John.

Variation: "I am dying," or words to that effect, "and when it is all over, I desire that no disturbance of any kind may be made in the house; lock the door, and let every one retire *quietly* to his apartment."

Source: *The Life of Sir Humphry Davy, Bart* by John Ayrton Paris (London, 1831). Paris's version, published two years after Davy's death, indicates the quotation was "or words to that effect" and has very minor variations from later published versions, such as the use of the words "own" and "quietly."

Day, Dorothy

(1897-1980) American peace activist, reformer, journalist. Convert to Roman Catholicism. A founder of *The Catholic Worker* and Pax Christi USA. Friend of the poor and downtrodden. Condemned war and oppression of workers. Jailed for acts of civil disobedience. Died at age 83 after a heart attack in New York City.

Different Last Words:

(1) "How good life can be at certain

moments." Spoken to her daughter Tamar who was at her side when she died.
Source: *Love is the Measure* by James H. Forest (New York, 1986).
(2) "Rise, clasp my hand, and come!" Whispered on her deathbed.
Source: *Meet Dorothy Day: Champion of the Poor* (Ann Arbor, MI, 2002).

Day, Leon
(1916-1995) American athlete. Professional baseball player in Negro Leagues. Noted right-handed fastball pitcher. Played for Baltimore Black Sox, Brooklyn and Newark Eagles and Baltimore Elite Giants. Pitched a perfect season in 1937 (13-0) while batting .320. Appeared in seven East-West All-Star Games; set All Star record striking out 14 batters and Negro League record striking out 18 batters, including Roy Campanella three times. Died at age 78 in Baltimore, Maryland, just six days after he learned he had been elected to the National Baseball Hall of Fame.
Last Words: "You promise?"
Source: "The Late Leon Day Has His Hall of Fame Dream Realized" by Dick Heller (*Washington Times*, July 30, 1995).

Dead (Per Yngve Ohlin)
(1969-1991) Swedish musician. Lead singer for black-metal band Mayhem. Known for occult stage antics. Died at age 22. Band mate discovered him dead with his wrists slit and a gunshot wound to the head. He left a suicide note.
Last Words (written): "Beklager alt blodet." (tr. "Excuse all the blood.") A band member later claimed the note included the following: "The knife was too dull to finish the job so I had to use the shotgun."
Source: *Lords of Chaos: The Bloody Rise of the Satanic Metal Underground* by Michael Moynihan and Didrik Søderlind (Venice, CA, 1998).

Dean, James
(1931-1955) American actor. Star of stage, screen and television. Was driving his Porsche Spider on a California two-lane highway with his mechanic Rolf Weutherich. Saw a car approaching the intersection. Killed in the collision at age 24. Received posthumous Academy Award nomination for Best Actor twice.

Last Words: "He'll see us." Dean's exact Last Words are debatable. Weutherich was thrown from the car and was seriously injured but he survived the impact. The driver of the other car had minor injuries.
Source: *James Dean in Death: A Popular Encyclopedia of a Celebrity Phenomenon* by Warren Beath with Paula Wheeldon (Jefferson, NC, 2005).

Dearing, James
(1840-1865) American military officer. U.S. Civil War Confederate general. Shot by General Theodore Read's orderly as Dearing and Read engaged in a saber (or pistol) duel at the Battle of High Bridge. Died at age 24 at Sayler's Creek, Virginia.
Last Words: "These belong on his collar." Spoken on his deathbed to Colonel Elijah White as Dearing pointed to the brigadier general's stars on his collar. Even as Dearing lay dying, he wanted to acknowledge the contribution of someone else to the war effort.
Source: *Touring Virginia's and West Virginia's Civil War Sites* by Clint Johnson (Winston-Salem, NC, 1999).

de Bary, Gerald
(1926-1964) Swiss-born American zoologist. Director of Hogle Zoological Gardens in Salt Lake City when he died at age 37. Fatally bitten when he fell into the cage of an African puff adder—one of the world's deadliest snakes—while preparing to clean it. Treated and hospitalized. He seemed to be recovering but took a turn for the worst and died 30 hours after he had been bitten. He did not want the snake destroyed.
Last Words: "Don't blame the snake. He was only protecting himself." Spoken shortly before he died.
Source: *Time* magazine, February 7, 1964.

Debs, Eugene Victor
(1855-1926) American labor leader, politician, socialist. One of the founders of the Industrial Workers of the World. Led the Pullman strike in 1895. Socialist Party of America candidate for U.S. President five times. Indicted for espionage and sentenced to 10 years in prison for opposing war. Released after nearly three years by U.S. President Harding. Died at age 70 in Elmhurst, Illinois.

Last Words (written): "It matters not how straight the gait. How charged with punishment the scroll. I am the master of my fate. I am the captain of my soul." His Last Words were a quotation from William Ernest Henley's poem *Invictus*. As he finished writing, his pencil fell from his hand. His wife took the paper and said the family would preserve it as his last utterance.

Source: "Eugene V. Debs Dies After a Long Illness. Socialist Leaders Succumbs to Heart Ailments After a Month in an Illinois Sanitarium. Once Leader of Rail Union. He Led Pullman Strike in 1895—Served Nearly Three Years in Prison For Opposing War" (*New York Times,* October 21, 1926).

Decatur, Stephen

(1779-1820) American military officer. U.S. naval officer. Distinguished himself during War of 1812, in Tripoli, Libya and against the Barbary States. Killed at age 41 in a duel by another naval officer, James Barron. Decatur's funeral was attended by a U.S. President, the Supreme Court, most of the U.S. Congress and 10,000 citizens. Five counties and at least a dozen U.S. towns and cities were named for him.

Last Words: "I am mortally wounded, I think."

Source: *Decatur* by Irvin Anthony (New York, 1931).

Variation: "I am a dying man." His response when asked if he was much injured. He told one of his bedside visitors: "You can do me no service. Go to my wife and do what you can to console her." The rest of what transpired during his last moments is treated by his biographer Alexander Slidell Mackenzie as a series of indirect quotations.

Source: *Life of Stephen Decatur, a Commander in the Navy of the United States* by Alexander Slidell Mackenzie (Boston, 1846).

Deffand, Marquise du

(1697-1780) French noblewoman. Birth name Marie Anne de Vichy Chamrond. Married Marquis du Deffand. Known for her correspondence and friendships with Voltaire, Montesquieu, Walpole. Reputed mistress of regent, Duke of Orleans. Died at age 83 in Paris, surrounded by close friends.

Different Last Words:

(1) "[She would] confess to my friend, the Duc de Choiseul." Her response when she was urged to confess.

Source: *Madame de Choiseul et son temps*: *étude sur la société française à la fin du XVIIIe siècle* by J. Grasset (Paris, 1874).

(2) "Do you love me then?" Spoken to her faithful secretary on her deathbed.

Source: *The Salon: A Study of French Society and Personalities in the Eighteenth Century* by Helen Clergue (New York, 1907).

(3) "Monsieur le Cure, I accuse myself of having broken God's Ten Commandments, and of having committed the seven mortal sins!"

Source: *Ho for Heaven. Man's Changing Attitude Toward Dying* by Virginia Moore (New York, 1946).

Defoe, Daniel

(1660-1731) English novelist, pamphleteer, journalist. Original surname: Foe. Changed his name in his 20s. Notable works*: Moll Flanders; Robinson Crusoe*. Died at age 70 alone and in debt in a London boarding house. His cause of death was recorded as "lethargy."

Last Words (doubtful): "I don't know which is most difficult in a Christian life—to live well or to die well."

Source: Various Last Words compilations and Internet websites.

These words first appeared in Defoe's *Compleat Tradesman* (published 1724), seven years before Defoe died.

Source: *Memoirs of the Life and Times of Daniel De Foe: Containing a Review of His Writings and His Opinions upon a Variety of Important Matters, Civil and Ecclesiastical* by Walter Wilson (London, 1830).

de Gaulle, Charles André Joseph Marie

(1890-1970) French military officer, politician, statesman, general. Wounded at Battle of Verdun during World War I. Leader of Free French Forces during World War II. First president of the Fifth Republic. Retired in 1969. Died the following year at age 79.

Last Words: "It hurts." Spoken to his wife when he suffered a heart attack.

Source: *Death, a New Perspective on the Phenomena of Disease and Dying* by M. L Kothari and L.M. Metha (New York, 1986).

Variation: "What is the matter with me? Yvonne, I hurt on my right side! Call a doctor!" A doctor and the family priest were summoned. de Gaulle was given the last sacraments, lost consciousness and died.

Source: "A Glimpse of Glory, a Shiver of Grandeur" (*Time* magazine, November 23,1970).

DeJarnette, Henry

(1921-1997) U.S. Army soldier. One of the liberators of Dachau concentration camp in Germany during World War II. Among the first Allied troops to go through Dachau's gate and see the horrors. His division discovered a death train at the edge of the camp. Of the 1,500 to 2,000 people packed into the boxcars, only one man was alive.

Last Words: "Call the Gilberts and let them know." (Mr. and Mrs. F.R. Gilbert had been liberated from Dachau by DeJarnette and other members of the U.S. Army's Rainbow Division on April 29, 1945.)

Source: "Henry DeJarnette: Death Camp Liberator Dies. Cedar Rapids Resident Was One of the 1st U.S. Soldiers to Enter Concentration Camp" (*Cedar Rapids* [Iowa] *Gazette*, November 14, 1997).

de Kalb, Baron Johann von Robaii

(1721-1780) German-born military officer. Major general in Continental Army during the American Revolution. Captured by the British after he had been wounded several times at the Battle of Camden in South Carolina. Died of injuries three days later at age 59. Monument at the Maryland state house honors his contributions to the independence struggle of colonists. His portrait was painted posthumously by Charles Willson Peale. Counties in Alabama, Georgia, Illinois, Indiana and Missouri are named for him; also towns in Mississippi and Illinois.

Last Words: "I thank you for your generous sympathy, but I die the death I always prayed for, the death of a soldier fighting for the rights of man." Spoken to a British officer.

Source: *Historic Camden: Colonial and Revolutionary,* Vol. I, by Robert M. Kennedy and Thomas J. Kirkland (Kershaw County, SC, 1905).

Dekker, Eduard Douwes ("Multatuli")

(1820-1887) Dutch writer, novelist, social reformer. Pen name Multatuli. Protested offenses in the Dutch colonial system. Wrote a novel to expose abuses in Java: *Max Havelaar* (1860). Died at age 66.

Last Words (written): "That you are still not crushed, I admit, but that will come a little later. And if this is too difficult for you, let it go, if you like; the game can wait." Written while playing chess by mail.

Source: *Der letzte Brief* by Friedrich Reck-Malleczewen (Frankfurt, Germany, 1949).

De Koven, Reginald

(1859-1920) American musician, composer, conductor, song writer, critic. Real name Henry Louis Reginald. Founded and conducted Washington Philharmonic Orchestra. Introduced more than 400 songs through his operas and operettas. Notable songs: "Oh Promise Me"; "The Spinning Song"; "Little Boy Blue"; "Do You Remember Love?"; "Gypsy Song." Died at age 61 in Chicago.

Last Words (written): "House sold out for Friday night, box office Vox Dei. Hurrah." Telegram to his wife.

Source: *A Musician and His Wife* by Mrs. Reginald De Koven (New York, 1926).

Delacroix, Ferdinand Victor Eugène

(1798-1863) French artist, painter. Leader of Romanticism in art. Notable works: *Self-Portrait; Dante and Virgil in Hell; Liberty on the Barricade.* Died at age 65 in Paris.

Different Last Words:

(1) His Last Words were printed in the newspaper *Le Figaro*. They included a request to have his eyes closed directly after he died.

Source: *At Home in Paris; and a Trip Through the Vineyards to Spain* by Blanchard Jerrold (London, 1864).

(2) He wanted his tomb to be copied from "classic forms with firm masculine mouldings, contrary to all that is now done in architecture." Part of his Last Words dictated in his will a few hours before he died.

Source: "The Barbizon School, First paper. Delacroix, Decamps and Diaz" by John LaFarge (*McClure's Magazine,* Vol. XXI, No. 2, June 1903).

(3) "Oh, if I get well, I will do wonderful things! My mind is bubbling with ideas!"

Source: *Last Words: A Dictionary of Deathbed Quotations* by C. Bernard Ruffin (Jefferson, NC, 1995).

Delahanty, Edward James ("Big Ed")

(1867-1903) American athlete. Professional baseball player. One of five famed Delahanty brothers. Played outfield mainly with Philadelphia Quakers/Phillies and Washington Senators. Led his league in slugging five times, RBI three times, homers twice, doubles five times, and steals once. Died at age 35. Found drowned in the Niagara River. He was inducted into the Baseball Hall of Fame in 1945.

Last Words: Cries for help. On the night of July 3, 1903, Delahanty was put off a train for disorderly conduct. He was spotted by Samuel Kingston, the night watchman of the Grand Trunk Rail Road Bridge over the Niagara River. Kingston was carrying a lantern. Delahanty said to him: "Take that light away or I'll knock your damned brains out!" Kingston asked why Delahanty was on the bridge and was met with a repeat of the earlier threat. Details about how Delahanty ended up in the water are not clear. By most accounts he fell. Kingston said the last he saw or heard of Delahanty was after he was in the water and his last words were cries for help.

Source: *Ed Delahanty in the Emerald Age of Baseball* by Jerrold Casway (Notre Dame, IN, 2004). Casway's source for this account came from an interview Ed's brother Frank Delahanty had done in 1963 (*Cleveland Plain Dealer*, May 26, 1963).

De La Mare, Walter John

(1873-1956) English poet, short-story writer, novelist. Pen name Walter Ramal. Notable works: *The Listeners and Other Poems; Peacock Pie; Memoirs of a Midget.* Died at age 83 in Twickenham, near London.

Last Words: "Too late for fruit, too soon for flowers." His response to his daughter when asked if he would like some fruit or flowers.

Source: *Oxford Book of Literary Anecdotes* by James Sutherland (Oxford, England, 1975).

De Lancey, Sir William Howe

(1778-1815) American-born British military officer. Colonel. Died from injuries received at Waterloo. He and his wife Magdalene had been married only a few months when he was called to serve at Waterloo. She spent a week with him and wrote *A week at Waterloo in 1815* about her experiences.

Last Words: "Magdalene, my love, the spirits." Spoken to his wife who was caring for him at a French farmhouse.

Source: *A Week at Waterloo in 1815. Lady De Lancey's Narrative: Being an Account of how She Nursed Her Husband, Colonel Sir William Howe De Lancey, Quartermaster General of the Army, Mortally Wounded in the Great Battle* by Lady Magdalene Hall DeLancey, ed. by Major B.R. Ward (London, 1906).

Delane, John Thadeus

(1817-1879) English editor, journalist. Editor of *The Times of London*. During his tenure, the *Times* grew in importance. He supported Florence Nightingale's attempt to reform military hospitals. Died at age 62 in Ascot, England.

Last Words: "It is better for me to die than to live."

Source: *John Thadeus Delane* by Arthur Irwin Dasent (London, 1908). The author was his nephew.

Delaney, Joe Alton

(1958-1983) American athlete. Professional football player who played two seasons with Kansas City Chiefs. Set four franchise records that would stand more than 20 years. AFC Rookie of the Year in 1981. Died at age 24 in Monroe, Louisiana, while attempting to rescue three children from drowning in a lake. Posthumously awarded Presidential Citizen's Medal from President Ronald Reagan.

Last Words: "I can't swim good, but I've got to save those kids. If I don't come up, get somebody." His response when asked if he could swim. He was the only person in the crowd who jumped in to try and save the children, two of whom also drowned.

Source: "Sometimes the Good Die Young–The Chiefs' Joe Delaney Would Have Been 25 Last Week Had He Not Given Up His Life Attempting to Save Two Drowning Boys" by Frank Deford (*Sports Illustrated*, November 7, 1983).

Delano, Jane Arminda

(1862-1919) American nurse, educator. Member of the New York Chapter of the American Red Cross during the Spanish-American War; served as secretary for enrollment of nurses. Superintendent of the U.S. Army Nurse Corps. President of American Nurses Association. Chair of National Committee of the Red Cross Nursing Service. Founded American Red Cross Nursing System by uniting American Nurses Association, Army Nurse Corps and American Red Cross. Died at age 57 in a French hospital after World War I.

Last Words: "What about my work? I must get back to my work."

Source: "Jane Arminda Delano" in *Dictionary of American Biography* (New York, 1936).

Delany, Mary Granville

(1700-1788) English artist, writer. Friend of British King George III and Queen Charlotte. Literary correspondent of Jonathan Swift. Some of her paper mosaics (collages) are now in the British Museum. Notable work: *Autobiography and Letters* (6 vol.; provides interesting insight into English society during her era). Died at age 87.

Last Words: "I have always had a presentiment that if bark were given, it would be my death. You know I have at times great defluxion on my lungs; it will stop that and my breath with it.—Oh, I never was reckoned obstinate, and I will not die so." Spoken when she was told that doctors had ordered bark to be administered.

Source: *Mrs. Delany (Mary Granville): A Memoir, 1700-1788* by George Paston (New York, 1900).

de la Torre, Lisandro

(1868-1939) Argentine lawyer, politician, political reformer. His writings on municipalities and communes laid the groundwork for the concept of municipal autonomy that was incorporated into the 1994 Argentine Constitution. Elected to provincial legislature as a representative of Santa Fe. As national senator, he investigated the meat trade. During the investigation, his disciple, senator-elect Enzo Bordavere, was murdered by a bullet that was meant for him. Economic problems and guilt over Bordavere's death troubled him. Committed suicide at age 70. Places named for him include a barrio in Buenos Aires, stadium, library and many streets. The 1984 film *Asesinato en el senado de la nación* dramatized the murder of Bordavere.

Last Words (written): "If you do not disapprove she would wish that my ashes be thrown to the wind, it seems to me to be an excellent way of disappearing into everything that dies in the Universe." Suicide note.

Source: *Lisandro de la Torre* by Dardo Cúneo (Buenos Aires, Argentina, 1986).

De Long, George Washington

(1844-1881) American explorer, military leader, U.S. Navy lieutenant commander. Set out to find way to North Pole via Bering Strait. Discovered and claimed three islands (De Long Islands). When his ship USS *Jeannette* became trapped in ice, he and his crew abandoned ship and set out for Siberia in three groups. De Long died of starvation near Mat Vay, Yakutsk, Siberia. A survivor, Chief Engineer George W. Melville, returned a year later and found the bodies of De Long and his group. His diary was found with him. Nineteen expedition members and rescuers died during the expedition and later. Two ships and De Long Mountains in northwest Alaska were named in his honor

Last Words (written): Sunday October 30, 140th Day. "Boyd and Gertz died during night. Mr. Collins dying." Last entry in his diary.

Source: *In the Lena Delta: A Narrative of the Search for Lieut.-Commander De Long and His Companions* by George Wallace Melville (Boston, 1885).

De Mille, Cecil Blount

(1881-1959) American film producer, director. Notable movies: *King of Kings; The Ten Commandments; The Greatest Show on Earth; The Buccaneer; Union Pacific*. Produced popular dramatic radio series: *The Lux Radio Theater* (1936 to 1945). Died at age 77 in Hollywood, California.

Last Words (written): "'The Lord giveth and the Lord taketh away. Blessed be the name of the Lord.' It can only be a short time until those words, the first in the Episcopal funeral services, are spoken over me. After those words are spoken, what am I? I am only what I have accomplished. How much good have I spread? How much evil have I spread? For what am I a moment after death—a spirit, a soul, a bodiless mind—I shall have to look back and forward, for I have to take both with me." Written the night before he died.

Source: *Cecil B. De Mille* by Charles Higham (New York, 1973).

Democratis Junior, see Burton, Robert.

De Molay, Jacques

(1244?-1314) Frankish nobleman, knight. Last Grand Master of the Knights Templar. Executed by burning at the stake by order of Pope Clement V and King Philip IV of France after the Knights were accused of heresy, blasphemy, thievery and more. De Molay declared his innocence. His Last Words were a prophecy.

Last Words: "Gentlemen at least let me join my hands and make a prayer to God for now the time is fitting. Here I see my judgment when death freely suits me. God knows who is wrong and who has sinned. Soon misfortune will come to those that have wrongly condemned us: God will avenge our death. Gentlemen, make no mistake, all those against us will have to suffer because of us. In that belief I wish to die. That is my faith; and I beg you to turn my face toward the Virgin Mary, of whom our Lord Christ was born." Known as the "Account of the Stake." Recorded by Geoffroi de Paris who wrote it in poetic form. From this poem, De Molay's Last Words were frequently shortened by later historians and writers to: "Let evil swiftly befall those who have wrongly condemned us. God will avenge us," often as part of the story of the "Curse of The Accursed Kings" said to have befallen the Capetian kings of France. The prophecy did come true: Pope Clement V died a month later. Then Philip IV was killed on a hunting trip, followed in rapid succession by the deaths of Philip IV's three sons between 1314 and 1328. They were the last direct line of the Capetian kings of France.

Source: *La chronique métrique attribuée à Geffroy de Paris* by Geoffroi de Paris, ed. by A. H. Diverres (Paris, 1956); original text in ms. fr. 146 of the Bibliothèque Nationale (Paris, 1314-1318).

Variation: "None of us have betrayed either our God or our country: we die innocent: the decree which condemns us is an unjust one, but there is in heaven an august tribunal where the oppressed never implore in vain; to that tribunal I cite thee, O Roman Pontiff, within forty days thou shalt be there; and thee, O, Philip, my master and my king: in vain do I pardon thee, thy life is condemned: within the year I await thee before God's throne."

Source: "The Knights Templars, Suppression of the Order March 22d 1312" (*The Eclectic Magazine of Foreign Literature*, Vol. 57, November 1862).

Demonax

(2nd century) Cyprus-born Greek philoso-

pher, educator, Cynic. Taught in Athens. Gave instructions that his body was to be thrown away with no burial so that wild animals could eat it.

Different Last Words:

(1) "I can see nothing out of the way in it, if even in death I am going to be of service to living things." Spoken after concern was raised about his exposure to birds and dogs.

Source: *Luciani Alexander, Demonax, Gallus, Icaromenippus, Philopseudes, Ad Hesiodum, Navigium,* by Lucian of Samosata; tr. from ancient Greek in 1453, from Latin 1826; English ed. *Lucian* by A. M. Harmon, K. Kilburn, M. D. Macleod (London, 1913).

(2) "You may go home, the show is over."

Source: "Saving the World. Hints to Young Reformers" (*The Eagle and the Serpent: A Journal of Egoistic Philosophy and Sociology*, No. 6. December 1, 1898). The author described this as a "Dying Saying" of Demonax.

De Morgan, William Frend

(1839-1917) English artist, potter, novelist. Worked in ceramics, pottery. Wrote several novels. Became delirious after a fall and never recovered enough to recognize his wife Evelyn who was at his bedside. Died at age 77, possibly of influenza.

Last Words (written; part of unfinished novel, *The Old Madhouse*): "Pinning her faith on this, she passed into the passage where he ought to have been; the import of her demeanor being, that her shrewder insight would at once discern the whereabouts of—."

Source: *The Old Madhouse* by William De Morgan, with Mrs. De Morgan (New York, 1919).

De Mornay, Philippe

(1549-1623) French writer, religious leader, soldier. Seigneur du Plessis Marly, usually known as Du-Plessis-Mornay or Mornay Du Plessis. French Protestant. Member of Monarchomaques ("killer of kings"). Joined army of Condé and participated in campaigns of Henry IV of France. Present at siege of Dieppe. Fought at Ivry. Was at the siege of Rouen. After Condé died, de Mornay's influence became so great he was known as the Huguenot pope. Died at age 74 at his estate in La Forêt-sur-Sèvre, France.

Last Words: "I fly, I fly to heaven. Let the angels carry me to the bosom of my Saviour.—I know that my Redeemer liveth, and

I shall see him with these eyes, hisce ocu-lis." He repeated several times the words "hisce oculis." (tr. "I saw with my own eyes.")

Source: *The Whole Works of the Reverend and Learned Mr. John Willison, Late Minister of the Gospel at Dundee* by John Willison (Edinburgh, 1798) taken from Willison's "Choice Sayings of Dying Saints," first published in *The Afflicted Man's Companion* (Belfast, Ireland, 1744).

Demosthenes

(385?-322 B.C.) Greek orator, statesman. Recognized as one of the ten greatest Attic orators. Praised by Cicero as "the perfect orator." Engaged in a struggle against Antipater. When it failed, he poisoned himself rather than face capture.

Last Words: "Now, as soon as you please, you may commence the part of Creon in the tragedy, and cast out this body of mine un-buried. But, O gracious Poseidon, I, for my part while I am yet alive will rise up and depart out of this sacred place; though Antipater and the Macedonians have not left so much as thy temple unpolluted."

Source: "Demosthenes" in *Lives of the Noble Grecians and Romans* by Plutarch, tr. by John Dryden (New York, 1932).

Variation: "Now you can play the part of Creon in the tragedy as soon as you like and cast forth my body unburied. But I, O gracious Poseidon, quit thy temple while I yet live; Antipater and his Macedonians have done what they could to pollute it."

Source: *Attic Orators from Antiphon to Isaeos,* Vol. 1, by Sir Richard Claverhouse Jebb (London, 1893).

Demps, Bennie

(1950-2000) American murderer. Sentenced to die for the murder of a fellow prisoner. When he was put to death in Florida, it took technicians 33 minutes to find suitable veins for his execution. Died at age 49.

Last Words: "They butchered me back there. I was in a lot of pain. They cut me in the groin; they cut me in the leg. I was bleeding profusely. This is not an execution, it is murder." Shouted into a microphone that hung over his head while he was being executed.

Source: "Death Trip: The American Way of Execution" by Robert Sherrill (*The Nation,* January 8, 2001).

Dennis, John

(1657-1734) English critic, playwright. Wrote nine plays. In one of them, he used a new kind of special-effect stage thunder. When it was later used in a production of *Macbeth* without his permission, he complained that they had "stolen his thunder." His complaint has come to mean ruining the impact of someone's idea or performance by anticipating it. Died at age 77 in London.

Last Words. "By God, they could be no one but that fool S—'s." Spoken when he heard someone had put out verses in his name.

Source: *The Life of Mr. John Dennis, the Renowned Critick. In Which Are Likewise Some Observations on Most of the Poets and Criticks, His Contemporaries* by Edmund Curll and John Dryden (London, 1734).

Denton, John

(1818?-1846) English-born American writer, gunsmith. Victim of the Donner party, a group of California-bound settlers who met with tragedy on their journey.

Last Words (written):
"I wish I could once more recall
That bright and blissful joy,
And summon to my weary heart
The feelings of a boy.
But now on scenes of past delight
I look and feel no pleasure,
As misers on the bed of death
Gaze coldly on their treasure." Last verse of a poem found next to Denton's body by the relief party.

Source: *The California Tragedy* by J. Quinn Thornton and Edwin Bryant (Oakland, CA, 1945). Bryant was a member of the Donner party. He died in 1869. Thornton wrote books about California and Oregon. He died in 1888. This book was published many years after their deaths.

Denver, John

(1943-1997) American singer, songwriter, actor, aviator. Birth name Henry John Deutschendorf Jr. Grammy and Emmy winner. Notable folk-rock hit songs: "Sunshine on My Shoulder"; "Annie's Song"; "Thank God I'm a Country Boy"; "Rocky Mountain High"; "Leaving on a Jet Plane." Wrote Werner Erhard's (EST) theme song: "Looking for Space." Killed at age 53 when the aircraft he was piloting crashed just off the California coast.

Last Words: "Do you have it now?" A query about whether he had transmitted a four-digit code clearly. Then controllers lost contact with him. Witnesses heard a pop then saw the plane drop straight down into the ocean.

Source: "Singer John Denver Killed in Plane Crash" by Louis Sahagun and Mary Curtius (*Los Angeles Times,* October 14, 1997).

De Porres, Saint Martin

(1579-1639) Peruvian holy man. Son of a Spanish nobleman and a freed black slave. Dominican Brother. Known during his lifetime for his miracles. Died at age 59 of fever. The first black saint in the Americas when canonized in 1962.

Last Words: "He is already here with St. Vincent Ferrer." Spoken to those at his deathbed who asked him to call upon the help of Saint Dominic.

Source: *St. Martin de Porres, Apostle of Charity* by Giuliana Cavallini (St. Louis, 1963).

De Quincey, Thomas

(1785-1859) English writer. Friend of Samuel Taylor Coleridge and William Wordsworth. Became an opium user in 1804. Wrote *The Confessions of an English Opium Eater* for *London Magazine* in 1821. Published it as a book the following year. Influenced Edgar Allan Poe and other writers. Berlioz loosely based his *Symphonie Fantastique* on *The Confessions of an English Opium Eater.* De Quincey died at age 74 in Edinburgh.

Last Words: "Sister! Sister! Sister!" He may have imagined that he saw a vision of his dead sister Elizabeth.

Source: *Thomas De Quincey: A Biography* by Horace Ainsworth Eaton (New York, 1936).

De Reszke, Jean

(1850-1925) Polish singer. Operatic tenor. Birth name Jan Mieczyslaw. One of the world's great tenors. Brother of operatic bass Eduoard De Reszke. Notable roles: Lohengrin; Walther; Tristan; Siegfried; Rodrigue *(Le Cid).* Retired in 1902. Taught in Paris and Nice, France. Died at age 75 in Nice.

Last Words: "Let me lie quietly. I am very tired." Spoken to his wife. After that, while delirious, he sung passages from *Tristan* before he died.

Source: *Jean De Reszke and the Great Days of Opera* by Clara Leiser (New York, 1934).

De Rosa, Anthony

(1724-1752) Portuguese-born English murderer, robber. Stabbed his victim during a mugging. A bloody knife proved his guilt yet he protested that he was innocent to the very end, even producing an alibi. He was hanged at Tyburn.

Last Words: "I am as innocent as the child unborn. Would you have me own myself guilty of what I know no more of than you do? I know, if I be guilty and deny it, I must send my soul to the bottom of hell, which I hope I know better than to do."

Source: *The Newgate Calendar: Comprising Interesting Memoirs of the Most Notorious Characters Memoirs of the Most Notorious Characters Who Have Been Convicted of Outrages on the Laws of England Since the Commencement of the Eighteenth Century with Occasional Anecdotes and Observations, Speeches, Confessions and Last Exclamation of Sufferers* by Andrew Knapp and William Baldwin (London, 1828).

Desaix de Veygoux, Louis
Charles Antoine

(1768-1800) French nobleman, military officer. Known as Chevalier de Veygoux. General in French Revolutionary wars. Commanded division in an Egyptian expedition. Killed at age 31 by a musket bullet at the Battle of Marengo, Italy. Statue in his honor stands at Place Dauphine, Paris.

Last Words: "Go tell the First Consul that my only regret in dying is, to have perished before having done enough to live in the recollection of posterity."

Source: "Napoleon Bonaparte" by John S. C. Abbott (*Harper's New Monthly Magazine,* Vol. V, June-November 1852).

Descartes, René

(1596-1650) French scientist, philosopher, mathematician. Latin name Renatus Cartesius. Founder of Cartesian coordinate system and analytic geometry, the bridge between algebra and geometry that was important for the foundation of calculus and analysis. Known by some as the Founder of Modern Philosophy and the Father of Modern Mathematics. Remembered for the familiar proposition "Cogito ergo sum" (tr. "I think therefore I am"). Notable works: *Discours de la Méthode; La Dioptrique, Les Météores, Le Géométrie (essays)*. His deliberations on mind and mechanism influenced the Turing Test (artificial intelligence determination). Died at age 54 of pneumonia in Stockholm, Sweden, where he went in 1649 at the invitation of Queen Christine.

Last Words: "My soul, thou has long been held captive; the hour has now come for thee to quit thy prison, to leave the trammels of this body; suffer, then, this separation with joy and courage."

Source: *Descartes: His Life and Times* by Elizabeth S. Haldane (London, 1905).

Variation: "A mon ame, it faut partair" (tr. "So my soul a time for parting.")

Source: *Chambers Biographical Dictionary* (Edinburgh, 1997).

Variation: "Oh, my dear Schluter, this is the fatal stroke. I must leave now." Spoken to his valet who helped him to bed. He died a short time later.

Source: *René Descartes: a Biography* by Jack Rochford Vrooman (New York, 1970).

DeShields, Kenneth Wesley

(1960-1993) American murderer. One of only 14 people executed in Delaware since 1976. He was against the death penalty and used his Last Words to express it.

Last Words: "It ain't worth it. It ain't worth taking a life. I just like to say I don't hate anybody. What I did was wrong. I just hope everybody is satisfied with what's about to happen."

Source: "Word for Word: The Condemned; As Executions Mount, So Do Infamous Last Words" by Tom Kuntz (*New York Times*, July 31, 1994).

De Smet Pierre-Jean

(1801-1873) Belgian-born clergyman, writer, Jesuit missionary in the American Midwest and Northwest. Spent much time among Native Americans. His many descriptive writings about the Native Americans expanded knowledge about them elsewhere in the U.S. and Europe. Died at age 72 in St. Louis, Missouri.

Last Words: "I am a lazy old fool after all." Spoken to an attendant as he lay dying.

Source: *Father De Smet, Pioneer Priest of the Rockies* by Helene Magaret (New York, 1940).

Desmoulins, Camille

(1760-1794) French revolutionary, lawyer. Full name Lucie Simplice Camille Benoit Desmoulins. Wrote pamphlet against aristocrats. Joined Danton during the French Revolution. Arrested by Robespierre. Given a mock trial. Executed at age 34 in Paris with Danton. Wife Lucile was guillotined two weeks later.

Last Words: "Thus, then, the first apostle of Liberty ends! Have this [a lock of his wife's hair] sent to my mother-in-law! O my poor wife." Spoken at his execution.

Source: *Camille Desmoulins and His Wife. Passages from the History of the Dantonists Founded Upon New and Hitherto Unpublished Documents* by Jules Claretie and Frances Cashel Hoey (London, 1876).

Variation: "Look at the first apostle of liberty. The monsters who murder me will not survive me long." The axe fell and he was dead.

Source: *The French Revolution of 1789, as Viewed in the Light of Republican Institutions* by John Stevens Cabot Abott (Boston, 1887).

Desmoulins, Lucile

(1771-1794) French revolutionary. Full name Anne-Lucile-Phillipe Desmoulins. Wife of Camille Desmoulins. Arrested during the French Revolution on the pretext that she tried to incite a prison riot to free her husband. Executed at age 23 by guillotine in Paris two weeks after her husband.

Last Words: "You insulted Antoinette when she was in the tumbrel; that does not surprise me. Had you not better keep a little of your courage to brave another queen, Death, to whom we are hastening?" Spoken to another prisoner.

Source: *Camille Desmoulins and His Wife. Passages from the History of the Dantonists Founded Upon New and Hitherto Unpublished Documents* by Jules Claretie and Frances Cashel Hoey (London, 1876).

De Soto, Hernando

(1496?-1542) Spanish explorer, conquistador. Joined Francisco Pizarro in the conquest of South America. In 1539, De Soto launched the largest of the early Spanish colonial expeditions throughout the southeastern U.S., searching for gold and a passage to China. Died of fever on the bank of the Mississippi River (near present-day Memphis). De Soto County, Mississippi (where he is thought to have died), county seat Hernando, De Soto Parish, Louisiana, and De Soto County, Florida, were named in his honor, as was a city in Texas and a national forest.

Last Words (doubtful): "Luis de Moscoso." De Soto did name Luis de Moscoso as his successor as he lay dying of fever; however, he lived until the following day and almost certainly spoke again. De Soto's Last Words are unknown.

Source: *The Last Words (Real and Traditional) of Distinguished Men and Women Collected from Various Sources* by Frederic Rowland Marvin (New York, 1901). He gave as his source "Bancroft." Likely: *History of the United States: from the Discovery of the American Continent* by George Bancroft (Boston, 1864-1875).

Despard, Edward Marcus

(1751-1803) Irish-born British military officer, conspirator. Colonel who turned revolutionary. Named by government informers and soldiers as the organizer of a conspiracy to seize the Tower of London and Bank of England and assassinate King George III. Despite having Lord Nelson as a character witness, Despard was found guilty of high treason and sentenced to die with six of his co-conspirators. They were the last in England to be sentenced to be hanged, drawn and quartered (the prescribed punishment for anyone who attempted regicide). Despard was hanged and decapitated on the roof of Horsemonger Lane Gaol gatehouse in front of 20,000 or more people.

Last Words: "I wish you all health, happiness and freedom, which I have endeavored, as far as was in my power, to procure for you, and for mankind in general."

Sources: "Obituary. Death of Colonel Despard" (*The Christian Observer*, No. 14, Vol. II, February 1803); *The Criminal Recorder: Or, Biographical Sketches of Notorious Public Characters,* Vol. I (Nottingham, England, 1815).

Devereux, Robert, 2nd Earl of Essex

(1566?-1601) English nobleman, military officer, conspirator. Held numerous titles including Earl Marshal, Lord Deputy of Ireland, Master of the Horse. Military hero and favorite of Queen Elizabeth. Eventually plotted against her. Caught, found guilty of high treason, executed. Died at age 34 or 35.

The opera *Roberto Devereux* by Gaetano Donizetti is loosely based on his life.

Last Words: "In humility and obedience to Thy commandment, in obedience to Thy ordinance, and to Thy good pleasure, O God, I prostrate myself to my deserved punishment. Lord be merciful to Thy prostrate servant.—Lord, into Thy hands I commend my spirit." Spoken on the scaffold.

Source: *The Annales, or, Generall Chronicle of England* by John Stow and Edmund Howes (London, 1615).

Dewey, George

(1837-1917) American military officer. U.S. Navy admiral. Known for the remarkable victory of his forces at the Battle of Manila Bay during the Spanish-American War without the loss of a single life. First and only person to attain rank of Admiral of the Navy, highest rank in U.S. Navy (by act of Congress). Died at age 79 in Washington, D.C. Three U.S. ships were named for him.

Last Words: "Gentlemen, the battle is done. The victory ours." Spoken while delirious.

Source: *The Admiral* by Laurin Hall Healy and Luis Kutner (Chicago, 1944).

De Witt, Cornelius

(1623-1672) Dutch statesman. Brother of Jan de Witt. Falsely accused of treason. Assassinated by the same lynch mob that killed his brother on the day he was to be released. Their bodies were horribly mutilated.

Last Words: "What do you want me to do? Where do you want me to go?" Spoken to the mob that tortured them.

Source: *John de Witt, Grand Pensionary of Holland; or, Twenty Years of a Parliamentary Republic* by Antonin Lefèvre Pontalis, tr. by S.E. and A. Stephenson (London, 1885).

De Witt, Jan, Johan or John

(1625-1672) Dutch statesman. Brother of Cornelius De Witt. Falsely accused of treason. Assassinated by the same lynch mob that killed his brother Cornelius on the day he was to be released. Their bodies were horribly mutilated.

Last Words: "What are you doing? This is not what you wanted." Spoken to the angry mob.

Source: *John de Witt, Grand Pensionary of Holland; or, Twenty Years of a Parliamentary Republic* by

Antonin Lefèvre Pontalis, tr. by S.E. and A. Stephenson (London, 1885).

Diaghilev, Sergei Pavlovich

(1872-1929) Russian ballet producer, art critic, ballet impresario. Founder of Ballets Russes from which many famous choreographers and ballet dancers would come. Collaborated with Stravinsky. Died suddenly at age 57 at the Lido in Venice.

Last Words: "Ah, Catherine—How beautiful you look—I am ill—very ill indeed—I feel so hot—light-headed." Spoken to Baroness Catherine d'Erlanger, one of the people at his bedside as he lay dying.

Source: *Diaghileff: His Artistic and Private Life* by Arnold L. Haskell, collaborator Walter Nouvel (New York, 1935).

Diana, Princess of Wales

(1961-1997) British princess. Full name Diana Frances Mountbatten-Windsor, née Spencer. Ex-wife of Prince Charles. Mother of Prince William and Prince Harry. Killed at age 36 in a car crash in Pont de l'Alma tunnel in Paris, along with Dodi Al-Fayed (Emad El-Din Mohamed Abdel Moneim Fayed) and their chauffeur, Henri Paul. Bodyguard Trevor Rees-Jones was the only survivor.

Last Words: Unknown. "Oh My God!" and "Leave me alone" have both been quoted by paparazzi at the scene. If she spoke any Last Words, Dr. Frédéric Mailliez, who was present at the accident scene when she lost consciousness, would probably have heard them. When questioned by *Newsweek*, Mailliez said: "I must respect the privacy of the patient."

Source: "The Diana File" by Rod Nordland (*Newsweek*, October 20, 1997).

Dickens, Charles John Huffam

(1812-1870) English novelist, social reformer. Pen name Boz. One of the world's most popular writers. Leading novelist and social campaigner of the Victorian era. Notable works: *The Pickwick Papers; Oliver Twist; The Life and Adventures of Nicholas Nickleby; The Old Curiosity Shop; Barnaby Rudge; A Christmas Carol; Martin Chuzzlewit; David Copperfield; Bleak House; A Tale of Two Cities; Great Expectations.* Spoke his Last Words at dinner at his home in Kent just before he had a stroke. He announced that he must go to London at once. When he stood up, he started to fall to the floor. His sister-in-law and friends urged him to lie down as they tried to move him to a sofa. He slumped to the floor, fell into a coma, and died the next day at age 58.

Last Words: "On the ground!" His response to those who were helping him to lie down.

Source: *The Life of Charles Dickens* by John Forster (London, 1872-1874). The author was a friend of Dickens and his first biographer.

Dickerson, Almeron

(1808-1836) American military officer. Captain. Died defending the Alamo in San Antonio, Texas, in 1836. Last Words are known because at one point he started to run with his wife, Susannah, but he went back to the Alamo to face and be killed by the enemy.

Last Words: "Great God, Sue, the Mexicans are inside our walls! If they spare you, save my child!" Susannah and her infant daughter Angelina were among the very few American Alamo survivors.

Source: *Alamo Sourcebook, 1836: A Comprehensive Guide to the Battle of the Alamo and the Texas Revolution* by Timothy J. Todish, Terry Todish, and Ted Spring (Austin, TX, 1998).

Dickinson, Charles

(1780-1806) American landowner, nationally famous duelist. Killed 26 people in duels. Killed by Andrew Jackson in a duel. Jackson's political opponents convinced Dickinson to insult Jackson's wife, assuming Jackson would not survive a duel with Dickinson. Both men agreed to the duel. Dickinson fired first and wounded Jackson, breaking two of his ribs. Jackson then took aim, fired and killed Dickinson. Jackson fought 103 duels during his lifetime and Dickinson was the only person he killed.

Last Words: "Great God, have I missed him?" Screamed in astonishment at Jackson.

Source: *Andrew Jackson: His Life and Times* by H.W. Brands (New York, 2005).

Dickinson, Emily Elizabeth

(1830-1886) American poet. Virtually unknown during her lifetime. Lived a reclusive life in Amherst, Massachusetts. Most of her poems were published after her death. Now

regarded as one of the great 19th-century American poets. Died at age 55 after lapsing in and out of consciousness for several days. Plays about her include *The Belle of Amherst* by William Luce and *Alison's House* by Susan Glaspel. Some of Dickinson's poems have been used as texts for art songs by composers such as Aaron Copland and Nick Peros. Simon and Garfunkel sing about her in "The Dangling Conversation."
Different Last Words:
(1) "I must go in, for the fog is rising."
Source: *The Life and Letters of Emily Dickinson* by her niece Martha Dickinson Bianchi (Boston, 1924).
(2) "Oh, is that all it is!" Her response when offered a glass of water.
Source: *Famous Last Words* by Barnaby Conrad (Garden City, NY, 1961). Conrad lists both (1) and (2) as versions of her Last Words.

Dickinson, Jonathan

(1688-1747) American clergyman, educator. Leader in the Great Awakening in the Middle Colonies. Supported Presbyterian revivalists ("New Sides"). One of the founders and first president of College of New Jersey (Princeton University). Died suddenly at age 59 after serving only five months.
Last Words: "Many days have passed between God and my soul, in which I have solemnly dedicated myself to Him; and I trust, what I have committed unto Him. He is able to keep until that day." Spoken to Dr. Johnes who asked him about his prospects.
Source: *A History of the Presbyterian Church in America: From Its Origin Until the Year 1760* by Rev. Richard Webster (Philadelphia, 1857).

Diddley, Bo

(1928-2008) American musician. Birth name Ellas Otha Bates. Rock and Roll pioneer. Known for the "Bo Diddley Beat," a syncopated rhythm that has been widely used since the 1950s. His music influenced the funk and rap genres. Also known for his innovative early electric "cigar-box" guitar and for an appearance on *The Ed Sullivan Show* when he did not play what Sullivan had scheduled for him, but instead used the show to introduce his famous Beat. Died at age 79 in McComb, Mississippi.
Last Words: "Wow." Spoken with a thumbs-up motion. His grandson Garry Mitchell

reported that Bo made a gesture that he was going to heaven. His response to "Walk around Heaven," a song that was playing in the room where many family members were gathered at his bedside when he died.
Source: "Bo Diddley: 1928-2008" by Alan Light (*Rolling Stone*, June 26, 2008).

Diderot, Denis

(1713-1784) French encyclopedist, writer, philosopher. Known as Pantophile. Prominent figure during the Enlightenment. Worked 20 years on *Encyclopédie*. (Encyclopedia) that drew suspicion and was suppressed. He earned very little money from it. Had to sell his library to raise money for his daughter's dowry. Died at age 70 at his daughater's home.
Different Last Words:
(1) "Mais que diable de mal veux-tu que cela me fasse?" (tr. "What possible harm could it do to me?") Also translated as: "But what the devil do you think that will do to me?" Spoken to his wife about eating an apricot.
Source: *Diderot and the Encyclopaedists* by Viscount John Morley (London, 1914).
(2) "The first step toward philosophy is incredulity."
Source: *Isaac Asimov's Book of Facts* by Isaac Asimov (New York, 1979).

Didius Severus Julianus, Marcus, Emperor of Rome

(137?-193) Roman ruler. Also known as Didius Salvius Julianus. Purchased the imperial office auctioned off to the highest bidder by the Praetorian Guards. Abused by the public. His rival Severus was proclaimed governor by his troops. Julianus was assassinated.
Last Words: "What harm have I done! Have I put anyone to death?" Spoken before he was killed.
Source: *The Roman Empresses, or The History of the Lives and Secret Intrigues of the Wives of the Twelve Caesars: with Historical and Critical Notes* by Jacques Roergas de Serviez (London, 1899).

Dieneces or Dienekes

(d. 480 B.C.) Spartan officer. Described as the bravest of all Spartans at Thermopylae.
Last Words: "Our Trachinian friend brings us excellent tidings. If the Medes darken the

sun, we shall have our fight in the shade."
His reply when told the enemy had so many
arrows they could darken the sun with their
numbers.

Source: *The History of Herodotus,* Book VIII, tr. by
George Rawlinson (Chicago, 1955).

Diesel, Rudolf Christian Karl

(1858-1913) German engineer, inventor.
Patented Diesel engine. Died at age 55 under
mysterious circumstances while crossing the
English Channel. Conflicting theories about
his death claim he either jumped or was
thrown into the water. His body was found
in the channel a few days after he disappeared.

Last Words (written): "Greetings and a kiss.
In fondest love, Your Father." Written in a
letter.

Source: *Life Stories of the Great Inventors* by Henry
and Dana Lee Thomas (New York, 1948).

Dietrich, (Marie) Marlene

(1901-1992) German actress. Star of stage
and screen. Nominated for Academy Award
and Golden Globe. Died at age 90 in her
Paris apartment. Annual Cannes Film Festival opened the next day and that year's festival was dedicated to her memory.

Last Word: "Maria." She spoke her daughter's name. Reported by her grandson Peter,
who was at her bedside. He said she simply
mentioned her daughter's name then "closed
her eyes, as if she wanted to have her afternoon nap."

Source: *The Hollywood Book of Death: The Bizarre,
Often Sordid, Passings of More Than 125 American
Movie and TV Idols* by James Robert Parish (Chicago,
2002). *People Magazine* also carried her Last Words in
1992.

Digby, Sir Everard

(1578-1606) English nobleman, conspirator.
Executed at age 28 for his role in the Gunpowder Plot of 1605, an attempt to assassinate King James I of England and members
of the English Parliament.

Last Words: "Thou liest." His response to
Sir Francis Bacon's remark that when the
executioner held up Digby's heart he said:
"Here is the heart of a traitor."

Sources: *Historia Vitae et Mortis with Naturall and
Experimentall for the Prolonging of Life* by Sir Francis
Bacon (London, 1638); *Brief Lives* by John Aubrey, ed.
by Oliver Lawson Dick (Ann Arbor, MI, 1957).

Dillon, Wentworth, 4th Earl of Roscommon

(1630?-1685) Irish-born English writer,
poet, critic. He was the first critic to admire
Milton's *Paradise Lost.* Buried in Westminster Abbey. His *Poems* were published posthumously in 1717.

Last Words: "My God, my father, and my
friend, do not forsake me in my end." He
spoke a line from his version of *Dies Irae.*

Source: *Lives of the English Poets and a Criticism of
Their Work* by Samuel Johnson (Oxford, England,
1825).

DiMaggio, Giuseppe Paolo, Jr. ("Joe")

(1914-1999) American athlete. Professional
baseball great. Spent his entire career with
the New York Yankees. Nicknames "Joltin'
Joe" and "The Yankee Clipper." Three-time
MVP winner and 13-time All-Star. His 56-
game hitting streak in 1941 may be the
greatest baseball feat of all time. Voted into
the National Baseball Hall of Fame in 1955.
Brothers Vince and Dom also played professional baseball. Joe died at age 84 of cancer
in Hollywood, Florida.

Last Words: "I'll finally get to see Marilyn,"
referring to his one-time wife film actress
Marilyn Monroe.

Source: "Final Days of Joe DiMaggio" based on a
series of interviews with Morris Engelberg (*Vanity
Fair,* September 2000). DiMaggio's attorney and friend
Morris Engelberg was at his bedside when he died and
heard his Last Words.

Diogenes

(412?-323 B.C.) Greek philosopher, Cynic.
Lived in a tub. Went through the streets
holding a lantern, looking for an honest
man. Captured by pirates, sold as a slave and
taken to Corinth. Died at age 88. Little is
known about his life except apocryphal stories told to illustrate his stellar character and
beliefs.

Different Last Words:

(1) "On my face—because after a little time
down will be changed to up." His response
when asked how he wanted to be buried.

Variation: "Everything will shortly be
turned upside down."

Source: *Diogenes Laertius: Lives of the Eminent Philosophers* by Robert Drew Hicks (New York, 1925)
from *Diogenes Laertius. De vita & moribus philosophorum* (Venice, 1431, tr. to Latin).

(2) "If that is the case, it is no matter whether they eat me or not, seeing that I shall be insensible to it."

Source: *The Last Words (Real and Traditional) of Distinguished Men and Women Collected from Various Sources* by Frederic Rowland Marvin (New York, 1901). Marvin said the last words of Diogenes are uncertain. A short time before he died he was asked where he would be buried when dead. Diogenes replied "in an open field." When asked if he was afraid of becoming feed for birds of prey and wild animals, he replied that it was no matter whether they eat him or not, seeing that he would be insensible to it.

(3) "One brother anticipates the other. Sleep before Death. Everything will shortly be turned upside down."

Source: *Famous Last Words* compiled by Jonathon Green (London, 2002).

Disney, Walter Elias ("Walt")

(1901-1966) American artist, cartoonist, producer, director. Creator of Mickey Mouse. Notable productions: *Snow White and the Seven Dwarfs; Pinocchio; Dumbo; Bambi; Cinderella; Alice in Wonderland* and more. Won 22 Academy Awards; nominated for many others. Died at age 65 of cardiac arrest and cancer in Los Angeles.

Last Words (spoken): "Raise my bed so I can look out the window and see my studio." Disney's deathbed at St. Joseph's Hospital in Burbank was across the street from the Disney Studios. His Last Words were about the studio's water tower. Adorned with the image of Mickey Mouse, it towered above the back lot and was visible from a nearby freeway.

Source: *Walt Disney: Hollywood's Dark Prince* by Marc Eliot (Secaucus, NJ, 1993).

Last Words (written): "Kurt Russell." For many years this circulated as what was thought to be an urban legend about actor Kurt Russell. In 2007, when interviewed on the *Jimmy Kimmel Show* and asked about the rumor, Russell replied: "It's true. I don't know what to make of that. I was taken into his office one time after he died and I was shown that." At the time of Disney's death, Russell was already a veteran child actor who had been signed to MGM and then Disney's studio. Disney released its first feature film with Russell in 1966, *Follow Me Boys,* two weeks before Disney died.

Source: Interview with Kurt Russell on *Jimmy Kimmel*

Live!, aired on ABC April 7, 2007).

Disraeli, Benjamin, 1st Earl of Beaconsfield

(1804-1881) British statesman, writer, politician. Viscount Hughenden. Twice prime minister of Great Britain. Close friend of Queen Victoria. Served in government for three decades. Created modern Conservative party after the 1846 Corn Laws schism. Died at age 76 in London.

Last Words: "I have suffered much. Had I been a Nihilist, I should have confessed all. I had rather live, but I am not afraid to die."

Source: *The Life of Benjamin Disraeli, Earl of Beaconsfield* by William Flavelle Monypenny and George Earle Buckle (London, 1929).

Dix, Dorothea Lynde

(1802-1887) American social worker. Devoted her life to prison reform and helping the mentally ill. Lived last six years at New Jersey State Hospital, first of the hospitals she helped establish years earlier. Although not strong enough to travel in her final years, she spent her time writing letters to gain help for the mentally ill. Died at age 85 in Trenton, New Jersey.

Last Words: "Please tell me when the time is near. I want to know." Spoken to her doctor.

Source: *Stranger and Traveler: The Story of Dorothea Dix, American Reformer* by Dorothy Clarke Wilson (Boston, 1975).

Dixon, Henry Hall

(1822-1870) English writer, lawyer. Pen name The Druid. Regular writer for *Sporting Magazine,* which published three of his novels. Published legal compendium, *The Law of the Farm* in 1858. Also wrote about herds and flocks of Scotland and England. Died at age 47 in London.

Last Words: "Oh, God, I thank Thee! I could not bear much more." His response when told the end was near.

Source: *Bits of Character: A Life of Henry Hall Dixon "The Druid"* by J.B. Booth (London, 1936).

Dobbin, James Cochran

(1814-1857) American politician, lawyer, statesman. Secretary of the navy. Member U.S. House of Representatives from North Carolina. Member North Carolina Legislature. Played decisive role in nominating dark horse Presidential candidate Franklin Pierce at the 1852 Democratic convention. His speech helped break a deadlock. Died at age 43 in Fayetteville, North Carolina. Ship was named in his honor.

Last Words: "Praise the Lord, oh my soul."

Source: *Cyclopedia of Eminent and Representative Men of the Carolinas of the Nineteenth Century* by Edward McCrady and Samuel A. Ashe (Madison, WI, 1892).

Dobbins, Oliver B.

(1870-1935) American lawyer. President of Illinois State Bar Association. Brother of U.S. Representative Donald C. Dobbins of Illinois. Died while presenting closing arguments in a trial in Champaign, Illinois.

Last Words: "Excuse me, judge."

Source: "Lawyer Dies in Court as He Closes Argument" (*New York Times,* October 25, 1935).

Dod, John

(1549?-1645) English clergyman. Nonconformist. Suspended from his ministry and silenced by the archbishop because of the popularity of his services. When King James succeeded to the throne, Dod was restored to his church. Died age 96.

Last Words: "I desire to dissolve and be with Christ."

Source: *Genealogies of the Male Descendants of Daniel Dod of Branford, Connecticut, a Native of England 1646 to 1863* (Newark, NJ, 1864).

Dodd, Westley Allan

(1961-1993) American child molester, serial killer. Raped, tortured and murdered young boys. Executed in Washington state. First person legally hanged in the United States since 1963. He chose hanging because that was how he killed one of his victims. The Dodd case is unusual in that Dodd was repeatedly released after convictions. He claimed he never was a victim of molestation or any unusual early sexual activity.

Last Words: "I was once asked by somebody, I don't remember who, if there was any way sex offenders could be stopped. I said no. I was wrong. I was wrong when I said there was no hope, no peace. There is hope. There is peace. I found both in the Lord, Jesus Christ. Look to the Lord and you will find peace."

Source: "Word for Word: The Condemned; As Executions Mount, So Do Infamous Last Words" by Tom

Kuntz (*New York Times*, July 31, 1994).

Dodd, William

(1729-1777) English clergyman, theologian, criminal. Nicknamed the Macaroni Parson for his extravagant lifestyle. Used forgery (including a bond in the name of Lord Chesterfield) in an effort to clear his debts. Friend of Samuel Johnson who tried to defend him. Caught, convicted and sentenced to be hanged. Despite a public campaign for a royal pardon (23,000 people signed the 37-page petition), he was executed. He was the last person to be hanged for forgery at Tyburn.

Last Words (written): "For this fraud I am to die; and I die declaring, in the most solemn manner, that, however I have deviated from my own precepts, I have taught others, to the best of my knowledge, and with all sincerity, the true way to eternal happiness. My life, for some few unhappy years past, has been dreadfully erroneous; but my ministry has been always sincere. I have constantly believed; and I now leave the world solemnly avowing my conviction, that there is no other name under Heaven by which we can be saved but only the name of the Lord Jesus; and I entreat all who are here to join with me in my last petition, that, for the sake of that Lord Jesus Christ, my sins may be forgiven, and my soul received into His everlasting kingdom. June 23, 1777. WILLIAM DODD." Written message.

Source: *A Famous Forgery; Being the Story of "the Unfortunate" Doctor Dodd* by Percy Hetherington Fitzgerald (London, 1865).

Doddridge, Philip

(1702-1751) English clergyman, writer, hymnist. Nonconformist. Notable work: *The Rise and Progress of Religion in the Soul.* Studied at and later ran an academy for Nonconformists or dissenters at Kibworth, Leicestershire. Helped to unite fellow dissenters.

Last Words: "My confidence is not that I have lived such or such a life, or served God in this or the other manner; I know of no prayer I ever offered, no service I ever performed, but there has been such a mixture of what was wrong in it, that instead of recommending me to the favor of God, I needed His pardon, through Christ for the same. Yet I am full of confidence and this is my confidence—there is hope set before me: I have fled, I still fly, for refuge to that hope."

Source: "Doddridge's Righteousness" by Edward Butt in *The Sunday School Teachers' Magazine and Journal of Education* (London, 1852).

Dode de la Brunerie, Vicomte Guillaume

(1775-1851) French military officer. Marshal of France. Fought in the Napoleonic Wars and later during the first and second restorations. Friend of French king Louis XVIII during the Bourbon accession. Also served under Charles X and Louis-Philippe. Died at age 75 in Paris. His name is on the south face of the Arc de Triomphe de l'Etoile in Paris.

Last Words: "The doctors still assert that the enemy is retreating; I believe on the contrary that we are, as it were, on the eve of a battle. God knows what tomorrow will bring!"

Source: *Notice sur le vicomte Dode De La Brunerie, maréchal de France* by General Moreau (Paris, 1852).

Dodge, Grace Hoadley

(1856-1914) American social worker, educator, philanthropist. Organized working girls' club that developed into Associations of Working Girls' Societies. Helped found New York Travelers Aid Societies. Instrumental in forming Kitchen Garden Association (became Industrial Education Association). Provided primary source of funds for New York College for the Training of Teachers (became Teachers College, and finally a school at Columbia University). Died at age 58 in New York City.

Last Words: "And were they happy?" She was speaking about students who were visiting as her guests.

Source: *Grace H. Dodge, Merchant of Dreams: A Biography* by Abbie Graham (New York, 1926).

Dodgson, Charles Lutwidge ("Lewis Carroll")

(1832-1898) English mathematician, logician. writer, poet, photographer. Pen name Lewis Carroll. Notable works: *Alice's Adventures in Wonderland* and its sequel *Through the Looking-Glass*. Made photographic portraits of luminaries such as Ten-

nyson, Ruskin, Rossetti. Contracted influenza. Died at age 65 at his sister's house in Guildford, Surrey, England.

Last Words: "Take away these pillows. I shall need them no more."

Source: *Victoria Through the Looking-Glass: The Life of Lewis Carroll* by Florence Becker Lennon (New York, 1945).

Dolet, Étienne

(1509-1546) French printer, scholar, humanist. Leader in early 16th-century intellectual renaissance in France. Advocated reading the Bible in the vernacular. Convicted of heresy. Executed at age 37 in Paris. Statue of Dolet was erected on Place Maubert, Paris, in 1889.

Last Words: "This is not doleful for Dolet, but it means dole for the good people." Spoken about the spectators at his execution.

Source: *Étienne Dolet, the Martyr of the Renaissance* by Richard Copley Christie (London, 1899).

Dollfuss, Engelbert

(1892-1934) Austrian statesman, politician. Conservative. Minister of agriculture and forestry. Appointed chancellor in 1932. Came into conflict with powerful Austrian National Socialist party, backed by Nazi Germany. Assassinated at age 41 by Austrian Nazis in the Chancellery building.

Last Words: "Children, you are so good to me. Why aren't the others? I have only desired peace—we have never attacked anyone—we have always had to defend ourselves. May God forgive them!"

Source: *Dollfuss and His Times* by J.D. Gregory (London, 1935).

Domenec, Michael

(1816-1878) Spanish-born American Roman Catholic prelate. Joined order of Vincentians in Spain and went to U.S. as missionary in 1838. Second bishop of Pittsburgh. First bishop of Allegheny. Became ill while visiting Barcelona. Given Last Rites by archbishop of Tarragona. Died at age 61 from pneumonia.

Last Words: "A thousand thanks, sir. You know my mission is not to incommode anybody." His reply to the archbishop's instruction to take him to the archbishop's house.

Source: *A History of the Catholic Church in the Dioceses of Pittsburgh and Allegheny: From Its Establish-*

ment to the Present Time by Andrew Arnold Lambing (New York, 1880).

Dominic, Saint

(1170-1221) Spanish-born Roman Catholic priest, holy man. Also known as Dominic of Osma or Dominic de Guzmán. Founder of Dominican order of friars. Spent time traveling and preaching to heretics. One of the Inquisitors who attacked the Albigensians. Died at age 51 in Bologna, Italy.

Last Words: "Let not my departure in the flesh trouble you, my sons, and doubt not that I shall serve you better dead than alive!"

Source: *The Golden Legend or Lives of the Saints.* Compiled by Jacobus de Voragine, Archbishop of Genoa, 1275, 1st ed., 1470. English ed. by William Caxton, 1483, ed. by F.S. Ellis (Edinburgh, 1900).

Donn-Byrne, Brian Oswald Patrick

(1889-1928) American novelist, short-story writer, poet. Pen name Donn Byrne. Born in New York of Irish parents. Family returned to Ireland in the 1920s. Notable works: *Messer Marco Polo; Hangman's House; Blind Rafferty and His Wife Hannah.* Killed at age 38 in a car accident.

Last Words: "I think I'll go for a drive before dinner. Anyone come along?"

Source: *Donn Byrne, Bard of Armagh* by Thurston Macauley (New York, 1929).

Donne, John

(1572-1631) English clergyman, metaphysical poet, Jacobean writer. Dean of St. Paul's Cathedral. Notable works: "Death be not Proud"; "Batter My Heart" (sonnets); "Devotions upon Emergent Occasions" (prose). He also wrote love and religious poems, Latin translations, epigrams, elegies, songs, satires and sermons. Died at age 58 in London, a few weeks after delivering his funeral sermon "Death's Due" at St. Paul's Cathedral.

Different Last Words:

(1) "I were miserable if I might not die. Thy Kingdom come, Thy Will be done."

Source: *Walton's Lives of Dr. John Donne, Sir Henry Wotton, Mr. Richard Hooker, Mr. George Herbert, and Dr. Robert Sanderson* by Izaak Walton and Thomas Zouch (York, England, 1796).

(2) "I repent of all my life except that part of it which I have spent in communion with God, and in doing good."

Source: "Infidelity" by Francis Douce (*The Recreative*

Review, or Eccentricities of Literature and Life, Vol. 3, 1822).

Donner, Elizabeth Blue Hook

(1800?-1847) American frontierswoman. Victim of the ill-fated Donner party. Wife of Jacob Donner and sister-in-law of team leader George Donner. Died on March 7, 1847. The body of her husband, who died before her, was exhumed and cannibalized.

Last Words: "O, save, save my children!" Spoken to William H. Eddy who set out with a relief party in mid December 1846. When he returned on March 13, 1847, only nine people were alive. Elizabeth's two sons Samuel and Lewis had died with her on March 7th. Three of her seven children survived the ordeal.

Source: *Woman on the American Frontier: A Valuable and Authentic History* by William Worthington Fowler (Hartford, CT, 1877).

Dooley, Thomas Anthony, III

(1927-1961) American physician, medical missionary, humanitarian, military officer. U.S. Navy physician in Southeast Asia. Resigned from Navy in 1956. Built hospitals in Laos. Profits from his books and personal appearances were used to fund sending medical teams to underdeveloped countries. Dooley wrote of his experiences in *Deliver Us From Evil; The Edge of Tomorrow; The Night They Burned the Mountain; Doctor Tom Dooley, My Story.* Died at age 34 of cancer in New York City.

Last Words: "I'll have a piece of that in about two hours." He was referring to a birthday cake in his hospital room. Spoken to his nurse just before he stuck his finger in the icing.

Source: *Before I Sleep: The Last Days of Dr. Tom Dooley* by James Monahan and Thomas Anthony Dooley (New York, 1961).

Doorman, Karel Willem Frederik Marie

(1889-1942) Dutch military officer. Rear admiral in Royal Netherlands Navy during World War II. Commanded combined U.S., British, Dutch and Australian naval force on virtual suicide mission. Died at age 52 when his ship the light cruiser *De Ruyter* was struck by a Japanese torpedo during the Battle of the Java Sea. He went down heroically with his ship. Several ships of the Royal

Netherlands Navy were named in his honor. Last Words: "Ik val aan, volg mij!" (tr. "All ships follow me!") Became Dutch naval hero because of these words to the fleet (inferred to mean "I'm attacking, follow me"). He issued the command to prevent confusion when the damaged HMS *Exeter* sailed back to the harbor. Doorman wanted to indicate that his ships should follow him and not the *Exeter*.

Source: *Ik val aan, volg mij; Militaire blunders in de twintigste eeuw* by Saul David (Amsterdam, The Netherlands, 2001).

Dorman or Doorman, Isaiah

(1820?-1876) American interpreter, trapper, trader, woodsman. Victim of Battle of Little Big Horn. Former slave of D'Orman family of Louisiana before escaping to become a trapper and trader. Married Santee Sioux woman and lived among her people until 1865, when he took work as a woodcutter at a white settlement. Later he served as an interpreter with the U.S. Army. His services were requested by Custer. Dorman was the only black man killed at Big Horn. After being mortally wounded, he made his last request to the Sioux with whom he had once been friendly.

Last Words: "Goodbye, Rutten." Spoken to Roman Rutten, a private who rode by shortly before Dorman was mortally wounded. "My friends, you have already killed me; don't count coup on me." Spoken to the Sioux who surrounded him. By some accounts he was given water and was spared briefly by Sitting Bull shortly before he died. His request was ignored and his body was mutilated.

Source: *Sitting Bull: Champion of the Sioux* by Stanley Vestal (Norman, OK, 1957).

Dornacker, Jane

(1947-1986) American radio personality, rock musician, disaster victim. Actress, comedian-turned-traffic reporter for New York radio station WNBC 66 AM (later WFAN 66). Had film role in *The Right Stuff*. Died at age 39 after the helicopter in which she was a passenger crashed into Hudson River as she was delivering an on-air traffic report.

Last Words: "Hit the water! Hit the water! Hit the water!" Shouted to the pilot. Dornacker and pilot Bill Pate were trapped in 15 to 20 feet of water. Pate survived. Dornacker died on the way to the hospital.

Source: Voice recording of incident furnished by Jeff McNeal Productions, San Diego, California, recorded October 22, 1986, 4:44 p.m., WNBC-AM 66 Radio, New York, New York.

Dorney, Henry

(1613-1683) English writer. Notable work: *Contemplations and Letters,* published after his death. Died at age 69.

Last Words: "I am almost dead; lift me up a little higher." Spoken to his wife.

Source: *The Last Words (Real and Traditional) of Distinguished Men and Women Collected from Various Sources* by Frederic Rowland Marvin (New York, 1901). Marvin described Dorney as a man of "peculiarly beautiful life and religious experience."

Dors or d'Ors, Diana

(1931-1984) English actress, sex symbol. Billed as Britain's Marilyn Monroe. Fought a long battle with cancer at the end of her life. Believed to have placed an estimated 2 million pounds in several banks. Locations were encoded and the key to the code was given to Alan Lake, her third husband. Dors died at age 53 in Windsor, Berkshire, England. Lake committed suicide before the money was retrieved. A computer company determined Dors used a Vigenère cipher to hide her money. It remains unfound.

Last Words: "Oh my darling, I love you, take care of the boys and say farewell to everyone concerned. This is not the way it was rehearsed." Spoken to Alan Lake.

Source: "Britain's Diana Dors Called 'Blond Bombshell'" (*Chicago Tribune,* May 5, 1984).

Dos Passos, John Roderigo

(1896-1970) American writer, essayist, novelist, historian, dramatist. Major American novelist who wrote about the exploitation of workers and the impact of commercialism on American life. Literary revolutionary who used experimental techniques to show social conflict and change. Notable work: trilogy *U.S.A.* Died at age 74 in Baltimore, Maryland.

Last Words: "I think I'd like to read the paper now." Spoken to his wife Betty. She hurried to a nearby store to buy one. When she returned less than ten minutes later, she found him on the floor unconscious.

Source: *Dos Passos: a Life* by Virginia Spencer Carr and Donald Pizer (Evanston, IL, 2004).

dos Santos, Lucia (Sister Lucia)

(1907-2005) Portuguese child visionary. Last survivor of the three children who experienced an apparition of the Virgin Mary at Fatima. Died at age 97 at a Carmelite convent in Coimbra, Portugal.

Last Words: "With Our Lord—Our Lady— and the little Shepherds." Her response to Mother Celina who asked with whom she was going to Heaven.

Source: "Sister Lucia's last words" by Richard Salbato. Our Lady of Fatima Conference Program (Salt Lake City, UT, 2005).

Dostie, Anthony Paul

(1821-1866) American dentist, abolitionist activist in New Orleans. After the U.S. Civil War, he agitated for enfranchisement of blacks. Was shot, beaten and left for dead during a riot. Died six days later.

Last Words: "I am dying. I die for the cause of Liberty. Let the good work go on."

Source: *Life of A.P. Dostie; or, the Conflict of New Orleans* by Emily Hazen Reed (New York, 1868).

Dostler, Anton

(1891-1945) German military officer. Nazi commander of German 75th Army Corps in northern Italy. Ordered the death of 15 Americans without a trial. Sentenced to execution by firing squad in Aversa, Italy. First high-ranking enemy officer to be executed for war crimes in Western Europe after World War II.

Last Words: "I give my life for my country and my soul to God." Spoken in German with a hood over his head to American Catholic chaplain, Captain H.B. Crimmins of St. Louis, Missouri.

Source: "Nazi General Dies Before U.S. Firing Squad. Ordered Death of 15 Yanks Captured in Italy" (*Chicago Tribune*, December 2, 1945).

Dostoevsky, Fyodor

(1821-1881) Russian writer, novelist, journalist. One of the great 19th-century Russian authors. Novels often featured characters living in poverty and explored socioeconomic conditions that created such situations. Exiled to Siberia several years for his liberal beliefs. Notable works: *The Brothers Karamazov; Crime and Punishment; The Idiot.* Died at age 59 of cerebral hemorrhage in Saint Petersburg.

Different Last Words:

(1) "Did you hear? Hold me not back. My hour has come. I must die." He had asked his wife to read a passage from the Bible at random. She chose: "And Jesus answering said unto him: Hold me not back for thus it becometh us to fulfill all righteousness."

Source: *Fyodor Dostoevsky* by John Arthur Thomas Lloyd (New York, 1947).

(2) "Call the children."

Source: *Reminiscences* by Anna Dostoevsky (New York, 1975).

Doughtie, Jeffery Carlton

(1961-2001) American murderer, drug addict. Fatally beat an elderly couple in their Corpus Christi, Texas, antiques shop after they refused to give him money to support his drug habit.

Last Words: "For almost nine years I have thought about the death penalty, whether it is right or wrong and I don't have any answers. But I don't think the world will be a better or safer place without me. If you had wanted to punish me you would have killed me the day after, instead of killing me now. You are not hurting me now. I have had time to get ready, to tell my family goodbye, to get my life where it needed to be. It started with a needle and it is ending with a needle.—If you don't see peace in my eyes you don't see me. I will be the first one you see when you cross over. They got these numbers that I called today. Calling my family. That is it. Ready, Warden."

Source: *Texas Death Row: Executions in the Modern Era* by Bill Crawford (New York, 2008).

Douglas, Alexander, 10th Duke of Hamilton

(1767-1852) Scottish nobleman. Eccentric aristocrat. Spent later years planning a tomb at Hamilton Palace befitting his peerage, which included three dukes, two marquises, two earls and eight barons. He outbid the British Museum in 1852 on the purchase of a stone sarcophagus that had been made for an Egyptian princess, then had it lengthened to accommodate his six-foot, six-inch frame.

He had constructed a colossal mausoleum with a 120-foot dome, inlaid marble floor with rare stones, and doors that replicated the Baptistry in Florence. He entombed the remains of the first nine noblemen there.

Last Words: "Double me up! Double me up!" His Last Words were instructions to increase the size of the sarcophagus again, when he feared he would not fit. He was right. His feet had to be removed and placed in the sarcophagus separately.

Source: *The Dukes: The Origins, Ennoblement and History of Twenty-Six Families* by Brian Masters (London, 2001).

Douglas, Lord Alfred Bruce

(1870-1945) English poet. Known as Bosie. Son of John Sholto Douglas, 8th Earl of Queensberry, who supervised formulation of Marquis of Queensberry Rules. Friend of Oscar Wilde. Founded and edited *Plain English* and *Plain Speech*. Notable works: *City of the Soul; Sonnets.* Died at age 74 in Lancing, West Sussex, England

Last Words: "Mixed bark doubles. Nicholson's mounts." Spoken to one of the Colmans, friends with whom he spent the last several months of his life. He was in the habit of having them place bets for him at Worthing during his stay. His choice lost.

Source: "Obituary: Sheila Colman" by Jonathan Fryer (*The* [London] *Independent,* November 27, 2001).

Douglas, George Norman

(1868-1952) Austrian-born British writer. Notable works: *Siren Land; South Wind; Old Calabria; Looking Back.* Also wrote travel books. Friend of Graham Greene. Died at age 83 in Capri, after a long illness.

Last Words: "God be with you, my dears. You keep the old bugger. I shan't need him." He went into a coma and died shortly afterward.

Source: *Norman Douglas, a Biography* by Mark Holloway (London 1976).

Douglas, Sir Howard, 3rd Baronet

(1776-1861) British military officer, engineer, artillery expert, writer. Served in Canada. Founded University of Fredericton. Lord high commissioner of Ionian Islands. Succeeded to baronetcy on the death of his half-brother Vice-Admiral Sir William

Douglas. Governor of New Brunswick during the 1828 Maine boundary dispute. Member of Parliament. Wrote numerous works on military bridges and warfare, including *Treatise on Naval Gunnery.* Died at age 85 at Tunbridge Wells, England.

Last Words: "All that I have said about armored ships will prove correct. How little do they know of the undeveloped power of artillery!"

Source: *The Life of General Sir Howard Douglas, Bart., G.C.B., G.C.M.G., F.R.S., D.C.L., from His Notes, Conversations, and Correspondence* by S.W. Fullom (London, 1863).

Douglas, Sir James

(1286?-1330) Scottish nobleman, military leader. Known as The Black Douglas. Also known as The Good Sir James. Won independence for Scotland at the Battle of Bannockburn. Died in battle in Andalusia, carrying the heart of Robert the Bruce in a silver casket. Bruce wanted him to take it to the Holy Land on one of the Crusades.

Last Words: "A Douglas! A Douglas! I follow or die!" Douglas's body was found lying on the ground over the casket. The heart never made it to the Holy Land. It reached Granada, Spain, and eventually was taken back to Scotland.

Source: *The Three Edwards* by Thomas Costain (Garden City, NY, 1958).

Douglas, Stephen Arnold

(1813-1861) American politician. Known as the Little Giant. Member U.S Senate and House of Representatives from Illinois. Important leader in Illinois in 1830s and 1840s and in Congress in 1850s. Wrote controversial Kansas-Nebraska Act of 1854 that reopened the slavery question. One of two Democratic party nominees for U.S. President in 1860. He and John C. Breckenridge both lost to Republican party candidate Abraham Lincoln. During the Presidential campaign, Douglas engaged in a series of platform debates with Lincoln on slavery. He became ill while on a speaking tour. Died at age 48 of typhoid fever in Chicago in June 1861.

Different Last Words:

(1) "Tell them to obey the laws and support

the Constitution of the United States." His response to his wife when she asked if he had any words for his sons.

Source: *Stephen A. Douglas: His Life, Public Services, Speeches and Patriotism* by Clark E. Carr (Chicago, 1909).

(2) "He is very comfortable." Spoken to his wife and his physician after they expressed concern that he was not comfortable.

Sources: *Abraham Lincoln, The War Years* by Carl Sandburg (New York, 1939); *The Eve of Conflict: Stephen A. Douglas and the Needless War* by George Fort Milton (Boston, 1934).

Douglass, Frederick

(1818-1895) American abolitionist, writer, editor, lecturer, diplomat, reformer. Born into slavery in Maryland. Escaped to Massachusetts. Wrote autobiography, *Narrative of the Life of Frederick Douglass, an American Slave* (1845). Sought refuge in England where he was able to collect enough money to buy his freedom. Returned to U.S. in 1847. Published abolitionist newspaper, *North Star*. Became one of the most prominent African-Americans of his era, and one of most influential lecturers and writers in U.S. history. Later served as Minister to Haiti. Died at age 77 in Washington, D.C.

Last Words: "Why, what does this mean?" Spoken after dinner. He had a massive heart attack, fell to his knees, uttered these words and died.

Source: *Frederick Douglass* by Booker T. Washington (Philadelphia, 1906).

Doumer, Paul

(1857-1932) French statesman, politician. President of France. Governor-general of French Indochina. Served in several cabinets after World War I. Assassinated at age 75 in Paris at the opening of a book fair by Russian émigré Paul Gorgouloff.

Last Words: "Est-ce possible? Est-ce possible?" (tr. "Is it possible? Is it possible?") Murmured as he was losing consciousness. Doumer had autographed a book just before he was shot.

Source: "Est-ce possible?" (*Time* magazine, May 16, 1932).

Dowson, Ernest Christopher

(1867-1900) English poet. Created vivid phrases such as "days of wine and roses" in

his poem *Vitae Summa Brevis* and "gone with the wind" in his most notable poem "Non Sum Qualis eram Bonae Sub Regno Cynarae" that also contained the popular line: "I have been faithful to thee, Cynara, in my fashion." Robert Sherard found him destitute and homeless in a bar and took him to his home. Dowson spent his last six weeks with the Sherard family. Died at age 33 in London of tuberculosis and complications of alcoholism.

Last Words: "You are like an angel from heaven. God bless you." Spoken to Mrs. Sherard.

Source: *Ernest Dowson* by Mark Longaker (Philadelphia, 1944).

Doyle, Sir Arthur Conan

(1859-1930) British ophthalmologist, novelist, writer. His stories about detective Sherlock Holmes and Professor Challenger were major innovations in mystery fiction. Also wrote science fiction stories, historical novels, plays, poetry and nonfiction. In later years, he was involved with spiritualism and psychic phenomena. Knighted in 1902. Died at age 71 of a heart attack in Crowborough, Sussex.

Last Words: "You are wonderful." Spoken to his wife. He then clutched at his chest and died in his family garden.

Source: *Arthur Conan Doyle, A Memoir* by Rev. John Lamond (London, 1931). Rev. Lamond, a spiritualist colleague of Doyle, wrote one of the earliest Doyle memoirs.

Drake, Sir Francis

(1540-1596) English military officer, navigator, privateer, pirate, slaver. First Englishman to circumnavigate globe. Knighted by Queen Elizabeth in 1581. Helped defeat Spanish Armada. Died of dysentery on his ship *Defiance* near Puerto Bello, Panama.

Last Words: "Help me dress and buckle on my armor that I might die like a soldier." He wanted to die in uniform, so he rose from his sickbed to put on his armor.

Source: *Sir Francis Drake* by John Sugden (New York, 1990).

Draper, Daniel James

(1810-1866) British-born Australian Methodist clergyman, missionary. First Wesley missionary to South Australia. Had 30-year ministry in New South Wales, South Australia and Victoria. He and his wife were on the ship *London* that sank in a fierce storm in the Bay of Biscay, killing all but 17 of 263 aboard. Survivors reported that before he died, Draper comforted other victims. Draper Memorial Church in Adelaide was named for him.

Last Words: "We may all make the port of heaven. O God! may those that are not converted be converted now; hundreds of them! In a few moments we must all appear before our Great Judge. Let us prepare to meet Him. Rock of ages cleft for me." Spoken as the ship was sinking. His wife was by his side.

Source: *Life of the Rev. Daniel James Draper, Representative of the Australasian Conference, Who Was Lost in the "London," January 11th, 1866: With Historical Notices of Wesleyan Methodism in Australia: Chapters Also on the Aborigines, and Education in Victoria* by Rev. John C. Symons (London, 1870). The author was an associate of Draper.

Drayton, Michael

(1563-1631) English poet known for pastorals, odes and sonnets. Friend of Shakespeare and Ben Johnson. Notable works: *England's Heroicall Epistles; Poly-Olbion; Nymphidia.* Died at age 68 in London. Buried in Westminster Abbey.

Last Words (written):

"So all my Thoughts are pieces but of you,
Which put together makes a Glass so true,
As I therein no other's face but yours can View." Last stanza of a poem about his undying love for Anne Rainsford that he wrote the night before he died.

Source: *The Works of Michael Drayton,* ed. by J.W. Hebel, Kathleen Mary Tillotson and Bernard H. Newdigate (Oxford, England, 1931).

Dreiser, Theodore Herbert Albert

(1871-1945) American writer, newspaper reporter. Politically active socialist. Known for stories that dealt with the gritty reality of life and American culture. Notable works: *An American Tragedy; Jennie Gerhardt; Sister Carrie.* Died at age 74 in Hollywood, California.

Different Last Words:

(1) (doubtful): "Shakespeare, I come!"

Source: Various Last Words compilations and Internet websites.

His reputed Last Words were written many years earlier, in a 1921 letter to H.L. Mencken. Mencken was making light of the prevailing newspaper practice of writing obituaries while the subjects were still alive. He asked Dreiser for his Last Words in case he was called upon to write his *New York Times* obituary.

Sources: *Disturber of the Peace: H. L. Mencken* by William Manchester (Ann Arbor, MI, 1951); *Last Words: Variations on a Theme in Cultural History* by Karl A. Guthke (Princeton, NJ, 1992).

(2) "You are beautiful." Spoken to his wife.

Source: *My Life with Dreiser* by Helen Patges Dreiser (Cleveland, OH, 1951).

Drelincourt, Charles

(1595-1669) French clergyman, writer. Protestant minister in Reformed Church of Paris almost 40 years. Notable work: *The Christian's Consolations Against the Fears of Death with Seasonable Directions on How to Prepare Ourselves to Die Well.* Died at age 74.

Last Words: "Yes." His response when asked if he knew his son. This is the last word he was heard to speak distinctly.

Source: *The Christian's Consolations Against the Fears of Death with Seasonable Directions on How to Prepare Ourselves to Die Well* by Charles Drelincourt (Wheeling, VA, 1824).

Dreux, Charles D.

(1832-1861) American military officer. Confederate lieutenant colonel. First Confederate field officer killed in battle in U.S. Civil War. Died at Young's Mill, Warwick, Virginia (now Newport News) while on a failed mission to capture Union officers at Smith's Farm. More than 30,000 mourners attended his funeral in New Orleans.

Last Words: "Boys, steady!"

Source: *Meynier's Louisiana Biographies* by Arthur Meynier (New Orleans, LA, 1883).

Drew, Andrew

(1885-1913) American aviator, flying instructor. Studied aviation under Orville Wright in Ohio. Aviation instructor for Max Lillie School. Winner of early aviation contest sponsored by Aero Club of St. Louis. Flying partner J. C. Branazon urged him not fly a biplane with which he was unfamiliar. He was killed when the plane crashed near Lima, Ohio.

Last Words: "Just a little joy ride." Spoken to Branazon as he left to try out the new plane.

Source: "Takes 'Joy Ride,' Aviator Killed. Andrew Drew, Well Known in Chicago Plunges to Death at Lima, O. Biplane 'Flaming Torch'" (*Chicago Tribune*, June 13, 1913).

Drew, John, Jr.

(1853-1927) American actor. Son of actor John Drew. Brother-in-law of Maurice Barrymore. Notable performances: *Rip Van Winkle; The Taming of the Shrew; Masked Ball*. Became ill. Died at age 73 of rheumatic fever in a San Francisco hospital. Had just completed a successful road tour performing in *Trelawny of the Wells*.

Last Words: "This is but another act, and I am playing my part."

Source: *Time* magazine, July 18, 1927.

Drew, Samuel

(1765-1833) English theologian, philosopher, writer. Methodist. Known as the Cornish Metaphysician. Wrote historical and biographical themes. Notable work: *The Immateriality and Immortality of the Soul*. Died at age 68 in Heiston, Cornwall.

Last Words: "Yes, my good sir, I trust I shall." His response when told: "Today, I trust, you will be with the Lord Jesus." Almost the last coherent words he uttered.

Source: *The Life, Character, and Literary Labours of Samuel Drew, A.M.* by Jacob Halls Drew (New York, 1835). The author was his eldest son.

Drexel, Saint Katharine

(1858-1955) American nun, religious founder, holy woman, philanthropist. Roman Catholic saint. Member of wealthy Drexel family of Philadelphia. Devoted her fortune to missionary and educational work among the neediest members of society. Founded Sisters of the Blessed Sacrament. Established schools for Native Americans and African-Americans, including Xavier University, the first African-American Catholic institution of higher learning in the U.S. Died at age 96 in Bensalem Township, Pennsylvania. Canonized in 2000.

Last Words: "You've come early." Spoken to a priest who came to her deathbed.

Source: *Saint Katharine Drexel: Friend of the Oppressed* by Ellen Tarry (San Francisco, CA, 2002).

Drucci, Vincent

(1898-1927) Sicilian-born American gangster, bootlegger, jewel thief, murderer. Birth name Vittorio D'Ambrosio. Known as The Schemer for his wild schemes to kidnap the wealthy or rob banks. Killed at age 29 when he was shot in a Chicago squad car by a policeman who was taking him to the Criminal Courts Building. Drucci had attempted to take the officer's revolver.

Last Words: "You take your gun off me or I'll kick hell out of you! I'll take you and your tool [pistol]. I'll fix you." Spoken before being shot while struggling to get the policeman's revolver.

Source: *Al Capone: The Biography of a Self-made Man* by Fred D. Pasley (New York, 1930).

Drummond, Henry

(1851-1897) Scottish educator, evangelist, explorer, geologist, theologian, writer. Notable work: *Natural Law in the Spiritual World* (proposed that the scientific principle of continuity extended from the physical world to the spiritual world). Died at age 46 of cancer.

Last Words (doubtful): "There's nothing to beat that, Hugh." He was referring to the lines that Dr. Barbour had just joined with him in singing: "I'm not ashamed to own my Lord, or to defend His cause, Maintain the glory of His cross, and honour all His laws."

Source: *Famous Sayings and Their Authors, A Collection of Historical Sayings in English, French, German, Greek, Italian, and Latin* by Edward Latham (New York, 1906).

Drummond lived a few more days. His biographer noted that he talked, half dreaming, about John's Gospel. He murmured a message to his mother, became unconscious and died.

Source: *The Life of Henry Drummond* by Sir George Adam Smith (New York, 1901).

Drummond, William

(1620-1676) Scottish-born American colonist, rebel. First colonial governor of Albemarle Sound settlement in Province of Carolina. In 1655, Drummond discovered a large lake in the center of the Great Dismal Swamp. It was renamed Lake Drummond in his honor. Executed by Governor Berkeley for participating in Bacon's Rebellion.

Last Words: "I expect no mercy from you. I have followed the lead of my conscience, and done what I might to free my country from oppression." Spoken when told he was to be hanged in a half hour.

Source: *John Harpers' Popular Cyclopaedia of United States History from the Aboriginal Period to 1876* (in two volumes) Vol. I, by Benson Lossing (New York, 1881).

Drusus, Marcus Livius, the Younger

(124?-91 B.C.) Roman statesman, tribune. Attempted to strengthen rule of senate and remove jury courts from jurisdiction of equestrians. Lost support of senators who did not want Italians to become citizens, and of wealthy Italian landlords who did not want to lose their land. Murdered at about age 33. Soon after his assassination, Italian allies revolted, starting a civil war.

Last Words: "When will the republic find again a citizen like me?"

Source: *Encyclopedia Britannica*, 9th ed. (New York, 1875-1889).

Du Barry, Marie-Jeanne Bécu, Comtesse

(1743?-1793) French courtesan. Mistress of Louis XV. Part of group that brought down Duc du of Choiseul, minister of foreign affairs. Arrested for conspiring against the Republic during French Revolution. Guillotined. She inspired "The Sleeping Beauty" wax figure at Madame Tussaud's Museum in London (oldest figure on display).

Last Words: "Just a moment, Mr. executioner, only one moment more—Help! Help!" Spoken on her way to the guillotine as she pleaded with her executioner.

Source: *The Du Barry* by Karl von Schumacher, tr. by Dorothy M. Richardson (London, 1932).

Du Bois, William Edward Burghardt ("W.E.B.")

(1868-1963) American civil rights leader, activist, historian, sociologist, educator, writer, poet, editor, scholar, socialist. First non-white person to receive Ph.D. from Harvard University. Taught at Wilberforce University, University of Pennsylvania. Established department of sociology at Atlanta (now Clark Atlanta) University. Notable works: *The Philadelphia Negro; The Negro; The Souls of Black Folk; John Brown; Black*

Reconstruction; Black Folk, Then and Now. Joined U.S. Communist party at age 93 and became a naturalized citizen of Ghana at age 95. Died in Accra, Ghana, shortly afterward.

Last Word (spoken): "Shirley." Spoken to his wife Shirley Graham Du Bois.

Source: *His Day is Marching On: A Memoir of W.E.B. DuBois* by Shirley Graham Du Bois (Philadelphia, 1971).

Last Words (written, doubtful): "As you live, believe in life. Always human beings will live and progress to greater, broader and fuller life. The only possible death is to lose belief in this truth simply because the great end comes slowly, because the time is long." From his "Last Message to the World" read at his funeral.

Source: *Journal of Negro History* (April 1964).

Du Bois wrote this message on June 26, 1957. It was released to the world when he died on August 27, 1963.

Source: *W.E.B. Du Bois on Sociology and the Black Community* by W. E. B. Du Bois, Edwin D. Driver and Dan S. Green (Chicago, 1980).

Dubos, Jean-Baptiste

(1670-1742) French theologian, historian, writer, statesman. Gave up theology for law and politics. Employed by M. de Torcy, minister of foreign affairs, and by regent and Cardinal Dubois in several secret missions. Later devoted himself to history and literature, gaining distinction as an author. Elected member of Académie Française. Died at age 71.

Last Words: "Death is a law and not a punishment. Three things ought to console us for giving up life. The friends whom we have lost, the few persons worthy of being loved whom we leave behind us, and finally the memory of our stupidities and the assurance that they are now going to stop."

Source: *Biographie universelle*, Book VII, by J. Fr. Michaud and Louis Gabriel Michaud (Paris, 1811-1862).

Dubroff, Jessica Whitney

(1988-1996) American child. At age seven she attempted to become the youngest person to pilot a plane across the U.S. Gained much media attention as television networks followed her progress at each stop. A day into the trip, her plane crashed after she took off in a rainstorm from Cheyenne Regional Airport in Wyoming. Her biography was later published by her mother. The accident generated a storm of negative publicity and led to federal legislation that prohibits anyone from flying who does not hold at least a private pilot certificate and a current medical certificate.

Last Words: "Do you hear the rain? Do you hear the rain?"

Source: *Slipping the Surly Bonds: Great Quotations on Flight* compiled by David English (New York, 1998).

Ducos, Jean-François

(1765-1793) French tradesman. Representative of Gironde in Legislative Assembly during the French Revolution. Tried as a traitor before a revolutionary tribunal. Guillotined at age 28 with other Girondists.

Last Words: "It is time that the convention decreed the inviolability of heads." Spoken as he laid his head on the block.

Source: *Geschichte der Französischen Revolution* by J.B. Weiss (Vienna, Austria, 1888).

Variation: "The Convention has forgotten one decree." Spoken to Fonfrede, who was beside him at the place of execution. When asked what he meant, he replied: "A decree on the indivisibility of heads and bodies."

Source: *Pierre Vergniaud Voice of the French Revolution* by Claude G. Bowers (New York, 1950).

Dudley, John,
1st Duke of Northumberland

(1502?-1553) English nobleman, conspirator. Named Master of the Armoury in Tower of London. Invited to be cup-bearer at coronation of Anne Boleyn. Led procession at christening of Princess Elizabeth. Named Viscount Lisle, Lord Admiral for life and Knight of the Garter. Admitted to Privy Council, and later given the title of Duke of Northumberland. Lead council in ousting Somerset. Ended wars with France and Scotland that Somerset had initiated. Led palace rebellion to place Lady Jane Grey on English throne. Son Guildford married Grey. Dudley encouraged Edward VI to sign letters changing the succession of Crown to fall to Grey. Executed for interfering with Mary's succession to throne.

Last Words: "I have deserved a thousand deaths."

Source: *The Annales, or, Generall Chronicle of England* by John Stow and Edmund Howes (London, 1615).

Duff, George

(1764-1805) British military officer. Naval leader. Fought in the American Revolution, French Revolution and Napoleonic Wars. Killed at age 41 by cannon fire on his ship HMS *Mars* at the Battle of Trafalgar.

Last Words (written): "My dearest Sophia, I have just had time to tell you we are just going into action with the combined (fleets). I hope and trust in God that we shall all behave as becomes us, and that I may yet have the happiness of taking my beloved wife and children into my arms. Norwich is quite well and happy. I have, however, ordered him off the quarter deck. Yours ever and most truly, Geo. Duff." Final note to his wife.

Source: *The Five Hundred Best English Letters*, ed. by Frederick Edwin Smith, Earl of Birkenhead (London, 1931) from *The Naval Chronicle*, Vol. XV, ed. by James Stanier Clarke, S. Jones and J. Jones (London, 1806).

Dulles, John Foster

(1888-1959) American lawyer, statesman. Named *Time* magazine's Man of the Year in 1954. U.S. secretary of state during Eisenhower administration. Resigned because of cancer in 1959. Died at age 71 in Washington, D.C. Dulles International Airport was named for him.

Last Words: "If the United States is willing to go to war over Berlin, there won't be war over Berlin." Spoken to a friend.

Source: *John Foster Dulles, The Last Year* by Eleanor Lansing Dulles (New York, 1963). The author was his sister.

Dumas, Alexandre (père)

(1802-1870) French novelist, playwright. Birth name Dumas Davy de la Pailleterie. Father of Alexandre Dumas, fils (son). Known as Alexandre Dumas, père (father). Notable historical novels: *The Count of Monte Cristo; The Black Tulip; The Corsican Brothers; The Three Musketeers* and its sequels (originally *D'Artagnan Romances*). Died at age 68 of a stroke in Puys, near Dieppe, France.

Different Last Words:

(1) "Tell me Alexandre, on your soul and

conscience, do you believe that anything of mine will live?" Spoken to his son.

Source: *The Fourth Musketeer: The Life of Alexander Dumas,* tr. from the French of J. Lucas-Dubreton by Maida Castelhun Darnton (New York, 1928).

(2) "What for, my boy?" His response to his son who had said to him: "Forgive me, Papa. Forgive me!"

Source: *Famous Last Words* by Barnaby Conrad (Garden City, NY, 1961). Conrad listed both (1) and (2) as versions of Dumas's Last Words.

(3) "See there! Fifty years ago when I came to Paris I had one louis in my possession. Why have people accused me of being prodigal? I have preserved it and possess it still—look, there it is!" Spoken to his son.

Source: *Alexandre Dumas (père) His Life and Work* by Arthur F. Davidson (Westminster, England, 1902).

Dumas, Thomas Alexandre

(1762-1806) Haitian military officer. Son of white father, Antoine-Alexandre Davy, and black mother, Marie-Cesette Dumas. Father of Alexandre Dumas (père). General in Napoleon's army. Died at age 44 of cancer at Villers-Cotterets, France.

Last Words: "Oh, must a general who at thirty-five was commander in chief of three armies, die at forty in his bed like a coward? Oh, my God! my God! What have I done to be condemned so young to leave my wife and my children?" Spoken in his deathbed. He saw a priest and confessed his sins, then died in his wife's arms.

Source: *Alexandre Dumas—A Great Life in Brief* by Andre Maurois (New York, 1971).

Dunant, Jean Henri

(1828-1910) Swiss philanthropist, businessman, social activist. Witnessed aftermath of Battle of Solferino (Italy); recorded memories and experiences in book *A Memory of Solferino* that inspired creation of the International Committee of the Red Cross (ICRC). Geneva Convention was based on Dunant's ideas. Shared first Nobel Peace Prize with Frédéric Passy in 1901. Died at age 82 in Heiden, Switzerland.

Last Words: "I wish to be carried to my grave like a dog without a single one of your ceremonies which I do not recognize. I trust to your goodness faithfully, to respect my last earthly request. I count upon your friendship that it shall be so. Amen. I am a

disciple of Christ as in the first century, and nothing more."

Source: *Dunant: The Story of the Red Cross* by Martin Gumpert (New York, 1938).

Dunbar, Paul Laurence

(1872-1906) American poet, short-story writer, novelist. Son of escaped slave. President of literary society at Howard University. Friend of Orville and Wilbur Wright, who invested in his newspaper, *Dayton Tattler*. First book of poems *Oak and Ivy* was published in 1892. Second book, *Majors and Minors,* published in 1895, brought him the patronage of William Dean Howells. The two books were combined as *Lyrics of a Lowly Life*, creating his literary reputation. Died at age 33 of tuberculosis in Dayton, Ohio.

Last Words: "Through the valley of the shadow." From the 23rd Psalm.

Source: *Paul Laurence Dunbar, Poet of His People* by Benjamin Griffith Brawley (Chapel Hill, NC, 1936).

Duncan, Isadora

(1877-1927) American dancer. Birth name Dora Angela Duncan. Regarded as the Mother of Modern Dance by many. Did not achieve the popularity in America that she received in Europe. Had a tragic personal life: her children, both illegitimate by different men, and their nanny died in a bizarre drowning incident. Her Russian ex-husband was institutionalized and committed suicide. She died at age 50 in a freak accident. After she left a hotel in Nice, France, her long scarf caught in the open-spoked wheel of a friend's automobile in which she was a passenger. No one noticed. As the car sped away, the other end of the scarf tightened around her neck and strangled her.

Last Words: "Adieu, mes amis. Je vais a la gloire!" (tr. "Farewell, my friends. I go on to glory.") Spoken to her friend Mary Desti outside the hotel just before she got into the car.

Source: *The Untold Story: The Life of Isadora Duncan 1921-1927* by Mary Desti (New York, 1929). Mary Desti (Mary Estelle Dempsey) was one of Duncan's closest friends. She was the mother of writer/director Preston Sturges.

Duncan, Joseph

(1794-1844) American politician. Member

U.S. House of Representatives from Illinois. Governor of Illinois. During his tenure as governor, the Illinois capital was moved from Vandalia to Springfield. Died at age 49 in Jacksonville, Illinois.

Last Words: "Ever precious, ever precious." His response when asked if Christ was precious to him at this hour.

Source: *Biographical Sketch of Joseph Duncan, Fifth Governor of Illinois* by Julia Smith Duncan Kirby (Chicago, 1888). The author was his daughter. The sketch was a printing of a paper read before the Historical Society of Jacksonville, Illinois, on May 7, 1885. Despite the title of her biography about him, Duncan was the sixth, not the fifth governor of Illinois.

Dundee, John Graham, see Graham, John of Claverhouse, 1st Viscount of Dundee.

Dunlap, James

(1744-1818) American clergyman, educator. Presbyterian. Second president of Jefferson College. Died at age 74 in Abington, Pennsylvania.

Last Words: "Take my watch and keep it as a memento of my love for you." His response to one of his daughters who leaned over his bed and asked him if he knew who she was.

Source: *Annals of the American Pulpit: Or, Commemorative Notices of Distinguished American Clergymen of Various Denominations,* Vol. III, William B. Sprague (New York, 1858).

Dunn, John J.

(1869-1933) American prelate. Roman Catholic Bishop Auxiliary and Vicar General of the Archdiocese of New York. Described as "right hand" to His Eminence Patrick Cardinal Hayes. Active in foreign missions. Bishop Dunn Memorial School at Mount Saint Mary College in Newburgh, New York, was named for him.

Last Words: "If the Lord wants me, I am ready to die."

Source: "Throngs Mourn Bishop J.J. Dunn" (*New York Times,* September 4, 1933).

Dunstan, Saint

(909?-988) English monk, holy man. Archbishop of Canterbury. Reformed monastic orders. Made them dominant over secular clergy. Banished by King Edward. Died at Canterbury, England.

Last Words: "The merciful and gracious Lord hath so done His gracious works that they ought to be had in remembrance. He hath given meat to them that fear Him." He died almost immediately after speaking these words.

Source: *Martyrs and Saints of the First Twelve Centuries* by Elizabeth Rundle Charles (London, 1887).

Dupanloup, Félix Antoine Philibert

(1802-1878) French prelate. Bishop of Orléans. Member of French Academy. His eulogizing about Joan of Arc in 1849 attracted attention to her in England and France. She was later canonized, partly because of his efforts. In *Illustrissimi*—a collection of 40 letters written by Pope John Paul I when he was Patriarch of Venice—Dupanloup is one of the "recipients" of letters to well-known fictional and historical characters such as Pinocchio, Charles Dickens, Hippocrates and Jesus. Died at age 76 at Lacombe, Savoy, France.

Last Words: "Yes, yes." His reply when told that a prayer for him was about to be offered to the Blessed Virgin.

Source: *Life of Monseigneur Dupanloup, Bishop of Orleans* by Abbé F. Lagrange (London, 1885).

Dupetit-Thouars, Aristide Aubert

(1760-1798) French military officer. Naval commander of ship-of-the-line *Le Tonnant*. A cannonball tore off his legs in the Battle of the Nile against Britain. He refused to be taken below for medical attention. Had his men place him in barrel. He continued to lead his men. When he realized he could do no more, he spoke his final words.

Last Words: "I might lose my head with my blood and do something foolish if I keep the command. It is time I gave it up." Spoken to a lieutenant. He died at his post on the quarterdeck at age 37.

Source: *Fighting Sail* by A.B.C. Whipple (Alexandria, VA, 1978)

Dupleix, Joseph François

(1697-1763) French administrator, statesman. Governor general of all French possessions in India. Engaged in a long struggle with Britain when he tried to secure French dominance in India. Was recalled to France. His services went unrecognized. He lost his fortune and died in obscurity at age 66. At least four French warships and two commercial ships were named for him.

Last Words (written): "I have sacrificed my youth, my fortune, my life to enrich my nation in Asia. Unfortunate friends, too weak relations, devoted all their property to the success of my projects. They are now in misery and want. I have complied with all the judiciary forms: I have demanded, as the last of the creditors, that which is due to me. My services are treated as fables, my demand is denounced as ridiculous, I am treated as the vilest of mankind. I am in the most deplorable indigence. The little property that remained to me has been seized. I am compelled to ask for decrees for delay in order not to be dragged to prison."

Source: *Dupleix* by Col. G. B. Malleson (Oxford, England, 1895).

Du Pont, Alfred Irénée

(1864-1935) American businessman, philanthropist. Along with two other family members, helped rescue Du Pont Company from being sold to a competitor. Served as vice president of the new corporation. Took over black powder manufacture, sat on executive committee and helped create research program. Died at age 71 in Jacksonville, Florida. His will provided that when he and his wife died, his entire estate was to go to the Nemours Foundation to treat crippled children and care for the indigent elderly of Delaware and Florida.

Last Words: "Thank you, doctors. Thank you, nurses. I'll be all right in a few days."

Source: *Alfred I. Du Pont: The Family Rebel* by Marquis James (Indianapolis, IN, 1941).

Duranti, Jean-Etienne

(1534-1589) French magistrate. President of Toulouse Parliament. Mobbed and killed at age 55 in Toulouse. His statue is in Toulouse. His death is the subject of a painting by French painter Paul Delaroche.

Last Words: "Adieu, my beloved; what God has granted me—life, goods, honors—I am presently to be stripped of. Death is the end, but not the punishment of life; innocent of the charges imputed me, my soul is to appear at the tribunal of the sovereign Judge.

Trust in Him. He will always help you [to the mob]. Yes, here I am. But what crime have I committed, what is the wrong, O people, I am guilty of in your eyes?— Lord God, receive my soul. Do not blame them for this wrong, for they know not what they do." Spoken to his wife and to the mob that attacked him.

Source: *Histoire véritable de ce qui s'est passé à Toulouse en la morte du Prèsident Duranti* (Toulouse, France, 1861).

Durham, James

(1622-1658) Scottish minister, writer. Popular preacher in Glasgow. Died at age 35 in Glasgow.

Last Words: "After all I've preached or written, there is but one Scripture I can remember, or dare grip: tell me if I dare lay the weight of my salvation on it? 'Whosoever cometh unto Me I will in no wise cast out.' " Spoken on his deathbed to Mr. Carstairs. Durham had been concerned about the state of his spirituality. Carstairs reassured him by replying: "You may depend upon it, if you had a thousand salvations as hazard."

Source: *Dictionary of Anecdote, Incident, Illustrative Fact, Selected and Arranged for the Pulpit and the Platform* by Walter Baxendale (New York, 1888).

Durocher, Blessed Marie-Rose

(1811-1849) Canadian holy woman, nun, educator. Birth name Eulalie Durocher. Founded Roman Catholic religious order: Sisters of the Holy Names of Jesus and Mary. The order established a school in Longueuil, Quebec. Died at age 38. Beatified in 1982.

Last Words (written): "I beg pardon, my sisters, for lacking sweetness and kindness in your regard. I beg pardon for having hurt anyone in conversation at recreation, for having spoken harsh or offensive words. I beg pardon for having lacked charity in not having towards you the heart of a mother. I beg pardon for my irregularities in spiritual exercises. I beg pardon for my shortcomings."

Source: *Saints of North America* by Vincent J. O'Malley (Huntington, IN, 2004).

Durrant, William Henry ("Theo")

(1871-1898) American murderer. Medical student. Sunday school superintendent, church librarian. Apprehended for the killing of two women. Tried and found guilty of murder. Executed by hanging in San Francisco, California.

Last Words: "Don't put that rope on, my boy, until after I talk." Spoken to the sheriff as he approached him. The sheriff ignored him and told the hangman to continue.

Source: *By the Neck, A Book of Hangings Selected from Contemporary Accounts* by August Mencken (New York, 1942).

Duse, Eleonora

(1858-1924) Italian actress. Gained fame in Italian versions of roles made famous by Sarah Bernhardt, who later became her fierce rival. Duse was the first woman on the cover of *Time* magazine (1923). Her relationship with Gabriel D'Annunzio ended when D'Annunzio gave the lead in a play to Bernhardt instead of Duse. Died at age 65 in a hotel in Pittsburgh, Pennsylvania, while on tour. Building is now part of the University of Pittsburgh campus.

Different Last Words:

(1) "We must stir ourselves. Move on! Work, work! Cover me! Must move on! Must work! Cover me!"

Source: *Eleonora Duse* by Arthur Symons (New York, 1927).

Variation: "We must start off again! Work again! Cover me up."

Source: *The Life of Eleonora Duse* by Emil Alphons Rheinhardt (London, 1930). Quotation described as "among her last words."

Variation: "I am cold. Cover me."

Source: *Age Cannot Wither: The Story of Duse and D'Annunzio* by Bertita Harding (Philadelphia, 1947).

(2) "At dawn we must leave. Hurry, we must leave."

Source: *Eleonora Duse in Life and Art* by Giovanni Pontiero (New York, 1986).

Duveen, Joseph, 1st Baron

(1869-1939) British international art dealer. Made fortune buying works of art from impoverished European aristocracies and selling them to wealthy American clients such as Henry Clay Frick, Henry E. Huntington, William Randolph Hearst, J.P. Morgan, Andrew Mellon and John D. Rockefeller. These works are now in America's top museums. Died at age 69 in London.

Last Words: "Well, I fooled 'em for five years." Spoken to his nurse, referring to his long illness.

Source: *Duveen* by S.N. Behrman (New York, 1952).

Dwight, Timothy

(1752-1817) American clergyman, educator, writer, politician. Congregationalist. Grandson of Jonathan Edwards. President of Yale. Son and nephew were also presidents of Yale. Address he gave in 1797 is credited with starting the Second Great Awakening. Headed Connecticut Federalist party. Coined term "Cape Cod house" in his book *Travels in New England and New York*. Died at age 64 in New Haven, Connecticut. Residential College at Yale and school in New York City were named for him.

Last Words: "There, I have done! Oh, what triumphant truth!" Spoken as he finished his last manuscript.

Source: *Timothy Dwight, 1752-1817, A Biography* by Charles E. Cunningham (New York, 1942).

Dwyer, R. Budd ("Budd")

(1939-1987) American politician. Member of Pennsylvania House of Representatives, Pennsylvania Senate. State treasurer. Died at age 48. Televised his suicide. Accused and convicted of agreeing to accept a kickback of $300,000. The day before his sentencing, he called a press conference to proclaim his innocence and announce he would not resign as state treasurer. After reading his statement, he took a .357 Magnum revolver from an envelope and told the crowd to "Please leave the room if this will offend you." The crowd pleaded with him to put down the gun.

Last Words: "Stay away, this thing will hurt someone." Spoken as people tried to get near him, just before he shot himself while five news cameras televised the event live. Cult film *Faces of Death* and Michael Moore's *Bowling for Columbine* feature footage of the press conference. Many references to him in punk and alternative songs.

Source: "PA. Treasurer Kills Self at News Conference" (*Associated Press*, January 23, 1987).

Dyer, Mary Barrett

(1611?-1660) English-born American martyr. Quaker. Expelled from Boston under law that outlawed Quakers. When she returned to Massachusetts, she was convicted and executed for defying the law. Hanged on Boston Common. Believed to be the only woman in the North American colonies to be executed in the name of religious freedom.

Different Last Words:

(1) "Nay, I cannot, for in obedience to the will of the Lord God I came, and in his will I abide faithful to the death." Spoken to her former pastor who urged her to repent of her errors.

Source: *Clothed With the Sun: Biblical Women, Social Justice and Us* by Joyce Hollyday (Louisville, KY, 1994).

(2) "Nay, first a child; then a young man, then a strong man, before an Elder of Christ Jesus." Her response when asked if one of the Elders should pray for her.

Source: *A Conspectus of American Biography: Being an Analytical Summary of American History and Biography, Containing also the Complete Indexes of the National Cyclopedia of American Biography* by George Derby (New York, 1906).

Eads, James Buchanan

(1820-1887) American engineer, inventor. Named for mother's cousin, future President James Buchanan. Invented diving bell to salvage scrap metal from sunken ships. Built Eads Bridge across the Mississippi River at St. Louis. First to use cantilever construction method. Built iron-clad ships for the Union in U.S. Civil War. Built jetty system for faster navigation in New Orleans. Died at age 66 in Nassau, Bahamas, while working on a ship railway design across Tehuantepec Isthmus that would be 2,000 miles shorter than the Panama Canal.

Last Words: "I cannot die; I have not finished my work."

Source: *James B. Eads* by Louis How (Boston, 1900).

Eagels, Jeanne

(1890-1929) American actress. Real name Amelia Jeannine Eagels. Ziegfeld Follies Girl. Died at age 39 in a private New York hospital. Cause of death uncertain; possibly from alcoholism or drug overdose. Posthumously nominated for Academy Award for best actress for role in 1929 film *The Letter.*

Last Words: "I'm going to Dr. Caldwell's for one of my regular treatments."

Source: *The Rain Girl, The Tragic Story of Jeanne Eagels* by Eddie Doherty (Philadelphia, 1930). Her biography was named for her first major hit, the 1922 play *Rain* by John Colton, based on a short story by W. Somerset Maugham.

Earhart, Amelia Mary

(1898-1937?) American aviator. Noted for accomplishments as an early female pilot. Lost with co-pilot Frederick J. Noonan when they attempted an around-the-world flight along the Equator. Plane disappeared after taking off from New Guinea as they were completing the last leg of the flight. Despite a massive naval search, their plane was never found.

Last Words: "We are on the line of position 157-337—will repeat this message on 6210. We are running North and South." Her final radio contact was at 8:45 a.m., New York time, July 2, 1937.

Source: *The Voyage of the Odyssey, Voice from the Sea* (PBS, December 11, 2000).

Early, Jubal Anderson

(1816-1894) American military officer. Fought in Mexican and U.S. Civil Wars. Confederate States brigadier general. Commanded brigade at Bull Run, division at Fredericksburg and Gettysburg. Defeated by Sheridan in 1864. Removed of his command. Died at age 77 in Lynchburg, Virginia, after he fell down a flight of stairs.

Last Words: Told Senator John W. Daniel he wanted to talk with him "about certain arrangements." Early was in so much pain he could not tell him what the arrangements were. He died with his hand resting quietly in Senator Daniel's hand.

Source: "Gen. Jubal A. Early Dead; Peaceful End to the Southern Leader's Life" (*New York Times,* March 3, 1894).

Earp, Morgan Seth

(1851-1882) American frontier lawman. Brother of Wyatt, Warren, Virgil, and James Earp. Killed at age 30 while playing billiards in Tombstone, Arizona, by an unknown assassin, possibly in retaliation for his participation in the Gunfight at the O.K. Corral. The *Tombstone Epitaph* (March 20, 1882) noted that before he died, Morgan whispered something into his brother Wyatt's ear.

Different Last Words:

(1) Morgan asked his brother: "Do you know who did it?" Wyatt is said to have responded: "Yes, and I'll get them." "That's all I ask," Morgan whispered. "But Wyatt, be careful." He then said: "Don't, boys, don't. I can't stand it. This is the last game of pool I'll ever play." Spoken as he was carried to the pool table.

Sources: *Tombstone Epitaph*, March 20, 1882; *Wyatt Earp: The Life Behind the Legend* by Casey Tefertiller (New York, 1997).

(2) "I guess you were right, Wyatt. I can't see a damned thing." After a few minute, he said: "Take care of yourself, Wyatt. They got me, Wyatt. Don't let them get you. Tell Ma and Pa goodbye. I expect to meet you in heaven." He then drew a deep breath and died.

Sources: *Wyatt Earp* by Stuart N. Lake (Boston, 1931); *I Married Wyatt Earp* by Josephine Sarah Marcus Earp (Tucson, AZ, 1976); "Wyatt Earp: Man Versus Myth" by Roger S. Peterson (*American History*, August 1994).

Earp, Warren Baxter

(1855-1900) American frontier lawman, cattle detective. Brother of Wyatt, Morgan, Virgil and James Earp. Shot and killed at age 45 by Johnnie Boyett in Brown's Saloon in Willcox, Arizona.

Different Last Words:

(1) "I have not got any arm. You have a good deal the best of this." Spoken to Boyett as he continued to walk toward him. Boyett warned him then fired a shot that hit Warren in the chest.

Source: *Henry Clay Hooker and the Sierra Bonita* by Lynn R. Bailey (Tucson, AZ, 1998). Hooker was a rancher in southeastern Arizona. The Sierra Bonita was his ranch. Johnnie Boyett is believed to have worked for Hooker.

(2) "Johnnie, go get your gun this time! We're going to shoot it out."

Source: *The Earp Brothers of Tombstone* by Frank Waters (Lincoln, NE, 1960).

Earp, Wyatt Berry Stapp

(1848-1929) American frontier lawman, saloon keeper, gunfighter. Brother of Warren, Morgan, Virgil and James Earp. Participated in the Gunfight at the O.K. Corral in Tombstone, Arizona, with Doc Holiday and brothers Virgil and Morgan Earp. Survived other gunfights. Eventually settled in California. His story was told in the 1994 movie *Wyatt Earp*. Died at age 80 in Los Angeles.

Different Last Words:

(1) "Suppose, suppose—." Spoken moments before he died.

Source: *Wyatt Earp: The Life Behind the Legend* by Casey Tefertiller (New York, 1997).

(2) "What are you two coyotes cooking up? Spoken to his wife and a friend. He later called for "water." Soon afterward, he died peacefully.

Source: *I Married Wyatt Earp* by Josephine Sarah Marcus Earp (Tucson, AZ, 1976).

Eastman, George

(1854-1932) American inventor, industrialist, philanthropist. Founded Eastman Kodak Company. Introduced flexible film in 1884 and the Kodak box camera in 1889, making photography accessible to all. His technology was the basis for motion picture film. He coined the phrase "You press the button, we do the rest." As a philanthropist under the name "Mr. Smith," Eastman gave away an estimated $100 million to the University of Rochester, Massachusetts Institute of Technology, Tuskegee Institute, Hampton Institute, Eastman School of Music, and other organizations. In his final years, he suffered from an excruciatingly painful incurable spinal disease that led to his taking his life at age 77.

Last Words (written): "To my friends: My work is done. Why wait? G.E." Suicide note.

Source: *Rochester* [NY] *Democrat and Chronicle,* March 15, 1932.

Eastman, Joseph Bartlett

(1882-1944) American government official, lawyer. Distant cousin of George Eastman. Member Interstate Commerce Commission. Federal coordinator of transportation. Director Office of Defense Transportation during World War II, when he was given authority to curtail travel by cars, trucks, buses. When his health began to fail while handling railway labor problems, he was obliged to rest. Died at age 61 in Washington, D.C.

Last Words (written): "I am glad to say that I seem to be making good progress, and from all prognostications I shall be back in circulation again before too long." Written in a letter.

Source: *Joseph B. Eastman: Servant of the People* by Claude Moore Fuess (New York, 1952).

Eaton, Margaret O'Neale Timberlake ("Peggy")

(1799-1879) American matron. Central figure in "The Petticoat Affair" scandal that caused the resignation of U.S. President Andrew Jackson's entire Cabinet and had ramifications on careers that affected history. First husband John Timberlake committed suicide. When she married John Henry Eaton, Cabinet wives and other members of Washington society gossiped that she had been involved with Eaton before Timberlake died. After John Eaton died in 1856, she married Antonio Buchignani, who later ran off with her teenage granddaughter. Died at age 79 in Washington, D.C. The 1936 movie *The Gorgeous Hussy* was based on her story.

Different Last Words:

(1) Died singing this hymn, while a minister was at her bedside:

"I would not live always, I ask not to stay/
Where storm after storm rises dark o'er the way/
The few lurid mornings that dawn on us here/
Are enough of life's woes, full enough of its cheer."

Source: *Peggy Eaton, Democracy's Mistress* by Queen Pollack (New York, 1931).

(2) (doubtful): "I am not in the least afraid to die, but this is such a beautiful world to leave."

Source: "Literary and Personal" column (*Arthur's Home Magazine*, Vol. 48, 1880).

Arthur's Home Magazine noted that she spoke these words the day before she died as she looked out at the sunlight.

Eaton, Theophilus

(1590-1658) English-born American colonist. One of the principal founders of New Haven, Connecticut. Elected first governor of New Haven colony in 1639; reelected every year for the rest of his life. Enforced Puritan laws strictly. Died at age 68 in New Haven.

Last Words: "Some time thou mayst go, but I shall die here. Goodnight."

Source: "A Puritan Indeed" (*Harper's Magazine*, Vol.

71, No. 428, October 1885).

Variation: "You may, but I shall die here." Spoken to his wife who proposed that they return to their native country.

Source: "Governor Eaton" (*The Connecticut Evangelical Magazine and Religious Intelligencer,* September 1812).

Eaton, William

(1764-1811) U.S. military officer, diplomat, adventurer. U.S. Army general. Consul at Tunis. Fought Barbary States in Tripolitan War, supporting the brother of Tripoli's Pasha Yussif Karamanli. Eaton captured Derna in 1805, an event that made him a hero. When he returned home, he was a major witness against Aaron Burr in Burr's treason trial. Died at age 47 in Brimfield, Massachusetts. Eatonton, Georgia, and Eaton, Ohio, are named for him.

Last Words: "Yes, sir, I thank you." His reply when asked if he wanted to have his head raised.

Source: *The Life of the Late Gen. William Eaton; Several Years an Officer in the United States Army, Consul at the Regency of Tunis on the Coast of Barbary, and Commander of the Christian and Other Forces that Marched from Egypt Through the Desert of Barca, in 1805—Principally Collected from His Correspondence and Other Manuscripts* by Charles Prentiss (Brookfield, MA, 1813).

Eddé, Raymond

(1913-2000) Lebanese statesman, cabinet minister. Son of former president Émile Eddé. Strong nationalist. Headed Lebanese National Bloc political party. Opposed French mandate and Syrian, Israeli and Palestinian intervention. Candidate for president. Left Lebanon in 1976 and went into self-imposed exile in France after attempts on his life. His sister was killed by sniper in Beirut in 1978. He died at age 87 in Paris.

Last Words: "I'm thinking. I'm thinking of Lebanon." His response when advised to go to sleep.

Source: "I am Thinking of Lebanon" by Sabine Darrous (*The* [Beirut] *Daily Star,* May 15, 2000).

Eddy, Mary Morse Baker Glover

(1821-1910) American theologian. Founder of Church of Christ, Scientist, chartered in 1879. Turned to the Bible when she experienced the sudden abatement of symptoms after a major injury in 1866. Devoted next few years to Biblical study and development of Christian Science and healing. She put her philosophy in her book *Science and Health* (later re-titled *Science and Health with Key to the Scriptures*), her textbook of Christian Science. Died at age 89 in Chestnut Hill, Massachusetts.

Last Words: "God is my life."

Source: *Mrs. Eddy, The Biography of a Virginal Mind* by Edwin Franden Dakin (New York, 1929).

Eddy, Nelson Ackerman

(1901-1967) American actor. Baritone. Stage, screen, radio and recording star. Appeared in musical movies during the 1930s and 1940s as well as in opera, and stage performances. Frequently paired with singer/actress Jeannette MacDonald. Earned three stars on Hollywood Walk of Fame, for film, recording and radio. Sang at the third inauguration of President Franklin Delano Roosevelt. Died at age 65 while performing in a Florida nightclub. When he forgot the lyrics of the song he was singing, he turned to his accompanist and asked him to play another song.

Last Words: "Would you play 'Dardanelle'? Maybe I'll get the words back." After a few minutes, he cried out: "I can't see. I can't hear." He collapsed of a stroke and died a few hours later.

Source: *The Hollywood Book of Death: The Bizarre, Often Sordid, Passings of More than 125 American Movie and TV Idols* by James Robert Parish (Chicago, 2002).

Edelstein, Morris Michael

(1888-1941) American politician. Member of U.S. House of Representatives from New York. Collapsed after completing a speech on the floor of the House. Taken to the House cloakroom in the Capitol Building, where he died at age 53.

Last Words: "We are living in a democracy."

Source: "15,000 Pay Tribute to M.M. Edelstein. Lawyers, Jurists, Colleagues in House and Neighbors at Rites for Representative. Eulogy by Dr. Bergman. Galbraith Post of American Legion and Jewish Veterans Escort Funeral Cortege" (*New York Times*, June 7, 1941).

Edgeworth de Firmont, Henry Essex

(1745-1807) Irish-born French clergyman.

Son of Robert Edgeworth, rector of Edgeworthstown, Ireland. Great-grandson of Archbishop Ussher. Became confessor to Princess Elizabeth, sister of Louis XVI, in 1791 and later was confessor to Louis XVI. Celebrated Mass for him and attended him on the scaffold. Chaplain for Louis XVIII, whom he accompanied to Russia.

Last Words (doubtful): "Fils de Saint Louis, montez au ciel!" (tr. "Son of Saint Louis, ascend to Heaven.")

Source: *The Popular Encyclopedia: Being a General Dictionary of Arts, Sciences, Literature, Biography, History and Political Economy* by Sir Daniel K. Sandford, Thomas Thomson and Allan Cunningham (Glasgow, Scotland, 1841).

These were not his Last Words. It is questionable whether he ever said them. Scholars claim he did not quote this line in his memoirs or in a letter written in 1796 to his brother, in which he described the death of the king. Furthermore, he declared to several people who asked him about it, that the words were not his. In the section "Historical Errors" in his book *All the Year Round*, Charles Dickens wrote that the phrase was "a later invention."

Sources: *All the Year Round* by Charles Dickens (London, 1890); *Letters from Abbé Edgeworth to His Friends Written Between the Years 1777 and 1807 with Memoirs of His Life, Including Some Account of the Late Catholic Bishop of Cork, Dr. Moylan, and Letters to Him from the Right Hon. Edmund Burke and Other Persons of Distinction* by Thomas R. England (London, 1818).

Edgeworth, Richard Lovell

(1744-1817) British writer, educational theorist, inventor. Did pioneering experiments on telegraphic communication between Dublin and Galway. Other inventions include velocipede, semaphore, land-measuring machine and pedometer. Daughter Maria, one of his 21 children, was her father's companion and assistant. She finished his memoirs when he died at age 73 in Edgeworthstown, Ireland.

Last Words: "I die with the soft feeling of gratitude to my friends, and submission to the God who made me."

Source: *Memoirs of Richard Lovell Edgeworth, Esq., Begun by Himself and Concluded by His Daughter, Maria Edgeworth* by Richard Lovell Edgeworth and Maria Edgeworth (London, 1820).

Edison, Thomas Alva

(1847-1931) American inventor, business-man. Known as The Wizard of Menlo Park. Operated well-equipped and well-staffed laboratory in Menlo Park, New Jersey. Invented or credited with many significant inventions, including phonograph, motion picture camera, stock ticker, electric light bulb, automatic telegraph and carbon telephone transmitter. Died at age 84 in West Orange, New Jersey. Edison, New Jersey, was named for him.

Last Words: "It is very beautiful over there." Spoken as he looked out his bedroom window at the valley near his home just before he died.

Source: *Thomas A. Edison, Benefactor of Mankind; The Romantic Life Story of the World's Greatest Inventor* by Francis Trevelyan Miller (Chicago, 1931).

Edmund or Eadmund, Saint ("The Martyr")

(840?-869) King of East Anglia. Defeated and slain by Danes at Hoxne. According to legend, he was tied to a tree, shot to death with arrows and decapitated. When his head was thrown into a forest, a wolf found it and protected it until it was given a proper burial with the rest of his body. Buried at Bury St. Edmunds, England.

Last Words: "Jesus, Jesus." Spoken while he refused to renounce his religion.

Source: *The Annales, or, Generall Chronicle of England* by John Stow and Edmund Howes (London, 1615).

Edward, Prince of Wales

(1330-1376) English royalty. Eldest son of King Edward III of England. Known as the Black Prince for the color of his armor. Strong, popular military leader. Fought in Hundred Years' War. Was made Duke of Cornwall before assuming title Edward, Prince of Wales. Died at age 45, a year before his father. Throne passed to his son Richard upon the death of Edward III.

Last Words: "I thank Thee, O Lord, for all Thy benefits. With all my power I ask for Thy mercy that Thou wilt forgive me for all the sins that I, in my wrongdoing, have committed against Thee. And I ask with my whole heart the grace of pardon from all men whom I have knowingly or unwittingly offended."

Source: *The Life of Edward the Black Prince, 1330-1376; the Flower of Knighthood Out of All the World* by Henry Dwight Sedgwick (Indianapolis, IN, 1932).

Variation: "I give thee thanks, O God, for all thy benefits, and with all the pains of my soul I humbly beseech thy mercy to give me remission of those sins I have wickedly committed against thee; and of all mortal men whom willingly or ignorantly I have offended, I ask forgiveness with all my heart."

Source: *The Lives of the Princesses of Wales,* Vol. I, by Barbara Clay Finch (London, 1883).

Edward I, King of England

(1239-1307) English monarch. Son of Henry III of England. Known as Longshanks. Ruled 35 years. Died at age 68 at Burgh-by-Sands, Cumberland, during expedition against Scots. Succeeded by son Edward II.

Last Words: "Carry my bones before you on your march, for the rebels will not be able to endure the sight of me, alive or dead." Edward wanted his body to be boiled so that his bones could accompany every army against the Scots until they were defeated. His wish was not carried out. In 1774, his tomb was opened and his body was found to be still intact.

Source: *The Last Words (Real and Traditional) of Distinguished Men and Women Collected from Various Sources* by Frederic Rowland Marvin (New York, 1901).

Variation: "Wrap my bones in a hammock and have them carried before the army so that I may still lead the way to victory." Spoken to his officers.

Source: *The Three Edwards* by Thomas Bertram Costain (New York, 1962).

Edward III, King of England

(1312-1377) English monarch. Elder son of Edward II and Isabella of France. Earl of Chester. Duke of Aquitaine. Ruled as king 50 of his 64 years. Successful monarch, credited with restoring strong royal authority after the disastrous reign of Edward II. Edward III helped transform England into an efficient military power. Succeeded by grandson Richard II.

Last Word: "Jesu, miserere." (tr. "Jesus, have mercy.") Spoken as his voice began to fail. He could scarcely pronounce the words.

Sources: *The Annales, or, Generall Chronicle of England* by John Stow and Edmund Howes (London, 1615); *The Three Edwards* by Thomas B. Costain (Garden City, NY, 1958).

Edward IV, King of England

(1442-1483) English monarch. Second son of Richard Plantagenet, 3rd Duke of York. His challenge to the ruling family marked the beginning of the Wars of the Roses. When Richard was killed at the Battle of Wakefield, Edward IV inherited his claim, establishing the House of York. He died at age 40 at Westminster.

Last Words: "Wherefore, in these last words that ever I look to speak with you, I exhort you and require you all, for the love that you have ever borne for me, for the love that I have ever borne to you, for the love that our Lord beareth to us all, from this time forward, all griefs forgotten, each of you love other. Which I verily trust you will, if ye any thing earthly regard, either God or your king, affinity or kindred, this realm, your own country, or your own surety." Spoken on his deathbed.

Source: *The History of King Richard the Third* (unfinished) by Master Thomas More (c. 1513), printed originally in 1557, reprinted in *The Library of the Old English Prose Writers* (Cambridge, England, 1831).

Edward VI, King of England

(1537-1553) English monarch. Only son of Henry VIII and Jane Seymour. Last Tudor king. Ascended throne when he was nine, died of tuberculosis at age 15. Short reign was marked by loss of control of Scotland, social unrest, unfavorable economic conditions, increasingly harsh Protestant reforms. and more conflicts with France.

Last Words: "I am faint; Lord have mercy upon me, and take my spirit."

Source: *Book of Martyrs and the Acts and Monuments of the Church* by John Fox (or Foxe). First published 1563, ed. by John Cumming (London, 1851).

Variation: "Lord God, deliver me out of this miserable and wretched life, and take me amongst Thy chosen; howbeit, not my will but Thy will be done. Lord I commit my spirit to Thee. O! Lord, thou knowest how happy it were for me to be with Thee: yet, for Thy chosen's sake, send me life and health, that I may truly serve thee. O! my Lord God, defend this realm from papistry,

and maintain Thy true religion, that I and my people pay praise Thy holy name, for Thy son Jesus Christ's sake. Amen." Dictated.

Source: *Literary Remains of King Edward the Sixth. Edited from His Autograph Manuscripts, with Historical Notes and a Biographical Memoir* by Edward, King of England and John Gough Nichols (London, 1857).

Edward VII, King of United Kingdom of Great Britain and Ireland

(1841-1910) British monarch. Known as the Peacemaker. Eldest son of Queen Victoria. Prince of Wales. Married Alexandra, daughter of King Christian IX of Denmark. Ascended to the throne in 1901 at age 59 upon the death of his mother. Edwardian era named for him. Died at age 68 at Buckingham Palace.

Last Words: On the day he died, he learned his filly Witch of the Air had won a race. When his son congratulated him, he replied: "Yes I have heard of it. I am very glad." He then fell into a coma. Believed to have said "No, I shall not give in; I shall go on; I shall work to the end" as he lost consciousness.

Source: *Edward VII: A Biography* by Sir Sidney Lee (New York, 1927).

Edward VIII, King of the United Kingdom of Great Britain and Northern Ireland

(1894-1972) British monarch. Son of King George V and Queen Mary. Ascended to the throne January 1936; abdicated December 1936 to marry American divorcée Wallis Simpson as Duke of Windsor. Died at age 77 of throat cancer in Paris.

Different Last Words:

(1) "Mama, Mama, Mama, Mama." Spoken just before he died. Heard by his valet Sydney Johnson, who was with him at the end.

Source: *The Windsor Style* by Suzy Menkes (Topsfield, MA, 1987).

(2) "No darling, I shall soon be asleep. Get some rest, please." Spoken to the duchess who had offered to sit up with him. He lapsed into unconsciousness as she left the room.

Source: *Royal Feud: The Queen Mother and the Duchess of Windsor* by Michael Thornton (London, 1985).

Edward the Confessor

(1003?-1066) English monarch. Last surviving son of King Ethelred (the Unready). Ruled from 1042 until he died. Married Edith, daughter of Earl Godwin. Her brother Harold later succeeded Edward as king. Edward built Westminster Abbey. Known for his holiness. Died during the Norman Conquest. Canonized in 1161.

Last Words: "Dear loyal friends,
It is a folly to lament my death;
When God wills it, one cannot remain."
Looking at his queen, he said:
"Weep not, dear one,
Grieve not for my death.
Since after this my death
I shall arrive at the sure port
Where I shall live with my Lord,
Always in joy and happiness.
Now I pray you all who are here,
My loyal people and my friends,
To my queen who is my wife,
Whose virtues I cannot number,
Who has been to me sister and dear,
Bear loyal company.
She has been my daughter and wife,
And of very precious life;
Honour her, as befits
So good and so exalted a matron;
Let her have her dowry in full
And her manors and her people,
Be they English, be they Norman,
Honour them all their life.
In the church of Saint Peter, to whom
Of old I made my vow, let me be buried.
To him I give myself, both living and dead,
Who was to me both aid and comfort."

Source: *Lives of Edward the Confessor* by Henry Richards Luard (London, 1858).

Edward Augustus, Duke of Kent and Strathearn

(1767-1820) English royalty. Fourth son of King George III. Married Princess Victoria of Saxe-Coburg-Saalfeld. Father of Queen Victoria. Died at age 52 in Sidmouth, Devon.

Last Words: "Do not forget me." Spoken to his wife.

Source: *The Letters of Queen Victoria: A Selection from Her Majesty's Correspondence Between the Years 1837 and 1861, Published by Authority of His Majesty the King* by Victoria, Arthur Christopher Benson, Reginald Baliol Brett Esher et al. (London, 1911).

Edwards, Edward

(1812-1886) English librarian, writer. Municipal library pioneer. Assistant at British Museum. Helped draw up rules of cataloging. Supported and encouraged William Ewart to pass free-library legislation for the United Kingdom in 1850. That year Edwards became the first librarian of Manchester Free Library. Notable works: *Life of Sir Walter Raleigh; Memoirs of Libraries* and *Lives of the Founders of the British Museum.*

Last Words: "I am much obliged to you—very." Spoken to his landlady after she bathed his feet.

Source: *Edward Edwards, The Chief Pioneer of Municipal Public Libraries* by Thomas Greenwood (London, 1902).

Edwards, Jonathan

(1703-1758) American clergyman, missionary, theologian, educator. Congregationalist. One of the great American evangelical theologians. Often associated with defending Calvinist theology and Puritan heritage. In Boston in 1731, he preached "Public Lecture," later published as *God Glorified—in Man's Dependence* (his first public attack on Arminianism, an anti-Calvin doctrine). It was followed by the Great Awakening. Edwards became president of the College of New Jersey (now Princeton University), a position he held only one month. He died at age 54 in Princeton after receiving an inoculation for smallpox.

Last Words: "Trust in God, and ye need not fear."

Source: *Jonathan Edwards* by Alexander V.G. Allen (Boston, 1890).

Egbert, Henry Clay

(1839-1899) American military officer. Brigadier general. Killed at age 60 near Manila during the Spanish-American War.

Last Words: "Goodbye, General; I'm done. I'm too old." Spoken to General Wheaton, who exclaimed "Nobly done, Egbert" as he bent over his wounded body.

Source: *New York Daily Sun*, March 27, 1899.

Egino or Egon, Gaugraf

(1002?-1050?) Frankish king. Between about 1030 and 1050, Gaugraf Egino and

Rudolf of Achalm built the castle known today as Ruine Achalm, near the town of Reutlingen in Baden-Württemberg, Germany. The name Achalm appears to refer to a nearby stream. However, there is reason to believe that it is derived from Egino's Last Words. He was killed breaking up a fight between two workers.

Last Words: "Ach Alm," his attempt to say "Ach Allmächtiger." (tr. "Oh! Almighty God.") His brother named the castle Achalm thinking he was honoring Egino's Last Words.

Source: *Schwäbische Alb: Burgen, Schlösser, Ruinen* by Gerd Dörr (Hamburg, Germany, 1988).

Egmont, Lamoral, Count of

(1522-1568) Flemish nobleman, military officer, statesman. General. Cousin of King of Spain. Member of Council of State with William of Orange and Count of Hoorn (or Horn). Protested introduction of the Inquisition in Flanders. Shortly afterward, resistance against Spanish rule in Netherlands increased. Egmont was arrested for treason and condemned to death. Beheaded in Brussels along with Hoorn. Their deaths led to protests in The Netherlands and contributed to resistance against the Spaniards. Died at age 45 in Brussels. He was the subject of the play *Egmont* by Goethe. Beethoven wrote an overture and incidental music for the drama.

Last Words: "Lord, into thy hands I commit my spirit."

Source: *The Rise of the Dutch Republic* by John Lothrop Motley (New York, 1855).

Eichmann, Karl Adolf

(1906-1962) German military officer. Nazi leader involved in transporting Jews to death camps during the Holocaust. Escaped to Argentina after World War II. Tracked down in 1960. Captured by Israeli agents. Tried and convicted as a war criminal in Jerusalem. Sentenced to death. Executed at age 56 by hanging.

Last Words: "I had to obey the laws of war and of my flag. After a short while, gentlemen, we all shall meet again. Such is the fate of all men. I have lived believing in God and, believing in God, I die." Spoken as the noose was placed around his neck.

Source: "No Time to Waste" (*Time* magazine, June 8, 1962).

Einstein, Albert

(1879-1955) German-born American theoretical physicist, philosopher, humanitarian, educator. Director of Kaiser Wilhelm Physical Institute in Berlin. Emigrated to the U.S. in 1933. Appointed a permanent member of the Institute for Advanced Study in Princeton, New Jersey. Deprived of his citizenship and property by Nazi German government in 1934. Became naturalized American citizen in 1941. Notable enunciations, among many: Special Theory of Relativity, General Theory of Relativity, Unified Field Theory. Won 1921 Nobel Prize for Physics. Einsteinium, radioactive element (Es), named for him. Declined presidency of Israel in 1953. Died at age 76 in a Princeton hospital.

Last Words (spoken): Unknown. A nurse in his room heard him murmuring in German. She did not understand him. She left his room to get a physician. When they returned, Einstein was dead.

Source: *Einstein: Profile of the Man* by Peter Michelmore (New York, 1962).

Eisenhower, Dwight David

(1890-1969) 34th President of the U.S. American military officer, educator. Birth name David Dwight Eisenhower. Nicknamed "Ike." As general and supreme allied commander, he led invasions of North Africa, Italy and France during World War II. First military commander of NATO. As U.S. President, he redirected the defense budget toward nuclear weapons, launched the space race, enlarged Social Security and began building an interstate highway system. President of Columbia University. Died at age 78 in Washington, D.C.

Last Words: "I've always loved my wife, my children, and my grandchildren, and I've always loved my country. I want to go. God, take me."

Source: *Strictly Personal* by John S.D. Eisenhower (Garden City, NY, 1974). The author was his son.

El-Batouti, Gamil

(1940-1999) Egyptian airline pilot, disaster victim. Co-pilot of EgyptAir Flight 990 that crashed off the coast of Nantucket,

Massachusetts. Some versions of the crash that took 217 lives indicate El-Batouti shut off the Boeing 767's engines in flight and pushed the jet into a fatal suicidal dive. Other versions indicate he did not cause the dive but instead was a victim of a mechanical malfunction.

Last Words: "Tawakalt ala Allah." (tr. "I rely on God.") His Last Words, which he repeated eleven times, were on the plane's voice recorder.

Source: *The Air Up There: More Great Quotations on Flight* by Dave English (New York, 2003), citing the NTSB, 13:50 EST October 31, 1999.

Elijah

(d. c. 850 B.C.) Hebrew biblical prophet. Lived in the Kingdom of Israel during the reign of King Ahab and Jezebel. Elijah was carried off to Heaven in a flaming chariot. His disciple Elisha, a minor prophet, continued his policies. According to Jewish tradition, Elijah is welcomed at every Passover Seder as the forerunner of the Messiah. Elijah's Last Words were spoken to Elisha. Suddenly a chariot of fire and horses of fire came between them and parted them. Elijah went up to Heaven on the fiery chariot in a whirlwind. Elijah's Last Words appear in the many versions of the Bible, but with slight variations, as shown here.

Last Words: "You have asked a hard thing; yet, if you see me as I am being taken from you, it will be granted you; if not, it will not."

Source: 2 Kings 2:10 (Latin Vulgate Bible).

Variation: "Thou hast asked a hard thing: nevertheless, if thou see me when I am taken from thee, it shall be so unto thee; but if not, it shall not be so."

Sources: 2 Kings 2:10 (King James Version); (21st Century King James Version); (American Standard Version).

Variation: "You have asked a hard thing. Nevertheless, if you see me when I am taken from you, it shall be so for you; but if not, it shall not be so."

Sources: 2 Kings 2:10 (New American Standard Bible); (New King James Version).

Variation: "You have asked a hard thing; yet, if you see me as I am being taken from you, it shall be so for you, but if you do not see me, it shall not be so."

Source: 2 Kings 2:10 (English Standard Version).

Variation: "You have asked a difficult thing, yet if you see me when I am taken from you, it will be yours—otherwise not."

Source: 2 Kings 2:10 (New International Version).

Variation: "Thou hast asked a hard thing: if thou see me when I am taken from thee, it shall be so to thee; but if not, it shall not be [so]."

Source: 2 Kings 2:10 (Darby Translation).

Variation: "Thou hast asked a hard thing; nevertheless, if thou see me when I am taken from thee, thou shalt have what thou hast asked: but if thou see me not, thou shalt not have it."

Source: 2: Kings 2:10 (Douay-Rheims Translation).

Variation: "Thou hast asked a hard thing; if thou dost see me taken from thee, it is to thee so; and if not, it is not."

Source: 2 Kings 2:10 (Young's Literal Translation).

El Habashy, Ahmed Mahmoud

(1941-1999) Egyptian airline pilot, disaster victim. Captain of EgyptAir Flight 990 that crashed off the coast of Nantucket, Massachusetts, taking 217 lives. Some versions of the crash indicate co-pilot Gamil El-Batouti shut off the Boeing 767's engines in flight and pushed the jet into a fatal suicidal dive. Other versions indicate the co-pilot did not cause the dive but instead was a victim of a mechanical malfunction.

Last Words: "What's happening, Gamil? What's happening? What is this? What is this? Did you shut the engines? Pull. Pull with me. Pull with me. Pull with me." Spoken when he returned to the cockpit.

Source: *The Air Up There: More Great Quotations on Flight* by Dave English (New York, 2003), citing the NTSB, 13:50 EST October 31, 1999.

Elia, see Lamb, Charles.

Eliot, Charles William

(1834-1926) American educator. President of Harvard 40 years. Served longest term as president in the university's history. Helped establish Radcliffe College. Credited with transforming Harvard College into a pre-eminent research university. Edited *The Harvard Classics*, known as "The Five Foot Book Shelf." Died at age 92 at Northeast Harbor, Maine.

Last Words: "I see Mother."

Source: *Charles W. Eliot, President of Harvard University, 1869-1909* by Henry James (Boston, 1930).

Eliot, George,
see Evans, Mary Ann or Marian.

Eliot, John

(1604-1690) British-born American clergyman, missionary, writer, political philosopher. Known as Apostle to the Indians. Learned Algonkian language and preached to Native Americans in their own language. Translated Bible into Algonkian. Published first Bible printed in North America (1661-1663). Much of Eliot's missionary work was destroyed during King Philip's War. Died at age 86 in Roxbury, Massachusetts.

Different Last Words:

(1) "You are welcome to my very soul. Pray retire into my study for me, and give me leave to be gone." Spoken to a friend.

Source: *Life and Labors of John Eliot, The Apostle Among the Indian Nations of New England, Together with an Account of the Eliots in England* by Robert Boodey Caverly (Boston, 1880).

(2) "O come in glory! I have long waited for Thy coming. Let no dark cloud rest on the work of the Indians. Let it live when I am dead. Welcome joy!"

Source: *The Last Words (Real and Traditional) of Distinguished Men and Women Collected from Various Sources* by Frederic Rowland Marvin (New York, 1901).

Eliot, Thomas Stearns ("T.S.")

(1888-1965) American-born British poet, playwright, critic, editor. Won Nobel Prize for Literature in 1948. Notable works: *Murder in the Cathedral; The Waste Land; The Four Quartets.* Worked for many years as editor for Faber & Faber, Ltd., British publishing house. Died at age 76 in London.

Last Words: "Valerie." He died whispering his wife's name.

Source: *Last Words: A Dictionary of Deathbed Quotations* by C. Bernard Ruffin (Jefferson, NC, 1995).

Elisabeth, Queen of Romania

(1843-1916) Romanian royalty. Writer, poet, essayist. Daughter of Herman Prinz von Wied. Queen consort of Carol I of Romania. Wrote extensively under pen name Carmen Sylva. Patron of arts. Encouraged higher education for women. Died at age 72

of pneumonia in Curtea de Arges, Romania.

Last Words: "Stop giving me injections. Let me go."

Source: *Carmen Sylva Queen and Woman* by Elizabeth Burgoyne (London, 1941).

Elisabeth Christine, Queen of Prussia

(1715-1797) Prussian royalty. Daughter of Ferdinand Albert II, Duke Braunschweig-Wolfenbüttel. Wife of Frederick the Great of Prussia. After Frederick became king in 1740, Elisabeth lived apart from him in Niederschönhausen Castle, north of Berlin. Died at age 81.

Last Words: "I know you will not forget me."

Source: *Elisabeth Christine, Königin von Preussen, Eine Biographie* by Friedrich Wilhelm M. von Hahnke (Berlin, Germany, 1848).

Elizabeth, Empress of Austria

(1837-1898) Austro-Hungarian royalty. Empress of Austria. Queen of Hungary. Married cousin Emperor Franz Joseph I of Austria. Assassinated at age 60 by Italian anarchist Luigi Lucheni.

Last Words: "Why, what has happened?" Spoken as she stepped aboard a steamer on Lake Geneva and was stabbed. She was rushed to a hospital where she died

Source: *Elizabeth, Empress of Austria* by Egon Caesar Corti Conte; tr. by Catherine Alison Phillips (New Haven, CT, 1936).

Elizabeth, Saint (of Hungary)

(1207-1231) Hungarian noblewoman, holy woman, philanthropist. Roman Catholic. Daughter of Andrew II, King of Hungary. Married at 14. Widow at 20. Gave her wealth to the poor and built hospitals. Became a symbol of Christian charity. Believed to have performed miracles. Died at age 24. Canonized in 1235.

Last Words: "The time has already arrived wherein God has called those that are His friends to the heavenly espousals!"

Source: *The Golden Legend or Lives of the Saints.* Compiled by Jacobus de Voragine, Archbishop of Genoa, 1275, 1st ed., 1470. English ed. by William Caxton, 1483, ed. by F.S. Ellis (Edinburgh, 1900).

Variation: "This is the moment when Almighty God calls His friends to Himself."

Source: *Saint Elizabeth of Hungary* by Nesta De Robeck (Milwaukee, WI, 1954).

Elizabeth of France, Madame

(1764-1794) French royalty. Full name Elizabeth Philippine Marie Hélène de France. Known as Madame Elizabeth. Daughter of Louis, Dauphin of France and Marie-Josèphe of Saxony. Sister of King Louis XVI of France. Captured with him. Executed at age 30 during the French Revolution's Reign of Terror.

Last Words: "In the name of your mother, monsieur, cover me." Spoken on her way to the guillotine when her kerchief fell from her neck.

Source: *Madame Élisabeth, Soeur de Louis XVI* by Marie Célestine Amélie de Ségur Comtesse d'Armaille (Paris, 1886).

Variation: "In the name of modesty, cover my bosom!"

Source: *Memoirs of the Private Life of Marie Antoinette, Queen of France and Navarre. To Which Are Added, Recollections, Sketches and Anecdotes, Illustrative of the Reigns of Louis XIV, Louis XV, and Louis XVI* by Mme. Campan and François Barrière (Philadelphia, 1823).

Variation: "I pray you, gentlemen, in the name of modesty, suffer me to cover my bosom."

Source: *Unusual Words and How They Came About* by Edwin Radford (New York, 1946).

Elizabeth of the Trinity, Blessed

(1880-1906) French nun, holy woman. Birth name Elizabeth Catez. Entered Discalced Carmelite order. Known for the spirituality of her writing. Died at age 26 of Addison's disease. Beatified in 1984.

Last Words: "I am going to Light, to Love, to Life." Her last audible words.

Source: "Two Flowers of Carmel" by William Vowles (*The Catholic World,* Vol. 97, September, 1913.)

Elizabeth I, Queen of England

(1533-1603) English monarch. Daughter of Henry VIII and Anne Boleyn. Known as The Virgin Queen. Elizabethan Era named for her: Golden Age of English playwrights that included William Shakespeare, Christopher Marlowe, Ben Jonson and Francis Bacon. Important era for English exploration and colonization. Francis Drake became the first Englishman to circumnavigate the globe. English colonization of North America began under Sir Walter Raleigh and Sir Humphrey Gilbert. Commonwealth of Virginia named for her. Died at age 69 at Richmond Palace. Her death ended the Tudor dynasty.

Different Last Words:

(1) "My Lord, the crown which I have borne so long has given enough of vanity in my time. I beseech you not to augment it in this hour when I am so near my death." Spoken to the Archbishop of Canterbury, who was reminding her of her great accomplishments as monarch.

Source: *The Private Character of Queen Elizabeth* by Frederick Chamberlin (New York, 1923).

(2) "Must! Is *must* a word to be addressed to princes? Little man, little man! Thy father, if he had been alive, durst not have used that word.—Thou art so presumptuous because thou knowest I shall die." Spoken to Sir Robert Cecil when he declared she must go to bed and receive medical attention. She rallied when she heard Lord Beauchamp was a possible successor. She said: "I will have no rogue's son in my seat." After that, she became incoherent.

Source: *A Short History of the English People in two volumes* by John Richard Green (London, 1902).

(3) "All my possessions for a moment of time."

Source: *Life and Labor or Characteristics of Men of Industry, Culture and Genius Life and Labor or Characteristics of Men of Industry, Culture and Genius* by Samuel Smiles (New York, 1888).

(4) "I have been a great queen, but I am about to die and must yield an account of my stewardship to the great King of Kings." She died holding the archbishop's hand.

Source: *Gloriana: the years of Elizabeth I* by Mary M. Luke (New York, 1973).

Ellery, William

(1727-1820) American statesman, politician. Rhode Island delegate to Continental Congress. Signer of Declaration of Independence. Collector at the port of Newport.

Last Words: "I know that I am dying."

Source: *A Conspectus of American Biography: Being an Analytical Summary of American History and Biography, Containing also the Complete Indexes of the National Cyclopedia of American Biography* by George Derby (New York, 1906).

Elliot, Andrew

(1719-1778) American clergyman. Preacher at New North Church, Boston. Was offered but declined presidency of Harvard. One of the group who vouched that Phillis, an African-American slave in the Wheatley household in Boston, was qualified to write the poems claimed to be hers. Elliot died at age 58 in Boston.

Last Words: "Come, Lord Jesus, come quickly—why are Thy chariot wheels so long in coming?" Spoken on his deathbed.

Source: *Annals of the American Pulpit: Or, Commemorative Notices of Distinguished American Clergymen of Various Denominations* by William Buell Sprague (New York, 1869).

Elliott, Ebenezer

(1781-1849) English poet. Known as the Corn Law Rhymer for blaming all national ills on the bread tax he denounced in his Corn Law Rhymes. Died at age 68. After his death, John Greenleaf Whittier wrote a poem in his memory, titled "Elliott." Statue of him by English sculptor Neville Northey Burnard is in Weston Park, Staffordshire.

Last Words: "A strange sight, sir: an old man unwilling to die!"

Source: *Life, Poetry, and Letters of Ebenezer Elliott, the Corn-law Rhymer, with an Abstract of His Politics* by John Watkins (London, 1850). The author was his son-in-law.

Elliott, Henry Venn

(1792-1865) English clergyman, traveler, writer. Founder and perpetual curate of St. Mary's Hall (Parish of St. Mary the Virgin, Brighton, Sussex). Fellow of Trinity College, Cambridge. His sister was hymnist Charlotte Elliot. His wife was hymnist Julia Anne Elliott. Died at age 73.

Last Words: "Suffer me not—for any pains of death—to fall from Thee."

Source: *The Life of the Rev. Henry Venn Elliott; with a Portrait and an Appendix Containing a Short Sketch of the Life of the Rev. Julius Elliott* by Josiah Bateman (London, 1870).

Elliott, John Lovejoy

(1868-1942) American social reformer. Associated with New York Society for Ethical Culture. Established Hudson Guild to organize "Hurly Burlies" in Chelsea. Established many programs and clubs for young boys and girls, working women and families that provided springboard for residents to organize and improve neighborhood living conditions. Among groups he established were

Neighborhood House, League of Mothers' Club and School for Printers' Apprentices.

Last Words: "The only things I have found worth living for, and working for, and dying for, are love and friendship."

Source: *The Faith of John Lovejoy Elliott; Selections from Addresses and Writings* by John Lovejoy Elliott (New York, 1948).

Ellis, Henry Havelock

(1859-1939) British psychologist, social reformer, writer, essayist, editor, literary critic. Gave up medical practice for research and writing. Interested in human biology. Notable work: *Studies in the Psychology of Sex*. Also wrote on art and literature. Created and edited *Mermaid Series,* works by Elizabethan and Jacobean authors. Died at age 80 at Hintlesham, Suffolk.

Last Words: "You must go to bed, you are so tired and I feel better. Perhaps I may sleep a little.—I shall ring if I need you."

Source: *Friendship's Odyssey* by François Roussel DeLisle and Havelock Ellis (London, 1946).

Éloi or Eligius, Saint

(588?-660) French prelate, holy man. Bishop of Noyon. Studied goldsmithing. Patron saint of goldsmiths and other metal workers. Also patron saint of British Army's royal electrical and mechanical engineers.

Last Words: "And now, O Christ, I shall render up my last breath in confessing loudly Thy name; receive me in Thy great mercy, and disappoint me not in my hope; open to me the gate of life and render the Prince of Darkness powerless against me. Let Thy clemency protect me, Thy might hedge me, and Thy hand lead me to the place of refreshment and into the tabernacle Thou hast prepared for Thy servants and them that stand in awe of Thee."

Source: *Vie de saint Éloi: évêque de Noyon et de Tournai* by Saint Ouen évêque de Rouen and M. l'Abbé François J. Parenty (Arras, France, 1851).

Elphinstone, Arthur, 6th Baron Balmerino

(1688-1746) Scottish nobleman, Jacobite, French army officer. Son of John Elphinstone, Took up Jacobite cause. Enlisted in French army. His father obtained a pardon from the English crown for him. He joined with Charles Edward Stuart. After being taken prisoner at Battle of Culloden, he was tried before Parliament, along with William Boyd, 4th Earl of Kilmarnock and George Mackenzie, 3rd Earl of Cromartie. Found guilty and beheaded.

Last Words: "O Lord, reward my friend, forgive my foes, bless King James and receive my soul!"

Source: *Treason: Famous English Treason Trials* by Alan Wharam (Far Thrupp, England, 1995).

Elwes, John

(1714-1789) British politician, money lender. Original surname Meggott. Member of British Parliament for Berkshire, England. Speculator, gambler. Eccentric miser. Inherited considerable wealth. Took great business risks involving vast sums of money but was obsessive about spending only small amounts for clothing or food. Dressed in ragged clothes and lived on scraps. Died at age 75 in Berkshire.

Last Words: "I hope I have left you as much as you wished." Whispered to his son who was at his bedside.

Source: *The Life of the Late John Elwes, Esquire: Member in Three Successive British Parliaments for Berkshire* by Edward Topham (London, 1790).

Emerson, Ralph Waldo

(1803-1882) American essayist, poet, philosopher. Lived in Concord, Massachusetts. Known as The Sage of Concord. Founded Transcendental Club in 1836. Published seminal transcendental work *Nature* anonymously in 1837. Edited *The Dial*, transcendentalist journal. Friend and American agent for Thomas Carlyle. Died at age 78 in Concord.

Different Last Words:

(1) "Good-bye my friend." Spoken to his friend Amos Bronson Alcott.

Source: *Life of Emerson* by Van Wyck Brooks (New York, 1932).

(2) "O, that beautiful boy!" Emerson may have been referring to a long-dead child.

Sources: *Emerson, Romanticism, and Intuitive Reason: The Transatlantic "Light of All Our day"* by Patrick J Keane (Columbia, MO, 2005); *The Last Words (Real and Traditional) of Distinguished Men and Women Collected from Various Sources* by Frederic Rowland Marvin (New York, 1901). Marvin gave as his source James Elliot Cabot, a long-time friend of Emerson who

served for a time as his secretary and was with him the day he died.

Emmet, Robert

(1778-1803) Irish patriot, nationalist. Led an unsuccessful rebellion against British rule in 1803. Captured, tried and hanged for high treason. Died at age 25. His romance with Sarah Curran was commemorated in verse by poet Thomas Moore, a boyhood friend of Emmet. Monument to Emmet is on Embassy Row in Washington, D.C.

Last Words: "Not—." Emmet was hanged as he spoke. The executioner had asked him twice if he was ready and did not intend to ask him a third time.

The Life and Times of Robert Emmet, Esq. by Richard Robert Madden (London, 1906).

Emmett, Belinda Jane ("Belle")

(1974-2006) Australian actress, singer. Married Australian television personality Rove McManus. Known for television series *Home and Away* and *All Saints*. Recorded duet with Marcia Hines. Hines album reached No. 10 on the Australian charts. Emmett died at age 32 of breast cancer in Sydney.

Last Words: "Are you all right?" Spoken when she woke up and found her sister Lesley Arthur weeping at her bedside and holding her hand.

Source: "Family Pays Tribute to Belinda Emmett" (ABC [Australia] News, July 24, 2007), citing the family's appearance on ABC TV's *Australian Story* on July 23, 2007.

Emmons, Nathanael

(1745-1840) American theologian, clergyman. Congregationalist. Described by *Harper's Monthly Magazine* (December 1856-May 1857) as one of the "greatest intellectual divines of modern times." Died at age 95. His *Collected Works* were published after he died.

Different Last Words:

(1) (doubtful): "I am ready."

Source: *The Last Words (Real and Traditional) of Distinguished Men and Women Collected from Various Sources* by Frederic Rowland Marvin (New York, 1901).

Emmons spoke these words when he was told that his death might not be too far in the future. However, that was in January 1838 and he died in 1840.

Source: *A Discourse on the Official Character of Nathanael Emmons* by Thomas Williams (Boston, 1851).

(2) "I have kept the faith; and cherish a comfortable hope, that I shall finally receive the crown of righteousness, which awaits all Christian ministers and followers of Christ." His last recorded statement, spoken when he was near death.

Source: *A Discourse on the Official Character of Nathanael Emmons* by Thomas Williams (Boston, 1851).

Empedocles

(490?-430 B.C.) Greek philosopher, statesman, poet. Lived in Sicily. Died in Greece at around age 60. Notable poems: "On Nature"; "Purifications." He claimed to have magical powers. Legend persists that he died by throwing himself into Mount Etna. However, there is evidence that he actually died in Greece. His sudden disappearance caused many to believe he was superhuman.

Last Words: "I am to you a deathless god: a mortal never more."

Source: *Diogenes Laertius: Lives of the. Eminent Philosophers* by Robert Drew Hicks (New York, 1925) from Diogenes Laertius, *De vita et moribus philosophorum* (Venice, 1431, tr. to Latin).

Engel, George

(1836-1887) German-born American labor activist, terrorist, anarchist. Member of Working People's Association. Executed along with fellow anarchists Albert Parsons, August Spies and Adolph Fischer for 1886 Haymarket bombing in Chicago.

Last Words: "Hurrah for anarchy! This is the happiest moment of my life." Fischer made a similar scaffold statement.

Source: "The Execution of Parsons, Spies, Engel, and Fischer" (*Chicago Daily News*, November 12, 1887).

Enghien, Duc d', Louis Antoine Henri de Bourbon-Contè

(1772-1804) French royalty, martyr. Prince. Only son of Louis Henry II. Last descendant of House of Condè. Seized on neutral territory and falsely accused of plotting against France while in the pay of England. Condemned by military tribunal on trumped-up charges and executed at age 31 by firing squad by order of Napoleon I. The circumstances surrounding d'Enghien's death became famous. Talleyrand said of his execution: "[It] was worse than a crime; it was a mistake." A similar quote is credited to Joseph Fouché, Napoleon's Minister of Police. He said the act was "worse than a crime, it was a blunder." The saying has also been attributed to Boulay de la Meurthe, who edited d'Enghien's *Correspondance* (1904-1913). *Macmillan Book of Proverbs, Maxims and Famous Phrases* (1965) says Fouché's claim is the most direct. It appeared in his *Mémoires.* Russian writer Leo Tolstoy mentioned d'Enghien's death in *War and Peace.*

Different Last Words:

(1) "Let us go, my friends."

Source: *Histoire des trois derniers princes de la maison de Condé; Prince de Condé—Duc de Bourbon—Duc d'Enghien* by J. Crétineau-Joly (Paris, 1867).

(2) "I die for my King and for France."

Source: "Dying Words of Distinguished Persons" in *The Encyclopedia of Death and Life in the Spirit-World,* Vol. I, by J.R. Francis (Chicago, 1895).

(3) "And time presses!" As the death sentence was read, d'Enghien wrote a message to his wife. He gave it to the officer in command and asked for a priest. When he was told no priest was in residence at the chateau, he uttered these Last Words. He then covered his face with his hands and prayed for a moment. As he raised his head, the officer gave the word to fire.

Source: *The Dungeons of Old Paris: Being the Story and Romance of the Most Celebrated Prisons of the Monarchy and the Revolution* by Tighe Hopkins (New York, 1897).

Epaminondas

(418?-362 B.C.) Theban military leader, statesman. Defeated Spartans and transformed Thebes into a preeminent position in Greek politics. His victory at Leuctra broke Spartan military power, and liberated enslaved Peloponnesian Greek Messenian helots. Mortally wounded in the battle.

Different Last Words:

(1) "Satis, vixi, invictus enim morior!" (tr. "I have lived long enough, since I die unconquered!")

Source: *Cornelii Nepotis Vitae excellentium imperatorum, quibus accedunt notulae anclicaet quaestioe* by Cornelius Nepos (London, 1832).

(2) "Now it is time to die." Spoken as he drew a javelin from his wound.

Source: *Real-Encyclopädie der classischen Altertumswissenschaft* by August Friedrich von Pauly and Georg

Wissowa (Stuttgart, Germany, 1893).

(3) "Then, all is well." Spoken immediately after a javelin had been removed from his body.

Source: *An Universal History from the Earliest Account of Time: Compiled from Original Authors and Illustrated with Maps, Cuts, Notes etc. With a General Index to the Whole 15 Volumes* (London, 1748).

Epicurus

(341?-270? B.C.) Greek philosopher, writer. Taught in Athens. Epicureanism, a popular school of thought in Hellenistic philosophy, is derived from his teachings. Prolific author who may have left as many as 300 volumes, but very little of his writing survives except in *De Rerum Natura,* the work of his disciple Lucretius. In his later years, Epicurus suffered from a painful urinary condition for which there was no cure. He accepted his pain serenely and left a detailed description of his symptoms so that others might learn from his illness.

Last Words: "Now farewell; remember all my words."

Source: *Diogenes Laertius, De vitis, dogmatis & apophthegmatis clarorum philosophorum,* Book X, by Laertius Diogenes, Alexandrinus Hesychius and Isaac Casaubon (Geneva, Switzerland, 1615).

Erasmus, Desiderius

(1465?-1536) Dutch humanist, theologian, writer, educator, clergyman. Birth name Gerrit Gerritszoon. Regarded as a leader of the renaissance of learning in northern Europe. Catholic priest who took Augustinian monastic vows. Studied at the University of Paris. Professor at Cambridge. Spent last 14 years of his life as rector of the university at Basel, Switzerland. Prepared Greek and Latin editions of New Testament. Notable works: *The Praise of Follie* (satire); *Handbook of a Christian Knight; On Civility in Children.* Hans Holbein the Younger painted his portrait and Albrecht Dürer made an engraving of him.

Last Words: "Dear God."

Source: *Erasmus of Rotterdam* by Stefan Zweig, Eden Paul and Cedar Paul (New York, 1934).

Variation: "Lord, free me! Lord, pity me! Lord, bring the end! Lord have mercy! Dear God!"

Source: *Erasmus of Christendom* by Ronald Herbert Bainton (New York, 1969).

Variation: "Domine! Domine! Fac finem! Fac finem! (tr. "Lord, Lord, make an end.")

Source: *The Mirror of Literature, Amusement, and Instruction* by Percy B. St. John (London, 1823).

Ericsson, John

(1803-1889) Swedish-born engineer, inventor. Moved to U.S. in 1839 where his inventions were better received than in Europe. Gained governmental backing. Introduced two-screw propeller on commercial ships. Built armored ships, including the *Monitor,* for the North during the U.S. Civil War. Also experimented with torpedo devices. Died at age 85 in New York City. His body was taken back to Sweden. Ericsson's national memorial is in Washington, D.C. His statue is in Battery Park, New York City. A naval ship was named in his honor.

Last Words: "I am resting. This rest is magnificent; more beautiful than words can tell!"

Source: *The Life of John Ericsson* by William Conant Church (London, 1892).

Ernst August or Ernest Augustus, Prince of Hanover

(1887-1953) German royalty. Last prince of House of Hanover. Duke of Brunswick-Lüneburg. Married Princess Victoria Louise, daughter of Kaiser Wilhelm II. Father of Queen Frederika of Greece. Died at age 65 of a liver ailment at Marienburg Castle, Hanover, Germany.

Last Words: "Now I must jump the final hurdle, but God will help me over it." Spoken to his wife.

Source: *The Kaiser's Daughter: Memoirs of H.R.H Viktoria Luise, Duchess of Brunswick and Lüneburg, Princess of Prussia,* tr. and ed. by Robert Vacha (Englewood Cliffs, NJ, 1977).

Errera, Léo Abram

(1858-1905) Belgian botanist, educator, writer. Professor at University of Brussels. Director of Botanical Institute of Brussels. Member of Académie Royale des Sciences de Belgique. Corresponded with Darwin. Notable work: *The Russian Jews: Extermination or Emancipation.* Also wrote a major work on the physiology of vegetables. Died at age 46 in Brussels.

Last Words: "It is nothing. A little dizziness."

Source: *Notice sur Leo Errera, membre de l'Académie* by Leon Fredericq and Jean Massart (Brussels, Belgium, 1908).

Erskine, Ralph

(1685-1752) Scottish clergyman, poet. Notable work: *Gospel Sonnets*. Also wrote numerous sermons and poetical paraphrases. Studied at University of Edinburgh. Ordained assistant minister at Dunfermline. Supported his brother Ebenezer's church protests. Seceded from Church of England with Ebenezer and several others and formed Seceder Church of Scotland. Erskine College in South Carolina was founded in 1839 by the Associate Reformed Presbyterian Church and is named for Ebenezer. Statue of Ralph Erskine stands in Dunfermline.
Last Words: "I shall be for ever a debtor to free grace. Victory, victory, victory."
Source: *The Erskines* by Alexander R MacEwen (Edinburgh, 1900).

Erskine, Thomas (of Linlathen)

(1788-1870) Scottish theologian, writer, educator. Member of Edinburgh Faculty of Advocates. Friend and supporter of theologian Rev. John McLeod Campbell. While visiting the sick and dying, he developed a theology that emphasized the loving side of God. Notable work: *Internal Evidence for the Truth of Revealed Religion*. Died at age 81 in Edinburgh.
Last Words: "You there!—To the end—O Lord my God—Jesus—Jesus Christ—love — the peace of God—for ever and ever, for Jesus' sake, Amen and Amen."
Source: *Letters of Thomas Erskine of Linlathen* by Thomas Erskine and William Hanna (Edinburgh, 1878).

Espinosa, Felipe Nerio

(1836?-1863) Mexican mass murderer. Espinosa began a reign of terror about 15 years after losing six family members when his native city was shelled by the U.S. Navy during the Mexican War. He sent a letter to Colorado Territorial Governor John Evans stating his intention to murder 600 Anglos or Gringos—one hundred for each member of his family killed during the war. Aided by two cousins, he killed 26 people in the Colorado Territory in 1863. They were finally stopped by legendary tracker Tom Tobin and three soldiers who found their camp and killed Espinosa and his cousins in a brief gunfight.
Last Words: "Jesus, favor me! Escape, I am killed!"
Source: "The Small But Deadly Espinosa Gang" by Ruth Willet Lanza (*Wild West*, December 1995).

Esposito, Joseph ("Diamond Joe")

(1872-1928) Italian-born American criminal. 19th Ward committeeman. Chicago Prohibition-era gangster. Organized crime figure. Primarily involved in prostitution, bootlegging, Black Hand extortion and labor racketeering with the Genna brothers. Became a rival of Al Capone. Gunned down at age 55 in front of his wife and three children who were looking out a window, waiting for him to come home.
Last Words: "Oh, my God!" Spoken after being gunned down by a member of Capone's gang, while walking home with his bodyguards. He was hit 58 times. All the slugs were dipped in garlic, according to police reports.
Source: *Bloodletters and Badmen: A Narrative Encyclopedia of American Criminals from the Pilgrims to the Present* by Jay Robert Nash (New York, 1995).

Estrampes, Francisco

(1827-1855) Cuban-born revolutionary. Took arms and gunpowder to Cuba to incite a revolution. Arrested and tried in Cuba. Claimed he had become a naturalized American citizen in New Orleans and that he deserved the protection of American citizenship. However, the Cuban court did not agree. He was condemned to death and executed at age 27 in Havana.
Last Words: "Death to royalty! Liberty forever!" Spoken in a loud clear voice in front of the prison just before he was executed.
Source: "The Execution of Estrampes" (*North American and United States Gazette*, April 12, 1855).

Etty, William

(1787-1849) English artist. Created very large paintings of religious and historical subjects and of nudes. Copied much from great masters. Studied at the Royal Academy in London. Member of the National Academy. Retired to York, England, in ill health. Died there at age 62.

Last Words: "Wonderful, wonderful, this death!" Spoken to a servant.

Source: *Life of William Etty, R.A.,* Vol. II, by Alexander Gilchrist (London, 1855).

Eugène, Prince of Savoy

(1663-1736) French-born Austro-Hungarian nobleman, military officer. Full name François-Eugène, Prince of Savoy-Carignan. Son of Prince Eugène-Maurice of Savoy-Carignan, Comte de Soissons. Grandson of Charles Emmanuel I, Duke of Savoy. Imperial general. Disliked Louis XIV for banishing his mother from France. Left France and served Hapsburgs against France and the Turks. Appointed governor of Austrian Netherlands. Died at age 72 in Vienna. Monument to him is at Heldenplatz in Vienna.

Last Words: "That is enough for today. We will reserve the rest for tomorrow—if I live that long." Spoken as he ended a conference.

Source: *Das Leben des Prinzen Eugen von Savoyen, hauptsächlich aus dem militärischen Geschtspunke, nach den zuverlässigsten und neusten* by Franz George Friedrich von Kausler (Freiburg, Germany, 1838-1839).

Eugenius IV, Pope

(1383-1447) Italian prelate. Birth name Gabriele Condolmero, Condolmieri or Condulmer. Elevated to cardinal in 1408. Ruled as pope from 1431 to 1447. Had long struggle with Council of Basel. Deposed by Council, creating a schism. Spent nine years of his pontificate living in Florence. His pontificate was so difficult and contentious that on his deathbed he regretted ever leaving the monastery.

Different Last Words:

(1) "Pray only that God will perform His will. We have often begged in our prayers for what would have been better not to have prayed.—I do not desire to live long, but to die quickly and that my soul may return to God."

Source: *Eugenius IV* by Joseph Gill, S.J. (Westminster, MD, 1961).

(2) "Oh Gabriel, how much better would it have been for thee, and how much more would it have promoted thy soul's welfare, if thou hadst never been raised to the pontificate, but hadst been content to lead a quiet and religious life in the monastery."

Source: *History of Latin Christianity: Including that of the Popes to the Pontificate of Nicolas V,* Vol. VI, by Henry Hart Milman (London, 1855). Milman gave as his source *Palatii Gesta Pontificum apud Weisenberg.*

Euler, Leonhard

(1707-1783) Swiss mathematician, physicist, educator. Professor in Berlin, Saint Petersburg. Made important discoveries in the fields of calculus, number theory, topology, mechanics, optics and astronomy. Created modern mathematical terminology and notation including notion of a mathematical function. Devised logarithms to facilitate musical calculations. Lost vision in one eye in 1735 and in the other in 1766. Was totally blind when he died at age 76 in Saint Petersburg.

Last Words: "I die." (Or: "I am dying.") Spoken while playing with his young grandson. The pipe he was smoking slipped from his hands and he fell to the floor dead.

Source: *Men of Mathematics* by Eric Temple Bell (London,1937).

Evans, Christmas

(1766-1838) Welsh clergyman. Baptist. Named Christmas to commemorate the day he was born. Lost his eye as a youth. Known as the One-Eyed Bunyan of Wales. Nonconformist. Had great skill as a powerful preacher. Died at age 71 at Swansea, Wales.

Last Words: "Good-bye—drive on."

Source: *Memoir of the Life, Labors and Extensive Usefulness of the Rev. Christmas Evans: A Distinguished Minister of the Baptist Denomination in Wales* by David Phillips and Christmas Evans (New York, 1843).

Evans, Daniel

(1854-1875) American frontier criminal. Accused of murder. Hanged with five others at Fort Smith in Indian Territory by order of notorious hanging judge Isaac C. Parker. (Parker sentenced 79 men to die at Fort Smith.)

Last Words: "There are worse men here than me."

Source: *Let No Guilty Man Escape: A Judicial Biography of "Hanging Judge" Isaac C. Parker* by Robert H. Tuller (Norman, OK, 2001).

Evans, Mary Ann or Marian ("George Eliot")

(1819-1880) English writer, novelist. Pen

name George Eliot. Used male pen name to ensure that her works were taken seriously. Novels were largely set in provincial England and were known for their realism and psychological insight. Notable works: *Adam Bede; The Mill on the Floss; Silas Marner; Middlemarch*. Involved with George Henry Lewes (1854-1878). When he died, she married John Walter Cross. Died at age 61 in London of complications of a kidney disease.

Last Words: "Tell them I have a great pain on the left side."

Source: *George Eliot's Life as Related in Her Letters and Journals* by George Eliot and J.W. Cross (New York, 1885).

Evarts, Jeremiah F.

(1781-1831) American lawyer, missionary. Christian. Native-American activist. Worked to secure and protect the rights of Native Americans. Opposed U.S. government's Indian removal policy. Employed religious arguments that were later used during slavery abolition movement. Father of William M. Evarts who was U.S. secretary of state, attorney general and U.S. senator. Died at age 50 in Charleston, South Carolina.

Last Words: "Wonderful, wonderful, wonderful glory. We cannot understand—we cannot comprehend—wonderful glory—I will praise Him, I will praise Him. Who are in the room? Call all in—call all—let a great many come—I wish to give directions—wonderful—glory—Jesus reigns."

Source: *Memoir of the Life of Jeremiah Evarts,* by E.C. Tracy (Boston, 1845).

Variation: "O, wonderful! Wonderful! Wonderful! Glory that cannot be comprehended! Wonderful glory! I will praise Him! I will praise Him! Wonderful glory! Jesus reigneth!"

Source: *Dying Testimonies of Saved and Unsaved: Gathered from Authentic Sources* by Solomon Benjamin Shaw (Chicago, 1898).

Everett, Edward

(1794-1865) American statesman, politician, clergyman, orator, educator. Unitarian. Member U.S. House of Representatives and U.S. Senate from Massachusetts. Governor of Massachusetts. Minister to Great Britain. President of Harvard University. Appointed U.S. secretary of state by President Fillmore to fill vacancy caused by the death of Daniel Webster. Unsuccessful candidate for U.S. Vice President in 1860. Delivered address dedicating the national cemetery at Gettysburg on the same day as Lincoln. Died at age 71 in Boston. Face appeared on the U.S. $50 bill in 1890-1891. City of Everett, Massachusetts, was named for him.

Last Words (written): "I have turned the corner, and as soon as I can get a little appetite, shake off my carking cough and get the kidneys to resume their action, and subdue the numbness of my limbs, and get the better of my neuralgic pain in the left shoulder, I hope to do nicely." Letter to his daughter.

Source: *Edward Everett, Orator and Statesman.* by Paul Revere Frothingham (Boston, 1925).

Evers, Medgar Wiley

(1925-1963) African American civil rights activist. Worked with NAACP campaign to desegregate University of Mississippi after being refused admission to its Law School in 1954. Later involved in a boycott against white merchants. In 1963, he became a target of racists by publicly investigating Emmett Till's murder and by supporting Clyde Kennard. Murdered by Ku Klux Klan member Byron De La Beckwith, who shot him in the back in the driveway of his home in Jackson after Evers attended a meeting with NAACP lawyers. Died at age 37 at a local hospital less than an hour later and just hours after President John F. Kennedy's speech on national television in support of civil rights.

Different Last Words:

(1) "Let me go. Let me go." Spoken as he was being rushed to the whites-only University Hospital, where he was initially refused admission. Eventually, he was admitted after being recognized, but it was too late.

Source: "Myrlie Evers" in *Contemporary Black Biography*, Vol. 8 (Farmington Hills, MI, 1994). Myrlie Evers was his widow.

(2) "Sit me up—turn me loose." Reportedly spoken in the ambulance on the way to the University of Mississippi Hospital.

Source: *Medgar Evers* by Jennie Brown (Los Angeles, 1994).

Ewell, Richard Stoddert

(1817-1872) American military officer. Lieutenant general in Confederate Army in U.S. Civil War. Known as Old Baldy. Fought in campaigns at Bull Run, Cedar Mountain, Shenandoah Valley, Gettysburg, Spotsylvania and more. Lost a leg in combat in 1862. Returned to battle the following year. Died at age 54 of pneumonia at his home near Spring Hill, Tennessee.

Last Words: "After all my fighting against the United States so long, it is strange that an old pair of infantry pantaloons should kill me at last." The U.S. Army surplus trousers he was wearing were thinner than what he usually wore. He felt that contributed to his illness.

Sources: *Richard S. Ewell: A Soldier's Life* by Donald C. Pfanz (Chapel Hill, NC, 1998); *General R.S. Ewell: Robert E. Lee's Hesitant Commander* by Paul D. Casdorph (Lexington, KY, 2004).

Ewing, Finis

(1773-1841) American clergyman, writer. Presbyterian. One of the leaders of the Second Great Awakening or the Great Revival in the early 19th century. Co-founder of Cumberland Presbytery in Kentucky. Preached for temperance and against slavery. Moved to Lexington, Missouri, in 1836. Died there at age 67.

Last Words: "I leave the world trusting in the merits of the Saviour whom I have loved and trusted."

Source: *A Conspectus of American Biography: Being an Analytical Summary of American History and Biography, Containing also the Complete Indexes of the National Cyclopedia of American Biography* by George Derby (New York, 1906).

Fairbanks, Douglas, Sr.

(1883-1939) American actor, director, screenwriter, producer. Birth name Douglas Elton Ulman. Noted for action movies such as *The Three Musketeers; Robin Hood; The Thief of Bagdad.* Second wife was movie star Mary Pickford. Died at age 56 of a massive coronary in Santa Monica, California.

Last Words: "I've never felt better." Spoken to his attending nurse. He died minutes later.

Source: *Douglas Fairbanks: The Making of the Fourth Musketeer* by Ralph Hancock and Letitia Fairbanks. (New York, 1953). Letitia Fairbanks was a niece of Douglas Fairbanks.

Fall, Bernard B.

(1926-1967) Austrian-born French war correspondent, historian, political scientist, writer. Professor of international relations at Howard University. Notable books: *The Two Viet-Nams; Hell in a Very Small Place.* Killed at age 40 by a landmine while accompanying a U.S. Marine patrol near Hue, South Vietnam.

Last Words: "It smells bad. [It] could be an amb—" Tape recorded.

Source: "Bernard B. Fall" in *Contemporary Authors* (Farmington Hills, MI, 2002).

Falletti di Barolo, Marchesa Giulia

(1785-1864) French-born Italian noblewoman, social activist, vineyard owner. Born Juliette Colbert de Maulévrier. Daughter of Marquis Edouard de Maulévrier and Countess Anna Maria Quengo de Cremolle. Known as Reformer of the Turin Prisons. Did much charitable and religious work. Also responsible for changes in the wines of the Barolo region that are now among the best in Italy. Married Marchesi Tancredi Falletti di Barolo. Died at about age 79 at her estate near Turin. At the time she was the single richest woman to have her estate pass through probate.

Last Words: "May the will of God be done in me and by me in time and for eternity."

Source: *The Life of the Marchesa Giulia Falletti di Barolo* by Silvio Pellico and Lady Georgiana Fullerton (London, 1866).

Fannin, James Walker

(1804-1836) American military officer. Colonel. Leader in Texas independence revolution of 1835-1836. Executed at age 32 by a Mexican firing squad on orders of General Antonio López de Santa Anna. All of Fannin's men were executed with him in what became known as the Goliad Massacre. Two U.S. counties and a military camp were named for Fannin.

Last Words: "Don't shoot me in the head and see that my body is decently buried." The firing squad was ordered to shoot him in the head.

Source: *A Conspectus of American Biography: Being an Analytical Summary of American History and Biography, Containing also the Complete Indexes of the National Cyclopedia of American Biography* by George Derby (New York, 1906).

Variation: Fannin made two requests when he learned he was to be executed: that he not be shot in the head and that his personal belongings be sent to his family. He was shot in the head and his executioners stole his personal effects.

Source: *Moon Austin, San Antonio and the Hill Country* by Justin Marler (Emeryville, CA, 2006).

Fanon, Frantz Omar

(1925-1961) Martinique-born French psychiatrist, activist, writer, anticolonialist. Lived in France. Influenced by the racism he encountered as a black man in a white culture. Notable works: *Black Skin, White Masks; The Wretched of the Earth* (had an impact on the black liberation movement). Died at age 36 of leukemia in Bethesda, Maryland.

Last Words: "They put me in the washing machine again last night." Referring to the blood transfusion equipment he was subjected to, that he jokingly said was trying to make him white.

Source: *The Wretched of the Earth* by Frantz Fanon (New York, 1965).

Faraday, Michael

(1791-1867) English chemist, physicist, educator. Professor of chemistry at Royal Institution. Made substantial discoveries in electricity, magnetic fields. Developed first dynamo. Discovered chlorides of carbon and benzene. Created new kinds of optical glass. Declined knighthood and presidency of the Royal Society. Died at age 75 in Hampton Court, London. Farad, Faraday constant, Faraday's law of induction were named for him.

Last Words: "He hath set His testimony in the heavens."

Source: *Golden Lives, Biographies for the Day* by Alexander Hay Japp (London, 1873).

Farina, Paolo (Paul)

(1525-1606) Italian artist, painter, architect, engraver. Active in Verona, Venice, Mantua. Gained fame for his frescos in Verona churches. Notable work: *The Miracle of the Loaves and Fishes,* painted when he was 79. Kept a journal for many years. Two sons and daughter were also artists. Died at around age 81, on the same day and in the same room as his wife.

Last Words: "I am going!" Spoken as he lay on his deathbed. His wife, who was ill in the same room, replied: "I will bear you company." She died as he drew his last breath.

Source: *The Bizarre Notes and Queries in History, Folk-lore, Mathematics, Mysticism, Art, Science, Etc.,* Vol. III (Manchester, NH, 1886).

Farley, John Murphy

(1842-1918) Irish-born American prelate. Roman Catholic cardinal. Made Archbishop of New York in 1902. Elevated to cardinal in 1911. Died at age 76 in Mamaroneck, New York.

Last Words: "Water." His response when asked if he wanted anything.

Source: "Cardinal a Leader of Loyal Americans" (*New York Times,* September 18, 1918).

Farnsworth, Elon John

(1837-1863) American military officer. Union Army cavalry brigadier general in the U.S. Civil War. Killed while leading a cavalry charge at Battle of Gettysburg a few days after he was promoted to general.

Last Words: "General, if you order the charge, I will lead it, but you must take the responsibility." His response to General Hugh Judson Kilpatrick, who had ordered him to lead a charge into the Confederate position that would result in sure death for his men. Kilpatrick then made a comment that was not heard. As Farnsworth turned away, he replied: "I will obey your order." Kilpatrick then said: "I take the responsibility." Their conversation was heard by Henry C. Parson and others nearby.

Source: "Farnsworth's Charge and Death" by Henry C. Parsons in *Battles and Leaders of the Civil War,* Vol. III, by Robert U. Johnson and Clarence C. Buel (New York, 1884-1904).

Farouk, King of Egypt

(1920-1965) Egyptian royalty. Son of King Faud I. Succeeded his father in 1936. Overthrown in a revolution in 1952. Forced to abdicate. Succeeded by son as King Faud II. Died at age 45 of a heart attack in exile in Rome, Italy.

Last Words (doubtful): "There will soon be only five kings left: The King of England, Diamonds, Hearts, Spades and Clubs."

Source: Various Last Words compilations and Internet websites.

The quote was a quip Farouk made to Lord Boyd Orr in 1948 at a conference in Cairo 17 years before he died.

Source: *As I Recall* by John Boyd Orr, Baron Boyd-Orr (Garden City, NY, 1967).

Farragut, David Glasgow

(1801-1870) American military officer. First rear admiral, vice admiral, full admiral of U.S. Navy. Commanded West Gulf Blockading Squadron in the U.S. Civil War. Known for his order given at the Battle of Mobile Bay: "Damn the torpedoes, full speed ahead." Died at age 69 in Portsmouth, New Hampshire.

Last Words: "This is the last time I shall ever tread the deck of a man-of-war." He had wandered on board an old dismantled ship, looked around, then stepped ashore. His foreboding was correct, he died a short time later.

Source: *The Life of David Glasgow Farragut: First Admiral of the United States, Embodying His Journal and Letters* by Loyall Farragut (New York, 1879). The author was his son.

Faulkner, William Cuthbert

(1897-1962) American writer, novelist, short-story writer. Notable works: *As I Lay Dying; The Sound and the Fury; Absalom, Absalom!; Light in August; The Reivers*. Won 1949 Nobel Prize for Literature. Awarded 1955 and 1963 Pulitzer Prizes for Fiction. Fell from a horse in June, 1962. Died a few weeks later at age 64 of a heart attack.

Last Words: "Yes Jim, I will." His response to his brother who had taken him to the hospital and wanted to be told when he could come to get him. Faulkner died in the hospital soon afterward.

Source: *Scenes from Yoknapatawpha: A Study of People and Places in the Real and Imaginary Worlds of William Faulkner* by Emma Jo Grimes Marshall (University, AL, 1976).

Faure, François Félix

(1841-1899) French statesman. Co-prince of Andorra. Succeeded to the presidency of France upon the death of President Casimair-Périer. Faure died suddenly at age 58 of a stroke while still in office.

Different Last Words:
(1) "Offensé! Pardon!" (tr. "May those I have offended pardon me!")
(2) "You see, my poor Bridier, what a poor thing man is, even when he is president of the Republic."

Source for (1) and (2): *Last Words of Famous Men* by Bega (London 1930), citing *Standard,* February 18, 1899).

Fauré, Gabriel Urbain

(1845-1924) French musician, organist. Composer. Wrote vocal and instrumental music for stage, church, orchestra. Notable works: *Pelléas et Mélisande* (incidental music for drama); *Requiem; Impromptu* (for harp). Pupil of Saint-Saëns. Deafness in later years forced him to retire as director of the Paris Conservatory. Died at age 79 in Paris.

Last Words: "Have my works received justice? Have they not been too much admired or sometimes too severely criticized? What of my music will live?—But then that is of little importance." Spoken on his deathbed. He died a few hours later, surrounded by his wife, sons and his physician.

Source: *Gabriel Fauré* by Charles Koechlin, tr. by Leslie Orrey (London, 1945).

Favras, Thomas de Mahy, Marquis de

(1744-1790) French nobleman. Plotted to help Louis XVI escape. Arrested, convicted of high treason and hanged. Refused to implicate any of the plotters. On his way to the scaffold, he was handed his official death sentence, written by the court clerk. He read the paper; shook his head in disgust and spoke his Last Words:

Different Last Words
(1) (doubtful): "Permit me to point out that you have made three mistakes in spelling."

Source: *Personal Characteristics from French History* by Baron Ferdinand James De Rothschild (London, 1896).

Variation: "I see, monsieur, that you have made three spelling mistakes." (Or a close variant.)

Source: *Bartlett's Book of Anecdotes* by Clifton Fadiman and André Bernard (Boston, 2000).

Several compilations of Last Words give a near-verbatim version, omitting "monsieur." In the Victor Hugo drama, *Marion Delorme*, first presented in 1831, the line—spoken by the character Gaspar de Saverny—appears as: "You have made three mistakes in spelling, sir." He took a pen and corrected them. The play takes place in the early 17th century and is about a French courtesan famous for her many distinguished lovers. The play is critical of the king's ancestor Louis XIII. It is not known whether Hugo was inspired by the line—which would have been spoken 30 years earlier—or later biographers erroneously attributed a line from a drama to a real person—Favras.

(2) "In that case, I will take my secret with me." His response when Favras learned a confession of names would not save him. He then walked toward his place of execution.

Source: *The History of the French Revolution* by M.A. Thiers and Frederick Shoberl (New York, 1854).

Fawcett, Henry

(1833-1884) British economist, statesman, educator. Accidentally blinded in a shooting accident in his 20s. Postmaster-general under Gladstone. Inaugurated parcel post. Professor of political economy at Cambridge. Died at age 51 of pleurisy.

Last Words: "The best things to warm my hands with would be my fur gloves. They are in the pocket of my coat in the dressing room."

Source: *A Beacon for the Blind, Being a Life of Henry Fawcett* by Winifred Holt (London, 1915).

Fawcett, John

(1740-1817) English clergyman, hymnist, educator. Baptist. Wrote many sermons, essays and more than 150 hymns, including "Blest Be the Tie That Binds" and "Lord, Dismiss Us with Thy Blessing." His hymns were written to be sung at the conclusion of worship service. Died at age 77 at Hebden Bridge, Yorkshire.

Last Words: "Come, Lord Jesus, come quickly. O receive me to Thy children!"

Source: *An Account of the Life, Ministry, and Writings of the Late Rev. John Fawcett* by John Fawcett (London, 1818). The author was his son.

Fawsitt, Amy

(1836-1876) English actress. Popular stage performer in Scotland and England for more than 25 years. Made her American debut in 1876 in *Life*, a play that also starred Maurice Barrymore and Georgiana Drew. Fawsitt was not popular in the U.S. When American audiences failed to accept her, she became so distraught she withdrew from the play. She then came completely under the control of a man who lived in her apartment house. He is now believed to have hastened her death by taking advantage of her weakness for liquor. Her jewelry and dresses were pawned and her money was stolen. Contemporary reports, including her *New York Times* obituary, indicate she died of tuberculosis, but later accounts questioned her mysterious sad death. She died destitute at age 40 in New York City.

Last Words: "I am hungry." Last words heard to have passed her lips. She died alone and unattended in her room.

Source: *A History of the New York Stage from the First Performance in 1732 to 1901,* Vol. III, by Thomas Allston Brown (New York, 1903).

Febronia of Sibapte, Saint

(286-304) Mesopotamian holy woman. Christian martyr. Lived at Nisibis during the reign of Diocletian. Refused to renounce her religion and marry her nephew. She was tortured, mutilated, then beaten to death.

Last Words: "My Lord! My God, see what I suffer, and receive my soul into Thy hands!" Spoken to the executioner.

Source: *The Lives of the Saints* by Sabine Baring-Gould (London, 1897).

Feldman, Andrea ("Whips")

(1948-1972) American actress. Part of Andy Warhol's stable of film performers during the late 1960s and early 1970s. Typically played characters that were out of control. Appeared in the movies: **** (*The 24 Hour Film); Imitation of Christ; Trash; Heat; Groupies* (documentary). Jumped from a window of her family's New York City apartment after arranging for ex-boyfriends to be waiting for her outside of the building. She was clutching a can of soda and a rosary.

Last Words (written): "I'm going for the big time. Heaven." (Suicide note to her mother.) "I was unique as an antique, you're going to miss me farewell." (Other suicide notes.)

Source: *The Life and Death of Andy Warhol* by Victor Bockris (London, 1989).

Félix, Rachel Elisa

(1821-1858) French actress. Tragedian. Used only the name Rachel professionally. Known as La Grande Rachel. Famed as the greatest actress of her era. Notable roles: Camille, Cleopatra, Lucrece, Phedre, Roxanne. Died at age 36 of tuberculosis in Cannes, France. Thousands of people attended her funeral. Inspiration for character Vashti in Charlotte Bronte's novel *Villette*.

Different Last Words:

(1) "My poor Rebecca, my dear sister, I am going to see thee! I am indeed happy."

Source: *Memoirs of Rachel* by Madame de Barrera,(New York, 1858).

(2) "I am happy to die on a Sunday. It is sad to die on a Monday."

Source: *Les Mots de la fin* by Claude Aveline (Paris, 1957).

Felix of Thibiuca, Saint

(247?-303) African prelate, holy man, martyr. Bishop. One of the first Christians martyred by Diocletian. When Felix refused to surrender sacred Scriptures to be burned, he was arrested and beheaded at Carthage.

Last Word: "God, I give you thanks. I have been fifty-six years on earth. I have preserved my virginity; I have observed the Gospels; I have preached faith and the truth. Jesus Christ, Lord God of heaven and earth who will remain for ever, I bend my neck in sacrifice to you."

Source: *Diocletian and the Tetrarchy* by Roger Rees (Edinburgh, 2004).

Felton, John

(1595?-1628) English military officer, assassin. Lieutenant who assassinated George Villiers, 1st Duke of Buckingham, because he believed he was unjustly passed over for promotion. Felton was hanged for the crime. His assassination of the Duke was fictionalized in Alexander Dumas's *The Three Musketeers*.

Last Words (doubtful): "Let not the innocent be thought guilty. I am the man." Spoken when he surrendered to the Duke's men.

Source: *The Naval History of Great Britain: With the Lives of the Most Illustrious Admirals and Commanders and Interspersed With Accounts of Most Important Discoveries Made in the Several Parts of the World from the Earliest Amount of Time to the Year 1761* by Sir John Barrow (London, 1776).

These were not Felton's final words. He spoke them at the time of his arrest in August 1628; however, he was not tried and executed until November 1628. He spoke at his trial and afterward.

Source: *Dictionary of National Biography,* Vol. 18, ed. by Sir Leslie Stephen (New York, 1889).

Fénelon, François de Salignac de La Mothe

(1651-1715) French prelate, theologian, poet, writer. Tutored the grandson of Louis XIV. Wrote fables, dialogs for instruction of his pupil. Fell into disgrace for publishing *Télémaque,* satirizing the king and his policies. Forced to give up the title of Archbishop of Cambrai when he wrote *Maximes des Saints*. Died at age 63 in Cambrai.

Different Last Words:

(1) "Lord, if I am still necessary to Thy people, I refuse not to labor for the rest of my days. Thy will be done!"

Source: *Life of Fénelon* by Alphonse de Lamartine in Fénelon's *Adventures of Telemachus*, ed. by O.W. Wight (Boston, 1882).

(2) "Father, if it be possible let his cup pass from me; nevertheless, not as I will, but as Thou wilt." He repeated the prayer three times, then pain cut short his words and bystanders continued the prayer for him. In a broken, feeble voice, he said: "Thy will, not mine."

Source: *Fénelon, Archbishop of Cambrai: A Biographical Sketch* by Henrietta Louise Sidney Lear (London, 1901).

Fennell, Frederick

(1914-2004) American musician, conductor, Innovative and influential band leader. Major figure in promoting wind ensembles as performing groups. Founded Eastman Wind Ensemble. The Frederick Fennell Collection at the Library of Congress includes more than 20,000 items. Died at age 90 in Siesta Key, Florida.

Last Words: "I cannot die without a drummer. I hear him. I'm O.K. now." Recounted by daughter Cathy Fennell Martensen.

Source: "Frederick Fennell, 90, Innovative Band Conductor" (*New York Times*, December 9, 2004).

Fenning, Elizabeth ("Eliza")

(d. 1815) English domestic servant, cook. Accused of killing her employer by putting arsenic into dumplings she served to the family. Convicted and condemned to death on weak evidence. Popular opinion found her innocent. She was executed by hanging on what was to have been her wedding day wearing what would have been her bridal gown.

Last Words: "In the name of God, then, I am innocent." Spoken in response to the magistrate who asked her: "Tell me in the name of God that you are innocent."

Source: *Should Women Hang?* by Bernard O'Donnell (London, 1956). He said there wasn't enough evidence against her to "have hanged a cat."

Ferdinand I, King of Romania

(1865-1927) Romanian monarch. Prince of Hohenzollern-Sigmaringen. Succeeded uncle Carol I as king. Ruled from 1914 to 1927. Died at age 61 in Sinaia, Romania. Succeeded by grandson Michael I when his son renounced the throne.

Last Words: "I am so tired." Spoken to his wife, Queen Marie.

Source: *The Last Romantic: A Biography of Queen Marie of Roumania* by Hannah Pakula (New York, 1984).

Ferguson, Adam

(1723-1816) Scottish writer, educator, philosopher, historian. Professor of philosophy and mathematics at University of Edinburgh. Major participant in Scottish Enlightenment. Influenced writers such as Marx and Hegel. Notable works: *Institutes of Moral Philosophy; The History of the Progress and Termination of the Roman Republic.* Died at age 92 at St. Andrews.

Last Words: "There is another world." Spoken to his daughters. The quote was described as "according to tradition."

Source: *Adam Ferguson: His Social and Political Thought* by David Kettler (New Brunswick, NJ, 2005).

Ferguson, Catherine Williams ("Katy")

(1779?-1854) American social activist. Born a slave. Became a child welfare worker. Founder of Murray Street Sabbath School. Katy Ferguson Home (for unwed mothers) in New York City is named for her. Died in her mid-70s of cholera in New York City.

Last Words: "All is well."

Source: "Ferguson, Katy" by Sheryl A. Kujawa, *American National Biography* (New York, 1999).

Ferguson, Samuel ("Champ")

(1821-1865) American Confederate guerrilla leader in U.S. Civil War. Operated mostly in Kentucky. Was captured, tried and found guilty of 23 charges of murder in 1865. Ferguson was the only man other than Henry Wirz to be found guilty and executed for war crimes in the Civil War. Died by hanging at age 43.

Last Words: "I repeat that I die a Rebel out and out and my last request is that my body be removed to White County, Tennessee, and be buried in good Rebel soil." Spoken to the press in his prison cell.

Source: *Champ Ferguson: Confederate Guerrilla* by Thurman Sensing (Nashville, TN, 1994).

Fergusson, Robert

(1750-1774) Scottish writer, poet. Works inspired Robert Burns. Injured his head when he fell down a flight of stairs. Placed in an Edinburgh insane asylum where he died the day before his 24th birthday.

Last Words: "What ails ye? Wherefore sorrow for me, sirs? I am very well cared for here —I do assure you. I want for nothing—but it is cold—it is very cold. You know, I told you, it would come to this at last—yes, I told you so. Oh, do not go yet, mother—I hope to be soon—oh, do not go yet—do not leave me!" Spoken while confined to a cell for the insane.

Source: "Robert Fergusson" in *Poetical Works.* Intro, notes and glossary by Robert Ford (Paisley, Scotland, 1904).

Fernandez, Raymond Martinez

(1914-1951) American murderer. He and Martha Beck were known as the Lonely Hearts killers. He was executed at age 36 in the electric chair at Ossining (Sing Sing) prison in New York.

Last Words (written): "People want to know if I still love Martha. But of course I do. I want to shout it out. I love Martha. What do the public know about love?" Written in a note he gave to the guard as he was about to be electrocuted.

Source: *Bloodletters and Badmen: A Narrative Encyclopedia of American Criminals from the Pilgrims to the Present* by Jay Robert Nash (New York, 1995).

Fernando, Gratien

(1915-1942) Sri Lankan freedom fighter,

mutineer. Birth name Wathumullage Gratien Hubert Fernando. Leader of the Cocos Islands Mutiny. Joined Ceylon Garrison Artillery during World War II to fight fascism. Shipped off to Cocos Islands where he persuaded a group to mutiny and seize the island. The rebellion was suppressed. He and two other ringleaders were court-martialed and condemned to death. Executed at Welikada Prison. The men were among the only British Commonwealth troops executed for mutiny during World War II.

Last Words: "Loyalty to a country under the heel of a white man is disloyalty."
Source: *The Cocos Islands Mutiny* by Noel Crusz (Fremantle, Western Australia, 2001).

Ferrar, Robert

(c. 1500-1555) English prelate. Bishop of Saint David's in Wales. Deprived of bishopric for being married. Persecuted, imprisoned and martyred for heresy. Burned at the stake in Carmarthen.

Last Words: "If I stir through the pains of my burning, believe not the doctrine I have taught." Spoken as he was being chained to the stake.
Source: *Athenae Cantabrigienses* by George John Gray, compiled by Charles Henry Cooper and Thompson Cooper (Cambridge, England, 1858).

Ferrell, Charles Wayne

(1918-1973) American pilot, instructor. Led 1945 search for legendary "Lost Squadron" in the Bermuda Triangle—five Navy TBM Avenger bombers that were lost on a routine practice flight led by one of Ferrell's fellow instructors from Fort Lauderdale naval training center. Died at age 55.

Last Words: "Turn out the lights, I want to fly." Spoken to his son-in-law Steve Morrill, a Reuters news service employee who was at his bedside.
Source: "Charles Ferrell, Led Search for 'Lost Squadron'" (*Miami Herald*, April 16, 1973).

Ferrer, Francisco

(1859-1909) Catalan-Spanish anarchist, revolutionary. Birth name Francisco Ferrer Guardia. Arrested on charges of complicity in an uprising. Convicted, executed by firing squad in Barcelona at age 50. His trial caused violent antagonism against Spain and Roman Catholicism.

Last Words: "I desire to be shot standing, without a bandage over my eyes. Look well, my children, it is not your fault. I am innocent. Long live the School." Spoken at his execution.
Source: *The Martyrdom of Ferrer, Being a True Account of His Life and Work* by Joseph McCabe (London, 1909).

Ferrie, David William

(1918-1967) American pilot, private investigator. Played a mysterious and enigmatic role in the assassination of John F. Kennedy. Knew some of the key players, including Lee Harvey Oswald, Clay Shaw, Guy Banister, Jack Ruby and Carlos Marcello. Portrayed in movies *JFK* (1991) and *Ruby* (1992). Found dead at age 48 in his New Orleans apartment.

Last Words (written): "To leave this life, to me, is a sweet prospect. When you read this I will be quite dead and no answer will be possible." Beginning of a typewritten letter found with his body.
Source: *Who's Who in the JFK Assassination: An A-To-Z Encyclopedia* by Michael Benson (New York, 1993).

Ferrier, Kathleen Mary

(1912-1953) English singer. Lyric contralto. Known for her interpretation of songs by Brahms, Schumann and Schubert as well as British folk songs. Among operatic roles created for her: Lucretia in *The Rape of Lucretia* by Benjamin Britten. Awarded the C. B. E. in 1953. Died at age 41 of breast cancer in London.

Different Last Words:
(1) "Now I'll have eine kleine pause."
Source: *Am I Too Loud?: A Musical Autobiography* by Gerald Moore (New York, 1962). Moore was a noted accompanist of Kathleen Ferrier.
(2) "Wouldn't it be lovely if I could go to sleep and not wake up again?"
Source: *The Life of Kathleen Ferrier* by Winifred Ferrier (London, 1955). The author was her sister.

Ferry, Noah Henry

(1831-1863) American industrialist, military officer. Active in Michigan lumber industry. Founded Montague, Michigan, named in honor of his father, missionary William Montague Ferry who founded Grand Haven and Ferrysburg, Michigan. His brother was U.S. Senator Thomas W. Ferry. Noah was a major in the Union Army in the U.S. Civil War. In 1862, he raised a company of more than 100 men for the 5th Michigan Cavalry, under the command of Colonel Russell A. Alger, who later became U.S. secretary of war. Noah Ferry was killed at the Battle of Gettysburg.

Different Last Words:

(1) "Rally Boys! Rally for the fence!" Reported by a witness who heard the cry and saw Ferry fall.

Source: *Obituary Discourse of the Death of Noah Henry Ferry, Major of the Fifth Michigan Cavalry, Killed at Gettysburg, July 3, 1863*, by David Mack Cooper (New York, 1863).

(2) "Onward."

Source: *Cyclopedia of Michigan: Historical and Biographical, Comprising a Synopsis of General History of the State, and Biographical Sketches of Men Who Have, in Their Various Spheres, Contributed Toward Its Development* (New York, 1900).

Fessenden, Reginald Aubrey

(1866-1932) Canadian-born American physicist, electrical engineer, radio technician, educator. Professor at Purdue and Pittsburgh. Worked for Edison at West Orange, New Jersey. Known as the Father of Radio Broadcasting. First person to prove voices and music could be heard over air without wires. Was granted many patents for his research. Died at age 65 in Bermuda.

Last Words: "That was a nice little party. I'm sure this summer is helping me, with all this rest and sunshine and the sunshine lamps—I ought to be able to find out something that will be helpful not only to me, but to others."

Source: *Fessenden: Builder of Tomorrows* by Helen M. Fessenden (New York, 1940). The author was his wife.

Fetterman, William Judd

(1833?-1866) American military officer. Captain in U.S. Civil War. Killed in Federal Massacre. Inexperienced Indian fighter who boasted he could lead an 80-man column through the Sioux nation. The Sioux were ready: Decoy raids and ambushes were set up by Crazy Horse, Yellow Eagle and High Back Bone. Fetterman fell for the ruse. He and his men were killed by a group of Sioux warriors led by Red Cloud.

Last Words (doubtful): "Give me 80 men and I'll ride through the whole Sioux nation."

Source: Various Last Words compilations and Internet websites.

Fetterman made this boast long before the fatal battle. His Last Words are not known. He marched to his death leading precisely 80 men.

Source: *Chief Red Cloud, 1822-1909* by Judy Monroe (Mankato, MN, 2004).

Feynman, Richard Phillips

(1918-1988) American physicist, educator, raconteur, musician, adventurer. Assisted in development of atomic bomb, expanded understanding of quantum electrodynamics, identified the cause of the Challenger disaster, translated Mayan hieroglyphics. Professor of physics at Cornell and California Institute of Technology. Shared 1965 Nobel Prize for Physics with Schwinger and Tomonaga. Early years are depicted in the movie *Infinity* (1996). *Genghis Blues* (1999), a documentary film, describes his efforts to travel to Tuva. Died at age 69 of cancer in Los Angeles.

Last Words: "This dying is boring."

Source: *Richard Feynman: A Life in Science* by John Gribbin and Mary Gribbin (New York, 1997).

Fichte, Johann Gottlieb

(1762-1814) German philosopher, nationalist, educator. Transcendental idealist. Tried to rally Germans against Napoleon. Professor at Jena. Notable work: *Science of Knowledge*. Died at age 51 of fever in Berlin.

Last Words: "Never mind that. I need no more medicine. I feel that I am cured." Spoken when medicine was brought.

Source: *Leben und literarischer Briefwechsel* by Immanuel H. Fichte (Leipzig. Germany, 1862). The author was his son.

Variation: "Indeed no more medicine; I am well."

Source: *The Last Words (Real and Traditional) of Distinguished Men and Women Collected from Various Sources* by Frederic Rowland Marvin (New York, 1901). Marvin cited a quotation that circulated as the "Dying Confession of Fichte" but noted he was unable to find the authority upon which it was published: "I know absolutely nothing of any existence, not even my own. Images there are, and they constitute all that apparently exists. I am myself one of those images; nay, not so much, but only a confused image of an image. All reality is converted into a marvelous dream, without a life to dream of, or a mind to dream; into a dream itself made up only of a dream. Perception is a dream; and thought, the source of all the existence, the reality of which I imagine to myself, is but the dream of that dream." Marvin's source for this quote was Adamson, *Life and Philosophy of Fichte.*

Field, Cyrus West

(1819-1892) American capitalist. Organized the company that laid the first successful transatlantic cable in 1866. Awarded Congressional Medal of Honor in 1867. Invested heavily in New York elevated railway. Lost almost his entire fortune in one day in 1887. Died at age 72 in New York City.

Last Words: "Hold those ships! I must make further experiments first!" Spoken while delirious.

Source: *New York Tribune,* July 13, 1892.

Field, Eugene

(1850-1895) American poet. Known as the Children's Poet. Notable works: "Wynken, Blynken and Nod"; "Little Boy Blue." Wrote "Sharps and Flats," a popular Chicago newspaper column. Died at age 45 in Chicago.

Last Words: "Good-night."

Source: *Life of Eugene Field* by Slason Thompson (New York, 1927).

Field, John

(1782-1837) Irish-born British musician, pianist, composer. Notable works: piano concertos, solos and duets for piano; chamber music. Originated and named the nocturne. Pupil of Clementi. Influenced Chopin. Lived in Saint Petersburg and Moscow, Russia, 17 years. Made his last professional appearance in Vienna in 1835. Became ill. Returned to Russia. Died at age 54 in Moscow.

Last Words: "Not a Calvinist, but a pianist." His response when his friends wanted to summon a minister as he lay dying. One friend asked if he was Catholic or Calvinist.

Source: "John Field" (*The Etude Magazine,* August 1915).

Field, Mary Katherine Keemle ("Kate")

(1838-1896) American writer, actress, lecturer, journalist. Inspiration for Henrietta Stackpole in Henry James's novel *The Portrait of a Lady.* Lived in Florence, Italy, in late 1850s. Knew the Brownings and Trol-

lopes. One of the first women writers to contribute to the *Atlantic Monthly.* Became ill in Hawaii while on assignment for the *Chicago Times-Herald* as a member of the Amherst Eclipse Expedition. Died at age 57 of pneumonia in Honolulu.

Last Words: "The Amherst Eclipse Expedition." The expedition was a scientific voyage to Japan aboard the schooner yacht *Coronet* to view a solar eclipse in 1896. The *Coronet* visited Hawaii in May.

Sources: "Kate Field Dead" (*New York Tribune,* May 31, 1896); *Kate Field: A Record* by Lillian Whiting (Boston, 1899).

Field, Marshall, II

(1868-1905) American merchant. Son of Marshall Field I who founded Marshall Field, the world's largest retail store. His death at age 37 from a gunshot wound in a shooting accident was officially ruled accidental.

Last Words: "I do not know how this happened. I can account for it in no way. It was an accident. What are the chances of my recovery, Doctor?"

Source: *The Marshall Fields: A Study in Wealth* by John Tebbel (New York, 1947).

Fields, W.C.

(1880-1946) American stage, screen and radio comedian. Birth name William Claude Dukenfield. Performed with Ziegfeld Follies. Notable movies: *David Copperfield; You Can't Cheat an Honest Man; Never Give a Sucker an Even Break; My Little Chickadee.* Died at age 66 of stomach hemorrhage in Pasadena, California. The movie *W.C. Fields and Me* (1976) and the television documentary *W.C. Fields: Straight Up* (1986) detail his life and career.

Different Last Words:

(1) "God damn the whole friggin' world and everyone in it but you, Carlotta. " Spoken to his long-time companion, Carlotta Marti.

Source: *W. C. Fields* by Robert Lewis Taylor (New York, 1949).

(2) (doubtful): "Looking for loopholes." Deathbed response when asked why he was reading the Bible.

(3) (doubtful): "Pool little urchins, no doubt ill-clad, improperly nourished, something's got to be done." He then closed his eyes.

Twenty seconds later, he opened them and said: "On second thought, screw 'em." Spoken as he lay on his deathbed when he heard newsboys outside hawking newspapers.

Source: *The Yale Book of Quotations* by Fred R. Shapiro (New Haven, CT, 2006).

Shapiro gives (2) and (3) as examples of Fields' reputed Last Words. In his book's Foreword, he quotes Joseph Epstein who singles out these as some of the quotes that are "still in the fluttering flux of controversy" and asks, "Were they really his last words?" Most sources give (1) as Fields's likely Last Words.

Fillmore, Millard

(1800-1874) 13th President of the U.S. American politician, lawyer, educator. U.S. Vice President; succeeded to Presidency when Zachary Taylor died in office. Ran for President as National American and Whig candidate but lost. Chancellor of University of Buffalo. Had a stroke and died at age 74 in Buffalo, New York.

Last Words: "The nourishment is palpable." His response to a question by his physician.

Sources: "Millard Fillmore's Obituary" (*New York Times*, March 9, 1874); *Millard Fillmore* by William E. Griffis (Ithaca, NY, 1915).

Variation: "The food tasted good."

Source: *Buffalo Commercial Advertiser*, March 9, 1874.

Variation: "The food is palpable."

Source: *A Conspectus of American Biography: Being an Analytical Summary of American History and Biography, Containing also the Complete Indexes of the National Cyclopedia of American Biography* by George Derby (New York, 1906).

Fink, Mike

(1770?-1822) American boatman. Known as the King of the Mississippi keel boatmen. Fink and his close friend Carpenter were great marksmen. They used to fill a tin cup with whiskey and take turns placing it on each other's heads, then shooting at it with a rifle at a distance of 70 yards. They did it to show their confidence in each other and never had an injury until the day Fink killed Carpenter. A man named Talbott was a witness to the shooting. He believed the killing was deliberate so he shot and killed Fink.

Last Words: "I didn't mean to kill my boy!" Spoken as Talbott shot him. A few weeks later, Talbott drowned while trying to cross the Missouri River.

Source: *Half Horse Half Alligator: The Growth of the Mike Fink Legend*. Edited and Introduction and Notes by Walter Blair and Franklin J. Meine (Chicago, 1956). They noted that more than a hundred accounts circulated about Mike Fink's death.

Finley, Samuel

(1715-1766) Irish-born American clergyman, educator. Presbyterian. Preached during the Great Awakening. President of Princeton University (then called College of New Jersey). Great-grandfather of Samuel Finley Breese Morse, developer of the telegraph. Died at age 51 in Philadelphia while seeking medical treatment.

Last Words: "Why move the tardy hours so slow?"

Source: "Biographical Sketch of Samuel Finley," ed. by Cortland Van Rensselaer (*Presbyterian Magazine*, March 1853).

Finney, Charles Grandison

(1792-1875) American clergyman, theologian, abolitionist, educator. Presbyterian minister who became at odds with conservative clergy. Withdrew from Presbytery and became a Congregationalist. Active in Second Great Awakening. Known as the Father of Modern Revivalism. President of Oberlin College. Died at age 82 in Oberlin, Ohio.

Last Words: "Perhaps this is the thirst of death." Spoken after he asked for water and drank it. He died a few moments later.

Source: "Charles Grandison Finney" (*The Congregational Quarterly*, Vol. LXXIII, January 1877).

Finucane, Brendan Eamon Fergus ("Paddy")

(1920-1942) Irish pilot, military officer. Spitfire ace during World War II Battle of Britain. Killed when his plane was hit by machine-gun fire over the English Channel.

Last Words: "This is it, chaps." Spoken over his plane's radio as he lost altitude.

Source: *Wing Commander Paddy Finucane [Brendan Finucane] R.A.F., D.S.O., D.F.C.* by James Reynolds (New York, 1942).

Fischer, Adolph

(1858-1887) German-born American labor union activist, terrorist, anarchist. Executed for his role in the Chicago Haymarket riot, along with Albert Parsons, August Spies and George Engel.

Last Words: "Don't draw it so tight. I can't breathe—Long live Anarchy—This is the happiest moment of my life." Spoken as a cap was being placed over his face at his execution.

Source: *By the Neck, A Book of Hangings Selected from Contemporary Accounts* by August Mencken (New York, 1942).

Fish, Albert

(1870-1936) American murderer, cannibal. Confessed to six murders. Admitted to molesting more than 400 children over a 20-year span. Electrocuted at age 65 at Ossining (Sing Sing) prison in New York.

Last Words: "What a thrill that will be if I have to die in the electric chair. It will be the supreme thrill. The only one I haven't tried." After his execution, the defense attorney met with reporters. He was holding Fish's last statement—several pages of obscenities that were so filthy he said he would never show them to any one.

Source: *The Cannibal: The Case of Albert Fish* by M. Heimer (New York, 1971).

Fisk, James, Jr. ("Big Jim")

(1834-1872) American financial speculator. Killed by ex-partner Edward S. ("Ned") Stokes when Stokes learned he had been found guilty of blackmailing Fisk. Stokes fired a gun at Fisk on a hotel stairway. The first shot hit his arm. The second shot hit him in the stomach. Died at age 37.

Last Words: "For God's sake, will anybody save me?" Despite his cry for help, no one came to his aid.

Source: *The Life of James Fisk, Jr., Including the Great Frauds of the Tammany Ring* by Willoughby Jones (Philadelphia, 1872).

Fisk, Wilbur

(1792-1839) American clergyman, educator. Methodist Episcopalian. First president of Wesleyan University. Had respiratory problems much of his life. Died at age 46 in Middletown, Connecticut, after a long illness

Last Words: "Yes, love, yes." Spoken to his wife when she asked if he knew her.

Source: *Wilbur Fisk* by George Prentice (Boston, 1890).

Fitzgerald, Francis Scott Key ("F. Scott")

(1896-1940) American writer, novelist. No-table novels: *The Great Gatsby; Tender is the Night; The Last Tycoon.* Had first heart attack few weeks before he died at age 44. Was living in the apartment of his companion Sheilah Graham in Hollywood when he had a second attack. The movie *Beloved Infidel* (1950) depicted his life during his final years in Hollywood.

Last Words: "Good enough. They'll be fine." His reply to Graham while waiting for his physician. She asked if there was anything sweet he wanted and told him she had some Hershey bars. She brought him two chocolate bars from a box she kept next to the bedside. Fitzgerald picked up the *Princeton Alumni Weekly* and sank down in a chair. He made some marginal notes about the 1941 football prospects but said nothing as a Beethoven symphony was playing. He got up at one point and clutched the mantelpiece before he collapsed and died.

Source: *Beloved Infidel: The Education of a Woman* by Sheilah Graham and Gerold Frank (New York, 1958).

Fitzgerald, George Robert

(1746?-1786) Irish duelist. Known as "Fighting Fitzgerald because of the number of duels he fought. Notorious even before committing the murder for which he was convicted in 1786. The rope broke the first time during his execution. A new rope and a new hangman had to be brought in.

Last Words (doubtful): "You see, I am once more among you unexpectedly!"

Source: Various Last Words compilations and Internet websites.

Fitzgerald did say these words on the scaffold after the first rope failed, but they were not his Last Words. Before he died, he made a comment about the quality of the rope: He told the sheriff it would not hang anybody. According to two 1786 accounts of his execution, his Last Words were prayers he said on the scaffold while waiting for another rope to be brought.

Sources: *The Trials of George Robert Fitzgerald, Esq., Timothy Brecknock, James Fulton and Others for the Murder of Patrick Randal Macdonnell and Charles Hipson, Esq.* by William Garrow, Esq. (Dublin, Ireland, 1786); *Memoirs of the Late George R. Fitzgerald and P. R. M'Donnel, Esqrs. Interspersed with Anecdotes Tending to Illustrate the Remarkable Occurrences of Their Lives* by A Gentleman of the Co. Mayo (Dublin, Ireland, 1786).

Flagstad, Kirsten

(1895-1962) Norwegian singer. Operatic soprano. One of the great Wagnerian singers. Notable roles: Isolde; Sieglinde; Brünhild; Alceste. Made her debut at the Metropolitan Opera in 1935. Appeared as herself in the movie *The Big Broadcast of 1938.* Died at age 67 in Oslo.

Last Words: "You must be strong like Else. There is nothing to cry about. I have sung my song." Spoken to her friend Leif Stake. After she spoke, she slipped into a coma. Else Dusenberry, her daughter, was with her in the hospital.

Source: *Flagstad: Singer of the Century* by Howard Vogt (London, 1987).

Flanders, Donald Alexander

(1900-1958) American mathematician, computer scientist. Brother of Ralph Flanders, U.S. senator from Vermont. Senior mathematician with Argonne National Laboratory. Played an important role in the development of digital computers: AVIDAC, ORACLE and GEORGE. Suffered from ulcers and other ailments. Felt pressure caused by speculation, investigations and testimony that he was a Communist. Committed suicide by taking an overdose of prescribed medications.

Last Words (written): "I can't bear to go back to the lab. There are many decisions to make, and I feel that I am not capable of making these decisions. I am worth more—in dollars—dead than alive." Suicide note left for his wife Sarah.

Source: "Donald Flanders Found Dead in Chicago; Senator's Brother Directed A.E.C. Unit" (*New York Times*, June 28, 1958).

Flaubert, Gustave

(1821-1880) French writer. Novelist. Notable works: *Madame Bovary; Salammbô; The Temptation of Saint Anthony.* Leading exponent of realism in French literature. Died at age 58 at Croisset, France, possibly of a cerebral hemorrhage.

Last Words: "Rouen—we're not too far from Rouen—Hellot—I know the Hellots." A newspaper interpreted his Last Words as a reference to Victor Hugo. But to a close friend the words seemed unquestionably to mean: "Go to Rouen, we're not far from Rouen, and bring Dr. Hellot. I know the Hellots."

Source: *The Letters of Gustave Flaubert: 1857-1880* by Gustave Flaubert and Francis Steegmuller (Cambridge, MA, 1982).

Flavel, John

(1627-1691) English clergyman, writer. Presbyterian. Ousted from pastorate at Dartmouth for being a Nonconformist. Became minister at a Nonconformist church there. Notable works: *Treatise on the Soul of Man; A Token for Mourners.* Died around age 64 in Exeter, Devonshire.

Last Words: "I know that it will be well with me."

Source: *The Sunday School Teacher: A Biblical and Educational Magazine,* Vol. VII, New Series, by Sunday School Union (London 1881).

Flecker, Herman James Elroy

(1884-1915) English writer, diplomat, playwright, poet. British vice-consul in Beirut, Lebanon. Wrote five books of poems, a novel and two plays. Notable works: *Hassan; Don Juan* (plays). Poems were published posthumously. Died at age 30 of tuberculosis in Switzerland.

Last Words: "Lord, have mercy on my soul."

Source: *The Life of James Elroy Flecker from Letters and Materials Provided by His Mother* by Geraldine Hodgson (Oxford, England, 1925).

Fleming, Sir Alexander

(1881-1955) British biologist, bacteriologist, pharmacologist. Isolated penicillin from fungus, introducing the age of antibiotics. Shared Nobel Prize for Medicine with Florey and Chain (1945). Knighted in 1944. Died at age 73 of a heart attack in London.

Last Words: "I'm covered in a cold sweat. And I don't know why I've got this pain in my chest. It's not the heart. It's going down from the esophagus to the stomach."

Source: *Alexander Fleming: The Man and the Myth* by Gwyn Macfarlane (Cambridge, MA, 1984).

Fleming, Marjory

(1803-1811) Scottish child prodigy. Died of meningitis at age 8. Kept a diary during her last 18 months that was first published in 1858, then edited and republished. The complete edition appeared in 1935.

Last Words: "Oh, mother, mother."

Source: *The Complete Marjory Fleming, Her Journals Letters & Verses,* ed. by Frank Sidgwick (New York, 1935).

Fletcher, Andrew

(1655-1716) Scottish politician, writer. Opposed British rule in Scotland and the 1707 Act of Union between Scotland and England. Drew up a set of limitations to restrict power of English crown and ministers in Scottish affairs. Died in London.

Last Words: "I have a nephew who has been studying the law. Make him a judge when he is fit for it." His response to Lord Sunderland who asked if there was anything he wished done.

Source: *Fletcher of Saltoun* by G.W.T. Omond (New York, 1897).

Flint, Frank Sylvester ("Silver Flint")

(1855-1892) American athlete. Professional baseball player. Made major league debut in 1875 with the St. Louis Red Stockings. During his 13-year career, he was star catcher for the Chicago White Stockings. Died of alcoholism at age 36 in Chicago, Illinois.

Last Words: "There's nothing in the life of years ago I care for now. I can hear the bleachers cheer when I make a hit that wins the game. But there is nothing that can help me now. And if the Umpire calls me out now, won't you say a few words over me, Bill." He died after speaking these words to former teammate preacher Billy Sunday.

Source: *Famous Conversions: The Christian Experience,* ed. by Hugh T. Kerr and John M. Mulder (Grand Rapids, MI, 1993).

Flowers, Theodore ("Tiger")

(1895-1927) American athlete. Professional boxer. Known as the Georgia Deacon. First African-American boxer to capture the middleweight boxing championship. First African American after Jack Johnson to hold the world title. Died at age 32 in New York City from complications following eye surgery.

Last Words: "If I should die before I wake, I pray the Lord my soul to take."

Source: *Time* magazine, November 28, 1927.

Floyd, Charles

(1782-1804) American military man. Sergeant. Member of Lewis and Clark expedition. Only member of the party who died on the expedition. Fell ill and died at age 22. May have had dysentery. Clark reported that nothing stayed in his stomach or bowels. A monument to him was placed over his remains at Sioux City, Iowa, near where he was born.

Last Words: "I am going away.—I want you to write me a letter." Spoken to Clark who reported it in his journal.

Source: *The Lewis and Clark Journals: An American Epic of Discovery: The Abridgment of the Definitive Nebraska Edition* by Meriwether Lewis, William Clark and Gary E. Moulton (Lincoln, NE, 2003).

Floyd, Charles Arthur ("Pretty Boy")

(1904-1934) American bank robber, murderer. Folk hero to some of his Oklahoma neighbors. Known as Robin Hood of Cookson Hills. Once claimed he robbed only men with money. Subject of Woody Guthrie's *The Ballad of Pretty Boy Floyd*. Killed at age 30 by FBI agents in an Ohio field.

Last Words: "I'm Floyd, all right. You got me this time."

Source: *The Life & Death of Pretty Boy Floyd* by Jeffery S. King (Kent, Ohio, 1998).

Flynn, Errol Leslie Thomson

(1909-1959) Australian-born American actor. Famed for romantic swashbuckler roles in Hollywood movies and a flamboyant heavy drinking lifestyle. Died at age 50 of heart failure in Vancouver, British Columbia.

Different Last Words:

(1) (doubtful): "I've had a hell of a lot of fun, and I've enjoyed every minute of it."

Source: Various Last Words compilations and Internet websites.

(2) "I shall return." Spoken while visiting a friend's apartment in Vancouver. He experienced leg pain and wanted to rest. He promised to be back in an hour to join guests for dinner. He then went into a bedroom and rested. A half hour later, his friend checked on him and found him suffering a massive heart attack. He died within minutes.

Source: *The Two Lives of Errol Flynn* by Michael Freedland (London, 1978).

Foch, Ferdinand

(1851-1929) French military leader, writer.

Marshal of France. Commanded Allied forces in World War I. Halted German offensive and helped bring about German defeat. Elected to the Academy of Sciences, French Academy. Died at age 77 in Paris. Aircraft carrier, Avenue Foch in Paris and several other places were named for him.

Last Words: "Let us go."

Source: *The Biography of the Late Marshal Foch* by Major General Sir George Aston (New York, 1929).

Foé, Marc-Vivien ("Marco")

(1975-2003) Cameroonian athlete. Professional soccer player. Died suddenly during a major international competition. In 2003, during the FIFA Confederations Cup tournament, Cameroon was facing Colombia in the semi-final in Lyons, France, when Foé collapsed in the 72nd minute of play. His death at age 28, which shocked the soccer world, was later determined to be heart-related. He was given a state funeral in Cameroon. Several streets were named for him, and some of his former clubs have retired his number.

Last Words: "Boys, even if it means dying on the pitch, we must win this semi-final." Spoken to his teammates immediately before the end of half time.

Source: "Foé Told Mates 'It's Do or Die'" (Reuters News, Ltd., June 27, 2003).

Foix, Gaston de, III

(1331-1391) French military leader. Member of House of Foix-Béam, prominent medieval French family. Identified himself as "Fébus" (Apollo). Wanted to create a state at Béarn. Became involved in a long war. Made peace with Charles V. Appointed lieutenant general of Languedoc but lost his office when Charles VI took the throne. Died at Béarn.

Last Words: "I am a dead man! Lord God, have mercy upon me!"

Source: *Chronicles of England, France, Spain and the Adjoining Countries,* Vol. II, by Sir John Froissant, tr. from French by Thomas Johnes, Esq. (London, 1862)

Foley, Thomas Patrick Roger

(1822-1879) American prelate. Coadjutor Bishop of Roman Catholic Diocese of Chicago. Died at age 56, before he could succeed the Bishop of Chicago.

Last Words: "I appoint you Administrator. I have tried to do my duty. I bow to the will of Almighty God."

Source: "Bishop Thomas Foley" (*New York Times*, February 20, 1879).

Fontaine-Martel, Madame de

(1662-1733) French noblewoman, countess. Friend of Voltaire who was a guest in her home in a very pleasant Palais-Royal neighborhood of Paris. When she died, he had to find another place to live. He lingered in her house three months then moved to a home on a dingy, obscure lane.

Last Words: "God be blessed! Whatever the hour, there is always a rendezvous going on." Response when asked what time it was.

Source: *Voltaire et la société au XVIIIe siècle* by Gustave Desnoiresterres (Paris, 1871).

Fontenelle, Bernard Le Bovier de

(1657-1757) French writer, scientist. Challenged dogma and superstition. Helped popularize Copernican and Cartesian science. Nephew of Corneille. Died in his 100th year.

Last Words: "I do not feel anything but a certain difficulty of existing."

Source: *Fontenelle, l'homme, l'oeuvre, l'influence* by Louis Maignon (Paris, 1906).

Variation: "I feel nothing except a certain difficulty in continuing to exist."

Source: *Famous Last Words & Tombstone Humor* by Gyles Brandreth (New York, 1989).

Variation: "I suffer nothing, but feel a sort of difficulty of living longer."

Source: *The Last Words (Real and Traditional) of Distinguished Men and Women Collected from Various Sources* by Frederic Rowland Marvin (New York, 1901).

Fonton, Francis

(d. 1790) English bank clerk, forger, counterfeiter. Bank of England employee who was executed for forgery and counterfeiting.

Last Words: "By a way which I knew not." Spoken on the scaffold. He announced that the Almighty had the right to lead him home.

Source: *Genuine and Impartial Memories of Francis Fonton, Late of the Bank of England* by a Student of the Law in the Inner Temple (London, 1790).

Foot, Solomon

(1802-1866) American politician, lawyer.

Member U.S. House of Representative and U.S. Senate from Vermont. Died at age 63 in Washington, D.C. Funeral services were held in the Chamber of the U.S. Senate.

Last Words "What, can this be death? Is it come already?—I see it! I see it. The gates are wide open! Beautiful! beautiful!" Spoken to his wife.

Source: *Proceedings on the Death of Hon. Solomon Foot, Including the Addresses Delivered in the Senate and House of Representatives on April 12, 1866. 39th Congress, 1st session, 1865-1866* (Washington, D.C., 1866).

Foote, Andrew Hull

(1806-1863) American military officer. Rear admiral in U.S. Navy. Wounded at Fort Donaldson in 1862 in U.S. Civil War. Died a year later in New York City as he was about to take command of South Atlantic Blockading Squadron.

Last Words: "We will have them, North and South. When his black servant Brooks asked what he meant, he replied: "The colored people, yes, we will have them. We must have charity, charity, charity."

Source: *Life of Andrew Hull Foote: Rear-admiral United States Navy* by James Mason Hoppin (New York, 1874).

Fooy, Sam

(1844-1875) American murderer, robber. Sentenced to death by Judge Isaac Parker in Fort Smith, Indian Territory for murdering a teacher. Hanged.

Different Last Words:

(1) "I am as anxious to get out of this world as the people who have come here today to see me. I will not delay you." His response to hangman George Maledon when asked if he had any Last Words.

Source: *Hanging Judge* by Fred Harvey Harrington (Norman, OK, 1996).

Variation: "I am as anxious to have this thing over with as these who have assembled to see it, and therefore will not delay matters. Farewell to all." Maledon's recollection of Fooy's last words.

Source: "Dropped Into Eternity George Maledon's Memories of Fifty-Two Executions — Sixteen Years' Experiences with Condemned Men on the Scaffold — Hanging Six Men at One Time — Curious Incident Attending the Taking Off of an Indian Murderer — Nervy Men Who Shed Tears — Indians Usually Make Less Trouble than White Men" (*Chicago Daily Tribune*, September 25, 1887).

(2) (doubtful): "I dreamed I was on the gallows before a great crowd of people. I was sick and weak and felt like fainting, and thought I could not face death. Just then a man stepped up in the crowd, came right up to me and said 'Look Sam, don't you be afraid to let them jump you. Jesus is standing under the floor and he will catch you in His arms.' That made me feel strong, when the drop came, and I felt no pain. I just fell asleep and woke up in the beautiful garden. It had running waters and stars were dancing on the waves."

Fooy did say this, but these were not his Last Words. They were spoken to a reporter about a dream he had the night before his execution. The *Fort Smith Independent* printed it on September 8, 1875, five days after the execution of Fooy and five others.

Source: *Pictorial History of The Wild West: A True Account of the Bad Men, Desperadoes, Rustlers, and Outlaws of the Old West—and the Men Who Fought Them to Establish Law and Order* by James David Horan and Paul Sann (London, 1954).

Ford, Arthur Augustus

(1896-1971) American psychic, spiritual medium. Founder of International General Assembly of Spiritualists. Did much to revive interest in spiritualism and psychic phenomena, especially in the 1960s. Several of his most famous performances were later shown to be faked. Died at age 74 of a heart attack in Miami, Florida.

Last Words: "Oh God, I can't take any more! God, help me!"

Source: *Arthur Ford: The Man Who Talked with the Dead* by Allen Spraggett with William V. Rauscher (New York, 1973). While researching this book, the authors discovered one of Ford's most famous séances was faked.

Ford, Henry

(1863-1947) American automobile manufacturer, industrialist. Founder of Henry Ford Motor Company. Pioneer in using assembly line method of manufacturing. Produced affordable cars. The night he died, he retired to his bedroom around 9 p.m. At 11:15, he called out to his wife Clara.

Different Last Words:

(1) He told his wife he had a headache and a "dry throat." The maid and Mrs. Ford

propped him up in bed. He died a short time later of a cerebral hemorrhage.

Source: *The Public Image of Henry Ford: An American Folk Hero and His Company* by David L. Lewis (Detroit, 1976).

(2) "I'll sleep well tonight. We're going early to bed." Spoken to his maid.

Source: *Last Words: A Dictionary of Deathbed Quotations* by C. Bernard Ruffin (Jefferson, NC, 1995).

Ford, John

(1894-1973) American film director. Birth name John Martin (or Sean Aloysius) Feeney (or O'Leary). Famed for westerns and film adaptations of American novels. Won four Academy Awards as best director: *The Informer; The Grapes of Wrath; How Green Was My Valley; The Quiet Man.* Earned American Film Institute Life Achievement Award (1973). Died at age 79 of cancer in Palm Desert, California, surrounded by family and friends.

Different Last Words:

Ford biographer Joseph McBride noted several variations of John Ford's Last Words. He listed:

"May I please have a cigar?" (or variant). As Ford neared death, Mass was said at his bedside each day. When Mass ended, he would often make this or a similar comment; which may be why the quote has been perpetuated as his Last Words.

"Now will someone give me a cigar."

"Will someone please give me a cigar."

"Holy Mary, mother of God."

"Cut."

However, McBride reported that interviews with Josephine Feeney and Woody Strode indicate Ford died silently. Feeney (Ford's sister) was present when he died. She said the "cigar" quote was not his Last Words but became widely circulated among Ford's colleagues.

Source: *Searching for John Ford: A Life* by Joseph McBride (New York, 2001).

Ford, Paul Leicester

(1865-1902) American novelist, biographer, editor. Great-grandson of Noah Webster. Physically disabled by a spinal injury when young. Edited: *Writings of Thomas Jefferson* (10 vol.); *Writings of John Dickinson* (2 vol.). Notable novels: *Janice Meredith; The*

Honorable Peter Stirling. Murdered at age 37 by his estranged brother Malcolm Webster Ford who then committed suicide.

Last Words: "I must die like a brave man." Spoken to his secretary as he was helped to his sofa after he was shot.

Source: "Obituary—Paul Leicester Ford" (*Canadian Bookseller and Library Journal,* Vol. 15-16, 1902-03).

Variation: "All right, I want to die bravely."

Source: *The Current Encyclopedia: a Monthly Record of Human Progress* (Chicago, 1902).

Ford, Robert

(1862-1892) American saloon owner. Killer of Jesse James. Shot and killed at age 30 in his saloon by Ed O'Kelly.

Last Words: "I'll raise him five." His response when he saw on a charity list that Soapy Smith had donated $5. He then wrote: "Bob Ford—Ten Dollars—Charity covereth a multitude of sins."

Source: *Knights of the Green Cloth: The Saga of Frontier Gamblers* by Robert K. DeArment (Norman, OK, 1990).

Fordyce, George

(1736-1802) Scottish physician, lecturer, chemist. Fellow of Royal Society and of the Royal College of Physicians. Notable work: *Elements of Agriculture and Vegetation.* Died at age 65.

Last Words: "Stop, go out of the room; I am about to die." Spoken to his daughter who was reading to him. She put down her book and called an attendant who went into the room and found Fordyce had died.

Source: *Five Dissertations on Fever* by George Fordyce and W. G. Palmer (Philadelphia, 1846).

Forrest, Edwin

(1806-1872) American actor. Notable roles: Hamlet; Lear; Macbeth; Mark Antony; Othello. Involved in a feud with English actor McCready that led to the disastrous 1849 Astor Place Opera House riot in New York City, where more than 20 people were killed and many more were injured. Forrest established a home for retired actors in Philadelphia. Died at age 66 in Philadelphia.

Last Words (written): "God bless you ever, my dear and much valued friend." Last line of a letter to James Oakes of Boston, written the day before he died. Forrest had a stroke in his bedroom the following morning.

When his servants reached him, he was unable to speak. He died a short time later.

Source: *The Life of Edwin Forrest; with Reminiscences and Personal Recollections* by James Rees (Philadelphia, 1874).

Forrest, Nathan Bedford

(1821-1877) American military officer. Confederate general. Tactician in U.S. Civil War. Skilled cavalry and guerrilla leader. One of the reputed founders of the Ku Klux Klan. Charged with committing war crimes by leading the massacre of unarmed black Union troops at Fort Pillow, Tennessee. He later changed his views after embracing Christianity and perceiving Klan's activities as wrong. In 1875, he became the first white man to speak to the Independent Order of Pole-Bearers Association, civil rights group made up of former slaves. He stated that blacks had the right to vote and that their role should be elevated. County in Mississippi, town in Arkansas and parks, schools and monuments in Tennessee were named for Forrest. In the movie *Forrest Gump* (1994), the title character said he was named for his ancestor General Nathan Bedford Forrest.

Last Words: "Call my wife."

Source: *Shrouds of Glory: From Atlanta to Nashville: The Last Great Campaign of the Civil War* by Winston Groom (New York, 2004). Groom also wrote the novel *Forrest Gump*.

Forrestal, James Vincent

(1892-1949) American banker, statesman. U.S. secretary of the navy. First U.S. secretary of defense. Believed he was victim of a vast conspiracy and that enemies were hiding nearby. Admitted to Naval Medical Center, Bethesda, Maryland. Committed suicide at age 57 by leaping from the 13th floor of the Center.

Last Words (written): His suicide note included part of "Chorus from Ajax" by Sophocles:

"Woe to the mother, in her close of day
Woe to her desolate heart, and temples gray.
When she shall hear
Her loved one's story whispered in her ear
'Woe, woe! Will be the cry—
No quiet murmur like the tremulous wail
Of the lone bird, the querulous night—"

He left unfinished the word "nightingale."

Source: *Bergen* [Hackensack, NJ] *Evening Record*, May 23, 1949.

Forster, Edward Morgan ("E.M.")

(1879-1970) British writer, novelist, essayist, literary critic. Notable works: *A Passage to India; A Room with a View; Howard's End*, all of which were made into popular movies. Received Order of Merit from Queen Elizabeth II on his 90th birthday. Died at age 91 in Coventry, England.

Last Words: "He's really nice, that old bore." Murmured after a talkative visitor left his sickroom.

Source: *E.M. Forster: Polycrates' Ring (1914-1970)* by Philip Nicholas Furbank (London, 1978).

Forster, Johann Georg Adam (Georg)

(1754-1794) German explorer, botanist, writer. Son of Johann Reinhold Forster whom he accompanied to England, Russia and on Captain Cook's second voyage. Notable work: *A Voyage Round the World*. Went to Paris as delegate of the Mainz Republic during the French Revolution. Arrested the summer of 1793. Declared an outlaw and banned from leaving the city. Became ill. Died at age 39 of stroke in Paris.

Last Words (written): "It's true, isn't it, my children, that two words are better than none? I haven't strength to write more. Good-bye. Keep away from illness. A kiss for my little darlings." Letter to his family.

Source: *Georg Forster, der Naturforscher des Volkes* by J. Moleschott (Frankfurt, Germany, 1854).

Forster, Johann Reinhold

(1729-1798) Prussian scientist, educator, naturalist, geographer, philologist. Notable works: *Introduction to Mineralogy; Flora of South America*. Father of Georg Forster, with whom he traveled to England, Russia and on Captain Cook's second voyage. Professor of natural history and mineralogy at Halle University. Died at age 69 in Halle.

Last Words: "This is a beautiful world."

Source: *The Last Words (Real and Traditional) of Distinguished Men and Women Collected from Various Sources* by Frederic Rowland Marvin (New York, 1901).

Forten, James

(1766-1842) American businessman, abolitionist. African-American who was born into a free black Philadelphia family. Served in the Continental Navy during the American Revolution. Was the leading sail maker in Philadelphia. Would not sell rigging for slave ships. Vice President of American Anti-Slavery Society. Loaned money to his friend William Lloyd Garrison to start up *The Liberator*.

Last Words: "Happy, happy, happy! I feel peace that passeth all understanding. Lord let thy kingdom come, thy will be done on earth as it is in heaven."

Source: *A Gentleman of Color: The Life of James Forten* by Julie Winch (New York, 2002).

Fosdick, Harry Emerson

(1878-1969) American clergyman, educator, writer. Professor of practical theology at Union Theological Seminary. Pastor of First Presbyterian Church and Riverside Church in New York City. Gained wide recognition with his sermons and radio addresses. Died at age 91 in Bronxville, New York.

Last Words: "Because you'll need someone to guide you up and by Saint Peter." Spoken to his daughter who wanted to know why she had to wait at the bottom steps of the pearly gates.

Source: *Harry Emerson Fosdick: Preacher, Pastor, Prophet* by Robert Moats Miller (New York, 1985).

Foster, John

(1770-1843) English clergyman, writer. Devoted his later years to writing. Known as The Essayist. Criticized the prevailing ecclesiastical institution. Died at age 73 at Stapleton, near Bristol, England.

Last Words (written): "I commend you to the God of mercy, and very affectionately bid you—Farewell." Written in a letter.

Source: *Life and Correspondence of John Foster,* ed. by J.E. Ryland (London, 1846).

Foster, Stephen Collins

(1826-1864) American song writer. Notable songs: "Oh, Susanna"; "Camptown Races"; "My Old Kentucky Home"; "Old Black Joe"; "Swanee River"; "Beautiful Dreamer"; "Massa's in the Cold, Cold Ground." Died at age 37 in a charity ward of Bellevue Hospital, New York City, three days after he was admitted.

Different Last Words:

(1) (spoken): Foster told his friend George Cooper that nothing had been done for him at the hospital and that he could not eat the food they brought him. When Cooper returned to Bellevue the following day, Foster was dead. All that is known about Foster's death comes from the letters and telegrams Cooper sent to Foster's family.

(2) (spoken; doubtful): "God bless you." Spoken to Mrs. Pankhurst Duer, who worked in a music store. In an article for *Etude* magazine, she described the day she met Foster. He spoke these words to her as he left the store. In her interview, she said she was sure they were his "Last Words on earth." Most likely they were not. Foster died three days later in a hospital.

Source for (1) and (2): *Stephen Collins Foster: A Biography of America's Folk-Song Composer* by Harold Vincent Milligan (New York, 1920).

(3) (written): "Dear friends and gentle hearts." Found on a note in his pocket after he died. It may have been a line or a title for a song he was working on. The note became the subject of a short story by Alexander Woollcott. Also found in Foster's pocket were thirty-five cents.

Source: *Swanee Ribber and a Biographical Sketch of Stephen Collins Foster* by Fletcher Hodges (Orlando, FL, 1958).

Foster, Vincent Walker, Jr.

(1945-1993) American lawyer. Deputy White House counsel, legal adviser to President and Mrs. Clinton during Whitewater and Travelgate scandals. Died from gunshot wound. Many conspiracy theories of a cover-up surfaced after his death, but investigations by U.S. Park Police, U.S. Congress and independent counsels Robert B. Fiske and Kenneth Starr concluded Foster's death was a suicide. He had been suffering from depression and was frustrated at what he saw as partisan lying and roadblocks put up to hinder his defense of the Clintons. He wrote a rough draft of a resignation letter or suicide note (depending on interpretation), leveling criticism against some government factions and media then tore it up. The note, found with his briefcase, contained his Last Words.

Last Words (written): "I was not meant for

the job or the spotlight of public life in Washington. Here ruining people is considered sport."

Source: *The Clinton Wars* by Sidney Blumenthal (New York, 2003).

Fothergill, Samuel

(1715-1772) English missionary. Quaker. Brother of English physician John Fothergill. Died at age 56 in Warrington, Lancashire.

Last Words: "All is well with me; through the mercy of God, in Jesus Christ, I am going to a blessed and happy eternity. My troubles are ended. Mourn not for me."

Source: *Memoirs of the Life and Gospel Labours of Samuel Fothergill, with Selections from His Correspondence. Also an Account of the Life and Travels of His Father John Fothergill, and Some Notices of His Descendants,* ed. by George Crosfield (New York, 1844).

Fothergill, William Edward

(1865-1926) British physician, gynecologist, educator. Professor of clinical obstetrics and gynecology, University of Manchester. Senior surgeon, St. Mary's Hospitals, Manchester, England. Designed Fothergill's operation, a surgical procedure for correcting a prolapsed uterus. Died suddenly at age 61 at the end of a speech he was making at a University of Manchester banquet.

Last Words: "I have enjoyed tonight one of the best dinners I can remember."

Source: "Dr. Fothergill Dies as He Ends Speech" (*New York Times,* November 6, 1926).

Four Bears (Mahto-Topa)

(1800?-1837) Native American leader. Mandan warrior. Portrait painted by Karl Bodner and George Catlin. His exploits were written down by German explorer/naturalist Prince Maximilian zu Wied. Shortly before he died, Four Bears blamed the white men for the smallpox epidemic that was killing his people. The last part of his statement is given here:

Last Words: "Listen well what I have to say, as it will be the last time you hear Me! Think of your Wives, Children, Brothers, Sisters, Friends, and in fact all that you hold dear, are all Dead, or Dying, with their faces all rotten, caused by those dogs, the whites! Think of all that My friends, and rise to-

gether and Not leave one of them alive! The Four Bears will act his Part!"

Source: *The Village Indians of the Upper Missouri* by Roy Willard Meyer (Lincoln, NE, 1977).

Fowler, Mark Andrew

(1965-2001) American robber, murderer. Convicted for 1985 killing of grocery store employees during a robbery. Admitted the robbery but blamed his accomplice Billy Ray Fox for the killing. Executed at age 35 by lethal injection at Oklahoma State Penitentiary on January 23, 2001. Fifth person executed that month in Oklahoma.

Last Words: "Hail Mary!" His response when asked if he had any final words. Recited until drugs took effect.

Source: *Death and Justice: An Expose of Oklahoma's Death Row Machine* by Mark Fuhrman (New York, 2003).

Fox, Billy Ray

(1965?-2001) American robber, murderer. Convicted for 1985 murders of grocery store employees during robbery. Admitted robbery but blamed accomplice Mark Andrew Fowler for the killing. Executed at age 35, by lethal injection at Oklahoma State Penitentiary on January 25, 2001. Sixth person executed that month in Oklahoma.

Last Words: "No." His response when asked if he had any final words.

Source: *Death and Justice: An Expose of Oklahoma's Death Row Machine* by Mark Fuhrman (New York, 2003).

Fox, Charles James

(1749-1806) British statesman, politician. Member of Parliament. Foreign secretary. Died at age 57 in Chiswick, Devon, after he made a speech in the House of Commons in favor of abolishing slave trade.

Different Last Words:

(1) "I die happy, but pity you. It doesn't signify, my dearest, dearest Liz." Spoken to his wife.

Source: *Charles James Fox* by John Drinkwater (New York, 1928).

Variation: "God's will be done. I have lived long enough and I shall die happy." His response when told he might not live another day. When his wife asked him to repeat what he had said. He told her: "It don't signify, dearest Liz."

Source: *The Last Words (Real and Traditional) of Distinguished Men and Women Collected from Various Sources* by Frederic Rowland Marvin (New York, 1901).

(2) "Trotter will tell you." Spoken to his wife.

Source: *Memoirs of the Latter Years of the Right Honourable Charles James Fox* by John Bernard Trotter (Philadelphia, 1812).

Fox, George

(1624-1691) English religious leader. Founder of Religious Society of Friends (Quakers). Died at age 66 in London.

Different Last Words:

(1) "I am glad I was here. Now I am clear, I am fully clear!...All is well; the Seed of God reigns over all and over death itself. And though I am weak in body, yet the power of God is over all, and the Seed reigns over all disorderly spirits." Spoken at the meeting of Friends.

Source: *The Story of George Fox* by Rufus M. Jones (New York, 1919).

(2) "Never heed; all is well. The seed or power of God reigns over all, and over death itself. Blessed be the Lord."

Source: *The British Friend. A Monthly Journal Chiefly Devoted to the Interests of the Society of Friends*, Vol. XLVI, Nos. I to XII (Glasgow, Scotland,1888).

Fox, Henry, 1ˢᵗ Baron Holland

(1705-1774) British statesman, politician. Member of Parliament. Pupil and supporter of Sir Robert Walpole. Made a baron in 1763. Died at age 68 in Holland House, Kensington.

Last Words: "If I am alive, I shall be glad to see him; and if I am dead, he would like to see me." He was speaking about his friend George Selwyn. If Selwyn called again, he was to be shown to his room.

Source: *Henry Fox, 1ˢᵗ Lord Holland: A Study of the Career of an 18th Century Politician* by Thad W. Riker (Oxford, England, 1911).

Fox, Henry Watson

(1817-1848) English missionary to the Telugu people of South India. Notable work: *Chapters on Missions in South India* (describing mission life and his views on the Hindu religion and manners). Wife died in Madras, India, in 1845. Ill health forced him to return to England in 1848. Died at age 31 at his mother's house in Durham.

Last Words: "Jesus, Jesus must be first in the heart." When asked: "He is the first in yours?" he replied: Yes, he is."

Source: *A Memoir of the Rev. Henry Watson Fox* by Rev. George Townshend Fox (London, 1853). The author was his father.

Fox, Margaret Askew Fell

(1614-1702) English writer. Quaker. First husband Thomas Fell died. Married religious leader George Fox. Played an important role in establishing Society of Friends (Quakers).

Last Words: "Take me in thy arms, I am in peace." Spoken to her daughter.

Source: *The Life of Margaret Fox, Wife of George Fox, Compiled from Her Own Narrative and Other Sources* (Philadelphia, 1859).

France, Anatole

(1844-1924) French writer, novelist, critic, poet, playwright. Pen name of Jacques Anatole François Thibault. Awarded Nobel Prize for Literature (1921). Notable works: *The Crime of Sylvestre Bonnard; At the Sign of the Reine Pédauque; Revolt of the Angels; Penguin Island.* Died at age 80 in Tours.

Last Words: "Maman!" (tr. "Mother.")

Source: *Anatole France* by Jacques Suffel (Paris, 1946).

Frances of Rome, Saint

(1384-1440) Italian holy woman. mystic. Known as Francesca Romana. Founded religious community of Benedictine nuns. Died at age 56 in Rome. Canonized in 1608.

Last Words: "The angel has finished his task. He stands before me. He beckons me to follow him."

Source: "A Guardian Angel" (*Spiritual Magazine*, Vol. VII, April 1872).

Francis, Willie

(1929-1947) American murderer, Constitutional challenger. Survived electrocution due to a loose connection in the electric chair. The event touched off a lawsuit claiming that executing him would be cruel and unusual punishment that is prohibited by the Eighth Amendment. Also, it placed him in double jeopardy. Francis was only 16. He went back to the electric chair in St. Martinville, Louisiana, and was executed on May 9, 1947, one year and six days after his first trip. Two hours before the execution, his lawyer told him he might be able to get him another stay. Francis turned it down saying he was ready to go.

Last Words: "Nothing at all." His response when asked by the executioner if he had anything to say.

Source: "Willie Francis Dies Smiling in 2d 'Execution'" (*Chicago Tribune*, May 10, 1947).

Francis of Assisi, Saint

(1182?-1226) Italian clergyman, holy man. Birth name Giovanni Francesco Bernardone. Founder of Franciscan order. Canonized in 1228.

Different Last Words:

(1) "Welcome, sister Death!"

Source: *The Golden Legend or Lives of the Saints.* Compiled by Jacobus de Voragine, Archbishop of Genoa, 1275, 1st ed., 1470. English ed. by William Caxton, 1483, ed. by F.S. Ellis (Edinburgh, 1900).

(2) "When you see that I am brought to my last moments, place me naked upon the ground, just as you saw me the day before yesterday; and let me lie there, after I am dead, for the length of time it takes to walk one mile unhurriedly."

Source: *St. Francis Assisi: First and Second Life of St. Francis, with Selections from Treatise on the Miracles of Blessed Francis* by Thomas Celano, Thomas Francis and Placid Hermann (Chicago, 1963).

(3) "The righteous wait expectant till I receive my recompense." Spoken to members of his order who knelt around his bed awaiting his death.

Source: *Francis of Assisi* by Margaret Oliphant (London, 1889).

Francis de Sales, Saint

(1567-1622) French prelate, writer, holy man. Roman Catholic bishop of Geneva, Switzerland. Doctor of the Church. Founded religious Order of the Visitation. Famed for his letters and devotional books. Notable works: *Introduction to the Devout Life; Treatise on the Love of God.* Died at age 55 in Lyon, France. Canonized in 1661.

Last Words: "Advesperascit, et inclinata est jam dies." (tr. "It is toward evening, and the day is far spent.") These were his last words, save that of the Name of Jesus.

Source: *S. Francis de Sales, Bishop and Prince of Geneva* by H.L. Sidney Lear (London, 1898).

Francis Xavier, Saint

(1506-1552) Spanish missionary in India and Japan, holy man. Roman Catholic Jesuit. Known as Apostle of the Indies. Died at age 46 on Changchun, an island off the coast of China, while waiting to be taken to Canton. Canonized in 1622.

Different Last Words:

(1) "In Thee, O Lord, have I hoped, let me never be confounded." He spoke the words of *"Te Deum,"* a hymn of joy and thanksgiving.

Source: *Lives of the Saints* by S. Baring-Gould (Edinburgh, 1914).

(2) "Jesus, Son of David, have mercy on me. O Virgin Mother of God, remember me." Repeated in a barely audible chant as he lapsed into and out of consciousness.

Source: *The Scents of Eden: a History of the Spice Trade* by Charles Corn (New York, 1999).

Francke, August Hermann

(1663-1727) German clergyman, educator, philanthropist. Protestant. Founder of Pietism. Died at age 64 in Halle, Brandenburg.

Different Last Words:

(1) "Of that there is no doubt." His response to his wife who asked if his Savior was still with him.

Source: *August Hermann Francke, der Mann und sein Werk* by Hellmuth Heyden (Stettin, Germany, 1927).

(2) "God will continue to support me. My soul has cast itself upon him; Lord, I wait for Thy salvation." Spoken from time to time in Hebrew and German.

Sources: *The Last Words (Real and Traditional) of Distinguished Men and Women Collected from Various Sources* by Frederic Rowland Marvin (New York, 1901); *Christian Biography*; Religious Tract Society (London, 1832).

Franco, Francisco

(1892-1975) Spanish military officer, dictator. Full name Francisco Paulino Hermenegildo Teódulo Franco Bahamonde. Led a revolt in 1936. Headed Falange party in 1937. Declared himself chief of state, prime minister, commander in chief in 1939. Reorganized government after World War II. Selected Prince Juan Carlos de Borbón as his successor. Died at age 82 Madrid. Juan Carlos was sworn in as king.

Last Words: "My God, how hard it is to die!"

Source: *Franco: A Biography* by J.P. Fusi (New York, 1987).

Francois, Marvin

(1945-1985) American mass murderer, thief. Convicted for execution-style murder of six residents in one Florida house during a drug-related robbery. All his victims were laid face-down with their hands behind their backs before he shot them. Electrocuted at age 39. His co-defendant, Beauford White was executed in 1987.

Last Words: "If there is such thing as an Anti-Christ, it ain't one man, but the whole white race."

Source: *Last Suppers: Famous Final Meals from Death Row* by Ty Treadwell and Michael Vernon (Port Townsend, WA, 2001).

Frank, Anne

(1929-1945) German-born Dutch Jewish diarist. Kept a diary from 1942 to 1944. Arrested and sent to a concentration camp in Germany. Died of typhoid fever in Bergen-Belsen at age 15, just three weeks before the camp was liberated.

Last Words (written): "And finally I twist my heart around again, so that the bad is on the outside and the good is on the inside, and keep on trying to find a way of becoming what I would so like to be, and what I could be if there weren't any other people living in the world." Last entry in her diary, written three days before she was arrested.

Source: *Anne Frank: The Diary of a Young Girl* (New York, 1952).

Frank, Hans

(1900-1946) German military officer. Governor of Nazi-occupied Poland. Nazi war criminal. Nuremberg Trial defendant. Known as the Gauleiter of Poland. One of 12 convicted by the International Military Tribunal at Nuremberg and sentenced to death by hanging. Converted to Roman Catholicism after his arrest. Executed at age 46 in Nuremberg.

Last Words: "I am thankful for the kind of treatment during my captivity and I ask God to accept me with mercy."

Source: "The Execution of Nazi War Criminals" by Kingsbury Smith (International News Service, October 16, 1946).

Frankfurter, Felix

(1882-1965) Austrian-born American lawyer, jurist. Associate justice of the U.S. Supreme Court. Received Presidential Medal of Freedom. Suffered heart attack. Died the next day, at age 82.

Last Words: "I hope I don't spoil your Washington's Birthday." Spoken to a visitor in George Washington University Hospital, where he died a short time later.

Source: *Brandeis and Frankfurter: A Dual Biography* by Leonard S. Baker (New York, 1984).

Franklin, Benjamin

(1706-1790) American statesman, scientist, writer, philosopher, printer, publisher, inventor. Published *Pennsylvania Gazette* and *Poor Richard's Almanack*. Agent in England. Minister to France. Member of Continental Congress. On committee that drafted Declaration of Independence. Member Constitutional Convention. Experimented with electricity. Invented a type of printing press, a chair and a stove. Helped negotiate peace after American Revolution. Died at age 84 in Philadelphia. *Autobiography* published a year after he died.

Last Words: "A dying man can do nothing easy." Spoken to his daughter who advised him to change his bed position to breathe more easily.

Source: *Benjamin Franklin* by Carl Van Doren (New York, 1938).

Franklin, Sir John

(1786-1847) British military officer, politician, explorer. Rear admiral. Arctic explorer. Governor of Tasmania. Made three Arctic explorations (1819, 1823, 1845-1847). Mapped almost two-thirds of North America's northern coastline. Disappeared while attempting to chart Northwest Passage. Crew perished from starvation, exposure, tuberculosis and lead poisoning. Some 30 search and recovery efforts were made and several found remnants of the Franklin expedition in various locations. One group of searchers found a paper in a can south of King William's Island in May 1859. It was one of the standard printed forms furnished by the Admiralty and was dated 28th of May 1847. It revealed that the ships *Erebus* and *Terror* wintered at Beechey Island. It closed with these words:

Last Words (written): "Sir John Franklin

commanding the expedition. All well. Party consisting of 2 officers and 6 men left on Monday 24th of May, 1847. [Signed] Gm [Graham] Gore, Lieut, Chas. F. Des Voeux, Mate." Someone later wrote on the margin of the paper: "Sir John Franklin died on the 11th June, 1847."

Source: *Sir John Franklin* by Augustus Henry Beesly (New York, 1881).

Franz, Robert

(1815-1892) German musician, organist, conductor, composer, songwriter, arranger. Birth name Robert Franz Knauth. He dropped his surname and used his middle name as his last name. Wrote almost 300 songs. Notable songs: "Schlummerlied"; "De Lotosblume"; "Die Widmung." Died at age 77 in Dessau.

Last Words: "There, take a good look at that! Such a face you will never see again!" Spoken to a friend about a picture of his late wife.

Source: *Composers of Yesterday* by David Ewen (New York, 1937).

Franz Ferdinand, Archduke of Austria

(1863-1914) Austrian royalty. Heir apparent to the Austro-Hungarian throne. Nephew of Emperor Franz Josef. His assassination and that of his wife by a Serbian revolutionary set off World War I. Franz Ferdinand was hit in the neck. His wife Sophie was hit in the abdomen. They both died within an hour.

Last Words (doubtful): "Sophie, Sophie, do not die. Live for our children."

Source: Various Last Words compilations and Internet websites.

Although this quote is often reported as his Last Words, researchers now tend to believe he said only "Sophie." The Archduke's Last Words may have been stretched and romanticized for propaganda purposes.

Sources: *Archduke of Sarajevo: the Romance and Tragedy of Franz Ferdinand of Austria* by Gordon Brook-Shepard (Boston, 1984); *The Road To Sarajevo* by Vladimir Dedijer (New York, 1966); *Thunder At Twilight: Vienna 1913-1914* by Frederick Morton (New York, 1989).

Franz Josef, Emperor of Austria

(1830-1916) Austrian monarch. King of Hungary. Nephew of Emperor Ferdinand I. Experienced several tragic deaths in his fam-

ily: brother Maximilian (executed), son Rudolph (suicide), wife Elizabeth (assassinated), nephew Archduke Franz Ferdinand (assassinated). Died at age 86 while World War I was being waged. His grand nephew Karl I assumed the throne but ruled only two years and was the last Hapsburg monarch.

Different Last Words:

(1) "I thank thee, Ketterl." Spoken to his personal valet.

Source: *Golden Fleece: The Story of Franz Joseph and Elisabeth of Austria* by Bertita Harding (Indianapolis, IN, 1937).

(2) "God preserve the Emperor!" Died while singing the song.

Source: *Famous Last Words* by Barnaby Conrad (Garden City, NY, 1961).

(3) "Fine." Murmured after drinking some tea. He fell into a coma and died three hours later.

Source: *Last Words: A Dictionary of Deathbed Quotations* by C. Bernard Ruffin (Jefferson, NC, 1995).

Fraser, Simon (12th Baron Lovat)

(1667?-1747) Scottish chief, Jacobite schemer. Captured after the Battle of Culloden. Impeached, beheaded for his role in fighting for the Pretender to the throne.

(1) (doubtful): "Dolce et decorum est pro patria mori" (tr. "It is sweet and proper to die for one's country"), quoting Horace. He then quoted Ovid: "Nam genus et proavos et quae non fecimus ipsi, vix ea nostra voco." (tr. "Birth and ancestry and that which we have not ourselves achieved, we can scarcely call our own.")

Source: *Dictionary of National Biography, from the Earliest Times to 1900,* by Sir Leslie Stephen, George Smith and Sir Sidney Lee (London, 1921-1922).

Fraser did speak these words at his execution, but they were not his Last Words. After he quoted Ovid and Horace, he said a prayer and gave a cane to his solicitor. His final words appear in (2).

(2) "My dear James, I am going to heaven, but you must continue to crawl a little longer in this evil world." Spoken to his friend James Fraser. He then gave his wig, hat and clothes to William Frazer and told him to see that the executioner did not touch them. He said a short prayer and gave the signal to the executioner by dropping his handkerchief.

Source: *The New Newgate Calendar Being a Series of Memoirs and Anecdotes of Notorious Characters Who Have Outraged the Laws of Great Britain from the Earliest Period to 1841,* Vol. I, by Camden Pelham (London, 1886).

Frederick II, King of Prussia ("Frederick the Great")

(1712-1786) Prussian monarch, writer. Known as Old Fritz. Prolific military, historical and political writer. Enlightened monarch who patronized the arts. Corresponded with Voltaire. Skilled musician, flutist, composer. Made Prussia an important European power. Streamlined the bureaucracy and civil service. Died childless at age 74 in Potsdam. Succeeded by nephew, Frederick William II of Prussia.

Last Words: "La montagne est passée, nous irons mieux." (tr. "We are over the hill, we shall go better now." Or, "The mountain is passed. We shall go better now.") Spoken while delirious.

Sources: *History of Frederick the Great: The Works of Thomas Carlyle* by Thomas Carlyle (New York, 1896); *The Last Words (Real and Traditional) of Distinguished Men and Women Collected from Various Sources* by Frederic Rowland Marvin (New York, 1901).

Frederick III, King of Prussia, German Emperor

(1831-1888) Prussian monarch. Son of William I of Prussia. Full name Frederick William Nicholas Charles. Known as Our Fritz. Married Victoria Adelaide Mary Louise, eldest daughter of Queen Victoria. Ruled three months. Died at age 56 of throat cancer. Succeeded by son Kaiser Wilhelm II.

Last Words: "Very, very."

Source: *Vicky: Princess Royal of England and German Empress* by Daphne Bennett (London, 1971).

Frederick V, King of Denmark and Norway

(1723-1766) Danish and Norwegian monarch. Son of Christian VII. Succeeded to the throne in 1746. Expanded commerce and industry. Died at age 42 in Copenhagen.

Last Words: "It is a great consolation to me in my last hour that I have never willfully offended any one and that there is not a drop of blood on my hands."

Source: "Last Words of the Learned" (*The United States Magazine and Democratic Review,* Vol. 20, No. 106, April 1847).

Frederick VI, King of Denmark and Norway

(1768-1839) Danish monarch. Son of Christian VII. Helped end serfdom and the slave trade. Lost Norway to Sweden in 1814 after defeat in Napoleonic Wars. Highly regarded conservative ruler.

Last Words: "It is getting cold; we must see that the poor folks have fuel."

Source: *Hans Christian Anderson: A Biography* by Robert Nisbet Bain (New York, 1895).

Frederick VIII, King of Denmark

(1843-1912) Danish monarch. Son of King Christian IX. Brother of Britain's Queen Alexandra. Succeeded to the throne when he was 63. Stopped in Hamburg, Germany, while returning from a trip to France. Went out walking incognito. Became ill. Collapsed on a park bench and died at age 68.

Last Words: "I am staying at the Hamburger Hof. I feel better. I will go on foot." Spoken to a bystander who saw that he was in distress. He walked a short distance then collapsed.

Source: *London Daily Telegraph*, May 16, 1912.

Frederick William I, King of Prussia

(1688-1740) Prussian monarch. Son of Frederick I. Father of Frederick the Great. Was practical and frugal. Encouraged agriculture, industry, and a large army but discouraged the arts and science. Introduced woolen manufacturing. Died at age 51 in Potsdam, Germany. Left a huge treasury for his son to draw upon.

Different Last Words:

(1) "Lord Jesus, to thee I live. Lord Jesus, to thee I die. In life and in death thou art my gain." Cried out to his physician M. Pitsche. He fainted then died after a few gasps.

Source: *History of Frederick the Second, Called Frederick the Great* by John S. C. Abbott (New York, 1871).

(2) (doubtful): "No, not quite naked. I shall have my uniform on." His response on hearing a favorite hymn that quoted the Bible (Job 1:21): "Naked came I into the world, and naked shall I go out of it."

Source: Various Last Words compilations and Internet websites.

This quote is often given as the Last Words of Frederick William I. He did say these words during his final days, but they were not his last. He discussed prayers, abdication and his health before dying. See (1) for his Last Words.

Source: *History of Frederick the Second, Called Frederick the Great* by John S. C. Abbott (New York, 1871).

Freeman, Edward Augustus

(1823-1892) English historian, educator. Regius professor at Oxford. Notable work: *History of the Norman Conquest.* Died at age 68 of smallpox in Spain while on one of his many travels abroad.

Last Words (written): "Very weak. Rail to La Encina and Alicante." His last journal entry.

Source: *The Life and Letters of Edward A. Freeman, C.D.L., LL.D.* by W.R.W. Stephens (London, 1895).

Frelinghuysen, Theodore

(1787-1862) American politician, educator. Member U.S. Senate from New Jersey. New Jersey attorney general. Mayor of Newark, New Jersey. Vice Presidential Whig candidate with Henry Clay. Chancellor of New York University. President of Rutgers College. Died at age 75 in New Brunswick. New Jersey township was named for him.

Last Words: "All peace, more than ever before."

Source: *Memoirs of Theo. Frelinghuysen* by Talbot W. Chambers (New York, 1863).

Frémont, John Charles

(1813-1890) American explorer, military officer, politician. Known as The Pathfinder. Led five expeditions to the American West. Helped take over California during Mexican War. Member U.S. Senate from California. Nominated but defeated for U.S. President. Governor of Arizona Territory. Died at age 77 of peritonitis in New York City.

Last Words: "California, of course." Spoken to his physician who asked him which home he meant when he said he would go home next week if he continued to be free of pain.

Source: *Fremont: Explorer for a Restless Nation* by Ferol Egan (Garden City, NY, 1977).

French, Daniel Chester

(1850-1931) American artist, sculptor. Neighbor and friend of Ralph Waldo Emerson and Alcott family. Notable works: *Min-ute Man* (Concord, Massachusetts); *Abraham Lincoln* (Lincoln Memorial, Washington D.C.); *John Harvard* (Harvard University, Cambridge, Massachusetts). Died at age 81 in Stockbridge, Massachusetts.

Last Words: "You're very good to me." Spoken to his nurse.

Source: *Journey into Fame: The Life of Daniel Chester French* by Margaret French Cresson (Cambridge, MA, 1947). The author was his daughter.

French, James D.

(1936?-1966) American murderer. Claimed his constitutional rights were violated because he was forced to wear prison clothes and was surrounded by prison guards during his trial. Murdered his cellmate. Executed by electrocution in Oklahoma.

Different Last Words:

(1) "How about this for a headline? French fries."

Source: *The Mammoth Book of Zingers, Quips and One Liners* by Geoff Tibbals (New York, 2004).

(2) "I'd kill your mother, your father, or your daughter. I love to kill. So you'll be doing society one of the best jobs you ever did."

Source: *Death Watch: A Death Penalty Anthology* by Lane Nelson and Burk Foster (Upper Saddle River, NJ, 2001).

Frere, Sir Henry Bartle Edward (Bartle)

(1815-1884) British colonial administrator. Made Knight Grand Cross of the Bath by Queen Victoria. High commissioner of Southern Africa. His treatment of the Zulu may have precipitated the 1879 Zulu War. He was recalled the following year. He published a defense of his actions in 1881. Died at age 69 in Wimbledon, England.

Last Words: "If they would only read the 'Further Correspondence' they would surely understand—they must be satisfied."

Source: *Life and Correspondence of the Right Hon. Sir Bartle Frere* by John Martineau (London, 1895).

Freud, Sigmund

(1856-1939) Austrian neurologist. Founder of psychoanalysis. His theories had great impact on psychiatry, psychology and other fields. Notable work: *The Interpretation of Dreams.* Bed-ridden and in agonizing pain with jaw cancer during his final days. Died at age 83 in London, England. In 1929, when Dr. Max Schur became Freud's physician, they agreed that if his cancer caused him to suffer needlessly, Schur would administer morphine.

Last Words: "Now it's nothing but torture and makes no sense any more." Spoken to Dr. Schur the day before he died.

Source: *Anna Freud: A Biography* by Elisabeth Young-Bruehl (New Haven, CT, 2008).

Frick, Henry Clay

(1849-1919) American industrialist, financier, philanthropist. Seriously wounded by an anarchist in his Pittsburgh office in 1892. Helped form United States Steel Corporation; served as director 1901 to 1919. Bequeathed his home, land, art treasures and a large endowment to the public. Died at age 69 in New York City.

Last Words: "That will be all; now I think I'll go to sleep."

Source: *Henry Clay Frick, the Man* by George Harvey (New York, 1928).

Frick, Wilhelm

(1877-1946) German military officer, Nazi War criminal. Nuremberg Trial defendant. Architect of Nazi system of concentration camps that resulted in the death of millions of people. One of 12 convicted at the International Military Tribunal in Nuremberg. Sentenced to death by hanging. Died at age 69 in Nuremberg. He remained unrepentant.

Last Words: "Long live eternal Germany!"

Source: *Hess: The Man and His Mission* by Joseph Bernard Hutton (New York, 1970).

Friedell, Egon

(1878-1938) Austrian critic, essayist, theater director. Birth name Egon Friedmann. Notable work: *A Cultural History of the Modern Age*. Opposed Nazi annexation of Austria. Killed when he jumped out of his apartment window to avoid capture by Gestapo agents.

Last Words: "Vorsicht bitte!" (tr. "Take care, please!") According to an anecdote.

Source: *Lexikon der letzten Worte: letzte Botschaften berühmter Männer und Frauen von Konrad Adenauer bis Emiliano Zapata* by Werner Fuld (Munich, Germany, 2002).

Frith, John

(1503-1533) English clergyman, martyr. Protestant. Helped translate New Testament with William Tyndale. Refused to yield on his views of transubstantiation, purgatory and papal infallibility. Imprisoned for heresy. Burned at the stake in London.

Last Words: "The Lord forgive thee."

Source: *Pioneers of the Reformation in England* by M.L. Loane (London, 1964).

Froebel, Friedrich Wilhelm August

(1782-1852) German educator. Founder of kindergarten system. Established training courses and opened kindergartens in Germany. Died at age 70 in Marienthal, Germany.

Last Words: "My friend, I have peeked at lovely Nature all my life. Permit me to pass my last hours with this enchanting mistress." He wanted to be placed by an open window, even though it might hasten his death.

Source: *Friedrich Froebel, Festschrift zur hundertjährigen Geburtstagsfeier* by Lina Morgenstern (Berlin, Germany, 1882).

Frohman, Charles

(1860-1915) American theater owner, manager, producer. Victim of *Lusitania* disaster. Owned theaters in U.S. and England. Produced several hundred shows. Died at age 54 when RMS *Lusitania* was sunk by a German submarine near Kinsale, Ireland. His body was later recovered and returned to the U.S. for burial.

Last Words: "Why fear death! Death is only a beautiful adventure." Spoken just before he drowned.

Source: *Charles Frohman: Manager and Man* by Isaac F. Marcosson and Daniel Frohman (New York, 1916). Daniel Frohman was Charles's brother.

Variation: "Why fear death? It is the most beautiful adventure in life."

Source: *Horrors and Atrocities of the Great War Including the Tragic Destruction of the Lusitania* by Logan Marshall (Philadelphia, 1915).

Frost, Robert Lee

(1874-1963) American poet. Won four Pulitzer Prizes. Participated in the inaugural ceremony of President John F. Kennedy in 1961 by reading "The Gift Outright," written for the occasion. Notable poems: "Stopping By Woods on a Snowy Evening"; "The Road Not Taken"; "Mending Wall." Died at age 88 of a pulmonary embolism in Boston.

Last Words: "I feel as though I were in my last hours."

Source: *Robert Frost, the Later Years, 1939-1963* by

Lawrence Thompson and R.H. Winnick (New York, 1976).

Froude, James Anthony

(1818-1894) English historian, educator, writer. Specialized in Reformation and Tudor history. Close friend and literary executor of Thomas Carlyle. Regius professor at Oxford. Died at age 76 in Kingsbridge, Devon.

Last Words: "Shall not the Judge of all the earth do right?"

Source: *The Life of Froude* by Herbert Paul (New York, 1906).

Fry, Elizabeth Gurney

(1780-1845) English social activist, philanthropist. Quaker. Known as Angel of the Prisons. Devoted her life to prison reform and rehabilitation at home and abroad. Helped women in halfway houses and on prison ships bound for the colonies. Died at age 65 at Ramsgate, England.

Last Words: "Oh! my dear Lord, help and keep Thy servant!"

Source: *Memoir of the Life of Elizabeth Fry: With Extracts from Her Journal and Letters,* ed. by two of her daughters Katherine Fry and Rachel Elizabeth Cresswell (London, 1856).

Fuller, Andrew

(1754-1815) English clergyman. First secretary of the Baptist Missionary Society. Pastor of Baptist Church in Kettering, Northamptonshire, for 32 years. Died at age 61 at Kettering.

Different Last Words:

(1) "Help me!" Spoken while praying.

Source: *Memoirs of the Life and Writings of the Rev. Andrew Fuller* by John Webster Morris (London, 1816).

(2) I have no religious joys; but I have a hope, in the strength of which I think I could plunge into eternity." Spoken to a young minister who was at his bedside.

Source: *The Work of Faith: The Labour of Love, and the Patience of Hope Illustrated in the Life and Death of the Rev. Andrew Fuller* by John Ryland and Andrew Fuller (London, 1818).

Fuller, Arthur Buckminster

(1822-1862) American clergyman. Union chaplain with 16th Massachusetts Volunteer Infantry in U.S. Civil War. Discharged for poor health but volunteered to stay with the regiments. Within a few minutes after he was posted in front of a store in Fredericksburg, Virginia, he was hit and killed by a Confederate sharpshooter. Arthur was the grandfather of 20th century architect and inventor Richard Buckminster Fuller.

Last Words: "Captain, I must do something for my country. What shall I do?"

Source: *Chaplain Fuller* by Richard F. Fuller (Boston, 1864). The author was his brother.

Fuller, Melville Weston

(1833-1910) American lawyer, jurist, politician. Managed 1860 U.S. Presidential campaign for Stephen Douglas. Chief justice of U.S. Supreme Court. Friend of Oliver Wendell Holmes. Died at age 77 in Sorrento, Maine.

Last Words: "I am very ill."

Source: *Melville Weston Fuller Chief Justice of the United States 1888-1910* by Willard L. King (New York, 1950).

Fuller, Sarah Margaret (Margaret)

(1810-1850) American critic, social reformer. Married Marquis Angelo Ossoli in Rome. Lost with her husband and child in a shipwreck off Fire Island, New York, on the way back to U.S. May have been the inspiration for character Zenobia in Hawthorne's *Blithedale Romance*.

Last Words: "I see nothing but death before me—I shall never reach the shore."

Source: *Margaret Fuller: A Psychological Biography* by Katherine Anthony (New York, 1920).

Furnivall, Frederick James

(1825-1910) English philologist, editor. Founded Early English Society, Shelley Society, National Amateur Rowing Association. Jointly founded Browning Society, London Working Men's College. Jointly founded and was second editor of *Oxford English Dictionary*. Died at age 85 in London.

Last Words: "I want the Club." His response to a question about how he wished to be commemorated.

Source: *Frederick James Furnivall: A Volume of Personal Record.* Reminiscences by forty-nine contributors, with a biography by John Munro (London, 1911).

Fuseli, Henry or Füssli, Johan Heinrich

(1741-1825) Swiss-born English artist,

painter, illustrator, writer, engraver. Member of Royal Academy. Painted stylized, surrealistic pictures. Illustrated Shakespeare's plays and Milton's *Paradise Lost*. Influenced William Blake. Died at age 84 in London.

Different Last Words:

(1) "Is it you, Samuel?" He was told Mr. Cartwright was in the house. Since he knew two men by that name, he wasn't sure who it was. When Samuel Cartwright approached his bed, Fuseli put out his hand and spoke these words.

Source: *The Life and Writings of Henry Fuseli* by John Knowles (London, 1831).

(2) "Is Lawrence come—is Lawrence come?" He seemed to be listening for the wheels of the carriage that bought his friend to see him each day from London.

Source: *Lights and Shadows of Artist Life and Character* by James Smith (London, 1853).

Gacy, John Wayne

(1942-1994) American serial murderer. Convicted of murdering 33 young men and boys but may have killed many more. Executed at age 52 by lethal injection at the Stateville penitentiary in Crest Hill, Illinois.

Last Words: "Yeah; kiss my ass." His response in the death chamber when someone asked if he had any Last Words.

Source: "Execution of Gacy Took 18 Minutes—Death Penalty Opponents Cite Malfunction in Lethal Injection" (*San Francisco Chronicle*, May 11, 1994).

Gadsden, Christopher

(1724-1805) American military officer, clergyman. Brigadier general in the American Revolution. Delegate to Continental Congress. Voted for ratification of U.S. Constitution. Grandfather of James Gadsden, for whom the Gadsden Purchase was named. Christopher designed the Gadsden flag with a coiled snake and the legend "Don't tread on me." Died from a fall at age 81 in Charleston, South Carolina.

Last Words: "I am reaching toward my inheritance." Spoken as he raised his arms toward heaven.

Source: *In Memoriam. Tributes to the Memory of the Rev. C.P. Gadsden, Late Rector of St. Luke's Church, Charleston, S.C. Mostly Delivered Shortly After His Decease; To Which Are Added at the Request of Many of His Friends, Thirteen of His Sermons* compiled by Rev. James H. Elliott (Charleston, SC, 1872).

Gainsborough, Thomas

(1727-1788) British artist. Major portrait and landscape painter. Influenced by the work of Van Dyck. Notable works: *The Blue Boy; Mrs. Siddons; The Market Cart; Mrs. Graham*. Died at age 61 of cancer in London.

Last Words: "We are all going to heaven, and Van Dyck is of the company." Recorded by his friend William Jackson.

Source: *Gainsborough and His Place in English Art* by Sir Walter Armstrong (New York, 1904).

Galba, Servius Sulpicius, Emperor of Rome

(3? B.C.-69 A.D.) Roman ruler. Joined in an insurrection against Nero. Made emperor by Praetorians when Nero died. Had a short, catastrophic reign. Assassinated at age 72 by Otho's loyalists.

Different Last Words:

(1) "Feri, si ex re sit populi Romani." (tr. "Strike, if it be for the good of Rome.")

Source: "Galba" in *Lives of the Noble Grecians and Romans* by Plutarch, tr. by John Dryden (Chicago, 1952).

(2) "Quid agitis commilitones? Ego vester sum et vos mei." (tr. "What mean you fellow soldiers? I am yours and you are mine.")

Source: "Galba" in *The Lives of the Twelve Caesars* by C. Suetonius Tranquillus, Book VII, tr. by Alexander Thomson, rev. by Thomas Forester (London, 1901).

Galgani, Saint Gemma

(1878-1903) Italian holy woman, mystic. Roman Catholic. Birth name Maria Gemma Umberta Pia Galgani. Claimed to have had extraordinary mystical experiences. Showed signs of the Stigmata in 1899 when she was 21. Miraculously healed of spinal meningitis. Died at age 25. Canonized in 1940.

Last Words: "Now it is indeed true that nothing more remains to me, Jesus. I recommend my poor soul to Thee—Jesus!"

Sources: *A Book of Unlikely Saints* by Margaret T. Monro (London, 1943); *The Life of the Servant of God, Gemma Galgani: An Italian Maiden of Lucca* by Father Germanus of Saint Stanislaus (London, 1913).

Galilei, Galileo

(1564-1642) Italian astronomer, mathematician, physicist. Forced to recant belief that Earth revolves around Sun and not vice versa as Roman Catholic Church claimed. Was working on addition to *Dialogues on*

Motion when he experienced fever and heart palpitations. Died at age 77 in Arcetri, near Florence. His actual Last Words are unknown.

Last Words (doubtful): "Eppur si muove" (or "E pur si muove"; tr. "Yet it moves"), referring to Earth. Often reported as Galileo's Last Words. He made his recantation in 1633, nine years before his death. Since 1761, he has been quoted as having said this immediately after his retraction. The quote may have originated with a 1640 painting of Galileo with the words "Eppur si muove" inscribed on it. (The inscription may have been added later.) The quote was widely published in *Querelles Litteraires* in 1761, based on a story told by an Italian living in London around that time. Modern historians and biographers doubt Galileo said these words. He ran the risk of being ritually executed by the Church for heresy. William J. Bernstein mentioned that the first assertion that Galileo even made the statement did not occur until 130 years later, and in that version Galileo said it as he stepped out of a carriage in Siena. Bernstein dismissed the story as "Apocryphal." Mary Allan-Olney noted that it would have been virtually impossible for Galileo to have uttered the phrase and not suffered horrific consequences. She attributed the statement to Galileo's biographers. Her research produced very few details on his last years under house arrest as his daughter with whom he corresponded had predeceased him.

Sources: *The Private Life of Galileo: Compiled Primarily from His Correspondence and that of His Eldest Daughter, Sister Marie Celeste* by Mary Allan-Olney (London, 1870); *The Birth of Plenty: How the Prosperity of the Modern World Was Created* by William J. Bernstein (New York, 2004); *Biographical Encyclopedia of Scientists* by John Daintith (New York, 1981); *Columbia Encyclopedia,* 3rd edition, ed. by William Bridgwater and Seymour Kurtz (New York, 1967).

Gallaudet, Thomas Hopkins

(1787-1851) American educator. Pioneer in education of the hearing impaired. Established first free American school for the deaf in Hartford, Connecticut. His son was a founder of Gallaudet College in Washington, D.C. Died at age 63 in Hartford.

Last Words: "I will go to sleep."

Source: *The Life and Labors of the Rev. T.H. Gallaudet* by Rev. Heman Humphrey (New York, 1857).

Galli-Curci, Amelita

(1882-1963) Italian operatic singer. Leading coloratura soprano of her era. Performed at the Metropolitan Opera. Notable roles: Juliette (Gounod's *Romeo et Juliette*); Lucia (Donizetti's *Lucia di Lammermoor*); title role in *Lakme*; Cio-Cio-San (Puccini's *Madame Butterfly*). A problem with a thyroid goiter led to unsuccessful throat surgery in 1935. She could no longer sing high notes. After a few recitals, she concentrated on teaching. Died at age 81 in La Jolla, California.

Last Words (written): "I am learning to make peace with my handicaps. I read a lot. I still have much to learn, and I enjoy fully this final, fascinating cycle of my life that prepares me for the exodus—The Great Adventure."

Source: *Galli-Curci's Life of Song* by C.E. LeMassena (Beverly Hills, CA, 1972).

Galois, Évariste

(1811-1832) French mathematician. His work laid the foundation for the Galois theory, a branch of abstract algebra. Stabbed at age 20 in a duel by a political enemy in Paris. He died a day later.

Last Words: "Don't cry, Alfred! I need all my courage to die at twenty." Spoken to his brother.

Source: *Men of Mathematics* by Eric Temple Bell (New York, 1937).

Galsworthy, John

(1867-1933) English novelist, playwright. Pen name: John Sinjohn. Won Nobel Prize for Literature in 1932. Notable works: *The Forsyte Saga* and its sequels; *A Modern Comedy; End of the Chapter*. His novels have been adapted into television miniseries. Died at age 65 in Hampstead, England.

Last Words (written): "Tax: two years, I've enjoyed two pleasant circumstances—a year—one draft" and "children, how do it not here with our home." Last Words were illegibly scribbled in a note. These were the only legible parts.

Source: *The Man of Principle: A View of John Galsworthy* by Dudley Barker (London, 1963).

Gambetta, Léon Michel

(1838-1882) French lawyer, statesman, politician. One of the chief founders of the French Third Republic. Opposed the government of Napoleon III. President of Chamber of Deputies. Prime minister of France less than three months. Killed at age 44 by a shot from a revolver that fired accidentally at his home near Sevres. He was a popular leader and had a very large funeral.
Different Last Words:
(1) "Good heavens! Has he hurt himself?" Spoken when someone fainted after seeing him.
Source: *Gambetta, Life and Letters* by P.B. Gheusi (London, 1910).
(2) "I am lost—it is useless to dissimulate,— but I have suffered so much it will be a deliverance."
Source: "Editor's Outlook–Gambetta" (*The Chautauquan: Organ of the Chautauqua Literary and Scientific Circle*, Vol. III, No. 5, February 1883).
Variation: "I am lost, and there is no use to deny it."
Source: *The Last Words (Real and Traditional) of Distinguished Men and Women Collected from Various Sources* by Frederic Rowland Marvin (New York, 1901).

Gammage, Jonny

(1964-1995) American police brutality victim. Black motorist who died at age 31 in Brentwood, a nearly all-white suburb of Pittsburgh, Pennsylvania, after being stopped by the police. His story made national headlines and led to a wide-ranging investigation into police conduct by the U.S. Justice Department.
Last Words: "Keith, Keith, I'm only 31." Uttered as he was being beaten.
Source: "Interview with Jonny Gammage Jury Foreman Richard Lyons" by Brian Connelly (*FOCUS Magazine*, Carnegie Mellon University, Pittsburgh, PA, 1995).

Gandhi, Indira

(1917-1984) Indian leader. Stateswoman. Prime minister of India. Daughter of Jawaharlal Nehru, India's first prime minister, and mother of another, Rajiv Gandhi. Assassinated at age 66 by her bodyguards in New Delhi while walking from her palace to a gate. She died in a hospital after surgery to remove the bullets.
Last Words: "Namaste" (in Hindi; tr.

"Greetings to you.") Spoken to two Sikh guards.
Source: "Indira Gandhi: Death in the Garden" by William E. Smith (*Time* magazine, November 12, 1984).

Gandhi, Mohandas Karamchand (Mahatma)

(1869-1948) Indian Hindu spiritual leader, lawyer, nationalist. Known as Mahatma (Sanskrit for Great Soul). Lived a simple life. Sought to end poverty and gain rights for the downtrodden. Preached nonviolence. Used peaceful civil disobedience to gain civil rights for Indians. Shot by a Hindu extremist fanatic who believed Gandhi was weakening India by befriending Muslims. Died at age 78 in New Delhi.
Last Words: "He Ram!" (tr. "Oh, God!")
Source: *Life of Mahatma Gandhi* by Louis Fischer (New York, 1950).

Garcia, Manuel ("Three-Fingered Jack")

(d. 1853) California criminal. Member of Joaquin Murrieta's gang of desperados responsible for cattle rustling, robberies and murders during the California Gold Rush. Killed by California Rangers.
Last Words: "I will throw up my hands for no gringo dog."
Source: *The Robin Hood of El Dorado* by Walter Noble Burns (New York, 1932).

Garcia Lorca, Federico

(1898-1936) Spanish writer, poet, playwright. Notable works: *Blood Wedding; The House of Bernarda Alba.* Shot to death without a trial at age 38 near Granada, Spain, by a member of a fascist paramilitary group known as the Black Squad during Spain's Civil War.
Last Words (written): "Father, please give this man a donation of 1,000 pesetas for the Army." The note, probably written under duress, was a request for money for a member of the Black Squad. His father carried the note in his wallet the rest of his life.
Source: *Federico Garcia Lorca* by Ian Gibson (New York, 1990).

Gardiner, Allen Francis

(1794-1851) English missionary. Naval commander. Protestant. Died at age 57, cold and starving with six followers in Patagonia.
Last Words (written): "My dear Mr. Wil-

liams, The Lord has seen fit to call home another of our little company. Our dear departed brother left the boat on Tuesday at noon, and has not since returned; doubtless he is in the presence of his Redeemer, whom he served so faithfully. Yet a little while, and through grace we may join that blessed throng to sing the praises of Christ throughout eternity. I neither hunger nor thirst, though five days without food! Marvelous loving kindness to me a sinner! Your affectionate brother in Christ. Sept. 6, 1851, Allen F. Gardiner." Written in a letter.

Source: *The Story of Commander Allen Gardiner, R.N. with Sketches of Missionary Work in South America* by John W. Marsh and W.H. Stirling (London, 1883).

Gardiner, James

(1687-1745) Scottish military officer. Colonel. Fought in a disastrous engagement with the Jacobites at the Battle of Prestonpans. Killed at age 57 by the Jacobite army. He is mentioned in Sir Walter Scott's historical novel, *Waverley.*

Last Words: "Fire on, my lads, and fear nothing." Spoken as a Highlander attacked him.

Source: *Some Remarkable Passages in the Life of Colonel James Gardiner* by Philip Doddridge (London, 1753).

Gardiner, Stephen

(1483-1555) English prelate, statesman. Bishop of Winchester. Renounced obedience to the Roman Catholic Church during the reign of Henry VIII but later disavowed his actions and became an arch prosecutor of Protestants. Died age 72 at Whitehall.

Last Words: "Erravi cum Petro, sed non flevi cum Petro." (tr. "I have sinned with Peter, but I have not wept with Peter.") Repeated frequently on his deathbed as he expressed great remorse.

Source: *The Visitor's Guide to Knole in the County of Kent* by John Henry Brady (Sevenoaks, England, 1839).

Gardner, Ava Lavinia

(1922-1990) American actress. Screen star. Listed as one of American Film Institute's greatest stars of all time. Nominated for an Academy Award for *Mogambo* and a Golden Globe for *The Night of the Iguana.* Died at age 67 of pneumonia in London.

Last Words: "I'm so tired." Spoken to her housekeeper Carmen Vargas.

Source: *Ava Gardner: Love is Nothing* by Lee Server (New York, 2006); "The Woman Who Shocked Sinatra" (*The* [London] *Daily Mail*, July 15, 2006).

Gardner, Thomas

(1724-1775) American military officer. Colonel in the American Revolution. Fatally wounded at Bunker's Hill (Breed's Hill). As his men carried him from the field, his son, a second lieutenant, saw him and offered to help in moving him. The father declined the help and retired from the field to die.

Last Words: "Think not of me, think not of me—I am well. Go forward to your duty." Spoken to his son.

Source: *The Library of American Biography,* Vol. 10: Joseph Warren by Jared Sparks (Boston, 1838).

Garfield, James Abram

(1831-1881) 20th President of the U.S. American politician, lawyer. Held office of President four months. Shot in a Washington, D.C., railroad station. Assassinated by disgruntled office seeker Charles Guiteau. Lingered more than two months. Died at age 49 of blood poisoning in Elberon, New Jersey.

Different Last Words:
(1) "Oh, Swaim there is a pain here!—Oh! oh! Swaim." Spoken in a whisper to General David Gaskill Swaim, his chief of staff.

Source: *Life of President Garfield: The Complete Record of a Wonderful Career* by William Ralston Balch (Philadelphia, 1881).

(2) "The people, the people, my trust." Cried out in his last languish.

Source: *The President's Death: a Discourse Delivered in the West Church on Sunday the 25th of September* by Cyrus Augustus Bartol (Boston, 1881).

Garibaldi, Giuseppe

(1807-1882) Italian patriot, soldier, writer. One of the creators of a united Italy. Championed racial equality, rights for women, abolition of capital punishment. Final years were spent living simply on a farm on the island of Caprera. Died there at age 74. Several Italian ships were named for him.

Last Words: "Maybe they are the souls of my little ones come to call me. Feed them when I am gone."

Sources: *Autobiography of Giuseppe Garibaldi* by Giuseppe Garibaldi, Alica Werner and Jessie White Mario (London,1889); *Joseph Garibaldi, Patriot and Soldier* by R. Corlett Cowell (London, 1897).

Variation: "Those are the spirits of my little girls, Rosa and Anita, who have come to see their father die. Be kind to them, and feed them when I am dead." Spoken about the two small birds on his windowsill.

Source: *The Last Words (Real and Traditional) of Distinguished Men and Women Collected from Various Sources* by Frederic Rowland Marvin (New York, 1901).

Garland, Samuel, Jr.

(1831-1862) American lawyer, military officer. Graduate of Virginia Military Institute and University of Virginia law school. Captain of Lynchburg Home Guard militia. Confederate brigadier general in U.S. Civil War. Killed in action at age 31 at Fox's Gap, Maryland.

Last Words: "I am killed; send for the senior colonel and tell him to take command."

Source: *The Military History of the Virginia Military Institute from 1839 to 1865* by Jennings C. Wise (Lynchburg, VA, 1915).

Garner, John Nance

(1868-1967) American politician. Known by his friends as Cactus Jack. Member U.S. House of Representatives from Texas for 30 years. Vice President of the U.S. for two of Franklin D. Roosevelt's terms (1932, 1936). In 1940 he ran against Roosevelt for the Presidential nomination and was defeated. Died at age 98 in Uvalde, Texas.

Last Words: "I love you." Spoken to his family.

Source: *Portland* [Maine] *Press Herald,* November 8, 1967.

Garnett or Garnet, Henry

(1555-1606) English clergyman, conspirator. Jesuit. Executed for involvement in the Gunpowder Plot, a conspiracy to blow up English Parliament and King James I.

Last Words: "Imprint the cross on my heart. —Mary, mother of grace."

Source: *The Dying Speeches and Behavior of the Several State Prisoners that Have Been Executed the Last 300 Years* (London, 1720).

Garnett, Robert Selden

(1819-1861) American military officer. Fought in Mexican War. Confederate brigadier general in U.S. Civil War. Killed at Corrick's (or Carrick's) Ford, Virginia (now West Virginia). First Civil War general to fall in battle.

Last Words: "The men need a little example." Spoken during his first military engagement as he walked slowly out in view of the enemy. Just as he gave the order to withdraw, he was shot and killed by Union sharpshooters.

Source: *Fighting for the Confederacy: The Personal Recollections of General Edward Porter Alexander* by Edward Porter Alexander and Gary W. Gallagher (Chapel Hill, NC, 1998).

Garnock, Robert

(1660?-1681) Scottish martyr. Covenanter. Was a smith in Stirling before being arrested for his beliefs. Held without charge for three years. Eventually he was executed by hanging in Edinburgh.

Last Words (written): "Farewell, all crosses of one sort or another; and so farewell, every thing in time, reading, praying and believing. Welcome eternal life and the spirits of just men made perfect: Welcome Father, son and Holy Ghost: into thy hands I commit my spirit."

Source: *The Scots Worthies: Containing a Brief Historical Account of the Most Eminent Noblemen, Gentlemen, Ministers, and Others, Who Testified or Suffered for the Cause of Reformation in Scotland: From the Beginning of the Sixteenth Century to the Year 1688* by John Howie (Glasgow, Scotland, 1829).

Garrett, Johnny Frank, Sr.

(1963-1992) American rapist, murderer. Accused of raping and killing a Roman Catholic nun when he was 17. Caught, tried, convicted and executed at age 28 by lethal injection in Texas. Garrett claimed he was innocent of the murder. His execution was protested by many human rights groups. Garrett was not only a minor when the crime was committed; he was also developmentally disabled.

Last Words: "I'd like to thank my family for loving me and taking care of me. And the rest of the world can kiss my ass."

Source: "Inside the Prison and Out, Execution Feelings Run High" by Kathy Fair (*Houston Chronicle*, February 12, 1992).

Garrett, Patrick Floyd ("Pat")

(1850-1908) American frontier lawman,

rancher. Believed to have killed Billy the Kid. Was shot and killed at age 57 at his New Mexico ranch after he got into an argument. Historians do not agree on who killed Garrett. Some believe it was Jessie Wayne Brazel, who confessed to the crime. Others believe the killer was a paid assassin. Last Words: "Well, damn you. If I don't get you off my property one way, I will another." Garrett's traveling companion Carl Adamson claimed to have overheard this argument between Brazel and Garrett about Brazel's animals grazing on his land.
Source: *Pat Garrett: The Story of a Western Lawman* by Leon Claire Metz (Norman OK, 1984).

Garrick, David

(1717-1779) English actor, theater manager. Pupil and friend of Samuel Johnson. Famed as one of the great English actors. One of the owners of Drury Lane Theater in London. Portrait was painted by Gainsborough. Died at age 61 in London. Buried in Poets' Corner, Westminster Abbey.
Last Words: "Oh! dear." Spoken softly immediately after he took his medicine then died.
Source: *Life of David Garrick: From Original Family Papers and Numerous Published and Unpublished Sources* by Percy Fitzgerald (London, 1899).

Garrick, Violette

(1724-1822) Austrian-born dancer. Birth name Eva Marie Veigel. Married David Garrick in 1749. Died at age 98 at her home in London. Her portrait by Hogarth is in Windsor Castle.
Last Words: "Put it down, hussy! Do you think I cannot help myself?" Spoken to a servant who offered her a cup of tea. She took the cup, tasted the tea, then died in her chair.
Source: *Life of David Garrick: From Original Family Papers and Numerous Published and Unpublished Sources* by Percy Fitzgerald (London, 1899).

Garrison, William Lloyd

(1805-1879) American abolitionist, journalist, social reformer. One of the founders of the American Anti-Slavery Society. Founder and editor of *The Liberator* in 1831. Continued publication until slavery was abolished. Died at age 73 of complications of kidney disease in New York City.

Last Words: "To finish it up." His response to his physician who asked if he wanted anything.
Source: *William Lloyd Garrison, 1805-1879): The Story of His Life Told by His Children* by Wendell Phillips Garrison and Francis Jackson Garrison (Boston, 1889).

Garth, Sir Samuel

(1661-1719) English physician, writer, poet. Had large practice in London. Friend of Addison. Court physician to King George I. Knighted in 1714. Notable work: *The Dispensary* (satire that ridiculed apothecaries and physicians). Died at age 58.
Last Words: "I am going on my journey. They have greased my boots already." Spoken as he pointed to the doctors. He had just received Extreme Unction (Last Rites) and was responding to a friend who asked how he was feeling.
Source: *Thesaurus of Anecdotes*, ed. by Edmund Fuller (New York, 1945). These Last Words are also attributed to Rabelais in *Apothegms Old and New* by Francis Bacon (1624) and *Joe Miller's Jests: or the Wits Vade-Mecum* (1739).

Gasparin, Comte Agénor de

(1810-1871) French nobleman, politician, minister plenipotentiary. One of the first investigators of table turning and telekinetic movements. Died at age 60.
Last Words: "No, you know I like to have you go before me." Spoken to his wife who wanted to walk behind him as he climbed the stairs.
Source: *Le Comte Agénor de Gasparin* by Theodore Borel (Lausanne, Switzerland, 1878).

Gassendi or Gassend, Pierre

(1592-1655) French philosopher, astronomer, mathematician. Friend of Galileo and Kepler. Advocate of empirical method. Attacked the teachings of Aristotle. Opposed Descartes. Revived epicurean doctrines. Died at age 63 in Paris. A lunar crater was named for him.
Different Last Words:
(1) "I pray you, say them softly, because speaking out loud disturbs me." Spoken to his confessor who offered to recite psalms aloud.
Source: *Pierre Gassendi* by Louis Andrieux (Paris, 1927).
(2) "You see what is man's life."

Source: *Universal Biography, Containing a Copious Account, Critical and Historical, of the Life and Character, Labor and Actions, of Eminent Persons,* Vol. I, by J. Lemprière (New York, 1810).

Gates, Sir John

(1504-1553) English statesman. Tried, sentenced and executed for treason. He had supported Lady Jane Grey's brief reign as queen of England.

Last Words: "I forgive thee with all my heart. —I will see how meet the block is for my neck. I pray thee strike not yet, for I have a few prayers to say, and that done, strike on God's name, good leave have thou." Spoken to his executioner.

Source: *The Annales, or, Generall Chronicle of England* by John Stow and Edmund Howes (London, 1615).

Gauguin, Eugéne Henri Paul

(1848-1903) French artist. One of the leading Post-Impressionist painters. Notable works: *Where Do We Come From? Who Are We? Where Do We Go; The White Horse; The Yellow Christ.* Spent final years in Tahiti and Marquesas Islands, French Polynesia. Died at age 54 of heart failure in the Marquesas.

Last Words (written): "Dear Monsieur Vernier: Would it be troubling you too much to ask you to come to see me? My eyesight seems to be going and I cannot walk. I am very ill. P.G." Letter to missionary Rev. Paul Vernier.

Source: *Paul Gauguin, the Calm Madman* by Beril Becker (New York, 1931).

Gaunt, Elizabeth

(d. 1685) English martyr. Baptist. Wife of William Gaunt of London. Sheltered James Burton during a rebellion against King James II. He later incriminated her. She was found guilty of high treason and burned at the stake four days later. She was the last woman in England to be executed for a political offense. She left a long testimony that she read before at her trial. It ended with the following:

Last Words: "O that you will be wise, instructed, and learn, is the desire of her that finds no mercy from you."

Source: "Trials of Fernley, Ring, Mrs. Gaunt, & Cornish" in *A Complete Collection of State Trials and Proceedings for High Treason and Other Crimes and Misdemeanors from the Earliest Period to the Present Time,* Vol. XI, 1680-1688. Compiled by T.B. Howell (London, 1811).

Gautama Buddha, see Buddha.

Gaveston, Piers
1st Earl of Cornwall

(1284?-1312) English nobleman. Royal favorite of Edward II who made him 1st Earl of Cornwall and arranged his marriage to his niece. Captured by the Earl of Warwick and other barons. Gaveston was viewed as a threat. He was beheaded at Warwick.

Last Words: "Oh! noble Earl, spare me." Spoken to Thomas, Earl of Lancaster.

Source: *Piers Gaveston: A Chapter of Early Constitutional History* by Walter Phelps Dodge (London, 1899).

Gaye, Marvin Pentz, Jr.

(1939-1984) American musician. Rock vocalist, composer. Notable hits: "I Heard It Through the Grapevine"; "How Sweet It Is"; "Ain't Nothing Like the Real Thing"; "Ain't No Mountain High Enough." Died at age 44 in Los Angeles, California. Gaye was killed by his father who shot him in the chest after a dispute. Inducted into the Rock and Roll Hall of Fame posthumously in 1987.

Last Words: "I ran my race. There's no more left in me." Spoken to his brother who held him until the paramedics arrived.

Source: *Marvin Gaye, My Brother* by Frankie Gaye and Frankie Basten (San Francisco, CA, 2003).

Gazuyeva, Elza, or Gazueva, Aiza

(1982?-2001) Chechnyan war victim, assassin. Assassinated Russian general Guider Gadzhiyev, commandant of the Urus-Martan military district in Chechnya. She had lost her husband, two brothers—one of whom was disabled—and a cousin in the war. Some accounts say Gadzhiyev was accused of atrocities against local civilians including summoning Gazuyeva to witness her husband's torture and execution. Other accounts indicate the general did summon her but only refused to tell her the fate of her husband who was being detained. Gazuyeva killed herself, Gadzhiyev and several of his bodyguards with a hand grenade. She became the first shahidka (Chechnyan suicide bomber).

Last Words: "Do you still remember me?" Spoken as she exploded the grenade.

Source: "Russia: Nord-Ost Anniversary Recalls Ascent of Female Suicide Bomber," Radio Free Europe (Prague, October 27, 2006).

Gehrig, Henry Louis ("Lou")

(1903-1941) American athlete. Professional baseball player, Major League first baseman. Known as the Iron Horse for playing in so many consecutive games. Played entire career for New York Yankees. Inducted into the National Baseball Hall of Fame in 1939. Diagnosed with amyotrophic lateral sclerosis (ALS, later known as Lou Gehrig's disease). Died of ALS at age 37 at his home in The Bronx.

Last Words: "Fifty-fifty." He mouthed his final words to his wife Eleanor.

Source: *Luckiest Man: The Life and Death of Lou Gehrig* by Jonathan Eig (New York, 2005).

Gellert, Christian Fürchtegott

(1715-1769) German writer, poet. Known for songs and fables. C.P.E. Bach, Haydn, Beethoven and others put his poems to music. Notable works: *Fables and Tales* (collection of fables and stories); *Spiritual Odes and Songs* (religious poems and hymns). Died at age 54 in Leipzig, Germany.

Last Words: "God be praised—only one more hour!" His response when he asked how long he had to live and was told that he had perhaps an hour.

Source: *Life of Professor Gellert Taken from a French Translation of the Original German* by Mrs. Douglas of Ednam House (London, 1805).

Genghis Khan

(1162-1227) Mongolian warlord, conqueror. Founder of Mongol Empire. Original name Temuchin (or Temüjin). Title Genghis Khan (universal ruler) was conferred on him. Became seriously ill and died at age 65, possibly of typhus, in the Ordos desert.

Last Words: "Let not my end disarm you, and on no account weep or keen for me, lest the enemy be warned of my death." Spoken when he knew his death was near.

Source: *Genghis Khan: His Life and Legacy,* tr. and ed. by Paul Ratchnevsky and Thomas Nivison Haining (Oxford, England, 1993).

Genna, Antonio ("Tony the Gentleman")

(d. 1925) Sicilian-born American gangster. One of six brothers of a crime family. Shot in the back by John Scalise and Albert Anselmi.

Last Words: "Cavallero." (tr. "The Cavalier.") His response to his mistress Gladys Bagwell who asked who shot him.

Source: *Capone: The Life and World of Al Capone* by John Kobler (Cambridge, MA, 2003).

Genna, Michael ("Mike the Devil")

(d. 1925) Sicilian-born American gangster. One of six brothers of a crime family. Shot in a Chicago police fight. Artery severed. Bled to death. Had just kicked a police ambulance stretcher bearer in the face.

Last Words: "Take that, you son of a bitch."

Source: *Capone: The Life and World of Al Capone* by John Kobler (Cambridge, MA, 2003).

Variation: "Take that, you dirty son of a bitch."

Source: *The Wicked City: Chicago from Kenna to Capone* by Curt Johnson and R. Craig Sautter (New York, 1998).

Variation: "Take that, you blue-coated bastard."

Source: *The One-way Ride; the Red Trail of Chicago Gangland from Prohibition to Jake Lingle* by Walter Noble Burns (Garden City, NY, 1931).

George III, King of Great Britain and Ireland

(1738-1820) British monarch. Grandson and successor of George II. Married Charlotte Sophia of Mecklenburg-Strelitz. Had 15 children. Reigned from 1760 to 1820. Lost the American colonies during the American Revolution. Eyesight began to fail around 1805. Became too unstable to rule in 1811. Son George acted as prince regent. Died in Windsor Castle at age 81. Play and movie *The Madness of King George* detail his battle with a condition modern medical science has identified as porphyria, a metabolic imbalance.

Last Words: "Do not wet my lips but when I open my mouth.—I thank you. It does me good."

Source: *Our Tempestuous Day: A History of Regency England* by Carolly Erickson (New York, 1986).

George IV, King of Great Britain and Ireland

(1762-1830) British monarch. Son of George III. King of Hanover. Became reclusive and delusional toward the end of his life. Died childless at age 67 at Windsor Palace, London. His brother succeeded him as William IV.

Different Last Words:

(1) "Good God, what do I feel? This must be death!" Exclaimed as he put his hand to his chest after a blood vessel burst in his stomach. He died a few minutes later.

Source: *Journal of Mrs. Arbuthnot,* Vol. II, cited in *The Oxford Book of Royal Anecdotes,* ed. by Elizabeth Longford (Oxford, England, 1991).

(2) "Watty, what is this? It is death, my boy. They have deceived me." Spoken to his physician Sir Wathen Waller.

Sources: *Life of George* IV by Percy Fitzgerald (New York, 1881); *A Portion of the Journal Kept by Thomas Raikes, Esq., from 1831 to 1847* by Thomas Raikes (London, 1856-1857).

George V, King of Great Britain and Northern Ireland and Emperor of India

(1865-1936) British monarch. Duke of York. Son of Edward VII. Grandfather of Queen Elizabeth II. Known as the Sailor King. Died at age 70 in Sandringham House, Norfolk.

Different Last Words:

(1) "How is the Empire?" Official Last Words reported to the nation the day after he died.

Source: Radio tribute by Prime Minister Stanley Baldwin. Also reported in *The* [London] *Times.*

(2) "God damn you." Lord Dawson, his physician, recorded in his journal that when he gave the king a small dose of morphine, the king replied with those words.

Sources: *Columbia World of Quotations* (New York, 1996); "1936 Secret is Out: Doctor Sped George V's Death" by Joseph Lelyveld (*New York Times,* November 28, 1986).

(3) "Bugger Bognor!" His doctor tried to cheer him up by saying: "Your Majesty, you will soon be at Bognor again." George replied: "Bugger Bognor" [an obscenity] just before he died. The King's Librarian Sir Owen Morshead gave a different version: A group of residents from Bognor went to see the king to request that their town be renamed Bognor Regis. They waited while the king's private secretary consulted with him in another room. George replied "Bugger Bognor." But the secretary told them George would be pleased to grant their request.

Source: *Kings, Queens And Courtiers: Intimate por-*

traits of The Royal House of Windsor From Its Foundation to The Present Day by Kenneth Rose (London, 1989), cited in *The Oxford Book of Royal Anecdotes,* ed. by Elizabeth Longford (Oxford, England, 1991).

(4) "Gentlemen, I am sorry for keeping you waiting like this. I am unable to concentrate."

Source: *King George the Fifth: His Life and Reign* by Harold Nicolson (New York, 1953). The official biography of George V.

George VI, King of Great Britain, Ireland, British Dominions, Emperor of India

(1895-1952) British monarch. Son of George V. Succeeded to the throne when his brother Edward VIII abdicated in 1936. Last emperor of India. Last King of Ireland. Ruled during World War II. Father of Queen Elizabeth II. Had lung cancer. Died at age 56 in his sleep at Sandringham House, Norfolk.

Last Words: "I'll see you in the morning."

Source: *Royal Feud: The Dark Side of the Love Story of the Century* by Michael Thornton (New York, 1985).

George I, King of the Hellenes

(1845-1913) Greek monarch. As a 17-years-old Danish prince, he was chosen by the Greek National Assembly to be king of Hellenes (Greece) after King Otto was deposed. His nomination was supported by Britain, France and Russia. His 50-year reign ended when he was shot in the back and killed by Alexandros Schinas while walking in Salonika. Schinas, thought to be insane, committed suicide while in custody. George I was succeeded by his son Constantine I.

Last Words: "Tomorrow I am to pay a formal visit to the dreadnought Goeben, the German battleship that is to honor a Greek king here in Salonika. That fills me with happiness and contentment."

Source: "King George of Greece Shot Dead. Bullet Fired by Crazed Man Enters Heart—Attacked from Behind as He Walks in Streets of Salonika. Constantine Rules. Slaying Shocks London; Queen Mother, Sister of Victim, Prostrated. All Europe Mourns Loss" (*Chicago Tribune,* March 19, 1913).

George II, King of the Hellenes

(1890-1947) Greek monarch. Son of Constantine I. Governor of Crete. Prince of Denmark. Duke of Sparta. Succeeded to throne in 1922 but was forced to step down by a military junta in 1923. Restored to power by a plebiscite in 1935. Fled Greece in 1941 during World War II. Returned in 1946. Died suddenly at age 56 in Athens after a heart attack. Succeeded by his brother Paul I.

Last Words: "Get me a glass of water." Spoken to a servant.

Source: *A Measure of Understanding* by Queen Frederica (New York, 1971). Frederica was married to King Paul I, who succeeded George II and reigned from 1947 to 1964.

George, Henry

(1839-1897) American economist, reformer, social philosopher, writer. Grandfather of choreographer Agnes de Mille. Developed basis for single tax theory. Notable work: *Progress and Poverty*. Ran for mayor of New York in 1886 and lost. Ran again in 1897 but became ill during the campaign. Died at age 58 in New York City.

Last Words: "Yes, yes, yes."

Source: *The Life of Henry George* by Henry George Jr. (New York, 1924).

Gérard, Baltazar or Balthasar

(1557-1584) Assassin. Killed William I of Orange (William the Silent). Admirer of Philip II, King of Netherlands and of Spain. When Philip offered a reward to the person who would kill William, Gerard took him up on the offer. After the murder, he was caught, tried, brutally tortured and executed.

Last Words: "Like David, I have slain Goliath of Gath."

Source: *History of the United Netherlands 1584-1609* by John Lothrop Motley (New York, 1861-1868).

Gershwin, George

(1898-1937) American musician, pianist, composer of popular and serious music. Notable scores for musical comedies: *Funny Face; Girl Crazy; Lady Be Good; Of Thee I Sing* (awarded Pulitzer Prize); *Strike Up the Band*. Other notable works: *Porgy and Bess* (opera); *Concerto in F; Rhapsody in Blue* (piano and orchestra); *Jazz Piano Preludes*. Brother Ira Gershwin wrote the lyrics for many of his musical comedies. George died of a brain tumor at age 38 in Los Angeles, California.

Last Words: "Astaire." Whispered to Ira in the hospital just before he lost consciousness. The last musical score Gershwin worked on was for the movie *A Damsel in Distress*, starring dancer/actor Fred Astaire.

Source: *The Poets of Tin Pan Alley: A History of America's Great Lyricists* by Philip Furia (New York, 1990).

Gerson, Jean Charlier de

(1362-1428) French theologian. Original surname Charlier. Chancellor of University of Paris and canon of Notre Dame. Tried to bring about church reforms. Wanted to resolve the Great Schism (three rival claims to the papacy). Died at age 65 in Lyons.

Different Last Words:

(1) "My God, my creator, have mercy on Thy poor servant, Jean Gerson."

Source: *Jean Gerson* by A.L. Masson (Lyons, France, 1894).

(2) "Now, O God, Thou dost let Thy servant depart in peace! The soul that is accompanied to eternity by the prayers of three hundred children may advance with humble hope into the presence of their Father and their God." His response when he realized the children for whom he had specially cared were praying for him.

Source: *Book of Catholic Quotations Compiled from Approved Sources Ancient, Medieval and Modern*, ed. by John Chapin (New York, 1956).

Gertrude of Delft, Saint

(d. 1358) Dutch servant-girl, Béguine, holy woman, mystic, stigmatic. Also known as Gertrude Van Der Oosten. Joined Béguines sisterhood. Stigmata appeared in 1340. Died at the Almshouse in Delft.

Last Words: "I am longing to go home." Whispered as she was dying.

Source: *Butler's Lives of the Saints, Complete Edition, Edited, Revised and Supplemented*, Vol. 1, by Alban Butler, ed. by Herbert Thurston and Donald Attwater (New York, 1956).

Gertrude of Helfta, Saint

(1256-1302) German nun, holy woman, scholar, writer, mystic. Benedictine nun. Known as Gertrude the Great. Wrote books on theology, prayer, meditation and her mystical experience.

Last Words: "When will Thou come? My soul thirsteth for Thee, O loving Father."

Source: *The Life and Revelations of Saint Gertrude, Virgin and Abbess of the Order of St. Benedict* by Sister M. Frances Clare (Whitefish, MT, 2006).

Gezmiş, Deniz

(1947-1972) Turkish political activist. In the 1960s, he was one of the most high-profile revolutionaries active in the Republic of Turkey and a Marxist-Leninist founder of the outlawed People's Liberation Army of Turkey. Arrested for participating in a bank robbery and sentenced to death for attempting to overthrow Constitutional order.

Last Words: "Long live the People of Turkey's independence, long live the great ideology of Marxist-Leninism, long live the brotherhood of Turkish and Kurdish people, damn imperialism."

Source: *Gülünün Solduğu Akşam* by Erdal Öz (Istanbul, Turkey, 1997).

Ghiyas ud-din Khilji

(1420?-1500) Khilji Sultan of Malwa. Second sultan of Khilji dynasty. Had many wives and concubines. Died at age 80. Succeeded by elder son.

Last Words: "O Lord! I have now arrived at the age of eighty. All this time I have passed in ease and prosperity, and in a state of pleasure such as has been the lot of no monarch. This moment is my last. This moment is my last, and I pray thee not to hold my son Nasir answerable for my blood. May my death be deemed a natural death, and may my son be not held answerable for it."

Source: *The History of India, as Told by Its Own Historians. The Muhammadan Period,* Vol. VI, by Henry Miers Elliot (London, 1875).

Giacometti, Alberto

(1901-1966) Swiss-born artist, sculptor, painter, printmaker. Surrealist. Eldest son of painter Giovanni Giacometti. Studied in Geneva, Italy. Settled in Paris in 1922. Known for his stark, thin, elongated human figures. Notable works: *Head of a Man; Man Pointing* (sculptures). Died at age 64 in Chur, Switzerland.

Last Words: "À demain." (tr. "Till tomorrow.") Spoken to his wife just before he lost consciousness.

Source: *Giacometti: A Biography* by James Lord (New York, 1983).

Giangir (or Giangar, Jihanger)

(d. 1552) Turkish nobleman. Son of Suleiman the Magnificent. Suleiman murdered his other son then offered Giangir the house and possessions of his dead brother. Giangir chose to kill himself.

Last Words: "Fie on thee thou impious and wretched dog, traitor, murderer, I cannot call thee father, take the treasures, the horse and armour of Mustapha to thyself." Spoken as he killed himself with his dagger.

Source: *Book of Martyrs, Or, A History of the Lives, Sufferings and Triumphant Deaths, of the Early Christian and the Protestant Martyrs* by John Foxe and Charles Augustus Goodrich (Cincinnati, OH, 1831).

Variation: "Oh cruell and wicked doge: yea, and if I may so call my father, Oh traytor most pestilent, do thou enjoy Mustapha his treasures, his horses, furnitures, and the sayd countrey to. Is thy heart so unnaturall, cruell, and wicked, to kill a yongue man so notable as Mustapha was, so good a warriour, and so worthy a gentleman as the Ottoman house never had or shall have the like, without any respect of humanity or zeale natural? By saynct Mary I need to take heede least heareafter in like maner thou as impudently do triumph of my death, being but a crokebacke and deformed man." Spoken when Giangir learned his father had killed his brother Mustapha and given him all Mustapha's treasures, apparel, horsemen, and other possessions. When he said these words, Giangir took out his dagger and killed himself.

Source: *The Second Tome of the Palace of Pleasure,* ed. by William Painter (London, 1566?).

Gibbon, Edward

(1737-1794) English historian, politician, member of Parliament. Notable work: *The History of the Decline and Fall of the Roman Empire.* Died at age 56 in London.

Different Last Words:

(1) "Pourquoi est ce que vous me quittez?" (tr. "Why are you leaving me?") Spoken to his valet. He then asked one of his servants to stay with him. These were the last words anyone heard him speak clearly.

Source: *Memoirs of Edward Gibbon Written by Himself and a Selection from His Letters with Occasional Notes and Narrative by John Lord Sheffield* by Edward Gibbon and Henry Morley (London, 1891).

(2) "All is now lost; finally, irrecoverably lost. All is dark and doubtful."

Source: "Death and Beyond" by Rev. John Y. Ewart, D.D. (*The Hearld of Gospel Liberty,* November 21,

1918). Ewart described the quote as spoken by Gibbon "in his last hours."

Gibbons, James

(1834-1921) American prelate, writer, educator. Roman Catholic Bishop of Richmond, Virginia, Bishop of Baltimore. Created cardinal in 1886. Instrumental in establishing Catholic University in Washington, D.C.; served as first chancellor. Friend of Theodore Roosevelt and Cleveland. Died at age 86 in Baltimore.

Last Words: "I have had a good day."

Source: *Life of Cardinal Gibbons, Archbishop of Baltimore* by Allen Sinclair Will (New York, 1922).

Gibbons, Jennifer

(1963-1993) West-Indian-born British eccentric and writer. One of Britain's so-called "silent twins," elective mutes since age 8 who lived in their own world and spoke to each other in a babble-like language only they understood. They were institutionalized at Broadmoor Hospital for 11 years after a spree of arson, drug-taking and burglary at their home in Wales. They were released at age 29. Jennifer died from a heart inflammation 12 hours after her release. June, the surviving sister, said they had determined that one of them must die to set the other free. They were prolific but secret writers. They became the subject of an opera, *Jumelle*, as well as a book and movie called *The Silent Twins*.

Last Words: "At last we're out of Broadmoor." Spoken to her sister June, just before she died.

Source: *Evil Twins: Chilling True Stories of Twins, Killing and Insanity* by John Glatt (New York, 1999).

Gibran, Kahlil or Khalil

(1883-1931) Lebanese-born American philosopher, poet, writer, artist. Family relocated from Lebanon to U.S. when he was 12. Essayist, novelist; wrote in both Arabic and English. Notable works: *The Madman; Sand and Foam; The Prophet* (series of poetic essays that became a best seller). Died at age 48 in New York City.

Last Words: "Don't be troubled. All is well."

Source: *Gibran, His Life and World* by Jean Gibran and Kahlil Gibran (New York, 1991).

Gide, André Paul Guillaume

(1869-1951) French novelist, poet, playwright, critic. Notable works: *Strait is the Gate; Isabelle; The Pastoral Symphony; The Counterfeiters*. Awarded 1947 Nobel Prize for Literature. Died at age 81 in Paris.

Last Words: "C'est bien." (tr. "It is well.")

Source: "Andre Gide: The Hazards of Immortality" by Albert J. Guerard (*The Nation*, April 21, 1951).

Gilbert, Ann Taylor

(1782-1866) English writer, poet, hymnist. Sister of poet Jane Taylor. Notable poem: "My Mother." Some of her works appeared in *Original Poems for Infant Minds* (1804). Died at age 84 in Nottingham, England.

Last Words: "That's for thank you. That's for good-night." Spoken as she gave two kisses to her daughter who was arranging her hair.

Source: *The Autobiography and Other Memorials of Mrs. Gilbert, Formerly Ann Taylor* by Ann Taylor (1782-1866), ed. by Josiah Gilbert (London, 1874). Josiah Gilbert was her son.

Gilbert, Sir Humphrey

(1539?-1583) English nobleman, soldier, navigator, member of Parliament. Half-brother of Sir Walter Raleigh. Established the first English colony in North America. Died when his ship, *Squirrel,* sank while returning home from his second voyage.

Last Words: "We are as near to Heaven by sea as by land!" Spoken to his crew as he tried to cheer them up.

Source: *Sir Humphrey Gilbert, Elizabeth's Racketeer* by Donald Barr Chidsey (New York, 1932).

Gilbert, Sir William Schwenck ("W.S.")

(1836-1911) British librettist, writer, lawyer. Collaborated with Sir Arthur Seymour Sullivan on comic operas. Notable works: *H.M.S. Pinafore; The Pirates of Penzance; The Mikado; The Yeoman of the Guards*. Knighted in 1907. Drowned at age 74 while rescuing a young woman who was drowning in a lake at his home in Harrow Weald, Middlesex, England. He suffered a heart attack during the rescue.

Last Words: "Put your hands on my shoulders and don't struggle."

Source: *W.S. Gilbert, His Life and Letters* by Sidney Dark and Rowland Grey (London, 1923).

Gilbert of Sempringham, Saint

(1083?-1187) English ecclesiastic, holy man. Founded Gilbertines, English religious order. Lived more than a century. Died in Sempringham. Canonized in 1202.

Last Words: "Tibi amodo incumbit." (tr. "Upon you the responsibility rests.") The barely audible words he spoke were final confirmation of the ministry of his son Roger of Malton.

Source: *The Book of St. Gilbert* by Raymonde Foreville and Gillian Keir (Oxford, England, 1987).

Gilder, Richard Watson

(1844-1909) American editor, poet. Co-founded *Newark Register.* Editor of *Hours at Home.* Editor of *Scribner's.* Editor of *Century Magazine.* Worked for civil service reform and international copyright protection. Died at age 65 in New York City.

Last Words (written): "He wrote some of his sagest and loveliest things in the last days— there seems to have been an otherworld light on these latest utterances. You see him standing serene in the afterglow, awaiting in tranquility the natural end." Written about Tennyson.

Source: *Letters of Richard Watson Gilder,* ed. by Rosamond Gilder (Boston, 1916). The editor was his daughter.

Gilfillan, George

(1813-1878) Scottish clergyman, writer. Presbyterian. Friend of DeQuincey, Carlyle. Notable work: *The Bards of the Bible.* Died at age 65.

Last Words: "I am dying, doctor? The will of the Lord be done. Yes, I believe in God, in Christ."

Source: *Letters and Journals, with Memoir* by Robert A. Watson and Elizabeth S. Watson (London, 1892).

Gilman, Charlotte Perkins

(1860-1935) American writer, social activist, lecturer. Notable works: *Women and Economics; Concerning Children.* Advocated right to choose when to die. Had incurable breast cancer. As death neared, she chose to take an overdose of chloroform. Committed suicide at age 75 in Pasadena, California.

Last Words (written): "When all usefulness is over, when one is assured of unavoidable and imminent death, it is the simplest of human rights to choose a quick and easy death in place of a slow and horrible one. I have preferred chloroform to cancer." Suicide note.

Sources: *To Herland and Beyond: The Life and Work of Charlotte Perkins Gilman* by Ann J. Lane (New York, 1990); *Ain't Nobody's Business if You Do: The Absurdity of Consensual Crimes in Our Free Country* by Peter McWilliams (Los Angeles, 1996).

Gilmore, Gary Mark

(1940-1977) American convicted murderer. Executed by firing squad in Salt Lake City, Utah, at age 36. First person legally executed in U.S. after the death penalty was reinstated in 1976. Norman Mailer's book *The Executioner's Song,* depicting events around Gilmore's execution, won the 1979 Pulitzer Prize.

Last Words: "Let's do it."

Source: "Today…Gilmore Has Quiet" by William Greider (*Washington Post,* January 18, 1977).

Ginsberg, Allen

(1926-1997) American writer, poet, politician, activist. Proponent of gay rights, free speech. Part of the Beat Generation. Notable works: *Howl; Kaddish* (poems). Died at age 70 in New York City.

Last Words: "Oh, yes." His response when asked whether he would sleep.

Source: *Screaming with Joy: The Life of Allen Ginsberg* by Graham Caveney (New York, 1999).

Giordano, Luca

(1634-1705) Italian artist, printmaker, painter. Notable works: Corsini Chapel (Florence), frescoes in the Escorial and cathedral (Toledo). Court painter in Spain. Died at age 70 in Naples.

Last Words: "O Napoli, sospiro mio!" (tr. "O Naples, my heart's love!")

Source: *Encyclopedia Britannica,* 11th ed. (New York, 1910-1911).

Gipp, George

(1895-1920) American collegiate football player who led Notre Dame to unbeaten seasons in 1919 and 1920. Died at age 25 of pneumonia.

Last Words (doubtful): "Some time, Rock, when the team's up against it, when things are wrong and the breaks are beating the boys—tell them to go in there with all they've got and win just one for the Gipper."

Spoken on his deathbed to Notre Dame coach Knute Rockne.

Source: Knute Rockne, "Gipp the Great" (*Collier's*, November 22, 1930).

George Gipp did not refer to himself as "the Gipper." And he did not make a deathbed plea to coach Knute Rockne. Also, there is no record of Gipp saying these Last Words. The "win one for the Gipper" speech was made by Rockne in 1928 when he was having a bad season. Notre Dame was playing Army and Rockne wanted to win. At half-time, he mentioned Gipp and his deathbed words. Notre Dame won the game by a score of 12 to 6. Two years later, his speech appeared in Rockne's autobiography.

Sources: *Shake Down the Thunder: The Creation of Notre Dame Football.* by Murray Sperber (New York, 1993); "Book Steals Irish Thunder" by Bob Harig (*St. Petersburg Times*, November 12, 1993).

Girard, Catelin

(d. c. 1500) French martyr. Executed at Revel, France. While standing at the stake, he asked his executioner for a stone. The executioner hesitated, but Girard convinced him he would not throw it at anyone.

Last Words: "When it is in the power of a man to eat and digest this solid stone, the religion for which I am about to suffer shall have an end, and not before." He threw the stone on the ground and was executed.

Source: *Book of Martyrs, Or, A History of the Lives, Sufferings and Triumphant Deaths, of the Early Christian and the Protestant Martyrs* by John Foxe, Charles Augustus Goodrich (Cincinnati, OH, 1831).

Girard, Stephen

(1750-1831) French-born American banker, merchant, philanthropist. Moved to U.S. in his 20s. Opened a bank in Philadelphia to take over the business of the Bank of the U.S. Helped U.S. government finance the War of 1812. Bequeathed funds for Girard College where poor white male orphans could be trained in the arts and trades. Contracted influenza that developed into pneumonia. Died at age 81 in Philadelphia.

Last Words: "How violent is this disorder! How very extraordinary it is!" Spoken when he rallied from a semiconscious state a short time before he died.

Source: *The Life and Character of Stephen Girard, Mariner and Merchant. With an Appendix, Descriptive*

of Girard College by Henry Atlee Ingram (Philadelphia, 1886).

Gissing, George Robert

(1857-1903) English writer, novelist. Wrote realistically about the middle class and the effect of poverty in late Victorian England. Notable works: *Demos; New Grub Street; Born in Exile.* Died at age 46 in Saint Jean-Pied-du-Port, France.

Last Words: "Patience, patience. God's will be done."

Source: *Letters of George Gissing to Members of His Family,* ed. by Algernon and Ellen Gissing (London, 1927). Algernon and Ellen Gissing were two of his four siblings.

Giustiniani, Laurence, Saint
(Lawrence Justinian)

(1381-1456) Venetian prelate, holy man. Bishop of Castello. Bishop of Venice. Canonized in 1690.

Last Words: "My Lord lay not on feathers, but on the hard wood." Spoken to his caregiver who tried to give him a featherbed while he was dying. He was restless until he was placed on straw. Before he died he said: "I have ever had this day before my eyes. Thou knowest, Lord, when I consider my life, it is rather a confusion than life. Yet I know Thy voice, not that of others. Bring me back, Lord, to Thy fold. I ask but for crumbs from Thy most sweet Table. Enough for me, and ah! more than enough, if Thou deny me not a place under the feet of the lowest of Thine Elect."

Source: *Sanctorale Catholicum; or Book of Saints: With Notes Critical, Exegetical and Historical* by Robert Owen (London, 1880).

Gladstone, William Ewart

(1809-1898) British statesman, writer. Member of Parliament more than six decades. Chancellor of the exchequer. Prime minister four times between 1868 and 1894. Leader of liberal reform movement. Died at age 88 of cancer at his home near Chester.

Different Last Words:

(1) "Amen."

Source: *William Ewart Gladstone the Man and His Work, A Biographical Study* by Frank Wakely Gunsaulus (Chicago, 1898).

(2) "God bless you. God bless you. May a good and silver light shine down upon your

path. I am quite comfortable, quite comfortable. I am only waiting, only waiting, but it is a long time, the end. Kindness, kindness, nothing but kindness on every side." Spoken to his daughter.

Source: *The Oak and the Ivy* by Joyce Marlow (Garden City, NY, 1977).

Glass, Jimmy L.

(1962?-1987) American murderer. Convicted of killing a couple in their home on Christmas Day. His case is notable in that he petitioned the U.S. Supreme Court claiming execution by electrocution is cruel and unusual punishment and a violation of the Eighth and Fourteenth Amendments to the U.S. Constitution. The Court ruled 5 to 4 that electrocution was an acceptable form of execution. Glass was executed by electric chair in Louisiana at age 25.

Last Words: "I'd rather be fishing." Spoken while he was sitting in the electric chair waiting to die.

Source: "The Poet of Death Row" by Helen Prejean (*St. Petersburg Times,* May 15, 1988).

Glatman, Harvey Murray

(1928-1959) American rapist, murderer. Killed three women. Fourth victim was rescued by a California highway patrolman as Glatman was about to kill her. Executed at age 31 in the gas chamber at San Quentin. Refused to cooperate with his lawyers in seeking appeals.

Last Words: "It's better this way. I knew this is the way it would be."

Source: *Bloodletters and Badmen: A Narrative Encyclopedia of American Criminals from the Pilgrims to the Present* by Jay Robert Nash (New York, 1995).

Glinka, Mikhail Ivanovich

(1804-1857) Russian musician, composer. Had profound effect on Russian music. Regarded by some as the founder of Russian symphonic music. Notable works: *A Life for the Tsar; Ruslan and Ludmilla* (operas); *Kamarinskaya* (orchestral fantasia). Had a seizure after attending a concert in Berlin, Germany, where part of *A Life for the Tsar* had been performed. Died at age 52 a short time later.

Last Words: "It is nonsense. I do not believe in eternity."

Source: *Glinka's Life in Music: A Chronicle* by Aleksandra Anatol'evna Orlova (Ann Arbor, MI, 1988).

Glossbrenner, Jacob John

(1812-1887) American prelate. Known familiarly as Brother Gloss by adults and Uncle Gloss by children. Bishop of The Church of the United Brethren in Christ. Among the earliest United Brethren ministers to give all their time to the ministry. Became bishop emeritus in 1885. Died at age 74 in Churchville, Virginia.

Last Words: "My Savior." Whispered on his deathbed.

Source: *Dying Testimonies of Saved and Unsaved: Gathered from Authentic Sources* by Solomon Benjamin Shaw (Chicago, 1898).

Glover, Robert

(d. 1555) English martyr. Embraced Protestant tenets along with brothers William and John. Taken from a sick bed, imprisoned in a dungeon then executed by order of the Bishop of Lichfield. Burned at the stake in Coventry. His two brothers escaped.

Last Words: "Austin, he is come. He is come." Spoken to his friend Augustine Bernher on his way to be executed. Earlier, Glover had entrusted the care of his wife and children to him.

Source: *Ecclesiastical Memorials Relating Chiefly to Religion and the Reformation of It, and the Emergencies of the Church of England, under King Henry VIII, King Edward VI and Queen Mary. With Large Appendixes Containing Original Papers, Records, &c.* (Oxford, England, 1822).

Goar, Saint (Goar of Aquitaine)

(d. c. 575) French-born holy man. Also known as Goar of Aquitaine. Became a hermit and lived near the town of Oberwesel on the Rhine. Was offered archbishopric of Treves but declined it.

Last Words: "Here shall my Saviour be known in all the simplicity of his doctrines. Ah! would that I might witness it; but I have seen those things in a vision. But I faint! I am weary! My earthly journey is finished! Receive my blessing. Go! and be kind to one another."

Source: *Christian Hermits or the Lives of Several Distinguished Solitaries from the Earliest Ages of the Christian Church until the Eighth Century, with Extracts, both in Prose and Verse, from Their Literary Remains* by Robert Blakey (London, 1845).

Godet, Frédéric Louis

(1812-1900) Swiss theologian, educator. Protestant. Tutor to Crown Prince Frederick William who became King Frederick William III of Prussia. Godet was one of the founders of the Evangelical Church of Neuchâtel. Professor of theology on its faculty. Died at age 88 in Neuchâtel.

Last Words: "I have carried you in my heart all my life, and I hope it will still be permitted to do the same up there." Spoken to his family.

Source: *Frédéric Godet (1812-1900) D'apres sa correspondance et d'autres documents inedits* by Philippe Godet (Neuchâtel, Switzerland, 1913). The author was his son.

Godolphin, Sidney

(1610-1643) English military officer, poet. Royalist. Member of Parliament. Friend of Lord Clarendon. Volunteered to fight in English Civil War. Killed at age 32 in a skirmish at Clagford, Devon.

Last Words: "Oh God, I am hurt." Spoken as he was shot by a musket. He fell from his horse and died.

Source: *The Life of Edward, Earl of Clarendon* by Himself (Oxford, England, 1759).

Godwin, Earl of Wessex

(1000?-1053) English nobleman. Earl of the West Saxons. Father of Harold II and Edith of Wessex who married Edward the Confessor. Had role in placing Edward the Confessor on the throne.

Last Words: "So might I safely swallow this morsel of bread, as I am guiltless of the deed." Spoken after he was accused by Edward the Confessor of murdering his brother.

Source: *Book of Martyrs and the Acts and Monuments of the Church* by John Fox (or Foxe). First published 1563, ed. by John Cumming (London, 1851).

Godwin, Frances Imlay ("Fanny")

(1794-1816) English woman. Illegitimate daughter of Mary Wollstonecraft and Gilbert Imlay. Elder sister of Mary Shelley. Committed suicide at age 22 by an overdose of laudanum at an inn in Swansea.

Last Words (written): "I have long determined that the best thing I could do was to put an end to the existence of a being whose birth was unfortunate, and whose life has only been a series of pains to those persons who have hurt their health in endeavoring to promote her welfare. Perhaps to hear of my death may give you pain, but you will soon have the blessing of forgetting that such a creature ever existed." Suicide note.

Source: *Shelley, His Life and Work* by Walter E. Peck (Boston, 1927).

Godwin, Mary Wollstonecraft

(1759-1797) English writer, feminist. Notable work: *Vindication of the Rights of Woman*. Mother of Mary Shelley who wrote the gothic novel *Frankenstein*. Died at age 38 of puerperal sepsis, shortly after the birth of her daughter Mary.

Different Last Words:

(1) "He is the kindest, best man in the world." Spoken about her husband, William Godwin.

Source: *Mary Wollstonecraft: A Critical Biography* by Ralph M. Wardle (Lawrence, KS, 1951).

(2) "I know what you are thinking of." Spoken to her husband. He needed instruction on the care of their children, but she was too weak to discuss it.

Source: *Mary Wollstonecraft: A Revolutionary Life* by Janet M. Todd (New York, 2000).

Godwin, William

(1756-1836) English philosopher, writer, novelist. Was a clergyman as a young man but had religious doubts; left the church. His wife Mary Wollstonecraft died after the birth of their only child Mary. Godwin was a friend of Coleridge, Thomas Paine, Lamb, Shelley. Notable work: *Enquiry Concerning Political Justice*. Died at age 80 in London.

Last Words (written): "Cough, snow." Written in his diary.

Source: *William Godwin: His Friends and Contemporaries* by C. Kegan Paul (London, 1876).

Goebbels, Joseph Paul

(1897-1945) German military officer, politician. Nazi leader. Minister of propaganda. Remained with Hitler to the end in a Berlin bunker. Committed suicide with his family as World War II in Europe ended.

Last Words: "This is the worst treachery of all. The generals have betrayed the Fuehrer. Everything is lost. I shall die, together with my wife and children. You will burn our bodies, can you do that?" Spoken to his

adjutant S.S. Hauptsturmfuehrer Guenther Schwaegermann.
Source: *The Rise and Fall of the Third Reich: A History of Nazi Germany* by William L. Shirer (New York, 1959).
Variation: "Everything is over. My wife and I will commit suicide. You will burn our bodies. Can you do that?—Here is a present for you." Spoken to his adjunct Guenther Schwaegermann to whom Goebbels handed a picture of Hitler.
Source: *Joseph Goebbels: A Biography* by Curt Riess (New York, 1948).

Goebbels, Madga

(1901-1945) German matron. Wife of Joseph Goebbels, German Nazi minister of propaganda. Suicide with husband and children rather than surrender. Remained with Hitler to the end in a Berlin bunker.
Last Words: "You see, we shall die an honorable death. If you should ever see Harald again, give him our best and tell him we died an honorable death." Spoken to S.S. Hauptsturmfuehrer Guenther Schwaegermann. Harald, her son by her first marriage, was a prisoner of war.
Source: *Joseph Goebbels: A Biography* by Curt Riess (New York, 1948).

Goebel, William

(1856-1900) American politician, businessman, lawyer. Kentucky Senate leader. Governor of Kentucky for three days. Shot by an assassin just after taking office. Died several hours later at age 44.
Last Words: "Tell my friends to be brave and fearless and loyal to the great common people."
Source: His Last Words are inscribed on the Gov. William Goebel Monument (sculpture) in Frankfort, Kentucky.

Goering, Hermann Wilhelm

(1893-1946) German politician, military officer. Nazi leader. Commander of Luftwaffe. Second in command of Third Reich during World War II. Tried for war crimes and crimes against humanity in Nuremberg, Germany. Sentenced to die by hanging. Committed suicide at age 53 by taking poison concealed in a capsule shortly before his scheduled execution.

Last Words: "Gute nacht." (tr. "Good night.")
Source: *Göring* by David Irving (New York, 1989).

Goethals, George Washington

(1858-1928) American civil engineer, military officer, politician. Chief engineer during Panama Canal construction. Promoted to major general. Governor of Canal Zone. Quartermaster general during World War I. Later worked as a consulting engineer. Died at age 69 in New York City. Goethals Bridge, Staten Island, was named for him.
Last Words: "Let me stay here. If I stay here, I'll be much nearer to West Point."
Source: *Goethals: Genius of the Panama Canal* by Joseph B. Bishop and Farnham Bishop (New York, 1930).

Goethe, Johann Wolfgang von

(1749-1832) German poet, playwright, novelist, natural philosopher. Regarded as the greatest German poet. Started Sturm und Drang literary movement. Notable works: *Faust; Egmont; The Sorrows of Young Werther*. Died at age 82 in Weimar, Germany.
Different Last Words:
(1) "Meir licht!" (tr. "More light!")
Source: *The Story of Goethe's Life* by George H. Lewes (Boston, 1872).
Variation: "Macht doch den Fensterladen im Schlafgemach auf, damit mehr Licht herein komme." (tr. "Open the shutters so that more light can come in.") Friedrich von Muller was at Goethe's deathbed. In describing Goethe's death later, he said Goethe made this request a half hour before he died. They were his last audible words.
Source: *Goethe: The Story of a Man: Being the Life of Johann Wolfgang Goethe as Told in His Own Words and the Words of His Contemporaries,* ed. by Ludwig Lewisohn (New York, 1949).
(2) "Come my little one and give me your hand." Spoken to his daughter Ottile.
Source: *Goethe's Tod* by Carl Schüddekopf (Leipzig, Germany, 1907).

Goffe, Goff or Gough, Thomas

(1591-1629) English writer, dramatist. Notable works: *Orestes; The Courageous Turk*.
Last Words: "Oracle, oracle, Thomas Thimble." Thomas Thimble, a friend at Oxford, had warned Goffe not to marry a certain woman because she would break his heart.

He did marry her and she made his life miserable. He died soon after the wedding.

Source: *Brief Lives* by John Aubrey, ed. by Oliver Lawson Dick (London, 1949).

Gogol, Nikolai Vasilyevich

(1809-1852) Russian writer, novelist, playwright, mystic. Notable works: *Dead Souls; Taras Bulba*. Practiced fanatical mysticism that required excessive fasting. It ruined his health and hastened his death. Died at age 42 in Moscow.

Different Last Words:

(1) "And I shall laugh a bitter laugh." Quote from the Old Testament.

Source: *Nicolas Gogol, écrivain et moraliste* by Raína Tyrnéva (Aix, France, 1901).

(2) "Go on! Rise up! Charge, charge the mill." Spoken while delirious.

Source: *Divided Soul: The Life of Gogol* by Henri Troyat (Garden City, NY, 1973).

(3) "Ah! if people knew how pleasant it was to die, they would not fear death."

Source: "Literary Miscellanies" in *Eclectic Magazine,* ed. by Walter Hilliard Bidwell and John Holms Agnew (London, 1852).

Goldberger, Joseph

(1874-1929) Austro-Hungarian-born American physician, medical researcher, epidemiologist. Worked with U.S. Public Health Service, specializing in preventive medicine. Discovered cause and remedy for pellagra. Died at age 54 of cancer in Washington, D.C.

Last Words: "Mary, don't leave me; you have always been my rock, my strength. Mary, we must have patience." Spoken to his wife.

Source: *Trail to Light: A Biography of Joseph Goldberger* by R.P. Parsons (Indianapolis, IN, 1943).

Goldsborough, Fitzhugh Coyle

(1880-1911) American murderer. When David Graham Phillips's novel *The Fashionable Adventures of Joshua Craig* was published, Goldsborough mistakenly believed one of the characters—a selfish, egocentric woman—was based on his sister and that his sister had been intentionally maligned by Phillips. Goldsborough shot and killed the writer on a New York City sidewalk as he shouted "Here you go." He then turned the gun on himself.

Last Words: "Here I go!" Shouted as he placed a gun to his head and killed himself.

Source: *The Great Pictorial History of World Crime* by Jay Robert Nash (Wilmette, IL, 2004).

Goldsby, Crawford ("Cherokee Bill")

(1876-1896) Oklahoma criminal. Hanged at age 20 for murder at Fort Smith.

Last Words: "I came here to die, not to make a speech." Spoken to one of the guards at the gallows before his execution when asked if he had any Last Words. He then called "Goodbye" to the crowd, and turned to one of the guards and said: "The quicker this thing is over, the better."

Sources: "Cherokee Bill" by Drew Gomber, Lincoln Heritage Trust Historian (*Tombstone Epitaph*, March 2002).

Variation: "Goodbye, all you chums down that way."

Source: *Marauders of the Indian Nations: The Bill Cook Gang and Cherokee Bill* by Glenn Shirley (Stillwater, OK, 1994).

Goldsmith, Oliver

(1728-1774) Irish-born English writer, poet, playwright, novelist, biographer, historian. Studied medicine but failed at the practice of it. Often plagued with debt, spending more than he earned. Friend of Dr. Samuel Johnson. Notable works: *The Vicar of Wakefield; She Stoops to Conquer; The Good Natur'd Man*. Died at age 45 of a chronic kidney ailment in London.

Last Words. "No, it is not." His response to a question about whether his mind was at ease.

Source: *Oliver Goldsmith* by Stephen Gwynn (New York, 1935).

Gompers, Samuel

(1850-1924) British-born American labor leader. Founder and first president of American Federation of Labor. Headed War Advisory Commission Council of National Defense during World War I. Died at age 74 in San Antonio, Texas.

Last Words: "God bless our American institutions. May they grow better day by day."

Source: *Samuel Gompers—Champion of the Toiling Masses* by Rowland Hill Harvey (Stanford, CA, 1935).

Gonne, Maud

(1866-1953) English-born Irish social and political activist, nationalist. Heroine in many of William Butler Yeats's plays and lyrics. Married John MacBride, who was later executed. Jailed in 1918 for her role in the Irish anti-conscription movement. Jailed again in 1923 by the Irish Free State government. Went on a hunger strike with other women. Wrote her autobiography in 1938. Died at age 86 in Roebuck, Clonskeagh. Her son Sean MacBride, a founder of Amnesty International, won the Nobel Peace Prize in 1974.

Last Words: "I feel an ineffable joy."

Source: *Lucky Eyes and a High Heart: The Life of Maud Gonne* by Nancy Cardozo (Indianapolis, IN, 1978).

Gooch, Arthur

(1900?-1936) American kidnapper, thief, larcenist. First person to be executed for violation of the Lindbergh kidnapping law. Died at age 36 at the Oklahoma State Penitentiary in McAlester. His execution took 15 minutes. Hangman's inexperience was blamed. The noose around Gooch's neck slipped. He choked to death rather than die of a broken neck. His execution was the first hanging in Oklahoma since 1911. The law was later changed to execute condemned prisoners by electrocution.

Last Words: "It's kind of funny—dying. I think I know what it will be like. I'll be standing there, and all of a sudden everything will be black, then there'll be a light again. There's got to be a light again—there's got to be."

Source: *Death Watch: A Death Penalty Anthology* by Lane Nelson and Burk Foster (Upper Saddle River, NJ, 2001).

Gooch, Mary

(1800?-1823) English woman. Suicide victim. Involved in a double suicide pact with her paramour John Spring. They both took a large dose of laudanum. Spring's dose was not sufficient to kill him and he recovered. He was with her when she died. Gooch was one of the last people in England to be buried beneath a crossroad—the traditional burial ground for suicides. The practice was abolished by Parliament in 1823.

Last Words: "My dear, pray give me that blue muslin handkerchief, that I may have it in my hand when I die. Pray don't you take

anything; but let me die, and you will get over." Her response when Spring told her he would buy more laudanum to take so that he would die with her. After she spoke these words, she placed her head on his shoulder and died almost immediately.

Source: *The Anatomy of Suicide* by Forbes Winslow (London, 1840).

Good, John Mason

(1764-1827) English physician, writer. Translator who spoke many languages. Notable work: *A History of Medicine* (helped bring about much-needed reforms in the pharmaceutical profession). Died at age 62 in Shepperton, Middlesex, England.

Last Words: "Which taketh away the sins of the world."

Source: *Memoir of John Mason Good* by Olinthus Gregory (Boston, 1829).

Good, Sarah

(1653-1692) American witchcraft victim. One of the first three people accused of witchcraft in Salem, Massachusetts. She was the first woman hanged for witchcraft at the Salem trials.

Last Words: "You are a liar! I am no more a witch than you are a wizard and if you take away my life, God will give you blood to drink." Spoken at her execution to Rev. Nicholas Noyes, who urged her to confess that she was a witch.

Source: *The Witchcraft Delusion in New England: Its Rise, Progress and Termination, as Exhibited by Dr. Cotton Mather, in The Wonders of the Invisible World; and by Mr. Robert Calef, in His More Wonders of the Invisible World* by Samuel Gardiner Drake, Cotton Mather and Robert Calef (Roxbury, MA, 1866).

Goodman, Benjamin David ("Benny")

(1909-1986) American musician, jazz and classical clarinetist, band leader. Known as the King of Swing, The Professor, Patriarch of the Clarinet and Swing's Senior Statesman. Credited with integrating jazz bands. Earlier career was the basis for the 1955 movie *The Benny Goodman Story*. He played in a club in Manhattan the night before he died. Died at age 77, while practicing a Brahms sonata in his New York City apartment.

Last Words: "Don't worry. It's all right." Spoken to friend Carol Phillips who found him slumped over a couch. Moments later he was dead.

Source: "Last Notes From Brahms" (*Bergen* [NJ] *Record*, June 15, 1986).

Gordon, Adoniram Judson ("A.J.")

(1836-1895) American clergyman, writer, hymnist. Boston minister who influenced Northern Baptists and the emerging Fundamentalist movement. Chairman of American Baptist Missionary Union committee. President of Baptist Pastors' Conference for Bible Study. Founded Boston Missionary Training School (now Gordon College). Composed more than 15 hymns, including "My Jesus, I Love Thee." Through his evangelical outreach, he established a Jewish ministry, Chinese church, ministry among African-Americans, rescue mission for women, and an industrial temporary home for recovering alcoholics. Died at age 58 in Boston.

Last Words: "Maria, pray." Spoken to a nurse at his deathbed. His response to a question asked by one of the physicians: "Have you a good word for us tonight?" This was followed by inaudible words. His last audible utterance is often given as "Victory."

Source: *Adoniram Judson Gordon: A Biography of A. J. Gordon with Letters and Illustrative Extracts Drawn from Unpublished or Uncollected Sermons & Addresses* by Ernest Barron Gordon D.D. (London, 1897). The author was the son of A.J. Gordon.

Gordon, Charles George

(1833-1885) Scottish-born British military officer. General. Known as Chinese Gordon. National hero for his exploits in China and his ill-fated defense of Khartoum. Went to Sudan to help evacuate Egyptians from Khartoum. Threatened by the Mahdi and his forces. Rebels attacked the city, killing Gordon at age 51. Chinese Gordon was depicted in the movie *Khartoum* in 1966.

Last Words: "Where is the Mahdi?"

Source: *Gordon: An Intimate Portrait* by H.E. Wortham (Boston, 1933).

Gordon, Elizabeth, Duchess of

(1794-1864) English noblewoman, philanthropist. Married George Gordon, who became the 5th Duke of Gordon. Known as The Good Duchess for her charitable works. En-

dowed institutions known as Gordon Schools.

Last Word: "Yes." Her response after she tried to ask for something and a companion repeated the words: "My Beloved is mine, and I am His." She then died in her sleep.

Source: *Life of Elizabeth, Last Duchess of Gordon* by Rev. A. Moody Stuart (London, 1865).

Gordon, George, see Byron, George Gordon, 6th Baron Byron ("Lord Byron").

Gordon, John, 1st Viscount of Kenmure

(1599?-1634) Scottish nobleman. Supporter of Stuart monarchy. Created Viscount of Kenmure by Charles I in 1633. Friend of preacher John Welsh in his youth, and of patron theologian Samuel Rutherford in later life. Important Presbyterian figure in Scotland. Founded town of New Galloway, near his home.

Last Words: "By no means." Spoken on his deathbed to a minister who asked him: "Will ye no sunder with Christ?"

Source: *The Scots Worthies: Containing a Brief Historical Account of the Most Eminent Noblemen, Gentlemen, Ministers, and Others, Who Testified or Suffered for the Cause of Reformation in Scotland: from the Beginning of the Sixteenth Century to the Year 1688* by John Howie (Glasgow, Scotland, 1829).

Gordon, Nathaniel

(1826-1862) American pirate, slave trader. Only American to be executed for engaging in slave trade under provisions of the Piracy Law of 1820. He loaded 897 slaves aboard his ship *Erie* at Sharks Point, Congo River, West Africa, in 1860. Captured by USS *Mohican* about 50 miles from port. Convicted and sentenced to death in New York. President Abraham Lincoln issued a stay of Gordon's execution. During this time, Gordon unsuccessfully attempted suicide, prompting authorities to move up his execution. He was hanged in 1862.

Last Words: "I did nothing wrong."

Sources: *New York Daily Tribune*, February 21, 1862; *Harper's Weekly*, March 8, 1862.

Goretti, Saint Maria

(1890-1902) Italian holy woman. Young girl who was stabbed and died in a sexually motivated attack by a 19-year-old man. She knew her attacker. Canonized in 1950.

Different Last Words:

(1) "May God forgive him. I want him in Heaven." Spoken about her killer.

Source: *St. Maria Goretti—In Garments All Red* by Rev. Godfrey Poage (Rockford, IL, 1988).

(2) "Carry me to bed! Carry me to bed, because I want to be nearer to the Madonna!"

Source: *St. Maria Goretti* by Marie Cecelia Buehrle (Milwaukee, WI, 1950).

Gorgas, William Crawford

(1854-1920) American military officer. Military physician. Brigadier general in U.S. Army. Surgeon general of U.S. Helped eradicate yellow fever mosquito, making possible construction of the Panama Canal. Died at age 65 in a London hospital. Received honorary knighthood from King George V shortly before he died.

Last Words: "Well, if this is dying, dying is very pleasant." Spoken after he received the Last Rites.

Source: *Physician to the World: The Life of General William C. Gorgas* by John M. Gibson (Durham, NC, 1950).

Gorguloff, Paul

(1895-1932) Russian assassin. Killed French President Paul Doumer at a book fair in Paris. Tried, convicted and beheaded at age 37 by guillotine in Paris.

Last Words: "Oh Holy Russia." An alternative version translates his Last Words as "Russia, my country!" However, the quotation "Oh Holy Russia" comes from his executioner's diary.

Source: *Carnets d'executions: 1885-1939* by Anatole Deibler (Paris, 2004).

Gosse, Sir Edmund William

(1849-1928) British poet, writer, biographer, translator, librarian. On the staff of the British Museum. Librarian to the House of Lords. Knighted in 1925. Recipient of French Legion of Honor. Notable work: *Father and Son* (autobiography). Died at age 78 in London.

Last Words (written): "You will think of me in this hour with sympathy and hope. There seems good reason to think I shall survive the shock. In any case I am perfectly calm and able to enjoy the love which has accompanied me through such long years and surrounds me still." Written in a letter before he had surgery.

Source: *Life and Letters of Sir Edmund Gosse* by Hon. Evan Charteris (London, 1931).

Gottschalk, Louis Moreau

(1829-1869) American musician, pianist, composer. One of the first American-born internationally famous concert pianists. Kept journals for the years 1857 to 1868 that provide valuable a first-hand account of that era in the U.S., Canada, Central and South America. Notable works: *The Banjo; Cuban Dances; Last Hope; Cakewalk*. Also wrote two symphonies and two operas. Died at age 40 of appendicitis and peritonitis in Rio de Janeiro, Brazil while on a concert tour.

Last Words: "I have traveled much, I have often been dangerously sick; but never have I found a friend as devoted as you. A father, a brother could not have done more, because your efforts are truly superhuman." Spoken on his deathbed to Dr. Severiano Martins his attending physician.

Source: *Notes of a Pianist: Louis Moreau Gottschalk* by Jeanne Behrend (New York, 1964).

Gouges, Marie-Olympe de

(1748-1793) French writer, playwright, journalist, feminist. Birth name Marie Gouze. Proponent of democracy who demanded the same rights for French women that French men were demanding for themselves. Notable work: *Declaration of the Rights of Woman and the Female Citizen* (challenged the practice of male authority and the notion of male-female inequality). Executed by guillotine for her beliefs.

Last Words: "Enfants de la Patrie, vous vengerez ma mort." (tr. "Children of the fatherland, you will avenge my death.")

Source: "Marie-Olympe de Gouges" by Gabrielle Verdier in *Dictionary of Literary Biography: Writers of the French Enlightenment* (Auburn, AL, 2005).

Gough, John B.

(1817-1886) English-born American lawyer, temperance lecturer. Delivered several thousand public talks on the evils of drink. Died in a Philadelphia church during a lecture on the dangers of alcoholism.

Last Words: "Young man, keep your record cl—." Spoken on the platform. The last word was inaudible but probably "clean."

Source: *John B. Gough: The Apostle of Cold Water* by Carlos Martyn (New York, 1893).

Gould, Glenn Herbert

(1932-1982) Canadian musician, pianist, composer. Notable recording: Bach's *Goldberg Variations* (one of the best-known classical recordings ever). Wrote and appeared in *Glenn Gould's Toronto* in 1979. Died at age 50 in Toronto, a week after suffering a massive stroke. Docudrama *32 Short Films About Glenn Gould* appeared in 1993.

Last Words: "Ray, where are you?" Spoken to a friend of Gould and his family.

Source: *Glenn Gould: A Life and Variations* by Friedrich Otto (New York, 1989).

Gounod, Charles François

(1818-1893) French musician, composer, organist. Notable works: *Faust; Romeo and Juliet* (operas); "Ave Maria" (religious song based on a Bach prelude). Died at age 75 in Saint Cloud, France.

Last Words: "Au revoir." (tr. "Goodbye.") Spoken to a friend just before he suffered a final stroke and died.

Source: *Gounod* by James Harding (London, 1973).

Gowanlock, John C.

(1857?-1885) Canadian sawmill operator. Killed at age 28 in Frog Lake Massacre, a Cree uprising in Canada. His wife Theresa was taken prisoner and kept in the camp of Cree chief Big Bear for two months. She later wrote a book describing her experience.

Last Words: "My dear wife, be brave to the end." Immediately after he spoke those words, he was shot and killed.

Source: *Two Months in the Camp of Big Bear. The Life and Adventures of Theresa Gowanlock and Theresa Delaney* (Parkdale, ON, 1885).

Grable, Elizabeth Ruth ("Betty")

(1916-1973) American actress. Screen star whose career spanned 44 years and included more than 80 movies. Gained popularity as poster pin-up girl during World War II. Died at age 56 of lung cancer in Los Angeles.

Last Words: "Marjorie isn't here." Marjorie was her older sister.

Source: *Betty Grable, the Reluctant Movie Queen* by Doug Warren (New York, 1974).

Grady, Henry Woodfin

(1851-1889) American journalist. Editor and part owner of the *Atlanta Constitution*. Prominent public speaker. Notable speech: "The New South" (delivered in 1886). Died suddenly at age 38 in Atlanta.

Last Words: "And the little children cried in the streets." He had just read a description of Jefferson Davis's funeral and repeated part of what he had read.

Source: *Spokesman of the New South* by Raymond B. Nixon (New York, 1943).

Graham, Barbara Elaine Wood

(1923-1955) American murderer. Convicted of beating an elderly woman to death in a botched robbery. Executed at age 31 in the gas chamber at San Quentin, California. Her story was told in the movie *I Want to Live!* (1958, remade 1983).

Last Words: "Good people are always so sure they're right."

Source: *Poetic Justice: Reflections on the Big House, the Death House & the American Way of Justice* by Robert Johnson (Thomaston, ME, 2003).

Graham, James, 1st Marquis and 5th Earl of Montrose

(1612-1650) Scottish nobleman, royalist leader. Known as the Great Marquis. Wanted to avenge the death of the king. Invaded Scotland in 1650 and was soon defeated. Executed at age 37 by hanging at Edinburgh Castle. Sir Walter Scott told his story in *A Legend of Montrose*.

Last Words: "May God have mercy on this afflicted kingdom."

Source: *Montrose* by Mowbray Morris (New York, 1892).

Graham, Sir James Robert George, 2nd Baronet of Netherby

(1792-1861) British politician, statesman, member of Parliament. First lord of the admiralty. Home secretary. Led Conservatives after death of Robert Peel. Graham Land, Antarctica, was named for him.

Last Words "Ah! I thought it was over then." Spoken after he had a heart spasm. Died at age 69 in Netherby, Cumberland.

Source: *Life and Letters of Sir James Graham, Second Baronet of Netherby, P.C., G.C.B., 1792-1861* by Charles Stuart Parker (London, 1907).

Graham, John of Claverhouse, 1st Viscount of Dundee

(1648-1689) Scottish nobleman, royalist,

soldier. Known as Bonnie Dundee. Descended from King Robert III. Elder son of Sir William Graham. Acquired estate of Claverhouse near Dundee, Scotland. Made Viscount Dundee by King James II. Supporter of Stuart cause and later Jacobite cause. Killed at age 41 at the Battle of Killiecrankie. Several legends surround his death; best known is that he was invulnerable to all bullets but was killed by a silver button from his own coat. The use of the epithet "Bonnie Dundee" began with Sir Walter Scott's song; the original old ballad of that name is about the town of Dundee.

Last Words: "How goes the day?" Spoken to a soldier. The man replied: "Well for King James, but I am sorry for your lordship." Graham then said: "If it goes well for him it matters the less for me."

Source: *Dictionary of National Biography, from the Earliest Times to 1900* by Sir Leslie Stephen, George Smith and Sir Sidney Lee (London, 1921-1922).

Grainger, George Percy Aldridge (Percy)

(1882-1961) Australian-born musician, pianist, composer, educator. Relocated to the United States in 1914. Dean of School of Music at New York University. Notable works: *Country Gardens; Lincolnshire Posy.* Died at age 78 in White Plains, New York. The 1999 film *Passion* was based on his life.

Last Words: "You're the only one I like." Spoken to his wife Ella, whom he married in 1928.

Source: *Percy Grainger* by John Bird (London, 1976).

Grandier, Urbain

(1580-1634) French clergyman. Roman Catholic. Assigned to parish of Sainte Croix, Loudun. Burned at the stake after being convicted of witchcraft.

Last Words: "My God, by the light I wait for you. My God forgive my enemies."

Source: *Urbain Grandier et les possédées de Loudun* by Gabriel Legué (Paris, 1884).

Grant, Cary

(1904-1986) English-born American actor. Screen star. Nominated for two Academy Awards. Received honorary Academy Award in 1970. Died at age 82 after a stroke in Davenport, Iowa, where he was scheduled

to perform his one-man show "An Evening with Cary Grant."

Last Words: "I love you Barbara. Don't worry." Spoken to his wife as he was wheeled into intensive care.

Source: *Cary Grant: A Touch of Elegance* by Warren G. Harris (Garden City, NY 1987).

Grant, Joe

(d. 1880) American gunfighter. Known as Texas Red. Killed by Billy the Kid in a saloon in Fort Sumner, New Mexico. Grant had confronted the Kid earlier and made a bet with him that he could kill a man before the Kid did. Grant then picked his target, John Chisum. The Kid told Grant his target was Jim Chisum (John's brother), the wrong person. Grant refused to believe him. Earlier, the Kid had gotten hold of Grant's gun and found three empty cartridges where Grant had used his gun but failed to reload it. The Kid spun the cylinder so that the three empties would come up the next time the gun was fired. Later, Grant fired a shot at the Kid, convinced that he had been lied to. The Kid heard the shot, turned around and shot Grant dead.

Last Words: "That's a lie." Spoken as Billy the Kid fired three shots at him.

Source: *Billy the Kid: A Short and Violent Life* by Robert M. Utley (Lincoln, NE, 1991).

Grant, Ulysses Simpson

(1822-1885) 18th President of the U.S. American military officer, politician. Birth name Hiram Ulysses Grant. General who led the Union Army in the U.S. Civil War. Wrote *Personal Memoirs of U.S. Grant* (2 vol.) during his last years while suffering from throat cancer. Samuel L. Clemens (Mark Twain) helped publish and promote the memoirs. Grant died at age 63 in Mount McGregor, New York.

Last Word: "Water." His response to his son who asked if he needed anything.

Source: *The Life of U.S. Grant* by Hamlin Garland (New York, 1898).

Granville, Augustus Bozzi

(1783-1872) Italian physician, obstetrician, writer. Practiced medicine in Greece, Portugal, Spain and Turkey. Joined British navy. Settled in England; had a practice in

London. Notable works: *Spas of Germany; Spas of England*. Died at age 88.

Last Words: "Light, all light."

Source: *Autobiography of A.B. Granville M.D. with a Brief Account of the Last Years of His Life by His Daughter*, ed. by Paulina B. Granville (London, 1874).

Grasso, Thomas J.

(1962?-1995) American murderer. Convicted of double murder. Executed at age 32 by lethal injection in Oklahoma.

Last Words: "I did not get my Spaghetti-O's; I got spaghetti. I want the press to know this."

Sources: "Grasso is Executed, Getting Death Wish Complains No Spaghetti-O's in Last Meal" (*The Record* [NJ], March 20, 1995); "Pulp Nonfiction" by Christopher Hanson (*Columbia Journalism Review*, July/ August 1995).

Grattan, Henry

(1746-1820) Irish statesman, nationalist, orator. Member of Irish and British Parliaments. Champion of Roman Catholic emancipation. Opposed the union of Ireland and Great Britain. Died at age 73 in London.

Different Last Words:

(1) "I die with a love of liberty in my heart, and this declaration in favor of my country in my head.—It will do. I should wish it to be read in the House; give my love to Plunket, he will do it." Last Words were dictated. William Conyngham Plunket was Grattan's successor in Parliament.

Source: *Memoirs of the Life and Times of the Right Hon. H. Grattan* by Henry Grattan (London, 1849). The author was his son.

(2) "I am perfectly resigned. I am surrounded by my family. I have served my country. I have reliance upon God, and am not afraid of the devil." Spoken to Crampton, the surgeon-general who saw him just before he died.

Source: *Sketches of the Irish Bar; with Essays, Literary and Political* by William Henry Curran (London, 1855).

Gray, Henry Judd

(1893-1928) American murderer. Killed Albert Snyder with the help of Snyder's wife Ruth. Gray and Snyder were tried, convicted and electrocuted at Ossining (Sing Sing) prison in New York. The crime is notable in that it created a media frenzy. The perpetrators were ordinary people who did

some stupid things the public found interesting. Known as the Dumb-Bell murder.

Last Words: "I am ready to go. I have nothing to fear."

Source: *The Lawless Decade; A Pictorial History of a Great American Transition: from the World War I Armistice and Prohibition to Repeal and the New Deal* by Paul Sann (New York, 1957).

Gray, Robert

(1809-1872) English clergyman. Anglican. First bishop of Cape Town, South Africa. The number of dioceses and educational institutions increased during his years there.

Last Words: "Well, dear fellows, I am ready when you like." His response when he learned Holy Communion the next day would be too late.

Source: *The Life of Robert Gray, Bishop of Cape Town and Metropolitan of Africa* by Henrietta Louisa Lear and Charles Norris Gray (London, 1876).

Gray, Thomas

(1716-1771) English writer, poet, educator. Spent most of his adult life at Cambridge University where he was professor of history. Notable works: "Ode on the Spring"; "Hymn to Adversity"; "An Elegy Written in a Country Church Yard" (his best known poem). Died at age 54 of gout in Cambridge.

Last Words: "Molly, I shall die!" Spoken to his niece.

Source: *The Works of Thomas Gray in Prose and Verse*, ed. by Edmund Gosse (New York, 1902).

Greble, John Trout

(1834-1861) American military officer. Union Army lieutenant. Shot at the Battle of Big Bethel, Virginia, during the first military land engagement of the U.S. Civil War. Died at age 27.

Last Words: "Sergeant! Take command. Go ahead." Spoken when he was hit by an exploding shell.

Source: *Memorial of Lieutenant John Trout Greble* by Benson J. Lossing (Philadelphia, 1870).

Greeley, Horace

(1811-1872) American journalist, newspaper editor, politician. Founder and editor of the *New York Tribune*. Often credited with coining the phrase "Go West, young man." John B. L. Soule used it first in an 1851 Indiana newspaper article. Greeley later used the expression. When he learned he was credited as the author, he set the record straight in a *New York Tribune* editorial. He ran unsuccessfully against Grant in the 1872 U.S. Presidential campaign. Depressed by attacks on his character during the campaign and the death of his wife in October 1872. Died at age 61 a month later in Pleasantville, New York. Two counties and two towns were named for him.

Different Last Words:

(1) "It is done."

Source: *A History: Greeley and the Union Colony of Colorado* by David Boyd (Greeley, CO, 1890).

(2) "I know that my Redeemer liveth." Earlier, Greeley had heard Clare Louise Kellogg sing the soprano aria "I know that my Redeemer liveth" from Handel's *Messiah*. She said his Last Words were these, whispered faintly to her. She sang the aria at his funeral.

Source: *Memoirs of an American Prima Donna* by Clare Louise Kellogg (New York, 1913).

Green, Hetty Howland Robinson

(1834-1916) American financier. Known as the Witch of Wall Street. Had a reputation for being shrewd, miserly, eccentric and antisocial. When she died at age 81 in New York City, she was the richest American woman of her era.

Last Words: "I am not worrying. I don't know what the next world is like, but I do know that a kindly light is leading me and that I shall be happy after I leave here."

Source: *Men of Wealth: The Story of Twelve Significant Fortunes from the Renaissance to the Present Day* by John T. Flynn (New York,1941).

Green, Joseph Henry

(1791-1863) British anatomist, surgeon, philosopher, educator, writer. Surgeon at St. Thomas's Hospital, London. Professor of surgery at King's College London. Had a long partnership with Samuel Taylor Coleridge and was his literary executor. Notable work: *Spiritual Philosophy Founded on the Teaching of the Late Samuel Taylor Coleridge* (1865).

Last Word: "Stopped." Spoken on his deathbed when he checked his pulse.

Source: *Spiritual Philosophy*, ed. by John Simon (London, 1865).

Greene, Henry Graham (Graham)

(1904-1991) English novelist, playwright, short-story writer, movie critic. On the staff of the London *Times*. Worked for the British foreign office. Notable works: *The Power and the Glory; Our Man in Havana; The Quiet American*. His stories have a Roman Catholic point of view. Died at age 86 in Vevey, Switzerland.

Last Words: "Will it be an interesting experience? Will I find out what lies behind the barrier? Why does it take so long to come?"

Source: *The Life of Graham Greene, Volume 3, 1956-1991* by Norman Sherry (New York, 2004).

Gregg, Maxey

(1814-1862) American military officer. Confederate provisional army colonel of the 1st South Carolina Infantry at the outbreak of the U.S. Civil War. Promoted to brigadier general in 1861. Killed a year later at age 48 at the Battle of Fredericksburg. He was one of two Southern brigadier generals killed in a battle that was viewed as a Confederate victory in terms of number of casualties.

Last Words: "Tell the Governor of South Carolina I cheerfully yield my life for the independence of my State!"

Source: *The Lost Cause: A New Southern History of the War of the Confederates* by Edward A. Pollard (New York, 1866). The term "Lost Cause" in the context of the U.S. Civil War was first used with this book. Pollard, a Virginia historian, sold the book by subscription only.

Grègoire, Henri

(1750-1831) French clergyman, statesman. Roman Catholic priest. Revolutionary leader during the French Revolution. First priest to take the oath of allegiance to the Civil Constitution of Clergy. Elected Bishop of Blois. Member of National Convention, Directory's Council of Five Hundred. Died at age 80 in Paris.

Last Words: "Monsieur Baradère, I have been tormented for eight days; I see a whole population of blacks isolated on an island which serves as their refuge. They are going to die of hunger!—I was told that some Protestants and Jews came to see me; although they are not of my church, I desire to make acknowledgments to them.—Let someone send theological books to Haiti. The poor

Haitians!—I see that my last hour is come.—Do not desert me in my last moments!" Spoken while he was delirious.

Source: *Memories de Grègoire, ancien Evoque de Blois, etc., prece de d'une notice historique sur l'auteur,* ed. by M.H. Carnot (Paris, 1857).

Gregory I, Pope, Saint

(540-604) Italian prelate, holy man. Roman Catholic pope. Known as Gregory the Great. Sent Augustine to Britain to convert Anglo-Saxons to Christianity. Tried to mitigate or end slavery. Fourth person to be named Father of the Church. Gregorian chant (plainsong choral chants) named for him. He was responsible for collecting and preserving the chants. Died at age 64. Canonized soon afterward.

Different Last Words:

(1) "I pray that the hand of Almighty God raise me from the sea of this present life and let me rest on the shores of eternal life."

Source: *The Chair of Peter* by Friedrich Gontard (New York, 1964).

(2) "How can a mind full of trouble clear up such dark sayings? The more the mind is engaged with worldly things, the less it is qualified to expound the heavenly."

Source: *The Makers of Modern Rome; in Four Books* by Mrs. Oliphant, Henry Parsons Riviere and Joseph Pennell (New York, 1895).

Gregory VII, Pope

(1020?-1085) Italian prelate. Benedictine monk. Real name Hildebrand. As Roman Catholic pope, he upheld papal authority in a dispute with Holy Roman Emperor Henry IV. Was driven from Rome by Henry. Died in exile in Salerno.

Last Words: "I have loved justice and hated iniquity; therefore I die in exile."

Source: *The History of the Christian Church: From the Birth of Christ to the Eighteenth Century, Including the Very Interesting Account of the Waldenses and Albigenses,* Vol. I, by William Jones (Philadelphia, 1832).

Gregory XII, Pope

(1327?-1417) Italian prelate. Birth name Angelo Correr. Roman Catholic pope during the Great Schism. While he was ruling, two other popes vied for authority. He was deposed by the Council of Pisa in 1409. Refused to step down. Eventually resigned at Council of Constance in 1415. Died in Recanati, Italy.

Last Words: "I have not understood the world and the world has not understood me."

Source: *The Three Popes* by Marzieh Gail (New York, 1969).

Gregory XV, Pope

(1554-1623) Italian prelate. Birth name Alessandro Ludovisi. Roman Catholic pope. Supported Emperor Ferdinand II during Thirty Years' War. Established Congregation of Propaganda. Became ill with "the stone." Died at age 69 in Rome.

Last Words: "We shall die with one consolation. Our successor may correct some errors in the administration of the Christian Republic. It will not be possible, my beloved brothers, for a successor to us to be chosen who will not be more worthy of the authority than we, and who will not better fill the exalted pontifical office." Spoken to the cardinals who were assembled around him.

Source: *The Lives and Times of the Popes* by the Chevalier Artaud De Montor (New York, 1911).

Gregory XVI, Pope

(1765-1846) Italian prelate. Birth name Bartolomeo Alberto Cappellari. Roman Catholic pope. Name as Camaldolese monk was Mauro Cappellari. Last monk to become a pope. Reigned 15 years. Died at age 80.

Last Words: "I wish to die as a monk and not as a sovereign."

Source: "The Last Moments of the Pope" in *The Living Age* by Eliakim Littell and Robert S. Littell (Boston, 1846).

Grellet, Stephen

(1773-1855) French missionary. Quaker. Son of counsel to King Louis XVI. Full French name Etienne de Grellet du Mobillier. Fled to New York to escape the French Revolution. Anglicized his name and settled in Burlington, New Jersey. Became a Quaker missionary. He is believed to have been the last living person able to identify the true Lost Dauphin of France. Died at age 82 in Burlington.

Last Words: "Not my will, but Thine be done."

Source: *Memoirs of the Life and Gospel Labours of Stephen Grellet,* ed. by Benjamin Seebohm (Philadelphia, 1870).

Grenville, Sir Richard

(1542-1591) English military officer. Admiral. Knighted prior to 1573. One of the Elizabethan "sea dogs." Commanded the fleet that colonized Virginia. Forced to leave his ship *Revenge* in a sea battle with the Spanish near the Azores. Killed at age 49. English poet Tennyson commemorated the event with his ballad "The Revenge." English writer Charles Kingsley noted the battle in his novel *Westward Ho*.

Last Words: "Here die I, Richard Grenville, with a joyful and a quiet mind, for that I have ended my life as a good soldier ought to do, who has fought for his country, Queen, religion, and honor. Wherefore my soul most joyfully departeth out of this body, and shall always leave behind it an everlasting fame of a valiant and true soldier who hath done his duty, as he was bound to do. But the others of my company have done as traitors and dogs, for which they shall be reproached all their lives, and leave a shameful name for ever." Spoken after he was taken aboard the Spanish flagship *San Pablo*.

Source: *Sir Richard Grenville; The Turbulent Life and Career of the Hero of the Little "Revenge"* by George Herbert Bushnell (London, 1936).

Grey, Lady Jane

(1537-1554) English monarch. Great-granddaughter of King Henry VII. Married Lord Guildford Dudley. Named queen when Edward VI died. After only nine days, she was ousted in favor of Mary Tudor. Lady Jane and her husband were imprisoned in the Tower of London and executed within a few months. She died at age 16.

Last Words: "What shall I do? Where is it?" Spoken after she had been blindfolded and could not find the execution block. A bystander led her to it. She laid her head on the block and said "Lord, into Thy hands I commend my spirit."

Source: *Book of Martyrs, Or, A History of the Lives, Sufferings and Triumphant Deaths, of the Early Christian and the Protestant Martyrs* by John Foxe and Charles Augustus Goodrich (Cincinnati, OH, 1831).

Grey, Pearl Zane (Zane)

(1872-1939) American novelist, dentist. Known for western stories. Notable works: *Riders of the Purple Sage; Lone Star Ranger; King of the Royal Mounted*. Many of his novels were best sellers and made into popular movies and television shows. Died at age 67 in Altadena, California.

Last Words: Went to bed complaining about "A slight case of indigestion." The following morning, he suffered a heart attack.

Source: *Zane Grey, Man of the West* by Jean Karr (New York, 1951).

Gridley, Charles Vernon

(1844-1898) American military officer. Captain. Commanded cruiser *Olympia*, flagship of Asiatic squadron. One of the heroes of the U.S. victory at Manila Bay in Philippines during the Spanish-American War. One of Admiral Dewey's chief advisers. It was to him that Dewey gave his famous command: "You may fire when you are ready, Gridley." Taken ill while in Asia. Sent home. Died en route at age 53 in Kobe, Japan.

Last Words: "Going to Manila killed me, but I would do it again if necessary."

Source: *Our Three Admirals, Farragut, Porter, Dewey; An Authentic Account of the Heroic Characters, Distinguished Careers, and Memorable Achievements of the Three Officers, Who Have Attained the Highest Rank in the Navy of the United States* by James E. Homans (New York, 1899).

Grieg, Edvard Hagerup

(1843-1907) Norwegian musician, composer. Considered Norway's greatest composer. Wrote nationalistic music. In frail health much of his life with respiratory problems. Notable works: *Piano Concerto in A Minor; Peer Gynt Suites; Holberg Suite*. Died at age 64 in Bergen, Norway.

Last Words: "Well, if it must be so." Spoken after he learned he might not survive a heart attack.

Source: *Edvard Grieg* by David Monrad-Johansen (Princeton, NJ, 1938).

Grimaldi, Joseph

(1778-1837) English comedian, mime. Performed as Joey the Clown. Known as the Father of Modern Clowning. Star performer at Sadler's Wells, Drury Lane and Covent Garden theatres. Charles Dickens edited his memoirs. In later years, Grimaldi became infirm and had difficulty getting about. He died at age 58 in London.

Last Words: "God bless you my boy! I shall be ready for you tomorrow night." Spoken to George Cook, the tavern keeper who helped him home from the Marquis of Cornwallis tavern each evening. He died that night.

Source: *Grimaldi, King of Clowns* by Richard Findlater (London, 1955).

Grimston, Robert

(1816-1884) British lawyer, sportsman. Son of James Walter Grimston, 1st Earl of Verulam. Died at age 67.

Last Words: "I don't think I shall join you at dinner; but I will punish your dinner for you. I will have a bit of your fish."

Source: *The Life of the Hon. Robert Grimston* by Frederick Gale (London, 1885).

Grindscobbe, William

(d. 1381) English peasant, rebel. Leader of Peasants' Revolt of 1381. He and Jack Straw led peasants as they forced their way into the Abbey at St. Alban's, Hertfordshire, demanding rights. Grindscobbe was arrested, hanged, drawn and quartered for his actions. He had been offered a pardon if he would surrender charters taken from the monks, but he refused to do so.

Last Words: "If I die, I shall die for the cause of the freedom we have won, counting myself happy to end my life by such a martyrdom. Do then today as you would have done had I been killed yesterday."

Source: *A Short History of the English People in Volumes* by John Richard Green (London, 1902).

Grisi, Giulia

(1811-1869) Italian opera singer. One of the great operatic sopranos. From a musical family: sister, aunt, father, cousin all sang professionally. Roles of Elvira in *I Puritani* (Bellini) and Norina in *Don Pasquale* (Donizetti) were created for her. Toured U.S. in 1854 with tenor Giovanni Matteo Mario. When her husband Count de Meley refused to divorce her, she had a common-law relationship with Mario. Died of pneumonia at age 58 while visiting Berlin.

Last Words: "Beautiful. — My beautiful." Her response to her daughter who asked if she wanted anything.

Source: *Mario and Grisi* by Elizabeth Forbes (London, 1985).

Griswold, Rufus Wilmot

(1815-1857) American editor, anthologist, critic. Named Poe's literary executor when he died. Griswold's biography of Poe was highly critical of him. Died at age 42 of tuberculosis in New York City.

Last Words: "Sir, I may not have been always a Christian, but I am very sure that I have been a gentleman."

Source: *Poe's Literary Executor* by Joy Bayless (Nashville, TN, 1943).

Groeneveld, Reinier, Seigneur de

(1588-1623) Dutch patriot. Champion of Dutch independence. Son of John of Barneveld. Condemned and executed as a traitor.

Last Words: "O God! What a man I was once, and what am I now? Patience." Muttered as he placed a red velvet cap over his eyes.

Source: *Life and Death of John of Barneveld* by John L. Motley (New York, 1904).

Grossinger, Asher Selig

(1867-1931) European-born American restaurateur, hotelier. Moved to America in 1897. Family settled in the Jewish community of Ferndale, New York, in the Catskills in 1914. Planned to be farmer but found renting rooms to city visitors more profitable. Grossinger's grew under the direction of his daughter, Jennie. Resort offered topline entertainers, excellent all-you-can-eat Kosher food, and recreational facilities that included a championship golf course and the world's first artificial snow for skiers. At its peak, Grossinger's was a massive complex of 35 buildings of more than 1,200 acres hosting 150,000 guests per year. The complex was sold in 1985 and closed in 1986.

Last Words: "Abie, make sure that everybody eats." Spoken to his maitre d'.

Source: *A Summer World: The Attempt to Build a Jewish Eden in the Catskills, from the Days of the Ghetto to the Rise and Decline of the Borscht Belt* by Stefan Kanfer (New York, 1992).

Grotius, Hugo

(1583-1645) Dutch writer, statesman, jurist. Brilliant scholar who wrote on history, theology, law, politics. Imprisoned 1619 for supporting Arminian heresy. Spent a few years in Paris as an exile. Swedish ambassador to France. Notable work: *On the Law of War and Peace* (on international law). Shipwrecked at Rostock, Germany, on his way home from Sweden. Died there at age 62.

Different Last Words:

(1) "By understanding many things, I have accomplished nothing."

Source: *The Life and Works of Hugo Grotius* by W.S.M. Knight (London, 1925).

(2) "Be serious."

(3) "I heard your voice; but did not understand what you said."

Source for (2) and (3): *The Last Words (Real and Traditional) of Distinguished Men and Women Collected from Various Sources* by Frederic Rowland Marvin (New York, 1901).

Variation: "I hear your voice well, but I understand with difficulty what you say." He died soon afterward, exactly at midnight.

Source: "Hugo Grotius, Diplomatist" by Hamilton Vreeland Jr. in *The American Journal of International Law* (Washington, D.C., 1917).

Groves, Anthony Norris

(1795-1853) English-born missionary in Middle East and India. Christian. Considered the Father of Faith Missions. Ill health forced him to return to England in 1852. Died at age 58 in England a year later.

Last Words: "Now, my precious boy, I am dying. Be a comfort to your beloved mother, as your dear brothers Henry and Frank have been to me. And may the Lord Himself bless you and make you His own. May the Lord give you the peace and joy in Himself that He has given me, for these are true riches. What would thousands of gold and silver be to me now? Now I give you a father's blessing." Spoken to his son.

Source: *Memoir of the Late A.N. Groves, Containing Extracts from His Letters and Journals* by his widow [H.N.] (London 1856).

Guay, Joseph-Albert

(1917-1951) Canadian bomber, mass murderer. Convicted of blowing up Canadian Pacific Airlines DC-3 airplane in 1949, killing all 23 on board, including his wife, to collect a $10,000 insurance policy. He and two accomplices were arrested and executed in Quebec for the crime.

Last Words: "Au moins, je meurs célèbre." (tr. "At least I die famous.").

Sources: "Fame of a Sort" (*Time* magazine, January 22, 1951); *Causes célèbres du Québec* by Dollard Dansereau (Montréal, QC, 1974).

Guérin, Saint Mother Théodore

(1798-1856) French-born American educator, nun, holy woman. Founded Sisters of Providence of Saint Mary-of-the-Wood, Roman Catholic order of nuns. Also founded several schools, notably Saint Mary-of-the-Woods College, near Terre Haute, Indiana. Died at age 57 at Saint Mary-of-the-Woods. Canonized in 2006.

Last Words: "And the Memorare." Her response to a plea from one of the sisters to have a group go to the chapel and recite the Miserere.

Source: The *Eighth American Saint: The Life of Saint Mother Theodore Guerin Foundress of the Sisters of Providence of Saint-Mary-of-the-Woods, Indiana,* by Katherine Burton (Skokie, IL, 2006).

Guesclin, Bertrand du

(c 1320-1380) French military officer, lawman. Known as the Eagle of Brittany. Constable of France. Fought for Charles of Blois against Brittany and England. Died during the siege of Châteauneuf de Randon.

Last Words: "Remember that your business is only with those who carry arms. The churchmen, the poor, the women and children are not your enemies—I commend to the king my wife—my brother—Farewell—I am at an end!"

Source: *Bertrand of Brittany: A Biography of Messire du Guesclin* by Roger Vercel (New Haven, 1934).

Guevara, Ernesto ("Ché")

(1928-1967) Argentinean revolutionary, physician. Communist. Birth name Ernesto Guevara de la Serna. Known as Ché. Helped Castro seize Cuba. Set up guerrilla post in Bolivia but failed to gain support of local Communists. Executed at age 39 by Bolivian soldiers.

Different Last Words:

(1) "Know this now, you are killing a man." Spoken to the soldier who shot him.

Source: "The Death of Che Guevara: Declassified" by Peter Kornbluh (Department of Defense Files. Declassified government documents. National Security Archive Electronic Briefing Book No. 5).

(2) "Do not worry, Captain. It is all over. I have failed." Spoken to a Bolivian captain

after he had been captured and shot.
Source: *Ché Guevara: a biography* by Daniel James (New York, 1970).

Guggenheim, Benjamin

(1865-1912) American businessman. Victim of *Titanic* disaster. Son of mining magnate Meyer Guggenheim. His Last Words were reported by one of *Titanic's* stewards, a survivor named Johnson, to whom Guggenheim gave a message for his wife.

Last Words: "Tell my wife, Johnson, if it should happen that my secretary and I both go down and you are saved, tell her I played the game out straight and to the end. No woman shall be left aboard this ship because Ben Guggenheim was a coward. Tell her that my last thoughts will be of her and of our girls, but that my duty now is to these unfortunate women and children on this ship. Tell her I will meet whatever fate is in store for me, knowing she will approve of what I do."
Source: *Sinking of the Titanic and Great Sea Disasters* by Logan Marshall (Philadelphia, 1912).
Variation: "If anything should happen to me, tell my wife I've done my best in doing my duty."
Source: *A Night to Remember* by Walter Lord and Nathaniel Philbrick (New York, 2005).

Guggenheim, Peggy

(1898-1979) American art patron, collector. Opened modern art gallery in London. Acquired a vast surrealist and abstract art collection. Donated her home in Italy and her collection to the Solomon R. Guggenheim Foundation, provided that it remain in Venice. Died at age 81 in Padua, Italy.
Last Words: "These nurses don't have any idea what's wrong with me. They haven't a clue."
Source: *Peggy, the Wayward Guggenheim* by Jacqueline Bograd Weld (New York, 1986).

Guiccioli, Countess Teresa

(1800-1873) Italian noblewoman. Birth surname Gamba Ghiselli. Married Count Alessandro Guiccioli in 1818. Met George Gordon, Lord Byron, in 1819. Became his mistress and close companion. Notable work: *My Recollections of Lord Byron* (memoir). Became Marquise de Boissy in 1851. Died at age 73 in Florence, Italy.

Last Words: "The more Byron is known, the better he will be loved." Believed to have been spoken on her deathbed.
Source: *The Last Attachment: The Story of Byron and Teresa Guiccioli* by Iris Origo (New York, 1949).

Guiteau, Charles Julius

(1841-1882) American lawyer, assassin. Embittered, disappointed office seeker who shot U.S. President James Garfield in a Washington, D.C., train station. Executed at age 40 by hanging in District of Columbia jail. On the scaffold, he read a poem he wrote that morning: "I am Going to the Lordy." He wanted it set to music and said it indicated his feelings at the moment of leaving the world.
Last Words (last lines of poem):
"Glory, hallelujah!
I wonder what I will see when I get to the Lordy,
I expect to see most glorious things,
Beyond all earthly conception,
When I am with the Lordy!
Glory hallelujah! Glory hallelujah!
I am with the Lord."
Source: *Dark Horse: The Surprise Election and Political Murder of President James A. Garfield* by Kenneth D. Ackerman (New York, 2004).

Guizot, François Pierre Guillaume

(1787-1874) French leader, statesman, historian. Notable work: *Histoire de la Civilisation en Europe.* Member of French Chamber of Deputies. Premier of France. Forced into exile in England in 1848 by a revolution in France. Returned a year later and spent the rest of his life in Normandy. Died at age 86 in Val-Richer.
Different Last Words:
(1) "No one is more convinced of that than I am!" His response to his daughter who said: "We shall meet again, my father."
Source: *Guizot in Private Life* by Madame de Witt (Boston, 1882). The author was his daughter.
(2) "God alone should speak by the side of the grave." He arranged his own funeral and did not want any oration at his tomb.
Source: *Wesleyan-Methodist Magazine*, July 1880.

Gulliver, Lemuel, see Swift, Jonathan.

Gunther, Mary

(1866?-1910) American courtroom defendant. Died in a Long Island, New York, courtroom, of cardiac arrest after hearing an allegation leveled against her by Lillian Sherman.

Last Words: "I never! I wouldn't do such a thing." Her response when she was accused by Sherman of stealing her husband. Gunther then shrieked, fainted into a policeman's arms and died.

Source: "Mortally Stricken in Court" (*New York Times*, April 17, 1910).

Gurney, Joseph John

(1788-1847) English banker, philanthropist. Quaker. Brother of Elizabeth Gurney Fry who was active in prison reform. He endeavored to free slaves, end capital punishment and bring about prison improvements. Died at age 58 at Earlham Hall, near Norwich.

Last Words: "I think I feel a little joyful, dearest." Spoken to his wife.

Source: *Memoirs of Joseph John Gurney; with Selections from his Journal and Correspondence*, ed. by Joseph Bevan Braithwaite (Philadelphia, 1855).

Gusenberg, Frank

(1893-1929) American gangster. Shot in a Chicago garage during the St. Valentine's Day massacre.

Last Words: "That's all I know. Coppers done it." His response in the hospital when asked: "Who shot you?" A few hours later he said to Lieutenant Tom Loftus: "It's getting dark Tom. I'm cold, awful cold. Pull the covers up over me." He then breathed his last.

Source: *The One-way Ride; the Red Trail of Chicago Gangland from Prohibition to Jake Lingle* by Walter Noble Burns (Garden City, NY, 1931).

Gussman, Charles J.

(1913-2000) American radio and television script writer, announcer. Wrote pilot script for *Days of Our Lives* and gave the series its name. Also wrote for *Search for Tomorrow; Young Doctor Malone;* and *Gilligan's Island,* among other shows. He said he wanted his Last Words to be memorable. His daughter reminded him of this as he was dying, so he slowly removed the oxygen mask and whispered:

Last Words: "And now for a final word from our sponsor—."

Source: "Charles Gussman, 87, Dies; Spinner of Soap Opera Webs" (*New York Times*, October 28, 2000).

Gustavus II, King of Sweden

(1594-1632) Swedish monarch. Known as Gustavus Adolphus. Called Lion of the North. Led Swedes during Thirty Years' War in Germany. Mortally wounded at the Battle of Lützen. Became separated from his troops while leading a cavalry charge. Died at age 37.

Different Last Words:

(1) "I am the King of Sweden, who do seal the religion and liberty of the German nation with my blood." Spoken when he identified himself to a group of soldiers.

Source: *Gustavus Adolphus* by C.R.L. Fletcher (New York, 1890).

(2) "I have had enough, brother; try to save your own life." Spoken in a feeble voice to the Duke of Lauenburg. He then fell from his horse and died a short time later.

Source: *A History of Germany, from Its Invasion by Marius Down to the Year 1867* by R. B. Paul and Mrs. Markham (London, 1876).

Variation: "Brother, I am gone. Look to your own life." Whispered to his guide.

Source: *Scandinavia, Ancient and Modern: being a History of Denmark, Sweden and Norway,* Vol. II, by Andrew Crichton, Henry Wheaton (New York, 1841).

Gustavus III, King of Sweden

(1746-1792) Swedish monarch. Son of King Adolf Frederick. Increased the power of the monarchy. Ruled as an enlightened despot. Founder of Swedish Academy. Wrote and produced dramas. Shot while attending a masquerade ball at the opera house by a member of a group of aristocrats who had plotted against him. Died at age 46 in Stockholm two weeks later.

Last Words: "'Tis all over."

Source: *Gustavus III and His Contemporaries, 1746-1792: An Overlooked Chapter of Eighteenth Century History* by Robert Nisbet Bain (London, 1894).

Guthrie, James

(1612?-1661) Scottish Presbyterian clergyman. Executed by hanging for publishing work that declared God's wrath was coming upon Scotland for setting up the King of England as head of the Church, a role only Christ could fill.

Last Words: "The Covenants, the Covenants, shall yet be Scotland's reviving!"

Cried out as the hangman placed the noose around his neck.
Source: *Lives of Alexander Henderson and James Guthrie* by the Committee of The General Assembly of the Free Church of Scotland (Edinburgh, 1846).

Gwenn, Edmund
(1877-1959) Welsh-born English actor. Screen star. Nominated for two Academy Awards for Best Supporting Actor; won for *Miracle on 34th Street* (1948). Won two Golden Globes: *Miracle on 34th Street* and *Mister 880* (1951). Died at age 81 in Woodland Hills, Los Angeles.
Last Words: "Yes, but not as hard as doing comedy." His deathbed response when visiting film director George Seaton asked if dying was difficult.
Source: *Lemmon: A Biography* by Don Widener (New York, 1975).

Haakon VII, King of Norway
(1872-1957) Danish monarch. Prince Carl of Denmark. Son of King Frederick VIII of Denmark. Birth name Christian Frederick Carl George Valdemar Axel. First King of Norway after dissolution of the union with Sweden. Ruled for 52 years, including five years of Nazi occupation during World War II. Died at age 85 in Oslo. He was succeeded by his only son Olaf V.
Last Words: "When I am gone, Norway will get its first Norwegian king." Spoken to his physician.
Source: *Haakon VII of Norway: The Man and the Monarch* by Tim Greve (London, 1983).

Hackman, James
(1752-1779) English murderer, soldier, clergyman. Indicted for the murder of Martha Ray, who apparently rejected his proposal. She was mistress of the 4th Earl of Sandwich, a member of George III's government. Hackman was executed at age 26 at Tyburn.
Last Words (written): "Farewell for ever in this world! I die a sincere Christian and penitent, and everything I hope that you can wish me. Would it prevent my example's having any bad effect if the world should know how I abhor my former ideas of suicide, my crime.—will be the best judge. Of her fame I charge you to be careful. My poor sister will—." Note he wrote to a friend before he was hanged.
Source: *The Love Letters of Mr. H and Miss R 1775-1779,* ed. by Gilbert Burgess (London, 1895).

Hackworth, David. H.
(1930-2005) American military officer, writer. Colonel. Known as the Champion of the Ordinary Soldier. Served in World War II, Korea and Vietnam. Wrote several books, including best-seller, *About Face*. Had a weekly column, "Defending America." Was military analyst on television. Ran two Internet websites devoted to helping troops to publicize issues such as the lack of proper armor and supplies, incompetence in high command, leadership by politics and self interest, and exposure to herbicide Agent Blue. Died at age 74 in Mexico.
Last Words: "If I die, tell Eilhys I was grateful for every moment she bought me, every extra moment I got to spend with her. Tell her my greatest achievement is the love the two of us shared." Spoken to his doctor about his wife.
Source: "Colonel David Hackworth, 'Soldier's Soldier' Dies at 74" by Ken Borsuk (*Greenwich* [Connecticut] *Post*, May 12, 2005).

Hadley, Samuel Hopkins
(1842-1906) American clergyman, missionary. Helped to sobriety by Jerry McAuley at Water Street Mission, New York City. Became a missionary. Died at age 63 after appendicitis surgery.
Last Words: "My poor bums! My poor bums! Who will look out for them for me?"
Source: *Record of Christian Work,* ed. by Alexander McConnell, William Revell and Arthur Percy Fitt (East Northfield, MA, 1906).

Hadrian, Emperor of Rome
(76-138) Roman ruler. One of the five Good Roman Emperors. Nephew of Trajan. Built Hadrian's Wall in England. Rebuilt and named city of Hadrianopolis (now Adrianople). Died at age 62 at his villa near Naples.
Last Words (said to have been composed while he was dying):
"Soul of mine, pretty one, flitting one,
Guest and partner of my clay,
Whither wilt thou hie away,
Pallid one, rigid one, naked one,

Never to play again, never to play?"
Source: *Translations, Literal and Free, of the Dying Hadrian's Address to His Soul* by Hadrianus and David Johnston (Bath, England, 1876).
Variation: "O blithe little soul, thou, flitting away,
Guest and comrade of this my clay,
Wither now goes thou, to what place
Bare and ghastly and without grace
Nor, as thy wont was, joke and play?"
Source: "Life of Hadrian," Part 2, in *Historia Augusta*, tr. by A. O'Brien-Moore (Boston, 1921).

Hagey, Joseph B.

(1810-1876) American-born Canadian clergyman, prelate. Bishop of Mennonite Church in Ontario. Served as bishop for 25 years. Presided over a group that was torn by a schism within the Mennonite Church in Canada. Married Sophia Bricker, daughter of Mennonite leader Samuel Bricker who helped settle what became the city of Waterloo, Ontario. Died at age 66 in Ontario. Hagey's great-grandson Joseph Gerald ("Gerry") Hagey founded the University of Waterloo.
Last Words: "O what a good and merciful Lord we have."
Source: A *Biographical History of Waterloo Township and Other Townships of the County: Being a History of the Early Settlers and Their Descendants, Mostly all of Pennsylvania Dutch Origin,* Vol. 1, by Ezra Eby (Berlin, ON, 1895).

Haggard, Mark

(1876-1914) British military officer. Captain 2nd Battalion, Royal Welsh Fusiliers. Killed at Aisne during World War I. Corporal William Charles Fuller was awarded the Victoria Cross for rescuing Haggard under heavy fire during the battle, but Haggard died later from his injuries. He was famous for his rallying cry "Stick it, the Welsh!"
Last Words (written): "Stick it, the Welsh!" Written in a letter by a Private Derry and in an article by a relative, H. Rider Haggard. His Last Words were widely published in British and U.S. newspapers
Source: "Capt. Mark Haggard's Death in Battle" by H. Rider Haggard (*New York Times Current History: A Monthly Magazine. The European War*, Vol. I, March, 1915).

Hahnemann, Christian Friedrich Samuel

(1755-1843) German physician. Founder of homeopathy. Notable work: *Organon der Rationellen Heilkunde* (explanation of his homeopathic system of medicine). Died at age 88 of bronchitis in Paris.
Last Words: "Every man on Earth works as God gives him strength, and meets from man with a corresponding reward; but no man has a claim at the judgment Seat of God. God owes me nothing: I owe Him much—yea, all."
Source: *Cleave's Biographical Cyclopædia of Homœpathic Physicians and Surgeons* by Egbert Cleave (Philadelphia, 1873).

Haig, Douglas, 1st Earl Haig

(1861-1928) Scottish-born British military officer. Field marshal. Created 1st Earl Haig in 1919. Fought in Sudan, Boer War, India. Commander in chief of all British forces on the Western Front during the last three years of World War I. Died at age 66 of heart failure in London.
Last Words (written): "I hope to see you on Tuesday at 10:30 a.m."
Source: *Haig* by Alfred Duff Cooper (London, 1936).

Haldane, James Alexander

(1768-1851) Scottish clergyman. First Congregational minister in Scotland. Pastor of large independent congregation in Edinburgh. Brother of evangelist Robert Haldane. Died at age 82.
Last Words: "Oh, yes." His response to his wife who said to him: "You are going to Jesus. How happy you will be soon."
Source: *Memoir of Robert Haldane and James Alexander Haldane; with Sketches of Their Friends, and of the Progress of Religion in Scotland and on the Continent of Europe* (New York, 1858).

Haldane, Robert

(1764-1842) Scottish evangelist, religious writer. Brother of James Alexander Haldane. Died at age 78.
Last Words: "For ever with the Lord. For ever. For ever."
Source: *Memoir of Robert Haldane and James Alexander Haldane; with Sketches of Their Friends, and of the Progress of Religion in Scotland and on the Continent of Europe* (New York, 1858).

Hale, Edward Everett

(1822-1909) American clergyman, writer. Unitarian. Nephew of Edward Everett. Chaplain of U.S. Senate. Notable work: *The

Man Without a Country. Died at age 87 in Roxbury, Massachusetts.

Last Words (written): "It was a lovely day and I spent all the time on the deck, from half past ten till five. Had a very good night." Written in his journal.

Source: *The Life and Letters of Edward Everett Hale* by Edward E. Hale, Jr. (Boston, 1917).

Hale, John ("Johnny")

(d. 1881) Texas rancher, cattle rustler. While drunk, Hale fired the first shot that ignited the bloodiest gunfight in El Paso, Texas history, known as the "Four Dead in Five Seconds Gunfight." Among those killed were Hale and El Paso Constable Gus Krempkau. El Paso Marshal Dallas Stoudenmire gunned down three men, one of them Hale, in five seconds while Krempkau was killed by Hale.

Last Words: "Turn loose, Campbell! I've got him covered!" Spoken to George Campbell, a former city marshal and friend of Hale who insulted Krempkau, causing Hale to grab Campbell's gun and fire. Campbell was one of the four killed, along with a Mexican bystander.

Source: *Dallas Stoudenmire El Paso Marshal* by Leon Claire Metz (Norman, OK, 1993).

Hale, Nathan

(1755-1776) American military officer, Revolutionary War hero. Officer in Continental Army. Hanged by the British as a spy a day after he was caught while on an espionage mission. Executed at age 21 by order of British general William Howe without a trial.

Different Last Words:

(1) "It is the duty of every good officer to obey any orders given him by his commander-in-chief." Hale's Last Words were recorded by British officer Captain Frederick Mackenzie in his diary.

Source: *Diary of Frederick Mackenzie, Giving a Daily Narrative of His Military Service as an Officer of the Regiment of Royal Welsh Fusiliers During the Years 1775-1781 in Massachusetts, Rhode Island and New York* by Frederick Mackenzie (Cambridge, MA, 1930).

(2) "I only regret that I have but one life to lose for my country." Spoken as he ascended the gallows: a paraphrase of lines from Addison's *Cato*.

Source: *Field-Book of the Revolution* by Benson Loss-ing (New York, 1850); *History of the United States* by George Bancroft (New York, 1896).

Halévy, Jacques

(1799-1862) French musician, composer, educator. Birth name Jacques Fromental Elie Lévy. Professor of harmony at the Paris Conservatory. Teacher of Bizet, Gounod. Notable operas: *La Juive; L'éclair*. Died at age 62 of tuberculosis in Nice, France.

Last Words: "Lay me down like a gamut." Spoken to his daughter. He wished to be turned on his bed and asked her to repeat "Do, re, mi," etc., until the turn was completed.

Source: The *Great Italian and French Composers* by George T. Ferris (New York, 1878).

Hall, Ben

(1837-1865) Australian bush wrangler. After his wife ran away, he turned to a life of crime. He began with armed robbery and stealing gold and was soon the leader of the infamous Gardiner Gang. From 1863 to 1865, his gang robbed 10 mail coaches, stole 23 race horses and held up 21 towns and stations. In 1865, Hall's friend, Mick Connolly, told police Hall would be visiting that night. In the early hours of the morning, eight policemen and tracker Billy Dargin, a former friend of Hall, descended on Hall. Hall fled without firing a shot. He was shot in the back 30 times.

Last Words: "Shoot me dead Billy! Don't let the traps take me alive." Spoken to tracker Billy Dargin. Hall then fell dead.

Source: *100 Famous Australian Lives* by Ure Smith (Sydney, Australia, 1977).

Hall, John Vine

(1774-1860) English book dealer, printer, publisher, temperance supporter. Gave up alcohol and became a teetotaler for nearly 40 years. Notable work: *The Sinner's Friend* (translated into 30 languages). Died at age 86.

Last Words: "Passing away, passing away— Jesus, Jesus!— He is! He is!— Pray— Amen."

Source: *Hope for the Hopeless, An Autobiography of John Vine Hall,* ed. by Rev. Newman Hall (New York, 1865).

Hall, Martha Wesley

(1707-1791) English matron. Methodist.

Younger sister of John and older sister of Charles Wesley. Known as Patty or Pat. Married the Reverend Westley Hall. Friend of Dr. Johnson and other learned men.

Last Words: "No, but a new feeling. I have the assurance which I have long prayed for. Shout!" Her response when a niece asked her if she was in pain.

Source: *Memoirs of the Wesley Family: Collected Principally from Original Documents* by Adam Clarke (New York, 1848).

Hall, Radclyffe

(1880-1943) British writer, poet. Birth name Marguerite Radclyffe-Hall. Notable novel: *The Well of Loneliness*. Wrote several other novels as well as poetry. Died at age 63.

Last Words: "What a life! But such as it is, I offer it to God!"

Source: *Radclyffe Hall: A Woman Called John* by Sally Cline (New York, 1998).

Hall, Robert

(1764-1831) English clergyman, writer. Baptist minister in Cambridge. Known for his preaching. Notable works: *Christianity Consistent with the Love of Freedom* (defense of political conduct of dissenters); *Apology for the Freedom of the Press* (banned in subsequent editions, largely due to an attack on a bishop in the work). Moved to a small congregation in Leicester and later Bristol after suffering mental issues. His statue by sculptor John Birnie Philip is located in Leicester.

Last Words: "Very comfortable, very comfortable. Come, Lord Jesus, come!" His response to his wife who asked if he was comfortable in mind.

Source: "Words on the Threshold: Being the Last Utterances of Illustrious Men and Women" (*The Quiver, an Illustrated Magazine for Sunday and General Reading*, Vol. XI, 1876).

Halleck, Fitz-Green or Fitz-Greene

(1790-1867) American writer, poet. Worked as clerk in John Jacob Astor's office. Notable works: "Alnwick Castle, with Other Poems"; "Marco Bozzaris"; "On the Death of Joseph Rodman Drake." Died at age 77 in Guilford, Connecticut.

Last Words: "Maria, hand me my pantaloons, if you please." Spoken to his sister.

Source: *Fitz-Green Halleck: An Early Knickerbocker Wit and Poet* by Nelson Frederick Adkins (New Haven, CT, 1930).

Haller, Albrecht von

(1708-1777) Swiss anatomist, physiologist, botanist, physician, educator, poet. Wrote first standard textbook of physiology. Helped found University of Göttingen, where he served as chairman of botany, surgery and anatomy. Died at age 69 in Bern, Switzerland. While researching Haller, Karl S. Guthke came across several versions of his "Last Words." One was a confession of faith, another was the opposite, a third was about his pulse, a fourth mentioned his calmness, and one mentioned that he was dying. Guthke wrote about the controversy over Haller's Last Words in *Das Abenteuer der Literatur*. Haller's Last Words and variations mentioning his pulse, calmness and dying are shown here:

Different Last Words:

(1) "My friend, the artery ceases to beat." Spoken to his medical attendant.

Source: *Dictionary of Phrase and Fable* by E. Cobham Brewer (Philadelphia, 1898).

Variation: "It's beating—beating—beating—it's stopped."

Source: *Last Words. Variations on a Theme in Cultural History* by Karl S. Guthke (Princeton, NJ, 1992).

(2) "Now I am dying. The artery ceases to beat." Spoken after he felt his pulse.

Source: *Famous Last Words* by Barnaby Conrad (Garden City, NY, 1961).

Variation: "My God! I am dying!"

Source: *Last Words. Variations on a Theme in Cultural History* by Karl S. Guthke (Princeton, NJ, 1992).

(3) "I am calm."

Source: *Das Abenteuer der Literatur* by Karl S. Guthke (Bern, Switzerland, 1981).

Halliburton, Richard

(1900-1939) American writer, adventurer. Global traveler. Best-selling adventure writer who attempted to sail the Chinese junk *Sea Dragon* from Hong Kong to San Francisco as a publicity stunt. *Sea Dragon* was not seaworthy and went down in a typhoon, apparently shortly after Halliburton sent his last signal. No one survived. Halliburton was 39.

Last Words: "Southerly gales, squalls, lee rail under water, wet bunks, hard tack, bully beef, wish you were here—instead of me!"

His last signal.

Sources: "Richard Halliburton: The Forgotten Myth" by Guy Townsend (*Memphis Magazine*, August 1977); *Halliburton, the Magnificent Myth: A Biography* by Jonathan Root (New York, 1965).

Halyburton, Thomas

(1674-1712) Scottish clergyman, theologian, educator, writer. Presbyterian. Professor of theology at St. Andrews, Scotland. Notable work: *The Great Concern of Salvation*. Fled to Holland to escape the persecutions against the Covenanters. When he returned to Scotland he was ill and unable to perform his ministerial duties. Died at age 38.

Last Words: "Pray, pray." Spoken to the clergymen present at his bedside.

Source: *Memoirs of the Life of Mr. Thomas Halyburton* (Glasgow, Scotland, 1838).

Hamerton, Philip Gilbert

(1834-1894) English artist, etcher, editor, writer. Edited *The Portfolio* (art periodical). Notable work: *Etching and Etchers*. Died at age 60 in Boulogne-sur-Seine, France.

Last Words (written): "If I indulge my imagination in dreaming about a country where justice and right would always surely prevail, where the weak would never be oppressed, nor an honest man incur any penalty for his honesty—a country where no animal would ever be ill-treated or killed, otherwise than in mercy—that is truly ideal dreaming, because however far I travel, I shall not find such a country in the world, and there is not any record of such a country in the authentic history of mankind."

Source: *Philip Gilbert Hamerton: An Autobiography, 1834-1858, and a Memoir by his Wife, 1858-1894* (Boston, 1898).

Hamilton, Alexander

(1757-1804) American politician, statesman, lawyer, military officer. Born in British West Indies. Member of the Continental Congress. First secretary of treasury. Coauthor of *The Federalist Papers*. Inspector general of the army. Died at age 47 in New York City, a day after being fatally wounded in a duel with Aaron Burr.

Last Words: "Remember, my Eliza, you are a Christian."

Source: *The Rise and Fall of Alexander Hamilton* by Robert A. Hendrickson (New York, 1976).

Hamilton, Edith

(1867-1963) American writer, educator, translator, historian. Headmistress at Bryn Mawr Preparatory School, Baltimore. Notable works: *Mythology; The Greek Way; The Echo of Greece; The Great Age of Greek Literature*. Received many honors and awards. Made honorary citizen of Athens in 1957. Died at age 95 in Washington, D.C.

Last Words: "You know, I haven't felt up to writing, but now I think I am going to finish that book on Plato."

Source: *Edith Hamilton: An Intimate Portrait* by Doris Fielding Reid (New York, 1967).

Hamilton, Louis McLane

(1844-1868) American military officer. Grandson of Alexander Hamilton. Captain, Seventh U.S. Cavalry. Killed at age 24 in the Battle of the Washita waged by cavalry under General Custer and Native Americans led by Big Kettle.

Last Words: "Now men, keep cool! Fire low and not too rapidly." Instructions yelled to his squadron. Hamilton was killed instantly by a Native American's rifle.

Source: *Spurs to Glory: The Story of the United States Cavalry* by James M. Merrill (Chicago, 1966).

Hamilton, Patrick

(1504-1528) Scottish reformer, martyr. Lutheran. Great-grandson of James II of Scotland. Abbot of Ferm. Met with Luther. Returned to Scotland, was arrested and tried by a church council. Found guilty of heresy. Burned at the stake at St. Andrews, becoming the first Protestant martyr in Scotland.

Last Words: "How long, O Lord, shall darkness oppress the realm! How long wilt Thou suffer this tyranny of men? Lord Jesus, receive my spirit!"

Source: *Memoirs of Literature*, Vol. IV (London, 1722). Later versions varied by a few words.

Variation: "How long, Lord, shall darkness overwhelm this kingdom? How long wilt Thou suffer this tyranny of men? Lord Jesus, receive my spirit!"

Source: *Patrick Hamilton* by Rev. Peter Lorimer (Edinburgh, 1857).

Variation: "How long, O Lord, shall darkness brood over this realm? How long wilt thou suffer this tyranny of man? Lord Jesus, receive my spirit."

Source: *Heroes and Heroines of the Christian Church* by Andrew Ritchie (New York, 1884).

Hamilton, William, 2nd Duke of Hamilton

(1616-1651) Scottish nobleman, royalist. Earl of Lanark. Secretary of state in Scotland. Died of wounds received at the Battle of Worcester.

Last Words: "I believe that though in the last hour of the day I have entered into my Master's service, yet I shall receive my penny." He was referring to the parable of the vineyard.

Source: *Lives of James and William, Dukes of Hamilton* by Gilbert Burnet (London, 1677).

Hamilton-Gordon, George John James, 5th Earl of Aberdeen

(1816-1864) British nobleman, politician. Known as Lord Haddo until he inherited his father's title in 1860. Died at age 47 at his home in Scotland.

Last Words: "Perfectly comfortable."

Source: *Memoir of Lord Haddo, Fifth Earl of Aberdeen,* ed. by E. B. Elliott (London, 1868).

Hamlin, Cyrus

(1811-1900) American missionary, educator. First president of Robert College, Constantinople (now Istanbul). President of Middlebury College, Vermont. Died at age 89 in Waterford, Massachusetts.

Last Words: "Put me there." Spoken as he pointed to a chair he used to sit in as a child.

Source: "Rev. Cyrus Hamlin, D.D., LL.D" (*Missionary Review of the World,* Vol. VIII, new series, October, 1900).

Hamlin, Henrietta Anna Lorraine Jackson

(1811-1850) American missionary. Married Cyrus Hamlin in 1838 and accompanied him to Turkey. Died at age 39 of influenza in Rhodes, Greece.

Last Words: "What child is this? It is little Carrie? Yes, it is little Carrie, and the room is full of them." Spoken while she was delirious.

Source: *Light on the Dark River; or, Memorials of Mrs. Henrietta A.L. Hamlin, Missionary in Turkey* by Margarette Oliver Woods Lawrence (Boston, 1854).

Hammerstein, Oscar, II

(1895-1960) American theatrical producer, writer, lyricist, director. Collaborated with composer Richard Rodgers. Notable works: *Oklahoma!; The Sound of Music; Carousel; South Pacific; King and I; Flower Drum Song.* Won two Academy Awards, two Pulitzer Prizes and five Tony Awards. Died at age 65 in Doylestown, Pennsylvania.

Last Words: "Ruth, Gehrig, Rizzuto—" Murmured the names of his three favorite baseball players. He died a few minutes later.

Source: *Getting to Know Him: A Biography of Oscar Hammerstein II* by Hugh Fordin (New York, 1977).

Hammond, Henry

(1605-1660) English clergyman, educator, writer. Teacher of William Temple and William Fulman. Although Hammond was nominated to the Westminster Assembly, he chose instead to take part in an unsuccessful rising at Tonbridge in favor of King Charles I. As a result, Hammond had to flee to Oxford in disguise. His writings include mostly controversial tracts and sermons. Notable work: translation of Blaise Pascal's *Provincial Letters.* Died at age 54 on the eve of his elevation to Bishop of Worcester.

Last Words: "Lord, make haste."

Source: *The Life of the Most Learned, Reverend and Pious Dr. H. Hammond* by John Fell (Oxford, England, 1856).

Hamnett, Nina

(1890-1956) Welsh artist, writer, musicologist. Expert on sailors' sea chanteys. Her interests along with her flamboyant, unconventional and openly bisexual lifestyle, earned her the nickname Queen of Bohemia. Was a close friend of Modigliani, Picasso, Diaghilev and Jean Cocteau, as well as many leading members of the avant-garde living at La Ruche (artists' residence in Montparnasse, Paris). Impaled on a railing when she fell 40 feet from her apartment window. Died at age 66 a short time later.

Last Words: "Why don't they let me die?"

Source: *Nina Hamnett: Queen of Bohemia* by Denise Hooker (London, 1986).

Hampden, John

(1594-1643) English clergyman, military officer, statesman. Puritan leader. His mother was Oliver Cromwell's aunt. Member of Parliament. Imprisoned for refusing to pay a forced loan, claiming it violated the Magna Carta. Died at age 49 of injuries sustained at the siege of Reading.

Variation: "O Lord, save my country! O Lord, be merciful too."

Source: "Death of John Hampden" (*The Mirror of Literature, Amusement, and Instruction*. Vol. 19, No. 536, March 3, 1832).

Hampton, Wade

(1818-1902) American politician, military officer, plantation owner. Confederate cavalry general in U.S. Civil War. Led Hampton's Legion at Bull Run. Promoted to the rank of lieutenant general. Commanded Cavalry of Army of Northern Virginia. Governor of South Carolina. Member of U.S. Senate from South Carolina. U.S. railroad commissioner. Died at age 84 in Columbia, South Carolina.

Last Words: "All my people, black and white, God bless them all!"

Source: *Wade Hampton: Confederate Warrior, Conservative Statesman* by Walter Brian Cisco (Washington, D.C., 2004).

Hancock, Winfield Scott

(1824-1886) American military officer. Union general in U.S. Civil War. Died at age 61 at Governors Island, New York, while in charge of the Army of the East.

Last Words: "O Allie, Allie, Myra.—Good." Spoken to his wife Almira Russell Hancock. Allie and Myra were his pet names for her.

Source: *Life of Winfield Scott Hancock: Major-general U.S.A. His Childhood, Youth, Education, Military Career, Social and Domestic Life* by Frederick Elizur Goodrich (Boston, 1886).

Hand, Daniel

(1801-1891) American merchant, philanthropist. Accumulated fortune in Georgia and South Carolina. Moved North after the U.S. Civil War where he became a philanthropist. Gave more than $1 million to the American Missionary Association and more than $1 million to the Daniel Hand Educational Fund for Coloured People to be used in states that recognized slavery in 1861. Died at age 90 in Guilford, Connecticut. Daniel Hand High School in Madison, Connecticut, was named for him.

Last Words (doubtful): "I hope I am ready to go when called."

Source: *A Conspectus of American Biography: Being an Analytical Summary of American History and Biog-*

raphy, Containing also the Complete Indexes of the National Cyclopedia of American Biography by George Derby (New York, 1906).

Hand was often heard to say: "I have now a very short time for this world, but I take no concern about that; no matter where or when I die, I hope I am ready to go when called."

Source: *Famous Givers and Their Gifts* by Sarah Knowles Bolton (New York, 1896).

Hanna, Marcus Alonzo ("Mark")

(1837-1904) American businessman, politician. Presidential adviser. Made his fortune in coal and iron. Member U.S. Senate from Ohio. Died at age 66 in Washington, D.C., while serving a second term as senator.

Last Words: "Yes, I would like one, but I suppose I cannot have it. My wife takes them all." His response when asked if he wanted a handkerchief.

Source: *Marcus Alonzo Hanna: His Life and Work* by Herbert Croly (New York, 1912).

Hannibal

(247?-183? B.C.) Carthaginian general. Left Spain and crossed the Alps into Italy with a large army that included elephants. Waged war for 15 years against Rome during the Second Punic War. Committed suicide by taking poison to avoid surrender to the Romans.

Last Words: "Let us ease the Romans of their continual dread and care, who think it long and tedious to await the death of a hated old man. Yet Titus will not bear away a glorious victory, nor one worthy of those ancestors who sent to caution Pyrrhus, an enemy, and a conqueror too, against the poison prepared for him by traitors." Spoken just before he drank poison.

Source: "Flaminius" in *Lives of the Noble Grecians and Romans* by Plutarch, tr. by John Dryden (Chicago, 1952).

Hansford, Thomas

(1646?-1676) American military officer, martyr. Colonel. One of Nathaniel Bacon's officers. Refused to surrender. Hanged by Governor William Berkeley for taking part in Bacon's Rebellion. Known as the First Martyr to American Liberty.

Last Words: "Take notice that I die a loyal subject and a lover of my country." Spoken on the gallows on Virginia's Eastern Shore where he was executed.

Source: *Introduction to the History of the Colony and Ancient Dominion of Virginia* by Charles Campbell and Samuel L. Campbell (Richmond, VA, 1847).

Hanway, Jonas

(1712-1786) English writer, philanthropist. Traveled in Europe, Russia and Persia. Partnered with a merchant in St. Petersburg, Russia. First Londoner to carry an umbrella in the city. Founded Magdalen Hospital for Woman. Did much to help poor children. Died at age 74. Street in London was named for him.

Different Last Words:

(1) "Christ."

Source: *Jonas Hanway: Philanthropist, Politician, Author, 1712–1786* by R. Everett Jayne (London, 1929).

(2) (doubtful): "If you think it will be of service in your practice, or to any one who may come after me, I beg you will have my body opened; I am willing to do as much good as is possible." This quotation is cited as Hanway's Last Words in some sources; others state that it was spoken on the day he died and that he did speak after this.

Sources: *The Georgian Era: Memoirs of the Most Eminent Persons, Who Have Flourished in Great Britain, from the Accession of George the First to the Demise of George the Fourth,* Vol. III (London, 1834); *The Power of Religion on the Mind* by Lindley Murray (New York, 1838).

Harden, Jacob S.

(1837-1860) American clergyman, murderer. Minister of Mt. Lebanon Methodist Episcopal Church, Hunterdon County, New Jersey. Convicted and executed for poisoning his wife after her mother coerced him into the marriage.

Last Words: "God have mercy upon me! Lord Jesus save me in Heaven." Spoken just before he was hanged.

Source: *Life, Confession and Letters of Courtship of Jacob S. Harden, of the M.E. Church, Mount Lebanon, Hunterdon Co., N.J.* (Hackettstown, NJ, 1860).

Harden-Hickey, James A.

(1854-1898) American soldier of fortune. Self-proclaimed James I, Prince of Trinidad. Wrote *Euthanasia: The Aesthetics of Suicide*, describing suicide as a powerful art form and "a privilege." Overdosed on morphine at age 43 in a hotel in El Paso, Texas,

when he could not sell his Mexican ranch.

Last Words (written): "My dearest—no news from you, although you have had plenty of time to write; Harvey has written me that he has no one in view at present to buy my land. Well, I shall have tasted the cup of bitterness to the very dregs, but I do not complain. Good-bye. I forgive you your conduct toward me and trust you will be able to forgive yourself. I prefer to be a dead gentleman to a living blackguard like your father." Suicide note to his wife.

Source: *Real Soldiers of Fortune* by Richard Harding Davis (New York, 1906).

Hardin, John Wesley

(1853-1895) American lawyer, murderer, frontiersman. Texas gunslinger. Killed at age 42. Shot in the back of his head by a constable as he was rolling dice in a saloon.

Last Words: "Brown, you've got four sixes to beat!"

Source: *John Wesley Hardin: Dark Angel of Texas* by Leon Claire Metz (El Paso, TX, 1996).

Harding, Florence Mabel Kling DeWolfe ("Flossie")

(1860-1924) American First Lady. Wife of Warren G. Harding. Died at age 64 in Marion, Ohio, 15 months after the death of her husband.

Last Words: "I am glad you are here, George. I want you to take care of this mail and see that every letter is acknowledged and thank them for their kind interest." Spoken to her husband's secretary George Christian a few days before she lost consciousness. She lost the ability to speak, but her last conscious act was a response to a letter from President and Mrs. Coolidge. She "smiled and nodded her head."

Source: *Washington Times*, November 24, 1924.

Harding, Warren Gamaliel

(1865-1923) 29th President of the U.S. American editor, publisher, politician. Editor and publisher of *Marion* [Ohio] *Star.* Member of Ohio state senate. Lieutenant governor of Ohio. Ran unsuccessfully for governor. Member U.S. Senate from Ohio. Suffered a stroke while on a train to Seattle. Taken to Palace Hotel in San Francisco. Died there at age 57.

Last Words: "That's good. Go on. Read some more." Spoken to his wife while she read aloud a complimentary article about him in the *Saturday Evening Post* titled "A Calm View of a Calm Man."
Source: *Incredible Era* by Samuel Hopkins Adams (Boston, 1939).

Hardy, Oliver Norvell

(1892-1957) American actor, comedian. Star of stage and screen. Half of the comedy team of Laurel and Hardy with Stan Laurel. Died at age 65 in North Hollywood, California, after a debilitating stroke.
Last Words: "I love you." Spoken to his wife.
Source: *Stan: The Life of Stan Laurel* by Fred Lawrence Guiles (New York, 1980).

Hardy, Thomas

(1840-1928) English novelist, poet. Notable works: *Tess of the D'Urbervilles; Jude the Obscure; Far from the Madding Crowd; The Mayor of Casterbridge; The Return of the Native.* Died at age 87 at his home in Dorchester, England. Many of his novels have been made into movies, television and stage productions.
Last Words: "Eva. Eva. What is this?" Spoken to Eva Dugdale, the sister of his second wife Florence Emily.
Source: *Thomas Hardy's Later Years* by Robert Gittings (Boston, 1978).

Harlan, John Marshall, I

(1833-1911) American lawyer, jurist, politician. Attorney general of Kentucky. Ran for governor twice and lost. Associate justice of U.S. Supreme Court. Lone dissenter in *Plessey v. Ferguson,* decision that established "separate but equal" by legalizing Southern segregation. Grandfather of John Marshall Harlan II, also associate justice of U.S. Supreme Court. Died at age 78 of pneumonia in Washington, D.C., after serving 33 years with the court.
Last Words: "Goodbye, I am sorry to have kept you all waiting so long." Spoken to visitors at his bedside.
Source: *New York Tribune,* October 15, 1911.

Harlan, John Marshall, II

(1899-1971) American lawyer, jurist. Grandson of John Marshall Harlan I. Associate justice of U.S. Supreme Court. Died at age 72 of cancer three months after retiring in Washington, D.C.
Last Words: "Why did this have to happen to me?" Spoken to an assistant.
Source: *John Marshall Harlan: Great Dissenter of the Warren Court* by Tinsley E. Yarbrough (New York, 1992).

Harley, John Pritt

(1786-1858) English actor, singer. Known as Fat Jack, even though he was thin. Popular comic actor. Artist Samuel de Wilde painted his portrait as Pedrillo in *The Castle of Andalusia.* Harley had a stroke while on stage performing in the *Merchant of Venice.* He was rushed home where he died a short time later at age 72.
Last Words: "I have an exposition of sleep come upon me." The words were those of Bottom in Shakespeare's *A Midsummer Night's Dream.* After uttering them, he remained speechless until he died.
Source: *Relics of Genius: Visits to the Last Homes of Poets, Painters and Players with Biographical Sketches* by T.P. Grinsted (London, 1859).

Harlow, Jean

(1911-1937) American actress. Screen star. Birth name Harlean Harlow Carpenter. Known as the Platinum Blonde and the Blonde Bombshell. Became ill during filming of *Saratoga.* Died at age 26 in a Los Angeles hospital. Two biographical movies about her, both titled *Harlow,* were released in 1965.
Last Words: "Where is Aunt Jetty? Hope she didn't run out on me."
Source: *Bombshell, The Life and Death of Jean Harlow* by David Stenn (New York, 1993).

Harmison, Frank

(d.1889) American gunfighter, vigilante mob member. Part of gang that attacked the Marlow clan, causing one of the American West's most famous gunfights. While Harmison's gang was in retreat, the Marlows accused him of cowardice, which prompted him to change direction. He died near Graham, Texas, shot by one of the Marlows. The 1965 movie *The Sons of Katie Elder* is based on their story.
Last Words: "Back to see it out!" His response to another mob member when asked

where he was going after he reversed direction.

Source: *The Fighting Marlows: Men Who Wouldn't be Lynched* by Glenn Shirley (Fort Worth, TX, 1994).

Harmsworth, Alfred Charles William, 1st Viscount Northcliffe

(1865-1922) British newspaper entrepreneur. Tabloid journalism pioneer. Known for resurrecting unprofitable newspapers and attracting a mass market for them. Older brother of Harold Harmsworth, 1st Viscount Rothermere. Started *London Daily Mail* and *Daily Mail* with Harold. Bought *The Times* in 1908 and modernized it. Created 1st Baronet Harmsworth in 1904. Created 1st Viscount Northcliffe in 1918. Died at age 57 in London without issue.

Last Words: "I wish to be laid as near Mother as possible at North Finchley and I do not wish anything erect from the ground or any words except my name, the year I was born and this year upon the stone. In the *Times* I should like a page reviewing my life work by someone who really knows, and a leading article by the best man available on the night."

Source: *The House of Northcliffe: A Biography of an Empire* by Paul Ferris (New York, 1971).

Harmsworth, Harold Sidney, 1st Viscount Rothermere

(1868-1940) British newspaper entrepreneur. Owner of Associated Newspapers. Started *London Daily Mail* and *Daily Mirror* with brother Alfred Harmsworth 1st Viscount Northcliffe. Highly respected in Hungary for supporting the treaty favoring that nation; was offered the crown of Hungary in 1927 but declined. Aircraft he owned was the basis for the development of superior aircraft for the Royal Air Force and was adapted into the Blenheim Mk.I. In the 1930s, he supported an alliance with Germany and corresponded secretly with Adolf Hitler; however, when war was imminent, his loyalties changed.

Last Words: "There is nothing more I can do to help my country now." Spoken shortly before losing consciousness. Died at age 72 in Bermuda.

Sources: *The Prerogative of the Harlot: Press Barons & Power* by Hugh Cudlipp (London, 1980); "Death of a Viscount" (*Time* magazine, December 9, 1940).

Harpe, William Micajah ("Big")

(1768-1799) American murderer. Several murders were attributed to him and his brother Wiley "Little" Harpe, who terrorized frontier settlers along the Wilderness Trail. He was shot off his horse by a large posse of frontiersmen in Ohio.

Last Words: "You are a God-damned rough butcher, but cut on and be damned!" Spoken to the posse that was attempting to cut off his head.

Source: *Pictorial History of the Wild West: A True Account of the Bad Men, Desperadoes, Rustlers and Outlaws of the Old West—and the Men Who Fought Them to Establish Law and Order* by James David Horan and Paul Sann (London, 1954).

Harper, Henry Albert

(1873-1901) Canadian journalist, civil servant. Friend of future prime minister William Lyon Mackenzie King. Journalist for *Montreal Daily Herald*. Assistant editor of *Labour Gazette*. In 1901, while at an ice skating party on the Ottawa River, a man and woman fell through thin ice. The man pulled himself out. Harper dove into the river in an attempt to save the woman, Bessie Blair, daughter of Canada's Minister of Railways and Canals. Both drowned. Harper's heroism was commemorated by a statue of Sir Galahad dedicated to Harper at Parliament Hill in Ottawa, Canada. It was placed there by King.

Last Words: "What else can I do?" His response to his companions who tried to dissuade his rescue attempt.

Source: *The Secret of Heroism: A Memoir of Henry Albert Harper* by W.L.M. King (New York, 1906).

Harrington, Calvin Sears

(1826-1886) American educator, writer. Professor of Latin language and literature at Wesleyan University. Died at age 59.

Last Words: "As it was in the beginning, is now, and ever shall be, world without end. Amen."

Source: *Memories of the Life of Calvin Sears Harrington, D.D.* by Mrs. Eliza C. Harrington (Middleton, CT, 1887). The author was his widow.

Harris, Henry B.

(1866-1912) American theatrical producer, theater owner and operator. Victim of

Titanic disaster. Produced more than 60 shows on Broadway. On the *Titanic*, Harris went to the side of his wife before the lifeboat was lowered away. Upon hearing "Women first" shouted to him by one of the ship's officers, Harris made his last known statement.

Last Words: "All right. Good-bye, my dear." He hugged and kissed his wife goodbye then climbed back to the deck of the *Titanic* where he drowned.

Source: *Sinking of the Titanic and Great Sea Disasters* by Logan Marshall (Philadelphia, 1912).

Harris, Jack

(d. 1882) American theater owner, shooting victim of western gunfighter Ben Thompson. Harris and Thompson had a long-running feud that involved an old gambling debt. When Thompson went to San Antonio, Texas, looking for him, Harris was waiting with a gun but Thompson shot him first.

Last Words: "He took advantage of me and shot me from the dark." Spoken to a doctor a few moments before he died.

Source: *Ben Thompson, Man With a Gun* by Floyd Benjamin Streeter (New York, 1957).

Harris, James Thomas ("Frank")

(1856-1931) Irish-born American journalist, writer, publisher, editor. Moved to America in 1869. Returned to England in 1882. Edited: *London Evening News; Fortnightly Review; Saturday Review.* Returned to U.S. in 1916. Became American citizen. Notable work: *My Life and Loves* (memoir widely banned for its sexual explicitness). Wrote biography of Oscar Wilde that was also criticized for its frankness. Founded Frank Harris Publishing Company in New York City in 1920s to publish his own works. Died at age 75 of a heart attack in France.

Last Words: "Nellie, my Nellie, I'm going!" Spoken to his wife in a hospital before losing consciousness.

Source: *Frank Harris* by Philippa Pullar (London, 1975).

Harris, Joel Chandler

(1848-1908) American writer, journalist, poet. On the staff of the *Atlanta Constitution* 24 years. Creator of Uncle Remus. Wrote ten collections of Uncle Remus stories start-

ing with *Uncle Remus: His Songs and His Sayings.* Died at age 59 in Atlanta, Georgia. Different Last Words:

(1) "I am about the extent of a tenth of a gnat's eyebrow better." His response when asked how he was feeling.

Source: *The Life and Letters of Joel Chandler Harris* by Julia Collier Harris (Boston, 1918). The author was married to his son Julian LaRose Harris.

(2) "I have always been curious to know what was on the other side. I am very tired." Spoken to his wife and children who were gathered at his bedside.

Source: " 'Uncle Remus' " Dead. Joel Chandler Harris's Last Words, 'I am Very Tired' " (*New York Times*, July 4, 1908).

Harris, Martin

(1783-1875) American farmer. Religious figure. Member of Latter Day Saints. Financed first printing of *The Book of Mormon*. One of Three Witnesses who testified they had seen the Golden Plates from which *The Book of Mormon* was transcribed. Died at age 92.

Last Testimony: "Yes, I did see the plates on which the Book of Mormon was written. I did see the angel; I did hear the voice of God: and I know that Joseph Smith is a prophet of God, holding the keys of the Holy Priesthood." The last testimony of Harris was recorded by friends William Pilkington and William H. Homer.

Source: "Play Magnifies Martin Harris' Testimony. His Words 'Shine Like sun,' Affirming Book of Mormon's Truthfulness to Thousands" (*Deseret* [Salt Lake City] *News,* April 19 1989).

Harris, Robert Alton

(1953-1992) American murderer. Convicted of the murder of two teenage boys. When he died in San Quentin's gas chamber in 1992, he was the first person to be executed in California since 1967.

Last Words: "You can be a king or a street sweeper, but everyone dances with the grim reaper." Recorded by Warden Daniel Vasquez.

Source: "Television Dances with the Reaper (Television Broadcasting of Analysis Following Execution of Robert Alton Harris)" by Lance Morrow (*Time* magazine, May 4, 1992).

Harrison, Benjamin

(1833-1901) 23rd President of the U.S.

American politician, lawyer. Grandson of U.S. President William Henry Harrison. Defeated for second term by Grover Cleveland. Member U.S. Senate from Indiana. Attorney for Venezuela in boundary dispute with Great Britain over British Guiana. Died at age 67 of influenza and pneumonia in Indianapolis.

Different Last Words:

(1) "Doctor— my lungs." The only words he uttered that could be understood. His Last Words were indistinct.

Source: "Benjamin Harrison Dead—Ex-President's Battle for Life Ended Yesterday Afternoon" (*New York World*, March 14, 1901).

(2) The last words he spoke were to Mrs. Harrison in answer to a question. His voice was almost inaudible and it required an effort to grasp the meaning of her question and frame a reply. His mind wandered often. He seemed occupied with the Boer War and the sufferings of the Boer people.

Source: *New York Sun*, March 14, 1901.

Harrison, Caroline Lavinia Scott

(1832-1892) American First Lady. First wife of Benjamin Harrison. Died at age 60 of tuberculosis and influenza in the White House while First Lady.

Last Words: "No, dear." Her response to her husband who asked if there was anything they could do for her. She had slipped into a coma then regained consciousness and spoke to her husband.

Source: *The First Ladies Fact Book: The Stories of the White House from Martha Washington to Laura Bush* by Bill Harris (New York, 2005).

Harrison, Carter H., III

(1825-1893) American lawyer, politician. Member U.S. House of Representatives from Illinois. Mayor of Chicago. Assassinated at age 68 in the mayor's residence, soon after giving the closing speech at the World Columbian Exposition. Shot and killed by Patrick Eugene Prendergast, disgruntled job seeker who was later executed for the crime.

Different Last Words:

(1) "Give me water. Where is Annie?" Annie Hall, the mayor's fiancée, was visiting nearby when the shooting occurred. She arrived as he died. About a half hour later,

Prendergast, who had escaped capture, walked into a police station and surrendered.

Source: "A Victorian Tragedy: The Strange Deaths of Mayor Carter H. Harrison and Patrick Eugene Prendergast" by Richard Allen Morton (*Journal of Illinois State Historical Society*, Spring 2003).

(2) "I have been shot in the heart and know I cannot live."

Source: *New York Tribune*, October 29, 1893.

Harrison, Thomas

(1606-1660) English military officer, conspirator. Cromwellian general. Convicted of regicide. Guarded King Charles I on his last journey to London. Was member of the court that tried him. Signed the king's death warrant. Following the Restoration, he was executed by being hanged, drawn and quartered. Died at age 54.

Last Words: "He hath covered my head many times in the day of battle. By God I have leapt over a wall, by God I have run through a troop, and by God I will go through this death, and He will make it easy to me. Now into Thy hands, O Lord Jesus, I commit my spirit."

Source: *Life of John Milton* by David Masson, Vol. 6 (New York, 1946).

Harrison, William Henry

(1773-1841) 9th President of the U.S. American politician, diplomat. Grandfather of U.S. President Benjamin Harrison. Governor of Indiana Territory. Member U.S. House of Representatives and U.S. Senate. U.S. minister to Colombia. Unsuccessful Whig candidate for President in 1836; elected in 1840. Served only a month as President. Died at age 68 of pneumonia in Washington, D.C. First President to die in office.

Last Words: "Sir, I wish you to understand the true principles of government. I wish them carried out. I ask nothing more." Spoken to Vice President Tyler while delirious.

Source: *Old Tippecanoe: William Henry Harrison and His Time* by Freeman Cleaves (New York, 1939).

Hart, Lorenz Milton

(1895-1943) American lyricist. Collaborator with composer Richard Rodgers on many Broadway shows. Notable works: *Babes in Arms; I Married an Angel; Pal Joey; By Jupiter; The Boys from Syracuse*. Rodgers ended his collaboration with Hart to form a team with Oscar Hammerstein. Hart died at age 48 of pneumonia in New York City.

Last Words: "What have I lived for?" Spoken on his deathbed.

Source: *Rodgers and Hart: Bewitched, Bothered and Bedeviled* by Samuel Marx and Jan Clayton (New York, 1976).

Harun al-Rashid or Haroun Alraschid

(765-809) Abbasid caliph immortalized in *The Arabian Nights.* During his reign, Baghdad was the artistic and intellectual center of the Middle East.

Last Words: "Sahl, remember in a moment like this what the poet has said—'Descended from a race so great, I firmly bear the hardest fate.'"

Source: *The Caliph Haroun Alraschid and Saracen Civilization* by E.H. Palmer (New York, 1881).

Harvey, Fred

(1835-1901) English-born American restaurateur. Developed the Harvey House chain of restaurants and hotels serving passengers on the Atchison, Topeka and Santa Fe Railway and other western rail lines. Story of the restaurant chain was featured in the 1946 movie *The Harvey Girls.* Harvey died at age 65 in Leavenworth, Kansas.

Last Words: "Don't cut the ham too thin, boys!" Said to have been spoken to his sons.

Sources: *Meals by Fred Harvey* by James D. Henderson (Fort Worth, TX, 1969); *The Harvey Girls: The Women Who Civilized the West* by Juddi Morris (New York, 1994).

Harvey, William Henry

(1811-1866) Irish botanist, educator. Authority on algae and South African flora. Professor of botany at Trinity College. Acquired a large natural history collection in Australia. Died at age 55 of tuberculosis in Torquay, Devonshire, England.

Last Words: "Yes, it has been a pleasant world to me."

Source: *Memoir of W.H. Harvey, M.D., F.R.S.* by L. Fisher (London, 1869).

Hašek, Jaroslav

(1883-1923) Czech writer, novelist, journalist, humorist, satirist. Notable work: *The Good Soldier Švejk* (*The Good Soldier Schweik*), a collection of satirical incidents about a soldier during the World War I era.

He also wrote 16 volumes of short stories. Died at age 39 of tuberculosis contracted during the war.

Last Words: "But you're cheating me!" Spoken to his doctor who refused him one final glass of brandy.

Source: *The Bad Bohemian. A Life of Jaroslav Hašek, Creator of The Good Soldier Švejk* by Cecil Parrott (London, 1978).

Hassler, Ferdinand Rudolph

(1770-1843) Swiss-born American engineer, educator. Taught at West Point and Union College. Head of U.S. Coast Survey. Standardized weights and measures in the U.S. Died at age 73 in Philadelphia.

Last Words: "My children! My papers!"

Source: *The Chequered Career of Ferdinand Rudolph Hassler* by Florian Cajori (Boston, 1929).

Hastings, Warren

(1732-1818) British statesman. Administrator in India. Governor of Bengal. Impeached for corruption and cruelty. Acquitted in 1795. Spent the rest of his life in retirement. Died at age 85 in Daylesford, Worcestershire.

Last Words: "Surely at my age it is time to go.—God only can do me good.—My dear, why wish me to live to suffer thus? None of you know what I suffer."

Source: *Memoirs of the Life of Warren Hastings, First Governor-General of Bengal. Compiled from Original Papers* by the Rev. G.R. Gleig, M.A. (London, 1841).

Hatfield, John

(1759-1803) British criminal. Known as the Keswick Imposter. Had a reputation as a notorious swindler and felon. Executed by hanging for forgery.

Last Words: "May the Almighty bless you all."

Source: *The Newgate Calendar: Comprising Interesting Memoirs of the Most Notorious Characters Memoirs of the Most Notorious Characters who have been Convicted of Outrages on the Laws of England Since the Commencement of the Eighteenth Century with Occasional Anecdotes and Observations, Speeches, Confessions and Last Exclamation of Sufferers* by Andrew Knapp and William Baldwin (London, 1828).

Hauff, Wilhelm

(1802-1827) German writer, editor, novelist, poet. Known for his fairy tales. Notable work: *Lichtenstein* (historical romance). Editor of *Stuttgart Morgenblatt.* Died at age

24 of fever in Stuttgart.

Last Words: "Father, into Thy hands I commend my immortal spirit!"

Source: *Eine Darstellung* by Hans Hofmann (Frankfurt, Germany, 1902).

Hauser, Kaspar

(1812?-1833) German foundling. He was discovered walking along a road in Nuremberg, Germany, in 1828. He was about 16 and apparently had been imprisoned more than 10 years. Some who observed him believed he was of noble birth. He was placed in the custody of Professor Daumer and later adopted by Lord Stanhope. Hauser died mysteriously from stab wounds in 1833. DNA tests in 2002 indicated he was of the House of Baden. Subject of the novel *Caspar Hauser* by Jacob Wasserman.

Different Last Words:

(1) "Tired—very tired—a long journey—to take."

Source: *The True Story of Kaspar Hauser, from Official Documents* by Catherine Lucy Wilhelmina Powlett, Duchess of Cleveland (London, 1893).

(2) "I didn't do it myself."

Source: *The World's Greatest Unsolved Mysteries* by Lionel and Patricia Fanthorpe (Toronto, ON, 1997).

Havelock, Sir Henry

(1795-1857) British military officer. Fought in Burmese War, Afghan War, Sikh campaign and at the relief of Luchnow during the Sepoy Mutiny. Knighted in 1842. Died at age 62 of dysentery in Luchnow. Havelock military gear—white cap and neck cover first worn during the Sepoy Mutiny—was later named for him. Street in west London was also named for him. Statue of him stands in Trafalgar Square.

Last Words: "Come, my son, and see how a Christian can die."

Source: *A Biographical Sketch of Sir Henry Havelock, K.C.B.* by Rev. William Brock (New York, 1860).

Haven, Gilbert

(1821-1880) American prelate, educator, abolitionist. Bishop of Methodist Episcopal Church. Early benefactor of Clark College (now Clark Atlanta University), which he envisioned as a university for the education of Methodist former slaves. Despite his vigorous support for Clark, he declined all honorary degrees offered to him. He succeeded

Bishop Davis W. Clark (namesake of Clark College) as president of the Freedman's Aid Society of the Methodist Episcopal Church. Died at age 58 in Massachusetts.

Different Last Words:

(1) "It is all bright and beautiful; there is no darkness; there is no river. I am upborne by angels. I am floating away into God."

Source: *"Graduated with Honor": Memorials of Gilbert Haven, Bishop of the Methodist Episcopal Church*, ed. by W. H. Daniels (Boston, 1880).

Variation: "There is no river here! All is beautiful."

Source: *National Repository Devoted to General and Religious Literature, Criticism and Art*, ed. by Daniel Curry, Vol. II (Cincinnati, OH, 1880).

(2) "Glory, glory, glory!"

Source: *The Life of Gilbert Haven: Bishop of the Methodist Episcopal Church* by George Prentice (New York, 1883).

Havergal, Frances Ridley

(1836-1879) English poet, musician, writer of religious verse. Began writing poetry at age seven. Died at age 42 in Swansea, Wales.

Last Words: "There, now it is over! Blessed rest!" She then tried to sing: "He—" but her voice failed.

Source: *Memorials of Frances Ridley Havergal by Her Sister* by M.V.G. Havergal (London, 1882). M.V.G. Havergal was Maria Vernon Graham Havergal.

Hawker, Robert Stephen

(1803-1875) British writer, poet, clergyman. Anglican Vicar of Morwenstow, Wellcombe, Magdalen College (Oxford). Converted to Roman Catholicism shortly before he died. Notable works: "Cornish Ballads & Other Poems"; "The Quest of the Sangraal"; "The Song of the Western Men" (has popular chorus line, "And shall Trelawney die?"). Died at age 71.

Last Words: "His banner over me was love."

Source: *The Life and Letters of R. S. Hawker (Sometime Vicar of Morwenstow)* by Charles Edward Byles (London, 1905).

Hawthorne, Nathaniel

(1804-1864) American novelist. Notable works: *Twice-Told Tales; The Scarlet Letter; House of Seven Gables; The Marble Faun*. Friend of Melville and Franklin Pierce. Died at age 59 in Plymouth, New Hampshire, while on a trip with Pierce.

Last Words: "What a boon it would be, if when life draws to its close, one could pass away without a struggle." Spoken to Pierce a few hours before he died in his sleep.
Source: *Nathaniel Hawthorne: A Biography* by Arlin Turner (New York, 1961).

Hawthorne, Sophia Amelia Peabody
(1809-1871) American matron. Wife of Nathaniel Hawthorne. Died at age 62 of typhoid pneumonia in England.
Last Words: "I am tired—too tired—I am—glad to go—I only wanted to live—for you—and Rose.—Flowers—flowers."
Source: *Nathaniel Hawthorne and His Wife* by Julian Hawthorne (Boston, 1892). The author was their son.

Hay, John Milton
(1838-1905) American statesman, diplomat. Private secretary to Abraham Lincoln. U.S. assistant secretary of state. U.S. ambassador to Great Britain. U.S. secretary of state. Negotiated Hay-Pauncefote Treaty that led to construction of the Panama Canal. Died at age 66 in Newbury, New Hampshire. Mount Hay, Alaska, was named for him.
Last Words: "Come." Spoken haltingly to his nurse. He died of a pulmonary embolism a short time later.
Source: *A Conspectus of American Biography: Being an Analytical Summary of American History and Biography, Containing also the Complete Indexes of the National Cyclopedia of American Biography* by George Derby (New York, 1906).

Haydn, Franz Joseph
(1732-1809) Austrian musician, composer. Wrote operas, masses, piano sonatas, oratorios and more than 100 symphonies. Sometimes known as Father of the Symphony for his pioneering work in that form. Had long friendship with Mozart. Was living in Vienna in 1809 during the Napoleonic War when the French bombed the city. The attack shocked him. He died at age 77 a short time later.
Last Words: "Children be comforted. I am well."
Source: *The Lives of the Great Composers* by Harold C. Schonberg (New York, 1997).
Variation: "Cheer up, children, I'm all right."
Source: *Haydn (Master Musician)* by Rosemary Hughes (London, 1950).

Haydon, Benjamin Robert
(1786-1846) English artist, painter, writer. Wordsworth and Keats addressed sonnets to him. He had a close friendship with Keats, then quarreled with him. Suffered from depression. Kept a diary for many years that was published in the 1960s. Committed suicide at age 60 in London.
Last Words (written): "22nd—God forgive me. Amen. Finis of B.R. Haydon. 'Stretch me no longer on this rough world.' Lear. End of Twenty-sixth Volume." Last entry in his diary, June 22, 1846. He paraphrased a quote from *King Lear*.
Source: *Life of B.R. Haydon, from His Autobiography and Journals*, ed. and compiled by Tom Taylor (London, 1855).

Hayes, Patrick Joseph
(1867-1938) American prelate. Appointed Roman Catholic Archbishop of New York in 1919. Named Cardinal of the Church in 1924. Died at age 70 in Monticello, New York. Interred in the crypt under the altar of St. Patrick's Cathedral.
Last Words: "Good night!" Spoken to his secretary.
Source: "Cardinal Hayes Dies at 70 in Sleep at Country Home" (*New York Times*, September 5, 1938).

Hayes, Rutherford Birchard
(1822-1893) 19th President of the U.S. American politician, lawyer, military officer. Union officer in Civil War. Brevetted major general in 1865. Member U.S. House of Representatives from Ohio. Governor of Ohio. Defeated Samuel J. Tilden by one electoral vote (185 to 184) after a disputed Presidential election in 1876. Died at age 70 in Fremont, Ohio, after an attack of angina.
Last Words: "I know that I am going where Lucy is." His wife Lucy Ware Webb Hayes was the first wife of a President to graduate from college and the first to be called First Lady. She died in 1889.
Source: *Life of Rutherford Birchard Hayes* by Charles Richard Williams (Boston, 1914).

Hayne, Isaac
(1745-1781) American military officer. Colonel in the American Revolution. Ordered by the British to join their forces. Refused and instead joined the South Carolina colonial militia. Captured by the British.

Tried and hanged as a spy. His execution created much anger among Americans.

Last Words: "Don't lay too much to heart our separation from you; it will be but short. 'Twas but lately your dear mother died. Today I die. And you, my son, though but young, must shortly follow us." Spoken to his son who accompanied him to his execution.

Source: *The Life of General Francis Marion: A Celebrated Partisan Officer in the Revolutionary War Against the British and Tories in South Carolina and Georgia* by M.L. Weems and P. Horry (Philadelphia, 1834).

Haynes, Lemuel

(1753-1833) American clergyman, writer, soldier. Indentured servant who purchased his freedom. Served in the American Revolution. Ordained by Congregational Church in 1785. First African-American ordained by a major denomination in the U.S. Had a 30-year pastorate in an integrated church in Rutland, Vermont. Spent his last 11 years with a congregation in Granville, New York. Died at age 80.

Last Words: "I love my wife, I love my children, but I love my Saviour better than all."

Source: *Sketches of the Life and Character of the Rev. Lemuel Haynes, A.M. for Many Years the Pastor of a Church in Rutland Vt., and Late in Granville, New York* by Timothy Mather Cooley (New York, 1837).

Hayward, Susan

(1917-1975) American actress. Screen star. Nominated for five Academy Awards. Won in 1959 for *I Want to Live*. Died at age 57 of cancer in Hollywood, California.

Last Words: "I love you." Spoken to her son.

Source: *Susan Hayward: Portrait of a Survivor* by Beverly Linet (New York, 1980.

Hayworth, Rita

(1918-1987) American actress. Screen star. Nominated for a Golden Globe in 1965 for *Circus World*. In her later years, Alzheimer's disease caused her to lose her mental faculties and the ability to speak. Died at age 68 in New York City.

Last Words: "He used to do that. He told me how to do that." Mumbled and perhaps openly addressed to her father.

Source: *If This Was Happiness* by Barbara Leaming (New York, 1989).

Hazen, Richard S.

(1943-1996) American airline pilot, disaster victim. First officer of ValuJet 592, a 27-year-old DC-9. The plane had an in-flight fire and crashed in the Florida Everglades en route from Miami International Airport to Hartsfield International Airport in Atlanta, Georgia. All 100 aboard were killed, including San Diego Chargers running back Rodney Culver, former University of Miami offensive lineman Robert Woodus and songwriter and musician Walter Hyatt. The television drama COPS was taping with the Miami-Dade Police Department when the accident occurred and documented some of the first 9-1-1 calls and the initial investigations into the accident.

Last Words: "Critter five-ninety-two, we need the, uh, closest airport available." Spoken just prior to crashing.

Source: *Mayday: Accident Reports and Voice Transcripts from Airline Crash Investigations* by Marion F. Sturkey (Plum Branch, SC, 2005).

Hazlitt, William

(1778-1830) English essayist, scholar, critic. Master of English prose; brilliant essayist. Friend of Coleridge, Wordsworth, Lamb, Leigh Hunt. Wanted to be a portrait painter but after nine years of trying, realized he lacked the talent. Turned to literature. Worked as journalist, magazine writer. Suffered a long time with stomach trouble. Died of cancer at age 52.

Last Words: "I have had a happy life." Spoken as he lay dying.

Source: *The Life of William Hazlitt* by Percival P. Howe (London, 1922).

Variation: "Well, I have led a happy life."

Source: *Soho and Its Associations: Historical, Literary & Artistic* by Edward F. Rimbault and George Clinch (London, 1895).

Variation: "Well, I've had a happy life!"

Source: *British Authors of the Nineteenth Century*, ed. by Stanley J. Kunitz and Howard Haycraft (New York, 1936).

Healy, James Augustine

(1830-1900) American prelate. Son of an ex-slave. Bishop in Portland, Maine. First African American to be ordained bishop in the American Roman Catholic Church. He suffered a long and painful illness before dying at age 70.

Last Words: "I wonder if heaven is worth it all? Yes! Yes! It is worth all this and infinitely more still!" Spoken to his physician before he died of a heart attack.

Source: *Bishop Healy: Beloved Outcaste* by Albert S. Foley (New York, 1954).

Hearn, Lafcadio

(1850-1904) Greek-born Irish writer. Born of Irish and Greek parents on Greek island of Santa Maura. Birth name Patricio Lafcadio Tessima Carlos Hearn. Raised in Ireland. Lived in the U.S. from 1869 to 1890. Settled in Japan in 1890. Known as Yakumo Kiozumi after he became Japanese citizen. Became a Buddhist. Notable works: *Glimpses of Unfamiliar Japan; Japan, An Attempt at Interpretation.* Died at age 54 in Tokyo.

Last Words: "Ah—because of sickness."

Source: *Lafcadio Hearn* by Vera McWilliams (Boston, 1946).

Heath, Neville George Clevely

(1917-1946) British murderer. Tried, convicted and executed for savagely mutilating and sexually assaulting his 21-year-old victim. Although prison doctors testified that he was a sadistic, psychopathic sexual pervert, he was not insane. Heath received the death penalty and was hanged by Albert Pierrepoint at Pentonville Prison. Heath asked Pierrepoint for a whiskey, and then spoke his Last Words, correcting himself.

Last Words: "You might make that a double."

Source: *A Lance for Liberty* by J.D. Casswell (London, 1961).

Heber, Reginald

(1783-1826) English prelate, poet, hymnist. Bishop of Calcutta. Notable work: "Palestine" (poem). Died suddenly at age of 42 while visiting Trichinopoly, India.

Last Words (written): "Trichinopoly, April 3, 1826."

Source: *Life of Reginald Heber, D.D., The Lord Bishop of Calcutta by His Widow with Selections, Correspondence, Unpublished Poems, and Private Papers* by Amelia Shipley Heber (New York, 1830).

Hecker, Isaac Thomas

(1819-1888) American clergyman. Member of Brook Farm Community. Member of Amos Bronson Alcott's Fruitlands. Friend of Thoreau, Ralph Waldo Emerson. Ordained Roman Catholic priest. Founded Paulist Fathers. Founded magazine *Catholic World.* Died at age 69 in New York City.

Last Words: "No, I will." He wanted to give his own blessing.

Source: *Celestial Homespun: The Life of Isaac Thomas Hecker* by Katherine Burton (London, 1943).

Heckewelder, John Gottlieb Ernestus

(1743-1823) English-born American missionary, writer. Moravian church missionary among Ohio Native Americans. He and wife Sarah were the first white couple to marry in Ohio. He aided in negotiating several treaties with Native Americans in western Ohio, Indiana and Michigan. Wrote of his experiences and recorded Native American customs. James Fenimore Cooper used his account as a historical source.

Last Words: "Golgotha, Gethsemane."

Source: *Life of John Heckewelder* by Rev. Edward Rondthaler (Philadelphia, 1847).

Hedgepath, Marion

(1856-1910) American murderer, train robber, bandit. Known as the Handsome Bandit, Debonair Bandit, Montana Bandit. Most infamous as a train robber. In 1890, he robbed a train in Glendale, Missouri, escaping with $10,000. He was later caught and arrested in San Francisco by the Pinkertons. He served less than 20 years of a 25-year sentence in the Missouri State Prison. After his release he was shot and killed in Chicago by a policeman. Died at age 54.

Last Words: "Never!" His response to the policeman who ordered him to surrender.

Source: *Bloodletters and Badmen: A Narrative Encyclopedia of American Criminals from the Pilgrims to the Present* by Jay Robert Nash (New York, 1995).

Hegel, Georg Wilhelm Friedrich

(1770-1831) German philosopher, writer, educator. Professor at University of Jena, Heidelberg, Berlin. Created system of philosophy known as Hegelianism. Notable works: *Phenomenology of the Mind; History of Philosophy; Philosophy of Religion.* Died at age 61 during a cholera epidemic in Berlin.

Last Words (doubtful): "Only one man ever understood me. And he didn't understand me."

Source: Various Last Words compilations and Internet websites.

These were not Hegel's Last Words. In *Schelling on Hegel*, Friedrich Engels said the quote was allegedly from Hegel but doubtless stemmed from Schelling: "Only one of my pupils understood me, and even he unfortunately understood me wrongly." Friedrich Wilhelm Joseph von Schelling was Hegel's college classmate, roommate and best friend.

Source: "Schelling on Hegel" by Friedrich Engels (*Telegraph für Deutschland*, Nos. 207/208, December 1841).

Heilbrun, Carolyn Gold

(1926-2003) American writer, feminist, educator, mystery novelist. Pen name: Amanda Cross. Professor of English and comparative literature at Columbia University. Wrote several best-seller mystery novels using as heroine Kate Fansler, a feminist professor of literature who solved crimes. Won Nero Wolfe Award for literary excellence in mystery genre in 1981. She also wrote nonfiction books. Committed suicide at age 77 by means of asphyxiation.

Last Words: (written): "The journey's over. Love to all. Carolyn." Suicide note.

Source: "Her Final Mystery, Author, 77, Acts Out Suicide Plot" (*New York Post*, October 11, 2003).

Heindel, Max

(1865-1919) Danish-American Christian occultist, astrologer, writer, mystic. Birth name Carl Louis von Grasshoff. Founder of Rosicrucians. After abandoning a career in engineering, he wrote many books related to the Rosicrucians and Christian occultism. Died at age 53 in Oceanside, California.

Last Words: "I am all right dear." Spoken to his wife.

Source: *The Rosicrucian Mysteries—An Elementary Exposition of Their Secret Teachings* by Max Heindel (Charleston, SC, 2008) His "Last Words" appear in the publisher's preface.

Heine, Heinrich

(1797-1856) German writer, poet, literary critic. Important figure in radical political journalism. Wrote many popular German lyrics, including "Die Lorelei." Some were set to music by Schumann, Brahms and Grieg. Bedridden last eight years of his life with an incurable disease of the spine. Died at age 58 in Paris.

Different Last Words:

(1) "Write—write! Paper—Pencil!"

Source: *That Man Heine: A Biography* by Lewis Browne with collaboration of Elsa Weihl (New York, 1927).

(2) "Bien sûr, il me pardonnera; c'est son métier." (tr. "God will forgive me, that's his job.") Spoken to a friend who came to see him and asked if he was on good terms with God.

Source: *Life, Work and Opinions of Heine* by William Stigand (London, 1875).

(3) "No, not even a play of Scribe." His response to a physician who placed a hand glass to his lips and asked "Can you hiss (siffler)?"

Source: *A History of the Nineteenth Century Year by Year* by Edwin Emerson Jr. (New York, 1902).

(4) "I am done for."

Source: *The Last Words (Real and Traditional) of Distinguished Men and Women Collected from Various Sources* by Frederic Rowland Marvin (New York, 1901). Marvin quoted Catherine Bourlois, Heine's nurse. She wrote in a letter to Mrs. Charlotte Emden that these were Heine's last words, spoken repeatedly.

Heinrich der Löwe see **Henry The Lion**.

Helm, Boone

(1823-1864) American murderer, cannibal, thief. Implicated in several killings. Also involved in a harsh winter episode that concluded when he and another man in his traveling party resorted to eating other members of the party to survive. His final depravity was when he teamed up with the notorious Montana Sheriff Henry Plummer. A vigilante committee was formed to deal with him. The committee hauled him in and tried him in secret. He was hanged with several others in the gang.

Last Words: "Kick away, old Jack; I'll be in hell with you in ten minutes. Every man for his principles—hurrah for Jeff Davis! Let her rip."

Source: "Biographical Notices of the Leading Road Agents of Plummer's Band and Others*" in *The Vigilantes of Montana* by Prof. Thomas J. Dimsdale (Helena, Montana, 1915).

Heloise

(1100?-1164) French nun, writer. Pupil and beloved wife of Abelard, who died in 1142. Heloise became a Benedictine nun and abbess. She died 22 years after Abelard and was buried in his coffin near Troyes, France, at her request. Their bodies were later moved Paris.

Last Words: "In death at last let me rest with Abelard."

Source: *Book of Catholic Quotations Compiled from Approved Sources Ancient, Medieval and Modern*, ed. by John Chapin (New York, 1956).

Helper, Hinton Rowan

(1829-1909) American abolitionist, writer. Friend of Horace Greeley. Notable work: *The Impending Crisis of the South, and How to Meet It* (published 1857; a book that aroused strong antislavery feelings before the Civil War). His condemnation of slavery was for economic, not humanitarian reasons. He argued that slavery was an economic threat to poor white Southerners. After the war, three of his books on "the Negro Question" were extremely racist. He worked as a Washington lobbyist. Became unbalanced after his wife died. Committed suicide at age 79 in a Washington, D.C., rooming house.

Last Words: "There is no justice in this world."

Source: *American Reformers*, ed. by Alden Whitman (New York, 1985).

Hemans, Felicia Dorothea Browne

(1793-1835) English poet. Pen name Clara Balfour. Often wrote about historical events. Published first book at age 15. Notable poem: "Casabianca" (well-known opening line: "The boy stood on the burning deck.") Died in Dublin at age 41, possibly of tuberculosis or a heart problem complicated by scarlet fever.

Last Words: "Well, do you like it?" Her response when her son told her what book he was reading. She then fell into a gentle sleep till evening and died between eight and nine without a struggle.

Source: *Memorials of Mrs. Hemans with Illustrations of Her Literary Character from Her Private Correspondence* by Henry F. Chorley (London, 1836).

Hemingway, Ernest Miller

(1899-1961) American novelist, short-story writer, reporter, essayist. Awarded 1953 Pulitzer Prize for Fiction and 1954 Nobel Prize for Literature. Notable works: *A Farewell to Arms; A Moveable Feast; The Old Man and the Sea; For Whom the Bell Tolls; The Sun Also Rises*. Many of his novels have been made into movies. Hospitalized for depression. Committed suicide at age 61 at his home in Ketchum, Idaho.

Last Words: "Goodnight my kitten." Spoken to his wife.

Source: *The Hemingway Women* by Bernice Kert (New York, 1963).

Henderson, Alexander

(1583?-1646) Scottish clergyman, Leader in developing Church of Scotland. Moderator of Glasgow Assembly.

Last Words (written): "...most of all obliged to the grace and goodness of God, for calling me to believe the promises of the Gospel, and for exalting me to be a preacher of them to others, and to be a willing, though weak instrument in this great and wonderful work of Reformation, which I beseech the Lord to bring to a happy conclusion."

Source: *Lives of Alexander Henderson and James Guthrie* by the Committee of The General Assembly of the Free Church of Scotland (Edinburgh, 1846).

Henderson, Ebenezer

(1784-1858) Scottish missionary, linguist, translator. Formed first Congregational church in Sweden. Spoke many languages, including Hebrew, Persian, Turkish and Manchu. Translated many books. Died at age 73 at Mortlake.

Last Words: "My flesh and my heart faileth; but God is the strength of my heart, and my portion for ever."

Source: *Memoirs of Ebenezer Henderson* by Thulia S. Henderson (London, 1859). The author was his daughter.

Hendricks, Thomas Andrews

(1819-1885) American politician. Member U.S. House of Representatives and Senate from Indiana. Governor of Indiana. Ran unsuccessfully for U.S. Vice President on the Tilden ticket. Elected 21st Vice President in the administration of Grover Cleveland. Served less than a year. Died at age 66 of heart disease in Washington, D.C. Poet Joseph Samuel Reed dedicated the poem

"To Thos. A. Hendricks, In Memoriam" to him in his collection *Winnowed Grasses.*
Last Words: "At rest at last."
Source: *The Miscellaneous Documents of the Senate of the United States for the First Session of the Forty-Ninth Congress* (Washington, D.C., 1886).
Variation: "I am free at last." Spoken to his physician.
Source: *Life and Public Services of Thomas A. Hendricks with Selected Speeches and Writings* by John Walker Holcombe and Hubert Marshall Skinner (Indianapolis, IN, 1886).

Henie, Sonja
(1912-1969) Norwegian-born ice skater, actress. Screen star. Three-time Olympic ice skating champion. Appeared in movies and ice shows in the 1930s and 1940s. Died at age 57 of leukemia, while traveling by plane from Paris to Oslo.
Last Words: "Oh, Niels, I am so tired." Spoken to her husband Niels Onstad.
Source: *Queen of Ice, Queen of Shadows: The Unsuspected Life of Sonja Henie* by Raymond Strait and Leif Henie (Chelsea, MI, 1985). Leif Henie was her brother.

Henley, John
(1800-1842) British clergyman, hymnist, journalist, editor. Methodist. Notable hymn: "Children of Jerusalem." Kept a journal for the years 1825 to 1830 that described his life work, travel, thought, prayers, schools, social reading and meetings in southwestern England, including Devon, Somerset.
Last Words: "Stay! Stay! Stay!"
Source: *Memorials of Rev. John Henley* compiled by his widow Mary Henley, ed. by John G. Avery (London, 1844).

Henley, William Ernest
(1849-1903) English writer, poet, journalist. Editor of *Scots Observer* and *National Observer*. Close friend of Robert Louis Stevenson. Lost a leg to tuberculosis. Was the inspiration for peg-legged Long John Silver in Stevenson's *Treasure Island.* Notable work: *Invictus* (poem that ends with the lines: "I am the master of my fate. I am the captain of my soul." American terrorist Timothy McVeigh chose *Invictus* as his final statement while awaiting execution for the Oklahoma bombings.) Henley died at age 53 in Woking, England.
Last Words (written): "Dear Boy—I'd give so much to see you just now. When can you come? I can't get to town; being kind of broken-hearted; or I'd tryst you there. But I want your advice and (if I can get it) your help. And I want the first of the things soon. The sooner the better. W.E.H." Letter to editor, journalist, critic Charles Whibley.
Source: *W.E. Henley* by John Connell (London, 1949).

Henrietta Anne, Duchess of Orléans
(1644-1670) English and French royalty. Daughter of Charles I and Henrietta Marie. Youngest sister of Charles II. Married Philip, Duke of Orleans (brother of Louis XIV). Worked for an alliance between England and France, and to convert Charles to Catholicism. Helped negotiate Treaty of Dover. The Jacobites claim to the throne following the death of Henry Benedict Stuart descends from her. Died at age 26 at Saint Cloud, France.
Last Words: "With all my heart." Her response when asked by the abbé: "Madame, you believe in God, you hope in God, you love God?"
Sources: *Madame: A Life of Henrietta, Daughter of Charles I and the Duchess of Orleans* by Julia Cartwright [Mrs. Henry Ady] (New York, 1907); *Bossuet and His Contemporaries* by H. L. Sidney Lear (London, 1874).

Henrietta Maria, Queen Consort of Charles I of England
(1609-1669) French-born English royalty, queen consort. Daughter of French King Henry IV and Marie de Medicis. Wife of Charles I of England. Fled to France in 1644 as the monarchy collapsed. Charles was executed in 1649. Henrietta Maria went back to England for five years during the Restoration. She then returned to France where she died at age 59.
Last Words: "Tell Duquesne that I cannot sleep and that I would like him to take me some new medicine."
Source: *Last Words: A Dictionary of Deathbed Quotations* by C. Bernard Ruffin (Jefferson, NC, 1995).
The queen was given a grain of laudanum. Doctor Duquesne remained at her side to watch the effects of the drug. When he noticed the profoundness of her sleep, he tried in vain to rouse her. She never woke up.
Source: *The Life of Queen Henrietta Maria* by Ida

Ashworth Taylor (London, 1905).
Her cause of death is described. This and other sources give no direct Last Words. They only indicate that she could not sleep and was administered a medicine.

Henry II, King of England

(1133-1189) English monarch. Grandson of Henry I. Son of Matilda and Geoffrey of Anjou. Known as Curtmantle. Founder of the Plantagenet dynasty. Married Eleanor of Aquitaine. Becket, whom he appointed archbishop, opposed his church reform plans and was murdered in 1170. Henry's sons conspired against him in later years. Died at age 56 in Chinon, France.

Last Words: "Shame, shame on a conquered king." Heartbroken comment made when he heard the news that even his youngest son John had betrayed him.

Source: *A Short History of the English People* by John Richard Green (London, 1874).

Henry IV, King of England

(1367-1413) English monarch. Known as Henry of Bolingbroke and Henry of Lancaster. Oldest surviving son of John of Gaunt. Established the House of Lancaster. An old prophecy predicted Henry would die in Jerusalem. He died in the Jerusalem Chamber in Westminster Abbey and was succeeded by his son Henry V.

Last Words: "Lauds be given to the father of heaven, for now I know that I shall die here in this chamber, according to the prophecy of me declared, that I should depart this life in Jerusalem." Spoken when told the chamber in which he was dying was called Jerusalem.

Source: *Chronicles of England, Scotland, and Ireland* by Raphael Holinshed (London, 1808).

Henry V, King of England

(1387-1422) English monarch. Son of Henry IV. Invaded France and won victory at Agincourt. Made heir of Charles VI of France with Treaty of Troyes. Married Catherine of France. Died at age 34 of dysentery in Bois de Vincennes, France. Succeeded by his son Henry VI.

Last Words: "Into Thy hands, O Lord—."

Source: *Henry the Fifth* by Alfred John Church (London, 1889).

Henry VII, King of England

(1457-1509) English monarch. First Tudor king of England. Defeated and killed Richard III at Bosworth Field. Married daughter of Edward IV. When he died of tuberculosis at age 52, his son Henry VIII ascended to the throne.

Last Words: "If it should please God to send me life, you should find me a new changed man."

Source: *Henry the Eighth* by Francis Hackett (New York, 1945).

Henry VIII, King of England

(1491-1547) English monarch. Son of Henry VII. Second Tudor monarch. Severed ties with Roman Catholic Church. Obtained from Parliament the Act of Supremacy creating a national church separate from Rome. Had six wives. Last wife was Catherine Parr, who took care of him during the final three years of his life. Died at age 55 in Whitehall Palace in London, after ruling for 37 years. He was succeeded by his nine-year-old son Edward VI, by his third wife Jane Seymour.

Different Last Words:

(1) "Monks, monks, monks!" It is said that he repeated the word several times. Probably a reference to when he abolished the monasteries and ousted the monks. He also looked at one of his friends and said: "All is lost."

Source: *History of the Protestant Reformation in Germany and Switzerland and in England, Ireland, Scotland, The Netherlands, France and Northern Europe in a Series of Essays* by M.J. Spalding (Baltimore, MD, 1860).

(2) "Cranmer, but he not yet." Spoken on his deathbed to Sir Anthony Denny, a gentleman of the chamber, in response to his inquiry: "Was there any learned man to confer withal and open his mind to?" Henry then said he would "take a little sleep and then, as I feel myself, I would advise upon the matter." Cranmer later entered the room and asked Henry: "Do you die in the faith of Christ?" But Henry was too close to death to respond. Cranmer was the Archbishop of Canterbury.

Sources: *Henry VIII* by A F. Pollard (London, 1905); *Henry the Eighth* by Francis Hackett (New York, 1929).

Henry III, King of France

(1551-1589) French monarch. Son of Henry II and Catherine de' Médici. Last member of the House of Valois. Had no children. Joined forces with the Huguenots against the Holy League. Forced to flee Paris. Assassinated at St. Cloud by Jacques Clement, a fanatical Dominican monk. Succeeded by Henry of Navarre.

Last Words: "You will have many troubles unless you make up your mind to change your religion. I exhort you to do this!" Spoken to Henry of Béarn. The king then lost consciousness and died three hours later.

Source: *The National History of France: The Century of the Renaissance* by Louis Batiffol, tr. by Elsie Finnimore Buckley (New York, 1916).

Henry IV, King of France

(1553-1610) French monarch. First Bourbon king of France. Known as Henry of Navarre. Succeeded Henry III. Popular monarch. Ended religious wars in France. Assassinated in Paris at age 56 by a fanatical Jesuit monk François Ravaillac. Succeeded by his son Louis XIII.

Different Last Words:

(1) "I am wounded." Spoken when stabbed by Ravaillac. The assassin then stabbed Henry again. He died almost instantly.

Source: *Memoirs of Maximilian de Bethune, Duke of Sully, Prime Minister to Henry the Great* by Maximilien de Béthune Duc de Sully and Charlotte Lennox (London, 1756).

(2) "It is nothing." He died immediately after he was stabbed in the heart.

Source: *Henry of Navarre: The King Who Dared* by Hesketh Pearson (New York, 1963).

Henry IV, Holy Roman Emperor and King of Germany

(1050-1106) German monarch. Son of Emperor Henry III. Forced to abdicate as emperor. Son Henry captured and imprisoned him in 1105. He escaped and went to Liege to raise an army. Died suddenly at age 55 in Liege before he could do so.

Last Words: "O how unhappy I am who squandered such great treasures in vain—how happy I could have been if I had given these things to the poor! But I swear before the eye of the All-Knowing that all my efforts have been only for the advancement of my Church."

Source: *Adalbert, Erzbischof von Hamburg* by Cosmar Grünhagen (Leipzig, Germany, 1854).

Henry, Bayard

(1857-1926) American financier, industrialist, politician. President of United New Jersey Rail Road & Canal Company. Director of Pennsylvania Railroad and numerous other corporations. Pennsylvania state senator. Trustee of Princeton University. Became ill with complications from diabetes while in Hawaii. Sailed to San Francisco where he died.

Last Words: "Don't worry about me. I am comfortable. If my time is to come, I am resigned to the inevitable." Spoken to his wife and son who were at his bedside when he died.

Source: "Bayard Henry Dies in San Francisco. Philadelphia Financier Was Director of the Pennsylvania Railway and Trustee of Princeton" (*New York Times*, September 18, 1926).

Henry, Matthew

(1662-1714) Welsh-born Nonconformist English clergyman. Minister of Presbyterian congregation in Chester. Biblical commentator. Son of Rev. Philip Henry. Died at age 51 suddenly of apoplexy in Nantwich, before he finished *Exposition of the Old and New*. Several ministers who were his colleagues completed it.

Last Words: "A life spent in the service of God and communion with Him is the most comfortable and pleasant life that anyone can live in this world."

Source: *An Account of the Life and Death of Matthew Henry* by W. Tong (London, 1716).

Henry, O., see **Porter, William Sydney**.

Henry, Patrick

(1736-1799) American lawyer, politician, statesman, jurist, orator. Initiated Committee of Correspondence. Member Continental Congress. Involved in ratification of Bill of Rights. Governor of Virginia. U.S secretary of state. Chief justice of U.S. Supreme Court. Came out of retirement in 1799 to run for Virginia legislature. Won but died at age 63 at his Virginia plantation before he could take his seat. Submarine, ship and several U.S. counties and schools named for him.

Different Last Words:

(1) "Be thankful for the kind God who allows me to go thus painlessly."

Source: *Living Biographies of Famous Americans* by Henry and Dana Lee Thomas (New York, 1946).

(2) "I trust in the mercy of God, it is not now too late."

Source: "Dying Words of Noted People" (*American Notes and Queries,* Vol. VII, No. 9, June 27, 1891).

Henry, Philip

(1631-1696) English Nonconformist clergyman. Father of Matthew Henry. Minister of gospel in Shropshire. Died at age 64. His sermons were published from his manuscripts in 1816.

Last Words: "O death, where is thy—."

Source: *Memoir of the Rev. Philip Henry* by Matthew Henry (London, 1848).

Henry Frederick, Prince of Wales

(1594-1612) English royalty. Henry Frederick Stuart, eldest son of James VI of Scotland/James I of England and Anne of Denmark. Died at age 18 of typhoid fever.

Different Last Words:

(1) "I would say somewhat, but I cannot utter it." Spoken to Sir David Murray.

Source: *The Life of Henry Prince of Wales, Eldest Son of King James I. Compiled Chiefly from His Own Papers, and Other Manuscripts, Never Before Published* by Thomas Birch, D.D. (London, 1790).

(2) "Where is my dear sister?"

Source: *Charles the First* by John Bowle (Boston, 1975).

Henry the Lion, Duke of Saxony and Bavaria

(1129-1195) German royalty. Prince. Son of Henry the Proud. Cousin of Emperor Frederick I (Barbarossa). Colonized northern Germany. Founder of Munich and Lübeck. Died at age 66 in Brunswick, Saxony.

Last Words: "God be merciful to me a sinner."

Source: *Heinrich der Löwe* by Hans Prutz (Leipzig, Germany, 1865).

Herbert, Edward, 1st Baron Herbert of Cherbury

(1583-1648) English courtier, historian, nobleman, diplomat. Metaphysical poet. Brother of poet George Herbert. Cousin of Earl of Pembroke. English ambassador to France. Died at age 65 in London.

Last Words: "Then an hour hence I shall depart." His response after asking what time it was.

Source: *Brief Lives* by John Aubrey, ed. by Oliver Lawson Dick (London, 1949).

Herbert, George

(1593-1633) Welsh-born English clergyman, nobleman. Metaphysical poet. Cousin of Earl of Pembroke. Brother of Edward Herbert (1st Baron Herbert of Cherbury). Wrote popular sacred poems. Favorite poet of Charles I. Notable work: *The Temple.* His works were published posthumously. Died at age 39 of tuberculosis in Bemerton, Wiltshire, England. Composers who have set his poetry to music include Randall Thompson, William Walton and Ralph Vaughan Williams.

Last Words: "I am now ready to die. Lord, forsake me not, now my strength faileth me: but grant me mercy for the merits of my Jesus. And now Lord, Lord, now receive my soul."

Source: *Walton's Lives of Dr. John Donne, Sir Henry Wotton, Mr. Richard Hooker, Mr. George Herbert, and Dr. Robert Sanderson* by Izaak Walton and Thomas Zouch (York, England, 1796).

Herbert, Sidney, Lord Herbert of Lea

(1810-1861) British politician, statesman, nobleman. Son of 11th Earl of Pembroke. Member of Parliament. Secretary of war. Illness forced him to retire in 1860. Died the following year at age 50, shortly after he was created Lord Herbert of Lea.

Last Words: "Well, this is the end. I have had a life of great happiness. A short one, perhaps; but an active one. I have not done all I wished; but I have tried to do my best."

Source: *Sidney Herbert, Lord Herbert of Lea* by Arthur Hamilton-Gordon Stanmore, Baron (London, 1906).

Herder, Johann Gottfried von

(1744-1803) German poet, critic, theologian, philosopher. Lutheran. Influenced Goethe. Held position at court at Weimar many years. Died at age 59 in Weimar.

Different Last Words:

(1) "My friend, my dearest friend, preserve me still, if that is possible." He was discussing work he had not finished.

Source: *Herders Leben* by Eugen Kühnemann (Munich, Germany, 1895).

(2) "Refresh me with a great thought." His last spoken words. He died writing an "Ode to the Deity." His pen had just reached the last line.

Sources: *Gleanings from the Harvest-Fields of Literature, Science and Art: A Mélange of Excerpta, Curious, Humorous, and Instructive* by Charles C. Bombaugh (Baltimore, MD 1860); *The Last Words (Real and Traditional) of Distinguished Men and Women Collected from Various Sources* by Frederic Rowland Marvin (New York, 1901).

Herrera, Leonel Torres

(1947-1993) American execution victim. Controversial appellant of U.S. Supreme Court decision. Executed in Texas not because he could not prove his innocence, but because he could not get a new trial, as the first trial was considered fair. Herrera was accused of killing two Texas police officers in 1981. In 1984, his brother Raul's attorney signed an affidavit stating Raul told him he had killed the officers. Raul's former cellmate signed a similar affidavit, as did Raul's son, Raul Jr. and Jose Ybarra, Jr. who claimed Raul confessed to him in 1983. Despite the four affidavits, Herrera was denied relief in state courts. On appeal in 1993, the U.S. Supreme Court ruled that Herrera's claim of innocence was not a bar to his execution. He had to show that there were procedural errors in his trial in order to gain relief. The only dissenting justice Harry Blackmun stood by reason over law, saying: "The execution of a person who can show that he is innocent comes perilously close to simple murder." Herrera was executed by lethal injection on May 12, 1993, four months after the ruling.

Last Words: "I am innocent, innocent, innocent. Make no mistake about this; I owe society nothing. Continue the struggle for human rights, helping those who are innocent, especially Mr. Graham. I am an innocent man, and something very wrong is taking place tonight. May God bless you all. I am ready."

Source: *Last Words from Death Row: The Wall Unit* by Norma Herrera (Mequon, TN, 2007). The author was his sister.

Herrick, Myron T.

(1854-1929) American banker, politician, lawyer, diplomat. Governor of Ohio. Unsuccessful candidate for U.S. Senate. U.S. ambassador to France twice: 1912 to 1914 and 1921 to 1929. Died at age 74 in office.

Last Words: "Do you really think so? Well, I will do my best!" His response to his wife who told him he had pulled through much worse things than this and would soon be all right.

Source: *Myron Herrick, Friend of France: An Autobiographical Biography* by Col. T. Bentley Mott (Garden City, NY, 1929).

Herschell, William Miller

(1873-1939) American poet, newspaper journalist. Wrote for the *Indianapolis News; Evansville Journal; Indianapolis Press; Terre Haute Tribune* and *Indianapolis Journal.* Notable work: *Ain't God Good to Indiana,* which is inscribed on a bronze plaque in the rotunda of the Indiana state house. Much of his poetry was inspired by the Indiana landscape and environment. Died at age 66.

Last Words: "I'll whip it yet, lo." Spoken to his wife Josephine.

Source: "William Miller Herschell" by Ray E. Boomhower, Indiana Journalism Hall of Fame (Greencastle, IN, 2003).

Hervey, James

(1714-1758) English clergyman, writer. Anglican. Notable works: *Meditations Among the Tombs; Reflections on a Flower Garden; Contemplations on the Night.* His writing was admired by William Blake who mentioned Hervey in his work. Died at age 44.

Different Last Words:

(1) "Lord, lettest now Thy servant depart in peace."

Source: *Méditations d'Hervey,* tr. from English by M. Le Tourneur (Paris, 1771).

(2) "Precious salvation!" Spoken two or three times. He leaned his head against the side of his chair, shut his eyes and died without a sigh or groan.

Source: *The Whole Works of the Late Rev. James Hervey, A.M.,* Vol. I (Philadelphia, 1810).

Herzl, Theodor

(1860-1904) Hungarian-born Viennese Jewish leader, journalist, publisher. Father of political Zionism. Notable work: *The Jewish State* (advocated theory of Jewish nationalism that led to creation of Zionist Movement). Died at age 44 of pneumonia and heart failure in Edlach, Austria.

Different Last Words:

(1) "Your brethren are dispersed throughout the whole world. If you want to, you will find them. I have found them, too, because I have been looking for them. Think of it and don't forget that your people need young, healthy strength and that you are the heir of the name Herzl." Spoken to his son.

Source: *Star Over Jordan* by Josef Patai (New York, 1946).

(2) "Well my dear ones, you saw me, and I saw you. Now go back."

Source: *Theodor Herzl: A Biographical Study* by Jacob de Haas (Chicago, 1927).

Hessus, Helius Eobanus

(1488-1540) German poet, humanist, educator. Original surname Koch. Professor of Latin at Erfurt University. Notable work: *Sylvae* (or *Silvae*; pastoral poems). His *Epistolae* were edited by his friend Camerarius, who also wrote his biography. Died at age 52. School, fire boat and a forest were named for him.

Last Words: "I want to ascend to my Lord."

Source: *Narratio de H. Eobano Hesso* by Joachim Camerarius, ed., J.T. Kreyssig (Meissen, Germany, 1843) Original edition published in Nuremberg, Germany, 1553.

Hewart, Gordon, 1st Viscount Hewart

(1870-1943) British politician, jurist. 1st Viscount Hewart. Solicitor general and attorney general. Given peerage in 1921 so that he could sit in the House of Lords as Lord chief justice. He held the position until 1940. At retirement, he was created Viscount Hewart. Died at age 73 in London.

Last Words: "Damn it! There's that cuckoo again!" He was referring to an annoying bird outside.

Sources: *Encounter* by Congress for Cultural Freedom, v. 17 (London, 1961); "A Dying Art: The Classy Exit Line" by Lance Morrow (*Time* magazine, January 16, 1984).

Hewitt, Abram Stevens

(1822-1903) American industrialist, reformer, politician, businessman. Member U.S. House of Representatives from New York. Mayor of New York City. Aided in overthrow of Tweed Ring. Son-in-law of Peter Cooper. Helped establish and manage Cooper Union. Died at age 81 in New York.

Last Words: "And now I am officially dead." Spoken in the hospital as an oxygen tube was removed.

Source: *Abram S. Hewitt: With Some Account of Peter Cooper* by Allan Nevins (New York, 1935).

Hexum, Jon-Erik

(1957-1984) American actor, model. Accidentally shot and killed himself with a prop gun. He died at age 26 on the set of the television series *Cover Up,* in which he was appearing in Century City, California.

Last Words: "Let's see if I get myself with this one."

Source: *The Hollywood Book of Death: The Bizarre, Often Sordid, Passings of More Than 125 American Movie and TV Idols* by James Robert Parish (Chicago, 2002). This version is quoted by *The Jon-Erik Hexum Fan Club and Archive* (who added "or words to that effect" after the quote).

Variation: "Let see if this will do it."

Source: Various Last Words compilations and Internet websites.

Hey, Johann Wilhelm (Wilhelm)

(1789-1854). German clergyman, hymnist. Author of fables, children's poems. Notable work: *Fabeln für Kinder*. Died at age 65 in Ichtershausen, Germany.

Last Words (written):

"So you, my nurses dear,
In these last difficult days,
In bitter parting here
Show me your loving ways.
The love so tenderly given—
And yet such strength behind:
A brief foretaste of heaven
Is what it brings to mind."

Verses were written to thank two villagers who helped him during his final days.

Source: *Wilhelm Hey nach seinem eigenen Briefen* by Theodor Hansen (Gotha, Germany, 1886).

Heyburn, Weldon Brinton

(1852-1912) American lawyer, politician. Member U.S. Senate from Idaho. Member of convention that framed Idaho constitution. Delegate to Republican conventions in Chicago, Minneapolis, Philadelphia and Chicago. Died at age 60 in Washington, D.C. while serving as senator. Heyburn, Idaho, and Mount Heyburn, in the Sawtooth

Mountains, were named for him.

Last Words: "I have lived my life as best I could within human limitations. I am worn out in the service of a great cause." Spoken to his brother Elwood.

Source: "Senator Heyburn Dies After Message" (*New York Times*, October 12, 1912).

Heylin or Heylyn, Peter

(1600-1662) English clergyman, historian, religious writer. Notable works: *History of the Reformation of the Church of England; Cosmographie* (encyclopedic description of the known world). Died at age 62.

Last Words: "I know it is church-time with you, and I know this is Ascension Day. I am ascending to the Church Triumphant. I go to my God and Saviour, unto joyous celestial, and to Hallelujahs eternal." Spoken to a minister.

Source: *Theologico-Historicus or the True Life of the Most Reverend Divine, and Excellent Historian Peter Heylyn* by John Barnard (London, 1683).

Hick, Samuel ("Sammy")

(1758-1829) English blacksmith, preacher. Gave up his blacksmithing business in 1825 to devote his life to preaching. His eccentricities and religious devotion were widely known, not only in England but also in other countries. A month before he died, he told his friends he was "going home." He then set about making funeral arrangements: choosing a sermon, placing his obituary in the newspaper, ordering food for the many people who would come to his interment. His last request was that his body be taken downstairs to be laid out as soon as he died. He reminded a friend that the stairway was too narrow and the windows of his room were too small for the coffin. He died at age 71.

Last Words: "I am going, get the sheets ready."

Source: *The Village Blacksmith, or, Piety and Usefulness Exemplified in a Memoir of the Life of Samuel Hick, Late of Micklefield, Yorkshire,* by James Everett (London, 1863).

Hickock, Richard Eugene ("Dick")

(1931-1965) American drifter, vagrant, murderer. Hickock and accomplice Perry E. Smith invaded the Clutter home in Kansas in

1959 and killed the parents and two children. Smith and Hickock were apprehended, tried, found guilty and sentenced to death. Both were executed by hanging in 1965. American writer Truman Capote wrote a best-selling book about the murders: *In Cold Blood.*

Last Words: "I just want to say I hold no hard feelings. You people are sending me to a better world than this ever was." He then shook hands with the four people who were responsible for his capture and conviction. He said "Nice to see you," then mounted the scaffold steps.

Source: *In Cold Blood* by Truman Capote (New York, 1965).

Hickok, James Butler ("Wild Bill)

(1837-1876) American scout, lawman. Frontier marshal. His shooting exploits made him a legend. Was shot and killed at age 39 by Jack McCall in a saloon in Deadwood, South Dakota. Hickok was holding a pair of aces and a pair of eights. After his killing it became known as the "dead man's hand." McCall was later hanged for the crime. The movie *Wild Bill* (1995) is a fictionalized version of his exploits.

Last Words (spoken): "The old duffer, he broke me on the hand."

Source: *They Called Him Wild Bill: The Life and Adventures of James Butler Hickok* by Joseph G. Rosa (Norman OK, 1964).

Last Words (written): "Agnes Darling: If such should be we never meet again, while firing my last shot, I will gently breathe the name of my wife—Agnes—and with wishes even for my enemies I will make the plunge and try to swim to the other shore. J.B. Hickok." Letter to his new wife shortly before he was shot.

Source: *Wild Bill Hickok: The Prince of Pistoleers* by Frank Wilstach (New York, 1937).

Hicks, William Melvin ("Bill")

(1961-1994) American comedian, satirist, social critic. Learned he had pancreatic cancer. Made final appearance at Caroline's in New York City in January 1994. Called friends to say good-bye.

Last Words: "I've said all I have to say." Spoken to fiancée Colleen and his family. He stopped speaking on February 14, 1994, and died two weeks later at age 32.

Source: "The Gospel According to Hicks" by Mike Sager (*GQ Magazine*, September 1994).

Higginson, Francis

(1587?-1630?) English-born American clergyman. Moved to Massachusetts Bay Colony as minister of a church in Salem. Died after a fever at age 42. He may have died of tuberculosis. His Last Words were reported by a bystander.

Last Words: "Though he [Higginson] shall leave his desolate wife and eight children whereof the eldest of whom was fourteen years old, in a low condition, yet he left them with his God, and he doubted not but the 'faithful God will graciously provide for them.'" After he said this final prayer, he fell asleep and died.

Source: *Life of Francis Higginson, First Minister in the Massachusetts Bay Colony, and Author of New England's Plantation* by Thomas Wentworth Higginson (New York, 1891).

Hilario, Saint (Brother) Jaime

(1889-1937) Spanish clergyman, holy man, martyr. Member of Institute of the Brothers of the Christian Schools. Birth name Manuel Barbal Cosan. Arrested during the Spanish Civil War. Tried and convicted for being a member of the Christian Brothers. Martyred by firing squad. Canonized in 1999.

Last Words: "My friends, to die for Christ is to reign!"

Source: *Catholic Martyrs of the Spanish Civil War 1936-1939* by Fray Justo Perez de Urbel (Kansas City, MO, 1993).

Variation: "To die for Christ, my young friends, is to live."

Source: De LaSalle Educational Institute, Casa Generalizia, Via Aurelia, 476 - 00165 Roma, Italia (Rome, 2007).

Hilary, Saint

(297?-367?) French prelate, holy man. Bishop of Poitiers. Doctor of the Church.

Last Words: "Soul, thou hast served Christ these seventy years, and art thou afraid to die? Go out, soul, go out!"

Source: "Death's Duel" in *Complete Poetry and Selected Prose* by John Donne, Dean of St. Paul's, ed. by John Hayward (London, 1936).

Hilda or Hild of Whitby, Saint

(614-680) English nun, holy woman. Abbess of Whitby. Suffered from fever for six years; continued to work until her death at age 66. In her last year she set up a monastery at Hackness, 14 miles from Whitby. Legend has it that at the moment she died, the bells of Hackness monastery tolled, and Begu, a nun, claimed to have witnessed Hilda's soul being borne to heaven by angels.

Different Last Words:

(1) "Live in evangelical peace with each other, and indeed with all, and while uttering them look cheerfully on death, or rather, if I may use the Lord's words, passed from death onto life."

Source: *Chapters of Early English Church History* by William Bright (Oxford, England, 1878).

(2) With her last words, she exhorted the "handmaids of Christ" who stood around her to "maintain the peace of the Gospel with each other and with all."

Source: *Dictionary of National Biography: from the Earliest Times to 1900* by George Smith, Leslie Stephen, Robert Blake, Christine S. Nicholls, Edgar T. Williams (London, 1900).

Hill, Ambrose Powell ("A.P")

(1825-1865) American military officer. Confederate general in U.S. Civil War. One of Stonewall Jackson's ablest subordinates. Gained early fame as commander of Hill's Light Division. Later in the war he commanded a corps under Robert E. Lee in the Army of Northern Virginia. Died at age 39 just before the war ended, near Petersburg Virginia, after approaching two skirmishers and ordering them to surrender.

Last Words: "Surrender, or I will shoot you!" Spoken to two privates who, not recognizing him for a general, shot and killed him.

Source: *To Appomattox* by Burke Davis (New York, 1959).

Hill, Benjamin Harvey

(1823-1882) American politician, lawyer. Helped organize government of the Confederacy. Member Confederate Provisional Congress in U.S. Civil War. After the war ended, he was a member of the U.S. House of Representatives and U.S. Senate from Georgia. Died at age 58 in Atlanta while serving in the Senate.

Last Words: "Almost home."
Source: *Senator Benjamin H. Hill of Georgia; His Life, Speeches and Writings* by Benjamin H. Hill Jr. (Atlanta, GA, 1893). The author was his son.

Hill, Daniel Harvey

(1821-1889) American military officer, educator. Brother-in-law of Stonewall Jackson. Fought in the Mexican War and Civil War. Confederate general. Saw action at Big Bethel, Fair Oaks, Fredericksburg, Antietam. President of University of Arkansas. President of Military and Agricultural College, Milledgeville, Georgia. Died at age 68 in Charlotte, North Carolina.
Last Words: "Nearly there." His children Harvey Jr. and Isabella were at his bedside and thought he murmured these final words.
Source: *Lee's Maverick General, Daniel Harvey Hill* by Hal Bridges (New York, 1961).

Hill, Joe

(1879-1915) Swedish-born American labor union activist. Real name Joel Emmanuel Hägglund. Also known as Joseph Hillström. Member of the Industrial Workers of the World (IWW; the Wobblies). Wrote political songs and poems, and made speeches supporting the IWW. Wrote "Casey Jones." Coined the phrase "pie in the sky" in his song "The Preacher and the Slave." Tried and convicted for the murder of a shop owner in Utah. Executed by firing squad. Inspiration for the song "I Dreamed I Saw Joe Hill Last Night."
Last Words (written): "Good-bye, Bill. I will die like a true blue rebel. Don't waste any time mourning. Organize." Written in a telegram to Big Bill Haywood the night before he was executed.
Source: *Joe Hill* by Wallace Stegner (New York, 1969).
Last Words (spoken): "I will show you how to die. I will show you how to die, I have a clear conscience. I am going now boys. Goodbye, Goodbye, boys. Fire! Go on and fire!" In keeping with his wishes, Hill was cremated and his ashes were sent to IWW groups in every state.
Source: *Joe Hill* by Gibbs M. Smith (Salt Lake City, 1969).

Hill, Paul

(1954-2003) American murderer, anti-abortion terrorist, ex-clergyman. Executed in Florida for the 1994 shooting slayings of a doctor and a volunteer at a Pensacola abortion clinic. Hill became the first American executed for anti-abortion violence.
Last Words: "If you believe abortion is a lethal force, you should oppose the force and do what you have to do to stop it. May God help you to protect the unborn as you would want to be protected." Spoken while strapped to a gurney.
Source "Ex-minister Executed for 1994 Murders Outside Abortion Clinic" by John Kennedy, John and Bob Mahlburg (*Orlando Sentinel*, September 3, 2003).

Hill, Rowland

(1744-1833) English clergyman, teacher. Popular but eccentric preacher. Issued several editions of *Village Dialogues* which sold in vast numbers. Actively promoted foreign Bible and missionary societies. Strong advocate of smallpox vaccinations. Personally vaccinated thousands of people. Died at age 88.
Last Words: "Christ also hath once suffered for sins, the just for the unjust, that he might bring us unto God."
Source: *Memoir of the Rev. Rowland Hill, M.A.* by William Jones, James Sherman (London, 1845).

Hill, Ureli Corelli

(1802-1875) American musician, conductor, impresario. Founder of Philharmonic Society of New York. Depressed by failure of his commercial ventures. Committed suicide at age 73 by swallowing an overdose of morphine.
Last Words (written): "Ha, Ha! I go, the sooner the better!" Suicide note found beside his body.
Sources: "Hill's Melody Boys" (*Time* magazine, December 14, 1942); *Sketches and Impressions, Musical, Theatrical, and Social (1799-1885) Including a Sketch of the Philharmonic Society of New York* by Thomas Goodwin (New York, 1887).

Hillary, Richard H.

(1919-1943). British military officer, pilot, writer. RAF fighter pilot. Flight lieutenant. Fought in World War II. Notable work: *The Last Enemy* (wartime classic based on his experiences during the Battle of Britain). Killed at age 23 when his plane crashed during a night-time training flight in England.
Last Words: "Moderately. I am continuing

to orbit." His response when he was asked: "Are you happy?" Spoken over radio-telephone as he rose above the airfield.
Source: *Richard Hillary* by Lovat Dickson (London, 1950).

Hillman, Sidney

(1887-1946) Lithuanian-born American labor leader. Founder and president of Amalgamated Clothing Workers of America. Died at age 59 of a heart attack on Bay Shore, Long Island, New York.
Last Words: "I feel like hell. I'm going to lie down again."
Source: *Sidney Hillman: Statesman of Labor* by Matthew Josephson (New York, 1952).

Hilton, John

(1880-1943) British journalist, educator, radio personality. Popular BBC broadcaster in London before World War II. Radio programs: *This and That; This Way Out; John Hilton Talking.* Instead of reading monotonous prepared scripts, he used what he called calculated spontaneity. He enlivened the words by making them sound like conversational speaking. Worked for Ministry of Labour. Was director of home publicity for the Ministry of Information. Professor of industrial relations at Cambridge. Died at age 63.
Last Words: "That was very good." Spoken as he managed to swallow a few drops of tea.
Source: *John Hilton: The Story of His Life* by Edna Nixon (London, 1946).

Hiltzheimer, Jacob

(1729-1798) German-born American, politician, artisan, diarist. Member of Pennsylvania Assembly. Died in yellow fever epidemic in Philadelphia. Twenty-eight volumes of his diary survive, giving a day-to-day view of an artisan's life in Philadelphia from 1765 to 1798.
Last Words (written): "Deaths today, 66." The last entry in his diary was the number of people who died that day during the yellow fever epidemic that would soon kill him.
Source: *Extracts from the Diary of Jacob Hiltzheimer of Philadelphia*, ed. by Joseph Cox Parsons (Philadelphia, 1893).

Himmler, Heinrich

(1900-1945) German military officer. Nazi commander of German Schutzstaffel (SS) in Germany during World War II. War criminal. Arrested in heavy disguise by British officer in Bremen. Committed suicide at age 44 by swallowing potassium cyanide before he could be interrogated.
Different Last Words:
(1) "Ich bin Heinrich Himmler!" (tr. "I am Heinrich Himmler!")
Source: "A Grave on the Heath" (*Time* magazine, June 4, 1945);
(2) "He does not know who I am." Spoken when an officer ordered him to strip. When the order was repeated, Himmler bit down on the cyanide capsule in his mouth.
Source: *Himmler Reichsführer-SS* by Peter Padfield (New York, 1990)

Hindenburg, Paul von

(1847-1934) German statesman, military officer, field marshal. Birth name Paul Ludwig Hans Anton von Beneckendorff und von Hindenburg. President of Germany. Zeppelin *Hindenburg* (air ship) named for him. Died at age 86 at Neudeck, Germany.
Last Words: "It is all right, Sauerbruch, now tell Friend Hein he can come in." (Freund Hein was German poet Matthias Claudius's euphemism for Death).
Source: *Wooden Titan* by John W. Wheeler-Bennett (New York, 1936).

Hindman, George Washington

(1849-1878) American cowboy, law enforcement officer. Part of the posse that pursued and murdered rancher John Tunstall. Hindman was hunted down by Billy the Kid and the Lincoln County Regulators and shot in the back. No one came to his aid as he lay dying in the street. Finally, a saloon keeper brought him some water that he carried in his hat. Hindman died at age 28 of his injury.
Last Words: "Water." He died moments later.
Source: *Billy the Kid: A Short and Violent Life* by Robert M. Utley (Lincoln, NE, 1991).

Hitchcock, Sir Alfred Joseph

(1899-1980) British-born filmmaker, producer. Hosted television anthology series of mysteries and melodramas (1955 to 1965). Known as Master of Suspense. Nominated for five Academy Awards. Knighted in

1979. Died at age 80 in Los Angeles.

Last Words: "One never knows the ending. One has to die to know exactly what happens after death, although Catholics have their hopes." Spoken not long before he died.

Source: *The Dark Side of Genius: The Life of Alfred Hitchcock* by Donald Spoto (Boston, 1983).

Hitler, Adolf

(1889-1945) German political and military leader. Chancellor and führer. Leader of Nationalsozialistische Deutsche Arbeiterpartei or NSDAP (Nazi Party). Committed suicide at age 56 in underground bunker in Berlin, with wife Eva Braun.

Last Words (written): Last Lines of Hitler's Political Last Will: "Above all I charge the leaders of the nation and those under them to scrupulous observance of the laws of race and to merciless opposition to the universal poisoner of all peoples, International Jewry.—Given in Berlin, this 29th day of April 1945, 4:00 a.m. —Adolf Hitler."

Last Lines of Hitler's Personal Testament: "I myself and my wife—in order to escape the disgrace of deposition or capitulation—choose death. It is our wish to be burnt immediately on the spot where I have carried out the greatest part of my daily work in the course of a twelve years' service to my people.—Given in Berlin, 29th April 1945, 4:00 a.m.—A. Hitler."

Sources: Copies of Documents: "Mein politisches Testament," Berlin, Germany, April 29, 1945; "Mein privates Testament," Berlin, Germany, April 29, 1945. [The Fall: Bunker Documents]; English Translations: Office of U.S. Chief of Counsel for the Prosecution of Axis Criminality, Nazi Conspiracy and Aggression, Vol. VI). (U.S. Government Printing Office, Washington, D.C., 1946-1948).

Hitler, Eva Anna Braun

(1912-1945) German long-time companion and brief wife of Nazi dictator Adolf Hitler. Died at age 33, a suicide with Hitler in a Berlin, Germany, bunker. They had married less than two days earlier.

Last Words: "Greet Munich for me." Spoken to one of the secretaries just before she walked into another room where she committed suicide with Hitler by swallowing a capsule of cyanide. Her Last Words were heard by someone who was in the bunker.

Source: *Adolf Hitler* by John Toland (New York, 1976).

Hoar, Ebenezer Rockwood

(1816-1895) American lawyer, jurist, politician. U.S. attorney general. Helped negotiate Treaty of Washington. Member U.S. House of Representatives from Massachusetts. Member of board of overseers at Harvard 14 years. Died at age 78 in Concord, Massachusetts.

Last Words: "I am engaged in the not disreputable, but far from attractive, business of dying, and I have one quality especially suitable for it—I have plenty of leisure to attend to it." Spoken to a visitor while in hospital, not long before he died.

Source: *Ebenezer Rockwood Hoar: A Memoir* by Moorfield Storey and Edward W. Emerson (Boston, 1911).

Hobbes, John Oliver, see Craigie, Pearl Mary Teresa Richards.

Hobbes, Thomas

(1588-1679) English philosopher, scientist, writer. Friend of Harvey and Ben Jonson. Spent many years as tutor and companion of the Cavendish family (Earl of Devonshire). Exiled to France for his politics. Notable works: *Leviathan, or The Matter, Form, and Power of a Commonwealth, Ecclesiastic and Civil; Human Nature.* Died at age 91 in Hardwick, Derbyshire, England.

Different Last Words:

(1) "I am about to take my last voyage, a great leap in the dark."

Sources: *Dictionary of Phrase and Fable* by E. Cobham Brewer (Philadelphia, 1898); *Thomas Hobbes* by John Laird (London, 1934).

Variation: "I am about to take a leap in the dark.—I shall be glad to find a hole to creep out of the world at."

Source: *Dying Testimonies of Saved and Unsaved: Gathered from Authentic Sources* by Solomon Benjamin Shaw (Chicago, 1898)

(2) "I shall be glad to find a hole to creep out of the world at." Last coherent words he uttered. Spoken when he learned he was about to die.

Source: *General Biographical Dictionary,* ed. by Alexander Chalmers (London, 1814).

Hoche, Louis Lazare

(1768-1797) French military officer. Revolutionary general. Died at age 29 of tuberculosis in Wetzler, Germany.

Last Words: "Good-bye, my friends, good-bye. Tell the government to keep a sharp eye in the direction of Belgium! Good-bye, my friends."

Source: *Vie de Lazare Hoche, général des armées de la République Française* by A. Rousselin (Paris, 1798).

Hodge, Charles

(1797-1878) American clergyman, theologian, educator. Major figure in American Protestantism and Presbyterianism. Professor of Oriental and Biblical Literature at Princeton Theological Seminary. Later taught theology. Married Sarah Bache, granddaughter of Benjamin Franklin. Died at age 80 in Princeton, New Jersey.

Different Last Words:

(1) "Why should you grieve, daughter? To be absent from the body is to be with the Lord, to be with the Lord is to see the Lord, to see the Lord is to be like Him." Spoken to his daughter who was crying.

Source: *The Life of Charles Hodge* by A.A. Hodge (New York, 1880). The author was his son Archibald Alexander Hodge.

(2) "My work is done. The pins of the Tabernacle are taken out." Spoken quietly on his deathbed. He then began saying the lines of a hymn but could not finish them. As his wife finished the stanza, he looked up at her and said: "Say, Jesus," then breathed his last.

Source: *Annotations Upon Popular Hymns* by Charles Seymour Robinson (New York, 1893).

Hodges, Gilbert Raymond ("Gil")

(1924-1972) American athlete. Professional baseball player. First baseman with Brooklyn and Los Angeles Dodgers. Managed Washington Senators, New York Mets. Died suddenly of a heart attack at age 47 in West Palm Beach, Florida.

Last Words: "Let's say 7:30." His response to one of his coaches about when they would meet for dinner. He dropped dead a few seconds later.

Source: "Hodges, Manager of the Mets, Dies of Heart Attack at Age 47" by Joseph Durso (*New York Times*, April 3, 1972).

Hodgeson, Benjamin H. ("Benny")

(1848-1876) American military officer. Second lieutenant Company B, Seventh Cavalry at Reno's Retreat, Little Big Horn, Montana.

Shot and killed at age 27 during a rescue attempt as a soldier dragged him from the river.

Last Words: "Don't abandon me! I'm shot in both legs!"

Source: *The End of Custer: The Death of an American Military Legend* by Dale T. Schoenberger (Surrey, British Columbia, 1995).

Hodgson, Francis

(1781-1852) English clergyman, educator, poet. Provost of Eton. Made many reforms at Eton that lessened the harshness of conditions there. Friend of Lord Byron. Notable works: Juvenal (translation); *Sir Edgar, A Tale.* Died at age 71 at Eton.

Last Words: "Charming.—God's mercy."

Source: *Memoir of the Rev. Francis Hodgson, B.D., Scholar, Poet, and Divine: With Numerous Letters from Lord Byron and Others* by his son Rev. James Thomas Hodgson (London, 1878).

Hoefle or Hoeffle, Hermann

(1898-1947) German military official. Nazi general during World War II. SS and police leader in Slovakia. Nazi war criminal. Executed by hanging in Czechoslovakia.

Last Words: "Dear Germany."

Source: *Berkeley* [CA] *Gazette*, December 9, 1947.

Hofer, Andreas

(1767-1810) Bavarian revolutionary, soldier. Led revolt against Bavarian government of Tyrol. Defeated by combined French and Bavarian army. Court-martialed and executed by firing squad at age 42 in Mantua, Italy.

Different Last Words:

(1) "I stand in the presence of my creator and standing I will render back my account to God who gave it. Fire!" Spoken as he stood before a firing squad.

Source: *Memoirs of the Life of Andrew Hofer,* tr. from the German by Charles Henry Hall (London, 1820).

(2) "Good-bye, wretched world, this death is easy!"

Source: *A History of the Nineteenth Century Year by Year* by Edwin Emerson Jr. (New York, 1902).

Hoffman, Abbott Howard ("Abbie")

(1936-1989) American social and political activist, writer. Used aliases while on the run for a cocaine conviction. Identified self as communo-anarchist. Co-founder of Youth International Party ("Yippies"). Tried for conspiracy and inciting to riot by leading protests during the 1968 Democratic National Convention, with others called "the Chicago Seven." Notable work: *Steal this Book* (a best-seller). Diagnosed as manic-depressive, he committed suicide at age 52 by taking an overdose of barbiturate with alcohol at his home in New Hope, Pennsylvania. Some question whether his death was suicide or foul play. He left a suicide note with his Last Words.

Last Words (written): "It's too late. We can't win, they've gotten too powerful."

Source: *Abbie Hoffman: American Rebel* by Marty Jezer (New Brunswick, NJ, 1993).

Hoffman, Eugene Augustus

(1829-1902) American clergyman, theologian, educator. Episcopalian. Dean of General Theological Seminary in New York City for many years. One of the wealthiest clergymen in the U.S. when he died.

Last Words: "Goodbye, Matapedia." Matapedia was his favorite retreat.

Source: *Memorial Biography of the Very Reverend Eugene Augustus Hoffman* by Theodore Myers Riley (New York, 1904).

Hoffmann, Ernst Theodor Amadeus ("E.T.A.")

(1776-1822) German novelist, composer, artist, jurist. Changed part of his name from Wilhelm to Amadeus to honor Mozart. Known for stories with fantastic and strange characters. Influenced other writers, including Poe and Dostoevsky. Notable works: T*he Nutcracker and the Mouse King* (on which Tchaikovsky based his ballet). The libretto for Offenbach's opera *The Tales of Hoffman* was based on Hoffmann's life and several of his tales. Two of his stories formed the basis for the ballet *Coppelia*. Hoffmann was stricken by a disease that caused degeneration of the spinal cord. Died at age 46 in Berlin.

Last Words: He dictated a story until almost the hour of his death. The last words he spoke were an instruction for his writer to read to him passages where he had broken off in *Der Feind.* He then turned his head to the wall. A death rattle was heard in his throat as he died.

Source: *Weird Tales* by Ernst Theodor Amadeus Hoffmann and John Thomas Bealby (New York, 1885).

Hofmannsthal, Hugo von

(1874-1929) Austrian writer, librettist, poet, playwright. Wrote libretto for several of Richard Strauss's operas, including *Der Rosenkavalier; De Frau ohne Schatten; Elektra.* Died at age 55 of a stroke, in Rodaun, near Vienna, two days after his eldest son Franz committed suicide.

Last Words (written): "Good friend, I sincerely hope it goes well with you. Yesterday afternoon a great misfortune visited our Rodauner House. During a bad, oppressive thunderstorm, our poor Franz took his life with a shot in the temple. The motive for this dreadful deed lies darkly deep: in the depths of character and of fate. There was no external motive. We had eaten together as usual, en famille. There is something infinitely sad and infinitely novel in the way the poor child went. He was never able to share his thoughts. So his departure was silent too—Raymond is with us. In all friendship, Hugo von Hofmannsthal." Letter written to a friend about his son's suicide.

Source: *Erinnerungen an Hofmannsthal und Briefe des Dichters* by Carl J. Burckhardt (Basel, Switzerland, 1944).

Hogg, James

(1770-1835) Scottish writer, poet, novelist. Known as the Ettrick Shepherd. Lived and worked most of his life in Ettrick Forest on the Scottish border. Friend of Scott, Byron, and Wordsworth. Notable work: *The Private Memoirs and Confessions of a Justified Sinner* (novel). Suffered from liver disease. Died at age 64 while he had severe, nonstop hiccups.

Last Words: "It is a reproach to the faculty that they cannot cure the hiccup."

Source: *The Ettrick Shepherd* by Henry T. Stephenson (Bloomington, IN, 1922).

Hokusai, Katsushika

(1760-1849) Japanese artist, woodcut print maker, illustrator. Influenced artists outside Japan. Notable works: *Hundred Views of Mount Fuji; Ten Thousand Sketches.* Died at about age 88 in Yedo.

Last Words: "If Heaven had only granted

me five more years, I could have become a real painter."

Source: *Hokusai* by C.J. Holmes (New York, 1901).

Holcroft, Thomas

(1745-1809) English writer, playwright, novelist, translator, actor. Self-educated. Notable works: *The Road to Ruin; Tale of Mystery* (novel written in 1802 and described as the first English melodrama). Translated Beaumarchais's play *Le Mariage de Figaro.* Holcroft was indicted along with a group known as the Twelve Reformers on a charge of high treason. Discharged without a trial. Died at age 63 in London.

Last Words: "How tedious. My affections are strong." Spoken while he was in pain.

Source: *Memoir of Holcroft Written by Himself and Continued Down to the Time of His Death, from His Diary, Notes and Other Papers,* ed. by William Hazlitt (London, 1816). Hazlitt was a friend.

Holden, Oliver

(1765-1844) American musician, composer, hymnist. Compiled and published many books of hymns. When President George Washington came to Boston in 1789, Holden wrote an ode and trained a choir to sing it as an official musical greeting at the Old State House. His popular tune "Coronation"—to Edward Perronet's hymn "All Hail the Power of Jesus' Name"—is considered America's earliest hymn tune still in general use.

Last Words: "I have some beautiful airs running through my head, if only I had the strength to note them down."

Source: "Oliver Holden, The Composer of Coronation" by Abram English Brown (*New England Magazine,* Vol. 22, No. 6, August 1897).

Holiday, Billie

(1915-1959) American musician, singer, actress. Jazz vocalist. Birth name Elinore Harris. Known as Lady Day. Notable performances: "God Bless the Child," "Lover Man," "Strange Fruit." Died at age 44 in a New York City hospital of drug- and alcohol-related problems. The movie *Lady Sings the Blues* (1972) tells the story of her troubled life and career. Inducted into Big Band and Jazz Hall of Fame in 1979 and Rock and Roll Hall of Fame in 2000.

Last Words: "Don't be in such a hurry!" Spoken to the hospital staff.

Source: *Lady Day: The Many Faces of Billie Holiday* by Robert G. O'Meally (New York, 1991).

Holland, Henry Scott

(1847-1918) English theologian, clergyman, educator, writer. Anglican. Canon of St. Paul's Cathedral. Canon of Christ Church Oxford. Regius professor of divinity at Oxford. Notable work: "Death is nothing at all" (essay). Died at age 71 at Oxford.

Last Words "Goodnight dear." Spoken to his nurse.

Source: *Henry Scott Holland: Memoir and Letters,* ed. Stephen Paget (New York, 1921).

Holliday, John Henry ("Doc")

(1851-1887) American dentist. Gunfighter in the Old West. Known as Doc Holliday. Famous for his friendship with Wyatt Earp and his brothers. Died at age 36 of tuberculosis in Glenwood Springs, Colorado. Fictional characterizations of Doc Holliday have appeared in several TV programs and movies, including *Gunsmoke; The Outlaw; Gunfight at the O.K. Corral; Tombstone;* and *Purgatory.*

Last Words: "This is funny." Spoken while he was lying in bed looking at his feet.

Source: *The Chronicles of Tombstone* by Ben T. Traywick (Tombstone, AZ, 1990).

Holmes, John

(1812-1899) American lawyer. Brother of Oliver Wendell Holmes Sr. During his final days, he fell into a coma and was motionless so long his attendants wondered if he was still alive.

Last Words: "John Rogers did." His response to a nurse who felt his feet to see if they were warm then said: "Nobody ever died with warm feet." Rogers was a Protestant martyr who was burned at the stake for heresy.

Source: *Yankee From Olympus: Justice Holmes and His Family* by Catherine Drinker Bowen (Boston, 1944).

Holmes, Oliver Wendell, Jr.

(1841-1935) American jurist, writer. Son of Oliver Wendell Holmes Sr. Associate justice, U.S. Supreme Court. Notable work: *The Common Law.* Died at age 93 in

Washington, D.C.

Last Words: "A lot of damn foolery." Spoken when an oxygen tent was put up around his bed.

Source: *Yankee From Olympus: Justice Holmes and His Family* by Catherine Drinker Bowen (Boston, 1944).

Holst, Gustav

(1874-1934) English musician, composer, teacher. Birth name Gustavus Theodore von Holst. Wrote in many formats including operas, ballets, incidental music, orchestral and choral music and more. Notable works: *Saint Paul's Suite; The Planets*. Died at age 59 of complications following surgery in London.

Last Words (written): "And I wish myself the joy of your Fellowship at Whitsuntide."

Source: *Gustav Holst* by Imogen Holst (London, 1938). The author was his daughter.

Holtby, Winifred

(1898-1935) English writer, novelist, journalist, pacifist, feminist. Notable work: *South Riding* (novel). Had been in love with Harry Pearson for 16 years. When she had only a few days to live, her friend Vera Brittain asked someone to tell Pearson. Holtby died at age 37 of Bright's disease.

Last Words: "Not an engagement—just an understanding." Spoken when she announced her intention to marry Pearson.

Source: *Testament of Friendship* by Vera Brittain (New York, 1940).

Hölty, Ludwig Heinrich Christoph

(1748-1776) German writer. Poet who strived to promote nationalism in German verse. Died at age 27 of tuberculosis in Hanover.

Last Words: "I am very ill. Send for Zimmermann. In fact, I think I'll die today."

Source: *Hölty, Sein Leben und Dichten* by Hermann Ruete (Guben, Germany, 1883).

Hood, Edwin Paxton

(1820-1885) English clergyman, writer, biographer. Congregationalist. Notable works: *World of Proverb and Parable* and *World of Anecdote*. Also wrote popular biographies of Wordsworth, Carlyle, Cromwell, Milton and others.

Last Words: "O God! O God!, my wife, my wife!"

Source: *Edwin Paxton Hood, Poet and Preacher: A Memorial* by George Henry Giddins (London, 1886).

Hood, John Bell

(1831-1879) American military officer. Confederate general in U.S. Civil War. Commanded Texas Brigade. He lost the use of one arm at Gettysburg and had to have a leg amputated after Chickamauga. Died in a yellow fever epidemic in New Orleans soon after his wife and oldest child died. Fort Hood, Texas, was named for him. Poet Stephen Vincent Benet wrote a passage of his 1930 poem *Army of Northern Virginia* about Hood.

Last Words: He told those around his bed that after he died he wanted the Texas Brigade to take care of his children. He was referring to his ten minor children who were left orphaned by the epidemic. Unfortunately, there was no one to care for them. The children were adopted by several families.

Source: *John Bell Hood and the War for Southern Independence* by Richard M. McMurry (Lincoln, NE, 1992).

Hood, Thomas

(1799-1845) English writer, poet, humorist. Used caricatures when dealing with current events. Wrote poems of social protest, such as *The Song of the Shirt*. Had a long struggle with poverty and illness. Suffered from throbbing headaches. Died at age 55 in London.

Last Words: "Remember, Jane, I forgive all, all, as I hope to be forgiven." Spoken to his wife Jane Reynolds Hood. He then whispered: "O Lord! say 'Arise, take up thy cross, and follow me.'" His final words were "Dying! dying!"

Sources: *The Complete Poetical Works of Thomas Hood,* ed. by Walter Jerrold (New York, 1919); *The Living Age* by Making of America Project, Eliakim Littell and Robert S. Littell (Boston, 1863).

Hook, Walter Farquhar

(1798-1875) English clergyman, writer. Anglican. Vicar of Leeds. Dean of Chichester. Notable work: *Lives of the Archbishops of Canterbury*.

Last Words (written): "I am old, 78, and very infirm. My contemporaries are passing away, and I expect soon to receive my summons. Pray for me." Written in a letter.

Source: *The Life and Letters of Dean Hook* by his son-in-law W.R.W. Stephens (London, 1879).

Hooker, Richard

(1554-1600) English clergyman, writer. Notable work: *Of the Laws of Ecclesiastical Polity*. Five volumes were published during his lifetime, three after he died at age 46.

Last Words: "Good Doctor, God hath heard my daily petitions, for I am at peace with all men, and He is at peace with me; and from that blessed assurance I feel that inward joy which this world can neither give nor take from me: my conscience beareth me this witness, and this witness makes the thoughts of death joyful. I could wish to live to do the church more service, but cannot hope it, for my days are past as a shadow that returns not."

Source: *Walton's Lives of Dr. John Donne, Sir Henry Wotton, Mr. Richard Hooker, Mr. George Herbert, and Dr. Robert Sanderson* by Izaak Walton and Thomas Zouch (York, England, 1796).

Hooker, Thomas

(1586-1647) English-born clergyman. Congregationalist. Emigrated to America in 1633. Active in securing Fundamental Orders that became the Constitution for Connecticut.

Last Words: "Brother, I am going to receive mercy!" His response to the comment: "You are going to receive the reward of all your labors."

Source: *Thomas Hooker, Preacher, Founder, Democrat* by George Leon Walker (New York, 1891).

Hooper, John

(1495-1555) English prelate, reformer, martyr. Bishop of Gloucester and Worcester. Fled to Zurich in 1539 after a religious crisis of conscience. Returned to England in 1549. Sentenced to die as a heretic. Burned at the stake in front of Gloucester Cathedral before a crowd of several thousand people.

Different Last Words:

(1) "Therefore strengthen me of Thy goodness, that in the fire I break not the rules of patience, or else assuage the terror of the pains, as shall seem most to Thy glory."

Source: *Book of Martyrs and the Acts and Monuments of the Church* by John Fox (or Foxe). First published 1563, ed. by John Cumming (London, 1851).

(2) "Lord Jesus, have mercy on me; Lord Jesus, receive my spirit." He died while praying.

Source: *The History of The Martyrs Epitomised: A Cloud of Witnesses, or, The Sufferers Mirrour: Made Up of The Swanlike Songs, and Other Choice Passages of a Great Number of Martyrs and Confessors, to the End of the Sixteenth Century, in Their Treatises, Speeches, Letters, Prayers, & c.* by Thomas Mall (Boston, 1747). Mall noted that before the fire was lit, a free pardon was offered to Hooper if he would recant. He scorned it, saying: "Away with it; if you love my soul, away with it."

Hoover, Herbert Clark

(1874-1964) 31st President of the U.S. American mining engineer, administrator, politician, humanitarian. Worked throughout the world as a mining engineer. Held several positions during World War I administering U.S. economic aid. U.S. secretary of commerce. Died at age 90 in New York City.

Last Words: "Lewis Strauss is one of my best friends." Spoken to the nurse who announced the arrival of Strauss, an old friend.

Source: *An Uncommon Man: The Triumph of Herbert Hoover* by Richard Norton Smith (New York, 1984).

Hope, James

(1801-1841) English physician. Leading authority on pathology and cardiac physiology. Hope's sign, a medical term, is named for him. Died of tuberculosis at age 40.

Last Words: "I thank God."

Source: *Memoir of the Late James Hope, M.D., Physician to St. George's Hospital by Mrs. Hope. To Which are Added Remarks on Classical Education* by Dr. Hope, ed. by Klein Grant, M.D. (London, 1844).

Hope, John

(1868-1936) American educator, social activist. One of the founders of the Niagara Movement (forerunner of NAACP). First African-American president of Morehouse College and Atlanta University. Died at age 67 of pneumonia in Atlanta, Georgia.

Last Words: "I'd like to live long enough to tell my successors what I'm trying to do."

Source: *The Story of John Hope* by Ridgely Torrence (New York, 1948).

Hope, Leslie Townes ("Bob")

(1903-2003) British-born American comedian. Stage, screen, radio and television actor. Grew up in Cleveland, Ohio. Starred in popular radio and television programs.

Won many awards including Emmy, Golden Globe, People's Choice. Entertained American troops in World War II and subsequent conflicts. Died at age 100 at Toluca Lake, California.

Last Words: "Surprise me." His response to his wife who asked where he wanted to be buried.

Source: "Thanks for the Memory" by Nicholas Wapshott (*The* [London] *Times*, July 23, 2003).

Hopkins, Gerard Manley

(1844-1889) English clergyman, writer, poet. Jesuit priest. Innovative poet who wrote about religion and nature. All his poems were published posthumously by his friends. Notable works: *Pied Beauty; Spring and Fall; The Caged Skylark; The Windhover.* Died at age 44 of typhoid fever in Dublin, Ireland.

Last Words: "I am so happy, so happy."

Source: *Gerard Manley Hopkins: A Life* by Eleanor Ruggles (New York, 1944).

Hopkins, Harry Lloyd

(1890-1946) American statesman. Government New Deal administrator. U.S. secretary of commerce. Personal representative and adviser to Franklin D. Roosevelt during World War II. Resigned as adviser to Truman for health reasons. Died at age 55 of cancer in New York City.

Last Words (written): "Do give my love to Clemmie and Sarah, all of whom I shall hope to see before you go back, but I want to have a good talk with you over the state of world affairs, to say nothing of our private lives." Letter to Winston Churchill.

Source: *Roosevelt and Hopkins: An Intimate History* by Robert E. Sherwood (New York, 1948). The book won the 1949 Pulitzer Prize for Biography.

Last Words (spoken): "You can't beat destiny."

Source: *Harry Hopkins: Ally of the Poor and Defender of Democracy* by George McJimsey (Cambridge, MA, 1987).

Hopkins, John Henry

(1792-1868) Irish-born American clergyman, writer, artist, architect. Emigrated to U.S. as a child. First Protestant Episcopal Bishop of Vermont. Accomplished engraver, artist and architect. Introduced Gothic architecture to U.S. Wrote more than a dozen theological works. Died at age 75 in Rock Point, Vermont.

Last Words: "I feel easier."

Source: *The Life of the Late Right Reverend John Henry Hopkins, First Bishop of Vermont, and Seventh Presiding Bishop* by John Henry Hopkins, Jr. (New York, 1873).

Hopkins, Johns

(1795-1873) American merchant, philanthropist. Died at age 78 without heirs. His estate of more than $7 million was used to create Johns Hopkins Hospital, Johns Hopkins University, Johns Hopkins Press and other namesake institutions.

Last Words: "Joe, it is very hard to break up an old habit. I've been living for seventy-eight years now and I find it hard to make a change in my ways." Spoken to his nephew.

Source: *Johns Hopkins: A Silhouette* by Helen Hopkins Thom (Baltimore, MD, 1929). The author was his grandniece.

Hopkins, Samuel

(1721-1803) American clergyman, theologian, abolitionist. Congregationalist. Close friend of Jonathan Edwards. Preached that slavery was wrong. Started successful campaign to outlaw slavery in Rhode Island. Died at age 82 in Newport, Rhode Island.

Last Words: "It is only my body; all is right in my soul." His response when a fellow minister asked why he was groaning.

Source: *Ten New England Leaders* by Williston Walker (Boston, 1901).

Hopper, Isaac Tatem

(1771-1852) American book seller, abolitionist, social reformer. Quaker. Known as the Father of the Underground Railroad. Began helping African-American fugitive slaves in the 1790s. Worked with Prison Association of New York. Died at age 80 in New York City.

Last Words: "Tell them I love them all." Spoken to Lydia Child. She had asked permission to write his biography. From this dying statement, she concluded that he wished her to tell his story.

Source: *Isaac T. Hopper: A True Story* by Lydia Maria Francis Child (Boston, 1853).

Horn, Tom

(1860-1903) American western lawman, detective, hired killer. Hanged at age 42 in

Cheyenne, Wyoming, for the murder of a 14-year-old boy. Many people believed he was innocent. The 1980 movie *Tom Horn* depicted him as a victim.

Last Words: "Joe, they tell me you're married now. I hope you're doing well. Treat her right." Spoken while waiting for the trap door on the gallows to open.

Source: *The Saga of Tom Horn* by Dean Krakel (Laramie, WY, 1954).

Horney, Karen Danielson

(1885-1952) German-born American psychoanalyst. Challenged Freud's assumptions about women. Recognized importance of early childhood experiences in the development of neuroses. Notable works: *The Neurotic Personality of Our Time; Neurosis and Human Growth; New Ways in Psychoanalysis*. Died of cancer at age 67 in New York.

Last Words: Shortly before she died she whispered that she was at last content to be leaving. There was just no point going on.

Source: *Karen Horney: Gentle Rebel of Psychoanalysis* by Jack L. Rubins (London, 1977).

Hotman, William

(1752?-1781) American soldier. Revolutionary War hero who gave his life to save others. While under attack by British troops, he spoke his Last Words. They are recorded with his story on a tombstone in a New London, Connecticut, cemetery.

Last Words: "We will endeavor to crawl to this line; we will completely wet the powder with our blood, thus will we with the little life that remains to us, save the fort and magazine, and perhaps a few of our comrades who are only wounded."

Source: "William Hotman" (*Tioga* [PA] *Eagle,* March 18, 1840).

Houdetot, Vicomtesse d'

(1758-1780) French noblewoman. Birth name Perrinet de Faugnes. Daughter-in-law of Rousseau's Madame d'Houdetot

Last Words: "Je me regrette." (tr. "I regret my life." Or, "I am sorry for myself.")

Source: *Nouveaux mélanges extraits de ses manuscrits,* Tome Second [Vol. 2] by Mme. [Suzanne] Necker (Paris, 1801).

Houdini, Harry

(1874-1926) American magician, escape artist, illusionist, writer, actor. Birth name Erik Weisz; used name Ehrich Weiss. Changed name to Harry Houdini. Known for ability to escape any kind of restraint. Campaigned against fraudulent mediums. Notable books: *Miracle Mongers and Their Methods; A Magician Among the Spirits.* Died at age 52 of acute appendicitis in Detroit, Michigan.

Last Words: "I'm tired of fighting. I guess this thing is going to get me." Spoken to his brother Theodore, who was with him when he died.

Source: *The Life and Many Deaths of Houdini* by Ruth Brandon (New York, 1993).

Hough, John

(1651-1743) English prelate, theologian, educator. Bishop of Oxford, Bishop of Worcester. President of Magdalene College, Oxford. Expelled by James II. Restored after protests. Died at age 92.

Last Words: "We part to meet again, I hope, in endless joys." Spoken to friends who were with him when he died.

Source: *Comforts of Old Age* by Sir Thomas Bernard, Bart. (London, 1818).

Houghton, John

(1487-1535) English clergyman, martyr. Roman Catholic priest. Prior of London Charterhouse. One of four men imprisoned in the Tower of London for refusing to take an oath recognizing the Act of Supremacy that named Henry VIII head of the Church of England. All four men were tortured and hanged at Tyburn.

Last Words: "Good Jesu, what will you do with my heart?" Spoken to the tormentor who was tearing out his heart.

Source: *Tyburn Tree: Its History and Annals* by Alfred Marks (London, 1908).

Housman, Alfred Edward ("A.E.")

(1859-1936) English classical scholar, writer, poet, educator. Professor of Latin at University College in London, and Trinity College in Cambridge. Brother of writer-illustrator Laurence Housman. Notable works: *A Shropshire Lad; Last Poems*. Died at age 77 in Cambridge.

Last Words: "Yes, that's a good one, and tomorrow I shall be telling it again on the Golden Floor." His response to a risqué story his doctor told him. He died the next morning.

Source: *A.E.H.: Some Poems, Some Letters and a Personal Memoir by His Brother* by Laurence Housman (New York, 1938).

Housman, Robert

(1759-1838) English clergyman, theologian. Evangelical divine of Church of England. Founded Saint Anne's in Lancaster.

Last Words: "I shall never again see the spot where those flowers grew. Give him my best thanks for the present." Spoken after he was given some violets.

Source: *Robert Housman* by Robert Fletcher Housman (New York, 1846). The author was his nephew.

Houston, Samuel ("Sam")

(1793-1863) American military officer, politician. Member U.S. House of Representatives from Tennessee. Governor of Tennessee. First president of Republic of Texas. Governor of Texas. Member U.S. Senate from Texas. Died at age 70 of pneumonia in Huntsville, Texas.

Last Words: "Texas—Texas!—Margaret." His wife Margaret Lea Houston was at his bedside when he died.

Source: *The Raven: A Biography of Sam Houston* by Marquis James (Indianapolis, IN, 1929).

How, William Walsham

(1823-1897) English clergyman, poet, hymnist. Anglican minister. First bishop of Cathedral of All Saints, Wakefield. Rector at Whittington, Shropshire. Wrote more than 50 hymns. Notable hymns: "Who is This So Weak and Helpless?"; "Lord, Thy Children Guide and Keep." Died at age 73 in Leenane, Ireland.

Last Words: "Good night. I don't want anything, thank you." Spoken to his family.

Source: *Bishop Walsham How, A Memoir* by Frederick Douglas How (London, 1899). The author was his son.

Howard, Catherine

(1520?-1542) English monarch. Daughter of Lord Edmund Howard. Fifth wife and queen of Henry VIII of England. Convicted of adultery and beheaded.

Last Words: "I die a Queen, but I would rather have died the wife of Culpepper. God have mercy on my soul. Good people, I beg you, pray for me." She then fell to her knees and began to pray.

Source: *Henry VIII's Fifth Wife, the Story of Catherine Howard* by Michael Glenne (New York, 1948); *Henry the Eighth* by Francis Hackett (New York, 1929).

Howard, John

(1726-1790) English prison reformer, philanthropist. Quaker. Contracted typhus while visiting Russian military hospitals.

Different Last Words:

(1) (doubtful): "Is not this comfort for a dying father?" His response to the news that his son was getting better.

Source: *John Howard and the Prison World of Europe* by Hepworth Dixon (London, 1850).

(2) (doubtful): "Suffer no pomp at my funeral, nor monumental inscription where I am laid. Lay me quietly in the earth and put a sundial over my grave and let me be forgotten."

Sources: *John Howard, and the Prison World of Europe. From Original and Authentic Documents* by Hepworth Dixon, with an Introductory Essay by Richard W. Dickenson, D.D. (New York, 1850); *The Last Words (Real and Traditional) of Distinguished Men and Women Collected from Various Sources* by Frederic Rowland Marvin (New York, 1901).

Howard spoke both (1) and (2) shortly before he died but they were not his Last Words. After he said them, he expressed repugnance at being buried by the rites of the Greek church and begged that there be no interference on the part of Russian priests. He asked the admiral who was at his bedside to read the burial service of the Church of England over his body. He then was seized with a fit. When asked if he wanted a physician, he nodded his head. He spoke no more. A death rattle began in his throat and he died the next morning.

Source: *Memoirs of the Public and Private Life of John Howard, the Philanthropist* by James Baldwin Brown (London, 1823)

Howard, Joseph W. ("Ragtime Joe")

(1896?-1924) American gangster. Bragged about how easy it would be to hijack a truck, especially if it was owned by Johnny Torrio, a friend of Al Capone. When Capone heard the boast, he got into a quarrel with Howard. Howard became angry about the way Capone was talking to him in front of his friends.

Last Words: "Aw, g'wan to your girls, you

dago pimp!" After Howard spoke these words, Capone pulled out a gun, placed it at Howard's temple and fired several times. Howard was killed at age 28.

Source: *The Wicked City: Chicago from Kenna to Capone* by Curt Johnson and R. Craig Sautter (New York, 1998). The authors indicated that this was "the gist of Howard's reply."

Howard, Moses ("Moe")

(1897-1975) American actor, comedian. Birth name Harry Moses Horwitz. One of the original Three Stooges. Appeared in movies and vaudeville. Died at age 77 of lung cancer in Los Angeles, California.

Last Words: "I've been really sick lately, so I'm sorry that I haven't answered yours and Ernie's letters, but I think about you daily."

Source: *Once a Stooge, Always a Stooge* by Joe Besser (Santa Monica, CA, 1988). Besser was the last surviving Stooge.

Howard, Oliver Otis

(1830-1909) American military officer. Union general in U.S. Civil War. Lost his arm at Fair Oaks, Virginia. Commissioner of Freedman's Bureau. Founder and president of Howard University. Died at age 78 in Burlington, Vermont.

Last Words: "Some day it will just stop and I will be on the other shore." Spoken after the physician returned with medication for his heart.

Source: *Last Words: A Dictionary of Deathbed Quotations* by C. Bernard Ruffin (Jefferson, NC, 1995), citing *Sword and Olive Branch: Oliver Otis Howard* by John Alcott Carpenter (Pittsburgh, 1964). Ruffin pointed out that the context of the question did not make it clear how long before the general's death the words were spoken —minutes, hours, even days or weeks.

Howard, Saint Philip, 20th Earl of Arundel

(1557-1595) English nobleman, holy man, martyr. 20th Earl of Arundel. Found guilty of Roman Catholic conspiracies against Queen Elizabeth. Arrested on charge of high treason for participating in a Mass for success of the Spanish Armada. Sentenced to death, but sentence was not carried out. Died at age 38 in the Tower of London. Canonized in 1970, one of the 40 Martyrs of England and Wales.

Last Words: "Jesus, Mary!"

Source: *The Life of Philip Howard Earl of Arundel,* *Saint and Martyr,* ed. by the Duke of Norfolk, E.M. (London, 1857).

Howard, Robert E.

(1906-1936) American writer. Wrote fantasy, horror, pulp, historical adventure stories. Published mainly in *Weird Tales* in 1930s. Movies based on Howard's creations include: *Conan the Barbarian; Conan the Destroyer; Red Sonja* and *Kull the Conqueror.* Committed suicide at age 30, when he learned his comatose mother would not regain consciousness. The 1996 movie *The Whole Wide World* is based on his life.

Last Words (written): "All fled—all done, so lift me on the pyre. The feast is over and the lamps expire." Paraphrase of "The House of Cæsar" by Viola Garvin, a poem found in his billfold.

Source: "The Note" by Rusty Burke (*The Cimmerian*, Journal of the Life and Writings of Robert E. Howard, 3:1, January 2006).

Howard, Blessed William, 1st Viscount Stafford

(1614-1680) English nobleman, martyr. Roman Catholic. Son of Sir Thomas Howard, Earl of Arundel. Accused by Titus Oates of complicity in a plot to assassinate the king. Convicted of treason. Executed by beheading at age 66 in London. Beatified in 1929.

Different Last Words:

(1) "I do forgive you." Spoken to the executioner who asked his forgiveness.

Source: *Notices of the Historic Persons Buried in the Chapel of St. Peter ad Vincula, in the Tower of London. With an Account of the Discovery of the Supposed Remains of Queen Anne Boleyn* by Doyne Courtenay Bell (London, 1877).

Variation: "I do." His response when asked by his executioner if he forgave him.

Source: *The Dying Speeches and Behaviour of the Several State Prisoners that Have Been Executed the Last 300 Years. With Their Several Characters, from Cambden, Spotswood, Clarendon, Sprat, Burner, &c. And a Table Shewing how the Respective Sentences were Executed, and which of Them were Mitigated, or Pardon'd. Being a Proper Supplement to the State-Trials* (London, 1720).

(2) "This block will be my pillow and I shall repose there well, without pain, grief or fear." Spoken to his brother who accompanied him to his place of execution.

Source: *Life of Cromwell* by Alfonse Marie Louis de Lamartine (New York, 1886).

Howe, George Augustus, 3rd Viscount Howe

(1724-1758) British military officer. Brigadier general. Killed in French and Indian War while trying to capture Fort Carillon. Brother of William Howe who commanded British forces in America. Brother of Richard Howe, British admiral famed for victory over French in 1794.

Last Words: "Putnam, your life is as dear to you as mine is to me, and I am determined to go. Lead on!" Spoken to Major Israel Putnam, who served as his scout and guide.

Source: *The Campaign of 1758: New Historical Light on the Real Burial Place of George Augustus Lord Viscount Howe* by James Austin Holden and Frank B. Wickes (Albany, NY, 1911).

Howe, Julia Ward

(1819-1910) American writer, poet, essayist, lecturer, social reformer, biographer. Wife of Samuel Gridley Ward, educator of the blind. She worked to end slavery. Helped initiate women's movement in many states. Worked for international peace. Gained fame for writing lyrics to "The Battle Hymn of the Republic." Died at age 91 of pneumonia in Newport, Rhode Island.

Last Words: "God will help me. I am so tired."

Source: *Julia Ward Howe* by Laura E. Richards and Maud Howe Elliott (Boston, 1915). The authors were her daughters.

Howell-Price, Owen Glendower

(1890-1916) Australian military officer. Lieutenant colonel. Birth name Owen Glendower Price. Part of distinguished Australian military family that served in World War I. Two brothers were also soldiers. Father, one of his brothers and he were awarded Distinguished Service Order. Died the day after he was shot in the head near Flers, France.

Last Words: "Give my love to the battalion."

Source: "Howell-Price, Owen Glendower" by D.M. Horner, in *Australian Dictionary of Biography*, Vol. 9 (Melbourne, Australia, 1983).

Howells, William Dean

(1837-1920) American writer, novelist, poet, editor, critic. Editor at *Atlantic Monthly* and *Harper's New Monthly Magazine*. Author of novels, dramas, comedies, travel sketches, poems. Notable works: *A Modern Instance;*
A Traveler from Altruria; The Rise of Silas Lapham. Died at age 83 in New York City.

Last Words (written): "Our walks by day were only in one direction and in one region. We were always going to Fresh Pond, in those days a wandering space of woods and water where people skated in winter and boated in summer." He was describing visits by Henry James.

Source: *Life in Letters of William Dean Howells,* ed. by Mildred Howells (New York, 1928). The author was his daughter.

Hubbard, Elbert Green

(1856-1915) American writer, editor, printer. Victim of *Lusitania* disaster. Founded Roycroft Press. Founded and published monthly magazines *The Philistine,* and *The Fra.* Died at age 58 with his wife on the *Lusitania.*

Last Words: "Well, Jack, they have got us. They are a damned sight worse than I ever thought they were!" Spoken to a friend when a German torpedo struck the *Lusitania.*

Source: *Elbert Hubbard of East Aurora* by Felix Shay (New York, 1926). Shay knew and worked closely with Hubbard.

Hudson, Rock

(1925-1985) American actor. Screen star. Birth name Roy Harold Scherer Jr. Nominated for Academy Award. Won four Golden Globes. Died at age 59 of AIDS in Beverly Hills, California.

Last Words: "No. I don't believe so." Spoken to Tom Clark, who asked if he wanted another cup of coffee.

Source: *Rock Hudson: Friend of Mine* by Tom Clark (New York, 1989).

Hudson, William Henry

(1841-1922) Argentinean-born British writer, naturalist, ornithologist. Conservationist concerned with protecting birds. Notable works: *Hampshire Days; Far Away and Long Ago.* His novel *Green Mansions: A Romance of the Tropical Forest* was made into a popular movie (1959). Died at age 81 in London. Several places in Argentina were named for him.

Last Words: "Good-bye."

Source: *W.H. Hudson, a Portrait* by Morley Roberts (New York, 1924). The author was a friend of Hudson.

Hügel, Friedrich von

(1852-1925) Italian-born theologian, religious writer. Son of Austrian diplomat. Lived and died in England. Baron of the Holy Roman Empire. Notable work: *The Mystical Element of Religion*. Died at age 72 in London.

Last Words: "Pray for me." Spoken to his nurse.

Source: *Selected Letters, 1896-1924,* ed. by Bernard Holland (London, 1927).

Hugh of Lincoln, Saint

(1135?-1200) English prelate, holy man. Augustinian and later Carthusian monk. Bishop of Lincoln. Wrote many philosophical and theological works. Rebuilt Lincoln Cathedral. Canonized in 1220.

Last Words: "God grant it." His response to a request to pray to God that his church might have a good pastor.

Source: *Magna Vita Sancti Hugonis, Episcopi Lincolniensis*, ed. by James F. Dimrock (London, 1864).

Hughes, Charles Evans

(1862-1948) American lawyer, jurist, politician, statesman. Governor of New York. Resigned to serve as associate justice of U.S. Supreme Court. Resigned to be a candidate for U.S. President. Lost to Woodrow Wilson by 23 electoral votes. Served as U.S. secretary of state under Harding and Coolidge. Appointed chief justice of U.S. Supreme Court by Hoover. Retired 1941. Died at age 86 in Osterville, Massachusetts.

Last Words: "I would rather be alone." His response when asked if he wanted to see his family.

Source: *Charles Evans Hughes* by Merlo J. Pusey (New York, 1951).

Hughes, John Joseph

(1797-1864) Irish-born American clergyman, prelate. First Roman Catholic archbishop of New York. Founder of Fordham University. In July 1863, at what would be his last public appearance, he addressed a crowd of 5,000 and called for an end to the violent draft riots that had created chaos in the city. Died at age 66 in New York.

Last Words: "Did they say so?" Spoken when he learned the physicians said he had no chance for a recovery.

Source: *Most Reverend John Hughes, First Archbishop of New York* by Henry Athanasius Brann (New York, 1892).

Hugo, Victor Marie

(1802-1885) French writer, poet, novelist, playwright. Notable works: *Les Misérables; Notre Dame de Paris; The Hunchback of Notre Dame*. Was very close to his grandchildren. Wrote *The Art of Being a Grandfather* in 1877. Died at age 83 in Paris.

Different Last Words:

(1) "Adieu, Jeanne, adieu." (tr. "Good-bye, Jeanne, good-bye.") Spoken to his granddaughter.

Source: *Victor Hugo: A Memoir and a Study* by James Cappon (Edinburgh & London, 1885). Cappon wrote that Hugo adored his grandchildren. They grew up in his house. These words were the last of many farewells Hugo made.

(2) (doubtful): "Je vois de la lumière noire." (tr. "I see the black light.")

Source: Various Last Words compilations and Internet sites.

The quote may have originated with a deathbed photograph French printer and photographer Paul Nadar took of Hugo. Hugo's last photograph shows him against a somber background with a black drapery tied across a window.

(3) (doubtful): "C'est ici le combat du jour et de la nuit." (tr. "Here is the battle between day and night.")

Source: *A Dream of Stone: Fame, Vision and Monumentality in Nineteenth-Century Literary Culture* by Michael D. Garval (Newark, DE, 2004).

Garval mentions (2) and (3), the supposed Last Words of Hugo, as examples of the many deathbed stories circulating that may be apocryphal and the product of "posthumous mythmaking."

Hull, Isaac

(1773-1843) American military officer. Naval commodore. Commanded the *Constitution* (*Old Ironsides*) during the War of 1812, when he defeated the British frigate *Guerrière*. Died at age 69 in Philadelphia.

Last Words: "I strike my flag."

Source: *Captain of Old Ironsides* by Bruce Grant (Chicago, 1947).

Humbert or Umberto I, King of Italy

(1844-1900) Italian monarch. Son of Victor Emmanuel II. Second king of Italy. Assassinated at age 56 by anarchist Gaetano Bresci at Monza, near Milan. He was succeeded by his son Victor Emmanuel III.

Different Last Words:

(1) "I believe I have been hit."

Source: *La Fine del Regno* by Ugo d'Andrea (Turin, Italy, 1951).

(2) "It is nothing." Spoken as he sank into the arms of his aide after receiving the third bullet from the revolver of his assassin.

Source: *The Last Words (Real and Traditional) of Distinguished Men and Women Collected from Various Sources* by Frederic Rowland Marvin (New York, 1901). Marvin devoted two and a half pages to the assassination and gave *Carriere Della Sera* as his source.

Humbert or Umberto II, King of Italy

(1904-1983) Italian monarch. Son of Victor Emmanuel III and Queen Helen. Married Princess Marie Jose of Belgium. Assumed throne when his father abdicated in May 1946. A month later, the monarchy was rejected by popular vote. Humbert was the last king of Italy. Died at age 78 in Geneva, Switzerland.

Last Words: "Italy."

Source: *Newsweek* magazine, March 28, 1983.

Humbert, Jean Joseph Amable

(1755-1823) French military officer, politician, educator. General who participated in several Caribbean campaigns for Napoleon. Governor of Port Au Prince (now in Haiti). After Napoleon fell, Humbert fled to the U.S. and settled in New Orleans. Worked as a school teacher. Died at age 67 in New Orleans.

Last Words: "I die far from my country, too far, alas, to rest one day in the cemetery of my village, beside my poor parents. There I should have wished to die—Ah! my friends—Let the will of God—."

Source: *Le Général Humbert* by H. Le Vosgien (Mirecourt, France, 1866).

Humboldt, Alexander von

(1769-1859) German scientist, explorer, diplomat, naturalist. Renowned for explorations of America and Asia. Humboldt Current was named for him. Known as the Father of Modern Geography. Spent many years writing *Kosmos,* a five-vol. encyclopedic survey of the Earth and universe. Died

at age 89 in Berlin.

Last Words: "Wie herrlich diese Strahlen, sie schienen, die Erde, zum Himmel zu rufen!" (tr. "How grand these rays; they seem to beckon Earth to heaven!")

Sources: "Biographie: Alexander von Humboldt. Sein wissenschaftliches Leben und Wirken den Freunden der Naturwissenschaften dargestellt" by W. C. Wittwer in *Leipziger Repertorium der Deutschen und ausländischen Literatur* (Leipzig, Germany, 1860); *The Life, Travels and Books of Alexander von Humboldt* by Richard Henry Stoddard (New York, 1859).

Hume, David

(1711-1776) Scottish philosopher, historian. Notable works: *A Treatise of Human Nature; History of England*. Died of cancer at age 65 in Edinburgh.

Last Words (written): "I go very fast to decline, and last night had a small fever, which I hoped might put a quicker period to this tedious illness; but unluckily, it has, in a great measure, gone off. I cannot submit to your coming over here on my account, as it is possible for me to see you so small a part of the day; but Doctor Black can better inform you concerning the degree of strength which may, from time to time, remain with me. Adieu." Letter to Adam Smith.

Source: *David Hume* by Henry Calderwood (New York, 1904).

Last Words (spoken): "Doctor, as I believe you would not care to tell anything but the truth, you had better tell him that I am dying as fast as my enemies, if I have any, could wish, and as easily and as cheerfully as my best friends could desire." His response to Dr. Dundas who optimistically told him he was much better and in a fair way of recovery.

Source: *Chamber's Cyclopaedia of English Literature* by Robert Chambers and David Patrick (Philadelphia, 1902-04).

Humphrey, Hubert Horatio

(1911-1978) American politician, statesman. Mayor of Minneapolis, Minnesota. Member U.S. Senate from Minnesota. U.S. Vice President under President Lyndon B. Johnson. Died at age 66 of cancer in Waverly, Minnesota.

Last Words: "I feel I have so much to do yet." Spoken to a friend shortly before he went into a coma.

Source: *Hubert: The Triumph and Tragedy of the Humphrey I Knew* by Edgar Berman (New York, 1979).

Hunt, James Henry Leigh (Leigh)

(1784-1859) English writer, critic, editor, essayist, journalist, poet. Friend and adviser of major poets, including Byron, Shelley, Hazlitt, Lamb. Imprisoned for publishing reformist weekly, *The Examiner.* Notable poems: "Abou Ben Adhem"; "Jenny Kissed Me." Skimpole, a character in Dickens' *Bleak House*, was based on him. Died at age 74 in Putney, near London.

Different Last Words:

(1) "I don't think I shall get over this."

Source: *Cyclopaedia of English Literature,* ed. by Robert Chambers (Philadelphia, 1860).

(2) (doubtful): "Deep dream of peace."

Source: *The Last Words (Real and Traditional) of Distinguished Men and Women Collected from Various Sources* by Frederic Rowland Marvin (New York, 1901).

These words are from the opening lines of Hunt's poem "Abou Ben Adhem." The *Notes and Queries* compiler agreed that the words came from Hunt's poem but doubted that they were Hunt's Last Words. He pointed out that although many of the sayings advanced by Latham are reputed Last Words of the authors, "nothing is much more fallacious than are such utterances." Even when the phrase has been used by the man to whom it is imputed, there is rarely any proof that it is his last utterance."

Source: *Notes and Queries: A Medium of Intercommunication for Literary Men, General Readers, etc.,* 10th Series, Vol. 8, Book 3 (Oxford, England, January 28, 1905). The article was a review of Latham's *Famous Sayings and Their Authors.*

Hunt, Vincent

(1823-1852) English writer. Youngest son of English essayist, poet Leigh Hunt. Died at age 29 of tuberculosis. His father described his son's death in his *Autobiography.*

Last Words: "I drink the morning!" Spoken as he sipped a glass of water.

Source: *Leigh Hunt and His Circle* by Edmund Charles Blunden (New York, 1930).

Hunter, William

(1718-1783) Scottish physician, anatomist, art collector, educator. Obstetrician to Queen Charlotte. Fellow of Royal Society. Professor of Anatomy to Royal Academy.

Hunterian Museum and Art Gallery at University of Glasgow hold his collections of anatomical specimens in pathology and obstetrics, coins and works of art. Died at age 64 in London.

Last Words: "If I had the strength to hold a pen, I would write down how easy and pleasant it is to die." Spoken to another physician after he fainted at a lecture.

Sources: *Two Great Scotsmen: The Brothers William and John Hunter* by George R. Mather (Glasgow, Scotland, 1893); *Dictionary of National Biography, from the Earliest Times to 1900* by Sir Leslie Stephen, George Smith and Sir Sidney Lee (London, 1921-1922).

Huntingdon, Selina, Countess of

(1707-1791) English religious leader. Wife of Theophilus Hastings, 9th Earl of Huntingdon. Active in Methodist movement in England and Wales. Founded sect of Calvinistic Methodists known as Countess of Huntingdon's Connection. Died at age 83 in London.

Last Words: "My work is done; I have nothing to do but to go to my Father."

Source: *The Life and Times of Selina, Countess of Huntingdon* by Aaron Crossley Hobart Seymour (London, 1840).

Husband, Rick Douglas

(1957-2003) American astronaut. Colonel in U S. Air Force. Died at age 45 aboard STS-107 *Columbia* Space Shuttle, a 16-day science and research mission. The *Columbia* crew was killed 16 minutes before the shuttle's scheduled landing.

Last Words: "Roger."

Source: "In Shuttle Disaster, Families Lost More Than Mere Heroes" by Sarah Kershaw (*New York Times*, February 16, 2003).

Huss or Hus, John

(1369?-1415) Bohemian clergyman. Priest who led religious reform movement. Arrested, imprisoned, accused of heresy before Council of Constance. Refused to retract. Condemned, burned at the stake in Constance, Switzerland.

Different Last Words:

(1) "No. I never preached any doctrine of an evil tendency; and what I taught with my lips I now seal with my blood." Spoken to the Duke of Bavaria who wanted him to abjure. Huss then said to the executioner:

"You are now going to burn a goose but in a century you will have a swan, whom you can neither roast or boil." The flames were lit and Huss sang a song in a loud, cheerful voice.
Source: *Death-Bed Scenes: Dying With and Without Religion: The Truth and Power of Christianity* by Davis W. Clark (New York, 1852).

(2) Sung at the stake: "Christ, son of the living God, have mercy on me; Christ, son of the living God, have mercy on me; Christ, son of the living God, have mercy on me; Who art born of the virgin Mary."
Source: *The Life & Times of Master John Hus* by Count Lützow (London, 1909).

(3) "Truth will prevail."
Source: Inscribed on his monument, Old Town Square, Prague, Czech Republic, erected 1915.

(4) "O sancta simpliciatas!" (tr. "O blessed simplicity!") Spoken when a peasant woman cast a bundle of sticks on the pile where Huss was being burned.
Source: *What is Modernism* by Leighton Parks (New York, 1924).

Hussein, Saddam Abd al-Majid al-Tikriti

(1937-2006) Iraqi leader, politician, military officer. Leading member of Ba'ath Party that came to power in the 1960s. Vice president then president of Iraq for nearly 24 years; was prime minister for all but three of those years. Led nation during Iran-Iraq War (1980-1988), first Persian Gulf War (1991) and part of Iraq War until his capture in 2003. Executed by hanging in Baghdad at age 69. His Last Words are in dispute.
Different Last Words:
(1) "Ashadu an la ilaha ila Allah, wa ash-hadu ana Mohammedun rasool Allah." (tr: "I witness there is no god but Allah and that Mohammed is His messenger.")
Source: Several Internet websites indicate that this is clearly audible in a video made of the execution.

(2) "Down with the traitors, the Americans, the spies and the Persians." Spoken on the gallows, immediately following a final prayer. Other versions claim he was hanged while praying.
Source: "On the Gallows, Curses for U.S. and 'Traitors'" by Marc Santora (*New York Times*, December 31, 2006).

(3) "Muqtada Al Sadr" (powerful Shiite Muslim cleric) spoken in a mocking tone. This version is said to be based on the report of witness Judge Munir Haddad after one of the other executioners shouted "Long live Muqtada Al Sadr."
Source: "Witness: Saddam Hussein Argued with Guards Moments Before Death" (CNN.com and CNN, December 30, 2006).

Husserl, Edmund Gustav Albrecht

(1859-1938) German philosopher, educator. Founder of phenomenology. Professor of philosophy at Gottingen and Freiburg, Germany. Notable works: *Logical Investigations; Philosophy as Rigorous Science.* Died at age 79 of pleurisy in Freiburg.
Last Words: "Oh, I have seen something wonderful. Quick, write it down!"
Source: *Edith Stein, A Biography* by Waltraud Herbstrith (San Francisco, 1985). Stein was a former student of Husserl.

Hutchinson, John

(1615-1664) English Puritan leader, military officer. Colonel. Prominent Roundhead in English Civil War. One of Cromwell's trusted officers. Arrested on suspicion of plotting against government. Died at age 49 while imprisoned.
Last Words: "'Tis as I would have it: 'tis where I would have it."
Source: *Memoirs of the Life of Colonel Hutchinson* by Lucy Hutchinson (London, 1906). The author was his wife.

Hutchinson, Thomas

(1711-1780) American-born statesman, merchant, writer. Last royal governor of Massachusetts. Went to England in 1774. Spent the rest of his life writing *History of Massachusetts*. Died at age 68 in London, England.
Last Words: "Help me!"
Source: *Life of Thomas Hutchinson* by James K. Hosmer (Boston, 1896).

Hutton, William

(1723-1815) English bookseller, historian, poet. Published several histories, including ones on Birmingham (England), the Birmingham riots and Hadrian's Wall. Died at age 92.
Last Words: "Oh, yes." His response when asked whether he sat easy.
Source: *The Life of William Hutton and the History of the Hutton Family*, ed. by Llewellyn Jewitt (London, 1872).

Huxley, Aldous Leonard

(1894-1963) English novelist, poet, essayist. Grandson of Thomas Huxley. Notable work: *Brave New World*. Advocated use of hallucinogens. Died at age 69 of cancer in Los Angeles, California.

Last Words (written): "LSD—try it intermuscular—100mm—." He was given an injection of LSD and then another. He died that afternoon. Note to his wife.

Source: *This Timeless Moment: A Personal View of Aldous Huxley* by Laura Archera Huxley (New York, 1968). The author was his widow.

Huxley, Thomas Henry

(1825-1895) English biologist, educator. Grandfather of Aldous Huxley. Strong defender of Darwin's theory of evolution. Professor at Royal College of Surgeons. Fullerian professor at Royal Institution. President of Royal Society. Died at age 70 of kidney disease in Eastbourne, Sussex.

Last Words (written): "My dear Hooker, The pessimistic reports of my condition which have got into the papers may be giving you unnecessary alarm for the condition of your old comrade. So I send a line to tell you the exact state of affairs. There is kidney mischief going on—and it is accompanied by very distressing attacks of nausea and vomiting, which sometimes last for hours and make life a burden. However, strength keeps up very well considering, and of course all depends upon how the renal business goes. At present I don't feel at all like 'sending in my checks,' and without being over sanguine I rather incline to think that my native toughness will get the best of it—Albuminuria or otherwise. Ever your faithful friend, T.H.H." Letter to Sir J.D. Hooker.

Source: *Huxley: Prophet of Science* by Houston Peterson (London, 1932).

Hyde, Anne, Duchess of York

(1637-1671) English royalty. Daughter of Edward Hyde, 1st Earl of Clarendon. First wife of James II. Mother of two queens: Mary II of England; Anne of Great Britain. Gave birth to eighth child in February 1671, died a month later. Converted to Roman Catholicism on her deathbed. Anglican Bishop of Oxford who visited her did not know about it. She died at age 33, probably of breast cancer.

Last Words: "What is truth?" Spoken to the Bishop of Oxford, who told her he hoped she continued in the truth. Then as her pain increased she repeated the word "truth."

Source: *Anne Hyde, Duchess of York* by J. R. Henslowe (London, 1915).

Hyde, John Nelson

(1865-1912) American missionary in India. Presbyterian. Served in Ferozepore district in the Punjab and later in Lahore. Assigned by Board of Foreign Missions of the United Presbyterian Church in North America. Returned to the U.S. for health reasons. Died at age 46 in Clifton Springs, New York.

Last Words: "Shout the victory of Jesus Christ!"

Source: *Praying Hyde: Glimpses of the Amazing Prayer-Life of a Missionary in India* by Francis A. McGaw (Minneapolis, MN, 1970).

Ibsen, Henrik

(1828-1906) Norwegian writer, playwright, poet. Notable works: *Peer Gynt; Ghosts; A Doll's House; Hedda Gabler*. Had a stroke in 1900; spent his last years bed-ridden. Died at age 78 in Christiania.

Last Words: "On the contrary." His response when he heard his caregiver tell a visitor he was feeling better. He then lost consciousness and died.

Source: *Ibsen, A Biography* by Michael Meyer (New York, 1971).

Variation: "Tvert imod!" (tr. "Not at all!")

Source: *Ibsen, the Norwegian: A Revaluation* by Muriel Clara Bradbrook (London, 1948).

Ignatius of Antioch, Saint

(30?-107?) Syrian-born prelate, holy man, martyr. Surname Theophorus. One of the immediate successors of the Apostles. Bishop of Antioch. Father of the Church. Known for his epistles. Condemned to death by Trajan. Ordered to be devoured by wild animals in Rome.

Last Words: "I am the wheat or grain of Christ. I shall be ground with the teeth of wild beasts that I may be found pure bread." Said to have been uttered when he heard the roar of the lions that were about to devour him.

Source: *Book of Martyrs and the Acts and Monuments*

of the Church by John Fox (or Foxe), first published 1563, ed. by John Cumming (London, 1851).

Ignatius of Loyola, Saint

(1491-1556) Spanish soldier, clergyman, holy man. Birth name Íñigo de Oñez y Loyola. Founder of Society of Jesus (Jesuits). Fought against the Protestant Reformation. Promoted the Counter Reformation. Died in Rome at age 64. Canonized in 1622.

Last Words (written): "Tell him that my hour has come, and that I ask his benediction. Tell him that if I go to a place where my prayers are of any avail, as I trust, I shall not fail to pray for him, as I have indeed unfailingly, even when I had most occasion to pray for myself." Message he wanted his secretary to deliver to the pope.

Source: *Lives of the Saints* by S. Baring-Gould (Edinburgh, 1914).

Illeppy, Solyman

(d. 1800) Turkish peasant, assassin. Killed General Jean-Baptist Kléber in Cairo, Egypt. Tortured by having his hand burned and by being impaled. Died without showing fear.

Last Words: "Tay hop!" (tr. "That is good!") Exclamation he made to his executioner from the beginning of his torture until he died.

Source: *Percy Anecdotes: Anecdotes of Crime and Punishment* by Sholto Percy and Reuben Percy (London, 1868).

Impey, Sir Elijah

(1732-1809) British jurist. Chief justice of Bengal. Impeached by the House of Commons for his conduct in India. Successfully defended himself. Acquitted. Served as member of Parliament. Died at age 77.

Last Words: "Did I hurt you, my dear?" Spoken on his deathbed when he leaned against a servant who was helping him.

Source: *Memoirs of Sir Elijah Impey (1732-1809)* by his son Elijah Barwell Impey (London, 1847).

Ingersoll, Ebon Clark

(1831-1879) American politician, lawyer. Member U.S. House of Representatives from Illinois. Elected to fill vacancy caused by death of Owen Lovejoy. Served 1856 to 1871. Lost 1870 election. Remained in Washington, D.C.; practiced law. Brother of Robert Green Ingersoll. Died at age 47.

Last Words: "I am better now." His response

to his wife who wanted to give him some medicine.

Source: *Letters* by Robert Green Ingersoll (New York, 1951).

Ingersoll, Robert Green ("Bob")

(1833-1899) American lawyer, orator, military officer. Colonel in Union Army in U.S. Civil War. Noted agnostic lecturer. Attorney general of Illinois. Brother of Ebon Clark Ingersoll. Died at age 65 in Dobbs Ferry, New York.

Last Words: "Oh, better." His response when asked how he was feeling.

Source: *Colonel Bob Ingersoll: A Biographical Narrative of the Great American Orator and Agnostic* by Cameron Rogers (New York, 1927).

Ings, James

(1785?-1820) English butcher, coffee-shop owner, conspirator. Member of the Cato Street Conspiracy, a failed attempt to assassinate members of the British Cabinet at a London dinner party. Conspiracy was thwarted by police. Eleven men were arrested. Ings was one of the five who were found guilty of high treason and executed.

Last Words: "I hope you'll give me a good character, won't you, Mr. Cotton." Spoken to the Tyburn vicar at his execution.

Source: *The Newgate Calendar: Comprising Interesting Memoirs of the Most Notorious Characters who have been Convicted of Outrages on the Laws of England Since the Commencement of the Eighteenth Century with Occasional Anecdotes and Observations, Speeches, Confessions and Last Exclamation of Sufferers* by Andrew Knapp and William Baldwin (London, 1828).

Innocent X, Pope

(1574-1655) Italian prelate. Birth name Giovanni Battista Pamfili. Elevated to cardinal. Nuncio to Court of Naples. Began pontificate at age 70. Condemned Jansenism. Died at age 80 in Rome.

Last Words: "You see where the grandeurs of the sovereign pontiff must end." Spoken to Cardinal Sforza after he was given news of his impending death and was administered the Last Rites.

Source: *The Lives and Times of the Popes* by The Chevalier Artaud De Montor (New York, 1911).

Innocent XI, Pope and Blessed

(1611-1689) Italian prelate. Birth name Benedetto Odescalchi. Roman Catholic pope. Pontificate of 12 years, 1676 to 1689. Died at age 78 in Rome. Beatified in 1956.

Last Words: "We have no house or family! God gave us the pontifical dignity, not for the advantage of our kindred but for the good of the Church and nations." Spoken to an ambassador who assured him his master would take care of his family.

Source: *The Lives and Times of the Popes* by Chevalier Artaud De Montor (New York, 1911).

Inskip, John Swanell

(1816-1884) English-born American clergyman, writer, editor. Methodist Episcopal preacher noted as an orator and conductor of camp meetings. Editor of *Christian Standard*. Notable works: *Remarkable Display of the Mercy of God in the Conversion of a Family from Infidelity; Life of Reverend William Summers, a Blind Man; Methodism Explained and Defended.* Died at age 67 in Ocean Grove, New Jersey.

Last Words: "Victory! Triumph! Triumph." Shouted as his friends gathered to sing and pray with him. As they sang, he took his wife's hand, raised it up with his, and spoke his Last Words.

Source: "Memoirs—John S. Inskip" by the Methodist Episcopal Church, New York East Conference (*Minutes of the New York East Conference of the Methodist Episcopal Church: Official Journal, 36th Session,* 1884).

Iqbal, Sir Muhammad

(1877-1938) Muslim poet, lawyer, politician, philosopher. Born in British India (now Pakistan). Known as Aliama Iqbal. Proponent of Islamic civilization especially in India. Envisioned independent state for Indian Muslims that led to the creation of Pakistan. Knighted in 1922. Health began to deteriorate in 1934. Stopped practicing law. Died at age 60 in Lahore (now in Pakistan).

Last Words: "Chaudhari Sahib, please see to it that he learns the passage 'Addressed to Javid' which appears near the end of my *Javid-Namab* (Book of Eternity)." Javid was his teenage son.

Source: *Eight Lives: A Study of the Hindu-Muslim Encounter* by Rajmohan Gandhi (Albany NY, 1986).

Irenaeus of Sirmium, Saint

(d. 304) Pannonian (now Sremska Mitrovica, Serbia) prelate, holy man. Bishop during reign of Diocletian. Martyred when he refused to offer pagan sacrifices. Beheaded. His body was thrown in a river.

Last Words: "Lord Jesus Christ, who deigned to suffer for the world's salvation, let your heavens open that your angels may take up the soul of your servant Irenaeus, who suffers all this for your name and for the people formed of your Catholic church of Sirmium. I ask and implore your mercy to receive me and to strengthen them in your faith."

Source: "Irenaeus of Sirmium" by David Hugh Farmer in *The Oxford Dictionary of Saints* (Oxford, England, 2003).

Irving, Edward

(1792-1834) Scottish clergyman. Involved in forerunner of Pentecostal movement. Condemned by Presbytery on charge of heresy. His followers were known as Irvingites. Founded Catholic Apostolic Church. Friend of Lamb, Carlyle and Coleridge. Died at age 42 in Glasgow while on a preaching tour of Scotland.

Last Words: "If I die, I die unto the Lord, Amen."

Source: *Life of Edward Irving, Minister of the National Scotch Church, London* by Mrs. Oliphant (London, 1862).

Variation: "In life and in death, I am the Lord's. Amen! Amen!"

Source: *The History and Doctrines of Irvingism, or the so-called Catholic and Apostolic Church* by Edward Miller (London, 1878), He cited Carlyle's *Essays,* v. 130, as his source.

Irving, Sir Henry

(1838-1905) English actor, theatrical manager. Birth name John Henry Brodribb. Known as the Governor. Major performer during the late Victorian era. Notable roles: Iago, Hamlet, Richard III, Mathias (*The Bells*), Mephistopheles. Manager of the Lyceum Theatre in London 21 years. First actor to be knighted (1895). Had a stroke while performing. Died a short time later at age 67 in London. Buried in Westminster Abbey.

Last Words: "Into Thy hands, O Lord, into Thy hands." Spoken on stage. These were also the last words Becket spoke in Tennyson's play of that name.

Source: *Sir Henry Irving, a Biography* by Percy Hetherington Fitzgerald (Philadelphia, 1906).

Irving, Washington

(1783-1859) American writer, essayist, poet, diplomat, biographer. Military officer in War of 1812. Lived and traveled in Europe extensively. Ambassador to Spain from 1842 to 1846. Notable works: *The Sketch Book* (contained two of his best-known short stories, "The Legend of Sleepy Hollow" and "Rip Van Winkle"); *A History of New York by Diedrich Knickerbocker.* Died at age 76 in Tarrytown, New York.

Last Words: "Well, I must arrange my pillows for another weary night! When will this end?"

Source: *The Life and Letters of Washington Irving* by Pierre M. Irving (New York, 1869). The author was the son of Washington's brother William Irving. He collaborated with his uncle on the book *Astoria* in 1836.

Isabella I, Queen of Spain

(1451-1504) Spanish monarch. Queen of Castile and Leon. Married Ferdinand II of Aragon. Financed Columbus's first expedition. Campaigned to expel Spanish Jews and defeat Muslims. During her final years, three of her children died and another showed signs of madness. Died at age 53 in Medina del Campo.

Last Words: "Do not weep for me, nor waste your time in fruitless prayers for my recovery, but pray rather for the salvation of my soul."

Source: *History of the Reign of Ferdinand and Isabella* by W.H. Prescott (Boston, 1938).

Isabella II, Queen of Spain

(1830-1904) Spanish monarch. Daughter of Ferdinand VII and Maria Christina of the Two Sicilies. Married Francis, Duke of Cadiz. Ruled from 1833 to 1868. Dethroned by revolution. In 1870 she renounced the throne in favor of her son Alfonso XII. Died at age 73 in exile in Paris.

Last Words: "Take my hand and pull my right arm as hard as you can. There is something very strange in my chest. I think I am going to faint." Spoken to her son-in-law.

Source: *Royal Vendetta: The Crown of Spain, 1829-1965* by Theo Aronson (Indianapolis, IN, 1966).

Isaiah

(fl. 700s B.C.) Hebrew prophet, martyr. Son of Amos (Amoz). According to tradition he was martyred by being sawn asunder while false prophets watched. He continued speaking until he died.

Last Words: "Go ye to the country of Tyre and Sidon, for the Lord hath mixed the cup for me alone." Spoken to the prophets who were with him before he was martyred with a wooden saw.

Source: *The Last Words* (*Real and Traditional*) *of Distinguished Men and Women Collected from Various Sources* by Frederic Rowland Marvin (New York, 1901).

Marvin mentioned the tradition that Isaiah suffered martyrdom by a saw and that the ancient book *The Ascension of Isaiah* accords with that tradition. The book has been discussed and debated in detail by scholars of theology, as in the study by R.H. Charles who presented a slightly different translation than Marvin: " 'Go ye to the region of Tyre and Sidon for me only hath God mingled the cup.' And when Isaiah was being sawn in sunder he neither cried aloud nor wept, but his lips spake with the Holy Spirit until he was sawn in twain. "

Source: *The Assumption of Moses: Translated from the Ethiopic Version, Which, Together with the New Greek Fragment, the Latin Versions and Latin Translation of the Slavonic, Is Here Published in Full Edited with Introduction, Notes and Indices* by R.H. Charles (London, 1900).

Ito, Prince Hirobumi

(1841-1909) Japanese royalty, statesman, political reformer. Encouraged modernization of Japan. Resident general of Korea. Killed at age 68 by a Korean assassin at a train station in Harbin, Manchuria.

Last Words: "The fellow is a fool." His response when he was told the identity of his assailant.

Source: *Prince Ito* by Kengi Hamada (Tokyo, 1936).

Iturbide, Agustín de

(1783-1824) Mexican military officer, ruler. Declared himself emperor as Agustín I. Forced to abdicate. Left Mexico, then returned. Was seized, tried and executed at age 40 in Padillo, Mexico.

Different Last Words:

(1) "I am no traitor! Such a stain will never attach to my children or to their descendants." Spoken at his execution.

Source: "Mexican Execution" (*New York Times*,

October 9, 1927).

(2) "Mexicans, I die because I came to help you. I die gladly, because I die among you, I die not as a traitor, but with honor."

Source: *A History of the Nineteenth Century Year by Year* by Edwin Emerson Jr. (New York, 1902).

Jackson, Andrew

(1767-1845) 7th President of the U.S. American lawyer, jurist, politician, military officer. Fought at the Battle of New Orleans in the War of 1812. Member U.S. House of Representatives, U.S. Senate from Tennessee. Judge, Tennessee Supreme Court. Governor of Florida. Died at age 78 in Nashville. Different Last Words:

(1) "Oh, do not cry. Be good children, and we shall all meet in Heaven."

Source: *The Life of Andrew Jackson* by Marquis James (Indianapolis, IN, 1938).

Variation: "I hope to meet each of you in heaven. Be good children all of you and strive to be ready when the change comes."

Source: *Facts About the Presidents* by Joseph Nathan Kane (New York, 1964).

(2) (doubtful): "I have only two regrets—that I have not shot Henry Clay or hanged John C. Calhoun."

Source: Various Last Words compilations and Internet websites.

Jackson did say this, but these were not his Last Words. He made the remark in 1837 when leaving office after eight years as President.

Source: *Anything for a Vote: Dirty Tricks, Cheap Shots and Other October Surprises in U.S. Presidential Campaigns* by Joseph Cummins (Philadelphia, 2007).

Jackson, George

(1942-1971) American revolutionary, writer. A leader of the Black Panthers. One of the Soledad Brothers. Author of best-selling book *Soledad Brother*. In 1970, while serving his ninth year at Soledad correctional facility in California, for a $70 burglary, he and two other black inmates were charged with the murder of a guard. In 1971, when he was moved at San Quentin after a visit from his lawyer, he produced a gun and ordered some inmates to be released. In the ensuing fight, three guards and three prisoners, including Jackson, were killed. Controversy has surrounded the circumstances of his death: prison officials said he was shot

by a guard from a tower as he ran across the prison yard but an autopsy showed he was shot in the back from a low angle.

Last Words: "It's me they want." Yelled as he ran onto the chapel plaza.

Source: *Who Killed George Jackson?* by Jo Durden-Smith (New York, 1976).

Jackson, Helen Hunt

(1830-1885) American social activist, writer. Birth name Helen Maria Fiske. After her first husband Edward Hunt died, she married William Jackson. Activist for Native American rights. Notable works: *Ramona; A Century of Dishonor.* Friend of Emily Dickinson and Harriet Beecher Stowe. Jackson affected U.S. policy toward Native Americans and aroused public sentiment with her writing. She moved from Colorado to California in 1884 to recuperate from a fall. Died at age 54 a year later in San Francisco. Branch of the Los Angeles Public Library and two schools were named for her.

Last Words (written): "Dear Sir: From my deathbed I send you a message of heart-felt thanks for what you have already done for the Indians. I ask you to read my Century of Dishonor. I am dying happier for the belief I have that it is your hand that is destined to strike the first steady blow toward lifting this burden of infamy from our country, and righting the wrongs of the Indian race. With respect and gratitude, Helen Jackson." Letter to President Cleveland urging him to read her book *A Century of Dishonor.*

Source: *Helen Hunt Jackson* by Ruth Odell (New York, 1939).

Jackson, Joseph Jefferson ("Shoeless Joe")

(1888-1951) American athlete. Professional baseball player. Played for the Chicago White Sox. Involved in 1919 Black Sox scandal. Banned from baseball. Always maintained his innocence. Died at age 63 of a heart attack in Greenville, South Carolina. Was one of the main characters in the movies *Field of Dreams* (based on W.P. Kinsella's book *Shoeless Joe*) and *Eight Men Out.* Immortalized as subject of the line: "Say it ain't so, Joe."

Last Words: "I'm about to meet the greatest

umpire of all and He knows I am innocent."
Source: "Time to Pardon Shoeless Joe" by David Rosenbaum (*CIO* magazine, October 15, 1999).

Jackson, Rachel Donelson Robards

(1767-1828) American matron. Would-be First Lady. Divorced first husband, Lewis Robards. When she and Andrew Jackson were married in 1791, they did not know her first marriage was still legal. Robards finally had the marriage dissolved two years later and the Jacksons quickly remarried. Their lives were troubled by charges of adultery and bigamy. Rachel died at age 61 at the Hermitage, near Nashville, Tennessee, in December 1828 a few months before Andrew Jackson was inaugurated 7th President of the U.S.
Different Last Words:
(1) "I would rather be a doorkeeper in the House of God than live in that palace in Washington."
Source: *The Shackles of Power: Three Jeffersonian Decades* by John Dos Passos (Garden City, NY, 1966). Dos Passos said she made the comment during her last illness.
(2) Her last sound was a long, low cry, after which she never spoke again. Earlier that evening the only words she spoke were to implore her husband to rest so that he would not be fatigued when he attended a banquet given by Nashville citizens to honor his recent election to President.
Source: "Mrs. Rachel Donelson Jackson, Wife of General Andrew Jackson" (*American Monthly Magazine*, Vol. VI, No. 1, January 1895).

Jackson, Thomas Jonathan ("Stonewall")

(1824-1863) American military officer. Confederate lieutenant general in U.S. Civil War. Known as Stonewall Jackson. Seriously wounded in an accident at the Battle of Chancellorsville. Died at age 39, a week after his arm was amputated.
Last Words: "Let us cross over the river and rest under the shade of the trees."
Source: *Life of Stonewall Jackson* by John Esten Cooke (New York, 1897). Cooke was an officer in the Confederate army.

Jackson, William

(1737-1795) Irish clergyman, educator, writer, revolutionary. Tried and found guilty of high treason. Died in a Dublin prison before his verdict was announced. He may have taken arsenic supplied by his wife.
Last Words: "We have deceived the senate." Whispered to one of his counsel. His Last Words were the dying words of Pierre, a character in Thomas Otway's *Venice Preserv'd,* a drama that was one of the great theatrical successes of that era.
Source: *A History of England in the Eighteenth Century* by William Edward Hartpole Lecky (New York, 1878-1890).

Jackson, William Ayrault

(1832-1861) American lawyer, military officer. Inspector general for New York. Colonel of the 18th Regiment New York Volunteers (New York State Rifles) in the U.S. Civil War. On active service less than three months when he was killed. He had just joined as one of the leaders of Newton's Brigade, Franklin's Division, Army of the Potomac.
Last Words: "I do believe in the Lord Jesus Christ, I trust in Him."
Source: *Memoir of William A. Jackson, a Member of the Albany Bar, and Colonel of the 18th Regiment, N.Y. Volunteers, Who Died at the City of Washington, November 11, 1861,* by Albany New York Bar (Albany, NY, 1862).

Jackson, William Henry ("Zip the Pinhead")

(1842-1926) American sideshow performer. Barnum circus entertainer. Had receding forehead and very small head. Inspiration for Zippy the Pinhead, comic strip character created by Bill Griffith. Although described as a microcephalic, he was not one. Died at about age 84 in New York City.
Last Words: "Well we fooled 'em a long time." Spoken to his sister shortly before he died in a New York City hospital.
Source: *Very Special People: The Struggles, Loves and Triumphs of Human Oddities* by F. Drimmer (New York, 1973).

Jacob

Biblical figure. Old Testament Hebrew patriarch. Younger son of Isaac and Rebekah. Jacob and his family sought refuge from a famine by going to Egypt. He died in Egypt at age 147. His body was taken back to Canaan and he was buried in the family tomb in the Cave of Machpelah.
Last Words: "Et praecepit eis dicens: Ego congregor ad populum meum: sepelite me

cum patribus meis in spelunca duplici quae est in agro Ephron Hetthei, contra Mambre in terra Chanaan, quam emit Abraham cum agro ab Ephron Hettheo in possessionem sepulchri. Ibi sepelierunt eum et Sarram uxorem eius: ibi sepultus est Isaac cum Rebecca coniuge sua: ibi et Lia condita iacet."
Source: Genesis 49:29-31 (Latin Vulgate Bible).

Variation: "I am to be gathered unto my people: bury me with my fathers in the cave that is in the field of Ephron the Hittite, In the cave that is in the field of Machpelah, which is before Mamre, in the land of Canaan, which Abraham bought with the field of Ephron the Hittite for a possession of a burying place. There they buried Abraham and Sarah his wife; there they buried Isaac and Rebekah his wife; and there I buried Leah. The purchase of the field and of the cave that is therein was from the children of Heth."
Sources: Genesis 49:29-32 (King James Version); (21st Century King James Version). Very similar within a few words (New American Standard Bible) and (New King James Version).

Variation: "I am to be gathered to my people; bury me with my fathers in the cave that is in the field of Ephron the Hittite, in the cave that is in the field at Machpelah, to the east of Mamre, in the land of Canaan, which Abraham bought with the field from Ephron the Hittite to possess as a burying place. There they buried Abraham and Sarah his wife. There they buried Isaac and Rebekah his wife, and there I buried Leah—the field and the cave that is in it were bought from the Hittites."
Source: *Genesis* 49:29-32 (English Standard Version).

Variation: "I am about to be gathered to my people. Bury me with my fathers in the cave in the field of Ephron the Hittite, the cave in the field of Machpelah, near Mamre in Canaan, which Abraham bought as a burial place from Ephron the Hittite, along with the field. There Abraham and his wife Sarah were buried, there Isaac and his wife Rebekah were buried, and there I buried Leah. The field and the cave in it were bought from the Hittites."
Source: Genesis 49:29-32 (New International Version).

Variation: "I am gathered to my people: bury me with my fathers in the cave that is in the field of Ephron the Hittite, in the cave that is in the field of Machpelah, which is opposite to Mamre, in the land of Canaan, which Abraham bought of Ephron the Hittite along with the field for a possession of a sepulchre. There they buried Abraham and Sarah his wife; there they buried Isaac and Rebecca his wife; and there I buried Leah. The purchase of the field, and of the cave that is in it, was from the children of Heth."
Source: Genesis 49:29-32 (Darby Translation).

Variation: "I am now going to be gathered to my people : bury me with my fathers in the double cave, which is in the field of Ephron the Hethite, Over against Mambre in the land of Chanaan, which Abraham bought together with the field of Ephron the Hethite for a possession to bury in. There they buried him, and Sara his wife: there was Isaac buried with Rebecca his wife: there also Lia doth lie buried."
Source: Genesis 49:29-31 (Douay-Rheims Translation).

Variation: "I am being gathered unto my people; bury me by my fathers, at the cave which [is] in the field of Ephron the Hittite; in the cave which [is] in the field of Machpelah, which [is] on the front of Mamre, in the land of Canaan, which Abraham bought with the field from Ephron the Hittite for a possession of a burying-place; (there they buried Abraham and Sarah his wife; there they buried Isaac and Rebekah his wife; and there I buried Leah); the purchase of the field and of the cave which [is] in it, [is] from Sons of Heth."
Source: Genesis 49:29-32 (Young's Literal Translation).

Jacobi, Johann Georg

(1740-1814) German writer, dramatist, lyric poet, educator. Professor at Halle and Freiburg. Notable works: *Poetical Essays; Dramatic Works*. Brother of philosopher Friedrich Heinrich Jacobi. Died at age 73.
Last Words. "I shall not in fact see the New Year which I have just commemorated.—I hope, at least, it is not apparent in the poem how elderly I am." He was referring to a poem he had written on New Year's Eve about New Year's Day.
Source: *Leben Joh. Georg Jacobi* by Joseph Albrecht von Ittner (Zurich, Switzerland, 1822).

Jacobs, Christian Friedrich Wilhelm

(1764-1847) German classical scholar, philologist, writer. Notable work: *Greek Anthology* (13 vol.). Died at age 82 in Gotha, Germany.

Last Words: "Who would wish, indeed, to prolong pain, the breath failing all too gradually? Better to die in death, than to drag out a dead life, the senses buried in the limbs."

Source: *Friderici Jacobsii Laudatio* by E.F. Wuestemann (Gotha, Germany, 1848).

James, son of Alphaeus
or James the Less, Saint

(d. 62) Biblical figure, holy man, martyr. One of the 12 Apostles. Often identified as James the Less. He is rarely mentioned in the New Testament, sometimes identified with James the Just, and is clearly distinguished from James, son of Zebedee, another one of the Twelve Apostles. Put to death by stoning.

Last Words: "O Lord God my Father, I beseech thee, forgive them, for they know not what they do."

Source: *The Epistle of St. James: The Greek Text with Introduction, Notes and Comments* by Joseph Bickersteth Mayor (London, 1897).

James, son of Zebedee
or James the Greater, Saint

(d. 44) Biblical figure, holy man, martyr. One of the 12 Apostles. Son of Zebedee and Salome, and brother of John the Apostle. Called James the Greater to distinguish him from James, son of Alphaeus, who is also known as James the Less. James the Greater was one of only three apostles Jesus selected to bear witness to his Transfiguration. James was beheaded by King Herod Agrippa I. He was the first of the Apostles to be martyred.

Last Words: "Peace be with thee." (Or "Peace be with you.") Spoken to a fellow martyr. Tradition states the other martyr had denounced James but after James gave testimony, this man was so moved that he converted to Christianity and the two were led away together. On the way, he begged James to forgive him and James said his Last Words. Both were beheaded at the same time.

Source: *The Ecclesiastical History of Eusebius Pamphilus, Bishop of Caesarea, in Palestine: in Ten Books*, tr. by Christian Frederic Crusé (Philadelphia, 1833).

James the Dismembered, Saint

(d. 421) Persian holy man, martyr. Known as James the Persian. Called the Dismembered because of the way he was martyred. His killer ordered his body to be dismembered at every joint of his arms and legs, then beheaded.

Last Words: "O Lord of lords, Lord of the living and the dead, give ear to me who am half dead. I have no fingers to hold out to Thee, O Lord, nor hands to stretch forth to Thee. My feet are cut off and my knees demolished, wherefore I cannot bend the knee to Thee, and I am like to a house that is about to fall because its columns are taken away. Hear me, O Lord Jesus Christ, and deliver my soul from its prison!"

Source: *The Golden Legend or Lives of the Saints.* Compiled by Jacobus de Voragine, Archbishop of Genoa, 1275, 1st ed., 1470. English ed. by William Caxton, 1483, ed. by F.S. Ellis (Edinburgh, 1900).

James I, King of England/
James VI, King of Scotland

(1566-1625) English monarch. Son of Mary Queen of Scots. Successor to Elizabeth I. First Stuart monarch to rule England. King James Bible was prepared during his reign and named for him. His severity toward Roman Catholics caused the Gunpowder Plot. Died at age 58 at Theobalds, Hertfordshire, England.

Different Last Words:

(1) "Come, Lord Jesus."

Source: *James I of England, The Wisest Fool in Christendom* by Clara and Hardy Steeholm (New York, 1938).

(2) "But in the dark way of the Church of Rome, I do defy it." After a bishop prayed the Creed, James said: "There is no other belief, no other hope!" He then spoke these Last Words after receiving absolution for his sins under the Anglican rites.

Source: *Charles I: A Biography* by John Bowle (London, 1975).

James II, King of England and Ireland/
James VII, King of Scotland

(1633-1701) English monarch. Duke of York. Son of Charles I. Ascended to throne as James II in England and Ireland, and

James VII in Scotland. Last male monarch in the direct Stuart line. Last Roman Catholic monarch to reign Kingdoms of England, Scotland and Ireland. Lost the throne in 1688. Died at age 67 in Saint-Germain, France.

Different Last Words:

(1) "Into Thy hands I commend my soul, O Lord; lay not this great sin to their charge."

Source: *A Collection of Scarce and Valuable Tracts* [Lord Somer's Tracts], ed. by Walter Scott (London, 1814).

(2) "Think of it Madam, I am going to be happy." Spoken to his wife.

Source: *The Life and Times of James II* by Peter Earle (London, 1972).

(3) "Grateful—in peace!" Said to have murmured these words to King Louis XIV, who visited him and told him he would acknowledge James's son as King of England, Ireland and Scotland.

Source: *The Last Words (Real and Traditional) of Distinguished Men and Women Collected from Various Sources* by Frederic Rowland Marvin (New York, 1901).

James V, King of Scotland

(1512-1542) Scottish monarch. Son of James IV of Scotland. Died at age 30 in Falkland, a week after his only heir, a daughter, was born (Mary Stuart; the future Mary Queen of Scots).

Last Words: "The devil go with it. It will end as it began. It came with a lass and will go with a lass." He was talking about the end of the Stuart line.

Source: *Dictionary of National Biography* by Sir Leslie Stephen, George Smith and Sir Sidney Lee (London, 1921-1922).

James, Alice

(1848-1892) American diarist. Lived in England. Younger sister of psychologist William James and novelist Henry James Jr. Suffered from several neurological disorders since childhood. Obsessed with dying. She kept a journal that detailed her life as an expatriate invalid. Died at age 44.

Last Words (written): "Tenderest love to all. Farewell. Am going soon." Telegram sent from London to her brother William in the U.S.

Source: *Epistolary Practices: Letter Writing in America Before Telecommunications* by William Merrill Decker (Chapel Hill, NC, 1998).

James, Henry, Jr.

(1843-1916) American writer, novelist, essayist. Brother of William James. Traveled extensively in Europe. Awarded British Order of Merit. Notable works: *The American; Daisy Miller; The Portrait of a Lady; The Turn of the Screw; The Golden Bowl*. Several of his stories have been made into movies and television dramas. Had stroke in December 1915. Died two months later at age 72 in London.

Different Last Words:

(1) "So here it is at last, the distinguished thing!"

Source: *Henry James* by F.W. Dupee (Garden City, NY, 1956).

(2) "Stay with me Alice! Stay with me! This is the end." Spoken to his sister-in-law.

Source: *Henry James, The Master, 1901-1916* by Leon Edel (Philadelphia, 1972).

James, Henry, Sr.

(1811-1882) American theologian, social theorist, lecturer. Father of novelist Henry James and psychologist William James. Friend of Thoreau, Emerson and Hawthorne. Died at age 71 in Boston.

Different Last Words:

(1) "I stick by Almighty God—He alone is, all else is death. Don't call this dying; I am just entering upon life."

Source: *The Elder Henry James* by Austin Warren (New York, 1934).

(2) "There's my Mary." Spoken about his dead wife.

Source: *The Jameses: A Family Narrative* by R.W.B. Lewis (New York, 1991).

James, Jesse Woodson

(1847-1882) American outlaw, robber. Leader of band of desperados who robbed banks and trains. Shot and killed at age 34 in his home in St. Joseph, Missouri, by Bob Ford, a gang associate of James.

Last Words (doubtful): "That picture looks awful dusty."

Source: Various Last Words compilations and Internet websites.

Many Last Words quotations are circulating for Jesse James, but none are documented. Even Ford, who was at his autopsy, did not provide any final words for James. Garry Radison noted in his book that a popular version—"That picture looks awful

dusty"—is a fabrication of author Carl W. Breihan, who wrote often about James. James was beginning to adjust the picture on the wall when Ford shot him in the back. According to witnesses, James spun around with a wild look, then toppled forward. Ford said the gun went off accidentally. More likely, Ford shot James deliberately because he feared what James would do if he learned of Ford's plans: Ford had notified the governor that he and his brother would deliver James in return for amnesty and reward money.
Source: *Last Words, Dying in the Old West* by Garry Radison (Austin, TX, 2002).

James, John Angell
(1785-1859) English clergyman, writer. Nonconformist Congregationalist. A founder of the Evangelical Alliance and of the Congregational Union of England and Wales. Died at age 74 in Birmingham, England.
Last Words: "Inasmuch as thou hast done it unto one of the least of these, thou has done it unto Me." He was quoting the Bible to his physician.
Source: *John Angell James: A Review of His History, Character, Eloquence, and Literary Labors* by John Campbell (London, 1860).

James, William
(1842-1910) American psychologist, writer, philosopher, educator. Professor at Harvard. Brother of author Henry James. Notable work: *The Principles of Psychology*. Became ill in Europe. Returned to the U.S. Died at age 68 of heart failure in Chocorua, New Hampshire.
Different Last Words:
(1) "Go to Henry when his times comes." Spoken to his wife Alice about his brother.
Source: *William James* by Gay Wilson Allen (New York, 1967).
(2) "It's so good to get home!"
Source: *Letters,* ed. by Henry James (Boston, 1920).

Janacek, Leos
(1854-1928) Czech musician, composer, conductor, organist, teacher. Notable works: *Jenufa; Taras Bulba; The Cunning Little Vixen; From the House of the Dead; The Makropulos Affair.* Died at age 74 in Ostrava.

Last Words: "Nurse, you probably don't know who I am!"
Source: *Leos Janacek: His Life and Work* by Jaroslav Vogel (New York, 1962). Vogel, a Czech conductor and composer, was acclaimed for his study of Janacek's life and work.

Janeway, Jacob Jones
(1774-1858) American clergyman, writer, educator. Trustee, vice president, professor of literature at Rutgers. Died at age 83 in New Brunswick, New Jersey.
Last Words: "I'm tired of eating—I want to go home!"
Source: *Memoir of Reverend Jacob J. Janeway* by his son Thomas L. Janeway (Philadelphia, 1861).

Jara, Saint Cristóbal Magallanes
(1869-1927) Mexican clergyman, holy man. Roman Catholic martyr. Opened a seminary in Totatiche. Falsely accused of promoting rebellion. Arrested. Executed at age 57 without trial, along with Agustín Caloca in Colotlán, Jalisco. Gave away his possessions to his executioners. Canonized in 2000.
Last Words: "I am innocent and I die innocent. I forgive with all my heart those responsible for my death, and I ask God that the shedding of my blood may bring peace to divided Mexicans." Spoken just before his executioners shot him.
Source: *Butler's Lives of the Saints: The Third Millennium* by Alban Butler and Paul Burns (London, 2005).

Jaricot, Pauline-Marie
(1799-1862) French religious leader. Founder of Society of the Propagation of the Faith and the Association of the Living Rosary. Died at age 62 in Lyons, France. Cause for her beatification and sainthood was been introduced in Rome.
Last Words: "Par— Par— Par—" She was attempting to say "Pardon our trespasses as we pardon those who…" The prayer was completed by a woman in the room.
Source: *Difficult Star: The Life of Pauline Jaricot* by Katherine Burton (New York, 1947).

Jarman, Michael Derek Elworthy (Derek)
(1942-1994) British writer, film maker, stage designer, painter, activist. Iconoclastic, controversial. Subject of Chumbawamba song, "Song for Derek Jarman." Died of an

AIDS-related illness at age 52 in London.
Last Words: "I want the world to be filled
with white fluffy duckies."
Source: *Life as Art: Derek Jarman* (movie, 2004),
directed by Andy Kimpton-Nye. His Last Words were
reported by Christopher Hobbs in the movie.

Jarry, Alfred

(1873-1907) French writer, playwright, novelist. Absurdist who influenced surrealists
and Dadaists. Creator of *Ubu Roi*. Abused
his body with alcohol and ether. Died at age
34 of tuberculosis in Paris.
Last Words: "Bring me a toothpick."
Source: *The Banquet Years: The Origins of the Avant
Garde in France; 1885 to World War I* by Roger Shat-
tuck (New York, 1968).

Jasper, William

(1750?-1779) American military soldier.
Sergeant of the Grenadiers, 2nd South Carolina Regiment during the American Revolution. Gained fame for bravery at Fort Moultrie (Fort Sullivan) when he recovered and
raised the fallen South Carolina flag under a
shower of cannon fire. The incident was
immortalized in a painting (*The Rescue*) by
Charleston artist John Blake White. Jasper
was killed three years later at about age 29
during the Siege of Savannah. Eight U.S.
counties and several southern cities were
named for him.
Last Words: "Tell Mrs. Elliott I lost my life
supporting the colors she presented to our
regiment." Mrs. Elliott, wife of a captain,
had presented the flag to the regiment after
the Battle of Fort Moultrie.
Source: *A History of the United States. For Families
and Libraries* by Benson John Lossing (New York,
1857).

Jay, John

(1745-1829) American statesman, diplomat,
jurist, politician. Negotiated Jay's Treaty
with Britain. Justice of U.S. Supreme Court.
Governor of New York. Died at age 83 in
Bedford, New York.
Last Words: "I would have my funeral decent, but not ostentatious. No scarfs—no
rings. Instead thereof, I give two hundred
dollars to any one poor deserving widow or
orphan of this town, whom my children shall
select."
Source: *John Jay: Defender of Liberty* by Frank Mona-
ghan (Indianapolis, IN, 1935).

Jay, William

(1769-1853) English clergyman. Nonconformist Accomplished pulpit orator. Had
important ministry at Bath, England. Notable work: *Morning and Evening Exercises*.
Died at age 83.
Last Words: "Oh, none of you know what it
is to die."
Source: *Recollections of William Jay, of Bath: with
Occasional Glances at Some of His Contemporaries
and Friends* by Cyrus Jay (London, 1859). The author
was his son.

Jefferies, Richard

(1848-1887) English writer, naturalist.
Known for descriptions of nature in his writ-
ings. Notable works: *The Gamekeeper at
Home; Red Deer; Bevis: The Story of a Boy.*
Ill during the last five years of his life. Died
at age 38 of tuberculosis at Gorning-on-Sea,
West Sussex, England.
Last Words: "Yes, yes; that is so. Help,
Lord, for Jesus' sake. Darling, good-bye.
God bless you and the children, and save
you all from such great pain."
Source: *The Eulogy of Richard Jefferies* by Walter
Besant (London, 1893).

Jefferson, Joseph

(1829-1905) American actor. Third family
member with the same name who went on
the stage. Noted for performing title role in
Rip Van Winkle and as Bob Acres in *The
Rivals*. Died at age 76 of pneumonia in Palm
Beach, Florida.
Last Words: "I feel that there are only a few
more hours for me. Good-bye."
Source: *A Conspectus of American Biography: Being
an Analytical Summary of American History and Biog-
raphy, Containing also the Complete Indexes of the
National Cyclopedia of American Biography* by George
Derby (New York, 1906).

Jefferson, Thomas

(1743-1826) 3rd President of the U.S.
American statesman, lawyer, politician, ar-
chitect, writer. Member House of Burgesses.
One of the initiators of the Committees of
Correspondence. Member of the Continental
Congress. Prepared first draft of Declaration
of Independence for Congress. Governor of
Virginia. U.S. secretary of state. A founder
of University of Virginia. Died at age 83 in

Monticello, his Virginia home.

Different Last Words:

(1) "This is the Fourth?—Ah, just as I wished." Or: "Is it the Fourth?" When Henry Stephens Randall wrote his biography of Jefferson, he examined accounts of three eye witnesses to the Last Words and death of Jefferson: Thomas Jefferson "Jeff" Randolph (the President's grandson); Nicholas Trist (Jefferson's private secretary who was married to Jefferson's granddaughter Virginia Randolph); and Dr. Robley Dunglison (Jefferson's personal physician). The accounts were written years apart and without one of the three having seen the statements of the other two. Randolph's account of Jefferson's closing scene was so similar to Trist's that it didn't require transcription. Trist and Dunglison's accounts varied as to who responded to Jefferson's question about the date. In Trist's account, Jefferson woke on the evening of July 3rd and asked Trist: "This is the Fourth?" Trist could not bear to say it wasn't. When Jefferson asked again, Trist nodded his head in assent. Jefferson replied: "Ah, just as I wished." Trist said Jefferson rose in his couch and imagined he was sending messages to the Revolutionary Committee of Safety. He used his hands as if writing on a tablet: "Warn the Committee to be on the alert." Randolph said the family knew how much Jefferson wanted to live until July 4th and they carefully noted the minute hand on a watch as it approached midnight. His grandfather lapsed in a stupor on July 3rd, but when the sun rose on July 4th, he was still alive. At 11 a.m. Jefferson moved his lips slightly. Randolph put a sponge to his mouth. This was Jefferson's last evidence of consciousness. In Dr. Dunglison's account, Jefferson asked: "Is it the Fourth?" when he woke on July 3rd. Dunglison replied: "It soon will be." These were the last words Dunglison heard him utter. Jefferson remained unconscious until the middle of July 4th. He died at 12:50 that afternoon on the 50th anniversary of the Declaration of independence. John Adams also died on that day. (See also Adams, John.)

Source: *The Life of Thomas Jefferson* by Henry Stephens Randall, 3 vol. (Philadelphia, 1888). First published in 1858. Randall was the only biographer permitted to interview the Jefferson family. His biography was praised for its thoroughness and objectivity. It did much to dispel many of the 19th century distortions about Jefferson that had been spread by his political enemies.

(2) "I have done for my country, and for all mankind all that I could do, and I now resign my soul, without fear, to my God, my daughter to my country." These were the last words he articulated. All that was heard from him afterward was a hurried repetition of "Nunc Dimittis, Domine—Nunc Dimittis, Domine" (tr. "Now dismiss me, Lord.") He breathed his last without a struggle at ten minutes before one o'clock on July 4th.

Source: *Sketches of the Life, Writings and Opinions of Thomas Jefferson: with Selections of the Most Valuable Portions of his Voluminous and Unrivaled Private Correspondence* by B.L. Rayner (New York, 1832).

Variation: "I resign my spirit to God, my daughter to my country."

Source: "Presidential Last Words, Thomas Jefferson," *White House Special Handbook: How to Rule the World in the 21st Century* by Mikhail Kryzhanovsky (New York, 2007).

Jeffrey, Francis, Lord Jeffrey

(1773-1850) Scottish critic, journalist. A founder of the *Edinburgh Review*. Literary critic of Keats, Wordsworth, Byron. Friend of Charles Dickens. Died at age 76 in Edinburgh.

Last Words (written): "I could conjure up the spectrum of a close printed political paper filled with discussions of free trade, protection, and colonies, such as one sees in the Times, the Economist and the Daily News. I read the ideal copies with a good deal of pain and difficulty owing to the smallness of the type, but with great interest, and I believe, often for more than an hour at a time; forming a judgment of their merits with great freedom and acuteness, and often saying to myself, 'this is very cleverly put, but there is a fallacy in it, for so and so.'" He was describing curious visions he had after three sleepless nights. He died the next day.

Source: *The Life of Lord Jeffrey, with a Selection from His Correspondence* by Lord Cockburn (Edinburgh, 1852). The author was a life-long friend of Jeffrey.

Jeffreys, Sir George, 1st Baron Jeffreys of Wem

(1645-1689) English jurist. Knighted in

1677. Named lord chancellor in 1685. Known as the Infamous Jeffreys or the Hanging Judge for the punishment he handed out in the trials of Duke of Monmouth supporters. When King James was dethroned, Jeffreys tried to flee England. He was captured and placed in the Tower of London, where he died at age 43 of kidney disease.

Last Words: "People call me a murderer for doing what at the time was applauded by some who are now high in public favour. They call me a drunkard because I take punch to relieve me in my agony."

Source: *The History of England,* Vol. I, by Thomas Babington Macaulay (London, 1848).

Jehoram or Joram, King of Israel

(d. 842 B.C.?) Biblical figure. King of the northern Kingdom of Israel. Son of Ahab and Jezebel. Aided by his nephew Ahaziah, king of Judah, fought unsuccessfully at Ramoth-Gilead against the army of Hazael, king of the Arameans. Jehoram was wounded. At Jezreel, his general Jehu incited a revolt and Jehoram was killed.

Last Words: "Insidiae Ahazia." Ahaziah was his nephew and King of Judah.

Source: 2 Kings 9:23 (Latin Vulgate Bible).

Variation: "There is treachery, O, Ahaziah."

Sources: 2 Kings 9:23 (King James Version); (21st Century King James Version); (New Standard American Bible).

Variation: "Treachery, Ahaziah!"

Source: 2 Kings 9:23 (New King James Version);

Variation: "Treachery, O Ahaziah!"

Source: 2 Kings 9:23 (English Standard Version). (New International Version); (Darby Translation).

Variation: "There is treachery, Ochozias."

Source: 2 Kings 9:23 (Douay-Rheims Translation).

Variation: "Deceit, O Ahaziah!"

Source: 2 Kings 9:23 (Young's Literal Translation).

Jenkins, John

(1808?-1834) Australian murderer. Jenkins and his accomplice Thomas Tattersdale were escaped prisoners. While together, Jenkins shot and killed Dr. Robert Wardell. Tattersdale did not know Jenkins was seeking revenge for floggings he received at Wardell's instigation. Both men were apprehended, tried, convicted and executed for the crime. Jenkins died at age 26.

Last Words: "Let every villain shake hands with himself." Shouted as the hangman let him drop.

Source: *Manning Clark's History of Australia* by Manning Clark, abridged by Michael Cathcart (Carlton South, Victoria, Australia, 1997).

Jenkins, Micah

(1835-1864) American military officer. Confederate brigadier general in U.S. Civil War. Shot and killed at age 28 at the Battle of the Wilderness in Virginia the same time Lieutenant General James Longstreet was struck.

Last Words: "I am happy; I have felt despair of the cause for some months, but am relieved, and feel assured that we will put the enemy back cross the Rapidan before night." Spoken to those around him. He was fatally wounded a few minutes later.

Source: *Lee and Longstreet at High Tide: Gettysburg in the Light of the Official Records* by Helen Dortch Longstreet (New York, 1969). The author was the wife of General Longstreet.

Jerome of Prague

(1360?-1416) Bohemian religious reformer, martyr. Pupil and friend of John Huss. Sought sweeping reforms in Roman Catholic Church. Condemned as a heretic by the Council of Constance. Burned at the stake.

Different Last Words:

(1) "O Lord God, Father Almighty, have mercy upon me and be merciful unto mine offenses, for Thou knowest how sincerely I have loved Thy Truth." Spoken at the stake before he was killed.

Source: *Book of Martyrs and the Acts and Monuments of the Church* by John Fox (or Foxe). First published 1563, ed. by John Cumming (London, 1851).

(2) "Come here and kindle it before my eyes; for if I had been afraid of it, I had not come to this place." Spoken to the executioner who was about to light the fire. His final words were "This soul in flames I offer, Christ, to thee."

Source: *Death-Bed Scenes: Dying With and Without Religion: The Truth and Power of Christianity* by Davis W. Clark (New York, 1852).

Variation: "Bring thy torch hither; do thine office before my face; had I feared death I might have avoided it." Spoken to his executioner who was about to kindle the fire in back of him.

Source: *The Last Words (Real and Traditional) of Distinguished Men and Women Collected from Various*

Sources by Frederic Rowland Marvin (New York, 1901). Marvin also found these given as his Last Words: "This soul in flames I offer, Christ, to thee" but gave no sources.

Jerrold, Douglas William

(1803-1857) English playwright, humorist, novelist, journalist. Editor of *Lloyd's Weekly Newspaper*. Contributor to *Punch*. Notable works: *Cakes and Ale* (papers and stories); *Black-eyed Susan; Bride of Ludgate* (plays*)*; *Mrs. Caudle's Curtain Lectures*. Died at age 54 in London.

Last Words: "This is as it should be." Spoken as each of his sons took his hand.

Source: *Douglas William Jerrold, Dramatist and Wit* by Walter Jerrold (London, 1914). The author was his grandson.

Jesus of Nazareth (Jesus Christ)

(c. 4 B.C.-c. 30 A.D.) Biblical figure, spiritual leader, teacher, healer, carpenter, martyr. The central figure of Christianity, which views him as the prophesied Messiah foretold in the Old Testament. Most Christian denominations believe Jesus to be the Son of God and God incarnate. Islam views him as a prophet. His life and teachings are known through the Gospels of Matthew, Mark, Luke and John. He was born in Bethlehem and died by crucifixion in Calvary, Judea. The Gospels state that after Jesus was crucified, he rose from the dead, appeared to his Apostles then ascended to Heaven.

Last Words (prior to death by crucifixion):
(1) "Eloi, Eloi, lama sabachthani?" (tr. "My God, my God, why have you (hast Thou) forsaken me!").

Sources: Mark 15:34 and Matthew 27:46 (Latin Vulgate Bible); (King James Version); (New King James Version); (21st Century King James Version); (New Standard American Bible); (English Standard Version); (New International Version); (Darby Translation); (Douay-Rheims Translation); (Young's Literal Translation).

(2) "Pater in manus tuas commendo spiritum."

Source: Luke 23:46 (Latin Vulgate Bible).

Variation: "Father, into thy [your] hands I commend [commit] my spirit."

Sources: Luke 23:46 (King James Version); (New King James Version); (21st Century King James Version); (New Standard American Bible); (English Standard Version); (New International Version); (Darby Translation); (Douay-Rheims Translation); (Young's Literal Translation).

(3) "Consummatum est."

Source: John 19:30 (Latin Vulgate Bible).

Variation: "It is (hath been) finished."

Sources: John 19:30 (King James Version); (New King James Version); (21st Century King James Version); (New Standard American Bible); English Standard Version); (New International Version); (Darby Translation); (Douay-Rheims Translation); (Young's Literal Translation).

Last Words (prior to Ascension): He gave his Apostles a parting blessing then ascended into Heaven and was soon lost from view. His Ascension took place on Mount Olivet forty days after his Resurrection.

Sources: Luke 24:46-49; Acts of the Apostles 1:12 (Latin Vulgate Bible); (King James Version); (New King James Version); (21st Century King James Version); (New Standard American Bible); (English Standard Version); (New International Version); (Darby Translation); (Douay-Rheims Translation); (Young's Literal Translation).

Jewel or Jewell, John

(1522-1571) English prelate. Puritan leader in the English Reformation. Fled England to escape persecution during Queen Mary's reign. Returned and became Bishop of Salisbury. Published *Apologia pro Ecclesia Anglicana* (*Apology of the Church of England*, first precise statement of the position of the English Church against the Church of Rome). He collapsed during a sermon in Wiltshire. Died soon afterward at age 49.

Last Words: "O Lord, confound me not. This is my Today! This day quickly let me come unto thee. This day let me see the Lord Jesus."

Source: *The Works of John Jewel, Bishop of Salisbury,* ed. by John Eyre (Cambridge, England, 1850).

Jezebel

(d. 842 B.C.?) Biblical figure. Daughter of Ethbaal, King of the Sidonians. Wife of King Ahab of Israel. Mother of Jehoram or Joram, King of Israel. Her Last Words were spoken to Jehu about another king who tried to take the throne. Jehu then had her thrown from a window. Dogs ate her corpse.

Last Words: "Et ait numquid pax esse potest Zamri qui interfecit dominum suum."

Source: 2 Kings 9:31 (Latin Vulgate Bible).

Variation: "Had Zimri peace, who slew his master?"

Sources: 2 Kings 9:31 (King James Version); (21st Century King James Version).

Variation: "Is it well, Zimri, your master's murderer?"
Source: 2 Kings 9:31 (New American Standard Bible).

Variation: "Is it peace, Zimri, murderer of your master?"
Source: 2 Kings 9:31 (New King James Version).

Variation: "Is it peace, you Zimri, murderer of your master?"
Source: 2 Kings 9:31 (English Standard Version).

Variation: "Have you come in peace, Zimri, you murderer of your master?"
Source: 2 Kings 9:31 (New International Version).

Variation: "Can there be peace for Zambri, that hath killed his master?"
Source: 2 Kings 9:31 (Douay-Rheims Translation).

Variation: "Is it peace, Zimri, murderer of his master?"
Source: 2 Kings 9:31 (Darby Translation).

Variation: "Was there peace [to] Zimri— slayer of his lord?"
Source: 2 Kings 9:31 (Young's Literal Translation).

Jinnah, Muhammad, Mohammad or Mahomed Ali

(1876-1948) Indian-born Pakistani politician, lawyer. President of All-India Muslim League. Founder and first president of Pakistan. Died at age 71 of tuberculosis and lung cancer in Karachi, Pakistan.
Last Words: "Fati, Khuda Hjafiz—La llaha ll Allah—Mohammad—Rasul—Allah." He whispered "Fati," his sister Fatima's nickname.
Source: *My Brother* by Fatima Jinnah and Sharif Mujahid (Karachi, Pakistan, 1987).

Joan of Arc or Jeanne d'Arc, Saint

(1412-1431) French holy woman, soldier, martyr. Known as the Maid of Orléans. Believed she had a mission to save Orléans and drive the English from France. Burned at the stake in Rouen at about age 19 for heresy and other charges. Later found innocent. Sentence was annulled. Canonized in 1920.
Last Words: "Ah, Rouen! I have great fear that you are going to suffer by my death!— Jesus, Jesus!" Spoken as she was about to be burned at the Old Market in Rouen.
Source: *Saint Joan of Arc* by V. Sackville-West (New York, 1936).

Jodl, Alfred

(1890-1946) German Nazi military officer. Chief of operations for the German High Command. Signed Act of Unconditional Surrender ending World War II in Europe. Tried, convicted and executed in Nuremberg at age 56 as a Nazi war criminal.
Last Words: "My greetings to you, my Germany." Spoken as he was about to be hanged.
Source: "The Execution of Nazi War Criminals" by Kingsbury Smith (International News Service, October 16, 1946).

Joffre, Joseph Jacques Césaire

(1852-1931) French military officer. Commander-in-chief of French armies and later Allied armies in World War I. Hero at the Battle of the Marne. Created field marshal. Died at age 78 in Paris.
Last Words: "I have not done much evil in my life, and I have sincerely loved my wife." Spoken to a priest.
Source: *Le Maréchal Joffre* by Lt. Col. Charles Bugnet (Tours, France, 1932).

Jogues, Saint Isaac

(1607-1646) French clergyman, missionary, holy man, martyr. Jesuit priest. Roman Catholic. Captured in Quebec and held prisoner in an Iroquois village. Escaped and returned to France. Later went back to Quebec. Asked permission to visit the Iroquois village where he had been held captive years earlier. During his visit he was murdered. Died at age 39. Canonized in 1930.
Last Words (written): "My heart tells me that, if I am the one to be sent on this mission, I shall go, but I shall not return." Written to his superiors in France just before he left to visit the village.
Source: *Saints of North America* by Vincent O'Malley (Huntington, IN, 2004).

John, King of England

(1167-1216) English monarch. Son of Henry II and Eleanor of Aquitaine. Known as John Lackland. Succeeded to throne when his brother Richard I died. Signed Magna Carta (Great Charter) in 1215, stating the rights and limitations of the king. Died at age 48 in Newark, England.
Last Words: "To God and St. Wulfstan I commend my body and soul." He was invoking the name of an 11th-century Bishop of Worcester.
Source: *A History of the Church of England:*

Pre-Reformation Period by Thomas Pownall Boultbee (London, 1879).

John XXIII, Pope and Blessed

(1881-1963) Italian prelate. Roman Catholic pope. Birth name Angelo Giuseppe Roncalli. Apostolic delegate to Greece and Turkey. Apostolic Nuncio to Paris, France. Patriarch of Venice. Elevated to cardinal in 1953. Elected pope in 1958. Convoked Second Vatican Council (1962 to 1965) but was taken ill and lapsed into coma before it was completed. Died at age 81 in Vatican City. Beatified in 2000.

Different Last Words:

(1) "Ut unium sint." (tr. "That they may be one.") Spoken to cardinals assembled at his deathbed.

Source: "A Liberal Pontiff; Church Council and Encyclical on Amity Marked Tenure" by Arnaldo Cortesi (*New York Times*, June 4, 1963).

(2) "Do you remember how I never thought of anything else in life but being a priest?—I embrace you and bless you—I am happy, because in a little while I shall see our mother and father in heaven—Pray—I wish to be dissolved and be with Christ—into thy hands, O Lord, I commend my spirit."

Source: *I Will Be Called John: A Biography of Pope John XXIII* by Lawrence Elliott (New York, 1973).

John of Austria

(1547-1578) Spanish military officer. General. Illegitimate son of Holy Roman Emperor Charles V. Given title Don John of Austria by his half-brother Philip II of Spain. Wanted to liberate England and free Mary Queen of Scots who was imprisoned there. Defeated Turks at the Battle of Lepanto. Died at age 33 of typhus near Namur, Belgium.

Last Words: "Aunt! Aunt! My lady Aunt!"

Source: *The Story of Don John of Austria* by Luis Coloma and Ada Margarette Smith Moreton (London, 1912).

John of Kronstadt, Saint

(1829-1908) Russian clergyman. Birth name Ivan Ilyich Sergiyev. Russian Orthodox archpriest. Member Synod of Russian Orthodox Church. Assigned to Saint Andrew's Cathedral in Kronstadt, where he spent 54 years. Charismatic priest known throughout Russia and Western Europe for his holiness.

Died at age 79. Canonized in 1964.

Last Words: "I cannot breathe." Three days earlier he predicted the date of his death. Died on the third day after uttering these words.

Source: *Father John of Kronstadt: A Life* by Aleksandr Semenov-Tian-Shanskii (London, 1979).

John of the Cross, Saint

(1542-1591) Spanish theologian, mystical poet. Birth name Juan de Yepis y Alverez. Collaborated with Sr. Teresa of Avila in reforming the Carmelite order. Died at age 49 in Ubeda, Andalusia, Spain. Canonized in 1726.

Last Words: "Into Thy hands, O Lord, I commend my spirit."

Source: *Carmelite and Poet: A Framed Portrait of Saint John of the Cross* by Robert E. Sencourt (New York, 1944).

John the Almoner, Saint

(550?-616?) Holy man. Son of governor of Cyprus. Known as the Almoner or Almsgiver for his generosity to the poor. Entered religious life when his wife and child died. Patriarch of Alexandria. Died at about age 66 in Aranthus, Cyprus.

Last Words: "I thank Thee, O my God, that Thy mercy has granted the desire of my weakness, which was that at my death I should possess naught but a single penny. And now this penny, too, can be given to the poor!"

Source: *The Golden Legend or Lives of the Saints.* Compiled by Jacobus de Voragine, Archbishop of Genoa, 1275, 1st ed., 1470. English ed. by William Caxton, 1483, ed. by F.S. Ellis (Edinburgh, 1900).

John the Dwarf, Saint

(d. 405) Holy man, hermit. Also known as John Kolobos or John Colobus. Spent his life in wilderness in northern Egypt praying and doing manual labor. Died in Mount Colzim, Egypt.

Last Words: "I never followed my own will, nor did I ever teach another what I had not practiced first myself."

Source: *New Oxford Dictionary of Saints* (New York, 2003).

John the Evangelist
or John the Divine, Saint

(c. 2.-c. 101) Biblical figure, holy man, evangelist. One of the 12 Apostles. Known as John the Divine. Son of Zebedee. Brother of James.

Last Words: "Thou hast invited me to Thy table, Lord; and behold I come, thanking Thee for having invited me, for Thou knowest that I have desired it with all my heart." Spoke these words after he dug his own grave and vanished.

Source: *The Golden Legend or Lives of the Saints.* Compiled by Jacobus de Voragine, Archbishop of Genoa, 1275, 1st ed., 1470. English ed. by William Caxton, 1483, ed. by F.S. Ellis (Edinburgh, 1900).

John Paul I, Pope

(1912-1978) Italian prelate. Roman Catholic pope. Birth name Albino Luciani. Died suddenly at age 65 in Vatican City after a reign of one month. He was found dead of an apparent heart attack. Since no autopsy was performed, many rumors and conspiracy theories circulated as to his cause of death.

Different Last Words:

(1) "Good night. Until tomorrow, if God is willing." Spoken to an aide as he retired for the night.

Source: *A Thief in the Night: the Mysterious Death of Pope John Paul I* by John Cornwell (New York, 1989).

(2) "They kill each other, even the young people." He was commenting on a news story about the Red Brigades.

Source: "The September Pope" (*Time* magazine, October 9, 1978).

Variation: "Are those young people shooting each other again? Really, it is terrible." His reaction to a news story about the Red Brigades.

Source: "John Paul's 34 Days" (*Newsweek* magazine, October 9, 1978).

John Paul II, Pope

(1920-2005) Polish-born prelate. Roman Catholic pope. Birth name Karol Jozef Wojtyla. First non-Italian Pope since the 1520s. First Polish Pope. Ruled more than 26 years. Died at age 84 in Vatican City.

Last Words: "Let me go to the house of the Father." Uttered about six hours before he died.

Source: "Vatican Releases Official Record of Pope John Paul's Final Days" by Brian Wingfield (*New York Times*, September 19, 2005).

Variation: "Let me go to the Lord." Heard by a nun during his final hours.

Source: "Aide to Pope John Paul Recalls Last Words" (*New York Times*, August 27, 2005).

Johnsen, Nicolaus

(1869-1932) German military officer. Naval commodore. Senior officer, Northern German Lloyd Line. Master of the SS *Europa*. Became ill at sea. Died at age 63 in a Brooklyn hospital after appendicitis surgery.

Last Words: "If the end is to come, turn my face to the sea." Spoken to Captain William Dreschel, marine superintendent of the North German Lloyd Line.

Source: "1,200 at Funeral of Captain Johnsen—'If End Comes, Turn My Face to Sea,' Last Words of Europa Master, Throng is Told" (*New York Times*, December 8, 1932).

Johnson, Andrew

(1808-1875) 17th President of the U.S. American politician. Member U.S. Senate and House of Representatives from Tennessee. Military governor of Tennessee. Elected Vice President of the U.S. in March 1865. Less than six weeks later, he succeeded to the Presidency when Lincoln was assassinated. Johnson was the first President to be impeached. He was also the first former President to be a Senator when he was re-elected to the U.S. Senate from Tennessee in 1875. Served only five months. Had a stroke and died at age 66 in Carter's Station, Tennessee.

Last Words (written):

"Greenville, Tenn., June 6, 1875.

John M. Carmack, Esq.

Dear Sir: Your letter of the 9th ult. has been received and read. I confess I was somewhat surprised when I received your account of Vice-President Wilson's conversation with Gov. Isham Harris and others in regard to what would have been the policy of President Lincoln, if he had lived, &c. In your letter you state that H. Wilson Vice President—." Johnson then had a fatal stroke and wrote no more. The letter was found on Johnson's desk by his family and sent to Judge Carmack. It was later placed in the Tennessee Historical Society.

Source: "Andrew Johnson's Last Written Word" (*Nashville* [Tennessee] *American,* February 4, 1884).

Last Words (spoken): "My right side is paralyzed." Spoken to his granddaughter who rushed to his aid when he fell to the floor. When she went to send for a doctor he said: "I need no doctor. I can overcome my troubles." Before he fell completely silent, no one could understand what he was saying.

Sources: *Memphis Avalanche,* August 1, 1875; *Nashville Union and American,* August 1, 4, and 5, 1875.

Johnson, George

(1889-1944) American clergyman, educator. Roman Catholic monsignor. Professor of education at Catholic University. Served as executive director of National Catholic Welfare Council. First Roman Catholic to be vice president of Religions Education Association. Collapsed and died while delivering Commencement speech at Trinity College (now Trinity University) in Washington D.C.

Last Words: "We must do more work in educating youth for Christ."

Source: "Mgr. Johnson Dies in Midst of Speech. Catholic University Professor is Stricken at Trinity College Commencement" (*New York Times,* June 6, 1944).

Johnson, John Graver

(1841-1917) American lawyer, art collector. Prominent and highly successful Philadelphia corporate attorney who avoided publicity and twice turned down a seat on the U.S. Supreme Court. He amassed a vast art collection of more than 1,200 paintings that he bequeathed to the citizens of Philadelphia. The collection is now in the Philadelphia Museum of Art. He also gave his mansion to the city. Died at age 77 of heart disease.

Last Words: "Good-night. I am going to sleep now."

Source: *John G. Johnson: Lawyer and Art Collector: 1841-1917* by Barnie F. Winkelman (Philadelphia, 1942).

Johnson, Lyndon Baines

(1908-1973) 36th President of the U.S. American politician. Member U.S. House of Representatives and Senate from Texas. Vice President of the U.S. Assumed Presidency when John F. Kennedy was assassinated in 1963. Served as President until 1969. Died at age 64 near Johnson City, Texas.

Last Word: "Send Mike immediately!" He was preparing for an afternoon nap when he was suddenly stricken. He grabbed his bed-room telephone and gave this one last order to his Secret Service detail. By the time help arrived from about 100 yards away, Johnson had collapsed on the floor.

Source: "Lyndon Baines Johnson: 1908-1973" (*Time* magazine, February 5, 1973).

Johnson, Samuel

(1709-1784) English lexicographer, writer, essayist, poet, biographer. Known as Dr. Johnson. Held LL.D degrees from Dublin and Oxford. Notable work: *Dictionary of the English Language.* Died at age 75 in London.

Last Words: "God bless you, my dear." Spoken to Miss Morris, a visitor.

Source: *Life of Samuel Johnson* by James Boswell (London, 1910). Boswell's biography was first published in 1791.

Johnson, Tom Loftin

(1854-1911) American politician, businessman. Member U.S. House of Representatives from Ohio. Mayor of Cleveland. Died at age 56 of acute nephritis in Cleveland.

Last Words: "It's all right. I'm so happy."

Source: *My Story* by Tom Loftin Johnson, ed. by Elizabeth J. Hauser (New York, 1911). Written during the last five months of his life.

Johnson, Sir William, 1st Baronet

(1715-1774) Irish-born British statesman, colonist, fur trader. Official in the American colonies. Commanded Iroquois and colonial militia forces in French and Indian War. His part in the victory at the Battle of Lake George earned him a baronetcy in 1755. He was commissioned superintendent of Indian affairs for the northern colonies. Settled in Mohawk Valley. Interacted peacefully among Native Americans of the Six Nations. Founded Johnstown, New York. Died at age 59 of a stroke in Johnstown during a Native American conference.

Last Words: "Joseph, control your people. I am going away." Spoken to Joseph Brant, a Mohawk negotiator.

Source: *Johnson of the Mohawks: A Biography of Sir William Johnson, Irish Immigrant, Mohawk War Chief, American Soldier, Empire Builder* by Arthur Pound in collab. with Richard E. Day (New York, 1930).

Johnston, Albert Sidney

(1803-1862) American military officer. Brigadier general in the Texas Army during

Texas's war for independence. Fought in the Mexican War. Confederate general in the U.S. Civil War. Killed at age 59 at the Battle of Shiloh.

Last Words: "Yes, and I fear seriously." His response when asked if he was wounded.

Source: *The American Iliad: The Epic Story of the Civil War as Narrated by Eyewitnesses and Contemporaries,* ed. by Otto Eisenschiml and Ralph Geoffrey Newman (Indianapolis, IN, 1947).

Johnston, Archibald, Lord Warriston

(1611-1663) Scottish jurist, statesman. Member of Parliament of Scotland. Fell out of favor for attributing recent misfortunes to Stuart opposition to the Reformation. Later became part of Cromwell's government. At the Restoration, he was singled out for punishment. Executed in Edinburgh. Read a prepared speech on the scaffold. Prayed, forgave and tipped the hangman.

Last Words: "O pray, pray! Praise, Praise, Praise." Spoken just before he died.

Source: *The Scots Worthies: Containing a Brief Historical Account of the Most Eminent Noblemen, Gentlemen, Ministers, and Others, Who Testified or Suffered for the Cause of Reformation in Scotland: From the Beginning of the Sixteenth Century to the Year 1688* by John Howie (Glasgow, Scotland, 1829).

Johnston, David A.

(1949-1980) American volcanologist, geologist, victim of Mount Saint Helens disaster. Worked for U.S. Geological Survey. Was camped in a monitoring-station trailer at Coldwater Ridge. Died at age 30 when Mount St. Helens erupted.

Last Words: "Vancouver, Vancouver, this is it!" Spoken over a radio link from Coldwater Observation Post.

Source: "Mount St. Helens: 25 Years Later" by Jim Barlow (News Bureau, University of Illinois, Urbana-Champaign, IL, 2005).

Jokai, Mór or Maurus or Móricz

(1825-1904) Hungarian dramatist, novelist, poet, journalist. Wrote chiefly political and social novels and stories. His work has been compared to that of Dickens, Sir Walter Scott and Alexander Dumas. Many of his books were translated and published abroad. Notable works: *A Hungarian Nabob; A Man of Gold.* Took an active part in Hungarian politics and engaged in political journalism. Died at age 79 in Budapest.

Last Words: "I want to sleep."

Source: *Dictionary of Last Words* compiled by Edward S. LeComte (New York, 1955). He cited *Budapest Daily Szabad Ifjusag,* May 4, 1954, on authority of Mr. Istan Csicsery-Ronay.

Jolson, Al

(1886-1950) Lithuanian-born American singer, entertainer. Birth name Asa Yoelson. Had starring role in *The Jazz Singer*, first full-length talking motion picture. Had heart attack in San Francisco while playing poker. Died at age 64. Posthumously awarded Congressional Medal of Merit for entertaining U.S. military forces. The movies *The Jolson Story* (1945) and *Jolson Sings Again* (1949) are about his career.

Last Words: "Oh! oh, I'm going." Spoken to his physician after he had a heart attack.

Source: *Jolson: The Legend Comes to Life* by Herbert G. Goldman (New York, 1988).

Variation: "This is it. I'm going, I'm going." Source: *New York Post,* October 24, 1950.

Jones, Sir Henry

(1852-1922) Welsh writer, educator, philosopher. Professor of moral philosophy at Glasgow. Knighted in 1912. Notable work: *Browning as a Religious and Philosophical Teacher.* Died at age 69.

Last Words: "The Lord reigneth. Let the earth rejoice."

Source: *The Life and Letters of Sir Henry Jones* by H.J.W. Hetherington (London, 1924).

Jones, Henry Arthur

(1851-1929) English playwright. Wrote about social relationships and problems. Notable works: *The Silver King; Michael and His Lost Angel.* Died at age 77 in Hampstead, England.

Last Words: "I'm so glad." His response to being told his daughter Gertie would be back.

Source: *Taking the Curtain Call: The Life and Letters of Henry Arthur Jones* by Doris Arthur Jones (London, 1930). The author was his daughter.

Jones, John Luther ("Casey")

(1864?-1900) American railroad engineer. Killed in a train collision on the Illinois Central while trying to deliver the mail on time. The train was running several hours late. Jones was determined to make up for lost time. His train was nearly back on schedule when it reached Vaughn, Tennessee, where the caboose on another train extended onto the track and was in his way. He plowed into it. Killed at age 37. Story of the crash inspired the ballad "Casey Jones" and a play. It is now part of American folklore.

Last Words: "Jump, Sim!" Shouted to his fireman Sim Webb after he shouted to Jones: "Look out! We're gonna hit something." Sim jumped and survived the crash. Jones died in the wreck.

Source: "Casey Jones" in *Long Steel Rail: The Railroad in American Folksong* by Norm Cohen (Urbana, IL, 1981).

Jones, Robert Reynolds, Sr. ("Bob")

(1883-1968) American clergyman, evangelist, educator. Known as Dr. Bob Jones Sr. Founded Bob Jones College (now Bob Jones University) in 1927. Leading spokesman for fundamental, conservative Scriptural position. Opposed modernism in orthodoxy and evangelicalism. Died at age 84 in Greenville, South Carolina.

Last Words: "Mary Gaston, get my shoes. I must go preach."

Source: *Builder of Bridges: The Biography of Dr. Bob Jones* by R.K. Johnson (Murfreesboro, TN, 1969). The author was his friend for many years.

Jones, Robert Tyre ("Bobby")

(1902-1971) American athlete. Professional golfer. Was one of five sports giants, along with Babe Ruth, Jack Dempsey, Red Grange and Bill Tilden in the 1920s. Famed as one of the world's greatest golfer. Won all four major championships in the same year. Diagnosed with a degenerative spinal cord disorder that caused paralysis in 1948. Spent rest of his life confined to a wheelchair. Died at age 69 in Atlanta, Georgia.

Last Words: "You know, if I'd known how happy this had made Mary I would have done it years ago." His response to a priest about having converted to Roman Catholicism about a week before he died.

Source: *Triumphant Journey: The Saga of Bobby Jones and the Grand Slam of Golf* by Dick Miller (New York, 1980).

Jones, Warren ("Jim")

(1931-1978) American cult leader. Founder of the People's Temple. Responsible for the mass suicide of more than 900 members in Jonestown, Guyana. Died at age 47 in Jonestown massacre.

Last Words: "Take our life from us. We laid it down. We got tired. We didn't commit suicide. We committed an act of revolutionary suicide protesting against the conditions of an inhumane world." Tape recording made before his death and mass suicide of his followers at Jonestown, Guyana, November 18, 1978.

Source: *History's Worst Decisions and the People Who Made Them* by Stephen Weir (Millers Point, New South Wales, 2005).

Joplin, Janis Lyn

(1943-1970) American musician, singer. Rock performer. Ranked 28 on list of 100 Greatest Singers of All Time by *Rolling Stone* magazine. Performed with Big Brother and the Holding Company. Formed and performed with backup group Kozmic Blues Band. Formed Full Tilt Boogie Band and made her last public performance with them in August 1970 in Boston. Battled heroin addiction. Died at age 27 in Los Angeles of heroin overdose and possibly the effects of alcohol.

Last Words: Joplin had a ten-minute conversation with the night clerk in the lobby of the Landmark Hotel where she had gone to buy cigarettes. She told him how her day was and how excited she was about a recording. He didn't really know who she was but he listened to her. She returned to her room where she was found dead the next day.

Source: *Scars of Sweet Paradise: The Life and Times of Janis Joplin* by Alice Echols (New York, 2000).

Jordan, Barbara

(1936-1996) American lawyer, politician, educator. Member U.S. House of Representatives from Texas. First African-American woman to hold that position. Keynote speaker at 1976 Democratic National Convention when Jimmy Carter was nominated. Professor at University of Texas. Voted one of the most influential women of the 20th century by National Women's Hall of Fame. Received Presidential Medal of Honor in 1994. Multiple sclerosis diagnosed in 1973. Died at age 59 in Austin, Texas.

Last Words: "Nothing is a secret anymore."

Source: *Barbara Jordan: American Hero* by Mary Beth Rogers (New York, 1998).

Jortin, John

(1698-1770) English clergyman, church historian, writer. Archdeacon of London. Notable works: *Remarks on Ecclesiastical History; Life of Erasmus.* Died at age 71 in Kensington.

Last Words: "No, I have had enough of everything." Spoken to a servant who offered him food.

Source: *The Georgian Era: Memoirs of the Most Eminent Persons Who Have Flourished in Great Britain. The Royal Family, The Pretenders and Their Adherents: Churchmen, Dissenters and Statesmen* by Clarke (London, 1832).

Joseph (Tuekakas)

(1785-1871) Native American leader. Nez Perce chief. Known as Old Joseph. Father of Chief Joseph. Buried at the forks of the Wallowa and Lostine rivers. Later reburied at Wallowa Lake.

Last Words: "When I am gone, think of your country. You are the chief of these people. They look to you to guide them. Always remember that your father never sold his country. You must stop your ears whenever you are asked to sign a treaty selling your home. A few years more, and white men will be all around you. They have their eyes on this land. My son, never forget my dying words. This country holds your father's body. Never sell the bones of your father and mother." Spoken to his son.

Source: "An Indian's View of Indian Affairs" by Young Joseph, Chief of the Nez Perces (*Rose-Belford's Canadian Monthly and National Review,* May 1879).

Joseph II, Holy Roman Emperor

(1741-1790) European monarch. Eldest son of Empress Maria Theresa and Francis I. King of Germany. Brother of Marie Antoinette. Gained control of Austria when his mother died. Enlightened despot who introduced many reforms. Abolished serfdom. Allowed liberty of conscience. Encouraged manufacturing and industry. Died without issue in Vienna at age 48. Succeeded by his brother Leopold II.

Different Last Words:

(1) "I do not know whether the poet who writes 'Fearful is the step from the throne to the grave' is right. I do not miss the throne. I feel at peace, but only a little hurt with so much painful effort to have made so few happy and so many ungrateful. But then, such is the fate of men on the throne. Now I see that the Almighty is destroying all my works in my lifetime."

Source: *The Revolutionary Emperor: Joseph II of Austria* by Saul Kussiel (Hamden, CT, 1967).

(2) "Here lies Joseph, who was unsuccessful in all his undertakings." Exclamation on his deathbed that this should be his epitaph.

Source: *Historical Sketches of Statesmen who Flourished in the Time of George III, to Which is Added, Remarks on Party, and an Appendix* by Henry Peter Brougham 1st Baron of Brougham and Vaux (London, 1839).

Joseph of Cupertino, Saint

(1603-1663) Italian holy man. Birth name Giuseppe Maria Desa. Born in Cupertino, Italy. Roman Catholic Franciscan friar. Had a learning disability. He could barely read or write. Known as the Flying Saint. In 1630, he soared for the first time: a crowd saw him fly into the sky and hover. He would fly again, especially when singing hymns, hearing the names of Jesus or Mary, or praying at Mass. He allegedly took flight in the presence of Pope Urban VIII. Died at age 60 in Osima, Italy. Canonized in 1767. A town in California was named for him.

Last Words: "Praised be God! Blessed be God! May the holy will of God be done!"

Source: *Last Words. Final Thoughts of Catholic Saints & Sinners* by Paul Thigpen (Cincinnati, OH, 2006).

Josephine, Empress of the French

(1763-1814) French empress. Born in Martinique. Birth name Marie-Rose de Tascher de la Pagerie. Married Vicomte Beauharnais who was executed in the French Revolution. Married Napoleon I in 1796. Crowned empress of the French in 1804. Divorced in 1809. Spent final years at Malmaison, chateau near Paris. Died at age 50 in the arms of her children Eugene and Hortense. Daughter Hortense's son became Napoleon III.

Last Words: "Bonaparte! Elba! Marie Louise!"

Source: "Memories of Trianon and Malmaison" (*The Gentleman's Magazine and Historical Review,* Vol. 222, May 1867).

Variation: "Napoleon! Elba! Marie Louise!"

Source: *The Last Words (Real and Traditional) of Distinguished Men and Women Collected from Various Sources* by Frederic Rowland Marvin (New York, 1901).

Variation: "Bonaparte—Elba—the King of Rome."

Source: *Dictionary of Phrase and Fable* by E. Cobham Brewer (Philadelphia, 1898).

Variation: "Elba—Napoleon."

Source: *Lectures, Illustrated and Embellished with Views of the World's Famous Places and People, Being the Identical Discourses Delivered During the Past Eighteen Years Under the Title of the Stoddard Lectures* by John Lawson Stoddard (Boston, 1896).

Jowett, Benjamin

(1817-1893) English clergyman, educator, theologian. Greek scholar. Master of Balliol College, Oxford. Regius professor of Greek. Vice chancellor. Died at age 76.

Last Words: "Mine has been a happy life. I thank God for my life. Bid farewell to the College."

Source: *Life and Letters of Benjamin Jowett, M.A., Master of Balliol College*, ed. by Evelyn A. Abbott and Lewis Campbell (Oxford, England, 1897).

Joyce, James Augustine Aloysius

(1882-1941) Irish writer, playwright. Pioneered literary technique known as stream of consciousness. Notable works: *Ulysses; A Portrait of the Artist as a Young Man; Finnegan's Wake*. Had a perforated stomach ulcer while living in Zurich. Died at age 58 of peritonitis.

Different Last Words:

(1) "Does nobody understand?"

Source: *Chamber Music by James Joyce; Intro and Notes* by William York Tindall (New York, 1954).

(2) "A good omen. I like Neuchâtel wine." His response when he learned he was receiving a blood transfusion from two soldiers in Neuchâtel, Switzerland.

Source: "Dublin's Prodigal Son" (*Time* magazine, November 9, 1959).

Juárez, Benito Pablo

(1806-1872) Mexican statesman, politician. Zapotec Indian. Governor of Oaxaca. Provisional president of Mexico (1857 to 1861); elected president of Mexico (1865 to 1867, 1867 to 1872). Term interrupted by warfare against Maximilian. Died at age 66 of a heart attack in Mexico City while in office.

Different Last Words:

(1) He asked for a portrait of his wife to be brought from an adjoining room. He looked at it fondly, folded the bed clothes around his face and died.

Source: *Life of Juarez Constitutional President of Mexico* by Ulick Ralph Burke (London, 1894).

(2) "Doctor, is my disease mortal?"

Source: *Juarez and His Mexico: A Biographical History* by Ralph Roeder (New York, 1947).

Judas Iscariot

(d. 33) Biblical figure. One of the 12 Apostles. Betrayed Jesus. Committed suicide.

Last Words: "Peccavi tradens sanguinem iustum."

Source: Matthew 27:3 (Latin Vulgate Bible).

Variation: "I have sinned in that I have betrayed the innocent blood."

Sources: Matthew 27:3 (King James Version); (21st Century King James Version).

Variation: "I have sinned by betraying innocent blood."

Sources: Matthew 27:3 (New King James Version); (New Standard American Bible); (English Standard Version).

Variation: "I have sinned for I have betrayed innocent blood."

Source: Matthew 27:3 (New International Version).

Variation: "I have sinned [in] having delivered up guiltless blood."

Source: Matthew 27:3 (Darby Translation).

Variation: "I have sinned in betraying innocent blood."

Source: Matthew 27:3 (Douay-Rheims Translation).

Variation: "I did sin, having delivered up innocent blood."

Source: Matthew 27:3 (Young's Literal Translation).

Judd, Sylvester

(1813-1853) American clergyman, writer. Unitarian. Pastor of church in Augusta, Maine. Transcendentalist writer. Expressed religious and social views in his novels and poems. Notable works: *Margaret; Richard Edney and the Governor's Family*. Died at age 39 in Augusta after a short illness.

Last Words: "Cover me up warm, keep my utterance clear.—I'm doing well."

Source: *Life and Character of Sylvester Judd* by Arethusa Hall (Boston, 1857). Author became a member of the Judd family when she was nine.

Judson, Adoniram, Jr.

(1788-1850) American missionary in Burma for 37 years. Baptist. Translated Bible and dictionary into Burmese. Became ill. Died at age 61 aboard a ship in the Bay of Bengal.

World War II U.S. Liberty ship was named for him.

Last Words: "Brother Ranney, will you bury me? Bury me? Quick! Quick!" He told a servant: "Take care of poor mistress."

Source: *A Memoir of the Life and Labors of the Rev. Adoniram Judson, D.D.* by Francis Wayland (Boston, 1853).

Judson, Ann Hasseltine

(1789-1826) American missionary in Burma. Baptist. Married Adoniram Judson Sr. in 1812. First American woman missionary to go overseas. Died at age 37 in Burma. Judson College, Alabama, named for her.

Last Words: "I feel quite well, only very weak."

Source: *Memoir of Mrs. Ann H. Judson, Late Missionary to Burma: Including a History of the American Baptist Mission in the Burman Empire* by James D. Knowles (Boston, 1831).

Judson, Emily Chubbuck

(1817-1854) American writer. Pen name Fanny Forester. Third missionary wife of renowned Baptist minister Adoniram Judson Jr. Spent five years in Burma. Returned to New England after her husband and son died. Died at age 36 of tuberculosis in Hamilton, New York.

Last Words: "Yes, my month to die." Her response to her sister who asked her if she knew it was the month of June. She died later that day.

Source: *The Life and Letters of Mrs. Emily C. Judson* by Asahel Clark Kendrick (New York, 1860).

Judson, Sarah Hall Boardman

(1803-1845) American missionary. Married George Boardman in July 1825 and joined American Baptist missionaries in Burma. Boardman died in 1831. In 1834 Sarah married Adoniram Judson Jr., also an American missionary in Burma. Sarah became ill in December 1844 after the birth of her eighth child and made the decision to return to the U.S. Died at age 41 aboard ship in the port of St. Helena.

Last Words: "Oh yes, I ever love the Lord Jesus Christ." Her response when asked if she still loved the Savior. Within the hour she died.

Source: *Memoir of Sarah B. Judson, of the American Mission to Burmah* by Emily Chubbuck Judson (New York, 1872). Emily was a professional writer who used the pen name Fanny Forester. She met Adoniram Judson in the U.S. after Sarah died. He asked her to write the *Memoir*. They were married in 1846.

Judy, Steven

(1956-1981) American murderer. Pretended to be a Good Samaritan. Killed a motorist and her three children who were stranded on the side of a highway. During his trial, he warned jurors that if he did not get the death penalty, he would kill again, and one of them or a member of their family might be his next victim. Executed in the electric chair in Indiana.

Last Words: "I don't hold any grudges. This is my doing. Sorry it happened."

Source: "The Problem with the Chair" by Carl M. Cannon (*National Review*, Vol. 52, No. 11, June 19, 2000).

Jugurtha, King of Numidia

(160?-104 B.C.) Berber King of Numidia. Defeated in war with Rome. Taken prisoner. Starved to death in Rome.

Last Words: "Oh Hercules! How cold your bath is!" Uttered as Romans threw him into a dungeon. He struggled with hunger for six days then died.

Source: "Caius Marius" in *Lives of the Noble Grecians and Romans* by Plutarch, tr. by John Dryden (Chicago, 1952).

Julian, the Apostate, Emperor of Rome

(331-363) Roman ruler. Anti-Christian. Was the last of the pagan Roman emperors. Birth name Flavius Claudius Julianus. Nephew of Constantine the Great. Called the Apostate for proclaiming he had converted to paganism in 361. Killed in a battle against the Persians.

Last Words: "O Galilean! Thou hast conquered."

Source: *Julian the Apostate and the Duke of Mercia* by Sir Aubrey deVere (London, 1858).

Julius II, Pope

(1443-1513) Italian prelate, military officer. Roman Catholic pope. Birth name Guiliano della Rovere. Patron of arts. Bramante, Raphael and Michelangelo were active during his reign. Julius laid the cornerstone for St. Peter's Basilica. Known as Il Papa Terribile (The Terrible Pope). Endeavored to end abuses such as nepotism and simony within the Church. Became involved in wars with Venice and France to regain lost papal territory. Reestablished Papal States. Died at age 69 in Rome.

Last Words: "Would to God that we had never been Pope, or at least that we could have turned all the arms of religion against the enemies of the Holy See." Spoken on his deathbed.

Source: *The Lives and Times of the Popes* by Chevalier Artaud de Montor (New York, 1911).

Jung, Carl Gustav

(1875-1961) Swiss psychiatrist, educator, writer. Studied with Freud. Broke with him in 1913 over Freud's views on sexuality and neuroses. Professor of psychology at Zurich. Notable works: *The Psychology of the Unconscious; Psychological Types*. Continued writing into his 80s. Died at age 86 in Zurich.

Different Last Words:

(1) "Let's have a really good red wine tonight." He didn't drink the wine; he died before evening.

Source: *Carl Gustav Jung: A Biography* by Frank McLynn (New York, 1996).

(2) "Quick, help me out of bed before she comes back or she will stop me."

Source: *Fragments on the Deathwatch* by Louise Harmon (Boston, 1998).

Justin de Jacobis, Saint

(1800-1860) Italian clergyman, missionary, holy man. Lazarist missionary. Established Abyssinian (Ethiopian) mission. Vicar Apostolic of Abyssinia. Bishop of Nilopolis. When the government began persecuting Catholics, he was harassed and hunted. Imprisoned for extending hospitality to the French political mission. Forced to endure long marches while he was ill. Died at age 59 in Ethiopia. Canonized in 1975.

Last Words: "Pray hard little ones, for I am going to die. I won't forget you—I am dying." Spoken to a group of monks and students en route to Halai after he left prison. Died of fever along the side of the road.

Source: *Butler's Lives of the Saints* by Herbert J. Thurston and Donald Attwater (Westminster, MD, 1956).

Justin Martyr, Saint

(100?-165?) Early Christian martyr, saint. Philosopher, writer. Also known as Justin the Philosopher and Justin of Caesarea. His father was Greek. Justin was born in what is now Nablus (Palestine). Converted to Christianity around 133. Moved to Rome and became a Christian philosopher and apologist. Punished for his pro-Christian writings. Sentenced to death during the reign of Marcus Aurelius for refusing to sacrifice to the Roman gods. Scourged and beheaded in Rome with six other Christians.

Last Words: "We desire nothing more than to suffer for our Lord Jesus Christ; for this gives us salvation and joyfulness before His dreadful judgment seat."

Source: *The Church in History* by B.K. Kuiper (Grand Rapids, MI, 1988).

Kafka, Franz

(1883-1924) Bohemian-born writer, poet, novelist. Born in Prague (now in Czech Republic). Earned law degree but did not practice law. Chose instead to write. Worked in an insurance office. Kafka's surreal stories focused on the frustrations, anxieties and isolation of 20th century man and gave rise to the term *Kafkaesque*. Had tuberculosis. Spent the last six weeks of his life in a TB sanatorium in Kierling, near Vienna. Died at age 40. He requested his manuscripts be burned unread. His request was disregarded by friend and biographer Max Brod, who recognized their value and published the novels *The Trial*, *The Castle* and *Amerika* posthumously.

Different Last Words:

(1) "Away, Elli. Not so near, not so near.— Yes, that's good." Spoken to his sister, whom he worried about infecting.

Source: *Franz Kafka: A Biography* by Max Brod (Prague, Czechoslovakia, 1937).

Variation: "Don't come so close, Elli. Not so close—yes, this is better."

Source: *The Nightmare of Reason: A Life of Franz Kafka* by Ernst Pawel (New York, 1992).

(2) "There will be no proof that I was ever a writer." Spoken just before he died. He had asked his friend Max Brod to burn all his writings.

Source: *Uncommon Sense: The World's Fullest Compendium of Wisdom* by Joseph Telushkin (New York, 1987).

Ka'iulani, Princess Victoria

(1875-1899). Hawaiian royalty. Crown Princess of the Kingdom of Hawaii. Daughter of

Princess Miriam Likelike and Archibald Cleghorn, niece of Queen Lili'uokalani. Friend of Robert Louis Stevenson. Educated in England. Health deteriorated soon after she returned to her native land. Died at age 23 in Honolulu.

Last Words: "Mama," "Papa," or "Koa." (Koa was a family name for her cousin David). She was hallucinating and becoming delirious when she gasped out one Last Word. Those present at her bedside did not agree on which of these three words she spoke last.

Source: *Kaiulani: The People's Princess* by Ellen Emerson White (New York, 2001).

Kalakaua, David, King of the Hawaiian Islands

(1836-1891) Hawaiian royalty. Last reigning King of Hawaii. Known as The Merrie Monarch for his enjoyment of the arts and fine living. Traveled the world to study other nations and learn how they were ruled. Strong supporter of native civil rights. Notable work: *Legends and Myths of Hawaii.* Built Iolani Palace in Honolulu. Died at age 54 of kidney disease in a San Francisco hotel while seeking medical help. Left no heirs. Sister Lili'uokalani succeeded him.

Different Last Words:

(1) "Tell my people I tried to restore our gods, our way of life."

Source: *The Last King of Paradise* by Eugene Burns (New York, 1952).

(2) "Well, I am a very sick man." Spoken as he emerged briefly from a coma. He received the Last Rites then mumbled something in Hawaiian that bystanders did not understand.

Source: *San Francisco Chronicle*, January 21, 1891.

Kaliayev or Kalyayev, Ivan

(1877-1905) Russian socialist revolutionary, writer, poet, assassin. Planted bomb in St. Petersburg in February 1905 that killed Grand Duke Sergei who was governor of Moscow and uncle of Tsar Nicholas. Kaliayev was executed by hanging at age 27 in St. Petersburg three months later. When French writer Albert Camus wrote his play *The Just Assassins*, he named the lead character Kaliayev.

Last Words: "I already told you that I am finished with life and prepared for death. I consider my death as the supreme protest against a world of blood and tears."

Source: *The Terrorists: The Story of the Forerunners of Stalin* by Robert Payne (New York, 1957).

Kaltenbrunner, Ernst

(1903-1946) Austrian military officer. Nazi chief of security police during World War II. Found guilty of war crimes at Nuremberg trial. Executed at age 43.

Last Words: "I have loved my German people and my fatherland with a warm heart. I have done my duty by the laws of my people and I am sorry this time my people were lead by men who were not soldiers and that crimes were committed of which I had no knowledge. Germany, good luck."

Source: "The Execution of Nazi War Criminals" by Kingsbury Smith (International News Service, October 16, 1946).

Kamehameha I, King of the Hawaiian Islands

(1758?-1819) Hawaiian royalty. King of Hawaii. Known as Kamehameha the Great. Unified the Hawaiian Islands. Died on the island of Hawaii. Succeeded by two sons, Kamehameha II, who died in 1824, and Kamehameha III, who ruled until 1854.

Last Words: "Move on in my good way and—." Spoken in the presence of high chiefs who were in his room when he died.

Source: *The Hawaiian Archipelago: Six Months Among the Palm Groves, Coral Reefs, and Volcanoes of the Sandwich Islands* by Isabella L. Bird [Mrs. Bishop] (Rutland, VT, 1974). Originally printed 1875.

Variation: "Keep on in my good way." Spoken to the chieftains at his bedside.

Source: "Memories of Hawaii" (*The United Service: A Monthly Review of Military and Naval Affairs*, May 1884).

Kamehameha V, King of the Hawaiian Islands

(1830-1872) Hawaiian royalty. Last of the Kamehameha line. Birth name Lot Kapuaiwa. Assumed throne when his brother Kamehameha IV died in 1863. Many major socioeconomic changes took place during his reign. Hawaii's economy moved away from whaling to crops such as sugar cane, bringing many Japanese and Chinese workers. Died on his 42nd birthday in Honolulu, unmarried and without naming an heir.

Last Words: "She was merely Queen by courtesy, having been the wife of a King." Spoken about his sister-in-law Emma, when he was urged to name a successor.

Source: *Emma: Hawaii's Remarkable Queen: A Biography* by George S. Kanahele (Honolulu, HI, 1999).

Kanidis, Yanis or
Kanidis, Ivan Constantinovich

(1930-2004) Greek-born Russian physical education teacher. Gave his life in the Beslan school hostage crisis. He was in the school when Chechen extremists took more than 1,200 people hostage in Beslan, North Ossetia, Russia, in September 2004. His insistence on remaining with the children is credited with saving many lives. In a crisis that lasted days, Kanidis guarded and fought for the lives of his students as best he could including staving off dehydration and moving explosives away from areas where children were concentrated. He died on day three. One account says the 74-year-old PE teacher was killed when he jumped on a grenade a terrorist threw at children trying to escape. Another account says he died trying to dismantle an explosive. When Russian troops stormed the building, at least 350 people were dead. Kanidis was posthumously awarded a medal—For Protection of Human Rights—by the Russian government. A school destroyed during the crisis was rebuilt and named in his honor.

Last Words: "Get the children out!"

Source: "The School" by C.J. Chivers (*Esquire*, March 14, 2007).

Kant, Immanuel

(1724-1804) German philosopher, educator, writer. Professor of logic and metaphysics at University of Königsberg. Notable work: *Critique of Pure Reason*. He never traveled more than 40 miles from his home. Died at age 79 in Königsberg, East Prussia.

Last Words: "Est ist gut." (tr. "It is enough.") His response when offered something to drink.

Source: "The Last Days of Immanuel Kant" in *The Collected Writings of Thomas De Quincey*, ed. by David Masson (Edinburgh, 1890).

Kaplitz, Sir Gaspar

(1329?-1415?) Bohemian nobleman, martyr. Condemned to die at age 86 during the Bo-

hemian persecutions. Was told that because of his age, he would be given a pardon if he asked for one. He refused and spoke the following at his place of execution.

Last Words: "Ask pardon, I will ask pardon of God, whom I have frequently offended; but not of the emperor, to whom I never gave any offense; should I sue for pardon, it might be justly suspected I had committed some crime for which I deserve this condemnation. No, no, as I die innocent, and with a clear conscience, I would not be separated from this noble company of martyrs." After speaking these words, he resigned his head to the block.

Source: *Book of Martyrs and the Acts and Monuments of the Church* by John Fox (or Foxe). First published 1563, ed. by John Cumming (London, 1851).

Karge, Joseph

(1823-1892) Polish-born military officer, educator. Cavalry officer who emigrated to the U.S. Union brevet brigadier general in U.S. Civil War. Professor of languages and literature at Princeton University. Died at age 69.

Last Words: "I have but one desire concerning it—that it come suddenly and without warning." He was talking about his death.

Source: *Joseph Karge: A Memorial Sketch* by William A. Packard (New York, 1893). The author was a professor at Princeton.

Kath, Terence Alan ("Terry")

(1946-1978) American musician, guitarist, composer. Member of rock band Chicago. Killed accidentally while playing Russian roulette at the home of a roadie in Los Angeles. He put the gun he believed was unloaded to his head and pulled the trigger. He was 31.

Last Words: "Don't worry, it's not loaded." Spoken to a friend who nervously asked him to stop putting the gun to his head and snapping the trigger.

Source: *The Tombstone Tourist: Musicians* by Scott Stanton (New York, 2003).

Katte, Hans Hermann von

(1704-1730) Prussian military officer. Lieutenant. Executed at age 26 for conspiracy with Frederick the Great when the latter was Crown Prince. Frederick was forced by his father to watch Katte's beheading.

Last Words: "Der Tod is süss für den Prinzen, den ich liebe." (tr. "Death is sweet for a Prince I love so well.")

Sources: *Lexikon der letzten Worte: letzte Botschaften berühmter Männer und Frauen von Konrad Adenauer bis Emiliano Zapata* by Werner Fuld (Munich, Germany, 2002); *History of Friedrich II of Prussia, Called Frederick the Great* by Thomas Carlyle (London, 1900).

Kauffmann, Maria Anna Angelica

(1741-1807) Swiss-born artist. Known for portraiture, mythological and classic paintings. Was also an accomplished singer. Died at age 66 in Rome.

Last Words: "Nein Johann, das will ich nicht hören. Lies mir das Gebel für die Kranken auf Seite 128 vor!" (tr. "No, Johann, I will not hear that. Read me the 'Hymn for the Sick' on page 128.") Spoken to her cousin as she began to sing a hymn for the dying.

Sources: *Angelica Kauffmann: A Biography* by Frances A. Gerard (London, 1893); *Lexikon der letzten Worte: letzte Botschaften berühmter Männer und Frauen von Konrad Adenauer bis Emiliano Zapata* by Werner Fuld (Munich, Germany, 2002).

Kaufman, George Simon

(1889-1961) American playwright, screenwriter, director. Member of Algonquin Round Table. Notable works and collaborations: *Animal Crackers; Night at the Opera; The Man Who Came to Dinner; You Can't Take It With You.* Shared 1932 Pulitzer Prize for Drama with Morrie Ryskind and Ira Gershwin for *Of Thee I Sing.* Shared second Pulitzer 1937 with Moss Hart for *You Can't Take It with You.* Won Tony in 1951 for directing *Guys and Dolls.* Died at age 71 in New York City.

Last Words: "I'm not afraid anymore."

Source: *George S. Kaufman and His Friends* by Scott Meredith (Garden City, NY, 1974).

Kazantzákis, Nikos

(1883-1957) Greek writer, novelist, poet, journalist. Born in Crete. Traveled widely and lived in many places—France, Germany, Italy, Russia, Spain, Cyprus, Egypt, Japan, China and more. Spoke many languages. Notable works: *Zorba the Greek; The Last Temptation of Christ.* Both were made into successful movies. Died at age 74 in Freiburg, Germany.

Last Words: "No. No. I'm thirsty." His response to his wife when she asked if he was suffering. When asked if his lips were irritated, he said "Yes."

Source: *Nikos Kazantzakis: A Biography Based on His Letters* by Helen Kazantzakis (New York, 1968). The author was his wife.

Kean, Edmund

(1789-1833) English actor. Famous as tragedian. Notable roles: Othello, Hamlet, Iago, Macbeth, Lear, Richard III. Collapsed on stage at Covent Garden, London, in March 1833. His son Charles, also an actor, was on stage with him. During his final weeks, he had spells of delirium. Died two months later at age 44 in Richmond, Surrey.

Last Words: "Give me another horse! Howard."

Source: *The Life of Edmund Kean* by Frederick William Hawkins (London, 1869).

Variation: "A horse, a horse, my kingdom for a horse!" He jumped out of bed to speak these words. After he was put back in bed he became lethargic. When he awoke he sighed then died.

Source: *The Life and Adventures of Edmund Kean, Tragedian 1787-1833* by Joseph Fitzgerald Molloy (London, 1897).

Kearny, Philip

(1815-1862) American military officer. Lost his arm in Mexican War. Served as major general in Union Army in U.S. Civil War. Led first New Jersey troops in the war. He devised a way of quickly identifying his men: he had each sew on his cap a diamond-shaped piece of red flannel. The idea spread and military patches are still in use today. Kearny died at age 47 in the Battle of Chantilly, Virginia. He was the first American awarded the Cross of the Legion of Honor. Towns in New Jersey and Arizona were named for him.

Different Last Words:

(1) "Whose troops are these?" Asked as he approached soldiers. They replied that they were the 49th Georgia. As he turned quickly to ride away, he was struck by a mini ball and killed instantly.

Source: *A Conspectus of American Biography: Being an Analytical Summary of American History and Biography, Containing also the Complete Indexes of the National Cyclopedia of American Biography* by George

Derby (New York, 1906).

(2) "Don't fire. I am a friend." At that point, an enemy bullet struck and killed him almost instantly.

Source: "Philip Kearny: Soldier and Patriot." Address delivered before the New Jersey Historical Society by Cortlandt Parker, January 17, 1867 (Newark, NJ, 1868).

(3) "The rebel bullet that can kill me has yet to be molded." Spoken laughingly to a general just before Kearny rode out and was hit by a bullet.

Source: *Kearny, the Magnificent: The Story of General Philip Kearny (1815-1862)* by Irving Werstein (New York, 1962).

Keating, Lawrence

(d. 1895) American law enforcement officer. Deputy U.S. marshal. Prison guard at the United States Jail, Fort Smith, Arkansas. Shot by Crawford Goldsby, alias Cherokee Bill, during a jailbreak. Cherokee Bill's escape attempt was not successful. He was apprehended and tried again for murder. He received a second death sentence for the murder of Keating.

Last Words: "Kill the dog, Will. He has killed me." Called to Will Lawson, another guard.

Source: *Marauders of the Indian Nation: The Bill Cook Gang and Cherokee Bill* by Glenn Shirley (Stillwater, OK, 1994).

Keats, John

(1795-1821) English poet. Famed for his Romantic, lyric poetry. Notable works: "Ode on a Grecian Urn"; "To a Nightingale"; "The Eve of St. Agnes"; "La Belle Dame sans Merci"; "On First Looking into Chapman's Homer." Became seriously ill with tuberculosis. Went to Rome, Italy, for his health in 1820. Died there at age 25.

Last Words: "Severn—I—lift me up, for I am dying. I shall die easy. Don't be frightened! Thank God it has come." Spoken to his friend artist Joseph Severn who stayed with him until he died. Keats needed help breathing.

Source: *John Keats* by Amy Lowell (Boston, 1925).

Keeler, William Henry ("Wee Willie")

(1872-1923) American athlete. Professional baseball outfielder. Member New York Giants. Birth name O'Kelleher. Batting champion 1897, 1898. Died at age 50 in Brook-lyn, New York. Elected to baseball's Hall of Fame in 1939.

Last Words: "I know that I am fighting a losing fight, but I want to live to see 1923 ushered in." He died shortly after midnight on New Year's Day.

Source: "Willie Keeler Dies of Heart Disease; Famous Oldtime Player Succumbs to Malady at Brooklyn Home" (*New York Times,* January 2, 1923).

Keffer, James

(1864-1903) American murderer. Executed by hanging for murder and robbery in Wyoming.

Last Words: "Good morning, boys! I have no ill feelings for any man in town, but do not think much of the judge, supreme court and the governor." When asked if he was ready, he replied "Yes."

Source: "His First Hanging" by Jean A. Mathisen (*True West,* April 1987).

Keitel, Wilhelm

(1882-1946) German Nazi field marshal. Senior military leader during World War II. Tried and convicted as a war criminal at Nuremberg. Executed by hanging at age 64.

Last Words: "I call on God Almighty to have mercy on the German people. More than two million German soldiers went to their death for the fatherland before me. I follow now my sons—all for Germany."

Source: "The Execution of Nazi War Criminals" by Kingsbury Smith (International News Service, October 16, 1946).

Keith, George

(1638?-1716) Scottish clergyman. Missionary. Persecuted (imprisoned) after he became a Quaker. Went to America. Surveyor-general of East Jersey. Schoolmaster in Philadelphia. Started group called Christian Quakers or Keithians. Entered Anglican Church. Ordained. Had many converts. Died in Elberton, Sussex, England.

Last Words: "I wish I had died when I was a Quaker, for then I am sure it would have been well with my soul." Spoken on his deathbed to Richard Hayler of Sussex.

Sources: *History of Philadelphia, 1609-1884* by John Thomas Scharf and Thompson Westcott (Philadelphia, 1884); *History of the People Called Quakers from Their First Rise to the Present Time* by John Gough (Dublin, Ireland, 1799).

Kelly, Edward ("Ned")

(1855-1880) Australian bushranger, bandit. Clashed with police; three police were killed. Tracked down by posse. Captured, tried and executed. Viewed by some as a folk hero for defying colonial authority. *Ned Kelly and His Gang* (1906) was the first full-length feature movie. Several fiction and nonfiction books have been written about the Kelly Gang, including *Saint Ned* and *The True History of the Kelly Gang*. The book *Our Sunshine* was the basis for the movie *Ned Kelly* (2003).

Last Words: "Such is life." Spoken as he was about to be hanged.

Source: *In a Sunburned Country* by Bill Bryson (New York, 2000).

Kelly, George Edward

(1887-1974) American playwright, screenwriter, director, actor. Uncle of Princess Grace of Monaco (Grace Kelly). Notable plays: *Craig's Wife* (won 1926 Pulitzer Prize); *The Show-Off*. Died at age 87 in Bryn Mawr, Pennsylvania.

Last Words: "My dear, before you kiss me goodbye, fix your hair. It's a mess." Spoken when a relative attempted to kiss him farewell on his deathbed.

Source: *Those Philadelphia Kellys with a Touch of Grace* by Arthur H. Lewis (New York, 1977).

Kelly, Michael Joseph

(1857-1894) American athlete. Professional baseball player, outfielder, catcher, mostly with the Chicago White Stockings and Boston Red Stockings. One of the first superstars of baseball. Inspired the song and movie *Slide, Kelly, Slide!* Hospitalized with pneumonia. Died at age 36 in a Boston hospital.

Last Words: "This is my last ride." Spoken while being taken to the hospital.

Source: *My Sixty-Six Years in the Big Leagues* by Connie Mack (Philadelphia, 1950).

Kemble, John Philip

(1757-1823) English actor, theater manager. Brother of Sarah Siddons. Manager of Drury Lane and Covent Garden theaters, London. Notable roles: Othello, Macbeth, Coriolanus. Retired in 1817. Died at age 66 in Lausanne, Switzerland.

Last Words: "Don't be alarmed, my dear, I have had a slight attack of apoplexy." Spoken to his wife.

Source: *Memoirs of the Life of John Philip Kemble* by James Boaden (Philadelphia, 1825).

Kemp, Francis Adrian van der

(1752-1829) Dutch-born American, intellectual, clergyman. Friend of John Adams, DeWitt Clinton, Thomas Jefferson, George Washington. Died at age 77.

Last Words (written): "Now I must close. I can scarcely distinguish one letter from another. Whatever may happen, I know you remain unalterably my friend, as, so long as I draw breath, shall I be yours. Once again, farewell." Written in a letter.

Source: *Francis Adrian van der Kemp, 1752-1829: An Autobiography, Together with Extracts from His Correspondence,* ed. by Helen L. Fairchild (New York, 1903).

Ken, Thomas

(1637-1711) English prelate, hymnist. Bishop of Bath and Wells. One of seven bishops committed to the Tower of London in 1688 for refusing to read Declaration of Indulgence. Tried, acquitted. Declined oath of allegiance to William and Mary. Deprived of bishopric. Notable hymns: "Awake, My Soul"; "Glory be to Thee, My God, This Night." Died at age 73 of apoplexy near Warminster, Wilshire.

Last Words:

(1) (written): "All glory be to God." Note found in his diary after he died.

Source: *Thomas Ken, D.D.* by E.H. Plumptre (London, 1890).

(2) (spoken; doubtful): "God's will be done."

Source: *The Prose Works of the Right Rev. Father in God, Thomas Ken: to Which are Added Some of His Letters (Never Before Published) and a Short Account of His Life* by Thomas Ken, William Hawkins, and James Thomas Round (London, 1838).

These words were an expression he uttered often. He did say them on his deathbed, but that was two days before he died. They also appeared on his gravestone among other lines.

Kennedy, John Fitzgerald

(1917-1963) 35th President of the U.S. American politician, writer. Member U.S.

House of Representatives, U.S. Senate from Massachusetts. Brother of Robert F. Kennedy, Edward M. Kennedy. Won Pulitzer Prize for Biography in 1957 for *Profiles in Courage*. Assassinated at age 46 while traveling in a motorcade through Dallas, Texas. Different Last Words:

(1) "That's very obvious." His response to a comment made by Nellie Connally, wife of Texas Governor John Connally: "Mr. President, you can't say Dallas doesn't love you."
Source: *Assassination: The Death of President John F. Kennedy* by Relman Morin (New York, 1968).

(2) "My God. I've been hit." Heard by U.S. Secret Service agent Roy H. Kellerman who was sitting in the front seat of the President's limousine.
Source: *The Radical Right and the Murder of John F. Kennedy: Stunning Evidence in the Assassination of the President* by Harrison E. Livingstone (Victoria, BC, 2004).

Kennedy, Robert Francis ("Bobby")

(1925-1968) American politician, lawyer. U.S. attorney general. Member U.S. Senate from New York. Brother of John F. Kennedy, Edward M. Kennedy. Assassinated at age 42 at the Ambassador Hotel in Los Angeles, California, after winning the California primary election.
Last Words: "Please don't. Please don't. Don't lift me." Spoken to ambulance attendant who tried to pick him up.
Source: *1968 in America: Music, Politics, Chaos. Counterculture and the Shaping of a Generation* by Charles Kaiser (New York, 1988).

Kenney, Douglas C.

(1947-1980) American writer, actor. Co-founded *National Lampoon* magazine in 1970. Edited the magazine and wrote much of its early material. Co-authored screenplay for *Animal House*. He next co-wrote *Caddyshack,* a movie that opened to negative reviews. After a combative press conference with reporters about the film, he spiraled into depression. Died at age 32 after falling from a cliff in Kauai, Hawaii. Director Harold Ramis later paid homage to Kenney by using the name Doug Kinney for the main character in the 1996 movie *Multiplicity.*
Last Words (written): "These last few days are among the happiest I've ever ignored."

Apparent suicide note written on the back of a hotel receipt. This note, some random thoughts that included the reasons why he loved Kathryn, and a gag line are considered his Last Words.
Source: *A Futile and Stupid Gesture: How Doug Kenney and National Lampoon Changed Comedy Forever* by Josh Karp (Chicago, 2006).

Kenny, Elizabeth

(1880-1952) Australian nurse. Known for her therapy used to treat polio patients. Brought her methods to the U.S. in 1940. Became a celebrity. Retired in 1952 when she was diagnosed with Parkinson's disease. Died at age 72 in Queensland, Australia. The movie *Sister Kenny* (1946) is about her polio treatment.
Last Words: Either "America" or "Mother." Bystanders were not sure what she said. Her speech had been impaired by a stroke.
Source: *Sister Kenny: The Woman Who Challenged the Doctors* by Victor Cohn (Minneapolis, MN, 1975).

Kent, James

(1763-1847) American lawyer, jurist, educator, writer. Chief justice of New York Supreme Court. New York State chancellor. Professor of law at Columbia University. Notable work: *Commentaries on American Law.* Died at age 84 in New York City.
Last Words: "Go, my children. My object in telling you this is that, if anything happens to me, you might know, and perhaps it would console you to remember, that on this point my mind is clear; I rest my hopes of salvation on the Lord Jesus Christ."
Source: *Memoirs and Letters of James Kent LL.D.: Late Chancellor of the State of New York* by William Kent (Boston, 1898). The author was his great-grandson.

Kent, John

(1766-1843) English shipwright, hymnist. Composed many hymns still sung today. Notable work: *Original Gospel Hymns* (10th edition with 264 hymns, published 18 years after he died). His hymns were used in Charles Haddon Spurgeon's *Our Own Hymn Book* and Charles B. Snepp's *Songs of Grace and Glory*. Died at age 76.
Last Words: "I am accepted."
Source: *English Hymns: Their Authors and History* by Samuel Willoughby Duffield (New York, 1886).

Kepler, Johannes

(1571-1630) German astronomer, mathematician, physicist. Went to Prague to work with Tycho Brahe; succeeded him as astronomer to Emperor Rudolf II. Made many discoveries in physics, optics, geometry. Kepler's Three Laws of Planetary Motion formed the framework of Newton's discoveries. Notable work: *Harmonice Mundi.* Died at age 58 in Regensburg.
Last Words: "Solely by the merits of Jesus Christ, Our Saviour." His response to a question about how he hoped to be saved.
Source: *Kepler and the Jesuits* by M.W. Burke-Gaffney, SJ (Milwaukee, WI, 1944).

Ker, Robert, of Kersland

(d. 1680) Scottish nobleman. Persecuted Covenanter. Imprisoned for religious beliefs. Forced to forfeit his fortune and land. Died in Utrecht, Holland. Memorial brass was later erected in his honor in Parish Church of Dalry, Ayrshire, Scotland.
Last Words: "This much I can say in humility, that through free grace, I have endeavored to keep the post that God has assigned to me. These 14 years I have not desired to lift one foot before God showed me where to set down the other."
Source: *The Scots Worthies: Containing a Brief Historical Account of the Most Eminent Noblemen, Gentlemen, Ministers, and Others, Who Testified or Suffered for the Cause of Reformation in Scotland from the Beginning of the Sixteenth Century to the Year 1688* by John Howie (New York, 1856).

Ker, William Paton ("W.P.")

(1855-1923) Scottish literary scholar, essayist, educator. Authority on medieval literature. Notable work: *Epic and Romance.* Taught at several major universities. Elected to Chair of Poetry at Oxford. Highly respected by J.R.R. Tolkien and W. H. Auden. Accomplished mountain hiker. Died at age 67 while mountain climbing in the Italian Alps. The W.P. Ker Memorial Lecture is held in his honor at Glasgow University.
Last Words: "I thought this was the most beautiful spot in the world, and now I know it." Spoken just before he had a heart attack at Macugnaga in the Italian Alps.
Source: *Reading, Writing, and Remembering: A Literary Record* by Edward Verrall Lucas (New York, 1932).

Kerr, Michael Crawford

(1827-1876) American politician, lawyer. Member of U.S. House of Representatives from Indiana. Speaker of House of Representatives. Died at age 49 in Rockbridge Alum Springs, Virginia.
Last Words: "I stand upon my record."
Source: *Memorial Addresses on the Life and Character of Michael Crawford Kerr, Speaker of the House of Representatives of the United States. 44th Cong., 1 Sess., 1877* (Washington D.C., 1877).

Kerr, Victor

(d. 1851) American military officer. Captain. Executed in Havana along with General Narciso Lopez, Colonel William Logan Crittenden and about 50 others. Lopez headed the Cuban party that favored annexation of Cuba to the United States. He led an expedition from New Orleans to Cuba.
Last Words (written): "My Dear Friends, I leave you forever, and I go to the other world. I am prisoner in Havana and in an hour I shall have ceased to exist. My dearest friends think often of me. I die worthy of a Creole, worthy of a Louisianan and of a Kerr."
Source: *Cuba in 1851: Containing Authentic Statistics of the Population, Agriculture and Commerce of the Island for a Series of Years, with Official and Other Documents in Relation to the Revolutionary Movements of 1850 and 1851* by Alexander Jones (New York, 1851).

Kershaw, John

(1792-1870) English clergyman, educator. Founding father of Strict Baptists of England. Established school for children of laborers and mechanics at Oxfordshire in 1820s. Also founded a private school. Died at age 77.
Last Words: "God is faithful! God is faithful!"
Source: *Sermons of John Kershaw* by John Kershaw and B.A. Ramsbottom (Harpenden, Hertfordshire, England, 1995).

Ketchel, Stanley

(1886-1910) American athlete. Professional boxer. Real name Stanislaw Kiecal. Known as the Michigan Assassin. Famed as one of the world's greatest middleweight champions. Shot while visiting R.P. Dickerson's ranch in Conway, Missouri, by ranch hand Walter Dipley, a navy deserter who used the assumed name Hurtz. Trouble between the two men had started the day before when Ketchel upbraided Hurtz for beating a horse. Dickerson chartered a train to rush Ketchel to a Springfield hospital, 40 miles away, but the boxer could not be saved. He died at age 24.

Different Last Words:

(1) Ketchel became unconscious not long after the shooting, but he was able to say that Hurtz had shot him. He later gained consciousness briefly before he died.

Source: "Stanley Ketchel Slain by Rancher; Champion Middleweight Pugilist Shot in Lung by Hurtz Whom He Had Reproved" (*New York Times*, October 15, 1910).

(2) "I'm so tired. Take me home to Mother."

Source: "Boxing Game Not Enjoying Successful Autumn Campaign. Small Turnouts and Numerous Snarls are Hurting Sport Here" by Jim Jab (*Pittsburgh Press*, October 25, 1925).

Ketchum, Thomas Edward ("Black Jack")

(1863-1901) American cowboy, cattle driver, outlaw. Captured, brought to trial and sentenced to death. Executed in Clayton, New Mexico. The people who hanged him were inexperienced and accidentally decapitated him, giving him the dubious distinction of being the only American criminal decapitated during a hanging.

Different Last Words:

(1) "The rope looks like a good one—Goodbye, please dig my grave very deep—All right, hurry up—Ready. Let 'er go."

Sources: "Black Jack Ketchum" by Jack DeMattos (*Real West*, June, 1984); *Encyclopedia of Western Gunfighters* by Bill O'Neal (Austin, TX, 1989).

(2) "I'll be in hell before you're finished breakfast, boys. Let her rip!"

Source: *Almanac of World Crime* by Jay Robert Nash (Garden City, NY, 1981).

Keyes, Emily

(1990-2006) American crime victim. One of six girls held hostage by Duane Morrison who stormed Platte Canyon High School in Bailey, Colorado, in September 2006, and took hostages at gun point. Emily Keyes was shot dead by Morrison when she tried to escape. She text-messaged her parents just before her attempted escape. Morrison killed himself after a SWAT team secured the classroom.

Last Words (written): "I love U guys." Text-message sent to her father. Her Last Words became the name of a foundation created "to restore and protect the joy of youth through educational programs and positive actions in collaboration with families, schools, communities, and government entities."

Source: "Emily Keyes: Teen Recalled as Person Who Saw the Good in All" (*The* [Colorado Springs] *Gazette* October 1, 2006).

Keyserling, William

(1869-1951) Lithuanian-born American Jewish businessman, philanthropist, communal leader. Came to U.S. in 1888. Settled in Beaufort, South Carolina. Did much to help needy and homeless Jews overseas. Died at age 82 while giving an address at a national United Jewish Appeal meeting in New York City.

Last Words: "We must save lives."

Source: *Against the Tide: One Woman's Political Struggle* by Harriet Keyserling (Columbia, SC, 2004). The author was his daughter-in-law.

Khayyam, Omar, see Omar Khayyam.

Kid Curry, *see* Logan, Harvey.

Kidd, William ("Captain Kidd")

(1645?-1701) Scottish ship owner, sea captain. Started as a privateer, became a pirate. Arrested in Boston, imprisoned. Sent to London. Found guilty of piracy and murder. Hanged. Much of his loot has not been recovered.

Last Words: "This is a very fickle and faithless generation." Spoken just before he was hanged.

Source: *The Real Captain Kidd: A Vindication* by Sir Cornelius Neale Dalton (New York, 1911).

Kieft, William

(1597-1647) Dutch statesman. Colonial governor of New Netherlands. Drowned at age 50 aboard the ship *Princess* off the coast of Wales en route to Holland.

Last Words: "Friends, I have been unjust toward you; can you forgive me?" Heard by other passengers as the ship was sinking.

Source: *The History of North America* by Guy Carleton Lee and Francis Newton Thorpe (Philadelphia, 1907).

Kierkegaard, Søren Aabye

(1813-1855) Danish philosopher, theologian. Earliest of the existential philosophers. Stricken with spinal disease. Died at age 42 in Copenhagen.

Last Words: "Yes, that is why I am very happy and very sad that I cannot share this happiness with anyone." His response when asked whether his life turned out as he wanted. He lost the ability to speak soon afterward. Lingered two weeks before he died.

Sources: *Søren Kierkegaard* by Johannes Hohlenberg (New York, 1954); *Kierkegaard* by Josiah Thompson (New York, 1973).

Kim, Alexandra Petrovna

(1885-1918) Russian-Korean Communist, revolutionary, political activist. Joined Bolsheviks in 1916. Recognized as the first Korean woman to become a Communist. Lenin sent her to Siberia in 1917 to mobilize Koreans against counter-revolutionary forces and the Allied Expeditionary Forces. She was in charge of external affairs at the Far-Eastern Department of the party. Co-founded Korean People's Socialist party in Khabarovsk in 1918. Captured along with many other Korean Communists later that year and executed.

Last Words: "Freedom and Independence for Korea!" (Shown as "reputed" in some sources.)

Source: *Kim Alexandra Petrovna (Stankevich), Leader of Korean Socialist Party* by Pak Hwan (Seoul, Korea, 1992).

King, James Gore

(1791-1853) American merchant, banker, politician, military officer. Son of American political leader Rufus King. Served in War of 1812. Member U.S. House of Representatives from New Jersey. Died at age 62 in Weehawken, New Jersey. His estate occupied the site where the Alexander Hamilton and Aaron Burr duel was fought.

Last Words: "Thy will be done!"

Source: *A Memoir of the Life of James Gore King* by his brother Charles King (New York, 1864).

King, Martin Luther, Jr.

(1929-1968) American clergyman, civil rights leader. Baptist minister. Leader of the American civil rights movement during much of the 1950s and 1960s. Believed in non-violence. Used passive resistance to achieve his goals. Winner of 1964 Nobel Peace Prize. Assassinated at age 39 in Memphis, Tennessee. National day honors him on the third Monday in January.

Different Last Words:

(1) "Ben, make sure you play "Precious Lord, Take My Hand." Play it real pretty— for me." Spoken to Ben Branch, a musician, as he stood on the balcony of the Lorraine Motel in Memphis a few minutes before he was shot.

Source: *King: A Critical Biography* by David L. Lewis (New York, 1970).

(2) "Okay I will." His response to the suggestion that he wear an overcoat. Seconds later he was shot.

Source: "Martin Luther King is Slain in Memphis; a White is Suspected, Johnson Urges Calm" by Earl Caldwell (*New York Times*, April 5, 1968).

King, Samuel

(1775-1842) American clergyman. Helped establish Cumberland Presbyterian Church near Nashville, Tennessee. First minister to Choctaw and Chickasaw.

Last Words: "Peace, peace, peace!"

Source: "Samuel King" in *Brief Biographical Sketches of Some of the Early Ministers of Cumberland Presbyterian Church* by Richard Beard, D.D. (Nashville, TN, 1867).

King, Thomas Starr

(1824-1864) American clergyman, writer, activist. Ordained Universalist. Became Unitarian. Influential California politician in U.S. Civil War. Organized West Coast branch of U.S. Sanitary Commission and helped raise more than $1.5 million. Died at age 39 in San Francisco. Mountain peak and schools were named for him.

Last Words: "Dear little fellow! He's a beautiful boy." Spoken about his young son who had been brought to see him.

Source: *A Tribute to Thomas Starr King* by Richard Frothingham (Boston, 1865).

Kingsley, Charles

(1819-1875) English clergyman, novelist, poet. Involved in social reform issues of his era. Notable works: *Hypatia; The Water Babies; Westward Ho!* Died at age 55 in Eversley, Hampshire, England.

Different Last Words:

(1) "Thou knowest, O Lord, the secrets of our hearts; shut not Thy merciful ears to our prayers, but spare us, O Lord most holy, O God most mighty, O holy and merciful Saviour. Thou most worthy Judge Eternal, suffer us not, at our last hour, for any pains of death to fall from Thee." After he was heard repeating the Burial Service, he turned on his side and never spoke again.

Source: *Charles Kingsley, His Letters and Memories of His Life,* ed. by Mrs. Kingsley (London, 1878).

(2) "It is all right—all under rule." Repeated again and again as he faced death.

Source: *The Victorian Frame of Mind, 1830-1870* by Walter Edwards Houghton (New Haven, CT, 1957).

Kipling, Rudyard

(1865-1936) English writer, poet, novelist, short-story writer. Notable works: *The Jungle Book; Kim; The Light That Failed; Just So Stories for Little Children; Captains Courageous.* Many of his stories have been made into movies. Won 1907 Nobel Prize for Literature. While staying in London in 1936, he became violently ill and was taken to a hospital. Died there at age 70 of a cerebral hemorrhage.

Last Words: "Something has come adrift inside." His response to the question: "What's the matter, Rud?"

Source: *Rudyard Kipling* by Lord Birkenhead [Frederick W.F. Smith] (New York, 1978).

Kirkpatrick, William James

(1838-1921) Irish-born American musician, hymnist. Composer of church music. Gospel music pioneer. Founded publishing company. Published 50 song books that sold several million copies. Notable hymns: "Jesus Saves"; "Tis So Sweet to Trust in Jesus." Died at age 83 of a heart attack in Philadelphia, Pennsylvania, while writing a hymn.

Last Words (written):

"Just as Thou wilt, Lord, this is my cry
Just as Thou wilt, to live or to die.
I am Thy servant; Thou knowest best;
Just as Thou wilt, Lord labour or rest.
Just as Thou wilt, Lord—Which shall it be?
Life everlasting, waiting for me?
Or shall I tarry here at Thy feet?
Just as Thou wilt, Lord, whatever is meet."

He was found dead at his desk the following morning. His Last Words were on a piece of paper on the floor.

Source: *The Romance of Sacred Song* by David J. Beattie (London, 1931).

Kitching, John Howard

(1840-1865) American military officer. Union Army colonel in U.S. Civil War. Brevet brigadier general. Wounded at the Battle of Cedar Creek. Died at age 24, several months later, at Dobb's Ferry, New York.

Last Words: "It will all be over in a few minutes, darling, and we will have such a nice talk afterward!" Spoken to his sister before surgery.

Source: *More Than Conqueror: Or Memorials of Colonel J. Howard Kitching, 6th NY Artillery, Army of the Potomac* by Theodore Irving (New York, 1873). The author was his brother-in-law.

Kivi, Aleksis

(1834-1872) Finnish writer, novelist, playwright, poet. Birth name Alexis Stenvall. Wrote first significant novel in Finnish language, *Seven Brothers.* Also wrote 12 plays and poetry collection. Schizophrenia became apparent in his thirties. Died at age 38 in Tuusula, near his birthplace. Finnish composer Einojuhani Rautavaara wrote an opera about Kivi's life: *Aleksis Kiva.* Director Jari Halonen made a movie about him: *The Life of Aleksis Kivi.* (Finnish title: *Aleksis Kiven elämä*).

Last Words: "Minä elän!" (tr. "I live!" or "I am alive!").

Source: *The American-Scandinavian Review* (New York, 1974).

Kléber, Jean-Baptiste

(1753-1800) French military officer. Revolutionary general. Defeated royalists at Vendée. Highly esteemed by Napoleon who placed Kléber in command of French forces when he returned to France. Kléber was killed at age 47 by a Turkish fanatic in Cairo.

Last Words: "I have been assassinated."

Source: *Kléber, sa vie, sa correspondance* by Count Charles Pierre Victor Pajol (Paris, 1877).

Kleist, Heinrich von

(1776-1811) German playwright, short-story writer. Poverty-stricken. Grew despondent when his work failed to find the recognition he thought it deserved. Killed himself in suicide pact with young woman friend, Henriette Vogel, who was dying of cancer.

Last Words (written): "I cannot die without, contented and serene as I am, reconciling myself with all the world and—before all others—with you, my dearest Ulrike. Give up the strong expressions which you resorted to in your letter to me: let me revoke them; truly, to save me, you have done all within the strength, not only of a sister, but of a man—all that could be done. The truth is, nothing on earth can help me. And now good-bye: may Heaven send you a death even half equal to mine in joy and unutterable bliss: that is the most heart-felt and profoundest wish that I can think of for you Your Henry. Stimmung, at Potsdam, on the morning of my death." Suicide letter to his sister.

Source: *Der letzte Brief* by Friedrich Percyval Reck-Malleczewen (Frankfurt, Germany, 1949).

Klopstock, Friedrich Gottlieb

(1724-1803) German poet, lyricist. Wrote first three cantos of *The Messiah* in 1748. Finished last cantos in 1773. Died at age 78 in Hamburg.

Last Words: "Can a woman forget her child, that she should not have pity on the fruit of her womb? Yes, she may forget, but I will not forget Thee!" From his ode *Der Erbarmer*.

Source: *Memoirs of Frederick and Margaret Klopstock* by Friedrich Gottlieb Klopstock, Margareta Klopstock, Jakob Mumssen and Elizabeth Smith (London, 1809).

Klopstock, Margaret Moller ("Meta")

(d. 1758) Wife of poet Friedrich Klopstock. She was the "Cidli" mentioned in his poems.

Last Words: "The blood of Jesus Christ cleanseth from all sin! O, sweet words of eternal life!"

Source: *Dying Testimonies of Saved and Unsaved: Gathered from Authentic Sources* by Solomon Benjamin Shaw (Chicago, 1898).

Variation: "It is over.—The blood of Jesus Christ cleanse thee from all sin." Spoken to her sister Eliza.

Source: *Memoirs of Frederick and Margaret Klopstock* by Friedrick Gottlieb Klopstock, Margareta Klopstock, Jakob Mumssen and Elizabeth Smith (London, 1809).

Kluge, Günther von

(1882-1944) German military officer. Nazi military leader. Field marshal. Tried to contact Allied commanders during World War II, possibly to organize a cease fire. When Hitler ordered him back to Germany, he committed suicide at age 61.

Last Words (written): "I depart from you, my Führer, as one who stood nearer to you than you perhaps realized in the consciousness that I did my duty to the utmost. Heil, my Führer, von Kluge, Field-Marshal, 18 August 1944." End of his suicide note to Hitler.

Source: *Defeat in the West* by Milton Shulman (London, 1947).

Knibb, William

(1803-1845) English missionary. Baptist missionary in Jamaica. Persecuted for his concern about slaves. Worked for their emancipation. Died at age 42 of fever. In 1988, on the 150th anniversary of the abolition of slavery in the British Empire, Knibb was granted the Order of Merit, Jamaica's highest civil honor.

Last Words: "The service is over; you may go—All is well."

Source: *Memoir of William Knibb, Missionary in Jamaica* by John Howard Hinton (London, 1847).

Knickerbocker, Cholly, see Paul, Maury Henry Biddle.

Knickerbocker, Diedrich, see Irving, Washington.

Knight, Patrick Bryan

(1968-2007) American murderer. Convicted of 1991 double murder and sentenced to die in Huntsville, Texas, on June 26, 2007. Held a controversial contest on the Internet to determine what joke he would use as his Last Words. He had a website called "Dead Man Laughing." With 1,300 entries, Knight told prison officials he still intended to deliver a joke up to his final hours, but would not tell them what he planned to say. He claimed this was to boost the spirits of his fellow condemned inmates who were also judging the jokes. He died at age 39, when his execution was carried out as scheduled.

Last Words: "Yes, I do. I thank the Lord for giving me my friends, for getting me the ones I love. Lord reach down and help innocent men on death row. Lee Taylor needs help, Bobby Hines, Steve Woods. Not all of us are innocent, but those are. Cleve Foster needs help. Melyssa, I love you girl. I know I wasn't going to say anything, but I've got to. Jack, Irene, Danny, Doreen, I love you guys. I said I was going to tell a joke. Death has set me free. That's the biggest joke, I deserve this. And the other joke is I am not Patrick Bryan Knight, and ya'll can't stop this execution now. Go ahead, I'm finished. Come on, tell me Lord. I love you Melyssa, take care of that little monster for me." (Fingerprints confirmed that he was Patrick Bryan Knight).

Source: "Date of Execution: June 26, 2007; Offender: Knight, Patrick," Texas Department of Criminal Justice (www.tdcj.state.tx.us). [Accessed 09/09/2009].

Knill, Richard

(1787-1857) English clergyman, missionary, diarist. Chaplain for English residents at St. Petersburg, Russia. His journal allowed outsiders to learn about life in Russia during the years 1823 to 1836. Later was a minister at Queen Street Congregational Chapel, Chester, England. Died at age 67 in Chester.

Last Words: "How are you, Mary?" Spoken to his daughter.

Source: "The Life of the Reverend Richard Knill of St. Petersburg" by Rev. Charles M. Birrell (*New Englander and Yale Review,* Vol. 18, No. 69, February 1860).

Knorr, Frances Lydia Alice Sutton ("Minnie")

(1868-1894) Australian murderer. Left to fend for herself with a child when her husband was sent to jail. She began "baby-farming"—taking care of usually illegitimate children. Many of these children died in circumstances that led to the suspicion that they had been murdered or neglected. Following discovery of three infant corpses at one of her former residences, she was arrested and convicted of murder. She wwas one of only five women hanged in Victoria, Australia.

Last Words: "The Lord is with me, I do not fear what man can do unto me, for I have peace, perfect peace."

Source: "Knorr, Frances Lydia Alice (Minnie)" by Kathy Laster in *Australian Dictionary of Biography,* Supplementary Vol. (Melbourne, Australia, 2005).

Knowlton, Thomas

(1740-1776) American military officer, spy. Served in the French and Indian War and as a colonel in the American Revolution. America's first intelligence professional. Commanded Knowlton's Rangers and gathered significant intelligence during the early part of the war. Killed in action at Battle of Harlem Heights. Military Intelligence Corps Association grants the Knowlton Award to individuals who have contributed significantly to the promotion of Army Intelligence.

Last Words: "Have we driven the enemy?"

Source: *New York: Not so Little and Not so Old* by Sarah M. Lockwood (Garden City, NY, 1926).

Knox, John

(1505-1572) Scottish religious reformer, writer, statesman. Protestant leader of Scottish Reformation. Died at age 67 in Edinburgh.

Last Words: "Now it is come." Spoken with a deep sigh in the presence of his secretary Richard Bannatyne. When he saw that Knox could not speak, he asked him to raise his hand. Knox did so, then died.

Source: *John Knox: The Hero of the Scottish Reformation* by Henry Cowan (New York, 1905).

Knox, Ronald Arbuthnott

(1888-1957) British clergyman, theologian, writer, novelist, radio personality. Roman Catholic chaplain at Oxford. Published Catholic interpretation of Bible known as Knox Version. Wrote several crime novels. Had BBC radio show. Created near panic in 1926 with one of his shows that mixed fact and fake news. Died at age 69 of cancer.

Last Words: "No. Awfully jolly of you to suggest it, though." His deathbed response to Lady Elton who saw that he was stirring slightly and asked if he would like her to read from the Knox Version of the Bible.

Source: *The Life of the Right Reverend Ronald Knox* by Evelyn Waugh (London, 1959). The author was his friend and literary executor.

Koerner, or Körner, Carl Theodore or Karl Theodor (Theodor)

(1791-1813) German playwright, poet, freedom fighter. Soldier during the Napoleonic Era. Notable work: *Farewell to Life,* written while he was seriously wounded. Killed at age 21 at the Battle of Leipzig.

Last Words: "There I have one; but it doesn't matter."

Source: *Theodor Koerner* by Karl Berger (Leipzig, Germany, 1912).

Korzeniowski, Josef Teodor Konrad, see Conrad, Joseph.

Korda, Alexander

(1893-1956) Hungarian-born British film director, producer. Notable movies: *The Thief of Bagdad; That Hamilton Woman; Perfect Strangers*. Died at age 62 of a heart attack in London.

Last Words: "If I say goodnight to you now, my friend, will you promise me that I won't wake up again?"

Source: *Charmed Lives: A Family Romance* by Michael Korda (New York, 1979). The author is the son of Korda's brother Vincent.

Kossuth, Louis or Lajos

(1802-1894) Hungarian statesman, revolutionary. Led national revolutionary struggle against Austria. Served briefly as governor of Hungary then was exiled for many years. Died at age 92 in Turin, Italy.

Last Words: "It grieves me that I have to perish in exile." His sister then said to him: "You are the most popular Hungarian." He responded: "Only your vanity holds this."

Source: *Dictionary of Last Words* compiled by Edward S. Le Comte (New York, 1955). Le Comte cited as his source *Budapest Daily Pesti Naplo*, March 20, 1914, on authority of Istvan Csicsery-Ronay.

Kraus, Christian Jacob

(1753-1807) German philosopher, educator, librarian. Professor of practical philosophy, law, natural science at University of Königsberg. Student of Kant. Advocated the theories of Hume and Adam Smith. Died at age 54 in Königsberg.

Last Words: "Sterben ist ganz anders als ich gedacht hatte." (tr. "Dying is different from what I thought.")

Source: *Das Leben des Professor Christian Jacob Kraus* by Johannes Voigt [from *Vermischte Schriften über staatswirthschaftliche, philosophische und andere wissenschaftliche Gegenstände*] (Königsberg, Germany, 1819).

Krause, William Henry

(1796-1852) Irish clergyman. Preached at Bethesda Episcopal Chapel, Dublin, for 13 years. Gained fame for his sermons. They were published after his death as *Sanctification in Christ Jesus*.

Last Words: "I am so restless, I can hardly think; but the Lord's hand is not shortened."

Source: *Memoirs of W.H. Krause, A.M.* by Charles Stuart Stanford (Dublin, Ireland, 1854).

Krüdener, Barbara Juliana von

(1764-1824) Russian novelist, mystic, political prophetess. Birth name von Vietinghoff. Lived in Germany, France, Switzerland, Russia. Married Baron Burckhard Alexis Constantin von Krüdener. Had a religious conversion around 1800. Devoted her life to preaching. Helped influence formation of Holy Alliance. Notable work: *Valérie* (autobiographical novel). Died at age 60 in the Crimea.

Last Words: "The good I have done will remain; but what I have done wrong the mercy of God will blot out."

Source: *The Court of the Tuileries from the Restoration to the Flight of Louis Philippe* by Lady Catherine Charlotte Jackson (Boston, 1897).

Kuang-Hsu or Kwang-Hsü, Emperor of China

(1871-1908) Chinese ruler of Ch'ing or Manchu dynasty. Appointed to the throne by his aunt in 1889. In 1898, she took over the throne and imprisoned him for the rest of his life. He died at age 37 in Peking [now Beijing]. Many believe he was murdered.

Last Words: "We were the second son of the Prince Ch'un when the Empress Dowager selected Us for the Throne. She has always hated Us. But for Our misery of the past ten years, Yuan Shi Kai is responsible and none other. When the time comes, I desire that Yuan be summarily beheaded."

Source: *The Last Empress* by Daniele Vare (New York, 1937).

Kudrinsky, El'dar

(1978-1994) Russian disaster victim. Teenage son of Aeroflot 593 captain. While visiting his father in the cockpit during a flight, he asked if he could sit in the captain's seat. His father turned on the autopilot and gave El'dar the seat. El'dar asked if he could turn the control wheel a bit. His father replied he could. Unknown to either of them or to the flight crew, this action disconnected part of the autopilot. The plane started to dive with such force El'dar was unable to get out of the seat so that his father could correct the direction. All 75 aboard were killed. The incident was featured on an episode of the Discovery Channel and National Geographic Channel's Canadian television program *Mayday* (known as *Air Emergency* in the U.S.) in an episode called "Kid in the Cockpit." When the events were discovered from flight recorder, sweeping changes were made as to who was permitted into the cockpit.

Last Words: "Why is it turning? Yes it is." Recorded on the flight recorder just before the jet crashed.

Source: *The Air Up There: More Great Quotations on Flight* by Dave English (New York, 2003).

Kuhlman, Kathryn Johanna

(1907-1976) American evangelist. Pentecostal Christian faith healer. Began preaching at age 16. Well known. Died at age 69 in Tulsa, Oklahoma, after open-heart surgery.

Last Words: "Love! Love! Love!"

Source: *Kathryn Kuhlman: The Life She Led, the Legacy She Left* by Helen Kooiman Hosier (Old Tappan, NJ, 1976).

Kurz, Toni

(1913-1936) German mountain climber. Member of a four-man team who attempted to be the first to ascend the North Face of the Eiger. They were caught in an avalanche. Climbers tethered on both sides of Kurz were killed and he was left hanging. After more than a day of manipulating the rope and within meters of rescue, the attempt to save Kurz failed.

Last Words: "Ich kann nicht mehr." (tr. "I can do no more.") Died after he spoke these words.

Source: *The White Spider: The Classic Account of the Ascent of the Eiger* by Heinrich Harrer (New York, 1960).

Kusakábé

(d. c. 1859) Japanese politician, dissident. Imprisoned and executed.

Last Words: "It is better to be a crystal and be broken, than to remain perfect like a tile upon the housetop." Chinese verse he quoted on the way to his execution.

Source: *Familiar Studies of Men and Books* by Robert Louis Stevenson (New York, 1917).

La Barre, Jean François Lefebvre, Chevalier de

(1747-1766) French nobleman. A wooden crucifix on the bridge of Abbeville had been defaced. LaBarre was accused of the crime without sufficient evidence. He was sentenced to be burned to death and was executed at age 19. Voltaire was angered by La Barre's execution and waged a campaign to clear his name. The sentence was technically reversed in 1794.

Last Words: "I did not think they would put a young gentleman to death for such a trifle."

Source: *The French Humorists from the Twelfth to the Nineteenth Century* by Walter Besant (Boston, 1874).

La Bédoyère, Charles Angélique François Huchet, Comte de

(1786-1815) French military officer. General with Napoleon at Waterloo. Arrested for treason while trying to escape. Tried, found guilty and shot.

Last Words: "Ne me manquez pas!" (tr. "This is what you must not miss!" Or, "Don't miss me!") Spoken to the firing squad as he showed them where his heart was.

Source: *Biographie universelle*, Book III, by J. Fr. Michaud and Louis Gabriel Michaud (Paris, 1811-1862).

Labouchère, Henry DuPré

(1831-1912) British journalist, politician. Radical who wrote for *The Daily News* and *The World* and exposed corruption. Died in Florence, Italy, at age 80.

Last Words: "Flames? Not yet, I think." His comment to his nephew and biographer A.L. Thorold when a burning spirit lamp overturned and flared up. He laughed and went to sleep.

Source: *The Life of Henry Labouchère* by Algar Labouchère Thorold (London, 1913). The author was his nephew.

Labouré, Saint Catherine

(1806-1876) French nun, holy woman. Roman Catholic. Member of Daughters of Charity. Declared that the Blessed Virgin instructed her to create the Miraculous Medal. Died at age 70 at Enghein-Reuilly, France. Canonized in 1947.

Last Words: "You shall see me, but I shall not see you, for I shall not be here." Her response to her niece who said she would come to wish her a happy New Year in the morning. She was dead by 7 that evening.

Source: *Saint Catherine Labouré of the Miraculous Medal* by Fr. Joseph Dirvin (New York, 1958).

Lacépède, Bernard Germain Étienne de la Ville, Comte de

(1756-1825) French naturalist, writer. Notable works: *Poetic of Music; Essay on Electricity*. Collaborated on Buffon's *Natural History*. Died at age 68 in Épinay-on-Seine.

Last Words: "Charles, write in large letters the word END at the foot of the page." Spoken to his son referring to his unfinished manuscript.

Source: *Biographie universelle,* Book XXII, by J. Fr. Michaud and Louis Gabriel Michaud (Paris, 1811-1862).

Lackey, Clarence Allen

(1954?-1997) American murderer. Executed by lethal injection in Texas. Lackey's case is notable for the legal challenge he put forward. He argued unsuccessfully that executing a prisoner who had spent 17 years on death row would violate the cruel and unusual punishment prohibition of the U.S. Constitution's Eighth Amendment.

Last Words: "I love you, Mom."

Source: "'The Agony of Suspense' How Protracted Death Row Confinement Gives Rise to an Eighth Amendment Claim of Cruel and Unusual Punishment" by Kathleen M. Flynn (*Washington & Lee Law Review*, Winter 1997).

Lacordaire, Jean Baptiste Henri (Henri)

(1802-1861) French clergyman. Converted to Roman Catholicism and became a Dominican monk. Known for his sermons at Notre Dame and for his funeral orations. Died at age 60 in Sorèze, France.

Last Words: "My God, my God! Open to me! Open to me!"

Source: *Henri Dominique Lacordaire: A Biographical Sketch* by H.L. Sidney Lear (London, 1887).

Laënnec, René Théophile Hyacinthe

(1781-1826) French physician. Inventor of the stethoscope. Died at age 45 at Ker-

louanec, France.

Last Words: "It would be necessary soon that another do me this service. I do not want anyone to have the bother of it." Spoken as he took off his rings and placed them on a table.

Source: *Le Docteur Laënnec* by Paul Sarradon (Paris, 1949).

Lafayette, Adrienne, Marquise de

(1760-1807) French noblewoman. Birth name Marie Adrienne Françoise de Noailles. Married Marquis de Lafayette in 1774 when she was 14 and he was 16. Shared husband's views on social issues such as abolition of slavery. Died at age 48 at La Grange, France.

Last Words: "Is it then true? You have loved me! How happy I am! Kiss me. What a blessing! How happy I am to be yours." Spoken to her husband.

Source: *The Wife of Lafayette* by M.M. Crawford (New York, 1908).

Lafayette, Marquis de

(1757-1834) French nobleman, military officer, politician. General. Full name Marie Joseph Paul Yves Roch Gilbert du Motier, Marquis de Lafayette. Helped promote French support for the American Revolution. Received enthusiastic welcome during his return visit to America in 1824 and 1825. Died at age 76 in Paris. More than 20 American towns and cities were named for him.

Last Words: "What do you expect? Life is like the flame of a lamp; when there is no more oil—zest! It goes out, and it is all over."

Source: *Lafayette* by Brand Whitlock (New York, 1929).

La Follette, Robert Marion, Sr.

(1855-1925) American politician, statesman. Ran unsuccessfully for U.S. President as Progressive party candidate. Member U.S. House of Representatives from Wisconsin. Governor of Wisconsin. Member U.S Senate from 1906 until he died at age 70 of a heart attack in Washington, D.C.

Last Words: "I am at peace with all the world, but there is still a lot of work I could do. I don't know how the people will feel toward me, but I shall take to the grave my love for them, which has sustained me through life." He took a sip of milk and said "It is good." He died two hours later.

Source: *The La Follettes and the Wisconsin Idea* by Edward N. Doan (New York, 1947).

Lagny, Thomas Fantet de

(1660-1734) French hydrologist, librarian, educator, mathematician, banker. Member of Academy of Sciences. Professor of hydrography at Rochefort Institute. Librarian at Bibliothéque du Roi and deputy director of the Banque Générale. Self-taught mathematician known for his contributions to computational mathematics such as calculating π to 120 places and developing method of giving approximate solutions for algebraic equations. Died at age 73 in Paris.

Last Words: "One hundred and forty-four." His deathbed response to the question: "What is the square of 12?" A test to see how far his faculties were gone.

Source: "Dying Words and Thoughts" (*New York Daily Times*, October 13, 1852).

LaGuardia, Fiorello Henry

(1882-1947) American politician, reformer. Known as the Little Flower. Member U.S. House of Representatives from New York. Mayor of New York City. Chief of U.S. Office of Civilian Defense during World War II. Died at age 64 of pancreatic cancer in The Bronx, New York. New York airport was named for him.

Last Words (doubtful): "I'm glad to meet an honest judge."

Source: Various Last Words compilations and Internet websites.

LaGuardia is said to have made this statement to Judge Learned Hand, who was one of the last people to see him alive. LaGuardia's Last Words were spoken to his wife and children, not Judge Hand. A week before he died, LaGuardia fell into a coma, slept deeply for several days, rousing only once to drink a little orange juice and speak a few words with his wife, Marie, and his two children, Jean and Eric.

Source: "Little Flower" (*Time* magazine, September 29, 1947).

La Harpe, Jean-François de

(1739-1803) French writer, poet, literary critic, educator, playwright. Professor of literature at the Lycée. Notable play: *Warwick,* his most successful drama. His other plays were failures. Contributed articles to the popular French magazine *Mercure de France*. Died at age 63 in Paris.

Last Words: "My friend, I thank Heaven for having left me a consciousness free to realize how consoling and beautiful these are." Spoken when he heard the prayer for the dying.

Source: *Recherches historiques, litteraires et bibliographiques sur la vie et les ouvrages de M. De La Harpe* by Etienne-G. Peignot (Dijon, France, 1820).

Variation: "I am grateful to Divine Mercy for having left me sufficient recollection to feel how consoling these prayers are to the dying." Spoken to M. Fontanes, who had called to see him.

Source: *The General Biographical Dictionary: Containing an Historical and Critical Account of the Lives and Writings of the Most Eminent Persons in Every Nation; Particularly the British and Irish; from the Earliest Accounts to the Present Time* by Alexander Chalmers (London, 1812-1814).

Lahr, Bert

(1895-1967) American entertainer, actor. Star of stage, radio, television and movies. Birth name Irving Lahrheim. Notable role: The Cowardly Lion (and farmer Zeke) in the movie *The Wizard of Oz*. Died at age 72 of pneumonia in New York City.

Last Words: "Hurt." Whispered two days before he died. Earlier he said: "Mildred, why aren't my clothes laid out? I've got a seven o'clock call." He was imagining he was still at work. Lahr lingered on the edge of consciousness for several days before he died. He was heard singing. His nurse thought he needed help, then realized he was doing an old routine.

Source: *Notes on a Cowardly Lion: The Biography of Bert Lahr* by John Lahr (New York, 1967). The author was his son.

Laing, Ronald David ("R.D.")

(1927-1989) Scottish psychiatrist, writer, reformer. Notable work: *The Divided Self* (study of schizophrenia). Sought to understand inner experience of mental disorder. Established therapeutic centers where patients and therapists lived together. Died at age 61 of a heart attack while playing tennis in St. Tropez, France.

Last Words: "No bloody doctors."
Source: *We've Had a Hundred Years of Psychotherapy and the World's Getting Worse* by James Hilman and Michael Ventura (New York, 1993).

Lakanal, Joseph

(1762-1845) French politician, educator. Name originally spelled Lacanal. Member of the French Council of Five Hundred. Held educational posts under Napoleon. Exiled to the U.S. in 1816. President of Louisiana State University. Returned to France in 1834. Died at age 82 in Paris.
Last Words: "Your attentions will not save me; I feel that there is no more oil in the lamp." Spoken to his physician.
Source: *Lakanal* by Paul Le Gendre (Paris, 1882).

Lalande, Joseph Jérôme Le Français de

(1732-1807) French astronomer, writer. Notable work: *Histoire Céleste Française* (cataloged nearly 50,000 stars). Died at age 74 in Paris.
Last Words: "Withdraw, I no longer have need of anything."
Source: *Jérôme Lalande et la Bresse au XVIIIe siècle* by M. Jarrin (Bourg, France, 1869).

Lamb, Charles

(1775-1834) English writer, essayist, critic. Pen name Elia. Notable work: *Essays of Elia*. Died at age 59 of infection contracted from fall that cut his face.
Last Words (written; doubtful): "My bedfellows are cramp and cough—we sleep three in a bed."
Source: Various Last Words compilations and Internet websites.
Lamb wrote these words in a letter to Mr. Moxon on April 27, 1833, 20 months before he died. His last letter was to a Mrs. Dyer about a book.
Last Words (written): "Dear Mrs. Dyer—I am very uneasy about a Book, which I either have lost or left at your house on Thursday. It was the book I went out to fetch from Miss Buffam's while the tripe was frying. It is called "Phillips' Theatrum Poetarum," but it is an English book. I think I left it in the parlor. It is Mr. Cary's book, and I would not lose it for the world. Pray, if you find it, book it at the Swan, Snow Hill, by an Edmonton stage immediately, directed to Mr.

Lamb, Church Street, Edmonton, or write to say you cannot find it. I am quite anxious about it. If it is lost, I shall never like tripe again. With kindest love to Mr. Dyer and all, yours truly, C. Lamb." Letter written December 22, 1834, five days before he died.
Last Words (spoken): Probably incoherent. Bryan Waller Procter (pen name Barry Cornwall)—who at the time thought he might be the last surviving person who knew Lamb well—published an account in 1866 stating: "At last his voice began to fail, his perceptions became confused, and he sank gradually, very gradually, until the 27th of December, 1834; and then—he died! It was the fading away or disappearance of life, rather than a violent transit into another world."
Sources: *The Complete Works and Letters of Charles Lamb* by Charles Lamb (New York, 1935); *Charles Lamb, a Memoir* by Barry Cornwall (Boston, 1866); *The Letters of Charles Lamb* by Charles Lamb and Alfred Ainger (New York, 1904).

Lamballe, Louise de Savoie-Carignan, Princesse de

(1749-1792) Italian-born royalty. French courtier, royalist. Married Prince de Lamballe. Friend of Marie Antoinette. Arrested when the French monarchy was overthrown during the French Revolution. Refused to denounce the monarchy. Released to those conducting September Massacres. Killed by mob. Died at age 42 in Paris.
Last Words: "Fie on the horror!" Her response when she was asked to shout: "Vive la Nation!"
Source: *Èpisodes de l'histoire de Paris sous La Terreur. Louise de Savoie-Carignan, Princesse de Lamballe, et la prison de la Force* by Paul Fassy (Paris, 1868).

Lambert, John

(d. 1538) English clergyman, martyr. Protestant martyr. Birth name John Nicholson. Changed name after a theological dispute. Condemned to die for heresy. Burned at the stake in Smithfield, London.
Last Words: "None but Christ, none but Christ." Spoken as the flames leaped from his raised hands.
Source: *Book of Martyrs and the Acts and Monuments of the Church* by John Fox (or Foxe). First published 1563, ed. by John Cumming (London, 1851).

Lamennais, Félicité Robert de

(1782-1854) French clergyman, philosopher, writer. Incurred censure and condemnation from the clergy for his liberal views on religious freedom. Refused to recant on his deathbed. Died at age 71 in Paris.
Different Last Words:
(1) "Let it come; it is coming for me." He saw the sun streaming into his room.
Source: *Lamennais: étude d'histoire, politique et religieuse* by E. Spuller (Paris, 1892).
(2) "Nous nous reverrons." (tr. "We shall meet again.")
Source: *Famous Sayings and Their Authors, A Collection of Historical Sayings in English, French, German, Greek, Italian, and Latin* by Edward Latham (New York, 1906).

La Mothe Le Vayer, François de

(1588-1672) French philosopher, historian. Appointed historiographer of France. Leader of 17th-century French skeptics. Tutored Duke of Orleans and King Louis XIV. Died at about age 83 in Paris.
Last Words: "Well, what news have you of the great Mogul?"
Source: *La Mothe le Vayer: sa vie et son oeuvre* by Florence L. Wickelgren (Paris, 1934).

Lamy, Jean-Baptiste

(1814-1888) French prelate. Roman Catholic bishop and first archbishop of Santa Fe, New Mexico Territory. Died at age 73 in Santa Fe. His life and career in the American Southwest provided inspiration for Willa Cather's novel *Death Comes for the Archbishop*.
Last Words: "Thank you. I was able to follow every word of the prayers you came to say for me. Keep praying for me, for I feel that I am going."
Source: *Lamy of Santa Fe* by Paul Horgan and Jill Christman (Middletown, CT, 2003).

Landis, Carole

(1919-1948) American actress, screen star. Birth name Frances Lillian Mary Ridste. Notable movie: *Four Jills in a Jeep,* based on her experiences as a USO entertainer during World War II. Committed suicide at age 29 by taking an overdose of a prescription drug in Hollywood.
Last Words (written): "Dearest Mommie— I'm sorry, really sorry to put you through this, but there is no way to avoid it. I love you darling, you have been the most wonderful Mom ever, and that applies to all our family. I love each and every one of them dearly. Everything goes to you. Look in the files and there is a will which decrees everything. Goodbye, my angel Pray for me— your baby." Suicide note left for her mother. A second note was reportedly found with instructions to her maid to care for her cat.
Source: "The Heartbreaking True Story of Carole Landis by Her Mother" (*True Story*, October 1948).

Landis, Kenesaw Mountain

(1866-1944) American jurist, baseball commissioner. Named for the U.S. Civil War battlefield where his father fought. U.S. District Judge for Northern District of Illinois. Presided over Standard Oil of Indiana rebate case. First baseball commissioner (1921 to 1944). Died at age 78, shortly after being elected to a new seven-year term. Named to National Baseball Hall of Fame.
Last Words: "The Judge is doing all right." His instruction to his nurses about what they were to say if anyone asked about his condition.
Source: *Judge Landis and Twenty-five Years of Baseball* by J.G. Taylor Spink (New York, 1947).

Landon, Michael

(1936-1991) American actor. Star of television and screen. Birth name Eugene Maurice Orowitz. Starred in TV series *Bonanza; Little House on the Prairie; Highway to Heaven*. Nominated for Golden Globe in 1979. Died at age 54 of cancer in Malibu, California.
Last Words: "You're right. It's time. I love you all." Spoken to his son who told him it was time to move on.
Source: *I Promised My Dad: An Intimate Portrait of Michael Landon* by Cheryl Landon Wilson (New York, 1992). The author was his daughter.

Landru, Henri-Désiré

(1869-1922) French murderer. Serial killer. Known as the French Bluebeard. Made a living selling magic skulls. Sent to the guillotine for murdering 10 women and the son of one of his victims. Inspired the character of Monsieur Verdoux in the movie *Monsieur Verdoux*.

Different Last Words:

(1) "I am very sorry, but I must not keep these gentlemen waiting." Spoken to the prison chaplain when the executioners came for him.

Source: *Secrets of the Sûreté: The Memoirs of Commissioner Jean Belin* by Jean Belin (New York, 1950).

(2) "Eh bien, it is not the first time that an innocent man has been condemned."

Source: *Murder Cases of the Twentieth Century: Biographies and Bibliographies of 280 Convicted or Accused Killers* by David K. Frasier (Jefferson, NC, 1996).

Lane, Franklin Knight

(1864-1921) Canadian-born American lawyer. Democratic politician from California. Member U.S. Interstate Commerce Commission. U.S. Secretary of the Interior. Died at age 56 in Rochester, Minnesota, soon after heart surgery.

Last Words (written): "But for my heart's content in that new land, I think I'd rather loaf with Lincoln along a river bank. I know I could understand him, I would not have to learn who were his enemies, what theories he was committed to, and what against. We could just talk and open out our minds, and tell our doubts and swap the longings of our hearts that others never heard of. He wouldn't try to master me nor to make me feel how small I was. I'd dare to ask him things and know that he felt awkward about them too. And I know I would find, I know I would, that he had hit his shin on those very stumps that had hit me. We'd talk of men a lot, the kind they call the great. I would not find him scornful. Yet boys that he knew in New Salem would somehow appear larger in their souls, than some of these that I called the great. His wise eyes saw qualities that weighed more than smartness. Yes, we would sit down where the bank sloped gently to the great stream and glance at the picture of our people, the Negroes being lynched, the miners' civil war, labor's hold ups, employers' ruthlessness, the subordination of humanity to industry." Written in a manuscript fragment.

Source: *The Letters of Franklin K. Lane, Personal and Political* by Franklin Knight Lane, ed. by Anne Wintermute Lane and Louise Herrick Wall (Boston, 1922). Anne Wintermute Lane was his wife.

Lane, Joseph or John Kendall or Thomas

(1838?-1863) English-born American sailor. Union soldier in U.S. Civil War. Member 3rd New Hampshire Volunteers. Executed on Morris Island, South Carolina, for attempted desertion. Little is known about him except that he was born in England, came from a respectable family, deserted the British navy, took his mother's maiden name Thomas to avoid detection and was about 25 years old. He affirmed that although he enlisted as John Kendall, his real name was Joseph Lane.

Last Words: "I die an Englishman."

Source: "Department of the South: Execution of Joseph Lane, alias John Kendall, alias Thomas, for Desertion, on Morris Island, S.C." (*New York Times,* December 27, 1863).

Langtry, Lillie

(1853-1929) British actress. Birth name Emilie Charlotte Le Breton. Married Edward Langtry. After he died, she married Hugo de Bathe. Known as The Jersey Lily. Judge Roy Bean of Texas admired her so much he changed the name of his town to Langtry and his bar and sometimes courthouse became the Jersey Lily Saloon. She had a close friendship with British Prince of Wales (later King Edward VII). Financially well off in later years. Owned successful race horses. Died at age 75 in Monte Carlo, Monaco.

Last Words: "I know I'm at the end. I shall never get better, dear."

Source: *Lillie Langtry: Manners, Masks and Morals* by Laura Beatty (London, 1999).

Lanier, Sidney

(1842-1881) American poet, soldier, musician, flutist. Played with Peabody Symphony Orchestra, Baltimore. Confederate soldier and prisoner of war in U.S. Civil War. Conducted a series of lectures at universities. Notable poems: "The Marshes of Glynn"; "Corn"; "The Song of the Chattahoochee." Died at age 39 of tuberculosis at his family's home in Lynn, North Carolina.

Last Words: "I can't." His response when he was offered a sip of cordial.

Source: *Sidney Lanier: A Biographical and Critical Study* by Aubrey Harrison Starke (Chapel Hill, NC, 1933).

Lannes, Jean, Duc de Montebello

(1769-1809) French nobleman, military officer. Fought in Revolutionary and Napoleonic armies. Was created marshal of France in 1804. Struck by cannon and lost both legs at the Battle of Aspern-Essling. Napoleon held Lannes in high regard and when he learned the duke was dying, he went to his litter to see him. He asked Lannes if he knew the general.

Last Words: "I am dying for you, like so many others. You will not mourn my loss any more than the rest. Make peace before it is your turn." Spoken to Napoleon. Eyewitness report of Cadet Gassicourt who attended Lannes.

Source: *A History of the Nineteenth Century Year by Year* by Edwin Emerson Jr. (New York, 1902).

Variation: "I am dying for you and my country. Do not mourn my loss. May you live and save the army." Spoken to Napoleon. Account of General Petit.

Source: *A History of the Nineteenth Century Year by Year* by Edwin Emerson Jr. (New York, 1902).

Lansky, Meyer

(1902-1983) Russian-born American criminal. Birth name Majer Suchowlinski. Helped develop organized crime in U.S. Friend of Lucky Luciano and Bugsy Siegel. Died at age 81 of lung cancer in Miami Beach, Florida. Several movies, novels and TV dramas have characters based on Lansky, including *Bugsy; The Godfather Part II; Lansky; The Gangster Chronicles* and *The Lost City.*

Last Words: "Let me go!" Cried out to his wife. He then fell into a deep sleep and never woke up.

Source: *The Little Man: Meyer Lansky and the Gangster Life* by Robert Lacey (Boston, 1991).

Lanza, Mario

(1921-1959) American operatic singer, screen star. One of the world's great tenors. Birth name Alfredo Arnold Cocozza. Made many top recordings. Notable movies: *The Great Caruso; The Toast of New Orleans; Because You're Mine; That Midnight Kiss.* Died at age 38 of a heart attack in Rome.

Different Last Words:

(1) "I love you Betty—Betty." Spoken to his wife on the telephone. He died after talking with her.

Source: *The Mario Lanza Story* by Constantine Callincos and Ray Robinson (New York, 1960).

(2) "Go to the house. Don't let anyone know what you're up to. Bring me something to wear and let's get the hell out of here before they kill me with all these injections." Spoken to his chauffer as he made the decision to leave a weight-loss clinic in Rome. He died a short time later.

Source: *Lanza; His Tragic Life* by Raymond Strait and Terry Robinson (Englewood Cliffs, NJ, 1980).

Laplace, Pierre Simon, Marquis de

(1749-1827) French astronomer, mathematician, writer. Known as the French Newton. Notable work: *Mécanique Céleste* (5-vol. study on celestial mechanics that summarized and extended the work of his predecessors, including Sir Isaac Newton). Named marquis in 1817. Died at age 77 in Paris. Laplace transform, Laplace's equation, Laplace theorem and Laplacian differential operator were named for him.

Different Last Words:

(1) (doubtful): "What we know is of small amount; what we do not know is enormous." Variation: "The knowledge we have of things is small indeed while that of which we are still ignorant is immense."

Source: Various Last Words compilations and Internet websites.

LaPlace may have spoken these words, but they were not the last he spoke. Most likely the following actually were his Last Words:

(2) "Man follows only phantoms." His response when told on his deathbed that his theoretical discoveries on satellites of Jupiter had been verified. He spoke these words to his favorite pupil, M. Poisson, who had been asked by his family to try to get Laplace to speak. After making this comment, Laplace never spoke again and died soon afterward.

Source: *The Budget of Paradoxes* by Augustus DeMorgan, ed. by Sophie DeMorgan (London, 1872) reprinted as "Assorted Paradoxes" in *The World of Mathematics,* Vol. IV (New York, 1956).

Larcom, Lucy

(1824-1893) American educator, writer, poet, editor. Collaborated with Whittier on editing anthologies. Notable work: *A New England Girlhood.* Died at age 69 in Boston. Larcom Mountain is named for her.

Last Word: "Freedom."

Source: *Lucy Larcom: Life, Letters, and Diary,* ed. by Daniel Dulany Addison (Boston, 1894).

Larkin, Michael, see Manchester Martyrs.

Larkin, Philip Arthur

(1922-1985) English librarian, poet, novelist, jazz critic. Spent much of his working life as librarian at University of Hull. Was offered poet laureateship following death of John Betjeman but declined post. Notable poems: "The Whitsun Wedding"; "An Arundel Tomb"; "This Be the Verse." Died at age 63 of cancer of esophagus. In 2003, the BBC aired *Love Again,* a play about the last 30 years of Larkin's life.

Last Words: "I am going to the inevitable." Spoken on his deathbed to his nurse.

Source: "Easter 2003: A Time When Larkin Comes into His Own" by Duke Maskell (*Words in Edgeways*, No. 1, 2003).

La Rochefoucauld, Madame de, Duchess of Doudeauville

(1764-1849) French noblewoman. Full name Bénigne Augustine Françoise Tellier de Louvois de Montmirail de la Rochefoucauld, Duchess of Doudeauville. Founder of Society of Nazareth. Married Viscount Ambroise-Polycarpe of Rochefoucauld who had been named Duke of Doudeauville by Louis XVIII in 1817.

Last Words: "Yes!" Her response to the question: "Do you love the good God?"

Source: *Life of Madame de La Rochefoucauld: Duchess of Doudeauville, Founder of the Society of Nazareth,* tr. from the French by Mrs. Cashel Hoey (Boston, 1878).

La Salle, Saint Jean Baptiste de

(1651-1719) French clergyman. educator, holy man. Educational reformer. Founder of Institute of the Brothers of the Christian Schools (Christian Brothers). Died at age 67 in Rouen. Canonized in 1900.

Last Words: "Yes. I adore in all things the designs of God in my regard." His response when asked if he accepted his sufferings with joy.

Source: *Blessed J.B. de la Salle, Founder of the Institute of the Brothers of the Christian Schools* by Armand Ravelet (Paris, 1890). French version was published in 1888.

Variation: "In all things I adore the will of God in my regard." His response to a question asked by Brother Bartholomew.

Source: *The Story of John Baptist de la Salle: Founder of the Institute of the Brothers of the Christian Schools* by Francis Meehan (New York, 1921).

Laski, Harold Joseph

(1893-1950) British political theorist, economist, writer, educator. Member of Fabian Society, Labour Party. Taught political science at London School of Economics. Strong proponent of Marxism. Notable work: *Reflections on the Revolution of Our Time.* Died at age 56 in London.

Last Words: "Isn't this incredible." Spoken to his wife. He developed a lung infection that killed him after a short illness.

Source: *Harold Laski: A Life on the Left* by Isaac Kramnick and Barry Sheerman (New York, 1993).

Latimer, Hugh

(1485?-1555) English prelate, martyr. Bishop of Worcester. Resigned as bishop when King Henry VIII refused to allow Protestant reforms Latimer sought. Arrested and taken to Oxford along with Thomas Cranmer and Nicholas Ridley, where they were tried, condemned to death and executed by burning at the stake.

Different Last Words:

(1) "Be of good comfort, Master Ridley, and play the man; we shall this day light such a candle by God's grace in England as I trust shall never be put out." Spoken to his companion Bishop Nicholas Ridley, who was at the next pyre.

Source: *Book of Martyrs and the Acts and Monuments of the Church* by John Fox (or Foxe). First published 1563, ed. by John Cumming (London, 1851).

(2) "In manua tuas, Domine, commendo spiritum meum; Domine, recipe spiritum meum." He then cried out in English as the flames leaped up toward his face: "Lord, Lord, receive my spirit; O Father of Heaven, receive my soul."

Source: *A Select History of the Lives and Sufferings of the Principal English Protestant Martyrs: Chiefly of Those Executed in the Bloody Reign of Queen Mary. Carefully Extracted from Fox, and Other Writers: Being Designed as a Cheap and Useful Book for Protestant Families of All Denominations. Adorned with Copper-plates, Showing the Different Kinds of Cruelties that were Exercised upon Them* by T. Gardner (London, 1746).

Latrobe, John Hazlehurst Boneval

(1803-1891) American lawyer, philanthropist, artist, writer, inventor. Son of prominent American architect Benjamin Henry Latrobe. Founded Maryland State Colonization Society. President of American Colonization Society. Active in the founding of the Republic of Liberia. Invented a stove that has his name. Died at age 88 in Baltimore.

Last Words: "The machine is worn out."

Source: *John H.B. Latrobe and His Times, 1803-1891* by John Edward Semmes (Baltimore, MD, 1917).

Laud, William

(1573-1645) English prelate, martyr. Archbishop of Canterbury during reign of Charles I. Found guilty of trying to subvert laws, overthrow Protestant religion and act as an enemy to Parliament. Judges used unconstitutional ordinance of attainder to condemn him to death by beheading.

Last Words: "Lord, I am coming as fast as I can. I know I must pass through the shadow of death before I can come to Thee. But it is but umbra mortis, a mere shadow of death, a little darkness upon nature. But Thou by Thy merits and passion hast broken though the jaws of death. So, Lord, receive my soul and have mercy upon me and bless this kingdom with peace and plenty and with brotherly love and charity, that there may not be this effusion of Christian blood among them, for Jesus Christ, His sake, if it be Thy will. Amen." Spoken just before he was executed.

Source: *Laud, Storm Center of Stuart England* by Robert P. Tristram Coffin (New York, 1930).

Laughton, Charles

(1899-1962) English-born American actor, director, writer. Stage and screen star. Nominated for three Academy Awards; won for *The Private Life of Henry VIII*. Died at age 63 of cancer in Hollywood, California.

Last Words: "Am I dying? What's the matter? Am I dying?"

Source: *Charles Laughton: A Difficult Actor* by Simon Callow (London, 1987).

Laurel, Stan

(1890-1965) English-born American actor, comedian. Star of stage and screen. Birth name Arthur Stanley Jefferson. Half of famous comedy duo Laurel and Hardy, whose careers lasted from silent movies until the early 1950s. Died at age 74 in Santa Monica, California.

Last Words: "No, but better be doing that than having those needles stuck into me." His response when a nurse asked if he was a skier (as she stuck him with a needle). When the nurse looked in on him a short time later, he was dead.

Source: *Stan: The Life of Stan Laurel* by Fred Lawrence Guiles (New York, 1980).

Laurier, Sir Wilfrid

(1841-1919) Canadian statesman, politician. Member Quebec legislature, Dominion House of Commons. First French-Canadian prime minister of Canada. Promoted development of western Canada. Knighted in 1897. Died at age 77 of a stroke in Ottawa. Wilfrid Laurier University is named for him.

Last Words: "It is finished."

Source: *Day of Sir Wilfrid Laurier: A Chronicle of Our Own Times* by Oscar D. Skelton (New York, 1922).

Laval, Pierre

(1883-1945) French statesman, lawyer, politician. Prime minister of France. Premier of Vichy government during World War II. Pursued policy of collaboration with Nazi Germany. Tried, convicted, executed before a firing squad for high treason and complicity with the enemy. Died at age 62 in Paris.

Last Words: "Vive la France!" (tr. "Long live France!")

Source: "Laval is Executed as Suicide Effort in Cell is Balked" by Lansing Warren (*New York Times*, October 16, 1945).

Laverock or Laverick, Hugh

(1488?-1556) English artist, martyr. Sentenced to be burned at the stake during the Puritan persecutions in the reign of Mary. Executed by burning when he was age 68 and disabled.

Last Words: "Be of good comfort, my brother; for my lord of London is our good physician. He will heal us both shortly; thee of thy blindness and me of my lameness." Spoken to his fellow martyr, John Apprice (or Apice) as he tossed away his crutch and was consumed by flames.

Source: *Book of Martyrs and the Acts and Monuments of the Church* by John Fox (or Foxe). First published 1563, ed. by John Cumming (London, 1851).

Lawless, Valentine Brown, 2nd Lord Cloncurry

(1773-1853) Irish nobleman, politician, landowner. Agitator involved in rebellions to establish an independent republic in Ireland. Died at age 80.

Last Words: "Ah, LeClerc, the closing scene!" Spoken to his physician.

Source: *Life, Times and Contemporaries of Lord Cloncurry* by William John Fitzpatrick (Dublin, Ireland, 1855).

Lawrence or Laurentius, Saint

(d. 258) Roman holy man, martyr. Deacon of Rome. Died during the persecutions of Emperor Valerian. Burned to death on a gridiron.

Last Words: "This side is now roasted enough, turn up, O tyrant great; assay whether roasted or raw thou thinkest the better meat."

Source: *Book of Martyrs and the Acts and Monuments of the Church* by John Fox (or Foxe). First published 1563, ed. by John Cumming (London, 1851).

Variation: "Assatus est; jam versa et manduca." (tr. "I am roasted—now turn me, and eat me.")

Source: *The Last Words (Real and Traditional) of Distinguished Men and Women Collected from Various Sources* by Frederic Rowland Marvin (New York, 1901). Marvin noted that according to some authorities Lawrence later said: "I thank thee O my God and Savior that I have been found worthy to enter into thy beatitude."

Variation: "Seest thou not, O thou foolish man, that I am already roasted on one side, and that, if thou wouldst have me well cooked, it is time to turn me on the other? I thank thee O my God and Savior that I have been found worthy to enter into thy beatitude."

Source: *Sacred and Legendary Art*, Vol. II, by Mrs. Jameson [Anna Brownell Jameson] (London, 1857).

Lawrence, David Herbert ("D.H.")

(1885-1930) British essayist, poet, novelist, short-story writer. Notable works: *Sons and Lovers; Lady Chatterley's Lover.* Suffered from malaria and tuberculosis. Died at age 44 in Vence, France.

Last Words: "I am better now. If I could only sweat I would be better. I am better now."

Source: *The Intelligent Heart: The Story of D.H. Lawrence* by Harry Thornton Moore (New York, 1954).

Lawrence, Ernest Orlando

(1901-1958) American physicist. Invented cyclotron (atom smasher) that produced uranium-235 and plutonium for the first atomic bomb. Won Nobel Prize for Physics in 1939 and Enrico Fermi Award in 1957. Became ill at a conference in Europe. Flown home. Died at age 57 in Palo Alto, California, after surgery. Ran Lab at University of California later renamed Lawrence Berkeley Laboratory for him.

Last Words: "I'm ready to give up now, Molly, I can't make it." Molly was his wife.

Source: *An American Genius: The Life of Ernest Orlando Lawrence* by Herbert Childs (New York, 1968).

Lawrence, Gertrude

(1901-1952) English actress. Birth name Gertrud Alexandra Dagmar Klasen. Appeared in Broadway dramas and musicals such as *Private Lives; Tonight at 8:30; Lady in the Dark.* Made her final appearance on Broadway in 1952 in Rogers and Hammerstein's *The King and I* with Yul Brynner. She became ill during a performance. Died at age 54 from cancer in New York City.

Last Words: "About the play—see that Connie Carpenter steps in. She has waited so long for her chance. See that she gets the role. And see that Yul gets star billing. He has earned it."

Source: *Gertrude Lawrence as Mrs. A: An Intimate Biography of the Great Star* by Richard Stoddard Aldrich (New York, 1954). The author was her husband.

Lawrence, James

(1781-1813) American military officer. Commanded U.S. frigate *Chesapeake* in naval battle with British ship HMS *Shannon* during War of 1812. *Chesapeake* was captured and taken to Canada by the British. Lawrence was mortally wounded. As he was carried below deck he gave his final command.

Last Words: "Tell the men to fire faster and not to give up the ship; fight her till she sinks." His Last Words are often shortened to "Don't give up the ship." The phrase was made the motto of the U.S. Navy.

Source: *Military and Naval Quotations* by Robert Debs Heinl (Annapolis, MD, 1967).

Variation: "Don't give up the ship. Blow her up."

Source: *James Lawrence Captain, United States Navy Commander of the "Chesapeake"* by Albert Gleaves (New York, 1904).

It is possible that these were not Lawrence's words but those of someone reporting the battle.

Sources: *Macmillan Book of Proverbs, Maxims, and Famous Phrases,* ed. by Burton Stevenson (New York, 1965); *Facts and Fancies for the Curious* by Charles Carroll Bombaugh (Philadelphia, 1905).

Lawrence, Thomas Edward ("T.E.")

(1888-1935) British soldier, adventurer, writer. Known as Lawrence of Arabia. Legally changed his surname to Shaw in 1927. Led Arab revolt against the Turks. Notable work: *The Seven Pillars of Wisdom* (account of his adventures). Killed at age 46 in a motorcycle accident. His story provided the basis for the 1962 movie *Lawrence of Arabia.*

Last Words (written): "Lunch Tuesday wet fine Cottage one mile north Bovington Camp. [signed] Shaw." Telegram sent to author Henry Williamson the morning of Lawrence's accident: The message meant Williamson was to come for lunch even if the weather was wet.

Source: *The Letters of T.E Lawrence,* ed. by David Garnett (London, 1938).

Lear, Edward

(1812-1888) English artist, illustrator, writer, poet. Landscape painter. Author of nonsensical poetry, songs and stories. Coined many nonsense words. Popularized the limerick. Notable works: "The Owl and the Pussy-Cat"; "The Jumblies." Had severe epilepsy. Died at age 76 at his home in San Remo, Italy.

Last Words: "My good Giuseppe, I feel that I am dying. You will render me a sacred service in telling my friends and relations that my last thought was for them, especially the Judge and Lord Northbrook and Lord Carlingford. I cannot find words sufficient to thank my good friends for the good they have always done me. I did not answer their letters because I could not write, as no sooner did I take a pen in my hand than I felt as if I were dying." Spoken to his servant.

Source: *Edward Lear: Landscape Painter and Nonsense Poet (1812-1888)* by Angus Davidson (London, 1938).

Leary, Timothy Francis

(1920-1996) American psychologist, writer, drug advocate, educator. Fired from Harvard after supplying students with drugs. Advocated widespread use of LSD and urged American youth to "Turn on, tune in, and drop out." In later years, he designed software and extolled the virtues of personal computers. He planned to die online, but instead died in his sleep at age 75 in Beverly Hills, California. Last Words were reported to the media by his son, Zachary. Leary's death was videotaped at his request, capturing his Last Words forever. On February 9, 1997, some of Leary's cremated remains were launched into space.

Last Words: "Why? Why not? Why not? Why not? Why not? Why not?" and later, "Beautiful." Variation frequently shortened to: "Yeah.–Why not?" (Sometimes reported in reverse order: "Why not? Yeah.")

Sources: "Timothy Leary, Pied Piper of Psychedelic 60's, Dies at 75" (*New York Times*, June 1, 1996); "Leary 'Tunes in' to Hereafter—Counterculture Guru Dead at 75" (CNN, May 31, 1996).

Le Clerc du Tremblay, François

(1577-1638) French prelate. Capuchin monk. Known as Father Joseph. Adviser to Richelieu who entrusted him with important diplomatic missions. Called "Grey eminence" from the color of his clerical robes in contrast to Richelieu's red garments. Died at age 61, shortly before he was to be elevated to cardinal.

Last Words: "Render an account, render an account!"

Source: *Grey Eminence* by Aldous Huxley (New York, 1941).

Lecouvreur, Adrienne

(1692-1730) French actress. One-time mistress of Count Maurice de Saxe. Died mysteriously at age 37 in Paris. A rumor circulated that she had been poisoned by her rival, the Duchess of Bouillon. The Roman Catholic Church refused to allow her to have a Christian burial; Voltaire wrote a poem about it: "On the Death of Adrienne Lecouvreur, a Celebrated Actress." Her story also became the plot for a drama by Eugene Scribe and Ernest Legouvé (1849) and an opera by Francesco Cilea (1902).

Last Words: "There is my universe, my hope, my deity." Spoken as she pointed to the bust of the Count de Saxe when a priest asked her to repent.
Source: *The Love Life of Adrienne Lecouvreur* by Cécile Sorel (Paris, 1925).

Ledbetter, Huddie William ("Leadbelly")

(1888-1949) American composer, singer, musician. Folk and blues guitarist. Diagnosed with amyotrophic lateral sclerosis (ALS; Lou Gehrig's disease) in 1949. Died at age 61 later that year in a New York hospital .
Last Words: "Doctor, if I put this here guitar down now, I ain't never gonna wake up." Spoken to the doctor who told him to put down his guitar and get some sleep.
Source: *The Midnight Special: The Legend of Leadbelly* by Richard M. Garvin and Edmond G. Addeo (New York, 1971).
Variation: "You put me in that bed and I'll never get out." Spoken to a physician who moved him to the bed anyway, thinking he was just depressed. He had been sitting in a wheelchair to help his breathing.
Source: *The Life and Legend of Leadbelly* by Charles Wolfe and Kip Lornell (New York, 1992).

Ledyard, William

(1738-1781) American military officer in American Revolution. Colonel of Connecticut militia. At the fall of Fort Griswold, British officer Major Bromfield asked who was in command. Ledyard replied that he was and then presented his sword. He was immediately run through with it and killed at age 42 by Bromfield. A massacre ensued and about a hundred men were killed or wounded.
Last Words: "I did command it, but you do now."
Source: *Philip Freneau: The Poet of the Revolution: A History of His Life and Times* by Mary Stanislas Austin (New York, 1901).

Lee, Charles

(1731-1782) British-born American military officer. Virginia planter. Major general of Continental Army in the American Revolution. Court-martialed, found guilty of disobedience, misbehavior for his action at the Battle of Monmouth. Suspended from com-

mand for a year. Discharged from the army. Died at age 50 of pneumonia in Philadelphia. Fort Lee, New Jersey, was named for him.
Last Words: "Stand by me, my brave grenadiers." Spoken while he was delirious.
Source: *General Charles Lee: Traitor or Patriot?* by John Richard Alden (Baton Rouge, LA, 1951).

Lee, Gideon

(1778-1841) American politician, merchant. Worked in leather trade. Mayor of New York. Member New York Assembly and U.S. Congress from New York. Died at age 63 in Geneva, New York.
Last Words: "I should like to stay with you a little longer to finish some work begun; but if it is the pleasure of God that I should die now, I am ready to go."
Source: *Lives of American Merchants,* Vol. I, by Freeman Hunt (New York, 1858).

Lee, Gypsy Rose

(1911-1970) American burlesque entertainer, actress, writer. Birth name Rose Louise Hovick. Notable work: *Gypsy: Memoir of America's Most Celebrated Stripper* (best-selling book that inspired *Gypsy,* the Broadway musical and popular movie). Hosted TV talk show. Died at age 59 of lung cancer in Los Angeles.
Last Words: "What do you mean?" Her response to her son who told her: "It'll be over soon."
Source: *My G-String Mother: At Home and Backstage with Gypsy Rose Lee* by Erik Lee Preminger (Boston, 1984). The author was her son.

Lee, Jesse

(1758-1816) American clergyman, writer. Methodist preacher. Chaplain of U.S. House of Representatives. Notable work: *History of Methodism in America.* Died at age 58 when a leg injury became inflamed and he developed a fever.
Last Words: "Glory! Glory! Glory! Hallelujah! Jesus reigns! Heaven is just before me!"
Source: *Reminiscences, Historical and Biographical, of Sixty-four Years in the Ministry* by Henry Boehm and J.B. Wakeley (New York, 1866).

Lee, John Doyle

(1812-1877) American clergyman, convicted murderer. Prominent early member of the Church of Jesus Christ of Latter-Day Saints (Mormons); member of the Council of 50. In 1857, Lee was involved in the massacre of the Fancher party, emigrants from Arkansas, while they were camped at Mountain Meadows, Utah. Lee convinced the Fancher party to hand over their property to the Mormons in return for safe passage to Cedar City. However, the group of Mormon militiamen with him—dressed as Native Americans—killed approximately 120 of the Fancher party, sparing only about 17 small children. In 1877, when Lee was brought to trial for his part in the massacre, he declared his innocence. He was convicted by an all-Mormon jury and executed by firing squad at age of 64 at Mountain Meadow, Utah. In 1961, his case was reconsidered and the LDS posthumously reinstated Lee's membership in the church.

Last Words (spoken): "Center my heart, boys. Don't mangle my body." Spoken to his executioners. Last lines of a long speech.

Source: *The Mountain Meadows Massacre* by Juanita Brooks (Norman, OK, 1992).

Last Words (written): "I hope to meet the bullets with manly courage. I declare my innocence. I have done nothing wrong. I have a reward in Heaven, and my conscience does not accuse me. This to me is a consolation. I place more value upon it than I would upon an eulogy without merit. If my work be finished on earth, I ask God in Heaven, in the name of His Son Jesus Christ to receive my spirit, and allow me to meet my loved ones who have gone behind the veil. The bride of my youth and her faithful mother; my devoted friend and companion, N.A.; my dearly beloved children, with whom I parted in sorrow, but shall meet in joy; I bid you farewell. Be true to each other. Live faithful before God, that we may meet in the mansion that God has prepared for His servants. Remember the last words of your most true friend on earth, and let them sink into your aching hearts. I leave my blessing with you. Farewell. John Doyle Lee." Written in a letter.

Source: *Mormon Menace Being the Confession of John Doyle Lee, Danite, an Official Assassin of the Mormon Church Under the Late Brigham Young* by John Doyle Lee (New York, 1905).

Lee, Robert Edward

(1807-1870) American military officer, educator. Son of Light Horse Harry Lee. Commander of Confederate Army in U.S. Civil War. Surrendered to Grant at Appomattox in 1865, ending war. Spent final days as president of Washington College (now Washington and Lee University). Suffered a stroke in October 1870. Died at age 63, two weeks later in Lexington, Virginia.

Last Words (doubtful): "Tell Hill he must come up. Strike the tent!"

Source: Various Last Words compilations and Internet websites.

Emory M. Thomas, Lee's biographer, said Lee was comatose before he died and said simply "I will give that sum."

Source: *Robert E. Lee: A Biography* by Emory M. Thomas (New York, 1995).

Leeuwenhoek, Anton van

(1632-1723) Dutch biologist, microscopist. Known as the Father of Microbiology. Fellow of the Royal Society. First person to describe red blood cells and spermatozoa of dogs, rabbits, fish, as well as humans and several other animals. First to see one-celled bacteria and protozoa. Died at age 90 in Delft, the Netherlands.

Last Words: "Hoogvliet, my friend, be so good as to have those two letters on the table translated into Latin. Send them to London to the Royal Society."

Source: *Microbe Hunters* by Paul de Kruif (New York, 1926).

Lefebure, Eugene

(1878-1909) French pilot, stunt man. Often considered the first real aerial stunt man. First pilot to die at the controls of his craft. He was piloting a French-made Wright Flyer when the controls jammed. He crashed at Juvisy, France.

Last Words: "Yes, I will succeed and I'll make some money, unless I break my neck." Spoken just before he departed on his fatal flight.

Source: *Slipping the Surly Bonds: Great Quotations on Flight* compiled by David English (New York, 1998), citing *Le Petit Parisien*, September 9, 1909.

Leger, Saint

(615-678) French prelate, holy man, martyr. Known also as Leodegarius. Christian

Bishop of Autun. Wrongly accused of murder of Childeric. Arrested, imprisoned, tortured and executed.

Last Words: "There is no need to weary yourselves longer, brothers! Do here the bidding of him that sent you!" Spoken as swordsmen led him to his execution.

Source: *The Golden Legend or Lives of the Saints.* Compiled by Jacobus de Voragine, Archbishop of Genoa, 1275, 1ˢᵗ ed., 1470. English ed. by William Caxton, 1483, ed. by F.S. Ellis (Edinburgh, 1900).

Lehár, Franz

(1870-1948) Hungarian-born Austrian musician, composer, conductor. Composer of operas, operettas, symphonic poems. Notable works: *The Merry Widow; The Count of Luxembourg.* Died at age 78 at Bad Ischl, Austria.

Last Words: "Now I have finished with all earthly business, and high time, too.—Yes, yes, my dear child, now comes death." Spoken to his housekeeper.

Source: *Franz Lehar, Seine Musik, Sein Leben* by Maria von Peteani (Vienna, Austria, 1950).

Leibniz, Gottfried Wilhelm von

(1646-1716) German philosopher, mathematician. Anglicized spelling: Godfrey William Leibnitz. Invented system of differential calculus that was clouded by controversy created by Isaac Newton's claims of discovery. Pioneer of symbolic logic. Died at age 70 in Hanover of complications of arthritis and gout.

Last Words: "Also are other men mortal." His response to his servant when reminded that he was hovering on the brink of eternity. Earlier, he declined partaking of the sacraments as he had done no wrong and had nothing to confess. He asked to be left in peace.

Source: "Godfrey William Leibniz," Part 3, by Sylvanus Urban (*The Gentleman's Magazine and Historical Review,* Vol. 192, September 1852). Urban gave as his source Eckhart, who was Leibniz's faithful secretary and the only mourner at his funeral.

Leichhardt, Friedrich Wilhelm Ludwig

(1813-1848?) Prussian explorer, naturalist. Studied rocks and wildlife in Australia. Tried to cross Australia from east to west but disappeared on the Coogoon River without a trace. The Australian municipality of Leichhardt was named for him.

Last Words (written): "The only serious accident that has happened was the loss of a spade, but we were fortunate enough to make it up on this station where the superintendent is going to spare us one of his. Though the days are still very hot, the beautiful clear nights are cool and benumb the mosquitoes, which have ceased to trouble us. Myriads of flies are the only annoyance we have. Seeing how much I have been favored in my present progress, I am full of hopes that our Almighty Protector will allow me to bring my darling scheme to a successful termination. Your most sincere friend, Ludwig Leichhardt." His last letter.

Source: *Travels with Dr. Leichhardt in Australia* by Donald Bunce and Ludwig Leichhardt (Melbourne, Australia, 1859).

Leighton, Frederick, 1ˢᵗ Baron Leighton of Stretton

(1830-1896) English painter, sculptor. President of the Royal Academy. Knighted in 1878. Created baronet and baron in 1886. Notable works: *And the Sea Gave Up the Dead Which Were In It; The Bath of Psyche.* Died at age 65 of angina in London, soon after he was made Lord Leighton of Stretton.

Last Words (doubtful): "My love to the Academy."

Source: Various Last Words compilations and Internet websites.

Leighton did speak these words just before he died, but they were not his last. He made the remark as he was dying after he signed his will leaving his entire estate to his sisters Alexandra and Augustine. His Last Words were spoken in German to his sisters and were meant only for their ears.

Source: *The Life, Letters and Works of Frederick Leighton,* Vol. 2, by Mrs. Russell Barrington (London, 1906).

Leisler, Jacob

(1640?-1691) German-born colonial American merchant. Military officer. Father-in-law of Jacob Milborne. Chief of New York City's militia. Given command of colony by New York General Assembly. Relinquished authority but Leisler and Milborne were tried and condemned for treason. Both were hanged and beheaded in New York City. Although Governor Sloughter believed the decision was unjust, he signed the death warrant while he was intoxicated. By the time he sobered up, the two men were dead.

Last Words (written): "All that for our dying comfort we can say concerning the point for which we are condemned, is to declare as our Last Words, before that God whom we hope before long to see, that our sole aim and object in the conduct of the government was to maintain the interest of our sovereign Lord and Lady and the reformed Protestant churches of these parts." Read on the scaffold.

Source: *The Dutch and Quaker Colonies in America* by John Fiske (Boston, 1902).

Last Words (spoken): "It is for the King and Queen I die, and the Protestant religion to which I was born and bred. I am ready. I am ready. Father, unto thy hands I recommend my soul." Spoken to the sheriff who asked if he would bless the King and Queen.

Source: *Genealogical Notes Relating to Lieut.-Gov. Jacob Leisler, and His Family Connections in New York* by Edwin Ruthven Purple (New York, 1877).

Lekeu, Guillaume

(1870-1894) Belgian musician, composer. Pupil of Franck and D'Indy. Died at age 24 of typhoid fever in Angers, Belgium.

Last Words: "So many works unfinished— my quartet!" The quartet and Lekeu's cello sonata were completed by D'Indy.

Source: *Great Composers 1300-1900* by David Ewen (New York, 1966).

Lenclos, Ninon de

(1620?-1705) French woman known for her beauty and wit. Birth name Anne de Lenclos. Her many lovers and friends included the Great Condé, La Rochefoucauld, Saint-Évremond, Madame de Lafayette, Christina of Sweden. Died about age 85.

Last Words (written): "Let no vain hope strike me at the core; I'm ripe for death— have business here no more."

Source: *Mémoires sur la vie de Mademoiselle de Lenclos [Et Lettres de Mademoiselle de Ninon de Lenclos au Marquis de Sévigné (par Louis Damours)]*, ed. by A Bret (Paris, 1756).

Lenin, Vladimir Ilych

(1870-1924) Russian revolutionary. Soviet leader. Communist leader of Russian Revolution. One of the founders of the Soviet Republic. Real surname Ulyanov. Died at age 53 in Gorki after a series of strokes that destroyed his faculties. Unable to utter more than a few one-syllable words after the stroke he had in 1923. City of Saint Petersburg was renamed Leningrad after he died. His embalmed body was placed in a mausoleum in Moscow's Red Square.

Last Words: "Vot sobaka." (tr. "Good dog.") Spoken to a dog that retrieved a bird. Lenin died from his final stroke soon afterward

Sources: *The Man Behind the Mask* by Ronald W. Clark (New York, 1988); *USSR: The Story of Soviet Russia* by Walter Duranty (Philadelphia, 1944).

Lennon, John Ono

(1940-1980) British musician, singer, songwriter, peace activist. One of the founders and primary songwriters of the Beatles. One of Rolling Stone's Immortals: the 50 Greatest Artists of All Time. Father of Julian Lennon and Sean Lennon. Added Ono to middle name to honor wife. Shot in the back and killed at age 40 at the entrance to his New York City apartment building by Mark David Chapman. Posthumously inducted into the Rock and Roll Hall of Fame.

Last Words "I'm shot. I'm shot." Uttered before he fell. He staggered a few yards and died soon afterward.

Source: *John Ono Lennon: Volume 2, 1967-1980* by Ray Coleman (London, 1984).

Leo X, Pope

(1475-1521) Italian prelate. Birth name Giovanni de Medici. Son of Lorenzo de Medici. Created cardinal in 1488 as a teenager. Reigned as pope 1513 to 1521. Failed to halt the Protestant Reformation that began in his reign with Luther's accusation of corruption within the Roman Catholic Church. Died at age 46 in Rome.

Different Last Words:

(1) "Jesus."

Source: *History of the Popes from the Close of the Middle Ages* by Ludwig Pastor (London, 1908).

(2) "Pray for me. I want to make you all happy."

Source: *White Robe, Black Robe, A Dual Biography of Pope Leo X and Martin Luther* by Charles L. Mee Jr. (New York, 1972).

(3) "I have been murdered; no remedy can

prevent my speedy death."

Source: *The Last Words (Real and Traditional) of Distinguished Men and Women Collected from Various Sources* by Frederic Rowland Marvin (New York, 1901). Marvin wrote that the circumstances surrounding Leo's death were "involved in mysterious and total obscurity." Subsequent accounts of his death by Varillas and similar writers were "the spurious offspring of their own imagination." Marvin used as his sources *The Life and Pontificate of Leo the Tenth* by William Roscoe (Liverpool, England, 1805) and *The Life of Michelangelo Buonarroti* by John Addington Symonds (London, 1893).

Leo XI, Pope

(1535-1605) Italian prelate. Birth name Alessandro Ottaviano de Medici. Bishop of Pistoja. Archbishop of Florence. Elevated to cardinal 1574. Became ill with fever and died after a pontificate of only 26 days.

Last Words: "Do not suggest to us any care for earthly interests. You must speak to us now only about eternal things." His response to his confessor who wanted him to name one of his nephews as cardinal. He refused.

Source: *The Lives of the Roman Pontiffs* by Alexis François Artaud de Montor (New York, 1897).

Leo XIII, Pope

(1810-1903) Italian prelate, writer, educator. Birth name Gioacchino Vincenzo Rafaello Luigi Pecci. Reigned for 25 years. Founded Catholic University, Washington, D.C. Notable encyclical: *Rerum novarum* (tr. *Of New Things;* it addressed the condition of the working classes). Author of several other encyclicals on marriage, education, Bible study, and more. Died at age 93.

Last Words: "Be this my last greeting." He blessed the several cardinals at his bedside and declared "This is the end." He then lapsed into a coma and died.

Source: *Life of Leo XIII from an Authentic Memoir Furnished by His Order* by Rt. Rev. Bernard O'Reilly, Domestic Prelate of the Papal Throne (London, 1903).

Leonardo da Vinci

(1452-1519) Italian artist, scientist, sculptor, architect, engineer. Notable works: *Mona Lisa; The Last Supper* (two of the world's most famous paintings). His many journals and notebooks provide insight into his scientific and engineering genius. He moved to France in 1516 as court painter to King Francis I. Died at age 67 in Chateau de Cloux, Amboise, France.

Last Words: "I have offended God and mankind because my work did not reach the quality it should have." Sometimes shown in third person reiteration of what a witness reported Leonardo said: "He offended God and mankind by not working harder at his art; as he should have done."

Sources: *Leonardo da Vinci* by Maurice Rowdon (Chicago, 1975); *Leonardo DaVinci: The Flights of the Mind* by Charles Nicholl (London, 2004).

Leopardi, Giacomo

(1798-1837) Italian writer, classical scholar, lyrical poet. Many of his works had a pessimistic quality. He had a cerebrospinal condition that afflicted him all his life. He felt his physical deformity left him unattractive. Also suffered from asthma and lost his sight in one eye. Died at age 38 at a friend's house in Naples.

Last Words: "I can't see you any more."

Source: *Leopardi: A Biography* by Iris Origo (London, 1935).

Leopold I, King of Belgium

(1790-1865) Belgian monarch. Son of Francis Duke of Saxe-Coburg Saalfeld. First king of independent Belgium. Ruled from 1831, when State of Belgium was established, until he died at age 74. Succeeded by his son Leopold II.

Different Last Words:

(1) "Don't leave me."

Source: *King Leopold I of the Belgians* by Dr. Egon Caesar Corti (London, 1923).

(2) "May God pardon all my sins." Spoken to his chaplain.

Source: *Leopold First, the Founder of Modern Belgium* by Louis, Comte de Lichtervelde (New York, 1930).

Leopold II, King of Belgium

(1835-1909) Belgian monarch. Succeeded father Leopold I to throne in 1865. Ruled till his death. Founder, sole owner of Congo Free State (Belgian Congo, Zaire, now the Democratic Republic of Congo). In his final days, he was concerned about a military threat from Germany. Died at age 74 in Laeken, Belgium. Succeeded by his nephew Albert I.

Different Last Words:

(1) "I am hot."

Source: *Leopold of the Belgians* by Louis, Comte de Lichtervelde (New York, 1929).

(2) "I am suffocating, doctor, I am suffocating!"

Source: *New York World*, December 17, 1909.

Lepelletier or Lepeletier de Saint-Fargeau, Louis Michel

(1760-1793) French politician, statesman. Member of States-General. President of the National Assembly. Member of the National Convention. Assassinated at age 32 in Palais Royal by a member of the king's bodyguard. Saint-Fargeau subway station on Paris Metro was named for him.

Last Words: "I am cold."

Source: *Nouvelle biographie générale depuis les temps les plus reculés jusqu'à nos jours, avec les renseignements bibliographiques et l'Indication des sources à consulter* by Jean Chrétien Ferdinand Hoefer (Paris, 1854).

Lépine, Marc

(1964-1989) Canadian murderer. Spree killer. Birth name Gamil Gharbi. Went on murdering spree at École Polytechnique de Montréal (engineering school at Université de Montréal), shooting 26 people, killing 14. All the victims were women.

Last Words: "Ah s**t." Spoken when someone set off the school fire alarm. He pointed his rifle at his head, and pulled the trigger.

Source: "The Montreal Massacre" (*The Guardian Unlimited*, September 15, 2006).

Lespinasse, Jeanne Julie Eleonore de

(1732–1776) French hostess known for her brilliant salon in Paris. Famous for her liaisons. Had emotional and physical collapse over her relationship with le Comte de Guibert. Died at age 44.

Last Words: "Am I still alive?"

Source: *A Star of the Salons* by Camilla Jebbs (London, 1908).

Lessing, Gotthold Ephraim

(1729-1781) German writer, librarian, dramatist, critic. Wrote on philosophy, aesthetics. Advocated religious tolerance. Regarded as one of the great intellectual lights of his era. His works brought German literature onto a world stage. Notable works: *Laocoön; An Essay on the Limits of Painting and Poetry; Minna von Barnheim, or, A Soldier's Fortune; Nathan the Wise*. His last

three years were saddened by the loss of his wife and son in childbirth. Died on his 52nd birthday in Brunswick, Germany.

Last Words: "Zwei und fünfzig." (tr. "Fifty-two.")

Source: *Lexikon der letzten Worte: letzte Botschaften berühmter Männer und Frauen von Konrad Adenauer bis Emiliano Zapata* by Werner Fuld (Munich, Germany, 2002).

Lewis, Clive Staples ("C.S.")

(1898-1963) Irish-born British writer, educator. Known familiarly as Jack. Professor at Magdalen College, Oxford. Professor at Cambridge University. Wrote many books on Christian apologetics, including *The Screwtape Letters*. In the 1950s, he gained international fame with his seven-part children's fantasy *The Chronicles of Narnia*. His relationship with poet Joy Gresham was the basis for part of the television drama (1985), stage play (1989) and movie *Shadowlands* (1993). Died at age 64 in Oxford.

Last Words (written): "Yes." Lewis's brother Warnie handled his correspondence. He jotted a note on a letter that had come for Jack: "Shall I tell him that your commercial acumen is a minus quantity?" Jack wrote "Yes" beside the question. It was the last word he wrote. He died that afternoon.

Source: *Sleuthing C.S. Lewis: More Light in the Shadowlands* by Kathryn Ann Lindskoog (Macon, GA, 2001).

Last Words (spoken): After lunch, Lewis fell asleep in a chair. His brother Warnie suggested he would be more comfortable in bed, so he went there. At 4 p.m., when Warnie took him tea, he found him drowsy but comfortable. The few words they spoke were Lewis's last. At 5:30 p.m., Warnie heard a crash and ran to the room to find him lying unconscious at the foot of his bed. He stopped breathing three or four minutes later.

Source: *Letters of C. S. Lewis (edited with a Memoir)* by W.H. Lewis. Revised and Enlarged Edition by Walter Hooper (Orlando, FL, 1993). The original edition of this book appeared as *Letters* in 1966.

Lewis, Ellis

(1798-1871) American lawyer, jurist, writer. Pennsylvania attorney general. Pennsylvania Supreme Court chief justice. Notable work: *The Romance of Matrimony: A Tale*

Founded on Fact. Died at age 72 in Philadelphia.

Last Words: "I believe I am dying now."

Source: *The Life of Chief Justice Ellis Lewis, 1798-1871: Of the First Elective Supreme Court of Pennsylvania* by Burton A. Konkle (Philadelphia, 1907).

Lewis, George

(1900-1968) American musician, clarinetist, band leader. Birth name George Louis François Zenon. One of the great New Orleans jazz clarinetists. Had a band for many years. Gained his greatest popularity in later years. Toured extensively. Notable recording: *Burgundy Street Blues.* Died at age 68 in New Orleans.

Last Words: "Departings are too hard. I'll be back after you."

Source: *George Lewis: A Jazzman from New Orleans* by Tom Bethell (Berkeley, CA, 1977).

Lewis, Helen Joy Davidman Gresham

(1915-1960) American writer, poet. Divorced from William Lindsay Gresham. Mother of David and Douglas. Second marriage was to C.S. Lewis. Their relationship was part of the basis for a television drama (1985), stage play (1989) and movie *Shadowlands* (1993). Died at age 45 of bone cancer.

Last Words: "Don't get me a posh coffin. Posh coffins are all rot." She then said to the chaplain: "I am at peace with God."

Source: *Jack: A Life of C.S. Lewis* by George Sayer and Lyle W. Dorsett (Wheaton, IL, 1994).

Lewis, Meriwether

(1774-1809) American statesman, politician, explorer. Secretary to Thomas Jefferson. Co-leader with William Clark of expedition to explore the Louisiana Purchase. First governor of Upper Louisiana. Was shot in the head and chest while staying at a tavern on the Natchez Trace en route to Washington, D.C. Died at age 35 of gunshot wounds. Some local people believed he was murdered in a botched robbery. Others believed the shooting was a suicide.

Last Words: "I am no coward. But I am so strong, so hard to die." He also begged a servant not to be afraid of him. He died about two hours later.

Source: "Meriwether Lewis Esq." (*The Ariel. A Literary Gazette*, Vol. 1, No. 1, May 5, 1827). This account

of Lewis's Last Words and death came from the first published description written by ornithologist Dr. Alexander Wilson. It was originally in an 1810 letter.

Lewis, Percy Wyndham

(1882-1957) Canadian-born British writer, essayist, artist. Co-founder of Vorticism art movement. Editor of Vorticism journal, *Blast.* Notable literary works: *Tarr; The Apes of God; The Human Age* (trilogy). A trained and accomplished artist, he had to give up painting in his late 60s when he began to lose his eyesight. Died at age 75 in London.

Last Words: "Mind your own business." Spoken on his deathbed to a nurse who asked about his bowels.

Source: *Critical Survey of Long Fiction* by Carl Rollyson (Englewood Cliffs, NJ, 2000).

Lewis, Sinclair

(1885-1951) American novelist, playwright, journalist, editor. Notable works: *Babbitt; Elmer Gantry; Dodsworth; Main Street.* Winner of 1926 Pulitzer Prize for Fiction but refused the prize. Won 1930 Nobel Prize for Literature. Died at age 65 of a heart attack in Rome.

Different Last Words:

(1) "I am happy. God bless you all." Spoken to the nun in attendance at the hospital.

Source: *Sinclair Lewis: An American Life* by Mark Schorer (New York, 1961).

(2) "Alec, I beg it of you, help me. I am dying." Spoken to his Italian secretary

Source: *Dictionary of Last Words* compiled by Edward S. Le Comte (New York, 1955). Reported to Le Comte by Mark Schorer who had an authorized biography in preparation. [*Sinclair Lewis: An American Life* by Mark Schorer (New York, 1961)].

Ley, Robert

(1890-1945) German Nazi physician, military officer, politician. Headed German Labor Front. Helped supervise recruitment of slave labor during World War II. Captured at end of war. Taken to Nuremberg for War Crimes trials. Committed suicide at age 55 by hanging in his cell before he was tried.

Last Words (written): "Farewell, I can't stand this shame any longer. Physically nothing is lacking; the food is good; it is warm in my cell; the Americans are correct and partially friendly. Spiritually, I have reading matter and write whatever I want. I

receive paper and pencil. They do care more for my health than is necessary, and I may smoke and receive tobacco and coffee. I may walk at least twenty minutes every day. Up to this point everything is in order, but the fact that I should be a criminal—that is what I can't stand." Suicide note.
Source: "Suicide Pact Implied" by Drew Middleton (*New York Times*, October 27, 1945).

Liaquat Ali Khan, Nawabzada

(1896-1951) Indian-born Pakistani politician. First prime minister of Pakistan. Assassinated in Rawalpindi, Pakistan, by Rafiq, member of Khaksars fanatical Muslim group calling for a jihad against India over Kashmir. Rafiq was killed by angry spectators who literally tore him apart.
Last Words: "There is no God but one, and Mohammed is His prophet." Liaquat's Last Words, a Moslem declaration of faith, were spoken in Arabic and heard by a photographer who stood nearby.
Source: "Fanatic Kills Liaquat Ali, Pakistan Chief" (*Chicago Tribune*, October 17, 1951).

Liberace, Walter Valentino

(1919-1987) American musician, pianist, entertainer, actor. Stage, screen and television star. Popular recording artist. Birth name Wladziu Valentino Liberace. Known for flamboyant costumes and theatrical performances. Had TV show in 1950s and 1960s. Made guest appearances on many other TV shows, including *Sesame Street* and *Batman*. Died at age 67 of complication of AIDS at his home in Palm Springs, California.
Last Words: "I wish I could. I'll just stay here and watch my shows." His response when asked if he wanted to go to church.
Source: *Liberace: The True Story* by Bob Thomas (New York, 1987).

Lieutaud, Joseph

(1703-1780) French physician. Physician to King Louis XV. Pioneer in pathological anatomy. Corrected many medical errors. Precisely described anatomy of the bladder. Notable work: *Précis de la medecine pratique* (classified diseases by the groups affected: men, women, children, etc.). Died at age 77 of pneumonia in Versailles. Lieu-

taud's triangle, Lieutaud's sinus, Lieutaud's uvula were named for him.
Last Words: "Ah, I shall die well enough without all that!" Spoken after his colleagues proposed different remedies.
Source: *Biographie universelle,* Book XXIV, by J. Fr. Michaud and Louis Gabriel Michaud (Paris, 1811-1862).

Lieven, Princess Dorothea von

(1785-1857) Russian noblewoman. Princess von Lieven. Birth name von Benkendorff. Wife of Russian ambassador to London. Maid of honor to Empress of Russia. Friends included Metternich, Wellington, Guizot. Kept a diary that has been published. Died at age 71 in Paris.
Last Words (written): "I thank you for twenty years of affection and happiness. Don't forget me. Good-bye, good-bye." Note to her friend François Guizot.
Source: *Portraits in Miniature and Other Essays* by Lytton Strachey (New York, 1931).

Ligne, Charles Joseph, Prince of

(1735-1814) Belgian-born Austrian soldier, military writer. Fought in Seven Years War. Corresponded with Frederick the Great, Voltaire, Goethe, Catherine II of Russia and other luminaries. Created field marshal. Died at age 79 in Vienna.
Different Last Words:
(1) "Advance! Long live Marie Theresa!"
Source: *The Prince of Ligne: A Gay Marshal of the Old Regime* by O.P. Gilbert, tr. by Joseph McCabe (London, 1923).
(2) "Close the doors! Away with it! There is the monster, the Grey Comrade."
Source: *Karl Josef Furst von Ligne: ein Genie des Lebens (1735-1814)* by Ernst Benedikt (Vienna, Austria, 1937).

Liguori, Saint Alphonsus Maria de

(1696-1787) Italian prelate, holy man, theologian, writer, lawyer. Abandoned legal career to enter seminary. Founded Congregation of the Most Holy Redeemer in 1732. Appointed Roman Catholic bishop of St. Agatha of the Goths near Naples in 1762. Died at age 90 in Pagani, Italy. Canonized in 1839. Declared Doctor of the Church in 1871.
Last Words: "Holy Mary, Mother of God pray for us sinners, now and at the hour of

our death. Amen." Prayed part of the *Hail Mary* or *Ave Maria* as he looked at a picture of the Virgin Mary.

Source: *The Life of St. Alphonsus Maria de Liguori, Bishop of St. Agatha of the Goths* by Antonio Maria Tannoja and Frederick William Faber (London, 1848-1849).

Lilienthal, Otto

(1848-1896) German pilot, aviation pioneer, engineer, mathematician. First person to make sustained repeatable flights. Suffered severe injuries when his glider stalled and went into a nosedive during a flight near Stollen, Germany. Died at age 48 of a broken spine in a Berlin hospital soon afterward.

Last Words (doubtful): "Opfer müssen gebracht werden!" (tr. "Sacrifices must be made!")

Source: Various Last Words compilations and Internet websites.

Lilienthal used this phrase often and it is the epitaph on his tombstone, but these were not his final words. A witness at his crash said he did not realize he was seriously injured and said the following:

Last Words: "Ich muss etwas ausruhen dann machen wir weiter." (tr. "I must rest a little, then we continue.")

Source: *Mechanics of Flight* by Warren G. Phillips (Hoboken, NJ, 2004).

Lili'uokalani, Lydia, Queen of the Hawaiian Islands

(1838-1917) Hawaiian monarch, songwriter. Last reigning royal ruler of Hawaii. Composed popular song "Aloha 'Oe" (tr. "Farewell to Thee"). Placed under house arrest at Iolani Palace in Honolulu for eight months in 1895 when her royalist supporters tried to revolt against the U.S.-established provisional government. Their revolt failed and she formally abdicated. Died at age 79 in Honolulu after she had a stroke.

Last Words: "Thank you. How are you?" Spoken to a friend.

Source: *Hawaiian Gazette,* November 12, 1917.

Lincoln, Abraham

(1809-1865) 16th President of the U.S. American lawyer, politician. Member Illinois State House of Representatives. Member U.S. House of Representatives from

Illinois. Held office as President during U.S. Civil War. Assassinated at age 56 by actor John Wilkes Booth at Ford's Theatre, Washington, D.C. while attending a performance of the play *Our American Cousin*.

Last Words: "She won't think anything about it." His response when his wife asked what Miss Harris—the woman sitting next to them in their box—would say if she saw them holding hands. Mrs. Lincoln repeated these Last Words to her friend Dr. Anson G. Henry five days later. He wrote a letter to his wife, mentioning what Mrs. Lincoln had told him.

Source: *The Real Abraham Lincoln* by Reinhard H. Luthin (Englewood Cliffs, NJ, 1960).

Lincoln, Nancy Hanks

(1784-1818) American mother of U.S President Abraham Lincoln. Became ill with milk sickness and died a few days later. The sickness came from drinking milk from cows affected with the "trembles" (poisoning caused by eating white snakeroot). When her aunt and uncle, Elizabeth and Thomas Sparrow, died of the disease and she began to show symptoms, she realized she too was dying.

Last Words: "I know you will be kind to your father." Spoken to her son Abraham.

Source: *Four Great Americans: Washington, Franklin, Webster, Lincoln* by James Baldwin (New York, 1897).

Variation: "I am going away from you, Abraham, and I shall not return. I know that you will be a good boy, that you will be kind to Sarah and to your father. I want you to live as I have taught you, and to love our Heavenly Father."

Source: *Lincoln's Youth: Indiana Years, 1816-1830* by Louis A. Warren (Indianapolis, IN, 1991).

Variation: "Be kind to each other and to your father and live as I have taught you."

Source: *The Raising of a President: The Mothers and Fathers of Our Nation's Leaders* by Doug Wead (New York, 2005).

Lind, Johanna Maria ("Jenny")

(1820-1887) Swedish singer. One of the world's great sopranos. Professional name after marriage: Madame Jenny Lind-Goldschmidt. Known as the Swedish Nightingale. Brought to America by P.T. Barnum to tour for two years. Settled in England.

Died at age 67 at her home, Malvern Hills.
Last Words: First bars of an old German song she loved: "An den Sonnenschein" ("Sunshine Song"). As she lay dying she sang when her daughter opened the shutters of her room to let in the sunlight.
Source: *Memoir of Madame Jenny Lind-Goldschmidt: Her Early Art-Life and Dramatic Career, 1820-1851* by Henry Scott Holland, W. S. Rockstro and Otto Goldschmidt (London, 1891). It was noted that these were the last notes she ever sang on earth.

Lindbergh, Charles Augustus

(1902-1974) American aviator. First man to fly the Atlantic Ocean solo. First to fly from New York to Paris in a heavier-than-air craft. Gained worldwide fame. Married Anne Spencer Morrow. Oldest of their six children was kidnapped and killed at age 2 in 1932, leading to enactment of the Lindbergh Act. Lindbergh won a Pulitzer Prize for his book *The Spirit of St. Louis* (1953). Awarded rank of brigadier general in Air Force Reserve in 1954. Died at age 72 in Kipahulu, Maui, Hawaii.
Last Words: "It's harder on you watching me die, than it is on me." Spoken to his wife.
Source: *Anne Morrow Lindbergh: A Gift for Life* by Dorothy Herrmann (New York, 1993).

Lindsay, Howard

(1889-1968) American actor, producer, director, playwright, librettist. Birth name Herman S. Nelke. Won 1946 Pulitzer Prize for Drama with Russel Crouse for their play *State of the Union*, later adapted into a movie by Frank Capra. Lindsay and Crouse also won a Tony Award for Best Musical for *The Sound of Music*. Lindsay often acted with his wife Dorothy Stickney in plays such as the long-running *Life with Father*. Died at age 78 in New York City.
Last Words: "It's been a wonderful journey. And I have had a wonderful companion. And I have enjoyed every moment of it."
Source: "Howard Lindsay Is Eulogized; 600 Attend Memorial Service" (*New York Times*, February 16, 1968).

Lindsay, Vachel

(1879-1931) American poet. Known as the Prairie Troubadour. Notable works: "The Congo"; "The Chinese Nightingale"; "Abraham Lincoln Walks at Midnight." Had serious mental problems. During his final days, he suffered from delusions of persecution. Committed suicide at age 52 by drinking disinfectant at his home in Springfield, Illinois. His poem "The Congo" was recited in the 1989 movie *Dead Poets Society*.
Last Words: "They tried to get me; I got them first." Spoken to his wife.
Source: *Vachel Lindsay: A Poet in America* by Edgar Lee Masters (New York, 1935). The author was Lindsay's friend.

Lindsey, Theophilus

(1723-1808) English theologian, writer. Founded first Unitarian church in England. Notable work: *An Historical View of the State of the Unitarian Doctrine and Worship from the Reformation to Our Own Time.* Died at age 85 in London.
Last Words: "God's will is best."
Source: *Life of Theophilus Lindsey* by Thomas Belsham (London, 1873).

Linton, Eliza Lynn

(1822-1898) English novelist, newspaper correspondent. Her articles were published in *Saturday Review* and *Harper's Magazine*. Notable work: *My Literary Life* (her reminiscences). Died at age 76 in London.
Last Words (written): "I am very forlorn at the present moment and wish I was at Malvern. Oh, don't I just." Written in a letter. She had retired to Malvern a few years earlier.
Source: *Mrs. Eliza Lynn Linton: Her Life, Letters, and Opinions* by George Somes Layard (London, 1901).

Lippard, George

(1822-1854) American writer, journalist, novelist. Visionary, social critic. Founded Brotherhood of the Union, secret charitable organization. Notable works: *The Quaker City or The Monks of Monk Hall* (Gothic novel about Philadelphia, one of the earliest best-sellers in the U.S.); *Legends of the American Revolution, or Washington and His Generals.* Friend of Edgar Allan Poe. Died at age 31 of tuberculosis in Philadelphia.
Last Words: "Is this death?" Spoken to his physician.
Source: *The Last Words (Real and Traditional) of Distinguished Men and Women Collected from Various*

Sources by Frederic Rowland Marvin (New York, 1901).

Lisle, Sir George

(1610?-1648) English royalist. Leader in English Civil War. Executed for treason without a trial at about age 38.

Last Words: "Oh how many do I see here about me, whose lives I have shed in hot blood: and now must mine be taken away in cold blood most barbarously! Sure the like was never heard of among the Goths and Vandals, or the veriest barbarians in the world in any age. But what dare not those rebels and traitors do, they have imprisoned and could willingly cut the throat of their King? for whose deliverance from his enemies and peace to this distracted kingdom, these my last prayers shall be presented. Now then rebels and traitors do your worst to me.—Jesus."

Source: *Royal and Loyal Sufferers* by Cecil Deedes (London, 1903).

Liszt, Franz

(1811-1886) Hungarian musician, pianist, composer. Famed for piano virtuosity. Notable works: *Les Preludes; Hungarian Dances;* two piano concertos; *Liebesträume.* Daughter Cosima married first Hans von Bulow then Richard Wagner. Liszt died at age 74 in Bayreuth, Bavaria, while attending a performance of *Tristan und Isolde* at a Wagnerian music festival.

Different Last Words:
(1) "Tristan." His daughter Cosima insisted this was her father's Last Word.

Source: *Franz Liszt* by James Huneker (New York, 1911).

(2) "I thank you; please continue sleeping." Spoken as he returned to his sickbed. Heard by Lina Schmalhausen, who took care of Liszt during his final ten days.

Source: *The Death of Franz Liszt: Based on the Unpublished Diary of His Pupil Lina Schmalhausen* by Lina Schmalhausen, ed. and annotated by Alan Walker (Ithaca, NY, 2002).

Little, Jacob

(1796?-1865) American investor, railroad industrialist. Major stock market investor. Nation's first major mid-19th-century investor in railroad expansion. Known as Napoleon of the Board for his ability to manipu-

late stock market. Invented short sale during the 1837 market collapse, making money in an otherwise bleak market. Little was considered the first professional "bear," but was ultimately destroyed financially in the "Western Blizzard" Crash of 1857.

Last Words: "I am going up. Who will go with me?"

Source: *Sunshine and Shadow in New York* by Matthew Hale Smith (Hartford, CT, 1869).

Litvinenko, Alexander Valterovich

(1962-2006) Russian military officer, dissident, spy, writer. Lieutenant colonel in Federal Security Service of Russian Federation. Worked for the KGB. Claimed superiors ordered the assassination of Russian billionaire Boris Berezovsky. Arrested but released. Fled to the United Kingdom, where he was granted political asylum and citizenship. Tried to release a book detailing Russian terroristic bombings of an apartment complex that killed 300 people. Died in London hospital from polonium-210 radiation poisoning. Source of his toxic exposure was never determined.

Last Words: "Marina, I love you so much." Spoken to his wife.

Source: "His Last Words to Me Were: 'Marina, I Love You So Much'" by David Leppard and Margarette Driscoll (*The* [London] *Sunday Times,* December 10, 2006).

Livingston, Charlie

(1962?-1997) American murderer. Career criminal caught and convicted for attempted murder. While on probation, he shot and killed a woman carrying groceries just to steal her purse. He was identified by the T-shirt he was wearing. Executed at age 35 by lethal injection in Huntsville, Texas.

Last Words: "You all brought me here to be executed, not to make a speech. Get on with it. That's it."

Source: *Last Suppers: Famous Final Meals from Death Row* by Ty Treadwell and Michael Vernon (Port Townsend, WA, 2001).

Livingston, Edward

(1764-1836) American statesman, diplomat, jurist, politician, legal reformer. Nephew of Philip Livingston. Served in War of 1812. Member U.S. House of Representatives from New York and Louisiana. Member

U.S. Senate from Louisiana. Wrote legal code for Louisiana. U.S. secretary of state. Minister to France. Died at age 71 in Barrytown, New York. Counties in Illinois, Michigan and Missouri and cities in Texas, Tennessee and Alabama were named for him.

Last Words (doubtful): "You were imprudent in coming upstairs, but I thank you for feeling anxious about me."

Source: *A Conspectus of American Biography: Being an Analytical Summary of American History and Biography, Containing also the Complete Indexes of the National Cyclopedia of American Biography* by George Derby (New York, 1906).

Livingston said this, but these were not his Last Words. For a few hours after he made this comment, he was delirious and spoke of his rural pursuits. His biographers wrote that his eyes sparkled as he dwelt proudly upon his success in transplanting a locust in full leaf and boasted that it would revolutionize horticulture. His speech then left him.

Source: *Life of Edward Livingston* by Charles Havens Hunt and George Bancroft (New York, 1864).

Livingston, Philip

(1716-1778) American merchant, statesman. Uncle of Edward Livingston. Member New York Committee of Correspondence. Delegate to Stamp Act Congress. Member Continental Congress. Signer of Declaration of Independence. Member New York State assembly and senate. Died suddenly at age 62 in York, Pennsylvania, while attending the Continental Congress.

Last Words (doubtful): "I must blot out all desires for the sake of the public good."

Source: *A Conspectus of American Biography: being an Analytical Summary of American History and Biography, Containing also the Complete Indexes of the National Cyclopedia of American Biography* by George Derby (New York, 1906).

This quote is from a letter Livingston wrote when he knew death was near. He was expressing his wish to die at home with family but he felt an obligation to stay and do his duty.

Source: *History of the American Nation* by William James Jackman, Jacob Harris Patton and Rossiter Johnson (Chicago, 1920).

Livingstone, David

(1813-1873) Scottish missionary, physician, explorer in Africa. Tracked down in 1871 by Henry M. Stanley who was hired by an American newspaper to find out if he was still alive. Livingstone died two years later at age 60 near Lake Bangweulu (now part of Zambia), while searching for the source of the Nile.

Last Words (written): "Knocked up quite, and remain—recover sent to buy milch goats. We are on the banks of R. Molilamo." Journal entry.

Source: *The Personal Life of David Livingstone* by W. Garden Blaikie (New York, 1880).

Last Words (spoken): "All right; you can go out now." Spoken to his personal servant Susi. The next morning he was found dead beside his bed.

Source: "Livingstone: The Last Days of the Great Explorer. Extracts From His Recently Published Journals—The Final Journey and Its Sad Conclusion—Life Dying Out Slowly—His Solitary Death in the Native Hut" (*New York Times,* December 28, 1874).

Lloyd, Thomas

(1640?-1694) Welsh-born American physician, politician. Arrested for being a Quaker. Moved to America in 1683. Appointed lieutenant governor of provincial Pennsylvania. Died at age 54 in Pennsylvania.

Last Words: "I die in unity and love with all faithful Friends. I have fought a good fight. I have kept the faith; which stands not in the wisdom of words, but in the power of God. I have sought not for strife or contention, but for the grace of our Lord Jesus Christ and the simplicity of the Gospel. I lay down my head in peace and desire you may all do so. Farewell." Spoken on his deathbed.

Source: *Memoirs of the Private and Public Life of William Penn: Who Settled the State of Pennsylvania, and Founded the City of Philadelphia* by Thomas Clarkson and William Penn (Dover, NH, 1827).

Lloyd George, David, 1st Earl Lloyd-George of Dwyfor

(1863-1945) British statesman. Member Parliament. Chancellor of the exchequer. Minister of munitions. Secretary of state for war. Prime minister. 1st Earl of Dwyfor, Viscount Gwynedd. Raised to peerage in 1945. Died at age 82 in Newydd, Wales, before he could take his seat in the House of Lords.

Last Words: "Have you been to chapel?" Spoken to his physician.

Source: *David Lloyd George: A Biography* by Peter Rowland (New York, 1975).

Locke, John

(1632-1704) English philosopher, politician scientist, writer. Known as the Father of English Empiricism. Notable works: *An Essay Concerning Human Understanding; Two Treatises of Government.* Died at age 72 in Oates, Essex, at the home of Sir Francis and Lady Masham.

Last Words: "Cease now." Spoken to Lady Masham, who was reading some of the Psalms to him (Romans 11:33).

Source: *Literature, Its Rise, Progress, Fortunes and Advantages* by Charles Spence (Liverpool, England, 1863).

Lockhart, Tim

(1928-1963) American radio disc jockey. Died at age 34 of a heart attack while broadcasting on WINN in Louisville, Kentucky.

Last Words: "Bill, help, help." Reported by listeners. He apparently was trying to summon Production Director Bill Gerson for help.

Source: "Disk Jockey Cries 'Help, Help' and Dies" (*Chicago Tribune*, March 27, 1963).

Lodge, Henry Cabot

(1850-1924) American politician, statesman, writer. U.S. delegate to the Washington Conference on the Limitation of Armaments. Member U.S. House of Representatives and U.S. Senate from Massachusetts.

Last Words (written): "The doctors promise prompt recovery. I shall be back in Washington well and strong, and I trust that I shall be able to be of some service to you when I get there." Letter to President Calvin Coolidge.

Source: *Henry Cabot Lodge: A Biography* by John A. Garraty (New York, 1953).

Lody, Carl Hans

(1877-1914) German military officer, spy. First German spy executed in Britain during World War I. Shot at age 37 for espionage at the Tower of London.

Last Words (written): "My dear Ones, I have trusted in God and He has decided. My hour has come, and I must start on the journey through the Dark Valley like so many of my comrades in this terrible War of Nations. May my life be offered as a humble offering on the altar of the Fatherland. A hero's death on the battlefield is certainly finer, but such is not to be my lot, and I die here in the Enemy's country silent and unknown, but the consciousness that I die in the service of the Fatherland makes death easy. The Supreme Court Marshal of London has sentenced me to die for Military conspiracy. Tomorrow, I shall be shot in the Tower. I have had just Judges, and I shall die as an Officer, not a spy. Farewell. God bless you. Hans." Letter to relatives in Stuttgart, Germany.

Source: *A History of Capital Punishment with Special Reference to Capital Punishment in Great Britain* by John Laurence (London, 1932).

Loeb, Richard A.

(1906-1936) American murderer. He and 19-year-old Nathan Leopold kidnapped and murdered 14-year-old Bobby Franks. Clarence Darrow defended them. The judge gave them life in prison rather than death. Loeb was killed in a prison shower room fight after he was slashed with a razor multiple times by another inmate.

Last Words: "I think I'm going to make it." Whispered to Leopold as he was dying.

Source: "Last of Loeb" (*Time* magazine, February 10, 1936).

Loewe, Frederick

(1901-1988) Austrian-born American musician, composer. Collaborated on musical shows with lyricist Alan Jay Lerner. Notable works: *Brigadoon; Paint Your Wagon; My Fair Lady; Gigi; Camelot.* Won three Tony Awards. Nominated for two Academy Awards; won for *Gigi.* Died at age 86 of lung cancer in Palm Springs, California.

Last Words: "I want to die." Murmured in German.

Source: *Inventing Champagne: The World of Lerner and Loewe* by Gene Lees (New York, 1990).

Loft, Robert

(1917-1972) American airline pilot, disaster victim. Captain of Eastern Air Lines Flight 401 that crashed into the Florida Everglades on December 29, 1972, causing 101 fatalities. The plane, a four-month-old Lockheed L-1011, left New York's JFK Airport en route to Miami International Airport. Flight 401 was the first crash of a wide-body aircraft. The flight later took on additional notoriety due to rumors of paranormal activity. It was the inspiration for the film *The Ghost of Flight 401*.

Last Words: "Hey! What's happening here?"

Source: *Slipping the Surly Bonds: Great Quotations on Flight* compiled by David English (New York, 1998).

Logan, Harvey ("Kid Curry")

(d. 1904) American criminal. Member of the Wild Bunch. Pursued and wounded by a posse in Colorado. Shot himself.

Last Words: "Yes, and I'm going to end it here." His reply when a gang member asked: "Are you hit?"

Source: *Encyclopedia of Western Gunfighters* by Bill O'Neal (Norman, OK, 1979).

Logan, John Alexander

(1826-1886) American military officer, politician, legislator, writer. Member Illinois and U.S. House of Representatives. Fought in Mexican War. Union general in U.S. Civil War. Member U.S. Senate from Illinois. Unsuccessful Republican candidate for Vice President of the U.S. Wrote partisan history of the Civil War. Died at age 60 in Washington, D.C. Several towns, highways and schools were named for him.

Different Last Words:

(1) "Mary." Spoke his wife's name.

Source: *Washington Post,* December 27, 1886.

(2) "No, not a merry Christmas, but I hope a quiet and peaceful one." Spoken slowly as if weighing the words to a visitor who had said to him: "General, it would be a mockery to wish you a merry Christmas, but I do wish you a quiet and peaceful one."

Source: *Life and Service of Gen. John A. Logan* by George Francis Dawson (Chicago, 1887).

Lombard, Carole

(1908-1942) American actress, screen star. Birth name Jane Alice Peters. Nominated for Academy Award for *My Man Godfrey*. Killed at age 33 with 21 others in a plane crash near Las Vegas, Nevada. Was on a U.S. War Bond Tour during World War II.

Last Words: "Before I say goodbye to you all, come on, join me in a big cheer. V for victory!" Spoken in Indiana, just before she boarded the plane.

Source: *Great Stars of Hollywood's Golden Age* by Frank Cheney Platt (New York, 1966).

Lombardi, Vincent Thomas ("Vince")

(1913-1970) American athletic coach. Football head coach, general manager. With Green Bay Packers, Washington Redskins. Career highlights include two Super Bowl wins, five NFL Championship wins. Appeared on the cover of *Time* magazine in 1962. Vince Lombardi Trophy (awarded to Super Bowl winners) named for him. Diagnosed with cancer. Died at age 57 in Washington, D.C.

Last Words: "Happy anniversary. I love you." Whispered to his wife.

Source: *Vince: A Personal Biography of Vince Lombardi* by Michael O'Brien (New York, 1987).

London, Jack Griffith

(1876-1916) American writer, novelist. Birth name John Griffith Chaney. Spent time in the Klondike. Wrote popular books and articles about his adventures there. Notable works: *The Call of the Wild*; *White Fang*; *The Sea Wolf*. Several of his stories have been made into popular movies. Died at age 40 in Glen Ellen, California. Cause of death is debated: uremic poisoning? deliberate or accidental morphine overdose?

Last Words (written): "I leave California Wednesday following, Daddy."

Source: *Jack London and His Times* by Joan London (Garden City, NY, 1939). The author was his daughter.

Last Words (spoken): "Thank God you're not afraid of anything!" Spoken to his wife.

Source: *The Book of Jack London* by Charmian London (New York, 1921). The author was his wife.

Lonergan, Tom and Eileen

Tom (1963-1998) and Eileen (1969-1998). American SCUBA-diving couple. Accidentally abandoned in the ocean near Australia's Great Barrier Reef by their diving boat. Most likely died of dehydration, drowning and/or shark attack. Their bodies were not found but some of their gear and the diver's slate were recovered. Their story inspired the 2003 movie *Open Water*.

Last Words (written): "Monday Jan 26; 1998, 08 am. To anyone [who] can help us: We have been abandoned on A[gin]court Reef by MV Outer Edge 25 Jan 98 3pm. Please help us [come] to rescue us before we die. Help!!!" Message written on a diver's slate that washed ashore miles from where they had been left.

Source: "Open Water: The True Story Behind the Disturbing Movie" by David Ficking (*Cyber Diver News Network,* July 23, 2004).

Long, Huey Pierce, Jr. ("The Kingfish")

(1893-1935) American lawyer, politician. Governor of Louisiana. Member U.S. Senate from Louisiana. Shot by Carl Weiss outside the governor's office at Baton Rouge. Died at age 42. Weiss, son-in-law of one of Long's political enemies, was killed by Long's bodyguard. Long's story was fictionalized in 1947 in the Pulitzer-Prize winning novel *All the King's Men* by Robert Penn Warren, which was made into two movies.

Different Last Words:

(1) "Don't let me die. I have so much to do."

Source: "Who Shot Huey Long?" by Ken Burns (*American Heritage,* Vol. 41, No. 8, December 1990).

(2) "I wonder why he shot me."

Source: *The Inside Story of Huey Long* by Carlton Beals (Philadelphia, 1935).

Longfellow, Henry Wadsworth

(1807-1882) American poet, educator, linguist. One of the five Fireside Poets (the others: James Russell Lowell, Whittier, Oliver Wendell Holmes Sr., William Cullen Bryant). Received honorary doctorates from Oxford and Cambridge. Notable works: "Evangeline: A Tale of Acadie"; "Tales of a Wayside Inn"; "The Song of Hiawatha"; "The Courtship of Miles Standish." Died at age 75 of peritonitis in Cambridge, Massachusetts.

Last Words: "Now I know that I must be very ill, since you have been sent for." Spoken when he learned his sister had arrived from Portland, Maine.

Source: *Life of Henry Wadsworth Longfellow* by Samuel Longfellow (Boston, 1891). The author was his brother.

Longfellow, Mary Storer Potter

(1812-1835) American first wife of Henry W. Longfellow. Accompanied her husband to Europe. Died at age 23 of complications from a miscarriage in Rotterdam, The Netherlands.

Last Words: "Dear Henry, do not forget me! Tell my dear friends at home that I thought of them at the last hour." She then said she

would like to see Dr. Bosworth, the Episcopalian clergyman. By the time he arrived that afternoon she had died.

Source: *Henry Wadsworth Longfellow* by Thomas Wentworth Higginson (Boston, 1902).

Longfellow, Samuel

(1819-1892) American clergyman, writer, hymnist. Minister at Second Unitarian Church, Brooklyn and pastor at Unitarian Church in Philadelphia, Pennsylvania. He belonged to a section of the church that held views the most variant from the evangelical. Wrote a biography of his brother Henry. Composed many hymns. Published a hymn book in 1859. Died at age 73 in Cape Elizabeth, Maine.

Last Words: He asked a young relative if she could recall the lines of Whittier's "Hampton Beach." He repeated the first stanza then added part of the following stanza: "Familiar as our childhood's stream, Or pleasant memory of a dream."

Source: *Samuel Longfellow: Memoir and Letters* by Joseph May (Boston, 1894).

Longley, William Preston

(1851-1878) American gunfighter, robber, murderer. Obsessed with the myth of the Old South. Hated carpetbaggers, Yankees, blacks. Killed more than 30 men, including posse members, gunslingers and several African-American police. Claimed he was protecting the honor and dignity of the defunct Confederacy. Executed at age 27 by hanging in Giddings, Texas.

Last Words: "I deserve this fate. It is a debt I owe for a wild and reckless life. So long, everybody!" Spoken while standing on the gallows.

Source: *Features and Fillers: Texas Journalists on Texas Folklore* by Jim Harris (Denton, TX, 1999).

Longstreet, James

(1821-1904) American military officer. Veteran of Mexican War. Confederate general in U.S. Civil War. His delay in carrying out Lee's orders to attack at Gettysburg is said to have contributed to the South's defeat. Became friend of Ulysses Grant after war. Served as his minister to Turkey. Commissioner of Pacific railways. When he died at age 82 in Gainesville, Georgia, he was the last of the Confederate high command.

Last Words: "Helen we shall be happier in this post." Spoken to Helen Dortch Longstreet, his second wife, whom he married in 1897. She later published *Lee and Longstreet at High Tide: Gettysburg in the Light of the Official Records,* in which she defended her husband's actions.

Source*: Lee's Tarnished Lieutenant: James Longstreet and His Place in Southern History* by William Garrett Piston (Athens, GA, 1987).

López, Francisco Solano

(1826-1870) Paraguayan leader. President of Paraguay. Involved in five-year War of the Triple Alliance against Argentina, Uruguay and Brazil. Paraguay was devastated: 300,000 casualties were lost in battle or died of starvation or disease. López was trapped and killed by a Brazilian soldier. He died at age 43.

Last Words: "¡Muero por mi patria!" (tr. "I die for my homeland!") Shouted at his Brazilian pursuers.

Source: *Woman on Horseback* by William E. Barrett (New York, 1938).

Lothair I, King of the Franks

(794-855) French monarch. Eldest son of Louis I the Pious. Crowned co-emperor 817; emperor 823. Partitioned his kingdom among his three sons when he died.

Last Words: "What manner of king is He above who thus doeth to death such great kings?"

Source: *History of the Franks* by Gregory of Tours, tr. by Ormonde M. Dalton (Oxford, England, 1927).

Louis, Dauphin of France

(1729-1765) French royalty. Son of Louis XV and Maria Leszczynska who was the daughter of King Stanislas of Poland. Father of three French kings: Louis XVI, Louis XVIII and Charles X. Died at age 36 of tuberculosis at Fontainebleau.

Last Words: "Ah! take the bishop's. What fortitude he has!" Spoken as he told his physician to take the pulse of the Bishop of Verdun.

Source: *Éloge de Louis, Dauphin de France* by M. l'Abbé de Boulogne (Paris, 1814).

Louis I, King of the Franks, f
Holy Roman Emperor

(778-840) French monarch. Son of Charle-

magne. Father of Charles the Bold. King of France and Germany. Holy Roman Emperor. Known as Louis the Pious. and Louis the Debonair. Reign marked by quarrels with sons. Deposed by them in 830, then restored.

Last Words: "I pardon him, but let him know that it is on his account that I am dying." Spoken when Louis heard that one of his sons had revolted against him.

Source: *Biographie universelle,* Book XXV, by J. Fr. Michaud and Louis Gabriel Michaud (Paris, 1811-1862).

Louis VI, King of France

(1081-1137) French monarch. Son of Philip I. Known as Louis the Fat. Died near Compiegne, France, after ruling 29 years. Succeeded by son Louis VII. Died at age 55.

Last Words: "Remember, my son, that royalty is but a public employment of which you must render a rigorous account to him who is the sole disposer of crowns and sceptres."

Sources: *Eunomus; or, Dialogues Concerning the Law and Constitution of England. With an Essay on Dialogue* by Edward Wynne and W. M. Bythewood (London, 1822). It cited "Abbe Velly's Hist. of France," Vol. III. [(*France depuis l'établissement de la monarchie, jusqu'au règne de Louis XIV* by Paul-Francois Velly, Paris, 1761-1774)].

Louis VIII, King of France

(1187-1226) French monarch. Known as the Lionheart. Led an unsuccessful expedition to England. Tried to destroy the Plantagenets and capture southern France. Ruled only three years. Died at age 39 of dysentery after a campaign against the Albigensians and capture of Avignon. Succeeded by his son as Louis IX.

Last Words: "Ah, no, it will not be so, young lady. I will not commit mortal sin for whatever reason!" His response after a doctor instructed him that a virgin would cure him and one was sent to his room.

Source: *Fleur de Lys: The Kings and Queens of France* compiled by Joy Law (New York, 1976).

Louis IX, Saint, King of France

(1214-1270) French monarch, Crusader, holy man. Son of Louis VIII. Known as Saint Louis. Participated in the Sixth Crusade. Planned to go on another Crusade. Died at age 56 of dysentery in Tunis soon after leaving France. Canonized in 1297. Several places in the U.S. were named for him including the city of Saint Louis, Missouri.

Last Words: I will enter into thine house, I will adore in thine holy temple, and will confess unto thy name, O Lord."

Source: *A History of the Church from Its Establishment to the Present Century,* Vol. 5, by Charles Constantine Pise (Baltimore, MD, 1830). English translations of the quote—usually shorter and differing in only a few words—have appeared in several sources.

Louis XI, King of France

(1423-1483) French monarch. Son of Charles VII. Acquired part of Burgundy for France. Died at age 60 in Plessis, France. Succeeded by son Charles VIII.

Last Words: "Lord, in Thee have I trusted, let me never be confounded." The words were from the Latin hymn "Te Deum Laudamus."

Source: *The Life of Louis XI* by Christopher Hare (New York, 1907).

Louis XII, King of France

(1462-1515) French monarch. Known as Father of the People. Invaded Italy. Overthrew Ludovico Sforza. Conquered Naples but was later driven out. Third wife whom he married in 1514 was Mary Tudor, daughter of Henry VII, King of England. Louis died at age 52 in Paris on New Year's Day.

Different Last Words:

(1) "Mignonne, je vous donne ma mort pour vos étrennes." (tr. "My Darling, as a New Year's present, I give you my death.") Spoken to Mary, his wife of less than three months.

Sources: *Les Dames Galantes* by Pierre de Bourdeille Brantôme, seigneur de; and Maurice Rat (Paris, 1965); *Famous Sayings and Their Authors: A Collection of Historical Sayings in English, French, German, Greek, Italian and Latin* by Edward Latham (London, 1906).

(2) "I am dying. I commend our subjects to your care."

Source: *The Life of Marguerite D'Angoulême. Queen of Navarre, Duchesse d'Alençon and de Berry* by Martha Walker Freer afterward Mrs. John Robinson (London, 1856).

Louis XIII, King of France

(1601-1643) French monarch. Son of Henry IV and Marie de Medici. Assumed throne at age nine. Ruled as King of France and Navarre. Married Hapsburg Princess Anne of Austria. Died at age 41 in Paris.

Last Words: "Dinet! Thoughts arise which trouble me!" Spoken to his confessor. Dinet was a French Jesuit who was Descartes' protector as well as Louis's confessor.

Source: *The Married Life of Anne of Austria* by Martha Walker Freer (London, 1912).

Louis XIV, King of France

(1638-1715) French monarch. Son of Louis XIII. Known as the Sun King. Called the Great. Succeeded to the throne at age of 5. Reigned 73 years, longest in European history. Died in his sleep three days before his 77th birthday. Louisiana was named for him in 1682.

Different Last Words:

(1) "Why do you weep? Did you think I was immortal?"

Source: *Biographie universelle*, Book XXV, by J. Fr. Michaud and Louis Gabriel Michaud (Paris, 1811-1862).

(2) "O God, come to mine aid! O Lord, make haste to help me!"

Source: *The Last Words (Real and Traditional) of Distinguished Men and Women Collected from Various Sources* by Frederic Rowland Marvin (New York, 1901). Marvin cited *La Cour de Louis XIV* by Imbert de Saint-Amand.

Variation: "O, my God, come to my aid, hasten to help me!" He then said "Nunc et in hora mortis" (tr. "Now and at the hour of death") just before he lost the ability to speak.

Source: "Last Words of Monarchs" (*The Queries Magazine*, Vol. 6, No. 2, February 1890).

(3) "My son, you are going to be a great king; be always a good Christian. Do not follow my example with regard to war; endeavour to live in peace with your neighbors. Render to God what you owe to Him; follow always the most moderate counsels; endeavour to reduce the taxes, and thus do that which I have unhappily not been able to do. Take notice my son: these are my Last Words and let them sink deep into your mind—remember that kings die like other men." Spoken to his grandson the Dauphin who stood by his bedside. Reported by Madame Maintenon who heard the king's Last Words.

Source: *Universal History from the Creation of the World to the Decease of George III, 1820,* by Alexander Fraser Tyler Woodhouselee and Edward Nares (New York, 1859).

Louis XV, King of France

(1710-1774) French monarch. Succeeded to the throne at age 5. Succeeded his great-grandfather, Louis XIV. Known as Louis the Well-Beloved. Died at age 64 of smallpox at Versailles. Succeeded by his grandson who became Louis XVI (husband of Marie Antoinette).

Different Last Words:

(1) "Oh, much!" His response when asked if he was suffering.

Source: *Louis XV intime* by Claude Saint-André (Paris, 1921).

(2) "Repeat those words Monsieur the almoner, repeat them." Spoken to Cardinal de la Roche-Aymon, the grand almoner who read Louis's public apology to his people. The king repented of having given an occasion for scandal to his subjects.

Source: *The Last Years of Louis XV*, tr. from the French of Imbert de Saint-Amand (Boston, 1893).

(3) "I have never felt better or more at peace." Spoken after he had been administered the Last Rites.

Source: *Louis the Beloved: The Life of Louis XV* by Olivier Bernier (Garden City, NY, 1984).

Louis XVI, King of France

(1754-1793) French monarch. Son of the Dauphin. Grandson of Louis XV. Became Dauphin in 1763. Husband of Marie Antoinette. Deposed during French Revolution. Tried for treason. Found guilty. Sentenced to death. Executed at age 38 by guillotine in Paris. Several places in the U.S. were named for him for his aid during the American Revolution.

Last Words: "Je meurs innocent de tous les crimes qu'on m'impute; je pardonne aux auteurs de ma mort, et je prie Dieu que le sang que vous allez répandre ne retombe jamais sur la France, et qu'il apaise la colere de Dieu." (tr. "I die innocent of all the crimes laid to my charge. I forgive the authors of my death, and I pray God that the blood which you are about to shed may never fall on France and that it appeases God's anger.")

Source: *Histoire Impartiale des Révolutions de France, Depuis la Mort de Louis XV* by Louis Marie Prud-homme (Paris, 1826).

Louis XVII, King of France

(1785-1795) French monarch. Son of Louis XVI and Marie Antoinette. Known as Louis Charles of France. Became Dauphin in 1789, after the death of his brother. Proclaimed King of France in 1793. Officially reported to have died of tuberculosis in prison at age 10. But rumors persisted that he was taken to a safe place by royal sympathizers. Over the next several decades, several men claimed to be Louis XVII, the Lost Dauphin. (See Williams, Eleazer.)

Last Words: "I am still in pain, but not nearly so much—the music is so beautiful!" When asked from where he heard the music, he replied: "Since you knelt down. Do you not hear it? Listen! Listen! Amongst all the voices I have distinguished that of my mother!"

Source: *Memoirs of the Private Life of Marie Antoinette, Queen of France and Navarre. To Which Are Added, Recollections, Sketches, and Anecdotes, Illustrative of the Reigns of Louis XIV, Louis XV, and Louis XVI* by Mme. Campan [Jeanne Louise Henriette Campan] and Fs Barrière (London, 1823).

Louis XVIII, King of France

(1755-1824) French monarch. Grandson of Louis XV. Brother of Louis XVI and Charles X. Full name Louis Stanislas Xavier. Returned to Paris as Bourbon King after Napoleon's defeat. Died at age 68 of complications from diabetes in Paris. Left no children. Succeeded by brother Charles X.

Different Last Words:

(1) "A king should die standing."

Source: "Dying Words of Distinguished Persons" in *The Encyclopedia of Death and Life in the Spirit-World,* Vol. I, by J.R. Francis (Chicago, 1895).

(2) "Adieu! May Providence be with you."

Source: *Memoires de Louis XVIII,* ed. by M. le duc de D. (Brussels, Belgium, 1833).

(3) "Saint Denis, Givet." He woke after hours in a comatose state and gave the password of the day to a guard. It was a play on words: Givet = j'y vais (tr. "I'm going"). The king had a reputation as a punster.

Source: "Reminiscences of Thomas Raikes" (*The Gentleman's Magazine and Historical Review,* Vol. XLV, May 1856).

Louis, Joe

(1914-1981) American athlete. Professional boxer. World Heavyweight Champion from

1937 to 1949. Birth name Joseph Louis Barrow. Known as the Brown Bomber. Retired undefeated in 1949 but returned briefly to the ring. In his last fight in 1951, Rocky Marciano defeated him in the eighth round. Died at age 66 in Las Vegas, Nevada.

Last Words: "I'm ready whenever God wants to take me. I've lived my life and I've done what I needed to do."

Source: *Joe Louis: 50 Years an American Hero* by Joe Louis Barrow, Jr. (New York, 1988). It was not clear how long before death he spoke his Last Words.

Louise, Queen of Prussia

(1776-1810) Prussian monarch. Daughter of Duke Karl Ludwig Friedrich von Mecklenburg-Strelitz and Princess Friederike Caroline Luise of Hesse-Darmstadt. Full name Auguste Wilhelmine Amalie Luise. Married Frederick William III. Died suddenly at age 34 of a pulmonary embolism while visiting her father in Strelitz.

Different Last Words:

(1) "Do not fear, dear friend. I am not going to die. I am dying, Jesu! Make it short!" Spoken to her husband.

Source: *Queen Louise of Prussia, 1776-1810* by Gertrude Aretz (New York, 1929).

(2) "I am a Queen but have no power to move my arms."

Source: *Best Thoughts of Best Thinkers: Amplified, Classified, Exemplified and Arranged as a Key to Unlock The Literature of All Ages* by Hialmer Day Gould and Edward Louis Hessenmueller (Cleveland, OH, 1904).

Louise Caroline Alberta, Marchioness of Lorne, Duchess of Argyll

(1848-1939) Daughter of Queen Victoria and Prince Albert. Married Marquis of Lorne, who served as governor general of Canada. She became Duchess of Argyll when her husband gained the title in 1900. Died at age 91 at Kensington Palace. Lake Louise and the province of Alberta, Canada, were named for her.

Last Words: "You will never need to bring any more flowers for me."

Source: *Princess Louise: Queen Victoria's Unconventional Daughter* by Jehanne Wake (London, 1988).

Louise de France, Madame, Venerable Therese of Saint Augustine

(1737-1787) French royalty. Daughter of King Louis XV and Queen Maria Leszczynska. Died at age 50 in Saint Denis, France. Her cause for sainthood was introduced at the Vatican. Pius IX declared her Venerable in 1873.

Last Words: "Au paradis! Vite! Au grand galop!" (tr. "To Paradise! Hurry! At a gallop!")

Source: *Madame Louise de France, la vénérable Thérèse de Saint-Augustin* by Geoffroy de Grandmaison (Paris, 1907).

Louise of Savoy, Duchess of Angouleme

(1476-1531) French royalty. Mother of King Francis I of France. Became ill after watching a comet. She believed God had sent it as a warning and that she should prepare to meet death. She died three days later.

Last Words: "Unless I had seen the sign of my death, I should have said the same, for I do not myself feel that I am sinking." Spoken to her physicians who tried to assure her she was not seriously ill.

Source: "The Physical Phenomena of Death," ed. by Walter Hilliard Bidwell and John Holmes Agnew (*Eclectic Magazine*, January 1850).

L'Ouverture, Toussaint, see Toussaint L'Ouverture, Pierre.

Lovat, 12th Lord, see Fraser, Simon.

Love, Christopher

(1618-1651) Welsh clergyman. Advocate of Presbyterianism at the time of the English Civil War. Arrested by Cromwell's men for involvement in a plot to restore the monarchy. Tried and convicted of treason. Executed at age 33 at Tower Hill, London.

Last Words: "I bless God, sir, I am full of joy and comfort as ever my heart can hold. Blessed be God for Jesus Christ." Spoken following a longer sermon on the scaffold when he said: "I do more good by my death that by my life, and glorify God more in my dying upon a scaffold than if I had died of a disease upon my bed." Love tipped the executioner three pence to encourage the swordsman to do a clean job with one blow.

Source: *A Spectacle unto God: The Life and Death of Christopher Love (1618-1651)* by Don Kistler (Morgan, PA, 1994).

Lovejoy, Elijah Parish

(1802-1837) American clergyman, abolitionist, newspaper publisher. Presbyterian.

First Amendment activist. Established newspaper, *St. Louis Observer*. Angry white mob destroyed his press after he published an account of the lynching of an African-American. Lovejoy was shot and killed defending another press when a mob set fire to his building in Alton, Illinois. He became the first martyr to freedom of the press in America.

Last Words: "Oh, God! I am shot! I am shot!" He died within a few minutes.

Source: *Memoir of the Rev. Elijah P. Lovejoy: Who Was Murdered in Defense of the Liberty of the Press at Alton, Illinois, Nov. 7, 1837* by Joseph C. Lovejoy, Owen Lovejoy and John Quincy Adams (New York, 1838). Owen and Joseph were brothers of Elijah.

Lowder, Charles Fuge

(1820-1880) English clergyman. Anglican. Founded Society of the Holy Cross. Became ill and died while on holiday in Austria, probably of a perforated ulcer.

Last Words: "You are witness that I died in the faith of the Anglican Church, for they may say that I die a Roman Catholic."

Source: *Charles Lowder: A Biography* by Maria Trench (New York, 1883).

Lowell, Amy

(1874-1925) American poet, biographer, critic, writer. Notable work: *John Keats* (2-vol. biography). Died at age 51 of cerebral hemorrhage in Brookline, Massachusetts.

Last Words: "Pete, a stroke.—Get Eastman."

Source: *Amy Lowell, a Chronicle, with Extracts from Her Correspondence* by S. Foster Damon (Boston, 1935).

Lowell, James Russell

(1819-1891) American poet, critic, writer, editor, diplomat, abolitionist. Editor of *Atlantic Monthly*. Co-editor of *North American Review*. One of the five Fireside Poets. (The others: Longfellow, Whittier, Oliver Wendell Holmes Sr., William Cullen Bryant). U.S. minister to Spain and Great Britain. Died at age 72 in Cambridge, Massachusetts. Notable works: *Poems; The Biglow Papers*. Schools were named for him in Massachusetts, Minnesota, Pennsylvania and California.

Last Words: "Oh! why don't you let me die?" He was ill for several months before he died.

Source: *Life of James Russell Lowell* by Emma Elizabeth Brown (Chicago, 1895).

Lowry, Robert Wadsworth

(1826-1899) American clergyman, musician, hymnist, educator. Baptist minister at churches in New York, Brooklyn, West Chester, and Lewisburg, Pennsylvania, and Plainfield, New Jersey. Music editor for Biglow Publishing Company. Wrote several hundred gospel songs. Professor of literature at University of Lewisburg (now Bucknell). Died at age 73 in Plainfield.

Last Words: "Fanny, I am going to join those who have gone before, for my work is now done." Spoken to friend Fanny Crosby.

Source: *Memories of Eighty Years* by Fanny Crosby (Boston, 1906).

Lucan

(39-65) Roman poet. Full name Marcus Annaeus Lucanus. One-time favorite of Nero who later joined in a conspiracy against the emperor. Was betrayed and ordered by Nero to commit suicide. Died at age 25 in Rome.

Last Words: "He was torn asunder and his blood gushed out, not trickling as from a wound, but raining on all sides from his severed arteries; and the free play of the life coursing through the different limbs was cut off by the water. No other victim's life escaped through so wide a channel—." He was quoting from his epic *Pharsalia* (or Civil War) as he bled to death while sitting in a warm bath with his veins opened.

Source: *Pharsalia, III Tacitus Annals XV, The Classical Epic Tradition* by John Kevin Newman (Madison, WI, 1966).

Lucas, Sir Charles

(1613-1648) English military officer. Royalist commander in English Civil War. Had prominent role in the seizure of Colchester. Executed with no formal court-martial. After restoration of the monarchy, his death was called murder. He became a martyr for the Royalist cause. Was awarded posthumous peerage in 1666.

Different Last Words:

(1) "Now, rebels, do your worst." Spoken as he was being executed.

Source: *Royal and Loyal Sufferers* by Cecil Deedes (London, 1903).

(2) "Soldiers, fire!" Spoken to the soldiers appointed to shoot him.

Source: *The Last Words (Real and Traditional) of Distinguished Men and Women Collected from Various Sources* by Frederic Rowland Marvin (New York, 1901).

Luce, Clare Boothe

(1903-1987) American editor, playwright, politician, social activist, journalist, diplomat. Known for her sharp wit and intellect. Married Henry Luce, founder of *Time, Life* and *Fortune* magazines. Ambassador to Italy. Member U.S. House of Representatives from Connecticut. Notable plays: *The Women; Kiss the Boys Goodbye; Margin for Error*. Awarded Presidential Medal of Freedom by President Ronald Reagan. Died at age 84 of a brain tumor in Washington, D.C. Last Words: "Do not defend me." Her farewell advice to her friends.

Source: *Henry and Clare: An Intimate Portrait of the Luces* by Ralph G. Martin (New York, 1991).

Luce, Henry Robinson

(1898-1967) American magazine publisher. Known familiarly as Harry. Founder and publisher of *Time, Life, Sports Illustrated, Fortune*. Also published *House and Home, Architectural Forum* and Time-Life books. Died at age 68 in Phoenix, Arizona.

Last Words: "Oh, Jesus." Spoken when he was stricken with a heart attack. His nurse rushed to him and found he had collapsed and died.

Source: *Henry R. Luce, Time, and the American Crusade in Asia* by Robert Edwin Herzstein (New York, 2005).

Luciano, Charles ("Lucky")

(1897-1962) Italian-born American racketeer. Real name Salvatore Luciana. Partner in Murder, Inc. Leader of organized crime in the Eastern U.S. Convicted and jailed in 1936. During World War II, at the request of the U.S. government, Luciano asked the Sicilian Mafia to cooperate with U.S. military forces when they landed there. The Mafia guided the troops safely through passes and rivers and provided important information, thus saving many American lives. In gratitude after the war ended, his 30-50 year sentence was commuted on the condition that he be permanently deported to Italy. He

made the move in February 1946. Luciano died at age 64 at Naples Airport while on his way to meet television and movie producer Martin Gosch. As Luciano walked across the runway to greet him he had a fatal heart attack. Gosch wrote the book *Last Testament of Lucky Luciano*. Movies about him include *Lucky Luciano* and *The Last Testament of Lucky Luciano*.

Different Last Words:

(1) "Marty."

Source: *Bloodletters and Badmen: A Narrative Encyclopedia of American Criminals from the Pilgrims to the Present* by Jay Robert Nash (New York, 1995).

(2) "Tell Georgie I want to get in the movies one way or another."

Source: *Dear Muffo* by Harold Conrad and Budd Schulberg (New York, 1982).

Lucy, Saint

(225?-304) Roman widow, holy woman, martyr. Executed for Christian activism during Diocletian's rule in Syracuse, Sicily.

Last Words: "I make known to you that peace is restored to the Church! This very day Maximian has died and Diocletian has been driven from the throne. And just as God has bestowed my sister Agatha upon the city of Catania as its protectress, so He has this moment entitled me to be the patroness of the city of Syracuse."

Source: *The Golden Legend or Lives of the Saints.* Compiled by Jacobus de Voragine, Archbishop of Genoa, 1275, 1st ed., 1470. English ed. by William Caxton, 1483, ed. by F.S. Ellis (Edinburgh, 1900).

Lukwiya, Matthew

(1957-2000) Ugandan physician. First doctor to die from Ebola during the 2000 outbreak. He was supervisor of St. Mary's Hospital Lacor, outside Gulu, on the forefront of the outbreak. Died at age 43. In February 2001, the American Medical Association named Lukwiya a role model. The annual Dr. Matthew Lukwiya Memorial Lecture, sponsored by the World Health Organization, started the year after he died.

Last Words: "We have fought the battle, but I shall die last."

Source: "Lacor Mourns Lukwiya" (Asia Africa Intelligence Wire, September 25, 2002).

Lully, Jean-Baptiste

(1632-1687) Italian-born French musician,

composer. Notable works: *Alceste; Armide; Psyché* (operas). Popular French song "Au clair de la lune" is attributed to him. He accidentally poked his foot with his baton (large heavy staff) while conducting in January 1687. An abscess formed and gangrene set in. Died at age 54 at his home in Paris in March.

Last Words: "There is nothing to worry about. You see, I had another copy in my desk." Spoken to a friend after he had thrown the manuscript for an opera into the fire to show a priest his sincerity in repenting his sins.

Source: *Composers of Yesterday* by David Ewen (New York, 1937).

Luna, Álvaro de

(1388?-1453) Spanish statesman. Minister of John II of Castile. King's wife was jealous of the influence he had. She urged her husband to get rid of him. Luna was arrested, tried, condemned and executed.

Last Words: "It does not matter what they do with my body and head after my death." Spoken when he was informed that the post and hook he saw were to be attached to his head so it could be paraded after he died.

Source: *Derniers sentiments des plus illustres personnages condamnés à mort* by Joseph Donzé de Verteuil (Paris, 1775).

Lunalilo, King of the Hawaiian Islands

(1835-1874) Hawaiian monarch. Born William Charles Lunalilo. Son of High Chiefess Miriam Auhea Kekauluohi and High Chief Charles Kana'ina. Succeeded his uncle Kamehameha V, who died without naming an heir. He was king of the Hawaiian Islands less than two years. Died at age 39 of tuberculosis.

Last Words: "I am now dying."

Source: "Our Late King" (*Hawaiian Gazette,* February 11, 1874).

Luther, Martin

(1483-1546) German clergyman, religious reformer. Augustinian friar who posted Ninety-five Theses in 1517 attacking the Roman Catholic Church's practice of selling indulgences, its stance on purgatory and the venality of the popes. He established the Reformation in Germany and inaugurated Protestantism. Died at age 62 while on a visit to Eisleben, Germany.

Last Words: "Yes." His response when asked if he would die firm in the doctrine he preached.

Source: *The Life and Letters of Martin Luther* by Preserved Smith (Boston, 1911).

Lux, Walter H.

(1927-1979) American airline pilot, disaster victim. Captain of American Airlines Flight 191 that crashed on May 25, 1979, causing 271 fatalities. The plane, a McDonnell Douglas DC-10, left O'Hare International Airport in Chicago en route to Los Angeles International Airport. It crashed about 30 seconds after taking off. In terms of people killed, Flight 191 was the deadliest plane crash incident on U.S. soil until the September 11, 2001 attacks. Among those killed were biomedical inventor Itzhak Bentov (cardiac catheter), writer Judith Wax and husband Sheldon Wax (managing editor of *Playboy* magazine), as well as *Playboy*'s fiction editor Vicki Haider and several senior executives of the accounting firm Coopers & Lybrand.

Last Words: "American 191 under way."

Source: *The Air Up There: More Great Quotations on Flight* by Dave English (New York, 2003).

Lyon, Mary Mason

(1797-1849) American educator. Founder of Mount Holyoke Female Seminary in Massachusetts. Died at age 52 in South Hadley, Massachusetts.

Last Words: "I should love to come back to watch over the seminary, but God will take care of it."

Source: *The Life of Mary Lyon* by Beth Bradford Gilchrist (Boston, 1910).

Lyon, Nathaniel

(1818-1861) American military officer. Brigadier general in Union Army in U.S. Civil War. Mortally wounded at Wilson's Creek, Missouri, when he was struck by a mini ball that severed his aorta.

Different Last Words:

(1) "I will lead you! Onward brave boys of Iowa!"

Source: *Gen. Nathaniel Lyon, and Missouri in 1861: A Monograph of the Great Rebellion* by James Peckham (New York, 1866).

Variation: "Forward, men! I will lead you!"

Spoken to the Iowans he was commanding. He was shot and killed within two minutes.

Source: *Last Political Writings of Gen. Nathaniel Lyon: With a Sketch of His Life and Military Services* by Nathaniel Lyon (New York, 1861).

(2) "Lehman, I am killed; take care of my body." Spoken to his orderly as he collapsed.

Source: *The Pictorial Book of Anecdotes and Incidents of the War of Rebellion* by R.M. Devens (Hartford, CT, 1866).

Lyttelton, George, 1st Baron Lyttelton

(1709-1773) English poet, statesman. Known as the Good Lord Lyttelton in contrast to his son Thomas, the Wicked Lord Lyttelton. Friend of Alexander Pope and Henry Fielding. Died at age 64.

Last Words: "Be good, be virtuous, my lord; you must come to this." Spoken to a friend who had come to see him.

Source: *Lives of the English Poets and a Criticism of Their Work* by Samuel Johnson (Oxford, England, 1825).

MacArthur, Douglas

(1880-1964) American military officer. General in U.S. Army. Fought in World War I, World War II, Korean War. Commands: Superintendent of West Point; Department of the Philippines; U.S. Army Forces Far East; Supreme Allied Commander Pacific. Died at age 84 in Washington, D.C.

Last Words: "I am going to do the very best I can." Spoken to his wife and physician after he had surgery. He lapsed into a coma and died a short time later.

Source: *Washington Post,* April 5, 1964.

Macaulay, Thomas Babington, 1st Baron Macaulay

(1800-1859) English writer, historian, poet, politician. Notable work: *History of England*. Raised to peerage in 1857. Died at age 59 in London.

Last Words: "I shall retire early; I am very tired." Spoken to his butler who asked if he wanted to rest on the sofa. He sat down and died a short time later.

Source: *The Life and Letters of Lord Macauley* by Sir George Otto Trevelyan (New York, 1876). Trevelyan was his nephew.

Maccabaeus, Judas

(fl. 100s B.C.) Biblical figure. Chief member of a family of Jewish patriots. Purified the Jewish temple in 163 B.C. and restored Jewish worship. Hero of Handel's oratorio, *Judas Maccabaeus*. Virtually all that is known about him is contained in the Books of the Maccabees and in the works of Josephus. His Last Words are contained in the first book of Maccabees, which was written by a Jewish author after the restoration of an independent Jewish kingdom, probably about 100 B.C.

Last Words: "Absit istam rem facere ut fugiamus ab eis et si adpropiavit tempus nostrum moriamur in virtute propter fratres nostros et non inferamus crimen gloriae nostrae."

Source: I Machabaeorum 9 (Latin Vulgate Bible).

Variation: "Far be it from me to do such a thing as to flee from them! If our time has come, let us die bravely for our kinsmen and not leave a stain upon our glory!"

Source: 1 Maccabees 9 (New American Bible).

Variation: "God forbid we should do this thing, and flee away from them: but if our time be come, let us die manfully for our brethren, and let us not stain our glory."

Source: 1 Maccabees 9 (Douay-Rheims Translation).

MacDonald, George Browne

(1805-1868) English clergyman. Methodist minister. Four of his daughters married well-known people: Daughter Alice married John Lockwood Kipling and was the mother of Rudyard Kipling. Georgiana married pre-Raphaelite painter Edward Burne-Jones. Agnes married Edward Poynter, head of the Royal Academy. Louisa married industrialist Alfred Baldwin and was the mother of British Prime Minister Stanley Baldwin.

Last Words: "Lord, what things I lie here and remember."

Source: *A Kipling Chronology* by Harold Orel (Boston, 1990).

MacDonald, Jeanette

(1903-1965) American actress, operatic soprano. Stage and screen star. Known for her 1930s and 1940s Hollywood musical movies, including several with baritone Nelson Eddy. Made her final movie in 1948 then went into semi-retirement. Died at age 61 in Houston, Texas, while waiting to have heart surgery.

Last Words: "I love you." Spoken to her husband actor Gene Raymond.

Source: *The Jeanette MacDonald Story* by James Robert Parish (New York, 1976).

Macdonough, Thomas

(1783-1825) American military officer. Commodore in U.S. Navy. Served with Decatur in Tripolitan War. Won a strategic naval victory against the British at Lake Champlain in War of 1812. Died at age 41 of tuberculosis at sea near Gibraltar en route from Europe to New York City. Four U.S. Navy destroyers were named for him.

Last Words: "I have an aversion to being thrown into the sea. I wish my body taken home for interment." His wish was granted. He was buried in Middletown, Connecticut.

Source: *Life of Commodore Thomas Macdonough* by Rodney Macdonough (Boston, 1909). The author was his grandson.

MacGregor, Robert ("Rob Roy")

(1671-1734) Scottish Highland outlaw. Known as Rob Roy for his red hair. Freebooter who made thieves pay protection. Rustled cattle. When his lands were seized by the Duke of Montrose for debt, he gathered his clansmen and engaged in open war against him. He surrendered, was tried and imprisoned. Received a pardon while awaiting exile to Barbados. Returned to his home at Balquhidder. Died there around age 63. Sir Walter Scott made him the central character in his novel *Rob Roy*.

Last Words: "Now it is all over. Let the piper play. Let the piper play 'We return no more.'" As he lay dying, one of his enemies came to see him. He did not want to be seen in a position of defeat. He got out bed and armed himself. After the man left, he is said to have made this comment. The piper appeared and played until he died.

Source: *Rob Roy* by Sir Walter Scott (London, 1912). Scott gave MacGregor's biography in the Introduction.

MacKenna, Stephen

(1872-1934) Irish translator, scholar. Translator of *The Enneads* by Plotinus. Active in Irish literary revival. Died at age 62 in a London hospital after surgery.

Last Words (written): "Dear Peggy, I cannot resist, tho' I meant to see no one, not never no more. But you mustn't bring me anything whatsoever: I abhor grapes, am worried by flowers, can't read magazines. I'm greatly touched by your goodness, Peggy. Probably you could come any hour, simply arranging things over telephone with the Sister—you know the ropes. But Regular Visiting Fixtures: Sunday 2-3^1/2. Tuesd. and Frid. 5-6. I wept when I got you—S.M.K. What a howling swell of an address you have acquired. Go vfoiri dia orainn." Letter.

Source: *Journal and Letters of Stephen MacKenna,* ed. with a Memoir by E.R. Dodds (New York, 1937).

Mackenzie, Alexander

(1822-1892) Scottish-born Canadian stone mason, builder, politician. Emigrated to Canada in 1842. Formed and led Liberal party. Second prime minister of Canada. Died at age 70 in Toronto, Ontario.

Last Words: "Oh, take me home."

Source: *The Hon. Alexander Mackenzie, His Life and Times* by William Buckingham and Sir George William Ross (Toronto, ON, 1892).

Mackenzie, Sir Morell

(1837-1892) British physician, laryngologist, writer. Author of several books on laryngoscopy and diseases of the throat. Knighted in 1887. Died at age 54 in London.

Last Words: "Yes, send for Stephen." His brother was prominent British physician Sir Stephen Mackenzie.

Source: *Sir Morell Mackenzie; Physician and Operator; A Memoir Compiled and Edited from Private Papers and Personal Reminiscences* by the Rev. H.R. Haweis (London, 1893).

Mackintosh, Sir James

(1765-1832) Scottish philosopher, historian, writer, educator, politician. Member of Parliament. Professor of law at Haileybury. Wrote many books on the history of England. Notable work: *History of the English Revolution, 1688.* Died at age 66.

Last Word: "Happy!"

Source: *Memoirs of The Life of The Right Honourable Sir James Mackintosh* by His Son, Robert James Mackintosh (Philadelphia, 1835).

Macmillan, Harold, 1st Earl of Stockton

(1894-1986) British politician, statesman, economist. Member of Parliament. Minister of defense. Chancellor of the exchequer. Prime minister. Died at age 92 at Chelwood

Gate, Sussex.

Last Words: "I think I will sleep now."

Source: *Harold Macmillan, Volume II 1957-1986* by Alistair Horne (New York, 1989).

Macpherson, James ("Jamie")

(1675-1700) Scottish freebooter condemned for various crimes. Sang a ballad he wrote in prison before he was hanged. Legend says he read his farewell poem on the scaffold then played a tune he wrote on his fiddle. He offered the fiddle to the crowd. When no one came forward, he smashed it then was executed.

Last Words: "I spent my time in rioting
Debauch'd my health and strength,
I pillag'd, plundered, murdered,
But now alas! at length
I'm brought to punishment condign,
Pale Death draws near to me,
The end I ever did project
To hang upon a Tree."

Source: Ballad entitled "The Last Words of James Macpherson Murderer" in *Scottish Ballads and Songs* by James Maidment (Edinburgh, 1859).

Madison, Dolly Payne Todd

(1768-1849) American First Lady. Wife of James Madison, 4th President of the U.S. Birth name Dorothea Dandridge Payne. Married John Todd in 1790. Had two children. Her husband died in the yellow fever epidemic of 1793 in Philadelphia, along with their son William Temple Todd and John Todd's parents. In 1794, she met and married James Madison. Although they had no children, they raised Dolly's son John Payne Todd. Died at age 81 in Washington, D.C.

Last Words: "My poor boy."

Source: *The Memoirs and Letters of Dolly Madison, Wife of James Madison, President of the United States* by Dolly Madison and Lucia Beverly Cutts, her grand-niece (Boston, 1886).

Madison, James

(1751-1836) 4th President of the U.S. American statesman, lawyer, politician, educator. Member Virginia legislature, Continental Congress. Signed Constitution. Helped write *The Federalist Papers* with John Jay and Alexander Hamilton. Member U.S. House of Representatives from Virginia. U.S. secretary of state. Rector at University of Virginia. When he died at age 85 in Montpelier, Virginia, he was the last survivor of the founders of the United States. Many American cities and counties were named for him.

Different Last Words:

(1) "Nothing more than a change of mind, my dear." His response to his niece when she asked if anything was wrong. He died a few minutes later.

Source: *James Madison: A Biography* by Ralph Louis Ketcham (New York, 1971).

(2) "I always talk better lying down."

Source: *Facts About the Presidents* by Joseph Nathan Kane (New York, 1964).

Maeterlinck, Count Maurice Polydore Marie Bernard

(1862-1949) Belgian poet, playwright, essayist, writer. Awarded 1911 Nobel Prize for Literature. Notable works: *The Blue Bird; Pelléas et Mélisande* (the setting for Debussy's opera). Raised to the rank of count on his 70th birthday. Died at age 86 of a heart attack at his home in Nice, France.

Last Words: "For me this is quite natural. It is for you that I am concerned." Spoken to his wife.

Source: *Maurice Maeterlinck: Mystic and Dramatist* by Patrick F. Mahony (Los Angeles, 1951).

Maginot, André Louis René

(1877-1932) French politician. Member of chamber of deputies. Served in World War I. Advocated military preparedness. Encouraged construction of Maginot Line—line of forts and guns across northeastern boundary of France—named for him. Died at age 54 of typhoid fever before the Line was completed.

Last Words: "For me, this is the end, but you—continue." Spoken to French Premier Pierre Laval.

Source: *He Might Have Saved France: The Biography of Andre Maginot* by Marguerite Joseph-Maginot (New York, 1941). The author was his sister.

Magruder, John Bankhead

(1807-1871) American military officer. Known as Prince John. U.S. Army officer in Second Seminole War and Mexican-American War. Confederate brigadier general in U.S. Civil War. His actions delayed Union troops during the 1862 Peninsular

Campaign with elaborate ruses that confused Major General George B. McClellan into thinking the Confederate army had more forces than it actually had. After the Civil War, Magruder went to Mexico and served Emperor Maximilian I as major general in the Imperial Mexican Army. By May 1867, the emperor's forces had been beaten and Magruder returned to Houston, Texas. Died at age 63 in Houston. Fort Magruder and Magruder Boulevard in Virginia were named for him.

Last Words: "I don't think I am long for this world." Spoken to a hotel employee where he was staying.

Source: "The Late Gen. Magruder; Particulars of His Illness and Death, His Last Words" (*New York Times,* February 21, 1871).

Mahan, Alfred Thayer

(1840-1914) American historian, military officer, naval strategist. Captain in U.S. Navy. President of the Naval War College. Notable work: *The Influence of Sea Power Upon History, 1660-1783.* Died at age 74 in Quogue, New York.

Last Words: "If a few more quiet years were granted me, I might see and enjoy these things, but God is just and I am content." Spoken as he looked at a tree outside his window.

Source: *Mahan: The Life and Work of Captain Alfred Thayer Mahan* by William D. Puleston (New Haven, CT, 1939).

Mahler, Gustav

(1860-1911) Bohemian-born Austrian musician, composer, conductor. Director of the Imperial Opera in Vienna. Conducted at Metropolitan Opera in New York one season. Notable works: 10 symphonies (No. 10 unfinished); *The Song of the Earth; Songs on the Death of Children.* Died at age 50 of a blood infection in Vienna. Spent his last days in a sanitarium.

Last Words: "Mozart!" Spoken as he started to conduct an invisible orchestra.

Source: *Gustav Mahler: Memories and Letters* by Alma Mahler (New York, 1946). The author was his wife. Her life is the subject of the movies *Bride of the Wind* (2002) and *Alma Mahler* (2001).

Maier, Heinrich

(1908-1945) Austrian clergyman, activist.

Roman Catholic priest. Member of the Austrian Resistance during World War II. Executed less than two months before the war ended. He was the last executed victim of Hitler's régime in Vienna. A street in Vienna was named for him, and in 1995 the *Heinrich Maier Oratorium* was composed in his honor by Gerald Spitzner.

Last Words: "Es lebe Christus, der König! Es lebe Österreich!" (tr. "Long live Christ, the King! Long live Austria!")

Source: *Tatsachen, Begegnungen und Gespräche: Ein Buch um Österreich* by Lois Weinberger (Vienna, Austria, 1948).

Main, Sylvester

(1817?-1873) American musician, music publisher, singing teacher. Well-known chorister at Norfolk Street Methodist Church in New York City. Partnered with Lucius Biglow in 1867 to form the music publishing firm of Biglow & Main. Died in New York.

Last Words: "The dear Lord is about to give me rest. If you love me, do not weep, but rejoice."

Source: *Memories of Eighty Years* by Fanny Crosby (Boston, 1906).

Maintenon, Françoise Amiable d'Aubigné, Marquise de

(1635-1719) French historical figure, court favorite. Known for her intelligence and beauty. First husband was poet Paul Scarron. Mistress and second wife of Louis XIV. Founded school at Maison Royales de Saint-Louis, Saint Cyr. Died there at age 83. Many of her letters were later published.

Last Words: "I am not worthy." Spoken when she was asked to bless her daughters.

Source: *Madame de Maintenon* by Madeleine Marie Louise Chevrillon Saint-René Taillandier (London, 1922).

Malcolm X

(1925-1965) American activist. Black Muslim leader. Birth name Malcolm Little. Changed surname to "X" to symbolize changes in his life: "Ex-smoker, Ex-drinker, Ex-Christian, Ex-slave." Founded Organization of Black Unity. Assassinated at age 39 at the podium in a Harlem ballroom while making a speech.

Last Words: "Hold it! Hold it! Let's cool it!

Let's be cool, brothers!" Spoken to the three assassins who shot him multiple times.

Sources: *The Life and Death of Malcolm X* by Peter Goldman (New York, 1975); *Malcolm X: The Man and His Times,* ed. by John Henrick Clarke (New York, 1969).

Variation: "Let's cool it brothers."

Source: *A Change is Going to Come: Music, Race and the Soul of America* by Craig Hansen Werner (Ann Arbor, MI, 2006).

Malherbe, François de

(1555-1628) French poet, critic, translator. Known as the Father of French lyric poetry. Court poet to Henry IV and Louis XIII. Had such a passion for grammatical purity that he would destroy an entire quire of scarce paper composing a single stanza. Died at age 73 in Paris.

Last Words: "Don't speak of it any more. Your bad style leaves me disgusted." Spoken to his confessor, whose description of heaven bothered him.

Source: *Biographie universelle*, Book XXVI, by J. Fr. Michaud and Louis Gabriel Michaud (Paris, 1811-1862).

Variation: "Hold your tongue; your wretched style only makes me out of conceit with them." Spoken to his confessor who was using trite phrases to describe the joys of Heaven.

Source: "The Value of Last Words" by John Paul Bocock (*Frank Leslie's Popular Magazine,* Vol. XXXVIII, No. 2, August 1894).

Malibran, Maria Felicita

(1808-1836) French-born Spanish opera singer. Mezzo-soprano. Fell from her horse in a riding accident and never recovered. Collapsed while singing at a festival in Manchester, England. Died at age 28, nine days later.

Last Words: "I am a slain woman! They have bled me." Spoken to her physician.

Source: *Great Singers: Malibran to Materna, Second Series* by George T. Ferris (New York, 1880).

Malraux, André

(1901-1976) French writer, statesman. Active in French politics and culture. Fought with French Army and was Resistance leader during World War II. French minister for information and minister of culture. Notable work: *The Voices of Silence* (explores the role art can play in ennobling people's

lives). Died at age 75 in Paris.

Last Words: "It's endless drudgery to die."

Source: "Life of Andre Malraux Explored on Channel 13" by Walter Goodman (*New York Times,* June 11, 1987).

Manchester Martyrs
William O'Mera Allen,
Michael Larkin and William O'Brien

(d. 1867) Irish nationalists. Also known as the Three Fenians. William O'Mera Allen, Michael Larkin and William O'Brien were executed by hanging in 1867 in Manchester, England, for murdering a policeman during a prison break.

Last Words: "God save Ireland!" Called out from the dock by the Manchester Martyrs as they were being executed.

Source: *The Bold Fenian Men* by Robert Kee (New York, 1989).

Mandel, Maria

(1912-1948) Austrian military officer. Top-ranking Nazi official at Auschwitz-Birkenau extermination camp. It is estimated that she was directly responsible for orders to kill more than 500,000 people. The U.S. Army arrested her in 1945. She was extradited to Poland in 1946. In 1947 she was tried in Kraków and sentenced to death. She was hanged at age 36 in January 1948.

Last Words: "Long live Poland!"

Source: *The Camp Women: The Female Auxiliaries Who Assisted the SS in Running the Nazi Concentration Camp System* by D. P. Brown (Atglen, PA, 2002).

Mandrin, Louis

(1725-1755) French highwayman. A Robin Hood who smuggled goods to the poor and freed prisoners from jail. Became a popular folk hero. Arrested, tried and executed. His confession condemned him to death by the wheel.

Last Words: "Ah! What a moment, great God, and one that I ought to have foreseen!" Spoken before his execution.

Source: *Histoire de Louis Mandrin depuis sa naissance jusqu'a sa mort* by Leon Regley (Amsterdam, 1756).

Manekshaw, Sam Hormusji Framji Jamshedji

(1914-2008) Indian military officer. General and field marshal. Known familiarly as Sam Bahadur. He was the first general of the modern Indian army to be made a field marshal. Awarded this honorary rank in 1973 after four years as chief of army staff. His career spanned four decades and five wars. He died at age 94 in Wellington, Tamil Nadu, India.

Last Words: "I am okay."

Source: "'I am Okay' Were the Last Words of Sam Manekshaw" (*The Times of India,* June 27, 2008).

Manet, Édouard

(1832-1883) French artist. Founder and leader of impressionism. Notable works: *The Execution of Emperor Maximilian; The Fife Player; Bar at the Folies-Bergère; Olympia.* Became ill around 1881. Leg was amputated in 1883. Gangrene set in. Died at age 51 in Paris.

Last Words: "Take care! You'll hurt my foot!" Spoken to visiting friend Claude Monet when he put his hat on Manet's bed.

Source: *Manet* by Henri Perruchot (Cleveland, OH, 1962).

Mankiewicz, Herman J.

(1897-1953) American producer, screenwriter. Wrote screenplay for *Citizen Kane.* Died at age 55 in Beverly Hills, California.

Last Words: "Well that finishes everything I've got to take care of before I go to meet my maker. Or in my case, should I say 'co-maker'?" Spoken after his brother, the last of many visitors, left.

Source: *Mank: The Wit, World, and Life of Herman Mankiewicz* by Richard Meryman (New York, 1978).

Mankiller, Smoker

(d. 1875) Native American accused murderer. An 18-year-old Cherokee convicted and hanged for killing a neighbor after borrowing a rifle from him. Mankiller was one of six men put to death on one day in Fort Smith, Arkansas, by Isaac C. Parker, known as the Hanging Judge.

Last Words: Mankiller, who spoke only Cherokee, told onlookers through an interpreter that he was innocent and that he stood before them "convicted by prejudice and false testimony."

Source: *Isaac C. Parker: Federal Justice on the Frontier* by Michael J. Brodhead (Norman, OK, 2003).

Mann, Horace

(1796-1859) American educator, politician. Known as the Father of American Educa-tion. Revolutionized organization and teaching in public schools. Member U.S. House of Representatives from Massachusetts. President of Antioch College. Died at age 63 in Yellow Springs, Ohio.

Different Last Words:

(1) "Sing to me if you have the heart." He wanted to hear his wife sing to him before he died.

Source: *Until Victory: Horace Mann and Mary Peabody* by Louise Hall Tharp (Boston, 1953).

(2) "Now I bid you all goodnight." Spoken to his family.

Source: "Horace Mann and Antioch College" by George Allen Hubbell (*Ohio Historical Quarterly,* Vol. XIV, 1905).

Manning, Henry Edward

(1808-1892) English clergyman, prelate. Roman Catholic cardinal. Converted from Anglicanism to Church of Rome. Archbishop of Westminster. Eloquent preacher. Author of several books on religion. Active in temperance, education and housing the poor. Died at age 83.

Different Last Words:

(1) "Is there any use in your coming tomorrow? Then mind you come, Sir Andrew, at nine tomorrow." Spoken to his physician Sir Andrew Clark.

Source: *Life of Cardinal Manning, Archbishop of Westminster* by Edmund Sheridan Purcell (London, 1895).

(2) "I have laid down the yoke. My work is done." Spoken in Latin.

Source: *Cardinal Manning* by Robert Gray (New York, 1985).

Manolete

(1917-1947) Spanish bullfighter. Birth name Manuel Laureano Rodríguez Sánchez. Considered by some to be the greatest bullfighter of all time. Died at age 30 after being gored in the leg as he killed the fifth bull of the day. General Francisco Franco, then ruler of Spain, ordered three days of national mourning, during which only funeral dirges were broadcast on the radio. Museum of Bullfighting in Cordoba is dedicated to him. The 2007 movie *Manolete* depicts his career.

Last Words: "¡Qué disgusto le voy a dar a mi madre! ¡Don Luis, que no veo, no veo nada¡" (tr. "What sorrow [displeasure/

chagrin] I am going to give to my mother! Don Luis, I do not see, I do not see any- thing!") Spoken to Dr. Luis Gimenez Guinea.

Source: *Exposición Virtual* "Manolete," Ayuntamiento de Alicante Municipal Archives, www.alicante-ayto.es/ [Accessed 9/9/2009.]

Variation: "I can't feel anything in my legs, doctor. I can't see you, Don Luis."

Source: *Bull Fever* by Kenneth Tynan (New York, 1955).

Variation: "I can't feel anything in my right leg. I can't feel anything in my left leg. I can't see!"

Source: *The Twentieth Century Treasury of Sports* by Al Silverman and Brian Silverman (New York, 1992).

Variation: "I can't feel anything in my right leg. I can't feel anything in my left leg. Doc- tor, are my eyes open? I can't see!"

Source: *The Ultimate Book of Useless Information: A Few Thousand More Things You Might Need to Know (But Probably Don't)* by Noel Botham (New York, 2007).

Manouchian, Missak or Michel

(1906-1944) Turkish-born Armenian French Communist militant, activist, poet. Wrote poetry and edited political and literary jour- nals. Leader in resistance movement against Nazis in France in World War II. His final letters inspired poet Louis Aragon to write a poem about the group that was later set to music by Leo Ferré. Manouchian was exe- cuted at age 38. His last letter was written to his wife. Excerpts are shown here:

Last Words (written): "My dear Melinée, my beloved little orphan, In a few hours I will no longer be of this world. We are go- ing to be executed today at 3:00.— What can I write you? Everything inside me is confused, yet clear at the same time.—I will soon die with 23 of my comrades, with the courage and the serenity of a man with a peaceful conscience; for, personally, I've done no one ill, and if I have, it was without hatred.—I forgive all those who did me evil, or who wanted to do so, with the exception of he who betrayed us to redeem his skin, and those who sold us out. I ardently kiss you, as well as your sister and all those who know me, near and far; I hold you all against my heart. Farewell. Your friend, your com- rade, your husband.— Manouchian Michel.

P.S. I have 15,000 francs in the valise on the rue de Plaisance. If you can get it, pay off all my debts and give the rest to Arméne. MM"

Source: *Lettres des Fusillés*, preface de Jacques Duclos (Paris, 1970).

Mansfield, Katherine

(1888-1923) New Zealand-born British short-story writer. Pen name of Kathleen Mansfield Beauchamp Murry. Notable works: *The Garden Party; Bliss; The Doves' Nest*. Suffered from tuberculosis many years. Died at age 34 of a pulmonary hemor- rhage in France while seeking a cure.

Last Words: "I believe—I'm going to die." Spoken to her husband when she began hemorrhaging as they returned to their quar- ters. Her husband summoned doctors but they were unable to help. She died that eve- ning.

Source: *Katherine Mansfield's Letters to J. Middleton Murry*, ed. by J. Middleton Murry (New York, 1951).

Mansfield, Richard

(1857-1907) German-born Anglo-American actor. Performed on the English stage five years, then spent the rest of his career in America. Notable performances: *Dr. Jekyll and Mr. Hyde; Cyrano de Bergerac; Henry V; Beau Brummell;* Shylock in *The Mer- chant of Venice*. Died at age 50 in New London, Connecticut.

Last Words: "God is love." Spoken to his wife who said to him "God is life."

Source: *The Life and Art of Richard Mansfield* by Wil- liam Winter (New York, 1910).

Manzoni, Alessandro

(1785-1873) Italian writer, poet, novelist. Notable works: "Il Cinque Maggio" (poem); *The Betrothed* (novel). Became very ill after the death of his son. Died less than a month later at age 88 in Milan.

Last Words: "If I knew why it was, I wouldn't get them mixed up." His reply when asked why he was mixing up his words.

Source: *Manzoni and His Times: A Biography of the Author of "The Betrothed"* by Archibald Colquhoun (London, 1954).

Mao Zedong or Mao Tse-Tung

(1893-1976) Chinese Communist leader. Led Red Army in overthrow of Chiang

Kai-Shek. Founded People's Republic of China. Launched Great Leap Forward and Cultural Revolution. Words and writings about communism summarized in *Little Red Book*. Became enfeebled as he neared death. Died at age 82 in Beijing.

Last Words: "Really? No one? I don't believe it." Response to being told no one hoped that reaching his eighties he would have died sooner. He had said earlier that he should have died already.

Source: *Mao: A Biography* by Ross Terrill (New York, 1980). Terrill, a historian and China specialist, also wrote a biography of Madame Mao.

Marat, Jean Paul

(1743-1793) Swiss-born physician. Leader in the French Revolution. Joined with Robespierre and Danton in overthrowing the Girondists. Carried out wholesale massacres in 1792. Assassinated by Charlotte Corday who came to his apartment claiming she had information about a counter-revolutionary group. When she was let in, she handed him a list of conspirators. He read it, then commented: "They shall all be guillotined." While he was talking, she took knife from her dress and stabbed him.

Last Words: "A moi, ma chère amie, à moi!" (tr. "Help, my dear, help!") Cried out to a female companion as he collapsed and died.

Sources: *Feuille de correspondance, ou Nouvelles patriotiques pour les habitans des campagnes* (Paris, 1793). Carlyle gave a similar version, mixing French with English: "A moi, chère amie, help dear!" (tr. "Help, my dear, help dear!") in *The French Revolution: A History* by Thomas Carlyle (London, 1837).

Variation: "A moi, mes amis, à moi!" (tr. "Help, friends, help!") Cried out to a female companion as he collapsed and died.

Source: *Histoire populaire de la France,* Vol. 4 (Paris, 1863).

Maravich, Peter Press ("Pistol Pete")

(1947-1988) American athlete. Professional basketball player. Inducted into Basketball Hall of Fame in 1987. Voted one of the 50 Greatest Players in NBA history. Collapsed during pickup game in Pasadena, California. Died a short time later at age 40. Autopsy revealed he had played basketball many years without a left coronary artery.

Last Words: "I feel great."

Source: *Book of Sports Legends: Profiles of 50 of This*

Century's Greatest Athletes by Joseph J. Vecchione (New York, 1991).

Marconi, Guglielmo, Marchese

(1874-1937) Italian electrical engineer, inventor. His experiments led to practical wireless telegraphy and radio. Sent first signals across the Atlantic Ocean in 1901. Shared Nobel Prize for Physics with Karl Braun in 1909. Created marchese in 1929. Died at age 63 in Rome.

Different Last Words:

(1) "I'm feeling awfully ill."

Source: *Marconi: Pioneer of Radio* by Douglas Coe (New York, 1943).

(2) "But I don't care. I don't care at all." Spoken to his physician after telling him he knew he was dying.

Source: *Marconi* by Giancarlo Masini (New York, 1995).

Marcus Aurelius Antonius, Emperor of Rome

(121-180) Roman ruler, writer. Roman emperor. Notable work: *Meditations* (precepts on morality). Died of an infection at age 58 at his headquarters near Vienna, during his campaign in northern Europe.

Last Words: "Go to the rising sun, for I am setting. Think more of death than of me." His response when a tribune asked for the watchword.

Source: *Marcus Aurelius, a Saviour of Men, Sixteenth Emperor of Rome* by F.H. Hayward (London, 1935).

Margaret or Marguerite of Angoulême, Queen of Navarre

(1492-1549) French royalty, writer. Sister of Francis I, King of France. Queen of Navarre. Second husband was Henry II, King of Navarre. Famed as brilliant Renaissance writer. Notable work: *Heptaméron* (collection of stories in French, modeled on the *Decameron* of Boccaccio). Died at age 57 in Odos en Bigorre, France.

Different Last Words:

(1) "Jesus! Jesus! Jesus!"

Source: *Margaret of Angoulême, Queen of Navarre* by A. Mary F. Robinson (Boston, 1886).

(2) "Farewell and remember me."

(3) "I never departed from the true church."

Source for (2) and (3): *The Last Words (Real and Traditional) of Distinguished Men and Women Collected from Various Sources* by Frederic Rowland Marvin (New York, 1901).

Margaret of Antioch, Saint

(255?-275?) Holy woman, martyr from Antioch. Christian who was born the daughter of a pagan. Refused to renounce Christianity. Tortured. Executed by beheading.

Last Words: "Brother, draw thy sword now, and strike!" Spoken to her executioner.

Source: *The Golden Legend or Lives of the Saints.* Compiled by Jacobus de Voragine, Archbishop of Genoa, 1275, 1st ed., 1470. English ed. by William Caxton, 1483, ed. by F.S. Ellis (Edinburgh, 1900).

Margaret of Austria or
Margaret of Hapsburg

(1480-1530) Austrian royalty. Daughter of Holy Roman Emperor Maximilian I. Regent of the Netherlands. Guardian of nephew Charles (later Holy Roman Emperor Charles V). Died at age 50.

Last Words (written): "I have made you my universal and sole heir, recommending you to fulfill the charges in my will. I leave you your countries over here which, during your absence, I have not only kept as you left them to me at your departure, but have greatly increased them, and restore to you the government of the same, of which I believe to have loyally acquitted myself, in such a way as I hope for divine reward, satisfaction from you, monseigneur, and the goodwill of your subjects; particularly recommending to you peace, especially with the Kings of France and England. And to end, monseigneur, I beg of you for the love you have been pleased to bear this poor body, that you will remember the salvation of the soul, and the recommendation of my poor vassals and servants. Biding you the last adieu, to whom I pray, monseigneur, and give you prosperity and a long life. From Malines, the last day of November 1530.—Your very humble aunt, Margaret." Letter to her nephew Charles.

Source: *The First Governess of the Netherlands, Margaret of Austria* by Eleanor E. Tremayne (New York, 1908).

Margaret of Scotland
or Margaret Stewart

(1425?-1445) Scottish royalty, poet. Daughter of James I of Scotland. Became Dauphine with marriage to Louis XI of France. Wrote rondeaus and laments. Had an un-

happy marriage. Felt alienated at court and was depressed at the time of her death. Died at about age 20 in Chalons Sur-Marne, France.

Last Words: "Fi de la vie! Qu'on ne m'en parle plus." (tr. "Shame on life! Speak no more of it to me.") Her response when urged to rise above the melancholy she had sunk into, and live.

Sources: *Histoire de Charles VII,* Vol. IV, by Gaston Louis Emmanuel du Fresne Beaucourt, marquis (Paris, 1881-1891); *Dictionary of National Biography*, Vol. XXXVI, by Sir Leslie Stephen, George Smith and Sir Sidney Lee (London, 1921-1922).

Maria Christina, Princess of the
Two Sicilies, Queen of Spain

(1806-1878) Sicilian and Spanish royalty. Daughter of Francis I, King of Two Sicilies. Consort and fourth wife of Ferdinand VII of Spain. When he died in 1833, she became regent for daughter Isabella II. Married low-ranking soldier; tried to keep marriage secret. Unpopular for her intrigues. Removed as regent in 1840. Driven from Spain in 1854. Died at age 72 in Le Havre, France.

Last Words: "Tell my Alfonso he must console himself and make Spain flourish." Alfonso was her son Alfonso XII who took the throne when Isabella II renounced it.

Source: *Royal Vendetta: The Crown of Spain, 1829-1965* by Theo Aronson (Indianapolis, IN, 1966).

Maria Theresa, Empress of Austria

(1717-1780) Austrian royalty. Holy Roman empress. Queen of Hungary and Bohemia. Archduchess of Austria. Only woman ruler in 650 years of Hapsburg dynasty. Her reign spanned 40 years. Had 16 children. Mother of Marie Antoinette. Spent final few days upright in a chair; she could not breathe lying down. Died at age 63 in Vienna.

Last Words: "Open the windows!" (The window was already open.) "To thee! I am coming!" Her response to her son Joseph who asked: "Where does your Majesty want to go?" She then collapsed in his arms.

Source: *Memoirs of the Court and Aristocracy of Austria*, Vol. 2, by Eduard Vehse, tr. by Franz K.F. Demmier (London, 1896).

Maria Theresa or Marie Thérèse,
Queen of France

(1638-1683) French monarch. Daughter of

Philip IV of Spain. Married Louis XIV of France. Only one of her six children survived her: Dauphin Louis, who died in 1711. She died at age 44 at Versailles.

Last Words: "Yes. it is indeed frightful weather for a journey as long as the one before me." Spoken to her son who commented that it was raining.

Source: *Marie Theresa: The Last Conservative* by Constance Lily Morris (New York, 1937).

Mariam of Jesus Crucified or Blessed Mary of Christ Crucified

(1846-1878) Palestinian-born, holy woman. Known as the Little Arab. Birth name Mariam Baouardy. Born in Galilee. Entered Carmelite order at age 21. Helped found monasteries in India and in Palestine. At age 32, she fell and broke her arm while working in a Carmelite convent in Bethlehem. Gangrene set in. Died several months later. Beatified in 1983.

Last Words: "My Jesus, mercy."

Source: "The Little Arab" by Doris C. Neger (*Sophia*, 31:1, January-February 2001).

Marianne Cope, Blessed

(1838-1918) German-born missionary, holy woman. Birth name Barbara Koob. Member of Sisters of the Third Order of Saint Francis, Roman Catholic religious order. Lived among the lepers of Kalaupapa, Molokai, Hawaii. Died at age 80. Beatified in 2005.

Last Words: "Now Sister, to my room."

Source: *Mother Marianne of Molokai* by L.V. Jacks (New York, 1935).

Marie, Queen of Romania

(1875-1938) British-born Romanian royalty. Full name: Marie Alexandra Victoria Saxe-Coburg and Gotha, Princess of Edinburgh. Granddaughter of Queen Victoria and Tsar Alexander II. Consort of Ferdinand I, King of Romania. Mother of Carol II, King of Romania. Spent later years writing informative autobiography, *The Story of My Life*. Died at age 62 in Sinaia, Romania.

Last Words: "Be a just and strong king."

Source: *Marie of Romania: The Intimate Life of a Twentieth Century Queen* by Terence Elsberry (New York, 1972).

Marie Adelaide, Princess of Sardinia, Princess of Versailles

(1685-1712) French royalty. Married Louis the Dauphin of France at age 12. Mother of Louis XV, King of France. She and her husband fell ill with measles and died within a few days of each other. She was 26. He was 29. Their son Louis, Duke of Brittany, also contracted measles and died within a month.

Last Words: "Yes, my aunt." Spoken to the Marquise de Maintenon after being told she was "going to God."

Source: *A Rose of Savoy* by Noel Williams (New York, 1909).

Marie Antoinette, Queen of France

(1755-1793) French monarch. Daughter of Austrian Emperor Francis I and Empress Maria Theresa. Her arranged marriage to Louis XVI of France was an endeavor to strengthen an alliance between Austria and France. Imprisoned during the French Revolution. Brought to trial as "the Widow Capet." Condemned and executed by guillotine at age 37 in Paris.

Last Words: "Pardonnez-moi, monsieur." (tr. "I beg your pardon, monsieur.") Spoken to the executioner when she accidentally stepped on his foot.

Source: *Marie Antoinette: The Tragic Queen* by Dorothy Moulton Mayer (New York, 1968).

Marie Leczinska, Queen Consort of France

(1703-1768) Polish nobility. Full name Maria Carolina Sofia Felicia Leczinska. Daughter of dethroned King Stanislaus Leczinska of Poland. Became Queen Consort of France when she married Louis XV, King of France, in 1725. Grandmother of Louis XVI, Louis XVIII and Charles X. Died at age 65 in Versailles.

Last Words: "Rendez-moi mon fils, et vous me guérirez." (tr. "Give me back my children and you shall cure me.") Spoken to the physicians who sought a remedy for her illness. She had lost six of her ten children and recently her father.

Source: "Etudes Historiques—Marie Leczinska, Renne de France" by Dondey-Dupré (*Musée des Familles: Lectures du Soir*, Vol. XXXIV, 1866-1867).

Marie Louise, Empress of the French

(1791-1847) Austrian-born French royalty. Archduchess of Austria, later Duchess of Parma, Piacenza and Guastalla and finally as

the second wife of Napoleon Bonaparte, Empress of the French. Grandniece of Marie Antoinette. Mother of Napoleon II, King of Rome. Died at age 56 in Parma.
Different Last Words:
(1) "I will not sleep; I wish to meet death wide awake."
Source: *Best Thoughts of Best Thinkers: Amplified, Classified, Exemplified and Arranged as a Key to Unlock The Literature of All Ages* by Hialmer Day Gould and Edward Louis Hessenmueller (Cleveland, OH, 1904).
(2) "Go on praying." Spoken to the bishop who prayed by her bedside. As he began the Litany of the Dying, she sank into a coma and died.
Source: *An Imperial Victim: Marie Louise, Archduchess of Austria, Empress of the French, Duchess of Parma*, Vol. II by Mrs. Edith E. Cuthell (London, 1912).

Marie Thérèse Charlotte, Duchess of Angoulême

(1778-1851) French royalty. Daughter of Louis XVI and Marie Antoinette. Imprisoned with parents from 1792 to 1795. Became known as "Orphan of the Temple." Married Duke of Angoulême. Died in Austria.
Last Words: "My God, I am going to beg pardon for my sins; help Thy humble servant in this moment which is to be decisive for me for all eternity."
Source: *Les Dernières Années de la Duchesse de Berry* by Imbert de Saint-Amand (Paris, 1891).

Marion, Francis

(1732?-1795) American military officer. Fought in the American Revolution. Known as the Swamp Fox for hiding in forests and swamps during the war. Member South Carolina State Senate. Member of South Carolina constitutional convention. Died at age 63 at Pond Bluff, South Carolina.
Last Words: "My dear, weep not for me, I am not afraid to die; for, thank God, I can lay my hand on my heart and say, that since I came to man's estate, I have never intentionally done wrong to any."
Source: *The Life of General Francis Marion, a Celebrated Partisan Officer, in the Revolutionary War, Against the British and Tories in South Carolina and Georgia* by Brig. Gen. Peter Horry and M. L. Weems (Philadelphia, 1852). Originally published in 1824. Horry was a member of Marion's brigade.

Maris, Roger Eugene

(1934-1985) American athlete. Professional baseball player. New York Yankee who broke Babe Ruth's 34-year single-season home-run record in 1961. Diagnosed with lymphatic cancer in 1983. Established annual celebrity golf tournament to raise money for cancer research and treatment. Died at age 51 in Houston, Texas, where he was undergoing treatment.
Last Words: "I want a radio in my room."
Source: *Roger Maris* by Maury Allen (New York, 1986).

Mark, Saint

(d. 67?) Biblical figure, martyr, evangelist. Mentioned by Peter in his first Epistle. Wrote the Gospel with his name that is part of the New Testament. Chosen by Peter to be first bishop of Alexandria. Martyred in Alexandria during the reign of Nero.
Last Words: "I render my spirit into thy hands, O my God!"
Source: *Life of the Apostle and Evangelist Mark* by Severus, Bishop of Al-Ushmunain (fl. c. 955-987), tr. from Arabic by B. Evetts from Patrologia Orientalis, first series.
Variation: "Into Thy hands, O Lord, I commend my spirit."
Source: "The Martyrdom of St. Mark" in *The Ecclesiastical History of England and Normandy* by Ordericus Vitalis, Thomas Forester, M. Guizot and Leopold Delisle (London, 1853-1856).

Marlborough, 1st Duke of, see **Churchill, John.**

Marquette, Jacques ("Pere")

(1637-1675) French clergyman, missionary, explorer. Accompanied Louis Jolliet on an exploration of Midwestern America. Became ill. Tried to return to mission at Sault Ste. Marie. Died at age 37 of tuberculosis en route. Four Michigan communities claim to be his final resting place. City in Michigan and counties in Michigan and Wisconsin were named for him.
Last Words: "Jesus, Mary."
Source: *Pere Marquette: Priest, Pioneer, and Adventurer* by Agnes Repplier (New York, 1929).

Marryat, Frederick

(1792-1848) British military officer, novelist. Commander in Royal Navy. Known as Captain Marryat. Named Fellow of the

Royal Society for the improvements he made in maritime flag signaling and for other accomplishments. Wrote popular novels based on his sea experiences. Notable works: *Mr. Midshipman Easy; Masterman Ready*. Died at age 56 in Norfolk, England.

Last Words (written): "After years of casual, and, latterly, months of intense thought, I feel convinced that Christianity is true, and the only religion that can be practiced on this earth; that the basis of Christianity is love; and that God is love. To attempt to establish any other creed will only, in the end, be folly. But Christianity must be implanted in the breast of youth; there must be a bias towards it given at an early age. It is now half-past nine o'clock. World, adieu!" Message was dictated.

Source: *Life and Letters of Captain Marryat* by Florence Marryat (London, 1872). The author was his daughter.

Marseille, Hans-Joachim ("Jochem")

(1919-1942) German military officer. One of the ten most highly decorated German Luftwaffe pilots of World War II. Known as the Eagle of Africa. On his last flight, his plane engine caught fire. Killed at age 22 as he bailed out.

Last Words: "I've got to get out." When he put his plane on its back, the roof flew away and his body was pulled out. His parachute failed to open and he died when he hit the ground.

Source: *The Luftwaffe War Diaries: The German Air Force in World War II* by Cajus Bekker (New York, 1994).

Marsh, John

(1799-1856) American physician, pioneer, adventurer, lexicographer. Believed to be the first physician to practice medicine in California. Compiled first dictionary of the Sioux language. Murdered at about age 57 by three of his employees over a wage dispute as he traveled from Contra Costa County to Martinez, California.

Last Words: "Do you want to kill me?" Spoken to his killer. Marsh's son tracked down the man who killed him and brought him to justice.

Source: *John Marsh, Pioneer* by George D. Lyman (New York, 1930).

Marshal, William, 1st Earl of Pembroke and Strigul

(1146?-1219) English politician, military leader. Served four kings. Regent of England for Henry III for three years. Crusader in the Holy Land. Died near Reading, England.

Last Words: "Summon the countess and the knights, for I am dying. I can wait no longer, and I wish to take leave of them.—I commend you to God. I can no longer be with you. I cannot defend myself from death." Spoken to John of Earley. He then confessed his sins, was absolved and died.

Source: *William Marshal, Knight Errant, Baron, and Regent of England* by Sidney Painter (Baltimore, MD, 1933).

Marshall, Peter

(1902-1949) Scottish-born American clergyman. Presbyterian minister. Pastor of New York Avenue Presbyterian Church in Washington, D.C. Died at age 46 of a heart attack while Chaplain of the U.S. Senate. His story was told in the book *A Man Called Peter* by his wife Catherine and the 1955 movie based on it. Some of his sermons have been recorded and made available to the public.

Last Words: "You might ask Cranny to take the Senate prayer tomorrow." Spoken to his wife. Cranny was his friend Dr. Clarence W. Cranford of Calvary Baptist Church in Washington, D.C.

Source: *A Man Called Peter: The Story of Peter Marshall* by Catherine Marshall (New York, 1951).

Marsiglia, Eliza H. Ballentine Charruaud

(1799-1856) Wife of Gerlando Marsiglia. Died at about age 57 from the shock of hearing that her son had died aboard the U.S. steamer *Pacific*. The loss of the *Pacific* was one of the major news events of 1856. It disappeared with from 190 and 290 people aboard.

Last Words: "Tis only a thin gauze veil that holds me from Jesus."

Source: *Romana, Carteret and Bryant genealogy* by Catherina Baetjer (New York, 1887).

Marti, José

(1853-1895) Cuban nationalist, playwright, journalist, novelist, poet. Founded Cuban Revolutionary party. Inspired Cuban revolt.

Notable literary works: *Ill-Omened Friendship* (novel); "Guantanamera" (poem; set to music). Moved to New York City in 1881 and spent the rest of his life there. Planned an invasion of Cuba. Landed there with other exiles in April 1895. Killed at age 42 a month later in a skirmish with Spanish troops at Dos Rios.

Last Words (written): "There are some affections which involve such delicate points of honor." Unfinished letter.

Source: *Marti, Martyr of Cuban Independence* by Felix Lizaso (Albuquerque, NM, 1953).

Martin, Alfred Manuel ("Billy")

(1928-1989) American athlete. Professional baseball manager, player. Played for seven teams in 12 years. Held nine manager jobs with five separate teams. Manager of the New York Yankees five times, winning two American League championships and leading four teams to division championships. Killed at age 61 in a pickup-truck crash in Binghamton, New York. William Reedy, who was in the truck, heard Martin's Last Words.

Last Words: "Hang on! Look out!" Shouted an instant before the pickup-truck crash that killed him.

Source: *The Last Yankee: The Turbulent Life of Billy Martin* by David Falkner (New York, 1992).

Martin, R.A.C.

(d. 1872) American bank cashier. Was working at a bank in Columbia, Kentucky, when Jesse James and his gang robbed it. When Martin hesitated to turn over the keys to the safe, Jesse James shot and killed him. Frank James gathered up $600 from the cash drawers. A large crowd of bystanders chased the gang out of the bank but they were able to escape their pursuers.

Last Words: "Bank robbers!"

Source: *Encyclopedia of Western Gunfighters* by Bill O'Neal (Norman, OK, 1983).

Martin of Tours, Saint

(315?-397) French prelate, holy man. Bishop of Tours. Founder of Marmoutier monastery. First person to attempt to convert pagan Gaul. Patron saint of France. First saint honored for his asceticism, not for martyrdom.

Last Words: "Why standest thou here, horrible beast? Thou hast no share in me. Abraham's bosom is receiving me." He thought he saw the Devil near him.

Source: *Lives of the Fathers* by Frederic W. Farrer (London, 1907).

Martineau, Harriet

(1802-1876) English writer, journalist, philosopher, reformer. Gained fame for stories about the need for social and political reform. Attracted the attention of Wordsworth, Malthus and Carlyle. Her hearing was impaired and she had to use an ear trumpet. In her will, she wanted to leave her ears to science so physicians could learn more about the "auditory apparatus." Died at age 74 in Clappersgate, England.

Last Words: "I have had a noble share of life, and I do not ask for any other life. I see no reason why the existence of Harriet Martineau should be perpetuated."

Source: *The Autobiography of Harriet Martineau with Memorials* by Maria Weston Chapman (Boston, 1877). American abolitionist Maria Weston Chapman was her lifelong friend. They met when Martineau traveled to the U.S.

Martinuzzi, Utjesenovic ("Friar George")

(1482-1551) Hungarian prelate, statesman, monk. Birth name George Utjesenovic; used mother's surname Martinuzzi. Described as the Wolsey of Hungary. Bishop of Nagyvarad. Cardinal and archbishop of Esztergom. Assassinated by order of Holy Roman Emperor Ferdinand I, who suspected him of disloyalty.

Last Words: "Jesu, Maria!" Uttered while he was being executed.

Source: *Papacy and the Levant: The sixteenth century from Julius III to Pius V* by Kenneth M. Setton (Philadelphia, 1984).

Marto, Blessed Francisco

(1908-1919) Portuguese child visionary. One of three children who said they saw an apparition of the Virgin Mary at Fatima, Portugal, in 1917. Died at age 11 during the Spanish influenza epidemic that also killed his sister Jacinta. Beatified in 2000.

Last Words: "Mother, look at that lovely light by the door." He later said "Now I can't see it anymore." Spoken to his mother Olympia Marto.

Source: *The Children of Fatima: Blessed Francisco & Blessed Jacinta Marto* by Leo Madigan (Huntingdon, IN, 2003).

Variation: "Look, Mama, what a pretty light there, near the door! Now I don't see it any more. Mama, bless me and forgive me for all the trouble I have caused you in my life."

Source: *Last Words: Final Thoughts of Catholic Saints & Sinners* by Paul Thigpen (Cincinnati, OH, 2006).

Marto, Blessed Jacinta

(1910-1919) Portuguese child visionary. One of three children who said they saw an apparition of the Virgin Mary at Fatima, Portugal, in 1917. Died at age 10 in Lisbon during the same Spanish influenza epidemic that killed her brother. Beatified in 2000.

Last Words: "I have seen Our Lady. She told me that she was going to come for me soon and take away my pains. I am going to die. I want the Sacraments." Spoken to her nurse. She died a few minutes later.

Source: *Last Words: Final Thoughts of Catholic Saints & Sinners* by Paul Thigpen (Cincinnati, OH, 2006).

Marty, Christian

(1946-2000) French airline pilot. Victim of the Concorde disaster. Captain of Air France 4590 Concorde, the only Concorde to experience a fatal crash. Air traffic controllers had just warned him: "Concorde zero — 4590. You have flames. You have flames behind you." His Last Words were spoken as his reply.

Last Words: "Too late. No time, no."

Source: "A Key Runway Inspection Was Skipped the Day of the Concorde Crash, Investigators Report" by Donald G. McNeil Jr. (*New York Times*, September 2, 2000).

Martyn, Henry

(1781-1812) English clergyman, translator, missionary. Chaplain in India with the East India Company. Translated New Testament into Hindustani and Persian. Died at age 31 in Tokat, Armenia. His cause of death is unknown; he may have died of a plague.

Last Words (written): "Oh! when shall time give place to eternity? When shall appear that new heaven and new earth wherein dwelleth righteousness? And none of that wickedness which has made men worse than wild beasts—shall be seen or heard of any more." Written in his journal.

Source: *Essays in Ecclesiastical Biography* by Sir James Stephens (London, 1875).

Marvell, Andrew, Sr.

(1586?-1641) English clergyman. Father of English poet, satirist Andrew Marvell. In 1641 Andrew Sr. drowned while crossing the Humber in a ferry.

Last Words: "Ho for Heaven." Spoken as he boarded the ferry just before it sank.

Source: *Andrew Marvell* by Augustine Birrell (New York, 1905).

Marx, Julius Henry ("Groucho")

(1890-1977) American comedian, actor. Star of stage, screen, radio, television. One of the Marx Brothers, along with Harpo, Chico, Zeppo, Gummo. Hosted popular radio and TV game show *You Bet Your Life*. Won Emmy Award in 1951. Received honorary Academy Award in 1974. Died at age 86 of pneumonia in Los Angeles, California.

Last Words: "This is no way to live!"

Source: *Groucho* by Hector Arce (New York, 1979).

Marx, Karl Heinrich

(1818-1883) German economist, social philosopher, revolutionary, writer. With Friedrich Engels, he formulated the theory of dialectic materialism, or economic determinism. Notable works (collaborated with Engels): *Das Kapital; Communist Manifesto*. When his work was suppressed in Germany, he moved to London in 1849, and remained there the rest of his life. In poor health during the last decade. Died quietly at age 64 in an armchair in his London home.

Last Words (doubtful): "Go on, get out! Last Words are for fools who haven't said enough!" Spoken to his housekeeper who had encouraged him to tell her his final words so that she could write them down for posterity.

Source: Various Last Words compilations and Internet websites.

Marx was recuperating from pneumonia and his quiet but sudden death sitting in an armchair caught his family by surprise. Engels wrote a letter later that day that mentioned the state of Marx's health: a few days earlier Marx's physician told him there was a good chance Marx would be as healthy as he had been before. Marx's family had the same housekeeper for 40 years: Helene (Lenchen) Demuth, who raised the Marx children. She and Marx's daughter Eleanor were home when he died. It is highly unlikely that Demuth would encourage Marx to dictate his Last Words to her when she had no idea he was about to die.

Sources: *Sidelights on Contemporary Socialism* by John Spargo (New York, 1911); *Karl Marx: Biographical Memoirs* by Wilhelm Liebknecht (Chicago, 1901).

Marx, Leonard ("Chico")

(1887-1961) American comedian, actor. Star of stage, screen, radio. One of the Marx Brothers, along with Groucho, Harpo, Zeppo, Gummo. Often played the piano as part of his act. Died at age 74 in Hollywood, California.

Last Words: "Remember, Honey, don't forget what I told you. Put in my coffin a deck of cards, a mashie niblick, and a pretty blonde."

Source: *Growing Up with Chico* by Maxine Marx (Englewood Cliffs, NJ, 1980). The author was his daughter.

Mary Magdalen de' Pazzi, Saint

(1566-1607) Florentine mystic, holy woman. Carmelite nun. Suffered painful illness three years before she died at age 41. Canonized in 1669.

Last Words: "The last thing I ask of you— and I ask it in the name of our Lord Jesus Christ—is that you love Him alone, that you trust implicitly in Him and that you encourage one another continually to suffer for the love of Him."

Source: *Butler's Lives of the Saints* by Herbert J. Thurston and Donald Attwater (Westminster, MD, 1956).

Mary of Modena, Queen Consort of England

(1658-1718) English royalty. Birth name Maria Beatrice Eleanor Anna Margherita Isabelle d'Este. Daughter of Duke of Modena. Consort and second wife of James II, King of England. When James was deposed, she went to France. Died at age 59 of breast cancer in Paris. Her son, known as The Old Pretender, tried to claim the throne as James III but was unsuccessful. Rumors had persisted that he was switched at birth and was not the legitimate son of James II.

Last Words: "Molza, I pray you, when I am dead, send this crucifix to the king, my son." Spoken to Countess Molza while dying of pneumonia.

Source: *Queen Mary of Modena: Her Life and Letters* by Martin Haile (London, 1905).

Mary Stuart, Queen of Scots

(1542-1587) Scottish monarch. Only legitimate surviving child of James V of Scotland. Mother of James I of England/James VI of Scotland. Was next in line to the throne after Henry VIII's children. Titular queen of Scotland for six days. Charged with being an accomplice in the Babington conspiracy against Queen Elizabeth I. Tried and condemned to death. Beheaded at age 44 at Fotheringhay. Her story has been told in several dramas including those of Schiller and Swinburne.

Different Last Words:

(1) "Lord, into Thine hands I commend my spirit."

Source: *In the End is My Beginning* by Maurice Baring (New York, 1932).

(2) "Sweet Jesus." Spoken after the executioner missed her neck and hit the back of her skull.

Source: *Mary, Queen of Scots* by Antonia Fraser (New York, 1969).

Mary Tudor, Mary I, Queen of England and Ireland

(1516-1558) English monarch. Daughter and only surviving heir of Henry VIII and Catherine of Aragon. Queen of England from 1553 to 1558. Known as Bloody Mary. Tried to end Protestantism in England and reestablish Roman Catholicism. Persecuted Protestants. Died at age 42 at Saint James Palace, London.

Different Last Words:

(1) "When I am dead and opened you shall find Calais lying upon my heart." Mary was deeply troubled about the recent loss of Calais. When the English were expelled in 1558, they lost their last holding in France.

Source: *Dictionary of National Biography, from the Earliest Times to 1900*, Vol. XXXVI, by Sir Leslie Stephen, George Smith and Sir Sidney Lee (London, 1921-1922).

(2) "Miserere nobis, miserere nobis, dona nobis pacem." (tr. "Have mercy on us, have mercy on us, give us peace.") Spoken to a

faithful few at her bedside as she received Extreme Unction (Last Rites). Her strength then left her and she remained speechless until she died.

Source: *Mary Tudor* by Beatrice White (New York, 1935).

Mary II, Queen of England, Scotland and Ireland

(1662-1694) English monarch. Eldest child of James II. Married William of Orange. Had no children. Died at age 32 of smallpox. Different Last Words:

(1) "For Dr. Radclyffe has put a Popish Nurse upon me; and she is always listening to what is said about me; that woman is a great disturbance to me." Dr. John Radclyffe was a well-respected physician.

Source: *Princess and Queen of England* by Mary F. Sandars (London, 1913).

(2) "My Lord, why do you not go on? I am not afraid to die." Spoken to Archbishop Tillotson who read the prayer for the sick and was so overcome by grief he was forced to pause.

Source: "Anecdotes of Illustrious and Extraordinary Persons Perhaps Not Generally Known" (*London Review and Literary Journal*, May 1797).

(3) "I have but a little time to live and I would spend it a better way." Spoken as she refused further medical aid.

Source: *William and Mary* by Henri and Barbara Van der Zee (New York, 1973).

Mas Canosa, Jorge

(1938?-1997) Cuban exile leader, businessman. His dedication to freeing his homeland of communism influenced years of U.S. policy toward Cuba. Served as consultant to U.S. Presidents Reagan, Bush, Clinton. Died at age 58 of lung cancer in Miami.

Last Words: "Forward, forward, forward." Spoken to his son Jorge Mas Canosa Jr.

Source: "Castro Foe Dies; Played Key Role in U.S. Policy" (*Seattle Times*, November 24, 1997).

Masaniello, Tommaso

(1623?-1647) Neapolitan revolutionist. Birth name Tommaso Aniello. Led revolt in Naples against taxes levied by Spanish viceroy. Assassinated by his own soldiers.

Last Words: "Ah, ungrateful traitors!" Spoken to his assassins.

Source: *Monthly Magazine and British Register*, Vol. 52, December 1, 1821.

Variation: He sought refuge in a church. When he heard his name called, he thought his friends were looking for him. He replied: "You seek me? Here I am, my people." A moment later he was shot four times in the chest. He cried "Ingrates" and fell dead.

Source: *The Cambridge Modern History* by John Emerich Edward Dalberg Acton Acton, Adolphus William Ward, G. W. Prothero, Stanley M. Leathes (Cambridge, England, 1902-12).

Mason, John

(1503-1566) English educator, statesman. Served four monarchs as privy counselor: Henry VIII, Edward VI, Mary I and Elizabeth I. Chancellor of Oxford. Died at age 63. Last Words: "Were I to live again, I would change the court for a cloister, my privy counselor's bustle for a hermit's retirement, and the whole life I have lived in the palace for an hour's enjoyment of God in the chapel. All things now forsake me, except my God, my duty and my prayers." Spoken to those gathered around his deathbed.

Source: *The Power of Religion on the Mind in Retirement, Affliction, and at the Approach of Death: Exemplified in the Testimonies and Experience of Persons Distinguished by Their Greatness, Learning or Virtue* by Lindley Murray (New York, 1838).

Massavetas, Athanasios Nikolaos, see Athanasios Diakos or Athanasios the Deacon.

Massenet, Jules Emile Frédéric

(1842-1912) French musician, composer, educator. Notable operas: *Thais* (includes the popular "Meditation"); *Manon; Werther; Don Quichotte*. He also wrote ballets, oratorios, cantatas and orchestral pieces. Professor of composition at the Paris Conservatory. Gained much fame in 1870s. Made member of Legion of Honor in 1876 and Académie des Beaux Arts in 1878. Died in Paris at age 70.

Last Words: "Saint-Saëns would wish a grand funeral, but I would be content with a plain hearse and no fuss at all. I have been embraced, right in the theater, by the Prince of Monaco, but Saint-Saëns has not."

Source: *Massenet: A Chronicle of His Life and Times* by Demar Irvine (Seattle, WA. 1974).

Masters, Edgar Lee

(1868-1950) American writer, poet, biographer. Notable work: *Spoon River Anthology*. Died at age 81 in Melrose Park, Pennsylvania. He was buried in Oak Hill Cemetery, Petersburg, Illinois, the graveyard he made famous in *Spoon River Anthology*.

Last Words (doubtful): "Here, world, I hand you like an orange to a child. I can no more with you; do what you will."

Source: Various Last Words compilations and Internet websites.

The lines are part of Masters' poem *Tomorrow is My Birthday*, published in 1918. His loved ones chose it as his epitaph.

Source: *Spoon River Anthology* by Edgar Lee Masters (New York, 2004).

Masterson, William Barclay ("Bat")

(1853-1921) American buffalo hunter, military scout, lawman, gambler, journalist. Died at age 67 in New York City. Was at his desk at *New York Morning Telegraph*, preparing his column when he had a heart attack. Television series *Bat Masterson* was loosely based on his adventures.

Last Words (spoken): "All right." His response to a co-worker who asked about his health just before he collapsed.

Last Words (written): "Yet there are those who argue that everything breaks even in this old dump of a world of ours. I suppose these ginks who argue that way hold that because the rich man gets ice in the summer and the poor man gets it in the winter, things are breaking even for both. Maybe so, but I'll swear I can't see it that way." Part of his column that was in his typewriter when he died.

Source: *Bat Masterson: The Man and the Legend* by Robert K. DeArment (Norman, OK, 1979).

Mata Hari

(1876-1917) Dutch dancer, spy. Real name Margaret Gertrude Zelle. Wife of a Dutch military officer. Left her husband, changed her name and moved to Paris. Gained fame as an exotic dancer. Accused by the French of being a German spy during World War I. Executed at age 41 by a French firing squad. Movies based on her experiences include: *Mata Hari* (1931); *Mata-Hari* (1964); *Mata Hari, la vraie histoire* (2003).

Different Last Words:

(1) "Must I wear that?" She was talking about a blindfold. Her attorney Maitre Clunet turned to the French officer who responded: "If Madame prefers not, it makes no difference."

Source: Henry Wales' eyewitness account published in newspapers for the International News Service (October 19, 1917).

(2) "Thank you, monsieur." Spoken to the officer in charge of the firing squad.

Source: *Mata Hari: Courtesan and Spy* by Major Thomas Coulson (New York, 1930).

Mather, Abigail Phillips

(1670-1702) American mother and housewife. First of the three wives of religious leader Cotton Mather. Mother of nine of his 15 children. Died at age 32 of cancer after a long illness.

Last Words: "Heaven, heaven will make amends for all."

Source: *The Life and Times of Cotton Mather, D.D., F.R.S. Or A Boston Minister of Two Centuries Ago 1663-1728* by Abijah P. Marvin (Boston, 1892).

Mather, Cotton

(1663-1728) American clergyman, theologian, writer. Congregationalist. Son of Increase Mather. Served with his father at Second Church in Boston from 1685 until he died. Author of many religious books. Notable work: *Magnalia Christi Americana* (ecclesiastical history of New England). Died at age 65 in Boston.

Different Last Words:

(1) "Is this dying? Is this all? Is this all that I feared when I prayed against a hard death? Oh, I can bear this! I can bear it! I can bear it! I am going where all tears will be wiped from my eyes." Spoken to his wife the day before he died.

Source: *The Life and Times of Cotton Mather, D.D., F.R.S. Or A Boston Minister of Two Centuries Ago 1663-1728* by Abijah P. Marvin (Boston, 1892).

(2) "Grace." Uttered moments before he died.

Source: *The Life and Times of Cotton Mather* by Kenneth Silverman (New York, 1984).

Mather, Increase

(1639-1723) American clergyman, writer. Father of Cotton Mather. Wrote many religious treatises, sermons and political pamphlets. Served at Second Church in Boston. During the Salem witch hysteria, Mather warned other ministers to exercise caution and not jeopardize the innocent. Notable work: *Conscience Concerning Evil Spirits* (helped end witchcraft trials). Showed interest in scientific study; encouraged use of smallpox inoculation. Died at age 84 in Boston.

Last Words: "I do! I do! I do!" His response when his son Cotton told him: "This day thou shalt be in Paradise. Do you believe it, Sir, and rejoice in the views and hopes of it?"

Source: *Increase Mather, The Foremost American Puritan* by Kenneth B. Murdock (Cambridge MA, 1925).

Mather, Richard

(1596-1669) English-born American clergyman. Father of Increase Mather, grandfather of Cotton Mather. Minister of Dorchester, Massachusetts, church, One of the authors of *Bay Psalm Book,* first book printed in America. Famed as a preacher. Defended and expanded Congregationalism in America. Died at age 73 in Dorchester.

Last Words: "Far from well, yet far better than my iniquities deserve." His response to questions about his health during his final sickness.

Source: *Last Hours, Or Words and Acts of the Dying* by Augustus Charles Thompson (Boston, 1851).

Mathew, Theobald

(1790-1856) Irish clergyman. Roman Catholic Capuchin priest. Temperance reformer. Preached total abstinence. Spent two years preaching in U.S. Invited to dine with U.S. President Zachary Taylor at the White House. Also invited to the House of Representatives and Senate. He is credited with adding 600,000 members to temperance ranks. Died at age 66 in Cork, Ireland.

Last Words: "Yes." His response when his brother Charles asked if he wanted to be buried in a certain cemetery. Then when asked if the spot was under the Cross, he smiled and pressed his hand. It was the place he had chosen as his resting place many years earlier.

Source: *Father [T.] Mathew, a Biography* by John Francis Maguire (London, 1882).

Mathews, Charles

(1776-1835) English comedian, entertainer, playwright, theater manager. Performed skits based on his travels to America, France and elsewhere. One of Charles Dickens' favorite performers. Died on his 60th birthday in Devonport, England.

Last Words: "I am ready."

Source: *Memoirs of Charles Mathews, Comedian* by Mrs. Mathews (Philadelphia, 1839). Mrs. Mathews was his second wife, Anne Jackson, an actress whom he married in 1803.

Mathewson, Christopher ("Christy")

(1880-1925) American athlete. Professional baseball player. Spent most of his 17-year career with the New York Giants. Won 373 games, including 80 shutouts. One of the first Baseball Hall of Famers. Died at age 45 of tuberculosis in Saranac Lake, New York.

Last Words: "It's nearly over. I know it and we must face it. Go out and have a good cry. Don't make it a long one. This is something we can't help." Spoken to his wife Jane on his deathbed.

Source: *Matty: An American Hero, Christy Mathewson of the New York Giants* by Ray Robinson (New York, 1993).

Mathis, June Beulah Hughes

(1889-1927) American writer, producer. Hollywood film executive. Influential screenwriter who laid the groundwork for screenwriters to become producers. Responsible for more than 100 movies in a 12-year career. Notable films: *Camille; The Four Horsemen of the Apocalypse; Blood and Sand.* Died at age 38 in New York after suffering a heart attack.

Last Words: "Oh Mother I'm dying!" Apparently spoken to her grandmother who was with her. Her mother had died a few years earlier.

Source: *The Valentino Mystique: The Death and Afterlife of the Silent Film Idol* by Allan R. Ellenberger (Jefferson, NC, 2005).

Maturin, Basil

(1847-1915) English clergyman, writer, victim of the *Lusitania* disaster. Roman Catholic chaplain at Oxford University. Author of several religious books. Died when the ocean liner *Lusitania* sank.

Last Words: "Find its mother." Spoken as he handed a child into the last lifeboat that was lowered as the ship sank.

Source: *Father Maturin: A Memoir* by Maisie Ward (London, 1920).

Maugham, William Somerset

(1874-1965) English novelist, short-story writer, playwright. Notable works: *Of Human Bondage; The Moon and Sixpence; Cakes and Ale; The Razor's Edge.* Died at age 91 of pneumonia in Nice, France. Many of his books have been dramatized as movies and television series.

Last Words: "Why Alan! I want to say thank you and goodbye." Spoken to his secretary.

Source: *Somerset Maugham, a Writer for All Seasons: A Biographical and Critical Study* by Richard Albert Cordell (Bloomington, IN, 1969).

Maurice, John Frederick Denison

(1805-1872) English clergyman, theologian, social reformer, educator. Professor of literature and English history, King's College, London. Professor of moral theology at Cambridge. Co-founder of Christian Socialism movement. Died at age 66 in London.

Last Words: "The knowledge of the love of God—the blessing of God Almighty, the Father, the Son, and the Holy Ghost, be amongst you—amongst us—and remain with us forever."

Source: *Life of Frederick Denison Maurice* by C.F.G. Masterman (London, 1907).

Maury, Matthew Fontaine

(1806-1873) American military officer, oceanographer, meteorologist, educator. Commander in Confederate Navy in U.S. Civil War. Professor of meteorology at Virginia Military Institute. One of the founders of oceanography. The information Maury gathered on sea bottom enabled Cyrus Field to lay the first transatlantic telegraph cable. Died at age 67 in Lexington, Virginia. Maury Hall, U.S. Naval Academy, Annapolis, was named for him.

Last Words: "Are my feet growing cold? Do I drag my anchors? All is well."

Source: *Matthew Fontaine Maury, the Pathfinder of the Seas* by Charles Lee Lewis (Annapolis, MD, 1927).

Maximilian, Emperor of Mexico, Archduke of Austria

(1832-1867) Austrian-born Mexican emperor. Archduke of Austria. Married Carlotta, daughter of Leopold, King of Belgium. Became Emperor of Mexico when Napoleon III sought to extend his empire. Captured by Benito Juarez. Condemned by court-martial. Executed at age 34 by firing squad at Querétaro, Mexico.

Different Last Words:

(1) "I die in a just cause. I forgive all, and pray that all may forgive me. May my blood flow for the good of this land. Long live Mexico.— Men!"

Source: *The Phantom Crown: The Story of Maximilian and Carlotta of Mexico* by Bertita Harding (Indianapolis, IN, 1934).

Variation: "Mexicans! May my blood be the last spilt for the welfare of the country, and if more should be shed, may it flow for its good, and not by treason. Viva Independencia! Viva Mexico! "

Source: *The Story of Mexico* by Susan Hale (New York, 1889).

(2) "Lottie." He called out the name of his wife, Carlotta, who had gone to Europe to seek aid for him.

Source: *The Last Words (Real and Traditional) of Distinguished Men and Women Collected from Various Sources* by Frederic Rowland Marvin (New York, 1901). Marvin gave as his source: "Lippincott."

Maximilian, Saint

(274-295) Italian Christian, pacifist, holy man, martyr. Chose to die rather than be a soldier. Martyred in Numidia at age 21 for refusing to join the Roman army.

Last Words: "Give the new uniform you intended for me to the soldier who strikes me." Spoken to his father at his execution.

Source: *The Lives of the Saints* by Omer Englebert (New York, 1951).

Maxwell, C. L. ("Gunplay")

(1860?-1909) American murderer, thief. Utah gunfighter and outlaw. Birth name James Otis Bliss. Used several names but was best remembered as Gunplay Maxwell. Involved in a number of shoot-outs, robberies and rustlings. Finally brought down by Deputy Sheriff Edward Black Johnstone in a gunfight outside a saloon in Price, Utah.

Last Words: "Don't shoot again Johnstone, you have killed me."

Source: "C.L. Maxwell is Killed by Deputy Sheriff Johnstone. Coroner's Jury Finds That Officer Shot Outlaw in Self Defense. As When The Missourian's Mother-in-Law Died, 'No Complaint, Everyone Satisfied'" (*Eastern Utah Advocate*, August 26, 1909).

Maxwell, James Clerk

(1831-1879) Scottish mathematician, physicist, educator. Professor of physics and astronomy at King's College, London. Professor of experimental physics at Cambridge. Notable works: *On the Stability of Saturn's Rings* (essay); *Treatise on Electricity and Magnetism*. Demonstrated that electromagnetic energy travels through space in waves similar to those of light. Did research on color perception, color blindness and optics. Supervised building of Cavendish Lab at Cambridge. Died at age 48 of cancer at Cambridge.

Last Words: "I have looked into most philosophical systems and I have seen none that will work without a God."

Source: *The Life of James Clerk Maxwell* by Lewis Campbell and William Garnett (London, 1882). Campbell was a life-long friend of Maxwell.

Mayakovsky, Vladimir Vladimirovich

(1893-1930) Russian poet. Founder of Russian Futurism movement. Stalin called him "the best and most talented Soviet poet." Notable poems: "A Cloud in Trousers"; "The Backbone Flute." Committed suicide at age 36 in Moscow. Left an unfinished poem in a suicide note.

Last Words (written): "It isn't a brave way to go out for a revolutionist, but there is no other way out and I can stand it no longer." Part of his suicide note.

Source: "Red Kipling" (*Time* magazine, April 28, 1930).

Mayer, Frank H.

(1850-1954) American soldier, surveyor, rancher, editor, buffalo hunter. Drummer boy in U.S. Civil War. One of the last surviving Civil War veterans and buffalo hunters. Died at age 103 in Fairplay, Colorado.

Last Words: "I'm the last of the hide hunters left alive." Spoken to his nurse. He then slipped into a coma and died.

Source: "Last of the Hide Hunters" by Norman B. Wiltsey (*True West*, October 1957).

Mayer, Louis Burt

(1884-1957) Russian-born American motion-picture producer, Hollywood executive. Formed Metro Pictures Corporation, a producing company that merged into Metro-Goldwyn-Mayer. First vice president in charge of production at MGM. Received a special Academy Award in 1951 for his contributions to the industry. Died at age 73 of kidney failure in Los Angeles.

Last Words: "Nothing matters. Nothing matters." Spoken while hallucinating under a morphine drip.

Source: *Hollywood Rajah: The Life and Times of Louis B. Mayer* by Bosley Crowther (New York, 1960).

Mayhew, Jonathan

(1720-1766) American clergyman. Pastor of West Church, Boston. Noted as a preacher. Spoke out against British colonial rule. Strongly opposed the Stamp Act. Said: "No taxation without representation." Was Dudleian lecturer at Harvard in 1765. Died at age 45 in Boston.

Last Words: "My integrity I hold fast and I will not let it go." Spoken to a college friend, Rev. Dr. S. Cooper, who asked if he still held to his particular theological views.

Source: *Memoir of the Life and Writings of Rev. Jonathan Mayhew D.D., Pastor of the West Church and Society in Boston, from June 1747 to July 1766* by Alden Bradford (Boston, 1838).

Mazarin, Jules

(1602-1661) Sicilian-born French prelate, statesman. Born Giulio Raimondo Mazzarini. Succeeded Richelieu as prime minister. Made cardinal in 1641. Amassed great private fortune. Died at age 58 in Paris.

Different Last Words:

(1) "Ah! blessed Virgin, have pity on me and receive my soul."

Source: *Mazarin et Colbert* by Comte de Cosnac (Paris, 1892).

(2) "Oh! my poor soul! What will become of thee? Whither wilt thou go! Were I to live again, I would be a capuchin, rather than a courtier."

Source: *A Plea for Religion and the Sacred Writings: Addressed to the Disciples of Thomas Paine, and Wavering Christians of Every Denomination* by David Simpson (Philadelphia, 1809).

Mazzini, Giuseppe

(1805-1872) Italian nationalist, revolutionist, reformer. Founder of Young Italy. Sought a democratic state in a united Italy. Inspired Italians and other nationalist groups, especially India. Died at age 66 in Pisa.

Last Words: "Yes! Yes! I believe in God."

Source: *Mazzini: Prophet of Modern Europe* by

Gwilym O. Griffith (New York, 1932).

McAuley, Jeremiah ("Jerry")

(1839-1884) Irish-born American reformed thief. Spent six years in Ossining (Sing Sing) prison in New York. Became a social service worker. Founded Water Street Mission. Wrote his autobiography. Died at age 45 of hemorrhage in New York City.

Last Words: "It's all right up there." Spoken to one of the converts at the Water Street Mission in New York City as he pointed upward.

Source: *Jerry McAuley, an Apostle to the Lost* by R. M. Offord and Jerry McAuley (New York, 1970).

McCall, John ("Jack")

(1853?-1877) American miner, hunter, murderer. Used many aliases, including Bill Sutherland. Executed in Yankton, Dakota Territory, for the murder of Wild Bill Hickok. He claimed he killed Hickok because Hickok shot his brother; however, that allegation was refuted. McCall was tried for the killing and found innocent. He then went to Wyoming, where officials refused to recognize the verdict since the first trial was held in Indian Territory. McCall was tried again in Yankton, found guilty and hanged.

Last Words: As the marshal adjusted the noose, McCall asked for a moment to pray. He then said "Draw it tighter, marshal." As the drop fell, he cried out "Oh God!"

Source: *They Called Him Wild Bill: The Life and Adventures of James Butler Hickok* by Joseph G. Rosa (Norman, OK, 1987).

McCandless, Christopher J.

(1968-1992) American wanderer, journalist. Used the name Alex Supertramp. Brilliant, well-educated young man who spurned material goods, money and honors such as Phi Beta Kappa as irrelevant. Kept a journal of his physical and mental quest. Died at age 24 in the Alaskan wilderness. His body was found in an abandoned bus near Denali National Park. His story is told in the book and movie *Into the Wild*.

Last Words (written): "Visitors. S.O.S. I need your help. I am injured. Near death, and too weak to hike out of here. I am all alone; this is no joke. In the name of God please remain to help me. I'm collecting berries close by and should return this evening. Thank you. Chris McCandless. August." Written on a note tacked to the door of the old bus he was using as shelter.

Source: *Into the Wild* by Jon Krakauer (New York, 1997).

McCann, William ("Reddy")

(d. 1892) American frontier gunslinger. Faro dealer in Creede, Colorado, who was gunned down in a saloon by Texas lawman William Sidney "Cap" Light after an argument. McCann had been shooting out streetlights when Light confronted him. The coroner's jury showed that Light had used self-defense, but Light was so distraught over the killing he quit his job.

Last Words: "I'm killed."

Source: *Wild West Magazine*, April, 2006.

McCarty, Henry, see Bonney, William H.

McClain, James

(1933-1970) American revolutionary. Accused of stabbing a San Quentin prison guard while serving a sentence for burglary. Shot and killed while trying to escape during the Soledad Brothers hostage drama in a Marin County court room. Three others were killed, including a judge.

Last Words: "You take all the pictures you want! We are the revolutionaries!" Spoken to a news photographer who almost collided with the fleeing gunmen.

Source: "Justice: A Bad Week for the Good Guys" (*Time* magazine, August 17, 1970).

McClellan, George Brinton

(1826-1885) American military officer, politician. Served in Mexican and U.S. Civil Wars. Union general. Governor of New Jersey. Ran for U.S. President in 1864; defeated by Lincoln. Died at age 58 in Orange, New Jersey.

Last Words: "Tell her I am better now." He was referring to his wife.

Source: *General McClellan* by General Peter S. Michie (New York, 1901).

Variation: "I feel easy now. Thank you."

Source: *George B. McClellan: The Young Napoleon* by Stephen W. Sears (New York, 1988).

McCormack, John Francis

(1884-1945) Irish-born American singer. World-renowned lyric tenor. Gave up opera for recitals and concerts. Became U.S. citizen in 1919. Named papal count in 1929. Retired to Ireland. Died at age 61 in Booterstown, near Dublin.

Last Words: "So, you're here. In my opinion, all women should be strangled at birth." Spoken to his nurse. Fell into a coma and died two days later.

Source: *I Hear You Calling Me* by Lily Foley McCormack (Milwaukee, WI, 1949). The author was his wife.

McCormick, Cyrus Hall

(1809-1884) American manufacturer, inventor, industrialist. Developed successful mechanical grain reaper. Manufactured it on a large scale. His company, The McCormick Harvesting Machine Company, merged with other firms to form International Harvester. Died at age 75 in Chicago.

Last Words: "It's all right. It's all right. I only want Heaven."

Source: *Cyrus Hall McCormick* by William T. Hutchinson (New York, 1935).

McDaniel, Hattie

(1895-1952) American actress, singer. Screen, radio and television star. First African American performer to be nominated for and to win an Academy Award: Best Supporting Actress for her performance in *Gone With the Wind*. Died at age 57 of breast cancer in Los Angeles. Her story is told in the AMC TV biography *Beyond Tara: The Extraordinary Life of Hattie McDaniel* (2001).

Last Words: "I'll be all right. I'll soon be up and back in harness."

Source: *Hattie: The Life of Hattie McDaniel* by Carlton Jackson (Lanham, MD, 1990).

McGraw, John Joseph

(1873-1934) American athlete. Professional baseball player, manager. Played and managed Baltimore Orioles and New York Giants. Known as Little Napoleon for his management style. Won ten National League titles for the Giants. Member of the Baseball Hall of Fame. Died at age 60 of uremic poisoning in New Rochelle, New York.

Last Words (written): "Thanks for your kindness and well wishes." Letter sent to fans two days before he died.

Source: "An Update on My Health" by John J. McGraw (*New York Times,* February 23, 1934).

McGraw, Thomas ("Tam")

(1952-2007) Scottish criminal. Known as The Licensee. Involved in organized crime, including extortion, narcotics and drug trafficking in Glasgow. Died of an apparent heart attack at his home. Was one of the wealthiest businesspeople in Scotland when he died.

Last Words: "Margaret, bring me a slice of toast and a cup of tea." Spoken to his wife. She found him slumped over.

Source: "He Called for Toast Then Died" by David Leslie (*News of the World*, August 5, 2007).

McGuffey, William Holmes

(1800-1873) American educator, writer. President of Ohio University. Professor at Miami University, University of Virginia. Notable work: *McGuffey's Eclectic Readers* (series of popular textbooks). More than 120 million copies were sold. Died at age 72 in Charlottesville, Virginia.

Last Words: "Oh that I might once more speak to my dear boys! But Thy will be done."

Source: *William Holmes McGuffey and the Peerless Pioneer McGuffey Readers* by Harvey C. Minnich (Oxford, OH, 1928).

McIntyre, Oscar Odd ("O.O.")

(1884-1938) American journalist. Syndicated column *New York Day by Day* appeared in hundreds of newspapers. Died at age 53 in New York City.

Last Words: "Snooks, will you please turn this way. I like to look at your face." Spoken to his wife Maybelle. She died in 1985 at age 101.

Source: *The Life of O.O. McIntyre* by Charles B. Driscoll (New York, 1938).

McKinley, Ida Saxton

(1847-1907) American First Lady. Wife of U.S. President William McKinley. Was in Buffalo with her husband but not in the Temple of Music with him when he was shot. Suffered from epileptic seizures. Died at age 59 in Canton, Ohio, after a long illness.

Last Words: "Why should I linger? Please God, if it is Thy will, why defer it? He is gone and life is dark to me."

Source: "McKinley, Mrs. Wm." (*Carlton County* [New Brunswick, Canada] *Press*, July 29, 1907).

McKinley, William

(1843-1901)   25th President of the U.S. American politician. Member U.S. House of Representatives from Ohio. Governor of Ohio. Shot by anarchist Leon Czolgosz at the Pan American Exposition, Buffalo, New York, on September 6, 1901. Died a week later at age 58.

Different Last Words:

(1) "We are all going, we are all going, we are all going. Oh, dear." Spoken to his wife.
Source: *The Life of William McKinley* by Charles S. Olcott (Boston, 1916).

(2) "It's God's way. His will, not ours, be done."
Source: *Encyclopedia of Religion in American Politics,* ed. by Jeffrey D. Schultz, John G. West Jr. and Iain Maclean (Westport, CT, 1999).

Variation: "Good-bye all, good-bye. It is God's way. His will be done." He made a feeble movement as if trying to clasp his wife's hand then lapsed into unconsciousness.
Source. *The Authentic Life of William McKinley: Our Third Martyr President Together with a Live Sketch of Theodore Roosevelt* by Alexander K. McClure and Charles Morris (1901).

McLaury, Thomas Clark

(1853-1881) American cowboy. Killed by Doc Holliday at OK Corral in Tombstone, Arizona. Brother Frank also killed.
Last Words: "I'm not armed!" Spoken as he opened his coat. Holliday then shot him.
Source: *Encyclopedia of Western Gunfighters* by Bill O'Neal (Norman, OK, 1979).

McLoughlin, John

(1784-1857) Canadian-American physician, fur trader, settler. Worked with Hudson's Bay Company. Contributed to settling of Oregon. Known as The Father of Oregon. Died at age 72 in Oregon City.
Last Words: "To God." His response when asked: "Comment allez-vous?"
Source: *The White-Headed Eagle* by Richard G. Montgomery (New York, 1934).

McMillan, Rachel

(1859-1917) American-born British educator, social worker. Family returned to Scotland when she was a child. She and her sister Margaret headed the campaign for school meals that led to the 1906 Provision of School Meals Act. They also opened Brit-

ain's first school clinic providing medical and dental help. Established Night Camp where underprivileged children could wash and wear clean nightclothes. Rachel suffered from poor health. Died on her 58th birthday.
Last Words: "Poor Little Peter...Totty."
Source: *Margaret McMillan: Portrait of a Pioneer* by Elizabeth Bradburn (New York, 2000).

McNeil, Hugh W.

(1830-1862) American military officer. Union colonel in U.S. Civil War. Killed in action near Sharpsburg, Maryland.
Last Words: "Forward Bucktails, forward!" He and his men had escaped Confederate fire by lying down every few paces. But when McNeil thought they were safe, he stood and shouted. He was shot and killed instantly. His men routed the Confederates.
Source: *History of the "Bucktails" Kane Rifle Regiment of the Pennsylvania Reserve Corps (13th Pennsylvania Reserves, 42nd of the Line)* by Osmond Rhodes, Howard Thomson and William H. Rauch (Philadelphia, 1906).

McPherson, James Birdseye

(1828-1864) American military officer. General in Union Army during U.S. Civil War. Commanded Army of the Tennessee. Killed in action near Atlanta, Georgia. Shot in the back while riding toward the battlefield with his orderly Jackson Thompson.
Last Words: "Oh, orderly, I am." His response when asked if he was hurt. Within minutes, he was dead.
Source: "Gen. M'Pherson's Death: The Detailed Story Told by His Orderly. Jackson Thompson's Interesting Narrative—How His Commander was Killed on the Battle-field" (*New York Times,* August 15, 1881).

McQueen, Terence Steven ("Steve")

(1930-1980) American actor. Screen star. Nominated for six Golden Glove awards; won twice as Male World Film Favorite. Died at age 50 of lung cancer in Juarez, Mexico.
Last Words: "Terry—Chad—Barbara." He called out the names of his daughter, son and wife.
Source: *Steve McQueen: Portrait of an American Rebel* by Terrill Marshall (New York, 1993).

McSween, Alexander Anderson ("Max")

(1843-1878) Canadian-born lawyer. Lived in Lincoln County, New Mexico. Formed business partnership with rancher John

Henry Tunstall. Accused of embezzlement by former employer, the Murphy-Dolan law firm. The firm harassed McSween and rustled Tunstall's cattle, triggering what became known as the Lincoln County War. McSween and Tunstall hired a group of gunmen—the Lincoln County Regulators—to protect themselves; one of them was Billy the Kid. Tunstall was murdered in February 1878. In July, McSween was trapped in his home with Billy the Kid and other Regulators. His enemies—Murphy/Dolan and the Seven Rivers Cowboys—set fire to the house to force them outside. McSween was shot and killed in the backyard of his burning house.

Last Words: "I shall never surrender." When he shouted these words, both sides opened fire, killing McSween and two others.

Source: *Buried Treasure: Famous and Unusual Gravesites in New Mexico History* by Richard Melzer (Santa Fe, NM, 2007).

McVeigh, Timothy

(1968-2001) American terrorist, soldier in U.S. Army, security guard. Bombed Alfred P. Murrah Federal Building in Oklahoma City in 1995, killing 168 people. Tried, convicted, executed by lethal injection at the federal penitentiary in Terre Haute, Indiana.

Last Words (written): McVeigh issued a handwritten copy of the poem "Invictus" by English poet William Ernest Henley that ends with the lines: "I am the master of my fate. I am the captain of my soul." McVeigh remained silent.

Source: "Defiant McVeigh Dies in Silence" (BBC News, June 11, 2001).

Mead, Margaret

(1901-1978) American anthropologist, writer, lecturer. Curator of the American Museum of Natural History. Notable works: *Coming of Age in Samoa; Growing Up in New Guinea.* One of most famous anthropologists in the world during her lifetime. Died at age 77 of cancer in New York City.

Last Words: "But this is different." Her response to the nurse who replied, "We will all someday," after she told the nurse she was dying.

Source: *Margaret Mead: A Life* by Jane Howard (New York, 1984).

Meade, George Gordon

(1815-1872) American military officer, civil engineer. Union general in U.S. Civil War. Commanded Army of the Potomac. Defeated Lee at Gettysburg. Died at age 56 in Philadelphia.

Last Words: "I am about crossing a beautiful wide river, and the opposite shore is coming nearer and nearer."

Source: *The Life and Letters of General George Gordon Meade* by George Meade (New York, 1913).

Meagher, Mike

(1843-1881) Irish-born stagecoach driver, saloon keeper, politician, lawman. Appointed deputy U. S. marshal in 1874. Mayor of Caldwell, Kansas. Killed in a shootout with Texan Jim Talbot and three other men.

Last Words: "Yes. Tell my wife I have got it at last." His response when asked if he had been hit. He was taken to a nearby barber shop where he died a half hour later.

Source: *Encyclopedia of Western Gunfighters* by Bill O'Neal (Norman, OK, 1983).

Médici, Catherine de'

(1519-1589) Italian-born French noblewoman, royalty. Daughter of Lorenzo de' Medici. Full name Caterina Maria Romola di Lorenzo de' Medici. Queen Consort of Henry II of France. Mother of three French kings: Francis II, Henry III and Charles IX. Planned St. Bartholomew's Day massacre of Huguenots in 1572. Died at age 69 at Blois, France.

Last Words: "Ah! My God, I am dead!" Cried out when she discovered the name of her confessor was one that a prophecy said she should fear. She was told she would die close to Saint Germain (a city near Paris). The confessor was Julien de Saint Germain. She died soon after learning his name.

Source: *Catherine de' Médici: ses astrologues et ses magiciens envoûteurs, documents inédits sur la diplomatie et les sciences occultes du XVIe siècle* by Eugene Defrance (Paris, 1911).

Medici, Lorenzo de'

(1449-1492) Florentine statesman, ruler, patron of arts. Known as Lorenzo the Magnificent. Died at age 43 in Careggi, Italy. His tomb was designed by Michelangelo.

Last Words: "As a dying man always does."

His response when asked how he enjoyed a bit of food. He then embraced his friends and submitted to the last ceremonies of the church. He repeated scripture and pressed a crucifix to his lips then calmly died.

Source: *Life of Lorenzo de' Medici, Called The Magnificent* by William Roscoe (London, 1895).

Medill, Joseph

(1823-1899) Canadian-born American publisher, politician. Business and managing editor of *Chicago Tribune*. Credited with securing political recognition for Abraham Lincoln while he was still a country lawyer. Mayor of Chicago. He was elected immediately after the great fire. Ill health and pressures of public office caused him to take a leave of absence. Died at age 75 in San Antonio, Texas, where he had gone for his health three months earlier.

Last Words: "My last words shall be 'What is the news?'" Spoken to his physician ten minutes before he died.

Source: "Joseph Medill is Dead; Editor of The Chicago Tribune Passes Away in San Antonio After Lingering Illness" (*New York Times*, March 17, 1899).

Medina, Pedro Luis

(1957-1997) Cuban-born American convicted murderer. Figure in Eighth Amendment case. Arrived in the U.S. during 1980 Mariel boat lift. Executed at Florida State Prison for stabbing and killing a teacher in Orlando in 1982. The electric chair malfunctioned, causing flames to shoot from Medina's head. His execution is noteworthy not only because of his maintained innocence, but because of the horrific way he was killed. Two years after he was executed, Medina's death played a key role in a legal argument in Florida that argued the electric chair was a cruel and unusual punishment. Medina's pastor and another witness testified that flames and smoke rose from Medina's head with an acrid smell and that it took three labored breaths after the electrical current was applied before he died.

Last Words: "I am still innocent."

Source: "Revenge and the Sixth Commandment" by Joe Sharkey (*New York Times*, June 22, 1997).

Meher Baba ("Compassionate Father")

(1894-1969) Indian guru. Birth name Mer-

wan Sheriar Irani. Stopped speaking in 1925. Maintained silence until shortly before he died at age 74 in Meherazad, India. One of his last utterances in 1925 was "Don't worry, be happy," popularized in a song by Bobby McFerrin in 1988.

Last Words: "How fortunate you are that you have heard my voice so many times today! This incident with the snake took place to allow you to hear me speak for the final time."

Source: *Meher Prabhu: Lord Meher* by Bhau Kalchuri (North Myrtle Beach, SC, 1997).

Meir, Golda

(1898-1978) Russian-born Israeli politician, stateswoman. Raised in U.S. Birth name Golda Mabovitz. Moved to Palestine in 1921. After creation of Israel, served as minister to Moscow, labor minister and foreign minister. Chosen prime minister in 1969. Resigned in 1974. Died at age 80 of cancer in Jerusalem.

Last Words: "About the afterworld." Her response when asking what she was thinking about.

Source: *My Mother Golda Meir: A Son's Evocation of Life with Golda Meir* by Menahem Meir (New York, 1983).

Melanchthon, Philip

(1497-1560) German scholar, religious reformer. Birth name Philip Schwarzert. Friend and collaborator with Martin Luther in Protestant Reformation.

Last Words: "Nothing but heaven. And therefore do not ask me such questions any more." His response when asked if he wanted anything. He then asked: "What are you doing? Why do you disturb my sweet repose? Let me rest unto the end, for it will not last very long." Then, when asked if he could hear the psalm that was read, he replied: "Yes."

Source: *Life of Melanchthon* by Karl Friedrich Ledderhose (Philadelphia, 1855).

Melba, Dame Nellie

(1861-1931) Australian musician, singer. World-renowned operatic soprano. Outstanding coloratura. Real name Helen Porter Mitchell. Took the name Melba from the city of Melbourne near where she grew up. Associated with Metropolitan Opera in New

York and London's Covent Garden. Notable roles: Lucia, Marguerite, Gilda, Desdemona, Violetta, Mimi. Created Dame of the British Empire in 1918. Died at age 69 in a hospital in Sydney, Australia. *Melba* (1953) is a fictionalized movie of her life. Melba toast, Melba sauce and peach Melba were named for her.

Last Words: "John, why must I be subjected to a lingering death?" Spoken to a friend. Later, when she tried to sing a few bars of Gounod's "Ave Maria," her voice failed her.

Sources: *I Am Melba: A Biography* by Ann Blainey (Melbourne, Australia, 2008); *Australia, Beyond the Dreamtime* by Thomas Keneally, Patsy Adam-Smith, and Robyn Davidson (London, 1987).

Melchior, Lauritz

(1890-1973) Danish-born American musician, singer. World-renowned operatic tenor, screen and television performer. Sang with Metropolitan Opera. Notable roles: Siegfried, Lohengrin, Siegmund, Parsifal, Tristan. Died at age 82 in Santa Monica, California.

Last Words: "Have a good life." Spoken to his granddaughter.

Source: *Tristanissimo: The Authorized Biography of Heroic Tenor Lauritz Melchior* by Shirlee Emmons (New York, 1990). Emmons, a singer and voice teacher, toured the U.S. and Canada with Melchior.

Mellon, Richard B. ("R.B.")

(1858-1933) American banker, industrialist, philanthropist. Known as R.B. President of Aluminum Company of America (Alcoa). He and his brother Andrew were multimillionaires who established Mellon Fund philanthropic foundations. They maintained ultraconservative, tight-lipped appearances; however, privately they played unending practical jokes on each other well into their eighties. One, an ongoing game of tag, explains Richard's Last Words. Using his last breath, he called his brother close to his bedside and whispered the words "last tag" just before he died, ostensibly leaving his brother Andrew permanently "it."

Last Words: "Last tag. "

Source: *Zanies—The World's Greatest Eccentrics* by Jay Robert Nash (Piscataway, NJ, 1982).

Melville, Herman

(1819-1891) American writer, novelist. Cus-

toms inspector for New York City for 19 years. Notable works: *Moby Dick; Billy Budd; Omoo; Typee.* Died at age 72 of heart failure in New York City, almost unknown.

Last Words: "God bless Captain Vere!" He was quoting from his novel *Billy Budd*, which was found in manuscript form on his desk after he died.

Source: *Herman Melville: A Study of His Life and Vision* by Lewis Mumford (New York, 1929).

Mencken, Henry Louis ("H.L.")

(1880-1956) American journalist, editor, writer, critic. Born, lived and died in Baltimore and spent most of his life in the same row house. Influential American literary critic. Co-founder and editor of *The American Mercury*. Had a stroke that impaired his speech and ability to write. Died at age 75 of heart failure in Baltimore.

Last Words: "Louis, this the last time you'll see me." Spoken to a friend. He was dead by the following day.

Source: *Mencken: A Life* by Fred Hobson (New York, 1994).

Mendeleyev or Mendeleev, Dmitri Ivanovich

(1834-1907) Russian chemist. Born in Siberia. Developed periodic table of the elements. Recognized that some elements still had to be discovered. Left spaces in his periodic table where he predicted they would fall. Professor of general chemistry at University of St. Petersburg. Notable work: *Principles of Chemistry* (textbook). Died at age 72 in St. Petersburg, Russia. The element mendelevium was named for him.

Last Words (doubtful): "Doctor, you have science. I have faith." Spoken to a physician treating him.

Source: Various Last Words compilations and Internet websites.

This quote is a line from Jules Verne's *A Journey to the North Pole* (1875). While it appeared in a biography of Mendeleyev, it was spoken originally by Captain Hatteras, one of Verne's characters, and is treated as such in the biography.

Source: *Mendeleyev, the Story of a Great Scientist* by Daniel Q. Posin (Chicago, 1948).

Mendelssohn-Bartholdy, Felix

(1809-1847) German musician, composer,

pianist, conductor. Full name Jacob Ludwig Felix Mendelssohn-Bartholdy. Notable works: *Fingal's Cave; A Midsummer Night's Dream* (overtures); *Reformation, Italian, Scottish, C Minor* (symphonies); violin and piano concertos. Died at age 38 in Leipzig after a series of strokes.

Last Words: "Ja, ich bin müde, schrecklich müde." (tr. "Yes, I am tired, awfully tired.") His response to his wife who had asked if he was tired. He then had another stroke, fell into a coma and died.

Source: *Grove's Dictionary of Music and Musicians*, Fifth Edition, ed. by Eric Blom (New York, 1973).

Variation: "Weary, very weary." His response when asked how he was feeling.

Source: *Mendelssohn-Bartholdy, Mensch und Werk* by Bernhard Bartels (Bremen, Germany, 1947).

Menelik II, Emperor of Ethiopia

(1844-1913) Ethiopian monarch. Ruled from 1889 to 1913. Created the modern nation of Ethiopia. Introduced national currency, rail, telephone, telegraph and postal service. Died at age 69 in Addis Ababa. Succeeded by his grandson Lij Yasu.

Last Words: "God, help my people!"

Source: *Haile Selassie: The Conquering Lion* by Leonard Oswald Mosley (Englewood Cliffs, NJ, 1965).

Mercer, Hugh

(1726-1777) Scottish-born American military officer, physician. Served in Jacobite Army at the Battle of Culloden. Fled England for America in 1747 after Prince Charles Edward was defeated. Mercer served in the French and Indian War and the American Revolution. Fatally wounded at the Battle of Princeton. Died nine days later. Some 30,000 mourners attended his funeral in Philadelphia. American artist John Trumbull made a portrait drawing of *The Death of General Mercer at the Battle of Princeton, January 3, 1777*. Seven U.S. counties and a city were named for Mercer.

Different Last Words:

(1) "My death is owing to myself.—To die as I had lived, an honored soldier in a just and righteous cause."

Source: *The Pattons: A Personal History of an American Family* by Robert H. Patton (Washington, D.C., 2004).

(2) "What is to be is to be! Good-bye dear native land. Farewell adopted country. Into

thy care, O America, I commit my fatherless family. May God prosper our righteous cause. Amen."

Source: *With Sword and Lancet: The Life of General Hugh Mercer* by Joseph M. Waterman (Richmond, VA, 1941).

(3) "This wound will surely cause my death."

Source: *A Conspectus of American Biography: Being an Analytical Summary of American History and Biography, Containing also the Complete Indexes of the National Cyclopedia of American Biography* by George Derby (New York, 1906).

Mercier, Désiré Joseph

(1851-1926) Belgian prelate, educator. philosopher. Professor of Thomistic philosophy. Archbishop of Malines, Belgium. Cardinal of the Roman Catholic Church. Leader of revival of interest in Thomistic scholasticism. Died at age 74 in Brussels.

Last Words: "Now there is nothing more to be done, except to wait." Spoken after he received the Last Rites.

Source: *The Life of Cardinal Mercier* by John A. Gade (New York, 1934).

Meredith, George

(1828-1909) English novelist, poet, writer. Friend of Rossetti, Swinburne. Notable works: *The Ordeal of Richard Feverel; Diana of the Crossways*. Disabled by paralysis and deafness in later years. Seldom left his home. Died at age 81 at his home in Box Hill, Surrey.

Last Words: "I am afraid Sir Thomas thinks very badly of my case."

Source: *The Ordeal of George Meredith* by Lionel Stevenson (New York, 1953).

Mergenthaler, Ottmar

(1854-1899) German-born American instrument maker, inventor. Developed Linotype composing machine that quickly replaced labor-intensive hand typesetting. Died at age 45 of tuberculosis in Baltimore.

Last Words: "Emma, my children, my friends, be kind to one another." Emma Lachenmayer was his wife and mother of his five children.

Source: *Life Stories of the Great Inventors* by Henry and Dana Lee Thomas (New York, 1948).

Mérimée, Prosper

(1803-1870) French writer, dramatist. Popular short-story writer. Wrote *Carmen* on which Bizet based his opera. Other notable stories: *Colomba; Mateo Falcone; Lokis.* Appointed inspector general of historical monuments. Traveled extensively. Became travel writer and authority on architecture and archaeology. Died at age 66 in Cannes, France.

Last Words: "Goodnight now, I want to go to sleep."

Source: *Prosper Mérimée* by Alan William Raitt (New York, 1970).

Messner, Tammy Faye LaValley Baker

(1942-2007) American evangelist, singer, television personality. Co-hosted PTL Club with televangelist husband Jim Baker. He was later convicted on felony charges. She divorced Baker and married Roe Messner. Died at age 65 in Kansas City, Missouri.

Last Words: "My hand is in the hand of Jesus." Spoken to her husband Roe Messner, who later recounted her Last Words on CNN's *Larry King Live.*

Source: "Roe Messner reflects on life, Tammy Faye" by Donald Bradley (*Kansas City Star*, August 27, 2007).

Metastasio, Pietro Antonio Domenico Bonaventura

(1698-1782) Italian writer, poet, librettist. Original surname Trapassi. Pen name Metastasio. Moved to Vienna in 1730 as court poet to Holy Roman Emperor Charles VI. His libretti were used by such notable composers as Mozart, Gluck, Handel, Mercadante and Meyerbeer. Died at age 84 in Vienna.

Last Words:

T'offro il tuo proprio Figlio,
Che già d'amore in pegno,
Racchiuso in picciol segno.
Si volle a noi donar.
A lui rivolgi il ciglio.
Guardo chi t'offro, e poi,
Lasci, Signor, se vuoi,
Lascia di perdonar.

(tr. "I offer to thee, O Lord, thy own Son, who already has given the pledge of love, enclosed in this thin emblem. Turn on him thine eyes. Ah, behold whom I offer to thee, and then desist, O Lord! If thou canst desist from mercy.") Uttered a few minutes before he died.

Source: *Curiosities of Literature,* Vol. I, by Isaac D'Israeli (London, 1824).

Metchnikoff, Élie

(1845-1916) Russian bacteriologist, microbiologist, zoologist, writer. Identified the role of white blood cells in fighting infection. Worked with Pasteur. Shared Nobel Prize for Physiology and Medicine with Paul Ehrlich. Notable works: *Immunity in Infectious Diseases; The Nature of Man; Comparative Pathology of Inflammation.* Died at age 71 in Paris.

Last Words: "You remember your promise? You will do my post-mortem? And look at the intestines carefully, for I think there is something there now." Spoken to Dr. Salimbeni. An autopsy revealed inflammation of the abdominal cavity, including the large intestines.

Source: *Life of Elie Metchnikoff 1845-1916* by Olga Metchnikoff (London, 1921). The author was his wife.

Mew, Charlotte Mary

(1869-1928) English poet, writer. Highly regarded by other writers, including Thomas Hardy, Ezra Pound, Virginia Woolfe and Marianne Moore. Notable poems: "The Farmer's Bride"; "The Rambling Sailor." Fell into a depression after the death of her sister. Became delusional. Placed in a nursing home. Committed suicide at age 58 in London by drinking disinfectant.

Last Words: "Don't keep me, let me go." Spoken to the doctors who tried to revive her.

Source: *Collected Poems of Charlotte Mew* (London, 1953).

Meyerbeer, Giacomo

(1791-1864) German musician, composer. Birth name Jakob Liebmann Beer. Composed operas, incidental music, choral works, songs and instrumental music. Notable operas: *Les Huguenots; Il Crociato in Egitto* (last opera for which a solo role was written for a soprano castrato). Died at age 72 in Paris, France.

Last Words: "I will see you in the morning. I bid you goodnight." Spoken cheerfully to his nephew Julius and one or two close friends. He died early the next day.

Source: *The Diaries of Giacomo Meyerbeer: The Last Years 1857-1864* by Giacomo Meyerbeer and Robert

Ignatius Le Tellier (Madison, NJ, 2004).

Meynell, Alice Christiana Gertrude Thompson

(1847-1922) English essayist, editor, publisher, critic, poet, writer. Married Wilfred Meynell. They produced *Merry England*, a monthly publication. Her writing was praised by Browning, Ruskin, Rossetti and Coventry Patmore. Died at age 75 in London.

Last Words: "This is not tragic. I am happy."

Source: *Alice Meynell: A Memoir* by Viola Meynell (London, 1929). The author was her daughter.

Michelangelo Buonarroti

(1475-1564) Italian sculptor, painter, architect, poet. Birth name Michelangelo di Lodovico Buonarroti Simoni. Notable works: *Pieta* (St. Peter's); *David; Moses; Madonna of Bruges; Pitti Madonna;* Julius Tomb; Medici Chapel; Dome of St. Peter's; Sistine Chapel. Wrote many sonnets and madrigals. Died at age 88 in Rome.

Last Words: "I give my soul to God, my body to the earth, and my worldly possessions to my nearest of kin, charging them to remember the sufferings of Jesus Christ."

Source: *Sketches of Great Painters for Young People* by Mrs. Colonna Murray Dallin (New York, 1902).

Variation: [He encouraged his nearest relatives] "When their hour came, to think upon the sufferings of Jesus Christ."

Source: *The Life of Michelangelo Buonarroti, Based on Studies in the Archives of the Buonarroti Family at Florence* by John Addington Symonds (London, 1893).

Variation: "Remember the death of Christ."

Source: *Purposes of Art* by Albert Edward Elsen (New York, 1962). Elsen stated that these are "reputedly his last words to a friend."

Variation: "In your passage through this life, remember the sufferings of Jesus Christ."

Source: *The Life and Literary Works of Michel Angelo Buonarroti* by R. Duppa (London, 1856).

Michelet, Jules

(1798-1874) French historian, writer, educator. Head of the historical section of the French National Archives. Notable work: *History of France* (17 vol.). Died at age 75 in Hèyres, France.

Last Words: "Linen, doctor, you speak of linen. Do you know what linen is? —the linen of the peasant, of the worker— Linen,

a great thing—I want to make a book of it." Spoken when the physician ordered his linen to be changed.

Source: *Jules Michelet* by Daniel Halévy (Paris, 1929).

Michelson, Albert Abraham

(1852-1931) Prussian-born American physicist. First to measure the speed of light. First American to win a Nobel Prize (Physics, 1907). Died at age 78 in Pasadena, California.

Last Words (written): "The following is a report on the measurement of the velocity of light made at the Irvine Ranch, near Santa Ana, California, during the period of September 1929 to—." Dictated. He stopped there, fell asleep and died.

Source: *The Master of Light: A Biography of Albert A. Michelson* by Dorothy Michelson Livingstone (New York, 1973). The author was his daughter.

Middleton, Frank, Jr.

(d. 1996) American murderer, rapist. Escaped from a prison road crew, raped and murdered two women in South Carolina. Executed by lethal injection. The case was controversial because he was mentally disabled. He had an IQ of 68-69.

Last Words: "What are you people looking at? I'm going to the Promised Land! Ha, ha, ha!"

Source: *Last Suppers: Famous Final Meals from Death Row* by Ty Treadwell and Michael Vernon (Port Townsend, WA, 2001).

Middleton, Richard Barham

(1882-1911) British poet, short-story writer. Notable work: *The Ghost Ship and Other Stories*. Committed suicide at age 29 with chloroform in Brussels, Belgium.

Last Words (written): "Goodbye, Harry. I'm going adventuring again, and thanks to you I shall have some pleasant memories in my knapsack. As for the many bitter ones, perhaps they will not weigh so heavy now as they did before. 'A broken and contrite heart, oh Lord, thou shalt not despise.' Richard." Suicide note.

Source: *Richard Middleton: The Man and His Work* by Henry Savage (London, 1922). Savage was a close friend of Middleton and the "Harry" he addressed in his suicide note.

Mihailovich, Draza

(1893-1946) Serbian military officer. Served

in World War I. Raised to rank of colonel in the Yugoslav army after the war. Helped wage guerrilla warfare against Axis during World War II. When Tito's Communists rose to power, Mihailovich allied against them. Tried by Tito government for high treason and war crimes against civilians. Found guilty. Executed at age 53 by firing squad in Belgrade. Given the Legion of Merit posthumously in 1948 by U.S. President Harry S. Truman for helping to rescue several hundred American airmen during World War II.

Last Words (doubtful): "I wanted much, I started much, but the gale of the world carried away me and my work."

Source: Various Last Words compilations and Internet websites.

These are sometimes shown as his Last Words, but they were not. They were his last public words. He spoke them at the end of his trial after a four-hour plea. Five days later he was sentenced to be shot by a firing squad.

Source: "Yugoslavia: The Gale of the World" (*Time* magazine, July 11, 1946).

Milborne, Jacob

(d. 1691) American military officer, merchant. Son-in-law of Jacob Leisler. Major in charge of company of soldiers sent to Albany to occupy fort. Milborne and Leisler—who was lieutenant governor—were charged with treason and condemned to be executed. Although Governor Sloughter believed the decision was unjust, he signed the death warrant while he was intoxicated. By the time he sobered up, the two men were dead. Sloughter died suddenly two months later.

Last Words: "Robert Livingston, I will implead thee at the bar of Heaven for this deed." Spoken on the scaffold to Livingston, whom he deemed was personally hostile to him.

Source: "Jacob Leisler: Mercantile Biography" (*Merchant's Magazine and Commercial Review,* Vol. 12, January-June 1845).

Miles, Dixon Stansbury

(1804-1862) American military officer. Colonel in Union Army during U.S. Civil War. Assigned to defend Harpers Ferry with 12,000 troops. With Confederate troops bombarding from three sides, he made the hasty decision to surrender. He was mortally wounded. A subsequent inquiry censured his decision to surrender. The loss of so many men at one time was the largest for Union forces during the Civil War.

Last Words: "Captain, I have done my duty to my country and I am ready to die. God bless you." Spoken to an attending physician.

Source: *Last Words of the Civil War: The Moment of Sacrifice* by Garry Radison (Yorkton, SK, 2001).

Milholland, Inez

(1886-1916) American suffrage activist, lawyer. Full name Inez Milholland Boissevain. Wore white robes and rode a white horse leading a parade of suffragists in Washington, the day before Wilson's inauguration. Went on women's rights tour to California later that year. She collapsed during her speech. Died at age 30 of pernicious anemia several weeks later in a Los Angeles hospital. She was one of the subjects of HBO Films *Iron Jawed Angel.*

Last Words (public): "Mr. President, how long must women wait for liberty?" When she spoke the word "liberty" she collapsed.

Source: *Napoleon's Glance: The Secret of Strategy* by William Duggan (New York, 2003).

Mill, John Stuart

(1806-1873) English philosopher, economist, writer, reformer. Notable works: *On Liberty; Considerations on Representative Government; Utilitarianism.* Spent his last years in France. Died at age 66 in Avignon.

Last Words: "My work is done." His response when told he would not recover.

Source: *Life of John Stuart Mill* by W.L. Courtney (London, 1889).

Variation: "You know that I have done my work." Whispered to his wife.

Source: *The Subjection of Women* by John Stuart Mill and Edward Alexander (New Brunswick, NJ, 2001).

Millay, Edna St. Vincent

(1892-1950) American writer, poet. Notable work: *The Harp-Weaver and Other Poems* (won Pulitzer Prize in 1923). Died at age 58 of heart failure in Austerlitz, New York.

Last Words (written): "It is 5:30, and I have been working all night. I am going to bed. Good morning—E. St. V. M." Note she left to her maid.

Source: *Letters of Edna St. Vincent Millay*, ed. by Allan
Ross Macdougall (New York, 1952).

Miller, Glenn

(1904-1944) American musician, bandleader, trombonist, military officer. Major,
U.S. Army Air Force Band during World
War II. Boarded a plane from England to
Paris to arrange concerts for troops on leave
in Europe. The plane failed to reach its destination. Presumed to have gone down in the
English Channel. Died at age 40. The movie
The Glenn Miller Story (1954) traced his
career from the late 1920s until he disappeared during the war.

Last Words: "Where the hell are the parachutes?" Spoken to his companion Colonel
Don Baesell as he took his seat on the plane.
Baesell replied: "What's the matter Miller,
do you want to live forever?" The plane
vanished over the English Channel. These
are the last words heard by anyone who was
not on the plane.

Source: "Flight to Eternity," *Reader's Digest Facts &
Fallacies: Stories of the Strange and Unusual* (Pleasantville, NY, 1988). Discusses the possibility that
Miller's plane was accidentally hit by a jettisoned British bomb.

Miller, Henry

(1859-1926) English-born American actor,
theater manager, director, producer. Managed, directed and starred at Henry Miller's
Theatre in New York City (now demolished). Died at age 67 in New York City.

Last Words: "Gilbert—poor Dodd." Spoken
to his son Gilbert Miller who was a well-
known theatrical producer.

Source: *Backstage with Henry Miller* by Frank P.
Morse (New York, 1938).

Miller, Hugh

(1802-1856) Scottish stone mason, geologist, writer, religious reformer. Wrote for
Inverness Courier. Notable work: *Old Red
Sandstone* (series of geological articles that
became a classic). Many of the fossils he
collected and identified are in the Royal
Museum in Edinburgh. Began experiencing
agonizing headaches and hallucinations in
1856. Feared he might harm his family.
Committed suicide at age 54 at his home in
Portobello, Scotland, on Christmas Eve.

Glacier in Alaska was named for him.

Last Words (written): "Dearest Lydia, My
brain burns, I must have walked; and a fearful dream rises upon me. I cannot bear the
horrible thought. God and Father of the Lord
Jesus Christ, have mercy upon me. Dearest
Lydia, dear children, farewell. My brain
burns as the recollection grows. My dear
wife, farewell. Hugh Miller." Suicide letter
to his wife.

Source: *Hugh Miller* by W. Keath Leask (New York,
1938).

Miller, James ("Killin' Jim")

(1861-1909) American murderer, outlaw.
Hired hit man. Hanged by a lynch mob in
Ada, Oklahoma.

Last Words: "Just let the record show that
I've killed fifty-one men.—I'd like to have
my coat. I don't want to die naked.—If I
can't have my coat, then how about my
hat?—I'm ready now; you couldn't kill me
otherwise. Let 'er rip." Spoken as he stepped
off the box at his hanging.

Source: *Shotgun for Hire* by Glenn Shirley (Norman,
OK, 1980).

Miller, Joaquin

(1837-1913) American poet. Birth name
Cincinnatus Hiner (or Heine) Miller. Wrote
about the American West. Known as The
Poet of the Sierras. Popular visitor in London in the 1870s wearing Western clothes,
sombrero and boots. Notable work: *Songs of
the Sierras* (published first in England).
Died at age 74 in Oakland, California. Park
named for him in Oakland.

Last Words: "Take me away; take me
away."

Source: *Joaquin Miller, Literary Frontiersman* by
Martin Severin Peterson (Stanford, CA, 1937).

Miller, Samuel

(1769-1850) American clergyman, educator,
writer. Moderator and official historian of
Presbyterian General Assembly. Professor at
Theological Seminary, Princeton. Trustee at
Columbia College and College of New Jersey (now Princeton University). Founder
and president of New York Bible Society.
Notable work: *Brief Retrospect of the Eighteenth Century*. Died at age 80 in Princeton.

Last Words: "We are to meet no more on

earth. But when thy servant shall follow his aged father to the grave, may we meet in Heaven, there to sit and shine, and sing with those who have turned many to righteousness, who have washed their robes and made them white in the blood of the Lamb. Amen."
Source: *The Life of Samuel Miller, D.D. LL.D.: Second Professor in the Theological Seminary of the Presbyterian Church at Princeton, New Jersey* by Samuel Miller (Philadelphia, 1869). The author was his son.

Milligan, John

(1864?-1895) American murderer. Raised as the adopted son of Gabe and Hannah Clark. Refused to work or earn his keep. Murdered the Clarks and attacked their six-year-old grandchild. Milligan was quickly caught, tried, convicted and executed. He was the first man legally hanged in Oklahoma Territory. He was hanged from the gallows on Main Street in Oklahoma City.
Last Words: "Not a word." His response when asked if he had anything to say.
Source: "The Homicide, the Healer and the Hangman" by Glenn Shirley (*Old West,* Winter, 1995).

Milosevic, Slobodan

(1941-2006) Serbian politician. President of Serbia and Yugoslavia. Leader of Serbia's Socialist party from its beginning in 1992. Indicted for crimes against humanity in the Kosovo War—for breaches of Geneva Conventions in Croatia and Bosnia and for genocide. Spent his final four years in jail at The Hague in a protracted trial. It was still going on when he died at age 64 of a heart attack.
Last Words: "Don't you worry. They will not destroy me or break me; I shall defeat them all." Spoken to Socialist party aide Milorad Vucelic during a telephone call. Milosevic was found dead in his cell the next day.
Source: Milosevic Party Aide Says Ex-president's Last Words Were: "They Will Not Break Me" by Katrina Kratovac (*America's Intelligence Wire*, March 11, 2006).

Milton, John

(1608-1674) English poet. Regarded by some as one of the greatest English poets. Notable works: *L'Allegro; Il Penseroso; Paradise Lost; Paradise Regained; Samson*

Agonistes. Lost his eyesight in later years. Died at age 65 in London.
Last Words (doubtful): "Death is the great key that opens the palace of eternity."
Source: Various Last Words compilations and Internet websites.
The wording of the quotation is similar to a passage in Milton's *Comus* (line 13) written in 1634, 40 years before he died: "golden key that opens the palace of eternity." In the Introduction to *Dictionary of Last Words,* Edward S. Le Comte mentioned noted people for whom no Last Words are on record. He said Milton, along with Chaucer, Shakespeare and Spenser would have to be included in the list of those for whom Last Words are completely missing.
Source: *Dictionary of Last Words* by Edward S. Le-Comte (New York, 1955).

Mineo, Sal

(1939-1976) American actor. Stage and screen star. Notable roles: *Rebel Without a Cause; Exodus.* Nominated for Academy Award for both films. Won Golden Globe for *Exodus.* Died at age 37 in West Hollywood, California.
Last Words: "Oh God! No! Help! Someone help!" Screamed as he was being stabbed to death outside his apartment. Neighbors heard Mineo's cries and chased the assailant. A drifter was later arrested, tried, convicted and sentenced for the murder.
Source: *Murder Among the Rich and Famous: Celebrity Slayings that Shocked America* by Jay Robert Nash (New York, 1983).

Mirabeau, Honoré-Gabriel, Comte de

(1749-1791) French writer, orator, revolutionary leader. Full name Honoré Gabriel Riqueti, Comte de Mirabeau. Known simply as Mirabeau. Elected president of the National Assembly three months before he died at age 42. The severe pain he suffered before he died caused speculation that he had been poisoned.
Different Last Words:
(1) "Remove from the bed all that sad apparatus. Instead of these useless precautions, surround me by the perfumes and the flowers of spring; dress my hair with care; let me fall asleep amid the sound of harmonious music." Spoken to his attendants. He then

implored them to give him laudanum to ease his pain.

Sources: *History of Europe from the Fall of Napoleon in 1815 to the Accession of Louis Napoleon in 1852* by Sir Archibald Alison (New York, 1855). Alison cited as sources: *Histoire de la Revolution Francaise* by Thiers (Paris, 1828); *Lettres sur 1'Angleterre* by Baron De Stael (Paris, 1825); *Histoire de France pendant*, viii, by Lacretelle (Paris, 1826) This quote appeared in numerous 19th-century sources; however, several later sources, beginning with Brewer's *Dictionary of Phrase and Fable*, printed it with shorter variations such as: "Let me fall asleep to the sound of delicious music."

(2) "Are you not my doctor and my friend? Did you not promise to save me from the pain of such a death? Do you wish me to carry away regret for having given you my confidence?" Spoken to his physician when he asked for laudanum to ease his pain.

Source: *The Stormy Life of Mirabeau* by Henry De Jouvenal (Boston, 1929).

Variation: "Vous aviez promis de m'épargner des souffrances inutiles." (tr. "You promised to spare me useless suffering.")

Source: *Famous Sayings and Their Authors: A Collection of Historical Sayings in English, French, German, Greek, Italian, and Latin* by Edward Latham (London, 1906).

(3) "Si ce n'est pas la Dieu, s'est du moins son cousin germain." (tr. "If it is not God. It is at least his German cousin.")

Source: *The French Revolution*, Vol. 2, by Thomas Carlyle (London, 1837). Carlyle cited *Journal de la maladie et de la mort de Mirabeau* by P. J. G. Cabanis (Paris, 1803).

Last Words (written): "To die is to sleep." Scribbled on a piece of paper as he lay dying. He was quoting *Hamlet*. In the last days of his life, Mirabeau could not speak. He wrote this note to his physician Cabanis to obtain opium from him.

Source: "Mad. de Staël on the French Revolution" (*The Eclectic Review,* Vol. 11, January-June, 1819).

Mishima, Yukio

(1925-1970) Japanese writer, novelist, playwright. Pen name of Hiraoka Kimitake. Notable works: *The Temple of the Golden Pavilion; The Sea of Fertility.* Committed ritual suicide (seppuku) at age 45 after failing to convince the Japanese military to overthrow the civilian government.

Last Words: "Tenno Heika banzai!" (tr. "Long live His imperial Majesty!") Shouted three times as he stood on a balcony. He went inside and said to his companion: "I don't think they even heard me." He then sat on the floor and committed ritual suicide.

Source: *Mishima: A Biography* by John Nathan (New York, 2000).

Mitchell, James

(1621?-1678) Scottish Covenanter, martyr. Attempted to assassinate Archbishop Sharp in 1668. Persecuted for two years; subjected to torture. Finally sentenced and executed at the insistence of Archbishop Sharp. Became a Presbyterian folk hero. While awaiting execution, he wrote a speech he wanted to deliver on the scaffold, if given the opportunity. Denied the opportunity, he threw the copies over the side of the scaffold. The last lines are included here:

Last Words (written): "Finally concerning a Christian duty, in a singular and extraordinary case, and anent my particular judgment, concerning both church and state, it is evidently declared and manifested elsewhere. Farewell all earthly employments; and welcome Father, son and Holy Ghost into whose hands I commit my spirit.—James Mitchell."

Source: *The Scots Worthies: Containing a Brief Historical Account of the Most Eminent Noblemen, Gentlemen, Ministers, and Others, Who Testified or Suffered for the Cause of Reformation in Scotland: From The Beginning of the Sixteenth Century to the Year 1688* by John Howie (Glasgow, Scotland, 1829).

Mitchell, Maria

(1818-1889) American astronomer, educator. Vassar's first astronomy professor. Discovered a comet. Mitchell crater on moon was named for her. First woman elected to the American Academy of Arts and Sciences. Died at age 70 in Lynn, Massachusetts, a short time after she retired.

Last Words: "Well, if this is dying, there is nothing unpleasant about it." Spoken during one of the intervals of consciousness she experienced as she was dying.

Source: "Maria Mitchell" by Harriet Prescott Spofford (*The Chautauquan,* Vol. 10, New Series Vol. 1, October 1889-March 1890).

Mitchell, Silas Weir

(1829-1914) American physician, writer. Specialized in nervous disorders. Union

Army surgeon in U.S. Civil War. Author of several historic novels. Notable works: *Hugh Wynne, Free Quaker; The Red City.* Died at age 84 in Philadelphia.

Last Words: "That leg must come off. Save the leg. Lose the life!" Spoken while he was delirious and reliving a wartime experience.

Source: *Weir Mitchell: His Life and Letters* by Anna R. Burr (New York, 1930).

Mitchell, William M. ("Billy")

(1879-1936) American military officer. U.S. Army officer. Served in Spanish-American War. Commanded AEF air forces in World War I. Planned and led nearly 1,500 aircraft in Battle of Saint-Mihiel. Court-martialed for insubordination for criticizing U.S. war and navy departments. Convicted, suspended from service five years. Resigned from the U.S. Army. Died at age 66 in New York City. Awarded Congressional Gold Medal and rank of major general posthumously. The movie *The Court-Martial of Billy Mitchell* is based on his experience.

Last Words (written): "Although I should like to be with the pilots and my comrades in Arlington, I feel it is better for me to go back to Wisconsin, the home of my family." Statement Mitchell issued about his burial wishes.

Source: *Billy Mitchell* by James J. Cooke (Boulder, CO, 2002).

Mitford, Mary Russell

(1787-1855) English novelist, playwright. Notable works: *Our Village* (popular series of stories about English country life); *Julian; Rienzi* (plays). Died at age 67 in Swallowfield, England.

Last Words (written): "Today I am better; but if you wish for another cheerful evening with your old friend, there is no time to be lost." Letter to a friend.

Source: *Mary Russell Mitford Correspondence With Charles Boner and John Ruskin*, ed. by Elizabeth Lee (London, 1914).

Mizner, Wilson ("Bill")

(1876-1933) American playwright, writer, restaurateur, actor. Co-owner, manager of Brown Derby restaurant in Los Angeles. Notable works: *The Deep Purple; The Greyhound.* Known for the witty remarks, schemes, scams and misadventures he undertook with his brother Addison Mizner. Credited with the line: "When you copy from one author it's plagiarism; if you copy from many, it's research." Died at age 56 in Los Angeles, California.

Different Last Words:

(1) "Well, Doc, I guess this is the main event." Spoken when an oxygen tent was brought to his room.

Source: *The Young Man from Denver* by Will Fowler (Garden City, NY, 1962).

(2) "Why should I talk to you? I've just been talking to your boss." His response to priest summoned to his bedside who said: "I'm sure you want to talk to me."

Source: *Zanies—The World's Greatest Eccentrics* by Jay Robert Nash (Piscataway, NJ, 1982).

M'Kail, Hugh

(1640?-1666) Scottish clergyman. Presbyterian Covenanter. Tried for treason. Executed at age 26 by hanging in Edinburgh.

Last Words: "Farewell father and mother, friends and relations, farewell the world and all delights, farewell meat and drink, farewell sun, moon, and stars! Welcome God and Father; welcome sweet Jesus Christ, the mediator of the new covenant; welcome blessed Spirit of grace, and God of all consolation; welcome glory, welcome eternal life, and welcome death! O Lord, into thy hands I commit my spirit, for thou hast redeemed me, O Lord God of truth."

Source: *The Scots Worthies: Containing a Brief Historical Account of The Most Eminent Noblemen, Gentlemen, Ministers, and Others, Who Testified or Suffered for the Cause of Reformation in Scotland: From The Beginning of the Sixteenth Century to the Year 1688* by John Howie (Glasgow, Scotland, 1829).

Mocenigo, Tommaso

(1343-1423) Venetian doge, statesman, politician. Uncle of Giovanni Mocenigo and Venetian admiral Pietro Mocenigo, both of whom later were also doges. Led a fleet that sacked Nikopol, Bulgaria, in 1396. As doge, he extended Venetian authority over Trentino, Friuli and Dalmatia. Died at age 80 in Venice.

Last Words: "You will lose your money and reputation. You will be at the mercy of the soldiery! I have found it impossible to forbear expressing to you thus my opinion.

May God help you to make the wisest choice! May He rule your hearts to preserve your peace!" End of a long deathbed speech about choosing his successor, in particular warning against Francesco Foscari.

Source: *History of the Venetian Republic: Her Rise, Her Greatness, and Her Civilization* by William Carew Hazlitt (London, 1860).

Modigliani, Amedeo Clemente

(1884-1920) Italian artist, painter, sculptor. Moved to Paris in 1906. Influenced by styles of Gauguin, Cézanne and Toulouse-Lautrec. Notable works: *Madame Pompadour; Jeanne Hébuterne in Red Shawl; Portrait of Jacques and Berthe Lipschitz*. Suffered from tubercular meningitis. Died at age 35 in Paris. His story is told in the movie *Modigliani* (2004).

Last Words: "Cara Italia, cara." (tr. "Dear Italy, dear.")

Sources: "Amadeo Modigliani: The Prince of Montparnasse" by Ante Glibota (*NY Arts Magazine*, January 2003); *Modern Art and the Idea of the Mediterranean* by Anne Elizabeth Dymond and Vojtěch Jirat-Wasiutyński (Toronto, ON, 2007).

Modigliani's daughter wrote that according to stories, he murmured these words on the way to the hospital. She was a small child when he died.

Source: *Modigliani: Man and Myth* by Jeanne Modigliani (New York, 1958).

Moffat, Robert

(1795-1883) Scottish missionary, translator. Missionary to South Africa for more than 50 years. Translated New Testament into Sechuana language. Returned to England in 1870. Spent his remaining years traveling and lecturing in Great Britain. Died at age 87 in Leigh near Tunbridge, England. His daughter Mary married missionary and explorer David Livingstone.

Last Words: "It is all a mystery. Will not the Judge of all the earth do right?"

Source: *The Lives of Robert and Mary Moffat* by their son John Smith Moffat (London, 1885).

Molière

(1622-1673) French playwright, theatrical manager, director, actor. Pen name of Jean Baptiste Poquelin. Famous comedy writer. Notable works: *Le Misanthrope; Le Tartuffe; Le Bourgeois Gentilhomme*. Seized by convulsions while acting in *Le Malade Imaginaire (The Imaginary Invalid)*. Although he insisted there was no cause for alarm, he asked that his wife be told. He died at age 51 in Paris a short time later.

Last Words: "Still, go call my wife." Spoken to the two nuns who were attending him.

Source: *Moliere, A Biography* by H.C. Chatfield-Taylor (New York, 1906).

Molineux, Thomas

(d. 1387) English law officer. Deputy constable of Chester during the reign of Richard II. Caught by his enemies. Made a request to fight for his life. His request was not granted. As he approached his enemies, he was hit on the head and killed.

Last Words: "If there be no other remedy, suffer me to come up, and let me fight with hand blows either with you or some other, and so die like a man."

Source: *The Annales, or, Generall Chronicle of England* by John Stow and Edmund Howes (London, 1615).

Molnar, John

(1873?-1895) American murderer. Executed by hanging for killing an old man in a dispute over money in what has been described as one of the most brutal murders in northern Ohio.

Last Words: "Das ist alles." (tr. "That is all.")

Source: *Historical Lights and Shadows of the Ohio State Penitentiary and Horrors of the Death Trap. Heart-rending Scenes and Sad Wailing as Wife Parts with Husband, and Weeping Children Kiss a Doomed Father for the Last Time: Word Sketches From Life of the Greatest Prison in the World* by Dan J. Morgan (Columbus, OH, 1896).

Moltke, Helmuth Carl Bernhard von ("Moltke the Elder")

(1800-1891) Prussian military officer. Field marshal, chief of staff. Great military strategist of late 1800s. Reorganized the Prussian army. Died at age 90 while visiting Berlin.

Last Words: "What?" His response when asked: "Uncle Helmuth, are you ill?"

Source: *Moltke: His Life and Character, Sketched in Journals, Letters, Memoirs, a Novel, and Autobiographical Notes* by Graf von Moltke, tr. by Mary Herms (New York, 1892).

Moncey, Bon Adrien Jeannot de, Duc de Conegliano

(1754-1842) French military officer in

Revolutionary and Napoleonic armies. Created marshal of France. Died at age 87 in Paris.

Last Words: "Let everyone fulfill and close his course like me."

Source: *Le maréchal Moncey duc de Conegliano 1754-1842—Lettres et Documents,* ed. by Calmann Levy (Paris, 1902).

Monica, Saint

(332?-387) Holy woman. Mother of Saint Augustine. Died on the way from Africa to Ostia, Italy.

Last Words: "Lay this body wherever it may be. Let no care of it disturb you: this only I ask of you that you should remember me at the altar of the Lord wherever you may be."

Source: *The Confessions,* Book IX, by St. Augustine, tr. by Edward Bouverie Pusey (Chicago, 1952).

Monod, Jacques Lucien

(1910-1976) French biologist, chemist, educator, writer. Professor of chemistry at Sorbonne. Director of Pasteur Institute. Shared 1965 Nobel Prize for Physiology or Medicine with François Jacob and André Lwoff. Died at age 66 in Cannes, France.

Last Words: "I am trying to understand."

Source: "Monod, Jacques" in *Nobel Prize Winners* (New York, 1987).

Monroe, James

(1758-1831) 5th President of the U.S. American lawyer, politician, statesman, diplomat. Member of the Continental Congress. Ratifier of the U.S. Constitution. Member U.S. Senate from Virginia. Governor of Virginia. U.S. minister to France and England. U.S. secretary of state, U.S. secretary of war. Helped negotiate Louisiana Purchase. Proclaimed Monroe Doctrine. Moved to New York City in 1831. Died at age 73 of tuberculosis and heart failure. Many American cities and counties were named for him.

Last Words: "I regret that I should leave this world without again beholding him." Spoken to a mutual friend about James Madison.

Source: *The Life of James Monroe* by George Morgan (Boston, 1921).

Monroe, Marilyn

(1926-1962) American actress. Screen star. Sex symbol. Original name Norma Jeane Mortensen Baker. Married and divorced James Dougherty, Joe DiMaggio, Arthur Miller. Nominated for four Golden Globe awards; won three. Died at age 36 in her house in Brentwood, California, possibly of a drug overdose. Death was ruled a suicide.

Last Words: "Say good-bye to Pat, say good-bye to Jack [Kennedy] and say good-bye to yourself, because you're a nice guy." Spoken by telephone to actor Peter Lawford, brother-in-law of President Kennedy.

Sources: "Official Report of Monroe's Suicide Released on September 23, 1985" (*U.S. News & World Report,* October 7, 1985); *Marilyn Monroe: The Biography* by Donald Spoto (New York, 1993).

Montagu, Lady Mary Wortley

(1689-1762) English aristocrat, poet, writer. Pen name Artemisia. Society leader and fashion trendsetter. Introduced into England inoculation for smallpox that she had observed in Turkey. Died at age 73 of cancer n London. Her descriptive letters were published after she died.

Last Words: "It has all been very interesting."

Source: *Portrait of Lady Mary Wortley Montagu* by Iris Barry (London, 1928).

Montaigne, Michel Eyquem de

(1533-1592) French writer, statesman. Courtier at court of Charles IX. Mayor of Bordeaux. Notable work: *Essays* (influenced French and English literature). Died at age 59 at his family estate in Aquitaine.

Last Words (doubtful): "I submit myself to Nature, confident that she is armed with claws and teeth to defend us against the assaults of maladies."

Source: Various Last Words compilations and Internet websites.

The quote is similar to a passage in Montaigne's *Essays,* Book 1, Chapter 23: "Various Events from the same Counsel," published in 1580: "I let nature work, supposing her to be sufficiently armed with teeth and claws to defend herself from the assaults of infirmity." It is unlikely that Montaigne could have spoken these words on his deathbed. During his final days, he suffered from quinsy, which caused his tongue to be paralyzed. Unable to speak, he had to make his wishes known by signs or written words.

His last instruction to his wife was in writing. He asked that a Mass be said in his room. He died while it was being celebrated.
Source: *Montaigne and Medicine* by James Spottswoode Taylor (New York, 1922).

Montcalm, Louis Joseph, Marquis de

(1712-1759) French military officer. Field marshal. Full name Louis Joseph de Montcalm de Saint-Véran. Commander of French troops in Canada. Defeated by Wolfe. Mortally wounded at Plains of Abraham during the Battle of Quebec. Died at age 47 the next day.
Different Last Words:
(1) "I have no more orders to give. I am busy with more important affairs, and the time which remains to me is short—.I die content. I leave the affairs of the king my master in good hands; I have always had a high opinion of M. de Lévis." François Gaston de Lévis succeeded him in Canada.
Source: *Le Marquis de Montcalm (1712-1759)* by Thomas Chapais (Quebec, Canada, 1911).
(2) "So much the better. I shall not live to see the surrender of Quebec." Spoken when told he could survive only a few hours.
Source: *The Annals of America: from the Discovery by Columbus in the Year 1492, to the Year 1826* by Abiel Holmes (Cambridge, MA, 1829).
(3) "It's nothing, it's nothing. Don't be troubled for me my good friends." His response when someone shrieked that he was mortally wounded.
Source: *Montcalm and Wolfe,* Vol. II, by Francis Parkman (Boston, 1884). While Montcalm did make this statement, some sources note that (2) followed it.

Montefiore, Sir Moses Haim, 1st Baronet

(1784-1885) Italian-born British Jewish financier, stockbroker, philanthropist. Sheriff of London. Given baronetcy in 1838. Made a fortune in the stock market. Retired and devoted his life to helping others. Founded hospital and girls' school in Jerusalem. Died at age 100 in London. Left no children.
Last Words: "Thank God! Thank Heaven!"
Source: *Friends' Review: A Religious, Literary and Miscellaneous Journal*, Vol. 39, October 17, 1885. The story noted that during his last two hours Montefiore was frequently heard praying and this quote was among his last.

Montessori, Maria

(1870-1952) Italian physician, educator. First Italian woman to become a doctor of medicine. Originator of Montessori Method for teaching young children. Her schools became established throughout the world. Died at age 81 while visiting friends in the Dutch coastal village of Noordwijk.
Last Words: "Am I no longer of use then?" Spoken to her son Mario in response to a suggestion that she might be too frail to travel to Africa. She died of a cerebral hemorrhage an hour later.
Source: *Maria Montessori: A Biography* by Rita Kramer (Reading MA, 1988).

Montez, Lola

(1818?-1861) Irish-born dancer, actress. Birth name Marie Dolores Eliza Rosanna Gilbert. Mistress of King Ludwig I of Bavaria. Given the title Countess of Landsfeld. Fled Bavaria when king abdicated. Performed in U.S. and Australia in 1850s. Settled in New York and worked to help fallen women. Had a stroke and died a year later.
Different Last Words:
(1) "Tell me more of my dear Saviour." Spoken to the priest who was caring for her.
Source: *Woman in Black: The Life of Lola Montez* by Helen Holdredge (New York, 1955).
(2) "I am very tired."
Source: *The Magnificent Montez: From Courtesan to Convert* by Horace Wyndham (New York, 1935).

Montezuma II or Moctezuma II

(1466?-1520) Aztec emperor. Held hostage by Cortes. When he appeared before his people and tried to address them, they stoned him. He was wounded and died at Tenochtitlan a few days later.
Last Words: "I confide to your care my beloved children, the most precious jewels I can leave you. The great monarch beyond the ocean will interest himself to see that they come into their inheritance, if you present before him their just claims. I know your master will do this if for no other reason than for the kindness I have shown the Spaniards, though it has occasioned my ruin. For all my misfortunes, Malinche, I bear you no ill will." Spoken to Cortes about allowing his children to have some portion of their rightful inheritance.
Source: *The Conquest of Mexico* by William Hickling Prescott (New York, 1922).

Montfort, Simon de, 6th Earl of Leicester

(1208?-1265) French-born English states-man, soldier. Married Eleanor, sister of King Henry III. Joined Crusade to Jerusalem in 1240-1242. Known as Simon the Righteous. Popularly revered as a saint and martyr. One of the signers of the Provisions of Oxford. Led a rebellion against all violators of the provisions in the Barons' War. Killed at Evesham in Worcestershire, England.

Different Last Words:

(1) "It is God's grace."

Source: *A Short History of the English People* by John R. Green (New York, 1898).

(2) "By the arm of St. James, they have not learnt that from themselves, but from me. Commend your souls to God, for our bodies are theirs."

Source: *Simon de Montfort, Earl of Leicester, the Creator of the House of Commons* by Reinhold Pauli and Una M. Goodwin (London, 1876),

Variation: "Commend your souls to God, for our bodies are the foes."

Source: *The Last Words (Real and Traditional) of Distinguished Men and Women Collected from Various Sources* by Frederic Rowland Marvin (New York, 1901).

Montgomery, Bernard Law, 1st Viscount Montgomery ("Monty")

(1887-1976) British military officer. Commander. Field marshal during World War II. Fought at El Alamein in North Africa. Died at age 88 in Alton, England.

Last Words: "I've got to meet God and ex-plain all those men I killed at Alamein." Spoken shortly before he lapsed into a coma.

Source: *Monty: Final Years of the Field-Marshal, 1944-1976* by Nigel Hamilton (New York, 1987).

Montgomery, Richard

(1736-1775) Irish-born American military officer. Appointed brigadier general of Continental Army when the American Revolution began. Captured Montreal. Killed during the first discharge of British artillery while leading assault on Quebec.

Last Words: "Men of New York, you will not fear to follow where your general leads—forward!"

Source: *Military Heroes of the United States from Lexington to Santiago* by Hartwell James (Philadelphia, 1899).

Montmorency, Anne, Duc de

(1493-1567) French military officer, law officer. Marshal of France. Constable of France. Mortally wounded in a battle at St. Denis. Died at age 74 two days later in Paris.

Last Words: "Do you think a man who has known how to live honorably for eighty years does not know how to die for a quarter of an hour?" His response to the urging by bystanders to die a good Christian.

Source: *Anne Duc de Montmorency* by Francis Decrue (Paris, 1889).

Montmorency, Henri II, Duc de

(1595-1632) French military officer. Marshal of France. Joined in a revolt against Richelieu. Captured and beheaded as a traitor at Toulouse.

Last Words: "Give a good stroke. Sweet Saviour, receive my soul."

Source: *Derniers sentiments des plus illustres personnages condamnés a mort* by Joseph Donze de Verteuil (Paris, 1775).

Moody, Arthur Edson Blair

(1902-1954) American reporter, writer, politician. Had newspaper, radio and television career. Was appointed member U.S. Senate from Michigan to fill vacancy created by the death of Arthur H. Vandenberg. Died at age 52 of a heart attack in Ann Arbor, Michigan, while campaigning for U.S. senator.

Last Words: "I feel better."

Source: *New York Daily News*, July 21, 1954.

Moody, Dwight Lyman

(1837-1899) American evangelist, educator, publisher. Founded Northfield Schools in Massachusetts, Moody Bible Institute, Moody Church in Chicago. Held crusades in America, Ireland, Scotland and England that attracted thousands of people. Died at age 62 in Northfield, Massachusetts.

Different Last Words:

(1) "Doctor, I don't know about this. Do you think it best? It is only keeping the family in anxiety." He was questioning the wisdom of having a hypodermic injection.

Source: *The Life of Dwight L. Moody by His Son* by William R. Moody (New York, 1930).

(2) "Earth recedes and heaven opens before me. If this is death, there is nothing awful here. It is sweet. This is bliss. Do not call me

back. God is calling me. I must go. There is no valley here. It is all beautiful."
Source: "Moody's Last Words" (*New York Times,* January 3, 1900).

Moon, Keith John

(1946-1978) British musician, drummer. Member of Rock and Roll group The Who. Gained fame for his high-spirited drumming style as well as his destructive lifestyle. Nicknamed Moon the Loon. Was one of the first to play the drums as an equal lead instrument when drums were almost exclusively used only to keep the back beat. Died at age 32 of a prescription drug overdose in London. Posthumously inducted into the Rock and Roll Hall of Fame.
Last Words: "If you don't like it, you can just f**k off." Spoken to his girlfriend after requesting that she cook him some steak and eggs for breakfast.
Source: *Ben Trovato's Art of Survival* by Ben Trovato (Cape Town, South Africa, 2008).

Moore, George

(1806-1876) English merchant, philanthropist, writer. Traveled for a lace manufacturer. Notable work: *Journal of a Voyage Across the Ocean*. Killed in a fatal accident in Carlisle, England.
Last Words: "Yes! I fear no evil. He will never leave me nor forsake me."
Source: *The Successful Merchant: The Story of the Life of George Moore, Merchant and Philanthropist* by Samuel Smiles (London, 1878).

Moore, James

(1847?-1875) American horse thief, murderer. Shot and killed Deputy U.S. Marshal William Spivey while resisting arrest. Moore was one of six accused murderers who were put to death on the same day in Fort Smith, Arkansas, by Isaac C. Parker, known as the Hanging Judge. Moore was hanged at age 28.
Last Words: "I have lived like a man, and I will die like a man. I am prepared.—I think I see men in this crowd who are worse than I have ever been. I hope you may make peace with God before brought to my condition." Spoken in a clear voice as he looked down on the crowd.
Source: *Hanging Judge* by Fred Harvey Harrington (Norman, OK, 1996).

Moore, Sir John

(1761-1809) Scottish-born British military officer. General. Served in West Indies, America, Ireland, Egypt, Sweden, Spain. Died at age 47 of injuries received at the Battle of Coruña in Spain.
Different Last Words:
(1) "Stanhope, remember me to your sister." Spoken to one of his aides-de-camp who was the brother of Lady Hester Stanhope, to whom Moore was romantically attached or engaged.
Source: *The Life and Letters of Sir John Moore* by Beatrice Brownrigg (New York, 1923).
(2) "It is well as it is. I would rather have my sword to go out of the field together with me. You know that I always wished to die thus—I hope the English people will be content." Moore had been hit by a cannon ball that caused his sword to become entangled in his wound. When an officer tried to remove it, Moore spoke these words, then he died in the arms of his friend Colonel Anderson.
Source: *A History of the Nineteenth Century Year by Year* by Edwin Emerson Jr. (New York, 1902).

Moore, Zephaniah Swift

(1770-1823) American clergyman, educator. Congregationalist. Taught at Dartmouth. President of Williams College. Founder and first president of Amherst College. Died at age 52 n Amherst, Massachusetts.
Last Words: "God is my hope, my shield, and my exceeding great reward." Whispered as he was dying.
Source: *A History of Amherst College During Its First Half Century, 1821-1871* by William S. Tyler (Springfield, MA, 1873).

Moran, Patrick Joseph ("Pat")

(1876-1924) American athlete, manager. Professional baseball player. Manager of Philadelphia Phillies and Cincinnati Reds. Catcher for Boston Braves, Chicago Cubs, Philadelphia Phillies. Died at age 48 of Bright's disease during spring training in Orlando, Florida.
Last Words: "Hello, John. Take me out of here." Spoken to John Evers, acting manager of the Chicago White Sox who came to see him.
Source: *Time* magazine, March 17, 1924.

Moran, Thomas B. ("Butterfingers")

(1892-1971) American thief. Dean of American pickpockets. May have lifted as many as 50,000 wallets. Targeted race tracks, subways, busy streets. Arrested in every state and Canada. Died in a charity bed at Miami Rescue Mission.

Last Words: "I've never forgiven that smart-alecky reporter who named me Butterfingers. To me, it's not funny."

Source: *Bloodletters and Badmen: A Narrative Encyclopedia of American Criminals from the Pilgrims to the Present* by Jay Robert Nash (New York, 1995).

Morant, Harry Harbord ("Breaker")

(1864-1902) English-born Australian soldier. Real name may be Edwin Henry Murrant. Joined South Australian Mounted Rifles to fight in the Boer War. Court-martialed for executing several Boer prisoners and a German missionary. Tried, convicted and executed by firing squad in Pretoria, on order of Lord Kitchener. Morant was 37. The story of his trial and execution was told in the movie *Breaker Morant* (1980).

Last Words: "Shoot straight you bastards. Don't make a mess of it." Spoken as he faced the firing squad.

Source: *1001 Australians You Should Know* by Toby Creswell and Samantha Trenoweth (North Melbourne, Australia, 2006).

Morata, Olympia Fulvia

(1526-1555) Italian religious and classical scholar, educator. Protestant. Tutor in the ducal house of Este. Lectured on the teachings of Luther and Calvin. Married Andreas Grundler, professor at Heidelberg. Became ill. Died at age 29. Within a month, her husband and brother died of plague.

Different Last Words:

(1) "I can scarcely see you my friends, but all around me there seem to be beautiful flowers."

Source: "A Decade of Italian Women" by Thomas Adolphus Trollope in *The Christian Remembrancer,* Vol. 37, ed. by William Scott (London, 1859).

(2) "For the last seven years Satan has not ceased to use every means to induce me to relinquish my faith, but now it would appear that he has lost his darts, for I have no other sensation in this hour of my departure than of undisturbed repose and tranquility of soul

in Jesus." Recorded by her husband.

Source: "Olympia Morata" (*The Evangelical Repository,* August, 1842).

More, Hannah

(1745-1833) English religious writer, philanthropist. Defended traditional values in her writing. Worked to improve the lives of those who needed help. Friend of Gladstone, Macaulay, Coleridge, De Quincey, Sarah Siddons. Died at age 88 in Bristol, England. Left most of her estate to churches and charities.

Last Word: "Joy."

Source: *Hannah More, a Biographical Study* by Annette M.B. Meakin (London, 1911).

More, Saint Thomas

(1478-1535) English statesman, lawyer, writer, scholar. Lord high chancellor of England. Leading humanist scholar. Notable work: *Utopia* (novel about communal ownership of land in an imaginary island nation). Refused to take oath of supremacy that upheld Henry VIII's divorce from Catherine of Aragon, legalized his marriage to Anne Boleyn and impugned the pope's authority. Found guilty of treason. Beheaded at age 57. Canonized in 1935.

Last Words: "Pluck up thy spirits, man, and be not afraid to do thine office. My neck is very short; take heed therefore thou strike not awry, for saving of thine honesty." Spoken to his executioner. He removed his beard from the block as he remarked that "it has never committed treason."

Source: *The History of England from the Invasion of Julius Caesar to the Revolution in 1688* by David Hume (London, 1832).

Variation: "Pity that should be cut that has never committeth treason." Remark he made as he moved his beard out of reach of the axe.

Source: *History of England from the Fall of Wolsey to the Death of Elizabeth* by James Anthony Froude (London, 1881).

Variation: "Good friend, let me put my beard out of the way, for that has committed no offense against the King."

Source: *Dictionary of Anecdote, Incident, Illustrative Fact* by Rev. Walter Baxendale (New York, 1898).

Variation: "Master lieutenant, see me up and for my coming down, let me shift for myself."

Source: *The Life of Sir Thomas More* by William Roper (London, 1822).

Moreau, Jean Victor

(1763-1813) French military officer. General of French Revolutionary and Napoleonic armies. Turned against Napoleon when the war ended. Convicted in royalist Cadoudal plot. Exiled to Spain and U.S. Entered service to Russia. Mortally wounded at the Battle of Dresden. His legs were amputated. Died at age 50 a week later. Last Words: "Say to the Emperor that I go to the tomb with the same feelings of veneration, of respect and devotion that he inspired in me the first time I saw him—I have nothing to reproach myself with."
Source: *L'exil et la mort du général Moreau* by Ernest Daudet (Paris, 1909).

Morehead, John Alfred

(1867-1936) American clergyman, educator. A founder of the Lutheran World Convention Movement. Professor and head of Lutheran Theological Seminary in South Carolina. President Roanoke College. Retired to Salem where he died a few days after his wife of more than 40 years, Nellie V. Fisher. Last Words: "Will you do me a favor? Will you kindly ask my physician how long before I shall join my Nellie?" Spoken on the day of his wife's burial.
Source: *John A. Morehead—Who Created Lutheranism* by Samuel Trexler (New York, 1938).

Morgan, Charles ("Blinky")

(1835-1888) American robber, murderer. One of several aliases of Charles Conklin. Killed a detective on a train to assist with a prisoner escape. Arrested, tried and convicted of murder. Executed by hanging at the Ohio State Penitentiary in Columbus. Last Words: "Good-bye, Nellie."
Source: *Historical Lights and Shadows of the Ohio State Penitentiary and Horrors of the Death Trap. Heart-rending Scenes and Sad Wailing as Wife Parts with Husband, and Weeping Children Kiss a Doomed Father for the Last Time: Word Sketches from Life of the Greatest Prison in the World* by Dan J. Morgan (Columbus, OH, 1896).

Morgan, John Pierpont, Sr. ("J.P.")

(1837-1913) American financier, philanthropist, art collector. Created an industrial and financial empire. Formed United States Steel Corporation. Benefactor to many churches, museums. President of Metropolitan Museum of Art. Died age 75 in Rome.
(1) "Don't baby me so!"
Source: *The House of Morgan: A Social Biography of the Masters of Money* by Lewis Corey (New York, 1930).
(2) "I've got to get up the hill." Heard by his son-in-law.
Source: *Outrageous Fortunes: The Story of the Medici, the Rothschilds and J. Pierpont Morgan* by Cass Canfield (New York, 1981).

Moriale or Moreale d'Albarno ("Fra Moriale")

(1300?-1354) French-born Italian outlaw. Brigand who fought in the service of Louis of Hungary and the pope. Notorious for the pillaging and destruction left by his troops. Roman dictator Cola de Rienzi ordered his execution. Died in Rome.
Last Words: "I die for your poverty and my wealth." Spoken on the scaffold to the spectators.
Source: *The Historians' History of the World* by Henry Smith Williams (London, 1908).

Morris, Gouverneur

(1752-1816) American statesman, diplomat, diarist, politician. Signer of Articles of Confederation. Member of Continental Congress. Member of Constitutional Convention. Assistant minister and minister to France. U.S. commissioner to England. U.S. senator. Chairman of Erie Canal Commission. Died at age 64 in Morrisania, New York. His diary and letters, published after he died, give a valuable first-hand account of events of his time.
Last Words: "Sixty-four years ago it pleased the Almighty to call me into existence—here, on this spot, in this very room, now I shall complain that He is pleased to call me hence." Spoken just before he died. On the day he died he asked his nephew what kind of day it was. His nephew replied: "It is a beautiful day." Morris responded: "A beautiful day, yes, but—" then he recited these lines from Gray's "Elegy Written in a Country Church Yard":
"Who to dumb forgetfulness a prey,
This pleasing anxious being e'er resign'd,
Left the warm precincts of the cheerful day,

Nor cast one longing, lingering look behind?"

Source: *American Eloquence: A Collection of Speeches and Addresses by the Most Eminent Orators of America* by Frank Moore (New York, 1857).

Morris, Thomas, Jr.

(1946-2001) American postal worker, victim of terrorism. Died in Washington, D.C., as result of anthrax attack. Last Words were recorded on 911 tape the morning he died. A coworker handled a letter containing powder. He hadn't handled the envelope but had been nearby. He wasn't sure if the powder was anthrax. Three days earlier, he went to a hospital and told doctors he might have been exposed to anthrax. He was diagnosed as having a virus, told to take Tylenol for his pain and released. Morris was the first postal worker to die from anthrax exposure. The day he died, the U.S. government began testing the postal facility. A second person at the facility also died. The facility was later named for the two victims.

Last Words (his breathing was labored throughout the call): "I don't know anything, I don't know anything. I couldn't even find out if the stuff was or wasn't. I was told that it wasn't but I have a tendency not to believe these people. But anyway, uh, the woman who found it, her name was Helen. She could probably tell you more about it than I could. And the supervisor who was involved, her name is Shirley... [911 operator asks questions]... For a while, I thought I was getting better. This was like yesterday. But like I said, the achiness went away and the feverishness was dying down. But right now, I'm [mumble] water, so I guess I still have the fever or whatever, or dehydrated, I don't know what it is...[911 operator asks questions]...[Mumbling] I'm trying to put my pants on. So what do I need for, just my, my health care is Kaiser. So just bring my card and my...[911 operator asks questions]...No, he just told me to take Tylenol for the achiness...[911 operator asks questions]....[Ambulance is dispatched]... okay... [911 operator asks questions]... All right...Thank you." The 11-minute call ended at 4:50 a.m., Morris died later that morning at age 55.

Source: "D.C. Anthrax Victim Called 911. Dying Words Caught on Tape" by Lauran Neergaard (Associated Press, November 8, 2001).

Morris, William

(1834-1896) English artist, craftsman, printer, publisher, poet, socialist. Interested in medievalism. Founded tapestry business. Started Kelmscott Press; revived hand printing and binding of books. Close friend of artists Edward Burne-Jones and Rossetti, with whom he founded *Oxford and Cambridge Magazine.* Died at age 62 in Hammersmith, London.

Last Words (spoken): "I want to get mumbo jumbo out of the world."

Source: *William Morris: His Life and Work* by Jack Lindsay (London, 1975).

Last Words (written): "Come soon. I want a sight of your dear face." Letter to Lady Burne-Jones.

Source: *The Life of William Morris* by John William Mackail (London, 1911).

Morse, Samuel Finley Breese

(1791-1872) American inventor, artist. Studied art in London. First president of National Academy of Design, New York. Developed telegraph, Morse code. Had to sue to defend his patent in a Kentucky court. His claim was upheld: the U.S. Supreme Court sustained the decision. Died at age 80 of pneumonia in New York City.

Last Words: "Very good." His response when someone said to him: "This is the way we doctors telegraph."

Source: *The American Leonardo: The Life of Samuel F.B. Morse* by Carlton Mabee (New York, 1943).

Morton, John

(1724-1777) American statesman, jurist. Signer of the Declaration of Independence. Associate judge of the Supreme Court of Pennsylvania. Chairman of committee that reported Articles of Confederation. President of Provincial Assembly. Represented Pennsylvania and cast deciding vote for independence in 1776. Died of fever eight months after signing the Declaration of Independence. First of signers of Declaration to die. His sympathies were originally with the British, but he voted for independence causing many friends, relatives and neighbors to turn against him. This may have hastened his death and may explain his Last Words.

Last Words: "Tell them, tell them that they will live to see the hour when they shall acknowledge it to have been the most glorious service that I ever rendered to my country."

Source: *Biography of the Signers to the Declaration of Independence*, Vol. III, by John Sanderson (Philadelphia, 1828).

Morton, Oliver P.

(1823-1877) American statesman, politician. Birth name Oliver Hazard Perry Throckmorton. Governor of Indiana. Member U.S. Senate from Indiana. Served from 1867 until his death. Paralyzed by a stroke. Died at age 54 in Indianapolis after a second stroke.

Last Words: "I am dying. I am worn out."

Source: *Life of Oliver P. Morton: Including His Important Speeches* by William Dudley Foulke (Indianapolis, IN, 1899).

Mosedale, Ken

(1950-2000) Australian pilot. Victim of an in-flight disaster. Pilot of "ghost flight" plane carrying seven passengers across Australia with everyone inside the plane dead. Pilot and passengers died of oxygen deprivation, either when the plane depressurized soon after takeoff or by inhaling toxic fumes. Plane flew on autopilot from Perth to northern Queensland before running out of fuel and crashing. The event occurred just 11 months after golfer Payne Stewart suffered a similar fate in the U.S. This incident was significant in leading to the recommendation that an audible warning siren in the cockpit supplement a visual alarm.

Last Words: "Sierra Kilo Charlie—um—standby." Spoken with labored breathing to Anthony Ayliffe, Melbourne air traffic controller.

Source: "Dead Men Flying—The Ghost Flight Across Australia" by Selina Day (Asia Africa Intelligence Wire, September 13, 2002).

Moses, Anna Mary Robertson ("Grandma Moses")

(1860-1961) American folk artist. Married Thomas S. Moses in 1887. Family moved to Eagle Bridge, New York, where she spent the rest of her life. In her 70s, her folk paintings of rural life caught worldwide attention when they were exhibited by an art dealer.

She spent her final days at a health center. When she died at age 101, she had painted more than 1,500 pictures.

Last Words: "You take me back to Eagle Bridge and you'll get back your stethoscope." Spoken to the physician whose stethoscope she took.

Source: *Grandma Moses (Women of Achievement)* by Tom Biracree (New York, 1989).

Mostel, Samuel Joel ("Zero")

(1915-1977) American actor, comedian, singer, artist. Stage, television and screen star. Blacklisted by the House Un-American Activities Committee in 1950. Later appeared in the movie *The Front* playing a victim of the blacklist. Won Tony Awards for roles in *Rhinoceros* and *A Funny Thing Happened on the Way to the Forum*. Nominated for Golden Globe 1969 for the movie *The Producers*. Became ill in Philadelphia during the tryout of a dramatic play. Was hospitalized and died six days later of cardiac arrest at age 62.

Last Words: "I feel dizzy. You better call a nurse."

Source: *Zero Mostel, A Biography* by Jared Brown (New York, 1989).

Motley, John Lothrop

(1814-1877) American historian, diplomat, writer. U.S. minister to Austria and to Great Britain. Notable works: *Rise of the Dutch Republic; History of the United Netherlands; Life of John of Barneveld*. Died at age 63 of a brain hemorrhage in Dorsetshire, England.

Last Words: "I am ill—very ill. I shall never recover."

Source: *The Last Words (Real and Traditional) of Distinguished Men and Women Collected from Various Sources* by Frederic Rowland Marvin (New York, 1901). Marvin gave as his source "Sir William W. Gull's account of Motley's death."

Mott, James

(1788-1868) American merchant, abolitionist, philanthropist. Quaker. Founded American Anti-Slavery Society along with wife Lucretia. Provided refuge in his Philadelphia home for runaway slaves. One of the founders of Swarthmore College. Taken ill with pneumonia. Died at age 79 in Brooklyn, New York.

Last Words: "I would like to go home, but I suppose I shall die here, and then I shall be at home. It is just as well." Spoken to his wife. She was with him when he died that night.
Source: *Life of Girls Who Became Famous* by Sarah Knowles Bolton (New York, 1886).

Mott, Lucretia Coffin

(1793-1880) American social reformer. Women's rights pioneer, abolitionist. Quaker. Helped organize first women's rights convention at Seneca Falls, New York, in 1848. Husband James Mott was one of the founders of Swarthmore College. Both were advocates of pacifism. Lucretia died at age 87 in Abington, Pennsylvania.
Last Words: "Oh, my, my, my!"
Source: *James and Lucretia Mott* by Anna Davis Hallowell (Boston, 1884).

Moule, Handley Carr Glyn

(1841-1920) English prelate, educator. Principal of Ridley Hall, Cambridge. Norrisian professor of divinity at Cambridge. Anglican Bishop of Durham. Died at age 78 in Cambridge, England.
Last Words: "I know it." His response when told: "The Lord Jesus is with thee."
Source: *Handley Carr Glyn Moule, Bishop of Durham: A Biography* by John Battersby Harford and Frederick Charles Macdonald (London, 1928).

Mozart, Wolfgang Amadeus

(1756-1791) Austrian musician, composer, pianist, conductor, prodigy. Birth name Johannes Chrysostomus Wolgangus Theophilus Mozart. Prolific composer of operas, symphonies, concertos, chamber and church music, sonatas, cantatas. Köchel catalog of his music lists more than 600 works. Notable operas: *Don Giovanni; Cosi Fan Tutte; The Magic Flute; The Marriage of Fiaero; Idomeneo*. Died at age 35 in Vienna. Cause of death unknown. Theories suggest typhus, kidney failure, food poisoning, rheumatic fever, endocarditis, purpura, and more. The 1984 Academy Award-winning movie *Amadeus* attracted much attention to his life and music.
Different Last Words:
(1) "You spoke of a refreshment, my Emilie. Take my last notes, sit down at the piano, sing them with the hymn of your sainted mother. Let me hear once more those notes which have so long been my solace and delight."
Source: *Notes and Queries in History, Folk-lore, Mathematics, Mysticism, Art, Science, etc.* Vol. III (Manchester, NH, 1886). The quote appeared in school journals in Indiana and Wisconsin in 1882. Part of the quote appeared in *Man All Immortal: Or, The Nature and Destination of Man as Taught by Reason and Revelation* by Davis Wasgatt Clark (Cincinnati, OH, 1864).
(2) "Did I not tell you that I was writing this for myself?" Spoken to his sister-in-law Sophie about his *Requiem*.
Source: *The Life of Mozart* by Edward Holmes (London, 1878).
(3) "Keep my death a secret until you have informed Albrechsberger." Spoken to his wife Constanze.
Source: *Mozart and Constanze* by Francis Carr (London, 1983).
(4) Mozart left no profound last words. On December 4, 1791, he had the score of his *Requiem* brought to him. He tried to sing alto along with the tenor, bass and soprano but when he reached the "Lacrimosa" he realized he would never finish it and broke down and cried uncontrollably. Later, Mozart gave his pupil Franz Sussmayr musical instructions about the *Requiem*. While dozing, Mozart puffed out his checks imitating the drums. He asked his wife Constanze to keep his death a secret until Albrechtsberger—who handled services at the cathedral—was informed. A physician visited and ordered cold compresses for Mozart's head. He then lost consciousness. Around midnight, he suddenly sat up, turned his head to the wall and seemed to fall asleep. By 1 a.m., December 5th he was dead.
Source: *Grove's Dictionary of Music and Musicians*, Fifth Edition, ed. by Eric Blom (New York, 1973).

Mudgett, Herman Webster

(1861-1896) American murderer. Also known as Harry Howard Holmes. Operated a hotel during the Columbian Exposition of 1893 in Chicago, where he committed many of his murders. First serial killer identified in the U.S. Arrested, tried and convicted in Philadelphia. Claimed he killed 27 people then later said he killed only two. Police found the remains of 200 people in the basement of his Chicago home. Executed at Moyamensing Prison in Philadelphia.

Last Words: "As God is my witness, I was responsible for the deaths of only two women. I didn't kill Minnie Williams. Minnie killed her—." The trap sprang open killing him before he could finish speaking.

Sources: *Bloodletters and Badmen: A Narrative Encyclopedia of American Crime from the Pilgrims to the Present* by Jay Robert Nash (New York, 1995); *The Devil in the White City, Magic and Madness at the Fair That Changed America* by Eric Larson (New York, 2003).

Mugford, James

(1749-1776) American military officer. Naval captain. Commanded schooner *Franklin* in Continental Navy as part of John Manley's squadron near Boston. Captured the British ship *Hope* that was filled with military stores and powder. Successfully sailed the ship to Boston, past the British fleet lying in wait in Boston's outer harbor. Later, the *Franklin* was attacked and Mugford died on board. Two U.S. Navy ships were named for him.

Last Words: "Don't give up the ship! You will beat them off!" Spoken as he lay dying on board the *Franklin* during the British attack in Boston Harbor.

Source: "Instructions of the Inhabitants of Malden, Mass. to Their Representative in Congress, May 27, 1776" in *Principles and Acts of the Revolution in America*, ed. by Hezekiah Niles (New York, 1876).

Muhammed, Mahomet, Mohammed, or Muhammad

(570-632) Prophet. Spiritual leader, teacher. Founder of Islam. Many transliterations of his name, including Mehmet, Mohamed, Mohamet, Mohammed, Mohammad and Muhammad. Unified the Arabian peninsula. Ended wars. Created a sense of unity among Arabian tribes. Declared Mecca the holiest place in Islam and made it the center of Muslim pilgrimage. Fell ill with a severe headache and died suddenly.

Different Last Words:

(1) "I have chosen the most exalted company in paradise."

Source: *Islam* by Ruqaiyyah Waris Maqsood (Oxford, England, 1995).

(2) "O Allah, pardon my sins. Yes, I come, among my fellow laborers on high."

(3) "Henceforth among the glorious host of paradise."

Source for (2) and (3): *The Last Words (Real and Traditional) of Distinguished Men and Women Collected from Various Sources* by Frederic Rowland Marvin (New York, 1901). Marvin gave *Chambers' Encyclopedia* as his source.

Variation: "Rather, God on high and paradise."

Source: *The Life of Muhammed* by Muhammed Husayn Haykal (Philadelphia, 1976).

Muhlenberg, William Augustus

(1796-1877) American clergyman. Protestant Episcopal. Founder of Episcopal Church School movement in U.S. Founder of Saint Luke's Hospital, New York. Notable hymn: "I Would not Live Always." Died at age 80 in New York City.

Last Words: "Good morning."

Source: *The Life and Work of William Augustus Muhlenberg* by Anne Ayres (New York, 1880).

Muir, Kenneth

(1912-1950) Scottish military officer, pilot. Major general. Member of Argyll and Sutherland Highlanders. Rallied small force when ammunition was dwindling. Helped keep thousands of North Koreans at bay while the wounded were evacuated. Killed in action at age 38 at Songlu, Korea. Posthumous recipient of first Victoria Cross awarded during Korean War.

Last Words: "The gooks will never drive the Argylls off this hill."

Source: "Britain Awards Its Highest Medal to Hero Killed in Korea" (*Chicago Tribune*, January 6, 1951).

Mukasa, Saint Joseph

(1860-1885) Ugandan holy man, martyr. One of the Ugandan Martyrs. Known as Balikuddembe (a man of peace). Died at about age 25 in Nakivubo, Uganda. Beheaded for rebuking King Mwanga when the monarch executed several Christian missionaries. Canonized in 1964.

Last Words: "Tell Mwanga I forgive him for putting me to death without a reason—but let him repent, otherwise, I shall accuse him in God's court."

Source: *New African Saints: The Twenty-two Martyrs of Uganda* by Francis Marion and René Follet (Rome, 1985).

Muller, Franz

(1841?-1864) German tailor, robber, murderer. London banker Thomas Briggs died of his injuries after he was beaten, robbed and thrown from a British train. Muller was identified as the perpetrator. He tried to elude Scotland Yard detectives by boarding a passenger ship to New York but was arrested upon arrival in New York and extradited.

Last Words: "Ich habe es gethan." (tr. "I did it.") Spoken shortly before he was publicly hanged. His reputed response to a question as to whether he was responsible for the death of Briggs.

Source: *Trial of Franz Muller* by George H. Knott (London, 1911).

Müller, George

(1805-1898) Prussian-born English clergyman, philanthropist. Christian evangelist. Established an orphanage in Bristol, England. Died at age 92 in Bristol.

Last Words: "We will say nothing about tomorrow." Spoken about his son-in-law who suggested some changes for the next day.

Source: *Müller* by Frederic G. Warne (New York, 1898).

Mulligan, James Adelbert

(1830-1864) American lawyer, military officer. Union Army colonel with Irish Brigade (23rd Illinois Regiment) in U.S. Civil War. Fatally wounded at the Battle of Winchester, Virginia.

Last Words: "Lay me down and save the flag!" Spoken as his men carried him from the field. He died of his wounds a few days later. His Last Words were put to music by George Frederick Root. The words also are carved on a monument in a Chicago cemetery.

Source: *Military and Naval Quotations* by Robert Debs Heinl (Annapolis, MD, 1967).

Mumford, William Bruce

(1820?-1862) American flag desecrator. Confederate civilian. Resident of New Orleans, Louisiana. Convicted of treason by military commission for removing the American flag and walking through city with a piece of it in his lapel. Publicly hanged at age 42 in New Orleans.

Last Words: "I consider that the manner of my death will be no disgrace to my wife and child; my country will honor them."

Source: *A Youth's History of the Great Civil War in the*

United States from 1861 to 1865 by Rushmore G. Horton (New York, 1868).

Muni, Paul

(1895-1967) Ukrainian-born American actor. Stage and screen star. Birth name Meshilem Meier Weisenfreund. Nominated for six Academy Awards; won for *The Story of Louis Pasteur*. Won Tony Award in 1955 for *Inherit the Wind*. Died at age 71 in Montecito, California.

Last Words: "Papa, I'm hungry." Spoken to a photograph of his father as he lay dying in a hospital bed.

Source: *Actor: The Life and Times of Paul Muni* by Jerome Lawrence (New York, 1971).

Munro, Hector Hugh ("Saki")

(1870-1916) British short-story writer, journalist soldier. Created tales with macabre or somber themes. Pen name Saki. Notable works: *Shredna Vashtar; The Open Window; Tobermory*. Fought in World War I as a member of the Royal Fusiliers. Killed in action at age 45.

Last Words: "Put that bloody cigarette out!" Spoken just before troops were to take part in an attack on Beaumont-Hamel, France, in November 1916. He was shot in the head.

Source: *Short Stories of Saki* by H.H. Munro (New York, 1930).

Munson, Thurman Lee

(1947-1979) American professional athlete. Major League Baseball catcher with the New York Yankees for ten years. Served as Yankee captain and was a multi-season All-Star. Only Yankee so far to win both the Rookie of the Year and Most Valuable Player Awards. He was killed at age 32 when the small jet he was piloting crashed in Canton, Ohio. Two others aboard survived; they could not get Munson out of the cockpit before the resulting fire took his life.

Last Words: "Hey, are you guys okay?" His fellow passengers responded, "Thurm, are you alright? " He replied: "No. I can't move. I can't move."

Source: *Munson: The Life and Death of a Yankee Captain* by Marty Appel (New York, 2009).

Münsterberg, Hugo

(1863-1916) German-born American psychologist, educator. Born in Danzig,

Germany, now Poland. Pioneer in field of applied psychology. Notable works: *Psychology and Social Sanity; Psychology and Industrial Efficiency.* Taught at Harvard. Died at age 53 of heart failure while on a lecture platform at Radcliffe.

Last Words: "By spring we shall have peace!" He was referring to World War I, which began in 1914. Peace would not come for two and a half more years.

Source: *Hugo Münsterberg His Life and Work* by Margaret Münsterberg (New York, 1922). The author was his daughter.

Murat, Joachim, King of Naples and Sicily or Joachim I Napoleon

(1767-1815) Neapolitan monarch. Military leader. Brother-in-law of Napoleon Bonaparte who made him marshal of France in 1804. Made King of Naples and Sicily in 1808 as Joachim I Napoleon. Grand Duke of Berg. Defeated by Austrian army. Captured and executed at age 48 in Calabria, Italy.

Last Words: "Soldiers, do your duty. Aim for the heart; but spare the face." Spoken to the men who were assigned to shoot him.

Source: *Les derniers mois de Murat* by Marquis de Sassenay (Paris, 1896).

Mürger, Henri

(1822-1861) French novelist, short-story writer. Full name Louis Henri Mürger. Among the first to depict Bohemian life. Notable work: *Scènes de la Vie de Bohème* (Puccini drew upon the story for his opera *La Bohème).* He based the character Rodolfo on himself. Died at age 38 in a Paris hospital.

Last Words: "No more music, no more commotion, no more Bohemia!"

Source: *Legend of The Latin Quarter, Henry Mürger and the Birth of Bohemia* by Arthur Moss and Evalyn Marvel (New York, 1946).

Murphy, Arthur

(1727-1805) Irish actor, writer, playwright, lawyer, biographer. Pen name Charles Ranger. Friend of Samuel Johnson. Wrote biographies of Johnson, Fielding and David Garrick. Died at age 77 in London.

Last Words: "Taught, half by reason, half by mere decay.

To welcome death, and calmly pass away."

He recited lines from Alexander Pope's *An*

Essay on Man.

Source: *Arthur Murphy: An Eminent Dramatist of the Eighteenth Century* by John P. Emery (Philadelphia, 1946).

Murphy, Francis William ("Frank")

(1890-1949) American politician, jurist. Governor of Michigan. U.S. attorney general. Associate justice of U.S. Supreme Court. Known for his defense of civil liberties. His dissent in the case of *Korematsu v. United States* attacked the wartime evacuation and internment of Japanese Americans as racist. Died at age 59 in Detroit.

Last words: "Have I kept the faith?"

Source: *Mr. Justice Murphy: A Political Biography* by J. Woodford Howard (Princeton, NJ, 1968).

Murphy, Mario Benjamin

(1972-1997) Mexican murderer, convict. One of six people charged with the 1991 murder-for-hire of a U.S. Navy petty officer. Although Murphy fully cooperated with the police, he was the only defendant not offered a plea bargain by the prosecution and the only one sentenced to death. He was also the only foreign national. Despite the intervention of the Mexican government and Amnesty International, the governor of Virginia allowed his execution.

Last Words: "Today is a good day to die. I forgive all of you. I hope God does too."

Source: "Killer Executed in Va. Despite Mexico's Protests" by Carrie Hedges (*USA Today,* September 18, 1997).

Murray, William, 1st Earl of Mansfield

(1705-1793) Scottish-born British lawyer, jurist, politician, scholar. Held a high position in the House of Lords. Parliamentary debater. Rewrote commercial law so that it was coherent. It became the basis of British mercantile law. Helped end slavery in England. Close friend of Alexander Pope. Died at age 88 in London.

Last Words: "Let me sleep—let me sleep."

Source: *Lives of Eminent British Lawyers* by Henry Roscoe (London, 1830).

Murrieta, Joaquin

(1829?-1853) Mexican bandit. Known as the Mexican Robin Hood. Traveled with Three-Fingered Jack (Manuel Garcia) and their gang. Blamed for cattle rustling, robberies and murders in California during the Gold

Rush. In 1853, the California legislature created the California Rangers. A reward was placed on Murrieta and Garcia's heads, captured dead or alive. The Rangers hunted them down and killed them.

Last Words: "It is enough. Shoot no more. The job is finished. I am dead."

Source: *The Robin Hood of El Dorado* by Walter Noble Burns (New York, 1932).

Murrow, Edward R.

(1908-1965) American radio and television reporter, commentator. Became widely known with radio broadcasts from London during World War II. Headed U.S. Information Agency. Introduced television programs *See It Now* and *Person to Person.* Awards include four Peabodys, an Emmy, Medal of Freedom and honorary Knight Commander of Order of the British Empire. Died at age 57 in Pawling, New York.

Last Words: "Well, Jan, we were lucky at that." Spoken to his wife as he patted her on the hand.

Source: *Prime Time: The Life of Edward R. Murrow* by Alexander Kendrick (London, 1970).

Musset, Alfred Louis Charles de

(1810-1857) French poet, dramatist, novelist, librarian. Wrote first modern dramas in French. Served as librarian to French Ministry and later Second Empire. Recipient of Légion d'honneur. Notable works: "The October Night" (poem); *The Confession of a Child of the Century* (autobiography about his celebrated love affair with George Sand); The book was made into the movie *Children of the Century.* Musset spent his last two years confined to his apartment with a rare heart condition now known as Musset's Syndrome. Died at age 46 in Paris.

Last Words: "Sleep! At last I am to sleep."

Source: *Life of Alfred de Musset* by Arvede Barine (New York, 1906).

Mussolini, Benito

(1883-1945) Italian leader. Dictator. Prime minister of Italy. Known as Il Duce. Led Italy into World War II on the side of Germany after the fall of France in 1940. Deposed in 1943. Imprisoned. Tried to escape during the last days of the war. Found hiding in a truck in northern Italy. Executed at age 61 at Giulino de Mezzegra by partisans.

Different Last Words:

(1) "But—but—Mr. Colonel." Spoken to the partisan officer whose court condemned him to death.

Source: *Mussolini: The Intimate Life of a Demagogue* by Paolo Monelli (New York, 1953).

(2) "Shoot me in the chest." Mussolini's Last Words as reported by an eyewitness.

Source: *Death of the Father: An Anthropology of the End in Political Authority* by John Borneman (New York, 2004).

Mussorgsky, Musorgski, or Moussorgsky, Modest

(1835-1881) Russian musician, composer. One of Russia's great composers. Member of an elite group of national composers known as The Five, or The Mighty Handful (along with Borodin, Cui, Balakirev and Rimsky-Korsakov). Notable works: *Boris Godunov; Night on Bald Mountain; Pictures from an Exhibition.* An alcoholic in later years. Unable to compose toward the end of his life. Died at age 42 in a St. Petersburg hospital. Left many works unfinished, including *Boris Godunov* and *Khovanshchina.* They were edited and published posthumously by his friend Rimsky-Korsakov.

Last Words: "It's the end. Woe is me!"

Source: *Modest Mussorgsky, His Life and Works* by Michel D. Calvocoressi, ed. by Gerald Abraham (London, 1946).

Nabokov, Vladimir

(1899-1977) Russian-born American novelist, screenwriter, educator, critic, lepidopterist. Became naturalized U.S. citizen in 1945. Wrote *Lolita,* and later the screenplay for the movie, for which he received an Academy Award nomination. Coined the word "nymphet." Wrote scientific studies on butterflies and had several named for him. Entomologist at Harvard, where some of his butterflies are part of the museum collection. Moved to Switzerland in 1960. Died at age 78 in Montreux.

Last Words: "A certain butterfly is already on the wing." Spoken to his son Dmitri after his eyes welled up with tears when his son kissed his forehead.

Source: *Vladimir Nabokov, The American Years* by Brian Boyd (Princeton, NJ, 1991). Boyd also wrote about his Russian years.

Nadir (or Nader) Shah, King of Persia

(1688-1747) Turkish-born Iranian ruler. Military and tactical genius. Known as the Persian Napoleon. Turkish conqueror. Assassinated in his tent as he was sleeping by some of his officers. He woke in time to kill two of his assassins before the others cut off his head.

Last Words: "Thou dog!" Spoken to one of the assassins.

Source: *Last Words (Real and Traditional) of Distinguished Men and Women Collected from Various Sources* by Frederic Rowland Marvin (New York, 1901). Marvin gave as his source *Predictions Realized in Modern Times* by Welby.

Nagle, Nano Honoria

(1718-1784) Irish nun, educator, social activist. Concerned about poor children. Set up her first school for them around 1749. She soon had seven. In 1776, she became a nun. The following year she opened the first convent in Ireland when she founded the Sisters of the Presentation of the Blessed Virgin Mary (also known as the "Presentation Sisters"). The work of the sisterhood is still carried on by lay people.

Last Words: "Look after the children, the children of the poor."

Source: *One Pace Beyond: The Life of Nano Nagle*, by M. Raphael Consedine (Victoria, Australia, 1977).

Napoleon I (Napoleon Bonaparte)

(1769-1821) Emperor of the French. Known as the Little Corporal. Spent his last six years in exile on the island of Saint Helena. Died there at age 51. Believed to have suffered from stomach cancer during his final days. Body moved to a tomb at Les Invalides in Paris in 1840.

Last Words: "France—Army—head of the Army—Josephine." Napoleon was delirious during his final nine days. Comte de Montholon, who was present during that time, believed these were the words he spoke.

Source: *Napoleon* by Emil Ludwig (New York, 1928).

Napoleon II, King of Rome

(1811-1832) French nobleman. Only legitimate son of Napoleon I and Marie Louise. Full name François Charles Joseph Bonaparte. Duke of Reichstat. King of Rome. Known as l'Aiglon (The Eaglet). Taken to Vienna after his father abdicated. Placed in the custody of his grandfather, Francis II, emperor of Austria. Died at age 21 of tuberculosis at Schonbrunn palace. Buried in Vienna. In 1940, Hitler had his coffin moved to Paris and placed near the tomb of Napoleon I at Les Invalides.

Last Words: "Call my mother. Call my mother.—Take the table away. I don't need anything any more.—Poultices."

Source: *Napoleon II, the King of Rome "L'Aiglon"* by Octave Aubry (London, 1932).

Napoleon III, Emperor of the French

(1808-1873) French nobleman. Nephew of Napoleon I. Third son of Napoleon's brother Louis. Mother was Hortense de Beauharnais, daughter of Empress Josephine. Full name Charles Louis Napoleon Bonaparte. Known as Carbonaro. President of Second Republic. Emperor as Napoleon III. Had one son, Napoleon IV. Began Franco-Prussian War in 1870. Captured at the Battle of Sedan. Deposed, exiled in England. Died there at age 64 after surgery.

Last Words: "Etiez vous a Sedan?" (tr. "Were you at Sedan?") Spoken to his physician and friend Dr. Conneau.

Source: *The Life of Napoleon III* by Archibald Forbes (New York, 1897).

Napoleon IV, Prince Imperial of the French

(1856-1879) French nobleman, military officer. Only legitimate son of Napoleon III and Empress Eugenie. Full title Imperial Highness Eugene Louis Jean Joseph Napoleon Bonaparte. Known as Louis. Killed at age 23 in an ambush by spears of Zulu warriors while fighting with the British army in the Zulu War in southern Africa.

Last Words: "He'll take very good care that nothing happens to me." His response to Major Francis Grenfell who cautioned him to: "Take care of yourself, Prince, and don't get shot." The prince was referring to Lieutenant Jahleel Brenton Carey of Her Majesty's 98th Regiment of Foot, who accompanied him on a reconnaissance task. They were saddling up to return to camp when the Zulus attacked and the prince was killed.

Source: *The Zulu War* by David Clammer (Newton Abbot, Devon, England, 1973).

Nares, Edward

(1762-1841) English clergyman, educator, writer, historian. Regius professor of modern history and modern language at Oxford. Rector at Biddenden and New Church in Kent. Notable works: *Thinks I to Myself; The Plurality of Worlds.* While tutor to family of 4th Duke of Marlborough, he met and fell in love with the duke's daughter Lady Georgiana Charlotte Spencer Churchill. They eloped and were banned from her home, Blenheim Palace. She died three years later. Died at age 79 in Biddenden.
Last Words: "Goodbye."
Source: *The Last Words (Real and Traditional) of Distinguished Men and Women Collected from Various Sources* by Frederic Rowland Marvin (New York, 1901).

Naruszewicz, Adam Stanislas

(1733-1796) Russian-born (now Belarus) Polish nobleman, poet, writer, translator, historian, prelate. Jesuit priest. Bishop of Lukow and Smolensk. Known as the Polish Tacitus. Notable work: *History of the Polish Nation* (6 vol.). Also wrote fables, satires, pastorals, odes. Translated Tacitus, Horace. Died at age 62 in Janów, Poland.
Last Words: "Must I leave it unfinished?" He was speaking about his history of Poland.
Source: *Who Are the Slavs?: A Contribution to Race Psychology,* Vol. 1, by Paul Rankov Radosavljevich (Boston, 1919).

Narváez, Ramón Maria

(1800-1868) Spanish military officer, politician. General, prime minister. Supported Isabella II against the Carlists. She was overthrown by a revolution soon after he died at age 68 in Madrid.
Last Words: "I do not have to forgive my enemies, because I killed them all." His response when his confessor asked him to forgive his opponents.
Source: *Un dictador liberal, Narváez* by Andrés Révesz (Madrid, Spain, 1953).

Nasser, Gamal Abd-al

(1918-1970) Egyptian statesman. Prime minister of Egypt. President of Egypt. Aswan High Dam built during his administration. Nationalized Suez Canal. Formed United Arab Republic with Syria (1958-

1961). Died at age 52 in Cairo.
Last Words: "I don't think I could eat a thing." Spoken to his wife.
Source: *Nasser: A Biography* by Jean Lacouture (New York, 1973).

Nast, Thomas

(1840-1902) German-born American artist, illustrator, political cartoonist, statesman. His illustrations appeared in *Frank Leslie's Illustrated Magazine, Harper's Weekly, Nast's Weekly* and many books. He used his cartoons to attack corruption in government and social injustices. Created the popular image of Santa Claus. Also created elephant and donkey emblems for the Republican and Democratic parties. Appointed consul general to Ecuador. Died at age 62 of yellow fever in Guayaquil six months later.
Last Words: "I feel much better." Spoken to his secretary and to the vice-counsel. Nast insisted he was not seriously ill. After he spoke these words, he lost consciousness and said no more. He died the next morning.
Source: *Thomas Nast: His Period and His Pictures* by Albert Bigelow Paine (New York, 1904).

Nation, Carry Amelia Moore

(1846-1911) American temperance advocate. Lectured on the evils of alcohol. Used a hatchet to smash liquor and bar fixtures. Frequently arrested. Collapsed while making a speech. Hospitalized. Died at age 64 in Leavenworth, Kansas.
Last Public Words: "I have done what I could." Spoken on stage just before she collapsed. Her gravestone in Belton, Missouri, carries the epitaph: "She Hath Done What She Could."
Source: "Carry Nation Your Loving Home Defender" by Jan Holden (*Old West,* Spring 1999).

Navratil, Edmond

(1869?-1912) Czech victim of *Titanic* disaster. Used alias: Louis Hoffman. Abducted his children and tried to take them to America aboard the *Titanic.* One of the children, Michel, lived to be the last male *Titanic* survivor. He was almost four years old in 1912 when his father left his mother and took Michel and his younger brother Edmond aboard the ship under an assumed name as the Hoffman twins. After the children were saved, they became known as "The Titanic Orphans." They were claimed by their mother, who came to New York when she realized they were her children. Edmond, the father, went down with the ship. His Last Words were spoken to his sons as they were taken to a lifeboat.

Last Words: "Tell your mother that I loved her dearly and still do."

Source: "Philosophic About His Titanic Ordeal" (*The Australian*, February 16, 2001).

Nayler or Naylor, James

(1619?-1660) English Quaker. In 1656 in Bristol, England, he reenacted the arrival of Jesus Christ in Jerusalem. Although he denied that he was impersonating Christ, he was tried for violating the Blasphemy Act. His punishment was severe. He was given multiple lashes, his forehead was branded with the letter "B" and a red hot iron was used to bore a hole through his tongue. In 1659, he was robbed and badly beaten. Died at age 44, two days later. During his last few hours, he wrote his testimony that ended with the following lines:

Last Words (written): "I have fellowship therein with them who live in dens and desolate places of the earth, who through death obtained this resurrection and eternal holy life." Written testimony.

Source: *The History of the Rise, Increase and Progress of the Christian People Called Quakers* by William Sewell (New York, 1844).

Neander, Johann August Wilhelm

(1789-1850) German church historian, theologian, educator, writer. Protestant, born of Jewish parents. Birth name David Mendel. Changed name when he converted to Christianity. Studied with Planck. Lectured at Heidelberg. Professor of church history at University of Berlin. Notable work: *General History of the Christian Religion and Church.* Died at age 61 in Berlin.

Last Words: "I am weary. Let us go home! Goodnight!"

Source: *Saint Augustin, Melanchthon, Neander: Three Biographies* by Philip Schaff (New York, 1886).

Nehru, Jawaharlal

(1889-1964) Indian politician, statesman. Father of Indira Gandhi. First minister of external affairs of India. Finance minister of India. First prime minister of independent India. Held post until he died at age 74 in New Delhi after a heart attack. The Nehru jacket was named in his honor.

Last Words: "I have disposed of all my files."

Source: *Profiles of Indian Prime Ministers: Nehru to Narasimha Rao* by Shashi Ahluwalia and Meenakshi Ahluwala (New Delhi, India, 1991); *The Image of Nehru* by Ghan Sham Jolly (Gurgaon, India, 1968); *Day by Day Account of Rajiv Gandhi, 1944-1991: 1944-1988* by S. K. Dhawan (New Delhi, India, 1993). While this quote is often cited as his Last Words, some sources indicate that these were merely "among" his Last Words. Others have small variations of a word or two.

Nelson, David

(1793-1844) American clergyman, writer, physician, educator. Originally practiced medicine. Surgeon in U.S. Army during the War of 1812. Founder and first president of Marion College, which eventually failed. Opened training school for missionaries that also failed. Much of the school's finances were drained supporting the Underground Railroad. Notable work: *Cause and Cure of Infidelity Including a Notice of Author's Unbelief and the Means of His Rescue.* Spent his last years in Quincy, Illinois, where he was president of the Presbyterian Theological Seminary. Died at age 51.

Last Words: "My Master calls, I am going home. It is well."

Source: *Dying Testimonies of Saved and Unsaved: Gathered from Authentic Sources* by Solomon Benjamin Shaw (Chicago, 1898).

Variation: "All is well."

Source: "David Nelson: Sketches of His Life and Character, as a Man, a Christian, and a Preacher" by Drs. Frederick A. Ross of Tennessee, Robert J. Breckenridge of Kentucky and William S. Potts of Missouri and J. A. Jacobs, Esq., of Danville; Collected and Published by Dr. William B. Sprague in *Annals of the American Pulpit*, Vol. 5 (New York, 1858).

Nelson, Earle Leonard

(1897-1928) American rapist, mass murderer who murdered his way across the country with a Bible in his hand. Killed 20 women. Captured in Canada, tried, convicted and condemned to death in Winnipeg.

Last Words: "I am innocent. I stand innocent before God and man. I forgive those who have wronged me and I ask forgiveness of those whom I have injured. God have mercy!" Spoken on the gallows, just before he was hanged.

Source: *Bloodletters and Badmen: A Narrative Encyclopedia of American Criminals from the Pilgrims to the Present* by Jay Robert Nash (New York, 1995).

Nelson, George ("Baby Face")

(1908-1934) American robber, murderer. Real name Lester Joseph Gillis. Robbed small-town banks in the Midwest. Killed three FBI agents in 1934: one near Rhinelander, Wisconsin, in April; two in November in a shootout near Fox River Grove, Illinois, where Nelson was fatally wounded. Died at age 25.

Last Words: "You'll have to drive. I'm hit pretty bad." Spoken to fellow outlaw John Paul Chase as he attempted to get into a G-men's car and flee. His body was found in a ditch the next day.

Source: *Baby Face Nelson: Portrait of a Public Enemy* by Steven Nickel and William J. Helmer (Nashville, TN, 2002).

Nelson, Horatio, 1st Viscount Nelson

(1758-1805) British naval officer. Admiral. Known as Lord Nelson. Struck by a musket ball that broke his spine aboard *Victory* during the Battle of Trafalgar. Died at age 47, soon after the battle ended victoriously for Britain. Nelson's statue stands in Trafalgar Square in London.

Last Words: "I have not been a great sinner. Remember that I leave Lady Hamilton and my daughter Horatia as a legacy to my country.—Never forget Horatia." His thirst increased and he called "Drink—drink—fan—fan—rub—rub" to the surgeon, Dr. Scott, who was massaging his chest. As the pain increased, it was more difficult for him to speak. He then uttered his last words: "Thank God I have done my duty." He repeated these words until he died.

Source: *Life of Lord Viscount Nelson: Duke of Bronte, &c.* by Joseph Allen (London, 1853).

Variation: "God, I have done my duty."

Source: *The Life of Nelson* by Robert Southey (London, 1830).

Variation: "God and my country!"

Source: *Life of Nelson: The Embodiment of the Sea Power of Great Britain* by Alfred T. Mahan (Boston, 1899).

Variation: "Don't throw me overboard, Hardy. Take me home that I may be buried by my parents, unless the king shall order otherwise. And take care of my poor Lady Hamilton, Hardy. Kiss me, Hardy." Hardy knelt and kissed him on the forehead. Nelson replied: "Now I am satisfied. Thank God I have done my duty." Nelson then said to his physician: "Remember that I leave Lady Hamilton and my daughter Horatia as a legacy to my country." His speaking became more difficult. He repeated the words "Thank God I have done my duty" again and again. Nelson had been speaking with Captain Thomas Hardy when he was hit. He died a few hours later.

Source: *Historical Tales, The Romance of Reality* by Charles Morris (Philadelphia, 1897).

Variation: "Well Hardy, how goes the battle? How goes the day with us?—Kiss me, Hardy."

Source: *Nelson and His Captains: Sketches of Famous Seamen* by William Henry Fitschett (London, 1902).

Variation (doubtful): "Kismet [fate] Hardy." This is an often-repeated variation or conjecture of what Nelson said (as opposed to "Kiss Me, Hardy"). However, the word "kismet" was not a part of the English language at that time. Nelson died in 1805 but 1849 is the earliest written use of "kismet" in the English language.

Source: *The Oxford English Dictionary*, 2nd ed. (Cary, NC, 1989).

Nelson, John Byron, Jr.

(1912-2006) American athlete, commentator. Professional golfer. Nicknamed Lord Nelson. Became a golfing legend with 52 wins, including five majors (and runner-up in six others) in an 11-year career. Won 11 consecutive tournaments and 18 tournaments in 1945. Retired in 1946 at age 34 to be a rancher. Later he became a commentator. EDS Byron Nelson Championship named for him—first PGA tour event named for professional golfer. Died at age 94 in Roanoke, Texas.

Last Words: "I'm so proud of you." Spoken to his wife Peggy as she left for a Bible study meeting.

Source: "Golf Legend Byron Nelson Dies" (Associated Press, September 26, 2006).

Nelson, William ("Bull")

(1824-1862) American military officer.

Union major general in U.S. Civil War. Held the distinction of being the only naval officer to achieve the rank of major general. Originally a U.S. Navy officer, he commanded the Army of Kentucky. Shot and killed at age 38 at his headquarters in Galt House, a Louisville, Kentucky, hotel, by fellow officer Union Brigadier General Jefferson Columbus Davis [Not to be confused with Jefferson Finis Davis, President of the Confederacy.] They had argued over defense preparations.

Last Words: "Send for a clergyman. I wish to be baptized. I have been basely murdered." Spoken to the proprietor of the hotel. General T.K. Crittenden, who was nearby, took Nelson's hand and asked if he was seriously hurt. Nelson replied: "Tom, I am murdered." He died within the hour. Davis was arrested but never tried for the crime.

Source: *Battles and Leaders of the Civil War, Vol. III, The Tide Shifts,* ed. by Robert Underwood Johnson and Clarence Clough Buel (New York, 1887).The editors noted that the facts of Nelson's killing appeared in a pamphlet by General James Fry entitled "Killed by a Brother Soldier." They presented a brief account of Fry's description of the crime.

Nero, Emperor of Rome

(37-68) Roman ruler. Full name Nero Claudius Caesar Drusus Domitius Ahenobarbus. Son of Roman consul Domitius Ahenobarbus and Agrippina, daughter of Germanicus Caesar. She poisoned Emperor Claudius and made Nero emperor. He ordered her assassination. Nero was accused of setting the fire that destroyed much of Rome. He persecuted Christians. Declared public enemy by Roman Senate. Fled Rome. Stabbed himself to death at age 30 to avoid capture.

Different Last Words:

(1) "Sero! Haec est fides?" (tr. "Too late! Is this your loyalty?") Spoken to a servant who tried to stop the flow of blood in his wound. Nero died immediately after he uttered these words.

Source: "Nero Claudius Caesar" in *The Lives of the Twelve Caesars* by C. Suetonius Tranquillus, tr. by Alexander Thomson, rev. by Thomas Forester (London, 1901).

(2) (doubtful): "Qualis artifex pereo!" (tr. "What an artist is now about to perish!" Or

"What an artist the world is now about to lose!")

Source: Various Last Words compilations and Internet websites.

These are the Last Words most often ascribed to Nero; however, they were probably not the final words he spoke. More likely they were those in (1).

Source: *Irony and Misreading in the Annals of Tacitus* by Ellen O'Gorman (Cambridge, England, 2000), citing Suetonius (*Nero,* 49.3-4).

Neu, Kenneth

(1910-1935) American murderer. Unemployed singer, dancer. Picked up a middle-aged man on the street. Neu strangled him in a hotel then stole and wore his victim's clothes. He burst into song when he heard his death penalty pronounced in the courtroom. Composed a farewell song he delivered on gallows.

Last Words: "I'm fit as a fiddle and ready to hang!"

Source: *Crime and Detection: An Illustrated History from 1840* by Julian Symons (London, 1966).

Neubauer, Kurt

(1899-1923) German Nazi. One of the first killed in Hitler's unsuccessful Beer Hall Putsch. Hitler dedicated *Mein Kampf* to him and 15 others he deemed "martyrs," people who were first to die in support of the Nazi party. Hitler had them interred in an ornate mausoleum in Munich in 1936. In 1947, after World War II ended, the Allied Control Commission demolished the mausoleum.

Last Words: "The people do not yet want to believe in Adolf Hitler, but the time will come when they will have to believe!"

Source: "Ihr Vermächtnis. Letzte Worte unserer Toten," in *Der Schulungsbrief,* 3 (1936).

Nevin, Ethelbert Woodbridge

(1862-1901) American musician, composer, pianist. Wrote mostly songs and short piano pieces. Notable works: "The Rosary" (sold several million copies); "Mighty Lak' a Rose"; "Narcissus." Suffered from increasingly poor health. Died at age 38 in New Haven, Connecticut.

Last Words: "Anne, I'm dying, and I don't want to leave you." Spoken to his wife.

Source: *Ethelbert Nevin: A Biography* by John Tasker Howard (New York, 1935).

Newell, Arthur Webster

(1854-1912) American banker. Victim of *Titanic* disaster. Died at age 58. President of Fourth National Bank of Boston when he took daughters Marjorie and Madeleine on a tour of the Holy Land and Egypt. They planned their return to America on the *Titanic*. Marjorie Newell Robb was 23 when she survived the *Titanic* sinking. She died at age 103 in 1992.

Last Words: "It does seem more dangerous for you to get into that boat than to remain here with me here but we must obey orders." Spoken to his daughter. When she last saw him, he was helping others in the boat.

Source: "Oldest Living Survivor of the Titanic Disaster Dies" (*Desert News* [Salt Lake City, UT,] June 14, 1992).

Newell, Harriet

(1793-1812) American missionary to India. Died shortly after she arrived in Mauritius at age 19. After she died, her husband compiled a memorial volume that included excerpts from her diaries and letters. Her *Memoirs* were published and widely read.

Last Words: "Oh the pains, the groans, the dying strife. How long, O Lord, how long!" Heard by her husband.

Source: *Memoirs of the Life of Mrs. Harriet Newell, Wife of the Rev. Samuel Newell, Missionary to India* by Harriet Newell, Timothy Dwight and Leonard Wood (Lexington, KY, 1815).

Newman, Ernest

(1868-1959) English writer, critic, biographer, musicologist. Music critic for *Manchester Guardian* and *London Sunday Times*. His biographies of composers include Wagner, Elgar, Richard Strauss, Beethoven, Liszt. Known for his wit, succinct writing and candor. Died at age 90 in Tadworth, Surrey, England.

Last Words: "Yes, I want my cup of tea." His response to his wife who asked if he wanted anything.

Source: *Ernest Newman: A Memoir by His Wife* by Vera Newman (New York, 1964).

Newman, Venerable John Henry

(1801-1890) English theologian, prelate, educator, writer. Anglican leader of Oxford Movement. Converted to Roman Catholicism, ordained priest. Established University College, Dublin. Created cardinal-deacon. Notable works: *Apologia pro vita sua; The Grammar of Assent*. Died at age 89 of pneumonia at Oratory of St. Philip Neri, Edgbaston, Birmingham, England. Proclaimed Venerable in 1891.

Last Words: "I feel bad. I hope to go to sleep." He died a few hours later.

Source: *Newman, Light in Winter* by Meriol Trevor (Garden City, NY, 1963).

Newman, Samuel

(1602-1663) English-born American clergyman, writer. Pastor in Weymouth and Rehoboth, Massachusetts. Compiled *Concordance of the Bible* that was published in London in 1643, 1650, and 1658. After his death, an improved version was published at Cambridge and took the name *Cambridge Concordance*. When he was 61, Newman had a premonition that he would soon die, even though he was in perfect health. He asked the deacon to pray for him as he had not long to live. As soon as the prayer was finished, he said the time had come and he must leave this world. His friends saw no sign of illness and thought it was his imagination. He turned around, uttered his Last Words and suddenly died. Accounts of his death were written about throughout New England and England.

Last Words: "Angels, do your office" or "Now ye angels of the Lord do your duty."

Source: *The History of Rehoboth, Bristol County, Massachusetts* by Leonard Bliss (Boston, 1836). Bliss said a tradition existed in Rehoboth that Newman spoke the words: "Now ye angels of the Lord do your duty." He then turned his eyes to a particular part of the room as though he saw angels present.

Newport, Francis

(1620-1708) English nobleman, infidel. Son of Lord Newport. 1st Earl of Bradford. Joined a group of infidels. Ridiculed Christianity then had a change of heart after he became ill. Felt much remorse. Died at age 88 in Twickenham, England.

Last Words: "Oh, the insufferable pangs of hell and damnation."

Source: *Plea for Religion and the Sacred Writing* by David Simpson (Baltimore, MD, 1807).

Newton, Sir Isaac

(1642-1727) English mathematician, scientist, physicist, astronomer, alchemist, writer. educator. Professor of mathematics at Trinity, Cambridge. Warden and later master of the Mint. President of the Royal Society. Developed theory of gravity. Notable works: *New Theory About Light and Color; Optics; Philosophiae Naturalis Principia Mathematica* (published his laws of motion). Died at age 84 in Kensington, Middlesex.

Last Words: "I don't know what I may seem to the world. But as to myself I seem to have been only like a boy playing on the seashore and diverting myself now and then in finding a smoother pebble or a prettier shell than the ordinary, whilst the great ocean of truth lay all undiscovered before me."
Source: *Never at Rest: A Biography of Isaac Newton* by Richard S. Westfall (Cambridge, England, 1983).

Newton, John

(1725-1807) English clergyman, hymnist. Notable work: "Amazing Grace" (hymn he wrote after converting to Christianity and abandoning his participation in the slave trade). Friend of Cowper. Wrote *Olney Hymns* with him. Died at age 82. Newton was portrayed in two movies entitled *Amazing Grace* (2006).

Last Words: "I am satisfied with the Lord's will."
Source: *Memoirs of the Rev. John Newton* by Richard Cecil (London, 1828).

Newton, Robert

(1780-1854) English clergyman. Methodist Episcopalian. Supporter of Wesleyan missionary and philanthropic efforts. Elected four times to the presidency of the Wesleyan Conference. Traveled six to eight thousand miles a year preaching. In 1840 he visited America as the official representative of the British conference to the Methodist Episcopal Church of England. Died in Easingwold, England.

Last Words: "Farewell. I am going to join the myriads of angels and archangels before the throne of God. Farewell sin, and farewell death. Praise the Lord. Praise Him forever." After an interval, he again made an effort to speak and said "Praise God—praise."
Source: *The Life of Rev. Robert Newton* by Thomas Jackson (London, 1855).
Variation: "My voice and speech are failing forever. I am going,—going,—going to glory. Farewell sin! farewell death! Praise the Lord!"
Source: *Life, Labours, and Travels of the Rev. Robert Newton, D.D.* by a Wesleyan preacher (London, 1855).

Ney, Michel, Duke of Elchingen, Prince of the Moskova

(1769-1815) French nobleman, military officer. Fought in Revolutionary and Napoleonic armies. Created marshal of France. Described by Napoleon as "the bravest of the brave." Created Duke of Elchingen in 1808. Named Prince of the Moskova in 1812. Last combatant soldier of Napoleon's army to leave Russia. Present at Waterloo. Arrested by ultraroyalists and tried for treason. Executed at age 46 by firing squad in Paris.

Different Last Words:
(1) "Soldats, droit au cœur!" (tr. "Soldiers, straight to the heart!")
Sources: *Causes célèbres de tous les peoples,* Vol. VII, by Armand Fouquier (Paris, 1864); "Michel Ney, Maréchal D'empire" (*L'Ambigu: ou Variétés littéraires, et politiques*, Vol. 51, 1815).
Variation: "Soldats, hâtez-vous et tirez là!" (tr. "Soldiers! Make haste, and aim there!")
Source: *Histoire complète du procès du maréchal Ney; contenant le recueil de tous les actes de la procédure instruite, soit devant le conseil de guerre de la 1re. division militaire, soit devant la Cour des Paris, avec le texte des Mémoires, requêtes, consultations, discours et plaidoyers, relatifs à cette sur la vie du maréchal* by Évariste Dumoulin (Paris, 1815).
(2) "Don't you know, Sir, that a soldier does not fear death? Frenchmen, I protest against my condemnation. My honor—." Spoken at his execution when he refused to wear a blindfold.
Source: *The Bravest of the Brave, Michel Ney, Marshal of France, Duke of Elchingen, Prince of the Moskowa 1769-1815* by A. Hilliard Atteridge (London, 1912).

Ngor, Chang My Huoy (Hoa)

(1956-1978) Cambodian Khmer Rouge victim. Pregnant wife of Haing S. Ngor She died malnourished in premature labor at Ngor's side in the Cambodian Killing Fields; the baby also died. Ironically, Ngor was a trained gynecologist and obstetrician, but he was unable to render aid in the fields. Ngor later appeared in a movie about his experiences: *The Killing Fields* for which he won an Academy Award for Best Actor in a

Supporting Role. He was shot and killed outside his home in Los Angeles, California, in 1996 by members of a street gang.

Last Words: "Take care of yourself, Sweet." Spoken to her husband.

Source: *Survival in the Killing Fields* by Haing Ngor (New York, 2003).

Nhat Chi Mai

(1945?-1967) Vietnamese protester, pacifist, student, martyr. Opposed Vietnam War. Buddhist Van-Hanh University student. Worked for School of Youth for Social Services. Immolated herself in the courtyard of Tu Nghiem Pagoda in Saigon, South Vietnam, on May 16, 1967.

Last Words (written): "I offer my body as a torch to dissipate the dark to waken love among men to give peace to Vietnam. The one who burns herself for peace." She also left behind poems and letters signed "the one who burns herself for peace." Suicide note.

Source: "They Who Burned Themselves for Peace: Quaker and Buddhist Self-Immolators During the Vietnam War" by Sallie B. King (*Buddhist-Christian Studies,* Vol. 20, 2000).

Nicholas I, Tsar of Russia

(1796-1855) Russian emperor. Son of Tsar Paul I. Younger brother of Alexander I of Russia and Grand Duke Constantine Pavlovich of Russia. Ruled from 1825 to 1855. Married Charlotte of Prussia, daughter of Frederick William III of Prussia and Louise of Mecklenburg-Strelitz. Died at age 58 of pneumonia in St. Petersburg after catching a chill but refusing to rest. Succeeded by his son Tsar Alexander II.

Last Words (spoken): "Now I go to pray for Russia and for you all. After Russia, I loved you above everything else in the world. Serve Russia." Spoken to his family.

Sources: *Nicholas I* by W. Bruce Lincoln (Bloomington, IN, 1978).

Last Words (written): "I thank the glorious loyal guard who in 1825 saved Russia; and I also thank the brave army and fleet, and I pray God to maintain the courage and spirits by which they have distinguished themselves under me. So long as the spirit remains upheld, Russia's tranquility is secured both in and out, and woe to her enemies! I

loved my troops as my own children, and strove as much as possible to improve their condition. If I am not entirely successful in that respect, it is from no want of will, but because I was unable to do anything better or to do more." Written in an official manifesto issued by Alexander II, who stated Nicholas's "last words were..." Nicholas ended the manifesto with "May these memorable words remain preserved."

Source: Manifesto reprinted in "Latest Intelligence by Telegraph to the New-York Daily Times" (*New York Daily Times*, March 31, 1855).

Nicholas II, Tsar of Russia

(1868-1918) Russian emperor. Son of Alexander III. Last emperor of Russia. Forced to abdicate in 1917. Last of the Holstein-Gottorp-Romanov line. He and his entire family were executed by Bolsheviks in July 1918. Nicholas was 50 years old.

Different Last Words:

(1) "What?" Spoken when he heard his sentence of death.

Source: *Le Tsar Nicolas et la Révolution* by Jean Jacoby (Paris, 1931).

(2) "Father, forgive them, for they know not what they do."

Source: *The Last Tsar: The Life and Death of Nicholas II* by Edvard Radzinsky (Garden City, NY, 1992).

Nicholas, Saint

(270?-343) Turkish Christian prelate. Born near Myra (now part of Turkey). Bishop of Myra. Attended first Council of Nicea in 325. Died in Myra. Gained much popularity in Middle Ages, especially in England where more than 400 churches were named for him. Known for his generosity and his miracles. Had reputation for giving away gifts secretly. 19th century writers Washington Irving and Clement C. Moore helped popularize him as a folk figure.

Last Words: "Into Thy hands, O Lord, I commend my spirit."

Source: *The Golden Legend or Lives of the Saints.* Compiled by Jacobus de Voragine, Archbishop of Genoa, 1275, 1st ed. 1470. English ed. by William Caxton, 1483, ed. by F.S. Ellis (Edinburgh, 1900).

Nichols, John

(1834?-1863) American Confederate soldier, bushwhacker, spy. Fought in U.S. Civil War. Captured and executed under U.S.

laws of court martial. Hanged in Jefferson City, Missouri, in November 1863. Described by the *St. Louis Dispatch* at that time as the first bushwhacker hanged in Missouri by sentence of military authorities.

Last Words: "Yes, I have threatened people, and people have threatened me." Spoken on the scaffold to a priest who had told him: "John you should forgive all for the wrongs done you, as you would expect them to forgive you."

Source: "Execution of a Missouri Bushwhacker" (*New York Times,* November 15, 1863, from *Saint Louis Dispatch*).

Nicholson, John

(1821-1857) Irish-born British military officer, administrator. General. Helped settle the Northwest frontier in India. Involved in the storming of Delhi during the Sepoy Mutiny. Known as The Hero of Delhi. Died at age 35 of wounds received at Delhi. Lingered nine days after being shot.

Last Words: "Tell my mother that I do not think we shall be unhappy in the next world. God has visited her with a great affliction but tell her she must not give way to grief."

Source: *Lives of Indian Officers* by John W. Kaye (London, 1867).

Nicoll, Sir William Robertson

(1851-1923) Scottish clergyman, editor. Free Church leader. Pen name Claudius Clear. Friend of Lloyd George. Founded *Bookman*, literary monthly. Editor of *The British Weekly*. Knighted in 1909. Died at age 72 in Hampstead, England.

Last Words: "I believe everything that I have written about immortality."

Source: *William Robertson Nicoll, Life and Letters* by T.H. Darlow (London, 1925).

Niebuhr, Barthold Georg

(1776-1831) German historian, statesman, philologist, writer. Notable work: *History of Rome*. Laid groundwork for modern historiography. Died at age 54 in Bonn, Germany.

Last Words: "What essential substance is this? Am I so far gone?" Asked when he was given medicine he knew was used only in extreme cases.

Source: *The Life and Letters of Barthold George Niebuhr and Selections From His Minor Writings. With Essays on His Character and Influence* by the Chevalier Bunsen and Professors Brandis and Loebell (London, 1852).

Nietzsche, Friedrich Wilhelm

(1844-1900) German philosopher, poet, writer. Had strong influence on early 20th-century thinkers and writers. Hitler propagandized him by declaring him the pioneer of National Socialism. Notable and most celebrated work: *Thus Spoke Zarathustra* (in which he put forth his concept of the superman). Had breakdown in 1889. His mental and physical degeneration—probably caused by an early infection of syphilis—continued until he died 11 years later at age 55. His mother cared for him until she died in 1897. His sister Elisabeth then took over his care.

Last Words: "Elisabeth." Spoken to his sister.

Source: *Das Leben Friedrich Nietzsche* by E. Förster-Nietzsche (Leipzig, Germany, 1904). The author was his sister Elisabeth.

Nijinsky, Vaslav

(1890-1950) Russian ballet dancer, choreographer. Famed as one of the greatest ballet artists. Lead dancer with Ballets Russes. Notable performances: *Petrushka; Les Sylphides; Shéhérazade; Daphnis and Chloe*. Choreographed Diaghilev productions. Career as performer ended 1919 with a mental breakdown. Suffered from schizophrenia. Later was institutionalized. Died at age 60 of kidney disease in England.

Last Words: "Mamasha!" (tr. "Mama!" or "Mother!")

Source: *The Last Years of Nijinsky* by Romola de Pulszky Nijinsky (New York, 1952). The author was his wife.

Nimitz, Chester William

(1885-1966) American military officer. Rear admiral, commander of 1st battleship division. Chief of U.S. Navy Bureau of Navigation. Commander in chief, admiral and fleet admiral U.S. Pacific Fleet during World War II. Chief of Naval Operations after the war. Died at age 80 on Treasure Island, California. USS *Nimitz* aircraft carrier was named for him.

Last Words: "Jack, you can have something stronger if you like." Spoken to a visitor about a glass of wine he was drinking.

Source: *Nimitz* by E.B. Potter (Annapolis, MD, 1976).

Nisbet, Charles

(1736-1804) Scottish-born American educator, clergyman. Moved to America in 1785 at the request of Dickinson College founder Benjamin Rush. Served as Dickinson president 18 years. Died at age 67 of pneumonia. Last Words: "Holy, holy, holy." Spoken after uttering the name of his wife. He fell asleep and died.

Source: *Memoir of the Rev. Charles Nisbet, D.D., Late President of Dickinson College, Carlisle* by Samuel Miller (New York, 1840).

Nixon, Richard Milhous

(1913-1994) 37th President of the U.S. American lawyer, politician. Member U.S. House of Representatives and Senate from California. Vice President of the U.S. in Eisenhower administration. Disengaged U.S. from Vietnam War. Improved U.S. relations with mainland China. Encouraged other nations to be responsible for a greater share of their defenses with Nixon Doctrine. First U.S. President to resign. Quit office in 1974 after Watergate scandal. Was granted full Presidential pardon by his successor, President Gerald Ford. Suffered a stroke at his Park Ridge, New Jersey, home. Taken to New York Hospital-Cornell Medical Center in New York City. Died at age 81, four days later of cerebral edema.

Last Words: Desperate calls for help to his housekeeper Heidi Retter while he was on his outdoor deck.

Source: "Nixon's Condition Worsens after Stroke, His Doctor Says" by Sam Roberts (*New York Times,* April 20, 1994).

Nobel, Alfred Bernhard

(1833-1896) Swedish chemist, inventor, industrialist, philanthropist. Invented dynamite and many other items, including blasting jelly and smokeless powder. Bequeathed money to fund Nobel Prizes in the fields of chemistry, physics, physiology or medicine, literature and peace. Died at age 63 of a cerebral hemorrhage in San Remo, Italy.

Last Words: "Telegram."

Source: *Alfred Nobel: A Biography* by Kenne Fant (New York, 1991).

Noble, John

(1874-1934) American artist, cowboy. Studied with Picasso and Matisse in Europe. Regarded as both Bohemian and old-time Western cowboy. Died at age 60 in Bellevue Hospital, New York City. Many famous artists attended his funeral. Pallbearers were led by the president of the National Academy.

Last Words: "I could lick you in ten minutes." Spoken to his son at his bedside.

Source: "Artist in Tribute at Noble Funeral. National Academy Members Are Pallbearers at Rites Here for Noted Bohemian. Body is Taken to Kansas. Former Cowpuncher to Be Buried With 'Ten-Gallon' Texas Hat Which He Always Wore" (*New York Times,* January 10, 1934).

Noble, Margaret Elizabeth ("Sister Nivedita")

(1867-1911) Irish-born Indian nationalist. Adopted Hinduism and became disciple of Swami Vivekananda. Moved to India in 1898. Spent the rest of her life there, serving the poor, especially the women of Calcutta. Died at age 44.

Last Words: "The ship is sinking but I shall see the sun rise."

Source: *Vivekananda: An Ancient Silence—Heart and a Modern Dynamism—Life* by Sri Chinmoy (Jamaica, NY, 1993).

Nodier, Charles

(1780-1844) French poet, journalist, librarian, writer. Early Romantic writer. Wrote fantastic and Gothic stories. Notable works: *Le Vampire* (inspired Dumas); *Trilby, ou le Lutin d'Argail* (inspired the ballet *La Sylphide*). Died at age 63 in Paris.

Last Words: "It is very hard, my children, I no longer see you. Remember me. Love me always."

Source: *Charles Nodier: Épisodes et souvenirs de sa vie* by Mme. Mennessier-Nodier (Paris, 1867). The author was Nodier's daughter Marie.

Nordica, Lillian

(1857-1914) American operatic soprano. Birth name Lillian Norton. Made debut at Paris Opera in 1882 and at Metropolitan Opera in 1891. First American to sing at Bayreuth. Notable roles: Isolde, Brunhilde, Violetta, Marguerite. Set out on a recital tour in 1913. Shipwrecked three days. Suffered exposure. Died at age 57 of complications of pneumonia in Batavia, Java.

Last Words: "I am coming, Mother."

Source: *Yankee Diva* by Ira Glackens (New York, 1963).

North, Frederick, 8th Lord North, 2nd Earl of Guilford

(1732-1792) British statesman. Known as Lord North. Chancellor of the exchequer. First lord of the treasury. Prime minister. Lost his eyesight in 1790. Died at age 60 of dropsy in London.

Last Words: "I feel no pain, nor have I suffered any."

Source: *Lord North, Second Earl of Guilford, K.G., 1732-1792* by Reginald Lucas (London, 1913).

Norton, Katherine

(d. 1746) Scottish woman. Known as a young and beautiful lady from a good family and with a handsome fortune. Betrothed to Jacobite rebel Captain James Dawson who had been tried and convicted of high treason. He was executed on the day they were to marry. She was determined to witness his last hour so she and two companions rode there in a hackney cab. She is "Kitty" and Dawson is "Jemmy" in Shenstone's melancholy but popular ballad that describes the incident ("The Ballad of Jemmy Dawson").

Last Words: "My dear, I follow thee, I follow thee! Sweet Jesus, receive both our souls together." Cried out when Dawson was dead. She died that very moment.

Source: *One Hundred Romances of Real Life,* ed. by Leigh Hunt (London, 1888).

Nostradamus

(1503-1566) French physician, astrologer, prophet. Real name Michel de Notre Dame. Wrote a book of rhymed prophecies. When he accurately predicted how Henry II would die, he became the patron of Henry's widow, Catherine de' Medici, queen of France. He suffered from gout. Became ill with edema. Died at age 62 in Salon, France.

Last Words: "Demain, au soleil levant, je ne serais plus." (tr. "Tomorrow, at sunrise, I shall no longer be here.") Spoken to a friend who had been visiting him. Nostradamus was dead the next morning.

Source: *The Story of Prophecy: In the Life of Mankind from Early Times to The Present Day* by Henry James Forman (New York, 1936).

Nothnagel, Carl Wilhelm Hermann

(1841-1905) German physician, neurologist.

Known for research on physiology and pathology of the nervous system. He suffered from angina pectoris. Documented his symptoms in detail just before he died at age 63 in Vienna, Austria.

Last Words (written): "Paroxysms of angina pectoris, with extremely violent pains. Pulse and attacks completely different, sometimes slow, about 56-60, entirely regular, very intense, then again accelerated, 80-90, rather even and regular, finally completely arrhythmic, entirely unequal, now palpitating, now slow, with differing intensity. The first sensations of these attacks date several—three or four—years back, in the beginning rather weak, becoming slowly more and more definite. Properly speaking, attacks with sharp pains have appeared only within the last five or six days. Written on July 6, 1905, late in the evening, after I had three or four violent attacks."

Source: *Der letzte Brief* by Friedrich Reck-Malleczewen (Frankfurt, Germany, 1949).

Nott, Eliphalet

(1773-1866) American clergyman, educator, inventor. President of Union College, Schenectady, New York, for 62 years. Had 30 patents related to heating. Invented a stove that could be adapted for burning anthracite coal. Established a company to manufacture the Union Furnace. A portion of the profits went to the college as part of the Nott Trust Fund.

Last Words: "One word! One word! Jesus Christ."

Source: "Address at the Funeral of Rev. Dr. Nott, Schenectady, February 2, 1866, in the Presbyterian Church" by J. Trumbull Backus (New York, 1866).

Novalis

(1772-1801) German poet. Pen name of Friedrich Leopold, Freiherr von Hardenberg. His Romantic poems influenced later writers. Notable works: *Hymns to the Night; Faith and Love; Henry of Ofterdingen*. Died at age 28 of tuberculosis in Weissenfels, Saxony.

Last Words: A request to his brother to play the harpsichord for him. While his brother was playing, Novalis fell asleep and died a short time later.

Source: *The Works of Thomas Carlyle* (complete) by

Thomas Carlyle (New York, 1897). Carlyle did not give a direct quote for Novalis's Last Words.

Noyes, John

(1521?-1557) English shoemaker, martyr. Condemned for heresy and executed by burning at the stake.

Different Last Words:

(1) "We shall not lose our lives in this fire, but change them for a better, and for coals have pearls."

Source: *The Works of Thomas Adams: Being the Sum of His Sermons, Meditations, and Other Divine and Moral Discourses* by Thomas Adams (Edinburgh, 1861-62).

(2) "Lord have mercy upon me! Christ have mercy upon me! Son of David have mercy upon me." Spoken to bystanders as the fire was kindled and burned about him.

Source: *Book of Martyrs and the Acts and Monuments of the Church* by John Fox (or Foxe). First published 1563, ed. by John Cumming (London, 1851).

Oates, Lawrence Edward Grace

(1880-1912) British soldier, explorer. Member of Captain Robert Falcon Scott's ill-fated expedition to the South Pole in 1911-1912. Severe weather and a lack of food and water endangered the return trip to base camp. When Oates's illness threatened to delay the rest of the party, he left them and walked to his death so that his comrades might have better chance to survive. He was never seen again.

Last Words: "I am just going outside and may be some time."

Sources: *The Epic of Captain Scott* by Martin Lindsay (New York, 1934); Robert Falcon Scott diary entry, March 16-17, 1912, in *Scott's Last Expedition* (New York, 1913).

Oates, Titus

(1610?-1705) English impostor, perjurer. Dismissed as chaplain in the English navy. Obsessed with the idea that Catholics were trying to take over England. Joined Jesuits, then left and rejoined Church of England. Announced there was a Papist plot and Catholics were planning to massacre Protestants, kill King Charles II and burn London. His misinformation caused the deaths of about 35 innocent people. Oates received a home and pension, but later his lies were discovered. He was convicted of perjury during the reign of King James and was pilloried, flogged and imprisoned for life.

When William III gained the throne, Oates was pardoned and given a pension. Many different dates are given for his birth year. The most common one is 1610, suggesting Oates lived to be 94.

Different Last Words:

(1) "It is all the same in the end."

Source: *The Last Words (Real and Traditional) of Distinguished Men and Women Collected from Various Sources* by Frederic Rowland Marvin (New York, 1901).

(2) Not recorded. According to biographer Jane Lane, "There was no admirer left, it seems, to write down his Last Words."

Source: *Titus Oates* by Jane Lane (London, 1949).

O'Bannion, Charles Dion ("Deanie")

(1892-1924) American gangster, murderer. Killer in Chicago during the 1920s. Believed to have murdered or been responsible for the deaths of 25 people. Operated a flower shop. In November 1924, three men came to the shop to pick up a flower order for the funeral of Mike Merlo.

Last Words: "Hello boys. You from Mike Merlo's?" One of the men said "Yes, for Merlo's flowers." He grabbed O'Bannion's hand and held him in a viselike grip. The men then shot him and fled. The executioners later were identified as Frankie Yale, John Scalise and Albert Anselmi.

Source: *Written with Lead: Legendary American Gunfights and Gunfighters* by William Weir (Hamden, CT, 1992).

Oberon, Merle

(1911-1979) Indian-born American actress. Screen star. Birth name Estelle Merle O'Brien Thompson. Academy Award nominee for *The Dark Angel* (1936). Died at age 68 after suffering a stroke in Malibu, California.

Last Words: "Thank you for the happiest years of my life." Spoken to her husband.

Source: *Princess Merle: The Romantic Life of Merle Oberon* by Charles Higham and Roy Moseley (New York, 1983).

O'Brien, William, see Manchester Martyrs.

O'Brien, William

(1852-1928) Irish journalist, editor, nationalist, social revolutionary, politician. Member of Parliament. Editor of *United Irishman*.

Active in land reform. Started No Reduction, No Rent campaign. Imprisoned. Initiated United Irish League (agrarian movement). Founded All for Ireland party. Died at age 75 while visiting London.

Last Words: "Well the night is so long and dreary, I think I will wait up a little longer." Spoken to his wife who had asked: "Willie, isn't it time to go to bed?"

Source: *The Life of William O'Brien, the Irish Nationalist: A Biographical Study of Irish Nationalism, Constitutional and Revolutionary* by Michael MacDonagh (London, 1928).

O'Carolan, Turlough or Torlogh

(1670-1738) Irish musician, harpist. Described as the Last of the Irish Bards. Blinded by smallpox at around age 18. Composed more than 200 songs, several of which were adapted by Thomas Moore. Died at age 68 in Alder Ford, Roscommon County.

Last Words: "It was a pity that two such friends should part, at least without kissing." He died with a container of whiskey in his hand, but had no strength left to drink it.

Source: *Poems of Carolan,* ed. by Tomas O Maille (London, 1916).

O'Connell, Daniel

(1775-1847) Irish nationalist leader, politician. Known as the Liberator. United Roman Catholics to urge Irish emancipation. Lord mayor of Dublin. Member British House of Commons. Arrested and tried for conspiracy and sedition. Sentenced to fine and imprisonment. Both were reversed by House of Lords. Went to Europe for his health. Died at age 71 in Genoa, Italy, on the way to Rome.

Different Last Words:

(1) "My dear friend, I am dying—Jesus—Jesus—Jesus."

Source: *King of the Beggars: A Life of Daniel O'Connell* by Sean O'Faolain (New York, 1938).

(2) "I hope my soul will pass through Ireland."

Source: "Ireland's Lost Leader" by Louis J. McQuilland (*The Living Age, 8th Series,* Vol. X, April 1918).

O'Connell, William Henry

(1859-1944) American prelate. Bishop of Portland, Maine. Papal envoy to Japanese emperor Meiji. Cardinal archbishop of Boston. Presided over the marriage of Joseph P. Kennedy and Rose Fitzgerald in 1914. Died at age 84 in Brighton, Massachusetts.

Last Words: "You need not read any more. Run along. Jerry will be here soon. I would like to sit here and think."

Source: *Cardinal O'Connell of Boston: A Biography of William Henry O'Connell, 1859-1944* by Dorothy Godfrey Wayman (New York, 1955).

O'Connor, Donald David Ronald

(1925-2003) American actor, dancer, singer. Star of stage, screen, television. Emmy award-winning performer. Awarded 1953 Golden Globe for *Singin' in the Rain.* Died at age of 78 of congestive heart failure. His family, who was by his side when he died, reported his Last Words, which were spoken tongue-in-cheek. Some sources state these were merely among his Last Words to his family.

Last Words: "I'd like to thank the Academy for my lifetime achievement award that I will eventually get."

Source: "Donald O'Connor: Star of 'Singin' in the Rain,' dead at 78" by Roger Ebert (*Chicago Sun-Times,* September 28, 2003).

O'Dea, Edward J.

(1856-1932) American prelate. First Roman Catholic Bishop of Seattle. Designated Knight Commander of the Throne of Italy in 1927. Known as Dean of Bishops of the Church in the U.S. Died at age 76 of cancer, two days after celebrating his golden jubilee as a priest.

Last Words: "God bless you all." Spoken from his deathbed.

Source: "Bishop O'Dea Dies in Seattle at 76. Dean of Catholic Prelates in the U.S. Marked Golden Jubilee of Ordination 2 Days Ago. Last Words Benediction. Pioneer of Church in the West Was Made Knight Commander of Throne of Italy in 1927" (*New York Times,* December 27, 1932).

Oei Tjie Sien

(1835-1909) Chinese businessman, entrepreneur. Founder of Kian Gwan Kong Si multinational trading company, first multinational conglomerate in Southeast Asia. Laid groundwork for his son Oei Tiong Ham to be the richest man in Southeast Asia.

Last Words: "Your mother has come for me and I must go."

Source: *Hui-lan Koo (Madame Wellington Koo): An*

Autobiography as Told to Mary Van Rensselaer Thayer by Hui-lan Oei Koo and Mary Van Rensselaer Thayer (New York, 1943).

Offenbach, Jacques

(1819-1880) German-born French musician, composer, conductor, cellist. Birth name Jacob Eberst. Composed many operettas. Created opera bouffe. Notable works: *La Belle Hélène; La Vie Parisienne; Le Grande Duchesse de Gérolstein; Orphée aux enfers (Orpheus in the Underworld)*. Spent last days working on his only grand opera, *The Tales of Hoffmann*, which was in the final stages of completion. Died at age 61 in Paris of gout of the heart.

Last Words: "It will be all over by tonight." Spoken to his family after he had a choking fit. He went through bouts of unconsciousness then died quickly. His friend Léonce, a comedian, commented that "M. Offenbach died without knowing anything about it. He'll be surprised when he finds out."

Source: *Offenbach* by Peter Gammond (London, 1986).

O'Folliard, Tom

(1858-1880) American outlaw. Known as Big Foot. Joined Billy the Kid. Became second in command in his gang. Shot by Pat Garrett at Fort Sumter, New Mexico, while they searched for Billy the Kid and his men. O'Folliard survived about 45 minutes.

Last Words: "Aw, go to hell, you long-legged son-of-a-bitch." Spoken to Garrett, who had admonished O'Folliard that he should not curse when he was so close to death.

Source: *Billy the Kid: A Short and Violent Life* by Robert M. Utley (Lincoln, NE, 1989).

Ogilvy, Margaret

(1819-1895) Scottish mother of novelist, playwright James M. Barrie. Daughter of a stonemason, wife of a poor weaver. James was the youngest of her ten children. Some did not reach adulthood. When her favorite child died, she developed an unusually close relationship with James that was often based in fantasy. When she died, he wrote a book that gave an account of her life and his bond with her.

Last Words: "God—love."

Source: *Margaret Ogilvy by Her Son* by J. M. Barrie (New York, 1896)

O'Hara, Miles F.

(1851-1876) American soldier. Victim of Little Big Horn disaster. Sergeant in Company M, Seventh U.S. Cavalry. Served under George A. Custer. Shot in the chest and killed at age 24. Unable to join the others in Reno's Retreat.

Last Words: "For God's sake, don't leave me!"

Source: *End of Custer: The Death of an American Military Legend* by Dale T. Schoenberger (Surrey, British Columbia, 1995).

O'Kane, Tullius Clinton

(1830-1912) American educator, composer. music instructor, hymnist. Wrote many anthems and hymns. Notable hymns: "To Him be All the Glory"; "Oh, How Precious"; "The Stranger at the Door"; "The Standard of the Cross." Died at age 81 in Delaware, Ohio.

Last Words: "Amen." Died of a heart attack soon after he got up to go to his room.

Source: *Biography of Gospel Song and Hymn Writers* by J.H. Hall (New York, 1914).

O'Kelley, Edward Capehart

(1858-1904) American criminal. Killed Robert Ford, the man who assassinated Jesse James. O'Kelley spent ten years in prison for the crime and was released in 1902. He was arrested as a suspicious character by police officer Joe Burnett then released in Oklahoma City in 1903. In January 1904, O'Kelley encountered Burnett on the street and drew a revolver. The two men struggled. Burnett fired two shots into O'Kelley and killed him.

Last Words: "You come with me. I'll arrest you, you son-of-a-bitch." Spoken to Burnett. As the two men fought, O'Kelley shouted to a bystander for help, saying: "We will murder this fellow!" A railroad baggage man ran to Burnett's aid. Burnett shot and killed O'Kelley.

Source: "Dead: The Man Who Killed the Man Who Killed Jesse James" by Jim Cloud (*Oklahombres*, Vol. III, No. 3, Spring 1992).

Oldfield, Anne

(1683-1730) English actress. Stage star. Known for her talent and beauty. Performed in comedies and tragedies. When she died, she was the only actress buried inside

Westminster Abbey.

Last Words: "Odious! in woollen? 'twould a saint provoke!" She was reciting Alexander Pope's *Moral Essays,* Epistle I. She was the Narcissa about whom Pope wrote:

"Odious! in wollen? 'twould a saint provoke!/

Were the last words that poor Narcissa spoke./

No, let a charming chintz and Brussels lace/

Wrap my cold limbs and shade my lifeless face./

One would not, sure, be frightful when one's dead—/

And Betty, give this cheek a little red."

"Betty" was her friend, ex-actress Mrs. Saunders who cared for her in her final days.

Source: *The Roll Call of Westminster Abbey* by A. Murray Smith (London, 1903).

Olga Alexandrovna, Grand Duchess of Russia

(1882-1960) Russian royalty, artist. Last surviving daughter of Tsar Alexander III. Sister of Tsar Nicholas II. Fled Russia after 1917 Revolution. Lived in Denmark and later Canada. Talented artist who painted her entire life, producing more than 2,000 watercolors and some oils. Died at age 78 in Toronto.

Last Words: "The sunset is over."

Source: *The Last Grand Duchess* by Ivan Vorres (New York, 1964).

Olgiati, Gerolamo

(1453-1477) Italian government official, political radical, assassin. One of three killers of Galeazzo Sforza, Duke of Milan, in 1476. Executed at age 23 in Milan with the two other conspirators.

Last Words: "My death is untimely, my fame eternal, the memory of the deed will last for aye."

Source: *Renaissance in Italy* by John Addington Symonds (New York, 1888).

Olinger, Robert ("Pecos Bob")

(1841?-1881) American law officer. Deputy U.S. marshal. The last victim of Billy the Kid. He saw the Kid looking at him from an upper window of the courthouse in Lincoln, New Mexico. The Kid had gotten a gun and killed sheriff's deputy J.W. Bell.

Last Words: "Yes, and he's killed me too." Spoken by Olinger just after he heard that the Kid had killed Bell. The Kid fired and killed Olinger instantly.

Source: *Pat Garrett: The Story of a Western Lawman* by Leon C. Metz (Norman, OK, 1974).

Oliphant, Laurence

(1829-1888) South African-born British writer, traveler, mystic. Newspaper correspondent during the Franco-Prussian War. Notable work: *Piccadilly: A Fragment of Contemporary Biography* (novel). Influenced by spiritualist prophet Thomas Lake Harris for many years. Left him in 1881 and settled in Palestine. Died at age 59 in Twickenham, Middlesex, England, on a visit.

Last Words: "More light."

Source: *Memoir of the Life of Laurence Oliphant and of Alice Oliphant, His Wife* by Margaret Oliphant (New York, 1891). The author was his cousin.

Oliphant, Margaret Oliphant Wilson

(1828-1897) Scottish-born British novelist, history writer, journalist, biographer. Married cousin Frank Wilson Oliphant who died young, leaving her to support herself and three children. Prolific author of more than 100 books. Wrote about small-town life. Notable works: *Salem Chapel; Chronicles of Carlingford; Passages in the Life of Mrs. Margaret Maitland.* Died at age 69 in Wimbledon, England.

Last Words: "I seem to see nothing but God and our Lord."

Source: *The Autobiography and Letters of Mrs. M.O.W. Oliphant,* ed. by Mrs. Harry Coghill (New York, 1899). Mrs. Harry Coghill was Anna Louise Walker Coghill, a cousin of Margaret Oliphant.

Oliver, François

(1497-1560) French leader. Chancellor of France. Overcome by melancholy and remorse after persecuting many Protestants. As he lay dying, he was concerned about the future of his soul.

Last Words: "Oh! Cardinal, thou wilt make us all damned." Spoken to the Cardinal of Lorraine, under whom he condemned to death many innocent men.

Source: *The History of France* by François Pierre G. Guizot, Henriette Elizabeth Witt, tr. by Robert Black (Philadelphia, 1874).

Olivier, Lord Laurence

(1907-1989) British actor. Stage and screen star. Nominated for Academy Awards as Actor, Supporting Actor, Best Picture, and Best Director. Won for Best Actor for *Hamlet* in 1948. Knighted in 1947. Made Life Peer in 1970. Awarded Order of Merit in 1981. Died at age 82 in Steyning, West Sussex, England.

Last Words: "This isn't Hamlet, you know, It's not meant to go into the bloody ear." Spoken to his nurse who spilled water on his head.

Source: *Famous Last Words: The Ultimate Collection of Finales and Farewells* by Laura Ward and Robert Allen (2004).

Olson, Barbara Kay Bracher

(1955-2001) American television personality, writer, victim of 9/11 attack. Conservative whose investigations of the Clinton-era Travelgate and Filegate scandals were turned into two books highly critical of the Clinton administration. Was passenger on American Airlines Flight 77 that was hijacked and flown into the Pentagon by al Qaeda terrorists.

Last Words (or approximation): "What shall I tell the pilot? What can I tell the pilot to do?" Spoken via cell-phone call to her husband, U.S. Solicitor General Ted Olson. Call was made from inside the airplane lavatory. She made two calls to her husband. Her precise Last Words are not known. In subsequent interviews, he conveyed the words slightly differently, such as "would" or "should" instead of "can." Olson faulted his memory and admitted he may have confused the two calls. However, he was consistent in his reports that she said these Last Words (or something extremely close) just before being cut off the last call.

Source: CNN, September 14, 2001 (Live television broadcast). Olson also spoke with CNN on September 12, 2001. Other interviews were quoted that week including *Washington Post* and *New York Times*.

Omar Khayyam or al-Khayyam

(1050?-1131) Persian astronomer, mathematician, poet. Published treatise on algebra and series of astronomical tables. Notable work: *Rubaiyat of Omar Khayyam* (a collection of poems widely known outside Persia).

Last Words: "Oh God, verily I have sought to know Thee to the extent of my powers. Forgive me, therefore. My knowledge of Thee is my recommendation to Thee."

Source: *Life of Omar al-Khayyámi* by J.K.M. Shirazi (Edinburgh, 1905).

Onassis, Jacqueline Bouvier Kennedy

(1929-1994) American First Lady, editor. Wife of John F. Kennedy, 35th President of the U.S. Eyewitness to her husband's assassination in Dallas, Texas. Married Greek tycoon Aristotle Onassis. Died at age 64 in New York City.

Last Words: Speaking to her dead children, she said: "My little angels—I'll be with you soon." She then said to her two living children: "Don't cry for me. I'm going to be with your father now."

Source: *Last Words: A Dictionary of Deathbed Quotations* by C. Bernard Ruffin (Jefferson, NC, 1995). Ruffin gave as his sources *The Globe* and the *National Enquirer*, June 7, 1994.

Oneby, John

(1677?-1727) English murderer, military officer. Rank of major conferred on him for his participation in several military campaigns. Killed William Gower in a brawl. Committed suicide in his Newgate jail cell.

Last Words (written): "Cousin Turvill,— Give Mr. Akerman, the turnkey belowstairs, half guinea, and Jack, who waits in my room, five shillings. The poor devils have had a great deal of trouble with me since I have been here." Suicide note for his jailers.

Source: *The Newgate Calendar: Comprising Interesting Memoirs of the Most Notorious Characters who have been Convicted of Outrages on the Laws of England Since the Commencement of the Eighteenth Century; with Occasional Anecdotes and Observations, Speeches, Confessions, and Last Exclamations of Sufferers* by Andrew Knapp and William Baldwin (London, 1824).

O'Neill, Eugene, Sr.

(1888-1953) American playwright. Earned Nobel and four Pulitzer Prizes. Notable works: *Desire Under the Elms; The Iceman Cometh; A Long Day's Journey into Night; Ah, Wilderness* (his only comedy). Spent last months in a Boston hotel suffering from a debilitating neurological illness that affected his coordination. Died there at age 65. The hotel later became Shelton Hall dormitory at Boston University.

Last Words: "I knew it! I knew it! Born in a hotel room and, goddam it, dying in a hotel room." Cried out as he was dying. He went into a coma and died a short time later.

Source: *O'Neill: Son and Artist* by Louis Sheaffer (Boston, 1973).

O'Neill, Eugene, Jr.

(1910-1950) American classical Greek scholar. Son of playwright Eugene O'Neill. Left academia to work in the war effort during World War II. Returned to Yale as a professor. Later taught at Princeton. Actively involved in radio in the late 1940s. Suffered from alcoholism. Committed suicide at age 40 in Woodstock, New York.

Last Words (written): "Never let it be said of O'Neill that he failed to empty a bottle. Ave atque vale." Suicide note.

Source: " Eugene O'Neill Jr. is Found a Suicide" (*New York Times*, September 26, 1950).

O'Neill, James

(1847-1920) Irish-born American actor. Father of Eugene O'Neill, who based the father character James Tyrone in *A Long Day's Journey into Night* on him. Specialized in one role—*The Count of Monte Cristo*—which he performed more than 6,000 times. Died at age 72 in New London, Connecticut.

Last Words: "This sort of life—here—all froth—no good—rottenness." Spoken to his son Eugene.

Source: *The Curse of the Misbegotten: A Tale of the House of O'Neill* by Croswell Bowen (New York, 1959).

O'Neill, William Owen ("Buckey")

(1860-1898) American military officer. Arizona lawyer, miner, cowboy, gambler, newspaperman, law officer. Member of Teddy Roosevelt's Rough Riders during the Spanish-American War. Recruited many volunteers and supervised their training in San Antonio while waiting to be deployed. Just prior to the Rough Riders' famous charge up Kettle Hill, O'Neill was standing under heavy fire from a nearby ridge, smoking a cigarette and joking with his troops. One of his sergeants shouted to him above the noise: "Captain, a bullet is

sure to hit you!" The reply he shouted back would be his Last Words:

Last Words: "Sergeant, the Spanish bullet isn't made that will kill me." He then turned to another officer. As he started to speak, a bullet struck him in the face. O'Neill was dead before he hit the ground. Private Tuttle, who was standing nearby, later recalled: "I heard the bullet. You usually can if you're close enough, you know. It makes a sort of spat."

Source: *Buckey O'Neill, He Stayed With 'Em While He Lasted* by Ralph Keithley (Caldwell, ID, 1949).

Opie, Amelia Alderson

(1769-1853) English novelist, poet, writer. Second wife of English artist John Opie. Notable works: *Lays for the Dead; Adeline Mowbray.* Died at age 84 in Norwich, England.

Last Words: "Tell them I have suffered great pain, but I think on Him who suffered for me. Say that I am trusting in my Saviour, and ask them to pray for me." Spoken in response to a request to leave a message for those who asked.

Source: *Amelia: The Tale of a Plain Friend* by Jacobine Menzies-Wilson and Helen Lloyd (London, 1937).

Oppenheimer, J. Robert

(1904-1967) American physicist, educator. Directed development of the atomic bomb during World War II. Supervised creation of Los Alamos Laboratory. Director of Institute for Advanced Study in Princeton, New Jersey, from 1947 to 1967. Died at age 62 of cancer in Princeton.

Last Words (written): "I am in some pain. My hearing and my speech are very poor." Written to a friend.

Source: *American Prometheus: The Triumph and Tragedy of J. Robert Oppenheimer* by Kai Bird and Martin J. Sherwin (New York, 2005).

O'Reilly, John Boyle

(1844-1890) Irish-born journalist, poet, editor, writer. Deported to Australia for inciting a riot. Escaped, settled in United States. Editor of Boston newspaper *Pilot.* Wrote novel *Moondyne* based on his experiences in Australia. Found dead at age 46 after he took some of his wife's sleeping medicine. Cause of death uncertain. Public was told he died of heart failure. Official record shows it was accidental poisoning.

Last Words: "Yes, Mamsie dear. I have taken some of your sleeping medicine. I feel tired now, and if you will let me lie down on that couch I will go to sleep right away. Yes, my love! Yes, my love!"

Source: *John Boyle O'Reilly, His Life and Poems* by James Jeffery Roche (New York, 1891).

Orléans, Charlotte Elisabeth, Duchesse d'

(1652-1722)   German-French   nobility. Daughter of Elector Palatine Karl Ludwig. Known as Lisolette. Married Philippe, Duc d'Orléans, brother of Louis XIV of France. Died at age 70.

Last Words (written): "Thank God I am prepared to die, and I only pray for strength to die bravely. It is not bad weather, although today a fine rain is setting in. But I do not think any weather will help me. Many complain of coughs and colds, but my malady lies deeper. Should I recover, you will find me the same friend as ever. Should this be the end, I die with full faith in my Redeemer." Letter.

Source: *A Lady of the Old Regime* by Ernest F. Henderson (New York, 1909).

Orléans Louis Philippe Joseph, Duc d'

(1747-1793) French nobleman, revolutionary. Great-grandson of Philippe II, Duc d'Orléans. Father of Louis Philippe Joseph the Citizen King. Earned name Philippe Égalité for support of French Revolution. Voted for death of Louis XVI. Worked with Mirabeau and Danton against the king. Accused of conspiring against republic. Sentenced to die by military tribunal at Paris. Guillotined at age 46.

Last Words: "You can do that more easily to my dead body. Come, be quick." Spoken to the executioner's assistant who wanted to take off his boots.

Source: *Prince of the Blood* by Evarts S. Scudder (London, 1837).

O'Rourke, Heather Michele

(1975-1988) American actress. Child screen star. Played leading role in three *Poltergeist* movies. Her tag line "They're here" became one of the most recognized phrases in American film history. She became ill with flu-like symptoms while filming *Poltergeist*

III and was eventually diagnosed with Crohn's disease. She went into cardiac arrest en route to the hospital and died of an intestinal blockage that had led to infection and septic shock.

Last words: "I love you too." Her response to her mother's comment "I love you." Spoken on the way to the hospital.

Source: "Heather O'Rourke's Grieving Mother Tells Why She's Suing Her Child's Doctor for Wrongful Death" by John Stark, Eleanor Hoover and Peter Keogh (*People* magazine, June 13, 1988).

Ortega y Gasset, José

(1883-1955) Spanish philosopher, writer, statesman, educator. Professor at Madrid. Civil governor of Madrid. Notable works: *The Dehumanization of Art; The Revolution of the Masses*. Died at age 72 in Madrid.

Last Words: "I have a great confusion in my head. I would like you to clear it up for me." Spoken to his wife.

Source: *Les Mots de la fin* by Claude Aveline (Paris, 1957).

Orwell, George

(1903-1950) British novelist, critic, essayist. Pen name of Eric Arthur Blair. Born in Bengal, India. Taken to England when he was one year old. Notable works: *Down and Out in Paris and London; Animal Farm; Nineteen Eighty-four*. Spent his last three years in and out of hospitals. Died at age 46 of tuberculosis.

Last Words (written): "At fifty, everyone has the face he deserves." Note in his manuscript notebook.

Source: *The Quote Verifier: Who Said What, Where and When* by Ralph Keyes (New York, 2006).

Oscar II, King of Sweden and Norway

(1829-1907) Swedish monarch. Succeeded to the throne when brother Charles XV died in 1872. Governed for almost 35 years. Was a popular monarch. Brought many cultural and economic changes to Sweden during his reign. Updated an antiquated army and navy. Norway, which had united with Sweden in 1814, became independent in 1905. Died at age 78 in Stockholm. His oldest son ascended to the throne as Gustav V.

Last Words: "Don't let them shut the theatres for me."

Source: *Something of Myself for My Friends Known*

and Unknown by Rudyard Kipling (Garden City, NY, 1937). Kipling qualified the comment by noting that "they said" these had been the last words of the old king. His words prompted Stockholm to "go soberly about her pleasures, all dumbed down under the snow."

Osler, Sir William, 1ˢᵗ Baronet

(1849-1919) Canadian-born physician, historian, educator, writer. Taught in Pennsylvania and Maryland. Regius professor of medicine at Oxford. Received baronetcy in 1911. Notable works: *The Principles and Practice of Medicine; A Concise History of Medicine*. Died at age 70 in Oxford, England.
Last Words: "Nighty-night, a-darling!" Spoken to his wife.
Source: *The Life of Sir William Osler* by Harvey Cushing (Oxford, England, 1925). The book earned a Pulitzer Prize for Cushing in 1926.

Osteen, John

(1921-1999) American clergyman, televangelist. Founder and pastor of Pentecostal Lakewood Church in Houston, Texas, which boasts 15,000 members, 8,200-seat sanctuary and television audiences in more than 100 countries. Died at age 77 of a heart attack in Houston. Succeeded as leader by his son Joel. His Last Words were spoken to Joel.
Last Words: "God's mercy endures forever."
Source: "He Has Trained a Family of Ministers and Leaders, and We Will Continue to Be Faithful to His Vision of the Lord" by Cecile S. Holmes and Eric Berger (*Houston Chronicle*, January 24, 1999).

Oswald, Lee Harvey

(1939-1963) American accused assassin. Arrested on suspicion of killing President John F. Kennedy and police officer J.D. Tippit in Dallas, Texas, on November 22, 1963. Kennedy was shot in a motorcade. Tippit was shot later that afternoon. Shortly afterward, Oswald was apprehended. Two days later, he was shot and killed at age 24 in Dallas police quarters by nightclub owner Jack Ruby.
Different Last Words:
(1) "I will be glad to discuss this proposition with my attorney, and that after I talk with one, we could either discuss it with him or discuss it with my attorney if the attorney thinks it is a wise thing to do, but at the present time I have nothing more to say to you." Spoken to Inspector Thomas J. Kelley of the U.S. Secret Service in the basement of Dallas police headquarters just before he was shot and killed by Ruby.
Source: *Conspiracy of One: The Definitive Book on the Kennedy Assassination* by Jim Moore (Ottawa, ON, 2007).
(2) "There ain't nobody gonna shoot me." Spoken while handcuffed to Detective James Leavelle.
Source: *Famous Last Words: Apt Observations, Pleas, Curses, Benedictions, Sour Notes, Insights from People on the Brink of Departure* by Alan Bisbort (San Francisco CA, 2001).

Otho, Marcus Salvius, Emperor of Rome

(32-69) Roman ruler. Deposed by Vitellius. Committed suicide after his soldiers were defeated in a battle near Cremona and his army was obliged to surrender.
Different Last Words:
(1) "Go then and show yourself to the soldiers, lest they should cut you to pieces for being accessory to my death." Spoken before he fell on his sword.
Source: "Otho" in *Lives of the Noble Grecians and Romans* by Plutarch, tr. by John Dryden (Chicago, 1952).
(2) "If you love me in reality, let me die as I desire and do not compel me to live against my will, but make your way to the victor and gain his good graces." Spoken just before he committed suicide.
Source: *Dio's Rome: An Historical Narrative Originally Composed in Greek During the Reigns of Septimus, Severus, Geta and Caracalla, Macrinus, Elagabalus and Alexander Severus and Now Presented in English Form* by Cassius Dio Cocceianus, tr. and ed. by Herbert Baldwin Foster and Joannes Zonaras (Troy, NY, 1906).

Oughtred, William

(1574-1660) English mathematician, writer. Anglican clergyman. Designed early form of slide rule. Invented trigonometric abbreviations and signs of multiplication, including "X" notation for multiplication and : : for proportion. Notable work: *Clavis mathematicae*. Died at age 86 in Albury, England.
Last Words: "And are ye sure he is restored? Then give me a glass of sack to drink his Sacred Majesty's health." He was reacting to news that King Charles II had returned to England from Scotland and had been restored to the English throne. Tradition has it

that Oughtred died of joy on hearing the news.

Source: *Brief Lives* by John Aubrey, ed. by Oliver Lawson Dick (London, 1950).

Ouida, see Ramée, Louise de la.

Ousley or Ouseley, Gideon

(1762-1839) Irish clergyman. Methodist. Mission rider and preacher in Ireland for 40 years. Died at age 76 in Dublin.

Last Words: "I have no fear of death. The Spirit of God sustains me. God is my support."

Source: "Methodism in Ireland: Life of Gideon Ousley" by W. Irwin (*The British and Foreign Evangelical Review*, April 1880).

Outlaw, B.L. ("Bass" or "Baz")

(1854-1894) American law officer, outlaw, gunfighter. Discharged from the Texas Rangers in 1892 but allowed to become a deputy U.S. marshal. Shot a Texas Ranger in El Paso, Texas. Tracked down by Constable John Selman and arrested. Mortally wounded, he died a short time later.

Last Words: "Go gather my friends around me, for I know that I must die."

Source: *Triggernometry, a Gallery of Gunfighters* by Eugene Cunningham (Caldwell, ID, 1941).

Owen, John

(1616-1683) English clergyman, theologian, educator, writer. Puritan Nonconformist Chaplain to Oliver Cromwell. Dean of Christ Church, Oxford. Vice chancellor of Oxford. Died at age 67 in Ealing, England.

Last Words: "I am glad to hear it; but O brother Payne! The long-wished-for day is come at last, in which I shall see the glory in another manner than I have ever done, or was capable of doing, in this world." His response to his friend William Payne, who was overseeing the printing of Owen's *Meditations on the Glory of Christ* and had assured him all was going well with the publication.

Source: *A Critical Dictionary of English Literature and British and American Authors* by S. Austin Allibone (Philadelphia, 1897).

Owen, Robert

(1771-1858) Welsh social reformer. Utopian. Restored failing New Lanark Mills in Manchester, England. Founded several colonies of Owenites, including New Harmony in Indiana. Notable work: *A New View of Human Society*. Died at age 87 in Newton, Montgomeryshire, Wales.

Last Words: "Relief has come."

Source: *Robert Owen, a Biography* by Frank Podmore (London, 1906).

Owen, Wilfred

(1893-1918) British poet, military officer. Company commander on the Western Front in France during World War I. Injured and sent home. Returned to the Front. Killed in action at age 25, a week before war ended. Notable works: "Anthem for Doomed Youth"; "Dulce et Decorum Est." His poems expressed anger over the cruelty of war and pity for its victims.

Last Words: "Well done! You are doing very well, my boy!" Spoken to a soldier under his command.

Source: *The Poems of Wilfred Owen*, ed. by Edmund Blunden (New York, 1931).

Ozanam, Blessed Antoine-Frédéric

(1813-1853) French educator, lawyer, historian. Roman Catholic writer. Professor at the Sorbonne. Published books on religion and history. Notable works: *Dante and Catholic Philosophy in the Thirteenth Century; Germanic Studies*. One of the founders of the Society of Saint Vincent de Paul. Died at age 40 of a kidney ailment in Marseilles, France. Beatified in 1997.

Last Words: "My God! My God! Have mercy on me!" Cried out in a loud voice.

Source: *Frederic Ozanam, Professor at the Sorbonne. His Life and Works* by Kathleen O'Meara (Edinburgh, 1876).

Packer, Alfred G. ("Alferd")

(1842-1907) American gold prospector, travel guide, reputed cannibal. Accused of shooting and eating five of his gold prospecting companions in the harsh winter of 1873. Tried and convicted for manslaughter and sentenced to 40 years. Conviction was overturned. He was eventually paroled. Many people were convinced Packer was innocent of the charge, including staff members of the *Denver Post* newspaper, who helped gain his parole. He spent his final years in and around Littleton, Colorado. Died at about age 65. When he was a young man, a tattoo artist misspelled his name "Al-ferd" on a tattoo he had placed on his arm. Amused by the mistake, he sometimes used that spelling.

Last Words: "I'm not guilty of the charge."

Source: *Littleton Independent.* Sixtieth Anniversary Edition, 1888-1948 (Littleton, CO, 1948).

Paderewski, Ignace Jan

(1860-1941) Polish leader, statesman, musician, composer. International concert pianist. Composed opera, concertos, symphony, piano and orchestral pieces. Notable work: *Minuet in G.* He was part of Poland's post World War I coalition government: prime minister, minister of foreign affairs. Appeared as himself in the movie *Moonlight Sonata* (1937). Died at age 80 of pneumonia in New York City during a Polish Relief Fund Tour.

Last Words: "Please." His response when asked if he wanted some champagne.

Source: *Paderewski As I Knew Him: From the Diary of Aniela Strakacz,* tr. by H. Chybowska (New Brunswick, NJ, 1949). Aniela Strakacz was the wife of Pad-erewski's secretary.

Paetus, Arria

(d. 42) Roman matron. According to legend, her husband Caecina Paetus was involved in a conspiracy against Emperor Claudius. He was ordered by the emperor to commit suicide for his part in the scheme but had difficulty doing so. Arria grabbed the dagger from Caecina and stabbed herself, then handed it back to her husband with her final words. The sculpture *Arria et Paetus* by Lepautre and Jean-Baptiste Théodon is in the Louvre in Paris.

Last Words: "Non dolet, Paete!" (tr. "It doesn't hurt, Paetus!") Spoken to her husband. Pliny the Younger obtained his information from Arria's granddaughter Fannia.

Source: *Pliny the Younger, Epistulae (Letters) 3.16, A.D. 97-107,* cited in *Gaiuis Plinius Caecilius Secundus. The Letters of the Younger Pliny,* tr. by Betty Radice (London, 1963).

Paganini, Niccolo

(1782-1840) Italian musician, violinist, composer. One of the greatest violin virtuosos. His astonishing virtuosity caused rumors to be spread that he collaborated with the devil. Notable works: *Concerto in D*

Major; 24 Caprices (for unaccompanied violin). Died at age 57 in Genoa of a diseased larynx ("consumption of the throat"). During his final days, he was unable to talk and barely able to swallow. The Roman Catholic Church would not permit his body to be buried on consecrated ground for many years.

Last Words (written): "I don't know the laxative red roses." He was referring to the buds of some roses that were used as a mild purgative.

Source: *Paganini, the Genoese* by Geraldine I.C. de Courcy (Norman, OK, 1957).

Page, Alvah B.

(d. 1863) American soldier, gunner. Artilleryman in Union Army in U.S. Civil War. Shot by a Confederate sharpshooter while sitting under a flag of truce. Two Confederate officers had been taken blindfold to General Grant's headquarters. The Confederate sharpshooter had ignored the truce flag. Page was shot in the head and died instantly.

Last Words: "I guess they are gone up." He was referring to the two officers.

Source: *An Artilleryman's Diary* by Jenkin Lloyd Jones, Private, Sixth Wisconsin Battery (Original Papers by Wisconsin History Commission, Madison, WI, 1908-1914).

Page, Thomas Nelson

(1853-1922) American lawyer, novelist, diplomat. U.S. ambassador to Italy. Wrote historical novels about the South. Notable works: *In Ole Virginia; Two Little Confederates.* Died at age 69 in Hanover County, Virginia.

Last Words: "Here Alfred, take this spade."

Source: *Thomas Nelson Page: A Memoir of a Virginia Gentleman, By His Brother* by Rosewell Page (New York, 1923).

Pahlavi, Mohammed Riza, Shah of Iran

(1919-1980) Persian monarch. Son of Reza Shah Pahlavi, founder of Pahlavi dynasty. Succeeded his father in 1941. Introduced parliamentary government. His power became absolute with his coronation in 1967. Fled Iran in 1979 when his government was overthrown. Died at age 60 of cancer in exile in Cairo, Egypt.

Different Last Words:

(1) "I don't want to live like Tito." Spoken to his physicians and reported by Dr. Abdel Meguid Lutfi. He was referring to the Yugoslav leader who died two months earlier after months of grave complications.

Source: "Mohammed Riza Pahlavi: Deposed Shah Dies in Egypt at 60: Iran Says Death Will Not Affect Fate of 52 American Hostages: Funeral Tomorrow: Sadat Lauds Exiled Leader and Vows that Family Can Stay in Egypt" (*New York Times*, July 28, 1980).

(2) "You don't understand. I am dying." His response to his valet who told him he would be better.

Source: *The Shah's Last Ride* by William Shawcross (New York, 1988).

Pahlavi, Riza Shah, Shah of Iran

(1878-1944) Persian monarch. Founder of the Pahlavi dynasty. Gained control of Iran in 1925, when he replaced the deposed Ahmad Shah. Forced to abdicate in favor of his son in 1941, during World War II. Died at age 66 in exile in Johannesburg, South Africa.

Last Words: "Do not fear difficulties. Go forward to meet them. Never try to avoid them. One must confront difficulties face to face in order to remove them."

Source: *Riza Shah Pahlavi: The Resurrection and Reconstruction of Iran, 1878-1944* by Donald N. Wilber (Hicksville, NY, 1975).

Paine, Thomas

(1737-1809) English-born American revolutionary, pamphleteer, deist, political philosopher. Notable works: *Common Sense; The Crisis; The Rights of Man; The Age of Reason*. In later years, his views on Christianity and the divinity of Jesus Christ made him unpopular. Died at age 72 in New York City and buried on his farm. William Cobbett had Paine's body disinterred and taken to England in 1817. When Cobbett's estate was sold in 1836, the auctioneer refused to sell the body. Over the years, it passed through a series of receivers but no one claimed the bones. The present location of Paine's body is uncertain.

Different Last Words:

(1) "I have no wish to believe on that subject." Spoken to his doctor who asked: "Do you wish to believe that Jesus Christ is the Son of God?"

Source: *Paine* by David F. Hawke (New York, 1974).

(2) "And yours augments." Reply to his doctor who said "Your belly diminishes."

Source: *Thomas Paine, Friend of Mankind* by Kesketh Pearson (New York, 1937).

(3) "Let me alone; good morning!" Spoken to two clergymen who had entered his room and prodded him on his religious beliefs. Then Madame Bonneville asked if he was satisfied with the treatment he had received in her house. "Oh yes," he replied. These were his Last Words.

Source: *The Life of Thomas Paine: With a History of His Literary, Political and Religious Career in America, France, and England* by Moncure Daniel Conway (New York, 1906).

Palissy, Bernard de

(1510?-1589) French Huguenot potter. Created a superior type of pottery known as Palissy ware. Wrote his autobiography in which he described his attempts to make white porcelain. Arrested as a Huguenot. Imprisoned in the Bastille in 1588 for his religious beliefs. Was offered freedom if he would abandon his faith but refused to recant. Condemned to death when he was nearly 80. Because Palissy's beautiful wares graced his palace, King Henry III would not allow him to be turned over to the Guises who probably would have executed him. Instead, Palissy languished in a Bastille dungeon until he died.

Last Words: "Sire, I am ready to give up the remainder of my life for the honour of God. You have told me several times that you pity me, and now in turn I pity you who have used the words 'I am compelled.' It is not spoken like a King, sire! and they are words which neither you, nor the Guises, nor the people shall ever make me utter. I can die!"

Source: *Memoirs of Celebrated Characters* by Alphonse de Lamartine (New York, 1854).

Pallotti, Saint Vincent

(1795-1850) Italian clergyman, theologian, holy man. Priest who founded the Society of the Catholic Apostolate. Died at age 54 in Rome. Canonized in 1963.

Last Words: "Jesus, bless the Congregation: a blessing of goodness, a blessing of wisdom."

Source: *Butler's Lives of the Saints* by Herbert J. Thurston and Donald Attwater (Westminster, MD, 1956).

Palm, Johann Philipp

(1768-1806) German book dealer, pamphleteer, publisher. Published a pamphlet that attacked Napoleon and the conduct of the French Army in Germany and called on Germans to resist the French. Arrested by order of Napoleon. Tried in military court and executed at age 37.

Last Words (written): "To you dear wife, I say a thousand thanks for your love. Trust in God, and do not forget me. I have nothing in the world to say but farewell, you and the children, God bless you and them. My regards to Mr. and Mrs. Schwägerin and all my friends, whom I thank for their goodness and love. Once more, farewell. Yonder we shall meet again. Your husband, and children's father, Johann Palm. Braunau, in prison, August 26, 1806, a half hour before my death." Last part of a letter to his wife and children.

Source: *Der letzte Brief* by Friedrich Reck-Malleczewen (Frankfurt, Germany, 1949).

Palmer, Courtlandt

(1843-1888) American merchant, free thought advocate. Founded 19th Century Club of New York to promote free discussion of religious and philosophical issues. Died at age 45 at Lake Dunmore, Vermont.

Last Words: "I want you to say that you have seen a free thinker die without fear of the future, and without changing his opinion."

Source: *Courtlandt Palmer: Tributes Offered by Members of the Nineteenth Century Club to Its Founder and First President* (New York, 1889).

Palmer, John

(1742-1798) English actor. Notable roles: Falstaff, Sir Toby Belch, Macbeth, Shylock. Died at age 56 on stage in Liverpool while performing in *The Stranger*.

Last Words: "There is another and a better world." The words he spoke were a line in *The Stranger*. Ironically, he had recently lost his wife and a son and was suffering from depression.

Source: *Off the Track in London* by George R. Smith (London, 1911).

Palmer, Roundell, 1st Earl of Selborne

(1812-1895) British lawyer, politician, statesman, hymnist, writer. Solicitor general. Attorney general. Lord chancellor. Edited a hymnal. Wrote liturgical articles. Died at age 82 of influenza in Hampshire, England.

Last Words: "Lord show me what thou wouldst have me to do, and help me to do it faithfully and well."

Source: *Memorials, Parts I and II*, ed. by Lady Sophia Palmer (London, 1898). The author was his daughter.

Palmer, William

(1824-1856) English physician, murderer. Known as Rugeley Poisoner and Prince of Poisoners. Convicted for strychnine poisoning of John Parsons Cook of Rugeley. Executed at age 31 before a large crowd of spectators.

Different Last Words:

(1) "God bless you." Spoken to his executioner.

Source: *Illustrated Life, Career, and Trial of William Palmer of Rugeley* by William Palmer (London, 1856).

(2) "Are you sure it's safe?" Spoken as he stepped on the trap of the gallows.

Source: *The New Book of Lists: The Original Compendium of Curious Information* by David Wallechinsky and Amy Wallace (New York, 2005).

Palmerston, Lord, see Temple, Henry John.

Pambo or Panbis the Hermit, Saint

(d. 375) Egyptian Christian holy man. Lived as a hermit in the desert. Founded many monasteries. Known for his wisdom.

Last Words: "I thank God that not a Day of my life has been spent in idleness. Never have I eaten bread that was not earned by the sweat of my brow. I do not recall any bitter speech I have made for which I ought to repent now."

Source: *The Lives of the Saints,* Vol. VII, by S. Baring-Gould (London, 1874).

Pancratius or Pancras, Saint

(290?-304) Roman Christian martyr. Fourteen-year-old orphan beheaded in Rome during the reign of Diocletian.

Last Words: "In body I am a child, but I bear a man's heart, and by the grace of my Master Jesus Christ, thy threats seem as vain to me as this idol which stands before me. And as for the gods whom thou desirest me to adore, they are naught but impostors, who sully the women of their own household, and spare not their own kin. If thine own slaves today behaved as these gods, thou wouldst be in haste to put them to death. And it wonders me much that thou dost not blush to adore such gods." Spoken to Emperor Diocletian.

Source: *The Golden Legend or Lives of the Saints.* Compiled by Jacobus de Voragine, Archbishop of Genoa, 1275, 1st ed., 1470. English ed. by William Caxton, 1483, ed. by F.S. Ellis (Edinburgh, 1900).

Pandithan, M.G.
(1940-2008) Malaysian-Indian politician, statesman. Former vice president of Malaysian Indian Congress. Member of parliament. Parliamentary secretary to Trade and Industry Ministry. President and founder of Indian Progressive Front (IPF). Died at age 68 of leukemia in Kuala Lumpur, Malaysia.

Last Words (written): "There is no death for me." Written in Tamil on a note handed to his wife at his hospital deathbed shortly before he lost consciousness. Although his wife said she did not understand what he meant, others interpret his words as a paraphrase of a verse by Tamil poet Subrahmanya Bharathi, and that the verse meant a person dies but his works will live on after him.

Source: "His Last Words–There Is No Death for Me" by V.P. Sujata and Mazwin Nik Anis (*The* [Selangor, Malaysia] *Star*, May 1, 2008).

Pang, Layman
(740-808) Chinese Buddhist. Lived in the Zen tradition of Vimalakīrti, contemporary of Buddha (Siddhārtha Gautama). Nonmonastic Buddhist model of how to live an exemplary Buddhist life.

Last Words: "I ask that you regard everything that is as empty, nor give substance to that which has none. Farewell. The world is like reflections and echoes." Spoken to the governor of Xiangzhou, who asked about his health.

Source: *Zen's Chinese Heritage–The Masters and Their Teachings* by Andrew Ferguson (Somerville, MA, 2000).

Panzram, Carl
(1891-1930) American serial killer. Murdered 21 people. Executed by hanging in Leavenworth, Kansas, at age 39. The movie *Killer: A Journal of Murder* (1996) is based on his final years.

Last Words: "Hurry it up, you Hoosier bastard! I could hang a dozen men while you're fooling around." Spoken to the hangman who asked if there were any Last Words he wanted to say.

Source: *Bloodletters and Badmen: A Narrative Encyclopedia of American Crime from the Pilgrims to the Present* by Jay Robert Nash (New York, 1973).

Pape, Klaus von
(1904-1923) German Nazi businessman. Early member of Nazi party. One of the first Nazis killed in Hitler's unsuccessful Beer Hall Putsch. Hitler dedicated *Mein Kampf* to him and 15 others he deemed "martyrs," people who were the first to die in support of the Nazi party. Hitler had them all interred in an ornate mausoleum in Munich in 1936. In 1947, after World War II ended, the Allied Control Commission demolished the mausoleum.

Last Words: "Is Hitler alive? Is Ludendorff? Then I gladly die for my fatherland!"

Source: "Ihr Vermächtnis. Letzte Worte unserer Toten" (*Der Schulungsbrief*, 3, 1936).

Park Chung-hee
(1917-1979) Korean politician, military officer. Brigadier general in the Korean Amy. Gained presidency of Republic of Korea (South Korea) in 1961 by staging a bloodless military coup. Held the presidency until he was assassinated. He was shot and killed along with the head of presidential security at a dinner party in Seoul. Five of his bodyguards were killed at the same time. He had escaped an earlier assassination attempt in 1974, when his wife was killed.

Last Words: "I'm all right." His response when someone asked if he was okay.

Source: "Assassin Sought Presidency, Korea Says" (*Los Angeles Times,* November 6, 1979).

Park, Edwards Amasa
(1808-1900) American clergyman, theologian, educator, writer, editor, translator. Congregationalist. Professor at Andover Theological Seminary. Editor of *Bibliotheca Sacra.* Died at age 91 in Andover, Massachusetts.

Last Words: "These passages may be found on the following pages." His mind was wandering; he thought he was in the classroom again.

Source: *The Last Words (Real and Traditional) of Distinguished Men and Women Collected from Various Sources* by Frederic Rowland Marvin (New York, 1901).

Parke, Harry ("Parkyakarkus")

(1904-1958) American comedian. Real name Harry Einstein. Father of comedians Albert Brooks and Super Dave Osbourne. Portrayed Parkyakarkus ("park your carcass"), luncheonette owner who garbled English on Eddie Cantor's radio show and in movies. Died of a heart attack at age 54, in Los Angeles, California, after finishing his toast at the Friar's Club Roast of Lucille Ball and Desi Arnaz.

Last Words: "So Desi, we sincerely hope that you'll be using the facilities of our club very often. And Lucy, while ladies nights at the Friars are traditionally Thursdays and Saturdays, we love you so you can come any time. Thank you very much." He slumped against Milton Berle and then leaned forward. Berle called for "a doctor in the house." Most people thought it was part of the act. Berle directed Tony Martin to sing, attempting to divert the crowd. Martin sang *There's No Tomorrow.*

Source: "Playboy Interview: Albert Brooks" with Bill Zehme (*Playboy*, August 1999).

Parke, Samuel

(1788-1869) American clergyman. Presbyterian. Member of pioneering family of Parkesburg, Pennsylvania. One of 15 members of Dickinson College 1809 graduating class along with James Buchanan, later U.S. President.

Last Words: "I have tried to serve God."

Sources: *A Bibliography of the Wyoming Valley, Pennsylvania* by Rev. H.E. Hayden (privately printed); *History of Centre Presbyterian Church, New Park, Pa., 1780-1903* by Robert L. Clark (Lancaster, PA, 1903).

Parker, Bonnie Elizabeth

(1910-1934) American criminal. Accomplice to murderer and robber Clyde Barrow. Last Words (written, doubtful): After she and Barrow escaped in 1933, her poem *The Story of Suicide Sal* was found and published in newspapers. The last stanza reads:

"Some day they will go down together,
And they will bury them side by side.
To a few it means grief,

To the law it's relief,
But it's death to Bonnie and Clyde."

Although often stated as her Last Words, they were not. Bonnie and Clyde were killed by a posse in Louisiana in 1934. The lawmen who killed her said she let out a long horrified scream just before she was shot and killed.

Source: *Ambush: The Real Story of Bonnie and Clyde* by Ted Hinton and Larry Grove (Austin, TX, 1979). Hinton was one of the six posse members.

Parker, Theodore

(1810-1860) American clergyman, abolitionist, social reformer. Transcendentalist. Unitarian. Supported John Brown in his raid on Harper's Ferry. Poor health ended his career as a preacher. Went to Italy for a warmer climate. Died at age 49 in Florence of TB and exhaustion.

Last Words (written): "My dear John Ayres, So I shall still call you. Will you come over tomorrow and see us; just after your dinner time? Bring me a last year's apple if you can, or any new melon." Letter.

Source: *Theodore Parker: Yankee Crusader* by Henry Steele Commager (Boston, 1936).

Last Words (spoken): "It is all one, Phillips and Clarke will come for my sake." He was talking about his funeral and that Wendell Phillips and James Freeman Clarke would attend.

Source: *Theodore Parker: A Biography* by Octavius Brooks Frothingham (Boston, 1874).

Parkman, Francis

(1823-1893) American historian, writer. Notable works: *France and England in North America; The Oregon Trail; Pioneers of France in the New World; Montcalm and Wolfe; A Half-Century of Conflict.* Afflicted many years with nervous and other disorders, partial blindness and severe headaches. Died at age 70 of peritonitis in Jamaica Plain, Massachusetts.

Last Words: He described a dream he had that he was killing a bear. (Direct quote not given).

Source: *A Life of Francis Parkman* by Charles Haight Farnham (Boston, 1901).

Parnell, Charles Stewart

(1846-1891) Irish politician, nationalist. Leader of 1880s Home Rule Movement in

Ireland. Ruined in 1890 when his adulterous affair with Katie O'Shea, wife of former follower William Henry O'Shea, became known. They married in 1891 but the Roman Catholic Church refused to recognize the union. Parnell's political career was negatively affected. He lost his support and was replaced as leader. Died at age 45 of a heart attack in Brighton, England, less than four months after his wedding.

Last Words: "Kiss me, sweet Wifie, and I will try to sleep a little."

Source: *Charles Stewart Parnell: His Love Story and Political Life* by Katherine O'Shea (New York, 1914). The author was his wife.

Parry, Sir William Edward

(1790-1855) British naval officer, explorer. Rear admiral. Made four expeditions to the Arctic searching for the Northwest Passage. Published a journal of each expedition. Knighted in 1829. Died at age 64 in Bad Ems, Germany, after a long illness.

Last Words: "The chariots and horses!"

Source: *Memoirs of Rear-Admiral Sir W. E. Parry* by his son Rev. Edward Parry (London, 1857).

Parsons, Albert Richard

(1848-1887) American labor activist, anarchist, terrorist. Executed at age 39 in Chicago along with fellow anarchists George Engel, August Spies and Adolph Fischer for the 1886 Haymarket bombing.

Last Words: "Will I be allowed to speak, O men of America? Let me speak, Sheriff Matson! Let the voice of the people be heard! O—" The signal to execute was given and his speech ended.

Source: *Life of Albert R. Parsons: With Brief History of the Labor Movement in America; Also Sketches of the Lives of A. Spies, Geo. Engel, A. Fischer and Louis Lingg* by Albert Richard Parsons, Lucy Eldine Parsons (Chicago, 1889). Lucy Eldine Parsons was the wife of Albert R. Parsons and an active American anarchist.

Parsons, Theophilus

(1750-1813) American jurist, lawyer, politician, writer. Chief justice of the Supreme Court of Massachusetts from 1806 until he died at age 63. Federalist leader. Delegate to the 1788 state convention that ratified the Federal Constitution. Believed to be the author of *Conciliatory Resolutions*: proposed amendments to the Constitution that

did much to win over Samuel Adams and John Hancock to the side of ratification. With John Hancock, Parsons secured three amendments to the Constitution, part of the *Bill of Rights*. Future President John Quincy Adams studied law in his office.

Last Words: "Gentlemen of the jury, the case is closed; and in your hands; you will please retire and agree upon a verdict." Spoken when he was dying with "some trouble in the head." He thought he was in a courtroom.

Sources: *The Memorial History of Boston: Including Suffolk County, Massachusetts, 1630-1880* (Boston, 1881-1883); *Memoirs of Theophilus Parsons, Chief Justice of the Supreme Judicial Court of Massachusetts; With Notices of Some of His Contemporaries* by His Son, Theophilus Parsons (Boston, 1859).

Pascal, Blaise

(1623-1662) French mathematician, physicist, philosopher, inventor, writer. Perfected first mechanical calculator and first syringe. Developed Pascal's law of pressure. Created Pascal's Wager, a philosophical argument for believing in God. Notable works: *Provincial Letters; Pensées* (published eight years after he died). Suffered from ill health most of his life. Died in Paris at age 39 in intense pain after a malignant growth in his stomach spread to his brain.

Last Words: "Que Dieu ne m'abandonne jamais!" (tr. "May God never forsake me!")

Sources: *Pensées de Pascal: précédées de sa vie par Mme. Périer, sa sœur; suivi d' un choix des Pensées de Nicole, et de son Traité de la paix avec les homes* by Blaise Pascal, Pierre Nicole and Gilberte Perier (Paris, 1842); *Scientists of Faith: Forty-eight Biographies of Historic Scientists and Their Christian Faith* by Dan Graves (Grand Rapid, MI, 1996). Graves stated these were "among his last words."

Variation: "May God never abandon me!"

Source: *Blaise Pascal: The Life of a Genius* by Morris Bishop (New York, 1936).

Pascin, Jules

(1885-1930) Bulgarian-born French artist, painter. Expressionist. Birth name Julius Mordecai Pincas. Traveled in the U.S. during World War I and became an American citizen. Returned to France in 1920. Committed suicide at age 45 in Paris on the opening day of his one-man exhibition.

Last Words (written): "Adieu Lucy." Written in blood on the wall of his studio before

he killed himself. Lucy was Cécile Vidil, a model with whom Pascin was obsessed.
Source: *Abschiedsbriefe* by Wilhelm Treichlinger (Berlin, Germany, 1934).

Pasternak, Boris

(1890-1960) Russian writer, poet, novelist. Notable work: *Doctor Zhivago* (novel about Russia's transition from tsarism to communism; made into a popular movie). Awarded 1958 Nobel Prize for Literature but was forced by the Soviets to decline it. Died at age 70 of cancer in Peredelkino, Russia.
Different Last Words:
(1) "I can't hear very well. And there's a mist in front of my eyes. But it will go away, won't it? Don't forget to open the window tomorrow."
Source: *A Captive of Time: My Years with Pasternak* by Olga Ivinskaya (Garden City, NY, 1978). The author was his inspiration for Lara in *Doctor Zhivago*.
(2) When a needle was inserted into a vein on his arm, he murmured to his wife Zinaida: "Dosvidanya" (tr. "Goodbye.") Moments later, blood gushed from his mouth. He asked her: "Why am I hemorrhaging?" Trying to reassure him, she replied: "It is because you have pneumonia." She said death came fast. She leaned over him, counted 25 gasping breaths, then he died.
Source: "Death of a Man" (*Time* magazine, June 13, 1960).

Pasteur, Louis

(1822-1895) French chemist, bacteriologist, educator. Professor of chemistry at the Sorbonne. Founder of the science of microbiology. Discovered that infectious diseases are caused by microbes. Showed that spoilage of perishable food can be prevented by destroying microbes present in them and by protecting sterilized food against further contamination. This process for preserving food was named for him: pasteurization. Also perfected the first vaccine against rabies. Died at age 72 in Villeneuve l'Etang, France.
Last Words: "I cannot." His response when he was offered a cup of milk.
Source: *The Life of Pasteur* by René Vallery-Radot (New York, 1937).

Paterson, Joseph

(d. 1758) English actor. Long-time entertainer in Norwich, England. Known for his versatility and talent. Died on stage while performing as the Duke in Shakespeare's *Measure for Measure.* He collapsed into the arms of an actor named Moody who was portraying Claudio. Moody died on stage some years later while again portraying Claudio and speaking an equally ironic line as his Last Words.
Last Words: "Reason thus with life: If I do lose thee I do lose a thing That none but fools would keep: a breath thou art." He died immediately after saying these lines. They are also engraved on his tomb at Bury St. Edmunds.
Sources: *Representative Actors: A Collection of Criticisms, Anecdotes, Personal Descriptions, Etc., Etc., Referring to Many Celebrated British Actors from the Sixteenth to the Present Century; With Notes, Memoirs, and a Short Account of English Acting* by William Clark Russell (London, 1872); "Shakespeariana" by Albert R. Frey (*The Bookmart*, Vol. IV, No. 46, June 1887). Frey, a librarian at Astor Library, detailed many examples of people dying on stage (with last lines) while performing Shakespeare.

Patmore, Coventry Kersey Dighton

(1823-1896) British librarian, poet, writer, literary critic. Assistant librarian at the British Museum. Notable works: *The Angel in the House* (novel in verse); *The Unknown Eros and Other Odes* (poetry). Died at age 73 from pneumonia in Lymington, Hampshire, England.
Last Words: "I love you dear, but the Lord is my life and my light." Spoken as he held his wife.
Source: *Portrait of My Family, 1783-1896* by Derek Patmore (London, 1935). The author was his grandson.

Paton, John

(d. 1684) Scottish Covenanter leader, military officer, martyr. Known as Captain John. Fought with Gustavus Adolphus of Sweden in wars in Germany. Was with the Scots army at the risings at Rullion Green and Bothwell Bridge. Declared a rebel. Captured, sentenced to die, executed in Edinburgh.
Last Words: "Farewell, sweet scriptures, preaching, praying, reading, singing, and all duties. Welcome, Father, Son, and Holy Spirit. I desire to commit my soul to Thee in well-doing. Lord, receive my spirit." Spoken

on the scaffold.

Source: *The Scots Worthies: Containing a Brief Historical Account of the Most Eminent Noblemen, Gentlemen, Ministers, and Others, Who Testified or Suffered for the Cause of Reformation in Scotland: From the Beginning of The Sixteenth Century to the Year 1688* by John Howie (Glasgow, Scotland, 1829).

Pattison, Dorothy Wyndlow ("Sister Dora")

(1832-1878) English nurse. Sister of English scholar Mark Pattison. Took the name Sister Dora when she joined the Anglican sisterhood of the Good Samaritan. Left the sisterhood to take charge of the municipal epidemic hospital in Walsall, England. Tended the sick and dying during the 1875 smallpox epidemic. Died at age 46 of breast cancer in Walsall.

Last Words: "I have lived alone, let me die alone, let me die alone."

Source: *Sister Dora, a Biography* by Margaret Lonsdale (New York, 1880).

Pattison, William

(1706-1727) English poet. Attended Sidney College, Cambridge, but left without earning his degree. Died at age 20 of smallpox. Notable work: *Poetical Works* (published posthumously the following year).

Last Words (written): "Sir, If you was ever touched with a sense of humanity, consider my condition: what *I am*, my proposals will inform you; what *I have been*, Sidney College, in Cambridge, can witness; but what *I shall be* some hours hence, I tremble to think! Spare my blushes! I have not enjoyed the common necessaries of life for these two days, and can hardly hold to subscribe myself, Yours, etc." Written in a note.

Source: *Annals of the Poets, Backgrounds, Private Lives, Habits of Composition, Characters, and Personal Peculiarities* by Chard Powers Smith (New York, 1935).

Patton, George Smith

(1885-1945) American military officer. Known as Old Blood and Guts. U.S. Army general in European Theater of Operations during World War II. Participated in North Africa, Sicily, France, Germany campaigns. Seriously injured in an automobile accident in Europe shortly after the war ended. Died at age 60 of an embolism 12 days later in Heidelberg, Germany.

Last Words: "It's too dark, I mean, too late." Whispered to his wife.

Source: *General Patton: A Soldier's Life* by Stanley P. Hirshson (New York, 2002).

Pauahi, Princess, see Bishop, Bernice Pauahi.

Paul, Maury Henry Biddle ("Cholly Knickerbocker")

(1890-1942) American writer, editor, journalist. Syndicated gossip columnist and society editor for the Hearst newspaper chain, in particular *The New York Journal American*. Pen name Cholly Knickerbocker. He coined the term "Café Society" to describe the restaurant/night club crowd. He also coined the expression "Old Guard" to describe members of old conservative New York families. Paul was replaced by Igor Cassini who used the same pen name.

Last Words: "Oh Mother, how beautiful it is!"

Source: *Champagne Cholly: The Life and Times of Maury Paul* by Eve Brown (New York, 1947).

Paul I, Emperor of Russia

(1754-1801) Russian ruler. Member of the House of Holstein-Gottorp-Romanov. Son of Catherine II the Great and Peter III. Succeeded his mother in 1796. Assassinated at age 46 in St. Michael's Palace. Strangled after refusing to sign his abdication. Succeeded by his son Alexander I.

Last Words: "Gentlemen, in heaven's name spare me. At least give me time to say my prayers." His plea to his assassins.

Source: *The Romanovs* by Edith Martha Almedingen (New York, 1966).

Paul III, Pope

(1468-1549) Italian prelate. Birth name Alessandro Farnese. Excommunicated English King Henry VIII. Approved establishment of Jesuits. Convened Council of Trent. Fell ill with fever. Died at age 81 in Rome.

Last Words: "Keep back thy servant also from presumptuous sins; let them not have dominion over me. Then I shall be blameless, and innocent of great transgression." As he lay dying, he repeated one of the Psalms of David.

Source: *The Lives and Times of the Roman Popes* by Chevalier Artaud de Montor (New York, 1911).

Paul VI, Pope

(1897-1978) Italian prelate. Birth name Giovanni Battista Enrico Antonio Maria Montini. Ruled during the final days of the Second Vatican Council. Notable encyclicals: *Sacerdotalis Caelibatus* (reaffirming priestly celibacy); *Humanae Vitae* (reaffirming Church's prohibition of artificial birth control). Also declared women could not become priests. First pope to board an airplane. First to travel outside Italy since 1809. Died at age 80 in the papal summer residence at Castel Gandolfo, Italy.

Last Words: "Our Father, who art in Heaven…"

Source: *Paul VI: The First Modern Pope* by Peter Hebblethwaite (New York, 1993).

Paul, Saint

(d. 67?) Biblical figure, holy man, writer. Born at Tarsus. Originally named Saul. Changed his name to Paul when he converted to Christianity. Founded many churches. Wrote epistles that are part of the New Testament. Beheaded in Rome during the reign of Emperor Nero.

Last Words: "Festina ante hiemem venire salutat te Eubulus et Pudens et Linus et Claudia et fratres omnes."

Source: 2 Timothy 4:21 (Latin Vulgate Bible).

Variation: "Do thy diligence to come before winter. Eubulus greeteth thee, and Pudens, and Linus, and Claudia, and all the brethren. The Lord Jesus Christ be with thy spirit. Grace be with you."

Source: 2 Timothy 4:21-22 (King James Version).

Variation: "Do your utmost to come before winter. Eubulus greets you, as well as Pudens, Linus, Claudia, and all the brethren. Farewell. The Lord Jesus Christ be with your spirit. Grace be with you. Amen."

Source: 2 Timothy 4:21-22 (New King James Version).

Variation: "Try with diligence to come before winter. Eubulus greeteth thee, and Pudens and Linus and Claudia and all the brethren. The Lord Jesus Christ be with thy spirit. Grace be with you. Amen."

Source: 2 Timothy 4:21-22 (21st Century King James Version).

Variation: "Make every effort to come before winter. Eubulus greets you, also Pudens and Linus and Claudia and all the brethren.

The Lord be with your spirit. Grace be with you."

Source: 2 Timothy 4:21-22 (New American Standard Bible).

Variation: "Do your best to get here before winter. Eubulus greets you, and so do Pudens, Linus, Claudia and all the brothers. The Lord be with your spirit. Grace be with you."

Source: 2 Timothy 4:21-22 (New International Version).

Variation: "Do your best to come before winter. Eubulus sends greetings to you, as do Pudens and Linus and Claudia and all the brothers. The Lord be with your spirit. Grace be with you."

Source: 2 Timothy 4:21-22 (English Standard Version).

Variation: "Use diligence to come before winter. Eubulus salutes thee, and Pudens, and Linus, and Claudia, and the brethren all. The Lord Jesus Christ with your spirit. Grace with you."

Source: 2 Timothy 4:21-22 (Darby Translation).

Variation: "Make haste to come before winter Eubulus and Pudens, and Linus and Claudia, and all the brethren, salute thee. The Lord Jesus Christ be with thy spirit. Grace be with you. Amen."

Source: 2 Timothy 4:21-22 (Douay-Rheims Translation).

Variation: "Be diligent to come before winter. Salute thee doth Eubulus, and Pudens, and Linus, and Claudia, and all the brethren. The Lord Jesus Christ [is] with thy spirit; the grace with you! Amen."

Source: 2 Timothy 4:21-22 (Young's Literal Translation).

Paul I, King of the Hellenes

(1901-1964) Greek monarch. Married Frederika of Hanover. Succeeded brother George II and reigned from 1947 to 1964. Died at age 62 in Athens, soon after surgery for stomach cancer. Succeeded by his son Constantine II.

Last Words: "I see the light! It is much larger now and the peace is getting stronger! Now we go!"

Source: *A Measure of Understanding* by Queen Frederica (New York, 1971). The author was his wife.

Paulinus, Saint

(353-431) Italian prelate, holy man, poet, writer. Bishop of Nola, Italy. Full name

Meropius Anicius Paulinus. Wrote songs, poems and poetic epistles. Many of his letters have been preserved.

Last Words: "Thy word is a lantern unto my feet and a light unto my path."

Source: *Works of Henry Vaughan,* ed. by L.C. Martin (Oxford, England, 1914).

Pausch, Randolph Frederick ("Randy")

(1960-2008) American educator, computer scientist, writer, Internet celebrity. Carnegie Mellon professor of computer science and human-computer interaction. When he learned he had terminal pancreatic cancer, he wrote an upbeat lecture—"The Last Lecture: Really Achieving Your Childhood Dreams"—that became a sensation on YouTube. This led to media appearances and an offer to co-author a book, *The Last Lecture.* The book became a best-seller. Pausch fulfilled a number of his dreams, including speaking a line in a Star Trek movie and joining the Pittsburgh Steelers for a day of practice. In 2008 *Time* magazine listed him as one of the World's Top 100 Most Influential People. Died at age 47 in Chesapeake, Virginia.

Last Words: "I'll get back to you on that." Spoken to close friend Steve Seabolt in response to Seabolt's comment: "It's important for you to feel like you can let go. It's okay." According to Seabolt, these were Randy Pausch's final words.

Source: "Randy Pausch's Last Words" by Tara Parker-Pope (*New York Times*, July 30, 2008).

Pavese, Cesare

(1908-1950) Italian novelist, poet, critic, translator, diarist. Translated writers such as Hemingway, Faulkner, Dos Passos, Steinbeck and Sherwood Anderson. Founded Einaudi, publishing house. Wrote several short stories and novels. Notable works: *The Moon and the Bonfires; The Beautiful Summer.* Suffered from recurring bouts of depression. Committed suicide at age 41 by barbiturate overdose in Turin. His diaries were published in 1952. Pavese Prize for literature was established in 1957.

Last Words (written): "The thing most feared in secret always happens. I write: o Thou, have mercy. And then? All it takes is

a little courage. The more the pain grows clear and definite, the more the instinct for life asserts itself and the thought of suicide recedes. It seemed easy when I thought of it. Weak women have done it. It needs humility, not pride. I am sickened by all this. No words. Action. I shall write no more." Final diary entry.

Source: *The Business of Living: Diaries, 1935-1950* by Cesare Pavese and John Taylor (New Brunswick, NJ, 2009).

Pavlova, Anna

(1881-1931) Russian ballerina. Danced with Nijinsky while in Ballet Russes. Founded her own company and toured the world. Dying Swan solo in *Swan Lake* was created for her. Notable roles: *Coppelia; Sleeping Beauty; The Dying Swan; Les Papillons.* Died at age 49 of pleurisy at a hotel in The Hague, three days after performing in Paris.

Last Words: "Get my 'Swan' costume ready."

Source: *Anna Pavlova* by Victor d'André (London, 1932). The author was her manager and husband.

Paxton, Elisha Franklin ("Bull")

(1828-1863) American lawyer, military officer. Confederate brigadier general in U.S. Civil War. The day before he was killed, he had a premonition he was going to die. Killed in action at age 35 at Chancellorsville, Virginia, while commanding the Stonewall Brigade.

Last Words: "Tie up my arm." After he was shot, he raised himself with his arms extended, then died.

Source: *Memoir and Memorial: Elisha Franklin Paxton, Brigadier General, C.S.A., Composed of His Letters from Camp and Field While an Officer In the Confederate Army, with an Introductory and Connecting Narrative Collected and Arranged by His Son, John Gallatin Paxton* (New York, 1907).

Payne, John

(1842-1916) English poet, translator. Pre-Raphaelite. Translated *Arabian Nights*, Boccaccio's *Decameron.* Member of Villon Society. Translated works of François Villon. Died at age 73.

Last Words: "Have you got the sheets? Did you get the pillowcases?"

Source: *The Autobiography of John Payne of Villon Society Fame, Poet and Scholar with Preface and Annotations* by Thomas Wright (London, 1919).

Payson, Edward

(1783-1827) American clergyman. Pastor of the Second Congregational Church in Portland, Maine. Died at age 44 of tuberculosis in Portland. Many of his sermons have been published.

Different Last Words:

(1) "Faith and patience, hold out!" Spoken in great pain with much difficulty.

Source: *Memoir, Select Thoughts and Sermons of the late Rev. Edward Payson* by Asa Cummings (Portland, ME, 1846).

(2) "I feel like a mote in the sunbeam."

Source: *The Last Words (Real and Traditional) of Distinguished Men and Women Collected from Various Sources* by Frederic Rowland Marvin (New York, 1901). Marvin listed both (1) and (2) as Payson's Last Words.

Payton, Walter Jerry

(1954-1999) American athlete. Professional football player. Running back with Chicago Bears. Member of National Football Hall of Fame. NFL Most Valuable Player three times. Played in nine Pro Bowls. Set numerous records. Died at age 45 of a rare liver disease. The NCAA's Walter Payton Award is named in his honor, as is the NFL's Walter Payton Man of the Year Award. Walter Payton College Prep School in Chicago was named for him.

Last Words: "Where have you been?" Spoken to his son Jarrett, also a football player.

Source: "Payton Dedicates Rest of Season to His Father, Will Wear His Number" by Mark Long (*Pittsburgh* [Pennsylvania] *Post-Gazette*, November 17, 1999).

Peabody, Endicott

(1857-1944) American clergyman, educator. Spent six months in Tombstone, Arizona, shortly after the gunfight at OK Corral. Helped build church there. Founder and headmaster at Groton School, Massachusetts. Mentor of Groton student Franklin Delano Roosevelt. Officiated at his wedding and at private services FDR held before his first three inaugurations as U.S. President. Peabody died at age 86.

Last Words: "Franklin must have been a very religious man." The person who was chatting with him at the time said Peabody died soon after he spoke these words.

Source: *The Chosen: The Hidden History of Admission and Exclusion at Harvard, Yale and Princeton* by Jerome Karabel (Boston, 2005).

Peabody, Everett

(1830-1862) American civil engineer, military officer. Union colonel in U.S. Civil War. Member 25th Missouri Volunteer Infantry. Shot and killed at Shiloh, Tennessee, when his camp was overrun by attacking Confederates.

Last Words: "Stand to it yet!" Shouted as he rode through the tents.

Source: *Shiloh: Bloody April* by Wiley Sword (New York, 1974).

Peabody, George

(1795-1869) American merchant, philanthropist. Born in Massachusetts. Moved to London in 1837. Founded and endowed Peabody Institutes in Maryland and Massachusetts; Peabody Museums at Yale, Harvard and Salem; Teachers College in Tennessee. Received many honors and awards for his generosity, including Congressional Medal of Honor in 1867. Died at age 74 in London. Body brought back to Massachusetts. Town of South Danvers, Massachusetts, changed its name to Peabody in his honor.

Last Words: "It is a great mystery, but I shall know all soon."

Source: *George Peabody: A Biography* by Franklin Parker (Nashville, TN, 1971).

Peace, Charles

(1832-1879) English burglar, murderer. Went to the gallows convinced he had been forgiven for his sins.

Last Words: "What is the scaffold? A shortcut to Heaven!" Spoken as he was about to be executed.

Source: *A Book of Scoundrels* by Charles Whibley (New York, 1897).

Peacock, Thomas Love

(1785-1866) English novelist, writer, poet. Friend of Shelley. Worked for the East India Company many years, serving as clerk and chief examiner. Notable works: *Nightmare Abbey; Headlong Hall* (satirical novels). Died at age 81 in Lower Halliford, Surrey, England.

Last Words: "By the immortal gods, I will not move!" Spoken when a fire broke out in his home and he refused to leave his library. He died soon after the fire was put out.

Source: *The Works of Thomas Love Peacock, with a Biographical Note* by Edith Nicolls (London, 1875). The author was Peacock's granddaughter.

Peale, Charles Willson

(1741-1827) American artist, naturalist. Served in American Revolution. One of the founders of the Pennsylvania Academy of the Fine Arts. Opened the first museum of natural history in the U.S. Notable works: *The Artist in His Museum;* many portraits of George Washington. Eleven of his 17 children survived to adulthood. Some became important artists. Died at age 86 in Philadelphia.

Last Words: "I thought not." Spoken to his daughter after he asked her to take his pulse and she replied that she could not feel one.

Source: *The Corpse: A History* by Christine Quigley (Jefferson, NC, 1996).

Variation: "I thought so. The law makes my will." Spoken to his daughter when she could not find his pulse.

Source: *Charles Willson Peale* by Charles Coleman Sellers (Philadelphia, 1947).

Pearson, Charles Henry

(1830-1894) British-born historian, statesman. Spent 20 years in Australia. Minister of education in Parliament of Victoria. Died at age 63 in London.

Last Words: "My life has been faulty, but God will judge me by my intentions."

Source: *Charles Henry Pearson; Memorials by Himself, His Wife, and His Friends,* ed. by William Stebbing (London, 1900).

Peckham, Rufus Wheeler

(1809-1873) American jurist, politician. Member U.S. House of Representatives from New York. Justice of New York Supreme Court. Associate judge of New York Court of Appeals. Lost at sea with 225 passengers and crew of the *Ville du Havre* when the steamer collided with the British ship *Loch Earn* in mid-ocean.

Last Words: "If we must go down, let us die bravely."

Source: *In Memory of Rufus W. Peckham: A Judge of the Court of Appeals Who Perished on the Wreck of the Steamer Ville du Havre on the Voyage from New York to Havre November 22, 1873* by the Bar of the State of New York (Albany, NY, 1874).

Peel, Sir Robert

(1788-1850) English statesman, politician. Member of Parliament. Home secretary. Prime minister. Helped overhaul London police force. London police subsequently became known as Peelers and Bobbies. Thrown from horse in Hyde Park, London. Died three days later at age 62.

Last Words: "Julia, you are not going without wishing me 'goodbye' or saying those sweet words 'God bless you'?" Spoken to his wife before he mounted his horse.

Source: *The Private Letters of Robert Peel,* ed. by George Peel (London, 1920). The editor was his grandson.

Peerson, Anthony

(d. 1543) English martyr. Protestant. A talented preacher. Condemned by Roman Catholics to die for his Protestant beliefs. Burned at the stake at Windsor along with three others.

Last Words: "This is God's hat; now I am dressed like a true soldier of Christ, by whose merits only I trust this day to enter into His joy." Spoken as he placed a bunch of straw on his head.

Source: *Book of Martyrs and the Acts and Monuments of the Church* by John Fox (or Foxe). First published 1563, ed. by John Cumming (London, 1851).

Péguy, Charles Pierre

(1873-1914) French poet, essayist, writer, military officer. Expounded causes of nationalism, socialism and Catholicism. Founded literary review *Cahiers de la quinzaine (Fortnightly Review)*. Notable works: *Notre jeunesse* (prose; about the Dreyfus case); "Joan of Arc"; "Mystery of the Holy Innocents" (poems). Killed at age 41 in first Battle of the Marne during World War I.

Last Words: "Keep firing."

Source: *Vie et mort de Charles Péguy* by René Johannet (Paris, 1950).

Variation: "I haven't one either! Go on firing!" Shouted to his men who warned him not to face enemy fire without a helmet. At that moment, he was shot through the forehead and fell dead.

Source: *Charles Péguy: A Study in Integrity* by Marjorie Villiers (New York, 1965).

Pellico, Silvio

(1789-1854) Italian writer, dramatist, political prisoner. Imprisoned for treason and sentenced to death. Later released. Notable works: *Le mie Prigioni* (*My Prisons;* memoirs written while he was imprisoned); *Francesca de Rimini; Laodamia.* Died at age 64 in Turin, Italy.

Different Last Words:

(1) "Here my God is." Spoken as he placed his hands on his heart.

Source: *Della vita e della opere di Silvio Pellico* by Ilario Rinieri (Turin, Italy, 1899).

(2) "In two or three hours I shall be in paradise. If I have sinned, I have also atoned. When I wrote 'My Prisons,' I had the vanity to believe myself a great man; but then I saw it was not true, and repented of my conceit." Spoken shortly before he died.

Source: *Biographical Essays: Essays, Biographical and Critical; or, Studies of Character* by Henry T. Tuckerman (Boston, 1857).

Pembroke, 1st Earl of, see Marshal, William.

Penfield, Wilder Graves

(1891-1976) American physician, writer, educator. World-famous brain surgeon. Professor of neurology, neurosurgery at McGill University. Turned to writing when he retired. Notable books: *The Difficult Art of Giving; Man and His Family; The Mystery of the Mind.* Died at age 85 of cancer.

Last Words (written): "Here I am." Note scribbled in his diary that he brought with him to the hospital.

Source: *Something Hidden: A Biography of Wilder Penfield* by Jefferson Lewis (Garden City, NY, 1981).

Penn, Gulielma Maria Springett

(1644-1694) English matron. Wife of English Quaker William Penn, proprietor of Pennsylvania. Died at age 50.

Last Words: "My dear Love to all Friends." She lifted her hands and eyes and prayed to the Lord to preserve them and bless them. She took leave of her husband, saying all that was fit on that solemn occasion. She then died in her husband's arms.

Source: "Gulielma Penn" (*The Friend,* Seventh Day, Eighth Month, 1903).

Variation: "I have cast my care upon the Lord. My dear Love to all Friends."

Source: *Gulielma: Wife of William Penn* by G.L.V. Hodgkin (London, 1947).

Penn, Springett

(1674-1696) English Quaker. Eldest son and one of three surviving children of William Penn and Gulielma Maria Springett. Died at age 21 at Lewes, England.

Last Words: "Let my father speak to the doctor and I'll go to sleep."

Source: "Springett Penn" (*The Friend,* Twenty-fifth Day, Seventh Month, 1903).

Penn, William

(1644-1718) English Quaker. Advocate of civil and religious freedom. Founder of Philadelphia and proprietor of the colony of Pennsylvania. Incapacitated by a paralytic stroke in 1712. Was unable to manage his proprietary affairs for the rest of his life. Died at age 73 in Ruscombe, England. Commonwealth of Pennsylvania named for his father Admiral Sir William Penn.

Different Last Words:

(1) "Son William, if you and your friends keep to your plain way of preaching, and keep to your plain way of living, you will make an end of the proud priests to the end of the world.—Bury me by my mother—live all in love—shun all manner of evil; and I pray God to bless you all! and he will bless you all."

Source: *The Life of William Penn, the Settler of Pennsylvania, the Founder of Philadelphia, and one of the First Lawgivers in the Colonies, now the United States, in 1682* by Mason Lock Weems (Philadelphia, 1829). Several biographies describe this quote as "almost" the Last Words he uttered.

(2) (doubtful): "To be like Christ, then, is to be a Christian."

Source: *Famous Sayings and Their Authors: A Collection of Historical Sayings in English, French, German, Greek, Italian, and Latin* by Edward Latham (London, 1906).

Penn did say this as part of a longer maxim but there is no indication these were his Last Words.

Penrose, Boise

(1860-1921) American politician, lawyer. Member Pennsylvania legislature. Member U.S. Senate from Pennsylvania from 1897 to 1921. Accompanied the Liberty Bell on a nationwide tour in 1915. Died at age 61 in Washington, D.C.

Last Words: "See here, William. See here. I don't want any of your damned lies. How do

I look? Am I getting any better? The truth now—All right, William. When you go to church tomorrow, pray for me, too." Spoken to his valet. He died the next day.

Source: *Power and Glory, the Life of Boise Penrose* by Walter Davenport (New York, 1931).

Penruddock, John

(1619-1655) English revolutionary. Led failed Royalist uprising in support of Charles II during the English Civil War. Beheaded at Exeter.

Last Words: "I am like to have a sharp passage of it, but my Saviour hath sweetened it unto me. If I would have been so unworthy as others have been, I suppose I might by a lie have saved my life, which I scorn to purchase at such a rate: I defy temptations and them that gave them to me. Glory be to God on high, on earth peace, good will towards men, and the Lord have mercy upon my poor soul. Amen." Spoken as he kissed the axe.

Source: *The Dying Speeches and Behaviour of the Several State Prisoners that Have Been Executed the Last 300 Years. With Their Several Characters, from Cambden, Spotswood, Clarendon, Sprat, Burner, &c. and a Table Shewing how the Respective Sentences Were Executed, and Which of Them were Mitigated, or Pardon'd. Being a Proper Supplement to the State Trials* (London, 1720).

Peponila

(d. c. 79) Roman matron. Wife of Julius Sabinus the Gaul, a rebel leader who was sentenced to death. She and her family had gone into hiding with him for nine years. She died with him.

Last Words: "These little ones, Caesar, I bore and reared in the monument [where her husband had hidden] that we might be a greater number to supplicate you." She pleaded with Vespasian for mercy for her family.

Source: *Dio's Rome: An Historical Narrative Originally Composed in Greek During the Reigns of Septimus, Severus, Geta and Caracalla, Macrinus, Elagabalus and Alexander Severus and Now Presented in English Form* by Cassius Dio Cocceianus, tr. and ed. by Herbert Baldwin Foster and Joannes Zonaras (Troy, NY, 1906).

Pepys, Margaret Kite

(1609?-1667) English matron. Sister of a Whitechapel butcher. She worked as a washwoman while young. Mother of English diarist Samuel Pepys who was the fifth of 11 children.

Last Words: "God bless my poor son Sam." Recorded in Samuel Pepys' Diary.

Source: *Masterworks of Autobiography,* ed. by Richard D. Mallery (Freeport, NY, 1977).

Pepys, Samuel

(1633-1703) English Admiralty official, statesman, diarist. Secretary of the admiralty. Compiled his diary—January 1, 1660, to May 31, 1669—using shorthand, foreign words and ciphers he invented. The diary provides a unique view of court and everyday life in England at that time. Pepys began to have trouble with his vision in 1664. By 1669 his eyesight had weakened so much it affected his diary-keeping. He bequeathed his diary to Magdalen College, Cambridge. Died at age 70 in London.

Last Words: "Be good friends. I do desire it of you." Spoken to his nephew and Mrs. Mary Skinner, his housekeeper and longtime companion.

Source: *Pepys: His Life and Character* by John Drinkwater (London, 1930).

Perceval, Spencer

(1762-1812) British statesman, politician. Solicitor general. Attorney general. Chancellor of the exchequer. Prime minister. Assassinated at age 49 in the lobby of the British House of Commons by John Bellingham, a bankrupt merchant.

Different Last Words:

(1) "O my God."

Source: *Assassination of the Prime Minister: The Shocking Death of Spencer Perceval* by Mollie Gillen (London, 1972).

(2) "Oh, I am murdered!" Whispered faintly as he fell to the floor at the feet of William Smith. The shooting happened so fast, no one realized what happened. Smith did not know who the victim was until he lifted the body. Bellingham surrendered immediately.

Source: *The Life of the Rt. Hon. Spencer Perceval: Including his Correspondence with Numerous Distinguished Persons* by Sir Spencer Walpole (London, 1874). Walpole was Perceval's grandson.

Percy, Walker

(1916-1990) American physician, writer. Wrote philosophical novels. Notable work:

The Moviegoer (won 1962 National Book Award for fiction). Died at age 73 of prostate cancer in Covington, Louisiana.

Last Words: "No. She understands." His response to the nurse when she asked whether she should awaken his wife.

Source: *Pilgrim in the Ruins: A Life of Walker Percy* by Jay Tolson (New York, 1992).

Pericles of Athens

(490-429 B.C.) Greek statesman. Important leader of Athens during Golden Age. Died at age 61 after he was stricken by plague.

Last Words: "No Athenian ever put on mourning for an act of mine!" Spoken as he lay dying. His friends were gathered around his bed talking about his great accomplishments. He interrupted them and reminded them that some of their praise was the result of good fortune common to him and many other commanders. But they had not mentioned what he was most proud of.

Source: "Pericles" in *Lives of the Noble Grecians and Romans* by Plutarch, tr. by John Dryden (Chicago, 1952).

Perkins, William

(1558-1602) English clergyman, writer. Cambridge theologian who was one of foremost leaders of the Puritan movement in Church of England. Wrote dozens of works, many published posthumously. Pupils included John Robinson (founder of Congregationalism in Leiden and pastor on the *Mayflower*), Samuel Ward (master of Sidney Sussex College), Phineas Fletcher (Cambridge poet), James Ussher (Archbishop of Armagh) and Richard Montagu (Bishop of Winchester). Died at age 44 of a disease described as "the stone" after several days of suffering.

Last Words: "Lord, especially forgive my sins of omission."

Source: *The Lives of the Puritans: Containing a Biographical Account of Those Divines Who Distinguished Themselves in the Cause of Religious Liberty, from the Reformation under Queen Elizabeth to the Act of Uniformity in 1662* by Benjamin Brook (London, 1813).

Perón, Juan Domingo

(1895-1974) Argentinean military officer, political leader. Husband of Eva Peron. President of Argentina from 1946 to 1955; forced to resign. Went into exile. Elected President again in 1973. Terminally ill when he returned to office. Died at age 78 in Buenos Aires, Argentina, the following year. He was succeeded as president by his third wife Isabel.

Last Words: "Taiana, I'm leaving this world —my people—my people—." Spoken to his colleague and physician, Dr. Jorge Alberto Taiana.

Source: *Peron and the Enigmas of Argentina* by Robert D. Crassweller (New York, 1987).

Perón, Maria Eva Duarte de ("Evita")

(1919-1952) Argentinean first lady, actress. Birth name María Eva Ibaguren. Wife of Juan Perón, Argentina's president. Died at age 33 of cancer. Her life provided the background for the Broadway musical and movie *Evita*.

Different Last Words:

(1) "I never felt happy in this life. That is why I left home. My mother would have married me to someone ordinary and I could never have stood it. Irma, a decent woman has to get on in the world." Spoken to her maid. Soon afterward she went into a coma and was dead by evening.

Source: *Eva Perón* by Nicholas Fraser and Marysa Navarro (New York, 1980).

(2) "Before they put me to sleep, if I do not wake—Viva Perón."

Source: "Saga of Eva Peron: 12 Years to Power" (*New York Times,* July 27, 1952).

Perpetua, Vibia

(180?-203) Roman-born noblewoman, diarist, martyr. Lived in Carthage. Condemned to die by Emperor Septimius Severus for refusing to renounce her Christianity. She and her servant Felicitas were sentenced to be mangled by a wild cow. When the animal did not kill them, a soldier was ordered to finish the job. Vibia died a martyr at age 22. Her story is known through the *Passion of Perpetua and Felicitas*, based on her diary. She is one of few women of her era whose writings have been preserved.

Last Words: "Continue firm in the faith, love one another and be not offended by our sufferings."

Source: *The History of the Church of Christ: The Three First Centuries* by Joseph Milner (York, England, 1794).

Variation: "Continue firm in the faith, love one another and be not scandalized at our sufferings." Spoken to her brother.

Source: *The Lives of the Primitive Fathers, Martyrs and Other Principal Saints: Compiled from Original Monuments and Other Authentic Records,* Vol. III, by Alban Butler and Charles Butler (Edinburgh, 1798).

Variation: "Stand fast in the faith and love one another." Spoken to her brother.

Source: *All You Need Is Love: The Way of Joy* by Ricardo C. Castellanos and Allienne R. Becker (New York, 2003).

Perrin, Abner Monroe
(1827-1864) American lawyer, military officer. Fought in the Mexican War as a lieutenant. Confederate brigadier general in U.S. Civil War. Shot and killed at age 37 in the Battle of Spotsylvania Court House.

Last Words: "I shall come out of this fight a live major general or a dead brigadier." Declared as he led his men into battle.

Source: *Generals in Gray: Lives of the Confederate Commanders* by Ezra J. Warner (Baton Rouge, LA, 1987).

Perry, Oliver Hazard
(1785-1819) American naval officer. Fought in a battle at Lake Erie during War of 1812. Had to abandon ship, the *Lawrence*. After winning the battle, he sent the famous message to his superior: "We have met the enemy and they are ours." Died at age 34 of yellow fever while on a mission in Venezuela.

Last Words: "Few people have greater inducements to make them wish to live than I, but I am perfectly ready to go if it pleases the Almighty to take me; the debt of nature must be paid." Recorded by Dr. M. Morgan who attended him during his final hours.

Source: *Oliver Hazard Perry* by Charles S. Dutton (New York, 1935).

Perugino, Pietro
(1446?-1523) Italian artist, painter. Birth name Pietro di Cristoforo Vannucci. Pupil of Raphael. Notable work: *Madonna and Child* (painted just before he died of plague in Fontignano, Italy, at about age 77).

Last Words: "I am curious to see what happens in the next world to one who dies unshriven [unconfessed]." Spoken as he lay dying. He refused to send for a priest so that

Roman Catholic Last Rites could be administered.

Source: *Ho for Heaven: Man's Changing Attitude Toward Dying* by Virginia Moore (New York, 1946).

Pestel, Pavel Ivanovich
(1794-1826) Russian military officer. Adjutant to Prince Wittgenstein. A key leader of the Decembrists who tried to seize control of Russia in December 1825 after Tsar Alexander I died. They hoped their revolt would gain civil liberties and greater participation in government. Pestel and four others were executed by hanging.

Last Words: "Stupid country, where they do not even know how to hang." Spoken when the rope broke that was to have been used to hang him.

Source: *Short Sayings of Great Men: With Historical and Explanatory Notes* by Samuel Arthur Bent (Boston, 1882).

Petacci, Claretta
(1912-1945) Italian woman. Member of upper class Roman family. Mistress of Italian dictator Benito Mussolini. Shot and killed at age 33 by Italian partisans near the end of World War II. Mussolini was executed at the same time.

Last Words: "Mussolini must not die!"

Source: *Mussolini: The Intimate Life of a Demagogue* by Paolo Monelli (London, 1953).

Pétain, Henri Philippe
(1856-1951) French military officer, politician. Hero in World War I. Marshal of France. Premier of Vichy government in World War II. Fled to Switzerland after Allied invasion. Returned to France in April 1945, stood trial, convicted of collaborating with the enemy. Death sentence commuted to life imprisonment by President Charles De Gaulle. Pétain spent his final years imprisoned on Île d'Yeu, an island off the coast of Brittany. Died there at age 95.

Last Words: "Do not weep, do not grieve." Spoken to his wife.

Source: *Le cri de la France* by Marquis Andre de Belleval (Paris, 1951).

Peter, Prince of Portugal ("Don Pedro")
(1392-1449) Portuguese royalty. Brother of Prince Henry the Navigator. Named Duke of Coimbra in 1415. Traveled widely through-

out Europe and the Middle East. Killed in a battle at Alfarrobeire, Portugal.

Last Words: "Oh, body of mine! I feel that you can do no more; and you my spirit, why should you tarry here? Fight on, comrades! And you, you villains, do your worst!"

Source: *The Golden Age of Prince Henry the Navigator* by J. P. Oliveira Martins (New York, 1914).

Peter, Saint

(d. 64?) Biblical figure. Prelate, holy man, martyr. Disciple of Jesus. Originally called Simeon or Simon. Known as Peter or Cephas. Founder, with St. Paul, of See of Rome. First pope. Died a martyr during persecutions of Nero.

Last Words: "Oh, thou, remember the Lord!" Words of comfort spoken to his wife who was killed first.

Source: *The Ecclesiastical History of Eusebius Pamphilus, Bishop of Cesarea, in Palestine: in Ten Books*, tr. by Christian Frederic Cruse (Philadelphia, 1833).

Peter I, Tsar and Emperor of Russia ("Peter the Great")

(1672-1725) Russian ruler. Son of Alexis. Known as Peter the Great. Moved Russian capital to St. Petersburg. Reorganized the government. Organized the army. Built the navy. Encouraged manufacturing and foreign trade. Died at age 52 without choosing an heir.

Last Words (written): "Give back all to—" Written on a piece of paper.

Source: *Peter the Great, A Life of Peter I of Russia* by Stephen Graham (New York, 1929).

Last Words (spoken): "Anna." He called his daughter's name but was unconscious when she returned to his room. He died the next morning.

Source: *Peter the Great* by Robert K. Massie (New York, 1980).

Peter III, Emperor of Russia

(1728-1762) Russian ruler. Grandson of Peter the Great. Deemed mentally unfit to rule. Assassinated by his guards six months after he succeeded to the throne. Died at age 34. Succeeded by wife Catherine II, the Great.

Last Words: "It was not enough then to prevent my reigning over Sweden, and to tear from my head the crown of Russia! They must have my life besides!"

Source: *Peter III, Emperor of Russia, the Story of a Crisis and a Crime* by R. Nisbet Bain (New York, 1902).

Peter Martyr or Peter of Verona, Saint

(1206-1252) Italian clergyman, holy man, martyr. Roman Catholic. Dominican Inquisitor in Lombardy, Italy, where he fought the Cather heresy. Killed by an assassin hired by the Cathers. One of the first Dominican martyrs. Canonized a year after he died.

Last Words: "Credo in unum Deum." (tr. "I believe in one God.") It is rumored that he wrote his Last Words on the dirt with his blood.

Source: *Ideology and Inquisition: The World of the Censors in Early Mexico* by Martin Austin Nesvig (New Haven, CT, 2009).

Peter of Alcantara, Saint

(1499-1562) Spanish clergyman, holy man. Franciscan who founded a stricter religious order. Members known as Alcantarines. Canonized in 1669.

Last Words: "I rejoiced at the things that were said to me: 'We shall go in the house of the Lord.'"

Source: *Butler's Lives of the Saints* by Alban Butler, Herbert J. Thurston and Donald Attwater (New York, 1956).

Peters or Peter, Hugh

(1598-1660) English clergyman. Puritan. Pastor of First Congregational Church in Salem, Massachusetts. Returned to England in 1641. Chaplain to Oliver Cromwell. Indicted of high treason when Charles II was restored. Hanged, drawn and quartered at age 62 for inciting the regicide of Charles I. Different Last Words:

(1) "Sir, you have here slain one of the servants of God before mine eyes, and have made me to behold it, on purpose to terrify and discourage me; but God hath made it an ordinance to me for my strengthening and encouragement." Spoken to the sheriff when he saw a fellow prisoner quartered.

Source: *A Complete Collection of State-Trials and Proceedings for High Treason and Other Crimes and Misdemeanors: Commencing with the Eleventh Year of the Reign of King Richard II and Ending with the Sixteenth Year of the Reign of King George III, with Two Alphabetical Tables to the Whole. to Which Is Prefixed a New Preface by Francis Hargrave*, Vol. II, by Francis Hargrave (London, 1797).

(2) (doubtful): "Friend, you do not well to trample on a dying man."

Peters spoke these words but they were not his Last Words. Peters was forced to look at the body of a prisoner who had just been executed. He was carried on a sledge to the scaffold and forced to watch the execution of a man named Cook. After Cook was cut down and brought to be quartered, Colonel Turner ordered the sheriff's men to bring Peters to see the body. The blood-soaked executioner came to Peters rubbing his bloody hands together and tauntingly asked Peters how he liked his work. This quote was Peters' response. Peters spoke his Last Words later, when he was on the ladder of the scaffold.

Source: *Principles of Penal Law* by Baron William Eden Auckland (London, 1771).

Pettit, Roger Alan

(1947-1982) American airline pilot, disaster victim. First officer and co-pilot on Air Florida Flight 90 that crashed into the 14th Street Bridge over the Potomac River in Washington D.C., in 1982. Seventy-four people were killed in one of the worst urban airway disasters in U.S. history. The crash was the basis for the made-for-TV movie *Flight 90: Disaster on the Potomac*.

Last Words: "Larry! We're going down, Larry!" Spoken to Captain Larry Wheaton who replied, "I know."

Source: *Mayday: Accident Reports and Voice Transcripts from Airline Crash Investigations* by Marion F. Sturkey (Plum Branch, SC, 2005).

Pheidippides

(530-490 B.C.) Greek courier, long-distance runner. According to marathon lore, in 490, when the Athenians learned the Persians had invaded Greece, they sent Pheidippides to get help from Sparta. He collapsed and died after running 26 miles to warn of an attack by the sea at the Battle of Marathon.

Last Words (doubtful): "Rejoice! We are victorious."

Source: Various Last Words compilations and Internet websites.

Although Pheidippides is mentioned in Greek tradition as a messenger, his story has been fictionalized over the centuries. The historian Herodotus, who was aware of Pheidippides for other running feats, recorded the Persian Wars in his *Histories* but made no specific mention of a messenger at the Marathon event or of a messenger dying. Some 500 years later, Plutarch—writing in the Roman era—did mention several messengers in full armor collapsing, including one from Marathon, but not Pheidippides by name. In the year 180, the writer Lucian, while discussing the term "Rejoice," misattributed the event to Pheidippides as dying after running from Marathon, and he assigned the quote "Rejoice! We are victorious" to him. In 1879 English poet Robert Browning made Pheidippides a hero in a poem he included in his *Dramatic Idylls*. This inspired Baron Pierre de Coubertin and others who re-established the Olympic Games in 1896 to create a race called the Marathon.

Sources: *26.2 Marathon Stories* by Kathrine Switzer, Roger Robinson (Emmaus, PA, 2006); "The Dubious Origins of the Marathon" by F.J. Frost (*American Journal of Ancient History*, Vol. 4, 1979).

Philby, Harry St. John Bridger

(1885-1960) British statesman, writer, spy. British Intelligence operative. Born in Ceylon (now Sri Lanka). Also known as Sheikh Abdullah, Jack Philby and Sinjin Philby. Served as minister of internal security in the British Mandate of Iraq. Chief head of secret service for British Mandate of Palestine and later Ibn Saud's chief adviser in dealing with British Empire and Western powers. Died at age 75 of a heart attack while visiting his son Kim in Beirut, Lebanon.

Last Words: "God, I'm bored." Spoken to his son who was at his bedside.

Source: *Children of the Sun: A Narrative of "Decadence" in England after 1918* by Martin Burgess Green (New York, 1987).

Philip, Saint

(3?-90?) Biblical figure, martyr, evangelist. One of the 12 Apostles. He preached in Greece, Syria, and Phrygia. He was said to have been martyred by crucifixion in the city of Hierapolis.

Last Words: "Let not their dark air cover me, that I may pass the waters of fire and all the abyss. Clothe me in thy glorious robe and thy seal of light that ever shineth, until I have passed by all the rulers of the world and the evil dragon that opposeth."

Source: *The Apocryphal New Testament: Being the Apocryphal Gospels, Acts, Epistles, and Apocalypses,* tr. by M. R. James (London, 1924).

Variation: "Come now, Jesus, and give me the everlasting crown of victory against every adverse dominion and power, and do not let their dark air hide me when I shall cross the waters of fire and all the abyss. O my Lord Jesus Christ, let not the enemy have ground to accuse me at Thy tribunal: but put on me Thy glorious robe, Thy seal of light that ever shines, until I shall pass by all the powers of the world, and the wicked dragon that lieth in wait for us. Now therefore, my Lord Jesus Christ, make me to meet Thee in the air, having forgiven me the recompense which I recompensed to my enemies; and transform the form of my body into angelic glory, and give me rest in Thy blessedness; and let me receive the promise from Thee which Thou hast promised to Thy saints to everlasting." Having thus spoken, he died while the multitudes looked upon him.

Source: *Ante-Nicene Christian Library; Translations of the Writings of the Fathers Down to A.D. 325.* Vol. 16, Apocryphal Gospels, Acts and Revelations, tr. and ed. by Reverend Alexander Roberts and James Donaldson (Edinburgh, 1870).

Philip II, King of Spain
Philip I, King of Portugal

(1527-1598) Spanish monarch. Only legitimate son of Holy Roman Emperor Charles V and Isabella. Ruled Portugal as Philip I. Responsible for sending the Spanish Armada against England in 1588. Showed little interest in governing. Spain's economy and industry diminished during his reign. Died at age 71 in Madrid.

Different Last Words:

(1) "Give it to me; it is time now." He requested a blessed candle.

Source: *Philip II of Spain* by Martin A.S. Hume (New York, 1897).

(2) "I die like a good Catholic, in faith and obedience to the Holy Roman Church." He remained unconscious for several hours before dying.

Source: *History of the United Netherlands, from the Death of William the Silent to the Twelve Years Truce* by John Lothrop Motley (New York, 1900).

Philip III, King of Spain
Philip II, King of Portugal

(1578-1621) Spanish monarch. Son of Philip II of Spain. Grandson of Charles V, Holy Roman Emperor. Married Margaret of Austria. Became heir to the throne after three older brothers died. Ruled Portugal as Philip II. His last moments were spent in sorrow and remorse. He deplored the results of his 23 years of rule and prayed continually for mercy. Died at age 42 in Madrid.

Last Words: "Ah, how happy it would have been for me had I spent these twenty-three years that I have held the kingdom, in retirement."

Source: *The Columbian Miscellany; Containing a Variety of Important, Instructive, and Entertaining Matter, Chiefly Selected out of the Philadelphian Magazines, Published in London in the Years 1788 and 1789, Calculated to Promote True Religion and Virtue* by Abner Kneeland (Keene, NH, 1804).

Variation: "Oh would to God I had never reigned. Oh, that those years I have spent in my kingdom I had lived a solitary life in the wilderness! Oh, that I had lived alone with God! How much more secure should I now have died! With how much more confidence should I have gone to the throne of God! What doth all my glory profit, but that I have so much the more torment in my death."

Source: *Cyclopedia of Moral and Religious Anecdotes; A Collection of Nearly 3000 Facts with Copious Topical and Scriptural Indexes* by Kazlitt Arvine (New York, 1849).

Variation: "Oh, if heaven would please to prolong my life, how different should my conduct be."

Source: *Spain: Its Greatness and Decay (1479-1788)* by Martin Andrew Sharp Hume, Introduction by Edward Armstrong (Cambridge, England, 1899).

Philip IV, King of Spain
Philip III, King of Portugal

(1605-1665) Spanish monarch. Son of Philip III and Margaret of Austria. Ruled Portugal as Philip III. He tried unsuccessfully to recover Portugal after it regained its independence in 1640. Reigned when Velasquez, Lope de Vego and Quevedo were flourishing. Succeeded by his son Charles II. Died at age 60 near Madrid.

Last Words: "Tell him to go back to Consuegra. It is now time for nothing but death."

Spoken about his bastard son Don John of Austria, who had made three attempts to see him.

Source: *Carlos, The King Who Would Not Die* (Englewood Cliffs, NJ, 1962).

Philippa of Hainault, Queen of England

(1314-1369) English royalty. Belgian-born Queen Consort of Edward III. Before she died at Windsor Castle, she asked her husband to grant her three requests. He asked her to name them.

Last Words: "My Lord, I beg you will fulfill whatever engagements I have entered into with merchants for their wares; as well on this as on the other side of the sea: I beseech you to fulfill whatever gifts or legacies I have made or left to churches wherein I have paid my devotions, and to all my servants; whether male or female, and when it shall please God to call you hence, you will choose no other sepulchre than mine, and that you will rest by my side in the cloisters of Westminster Abbey." When the king heard her request, he replied "Lady, all this shall be done."

Source: *Lives of the Queens of England from the Norman Conquest* by Agnes Strickland and Elizabeth Strickland (London, 1864).

Phillips, David Graham

(1867-1911) American writer, novelist, journalist, social activist. Pen name John Graham. Known for early 20th-century muckraking writing. His series "The Treason of the Senate" appeared in *Cosmopolitan* magazine. He wrote 20 novels exposing social problems and political corruption. Notable work: *Susan Lenox: Her Fall and Rise.* Murdered at age 43 in New York City by a man who believed his family was slandered in Phillips' novel, *The Fashionable Adventures of Joshua Craig.*

Last Words: "It's of no use. I could have won against two bullets but not against six."

Source: *David Graham Phillips and His Times* by Isaac F. Marcosson (New York, 1932).

Phillips, Ulrich Bonnell

(1877-1934) American historian, writer, educator. Wrote about the antebellum South and the economic value of slavery. Taught at University of Wisconsin, Tulane, University of Michigan and Yale. Died at age 56 of cancer.

Last Words (written): "In body I'm down but not out; in mind, as lively as ever—a cricket!" Last part of a letter.

Source: *Ulrich Bonnell Phillips: Historian of the Old South* by Merton L. Dillon (Baton Rouge, LA, 1985).

Phillips, Wendell

(1811-1884) American abolitionist, orator, social reformer. Brahmin. Active in anti-slave movement. Member of American Anti-Slavery Society. After the Civil War ended, he turned his attention to temperance, women's rights, universal suffrage and equal rights for Native Americans. Died at age 72 in Boston.

Different Last Words:

(1) "Poor Ann." He was speaking about his wife Ann Terry Greene Phillips, an invalid for almost 50 years. She died two years after her husband.

Source: *Wendell Phillips, Brahmin Radical* by Irving H. Bartlett (Westport, CT, 1973).

(2) "I have no fear of death. I am as ready to die today as at any time." His response when the doctor acknowledged that the end was approaching.

Source: *The Life and Times of Wendell Phillips* by George Lowell Austin (Boston, 1888). Austin said Phillips also expressed a desire to outlive his wife so that he might care for her.

Philopœmen

(253?-183 B.C.) Greek military leader. General. Leading figure of Achaean League. Captured after a revolt. Forced to kill himself by drinking poison.

Last Words: "It is well that we have not been every way unfortunate." Spoken when he saw a man with poison nearby. He took the cup and asked him if he knew anything about his men. He was told some of them had escaped. After he spoke, he drank the poison and died.

Source: "Philopœmen" in *Lives of the Noble Grecians and Romans* by Plutarch, tr. by John Dryden (Chicago, 1952).

Phipps, Thomas

(1741?-1789) English accused forger. Father, age 48, and his son, age 20, were executed together although the forgery was committed only by the son who had exonerated his father. The forgery was for a twenty-pound note.

Last Words: "Tommy, thou hast brought me to this shameful end, but I freely forgive thee." Spoken to his son who made no reply. Then as he reached the gallows ladder, the father said: "You have brought me hither, do you lead the way?" They embraced each other and died hand-in-hand as the scaffold fell.

Source: *The Newgate Calendar: Comprising Interesting Memoirs of the Most Notorious Characters who have been Convicted of Outrages on the Laws of England Since the Commencement of the Eighteenth Century; with Occasional Anecdotes and Observations, Speeches, Confessions, and Last Exclamations of Sufferers* by Andrew Knapp and William Baldwin (London, 1824).

Phocion

(402?-317 B.C.) Greek military officer, statesman. Athenian. Elected general 45 times. Famed for his incorruptible reputation. Fought and won his last battle when he was 80. Was ordered to defend the Piraeus, but was misinformed and did not do so. Without allowing him to argue his case, he was condemned on a charge of treason and ordered to be killed. He was turned over to his enemies who executed him by forcing him to drink hemlock.

Different Last Words:

(1) "I bid him cherish no resentment against the Athenians." His response when asked if he had any message for his son. After his death, people repented their actions. His principal accuser was put to death and others were driven into exile.

Source: *The Library of Historic Characters and Famous Events of All Nations and All Ages* by Ainsworth Rand Spofford, John Porter Lamberton and Frank Weitenkampf (Philadelphia, 1894).

(2) "Yes. But not surprising—this is what usually happens at Athens to her great men." Spoken to a friend who had exclaimed how unworthy his treatment was as he was being led away to die.

Source: *Lives of Eminent Commanders* by Cornelius Nepos, tr. by J.S. Watson (London, 1885).

Phoenix, River

(1970-1993) American actor. Screen star. Birth name River Jude Bottom. Nominated for Academy Award and Golden Globe. Died at age 23 of drug-induced heart failure.

Different Last Words:

(1) "No paparazzi, I want anonymity." Spoken to a reporter who tried to help him outside the Viper Room in Los Angeles, California

Source: *Lost in Hollywood: The Fast Times and Short Life of River Phoenix* by John Glatt (New York, 1995).

(2) "I'm gonna die Dude!" Supposedly spoken to the doorman.

Source: *River Phoenix: A Short Life* by Brian J. Robb (London, 1995). Also reported in *National Enquirer*, November 16, 1993.

Piaf, Édith

(1915-1963) French singer, lyricist, actress. Birth name Edith Giovanna Gassion. Known as The Little Sparrow. Closely identified with the song "La vie en rose." Died at age 47. Her story is the subject of the 2007 movie *La Môme*.

Last Words: "I can die now; I've lived twice. Be careful, Momome. All the damned fool things you do in life you pay for." Spoken to her sister after they spent hours talking about the past.

Source: *Piaf: A Biography* by Simone Berteaut (New York, 1972).

Picasso, Pablo Ruiz y

(1881-1973) Spanish artist, painter, sculptor, ceramist. One of the great masters of modern art. Founder of Cubism. Spent final years in southern France. Died at age 91 in Mougins, near Cannes.

Different Last Words:

(1) "And now I must go back to work." Spoken to friends he had entertained that evening. He stayed up painting until 3 a.m. He woke the next morning at 11:30 and died a few minutes later.

Source: "Art: Pablo Picasso's Last Days and Final Journey" (*Time* magazine, April 23, 1973).

(2) "Drink to me, drink to my health. You know I can't drink any more." Sometimes shortened to "Drink to me." Became a song by Paul McCartney and Wings after McCartney had been told that "Drink to me" were Picasso's Last Words and was challenged to write a song on the spot. He did.

Source: *The Rough Guide to the Beatles* by Chris Ingham (London, 2003).

(3) "You are wrong not to marry. It's useful." Spoken to his physician who was a bachelor. As he spoke he reached his hand

to his wife Jacqueline.

Source: *Pablo Ruiz Picasso: A Biography* by Patrick O'Brian (New York, 1976).

Piccolo, Louis Brian

(1943-1970) American athlete. Professional football player. Chicago Bears running back. Died at age 26 of cancer. Went through many months of chemotherapy and radiation. Story of his battle with cancer and his friendship with team mate Gale Sayers told in the 1971 movie *Brian's Song*.

Last Words: "Can you believe it, Joy? Can you believe this s**t!" Spoken to his wife. He died three hours later in his sleep.

Source: *Brian Piccolo: A Short Season* by Jeannie Morris (Chicago, 1971).

Pickford, Mary

(1892-1979) Canadian-born American actress, screen star. Birth name Gladys Louise Smith. At her peak, she was the world's most famous screen actress. Co-founder and part owner of United Artists. Won Academy Award in 1929. Retired from acting in 1933. Given honorary Academy Award in 1976. Died at age 87 in Santa Monica, California. Her story was told in the 1997 movie *Mary Pickford: A Life on Film*.

Last Words: "There's Mama and Papa. And there's Jesus."

Source: *Mary Pickford: America's Sweetheart* by Scott Eyman (New York, 1990).

Pike, Albert

(1809-1891) American lawyer, soldier, military officer, writer, poet. Confederate general in U.S. Civil War. Freemason. Engaged for many years in rewriting the rituals of the society. Died at age 81 in Washington, D.C.

Last Words: "Shalom, Shalom, Shalom." (tr. "Peace, peace, peace.")

Source: *Albert Pike, a Biography* by Fred W. Allsopp (Little Rock, AR, 1928).

Pike, Zebulon Montgomery

(1779-1813) American explorer, military officer. Led expedition to Southwest for President Thomas Jefferson. Discovered Pikes Peak. Brigadier general during War of 1812. Killed at age 34 in the Battle of Lundy's Lane near Toronto when a magazine exploded. Ten U.S. counties and two cities are among the places named for him.

Last Words: "What does it mean?" Spoken to a sergeant who replied: "Victory. The British Union Jack is down and the Stars and Stripes are going up!" The captured British flag was placed under his pillow as he had requested, then he died.

Source: *The Expeditions of Zebulon Montgomery Pike: Memoir of the Author* by Zebulon Montgomery Pike and Elliott Coves (New York, 1895).

Pilkington, George Lawrence

(1865-1897) English writer, bicyclist. Missionary to Uganda. Notable work: *Handbook of Luganda*. Known for riding his bicycle from Mombasa to Uganda. Killed at about age 32 by Sudanese mutineers in Lubwa.

Last Words: "Thank you my friends. You have done well to take me off the battlefield; and now give me a rest."

Source: *Pilkington of Uganda* by Charles F. Harford-Battesby (New York, 1899).

Pindar, Peter, see Wolcot, John.

Pinza, Ezio Fortunato

(1892-1957) Italian singer, actor. One of the great operatic basses. Notable opera roles: Boris, Sarastro, Don Giovanni, Mephistopheles, Don Basilio, Figaro. Sang with Metropolitan Opera then appeared on Broadway, notably in *South Pacific*. Made several films and appeared often on television. Died at age 64 in Stamford, Connecticut, after suffering a stroke.

Last Words: "I want—I want." Spoken to his wife while he was paralyzed by a stroke.

Source: *Ezio Pinza: An Autobiography,* ed. by Robert Magidoff (New York, 1958).

Pio of Pietrelcina, Saint (Padre Pio)

(1887-1968) Italian friar, holy man. Birth name Francesco Forgione. Member of the Order of Friars Minor Capuchin. Became ill on 50th anniversary of when he received the Stigmata. Died early the next morning in his cell in San Giovanni Rotondo. He was 81. Canonized in 2002.

Last Words: "Gesú, Maria—Gesú, Maria." (tr. "Jesus, Mary—Jesus, Mary.") Whispered over and over.

Source: *Padre Pio* by Rev. John A. Schug (Chicago, 1983).

Piozzi, Hester Lynch (Mrs. Thrale)

(1741-1821) English matron. Known mostly

as Mrs. Thrale. Friend of Dr. Samuel Johnson, who lived and traveled with her family and saved one of her husbands from bankruptcy. Broke her leg while traveling to Clifton, Bristol. Died ten days later at age 80 in Clifton.

Last Words: "I die in the trust and the fear of God." Mrs. Pennington, a Clifton neighbor, reported her dying words.

Source: *Mrs. Thrale, Afterwards Mrs. Piozzi. A Sketch of Her Life and Passages from Her Diaries, Letters & Other Writings,* ed. by Leonard Benton Seeley (London, 1908).

Pirandello, Luigi

(1867-1936) Italian playwright, novelist, short-story writer. Notable works: *Six Characters in Search of an Author; Right You Are If You Think You Are* (dramas that explored identity and the relativity of truth). Won 1934 Nobel Prize for Literature. Died at age 69 in Rome.

Last Words: "The hearse, the horse, the driver, and—enough!" His instructions for his funeral. He wanted no pomposity or show.

Source: *Twentieth Century Authors, A Biographical Dictionary of Modern Literature* by Stanley J. Kunitz and Howard Haycraft (New York, 1942).

Pissarro, Lucien

(1863-1944) French artist, painter, publisher. Impressionist. Eldest son of French Impressionist painter Camille Pissarro. Spent much time in England. Became naturalized British subject in 1916. Founded Eragny Press in Hammersmith and published limited editions of ornately illustrated books. Died at age 81 in London.

Last Words: "What's the use?"

Source: *Lucien Pissarro: Un coeur simple* by William Sutton Meadmore (London, 1962).

Pitman, Sir Isaac

(1813-1897) English phonographer, educator. Designed first commercially successful phonic shorthand system. Knighted in 1894. Died at age 84 in Bath, England.

Last Words: "To those who ask how Isaac Pitman passed away, say, Peacefully, and with no more concern than in passing from one room into another to take up some further employment."

Source: *The Life of Sir Isaac Pitman (Inventor of Pho-*

nography) by Alfred Baker (London, 1908).

Pitt, William, the Elder, 1st Earl of Chatham

(1708-1778) British statesman, politician. Prime minister during the French and Indian War (Seven Years' War). Had a seizure in the House of Lords when he rose to speak. Died four days later at age 69.

Last Words: "Go, my son, go whither your country calls you: let her engross all your attention; spare not a moment, which is due to her service, in weeping over an old man, who will soon be no more."

Source: *The Life of William Pitt, Earl of Chatham,* by Basil Williams (London, 1913).

Pitt, William, the Younger

(1759-1806) British statesman, prime minister, politician. Son of 1st Earl of Chatham. Unmarried, no children. Died at age 46 at his home in Putney, an hour after speaking his Last Words.

Different Last Words:

(1) "Oh, my country! How I love my country."

Source: *Life of the Right Honourable William Pitt* by Lord Stanhope (London, 1862). The author was his nephew.

Variation: "Oh, my country! How I leave my country!" Pitt was very much aware of England's perilous situation following Napoleon's victory at Austerlitz when he spoke his Last Words.

Sources: *Life of the Rt. Hon. William Pitt* by Lord Stanhope (London, 1879); *William Pitt and National Revival* by J. Holland Rose (London, 1911).

Variation: "My country! Oh, my country!"

Source: *G. Rose Diary* (Entry for January 23, 1806). *The Diaries and Correspondence of the Right Hon. George Rose,* ed. by Leveson Vernon Harcourt (London, 1860). Rose was a British statesman and political writer.

Variation: "Alas, my country!"

Source: *Harper's New Monthly Magazine,* Vol. 6, December 1852 to May 1853.

(2) (doubtful): "I think I could eat one of Bellamy's veal pies."

Source: *The Concise Oxford Dictionary of Quotations* 2nd ed. (Oxford, England, 1987). Describes the quote as "oral tradition."

Bellamy may have been a House of Commons courier. Pitt may actually have said: "I think I have eaten one of Bellamy's veal pies."

Pius II, Pope

(1405-1464) Italian prelate, writer. Birth name Enea Silvio de Piccolomini. Used pen name Aeneas Silvius. Wrote poetry, prose, autobiography. Succeeded to the papacy in 1458. Called for a Crusade in 1463. Got as far as Ancona on the Adriatic Sea where he died at age 58.

Last Words: "One of the miseries of princes is to have flatterers even around their deathbed." Spoken to his physician.

Source: *The Lives and Times of the Popes: Including the Complete Gallery of Portraits of the Pontiffs Reproduced from Effigies pontificum Romanorum Dominici basae* by Artaud de Montor (New York, 1911).

Pius IV, Pope

(1499-1565) Italian prelate. Birth name Giovanni Angelo d' Medici. Named Archbishop of Ragusa in 1545. Elevated to cardinal in 1549. Elected pope in 1559. Council of Trent held during his reign. Patron of the arts. Commissioned buildings in Vatican and in Rome. A contemporary of Michelangelo. Died at age 66 in Rome.

Last Words: "Lord, now lettest Thou Thy servant depart in peace."

Source: *The Lives of the Fathers, Martyrs and Principal Saints* by Alban Butler (New York, 1846).

Pius V, Pope and Saint

(1504-1572) Italian prelate. Birth name Michele Ghislieri. Elected pope in 1566. Led an austere life. Banned luxury from court. Called for excommunication of Queen Elizabeth of England. Died at age 68 in Rome. Canonized in 1710.

Last Words: "Lord, increase my pain, but may it please you also to increase my patience!" Prayed on his deathbed.

Source: *St. Pius V: A Brief Account of His Life, Times, Virtues and Miracles* by Robin Anderson (Rockford, IL, 1989).

Variation: "Lord, increase the suffering, but if it please Thee, increase the patience also."

Source: *The Lives and Times of the Popes: Including the Complete Gallery of Portraits of the Pontiffs Reproduced from Effigies pontificum Romanorum Dominici basae* by Artaud de Montor (New York, 1911).

Pius VI, Pope

(1717-1799) Italian prelate. Birth name Giovanni Angelo Braschi. Elected cardinal in 1771 and pope in 1775. In 1799, Napoleon's army occupied the Papal States and established a republic. When the pope refused to relinquish his temporal authority, he was taken to Valence, France, where he was imprisoned. Died at age 81, six weeks later.

Last Words: "Lord, forgive them!" His last act was to raise his right arm and impart a triple benediction.

Source: *Studies in Church History* by Reuben Parsons (Philadelphia, 1886-1909).

Pius VII, Pope

(1742-1823) Italian prelate. Birth name Luigi Barnaba Chiaramonti. Created bishop of Tivoli and Imola. Created cardinal in 1785. Elected to the papacy in 1800. During Napoleon's occupation of Italy, he refused to ally himself with him. In 1808, Pius was imprisoned in Grenoble and Savona. In 1812, he was taken to Fontainebleau, where he remained a prisoner until Napoleon was defeated two years later. Died at age 81 in Rome after a pontificate of 23 years.

Last Words: "Savona—Fontainebleau."

Source: *The Life of Pope Pius the Seventh* by Mary Helen A. Allies, ed. by T. W. Allies (London, 1875).

Pius IX, Pope and Blessed

(1792-1878) Italian prelate. Birth name Giovanni Maria Mastai-Ferretti. Pontificate of almost 32 years. Defined dogma of the Immaculate Conception. Organized first Vatican Council. Died at age 85 at the Apostolic Palace in Rome. Beatified in 2000.

Different Last Words:

(1) "Yes, depart." Spoken as the Profiscere was said.

Source: *Pio IX e il suo pontificato,* tr. by Giuseppe Sebastiano Pelczar (Turin, Italy, 1911).

(2) "Guard the Church I have loved so well."

Source: *Leo XIII, and His Probable Policy* by Bernard O'Reilly (New York, 1878).

Pius X, Pope and Saint

(1835-1914) Italian prelate, holy man. Birth name Giuseppe Melchiorre Sarto. Died at age 79 in Rome as World War I began. Canonized in 1954.

Different Last Words:

(1) (doubtful): "Get out of my sight! We grant blessing to no one who provokes the world to war!"

Source: Various Last Words compilations and Internet websites.

Pius X did speak these words in 1914 when Emperor Franz Josef's ambassador came to seek an apostolic blessing for the Austrian Army, but they were not his Last Words.

Source: *Speaking of Cardinals* by Thomas Brynmor Morgan (New York, 1946).

(2) "I resign myself completely." These words were spoken to his confessor as he received the Last Rites. They were the last consecutive words he said.

Source: *Life of Pius X* by Francis Alice Forbes (New York, 1918).

Pius XI, Pope

(1857-1939) Italian prelate. Birth name Achille Amborgio Damiano Ratti. Ruled for 17 years. Independent Vatican City created during his pontificate. Notable among 30 encyclicals he issued: *Quadragesima Anno* (upholding rights of labor, condemning un-bridled capitalism and communism).

Last Words: Those at his deathbed said he mumbled something that sounded like: "Je-sus and Mary. Peace to the world." Others thought he said "In our Last Rites—Sister Therese of the Infant Jesus—art near to us. God is merciful. May his will be done." All agree the last articulate words he spoke were: "I still have so many things to do."

Source: "Death of a Pope" (*Time* magazine, February 20, 1939).

Pius XII, Pope

(1876-1958) Italian prelate. Birth name Eugenio Pacelli. Ruled during World War II. Died at age 82 at the papal summer palace in Castel Gandolfo, near Rome.

Different Last Words:

(1) "We must finish the Rosary we began."

Source: "How Pius XII Died" by Philip S. Land (*America*, November 8, 1959).

(2) "Pray, pray that this regrettable situation for the Church may end."

Source: "As Cardinal Pacelli, the Pope Visited D.C. in 1936. A Lithe, Ascetic Church Envoy with a Benign Smile" by Edward T. Folliard (*Washington Post and Times Herald*, October 9, 1958).

Pizarro, Francisco

(1471?-1541) Spanish explorer, conquista-dor. Conquered the Inca Empire. Claimed most of South America for Spain. Founded the city of Lima, Peru. Waged civil war with Diego de Almagro, who was defeated and killed. Pizarro was killed in revenge in Lima by Almagro's followers.

Last Word: "Jesu."

Source: *Pizarro and the Conquest of Peru* by Frederick A. Ober (New York, 1906).

Platt, Orville Hitchcock

(1827-1905) American politician. Member Connecticut State Senate and U.S. Senate from Connecticut. Author of the Platt Amendment. Died at age 77 in Meriden. Platt National Park, Oklahoma, was named for him.

Last Words: "You know what this means, Doctor, and so do I."

Source: *An Old Fashioned Senator: Orville H. Platt* by Louis A. Coolidge (New York, 1910).

Plotinus

(205?-270) Roman philosopher. Founder of Neoplatonist school. His writings were pub-lished as *Enneads*. Born in Egypt. Died near Minturnae, Italy.

Last Words: "I am endeavouring to rejoin that which is divine in me to that which is divine in the Universe."

Source: *On the Philosophy of the Mind* by James Doug-las of Cavers (Edinburgh, 1839).

Plowman, Max

(1883-1941) English writer, poet. Wounded in World War I. Wrote of his experiences. Notable work: *The Right to Life* (antiwar protest). Died at age 57.

Last Words (written): "Good wishes to you very sincerely. Do come & see us here someday, even tho' we are bunged up at the moment. And let me know if the enclosed needs revision. Yours ever, Max P." Letter to his editor.

Source: *Bridge Into the Future: Letters of Max Plow-man*, ed. by Dorothy Lloyd Plowman (London, 1944). The editor was his wife.

Plumb, Preston Bierce

(1837-1891) American newsman, lawyer, politician, settler. Helped lay out town of Emporia. Kansas. Established *Kansas News*. Member U.S. Senate from Kansas. Died at age 52 in Washington, D.C., during his third term.

Last Words (written): "Dear Frank, Please come to my room tomorrow (Sunday) about ten o'clock. Yours truly P.B.P." Note to his former private secretary.

Source: *The Life of Preston B. Plumb* by William E. Connelly (Chicago, 1913).

Plummer, Henry

(1832-1864) American murderer, robber. Elected sheriff of Bannock, Washington. Vigilantes rounded up some of the crooks who worked for him. When the vigilantes learned Plummer was the leader, they lynched him.

Last Words: "You wouldn't hang your own sheriff, would you?"

Source: *Bloodletters and Badmen: A Narrative Encyclopedia of American Criminals from the Pilgrims to the Present* by Jay Robert Nash (New York, 1995).

Poe, Edgar Allan

(1809-1849) American short-story writer, poet, critic. One of the first to write detective stories. Known for macabre mystery stories. Notable works: *The Murders in the Rue Morgue; Fall of the House of Usher; The Pit and the Pendulum*; *The Raven; The Cask of Amontillado; The Tell-Tale Heart.* Found in distress in Baltimore; taken to Washington College Hospital. Was wearing clothes that were not his. Died at age 40.

Last Words: "Lord help my poor soul." The informant for Poe's Last Words was Dr. J.J. Moran, who was at Washington College Hospital when Poe died. Moran mentioned the author's final words in a letter to Poe's aunt/mother-in-law Maria Clemm. He also said Poe repeatedly called out a name that sounded like "Reynolds" the night before his death.

Source: *Israfel: The Life and Times of Edgar Allan Poe* by Hervey Allen (New York, 1926).

Polk, James Knox

(1795-1849) 11th President of the U.S. American lawyer, planter, politician. Known as Young Hickory. Member Tennessee legislature. Member U.S. House of Representatives from Tennessee. Governor of Tennessee. Died at age 53 in Nashville.

Last Words: "I love you, Sarah. For all eternity, I love you." Spoken to his wife Sarah Childress, whom he married in 1824.

Source: *Young Hickory, The Life and Times of President James K. Polk* by Martha McBride Morrel (New York, 1949).

Polk, Sarah Childress

(1803-1891) American First Lady. Wife of 11th U.S. President James J. Polk. First First Lady to be photographed on the grounds of the White House and first to be photographed with her husband. Died at age 87 in Nashville, Tennessee.

Last Words: "The Lord bless thee, and keep thee, and make His face shine upon thee and give thee happiness and love and everlasting peace." Spoken while she placed her hands on the heads of everyone in the room. After she gave her blessing she said nothing for a while. Then she said "I do, I do" when her niece Sallie asked if she loved her. She asked for ice. When her niece faltered while trying to feed it to her, she said "I am not a baby, my dear." A few minutes later she died.

Sources: *Memorials of Sarah Childress Polk: Wife of the Eleventh President of the United States* by Anson Nelson and Fanny Nelson (New York, 1892); *Nashville Daily American,* August 14, 1891.

Polycarp, Saint

(69?-155) Near Eastern prelate, holy man, martyr. Bishop of Smyrna. A leading Christian who was persecuted under Marcus Aurelius. Condemned to be burned alive, but when the flames did not reach him, he was killed with a sword. He was in his 80s. His trial and execution were described in a letter written by his church and are believed to be the oldest church account of a martyr's death.

Last Words: "I give Thee thanks that thou hast vouchsafed to grant me this day, that I may have my part among the number of the martyrs in the cup of Christ, unto the resurrection of eternal life, both of body and soul, through the operation of Thy Holy Spirit; among whom I shall this day be received into Thy sight for an acceptable sacrifice: and as Thou hast prepared and revealed the same before this time, so Thou hast accomplished the same. O Thou most true God, which canst not lie. Wherefore I in like case for all things praise Thee, and bless Thee, and glorify Thee by our everlasting Bishop, Jesus Christ, to whom be glory evermore. Amen."

Source: *Book of Martyrs and the Acts and Monuments*

of the Church by John Fox (or Foxe). First published, 1563, ed. by John Cumming (London, 1851).

Pompadour, Marquise de ("Madame de Pompadour")

(1721-1764) French noblewoman. Mistress of King Louis XV of France. Birth name Jeanne Antoinette Poisson. Died at age 42 of bronchial pneumonia at Versailles.

Last Words: "One moment, Monsieur le curé, and we will leave together." Spoken to her confessor who had gotten up to leave.

Source: Madame de Pompadour by Edmond and Jules de Goncourt (Paris, 1906).

Pompey

(106-48 B.C.) Roman military officer, politician. Full name Gnaeus Pompeius Magnus. Known as Pompey the Great. After he lost the Battle of Pharsalius, Ptolemy ordered his death. Pompey fled to Egypt. Suspicious when no one aboard ship spoke friendly to him he spoke his Last Words to Septimus.

Last Words: "I am not too mistaken surely, in believing you to have been formerly my fellow soldier?" Septimus nodded without speaking then stabbed him with a sword.

Source: "Pompey" in The Lives of the Noble Grecians and Romans by Plutarch, tr. by John Dryden (Chicago, 1952).

Pompidou, Georges Jean Raymond

(1911-1974) French statesman, banker, educator. Taught French literature in Paris and Marseilles. Prime minister of France. President of the Fifth Republic. Died at age 62 of cancer in Paris. Centre Beaubourg renamed in his honor.

Last Words: "You cannot know what I am suffering." Spoken to a friend.

Source: "After Pompidou: France in Flux" (Newsweek magazine, April 15, 1974).

Poniatowski, Józef Antoni

(1763-1813) Polish royalty. Prince, military officer. General, minister of war. Commander in Napoleon's army. Fought against Russia. Made marshal of France by Napoleon. Nephew of Stanisław Poniatowski, the last king of Poland. Cut off from aid in a battle near Leipzig, Germany, he and his horse jumped into a river and were drowned. Died at age 50.

Last Words: "Gentlemen, it behooves us

now to die with honor."

Source: The Czar, His Court and People: Including a Tour in Norway and Sweden by John S. Maxwell (New York, 1848).

Ponselle, Rosa

(1897-1981) American singer. Operatic soprano. Birth name Rose Melba Ponzello. Made Metropolitan Opera debut in 1918 with Enrico Caruso. Notable roles: Leonora, Norma, Violetta, Carmen. Retired in 1937 while in her prime. Settled in Baltimore, Maryland. Became art director of Civic Opera. Died at age 84 at Villa Pace, her home near Baltimore.

Last Words: "La Forza del Destino. It's ironic. It is as if my whole life has been the Force of Destiny."

Source: Ponselle, A Singer's Life by Rosa Ponselle and James A. Drake (New York, 1982).

Poole, William ("Bill the Butcher")

(1821-1855) American gang member. Leader of the Bowery Boys gang. Member of the Know Nothing party that hated foreigners. Shot in a New York City saloon in a revenge killing. Died at age 33. Inspiration for the character William "Bill the Butcher" Cutting in Martin Scorsese's movie Gangs of New York.

Last Words: "Goodbye boys! I die a true American!"

Source: "The Death of William Poole" (New York Daily Times, March 10, 1855).

Pope, Alexander

(1688-1744) English poet, satirist, writer, essayist. Had spinal curvature. Experienced pain much of his life. Friend of Swift. Gained fame for his mock-heroic poem The Rape of the Lock. Other notable works: Duncaid; Essay on Criticism. Died at age 56 in Twickenham, Middlesex, England.

Different Last Words:

(1) "There is nothing that is meritorious but virtue and friendship, and indeed friendship itself is only a part of virtue."

Source: Lives of the English Poets and a Criticism of Their Work by Samuel Johnson (Oxford, England, 1825).

(2) (doubtful): "I am dying sir, of one hundred good symptoms."

Source: The Last Words (Real and Traditional) of Distinguished Men and Women Collected from Various Sources by Frederic Rowland Marvin (New York,

1901). Marvin noted that some writers give Pope's Last Words as: "Friendship itself is but a part of virtue." Pope did make a comment about "dying with one hundred good symptoms" the morning of his death but he said more later.
Source: *Testimony of the Gods* by Castleton (London, 1881).

Poquelin, Jean-Baptiste, see **Molière**.

Porcaro, Stefano
(d. 1453) Italian scholar, activist, revolutionary, republican ringleader. Executed for plotting to overthrow the papal government of Pope Nicholas V and establish a republic in Rome.
Last Words: "O my people, your deliverer dies today!"
Source: *Molders of Destiny (Renaissance Lives and Times)* by Lloyd W. Eshleman (New York, 1938).

Porter, Katherine Anne
(1890-1980) American short-story writer, novelist, critic, poet. Birth name Callie Russell Porter. Notable works: *Ship of Fools; Pale Horse, Pale Rider.* Awarded Pulitzer Prize and National Book Award in 1966. Died at age 90 in Silver Spring, Maryland.
Last Words: "Yes, I know that." Her response to a priest who told her eternity would be better than this world.
Source: *Katherine Anne Porter: A Life* by Joan Givner (New York, 1982).

Porter, Noah
(1811-1892) American clergyman, educator, lexicographer, philosopher. Congregational minister. Last clergyman president of Yale. Edited several editions of *Webster's Dictionary.* Died at age 80 in New Haven, Connecticut.
Last Words: "Go call your mother. Wake her up. I want to consult with her."
Source: *Noah Porter: A Memorial By Friends,* ed. by George S. Merriam (New York, 1893).

Porter, William Sydney ("O. Henry")
(1862-1910) American short-story writer. Pen name O. Henry. Known for ironic or humorous short stories. Notable works: "The Gift of the Magi"; "The Ransom of Red Chief." Spent three years in prison for embezzlement while working as a bank teller in Texas. Moved to New York in 1902 and devoted the rest of his life to writing. His stories appeared in magazines. Suffered from alcoholism and ill health. Died at age 47 of cirrhosis of liver in New York City.
Different Last Words:
(1) "Turn up the lights. I don't want to go home in the dark." Spoken to a nurse in the hospital. His words were taken from a song by Harry Williams that was popular when Porter died: "I'm afraid to come home in the dark." Porter died the following morning.
Source: *The Quiet Lodger of Irving Place* by William W. Williams (New York, 1936).
(2) "Send for Mr. Hall." Spoken to his physician just before he died. Gilman Hall was one of his editors.
Sources: *O. Henry* by Eugene Current-Garcia (New York, 1965); *Caliph of Bagdad: Being Arabian Nights Flashes of the Life, Letters and Work of O. Henry* by Robert H. Davis and Arthur B. Maurice (New York, 1931).

Porteus, Beilby
(1731-1808) English prelate, abolitionist, reformer. Anglican Bishop of Chester. Bishop of London. Chaplain to George III. Abolitionist who challenged the church position on slavery. Died at age 78 in Fulham, England.
Last Words: "O, that glorious sun!"
Source: *The Works of the Right Reverend Beilby Porteus, D.D. Late Bishop of London: with His Life* by the Rev. Robert Hodgson, A.M. F.R.S. (London, 1823).

Pothinus, Saint
(87?-177) French prelate, holy man, martyr. Christian. Disciple of Polycarp of Smyrna. Founded church in Lyons and presided over it 20 years, until he was persecuted by Marcus Aurelius. Died at age 90 in prison.
Last Words: "If you are worthy, you will know him." His response when brought before the governor and asked who was the God of Christians. He was beaten so severely he died two days later.
Source: *Cyclopaedia of Biblical, Theological and Ecclesiastical Literature* by John McClintock and James Strong (New York, 1891).

Potter, Helen Beatrix (Beatrix)
(1866-1943) English writer, illustrator of picture books for children. Creator of Peter Rabbit stories. Died at age 77 in Sawrey, England. Her life was the subject of the movie *Miss Potter* (2006).
Last Words (written): "Dear Joe Moscrop,

Still some strength in me. I write a line to shake you by the hand, our friendship has been entirely pleasant. I am very ill with bronchitis. With best wishes for the New Year." Letter to neighbor Joseph Moscrop.

Source: *The Tale of Beatrix Potter* by Margaret Lane (London, 1946).

Poundmaker (Opeteca-hanawaywin)

(1842-1886) Native American leader. Plains Cree chief. Responsible for having Canadian government add a famine clause to a treaty. In 1885, he stopped the movement of his people who had grown restless. Was arrested and found guilty of treason-felony. Released from jail for ill health after serving less than year of a three-year sentence. Died a few months later.

Last Words: "It would be so much easier just to fold our hands and not make this fight—to say, I, one man, can do nothing. I grow afraid only when I see people thinking and acting like this. We all know the story about the man who sat beside the trail too long, and then it grew over and he could never find his way again. We can never forget what has happened. But we cannot go back nor can we just sit beside the trail."

Source: *Poundmaker* by Norman Sluman (Toronto, ON, 1967).

Powell, Adam Clayton, Jr.

(1908-1972) American politician, clergyman, writer. Member of U.S. House of Representatives from New York. Defeated in 1970. Retired to Bimini in the Bahamas. Died in a Miami hospital at age 63. His story was told in the 2002 television movie *Keep the Faith, Baby*.

Last Words: "Sweetheart, I just don't feel up to it now. Come back later." Spoken to a female reporter who went to hospital to seek an interview.

Source: *King of the Cats: The Life and Times of Adam Clayton Powell* by Wil Haygood (Boston, 1993).

Powell, Lewis Thornton
(or Lewis Paine or Lewis Payne)

(1844-1865) American conspirator. Tried to assassinate U.S. Secretary of State William Henry Seward at Seward's home at the same time that Booth was assassinating Lincoln. He was arrested, charged with attempted murder and conspiracy, found guilty and sentenced to die. Hanged with three other conspirators. Powell, age 21, was the first of the four to be executed.

Last Words: "You know best." Spoken to his executioner, Captain Rath, who wished him a quick death. Powell then murmured to Rath: "I thank you. Goodbye."

Source: *Alias "Paine": Lewis Thornton Powell, the Mystery Man of the Lincoln Conspiracy* by Betty J. Ownsbey (Jefferson, NC, 1993).

Power, Tyrone Edmund, Jr.

(1914-1958) American actor. Stage and screen star. Appeared in more than 50 movies. Died at age 44 of a massive heart attack in Madrid, Spain, while filming *Solomon and Sheba*.

Last Words: "Don't worry. The same thing happened a week ago." Spoken to a friend.

Source: *Tyrone Power: The Last Idol* by Fred Lawrence Guiles (Garden City, NY, 1979).

Pratt, Daniel Darwin

(1813-1877) American politician, lawyer. Member Indiana State House of Representatives. Member U.S. House of Representatives from Indiana; resigned 1869. Member U.S. Senate from Indiana. Chairman, Committee on Pensions. Appointed Commissioner of Internal Revenue by President Grant. Died at age 63 in Logansport, Indiana.

Last Words: "Away over rivers and mountains, a thousand miles distant, in a humble farm house, on a bench, an aged mother reading to her boy from the Oracles of God!" His head fell back and he died after speaking these words.

Source: *History of Cass County, Indiana: From the Earliest Time to the Present* by Thomas B. Helm (Chicago, 1886).

Prejean, Dalton

(1959-1990) American murderer. Electrocuted in 1990 in Louisiana for shooting a state trooper in 1977. Prejean's case is unusual because all his crimes were committed while he was 17 years old or younger. He had also been found to have a mental age lower than that of a 13-year-old. A later Supreme Court ruling abolished juvenile executions as unconstitutional.

Last Words: "Nothing is going to be accomplished. I have peace with myself. I'd like to thank all of those who supported me all these years. I'd also like to thank my loved ones for being strong.—My son will be a better person for not letting something like this bring down his life.—Keep strong, keep pushing, keep praying. They said it wasn't for the revenge, but it's hard for me to see, to understand. I hope they're happy. So I forfeit my life. I give my love to all. God bless."

Source: *Death Watch: A Death Penalty Anthology* by Lane Nelson and Burk Foster (Upper Saddle River, NJ, 2001).

Prentiss, Elizabeth Payson

(1818-1878) American writer, poet, hymnist. Author of children's stories and poems such as "Little Susy's Six Birthdays" and "Little Susy's Six Teachers." Notable works: "The Flower of the Family"; "Golden Hours." Wrote the popular hymn "More Love to Thee O Christ." Experienced much pain during her final days. Died at age 59 in Dorset, Vermont.

Last Words: "Geduld Mein Herz! Stille Mein Wille!" (tr. "Patience, My Heart! Be still my Will!"). Her Last Words were two favorite German mottoes that were on the wall over her bed.

Source: *The Life and Letters of Elizabeth Prentiss* by E. Prentiss and George Lewis Prentiss (New York, 1882). George was her husband.

Prescott, William Hickling

(1796-1859) American historian, writer. Nearly blind much of his life. Lost the vision in his left eye in an accident; inflammation weakened his right eye. Notable works: *History of the Conquest of Mexico; The Conquest of Peru.* Died at age 62 of apoplectic shock in Boston.

Last Words: "How came you to remember?" Spoken to his wife. He was surprised she could recall the name of a diplomat he had forgotten.

Source: *Life of William Hickling Prescott* by George Ticknor (Boston, 1864).

Presley, Elvis Aaron

(1935-1977) American musician, entertainer, actor. Recording, screen, stage and television star. Cultural icon. Known as the King of Rock and Roll. Member of four major music Halls of Fame: Rock and Roll; Rockabilly; Country Music; Gospel Music. Won three Grammys. Died suddenly at age 42 at Graceland, his home in Memphis, Tennessee.

Last Words (doubtful): "I'm going to the can" (or a comment similar to this). Presley supposedly told his companion Ginger Alden he was not able to sleep and was going to the bathroom to read. She discovered him dead on the floor of his bathroom.

Source: Various Last Words compilations and Internet websites.

Ginger Alden was asleep when Elvis went to the bathroom around 9 a.m. He said nothing to her. She woke around 2 p.m. and found him lying on the bathroom floor.

Source: *The Hollywood Book of Death: The Bizarre, Often Sordid, Passing of More Than 125 American Movie and TV Idols* by James Robert Parish (New York, 2001).

Preston, John

(1587-1628) English clergyman, writer, educator. Notable work: *Treatise on the New Covenant.* Chaplain to Charles I. Master of Emmanuel College, Cambridge. Became a staunch Puritan in later years. Died at age 41 at Preston Capes, Northamptonshire.

Different Last Words:

(1) "I feel death coming to my heart, my pain shall now be quickly turned into joy."

Source: *The Life of the Renowned Doctor Preston* by Rev. Thomas Ball (1628), abridged and first published by Samuel Clarks (London, 1885).

(2) "Blessed be God, though I change my place, I shall not change my company; for I have walked with God while living, and now I go to rest with God."

Source: "A Happy Death" by Dr. Calamy (*The Christian Gleaner and Domestic Magazine,* Vol. I, No. 12, December 1824).

Prestwood, 1st Earl Attlee and Viscount, see Attlee, Clement Richard, 1st Earl Attlee and Viscount Prestwood.

Price, Sterling

(1809-1867) American military officer, politician. Elected member U.S. House of Representative from Missouri but resigned to participate in the Mexican War. While military governor of New Mexico, he put down the Taos Revolt. Promoted to brigadier general in 1847. Price commanded the Army of the West at the Battle of Santa Cruz de Rosales, Chihuahua—a battle that took place six days after the Treaty of Guadalupe Hidalgo ended the Mexican War. He was later elected governor of Missouri. Confederate major general in U.S. Civil War. Led his army back into Missouri in 1864 in an attempt to recapture his state for the Confederacy. Took his remaining troops to Mexico after the war rather than surrender to the Union Army. Established a failed Confederate exile colony in Veracruz. Returned to Missouri. Died at age 58 soon afterward. Several monuments in Missouri honor Price.

Last Words:

"Teach me to feel another's woe,
To hide the faults I see,
That mercy I to others show,
That mercy show to me."

After reciting this poem by Alexander Pope on his deathbed, he sank into unconsciousness and died.

Source: "Gen. Sterling Price's Last Words" (*New York Times,* October 10, 1879).

Pride, Sir Thomas

(c. 1610-1658) English military officer, law man. Lieutenant general in the parliamentary army. In 1648, he was responsible for the expulsion of Presbyterians from the English House of Commons; known as Pride's Purge. Commissioner for the trial of Charles I in 1649 and signed his death warrant. Served as high sheriff of Surrey and was knighted in 1655 at Whitehall, three year before he died. He acquired large estates, including Nonsuch, a palace previously owned by Henry VIII. After the Restoration, his estates were confiscated and returned to the Crown.

Last Words: "I am very sorry for these three nations, whom I see in a most sad and deplorable condition."

Source: *The Dictionary of National Biography* by George Smith, Leslie Stephen, Sidney Lee, Robert Blake, C. S. Nicholls (London, 1921-1922). Their information came from *The Weekly Intelligencer,* 1-8, November 1659.

Priestley, Joseph

(1733-1804) English clergyman, political theorist, physical scientist, chemist. Unitarian. Discovered oxygen. Friend of John Ad-

ams, Thomas Jefferson. In 1794, he and his wife moved to Northumberland, Pennsylvania, where he built a house and laboratory. Died at age 71 in Northumberland.

Different Last Words:

(1) "That is right. I have now done." Spoken after he dictated to his son Joseph revisions to a manuscript he was writing and was satisfied with the changes. About a half hour later, in a faint voice, he asked to be moved to a cot. He died ten minutes after he was moved.

Source: *Memoirs of Dr. Joseph Priestley to the Year 1795, Written by Himself with a Continuation to the Time of His Decease by His Son, Joseph Priestley* (London, 1807).

(2) "I am going to sleep like you, but we shall all awake together, and I trust to everlasting happiness." Spoken to his grandchildren who were brought to his bedside.

Source: *Annual Report of the Board of Regents of the Smithsonian Institution: Showing the Operations, Expenditures, and Condition of the Institution for the Year 1867* by Smithsonian Institution Board of Regents (Washington, D.C., 1868).

Prinze, Freddie

(1954-1977) American actor, comedian. Starred in television sitcom *Chico and the Man.* Shot himself in the head in front of his business manager while under the influence of an overdose of prescription drug in Los Angeles, California. Rushed to hospital, where he died.

Last Words (written): "I must end it. There's no hope left. I'll be at peace. No one had anything to do with this. My decision totally. Freddie Prinze P.S. I'm sorry. Forgive me. Dusty's here. He's innocent. He cared." Suicide note.

Source: *The Freddie Prinze Story as Told by His Mother* by Maria Pruetzel and John A. Barbour (Kalamazoo, MI, 1978).

Protasius, Saint

(fl. mid-1st century) Italian martyr, holy man. Christian. Twin brother of Gervasius, son of Saint Vitalis. The pagans in Milan feared the gods would not protect them unless Protasius and Gervasius were put to death. When the brothers refused to sacrifice to idols, Gervasius was beaten to death and Protasius was beheaded.

Last Words: "I bear thee no anger, Count,

for I know that thou are blind in thy heart, but rather do I pity thee, for thou knowest not what thou dost. Cease not to torture me, that I may share with my brother the good countenance of our Master." His response to Count Astasius, whom he accused of fearing him.

Source: *The Golden Legend or Lives of the Saints.* Compiled by Jacobus de Voragine, Archbishop of Genoa, 1275, 1st ed., 1470. English ed. by William Caxton, 1483, ed. by F.S. Ellis (Edinburgh, 1900).

Proust, Marcel

(1871-1922) French novelist, essayist, writer, critic. Notable work: *In Search of Lost Time (À la recherche du temps perdu,* translated previously as *Remembrance of Things Past*). Ill much of his life with asthma and anxiety attacks. Spent his last three years confined mostly to his bedroom. Died at age 51 in Paris.

Last Words: "Yes, Robert dear, you are." His response to his brother who asked: "Am I hurting you?"

Source: *The Quest for Proust* by André Maurois (New York, 1950).

Publius Vergilius Maro, see Virgil.

Puccini, Giacomo

(1858-1924) Italian musician, composer. Wrote twelve operas; died before he could complete the last, *Turandot.* Notable works: *La Bohème; Tosca; Madame Butterfly; Manon Lescaut; Girl of the Golden West; Sister Angelica.* Died at age 65 of a heart attack in Brussels, Belgium, after surgery for throat cancer.

Different Last Words:
(1) "My poor Elvira. My poor wife." Spoken to his wife Elvira Gemignani, whom he married in 1904.

Source: *Immortal Bohemian* by Dante del Fiorentino (New York, 1952).

(2) "Remember that your mother is a remarkable woman."

Source: *Puccini: A Critical Biography* by Mosco Camer (New York, 1974).

Pulitzer, Joseph

(1847-1911) Hungarian-born American journalist, publisher, philanthropist. Owner, publisher of *New York World.* During his final year, he was highly sensitive to sound, was almost totally blind and suffered from respiratory and digestive problems. Left $2 million to establish and endow a school of journalism at Columbia University and establish the Pulitzer Prizes. Died at age 64 on his yacht off Charleston, South Carolina.

Last Words: "Leise, ganz leise, ganz leise." (tr. "Softly, quite softly, quite softly.") Spoken to his secretary.

Source: *Joseph Pulitzer, His Life and Letters* by Don C. Seitz (New York, 1924).

Pulliam, Eugene Collins ("Gene")

(1889-1975) American publisher. During his career, he owned 46 newspapers, including *Indianapolis Star, Indianapolis News, Arizona Republic* and *Phoenix Gazette.* Formed Fellowship Program to help outstanding college graduates pursue careers in journalism. Died at age 86.

Last Word (written): "Goldwater." Written on a note tablet in a hospital before he died.

Source: *Publisher: Gene Pulliam: The Last of the Newspaper Titans* by Russell Pulliam (Ottawa, IL, 1984). The author was his grandson.

Pusey, Edward Bouverie

(1800-1882) English theologian. Anglican. One of the leaders of the Oxford Movement that endeavored to reconcile the Church of England with the Roman Catholic Church. Canon of Oxford Cathedral for 54 years. Died at age 82.

Last Words: "My God."

Source: *Life of Edward Bouverie Pusey* by Canon Henry Parry Liddon, completed by J.C. Johnston and R.J. Wilson (London, 1897).

Pushkin, Aleksander Sergeyevich

(1799-1837) Russian poet, playwright, novelist, short-story writer. Notable works: *Ruslan and Ludmilla; Boris Godunov; Eugene Onegin; The Queen of Spades.* Several operas have been based on his works. He was wounded in a duel with a French émigré nobleman accused of being his wife's lover. Pushkin died at age 37 of injuries two days later.

Different Last Words:
(1) "Life is finished—Life is finished!—I can't breathe—I am stifling!"

Source: "The Last Hours of Pushkin, Letter from Jukovskii to Sergei Pushkin, the Poet's Father, February 15/24, 1837" (*Blackwood's Edinburgh Magazine*, Vol. 57, January-June, 1845).

Variation: "Life is over." His friend misunderstood what he said and replied: "Yes it's over. We're finished turning you over." Pushkin responded: "It is life that is over. I can hardly breathe. Something is crushing me."

Source: *Pushkin: A Biography* by Henri Troyat (New York, 1950).

(2) (doubtful): "Farewell, my friends!"

Source: Various Last Words compilations and Internet websites.

Pushkin did say this on his deathbed, but these were not his Last Words. He went on to say much more. Most sources give (1) or a close variation as Pushkin's Last Words.

Pushmataha

(1764-1824) Native American leader. Choctaw chief, warrior, diplomat. Served with Andrew Jackson. Negotiated several treaties with the U.S. Died at age 60 in Washington, D.C. Buried at Congressional Cemetery at Washington. Station on Alabama, Tennessee & Northern Railroad and a county in Oklahoma were named for him.

Last Words: "I shall die, but you will return to our brethren. As you go along the paths, you will see the flowers and hear the birds sing, but Pushmataha will see them and hear them no more. When you shall come to your house, they will ask you, 'Where is Pushmataha?' And you will say to them, 'He is no more.' They will hear the tidings like the sound of the fall of a mighty oak in the stillness of the woods."

Source: *Alokoli* (Choctaw word; tr. "a cluster or collection"), Choctaw County bicentennial book by Josephine D. Evans and Ann H. Gay (Choctaw County, AL, 1976).

Putnam, Israel ("Old Put")

(1718-1790) American military officer, politician. Major general. Participated in French and Indian War campaigns. American commander at Bunker Hill (Breed's Hill) during the American Revolution. Served in Connecticut General Assembly. A founder of the Connecticut Sons of Liberty. Portrait painted by John Trumbull. Died at age 72 in Brooklyn, New York. Nine U.S. counties and a city were named for him.

Last Words: "I am resigned to the will of God and am willing to die now."

Source: *A Conspectus of American Biography: Being an Analytical Summary of American History and Biog-*

raphy, Containing also the Complete Indexes of the National Cyclopedia of American Biography by George Derby (New York, 1906).

His biographer did not give Putnam's Last Words as a direct quote. He reprinted a sermon given immediately after Putnam died. It indicated that when Putnam was asked whether his hope of the future attended him, Putnam "answered in the affirmative with a declaration of his resignation to the will of God and his willingness even then to die."

Source: *The Life of Israel Putnam, Major-General in the Army of the American Revolution* by William Cutter (New York, 1848).

Pyle, Ernest Taylor ("Ernie")

(1900-1945) American journalist, writer. World War II correspondent for Scripps-Howard newspapers. Known for his folksy, familiar style of writing. Wrote about ordinary soldiers and their reactions to war. Won Pulitzer Prize in 1944 for distinguished war correspondence. Died at age 44 of a Japanese sniper's machine gun shot on Ie Shima island near Okinawa. His story was told in the 1945 movie *The Story of G.I. Joe* and the 1998 TV movie *G.I. Joe: The Ernie Pyle Story*.

Last Words: "Are you all right?" Spoken to friends nearby just before the bullet hit the side of his head.

Source: "None Today Can Hold a Candle to Ernie Pyle" by Russell Smith (*Sweetwater Reporter*, April 6, 1991).

Quarles, Francis

(1592-1644) English poet, writer, pamphleteer. Notable work: *Emblems* (illustrated book). Wrote pamphlets in favor of Charles I. The Long Parliament ordered his house to be searched for subversive writings. All his manuscripts were burned. Died at age 52 in London.

Last Words: "Oh sweet Savior of the world, let Thy last words upon the cross be my last words in this world: Into Thy hands, Lord, I commend my spirit And what I cannot utter with my mouth, accept from my heart and soul."

Source: *Collected Works of Francis Quarles* by A.B. Grosart (London, 1881).

Quezon y Molina, Manuel Luis

(1878-1944) Philippine statesman, politician. President of the Philippines. Escaped from Luzon in U.S. submarine after Philippines fell to Japanese in World War II. Died at age 65 of tuberculosis in Saranac, New York, while the Philippines were still occupied.

Last Words: "Just six hundred miles!" Spoken in response to radio news that MacArthur's liberation forces had landed at Sansapor in Dutch New Guinea.

Source: *Manuel L. Quezon, His Life and Career: A Philippine President Biography* by Sol H. Gwekoh (Manila, Philippines, 1948).

Quick, John

(1748-1831) English actor. Celebrated comedian. The original Tony Lumpkin in Goldsmith's comedy *She Stoops to Conquer*. A favorite actor of George III. Lived and worked in London. Amassed fortune of 10,000£. Daughter was well-known actress Mrs. Davenport. Died at age 83.

Last Words: "Is this death?"

Source: *Famous Sayings and Their Authors: A Collection of Historical Sayings in English, French, German, Greek, Italian, and Latin* by Edward Latham (London, 1906).

Quijano, Alfredo Rueda

(1890-1927) Mexican military officer. General. Involved in the Mexican Revolution in 1927. Apprehended in Texcoco, Mexico. Tried, convicted and executed in Mexico City.

Last Words: "Still a little closer. Spoken to the firing squad after he asked them to move close. When they did, he called out "Goodbye" in English to three U.S. newspaper correspondents,

Source: "Mexico: Revolt" (*Time* magazine, October 17, 1927).

Quin, James

(1693-1766) English actor, comedian. Excelled in tragic roles. Convicted of manslaughter for killing another actor in a duel. Quin was not severely punished. The duel was regarded as more an accident than a crime. Retired in 1757. Died at age 72 in Bath, England.

Last Words: He wished "this tragic scene were over," but he hoped to "go through it with becoming dignity."

Source: *The Life of Mr. James Quin, Comedian* by

Anonymous (London, 1887).

Quincy, Josiah

(1772-1864) American lawyer, politician, educator. Member U.S. House of Representatives from Massachusetts. Mayor of Boston. President of Harvard. Died at age 92 in Boston.

Last Words: "I am sorry to leave you, but I wish to go. I have had a remarkably long, prosperous, and happy life, blessed in my children, grandchildren, and great-grandchildren. It is time that I should go. Weep not, mourn not for me." Spoken to his daughters after he thanked them for their affectionate attention.

Source: *Life of Josiah Quincy of Massachusetts* by Edmund Quincy (Boston, 1867).

Quisling, Vidkun

(1887-1945) Norwegian politician. President of a puppet government while the Nazis occupied Norway during World War II. Tried for high treason when the war ended. Executed by a firing squad in Oslo. Before he was executed, he asked to be allowed to shake hands with the ten-man firing squad. He told them not to let their consciences bother them in later years.

Last Words: "You are acting under orders and only doing your duty as soldiers, like myself." Spoken to the firing squad.

Source: *Quisling, Prophet Without Honor* by Ralph Hewins (London, 1965).

Quitman, John Anthony

(1798-1858) American planter, politician, military officer. Brigadier general and major general during Mexican War. Governor of Mississippi. Member U.S. House of Representatives from Mississippi. Believed to have been deliberately poisoned by food served at a banquet at the National Hotel, Washington, D.C., during the inauguration of President James Buchanan. Died at age 59 at his plantation near Natchez. Quitman, Texas, is named for him.

Last Words: "Yes, yes, I know it; He is my trust." Spoken to his daughter who told him: "My father, look to Jesus; He is your only hope."

Source: *Life and Correspondence of John A. Quitman: Governor of the State of Mississippi* by J.F.H. Claiborne (New York, 1860).

Rabelais, François

(1494?-1553?) French writer, humorist, satirist. Had been a Franciscan novice and later a Benedictine, but left the clergy. Studied medicine. Considered by many to be one of the greatest Renaissance writers. Notable works: *Gargantua* and *Pantagruel* (satires). Died at about age 59 in Paris.

Different Last Words:

(1) (doubtful): "Je m'en vais chercher un grand peut-être." (tr. "I go to seek a great Perhaps." or "I am going to the Great Perhaps.")

Sources: *Life of Rabelais* by Peter Anthony Motteux (ed. and tr. 1693-1708); *Oxford Dictionary of Quotations* 2nd ed. (Oxford, England, 1953).

Variation (doubtful): "Je vais quérir un grand peut-être." (tr. "I am going in search of a great maybe.")

Source: *Oeuvres de François Rabelais: contenant la vie de Gargantua et celle de Pantagruel, augmentées de plusieurs fragments et de deux chapitres du Ve livre restitués d'après un manuscrit de la Bibliothèque impériale, précédées d'une notice historique sur la vie et les ouvrages de Rabelais, augmentée de nouveaux documents par P. L. Jacob* by François Rabelais, Gustave Doré, Jacob Le Duchat, M. de L'Aulnaye and P. L. Jacob (Paris, 1857).

(2) (doubtful): "Tirez le rideau. La farce est jouée." (tr. "Bring down the curtain, the farce is played out.")

Variations:

"Let down the curtain, the farce is over."

"Draw the curtain: the farce is ended."

"Ring down the curtain, the farce is over."

Sources: *Dictionary of Phrase and Fable* by E. Cobham Brewer (Philadelphia, 1898); *Titans of Literature, from Homer to the Present,* by Burton Rascoe (New York, 1932); *Oxford Dictionary of Quotations,* 2nd ed. (Oxford, England, 1953).

(3) (doubtful): "Even going my journey, they have greased my boots already." Spoken on his deathbed after receiving Extreme Unction (Last Rites of dying Christians).

Sources: *Apothegms Old and New* by Francis Bacon (1624); *Joe Miller's Jests: Or the Wits Vade-Mecum* (London, 1739).

(4) (doubtful): "Hélas! oui, je le reconnais à sa monture." (tr. "Alas! yes, I recognize him by his steed.") His response when asked: "Voilà votre Sauveur et votre maître, qui veut bien s'abaisser jusqu'à venir vous trouver; le reconnaissez-vous?" (tr. "There is your Saviour and Master, who is kind enough to stoop to come and see you; do you recognize him?") The author noted that the phrase is more accurately attributed to Pierre Bayle (1647-1706).

Source: *Famous Sayings and Their Authors: A Collection of Historical Sayings in English, French, German, Greek, Italian, and Latin* by Edward Latham (London, 1906). Latham gives (1), (2) and (4) as Rabelais' Last Words.

Some sources for Rabelais' Last Words cite Cardinal du Bellay; others cite Cardinal de Chatillon. Accounts include the Cardinal sending a page to inquire about his condition. In Michaud's *Biographie universelle*, Rabelais is reported to have replied: "Dis à monseigneur l'état où tu me vois. Je m'en vais chercher un grand peut-être. Il est au nid de la pie: dis-lui qu'il s'y tienne; et, pour toi, tu ne seras jamais qu'un fou. Tire le rideau, la farce est jouée." (tr. "Tell my lord the state in which you find me. I am in search of a great may-be. He is at the top of the tree: tell him to keep there. As for you, you'll never be aught but a fool. Let the curtain fall, the farce is played out.")

Source: *Biographie universelle,* Book XVI, by J. Fr. Michaud and Louis Gabriel Michaud (Paris, 1811-1862).

All the Last Words attributed to Rabelais are more legend than fact. Historians know very little about Rabelais after 1552. There is no authentic account of his death. Even his death date is uncertain. Although May 3, 1553, is traditionally named as the day he died, he may have died in 1554.

Source: *Exit Lines: Famous (and Not-So-Famous) Last Words* by Brian O'Kill (Essex, England, 1986).

Rabelais' Last Words took on wider popularity and discussion when they were prominently used in John Green's 2006 Printz Award-winning novel *Looking for Alaska*. Miles "Pudge" Halter, the protagonist, has an unusual interest in learning the Last Words of famous people. Of particular interest is his affinity for and interpretation of Rabelais' comment: "I go to seek a Great Perhaps." Pudge leaves home and goes to a boarding school in search of his own "Great Perhaps."

Source: *Looking for Alaska* by John Green (New York, 2005).

Rachel, see **Félix, Rachel Élisa.**

Rachmaninoff, Sergei

(1873-1943) Russian-born musician, composer, conductor, pianist. Notable works: *Rhapsody on a Theme of Paganini; Symphonic Dances;* operas, concertos for piano and orchestra; symphonies, chamber music. After 1918, he spent most of his time in the U.S. Became ill on a farewell tour in 1943; proceeds were to go to war relief. Returned to his home in Beverly Hills and died at age 69, just two months after his tour had started.

Last Words: "Aa-ah! That means it's playing in my head." Spoken to his wife Natalia, who responded, "No one" after he asked her: "Who is it who keeps playing? Why do they keep playing?"

Source: *Sergei Rachmaninoff: A Lifetime in Music* by Sergei Bertensson, Jay Leyda and Sophia Satina (New York, 1956).

Racine, Jean Baptiste

(1639-1699) French poet. Member of the court that included Boileau, La Fontaine, Molière. Notable works: *Andromaque; Bérénice; Phèdre; Iphigénie; Britannicus.* Died at age 59 of cancer in Paris.

Last Words: "I can assure you that, did He grant me the option, living or dying at choice, I should not know which to choose. I have paid the price of death."

Source: *The Life of Racine* by Agnes Mary Frances Robinson (Port Washington, NY, 1972).

Radcliffe, Ann Ward

(1764-1823) English writer, poet. Original surname Ward. First two novels were published anonymously. Used terror and suspense in her plots. Notable works: *The Mysteries of Udolpho; The Italian* (Gothic novels). Suffered from asthma. Died at age 58 in London during an attack that may have been worsened by pneumonia.

Last Words: "There is some substance in that." Spoken after she was given food.

Source: *Ann Radcliffe, a Biography* by Aline Grant (Denver, CO, 1951).

Radcliffe, James,
3rd Earl of Derwentwater

(1689-1716) English nobleman. Companion of Prince James Edward (Old Pretender). Jacobite leader in Stuart rising. Imprisoned, sentenced to death. Executed by beheading at age 26 on Tower Hill.

Last Words: "I am but a poor man; there's ten guineas for you; if I had more, I would give it you; I desire you to do your office so as to put me to the least misery you can." Spoken to the executioner.

Source: *Dilston Hall* by William Sidney Gibson (London, 1850).

Radcliffe, John

(1652-1714) English physician, philanthropist. Physician to Queen Anne. Bequeathed money to Oxford to form a public medical library. Founded an observatory and infirmary there. Died at age 62 at his home in Carshalton, England.

Last Words (written): "I have nothing further than to beseech the Divine Being who is the God of the living to prosper you and all my relations with good and unblameable lives, that when you shall change the world you are now in for a better, we may all meet together in glory and enjoy those ineffable delights which are promised to all that love Christ's coming. Till then, my dear, dear, Milly, take this as a last farewell from your most Affectionate and Dying Brother, J. Radcliffe. N.B. The Jewels and Rings in my gilt cabinet, by my great scrutore, not mentioned in my will, I hereby bequeath to you." Letter to his sister.

Source: *The Five Hundred Best English Letters* by Frederick Edwin Smith, Earl of Birkenhead (London, 1931).

Raleigh, Sir Walter

(1552-1618) English poet, courtier, historian, explorer. Charged with treason. Granted a reprieve that was later revoked. Imprisoned 13 years. Freed to head an expedition to South America. When he returned to England, he was executed.

Different Last Words:

(1) "What dost thou fear? Strike, man, strike!" Spoken to his executioner when Raleigh saw that he was hesitant.

Source: *Sir Walter Raleigh* by Milton Wadman (New York, 1928).

Variation: "Why doth thou not strike? Strike, man!"

Source: "Sir Walter Raleigh" (*The National Magazine,* Vol. IX, No. 1, July 1856).

Variation: "This is a sharp but sure remedy against all miseries and disease." Spoken on the scaffold when he was permitted to feel the edge of the axe. He knelt down, recited a short prayer then said the agreed-upon word to his executioner: "Strike!" His head was severed with two blows.
Source: *Life of Sir Walter Raleigh:1552-1618* by James Augustus St. John (London, 1868).

(2) (doubtful): "So the heart be right, it is no matter which way the head lies." Spoken to the executioner who asked which way he would lay his head.
Source: *Death-bed Scenes: or, Dying With and Without Religion, Designed to Illustrate the Truth and Power of Christianity* by Davis Wasgatt Clark (New York, 1852). Raleigh did speak these words, but they were not his last. After he said them, he told his executioner not to hesitate. See (1).

Ralston, William Chapman

(1826-1875) American businessman, financier. Major investor in the Comstock Lode. Founder of Bank of California. Known as The Man Who Built San Francisco. Soon after his financial empire collapsed, his body was found in San Francisco Bay. A coroner's inquest found evidence Ralston had a stroke.
Last Words: "Keep these [his clothes] for me. There are valuable papers in my pocket."
Source: *Ralston's Ring: California Plunders the Comstock Lode* by George Dunlap Lyman (New York, 1937).

Ramakrishna Paramahamsa

(1836-1886) Hindu philosopher, religious leader. Mystic. Birth name Gadadhar Chatterji. Spent much of his life as a priest in a suburban Calcutta temple dedicated to the goddess Kali. Died at age 50 of throat cancer at Cossipore. His disciples, guided by Swami Vivekananda, have established Ramakrishna centers outside India.
Last Words: "Kali! Kali Kali!"
Source: "Women as Aspects of Mother Goddess in India: A Case Study of Ramakrishna" by M.D. McLelan (*Religion*, Vol. 19, No. 1, February 1969).

Ramal, Walter, see
De La Mare, Walter John.

Rameau, Jean-Philippe

(1683-1764) French musician, composer, organist, harpsichordist. Musical theorist. His book *Traité de l'harmonie* (tr. *Treatise on Harmony*) set the standard for musical style. Wrote baroque operas, motets, cantatas and instrumental music, especially for harpsichord. Notable works: *Hippolyte et Aricie; Castor et Pollux* (operas); *Rigadon; Sarabande; Tambourin; Allemande; Gigue* (harpsichord music). Died at age 80 at his home in Paris after suffering from a fever.
Last Words: "What the devil do you mean to sing to me, priest. You are out of tune."
Source: "Rameau" by Julien Tiersot (*Musical Quarterly,* Vol. XIV, No. 1, 1928).

Ramée, Louise de la ("Ouida")

(1839-1908) English writer. Pen name Ouida. Notable works: *Under Two Flags* (romantic novel); *A Dog of Flanders* (children's story). Died at age 69 of pneumonia in Viareggio, Italy.
Last Words (written): "I have been very ill these days, and my maid is of the opinion that I shall never get well. The weather is intensely cold; and at St. Remo it is so warm and brilliant; it is odd there should be so great a difference. Excuse this rough word; I am ill and cannot write well." Letter.
Source: *Ouida, the Passionate Victorian* by Eileen Bigland (New York, 1951).

Ramsay, David

(1749-1815) American physician, historian, writer, politician. Brother of Congressman Nathaniel Ramsay. South Carolina delegate to Continental Congress. Served as President pro tem during the last term. Served as surgeon in South Carolina militia. Practiced medicine in Charleston, South Carolina. One of the first major historians of the American Revolution. State historian. Wrote several historical works. Member and president of state senate of South Carolina. Shot and killed at age 66 by a demented man in Charleston.
Last Words: "I am not afraid to die; but should that be my fate, I call on all here present to bear witness that I consider the unfortunate perpetrator of this deed a lunatic and free from guilt."
Source: *Historical Papers and Addresses of the Lancaster County Historical Society* by Lancaster County Historical Society, PA (Paper read February 1921).

Ramseur, Stephen Dodson ("Dod")

(1837-1864) American military officer. Major general in Confederate Army in U.S. Civil War. Youngest general in the army. Killed at age 27 in the Battle of Cedar Creek in the Shenandoah Valley.

Last Words (written): "Bear this message to my precious wife: I die a Christian and hope to meet her in Heaven." Dictated in a letter.

Source: *Cyclopedia of Eminent and Representative Men of the Carolinas of the 19th Century*, Vol. II, by Edward McCrady and Samuel A'Court Ashe (Madison, WI, 1892).

Randolph, John ("John Randolph of Roanoke")

(1773-1833) American statesman, politician, diplomat. Known as John Randolph of Roanoke. Member U.S House of Representative and Senate from Virginia. Minister to Russia briefly; resigned for poor health. Erratic speech and behavior began in his mid 40s, indicating a mental abnormality. Died at age 59 of tuberculosis in Philadelphia.

Different Last Words:

(1) "Dying. Home.—Randolph and Betty, my children, adieu! Get me to bed at Chatham or elsewhere, say Hugh Mercer's or Minor's. To bed I conjure you all."

Source: *John Randolph of Roanoke, 1773-1833, a Biography Based Largely on New Material* by William Cabell Bruce (New York, 1922).

(2) "Yes. The two gentlemen will remain with me." Witnesses to his will had come to his bedside. He spoke these words when he was sure they understood manumission and that he confirmed all the conditions of his will respecting his slaves.

Source: *The Life of John Randolph of Roanoke* by Hugh A. Garland (Philadelphia, 1850).

Raphael

(1483-1520) Italian artist, architect. Real name Raffaello Sanzio (or Santi). Studied under his father Giovanni Santi. Assistant to Perugino. One of the great Renaissance artists. Important Italian architect. Appointed chief architect of Saint Peter's. Notable works: *St. George and the Dragon; Sistine Madonna; Transfiguration; Julius II.* Died of fever possibly on his 37th birthday in Rome.

Last word: "Happy." He tried to finish the sentence but could not speak.

Source: *The Last Words (Real and Traditional) of Distinguished Men and Women Collected from Various Sources* by Frederic Rowland Marvin (New York, 1901). Marvin gave as his source "Cardinal Gigiena in a letter to his niece Maria de Bibiena."

Rapp, Johann George

(1757-1847) German-born religious leader. Founder of a sect of Harmonists, or Harmonites, a communal group, and ultimately founder of the towns of Ambridge (Economy, Pennsylvania) and New Harmony (Harmony, Indiana). Rapp died at age 89 in Economy. The communal sect collapsed in 1904.

Last Words: "If I did not so fully believe that the Lord has designed me to place our society before his presence in the land of Canaan, I would consider this my last."

Source: *The Angel and the Serpent: The Story of New Harmony* by William E. Wilson (Bloomington, IN, 1984).

Rasputin, Grigori

(1871-1916) Russian monk, mystic. Known as The Mad Monk. Had so much influence over the court of Tsar Nicholas II that conservatives saw him as a threat. Prince Felix Yusupov and four others tried to kill him by feeding him poisoned food. When that did not work, they shot him then threw him in the Neva River.

Different Last Words:

(1) "What do they want of me! What do they want?"

Source: *Rasputin: The Man Behind the Myth, A Personal Memoir* by Maria Rasputin and Patte Barham (Englewood Cliffs, NJ, 1977). Maria Rasputin was his daughter.

(2) "Felix, Felix, I'll tell the tsarina." Shouted as he ran across a courtyard. Yusupov had just shot him in the chest. Another of his pursuers shot him four times and hit him twice. The group then threw Rasputin's body in the river.

Source: *The Life and Times of Grigorii Rasputin* by Alex de Jonge (New York, 1982).

Ravachol

(1859-1892) French anarchist, terrorist. Real name François Claudius Koenigstein. Used his mother's maiden name, Ravachol. Involved in dynamite bombings against the government. Arrested in 1892. Publicly guillotined at Montbrison, France.

Last Words: "Goodbye, you pigs! Long live anarchy." Cried out as he went to his death.

Source: *Written in Blood: A History of Forensic Detection* by Colin Wilson and Damon Wilson (New York, 2003).

Ravaillac, François

(1578-1610) French assassin. Killed Henry IV of France by stabbing the king in the heart as he sat in his carriage in Paris. Ravaillac was instantly seized and tortured. His body was torn limb from limb by horses.

Last Words: "I receive absolution upon this condition." The condition was that if he were concealing any accomplices he would be eternally damned.

Source: *Biographie universelle*, Book XXXV, by J. Fr. Michaud and Louis Gabriel Michaud (Paris, 1811-1862).

Ravel, Maurice Joseph

(1875-1937) French musician, composer, pianist. Notable works: *La Valse; Daphnis et Chloé; Rhapsodie Espagnole; Mother Goose Suite; Introduction and Allegro* (harp, string quartet, flute and clarinet); *Boléro;* piano concertos. A taxi accident in Paris in 1932 seriously affected his health. He did very little composing afterward. Had brain surgery in 1937 to restore his well-being. The surgery was a failure. Died at age 62.

Different Last Words:

(1) "I look like a Moor." Spoken after he saw his bandaged head in a mirror.

Source: *Bolero: The Life of Maurice Ravel* by Madeleine Goss (New York, 1940).

(2) "Ah! Yes indeed!" His response two days after surgery, when asked if he wanted to see his brother. These were apparently his Last Words as he then lapsed into a coma.

Source: *A Ravel Reader: Correspondence, Article, Interviews* by Arbie Orenstein and Maurice Ravel (New York, 1990).

Ray or Wray, John

(1627-1705) English naturalist, writer. Spelled his name "Wray" until 1670. Known as the Father of English Natural History. Spent his lifetime studying then writing about nature. Published botanical and zoological writings, as well as theological works and proverbs. Notable work: *The Wisdom of God Manifested in the Works of*

the Creation. Died at age 77 in Black Notley, Essex, England.

Last Words: "When you happen to write to my singular friend Dr. Hutton, I pray tell him I received his most obliging and affectionate letter for which I return thanks and acquaint that I am not able to answer it."

Source: *John Ray Naturalist: His Life and Works* by Charles E. Raven (Cambridge, England, 1942).

Raymond, John Howard

(1814-1878) American clergyman, educator. Baptist minister. Professor at Colgate, University of Rochester. President of Brooklyn Collegiate and Polytechnic Institute. President of Vassar College. Died at age 64.

Last Words: "How easy—how easy—how easy—to glide from the work here to the work—." He seemed to want to add the word "there" but did not have enough strength to say it.

Source: *Life and Letters of John Howard Raymond* by John Howard Raymond and Harriet Raymond Lloyd (New York, 1881). Harriet was his daughter.

Read, Thomas Buchanan

(1822-1872) American poet, artist. Portrait painter by profession. Painted Longfellow, William Henry Harrison, George Peabody, Notable poems: "Sheridan's Ride"; "Drifting"; "The Angler." Died at age 50 in New York City.

Last Words: "Sweet are the kisses of one's friends."

Source: *A Conspectus of American Biography: Being an Analytical Summary of American History and Biography, Containing also the Complete Indexes of the National Cyclopedia of American Biography* by George Derby (New York, 1906).

Variation: "Your kisses are very sweet to me." He then died calmly.

Source: *The Poetical Works of T. Buchanan Read* by Thomas Buchanan Read and Frederick Dielman (Philadelphia, 1890). Described as "among his last words."

Reade, Charles

(1814-1884) English novelist, playwright. Trained as lawyer but did not practice law. Notable works: *Peg Woffington; The Cloister and the Hearth; Christie Johnstone; Put Yourself in His Place.* Died at age 69 in London.

Different Last Words:

(1) "I have no hope but in God. God only can create; and God only can re-create."

Source: *Charles Reade,* by Malcolm Elwin (London, 1931).

(2) "Amazing, amazing glory! I am having Paul's understanding." He was referring to Saint Paul, 2 Corinthians 12:1-4, which he had recently discussed.

Source: *Heaven, Home and Happiness,* ed. by Mary Lowe Dickinson and Myrta Avary (New York, 1901).

Récamier, Jeanne Françoise Julie Adélaïde ("Madame Récamier")

(1777-1849) French hostess. Known as Madame Récamier. Her charm and wit attracted many social and political leaders to her salon. Friend of Chateaubriand. Had no money in later years. Lived in rooms in a convent. Became totally blind. Died at age 71 in the 1849 cholera epidemic. Painting of her by J.L. David hangs in the Louvre.

Last Words: "We shall meet again!"

Source: *Madame Récamier and Her Friends* by H. Noel Williams (London, 1907).

Red Jacket (Sagoyewatha)

(1758?-1830) Native American leader, orator. Chief of the Seneca. Known as Red Jacket for the red jacket the British gave him that he often wore. Died of cholera at Buffalo Creek Reservation.

Last Words: "Where is the missionary?" Spoken to his family. A few days before he died, he sent a message to Rev. Mr. Harris, the chief missionary, requesting a meeting. He wanted to die in peace with him. But the missionary was away and did not get the message until after Red Jacket died.

Sources: *Life and Times of Sa-go-ye-wat-ha, or Red Jacket: With a Memoir of the Author by His Son* by William Leete Stone (New York, 1866); *An Account of Sagoyewatha or Red Jacket and His People* by John Niles Hubbard (New York, 1971).

Reed, John

(1887-1920) American journalist, poet. Communist activist. Founded the Communist Labor party. Indicted for sedition. Went to Russia. Notable work: *Ten Days That Shook the World* (his account of the 1917 Bolshevik revolution). Became ill with typhus; was paralyzed and could no longer speak. Died five days later at age 32 in Moscow. His story was told in the movie *Reds* (1981).

Last Words: "You know how it is when you go to Venice. You ask people, 'Is this Venice?' just for the pleasure of hearing the reply."

Sources: "The Last Days with John Reed. A Letter to Max Eastman in New York from Louise Bryant in Moscow, November 14, 1920" (*The Liberator* [NY], 4:2.35, February 1921); *The Lost Revolutionary* by Richard O'Connor and Dale L. Walker (New York, 1967).

Reed, Thomas Brackett

(1839-1902) American politician, lawyer. Member and Speaker of U.S. House of Representatives from Maine. Reed Rules, adopted in 1890, were named for him. Resigned from Congress. Practiced law in New York City. Died at age 63 in Washington, D.C.

Last Words: "Doctor, you have no legal right to do that. It is the third time you have taken that liberty. I will have you to understand that the citizen is not obliged to submit to the dictation of the man with the hoe." Spoken to his physician.

Source: *The Life of Thomas Brackett Reed* by Samuel W. McCall (Boston, 1914).

Reed, Walter

(1851-1902) American physician, military officer. Major in U.S. Army. Head of the commission that identified the cause and transmission of yellow fever, making it possible to control the disease. Died at age 51 of peritonitis after surgery for a ruptured appendix. Walter Reed General Hospital, Walter Reed Army Medical Center, Walter Reed Army Institute of Research were named for him. The story of his discovery has been told in *Yellow Jack* (play, movie, television dramas).

Different Last Words:

(1) "I care nothing for that now." His response to a comment he heard that he had been recommended for promotion to colonel.

Source: *Walter Reed and Yellow Fever* by Howard Atwood Kelly (New York, 1906).

(2) "I leave so much."

Source: *Last Words: A Dictionary of Deathbed Quotations* by C. Bernard Ruffin (Jefferson, NC, 1995).

Rees, Goronwy

(1909-1979) Welsh-born journalist, writer, educator, Soviet spy. Oxford-educated Marxist intellectual who became an academic then a journalist for the *Manchester Guardian* and the *Spectator*. Close friends of known defector-spy Guy Burgess and member of Cambridge-5 spy ring. He was recruited by MI5 as a secret agent. Rees was appointed principal at University College of Wales at Aberystwyth in 1953; however, revelations about his relationship with Guy Burgess caused his resignation in 1957. He published his autobiography and several other books. In 1979, he gave a deathbed confession that he had been a Soviet spy. He also confirmed that other known figures were part of a spy ring.

Last Words: "What shall I do next?" Spoken to his son Daniel.

Source: *The Oxford Book of Death* by Dennis Joseph Enright (Oxford, England, 1983).

Reeves, George

(1914-1959) American actor. Birth name George Keefer Brewer. Best known for playing Superman on television in the 1950s. Died suddenly at age 45 at his home in Benedict Canyon, Beverly Hills, California.

Last Words: "I'm tired. I'm going to bed." He went upstairs. A shot was heard. Reeves was found dead on his bed with a bullet in his head. Whether his death was suicide or murder is debated. The mystery surrounding his death was examined in the movie *Hollywoodland* (2006).

Source: *They Went That-a-Way: How the Famous, the Infamous and the Great Died* by Malcolm Forbes with Jeff Bloch (New York, 1988).

Reinhardt, Julia

(1844-1924) American actress, suffragette. Stage star. Appeared in the first play staged at Belasco Theatre in New York City: David Warfield's *A Grand Army Man*. Toured the U.S, for woman's suffrage. Her suffrage speeches inspired Arlie Hines to write the Broadway play *Her Honor the Mayor* in which Reinhardt also starred. Her career was ending as motion pictures were coming of age. She made only one movie. Died at age 80 in New York City.

Last Words: "The Lord is my shepherd, I shall not want."

Source: "Last Curtain Rings on Julia Reinhardt" (*New York Times*, August 31, 1924).

Remington, Frederic Sackrider

(1861-1909) American artist, painter, illustrator, sculptor. Known for his depiction of the American West. Notable works: *The Bronco Buster* (sculpture); *Wounded Bunkie* (sculpture); *Roping Horses in the Corral* (painting). Died at age 48 in Ridgefield, Connecticut.

Last Words: "Cut her loose, Doc." Spoken to the surgeon just before he had an emergency appendectomy. He died of peritonitis and other complications following the surgery.

Source: *Frederic Remington, Artist of the Old West* by Harold McCracken (Philadelphia, 1947).

Renan, Joseph Ernest (Ernest)

(1823-1892) French philosopher, philologist, Orientalist, historian. Leader of French school of critical philosophy. Denied the existence of the supernatural. Questioned the divinity of Christ. Notable work: *Origins of Christianity* (series). Died at age 69 in Paris after a brief illness.

Different Last Words:

(1) "Remove that sun from off the Acropolis!"

Source: *Renan d'après lui-même* by Henriette Psichari (Paris, 1937).

(2) "I have done my work. I die happy. It is the most natural thing in the world to die; let us accept the Laws of the Universe—the heavens and the earth remain."

Source: *La Vie de Ernest Renan* by Madame James Darmesteter (Paris, 1898).

Variation: "Let us submit to the Laws of Nature of which we are one of the manifestations. The heavens and the earth abide."

Source: *Life of Ernest Renan* by Francis Espinasse (London, 1895). Described as "among the last words" Renan spoke to his wife.

Renforth, James

(1842-1871) British athlete. Professional oarsman. One of the four great Tyneside professional oarsmen—along with Harry Clasper, Robert Chambers and Harry Kelly—who elevated the sport of crew. World Sculling Champion in 1868. Formed crew to compete in a race in St. John, New Brunswick, Canada, in 1871. Collapsed midway through the race. Speculation is that it was heart failure or the result of an epileptic fit. He was taken ashore and gained consciousness briefly before dying in a nearby house. The New Brunswick community where he had his last race was renamed Renforth in his honor.

Different Last Words:

(1) "It is not a fit I have had—I will tell you all about it directly." Spoken to his crew mate Harry Kelly.

Source: *Newcastle* [Upon Tyne] *Daily Chronicle*, July 12 1871.

(2) (doubtful): "Harry, I have had something—. (fell back). What will they say in England?"

Source: Various Last Words compilations and Internet sites.

This is most common version of his Last Words. And there is good testimony that he did say this, but it is doubtful that these were his Last Words, because he briefly regained consciousness within the hour before dying, and spoke briefly while conscious.

Source: "James Renforth: A Mystery that is Unsolved" by Clarence R. Walton (*Old Gateshead* No. 322, December 19, 1952).

Variation: "Oh Harry, I have had something given me." This version, reported in some papers, led to speculation that he had been poisoned.

Source: "The Death of Renforth; Inquest on the Body at St. Johns—His Last Words" (*New York Times*, August 25, 1871).

Reno, Jesse Lee

(1823-1862) American military officer. Major general in Union Army in U.S. Civil War. Graduate of West Point, where he became a close friend of Stonewall Jackson. Career officer described as a soldier's soldier. Served in Mexican War. Shot in the chest by a Confederate sharpshooter's bullet near Boonsboro, Maryland. He was posthumously promoted to major general. City of Reno, Nevada, and a county in Kansas were named for him.

Last Words: "Hallo, Sam I'm dead!" He repeated, "Yes, Yes, I'm dead—good bye!" Spoken to Brigadier General Samuel Sturgis. Reno had been taken to Sturgis's command post when he was wounded. Died a few minutes later.

Source: *Remember Reno: A Biography of Major General Jesse Lee Reno* by William F. McConnell (Shippensburg, PA, 1996).

Renoir, Pierre-Auguste

(1841-1919) French artist, painter, sculptor. Leading 19th-century Impressionist. Notable works: *The Luncheon of the Boating Party; The Bathers; Woman with a Parasol*. Developed crippling arthritis. By his early 70s, he was confined to a wheelchair. Had to have his brushes strapped to his hand. Died at age 78 in Cagnes-sur-Mer, France.

Last Words: "I am still progressing."

Source: *Renoir et Ses Amis* by Georges Rivière (Paris, 1921). The author was a friend of Renoir.

Retzius, Anders Jahan

(1742-1821) Swedish chemist, botanist, entomologist. Pupil of Linnaeus. Discovered and classified many new species of insects. Died at age 79 in Stockholm. His Last Words were his observation of the progressive dissolution of his body.

Last Words: "Now the legs are dead; now the muscles of the bowels cease their functions. The last struggle must be heavy, but for all that, it is highly interesting."

Source: *Life and Labor, or Characteristics of Men of Industry, Culture and Genius* by Samuel Smiles (Chicago, 1891).

Revel, Bernard

(1885-1940) Lithuanian-born American Orthodox rabbi, scholar. Imprisoned during the Russian Revolution of 1905. Emigrated to the U.S. in 1906 when released. First president of Yeshiva University from 1915 until he died. Bernard Revel Graduate School of Jewish Studies was named for him. Died at age 55 in New York City. Appeared on $1 U.S. postage stamp as part of the Great Americans series.

Last Words: "You don't measure life by the yardstick of years, but by accomplishments and achievements. It was my privilege to serve God, the Torah, and the children of the Torah."

Source: *Bernard Revel: Builder of American Jewish Orthodoxy* by Aaron Rakeffet-Rothkoff (Philadelphia, 1972).

Reynolds, John Fulton

(1820-1863) American military officer. Fought at Monterrey and Buena Vista in Mexican War. Major general in Union Army in U.S. Civil War. Saw action at Bull Run, Chancellorsville, Fredericksburg. Killed at age 42 in the Battle of Gettysburg.

Last Words: "Forward, forward, men! Drive those fellows out of that! Forward! For God's sake forward." Shot in the head by a Confederate sharpshooter as he shouted these words. He fell from his horse and died.

Source: *The Civil War: A Book of Quotations* by Robert Blaisdell (Mineola, NY, 2004).

Reynolds, Sir Joshua

(1723-1792) English artist, painter, writer. First president of the Royal Academy of Arts. Painted portraits of luminaries of his era, including Samuel Johnson, Goldsmith, Gibbon, Burke, Fox, Garrick, Mrs. Siddons. Knighted in 1769. Career was severely curtailed when he lost sight in one eye in 1789. Died at age 68 in London.

Last Words: "I have been fortunate in long good health and constant success and I ought not complain. I know that all things on earth must have an end, and now I am come to mine."

Source: *The Life and Discourses of Sir Joshua Reynolds* by Sir Joshua Reynolds and Allan Cunningham (Hudson, OH, 1853).

Reynolds, Stephen

(1881-1919) English writer, essayist. Wrote about working class life. Notable works: *A Poor Man's House; The Holy Mountain.* Died at age 37 in Sidmouth, England, during the Spanish influenza epidemic.

Last Words (written): "Reference my letter of last night. Have got influenza myself now. Stop. Pretty sure unable to come to London next week." Sent in a telegram.

Source: *Letters of Stephen Reynolds,* ed. by Harold Wright (London, 1923).

Rhodes, Cecil John

(1853-1902) British administrator, businessman, philanthropist. Emigrated to South Africa. Made a fortune from gold and diamond mining. Died at age 48 from heart disease near Cape Town. Left much of his fortune to establish Rhodes Scholarships.

Different Last Words:

(1) "So little done, so much to do." Told by his physician to a crowd waiting outside his cottage.

Sources: *Cecil Rhodes: The Anatomy of Empire* by John Marlowe (London, 1972); *Who's Who in British History* (New York, 1998).

(2) "Turn me over, Jack."

Source: *Cecil Rhodes* by Sarah Gertrude Millin (New York, 1933).

(3) He spoke the names of his brother and some others present.

Source: "Death of Cecil Rhodes" (*New York Times* March 27, 1902).

Ribault or Ribaut, Jean

(1520-1565) French military officer, navigator, explorer, colonizer. Sent by France to explore and colonize southeastern North America. Built Charlesfort for colonists in present-day South Carolina. He returned to France for more supplies. While he was gone, the colony fell on hard times. Some colonists returned to France. Others deserted. The French government sent Ribault back to America to save the settlement. Soon after he arrived, the Spanish attacked, killing 350 men, including Ribault.

Last Words (doubtful): "Spare the lives of defenseless men who have confided in your honor."

Source: *A Conspectus of American Biography: Being an Analytical Summary of American History and Biography, Containing also the Complete Indexes of the National Cyclopedia of American Biography* by George Derby (New York, 1906).

Ribault's Last Words were most likely an indirect quote drawn from the writings of artist and mapmaker Jacques Le Moyne de Morgues, one of the few survivors. He published an account of his experiences in *Brevis narratio eorum quae in Florida Americal provincia Gallis acciderunt* (Frankfurt, Germany, 1591).

Ribbentrop, Joachim von

(1893-1946) German politician, diplomat. Nazi foreign minister during World War II. Found guilty at Nuremberg War Crimes Trial. Executed at age 53 by hanging.

Last Words: "God save Germany! My last wish is that Germany rediscover its unity and that an alliance be made between the East and West and that peace reign on earth."

Source: *New York Times,* October 16, 1946.

Rice, Henry Grantland

(1880-1954) American sportswriter. Successor to Walter Camp in selecting college football All-America teams beginning 1925.

Gave backfield of Notre Dame 1924 team the name "Four Horsemen" in the *New York Herald Tribune* story reporting on their game with Army at the Polo Grounds. Died at age 73 of a stroke in New York.

Last Words (written): "Willie, at least, has a golden start." Printed at the end of his final sports column.

Source: *New York Sunday Mirror,* July 18, 1954.

Rice, James Clay

(1829-1864) American military officer. Brigadier general in Union Army in U.S. Civil War. Leg shattered at Spotsylvania, Virginia. Died soon after he was wounded.

Last Words: "Tell the Forty-fourth I am done fighting. Turn me over and let me die with my face to the foe. Pray for me, Lieutenant." He was referring to his regiment, the 44th New York Volunteer Infantry,

Source: *A History of the Forty-fourth Regiment, New York Volunteer Infantry, in the Civil War, 1861-1865* by Eugene Arus Nash (Chicago, 1911).

Rice, John Holt

(1777-1831) American clergyman, educator, publisher. Presbyterian. Known as a powerful and fervent preacher. Earned a D.D. from Princeton in 1819. Published periodicals: *Christian Monitor; Virginia Evangelical and Literary Magazine.* Founder of Union Theological Seminary in Virginia. Died at age 53 in Hampton Sidney, Virginia.

Last Words: "Mercy is triumphant." Spoken on his deathbed. Several people were in his room waiting to document his Last Words. Mrs. Goodrich was not sure of his final word. She thought it was "great." Mrs. Rice said she thought it was a longer word: The dying man said the word "triumphant." He then put his head down and died.

Source: *A Memoir of the Rev. John Holt Rice, D.D, First Professor of Christian Theology in Union Theological Seminary, Virginia* by William Maxwell and John H. Rice (Philadelphia,1835).

Rich, Bernard ("Buddy")

(1917-1987) American musician. Jazz and Big Band drummer, bandleader. Known for his virtuoso technique, power, speed, improvisation. Often billed the "Best Drummer in the World." Died at age 69 of heart failure following surgery in Los Angeles.

Last Words: "Yeah, country music." Spoken prior to heart surgery while losing consciousness, in response to a question asked by a nurse: "Is there anything you can't take?" She was referring to drugs to which he might have an allergy. He went under anesthesia and never regained consciousness.

Source: "Metro" by John Hall (*Orange County* [California] *Register*, June 23, 1989).

Rich, Mary, Countess of Warwick

(1625-1678) Irish-born aristocrat, writer, diarist. Puritan. Wrote on religious themes. Daughter of Richard Boyle, Earl of Cork. Wife of Charles Rich, 4th Earl of Warwick.

Last Words: "Ladies, if I were but one hour in Heaven, I would not be again with you, well as I love you." Spoken to her attendants.

Source: *Mary Rich, Countess of Warwick (1625-1678): Her Family and Friends* by Charlotte F. Smith (London, 1901).

Richard I, King of England

(1157-1199) English monarch, Crusader. Son of Henry II of England and Eleanor of Aquitaine. Known as the Lion-Hearted. Participated in the Third Crusade. Fatally wounded by an archer during a siege in central France. He had the archer brought before him, forgave him, then died at age 41.

Different Last Words:

(1) "Youth, I forgive thee." Spoken to the archer who hit him with an arrow. Richard then told his attendants: "Loose his chains and give him one hundred shillings." One of his captains had the archer killed after Richard died.

Source: *The Comprehensive History of England: Civil and Military, Religious, Intellectual and Social: From the Earliest Period to the Suppression of the Sepoy Revolt* by Charles MacFarlane and Thomas Thomson (London, 1861).

(2) "I place all my trust, after God, in thee, that thou wilt make provision for my soul's welfare with motherly care, to the utmost of thy power." Spoken to his mother, Eleanor of Aquitaine.

Source: *Richard the Lion Hearted* by Kate Norgate (London, 1924).

Richard III, King of England,

(1452-1485) English monarch. King of the House of York. Duke of Gloucester. Killed at age 32 at Bosworth Field ending the War of the Roses. Died while he was attacking Henry Tudor who became Henry VII, first monarch of the Tudor line. His story was adapted by Shakespeare in *Richard III.*

Last Words: "I will die King of England. I will not budge a foot.—Treason! Treason!" Spoken at the Battle of Bosworth Field.

Source: *The Life and Reign of Richard the Third to Which Is Added the Story of Perkin Warbeck* by James Gairdner (Cambridge, England, 1898).

Richelieu, Armand Jean du Plessis, Cardinal, Duc de

(1585-1642) French statesman, prelate. Known as Eminence Rouge (Red Eminence) from the color of his cardinal's robes. Chief minister of Louis XIII. Bishop of Luçon. Created cardinal in 1622. Chief minister of Louis XIII. Established royal absolutism in France. Died at age 57 in Paris.

Different Last Words:

(1) "Niece, there are no truths but those in the Gospels. One should believe in them alone." Spoken to a niece who brought him a holy relic.

Source: *Richelieu* by D.P. O'Connell (Cleveland, OH, 1968).

(2) "I have had no enemies save those of the State." Spoken when he was asked if he pardoned his enemies.

Source: *Richelieu: A Study* by Hilaire Belloc (Philadelphia, 1929).

(3) "Absolutely, and I pray God to condemn me, if I had any other aim than the welfare of God and the state." His response when asked whether he pardoned his enemies.

Source: *Book of Catholic Quotations Compiled from Approved Sources Ancient, Medieval and Modern*, ed. by John Chapin (New York, 1956).

Richelieu, Louis François Armand du Plessis, Duc de

(1696-1788) French nobleman, diplomat, military officer. Lieutenant general. Marshal of France. Grandnephew of Cardinal Richelieu. Died at age 92 in Paris.

Last Words: "What would Louis XIV have said?" Spoken as he lay dying on the eve of the French Revolution.

Source: *The French Revolution: A History* by Thomas Carlyle (London, 1837).

Richmond, Legh

(1772-1827) English clergyman, writer, editor. Rector of Turvey Church in England. Published books about village life that were best sellers in his lifetime. They were combined into one volume, *Annals of the Poor,* in 1814. He also edited a collection of Reformation biographies: *Fathers of the English Church.* Died at age 55 in Turvey, Bedfordshire, England.

Last Words: "It will be all confusion." His wife asked him what would be confusion. He replied: "The church! There will be such confusion in my church!"

Source: *A Memoir of the Rev. Legh Richmond* by T.S. Grimshawe (Boston, 1829).

Richter, Jean Paul Friederich

(1763-1825) German writer, humorist, novelist. Pen name Jean Paul. His excessively sentimental books were widely read in his lifetime then faded in popularity. Lost his eyesight in 1824. Died at age 62 of dropsy in Bayreuth, Germany.

Different Last Words:

(1) "We'll let it go." Spoken when he found he was not understood.

Source: *Jean Paul* by Walther Harich (Leipzig, Germany, 1925).

(2) "My flowers. My lovely flowers." He was acknowledging a wreath of flowers brought to him by a well-wisher. Although he could neither see nor smell them, he enjoyed touching them.

Source: "Jean Paul Richter" by Julia Colman (*The Ladies' Repository, Monthly Periodical Devoted to Literature, Arts and Religion,* Vol. 19, No. 2).

Richthofen, Freiherr Manfred von ("Red Baron")

(1892-1917) German military officer, airman. Fighter pilot. Most successful flying ace of World War I. Had 80 combat victories. Killed at age 25 when his plane was shot down behind British lines while flying near the Somme River in France.

Last Words: "What's the hurry? Are you afraid I won't come back?" Spoken to a bystander who asked for an autograph as the Baron climbed into his plane.

Source: *Slipping the Surly Bonds: Great Quotations on Flight* compiled by David English (New York, 1998).

Rickey, Branch Wesley

(1881-1965) American professional baseball executive. Helped break the major league color barrier by signing Jackie Robinson to the Brooklyn Dodgers in 1946. Had a heart attack in Columbia, Missouri, while making an acceptance speech at Missouri Sports Hall of Fame. Lingered in a coma nearly a month. Died at age 83.

Last Words: "I don't believe that I'm going to be able to speak any longer." He collapsed into a chair next to his wife on the stage.

Source: *Branch Rickey: Baseball's Ferocious Gentleman* by Lee Lowenfish (Lincoln, NE, 2007).

Ridley, Nicholas

(1500?-1555) English prelate, reformer, martyr. Protestant. Bishop of London. Tried to help Lady Jane Grey secure the English throne. With Mary Tudor's accession to the throne, Ridley was declared a heretic, excommunicated, condemned and burned at the stake along with Hugh Latimer in front of Balliol College.

Last Words: "Let the fire come unto me, I cannot burn. Lord, have mercy on me." The fire under him was poorly made and the flames were not high enough. When Ridley called out, a bystander made the flames higher to hasten his death.

Source: *Fathers of the English Church,* ed. by Legh Richmond (London, 1809).

Riker, John Lafayette

(1822-1862) American lawyer, military officer. Colonel in Union Army in U.S. Civil War. Original commander of the Anderson Zouaves. Killed in action at age 39 at the Battle of Fair Oaks during the Peninsular Campaign.

Last Words: "Boys, we're surrounded—give them the cold steel!"

Source: *The Honors of the Empire State in the War of the Rebellion* by Thomas S. Townsend (New York, 1889).

Riley, James Whitcomb

(1849-1916) American poet, editor, writer. Known as the Poet of the Common People. Worked briefly as local editor for the *Anderson* [Indiana] *Democrat*. Often wrote in dialect. Notable poems: "When the Frost is on the Punkin"; "Little Orfant Annie." Had a stroke. Died at age 66 in Indianapolis.

Last Words: He asked the nurse for a glass of water then fell asleep and never woke up. His body lay in state in the Indiana capitol, while thousands of people filed by.

Source: *James Whitcomb Riley: The Poet as Flying Island of the Night* by Thomas E.Q. Williams (Greenfield, IN, 1997).

Rilke, Rainer Maria

(1875-1926) Bohemian-born poet, writer, novelist. Birth name René Karl Wilhelm Johann Josef Maria Rilke. Lived in Paris 12 years while writing Rodin biography. Notable works: *Sonnets to Orpheus; Duino Elegies*. Died at age 51 of leukemia at a sanatorium in Valmont, Switzerland.

Last Words (written): "My dear, dear Supervielle, gravely ill, painfully, miserably, humbly ill, I find myself again a moment in the comfortable knowledge that even there, in that untenantable and inhuman plane, your message and all the influences it brings could reach me, I think of you, poet, friend, and in so doing I still think of the world— poor shard of a vessel that remembers being of the earth. (But how it abuses our senses and their 'dictionary,' the pain that turns their pages!) R." Written in a letter. Jules Supervielle was a French poet.

Source: *Rilke, Man and Poet: A Biographical Study* by Nora Wydenbruck (London, 1949).

Last Words (spoken): "I don't want the doctor's death. I want to have my own freedom."

Source: *Rilke: A Life* by Wolfgang Leppman (New York, 1984).

Rimbaud, Jean Nicolas Arthur

(1854-1891) French poet. Influenced modern poetry with subject matter, imagery and verse form. Close friend of Paul Verlaine for a time. Notable works: *The Drunken Boat; Illuminations; A Season in Hell*. Died at age 37 in Marseilles, France.

Last Words (written): "To the Harbormaster: Please therefore send me the tariff of services from Aphinar to Suez. I am completely paralyzed, and so I wish to embark in good time. Tell me at what time I must be carried on board." Dictated to his sister Isabelle the day before he died.

Source: *Rimbaud: A Biography* by Graham Robb (New York, 2000).

Ripley, Robert LeRoy

(1890-1949) American entrepreneur, cartoonist, traveler, collector of curiosities.

Created *Ripley's Believe It or Not!* series that appeared in 3,000 newspapers in 14 languages during the first half of the 20th century. Series was a highly successful radio show beginning in 1933. Moved to television in 1949. Ripley suffered from hypertension. Died at age 58 in New York City less than three months after the TV series began. Last Words: "I'll be out to the farm to see you tomorrow." Spoken to friend Bugs Baer on the phone from a New York medical center where he had gone for a checkup. When he hung up, he collapsed and died of a heart attack.

Source: *Ripley The Modern Marco Polo: The Life and Times of the Creator of "Believe It or Not"* by Bob Considine (Garden City, NY, 1961).

Rita of Cascia, Saint

(1381-1457) Italian widow, holy woman, nun. Became an Augustinian nun after her husband was murdered and twin sons died. Served her order 40 years at the monastery of Saint Mary Magdalen in Cascia. Developed signs of Stigmata. Died at age 76. Canonized in 1900.

Last Words: "May God bless you and may you always remain in holy peace and love with your beloved Spouse Jesus Christ." Spoken to the nuns who were with her when she died.

Source: *Life of Saint Rita of Cascia of the Order of Saint Augustine: Advocate of the Impossible; Model of Maidens, Wives, Mothers, Widows and Nuns* by José Sicardo and Daniel Joseph Murphy (Chicago, 1916)

Rittenhouse, David

(1732-1796) American astronomer, mathematician, surveyor, educator. Inventor, clockmaker and scientific instrument craftsman. Vice-provost, trustee, and professor at what would become the University of Pennsylvania. Built one of the first telescopes in the U.S. Member of American Philosophical Society, succeeding Benjamin Franklin as leader. First director of U.S. Mint. Part of the team that surveyed Mason-Dixon line. Died at age 64 of cholera in Philadelphia. Rittenhouse Square in Philadelphia was named for him.

Last Words: "Yes, you have made the way to God easier." Spoken to his nephew after receiving a poultice of meal and laudanum

to relieve his pain.

Source: *Memoirs of the Life of David Rittenhouse, LLD. F.R.S. Late President of the American Philosophical Society, &c Interspersed with Various Notices of Many Distinguished Men: With an Appendix, Containing Sundry Philosophical and Other Papers, Most of Which Have Not Hitherto Been Published* by William Barton (Philadelphia, 1813). The author was Rittenhouse's nephew.

Rivarol, Antoine de

(1753-1801) French writer, journalist, epigrammatist. Royalist supporter during the French Revolution. Left France in 1792. Died at age 47 in exile in Berlin, Germany. Known for maxims such as: "The most civilized people are as near to barbarism as the most polished steel is to rust." "Nations, like metals, have only a superficial brilliancy." The complete works of Antoine de Rivarol were published in five volumes in 1805.

Last Words: "My Friends, it comes. These roses will change into poppies. It is time to contemplate eternity."

Source: "The Odd Chair of the French Academy" (*Titan: A Monthly Magazine*, Vol. XXIV, January–June, 1857).

Variation: "My Friends, behold the great shadow approaches. These roses will change into poppies. It is time to contemplate eternity"

Source: *Men and Women of the Eighteenth Century*, Vol. I, by Arsène Houssaye (New York, 1857).

Rivera, Diego

(1886-1957) Mexican artist, muralist, painter. Notable works: *Creation; Mother Earth; Detroit Industry*. Commissioned to do mural *Man at the Crossroads* for Rockefeller Center. Rivera's portrait of Lenin in the painting led to its removal in 1934. Rivera did a new version of the painting in Mexico City. Died at age 70 in Mexico City.

Last Words: "On the contrary. Lower it." Spoken to his wife, Emma Hurtado, who had come into his room and asked if she should raise his bed.

Source: *Diego Rivera: My Art, My Life: An Autobiography* by Diego Rivera with Gladys March (New York, 1991).

Rizal, José

(1861-1896) Philippine national leader, physician, poet, sculptor, writer, novelist. Full name José Protasio Rizal Mercado y Alonso

Realonda. Exiled for writing the political novel *Noli me tangere*. Arrested in Cuba in 1896 and returned to Philippines. Executed at age 35 by firing squad in Manila for alleged revolutionary activities.

Last Words: "O Father, how terrible it is to die! How one suffers! Father, I forgive every one from the bottom of my heart; I have no resentment against any one: believe me, your Reverence."

Source: *The Hero of the Filipinos: The Story of Jose Rizal, Poet, Patriot and Martyr* by Charles Edward Russell and E.B. Rodriguez (New York, 1923).

Rizzo, Francis Lazzaro ("Frank")

(1920-1991) American law officer, politician. Dominant political force in Philadelphia for a quarter century. First Italian-American Philadelphia police commissioner. Mayor of Philadelphia. Died at age 70.

Last Words: "Hello, there, Jodi." Spoken to his secretary at lunchtime in his downtown campaign headquarters. He then went into a restroom where he collapsed of a massive heart attack. Pronounced dead at a hospital a short time later.

Source: *Frank Rizzo: The Last Big Man in Big City America* by S.A. Paolantonio (Philadelphia, 1993). The author was a political reporter who covered Rizzo's career for the *Philadelphia Inquirer*.

Rob Roy, see MacGregor, Robert.

Robert I, King of the Scots ("The Bruce")

(1274-1329) Scottish monarch. Known as Robert the Bruce. Fought the English in Ireland and along the Scottish border until England formally recognized an independent Scotland with the Treaty of Northampton in 1328. Died at age 54 in Dumbarton, Scotland. His body was buried at Dunfermline Abbey. His heart was buried at Melrose Abbey.

Last Words: "Thanks be to God! For I shall now die in peace, since I know that the most valiant and accomplished knight of my kingdom will perform that for me which I am unable to do for myself." His response to the promise Lord James Douglas made to remove his heart from his body when he died, embalm it and take it to the Holy Sepulchre where Christ was buried. The king had vowed to go on a Crusade. Despite Douglas's promise, Robert's heart never made it to the Holy Land. It was carried in one of the Crusades and reached Granada in Spain, but went no farther. It eventually was taken back to Scotland.

Source: *Chroniques* (*Chronicles of England, France, Spain, and the Adjoining Countries*) by Jean Froissart (London, 1839).

Robertson, Frederick William

(1816-1853) English theologian, clergyman. Gained reputation as a preacher. Sermons were published in 1855. He was crippled by an illness that caused agonizing pain. Died at age 37 of tuberculosis in Brighton.

Last Words: "I cannot bear it. Let me rest. I must die. Let God do His work." Spoken when his caregivers tried to change his body position in bed.

Source: *Life and Letters of Fred. W. Robertson, M. A., Incumbent of Trinity Chapel, Brighton, 1847-53* by Stopford A. Brooke (Boston, 1865).

Robertson, James

(1839-1902) Scottish-born clergyman. Pastor of Norwich. First pastor of Knox Church, Winnipeg. Superintendent of missions in Manitoba, Northwest and British Columbia.

Last Words: "I am done out." Spoken just before he fell asleep.

Source: *The Life of James Robertson, Missionary Superintendent In the Northwest Territories* by Charles W. Gordon (New York, 1908).

Robertson, Thomas William

(1829-1871) English actor, playwright, stage manager. Gained fame as the author of mid-Victorian era society plays. Notable plays: *David Garrick; Society; Ours*. Died at age 42 in London.

Last Words: "Good-bye, my son, and God bless you. Come and see me tomorrow. If I don't speak to you, don't be frightened, and don't forget to kiss your father."

Source: *Thomas William Robertson: His Plays and Stagecraft* by Maynard Savin (Providence, RI, 1950).

Robertson, Walford Graham

(1866-1948) British writer, artist, illustrator. Born into a wealthy London family. Worked in many forms and styles. Notable works: *Gold, Frankincense, & Myrrh, & Other Pageants for a Baby Girl; Pinkie and the Fairies*. His portrait, painted when he was 28, is one of John Singer Sargent's most famous works. Died at age 82.

Last Words (written): "I should like the ashes to be buried or otherwise disposed of at the crematorium, with no tombstone nor inscription to mark the place of burial. No funeral, no mourning, no flowers. By request. If these arrangements are carried out one may perhaps manage to die without making a public nuisance of oneself. W. Graham Robertson."

Source: *Letters from Graham Robertson* by W. Graham Robertson, ed. by Kerrison Preston (London, 1953). The editor was a close friend of Robertson.

Robespierre, Maximilien François Marie Isidore de

(1758-1794) French revolutionist. Was crowned, along with Pétion Villeneuve, by the people of Paris as "incorruptible patriots." Opposed the Girandists. Leader of the Jacobin Club. Inaugurated and led Reign of Terror. Overthrown by the 9th Thermiador, arrested. Executed by guillotine the next day at age 36. His death is depicted in a painting by J. Beys.

Last Words: "Thank you, sir." Spoken to one of his executioners when a tight belt that was constricting him was loosened.

Source: *Robespierre: A Study* by Hilaire Belloc (New York, 1908).

Robinson, Edwin Arlington

(1869-1935) American poet. Won first Pulitzer Prize awarded for poetry for *Collected Poems* (1922). Won a second Pulitzer Prize for *The Man Who Died Twice* (1925) and a third Pulitzer for *Tristram* (1928). Died at age 65 in a New York City hospital while revising galleys of his last work, *King Jasper*.

Last Words: "We'll have our cigarettes together. Good night." Spoken to a friend who visited him in the hospital.

Source: *Edwin Arlington Robinson, a Biography* by Hermann Hagedorn (New York, 1938).

Robinson, Henry Crabb

(1775-1867) English diarist, journalist, lawyer. His diaries provide valuable information on life in the early Romantic era among his friends and acquaintances who included Goethe and Wordsworth. Died at age 91.

Last Words (written): "He [Matthew Arnold] thinks of Germany as he ought, and of Goethe with high admiration. On this

point I can possibly give him assistance, which he will gladly—But I feel incapable to go on." Entry in his diary.

Source: *Diary, Reminiscences and Correspondence of Henry Crabb Robinson,* selected and ed. by Thomas Sadler (Boston, 1869).

Robinson, William

(d. 1659) American martyr. Quaker who was tried, condemned to death and executed by hanging in Boston, Massachusetts, along with Marmaduke Stevenson and Mary Dyer for their religious beliefs.

Last Words: "I suffer for Christ, in whom I live, and for whom I die." Spoken after he ascended the ladder to be executed.

Source: *The History of the Society of Friends in America* by James Bowden (New York, 1972).

Robota, Rosa (Rojza, Rozia or Róza)

(1921-1945) Polish concentration camp rebel. Part of Sonderkommando revolt in 1944. While working at Birkenau Effektenlager adjacent to Crematorium IV at Auschwitz, she smuggled gunpowder collected by women in the munitions factory and transferred it to a member of the Sonderkommando. The gunpowder was used to manufacture weapons and blow up the crematorium. Robota, age 23, and three other women were arrested by the Gestapo, interrogated under torture, and hanged. The Rosa Robota Gates at Montefiore Randwick (Sydney, Australia) are named in her memory.

Last Words: "Be strong. Have courage." Spoken as the trap door opened.

Source: "Unorthodox Tribute" by Joe Drape (*New York Times*, June 24, 2000).

Rochambeau, Jean-Baptiste Donatien de Vimeur, Comte de

(1725-1807) French military officer. Brigadier general. Commanded French forces in the American Revolution. His troops forced Cornwallis to surrender. After the war, he returned to France and was created marshal of France. Died at age 81 at his castle in Thore. His statue, a gift from France, is in Lafayette Square, Washington D.C. Bridge over Potomac River named for him. French and U.S. navies named ships for him.

Last Words: "You must agree that I would have cut a pretty figure at the marriage yesterday." Spoken to his wife, Madame de Rochambeau, about the wedding of his apprentice he had to miss as he was not well enough to attend.

Source: *Rochambeau, Father and Son: A Life of the Maréchal de Rochambeau* by Jean-Edmond Weelen, tr. Lawrence Lee (New York, 1936).

Rockefeller, John Davidson, Sr.

(1839-1937) American oil magnet., industrialist, philanthropist. Founded Standard Oil Company in 1879. Remained active in oil until he retired in 1911. Founder of Rockefeller dynasty. Endowed several philanthropic institutions. Grandfather of Nelson A. Rockefeller who served as U.S. Vice President under Gerald Ford. Died at age 97 at his home in Ormond Beach, Florida.

Last Words: "Raise me up a little." His cousin, valet and night nurse were at his bedside.

Source: "Last Titan" (*Time* magazine, May 31, 1937).

Rockne, Knute Kenneth

(1888-1931) Norwegian-born American athlete. Football player, coach. Head coach of Notre Dame football team from 1918 to 1931. Killed at age 43 aboard F-10 Fokker monoplane en route to California with five other passengers. Plane went down in a storm near Bazaar, Kansas.

Last Words: "I suggest you buy some reading material. These plane engines make an awful racket and just about shut off most conversation." Spoken to another passenger just before boarding the plane.

Source: *Rockne: The Coach, The Man, The Legend* by Jerry Brondfield (New York, 1976).

Rodgers, James Charles ("Jimmie")

(1897-1933) American musician, country music singer. Notable recording: *Blue Yodel No. 9* (with Louis Armstrong in 1930). Contracted tuberculosis in his late 20s. Died at age 35 of a lung hemorrhage in New York City. Made a number of recordings in New York City a few days before he died, including *Mississippi Delta Blues* and *Years Ago*. Inducted into Country Music Hall of Fame and Rock and Roll Hall of Fame.

Last Words: "Let me take a blow." Spoken to his brother-in-law Alex Larson as he was gasping for air.

Source: *The Guinness Encyclopedia of Popular Music* by Colin Larkin (Enfield, Middlesex, England, 1995).

Rodgers, James W.

(1911-1960) American murderer. Executed by firing squad in Utah. Notable mostly for his Last Words.

Last Words: "Bring me a bullet-proof vest." His response when asked if he had a final request.

Source: *Low Man Rides Again* by H. Allen Smith (Garden City, NY, 1973).

Rodgers, John

(1772-1838) American military officer. Naval commodore in the War of 1812. Died at age 66 in Philadelphia. His son John Rodgers served in the U.S. Civil War, and his great-grandson John Rodgers served in World War I. Six ships have been named in their honor, three as USS *John Rodgers* and three as USS *Rodgers*.

Last Words: "Butler, do you know the Lord's Prayer? Then repeat it for me." Spoken to his servant.

Source: *Commodore John Rodgers, Captain, Commodore, and Senior Officer of the American Navy, 1773–1838: A Biography* by Charles Oscar Paullin (Cleveland, OH, 1910).

Rodin, François Auguste René

(1840-1917) French artist, sculptor. Notable works: *The Thinker; The Burghers of Calais; The Kiss;* portrait busts of Victor Hugo, George Bernard Shaw, Mahler, Proust and others. Gave his art to the French government. Rodin Museum was created in Paris. Works are also represented at the Rodin Museum in Philadelphia, Pennsylvania. Died at age 77 at Meudon near Paris.

Last Words: "And people say that Puvis de Chavannes is not a fine artist!" Pierre Puvis de Chavannes was a major French mural painter who decorated many public buildings in France.

Source: *Rodin: The Man and His Art with Leaves from His Note-Book* by Judith Cladel (New York, 1937). The author was a close friend.

Rodin, Rose Beuret

(1845?-1917) French woman. Legally became the wife of sculptor Auguste Rodin in 1917. Their relationship began 53 years earlier. Died at age 72.

Last Words: "I don't mind dying, but it's leaving my man. Who will look after him?

What will happen to the poor thing?"
Source: *Rodin: Immortal Peasant* by Anne Leslie (New York, 1937).

Rodney, George Brydges, 1st Baron Rodney

(1718-1792) British military officer. Naval admiral. Served in Seven Years War. Destroyed the Spanish fleet. Captured Dutch West Indies Islands. Defeated the French fleet under deGrasse. Received barony in 1782. Died at age 73 in London. At least four British warships were named for him.
Last Words: "I am very ill indeed."
Source: *Life of Rodney* by David Hannay (London, 1891).

Rodriguez, Blas de

(d. 1597) Spanish holy man, martyr, friar. Left Spain for Florida in 1580. One of five Franciscan friars martyred there in 1597. Martyred for insisting on monogamy in Christian marriages. Killed by chief's son known as Juanillo and his followers in the village of Tupiqui, later part of the Georgia coast.
Last Words: "My sons, for me it is not difficult to die. Even if you do not cause it, the death of this body is inevitable. We must be ready at all times, for we, all of us, have to die someday. But what does pain me is that the Evil one has persuaded you to do this offensive thing against your God and Creator. It is a further source of deep grief to me that you are unmindful of what we missionaries have done for you in teaching you the way to eternal life and happiness." Spoken to the Indians who informed him they had come to kill him. He was allowed to say Mass before he was tomahawked to death.
Source: *Saints of North America* by Vincent J. O'Malley (Huntington, IN, 2004).

Rogers, John

(1500-1555) English clergyman, translator, commentator, martyr. Divinity lecturer at St. Paul's London. First English Protestant martyr. Executed during the reign of Mary I of England. Sent to Newgate Prison for preaching against Catholicism. Sentenced to death. Taken to Smithfield to be executed. Refused to revoke his doctrine. Burned at the stake.
Different Last Words:

(1) "Lord, receive my spirit."
Source: *A Pictorial History of England: Being a History of the People, as Well as a History of the Kingdom* by George Lillie Craik (London, 1838-1841).
(2) "But I will pray for thee." Spoken on his way to the stake to the sheriff who called him a heretic. Rogers responded: "That shall be known on the day of judgment." The sheriff replied: "Well, I shall never pray for thee."
Source: *Book of Martyrs and the Acts and Monuments of the Church* by John Fox (or Foxe). First published 1563, ed. by John Cumming (London, 1851).

Rogers, Nathaniel Peabody

(1794-1846) American lawyer, abolitionist, editor. Radical proponent of many causes including abolition, Native American rights and temperance. Edited anti-slave newspaper *Herald of Freedom* in Concord, New Hampshire. Henry David Thoreau wrote an essay about him: entitled "Herald of Freedom." Died at age 52 in Concord.
Last Words: "Oh, it sustains me unspeakably—the reflection that I have done right." His response to a friend who asked if it consoled him that he had not labored in vain.
Source: *Modern Agitators: Or, Penn Portraits of Living American Reformers* by David W. Bartlett (New York, 1855).

Rogers, William Penn Adair ("Will")

(1879-1935) American actor, humorist. Popular newspaper columnist, movie star. Killed at age 55 in a plane crash near Point Barrow, Alaska. Plane was piloted by pioneer aviator Wiley Post, who was also killed.
Last Words: "Well, Wiley's got her warmed up. Let's go." Message broadcast by radio.
Source: *Will Rogers Scrapbook* by Will Rogers and Bryan B. Sterling (New York, 1976).

Rohan-Chabot, Louis-François-Auguste, Duc de

(1788-1833) French nobleman, prelate. Entered a seminary after his wife died. Ordained in 1822. Archbishop of Auch. Archbishop of Besançon. Elevated to cardinal in 1830. Died at age 44 in Besançon, France.
Last Words: "I am nothing, nothing, less than nothing!"
Source: *Le Cardinal de Rohan-Chabot, Archeveque de Besançon, 1788-1833* by Charles Baille (Paris, 1904).

Röhm, Ernst

(1887-1934) German military officer. Head of the Nazi Sturmabteilung (SA). Killed on Hitler's order with other SA leaders in a massive purge known as the Night of the Long Knives. The growing size and power of the SA had concerned Hitler.

Last Words: "If I am to be killed, let Adolf do it himself." Hitler had ordered that Röhm be allowed to commit suicide. When he refused, he was shot and killed by two Schutzstaffel (SS) men.

Source: *The Great Pictorial History of World Crime* by Jay Robert Nash (Wilmette, IL, 2004).

Roland de la Platière, Marie-Jeanne Philipon ("Madame Roland")

(1754-1793) French matron. Wife of former government official Jean-Marie Roland de la Platière, who led the Girondist party during the French Revolution. When the Girondists fell, she was arrested, tried before a Revolutionary Tribunal, condemned and guillotined at age 39. Her husband committed suicide when he learned of her death.

Different Last Words:

(1) "O Liberty, how you are mocked!" As she spoke, she nodded to a nearby statue of Liberty.

Source: *The Private Memoirs of Madame Roland* by Marie Roland, ed. with Introduction by Edward Gilpin Johnson (Chicago, 1900).

Variation: "O Liberté! O Liberté! Que de crimes on commet en ton nom!" (tr. "O Liberty! O Liberty! What crimes are committed in thy name!")

Source: *The French Revolution: A History* by Thomas Carlyle (London, 1837). This translation was published in the *Universal Biography* by John Lemprière soon after the revolution ended (New York, 1810).

(2) (doubtful): "Go first; I can at least spare you the pain of seeing my blood flow." Spoken at the foot of the scaffold to her companion, an old man whom she had been encouraging along the way.

Source: *The Last Words (Real and Traditional) of Distinguished Men and Women Collected from Various Sources* by Frederic Rowland Marvin (New York, 1901).

She did say something similar: "Go first. You would not have courage enough to see me die!" Spoken to Lamarche, an old man. They were not her Last Words. After this, she spoke a version of (1).

Source: *France and Its Revolutions: A Pictorial History 1789-1848)* by George Long (London, 1849).

Roland de la Platière, Jean Marie

(1734-1793) French politician, statesman. Husband of Madame Roland. Was Girondist during the French Revolution. Committed suicide at age 59 soon after his wife was executed.

Last Words (written): "Whoever thou art that findest me lying, respect my remains: they are those of a man who consecrated all his life to being useful; and who has died as he lived, virtuous and honest. Not fear, but indignation made me quit my retreat, on learning that my wife had been murdered. I wish not to remain longer on an Earth polluted with crimes." Suicide note.

Source: *The French Revolution: A History* by Thomas Carlyle (London, 1837).

Romaine, William

(1714-1795) English clergyman, theologian, writer. Anglican rector of St. Anne's Blackfriars for 30 years. Wrote works popular with evangelicals. Notable works: *Walk of Faith; Discourses Upon Law and Gospel.* Died at age 80 in London.

Last Words: "Holy! Holy! Holy blessed Jesus, to Thee be endless praise!"

Source: *Rev. William Romaine, Works and Life,* ed. W.B. Cadogan (London, 1813).

Romanes, George John

(1848-1894) Canadian-born British scientist, naturalist, psychologist, educator. Friend of Charles Darwin. Researched animal intelligence. Notable works: *Mental Evolution in Animals; Animal Intelligence.* Established Romanes Lectures at Oxford. Died at age 46 of a brain tumor in Oxford.

Last Words: Romanes went to his bedroom and complained of feeling ill. He spoke a few loving words to one of his family members then lost consciousness. He died less than an hour later. His exact Last Words were not given.

Source: *The Life and Letters of George John Romanes* by George John Romanes and Ethel Duncan Romanes (London, 1896). Ethel was his wife.

Romero y Galdames, Blessed Oscar Arnulfo

(1917-1980) Salvadorian prelate, activist. Archbishop of El Salvador who repeatedly called for a nonviolent end to the Salvadoran civil war. Nominated for 1979 Nobel Peace Prize. Murdered at age 62, while saying Mass at a hospital for terminally ill cancer patients. His murder caused an international outcry. Beatified in 2005.

Last Words: "May God have mercy on my assassin." Spoken as he lay dying.

Source: "Assassinated Left-Wing Archbishop on the Road to Sainthood" by Richard Owens (*The* [London] *Times,* March 31, 2005).

Rommel, Erwin Johannes Eugen

(1891-1944) German military officer. Nazi field marshal in World War II. Known as The Desert Fox. Led German Afrika Korps in North Africa. Defeated by British at El Alamein, Egypt. Given choice by Hitler: public execution for treason or private self-inflicted death by cyanide. He chose suicide. Died at age 52 in Ulm, Germany.

Last Words (written): "I have spoken to my wife and made up my mind. I will never allow myself to be hanged by that man Hitler. I planned no murder. I only tried to serve my country, as I have done all my life, but now this is what I must do. In about half an hour there will come a telephone call from Ulm to say that I have had an accident and am dead." Suicide note.

Sources: *Rommel: The Desert Fox* by Desmond Young (New York, 1950); *The Rommel Papers,* ed. by B.H. Liddell Hart (London, 1953).

Last Words (spoken): "Come outside with me....I have just had to tell your mother that I shall be dead in a quarter of an hour. To die by the hand of one's own people is hard. But the house is surrounded and Hitler is charging me with high treason. In view of my services in Africa, I am to have the chance of dying by poison. The two generals brought it with them. It's fatal in three seconds. If I accept, none of the usual steps will be taken against my family, that is against you. They will also leave my staff alone." Conversation with his son Manfred.

Source: "The Suicide of Field Marshal Erwin Rommel, Germany, 14 October 1944" by Manfred Rommel in *The Mammoth Book of Eyewitness World War II* by Jon E. Lewis (New York, 2002).

Roosevelt, Anna Eleanor (Eleanor)

(1884-1962) American First Lady, lecturer, writer, humanitarian. Daughter of Elliott Roosevelt who was the younger brother of U.S. President Theodore Roosevelt. Wife of U.S. President Franklin Delano Roosevelt. Had syndicated newspaper column, "My Day." Spoke out for rights of African Americans, working-class whites. U.S. spokesperson in United Nations. Helped draft UN Declaration on Human Rights. Died at age 78 in New York City.

Last Words: "Utter nonsense." Spoken to the nurse who told her she would die when the reason God put her on earth was fulfilled.

Source: *Eleanor: The Years Alone* by Joseph P. Lash (New York, 1972). The author was a close friend. This book was Vol. 2 of the work *Eleanor and Franklin* for which he won a Pulitzer Prize for Biography and a National Book Award.

Roosevelt, Franklin Delano

(1882-1945) 32nd President of the U.S. American statesman, politician, lawyer. Stricken with polio at age 39. U.S. Assistant secretary of navy. Governor of New York. President during the Great Depression and World War II. Only U.S. President elected for four terms. Died at age 63 of a cerebral hemorrhage at the Little White House, Warm Springs, Georgia.

Last Words: "I have a terrific headache!" Spoken to naval physician Commodore Howard E. Bruen while an artist was sketching him.

Source: "Roosevelt, Franklin Delano" in *1946 Britannica Book of the Year* (Chicago, 1946).

Roosevelt, Theodore

(1858-1919) 26th President of the U.S. American statesman, politician. Tried unsuccessfully to regain the presidency with a new Progressive party. Led Rough Riders during Spanish-American War. First American recipient of a Nobel Prize. Had recurring bouts of malaria. Also treated for inflammatory rheumatism. Died at age 60 in his sleep at Oyster Bay, New York.

Last Words "Please put out the light, James." Spoken to his valet James Amos.

Sources: *Theodore Roosevelt and His Time, Shown In His Own Letters* by Joseph B. Bishop (New York, 1920); "Theodore Roosevelt Dies at Oyster Bay Home; Nation Shocked, Pays Tribute to Former President; Our Flag on All Seas and in All Lands at Half Mast" (*New York Times,* January 6, 1919).

Roosevelt, Theodore, Sr.

(1831-1878) American businessman, importer, philanthropist. Father of U. S. President Theodore Roosevelt. Grandfather of American First Lady Eleanor Roosevelt. Suffered several months from a gastrointestinal tumor that caused much pain. Died at age 46 in New York City.

Last Words: "Call the doctor! Bamie! Corinne! Mother, come here for God's sake—quick."

Source: *Mornings on Horseback: The Story of an Extraordinary Family, a Vanished Way of Life and the Unique Child Who Became Theodore Roosevelt* by David McCullough (New York, 1982).

Root, Elihu

(1845-1937) American statesman, politician, diplomat, lawyer. U.S. secretary of war, U.S. secretary of state. Member U.S. Senate from New York. Won 1912 Nobel Peace Prize for initiating international arbitration agreements. Died at age 92 in Clinton, New York.

Last Words: "I have devoted considerable thought to the question, with the result that, while as a lawyer I cannot prove a case for the existence of God, as an individual I firmly believe that there is a God and I have no fear of death." His response when asked if he believed in God.

Source: *Elihu Root* by Philip C. Jessup (New York, 1938).

Rosa, Salvator

(1615-1673) Neapolitan artist, etcher, actor, musician. Known as Salvatoriello. Famed for landscapes, battle scenes. Leading artist of the Neapolitan School. Studied in Naples. Notable works: *Landscape with a Bridge; Witch of Endor.* Died at age 57 in Rome.

Last Words: "To judge by what I now endure, the hand of death grasps me sharply."

Source: *The Life and Times of Salvator Rosa* by Lady Sydney Morgan (London, 1855).

Roscommon, 4th Earl of,
see **Dillon, Wentworth.**

Rose of Lima, Saint

(1586-1617) Peruvian nun, holy woman. Member of Dominican order. Died at age 31 in Lima, Peru. Canonized in 1671. First American saint. Several churches and schools were named for her.

Last Words: "Jesus be with me."

Source: *The Life of Saint Rose of Lima* by Jean Baptiste Feuillet and Leonhard Hansen (New York, 1855).

Rosenberg, Alfred

(1893-1946) German politician, propagandist. Member of Adolf Hitler's Nazi cabinet during World War II. Tried as a war criminal at Nuremberg. Found guilty. Executed at age 53 by hanging.

Last Words: "No." His response when he was asked if he had any Last Words.

Source: "The Nuremberg Trials: The Execution of Nazi War Criminals" by Kingsbury Smith (International News Service, October 16, 1946).

Rosenberg, Ethel Greenglass

(1915-1953) American Communist. Ethel and husband Julius were charged with conspiracy to commit espionage. Both were tried, found guilty and executed in the electric chair in Ossining (Sing Sing) prison, New York. Ethel was 37; Julius was 35.

Last Words (written): "We are the first victims of American fascism. Love you, Ethel." Letter released by their attorney the day they were executed. The last penciled notes in Ethel's handwriting were on a scrap of paper attached to the letterhead: "George Eliot said: This is a world worth abiding in while one man can thus venerate & love another." Ended with: "My best to Pop Bloch."

Source: *The Rosenberg Letters: A Complete Edition of the Prison Correspondence of Julius and Ethel Rosenberg,* ed. by Michael Meccopol (New York, 1994).

Ross, Harold Wallace

(1892-1951) American publisher, editor. Founded *The New Yorker.* Member of the Algonquin Round Table (exclusive group of writers who lunched at the Algonquin Hotel in New York City and exchanged wit and wisdom). Diagnosed with cancer in 1951. Died at age 59 of heart failure during surgery to remove a lung.

Last Words: "I'm up here to end this thing, and it may end me, too. But that's better than going on this way. God bless you. I'm half under the anesthetic now." Spoken in a phone call to friend George S. Kaufman.

Source: *The Years With Ross* by James Thurber (Boston, 1959). The author worked with Ross at *The New Yorker* for many years.

Rossetti, Christina Georgina

(1830-1894) English poet. Pen name Ellen Alleyne. Sister of Dante Gabriel Rossetti. Afflicted with Graves disease in her early 40s. Illness caused her to become increasingly reclusive. Died at age 64 of cancer in London.

Last Words: "I love everybody. If ever I had an enemy I should hope to meet and welcome that enemy in Heaven."

Source: *Christina Rossetti: A Portrait with Background* by Marya Zaturenska (New York, 1949).

Rossetti, Dante Gabriel

(1828-1882) English poet, painter. Brother of Christina Rossetti. A founder of the Pre-Raphaelite movement. Notable work: *Annunciation.* Addicted to chloral hydrate after the tragic death of his wife. Final years spent in declining health. Became increasingly withdrawn physically and mentally. Died at age 53 at the home of a friend on the Isle of Thanet, Kent, trying to battle his addiction.

Different Last Words:

(1) "Perhaps later." Spoken to his brother who asked if he could read to him a passage from the Bible.

Source: *Dante Gabriel Rossetti* by William Michael Rossetti (Boston, 1895). The author was his brother.

(2) "Then you really think I'm dying. At last you think so; but I was right from the first."

Source: *Rossetti: His Life and Works* by Evelyn Waugh (New York, 1928).

(3) "I think I shall die tonight."

Source: *The Last Words (Real and Traditional) of Distinguished Men and Women Collected from Various Sources* by Frederic Rowland Marvin (New York, 1901). Marvin noted that these were Rossetti's "last recorded words."

Variation: "I believe I shall die tonight." Reported by his brother who indicated that Rossetti spoke a few other comments, making this among his Last Words.

Source: *Dante Gabriel Rossetti: His Family Letters* by Dante Gabriel Rossetti and William Michael Rossetti (London, 1895).

Rossini, Gioacchino

(1792-1868), Italian musician, composer. Wrote 39 operas. Notable works: *The Thieving Magpie; Semiramide; Barber of Seville; William Tell.* His last days were spent in much pain. Died at age 76 of cancer in Paris. Last Words: "Olympe." Spoke his wife's

name. He married his second wife Olympe Pelissier in 1846.

Source: *Rossini: The Man and His Music* by Francis Toye (London, 1934).

Rothschild, Mayer Amschel

(1744-1812) German financier. Birth name Mayer Amschel Bauer. Changed name to Rothschild (red shield). Founder of a dynasty of bankers. Established bank in Frankfurt, Germany. Five sons were placed in charge of bank branches in European financial centers. Rothschild died at age 69 in Frankfurt.

Last Words: "Observe these three points, and you will soon be rich among the richest and the world will belong to you." He asked his five sons to be faithful to the law of Moses, to remain united to the end, and undertake nothing without consulting their mother.

Source: *The Rothschilds: The Financial Rulers of Nations* by John Reeves (Chicago, 1887).

Rothschild, Nathan Mayer

(1777-1836) German financier. One of five sons of Mayer Amschel Rothschild, founder of banking dynasty. Established branch in London. Died at age 59.

Last Words: "Poor unhappy me! A victim to nervousness and fancied errors! And all because of my money."

Source: *The Rothschilds: The Financial Rulers of Nations* by John Reeves (Chicago, 1887).

Rothstein, Arnold

(1882-1928) American gambler. Known as Mr. Big and as A.R. Called before a grand jury on suspicion of fixing the 1919 World Series; dismissed without indictment. Financed illegal speakeasies during Prohibition. Shot while playing poker in a New York City hotel. Taken to a hospital. Refused to identify his assailant. Died the following day at age 46. Inspiration for fictional characters in F. Scott Fitzgerald and Damon Runyon novels.

Different Last Words:

(1) "I won't tell and please don't ask me any more questions." Spoken when police asked who shot him.

Source: *Trials and Other Tribulations* by Damon Runyon (Philadelphia, 1947).

(2) "Don't go away. I need you. I don't want

to be alone. I can't stand being alone. I've got to get home." Spoken to his wife.

Source: *The Life and Times of Arnold Rothstein* by Leo Katcher (New York, 1958).

Rousseau, Jean-Jacques

(1712-1778) French writer, philosopher. Expounded political philosophy in *The Social Contract*; educational philosophy in *Émile*. Other notable works: *La Nouvelle Héloise; The Reveries of a Solitary Stroller; Confessions.* His nemesis Voltaire died May 30, 1778. Rousseau predicted he would not survive him by very long. On July 1 Rousseau had a stroke at the country home of Marquis René de Girardin. He fell to the floor, was lifted to a bed, then fell again, hit the hard tile floor and died at age 66. French artist Jean Michel Moreau the Younger painted *The Last Words of Jean-Jacques Rousseau at Ermenonville in 1778.*

Last Words: "See the sun, whose smiling face calls me; see that immeasurable light. There is God! Yes, God Himself, who is opening His arms and inviting me to taste at last that eternal and unchanging joy that I had so long desired."

Source: *La vie et les œuvres de Jean-Jacques Rousseau* by Henri Beaudouin (Paris, 1891).

Variation: "Throw up the window that I may see once more the magnificent scene of nature."

Source: *The Last Words (Real and Traditional) of Distinguished Men and Women Collected from Various Sources* by Frederic Rowland Marvin (New York, 1901).

Variation: "See how pure the sky is! There is not a single cloud on it! I hope the Almighty will receive me there." He fell forward dead just after he spoke these words to his wife after she opened a window for him.

Source: "Rousseau, Jean-Jacques" in *Penny Cyclopaedia of the Society for the Diffusion of Useful Knowledge,* Vol. XX, by Society for the Diffusion of Useful Knowledge (London, 1841).

Routh, Martin Joseph

(1755-1854) English classical scholar, writer, educator. Authority on patristic literature. President of Magdalen College for 63 years. Last man to wear a wig at Oxford. Notable work: *Reliquiae Sacrae* (collection of early church writings). Died at age 99 after he collapsed while taking a heavy book from a high shelf in his library.

Last Words: "A worthless volume, sir! A worthless volume!"

Source: "Martin Joseph Routh: The Learned Divine" in *Lives of Twelve Good Men* by Joseph William Burgon (London, 1888). Described as his "alleged last words." The author was one of his associates at Magdalen College.

Royer-Collard, Pierre-Paul

(1763-1845) French statesman, politician, philosopher. Member Council of Five Hundred. Advocate of constitutional monarchy after the French Revolution. Member Chamber of Deputies. Died at age 82 in Châteauvieux.

Last Words: "There is nothing substantial in the world but religious ideas. Never give them up, or if you do, come back to them."

Source: *Royer-Collard* by E. Spuller (Paris, 1895).

Rubinstein, Anton Grigorevich

(1829-1894) Russian musician, pianist, composer, conductor. Among the greatest pianists of his era. Founded St. Petersburg Conservatory of Music. Brother of Russian composer Nicholas Rubinstein. Wrote operas, symphonies, concertos, chamber music and songs. Notable works: *Melody in F* (for piano); *Ocean Symphony.* Died at age 64 in Peterhof, Russia.

Last Words: "I am suffocating. A doctor! Quick! A doctor!"

Source: *Free Artist: The Story of Anton and Nicholas Rubinstein* by Catherine Drinker Bowen (New York, 1939).

Rubinstein, Helena

(1870-1965) Polish-born American cosmetics manufacturer. Opened her first beauty salon in Melbourne, Australia, then in London, Paris and New York. Founded Helena Rubinstein, Incorporated. Died at age 94 in New York City.

Last Words: "Not in the least now. But I've waited too long. It should be an interesting experience." Her response to a query about being afraid of death.

Source: *Madame: An Intimate Biography of Helena Rubinstein* by Patrick O'Higgins (New York, 1971). The author was her personal secretary.

Rubinstein, Nicholas or Nikolai Grigorevich

(1835-1881) Russian musician, pianist,

educator. Founded and operated Moscow Conservatory. Brother of Anton Rubenstein. Friend of Tchaikovsky. Died at age 45 in Paris.

Last Words: "Oysters! Nothing, Helen Andreyevna, will do me so much good as a dozen cold oysters. And an ice afterward." As he began to eat, he suddenly became ill, passed out and died a short time later.

Source *Free Artist: The Story of Anton and Nicholas Rubinstein* by Catherine Drinker Bowen (New York, 1939).

Rückert, Friedrich

(1788-1866) German poet, writer, educator, Professor of Oriental languages at University of Erlangen. Privy councilor in Berlin. Died at age 77 near Coburg, Germany.

Last Words: "In such weather, in such tempest, in such a storm, they are resting, as if in their mother's house, where no storm can frighten them, sheltered by God's hand."

Source: "Kindertotenlieder Exhibition," A collaboration of Opera North, Picture This, Impressions Gallery and Nottingham Trent University, 2006. The last room of the exhibit was a small empty unentered chamber that contained only Rückert's Last Words.

Rudolf of Hapsburg, Crown Prince of Austria

(1858-1889) Austrian royalty. Archduke and crown prince. Only son of Emperor Francis Joseph. Married Princess Stephanie of Belgium. Became romantically involved with Baroness Mary Vetsera. His family ordered him to terminate the relationship. When their bodies were found in his hunting lodge Mayerling, near Vienna, their deaths were ruled a double suicide. Rudolf was 30. (See also Vetsera, Marie ("Mary").

Last Words (written): "Dear Stephanie, You are freed henceforward from the torment of my presence. Be happy, in your own way. Be good to the poor little girl who is the only thing I leave behind. Give my last greetings to all my acquaintances, especially to Bombelles, Spindler, Latour, Nowo, Gisela, Leopold, etc., etc. I face death calmly; death alone can save my good name. With warmest love from Your affectionate Rudolf." Letter to his wife.

Source: *I Was to be Empress* by H.R.H. Princess Stephanie of Belgium (London, 1937). The author was Rudolf's wife.

Rumbold, Richard

(1622?-1685) English Puritan leader who supported Cromwell. Member of the Rye House Conspiracy in 1682. When the Stuarts returned to power, he was executed for his actions against the monarchy. On the scaffold, Rumbold gave a long speech that was interrupted by drum beating. He accused the perpetrator of being disingenuous for interrupting a dying man. He ended his speech with these words:

Last Words: "I am sure there was no man born marked of God above another; for none comes into the world with a saddle on his back, Neither any booted and spurred to ride him; not but that I am well satisfied that God hath wisely ordered different stations for man in the world, as I have already said: kings having as much power as to make them great and the people as much property as to make them happy. And to conclude, I shall only add my wishes for the salvation of all men who were created for that end."

Source: *Lend Me Your Ears: Great Speeches in History* by William Safire (New York, 1992).

Runyon, Alfred Damon (Damon)

(1884-1946) American journalist, playwright, short-story writer. Famed for colorful characters such as Harry the Horse and Apple Annie. Many of his stories have been adapted for stage and movies. The musical *Guys and Doll* was based on two of them. Died at age 62 of throat cancer in New York City.

Last Words (written): "You can keep the things of bronze and stone and give me one man to remember me just once a year." Note to his friend Walter Winchell.

Source: *The Damon Runyon Story* by Edward Horace Weiner (New York, 1948).

Ruppert, Jacob ("Jake")

(1867-1939) American politician, brewer, professional baseball club owner. Known as Colonel Ruppert (was colonel in National Guard). Member U.S. House of Representatives from New York. Inherited brewing company from father. President of New York American League Baseball Club (Yankees) 1914 until his death. Died at age

71 in New York City.

Different Last Words:

(1) "Babe." George Herman (Babe) Ruth was the last one to see him alive aside from family members and brewery officials. Ruppert was able to say just one word. Ruth said later that it was the only time in his life that Ruppert ever called him Babe to his face.

Source: *The House That Ruth Built: A Biography* by Marshall Smelser (Lincoln, NE, 1993).

(2) "Good morning." Whispered to his personal secretary Albert Brennan a few hours before he died.

Source: "Ruppert, Owner of Yankees and Leading Brewer, Dies; Rise of Ruppert in Business Rapid. In His 20s He Became Manager of Brewery Founded in 1851 by His Father. Bought Yankees in 1915 with Huston. He Paid $450,000 for Club Now Valued in Millions" (*New York Times,* January 14, 1939).

Rush, Benjamin

(1746-1813) American physician, politician, educator. Professor of chemistry. Member of Continental Congress. Surgeon in Continental Army. Signer of Declaration of Independence. Died at age 67 of typhus in Philadelphia.

Last Words: "Be indulgent to the poor." Spoken to his son on his deathbed.

Source: *Benjamin Rush: Physician and Citizen: 1746-1813* by Nathan G. Goodman (Philadelphia, 1934).

Russell, Charles, Lord Russell of Killowen

(1832-1900) Irish-born British jurist, politician, statesman. Member of Parliament. Attorney general. Lord chief justice. Counsel in Bering Sea Fur-Seal Controversy. Member of Venezuela Boundary Arbitration Tribunal. Died at age 67 in London.

Last Words: "My God, have mercy upon me."

Source: *The Life of Lord Russell of Killowen* by R. Barry O'Brien (New York, 1901).

Russell, Charles Marion

(1864-1926) American painter, sculptor. One of the great western artists. Specialized in cattle roundups, Native Americans, cowboys and other frontier scenes. Completed about 4,000 works of art during his lifetime. Died at age 62 of a heart attack in Great Falls, Montana. Schools, parks and national wildlife refuge were named for him.

Last Words: "Doc, I guess I ain't goin' to make the grade this time for you."

Source: *Charles M. Russell, the Cowboy Artist* by Ramon Frederick Adams, Homer Elwood Britzman and Karl Yost (Pasadena, CA, 1948).

Russell, George William ("A.E.")

(1867-1935) Irish writer, poet, artist, mystic, nationalist. Pen name Æ or A.E. Founding member of the Dublin Lodge of Theosophical Society. Notable works: *The Candle of Vision; Deirdre; The Living Torch.* Died at age 68 of cancer in Bournmouth, England.

Last Words: "Yes, I am not in pain. I have realized most of my ambitions. I have had an outstanding interest in life. I've got friends. What more can a man want?" Spoken to Senator Gogarty who visited Russell a few hours before he died.

Source: "George William Russell—AE, April 10, 1867-July 17, 1935" (*Canadian Theosophist*, 16:6, August 15, 1935).

Russell, John, Viscount Amberley

(1842-1876) British statesman, writer. Member of Parliament, politician. Son of John Russell, 1st Earl Russell. He chose not to inherit the earldom. Father of Bertrand Russell. Friend of John Stuart Mill. Wife and daughter died of diphtheria in 1874. He died at age 33 of bronchitis.

Last Words: "It is all done—Goodbye my little dears for ever."

Source: *The Amberley Papers: The Letters and Diaries of Lord and Lady Amberley,* ed. by Bertrand Russell and Patricia Russell (New York, 1937). The editors were his grandson and his grandson's wife.

Russert, Timothy John, Jr. ("Tim")

(1950-2008) American journalist, television host, writer, lawyer. Hosted NBC's *Meet the Press* and was Washington Bureau Chief for *NBC News,* as well as correspondent and guest on other NBC News programs including *The Today Show* and *Hardball.* Wrote a best-selling book about his father. Co-hosted the disputed 2000 Presidential Election Night coverage. Earned several awards including an Emmy. Died at age 58 in Washington, D.C.

Last Words: "What's happening?" He greeted NBC's Washington bureau editing supervisor Candice Harrington then collapsed without making another sound. His

Last Words were made public at his memorial service during a eulogy by NBC Nightly News Anchor, Brian Williams.

Source: Brian Williams Video at Tim Russert Memorial (MSNBC, June 18, 2008).

Ruth, George Herman ("Babe")

(1895-1948) American athlete. Professional baseball player. Known as the Sultan of Swat, the Big Bambino, the Babe. One of the great sports icons of the 20th century. Set numerous records that stood for decades. First player to hit 60 home runs in one season. Voted American League Most Valuable Player in 1923. One of the first players elected to the National Baseball Hall of Fame. Retired in 1935. Died of throat cancer at age 53 in New York City. *Headin' Home* (1920), *The Babe Ruth Story* (1948) and *The Babe* (1992) are among the movies that explore the Babe Ruth legend.

Last Words: "Not far. I'm just going over the valley." His response to the doctor who asked where he was going when he started to wander around his hospital room. A short time before he died, he uttered "My Jesus mercy" three times.

Sources: *One Hundred Greatest Sports Heroes* (New York, 1954); *New York World Telegram*, August 19, 1948.

Rutherford, Samuel

(1600?-1661) Scottish clergyman, theologian, writer, Covenanter. Banished for nonconformity. Published a book defending doctrines of grace that put him in conflict with Church authorities. Charged with treason. Exiled to Aberdeen. Died before he could be tried.

Different Last Words:

(1) "Glory, glory dwelleth in Immanuel's land!"

Source: *Letters of Samuel Rutherford,* ed. by the Rev. A. A. Bonar (Edinburgh, 1848).

(2) "Tell the Parliament that I have received a summons to a higher bar. I must needs answer that first; and when the day you name shall come, I shall be where few of you shall enter." Spoken as he was dying to a messenger from Parliament who brought a summons for Rutherford to appear for trial.

Source: *The Golden Dawn: Or, Light on the Great Future: In This Life, Through the Dark Valley, and in*

the *Life Eternal, as Seen in the Best Thoughts of Over Three Hundred Leading Authors and Scholars* by James Henry Potts (Philadelphia, 1883).

Ruthven, Alexander

(1580?-1600) Scottish nobleman. Alexander and his brother John, 3rd Earl of Gowrie, opposed King James VI. They persuaded him to come to their home in Perth with the intention of dethroning him. Known as the Gowrie Conspiracy, the plot was frustrated and Alexander and John were both killed at their house in Perth.

Last Words: "Alas! I had na wyte [blame] of it!"

Source: *James I* by Charles Williams (London, 1951).

Ryan, Cornelius

(1920-1974) Irish-born American journalist, writer. Wrote carefully researched books about World War II. Notable works: *The Longest Day; The Last Battle; A Bridge Too Far*. Died at age 54 of prostate cancer while on tour to promote *A Bridge Too Far*.

Last Words: "Katie, I'm so damned tired." Spoken to his wife.

Source: *A Private Battle* by Cornelius Ryan and Kathryn Ryan (New York, 1979). Kathryn was his wife. The book details Ryan's battle with cancer and uses notes Ryan left for that purpose.

Ryland, John

(1753-1825) English clergyman, hymnist. Pastor of Broadmead Church in Bristol, England. Played key role in founding what would become Baptist Missionary Society. Wrote about 100 hymns that he intended to be sung with his sermons. Many were widely circulated. Died at age 72 in Bristol.

Last Words: "No more pain."

Source: *Hymns and Verses on Sacred Subjects with a Brief Biographical Sketch* by John Ryland (London, 1862).

Sabatier, Raphael Bienvenu

(1732-1811) French surgeon, educator. Associate of Institute and of Academy of Sciences. Held chair of operative surgery at École de Santé in Paris. Wrote books on anatomy. Notable works: *On the Various Methods of Extracting the Cataract; De la Médicine Opératoire*. Died in Paris. During his last days, he became ashamed of his bodily weakness. He asked his wife and son to hide him from the world so that his family would be the only witnesses to the decay he felt.

Last Words: "Contemplate the state in which I am fallen, and learn to die." Spoken to his son.

Source: *The General Biographical Dictionary: Containing an Historical and Critical Account of the Lives and Writings of the Most Eminent Persons in Every Nation, Particularly the British and Irish, from the Earliest Accounts to the Present Time* by Alexander Chalmers (London, 1812-1817).

Sacco, Nicola

(1891-1927) Italian-born American political activist. Convicted along with Bartolomeo Vanzetti for the murder of the paymaster and guard at a Massachusetts shoe factory during a robbery. Many prominent people protested the verdict, including Dorothy Parker, Upton Sinclair, George Bernard Shaw and Jane Addams, but Sacco and Vanzetti's convictions and sentences were upheld. Both were executed in 1927. Maxwell Anderson's plays *Gods of the Lightning* and *Winterset,* Upton Sinclair's novel *Boston,* Edna St. Vincent Millay's poem *Justice Denied in Massachusetts* among others, were based on the case. In 1977, Michael Dukakis, governor of Massachusetts, vindicated Sacco and Vanzetti by official proclamation.

Last Words: "Viva Il Anarchismo! Farewell my wife and child and all my friends! Good evening gentlemen. Addio Mamma mia, addio Mamma mia."

Source: *I Killed for the Law, the Career of Robert Elliott and Other Executioners* by Leo W. Sheridan (New York, 1938).

Sadat, Mohammed Anwar Al

(1918-1981) Egyptian military officer, politician. Field marshal. President of Egypt from 1970 until his assassination. Killed at age 62 while watching an aerial display at a military parade. Assassins were part of an Egyptian Islamic Jihad organization that opposed his negotiations with Israel and the use of force a month earlier.

Last Words: "No." Reported by his wife who was sitting with her grandchildren in another box of the reviewing stand where he was shot. Sadat previously said he expected to be killed eventually and never wore a bulletproof vest.

Source: "Jihan Sadat Looks on Calmly at Rites for Her Husband" by Ann Crittenden (*New York Times*, October 11, 1981).

Saint-Edme, Bourg

(1785-1852) French political writer. Birth name Edme Théodore Bourg. Notable work: *Biographie des hommes du jour (Biography of Living Men,* 6 vol.) Committed suicide at age 66 in Paris.

Last Words (written): "At four o'clock or at 4:15 I will carry out my design, if everything goes right. I am not afraid of death, since I am seeking it, since I desire it! But prolonged suffering would be frightful. I walk; all ideas vanish. I think only of my children. The fire is dying out. What a silence all around. Four o'clock. I hear the chimes. Soon comes the moment of sacrifice. I put my snuff box in my desk drawer. Goodbye my dearest daughters. God will pardon my sorrows. I put my spectacles in the drawer. Goodbye once more, goodbye, my darling children!—My last thought is yours, for you are the last flutterings of my heart." Suicide note to his children.

Source: *Le requiem des gens de lettres* by Firmin Maillard (Paris, 1901).

Saint-Evremond, Charles de Marguetel De Saint Denis, Seigneur de

(1610-1703) French poet, essayist, courtier, nobleman. Notable work: *Maxims.* Forced into exile in England. Died at age 93 in London. Buried in Westminster Abbey.

Last Words: "With all my heart; I would fain be reconciled to my stomach which no longer performs its usual functions." Spoken to a priest who has asked if he was reconciled with Christ.

Source: *The Wits and Beaux of Society* by Grace Wharton and Philip Wharton (London, 1871).

Saint-Gaudens, Augustus

(1848-1907) Irish-born American artist, sculptor. Notable works: Lincoln Memorial, Washington, D.C.; double eagle coin, statues of Admiral Farragut, Lincoln, General Sherman. Diagnosed with cancer in 1900. Died at age 59 in Cornish, New Hampshire.

Last Words: "It's very beautiful, but I want to go farther away." Spoken while he was watching a sunset.

Source: *Reminiscences of Augustus Saint-Gaudens,*

ed. by Homer Saint-Gaudens (New York, 1913). The editor was his son.

Saint-John, Henry, see Bolingbroke, 1st Viscount.

Saint-Pierre, Charles, Abbé de

(1658-1743) French social philosopher, writer, reformer. Full name Charles Irénée Castel, Abbé de Saint-Pierre. Advocate of natural religion and toleration. Died at age 85 in Paris.

Last Words: "I am only to be reproached for this action. I do not believe a word of all this. It was a vile concession for the family and for the house, but I wanted to be the confessor of the truth all my life." Spoken to a priest after he consented to and went through Last Rites for his family's sake.

Source: *L'abbé de Saint-Pierre, l'homme et l'œuvre* by John Drouet (Paris, 1912).

Saint-Saëns, Camille

(1835-1921) French musician, composer, conductor, pianist, organist. Notable works: *Samson and Delilah; Carnival of the Animals; Danse Macabre.* Also known for symphonies, concertos, choral and chamber music. Died at age 86 in Algiers while on vacation.

Last Words: "This time I think it's really the end."

Source: *Saint-Saëns and the Organ* by Rollin Smith (Stuyvesant, NY, 1992).

Saint-Simon, Henri de

(1760-1825) French philosopher, utopian socialist. Full name Claude-Henri de Rouvroy, Comte de Saint-Simon. Founder of French socialism. Founder of sect of Saint Simonians. Fought on the American side in the American Revolution. Became destitute in 1823. Befriended by Olinde Rodrigues, who supported him until he died in Paris at age 64.

Last Words: "The future belongs to us."

Source: *Henri de Saint-Simon: die Persönlichkeit und ihr Werk* by Friedrich Muckle (Jena, Germany, 1908).

Sakharov, Andrei

(1921-1989) Russian scientist, physicist, social activist, politician. Spoke out against nuclear proliferation and atmospheric testing of the hydrogen bomb. Awarded Nobel Peace Prize in 1975 but was not permitted to accept it. Sentenced to internal exile at Gorky in 1980 for his stance on nuclear arms reduction and human rights. Permitted to return to Moscow in 1986. Remained a strong advocate of political reform and human rights the rest of his life. Elected to Soviet legislature. Died at age 68 of a heart attack in Moscow.

Last Words: "Tomorrow there will be a big fight." Spoken to his wife about an upcoming quarrelsome meeting of the legislature. He died a short time later.

Source: *Perils of Perestroika: Viewpoints of the Soviet Press, 1989-1991*, ed. by Isaac J. Tarasulo (Wilmington, DE, 1992).

Variation: "Tomorrow will be a battle." Spoken to his wife.

Source: *The Decline and Fall of the Soviet Empire: Forty Years That Shook the World, from Stalin to Yeltsin* by Fred Coleman (New York, 1997).

Variation: "Tomorrow there will be a battle!" Spoken to his wife and friends in his Moscow apartment. He went to his study to rest and was found dead two hours later.

Source: "At Last, a Tomorrow Without Battle: Andrei Sakharov, 1921-1989" by Patricia Blake and Ann Blackman (*Time* magazine, December 25, 1989).

Saki, see Munro, Hector Hugh.

Sakuma, Tsutomu

(1876-1910) Japanese military officer. Lieutenant commander in charge of a submarine that sank in Hiroshima Bay during maneuvers. His log recorded the approach of a slow but certain death as the crew of 15 suffocated. A malfunction had caused their air supply to run out.

Last Words (written): "12:30. I feel great pain in breathing. I thought I had blown out gasoline, but I have become intoxicated by gasoline. Commander Nakano—It is now 12:40—." Entry in his log.

Source: *Life and Death: Being an Authentic Account of the Deaths of One Hundred Celebrated Men and Women with Their Portraits* collated and retold by Colonel Thomas H. Lewin (London, 1910).

Saladin

(1137-1193) Egyptian leader. Sultan of Egypt and Syria. Arabic name Salah al-Din Yusuf Ibn Ayyub. Founder of Ayyubid dynasty. Known for his chivalry and humane treatment of Crusaders. Became ill while returning to Damascus from a trip.

Bedridden with pain and fever. Went into coma and died at age 55.

Last Word: "True." Spoken in response to hearing the passage: "He is God, than whom there is no other God—who knoweth the unseen and the seen, the Compassionate, the Merciful."

Source: *Saladin and the Fall of the Kingdom of Jerusalem* by Stanley Lane-Poole (New York, 1898).

Salomon, Haym

(1740-1785) Polish-born American financier. Made loans to help finance the American Revolution. Died at age 45 in Philadelphia, probably of tuberculosis. He was deeply in debt.

Last Words: "Take care of them, McCrae. There will be very little, very little for them." He was expressing concern about providing for his wife and four young children.

Source: *Haym Salomon: Son of Liberty* by Howard Fast (New York, 1941).

Saltus, Edgar Evertson

(1855-1921) American novelist, short-story writer. Notable works: *The Anatomy of Negation; The Philosophy of Disenchantment; Vanity Square; The Monster; Daughters of the Rich.* Died at age 65 in New York City.

Last Words: "Mowgy." Spoken to his wife, his pet name for her.

Source: *Edgar Saltus, the Man* by Marie Giles Saltus (Chicago, 1925). The author was his wife.

Salvini, Tommaso

(1829-1915) Italian actor. Tragedian. Made five trips to U.S. between 1872 and 1889. Retired in 1890. Notable roles: Othello, Macbeth, King Lear. Died at age 86 in Florence, Italy.

Last Words: "I do not want to die—absolutely."

Source: *Ho for Heaven. Man's Changing Attitude Toward Dying* by Virginia Moore (New York, 1946).

Samson

(d. 1155? B.C.) Biblical figure. Hebrew judge. Man of great physical strength who performed heroic deeds against the Philistines. Delilah, a Philistine woman, found the source of his strength was his hair and had it cut off while he slept. Samson was captured by his enemies and his eyes were put out.

The story of Samson and Delilah formed the basis for an opera by Saint-Saëns.

Last Words: "Ait moriatur anima mea cum Philisthim."

Source: Judges 16:30 (Latin Vulgate Bible).

Variation: "Let me die with the Philistines!"

Sources: Judges 16:30 (King James Version); (New King James Version); (21st Century King James Version); (New Standard American Bible); (English Standard Version); (Darby Translation); (Douay-Rheims Translation); (New International Version); (Young's Literal Translation).

San Martín, José de

(1778-1850) Argentine military officer. General. Full name José de San Martin Matorras. Known as Liberator of the South. Major leader of South America's independence movement. Went into voluntary exile in Europe in 1824. Died at age 72 in Boulogne-sur-Mer, France.

Last Words: "Mariano, back to my room." Spoken to his brother-in-law.

Source: *Captain of the Andes: The Life of Don Jose de San Martin Liberator of Argentina, Chile and Peru* by Margaret H. Harrison (New York, 1943).

Sanctus of Vienne

(d. 177) Gallic martyr. Christian. Deacon of Vienne. Tormented during Roman persecution of Gallic Christians. He refused to give his name or any other information. He died a martyr in an iron chair under which a fire had been lit.

Last Words: "I am a Christian. I am a Christian." His response to all questions. He answered repeatedly in Latin with these words.

Source: *Book of Martyrs and the Acts and Monuments of the Church* by John Fox (or Foxe). First published 1563, ed. by John Cumming (London, 1851).

Sand, George

(1804-1876) French novelist. Pen name of Amandine Aurore Lucie Dupin, Baroness Dudevant. Supported herself and two children mainly by her writing. Was one of the most widely read novelists in 19th-century Europe. Many rumors circulated about her behavior, masculine dress, cigar smoking. Had liaisons with French writer Alfred de Musset, Polish composer Frédéric Chopin and others. Friend of Liszt, Balzac, Flaubert. Died at age 71 after a short, painful illness.

Last Words: "Laissez la verdure." (tr. "Leave the greenery.")   She wanted her burial plot left green and with no covering of bricks or stone on the grave. After she spoke these words, she said goodbye to her grandchildren. "Farewell, I am going to die. Goodbye Lina, goodbye Maurice, goodbye Lolo, good..."

Sources: *The Life of the Heart, George Sand and Her Times* by Frances Winwar (New York, 1945); *Lélia, the Life of George Sand* by André Maurois (New York, 1953).

Sandburg, Carl

(1878-1967) American poet, historian, biographer, reporter, writer. Won three Pulitzer Prizes; one for history, two for poetry. Won a Grammy for his performance of Aaron Copland's *A Lincoln Portrait*. Served in U.S. Army during Spanish-American War. Worked as a reporter for the *Chicago Daily News*. Notable works: "Chicago" (well-known poem); *Abraham Lincoln: The Prairie Years; Abraham Lincoln: The War Years* (won 1940 Pulitzer for history)*; Rootabaga Stories* (4 vol., children's stories). Died at age 89 at his home, Connemara Farm, North Carolina.

Last Words: "Paula." Spoken to his wife when she touched his hand. "Paula" was Lilian Steichen, sister of renowned photographer Edward Steichen.

Source: *The Carl Sandburg Home: Connemara* by Galin Reuther (Charleston, SC, 2006).

Sanders, George

(1906-1972) British actor. Screen star. Film career spanned four decades and included *All About Eve*, for which he won the Academy Award for Best Supporting Actor. Often portrayed a cad. In 1972, at age 65, he checked into hotel in Barcelona, Spain, wrote a short suicide note and took an overdose of barbiturates.

Last Words (written): "Dear World. I am leaving you because I am bored. I feel I have lived long enough. I am leaving you with your worries in this sweet cesspool. Good luck." Suicide note.

Source: *The Hollywood Hissables* by George W. Mark (Metuchen, NJ, 1989).

Sanderson, Frederick William

(1857-1922) English educator. Popular schoolmaster who taught at Oundle, England. Dropped dead on a platform at the end of a major lecture to an assembly of scientists at University College, London. Chairman H.G. Wells had just proposed a vote of thanks to him and called for the first question from the floor.

Last Words: "No, no." His response to H.G. Wells, who asked if he was too tired to answer a few questions.

Source: *The Story of a Great Schoolmaster: Being a Plain Account of the Life and Ideas of Sanderson of Oundle* by H.G. Wells (New York, 1924).

Sanderson, Robert

(1587-1663) English prelate, educator. Chaplain to Charles I. Regius professor of divinity at Oxford. Deposed during England's Civil War. Reinstated during the Restoration. Bishop of Lincoln. Died at age 75.

Last Words: "My heart is fixed, O God, my heart is fixed where true joy is to be found."

Source: *Walton's Lives of Dr. John Donne, Sir Henry Wotton, Mr. Richard Hooker, Mr. George Herbert, and Dr. Robert Sanderson* by Izaak Walton and Thomas Zouch (York, England, 1796).

Sandoz, Jules Ami

(1856-1928) Swiss-born American pioneer, settler, trapper, land promoter, fruit grower. Settled in the Nebraska Sandhills. Died at age 72 in Alliance, Nebraska.

Last Words: "The whole damn sandhills is deserted. The cattlemen are broke, the settlers about gone. I got to start all over, ship in a lot of good farmers in the spring, build up, build, build."

Source: *Old Jules* by Mari Sandoz (Boston, 1935). Mari Susette Sandoz, his daughter, wrote historical narratives and novels. She is known especially for this biographical account of her immigrant father.

Sandri, Sandro

(d. 1937) Italian fascist war correspondent. While reporting the Sino-Japanese war for *Turin Stampa*, Sandri and several others sought refuge on the American gunboat *Panay* in the Yangtze river. When the boat was 25 miles upriver, Japanese planes strafed and sank it. Sandri sustained a serious injury.

Last Words: "They've killed me this time. What an end! In another nation's ship, in this country." Spoken to Luigi Brazini, another war correspondent. Sandri died of a stomach wound the next day.

Source: *The First Casualty: The War Correspondent as*

Hero and Myth-Maker from the Crimea to Iraq by Phillip Knightley (Baltimore, MD, 2004).

Sanger, Margaret Higgins

(1879-1966) American nurse, social activist, birth control advocate. Emphasized making contraception available to all women to enable them to control their lives and health. Founded the organization that evolved into Planned Parenthood. Died at age 86 of arteriosclerosis in Tucson, Arizona.

Last Words: "A party! Let's have a party."

Source: *Margaret Sanger: A Biography of the Champion of Birth Control* by Madeline Gray (New York, 1979).

Sankey, Ira David

(1840-1908) American evangelist, gospel singer, hymnist. Conducted revivals in U.S., England, Ireland, Scotland with evangelist Dwight L. Moody. Compiled and published hymn collections. Blinded by glaucoma in later years. Died at age 67 in Brooklyn, New York.

Last Words:

"Some day the silver cord will break

And I no more as now shall sing.

But, oh, the joy when I shall awake,

within the palace of the king!" He sang the hymn "Saved by Grace" as he lost consciousness. The hymn, by Fanny Crosby, was a favorite of Sankey's ministry and was sung at every service.

Source: "Ira Sankey's Funeral: Four of His Own Hymns Sung at Services. Dwight L. Moody's Son Present" (*New York Times,* August 16, 1908).

Santa Anna, Antonio López de

(1794-1876) Mexican military officer, politician. General. President of Mexico. Tried to end the Texas Revolution. Captured but lost the Alamo. Driven out of Mexico City during the Mexican War. Exiled then made president and exiled again. Granted amnesty in 1874. Allowed to return to Mexico. Died at age 82 in Mexico City, destitute, disillusioned, disabled and almost blind from cataracts.

Last Words: "Leave me alone so I can get some rest." Spoken to his wife.

Source: *Santa Anna* by Oakah L. Jones (New York, 1968).

Santayana, George

(1863-1952) Spanish-born American writer, poet, philosopher, educator. Professor of philosophy at Harvard. Lived in the U.S. from 1872 to 1912, then returned to Europe. Notable works: *The Last Puritan*; *The Realms of Being; The Life of Reason* (in which he wrote the much-quoted phrase: "Those who cannot remember the past are condemned to repeat it"). Died at age 88 in Rome.

Last Words: "Yes, my friend. But my anguish is entirely physical. There are no more difficulties whatsoever." His response when asked if he was suffering.

Source: *Santayana: The Later Years* by Daniel Corey (New York, 1963). Corey was a close friend, literary secretary and assistant of Santayana for the last 25 years of his life. His wife was Santayana's literary executor.

Sappho

(fl. from late 7th to 8th centuries B.C) Greek poet. Born on island of Lesbos. Little is known with certainty about her life. Her death date is unknown. Some of her poetry has survived.

Last Words: "For it is not right that in the house of song there be mournings. Such things befit not us." A poem to her daughter.

Source: *The Songs of Sappho, Including the Recent Egyptian Discoveries,* ed. and tr. by Marion Mills Miller and David Moore Robinson (New York, 1925).

Sarber, Jess L.

(1886-1933) American law officer. Sheriff in Lima, Ohio. Shot and killed by gunmen who were freeing John Dillinger from jail.

Last Words: "Mother, I believe I'm going to have to leave you." Spoken to his wife Lucy. He died 90 minutes later.

Source: *The Dillinger Days* by John Toland (New York, 1995).

Saro-Wiwa, Kenule Beeson ("Ken")

(1941-1995) Nigerian poet, novelist, television producer, environmental activist. Son of Chief Jim Wiwa of the Ogoni people of the Niger Delta, whose lands were under continual threat by oil companies. Became spokesman and later president of Movement for the Survival of the Ogoni People (MOSOP). In 1994, he was charged by a military tribunal for involvement in the murder of Ogoni elders. Witnesses were bribed to testify against him. He and eight other MOSOP leaders ("Ogoni Nine") were executed by hanging. The executions provoked international outrage. The Ken Saro-Wiwa Foundation honors his memory.

Last Words: "Lord take my soul, but the struggle continues." Spoken just a moment before he was hanged.

Sources: *Daily Telegraph*, November 13, 1995; "Nigeria, Permanent Transition" (*Human Rights Watch Africa*, Vol. 8, No. 3, September 1996).

Saroyan, William

(1908-1981) American writer. Playwright, short-story writer, novelist. Notable work: *The Time of Your Life* (play for which he won the 1940 Pulitzer Prize). He declined the prize, believing the arts should not be patronized. Died at age 72 of cancer in Fresno, California.

Different Last Words:

(1) "It's the most beautiful time in my life—and death."

Source: *Saroyan: A Biography* by Lawrence Lee and Barry Gifford (New York, 2005).

(2) (doubtful): "Everybody has to die, but I have always believed an exception would be made in my case. Now what?"

Source: *Brewer's Dictionary of Twentieth-Century Phrase and Fable* (Boston, 1992).

Saroyan dictated this quote to the Associated Press by phone shortly before he died. He requested that it be published posthumously.

Source: *William Saroyan: The Man and the Writer Remembered* by Leo Hamalian (Rutherford, NJ, 1987).

Sarpi, Paolo or Paul

(1552-1623) Venetian monk, historian, church reformer. Servite monk known as Fra Paolo (Father Paul). Friend of Galileo. Opposed the papacy in his *History of the Council of Trent.* Supported state supremacy. Died at age 70 in Venice.

Last Words: "Esto perpetua." (tr. "May thou last for ever" or "Be thou everlasting.") He was devoted to Venice. His Last Words were a prayer for its prosperity.

Source: "Reviews, Political Tracts, and Lives of Eminent Persons: Father Paul Sarpi, Boerhaave, Blake, Drake, Barretier" in *The Works of Samuel Johnson* (Oxford, England, 1825).

Sarsfield, Patrick, Earl of Lucan

(1650?-1693) Irish nobleman, military officer. Jacobite commander. Wounded in service to France at the Battle of Landen. Taken

to village of Huy, Belgium, where he died a few days later of fever.

Last Words: "Would to God this were shed for Ireland!" Spoken as he lay on the ground wounded. He covered his hand with his blood then exclaimed these words.

Source: *Life of Patrick Sarsfield, Earl of Lucan: With a Short Narrative of the Principal Events of the Jacobite War in Ireland* by John Todhunter (London, 1895).

Sartre, Jean-Paul

(1905-1980) French philosopher, writer, playwright. Existentialist. Founded *Les Temps Modernes* (monthly literary and political review). Notable works: *Critique of Dialectical Reason; Being and Nothingness; No Exit.* Awarded Nobel Prize for Literature in 1964 but declined it. Died at age 74 in Paris.

Last Words: "I love you very much, my dear Beaver." Spoken to his long-time companion, Simone de Beauvoir.

Source: *Sartre: A Life* by Ronald Hayman (New York, 1987).

Satank (Setangya)

(1800?-1871) Native American leader. Kiowa chief, medicine man. Kiowa name: Setangya. Also known as Sitting Bear. Arrested for his role in an attack on a wagon train in Texas that led to the deaths of seven teamsters. While being transported from Fort Sill to Texas, he attempted to escape and was killed.

Last Words: "O Sun, you remain forever, but we Kaitsenko must die. O Earth, you remain forever, but we Kaitsenko must die." After he finished his death song, he attacked one of the guards. He was shot and killed in the ensuing skirmish.

Source: "The Significance of the Jacksboro Indian Affair of 1871" by C. C. Rister (*Southwestern Historical Quarterly*, Vol. XXIV, No. 3, January 1926), citing *Calendar History of the Kiowa Indians* by James Mooney (Washington, D.C., 1878).

Sauckel, Ernst Friedrich Christoph ("Fritz")

(1894-1946) German official. Nazi who recruited forced laborers from German-occupied territories during World War II. Tried, convicted and executed as a Nazi war criminal at Nuremberg trial.

Last Words: "I pay my respects to American

officers and American soldiers but not to American justice!"
Source: *New York Times,* October 16, 1946.

Saul, King of Israel

(fl. 1020-1000 B.C.) Biblical figure. Son of Kish, First King of Israel. Defeated and wounded by the Philistines in the Battle of Mount Gilboa. Succeeded by David.

Last Words: "Sta super me et interfice me quoniam tenent me angustiae et adhuc tota anima in me est"
Source: 2 Samuel 1:9 (Latin Vulgate Bible).

Variation: "Stand I pray thee, upon me, and slay me; for anguish is come upon me, because my life is yet whole in me."
Sources: 2 Samuel 1:9 (King James Version); (21st Century King James Version).

Variation: "Please stand over me and kill me, for anguish has come upon me, but my life still remains in me."
Source: 2 Samuel 1:9 (New King James Version).

Variation: "Please stand beside me and kill me, for agony has seized me because my life still lingers in me."
Source: 2 Samuel 1:9 (New American Standard Version).

Variation: "Stand beside me and kill me, for anguish has seized me, and yet my life still lingers."
Source: 2 Samuel 1:9 (English Standard Version).

Variation: "Stand over me and kill me! I am in the throes of death, but I'm still alive."
Source: 2 Samuel 1:9 (New International Version).

Variation: "Stand, I pray thee, over me, and slay me; for anguish has seized me; for my life is yet whole in me."
Source: 2 Samuel 1:9 (Darby Translation).

Variation: "Stand over me, and kill me: for anguish is come upon me, and as yet my whole life is in me."
Source: 2 Samuel 1:9 (Douay-Rheims Translation).

Variation: "Stand, I pray thee, over me, and put me to death, for seized me hath the arrow, for all my soul [is] still in me."
Source: 2 Samuel 1:9 (Young's Literal Translation).

Saunders, Laurence

(d. 1555) English martyr. Condemned for heresy during the reign of Queen Mary. Burned at the stake in Coventry.

Last Words: "Welcome the cross of Christ, welcome everlasting life." Spoken as he took into his arms the stake to which he was to be chained and kissed it.
Source: *Book of Martyrs and the Acts and Monuments of the Church* by John Fox (or Foxe). First published 1563, ed. by John Cumming (London, 1851).

Savage, Richard

(1697-1743) English poet, playwright. Claimed to be the illegitimate son of 4th Earl Rivers and the Countess of Macclesfield. Subject of Dr. Samuel Johnson's *Life of Savage.* Killed a man in a tavern brawl. Escaped hanging. Died at age 46 in debtors' prison in Bristol, England.

Last Words: "I have something to say to you, sir. ''Tis gone!'" Spoken to his jailer.
Source: *Lives of the English Poets and a Criticism of Their Work* by Samuel Johnson (Oxford, England, 1825).

Savina, Saint

(d. 311) Italian holy woman, martyr. Sister of Saint Savinianus. Aided prisoners of Emperor Diocletian. Helped bury them after they were executed. Died in Milan, Italy.

Last Words: "O Lord, Who hast ever preserved me in chastity, suffer me not longer to be wearied with journeying! Command me not to go beyond this place! Let my body here find rest! I commend to Thee my servant, who has borne so much for me, and let me be worthy to see my brother in Thy Kingdom, whom I have not seen here!"
Source: *The Golden Legend or Lives of the Saints.* Compiled by Jacobus de Voragine, Archbishop of Genoa, 1275, 1st ed., 1470. English ed. by William Caxton, 1483, ed. by F.S. Ellis (Edinburgh, 1900).

Savinianus, Saint

(d. 275) Italian holy man. Apostle of Troyes, France. Brother of Saint Savina.

Last Words: "Fear not to strike me down; and do ye bear away some drops of my blood to the emperor, that he may receive his sight, and acknowledge the power of God!"
Source: *The Golden Legend or Lives of the Saints.* Compiled by Jacobus de Voragine, Archbishop of Genoa, 1275, 1st ed., 1470. English ed. by William Caxton, 1483, ed. by F.S. Ellis (Edinburgh, 1900).

Savio, Saint Dominic

(1842-1857) Italian student, holy man. Pupil of Saint Don Bosco. Died at age 14 of pneumonia while studying to be a priest. Canonized in 1954.

Different Last Words:

(1) "Goodbye father, goodbye; the priest wanted to tell me something else, but I cannot remember it now. Oh, what a beautiful sight I behold." He died soon afterward.
Source: *The Life of Dominic Savio,* tr. from work of Don Bosco (London, 1914).

(2) "Surely you're not crying, Mom, at seeing me go to heaven? Look, Dad, look! Can't you see? The wonderful! The beautiful!"
Source: *The Life of Dominic Savio* by Peter Lappin (New Rochelle, NY, 1954).

Savonarola, Girolamo Maria Francesco Matteo

(1452-1498) Italian religious reformer. Dominican monk. Preached reform. Imprisoned for sedition, disobedience, and heresy. Tortured, executed at age 45 with two other Dominicans by burning at the stake in Florence, Italy. Leading character in George Eliot's *Romola.* Also a character in Harriet Beecher Stowe's *Agnes of Sorrento.*
Different Last Words:

(1) "The Lord hath suffered as much for me." Spoken to a priest who asked him: "In what spirit dost thou bear martyrdom?"
Source: *Life and Times of Girolamo Savonarola* by Pasquale Villari (New York, 1896).

(2) "O Florence, what hast thou done this day?"
Source: *Dawn of the Reformation. Savonarola* by Rev. William H. Rule (London, 1855).
Variation: "O Florence, what hast thou done today?"
Source: *The Last Words (Real and Traditional) of Distinguished Men and Women Collected from Various Sources* by Frederic Rowland Marvin (New York, 1901). Marvin mentioned (1) was sometimes given as his Last Words.

Saxe, Hermann Maurice, Comte de

(1696-1750) German military officer. Illegitimate son of Augustus II, Elector of Saxony. Created marshal of France. Known as Marshal de Saxe. Regarded as among greatest generals of his age. Defeated English and Hanoverians at Fontenoy. Captured at Maastricht. Died at age 54 in Chambord, France.
Last Words: "Doctor, life is but a dream. Mine has been beautiful but it has been brief."
Source: *Maurice de Saxe, étude historique d'après les documents des archives de Dresden* by Saint-René Taillandier (Paris, 1865).

Scarron, Paul

(1610-1660) French writer, poet, playwright, novelist. Married Françoise d'Aubigne who later became Madame de Maintenon. Notable work: *The Comic Novel.* Suffered from rheumatism; was paralytic the last 22 years of his life. Died at age 50 in Paris.
Last Words: "Ah, my children, you will never weep for me so much as I have made you laugh." Spoken to his family and servants shortly before his death. A few minutes before he died he said he never thought it was "so easy a matter to laugh at the approach of death."
Source: *Curiosities of Literature* by Isaac D'Israeli (London, 1893).

Schaft, Jannetje Johanna ("Hannie")

(1920-1945) Dutch antiwar activist. Resistance fighter during World War II. Nickname "Het meisje met het rode haar" ("Girl with the red hair") later became the title of a book and movie about her. Her secret name in the resistance movement was Hannie. She was captured at the end of the war and executed at age 24 despite a ban on executing women. Several streets and schools were named in her honor, as was the foundation Stichting Nationale Hannie Schaftherdenking.
Last Words: "Ik schiet beter." (tr. "I shoot better than you.") Spoken to her executioner after she was shot the first time and only wounded. This quote is questionable. Many sources say it was "supposedly spoken."
Source: *Hannie Schaft: het levensverhaal van een vrouw in verzet tegen de nazi's* by T. Kors (Amsterdam, The Netherlands, 1980).

Schell, Augustus

(1812-1884) American politician, lawyer, industrialist. Joined Tammany Hall. After William M. Tweed's downfall, Schell was named Grand Sachem. Served as Chairman of the Democratic National Committee. Reorganized Tammany Hall but was an unsuccessful candidate for several offices. Was an early expert in the new field of corporate law and active in railroad management. Friend of Cornelius Vanderbilt. Gradually expanded his railroad connections through investments and legal counsel. Died at age 72 in New York.

Last Words: "My dear brother Edward." Spoken to his brother who was at his bedside along with another brother Robert and nephews Austin G. Fox and James W. Fellowes.

Source: "Funeral of Augustus Schell" (*New York Times*, March 28, 1884).

Schiele, Egon

(1890-1918) Austrian artist, painter. Expressionist who used sharp lines and bright colors. He was influenced by the works of Austrian artist Gustave Klimt. Died at age 28 of Spanish influenza during the last days of World War I.

Last Words: "The war is over and I must go. My paintings should be seen in museums worldwide." Spoken as he was dying.

Source: *Egon Schiele* by Serge Sabarsky, Egon Schiele and Robert Waissenberger (New York, 1984).

Schiller, Johann Christophe Friedrich von

(1759-1805) German writer, playwright, poet, historian. Friend of Goethe. Notable works: *William Tell; Mary Stuart; The Maid of Orleans; The Song of the Bell; Wallenstein.* Died at age 45 of tuberculosis in Weimar.

Different Last Words:

(1) "Judex!" (tr. "The judge.")

Source: *Schiller, Sein Leben und seine Werke* by Karl Berger (Munich, Germany, 1923).

(2) "Many things are growing plain and clear to my understanding." He closed his eyes, and fell into a sleep that deepened into death.

Sources: "The Life of Friedrich Schiller, Comprehending an Examination of his Works" (*American Quarterly Review*, Vol. XIII, No. 25, March 1833); "Studies in German Literature, 1770-1832" (*Monthly Packet of Evening Readings for Members of the English Church*, Vol. I, ed. by Charlotte M. Yonge, January 1891).

(3) "Liebe, gute." (tr. "Dear, good one.") Spoken to his wife Lotte.

Source: *The Life of Schiller* by Heinrich Düntzer and Percy Pinkerton (London, 1883).

(4) "Better and better, calmer and calmer." Spoken to his sister-in-law when she asked how he felt. That night his sleep was disturbed and his mind wandered. The next day, he tried to say the word "naphtha" but could not pronounce the last syllable. He tried to write but could trace only three letters that were not distinct. His wife, sister-in-law and physician were with him when he died soon afterward.

Source: *The Poems and Ballads of Schiller, with a Brief Sketch of the Author's Life,* tr. by Edward Bulwer-Lytton (Leipzig, Germany, 1844).

Schimmelpenninck, Mary Anne Galton

(1778-1856) English writer, theologian, abolitionist. Notable work: *Select Memoirs of the Port Royal.* Died at age 77 in Bristol.

Last Words: "Rejoice with me, rejoice with me! I am entering my Father's house. Do you not hear the voices? And the children's are the loudest!"

Source: *Life of Mary Anne Schimmelpenninck,* ed. by Christiana C. Hankin (London, 1858).

Schlageter, Albert Leo

(1894-1923) German soldier, saboteur. Fought in World War I. Later was a member of the German Freikorps. Executed by a French firing squad in Ruhr. Became martyr figure for National Socialists (Nazis). German Communist party sought to counter growing mythology of Schlageter by publicizing a speech by Karl Radek that portrayed Schlageter as misguided. But the Nazis exploited his story. Ceremonies were created to commemorate his death. By the mid-1930s, Schlageter had become a Nazi folk hero and martyr. Playwright Hanns Johst wrote the heroic drama play *Schlageter* in 1933. It was performed on the anniversary of the date Hitler took power. Among items named for Schlageter were the Jagdgeschwader 26 Schlageter fighter-wing of the Luftwaffe and the sailing ship *Albert Leo Schlageter.*

Last Words: "I find some satisfaction in dying. Perhaps I can help through my example. —From 1914 until this day, I have sacrificed all my strength and labor, out of love and loyalty, to my German homeland. Where it was in need, I sought to help.— Greet my parents, brothers and sisters, relatives, my friends, and my Germany!"

Source: "Ihr Vermächtnis. Letzte Worte unserer Toten" (*Der Schulungsbrief*, 1936).

Schlegel, Karl Wilhelm Friedrich von

(1772-1829) German writer, poet, philosopher, critic. Notable work: *Lucinde* (semi-autobiographical novel). Schlegel died at age 56 of a stroke in Dresden, Germany.

Last Words (written): "But the consummate and perfect knowledge—." The words were part of an unfinished lecture.

Source: *Sämmtliche Werke* by Friedrich von Schlegel (Vienna, Austria, 1846).

Schleiermacher, Friedrich Ernst Daniel

(1768-1834) German theologian, educator, orator, philosopher. Professor at Halle and Berlin. Notable work: *Der christliche glaube* (*The Christian Faith*). Died at age 65 of pneumonia in Berlin.

Last Words: "Now I can no longer remain here. —Place me in another position." Spoken to his family. He was placed on his side, breathed a few times then died.

Source: *Life of Schleiermacher as Unfolded in His Autobiography and Letters*, tr. by Frederica Rowan (London, 1860).

Schmidt, Hans-Theodor

(1899-1951) German military officer. Nazi lieutenant. An adjutant at Buchenwald concentration camp during World War II. Tried at the end of war as a Nazi war criminal. Found guilty, sentenced to death in 1948. His execution and those of six others were delayed several years due to court battles. Died at age 51.

Last Words: "Like me, you are obeying orders.—I am dying innocent." Cried out to the hangman.

Source: "Case Closed" (*Time* magazine, June 16, 1951).

Schmitt, Aloysius Herman

(1909-1941) American military chaplain. Assigned to the USS *Oklahoma* at Pearl Harbor when it was attacked on December 7, 1941. He pushed sailors through a porthole to safety while the *Oklahoma* sank. Responsible for saving many lives. Died at age 32 aboard ship.

Last Words: "Go ahead boys, I'm all right." Spoken after he insisted on being the last through the porthole, then his shoulders became wedged.

Source: *Heroes of the Pacific* by Ted Shane (New York, 1944).

Schnorr von Carolsfeld, Ludwig

(1836-1865) German singer. Operatic tenor.

Son of German artist Julius Schnorr von Carolsfeld. Made his operatic debut in 1855. His voice impressed German composer Richard Wagner, who asked him to create the role of Tristan in 1865. Schnorr died suddenly in Dresden at the age of 29, six weeks after the premiere. His cause of death, mysterious at the time, is believed to have been typhoid or meningitis.

Last Words: "Farewell, Siegfried! Console my Richard!"

Source: *The Dream King, Ludwig II of Bavaria* by Wilfrid Blunt (New York, 1970).

Schoenberg, Arnold

(1874-1951) Austrian-born American musician, composer, educator, conductor, painter. Emigrated to U.S. in 1933; became U.S. citizen in 1940. Professor at University of California, Los Angeles. Musical revolutionary: Abandoned traditional tone system and wrote much of his music in a 12-tone idiom. Composed for chorus, orchestra, piano. Wrote books on harmony. Notable works: *String Quartets Nos. 3 and 4; Gurre-lieder; Pierre Lunaire*. Died at age 76 in Los Angeles.

Different Last Words:

(1) "Harmony." His wife and a nurse were at his side.

Source: *Schoenberg: A Critical Biography* by Willi Reich (New York, 1971).

(2) "Has Ronny won?" He was asking about his son who was participating in a tennis match.

Source: *Schoenberg* by J.H. Stuckenschmidt (London, 1977).

Scholl, Art

(1931-1985) American aerobatic pilot, aerial cameraman. Multiple-time member of the U.S. Aerobatics team. Frequent contender at National Air Races in Reno. Formed own film production company. Killed during the filming of *Top Gun* when his camera plane went into a fatal flat spin and plunged into the Pacific Ocean. His camera work can be seen in *The Right Stuff; The Great Waldo Pepper; Blue Thunder; The A-Team* and *CHiPS*. The movie *Top Gun* is dedicated to his memory. Scholl's estate donated his DeHavilland DHC-1A Chipmunk Pennzoil Special to the Smithsonian Air and Space

Museum. Art Scholl Memorial Field in Rialto, California, and the Art Scholl Showmanship Award were named for him.
Last Words: "I've got a problem. I've really got a problem." His last recorded words.
Source: *Slipping the Surly Bonds: Great Quotations on Flight* compiled by David English (New York, 1998).

Scholl, Hans

(1918-1943) German World War II antiwar protestor, activist. Prominent member of White Rose nonviolent anti-Nazi resistance movement in Germany. Scholl and his sister Sophie were executed by guillotine after they were convicted of treason for distributing antiwar leaflets at the University of Munich. He was executed immediately after his sister. German literary prize, Geschwister-Scholl-Preis, was named for them.
Last Words: "Es lebe die Freiheit!" (tr. "Long live freedom!")
Source: *Sophie Scholl and the White Rose* by Jud Newborn and Annette Dumbach (Oxford, England, 2006).

Scholl, Sophia Magdalena

(1921-1943) German World War II antiwar protestor, activist. Prominent member of White Rose nonviolent anti-Nazi resistance movement in Germany. Scholl and her brother Hans were executed by guillotine after they were convicted of treason for distributing antiwar leaflets at the University of Munich. Since the 1970s, she has been celebrated as a great hero for actively opposing the Third Reich. In 1991, she was featured on a German postage stamp. The 2005 Academy Award-nominated movie *Sophie Scholl–Die letzten Tag* (tr. *Sophie Scholl – The Last Days*) is about the end of her life.
Different Last Words:
(1) "Your heads will fall as well!" Her Last Words are also given as "God, you are my refuge into eternity" but there is dispute over whether Sophie or her brother Hans said either or both of these statements.
Source: *Sophie Scholl and the White Rose* by Jud Newborn and Annette Dumbach (Oxford, England, 2006).
(2) (doubtful): "Die Sonne scheint noch." (tr. "The Sun still shines.") These were the Last Words she spoke in the movie. Much of the material was based on Gestapo documents in East Germany that were not released until 1990.
Source: *Sophie Scholl–Die letzten Tag* (tr. *Sophie Scholl –The Last Days*), movie, 2005.

Schreiner, Olive Emilie Albertina

(1855-1920) South African writer, essayist, novelist. Her novel *The Story of an African Farm* was published in 1883 under a man's name: Ralph Iron. When the book became a sensation and her identity was learned, she became a public figure. She wrote much but published little. Suffered from asthma in later years. Died at age 65 of heart failure in Cape Town.
Last Words (written): "I long to see the stars and the veld: one day I will go up to Matjesfontein just for one day, if I can find anyone to take me. It doesn't seem to me this is Africa. A Happy New Year, my dear one." Letter. Matjesfontein was a small settlement in Cape Colony where she lived for a while.
Source: *The Life of Olive Schreiner* by S. C. Cronwright-Schreiner (Boston, 1924). The author was her husband.

Schreuder, Willem

(1928-1977) Dutch pilot. Airline tragedy victim. Flight engineer of KLM Royal Dutch Airlines Boeing 747-206B that collided with a Pan-Am Boeing 747 on the ground in the Canary Islands. It was one of the worst aviation disasters ever with 583 people killed. The KLM plane had taken off without take-off clearance due to a misunderstanding between the tower and the aircraft.
Last Words: "Is he not clear, that Pan-American?") Transcription of the cockpit voice recorder.
Source: *JAR Professional Pilot Studies* by Phil Croucher (Morrisville, NC, 2004).

Schrödinger, Erwin

(1887-1961) Austrian physicist. Known for his work on wave theory and quantum mechanics. Devised Schrödinger's cat paradoxical thought experiment. Shared 1933 Nobel Prize for Physics with Paul Dirac. Died at age 73 of tuberculosis in Vienna.
Last Words: "Annikin, stay with me—so that I don't crash." Spoken to his wife after she gave him a sip of orange juice. He died later that evening.

Source: *Schrödinger: Life and Thought* by Walter Moore (Cambridge, England, 1989).

Schubert, Franz Peter

(1797-1828) Austrian musician, composer, pianist. Perfected German lied, or art song. Wrote more than 600 songs, including "Hark, Hark the Lark" and "Who is Sylvia?" Other notable works: symphonies, sonatas, chamber music, and more. Died at age 31 of typhus in Vienna.

Last Words: "Hier, hier ist mein Ende." (tr. "Here, here is my end.")

Source: *Franz Schubert: The Man and His Circle* by Newman Flower (New York, 1928).

Schultz, Dutch

(1902-1935) American mobster, bootlegger. Real name Arthur Flegenheimer. Ambushed, shot and fatally wounded in a restaurant. Died in a Newark, New Jersey, hospital. Police stenographer took down his Last Words. When asked who shot him, he said he didn't get a look and didn't know who could have done it. Schultz's Last Words have become famous for being a collection of irrational ramblings. But when he spoke them, he was suffering from a serious wound and delirious with a high fever.

Last Words: "Turn your back to me, please. Henry. I am so sick now. The police are getting many complaints. Look out. I want that G-note. Look out for Jimmy Valentine, for he is an old pal of mine. Come on, come on, Jim. Okay, okay. I am all through. Can't do another thing. Look out, Mama. Look out for her. You can't beat him. Police, Mama, Helen, mother, please take me out. I will settle the indictment. … Shut up. You got a big mouth. Please help me get up, Henry! Max! Come over here. French Canadian bean soup. I want to pay. Let them leave me alone." He fell asleep and died two hours later. His Last Words were recorded by F.J. Long, clerk-stenographer, Newark Police Department.

Source: *A Century of Journalism. An Anthology of Outstanding Feature Articles from the* New York Post, *New York's Oldest Newspaper, Founded in 1801* (New York, 1943).

Schumann, Clara Josephine Wieck

(1819-1896) German musician, pianist, teacher, composer. Child prodigy. Wife of German composer Robert Schumann. Devoted friend of Johannes Brahms. Taught many years at a conservatory in Frankfurt, Germany. Concertized extensively. Suffered a stroke in March 1896; died two months later at age 76.

Last Words: "You two must go to a beautiful place this summer." Spoken to her children.

Source: *Clara Schumann: A Romantic Biography* by John N. Burk (New York, 1940).

Schumann, Robert Alexander

(1810-1856) German composer, conductor, pianist, critic. Married pianist Clara Wieck. Composed symphonies, concertos. chamber music, songs, song cycles, piano solos and more. Notable works: *Rhenish Symphony; Piano Concerto in A Minor; Kinderscenen* (for piano). Showed signs of mental instability in his early 40s. Institutionalized during his final two years after he tried to kill himself. Died at age 46 in Endenich, Germany.

Last Words: "My Clara—I know." Spoken to his wife Clara.

Source: *Schumann and the Romantic Age* by Marcel Brion (London, 1956).

Schurz, Carl

(1829-1906) German-born American military officer, politician, reformer, writer, editor, diplomat. U.S. minister to Spain. General in Union Army in U.S. Civil War. Member U.S. Senate from Missouri. U.S. secretary of the interior. Died at age 77 in New York City.

Last Words: "It is so simple to die."

Source: *Carl Schurz, Reformer: 1829-1906* by Claude M. Fuess (New York, 1932).

Schwarzenberg, Felix, Prince of Austria

(1800-1852) Austrian statesman, military officer, prime minister. Nephew of Prince Karl Philip. Served in the army and diplomatic corps. Helped Josef Radetzky defeat rebels in Italy. Restored Hapsburg power in Europe. Died at age 51 suddenly of apoplexy.

Last Words: "That manner of death meets with my full approval." Spoken to his doctor who warned him he would have a stroke if he continued carrying on in the same way.

Source: *Prince Felix zu Schwarzenberg, Prime Minister of Austria 1838-1852* by Adolph Schwarzenberg (New

York, 1946). The author was a member of the wealthy and influential family.

Schweitzer, Albert

(1875-1965) French clergyman, physician, humanitarian, music scholar, writer, medical missionary. Protestant. Founded hospital at Lambaréné, French Equatorial Africa. Awarded Nobel Peace Prize (1952). Died at age 90 at Lambaréné.

Last Words (doubtful): "I'm tired, very tired." Spoken to his daughter.

Source: *Last Words: A Dictionary of Deathbed Quotations* by C. Bernard Ruffin (Jefferson, NC, 1995).

Life magazine reported that Schweitzer left no Last Words. No messages, no prophesies. He went to bed, fell into a coma and died.

Source: "Albert Schweitzer is Buried at His Jungle Mission. Goodbye at Lambarene" by Rudolph Chelminski (*Life* magazine, September 17, 1965).

Schwerin, Kurt Christoph, Graf von

(1684-1757) Prussian nobleman, military officer. Count. Field marshal. One of the top commanders of Frederick the Great. Distinguished leader in the Battle of Mollwitz, Second Silesian War and Seven Years' War. Shot and killed at age 72 while leading his regiment after the Battle of Prague.

Last Words: "Let all brave Prussians follow me." Spoken just before he died in battle.

Source: *Percy Anecdotes: Original and Select* by Sholto Percy and Reuben Percy (London 1823).

Schwind, Moritz von

(1804-1871) Austrian artist, painter, Close friend of Schubert. Illustrated his songs. Illustrated works of Goethe and other German writers. Versatile artist who also did murals, church altars and windows. Notable works: S*ingers' Contest; Honey Moon;* Glasgow Cathedral (designs for stained glass). Died at age 67 in Bavaria.

Last Word: "Excellent." His response when asked how he felt.

Source: *Franz Schubert: The Man and His Circle* by Newman Flower (New York, 1928).

Scipio Nasica (Quintus Caecilius Metellus Pius Scipio Nasica)

(100?-46 B.C.) Roman military officer, politician, general. Tribune and later consul with Pompey the Great. Fought against Caesar and Marcus Antonius. Was at the Battle of Pharsalus. Fled to Africa and commanded an army with Cato the Younger. Lost the Battle of Thapsus. Committed suicide by stabbing himself so he would not be captured.

Last Words: "Bene se habet imperator!" (tr. "All is well with the general!") Spoken as he stabbed himself.

Source: *L. Annaei Flori Epitome rerum Romanarum* by Lucius Annaeus Florus (London, 1818).

Scobee, Francis Richard ("Dick")

(1939-1986) American astronaut. Victim of *Challenger* disaster. NASA commander of *Challenger* mission STS-51-L. One of seven astronauts killed in the explosion of the Shuttle *Challenger*. Died at age 46. Seconds before the crash, ground control radioed him: "You're go for throttle up."

Last Words: "Roger, Houston, go at throttle up." The explosion followed within seconds.

Source: "Challenger Explodes/Shuttle Falls into Ocean; Crew Apparently Killed" by Carlos Byars (*Houston Chronicle,* January 28, 1986).

Scott, James, 1st Duke of Monmouth

(1649-1685) English nobleman. Known as James Fitzroy and James Crofts. Claimant to the throne. 1st Duke of Monmouth and of Buccleuch. Illegitimate son of Charles II. Led an unsuccessful rebellion against Charles's successor, James II. Executed on Tower Hill after losing the Battle of Sedgemoor. His executioner was Jack Ketch.

Last Words: "There are six guineas for you, and do not hack me as you did my Lord Russell. I have heard that you struck him three or four times. My servant will give you more gold if you do your work well." Spoken to his executioner, Jack Ketch.

Source: *Famous Sayings and Their Authors: A Collection of Historical Sayings in English, French, German, Greek, Italian, and Latin* by Edward Latham (London, 1906).

Variation: "Prithee, let me feel the axe. I fear it is not sharp enough. Do not hack me as you did my Lord Russell." Spoken to his executioner Jack Ketch. When Ketch executed Lord Russell in 1683, the beheading was clumsy and drew the criticism of Monmouth. Despite the duke's plea, Ketch did a terrible job of removing Monmouth's head. It required at least five blows with an axe

and finally some cutting with a knife. Legend persists that after Monmouth died, his executors realized there was no official portrait of him, so they sewed his head back on his body and posed the corpse for a painting.
Source: *Tyburn Tree: Its History and Annals* by Alfred Marks (London, 1910).

Scott, John, 1st Earl of Eldon

(1751-1838) English nobleman, jurist, politician. Member of Parliament. Lord high chancellor of England. As justice, in 1816, he refused to grant to Percy Bysshe Shelley custody of Shelley's two children because of his atheism. Died at age 86 in London.
Last Words: "It matters not to me, where I am going, whether the weather here be hot or cold." His response when someone commented that it was a cold day.
Source: *Lives of the Lord Chancellors and Keepers of the Great Seal Of England, from the Earliest Times Till the Reign of Queen Victoria* by Baron John Campbell and John A. Mallory (Boston, 1874-1875).

Scott, Robert Falcon

(1868-1912) English Antarctic explorer. Arrived at the South Pole with his team on January 18, 1912, only to find Norwegian explorer Roald Admundsen and his party had reached it a month earlier. Scott and his companions became lost on the return trip and died. Search party later found their bodies on the Ross Ice Shelf.
Last Words (written): "For God's sake look after our people." Final entry in Scott's diary, written Thursday March 29, 1912.
Source: *The Epic of Captain Scott* by Martin Lindsay (New York, 1934).

Scott, Sir Walter

(1771-1832) Scottish poet, novelist, historian, biographer. Knighted in 1820. Notable works: *The Lady of the Lake; Rob Roy; The Heart of Midlothian; Ivanhoe*. He was left with a massive debt when the printing/publishing firms in which he was partner failed. He accepted responsibility and spent the rest of his life paying his debts. He suffered debilitating strokes during the last two years. Died at age 61 in Abbotsford, Scotland.
Different Last Words:
(1) "God bless you all; I feel myself again."

Spoken to his family.
Source: *Memoirs of the Life of Sir Walter Scott* by John Gibson Lockhart (Edinburgh, 1837). The author was married to Scott's daughter Charlotte Sophia.
(2) "Lockhart, be a good man—be virtuous—be religious—be a good man. Nothing else will give you any comfort when you come to lie here."
Source: *Hours at Home: Popular Magazine*, ed. by J.M. Sherwood, Vol. 1, May-October 1865.
(3) "There is but one book. Bring me the Bible." Spoken to Lockhart when asked what book he wished to have read to him.
Source: *Lost Forever* by Luther Tracy Townsend (Boston, 1875). Townsend noted that Scott spoke these words "while death was approaching."

Scott, Walter Edward ("Death Valley Scotty")

(1872-1954) American mining prospector, adventurer, con man. Worked with Buffalo Bill Cody's Wild West Show as a stunt rider. Gained fame by staging a race to break the cross-country train speed record. Convinced many people to invest in a gold mine he said he found in Death Valley, California. Built Scotty's Castle that became a tourist attraction. Died at age 81 in Death Valley.
Last Words (doubtful): "I got four things to live by: Don't say nothing that will hurt anybody; Don't give advice—nobody will take it anyway. Don't complain. Don't explain."
Source: Various Last Words compilations and Internet sites.
These are the words on his epitaph. Scott died in an ambulance on the way to a Las Vegas hospital. He wanted a simple message on his tombstone: "Here he is." Instead, his favorite motto is there.
Source: *Southern California's Best Ghost Town: A Practical Guide* by Philip Varney (Norman, OK, 1994).

Scott, Winfield

(1786-1866) American military officer, lawyer, politician. Known as Old Fuss and Feathers for his dress and decorum. General in chief of U.S. Army. Fought in War of 1812, Mexican War. Whig U.S. Presidential candidate. Retired 1861. Died at age 79 in West Point, New York.
Last Words: "Peter, take good care of my horse."

Source: *General Scott* by General Marcus J. Wright (New York, 1894).

Variation: "James, take good care of the horse." Spoken to his servant.

Source: *Appleton's Cyclopaedia of American Biography*, Vol. 5, ed. by James Grant Wilson and John Fiske (New York, 1886-1891).

Scriabin, Alexander

(1872-1915) Russian musician, composer. Wrote mainly for orchestra and piano. Notable work: *Poem of Ecstasy*. Died at age 43 in Moscow of septicemia from an insect bite.

Last Words: "Suffering is necessary. It is good. I have a sense of well-being in suffering."

Source: *Milton Cross's Encyclopedia of the Great Composers and Their Music* by Milton Cross and David Ewen (Garden City, NY, 1962).

Scripps, Edward Wyllis

(1854-1926) American newspaper publisher, philanthropist. Founded E.W. Scripps Co. and United Press International. Scripps School of Journalism at Ohio University, Scripps Institution of Oceanography in La Jolla, California, were named for him. Died at age 71 aboard his yacht.

Last Words: "Too many cigars this evening, I guess." Spoken after complaining about not feeling well. He was a heavy cigar smoker.

Source: *Lusty Scripps: The Life of E.W. Scripps* by Gilson Gardner (New York, 1932).

Sedgwick, John

(1813-1864) American military leader. General in Union Army in U.S. Civil War. Admired by officers and men who called him Uncle John. Scoffed as a Confederate sharpshooter started firing from out of sight. His men began ducking. He was killed at age 50 at the Battle of Spotsylvania, Virginia.

Last Words: "Why, my man, I am ashamed of you, dodging that way. They couldn't hit an elephant at this distance." The soldier rose, saluted and told the general he had dodged a shell once. If he hadn't, it would have taken off his head. The general laughed and said: "All right, my man; go to your place." Sedgwick was then hit by a bullet as he spoke with another officer.

Source: "The Death of General John Sedgwick" by General Martin T. McMahon in *Battle and Leaders of the Civil War*, ed. by Robert Underwood Johnson and Clarence Clough Buel (New York, 1887).

Segrave, Sir Henry O'Neal de Hane

(1896-1930) British sportsman, speedboat racer. Published *The Lure of Speed* in 1928. Knighted in 1929. Killed at age 33 at Lake Windemere, Cumbia, England, while attempting to break a world speedboat record. His boat *Miss England II* swerved and turned over. He punctured a lung and died that night. The Segrave trophy was established to commemorate him.

Last Words: "Did we do it?" His wife told him he had broken the record. He died a few minutes later.

Source: *Speedboat Kings: 25 Years of International Speedboating* by J. Lee Barrett (Detroit, 1939).

Selwyn, George Augustus

(1809-1878) British prelate, missionary. First Anglican Bishop of New Zealand. Studied Maori language. Returned to England in 1867 to become Bishop of Lichfield. Died at age 69. Selwyn College at Cambridge was named for him.

Last Words: "It is all light." Spoken just before he died.

Sources: *Memoir of the Life and Episcopate of George Augustus Selwyn, D.D., Bishop of New Zealand, 1841-1867; Bishop of Lichfield, 1867-1878* by H.W. Tucker (New York, 1879).

Selznick, David Oliver

(1902-1965) American movie producer. Notable movies: *Gone With the Wind; Rebecca; Spellbound; Since You Went Away*. Nominated for six Academy Awards for Best Picture. Won for *Rebecca* and *Gone With the Wind*. Won Irving G. Thalberg Memorial Award. Suffered several heart attacks. Died at age 63 in Hollywood, California.

Last Words: "Mind if I sit down?" He died of a heart attack immediately afterward.

Source: *Showman: The Life of David O. Selznick* by David Thompson (New York, 1992).

Seneca, Lucius Annaeus

(4 B.C.-65 A.D.) Roman philosopher, orator, statesman, tragedian. Stoic. One of the brilliant minds of mid-1st century A.D. Rome. Tutor of Nero who later turned against him and ordered him to take his own life.

Last Words: "I offer this liquid as a libation

to Jupiter the Deliverer." Spoken as he opened veins on his arms. Bleeding, he entered a pool of heated water and died.

Source: *The Annals of Imperial Rome* by Cornelius Tacitus, Book XV, tr. by Michael Grant (New York, 1973).

Seraphim of Sarov, Saint

(1759-1833) Russian priest, hermit, mystic, monk, holy man. Birth name Prokhor Moshnin. Known for mystical powers. Took monastic vows at age 27. Became a hermit. Lived in a forest. Canonized by the Russian Orthodox Church in 1903.

Last Words: "O Passover, great and most Holy, O Christ, O Wisdom, Word, and Power of God. Grant that we may more perfectly partake of you in the day that knows no end, in Your kingdom."

Source: *The Royal Road to Joy: The Beatitudes and the Eucharist* by David Bird (Chicago, 2003).

Şerbănescu, Alexandru ("Alecu")

(1912-1944) Romanian military officer, pilot. One of the leading Romanian fighter pilots and flying aces of the Romanian Royal Aeronautics in World War II. Credited with 47 confirmed victories (and 8 probable). On August 18 1944, he and his 12 wingmen attacked a swarm of American planes. Two of his squadron attempted to clear his tail, but it was too late and he was killed. Five days later, Romania signed the armistice.. A boulevard in Bucharest was named in his honor.

Last Words: "My boys, I'm going down…"

Source: *Un nume de legenda—Cpt. av. erou Alexandru Serbănescu* by Vasile Tudor (Bucharest, Romania, 1998).

Serling, Rodman Edward ("Rod")

(1924-1975) American writer, actor, educator, producer, director. Wrote and hosted television shows. More than 200 of his teleplays were produced. He wrote 92 of the 156 episodes of *The Twilight Zone*. Won six Emmy Awards. Did voice-overs and narrations. Taught at Ithaca College, New York. Had two heart attacks. Died at age 50 in Rochester, New York after surgery.

Last Words (spoken): "That's what I anticipate death will be: a totally unconscious void in which you float through eternity with no particular consciousness about any-

thing."

Source: *Rod Serling: The Dreams and Nightmares of Life in the Twilight Zone* by Joe Engel (Chicago, 1989).

Last Words (written): "You can't kill this tough Jew." Written from his hospital bed to former *Twilight Zone* colleague Owen Comora.

Source: *Serling: The Rise and Fall of Television's Last Angry Man* by Gordon F. Sander (New York, 1992).

Serment, Louise-Anastasia

(1642-1692) French natural philosopher, poet. Disciple of Descartes. Known as The Philosopher because of her rare attainments in ethics in literature. Died of breast cancer.

Last Words:
"Soon the light of the skies
Will be gone from my eyes.
Soon the black night will creep,
Bringing smooth dreamless sleep.
Gone—the struggle and strife
Of the sad dream of life!"

Source: *Biographie universelle*, Book XXXIX, by J. Fr. Michaud and Louis Gabriel Michaud (Paris, 1811-1862).

Serra, Miguel José ("Junípero")

(1713-1784) Spanish-born clergyman. Franciscan missionary. Helped with Spanish conquest and colonization of California. Founded San Diego mission in 1769, followed by eight others. Died at age 70 in his sleep at Mission San Carlos Borromeo of Carmel, near Monterey, California.

Last Words: "Now I shall rest."

Source: *Junipero Serra* by Agnes Repplier (New York, 1933).

Servetus, Michael

(1511-1553) Spanish theologian, physician, heretic, martyr. Killed during the Reformation for criticizing doctrine of the Trinity, infant baptism and original sin. Burned at the stake in Geneva, Switzerland, when he refused to retract his beliefs.

Last Words: "Jesus Christ, thou Son of the eternal God, have mercy upon me."

Source: *History of the Christian Church* by Philip Schaff (New York, 1910).

Seton, Saint Elizabeth Ann Bayley

(1774-1821) American nun, holy woman. Founder and first superior of Sisters of Charity of St. Vincent de Paul in U.S. Known as Mother Seton. Died at age 46 of tuberculosis in Emmitsburg, Maryland. Canonized in 1975. First native-born North American saint. Seton Hall University was named for her.

Last Words: "Jesus, Mary, Joseph."

Source: *His Dear Persuasion: The Life of Elizabeth Ann Seton* by Katherine Burton (New York, 1944).

Seume, Johann Gottfried

(1763-1810) German writer, traveler. Described his nine-month walk to Sicily in *Spaziergang nach Syrakus*. Later, he visited Russia, Finland and Sweden and wrote about his journey in *Mein Sommer im Jahr 1805*. Died at age 47.

Last Words: "Nothing, dear Weigel. I only wanted to tell you that you shouldn't be annoyed if I should say some things I wouldn't say in a different situation. I take a guilt with me. You I cannot repay. My eyes grow dim." His response when asked if he wanted anything.

Source: *J.G. Seume. Geschichte seines Lebens and seiner Schriften* by Oskar Planer and Camillo Reismann (Leipzig, Germany, 1898).

Severus, Lucius Septimus, Emperor of Rome

(146-211) Roman ruler, military officer. General, consul. Waged successful war against Parthians. Went to England to suppress revolt of Caledonians in the year 207. Became ill on an expedition to Scotland. Died at age 65 in York, England.

Different Last Words:

(1) "Make haste, if there is anything more for me to do."

Source: *Dio's Rome: An Historical Narrative Originally Composed in Greek During the Reigns of Septimus, Severus, Geta and Caracalla, Macrinus, Elagabalus and Alexander Severus* by Cassius Dio Cocceianus, tr. and ed. by Herbert Baldwin Foster and Joannes Zonaras (Troy, NY, 1906).

(2) "I have been all things, and it has profited nothing."

Source: *Septimus Severus: The African Emperor* by Anthony Richard Birley (London, 1971).

Variation: "I have been everything, and everything is nothing!" He then ordered the urn to be brought to him in which his ashes were to be enclosed. "Little urn thou shalt contain all that remains of one for whom the whole world was too little."

Source: *The Preacher's Commentary on the Book of*

Jeremiah by Richard D. Dickinson (London, 1882).

Sévigné, Françoise Marguerite de

(1646-1705) French writer. Comtesse de Grignan. Known as Madame de Grignan. Daughter of Marquise de Sévigné. Letters from her mother recorded the daily events of their lives. Died at age 58 in Marseille.

Last Words: "Yes, but I am not yet dust and ashes." Spoken to the Abbé La Mousse who chided her on her vanity by saying "Remember that all your beauty will turn to dust and ashes."

Sources: *Aspects of Death and Correlated Aspects of Life in Art, Epigram and Poetry: Contributions Towards an Anthology and an Iconography of the Subject* by Frederick Parkes Weber (New York, 1918); *Madame de Sévigné* by Lady Ritchie [Anne Isabella Thackeray] (Edinburgh, 1881).

Seward, William Henry

(1801-1872) American politician, lawyer, statesman, diplomat. Member U.S. Senate from New York. U.S. secretary of state. Arranged the purchase of Alaska from Russia. Stabbed on the neck and face at his home by a Lincoln conspirator the night Lincoln was killed in 1865. Survived the injury. Died at age 71 in Auburn, New York.

Last Words: "Nothing, only 'love one another.'" Spoken when his daughter-in-law asked if he had anything to say.

Source: *William H. Seward: An Autobiography from 1801 to 1834, with a Memoir of his Life and Selections from his Letters*, ed. by Frederick W. Seward (New York, 1891). The editor was his son.

Seymour, Lady Catherine Grey, Countess of Hertford

(1540-1568) English nobility. Countess of Hertford. Daughter of Henry Grey, 1st Duke of Suffolk. Younger sister of Jane Grey. When Elizabeth I ascended to the throne Catherine was next in line. Her marriage to Edward Seymour in 1560 angered the Queen so much that Catherine was imprisoned in the Tower of London from 1561 to 1563. Catherine died at age 27 of tuberculosis.

Last Words: "Lo, He comes! Yea, even so come, Lord Jesus! Welcome death! O Lord for thy manifold mercies, blot out of Thy book all of my offenses." Sir Owen Hopton saw that her death was near and asked if the bell may be rung to mark her passing. She overheard him and said: "Good Sir Owen, let it be so." Immediately after this conversation she said: "O Lord! into thy hands I commend my spirit." She closed her eyes and died at 9 a.m.

Source: *Lives of the Tudor Princesses Including Lady Jane Grey and Her Sisters* by Agnes Strickland and Elisabeth Strickland (London, 1868).

Seymour, Edward, Duke of Somerset

(1506?-1552) English statesman. Earl of Hertford before he was raised to Duke of Somerset. Brother of Jane Seymour, wife of Henry VIII. Lord protector of England. Views on constitutional liberty differed from council. Indicted by Earl of Warwick and deposed from protectorate. Condemned on the charge of conspiring to murder Warwick. Beheaded at Tower Hill.

Different Last Words:

(1) "Lord Jesus, save me!" He laid his head on the block, repeated this prayer three times and was beheaded.

Source: *Book of Martyrs and the Acts and Monuments of the Church* by John Fox (or Foxe). First published 1563, ed. by John Cumming (London, 1851).

(2) "Masters and good fellows. I am come here to die; but a true and faithful man as any unto the King's Majesty and to his realm. But I am condemned by a law whereunto I am subject, as we all, and therefore to show obedience, I am content to die; wherewith I am well content, being a thing most heartily welcome to me; for the which I do thank God, taking it for a singular benefit as ever might have come to me otherwise."

Source: *History of England from the Fall of Wolsey to the Death of Elizabeth* by James Anthony Froude (New York, 1871). Froude noted that there were several reports of the Duke of Somerset's Last Words. The ones he used were from a manuscript printed by Sir Henry Ellis.

Seyss-Inquart, Artur

(1892-1946) German military officer. Nazi official responsible for deporting Dutch to Germany for labor and Dutch Jews to the east during World War II. Convicted and executed of Nazi war crimes by International Military Tribunal at Nuremberg.

Last Words: "I hope that this execution is the last act of the tragedy of the Second World War and that the lesson taken from this world war will be that peace and understanding should exist between peoples. I believe in Germany."

Source: "The Execution of Nazi War Criminals' by Kingsbury Smith, International News Service (October 16, 1946).

Sforza, Galeazzo Maria, Duke of Milan

(1444-1476) Italian nobleman. Member of the family that ruled Milan in the late 15th and early 16th centuries. Had a reputation for being dissolute and cruel. Assassinated at age 32 by republican conspirators in the Church of San Stefano in Milan. The popular uprising anticipated by the assassins did not materialize.

Last Words: "Oh, God!"

Source: *Renaissance in Italy: The Age of Despots* by John Addington Symonds (New York, 1888).

Shackleton, Sir Ernest

(1874-1922) Irish-born British Antarctic explorer. Member of Robert F. Scott's National Antarctic Expedition in 1901-1904. Knighted in 1909. He was with Scott again in 1909. On his third expedition in 1914-1917, his ship the *Endurance* was caught in an ice pack and sank. While 22 of his men were marooned on Elephant Island, Shackleton and five others went for help. A Chilean ship rescued them in August 1916. He returned to Antarctica for the last time in 1921-1922. Had a heart attack and died at age 47 aboard his ship *Quest* near South Georgia Island.

Last Words: "You are always wanting me to give up something. What do you want me to give up now?" His response to his physician when he was told to take it easy.

Source: *Shackleton's Last Voyage* by Frank Wild (London, 1923). Wild was second in command on the *Endurance* and *Quest* expeditions.

Shakespeare, William

(1564-1616) English playwright, poet. Considered by many to be the world's greatest dramatist. Wrote 37 plays: comedies, romances, histories (based on English royalty) and tragedies. Composed 154 sonnets. Active in London theater from around 1584 to around 1612. Retired to Stratford-upon-Avon, his birthplace. Died at age 52.

Last Words. Unknown. Shakespeare left no recorded Last Words. He drew up his will in

March 1616, leaving most of his estate to his daughter Susanna, with whom he and his wife lived. His wife received the "second-best bed" and furniture. Shakespeare died a month later and was buried in the chancel of Holy Trinity Church in Stratford-upon-Avon. His grave is inscribed with the following epitaph that 17th-century legend claims he wrote:
"Good friend, for Jesus' sake forbear,
To dig the dust enclosed here.
Blest be the man that spares these stones.
And curst be he that moves my bones."
Source: *The Tale of the Shakspere Epitaph* by Edward Hewes Gordon Clark (New York, 1888).

Shakur, Tupac Amaru ("2 Pac")

(1971-1996) American musician, rapper, actor, artist, poet. Birth name Lesane Parish Crooks. Shot four times. Killed at age 25 in Las Vegas, Nevada. Died just as he was establishing a successful movie and music career.
Last Words: "I'm dying. I'm dying." Spoken as he was bought into University Medical Center intensive care unit. He died after undergoing emergency surgery
Source: "Ready to Die" (*Vibe* magazine, Vol. 4, No. 9, November 1996).

Sharp, Cecil James

(1859-1924) English teacher, musicologist, anthologist. Noted collector of English and Appalachian folk songs and dances. Founded English Folk Dance Society. Died at age 64 in Hampstead, England.
Last Words: "Never again." Spoken after he was given an injection and told he would feel no more pain.
Source: *Cecil Sharp* by A.H. Fox Strangways (London, 1933).

Sharp, William ("Fiona Macleod")

(1855-1905) Scottish poet. Pen name Fiona Macleod. Never acknowledged his pseudonym, even when writing a mock biography of Fiona Macleod for *Who's Who*. General editor of "Canterbury Poets" series. Died at age 50 in Castello di Maniace, Sicily.
Last Words: "Oh, the beautiful 'Green Life' again! Ah, all is well."
Source: *William Sharp (Fiona Macleod): A Memoir* compiled by Elizabeth A. Sharp (New York, 1910). The compiler was his wife.

Shastri, Lal Bahadur

(1904-1966) Indian statesman, politician, philanthropist. Prime minister of India. Had key role in Indian independence movement. Had reputation as a peace-loving, generous man who lived simply and donated much of his earnings to the Servants of India Society. Died at age 61 of a heart attack in Tashkent, Uzbekistan. His sudden death caused speculation that he may have been assassinated. He was in Tashkent to sign a treaty ending war between India and Pakistan.
Last Words: "Mere Baap. Hai Ram" (tr. "My father. Oh God.")
Source: *Lal Bahadur Shastri: An Illustrated Biography* by Mithrapuram K. Alexander (New Delhi, India, 1967).

Shave Head, Charles

(d. 1890) Native American law enforcer. Sioux police sergeant. Died after a fight attempting to arrest Sitting Bull at Standing Rock Reservation, North Dakota. Fourteen men were killed during the fight, including six members of the police force.
Last Words: "Send for my wife that we may be married by the Black Gown before I die." He died before she arrived.
Source: *The Lance and the Shield: The Life and Times of Sitting Bull* by Robert M. Utley (New York, 1993).

Shaw, George Bernard

(1856-1950) Irish playwright, novelist, critic, social reformer. Active in the Fabian Society. Notable works: *Pygmalion; Major Barbara; Arms and the Man; Man and Superman.* Won 1925 Nobel Prize for Literature. Won 1939 Academy Award for *Pygmalion* (best writing, screenplay). Died at age 94 at Ayot St. Lawrence, Hertfordshire, England.
Last Words: "Sister, you're trying to keep me alive as an old curiosity, but I'm done, I'm finished, I'm going to die." Spoken to his nurse.
Source: "War: G.B.S. 1856-1950" (*Time* magazine, November 13, 1950).

Shaw, Henry Wheeler ("Josh Billings")

(1818-1885) American humorist, writer, lecturer. Pen name Josh Billings. Also used the pen name Uncle Esek. Started as an auctioneer and real estate dealer. Published *Josh Billings' Farmeres' Allminax*. Died at age 67 in Monterey, California.

Last Words: "My doctors East ordered a rest of brain, but you can see I do not have to work my brain for a simple lecture, it comes spontaneously." Spoken a few minutes before he died.

Source: *Josh Billings, Yankee Humorist* by Cyril Clemens (Webster Groves, MO, 1932).

Shaw, Irwin

(1913-1984) American writer, playwright, screenwriter, novelist. Birth name Irwin Gilbert Shamforoff. Notable works: *The Young Lions; Two Weeks in Another Town; Rich Man, Poor Man; Beggarman, Thief.* Many of his novels have been made into movies and television miniseries. Died at age 71 of cancer in Davos, Switzerland.

Last Words: "Not very good." His response when asked how he was.

Source: *Irwin Shaw: A Biography* by Michael Shnayerson (New York, 1989).

Shaw, Robert Gould

(1837-1863) American military officer. Colonel who commanded the all-black 54th Massachusetts Volunteer Infantry in Union Army in U.S. Civil War. Killed in action at the Battle of Fort Wagner in South Carolina. Shaw's military experience with the 54th was depicted in the (1989) movie *Glory.*

Last Words: "Forward, Fifty-fourth." He was shot and killed as he shouted from a parapet urging his men forward.

Source: *Life and Letters of Henry Lee Higginson* by Henry Lee Higginson and Bliss Perry (Boston, 1921).

Variation: "We shall take the fort or die there." He waved his sword, cried out "Forward, Fifty-fourth!" and fell dead.

Source: "Topics of the Time" (*The Century Illustrated Magazine,* Vol. 54, May-October 1897).

Shaw, Samuel

(1754-1794) American merchant, diplomat, military officer. Major. Made several voyages to Canton, China. In 1786 he was appointed U.S. consul to Canton. Died at age 39 aboard the ship *Washington* near the Cape of Good Hope. He was traveling home to seek medical aid for an illness that had worsened in recent months.

Last Words: "God's will be done." Spoken to the ship surgeon James Dodge. The doctor could not suppress a tear. When Shaw

saw it fall on his check, he said: "My dear friend, you know I am dying, speak comfort for me."

Sources: *The Journals of Major Samuel Shaw: The First American Consul at Canton* by Samuel Shaw and Josiah Quincy (Boston, 1847); *Yankee Ships in China Seas* by Daniel Henderson (New York, 2007).

Shawn, Dick

(1923-1987) American actor, comedian. Birth name Richard Schulefand. Notable roles: Sylvester Marcus, the Bohemian beach bum son in *It's a Mad, Mad, Mad, Mad World* and Lorenzo St. DuBois/Adolf Hitler in the musical "Springtime for Hitler" within *The Producers.* Died at age 63 while performing on stage at the University of California at San Diego.

Last Words: "And I would be your leader!" While doing a bit about nuclear war, he explained that no one would survive except the audience in the little sheltered theater. He fell forward and the audience laughed, thinking it part of the show. His son Adam was in the audience and knew it was no act.

Source: "Comic Actor Dick Shawn Dies at Age 57" (*Washington Post,* April 19, 1987).

Sheed, Francis Joseph (Frank)

(1897-1981) Australian-born British publisher, writer, apologist. Roman Catholic religious publisher. Soapbox preacher in Hyde Park, London and elsewhere. Notable works: *Theology and Sanity; Theology for Beginners.* Died at age 84.

Last Words: "I fancy I'll let it live. His reaction to the hospital food he had been given. Spoken as he pushed a flabby piece of fish around his plate with his fork.

Source: *Frank and Maisie: A Memoir with Parents* by Wilfrid Sheed (New York, 1985).

Shepard, Thomas

(1605-1649) English-born American clergyman. Silenced for nonconformity twice. After the second time, he sailed for America in 1635. Became pastor of a church in Cambridge, Massachusetts, the rest of his life. Was active in founding Harvard and placing it in Cambridge. Involved in Antinomian controversy. Died of quinsy at age 43 in Cambridge.

Last Words: "Oh! love the Lord Jesus very dearly. That little part which I have in Him is no small comfort to me now." Spoken to his friends while on his deathbed.

Source: *The Lives of the Puritans: Containing a Biographical Account of Those Divines, Who Distinguished Themselves in the Cause of Religious Liberty from the Reformation Under Queen Elizabeth to the Act of Uniformity in 1662* by Benjamin Black (London, 1813).

Sheppard, Jack

(1702-1724) English highwayman, burglar, thief. Notorious but popular. Apprehended by Jonathan Wild, an infamous London thief. Executed at age 22 by hanging. Hero in books by Defoe and William H. Ainsworth. Character of Macheath in John Gay's *The Beggar's Opera* is based on him.

Last Words: "Of two virtues I have ever cherished an honest pride: never have I stooped to friendship with Jonathan Wild, or with any of his detestable thief-takers; and, though an undutiful son, I never damned my mother's eyes."

Source: *A Book of Scoundrels* by Charles Whibley (London, 1897).

Sheridan, Philip Henry

(1831-1888) American military leader, politician. One of the top U.S. Union Army generals in Civil War. Known as Little Phil. Saw much action: Spotsylvania, Chickamauga, Wilderness, Cold Harbor, Appomattox and more. His historic ride from Winchester to Petersburg to rally troops in 1865 was celebrated in a poem by Thomas Buchanan Read: *Sheridan's Ride.* Governor of Louisiana and Texas military district after war. Commander-in-chief of U.S. Army. Helped protect Yellowstone. Had heart disease. Died age 57 in Nonquit, Massachusetts. Counties in Kansas, Montana, Nebraska, North Dakota and Wyoming were named for him, as well as towns in Arkansas, Colorado and Wyoming.

Last Words: "I hope that some of my old boys will find the book worth the purchase." He was referring to his *Memoirs*.

Source: *Personal Memoirs of P. H. Sheridan, General, United States Army* by Philip H. Sheridan (New York, 1888).

Sheridan, Richard Brinsley

(1751-1816) Irish-born British playwright, politician, parliamentary orator, statesman.

Member of Parliament. Undersecretary of state. Secretary of treasury. Treasurer of navy. Confidential adviser to George, Prince of Wales. Notable works: *The School for Scandal; The Rivals* (comedies). The term "malapropism" derived from the character Mrs. Malaprop in *The Rivals* who unintentionally misused words. A fire at Drury Lane Theater in 1809 plus accumulated debt put Sheridan in financial stress that stayed with him until he died at age 64 in London.

Different Last Words:

(1) "Tell her that my eyes will look up to the coffin lid as brightly as ever." "Her" was Lady Bessborough, a friend.

Source: *Here Lies Richard Brinsley Sheridan* by Kenelm Foss (New York, 1940).

(2) "Did you know Burke?" He was referring to statesman, orator Edmund Burke.

Source: *The Last Words (Real and Traditional) of Distinguished Men and Women Collected from Various Sources* by Frederic Rowland Marvin (New York, 1901).

(3) (doubtful): "I am absolutely undone."

Source: Various Last Words compilations and Internet websites.

This quote was part of a note Sheridan wrote in May 1816, a few month before he died.

Source: *Memoirs of the Life of the Rt. Hon. Richard Brinsley Sheridan,* Vol. 2, by Thomas Moore (New York, 1866).

Sherman, John

(1823-1900) American lawyer, statesman, politician. Member House of Representatives and Senate from Ohio. U.S. secretary of treasury. U.S. secretary of state. Ran for U.S. President in 1880, 1884 and 1888. Author of Sherman Antitrust Act. Brother of William Tecumseh Sherman. Died at age 77 in Washington, D.C.

Different Last Words:

(1) "Oh, Mamie." Spoken to his daughter when he recognized her.

Source: *John Sherman, His Life and Public Services* by Winfield S. Kerr (Boston, 1908).

(2) "I think you had better send for the doctor—I am so faint."

Source: *Albany Evening Journal,* October 22, 1900.

(3) "You must show them hospitality." Spoken to his daughter about the visitors and friends in their house.

Source: *John Sherman* by Theodore E. Burton (Boston, 1906).

Sherman, William Tecumseh

(1820-1891) American military officer. Brother of John Sherman. Union general in U.S. Civil War. Led destructive March to the Sea. Was commissioned lieutenant general and full general after the war. Given command of the entire U.S. Army. Retired in 1883. Died at age 71 of pneumonia in New York City.

Last Words: "Faithful and honorable, faithful and honorable." His response to his daughter who asked about the inscription he wished to have on his monument.

Source: *Sherman: A Soldier's Passion for Order* by John F. Marszalek (New York, 1993).

Sherwood, Mary Martha Butt

(1775-1851) English writer. Author of juvenile books. Notable works: *Little Henry and His Bearer; The History of Henry Milner*. Married Captain Henry Sherwood and accompanied him to India in 1805. Returned to England in 1816 for children's health reasons. Died at age 76 in Twickenham, England.

Last Words: "God is very good. Remember this, my children, that God is love. He that dwelleth in love dwelleth in God, and God in him."

Source: *The Life and Times of Mrs. Sherwood (1775-1851). From the Diaries of Captain and Mrs. Sherwood*, ed. by F.J. Harvey Darton (London, 1910).

Shirley, Laurence, 4th Earl Ferrers

(1720-1760) British aristocrat, murderer. Eccentric, violent womanizer who abused his wife. When she left him, he shot and killed his chief family steward Johnson because he believed Johnson was planning to give evidence on his wife's behalf. Ferrers was tried, convicted and sentenced to die. He was hanged wearing his white wedding clothes and silk stockings. At his request, the rope used to hang him was made of silk.

Last Words: "I freely forgive you as I do all mankind and hope myself to be forgiven."

Source: *Cobbett's Complete Collection of State Trials and Proceedings for High Treason and Other Crimes and Misdemeanors from the Earliest Period to the Present Time... from the Ninth Year of the Reign of King Henry, the Second, A.D. 1163, to George IV, A.D. 1820* by Thomas Bayly Howell, Thomas Jones Howell, William Cobbett and David Jardine (London, 1809-1826).

Sibelius, Johan Julius Christian ("Jan" or "Jean")

(1865-1957) Finnish musician, composer. Notable works: *Finlandia; The Swan of Tuonela; Valse Triste*. Also known for symphonies, violin concerto, vocal and theatrical music. Retired to Ainola, his country home at Järvenpää, near Helsinki, Finland, in 1904. Spent the rest of his life there. Died there at age 91.

Last Words: "I think that the cranes have taken leave of me. I was on my usual walk. The cranes were flying low over Ainola—I have never seen them fly that low before. Straight above Ainola one of them parted with a sad cry and banked in a steep curve around the hill, almost as if it meant to say goodbye." Spoken to his wife. Ainola is now a museum.

Source: *Sibelius* by Harold E. Johnson (London, 1960).

Sickingen, Franz von

(1481-1523) German military officer, statesman, knight. Supporter of Luther and the Reformation. Helped elect Charles V as Holy Roman Emperor. Was appointed imperial chamberlain and councilor. Later was defeated by an alliance for his forays along the Rhine. Fatally injured at age 42 while defending his castle at Landstuhl.

Last Words: "I have confessed God in my heart. He is the one to give absolution and administer the Sacrament." Spoken to a chaplain who asked if he wanted to confess.

Source: *Franz von Sickingen* by H. Ulmann (Leipzig, Germany, 1872).

Siddons, Sarah Kemble

(1755-1831) English actress. Daughter of actor Roger Kemble. Known as Mrs. Siddons. Played all the major female tragic roles during her 30-year career. Joshua Reynolds painted her portrait as *Tragic Muse*. Gainsborough also painted her portrait. Died at age 75 in London.

Last Words (doubtful): "She had health to sell."

Source: *Last Words of Famous Men* by Bega (London, 1930).

Siddons made this remark in April 1831 to Mr. Bushnell, her medical attendant, after he treated her. Her symptoms disappeared, and she decided she needed no more visits from him. She had a relapse in late May and died on June 8.

Source: *Life of Mrs. Siddons* by Thomas Campbell (New York, 1834).

Sidney or Sydney, Algernon

(1622-1683) English jurist, politician. Judge at trial of Charles I. Assisted his friend William Penn in drafting the Constitution of Pennsylvania in 1682. Suspected of complicity in Rye House Plot. Convicted of high treason on faulty evidence. Beheaded at about age 60 despite efforts to save his life.

Last Words: "Not till the general resurrection—strike on!" Spoken in response to the headsman's questions: "Are you ready, sir?" and "Will you rise again?"

Source: *The Life and Times of the Hon. Algernon Sydney, 1622-1683* by Alexander Charles Ewald (London, 1873).

Sidney, Sir Philip

(1554-1586) English military officer, statesman, poet, diplomat. Ambassador to Vienna. Notable works: *Arcadia; Defense of Poesy; Astrophel and Stella.* Wounded at the Battle of Zutphen, The Netherlands. Died at age 31 at Arnhem several weeks later.

Different Last Words:

(1) "I would not change my joy for the empire of the world."

Source: *Sir Philip Sidney* by Mona Wilson (London, 1931).

(2) "Love my memory, cherish my friends; their faith to me may assure you that they are honest. But above all, govern your will not your affections by the will and word of your Creator; in me beholding the end of this world with all her vanities." His message to his two younger brothers who came to say farewell.

Source: "Death of Sir Philip Sidney" in *English Writers: An Attempt Towards a History of English Literature* by Henry Morley and William Hall Griffin (London, 1892).

Variation: "In me behold the end of the world and all its vanities."

Source: *The Golden Dawn: Or, Light on the Great Future: In This Life, Through the Dark Valley, and in the Life Eternal, as Seen in the Best Thoughts of Over Three Hundred Leading Authors and Scholars* by James Henry Potts (Philadelphia, 1883).

(3) "Thy necessity is yet greater than mine." Spoken to a wounded soldier as he gave him a bottle of water.

Source: *A History of England and Greater Britain* by Arthur Lyon Cross (New York, 1914).

Sigourney, Lydia Howard Huntley

(1791-1865) American writer, poet. Wrote nearly 60 books on moral or religious themes. Notable work: *Moral Pieces in Prose and Verse.* Died at age 73 in Hartford, Connecticut. Town in Iowa was named for her. Several literary societies were also named for her.

Last Words: "I am so tired, so tired." She said the soul was weary of its burden of the flesh and she longed for "rest that remaineth for the people of God." She took a few drops of wine and said "Thank you" before she died.

Source: *Letters of Life* by Lydia Howard Sigourney (New York, 1866).

Simeon, Charles

(1759-1836) British clergyman, writer, educator, missionary, evangelical. Fellow of King's College, Cambridge. One of the founders of the Church Missionary Society and adviser to the British East India Company in the choice of chaplains for India. Published hundreds of sermons that are still in print. On his deathbed, he asked the people gathered in his room a question, then spoke his Last Words.

Last Words: "What do you think especially gives me comfort at this time?" When no one replied, he exclaimed, "The creation! I ask myself, 'Did Jehovah create the world or did I?' He did! Now if He made the world and all the rolling spheres of the universe, He certainly can take care of me. Into Jesus' hands I can safely commit my spirit!"

Source: "Great God" (*Our Daily Bread*, January 1, 1994).

Simon

(d. 1216) English martyr. Monk of Swinsted Abbey in Lincolnshire, England. Died after he drank poisoned wine in order to get King John to drink it.

Last Words: "If it shall like your princely majesty, here is such a cup of wine as ye never drank a better before in all your lifetime; I trust this wassail shall make all England glad."

Source: *Book of Martyrs and the Acts and Monuments*

of the Church by John Fox (or Foxe). First published 1563, ed. by John Cumming (London, 1851).

Simpson, Sir James Young

(1811-1870) Scottish physician, obstetrician. Discovered anesthetic properties of chloroform; first to use it in the field of obstetrics. Knighted in 1866; first person knighted for services to medicine. Died at age 58 in Edinburgh.

Last Words: "Oh, Sandy, Sandy." Spoken to his brother. Simpson died with his head in his brother's arms. His pain was allayed by chloroform.

Source: *Memoir of Sir James Y. Simpson* by John Duns (Edinburgh, 1873).

Sinatra, Francis Albert ("Frank")

(1915-1998) American singer, actor, entertainer. Stage, radio, television and screen star. Popular recording artist. Notable hits: "Strangers in the Night"; "That's Life"; "My Way"; "It Was a Very Good Year." Had television series from 1950 to 1952 and 1957 to 1958. Star of many films. Nominated for Best Actor Academy Award for *Man with the Golden Arm*. Won Academy Award for Best Supporting Actor for *From Here to Eternity*. Nominated for four Emmy Awards and one Grammy Award. Received Grammy Lifetime Achievement Awards. Nominated for four Golden Globes; won three. Died at age 82 in Los Angeles, California.

Last Words: "I'm losing it."

Source: *Sinatra: The Life* by Anthony Summers and Robbyn Swan (New York, 2005).

Sinjohn, John, see Galsworthy, John.

Sisera

Biblical figure. Canaanite leader. Cruel ruler of the Israelites for 20 years. Defeated by a surprise Israelite attack. After escaping, he took refuge in the tent of Jael, wife of Heber the Kenite. After he spoke his final words to Jael, he went to sleep. Jael crept up to him and killed him by driving a tent peg through his head. His story is told in the Song of Deborah, Judges 5 and in prose in Judges 4.

Last Words: "Sta ante ostium tabernaculi et cum venerit aliquis interrogans te et dicens numquid hic est aliquis respondebis nullus est."

Source: Judges 4:20 (Latin Vulgate Bible).

Variation: "Stand in the door of the tent, and it shall be, when any man doth come and inquire of thee and say, 'Is there any man here?' that thou shalt say, 'No.'"

Sources: Judges 4:20 (King James Version); (21st Century King James Version—spelling and punctuation difference only).

Variation: "Stand at the door of the tent, and if any man comes and inquires of you, and says, 'Is there any man here?' you shall say, 'No.'"

Sources: Judges 4:20 (New King James Version).

Variation: "Stand in the doorway of the tent, and it shall be if anyone comes and inquires of you, and says, 'Is there anyone here?' that you shall say, 'No.'"

Source: Judges 4:20 (New American Standard Bible).

Variation: "Stand at the opening of the tent, and if any man comes and asks you, 'Is anyone here?' say, 'No.'"

Source: Judges 4:20 (English Standard Version).

Variation: "Stand in the doorway of the tent. If someone comes by and asks you, 'Is anyone here?' say 'No.'"

Source: Judges 4:20 (New International Version).

Variation: "Stand before the door of the tent, and when any shall come and inquire of thee, saying: 'Is there any man here?' thou shalt say: 'There is none.'"

Source: Judges 4:20 (Douay-Rheims Translation).

Variation: "Stand in the door of the tent, and it shall be if any one come and inquire of thee, and say, 'Is there any man here?' that thou shalt say, 'No.'"

Sources: Judges 4:20 (Darby Translation).

Variation: "Stand at the opening of the tent, and it hath been, if any doth come in, and hath asked thee, and said, 'Is there a man here?' that thou hast said, 'There is not.'"

Source: Judges 4:20 (Young's Literal Translation).

Sitting Bull (Tatanka Yotanka)

(1831?-1890) Native American leader, medicine man. Chief of Hunkpapa Sioux. Defeated Custer at Little Big Horn. Later confined to Standing Rock Reservation, North Dakota. Native American constabulary was sent by federal authorities to arrest him. He was shot and killed along with his son Crow Foot in a scuffle that followed an arrest attempt.

Last Words: "I am not going. Do with me

what you like. I am not going." To his followers he shouted in the Sioux language: "Come on! Come on! Take action! Let's go!"

Source: *Sitting Bull* by Stanley Vestal (Norman, OK, 1957).

Sitwell, Dame Edith

(1887-1964) English novelist, poet, biographer, critic. Member of a distinguished literary family. Sister of writers Sacheverell and Osbert Sitwell. Named Dame of the British Empire in 1954. Notable works: *The Mother and Other Poems; Street Songs; Fanfare for Elizabeth.* Died in London at age 77.

Last Words: "I'm afraid I'm being an awful nuisance."

Source: *The Last Years of a Rebel: A Memoir of Edith Sitwell* by Elizabeth Salter (London, 1967). The author was her secretary from 1957 until Sitwell's death.

Siward (the Dane), Earl of Northumberland

(d. 1055) Danish warrior in England. Known as Siward the Dane. Murdered his wife's uncle and became Earl of Northumberland. Invaded Scotland and ousted Macbeth who dominated the region. Installed Malcolm III as king. Reputed to have risen from his deathbed and put on his armour so that he could die in the appropriate garb of a warrior. He died in York, England.

Last Words: "Shame on me that I did not die in one of the many battles I have fought, but am reserved to die with disgrace the death of a sick cow! At least put on my armour of proof, gird the sword by my side, place the helmet on my head, let me have my shield in my left hand, and my gold-inlaid battle axe in my right hand that the bravest of soldiers may die in a soldier's garb."

Source: *The Chronicle of Henry of Huntingdon*, tr. by Thomas Forester (London, 1853).

Sixtus or Zystus II, Pope, Saint

(d. 258) Italian prelate, holy man, martyr. Arrested and executed in a cemetery where he had been holding services during the persecutions of Emperor Valerian. Martyred along with seven deacons of the Roman Catholic Church. Sixtus appears in Raphael's *Sistine Madonna* (*Our Lady and Child with Saints Sixtus and Barbara*).

Last Words: "I forsake thee not, my son; a harder strife, and a grander triumph await thee. Cease to weep, after three days wilt thou follow me." Spoken to Lawrence, one of the deacons, who asked him: "Whither goest thou without thy son?"

Source: *The Ecclesiologist* by Ecclesiological Society (Cambridge, England, 1868).

Smalridge, George

(1663-1719) English prelate. Bishop of Bristol. Dean of Carlisle Cathedral. Sermons were highly regarded by Dr. Johnson, Steele, Swift and other luminaries. Many were published. Died at age 57.

Last Words: "God be thanked. I have had a very good night." Spoke these words   then died.

Source: "The Church Review" by Henry Mason Baum (*American Quarterly Church Review and Ecclesiastical Register,* Vol. XIX, July 1867).

Smedley, Edward

(1788-1836) English clergyman, editor, writer, poet. Editor of *Encyclopaedia Metropolitana.* Contributor to *British Critic* and *Penny Cyclopedia.* Became totally deaf. Died at age 47, after a lingering illness.

Last Words: "Be—always—thankful."

Source: *Poems, with a Selection from His Correspondence and a Memoir of His Life* by Rev. Edward Smedley (London, 1837).

Smith, Abigail Amelia Adams ("Nabby")

(1765-1813) American matron. Only daughter of John Adams. Married William Stephens Smith in 1786. Mother of four children. Diagnosed with breast cancer in 1810. Had mastectomy in 1811. Died at age 48.

Last Words: She found her favorite hymn, "Longing for Heaven," in a hymnal and asked her family to sing along with her.

"O could I soar to worlds above/
That blessed state of peace and love/
How gladly would I mount and fly/
On angels' wings to joys on high." She died a few hours later.

Source: The *Adams Women: Abigail and Louisa, Their Sisters and Daughters* by Paul C. Nagel (New York, 1987).

Smith, Adam

(1723-1790) Scottish economist, writer. Notable work: *Inquiry into the Nature and Causes of the Wealth of Nations* (formed the basis for the study of political economics). Died at age 67 in Edinburgh.

Last Words: "I love your company, gentlemen, but I believe we must adjourn this meeting to go to another world." Reported by writer Henry Mackenzie who was present when Smith spoke these words.

Variation: "I love your company, gentlemen, but I believe we must adjourn this meeting to some other place." Reported by geologist James Hutton who was also present.

Source for both quotes: *Life of Adam Smith* by John Rae (London, 1895).

Smith, Alfred Emanuel ("Al")

(1873-1944) American politician, businessman. Four-term governor of New York. Candidate for U.S. President. President of Empire State, Inc., the company that built and operated the Empire State Building in New York City. Died at age 70 in New York City. New York schools named for him.

Last Words: "Start the Act of Contrition." Spoken to a priest.

Source: *Al Smith American: An Informal Biography* by Frank Graham (New York, 1945).

Smith, Bessie

(1894-1937) American musician, vocalist. One of the top blues singers of the 1920s. Recorded with the great jazz musicians of that era. Notable recordings: *Downhearted Blues; Saint Louis Blues; Empty-Bed Blues.* Died at about age 43 from injuries sustained in an automobile accident in Clarksdale, Mississippi. Inducted into Rock and Roll Hall of Fame in 1989.

Last Words: "I'm going, but I'm going in the name of the Lord."

Source: *Somebody's Angel Child. The Story of Bessie Smith* by Carman Moore (New York, 1969).

Smith, Donald Alexander, 1st Baron of Strathcona and Mount Royal

(1820-1914) Scottish-born Canadian businessman, politician, philanthropist. Fur trader, railroad magnate. With Hudson's Bay Company 75 years. Served in Canadian House of Commons. Died at age 93. Lord Strathcona Medal named for him.

Last Words: "O God of Bethel, by whose hand Thy people still are fed."

Source: *The Life of Lord Strathcona and Mount Royal* by Beckles Willson (Boston, 1915).

Smith, Edward John

(1850-1912) British ocean liner captain, victim of *Titanic* disaster. White Star Line's most senior commander. Captain of the *Titanic*. Died at age 62 when the ship sank. Eyewitnesses gave different accounts of Smith's Last Words and death.

Different Last Words:

(1) "Let me go." Spoken as he declined to be helped into a lifeboat to which he had just swum with a child.

Source: *Titanic* by Filson Young (London, 1912). First book about the *Titanic*. It appeared within weeks of the disaster.

(2) "You have done your duty boys. Now every man for himself." Reported by survivor W.J. Mellers.

Source: *Sinking of the Titanic and Great Sea Disasters...Constructed From The Real Facts as Obtained from Those Aboard Who Survived...Including Descriptions of the Development of Safety and Life-Saving Appliances* by Logan Marshall (Philadelphia, 1912).

(3) (doubtful): "Be British, boys, be British!" Quote appears on many Internet websites.

Source: *The Myth of the Titanic* by Richard Howells (New York, 1999).

(4) (doubtful): "Good-bye boys, I'm going to follow the ship." Smith's response when he was offered a hand. Reported by lookout G.A. Hogg who thought he saw Captain Smith swimming alongside Boat 7.

(5) (doubtful): "Good boys, good lads." Survivor crewman Walter Hurst heard a voice in the water shouting these words. He was convinced for the rest of his life that it was the voice of Captain Smith.

(6) (doubtful): "Don't mind me, men. God bless you." A seaman claimed to have heard Captain Smith speaking these words to crewmen before he vanished in the water.

Source for (4), (5), (6): *Titanic: A Night Remembered* by Stephanie Barczewski (London, 2006).

Barczewski devoted an entire chapter to Smith. She wrote that the last reliable sighting of *Titanic's* captain was by Edward Brown, a steward, who reported seeing Smith on the bridge only minutes before the ship sank. G.A. Drayton, a crewman, corroborated this sighting. He said he saw Smith swept off the bridge by onrushing water but the captain swam back to the *Titanic* and went down with it.

Smith, Elliott

(1969-2003) American singer, songwriter, musician. Birth name Steven Paul Smith. Gained mainstream success in 1997 with Academy Award-nominated song "Miss Misery" from the movie *Good Will Hunting*. Suffered from depression and addictions. Died at age 34 an apparent suicide in Los Angeles.

Last Words (written): "I'm so sorry—love, Elliott. God forgive me." Suicide note written on a Post-It.

Source: "Smith Autopsy Inconclusive—Police Keep Investigation of Singer-Songwriter's Death Open" by Andrew Dansby (*Rolling Stone*, December 31, 2003).

Smith, Erastus ("Deaf")

(1787-1837) American frontiersman, military officer, spy. Hearing impaired. Known as "Deaf" Smith. Was a spy in the Texas War for Independence. Cut off Santa Anna's retreat at the Battle of San Jacinto. Member of the Texas Rangers. Died at age 50 in Richmond, Texas. Deaf Smith County, Texas, was named for him. He is depicted in the movie *Los Amigos* (1972).

Last Words: "When I die, bury me standing on my head, because I came into this world feet first and I've had bad luck ever since."

Source: *Deaf Smith: Incredible Texas Spy* by Cleburne Huston (Waco, TX, 1973).

Smith, Frederick Edwin, 1st Earl of Birkenhead,

(1872-1930) British statesman, politician, lawyer, orator. Birth name Frederick Edwin Smith. Gained title 1st Earl of Birkenhead in 1922. Member of Parliament. Attorney general. Lord chancellor. Secretary of state for India. Close friend of Winston Churchill. Died at age 58. Character in film *Chariots of Fire*. His son wrote biographies of him: *Frederick Edwin, Earl of Birkenhead: The First Phase;* and *Birkenhead, The Last Phase.*

Last Words: "I'm afraid, Peteil." J.E. Peteil was his clerk who was with him throughout his legal career.

Source: *F.E. Smith First Earl of Birkenhead* by John Campbell (London, 1983).

Smith, Jefferson Randolph, II ("Soapy")

(1860-1898) American criminal, con man. Operated in Denver and Creede, Colorado, and Skagway, Alaska, during the 1880s and 1890s. Was one of the most famous bunko men of the Old West. Got into an argument when his path to the Skagway wharf was blocked by four guards. A gunfight broke out with one of the guards and he was killed.

Last Words: "My God, don't shoot!"

Source: *The Skagway News*, July 15, 1898.

Smith, John Eldon

(1930?-1983) American criminal, murderer. Executed in electric chair in Georgia for the murder of Ronald and Juniata Akins. First person executed in Georgia after the death penalty was reinstated in 1976. Died at around age 53.

Last Words: "Well, the Lord is going to get another one."

Source: "Word for Word: The Condemned; As Executions Mount, So Do Infamous Last Words" by Tom Kuntz (*New York Times,* July 31, 1994).

Smith, Joseph

(1805-1844) American religious leader. Principal founder and leader of The Church of Jesus Christ of Latter-Day Saints (Mormon Church). Shot and killed at age 39, along with his brother, by a mob that broke into a Carthage, Illinois, jail where they were confined.

Different Last Words:

(1) "Is there no help for the widow's son? Oh Lord, my God!"

Source: *No Man Knows My History: The Life of Joseph Smith The Prophet* by Fawn M. Brodie (New York, 1945).

(2) "That's right Brother Taylor; parry them off as well as you can." Spoken to Mormon apostle John Taylor who was defending Smith and trying to drive back the mob.

Source: *History of Utah* by Herbert Howe Bancroft (San Francisco, CA, 1894).

Smith, Logan Pearsall

(1865-1946) American-born writer, essayist, critic. Settled in London, England. Notable works: *Unforgotten Years* (autobiography); *Afterthoughts.* Died at age 80 in London.

Last Words (doubtful): "Thank heavens the sun has gone in and I don't have to go out and enjoy it."

This quote appeared in Smith's writings in 1930, 1931 and 1933, many years before he died.

Sources: *The Miscellany,* July 1930, reprinted in *Life and Letters Today,* Vol. 5, 1930; *All Trivia (Including Trivia. More Trivia, Afterthoughts, Last Words)* by Logan Pearsall Smith (London, 1934).

Smith, Michael John ("Mike")

(1945-1986) American test pilot, astronaut, victim of the *Challenger* disaster. Fighter pilot during the Vietnam War, earning Distinguished Flying Cross. Selected for the shuttle program in 1980. Also slated to be part of a fall 1986 mission. Pilot of the NASA Space Shuttle *Challenger* (STS-51-L) that exploded shortly after take-off. All seven crew members were killed. Airfield in Beaufort, North Carolina, and a Chair at the U.S. Navy Postgraduate School were named for him.

Last Words: "Uh-oh—." Spoken in response to Commander Dick Scobee's order: "Roger Houston, go at throttle up."

Source: *The Air Up There: More Great Quotations on Flight* by Dave English (New York, 2003).

Smith, Perry Edward

(1928-1965) American murderer, robber. Smith and Richard E. Hickock terrorized and killed the Clutter family of Holcomb, Kansas, in 1959. Executed by hanging at age 36. The crime was the subject of the best-selling book *In Cold Blood* by Truman Capote and two major films.

Last Words: "I think it is a hell of a thing that a life has to be taken in this manner. I say this especially because there's a great deal I could have offered society. I certainly think capital punishment is legally and morally wrong. Any apology for what I have done would be meaningless at this time. I don't have any animosities toward anyone involved in this matter. I think that is all."

Source: "Truman Capote" (*Contemporary Literary Criticism,* Vol. 58, 1990).

Smith, Sydney

(1771-1845) English clergyman, writer, humorist. Originated the character Mrs. Partington later made famous by Benjamin P. Shillaber. Wrote articles for *Edinburgh Review.* Died at age 73 in London.

Last Words: "Then bring me all the blotting paper there is in the house." Spoken after he jokingly told the nurse who was looking for his medicine but found instead a half bottle of ink, that he probably drank the ink by mistake.

Source: *The Smith of Smiths, Being The Life, Wit and Humour of Sydney Smith* by Hesketh Pearson (London, 1934).

Smith, William

(1727-1803) Scottish-born American clergyman, educator, statesman, politician. Anglican founder of the school that evolved into the University of Pennsylvania. Member of First Continental Congress. Wrote eulogy for Benjamin Franklin. Died at age 75 near Philadelphia.

Last Words: "By the Lord God, if you don't stay longer with me, I will send for another doctor."

Source: *A Pair of Lawn Sleeves* by Thomas Firth Jones (Philadelphia, 1972).

Smollett, Tobias George

(1721-1771) Scottish novelist, surgeon. Gave up practice of medicine to write. Notable works: *Ferdinand Count Fathom; The Adventures of Peregrine Pickle; The Expedition of Humphry Clinker.* His stories were known for their use of satire and carefully defined characters. He went to Italy in 1770 for his health. Died at age 50 a year later in Leghorn, Italy.

Last Words: "All is well, my dear." Spoken to his wife. Earlier, he wrote in a letter to his friend John Hunter: "I am already so dry and emaciated that I might pass for an Egyptian mummy without any other preparation than some pitch and painted linen."

Source: *Smollett: His Life and a Selection From His Writings* by Robert Chambers and Sir James Smollett (London, 1867).

Snow, Catherine Mandeville

(1793?-1834) Canadian accused murderer. Last woman hanged in Newfoundland, Canada. Convicted for the murder of her husband John William Snow. She was pregnant at the time. Her execution was delayed until she gave birth. It is now believed that she was innocent and that the murder was committed by two men whom she knew.

Last Words: "I was a wretched woman, but I am as innocent of any participation in the crime of murder as an unborn child."

Source: *The Newfoundlander,* July 24, 1834.

Snow, Edgar Parks

(1905-1972) American writer, journalist. Expert on China. First American journalist to interview Mao Tse-tung after he set up headquarters in Shensi Province in 1935. Snow wrote several books on China. His last one, *The Long Revolution*, was published the year he died. He helped pave the way for President Richard Nixon's visit China. Died of cancer at age 66 at his home in Eysins, Switzerland.

Last Words: "Well, we three old bandits!" Spoken to two friends before he slipped into a coma and died.

Source: *Edgar Snow: A Biography* by John Maxwell Hamilton (Bloomington, IN, 1988).

Snow, William ("Skitch")

(d. 1789) English criminal. Sentenced to be executed for burglary. While he was suspended from the gallows, the rope slipped and he fell to the ground. To finish the job, the hangman took some rope from the arms of another criminal who had been executed at the same time.

Last Words: "Good people, be not hurried. I can wait a little." Spoken to the spectators who seemed disappointed by the delay.

Source: *The Newgate Calendar: Comprising Interesting Memoirs of the Most Notorious Characters who have been Convicted of Outrages on the Laws of England Since the Commencement of the Eighteenth Century; with Occasional Anecdotes and Observations, Speeches, Confessions, and Last Exclamations of Sufferers* by Andrew Knapp and William Baldwin (London, 1824).

Snyder, Adam Wilson

(1799-1842) American politician, military officer. Served as captain in the Illinois militia in Black Hawk War. Member of the Illinois legislature. Member U.S House of Representatives from Illinois. Presidential elector on Democratic ticket of Van Buren. Nominated as candidate for governor of Illinois. Died at age 42 in Belleville, Illinois, before the election.

Last Words: "Thompson, is it not hard that now I am prepared to live and serve my country, I must die." Spoken to Amos Thompson, a friend.

Source: *Adam W. Snyder and His Period in Illinois History, 1817-1842* by John Francis Snyder (Virginia, IL, 1906). The author was his son.

Snyder, Ruth Brown

(d. 1928) American murderer. When she tried and failed to kill her husband Albert, she involved salesman Henry Judd Gray in the crime. After a few botched attempts, they managed to kill him. Both Snyder and Gray were electrocuted in Ossining (Sing Sing) prison, New York. Author James M. Cain modeled his novel *Double Indemnity* on the case.

Last Words: "Oh, Father, forgive them, for they know not what they do!—Father, forgive me. Oh Father, forgive me!—Father, forgive them, Father, oh Father, forgive them." Spoken while sitting in the electric chair.

Source: *I Killed for the Law, the Career of Robert Elliott and Other Executioners* by Leo W. Sheridan (New York, 1938).

Sobhuza II, King of Swaziland

(1899-1982) Swazi monarch. King of the Swazi. Son of King Ngwane. Ascended the throne in 1921. Died at age 83. At the time of his death, he was the world's longest-reigning monarch, having ruled 61 years.

Last Words: "I am going." Spoken at a meeting of his advisers assembled to discuss political relations with other African states. He dismissed everyone but his minister of health who asked where he was going. The king smiled, then died.

Source: *Nearing Death Awareness: A Guide to the Language, Visions and Dreams of the Dying* by Mary Anne Sanders (London, 2007).

Socorro Nieves, Blessed Elias del

(1882-1928) Mexican clergyman, martyr. Birth name Mateo Elias Nieves del Castillo. Roman Catholic priest whom the government outlawed for saying Mass. Executed along with companions by soldiers. He forgave and prayed for his killers and spoke the Creed among his Last Words. Died at age 45 near Cortazar, Mexico. Beatified in 1997.

Last Words: "You have spoken the truth, because to die for the faith is a sacrifice pleasing to God." His response to a remark by the captain of the soldiers: "Now it is your turn. Let us see if dying is like saying Mass.—Long live Christ the King."

Source: *Saints of North America* by Vincent J. O'Malley (Huntington, IN, 2004).

Socrates

(470?-399 B.C.) Greek philosopher, moralist. Left no writings. What is known about him comes from secondary sources. Convicted by a jury for corrupting young people of Athens with his teaching. Sentenced to die by drinking poison (hemlock). Given a chance to escape but refused to break the law. He drank the hemlock and died.

Last Words: "Crito, I owe a cock to Asclepius; will you remember to pay the debt?" Asclepius was the Greek god of healing.

Source: *Dialogues of Plato,* tr. by Benjamin Jowett (New York, 1937).

Soleyman El-Haleby

(d. 1800) Egyptian assassin. Killed General Jean Baptiste Kléber, who had been appointed commander-in-chief in Egypt when Napoleon returned to France in 1799.

Last Words: "There is no God but God, and Mahomet is his prophet."

Source: *Kleber: sa vie, sa correspondance* by Charles Pierre Victor Pajol (Paris, 1877).

Somerset, 3rd Duke of,
see Beaufort, Henry.

Sonnier, Elmo Patrick ("Pat")

(1951-1984) American murderer, rapist. Executed by electrocution in Angola State Prison, Louisiana. One of the Death Row inmates featured in the book *Dead Man Walking: An Eyewitness Account of the Death Penalty in the United States* by Sister Helen Prejean. While acting as his spiritual adviser, she became aware of Louisiana's execution process and put her experiences into the book. The book became a best seller was made into a major film and an opera. Sonnier's Last Words were directed at Lloyd LeBlanc, father of one of his victims and to Sister Helen.

Last Words: "Mr. LeBlanc, I can understand the way you feel. I have no hatred in my heart, and as I leave this world, I ask God to forgive what I have done. I ask you to have forgiveness." LeBlanc nodded and said "Yes." Sonnier then said to Sister Helen, "I love you."

Sources: *Death Watch: A Death Penalty Anthology* by Lane Nelson and Burk Foster (Upper Saddle River, NJ, 2001); *Angolite* by Louisiana State Penitentiary, Vol. 25-26 (Angola, LA, 2000).

Soo, Jack

(1917-1979) American-born entertainer, actor of Japanese ancestry. Stage, screen and television star. Birth name Goro Suzuki. Spent time in a Japanese American internment camp in Utah during World War II. Played Detective Nick Yemana on the TV show *Barney Miller.* Died at age 61 of cancer of the esophagus, in Los Angeles.

Last Words: "It must have been the coffee." Spoken to his *Barney Miller* co-star Hal Linden as Soo was being wheeled into the operating room. His words referred to running gag: his character Nick Yemana had a reputation for making horrible coffee.

Source: "Esophageal cancer," ed. by Guy D. Eslick (*Gastroenterology Clinics of North America,* Vol. 38, No. 1, March 2009).

Sophia, Saint

(d. 126?) Italian holy woman, martyr. Mother of three saints: Faith, Hope and Agape, who were martyred during the reign of Emperor Hadrian. She died three days after she buried her daughters.

Last Words: "I yearn, my dearest children, to be with you!" Spoken as she lay on the grave of her three martyred daughters.

Source: *The Golden Legend or Lives of the Saints.* Compiled by Jacobus de Voragine, Archbishop of Genoa, 1275, 1st ed. 1470. English ed. by William Caxton, 1483, ed. by F.S. Ellis (Edinburgh, 1900).

Sophie Charlotte, Duchess of Alençon

(1847-1897) Bavarian noblewoman. Daughter of Bavarian Duke Maximilian Joseph. Married Ferdinand Philippe Marie, Duke of Alençon. Died at age 50 when a fire broke out at a charity bazaar in Paris. Burned to death with more than 140 others. She insisted the girls working with her be rescued first. Memorial chapel, Notre Dame de Consolation, now stands on the spot.

Last Words: "Because of my title, I was the first to enter here. I shall be the last to go out."

Source: *Winged Words* by Philip Howard (New York, 1988).

Sophonisba

(d. 204? B.C.) Carthaginian noblewoman. Daughter of Hasdrubal of Carthage. Sister of Hannibal. Engaged to Prince Masinissa of

Numidia. Married Syphax for political reasons. Masinissa defeated Syphax and captured Sophonisba but was forced to give her up. He sent her poison to save her from falling into the hands of Romans. She died by suicide. Her story is the theme of tragedies by Alfieri, Corneille, Voltaire, Mairet and others.

Last Words: "Accipio inquit nuptiale munus, neque ingratum, si nihil maius vir uxori praestare potuit: hoc tarnen nuntia, melius me morituram fuisse, si non in funere meo nupsissem." (tr. "I accept this wedding gift, no unwelcome one if my husband can do nothing more for his wife. But tell him that I should have died more happily had not my marriage bed stood so near my grave.")

Sources: *Titi Livi ab urbe condita libri* 6. Buch XXVII–XXX by Titus Livius (Berlin, Germany, 1863); *The History of Rome*, Vol. 4. by Livy, ed. and tr. by Ernest Rhys (London, 1921).

Variation: "I accept this nuptial present; nor is it an unwelcome one, if my husband can render me no better service. Tell him, however, that I should have died with greater satisfaction had I not married so near upon my death."

Source: *The History of Rome*, Books Twenty-seven to Thirty-six by Livy, ed. and tr. by Cyrus Edmonds (London, 1850).

Soubirous, Saint Bernadette

(1844-1879) French nun, holy woman. Known as Bernadette of Lourdes. Saw first of many apparitions of Virgin Mary at Lourdes in southern France at age 14. Joined Sisters of Charity of Nevers at age 22. Spent the rest of her life at a convent. Died at age 35 of tuberculosis. Canonized in 1933. The movies *Song of Bernadette* (1943) and *Bernadette* (1988) were based on her life.

Last Words: "All this is good for heaven! Blessed Mary, Mother of God, pray for me—a poor sinner, a poor sinner."

Source: *Bernadette of Lourdes* by Margaret Gray Blanton (New York, 1939; reissued 1958 as *The Miracle of Bernadette*).

Soucek, Karel

(1948-1985) Czech-born Canadian professional stunt man. Described himself as The Last of Niagara's Daredevils. To pay for his Niagara Falls Museum, he agreed to do a stunt at the Houston Astrodome—a danger-ous barrel drop of 180 feet from the top of the dome into a tank of water. The barrel was released too soon. It hit the rim of the tank instead of the tank's center, killing Soucek.

Last Words: "There is no heaven or hell; there is no God. It's all a myth. You're born, you live, one day you die and that's it." Spoken in response to a reporter who asked if he believed in an afterlife.

Source: "Niagara Falls: Niagara Daredevil Tells Reporter…You Die and That's It" by FPC Tract Society (Scarborough, ON, 1998).

Sousa, John Philip

(1854-1932) American musician, composer, bandmaster. Known as the March King. Head of U.S. Marine Corps band from 1880 to 1892. Formed his own band and toured widely with it. Notable marches: "The Stars and Stripes Forever"; "Washington Post"; "Semper Fidelis"; "El Capitan." Also composed several songs and operettas. Sousaphone was invented for him. Died at age 77 while on tour with the Ringgold Band in Reading, Pennsylvania. The movie *Stars and Stripes Forever* (1952) is loosely based on his career.

Last Words: "Oh, I don't need a doctor." Spoken in a hotel room when he was seized with chest pains.

Source: *Last Words: A Dictionary of Deathbed Quotations* by C. Bernard Ruffin (Jefferson, NC, 1995).

Sousa was discovered unconscious in his room by his secretary who went to check on him during the night. She summoned a physician who pronounced him dead. Sousa had died of a heart attack.

Source: "Remembering Sousa" by Vincent Patterson (*The Instrumentalist*, July 2009).

Southcott, Joanna

(1750?-1814) English domestic servant, religious imposter. Claimed she heard a voice that gave her solutions to social problems. She believed she was a prophetess. Published pamphlets. Gathered disciples. Announced she would give virgin birth to the new Messiah in November 1814 when she was in her 60s. The birth never took place. She died a month later. Some of her followers refused to believe she was dead.

Last Words: "If I have been deceived,

doubtless it was the work of a spirit; whether that spirit was good or bad I do not know." Spoken during a lucid interval shortly before she died.

Source: *The Book of Days: A Miscellany of Popular Antiquities in Connection with the Calendar, Including Anecdote, Biography & History, Curiosities of Literature and Oddities of Human Life and Character* by Robert Chambers (London, 1832).

Southey, Robert

(1774-1843) English poet, writer. Poet laureate of England. One of the Lake poets. Notable works: *Life of Nelson* (biography); *The Story of the Three Bears* (children's fable). Died at age 68 in Keswick, Cumberland, England.

Last Words: "Memory, memory, where art thou gone?" Spoken as he put his books away.

Source: "Memoirs of the Authors of the Age" (*Eclectic Magazine of Foreign Literature, Science, and Art*, January-June 1866).

Spafford, Horatio Gates

(1828-1888) American religious leader, hymnist. Lost most of his possessions in 1871 Chicago fire. Four daughters died in a shipwreck in 1873. After the tragedy, he and his wife had two more children. One, a son died of scarlet fever in 1880. Spafford moved to Jerusalem in 1881; founded Christian utopian society known as the American Colony. Died at age 59 of malaria in Jerusalem.

Last Words: "Annie, I have experienced great joy! I have seen wonderful things!" Spoken to his wife.

Source: *Our Jerusalem* by Bertha Spafford Vester (Garden City, NY, 1950). The author was his daughter, born in 1878.

Speaker, Tristram ("Tris")

(1888-1958) American athlete. Professional baseball player. Known as Spoke, Tris and Gray Eagle. Played with the Red Sox, Cleveland Indians, Washington Senators, Philadelphia Athletics. Regarded as one of the best offensive and defensive center fielders. Elected to Baseball Hall Fame in 1937. Died at age 70 of a heart attack in Lake Whitney, Texas, while on a fishing trip.

Last Words: "My name is Tris Speaker." He died after he whispered his name to a physician who had been summoned to the scene.

Source: *Tris Speaker: The Rough-and-Tumble Life of a Baseball Legend* by Timothy M. Gay (Lincoln, NE, 2006).

Spellman, Francis

(1889-1967) American prelate, writer. Roman Catholic archbishop assigned to the archdiocese of New York in 1939. Elevated to cardinal in 1946. Influential Catholic leader in America. Wrote a popular novel: *The Foundling*. Died at age 78 in New York City.

Last Words: "Now don't you worry about anything." Spoken to his doctor after he suffered a heart attack.

Source: *The American Pope: The Life and Times of Francis Cardinal Spellman* by John Cooney (New York, 1984).

Spencer, Herbert

(1820-1903) English social philosopher, biologist, writer. Created model for Social Darwinism. His theory of evolution predated Darwin's. Popularized the term "evolution." Coined phrases "struggle for existence" and "survival of the fittest." Died at age 83 in Brighton, England.

Last Words: "Now I take this step for the benefit of those who are to be my executors; my intention being that after death this my body shall be conveyed by sea to Portsmouth."

Source: *Life and Letters of Herbert Spencer* by David Duncan (New York, 1908).

Spencer, Sir Stanley

(1891-1959) British artist. Member of the Royal Academy. Knighted in 1959, shortly before he died. Notable work: *The Resurrection, Cookham*. The Methodist Chapel he attended in Cookham is now the Stanley Spencer Gallery, dedicated to his art. His younger brother, Gilbert Spencer was also a talented painter. Stanley died at age 68 at Cliveden, in Buckinghamshire, England.

Last Words: "Beautifully done." Spoken to the nurse who had injected him, just before he died.

Source: *Stanley Spencer; a Biography* by Maurice Collis (London, 1962).

Spenkelink, John Arthur

(1949-1979) American murderer. First

inmate to be executed in Florida after resumption of the death penalty in 1976. Claimed he killed a traveling companion in self-defense.

Last Words: "Capital punishment means those without the capital get the punishment." He spent his final days answering his mail and inscribing envelopes with this message.

Source: "At Issue: Crime and Punishment" (*Time* magazine, June 4, 1979).

Spicer, John Lester ("Jack")

(1925-1965) American educator, poet, linguist. Researcher at Berkeley. Identified with San Francisco (or Berkeley) Renaissance of the 1950s and 1960s. Co-founded Six Gallery while at Berkeley. Died at age 40 in San Francisco from complications of alcoholism.

Last Words: "My vocabulary did this to me. Your love will let you go on." Spoken to Robin Blaser.

Variation: Sometimes quoted only as "My vocabulary did this to me."

Source: *The Collected Books of Jack Spicer*, ed. and with commentary by Robin Blaser (Santa Rosa, CA, 1975).

Spies, August Vincent Theodore

(1855-1887) German-born American labor union activist. One of four men executed in the Haymarket Affair in Chicago. The others were Adolph Fischer, George Engel and Albert Parsons. The fifth man sentenced, Louis Lingg, committed suicide.

Last Words: "Our silence will be more powerful than the voices they are going to strangle today."

Source: *By the Neck, A Book of Hangings Selected from Contemporary Accounts* by August Mencken (New York, 1942).

Spinoza, Baruch or Benedictus

(1632-1677) Dutch philosopher. Born in Amsterdam of Portuguese-Jewish parents. Leading exponent of rationalism. Died at age 44 of tuberculosis in The Hague.

Last Words (doubtful): "God have mercy upon me and be gracious to me, a miserable sinner."

Frederic Rowland Marvin said this quote prevailed for a time as Spinoza's Last Words. A report, equally without foundation, said Spinoza committed suicide as death neared. More likely, he died quietly in his room. In his final days, he would come downstairs and talk with his companions about sermons they had just heard. The night he died, he went to bed early. His physician, Dr. Ludwig Meyer, asked the landlady to make him chicken soup for dinner. Dr. Meyer was the only person with him when he died later that evening, and Meyer did not reveal Spinoza's Last Words. Marvin gave as his source: "Kuno Fischer's Lecture on 'The Life and Character of Spinoza.'"

Source: *The Last Words (Real and Traditional) of Distinguished Men and Women Collected from Various Sources* by Frederic Rowland Marvin (New York, 1901).

Spruance, Raymond Amos

(1886-1969) American diplomat, military officer. Admiral in the U.S. Navy. Held many important commands during World War II, including task force commander at Midway; head of Central Pacific command; commander of U.S. 5th Fleet; commander in chief of U.S. Pacific Fleet. Ambassador to Philippines. Died at age 83 in Monterey, California. The USS *Spruance* (DD-963) was named for him.

Last Words: "I want to say goodnight to my wife." Spoken to his nurse.

Source: *The Quiet Warrior: A Biography of Admiral Raymond A. Spruance* by Thomas B. Buell (Boston, 1974).

Spurgeon, Charles Haddon

(1834-1892) English clergyman, preacher, writer, editor. Reformed Baptist. Preached the rest of his life at the 6,000-seat Metropolitan Tabernacle built for him in London. His sermons were translated into many languages. Notable works: *John Ploughman's Talks; John Ploughman's Pictures* (books of sayings). Died at age 57 in Menton, France, while seeking relief from gout, rheumatism and Bright's disease.

Last Words: "Oh, Wifie, I have had such a blessed time with my Lord." Spoken to his wife Susannah just before he died.

Source: *The Autobiography of Charles H. Spurgeon* by Charles Haddon Spurgeon, Susannah Spurgeon and Joseph Harrald (Philadelphia, 1898). Susannah Spurgeon was his wife. Joseph Harrald was his secretary.

Squanto (Tisquantum)

(1580?-1622) Native American leader. Pawtuxet interpreter, teacher to Pilgrims. Little is known about his early life. He may have been kidnapped and taken to England for nine years, returning in 1613. Helped English colonists in Massachusetts with farming techniques. Died at Chatham Harbor, Plymouth Colony, of fever he contracted while scouting.

Last Words: "Pray for me, pray for me, that I may go to the Englishmen's God in Heaven." Spoken to William Bradford, Pilgrim leader and governor of Massachusetts, who was kneeling by his bedside. Governor Bradford reported Tisquantum's dying words in his journal: *Of Plymouth Plantation, 1620-1647.*

Source: *Plymouth and the Pilgrims: or Incidents of Adventure in the History of the First Settlers* by Joseph Banard, Richard Law Hinsdale and Alonzo Hartwell (Boston, 1851).

Staaps, Frederick

(1791?-1809) German student, assassin. Attempted to kill Napoleon during a military review at Schoenbrunn. Napoleon offered to spare his life if he would be grateful. Staaps expressed regret that he had failed in his attempt and told the general he would kill him even if his life was spared. He was executed a few days later.

Last Words: "Long live Germany! Death to the tyrant!" Cried out as he walked to his place of execution.

Source: *A History of the Nineteenth Century Year by Year* by Edwin Emerson Jr. (New York, 1902).

Staël, Madame Germaine de

(1766-1817) French novelist, writer. Full name Anne Louise Germaine Necker, Baronne de Staël-Holstein. Fled France during the French Revolution. Returned after the fall of Napoleon's empire. Wrote a book about her experience: *Ten Years of Exile.* Died at age 51 in Paris after a stroke.

Different Last Words:

(1) "Deeply and profoundly." Her response when asked if she thought she would be able to sleep.

Source: *Germaine de Staël: The Woman of Affairs* by R. McNair Wilson (London, 1931).

Variation: "Yes, heavily, like a big peasant woman." Her response to an attendant who gave her opium then asked if she would now sleep.

Sources: *Mistress to an Age: A Life of Madame de Staël* by J. Christopher Herold (Indianapolis, IN, 1958); *Germaine: Portrait of Madame de Staël* by Wayne Andrews (New York, 1963).

(2) "I have loved God, my father and liberty."

Source: *The Golden Dawn: Or, Light on the Great Future: In this Life, Through the Dark Valley, and in the Life Eternal, as Seen in the Best Thoughts of Over Three Hundred Leading Authors and Scholars* by James Henry Potts (Philadelphia, 1883).

Stafford, 1st Viscount,
see Howard, Blessed William.

Stahl, Charles Sylvester ("Chick")

(1873-1907) American athlete. Professional baseball player, manager. Major League outfielder. Ended his playing career in 1906. Became player manager for Boston Red Sox. Suffered from depression and stress. Felt his job was too much for him. Committed suicide at age 34 by drinking acid.

Last Words: "I couldn't help it. I did it, Jim. It was killing me and I couldn't stand it." Spoken —just after he drank the acid—to Jim Collins with whom he was sharing a suite while on tour. By the time Collins was able to get help, Stahl was dead.

Source: *The 1903 World Series: The Boston Americans, the Pittsburgh Pirates and the "First Championship of the United States"* by Andy Dabilis and Nick Tsiotos (Jefferson City, NC, 2006).

Stallings, George Tweedy

(1867-1929) American athlete. Professional baseball player and manager. Managed 1914 Boston Braves when they went from last place to World Champions. Died at age 61 of heart disease in Haddock, Georgia.

Last Words: "Oh, those bases on balls." His response when asked what caused his heart to fail.

Source: *The Braves Encyclopedia* by Gary Caruso (Philadelphia, 1995).

Stambuloff or Stambulov, Stefan Nicolas

(1855-1895) Bulgarian statesman. Prime minister of Bulgaria. Known as the Bismarck of Bulgaria. Assassinated at age 41 in Sofia.

Last Words: "God protect Bulgaria."

Source: " 'God Protect Bulgaria'; The Dying Words of

Her Bismarck, Stefan Nicolas Stambuloff. Russia Loses an Implacable Foe. Prince Ferdinand Charged with Conniving at the Crime—The Men Who May Now Come in the Front" (*New York Times,* July 19, 1895).

Stanford, Jane Eliza Lathrop

(1828-1905) American educator. Wife of capitalist politician Leland Stanford. They founded Leland Stanford Junior University in their son's memory. After he died, she took over management and opened Stanford to women. Survived strychnine poisoning in San Francisco. Died in Honolulu, Hawaii. Persistent stories circulated suggesting she may have been poisoned.

Last Words: "May God forgive me my sins."

Source: *Mrs. Leland Stanford: An Intimate Account* by Bertha Berner (Stanford, CA, 1935). The author was Jane Stanford's personal secretary.

Stanford, Philip Dormer,
see Chesterfield, 4th Earl of.

Stanislas I, King of Poland

(1677-1766) Polish monarch. Full name Stanislas Leszczynski. Duke of Lorraine. Daughter Maria Leszczynski was the wife of King Louis XV of France. Died at age 88 in a fire in his bedroom at Lunéville, France.

Last Words: "You gave it to me to warm me, but it has kept me too hot." Spoken when the robe he was wearing caught fire.

Source: "Les derniers moments du Roi Stanislas" by Pierre Boyé, in *Mémories de la Société d'Archéologie Lorraine* (Nancy, France, 1898).

Stanislavsky

(1863-1938) Russian drama teacher, actor, director, producer. Full name Konstantin Sergeyevich Alekseyev Stanislavsky. Used only his surname professionally. A founder and director of Moscow Art Theater. Creator of "Stanislavsky method" of dramatic character development. Died at age 75 in Moscow.

Last Words: "I've lots to say to her, not just something. But not now. I'm sure to get it all mixed up." His response when asked by a nurse if he wished to say something to his sister in a letter the nurse was writing.

Source: *Stanislavsky: A Life* by David Magarshack (London, 1950).

Stanley, Arthur Penrhyn

(1815-1881) English clergyman, theologian, writer. Known as Dean Stanley. Canon of Canterbury. Dean of Westminster. Head of Broad Church party. Writer of ecclesiastical history, biographies. Died at age 65.

Last Words: "I wish Vaughan to preach my funeral sermon because he has known me longest." Earlier he said: "I wish to send a message of respect to the Queen. As far as I understand what the duties of my office were supposed to be, in spite of every incompetence, I am yet humbly trustful that I have sustained before the mind of the nation the extraordinary value of the Abby as a religious, national and liberal institution." Last recorded words, heard by Lady Frances Baillie and written down by Dr. Farrar.

Source: *The Life and Correspondence of Arthur Penrhyn Stanley: Late Dean of Westminster* by Baron Rowland Edmund Prothero Ernie, George Granville Bradley (London, 1894).

Stanley, Sir Henry Morton

(1841-1904) Welsh-born American journalist, writer. Original name John Rowlands. Adventurer who accepted *New York Herald's* offer to locate missing Scottish missionary, explorer David Livingstone. Stanley found Livingstone in Africa in 1871. After Livingstone's death, Stanley undertook his own explorations of Africa. The local people named him Bula Matari ("Breaker of Rocks" in Congolese). Knighted in 1899. Died at age 63 in London. The Stanley-Livingstone story provided background for several movies including *Stanley and Livingstone* (1939); *The Search for the Nile* (1971); *Forbidden Territory: Stanley's Search for Livingstone* (1995).

Last Words: "Four o'clock? How strange! So that is time! Strange!—Enough." Spoken as Big Ben struck four. Stanley died of pleurisy. Toward the end, his mind wandered.

Source: *Bula Matari. Stanley, Conqueror of a Continent* by Jacob Wassermann (New York, 1933).

Stanton, Charles Tyler

(1811?-1846) American frontiersman, guide. Member of ill-fated California-bound Donner Party. Guided a group until he became too weak to keep up. He was left behind. Died of starvation, exhaustion and exposure. His body was found later by a rescue party.

Last Words: "Yes, I am coming soon."

Spoken while sitting by a campfire after having led members of his party across the Donner Pass three times in the snow. He had returned to rescue more of the stranded Donner party.

Source: *Ordeal by Hunger: The Story of the Donner Party* by George R. Stewart (New York, 1936).

Stanton, Elizabeth Cady

(1815-1902) American social activist, suffrage leader. Prominent proponent of women's legal and social equality. Died at age 86 in her sleep after writing to President Theodore Roosevelt, urging him to declare himself in favor of women's right to vote.

Last Words (written): "Abraham Lincoln immortalized himself by the emancipation of four million Southern slaves. Speaking for my suffrage coadjutors, we now desire that you, Mr. President, who are already celebrated for so many honorable deeds and worthy utterances, immortalize yourself by bringing about the complete emancipation of thirty-six million women." Plea sent to President Theodore Roosevelt.

Source: *Five for Freedom: Lucretia Mott, Elizabeth Cady Stanton, Lucy Stone, Susan B. Anthony, Carrie Chapman Catt* by Constance Buel Burnett (New York, 1953).

Last Words (spoken): "Now I'll be dressed." Spoken after her maid fixed her hair. She stood a few minutes, then sat down, fell asleep and died.

Source: *In Her Own Right: The Life of Elizabeth Cady Stanton* by Elisabeth Griffith (New York, 1984).

Starkweather, Charles

(1938-1959) American spree killer. Murdered 11 people in Nebraska and Wyoming with his girlfriend Caril Ann Fugate. Electrocuted at age 20 at Nebraska State Penitentiary. Fugate was sentenced to life in prison and paroled in 1976. The crimes and criminals provided background for movies and television miniseries, including *Badlands* (1973) and *Murder in the Heartland* (1993).

Last Words: "Hell no! No one ever did anything for me. Why in the hell should I do anything for anyone else?" His response to being asked if he wanted to donate his eyes to the Lions Club eye bank.

Source: *Death Watch: A Death Penalty Anthology* by Lane Nelson and Burk Foster (Upper Saddle River, NJ, 2001).

Starr, Belle

(1848-1889) American outlaw. Birth name Myra Belle Shirley. Known as the Bandit Queen. Married Sam Starr. Husband was killed in gunfight in 1886. In 1889, she was shot while riding home. Her daughter Pearl and neighbors rushed to her aid. Starr died at age 40 at her cabin in the Choctaw Nation. She gained widespread publicity when the *National Police Gazette* wrote about her exploits. Depicted in movies *Belle Starr* (1941) and *Daughter of Belle Starr* (1946).

Last Words: "Baby, your brother Eddie shot me. I turned and seen him cross the fence, after he cracked down on me the second time." Spoken to her daughter Pearl who had rushed to her side.

Sources: *Doctor in Belle Starr Country* by Charles W. Mooney (Oklahoma City, OK, 1975); *Belle Starr* by Glenn Shirley (Norman, OK, 1982).

Stauffenberg, Count Claus Philipp Maria Schenk von

(1907-1944) German nobleman, military officer, assassination conspirator. Colonel in German Army in World War II. One of the leaders in July 20, 1944, attempt to kill Adolf Hitler at his headquarters in East Prussia. Executed that evening at age 36 in Berlin. Hitler had the execution filmed. His story is told in the movie *Valkerie* (2008).

Last Words: "Es lebe unser heiliges Deutschland!" (tr. "Long live our sacred Germany!")

Source: *World War II Almanac, 1931-1945: A Political and Military Record* by Robert Goralski (New York, 1981).

Stedman, Edmund Clarence

(1833-1908) American businessman, stock broker, poet, critic, anthologist. Notable works: *Poets of America; Victorian Poets.* Renowned for his Victorian and American anthologies and for his books of criticism. Died at age 74 in New York City.

Last Words: "Twenty-seven letters! What is the use?" He was referring to the amount of the mail that came that morning. He died that afternoon.

Source: *Life and Letters of Edmund Clarence Stedman* by Laura Stedman and George M. Gould (New York, 1910). Laura Stedman was his granddaughter.

Stein, Edith see Teresa Benedicta of the Cross, Saint.

Stein, Gertrude

(1874-1946) American writer, poet, feminist, playwright. Known for experimental prose. Died at age 72 of stomach cancer in Neuilly-sur-Seine, France.

Last Words: "What is the answer?" When she received no answer, she asked: "In that case what is the question?" Her comments were directed at her secretary and companion Alice B. Toklas as Stein was being wheeled into an operating room for surgery.

Source: *Gertrude Stein, A Biography of Her Work* by Donald Sutherland (New Haven, CT, 1951).

Steinbeck, John Ernst

(1902-1968) American writer, novelist. Notable works: *The Grapes of Wrath; Tortilla Flats; Of Mice and Men; Cannery Row; The Red Pony.* Many of his stories have been made into movies. Won Pulitzer Prize for Fiction in 1940 and Nobel Prize for Literature in 1962. Awarded U.S. Presidential Medal of Freedom in 1964. Died at age 66 of heart failure at Sag Harbor, New York.

Last Words: "Maybe it's just Shirley playing the bagpipes." His response to his wife about sounds they heard. "Shirley" was friend Shirley Fisher.

Source: *The True Adventures of John Steinbeck, Writer* by Jackson J. Benson (New York, 1984).

Steinberg, Milton

(1903-1950) American rabbi, philosopher, theologian, writer, lecturer. Conservative Jewish leader at Park Avenue Synagogue in New York City. Died at age 46.

Last Words: "I have to apologize to my wife and children for leaving them in such a spot." Spoken to a nurse.

Source: *Milton Steinberg: Portrait of a Rabbi* by Simon Noveck (New York, 1978).

Steinmetz, Charles Proteus

(1865-1923) German-born American electrical engineer, inventor, educator, writer. Birth name Karl August Rudolf Steinmetz. Born with curvature of spine and hip deformities. Had more than 100 patents for his inventions, including improvements on generators and motors. Worked on alternating-current and other electrical phenomena. Developed lightning arresters for high-power transmission lines. Professor at Union College. Consulting engineer with General Electric for 30 years. Died at age 58 of heart failure.

Last Words: "All right. I'll lie down." Spoken a few minutes before he died.

Source: *Loki, The Life of Charles Proteus Steinmetz* by Jonathan Norton Leonard (New York, 1929).

Stengel, Charles Dillon ("Casey")

(1890-1975) American athlete. Professional baseball player, manager. Nicknamed "Casey" (for K.C., Kansas City, his hometown, as well as the allusion to "Casey at the Bat") and later "The Old Perfessor." Managed the Yankees, Mets and Brooklyn Dodgers and played with the New York Giants. With the Yankees, he was the first person to manage a team to five consecutive World Series championships, as well as two additional world championships and three more league pennants. In his 70s, he managed the first years of the Mets, the worst team in baseball history, which along with his "Stengelese" (his wit and personality), added to his legend. Inducted into the National Baseball Hall of Fame in 1966. Died at age 85 of cancer in Glendale, California.

Last Words: "I might as well do this one last time." He put his legs over the side of his bed, got to his feet and stood at attention with his hand over his heart while the National Anthem was played on television.

Source: *Stengel: His Life and Times* by Robert W. Creamer (Lincoln, NE, 1996).

Stephen, Saint

(d. 35?) Biblical figure, holy man. Christian martyr. Deacon of church in Jerusalem. Falsely accused of violating Jewish laws and customs. Dragged outside the city by a mob and stoned to death.

Last Words: "Domine ne statuas illis hoc peccatum."

Source: Acts 7:59 (Latin Vulgate Bible).

Variation: "Lord, lay not this sin to their charge."

Sources: Acts 7:60 (King James Version); (New King James Version); (Darby Translation); (Douay-Rheims Translation).

Variation: "Lord, do not hold this sin against them."

Sources: Acts 7:60 (New Standard American Bible); (English Standard Version).

Variation: "Lord, mayest thou not lay to

them this sin."
Source: Acts 7:60 (Young's Literal Translation).

Stephens, Alexander Hamilton

(1812-1883) American statesman, politician, lawyer. Vice President of Confederate States during U.S. Civil War. Member U.S. House of Representative from Georgia. Elected governor of Georgia in 1882. Taken ill. Died at age 71 in Atlanta, shortly after taking office.
Different Last Words:
(1) "But I carried it individually by six hundred majority." Muttered in a final stupor.
Source: *Alexander H. Stephens: A Biography* by Rudolph von Abele (New York, 1946).
(2) "Get ready. We are nearly home." Spoken while delirious.
Source: *Little Aleck: A Life of Alexander H. Stephens, the Fighting Vice-President of the Confederacy* by Eudora Ramsey Richardson (Indianapolis, IN, 1932).

Stephenson, Marmaduke

(d. 1659) American martyr. Quaker. Tried, condemned to death and executed by hanging in Boston, Massachusetts, along with William Robinson and Mary Dyer for their religious beliefs.
Last Words: "Be it known to you all this day, that we suffer not as evil-doers, but for conscience' sake." Spoken to spectators after he climbed the ladder to be hanged.
Source: *The History of the Society of Friends in America* by James Bowden (New York, 1972).

Sterne, Laurence

(1713-1768) English clergyman, novelist, humorist. Notable works: *The Life and Opinions of Tristram Shandy; A Sentimental Journey Through France and Italy*. Died at age 55 of tuberculosis in London.
Last Words: "Now it is come."
Source: *The Life and Times of Laurence Sterne* by Wilbur L. Cross (New Haven, CT, 1925).

Steuben, Frederick William von ("Baron")

(1730-1794) Prussian engineer, military officer. General staff office and aide de camp to Frederick the Great. Grand marshal in court to Prince of Hohenzollern-Hechingen. Made honorary baron by Margrave of Baden. Benjamin Franklin arranged his passage to the U.S. Steuben served as a volunteer to the American Congress. Was commissioned inspector general. Organized and trained Continental troops at Valley Forge. Retired in 1784. Spent the rest of his life in America. Died in Remsen, New York. Steubenville, Ohio, and counties in New York and Indiana were named for him.
Last Words: "Don't be alarmed my son." His last coherent words were spoken to John W. Mulligan, who had served as his private secretary since he graduated from college in 1791. Mulligan regarded the Baron as a father figure.
Source: *Frederick William von Steuben and the American Revolution: Aide to Washington and Inspector General to the Army; with Account of Posthumous Honors at Various Places* by Joseph Beatty Doyle (Steubenville, OH, 1913).

Stevens, Thaddeus

(1792-1868) American politician, lawyer, abolitionist. Member U.S. House of Representatives from Pennsylvania. Opponent of slavery. Led Radical Republicans. Died at age 76 in Washington, D.C.
Last Words: "Nothing more in this world." His response to his housekeeper when asked if there was anything more he wanted.
Source: *I Speak for Thaddeus Stevens* by Elsie Singmaster (Boston, 1947).

Stevenson, Adlai Ewing, II

(1900-1965) American politician, lawyer, diplomat. Governor of Illinois. Ran twice unsuccessfully for U.S. President. Ambassador to the United Nations. Died at age 65 after a heart attack in London, England.
Last Words: "I feel faint." Spoken to his companion just before he collapsed on the steps of the U.S. Embassy in London. He died a short time later in a London hospital.
Source: *Adlai Stevenson and American Politics: The Odyssey of a Cold War Liberal* by Jeff Broadwater (New York, 1994).

Stevenson, Robert Louis Balfour

(1850-1894) Scottish novelist, poet, essayist. Notable works: *Treasure Island; Kidnapped; Dr. Jekyll and Mr. Hyde*. Suffered from tuberculosis. Moved to Samoa in 1889. Died at age 44 of cerebral hemorrhage in Vailima, Samoa.
Different Last Words:
(1) "My head, my head!"

Source: *Robert Louis Stevenson: A Critical Biography* by John A. Steuart (Boston, 1924).

(2) "What's that? Do I look strange?" Spoken to his wife as they were standing on the verandah at Vailima, just before he had the hemorrhage that killed him. A physician on an English ship in the harbor came to help him but it was too late.

Source: *Treasure Island* by Robert Louis Stevenson, ed. by Edmund Kemper Broadus (Chicago, 1907).

Stewart, James Maitland

(1908-1997) American actor. Screen star. Notable movies: *Mr. Smith Goes to Washington; It's a Wonderful Life; Rear Window.* Nominated for five Academy Awards. Won in 1941 for *The Philadelphia Story.* Given Honorary Award in 1985 for 50 years of memorable performances. Died at age 89 in Los Angeles of cardiac arrest and pulmonary embolism.

Last Words: "I'm going to be with Gloria now." He was referring to his wife who died in 1994.

Source: *Where Are They Buried? How Did They Die? Fitting Ends and Final Resting Places of the Famous, Infamous and Noteworthy* by Tod Benoit (New York, 2003).

Stewart, Robert, 2nd Marques of Londonderry ("Viscount Castlereagh")

(1769-1822) British statesman. Viscount Castlereagh. Foreign secretary. Leader of House of Commons. Became paranoid. Committed suicide at age 53 in London by slitting his throat.

Last Words: "Oh, Bankhead, it is all over." Spoken to his physician who arrived as he was dying. "Bankhead" was Dr. Charles Bankhead, personal physician to Lord Castlereagh.

Sources: *Castlereagh* by Ione Leigh (London, 1951); *The Strange Death of Lord Castlereagh* by H. Montgomery Hyde (London, 1958).

Stiles, Ezra

(1727-1795) American clergyman, educator, lawyer. Pastor of Second Congregational Church, Newport, Rhode Island, and of Congregational Church at Portsmouth, New Hampshire. President of Yale College. Died at age 67 in New Haven. Ezra Stiles College at Yale University was named for him.

Last Words: "Above all, seek religion, read the Bible and follow the example of Christ. What I now say to you I say to all the college. Tell the scholars what I tell you, that I wish them happy, and hope they have a better president than I have been." Spoken to two students who were at his deathbed. He died later that evening.

Source: *The American Quarterly Register,* Vol. VII, conducted by B.B. Edwards, American Education Society (Boston, 1835).

Stolberg-Stolberg, Count Friedrich Leopold von

(1750-1819) German poet, translator. Poet of Sturm und Drang (Storm and Stress) and early Romantic periods. Born in Holstein when it was part of Denmark. Wrote ballads, odes, satires, dramas. Translated Homer, Plato, Aeschylus. Died at age 69 near Osnabrück, Hanover. Germany.

Last Words: "Tell me, will it truly all be over tomorrow or the next day?—Praise God! Thanks, thanks! I thank you with all my heart. Jesus Christ be praised." Spoken to the doctor.

Source: *Der Graf Friedrich Leopold Stolberg und seine Zeitgenossen* by Theodor Menge (Gotha, Germany, 1862).

Stolypin, Pyotr Arkadyevich

(1863-1911) Russian statesman, lawyer. Prime minister. Interior minister. Shot by leftist radical terrorist assassin Dmitri Bogrov while attending a performance at the Kiev Opera House with Tsar Nicholas II. Stolypin died three days later at age 49. His death was allegedly prophesied by Grigori Rasputin the day it happened.

Last Words: "Give me the letter. Take it away! Give me a red pencil. Lift me. Light up." Spoken while delirious.

Source: "M. Stolypin Dead; Kieff Fears Riots; Thirty Thousand Troops Poured Into City to Keep Order, But Jews Are Fleeing" (*New York Times*, September 19, 1911).

Stone, Harlan Fiske

(1872-1946) American lawyer, jurist. U.S. attorney general. Associate and chief justice of U.S. Supreme Court. Died suddenly at age 73 in Washington, D.C.

Last Words: "The case should be stayed; we decided to send this case back to conference for reconsideration." As he spoke, he was

stricken with a massive cerebral hemorrhage. He was taken home and died a few
hours later.
Source: *Harlan Fiske Stone: Pillar of the Law* by Al-
pheus Thomas Mason (New York, 1956).

Stone, Lucy

(1818-1893) American reformer, suffrage
leader. Women's rights pioneer. Mrs. Henry
Brown Blackwell (retained maiden name).
Made her last public speech at the Congress
of Women, Columbian Exposition, Chicago.
Died at age 75 of a stomach tumor in Dor-
chester, Massachusetts.
Last Words: "Make the world better!" Spo-
ken to her daughter.
Source: *Lucy Stone: Pioneer of Woman's Rights* by
Alice Stone Blackwell (Boston, 1930). The author was
her daughter.

Stonehouse, Sir James

(1716-1795) English physician, clergyman,
writer. Practiced medicine in Northampton.
Founded infirmary. Wrote book of advice
for patients. Died at age 79 in Bristol, England.
Last Words: "Precious salvation."
Source: *Man All Immortal: Or, The Nature and Destination of Man as Taught by Reason and Revelation* by
Davis Wasgatt Clark (Cincinnati, OH, 1864).

Story, Joseph

(1779-1845) American lawyer, jurist, educator. Member U.S. House of Representatives
from Massachusetts. Associate Justice, U.S.
Supreme Court. Professor of law at Harvard.
Died at age 65 in Cambridge, Massachusetts.
Last Words: "God." The last word he ever
spoke.
Source: *Life and Letters of Joseph Story,* ed. by his
son, William Wetmore Story (Boston, 1851).

Stowe, Harriet Beecher

(1811-1896) American writer, novelist, abolitionist. Sister of Henry Ward Beecher. Notable work: *Uncle Tom's Cabin, or Life
Among the Lowly* (published serially 1851-
1852; intensified Northern sentiment against
slavery). Died at age 85 in Hartford, Connecticut.
Last Words: "I love you." Spoken to her
nurse.
Source: *Crusader in Crinoline* by Forrest Wilson
(Philadelphia, 1941).

Strachey, Giles Lytton

(1880-1932) English writer, biographer.
Member of the Bloomsbury Group of artists,
intellectuals, writers in England after World
War I. Died at age 51 of stomach cancer
near Hungerford, England.
Last Words: "If this is dying, then I don't
think much of it."
Source: *Lytton Strachey: A Critical Biography* by Michael Holroyd (New York, 1968).

Strathcona and Mount Royal, 1st Baron see Smith, Donald Alexander.

Straus, Oscar

(1870-1954) Austrian composer, musician,
conductor. Family name originally spelled
Strauss. Wrote for operetta, ballet, movies,
and orchestra. Notable works: *A Waltz
Dream; The Chocolate Soldier; The Last
Waltz*. Fled Europe in 1940 to escape Nazi
persecution because of his Jewish background. Lived in U.S. several years. Returned to Austria in 1948. Died at age 83 in
Bad Ischl, Austria.
Last Words: "Well, good." His response
when asked how he was.
Source: *Prince of Vienna: The Life, the Times, and the
Melodies of Oscar Straus* by Bernard Grun (New York,
1957).

Straus, Rosalie Ida Blun

(1849-1912) American socialite, victim of
the *Titanic* disaster. Wife of Isidore Straus,
American department store magnate, politician, tycoon. Both were passengers on the
fatal voyage of the *Titanic*. She refused to
leave her husband to board a lifeboat as the
ship sank. Died with him.
Last Words: "We have been together for
forty years and we will not separate now."
Source: *Titanic* by Filson Young (London, 1912). First
book on the *Titanic*. It appeared within weeks of the
disaster.
Variation: We have lived together for many
years. Where you go, I go."
Source: *Titanic: Book of Fascinating Facts* by Janet
Palazzo-Craig (Mahwah, NJ, 1999).

Strauss, Johann, Jr.

(1825-1899) Austrian musician, composer,
conductor. Known as the Waltz King. Son
of composer/conductor Johann Strauss Sr.
Composed polkas, marches, operettas and

more than 170 waltzes. Notable works: *Blue Danube*; *Roses from the South; Tales from the Vienna Woods*. Died at age 73 of pneumonia in Vienna.

Last Words: "I will, whatever happens." Spoken in response to a request to go to sleep.

Source: *Johann Strauss, Father and Son: A Century of Light Music* by H.E. Jacob, tr. Marguerite Wolff (New York, 1940).

Strauss, Richard

(1864-1949) German musician, composer, conductor. Wrote operas, ballets, chamber music, choral music, songs. Notable works: *Don Juan; Death and Transfiguration; Till Eulenspiegel's Merry Pranks; Thus Spake Zarathustra*. Died at age 85 in Garmisch-Partenkirchen, Germany.

Last Words: "Funny thing, Alice, dying is just as I composed it in *Death and Transfiguration*." Spoken to his daughter-in-law. Strauss had composed the work 60 years earlier as a musical depiction of an artist on his deathbed.

Source: *Richard Strauss* by Norman Del Mar (Philadelphia, 1962).

Stravinsky, Igor

(1882-1971) Russian-born American composer. One of the great composers of modern music. Notable works: *Symphony of Psalms; Firebird; Petrouchka; The Rite of Spring; Oedipus Rex*. Died at age 88 of pneumonia in New York City.

Last Words: "How lovely. This belongs to me, it is my home." Heard by his personal manager, Lillian Libman. He was referring to his new apartment on Fifth Avenue overlooking Central Park that he occupied the previous week.

Source: "Igor Stravinsky, the Composer, Dead at 88" by Donal Henahan (*New York Times*, April 7, 1971).

Straw, Jack

(d. 1381) English peasant, activist. Leader of 1381 Peasants' Revolt against England's feudal system. "Jack Straw" may have been a nickname. He made his confession at the gallows.

Last Words: "Against the same day that Wat Tyler was killed, we purposed that evening—because that the poor people of Lon-

don seemed to favor us—to set fire in four corners of the city and so to have burnt it, and to have divided the riches at our pleasures amongst us." Wat Tyler, leader of the Peasants' Revolt, was killed in London on June 15, 1381, the day after he killed the Archbishop of Canterbury.

Source: *The Annales, or, Generall Chronicle of England* by John Stow and Edmund Howes (London, 1615).

Streicher, Julius

(1885-1946) German military officer, publisher, propagandist. Nazi publisher of World War II Nazi propaganda newspaper *Der Stürmer*. Convicted of crimes against humanity at Nuremberg war crimes trial. Executed by hanging.

Last Words: "I am now with God my Father. Adele, my dear wife." Spoken as the hood was placed over his head.

Source: *The Nuremberg Trials* by Earle Rice (San Diego, CA, 1997).

Stresemann, Gustav

(1878-1929) German statesman, politician. Regarded as one of the most important leaders of Germany during the Weimar Republic. Chancellor. Foreign secretary. Led Deutsche Volkspartei (People's Party). Ended Germany's hyperinflation. Shared Nobel Peace Prize with Aristide Briand in 1926. Died at age 51 of a heart attack in Berlin.

Last Words: "But I'm all right now. I'll just rest for a bit." Spoken to his doctor.

Source: *Stresemann* by Antonina Vallentin, tr. by Eric Sutton (New York, 1931).

Stribling, Young

(1904-1933) American athlete. Professional heavyweight boxer. Birth name William Lawrence Stribling Jr. Challenged Max Schmeling for National Boxing Association World Heavyweight Title in 1933 and lost via TKO in the 15th round. The Stribling-Schmeling fight was named *Ring Magazine* Fight of the Year. Stribling died at age 28, after his motorcycle collided with an automobile near Macon, Georgia. At the hospital he had a foot amputated and clung to life for a short time. Inducted into International Boxing Hall of Fame posthumously in 1966. Different Last Words:

(1) "Hello, baby." Spoken to his wife from his hospital bed.

Source: "Young Stribling" in *Boxrec Boxing Encyclopaedia* (www.boxrec.com). [Accessed 10/29/ 2009.]

(2) "Can I have a small glass of beer, Doc? It gives a fellow strength to die." Spoken to a doctor at his bedside.

Source: "The Long and The Short of Young Stribling" by Mike Case (*Boxing Scene*, December 18, 2006).

Strindberg, Johan August

(1849-1912) Swedish playwright, novelist, short-story writer, artist. Notable works: *The Father; Miss Julie; The Secret of the Guild; The Red Room.* Died at age 63 of stomach cancer in Stockholm.

Last Words: "Everything is atoned for." Spoken as he held a Bible.

Source: *The Strange Life of August Strindberg* by Elizabeth Sprigge (New York, 1949).

Stroheim, Erich von

(1885-1957) Austrian actor, writer, director. Screen star. Nominated for Academy Award and Golden Globe for Best Supporting Actor for *Sunset Boulevard.* Died at age 71 in Maurepas, France.

Last Words: "This is not the worst. The worst is that they stole twenty-five years of my life." Spoken to his biographer while on his deathbed. He was talking about how Hollywood treated artists.

Source: *Movieland: Hollywood and the Great American Dream Culture* by Jerome Charyn (New York, 1996).

Strong, Nathan

(1748-1816) American clergyman, writer, publisher, hymnist. Had begun to study law at Yale but abandoned it for the clergy. Earned D.D. at Princeton. Published *Connecticut Evangelical Magazine* for 15 years. A founder of the Connecticut Missionary Society. One of the compilers of the *Hartford Collection of Hymns,* several of which he wrote. Died at age 68 in Hartford, Connecticut.

Last Words: "Death is to me but as going into the next room and to that next room most of my friends have already gone— many more than are here among the living."

Source: "Nathan Strong" by Rev. Daniel Waldo in *Annals of the American Pulpit or Commemorative Notices of Distinguished American Clergymen of the Various Denominations,* Vol. II (New York, 1906).

Strozzi, Filippo, II

(1489-1538) Florentine statesman. Known as "the Younger." Opposed Medici dukes of Florence, Alessandro and Cosimo. Driven out of Florence; chosen leader of exiled Florentines. Taken prisoner by Cosmo de' Medici who tortured him to force him to implicate others. Committed suicide after being imprisoned 17 months.

Last Words (written): "If I have not known how to live, I shall know how to die." While he was dying, he carved a line from Virgil on the mantelpiece with his sword: "Exari-are alquis nostris ex ossibus ultor!" (tr. "May some avenger rise from my bones!")

Source: *Biographie universelle,* Book XL, by J. Fr. Michaud and Louis Gabriel Michaud (Paris, 1811-1862).

Stuart or Stewart, Henry, Lord Darnley

(1545-1567) Scottish nobleman. Son of 4th Earl of Lennox. Second husband of Mary, Queen of Scots. Father of James I. Murdered at age 21 in the house where he had been staying with Mary in Edinburgh.

Last Words: "It is not an open enemy that hath done me this dishonor, for then I could have borne it. It was even thou, my companion, my guide, and my own familiar friend."

Source: *History of England from the Fall of Wolsey to the Death of Elizabeth* by James Anthony Froude (London, 1898).

Stuart, James Ewell Brown ("Jeb")

(1833-1864) American military officer. General in Confederate Army in U.S. Civil War. Famed for his brilliant command as cavalry officer. Mortally wounded in action near Richmond, Virginia. Died at age 31 in Richmond the following day.

Last Words: "I am going fast now; I am resigned. God's will be done." Earlier that afternoon, he asked Dr. Brewer if it was possible for him to survive the night. Brewer told him death was close at hand.

Source: *I Rode With Jeb Stuart: The Life and Campaigns of Major General J.E.B. Stuart* by Major Henry Brainerd McClellan, contributor Burke Davis (New York, 1994).

Stuart, Jesse Hilton

(1907-1984) American writer, poet, novelist, short story writer, educator. Taught school and served as school superintendent and principal. Notable works: *The Thread That Runs So True; Taps for Private Tussie; The Years of My Rebirth*. Donated 700 acres to Kentucky for a nature preserve named for him. Died at age 76 in Ironton, Ohio.

Last Words: "Amen." Spoken after praying with his wife and friend. Suffered a stroke and spoke no more.

Source: *Jesse: The Biography of an American Writer* by H. Edward Richardson (New York, 1984).

Suárez, Francisco

(1548-1617) Spanish clergyman, philosopher, theologian, educator, writer. Jesuit. Taught philosophy at Segovia and theology at Valladolid, Rome, Salamanca, Coimbra and Alcalá. Wrote 5-vol. commentary on *Summa Theologica* by Thomas Aquinas. Died in Lisbon, Portugal.

Last Words: "I would never have thought it was so sweet to die."

Source: "Francisco Suárez" in *Oxford Dictionary of Philosophy* (Oxford, England, 1994).

Suárez, San Miguel Augustine Pro

(1891-1927) Mexican clergyman, radical. Roman Catholic. Arrested for involvement in a bombing and assassination attempt on General Álvaro Obregón. Was connected to the crime when his brother sold a car that was used in the attempt. Suarez was one of four executed for the crime.

Last Words: "Long live Christ the King." Heard by his firing squad.

Source: "Il Beato Michele Agostino Pro, Martire della Fede" by Paolo Molinari, S.J., tr. by José María Fuentes, S.J. (Manila, Philippines, 1988).

Sudbury, Simon of

(d. 1381) English prelate. Archbishop of Canterbury. Murdered during 1381 Peasants' Revolt by rebels who blamed him for their problems. Beheaded.

Last Words: "Aha, it is the hand of God." Spoken after he survived being hacked on the neck by one of the rebels.

Source: *The Annales, or, Generall Chronicle of England* by John Stow and Edmund Howes (London, 1615).

Suleiman I or Suleyman, Sultan of Turkey

(1494-1566) Turkish ruler. Known as the Magnificent and as the Law Giver. Expanded land and wealth of Ottoman Empire. Died at age 71 of a stroke while in battle.

Last Words: "The drums of victory have not yet been beat." Lamented, just before he died.

Source: *The Turks in Europe: A Sketch Study* by William Edward David Allen (London, 1919).

Sullivan, Sir Arthur Seymour

(1842-1900) British musician, composer. Collaborated with librettist William Schwenck Gilbert. Composed the music for 14 Gilbert and Sullivan comic operas. Notable works: *The Pirates of Penzance; Iolanthe; The Mikado; H.M.S. Pinafore*. Knighted in 1883. Died at age 58 of bronchitis in London.

Last Words: "My heart! My heart!"

Source: *Sir Arthur Sullivan: His Life, Letters and Diaries* by Herbert Sullivan and Newman Flower (London, 1927). Herbert Sullivan was his nephew. Arthur Sullivan, who never married, adopted him and made him his heir.

Sullivan, John Lawrence

(1858-1918) American athlete. Professional heavyweight boxer. Known as Boston Strong Boy. Last bare-knuckle heavyweight champion. First athlete to earn more than $1 million. Died suddenly at age 59 at his home in Abington, Massachusetts. Inducted into International Boxing Hall of Fame in 1990.

Last Words: "I'll be all right in a little while."

Source: *John the Great: The Times and Life of a Remarkable American, John L. Sullivan* by Donald Barr Chidsey (Garden City, NY, 1942).

Sullivan, Robert

(1947-1983) American murderer, robber. Killed a man in Dade County, Florida, in 1973. Executed in 1983 after death penalty reinstated. On Death Row 10 years, longer than any other inmate in the U.S.

Last Words: "May God bless us all."

Source: *To Kill and Be Killed: Case Studies from Florida's Death Row* by Kent S. Miller and Betty Davis Miller (Pasadena, CA, 1989).

Sumner, Charles

(1811-1874) American lawyer, statesman, politician, abolitionist. Member U.S. Senate from Massachusetts. Opponent of slavery. Advocated Civil Rights Bill that would protect freed slaves from black codes (such as laws banning them from voting). In 1856, he was beaten on the head with a heavy cane by

Representative Preston Smith Brooks of South Carolina for his stand on slavery. Sumner died at age 63 of a heart attack in Washington, D.C.

Different Last Words:

(1) "My book, my unfinished book!—You must take care of the Civil Rights Bill, my bill, the Great Civil Rights Bill, and don't let it fail! — Judge, tell Emerson how much I love and revere him." A few hours before he died, Sumner was given a message from Ralph Waldo Emerson. His Last Words were his reply, spoken to his friend Judge Ebenezer Rockwood Hoar.

Source: *Charles Sumner* by George H. Haynes (Philadelphia, 1909).

(2) "Sit down." Spoken to his friend Hon. Samuel Hooper. As he said these words, he died of a convulsion.

Source: *Memoirs and Letters of Charles Sumner*, Vol. 4, by Edward Lillie Pierce and Charles Sumner (Boston, 1893).

Sun Yat-Sen

(1866-1925) Chinese statesman, revolutionary leader, national hero. Known as Father of the Revolution. Planned revolution against Manchus. Founded Kuomintang. Provisional president of Chinese Republic in 1911-1912. Died at age 58 of cancer in Beijing.

Last Words: "Peace. — Struggle. — Save China."

Source: *Sun Yat Sen, A Portrait* by Stephen Chen and Robert Payne (New York, 1946).

Sunday, William Ashley ("Billy")

(1862-1935) American evangelist, professional athlete. Baseball outfielder in 1880s National League. Signed to the Chicago White Stockings. Converted to evangelical Christianity by a street-preaching team from a Chicago homeless shelter around 1887. Took leave of absence from the Philadelphia Phillies in 1891 to preach. Became a celebrated and influential evangelist during the early decades of the 20th century. Known for his colloquial sermons and frenetic delivery.

Last Words: "I'm getting dizzy Ma."

Source: *Billy Sunday and the Redemption of Urban America* by Lyle W. Dorsett (Grand Rapids, MI, 1991).

Surratt, Mary Elizabeth Eugenia Jenkins

(1823-1865) American conspirator. Accused of being one of the Lincoln assassination conspirators who met in her Washington, D.C., boarding house. Convicted by a military court. Hanged at age 42. First woman executed by the U.S. government.

Last Words: "Please don't let me fall." Spoken to those standing nearby on the scaffold.

Source: *American Brutus: John Wilkes Booth and the Lincoln Conspiracies* by Michael W. Kauffman (New York, 2004).

Susann, Jacqueline

(1918-1974) American writer. Television personality. Literary phenomenon. Three novels *Valley of the Dolls*; *Once Is Not Enough; The Love Machine* all best-sellers and made into popular movies. Died at age 56 of cancer in New York City.

Last Words: "Good-bye my darling." Spoken to a friend.

Source: *Lovely Me: The Life of Jacqueline Susann* by Barbara Seaman (New York, 1987).

Sutter, John Augustus

(1803-1880) German-born California pioneer. Gold discovered on his property spurred the 1849 gold rush. Workers deserted him. His livestock was stolen and his land was occupied by squatters. Bankrupt by 1852. Tried to seek reimbursement from U.S. Congress for his help in colonizing California, aiding emigrants and for losses sustained when his land grant was declared invalid. Congress adjourned in 1880 without passing the bill that would have paid him $50,000. Sutter died two days later of heart failure in Washington, D.C.

Last Words: "Next year, next year they will surely—" He lapsed into a coma and died.

Source: *Sutter of California: A Biography* by Julian Dana (New York, 1934).

Svevo, Italo

(1861-1928) Italian novelist, short-story writer. Pen name of Aron Ettore Schmitz. Pioneered the psychological novel in Italy. Used psychoanalysis as a plot in *Confessions of Zeno*. Died at age 66, a few days after he was hit by a car while crossing a street in Motta de Livenza.

Last Words: "When you haven't prayed all your life, it's no use at the last moment." Spoken to a nurse just before he died of a heart attack.

Source: *Vita di mio marito* by Livia Veneziani Svevo (Milan, Italy, 1976). The author was his widow.

Swartz, Christian Frederick

(1726-1798) Prussian-born clergyman, missionary. Member of London-based Society for Promoting Christian Knowledge. Early missionary in India. Died at age 71.

Last Words: "Had it pleased my Lord to spare me longer I should have been glad: I should then have been able to speak yet a word to the sick and poor; but His will be done! May he but in mercy receive me! Into thy hands I commend my spirit; thou hast redeemed me, O God of Truth!" His native assistants then sang the last verse of a hymn in which he frequently joined. He died soon afterward.

Source: *Memoirs of the Life and Correspondence of the Reverend Christian Frederick Swartz: To Which is Prefixed a Sketch of the History of Christianity in India* by Christian Frederick Swartz and Hugh Pearson (New York, 1835).

Swedenborg, Emanuel

(1688-1772) Swedish scientist, philosopher, theologian, writer. Surname was originally Swedberg or Svedberg. Devoted time to psychic and spiritual research. Followers are known as Swedenborgians. Their organization is known as the Church of the New Jerusalem. He died at age 84 in London.

Last Words: "That is good, thank you. God bless you." Spoken after learning what time it was.

Source: *The Life and Mission of Emanuel Swedenborg* by Benjamin Worcester (Boston, 1883).

Sweeney, Brian D.

(1963-2001) American business consultant, victim of 9/11 disaster. Passenger on United Airlines Flight 175 en route from Boston, Massachusetts, to Los Angeles, California, September 11, 2001. Plane struck the South Tower of the World Trade Center in New York City. Died at age 38.

Last Words: "Hi, Jules. It's Brian. I'm on a plane and it's hijacked, and it doesn't look good. I just wanted to let you know that I love you, and I hope to see you again. If I don't, please have fun in life and live your life the best you can. Know that I love you,

and no matter what I'll see you again." Message to his wife left on his answering machine.

Source: *Sept. 11, 2001: A Time for Heroes: A Tribute to American Faith, Guts and Patriotism* by Lance Wubbels (Shippensburg, PA, 2001).

Swetchine or Svetschine, Madame Sophie Soymonof

(1782-1857) Russian writer, mystic. Known as Madame Swetchine. Settled in Paris in 1812. Lived there the rest of her life. Entertained at a famous salon. Died at age 75 in Paris.

Last Words: "It will soon be time for Mass. They must raise me." Spoken when she learned it was 5:30 a.m.

Source: *Life and Letters of Madame Swetchine* by Count de Falloux, tr. by H. W. Preston (Boston, 1867).

Swift, Gustavus Franklin

(1839-1903) American manufacturer, philanthropist. Founder of Swift & Co. Revolutionized meatpacking industry by using automation, refrigerated rail cars, large-scale slaughtering and processing. Died at age 63 in Chicago after surgery.

Last Words: "I like to hear you read." Spoken to his wife.

Source: *My Father and My Mother* by Helen Swift (Chicago, 1937).

Swift, Jonathan

(1667-1745) Irish-born English satirist, poet, political writer, clergyman. Cousin of John Dryden. Published works under the pen names Lemuel Gulliver, Isaac Bickerstaff and M.B. Drapier. Wrote tracts that championed grievances of people. Notable works: *A Modest Proposal; A Tale of a Tub; Gulliver's Travels*. Friend and collaborator with John Gay. In later years, Swift feared the onset of insanity. His health failed him in 1743. He may have had a stroke. Lost his mental acuity. Became paralyzed. Although he could speak, he could not express his meaning. When he died at age 77, he left much of his estate to establish a hospital for the mentally ill.

Different Last Words:

(1) (doubtful): "Ah, a German and a genius! a prodigy, admit him." Spoken when his visitor, the composer Handel, was

announced. The quote originated in Pilking-ton's *Memoirs* (1754) and is fiction.

Source: *Jonathan Swift and Popular Culture: Myth, Media, and the Man* by Anne Cline Kelly (New York, 2002).

(2) (doubtful): "It is folly; they had better leave it alone." He was referring to preparations being made to honor his birthday anniversary that included bonfires and illuminations. Quote was spoken two years before Swift died when he learned the citizens of Dublin were planning a celebration.

Source: "Swift" in *Johnson's Lives of the Poets* (London, 1890).

(3) (doubtful): "I am what I am, I am what I am." Jonathan Swift spoke these words a year and a half before he died. A letter written by Deane Swift in April 1744 discussed Swift's mental state. He said when a knife was taken from Jonathan's reach by his housekeeper, he shrugged his shoulders, rocked back and forth and spoke these words. He repeated them a few times over the next few minutes.

Source: *Remarks on the Life and Writings of Dr. Jonathan Swift, Dean of St. Patrick's Dublin* by John Boyle Orrery (London, 1752).

Swift, Sir Rigby Philip Watson

(1874-1937) British jurist, politician. Member of Parliament. Judge of High Court of Justice. Awarded honorary degree from University of Liverpool. Died at age 63.

Last Words (written): "My dear Chief, Your most kind and sympathetic letter has been a wonderful tonic and I already feel much better. Yours very faithfully, Rigby Swift."

Source: *The Life of Mr. Justice Swift* by Edgar Stewart Fay (London, 1939).

Switzer, Carl Dean ("Alfalfa")

(1927-1959) American actor. Child screen star. Played character Alfalfa in Our Gang comedies. Shot and killed at age 31 in a brawl over reward money with Moses ("Bud") Stiltz at Stiltz's home in Mission Hills, California. Switzer's death was ruled justifiable homicide (self-defense). What actually happened is one of Hollywood's unsolved mysteries.

Last Words: "I want that fifty bucks you owe me and I want it now!" Spoken to Stiltz when he opened the door.

Source: "Alfalfa. 'Our Gang' Star, Is Killed in Fight with Friend Over $50 Debt" ([California] *Evening Bulletin*, January 22, 1959).

Symons, Sir William Penn

(1843-1899) British military officer. General in Boer War. Knighted in 1898. Ignored warnings when he stood on a rampart to survey the scene. Killed at the Siege of Ladysmith.

Last Words: "I am severely—mortally—wounded in the stomach." Spoken calmly to his aide-de-camp. The general was placed on his horse and taken back to camp where he died.

Source: *The Times History of the War in South Africa, 1899-1902,* Vol. 2, by Leopold Stennett Amery, Erskine Childers and G.P. Tallboy (London, 1902).

Synge, John Millington

(1871-1909) Irish playwright, director. Wrote about rural Irish life. Notable works: *The Playboy of the Western World; Riders to the Sea; The Aran Islands.* Director at Abbey Theatre. Had an inoperable tumor. Died at age 37 in Dublin, Ireland.

Last Words: "It is no use fighting death any longer."

Source: *John Millington Synge and the Irish Theatre* by Maurice Bourgeois (London, 1913).

Tabor, Horace Austin Warner

(1830-1899) American businessman, mining magnate, politician. Known as the Bonanza King of Leadville. Lieutenant governor of Colorado. Member U.S. Senate from Colorado. Lost a fortune in the Silver Crash of 1893. His mine holdings became worthless. Was postmaster of Denver when he died at age 68 of appendicitis.

Last Words: "Hang on to the Matchless [mine]. It will make millions again." Spoken to his wife Baby Doe. She held onto the mine for 35 years and died a pauper and recluse in 1935. The opera *The Ballad of Baby Doe* (1956) by Douglas Moore is based on her story.

Source: *Photo Story of the Matchless Mine and Baby Doe Tabor* by Carolyn Bancroft (Denver, CO, 1953).

Taft, Robert Alphonso

(1889-1953) American lawyer, politician. Son of U.S. President William Howard Taft. Member Ohio House of Representatives. Member U.S. Senate from Ohio. Unsuccessful when he sought the 1952 Republican nomination for U.S. President. Died at age 63 of cancer in New York City.

Last Words: "Well, Martha. —Glad to see you looking so well." Spoken to his wife.

Source: *Eight Weeks to Live: The Last Chapter in the Life of Robert A. Taft* by Jhan and June Robbins (Garden City, NY, 1954).

Taft, William Howard

(1857-1930) 27th President of the U.S. American lawyer, jurist, statesman, educator. Father of Robert Alphonso Taft. U.S. solicitor general, U.S. secretary of war. Professor of law at Yale. Chief justice of U.S. Supreme Court. Died at age 72 of a heart attack in Washington, D.C.

Different Last Words:

(1) "Good morning."

Source: *Washington Herald,* March 9, 1930.

(2) Unknown.

Source: *Facts About the Presidents from Washington to Johnson* by Joseph Nathan Kane (New York, 1964). In his list of Last Words, Kane excluded Taft, indicating there were no generally accepted Last Words for the President.

Tagore, Sir Rabindranath

(1861-1941) Indian writer, poet, playwright, composer, artist. Hindu. Established a school in Shantiniketan that grew into a university. Won Nobel Prize for Literature (1913). Knighted by British Crown in 1913; resigned title in 1919 to protest a massacre. Composed national songs for two countries. In July 1941, he was taken to Calcutta for surgery. Before he went into the operating room, he dictated this poem. He did not live long enough to read what he dictated or to revise the text.

Last Words:

"Your Creation's path you have covered

With a varied net of wiles

Thou Guileful one.

False belief! Snare you have

Laid with skillful hands

In simple lives.

With this deceit have you left a mark on greatness

For him kept no secret night....

He who has carefully borne your wile

Gets from your hands

The unwasting right to peace."

Source: *Rabindranath Tagore: A Biography* by Krishna Kripalani (New York, 1962).

Tait, Archibald Campbell

(1811-1882) Scottish-born prelate. Anglican. Headmaster of Rugby School. Archbishop of Canterbury. Died at age 70 in Addington, Surrey, England.

Last Words (written): "A last memorial of twenty-six years of devoted service: with earnest love and affectionate blessing on the Queen and her family—A.C. Cantuar." Note to Queen Victoria. (Cantuar is the title an archbishop is permitted to use when officially signing his name.)

Source: *Life of Archibald Campbell Tait* by Randall T. Davidson and William Benham (London, 1891). Davidson was Tait's son-in-law.

Last Words (spoken): "It is coming. It is coming." Spoken in the presence of his three daughters, son-in-law Mr. Davidson, Canon Knollys and Dr. Carpenter. He was then seized by a spasm and did not speak again.

Source: "Obituary–The Archbishop of Canterbury" (*New York Times*, December 4, 1882).

Talfourd, Thomas Noon

(1795-1854) British jurist, writer. Introduced important copyright bill in House of Commons in 1837. Wrote for *London Magazine; Edinburgh Review and Quarterly Review; New Monthly Magazine; The* [London] *Times* and other periodicals. Notable works: *Ion; The Athenian Captive;* and *Glencoe, or the Fate of the Macdonalds* (dramas). Talfourd also wrote *The Letters of Charles Lamb, with a Sketch of his Life* and *Final Memorials of Charles Lamb*. Dickens dedicated *The Pickwick Papers* to him. Talfourd died at age 58 in court delivering a charge to the grand jury at Stafford, England.

Last Words: "That which is wanted to bind together the bursting bonds of different classes of this country is not kindness, but sympathy." Spoken just before he collapsed.

Source: "Last Words of Great Men" in *Chambers Journal* by John Holmes Agnew and Walter Hilliard Bidwell (*The Eclectic Magazine*, June 1863).

Talleyrand-Perigord, Charles Maurice de, Prince of Bénévent

(1754-1838) French nobleman, statesman, diplomat, clergyman. Quarreled with Napoleon over his Russian and Spanish policy. After Napoleon's fall, he helped restore the

Bourbons to power. Formed Confederation of the Rhine. Ambassador to Britain.

Different Last Words:

(1) "He can find a much better use for it." Spoken when he heard the Archbishop of Paris would willingly give his life for him.

Source: *Talleyrand the Man* by Bernard de Lacombe, tr. by A.D. Alberti (London, 1911).

(2) "I am suffering the pangs of the damned." Spoken to King Louise Philippe, who asked about his condition, at which the king said under his breath: "Quoi, déjà?" (tr. "What, already?")

Source: *Histoire de dix ans, 1830-1840* by Louis Blanc (Paris, 1844).

Talleyrand-Perigord, Henri de, Comte de Chalais

(1599-1626) French nobleman, conspirator. Member of the household of French King Louis XIII. Master of the Wardrobe. Conspired against the king. Beheaded.

Last Words: "Do not keep me in suspense." Spoken to the executioner who was clumsy and cruel.

Source: *Derniers sentiments des plus illustrares personnages condemnés à mort* by Joseph Donzé de Verteuil (Paris, 1775).

Talma, François Joseph

(1763?-1826) French actor, tragedian, theatrical company manager. Favorite actor of Napoleon and Louis XVIII. Known as The Garrick of the French Stage. Notable roles: Henry VIII, Nero, Othello, Hamlet, Macbeth. French sculptor David d'Angers created a marble statue of him. Talma made his last stage appearance in Delaville's *Charles VI* in June 1826. He was taken ill in Paris. Died a few months later at about age 63. Talma was evasive about his age, saying that actors and women should never be dated.

Last Words: "The worst is I cannot see." He did not suffer acute pain. He complained only of a cloud before his eyes.

Sources: *Mémoires sur Talma. Avec notices et notes par Henri d'Alméras* by Jean-Baptiste Regnault-Warin (Paris, 1904); *Lady Morgan's Memoirs: Autobiography. Diaries and Correspondence* by Morgan (Sydney) and William Hepworth Dixon (London, 1863).

Tamerlane, Tamburlaine or Timur

(1336-1405) Tarter warlord. Descendent of Genghis Khan. Persian name: Timur-i Lang

(Temur the lame). Name distorted by westerners into Tamerlane. Conquered Persia and subdued Turks of Asia Minor. Founded the Mogul dynasty in India. Built a powerful empire. Was the last of the nomadic rulers. Died at age 68.

Different Last Words:

(1) "I would like nothing except to see Shah Rukh again. But that is—impossible." Shah Rukh was his son.

Source: *Tamerlane, The Earth Shaker* by Harold Lamb (New York, 1928).

(2) "Allah has not willed it so I must wait for the day of the last judgment before my wish can be fulfilled."

Source: *The Mongol Empire: Its Rise and Legacy* by Michael Prawdin (New Brunswick, NJ, 2006).

Taney, Roger Brooke

(1777-1864) American lawyer, jurist, statesman. U.S. secretary of the treasury. U.S. attorney general. Chief justice of U.S. Supreme Court. One of the justices who ruled in the Dred Scott case. Brother-in-law of Francis Scott Key. Died at age 87 in Washington, D.C.

Last Words: "Lord Jesus receive my spirit."

Source: *Roger B. Taney* by Carl B. Swisher (New York, 1935).

Tanner, Henry Ossawa

(1859-1937) American artist. Studied with Thomas Eakins at Philadelphia Academy of Fine Art. First African-American artist to receive international recognition. Known for his Biblical paintings. Notable works: *Destruction of Sodom and Gomorrah; The Seine*. Moved to France in the 1890s. Died at age 77 at his home in Paris.

Last Words: "How beautiful springtime is in Paris!"

Source: *Henry Ossawa Tanner: American Artist* by Marcia M. Matthews (Chicago, 1969).

Tarakin, Vasilij Egorovich

(d. 1919) Russian pacifist, conscientious objector. Shot by a firing squad for refusing to join the revolution and fight.

Last Words: "Know it, brethren and always remember that by shooting my body you are killing your own soul. My body shall perish but my spirit will live, because I die for love and brotherhood." He remained firm in his convictions until the last minute.

Source: *Modern Martyrs, Documents* by War Resisters' International (Enfield, Middlesex, England, 1928).

Tarbell, Ida Minerva

(1857-1944) American writer, journalist. Known for her muckraking exposés in *McClure's Magazine*. One of the founders of *American Magazine*. Notable work: *History of the Standard Oil Company*. Died at age 86 in Bridgeport, Connecticut.

Last Words: "Hark, the Herald Angels Sing." Her response when carolers asked her what carol she wanted to hear. She lost consciousness and died several days later.

Source: *Ida Tarbell: Portrait of a Muckraker* by Kathleen Brady (New York, 1984).

Tasso, Torquato

(1544-1595) Italian poet. Named by Longfellow as one of the Immortal Four of Italy (along with Dante, Ariosto and Petrarch). Notable work: *Jerusalem Delivered* (epic poem). Had panic attacks fearing some of the poem contradicted the teachings of the Roman Catholic Church. Became delusional. Had to be institutionalized. Spent several years in a hospital. Died at age 51 in Rome.

Last Words: "Into Thy hands O lord—."

Source: *The Life of Torquato Tasso* by Rev R. Milman (London, 1850).

Tatum, Art

(1909-1956) American musician, pianist. Birth name Arthur Taylor Jr. Visually handicapped. Had no sight in one eye and only partial sight in the other. His astonishing ability as a jazz pianist is legendary. Died at age 47 in Los Angeles. Was awarded Grammy Lifetime Achievement Award posthumously in 1989.

Last Words: "I'll be looking for you." Spoken to his sister on the phone.

Source: *Too Marvelous for Words: The Life and Genius of Art Tatum* by James T. Lester (New York, 1994).

Taylor, Edward T.

(1793-1871) American clergyman, sailor. Known as Father Taylor and as the Sailor Preacher. Chaplain at Seamen's Bethel, Boston. Died at age 77. The book *Incidents and Anecdotes of the Rev. Edward T. Taylor for Over Forty Years Pastor of the Seamen's Bethel, Boston* by Gilbert Haven and Tho-

mas Russell was published in 1872.

Last Words: "Why certainly, certainly." His response when asked if he knew Jesus and if He was precious.

Source: *Life of Father Taylor, the Sailor Preacher* by Boston Port and Seamen's Aid Society (Boston, 1904).

Taylor, James Bayard

(1825-1878) American diplomat, writer, journalist, poet, novelist, translator. Traveled extensively. Wrote about Europe for *The New York Tribune, Saturday Evening Post* and *The United States Gazette*. Translated Goethe's *Faust*. Died at age 53 in Berlin, a few months after he was appointed U.S. minister to Germany.

Last Words: "I want, I want, oh, you know what I mean, that stuff of life!"

Source: *Life and Letters of Bayard Taylor*, ed. by Marie Hansen-Taylor and Horace E. Scudder (Boston, 1884). Marie Hansen-Taylor was his wife.

Taylor, Jane

(1783-1824) English writer. Known for her children's literature. Wrote the words for the song "Twinkle, Twinkle, Little Star" (published originally under the title "The Star"). Sister of writer Ann Taylor Gilbert. Died at age 40 of breast cancer in Ongar, England.

Different Last Words:

(1) "Well, I don't think now I shall see Ann again, I feel I am dying fast." Spoken to her brother who told her their sister was on her way to see her. After speaking these words, she said nothing that could be understood. She died a few hours later.

Source: *Memoirs, Correspondence and Poetical Remains of the Late Jane Taylor* by Jane Taylor and Isaac Taylor (London, 1826). Isaac Taylor was her brother.

(2) "Are we not children, all of us?"

Source: *The Homiletic Review*, Vol. 94, 1927.

Taylor, Jeremy

(1613-1667) English prelate, scholar, writer, orator. Anglican. Known as the Shakespeare of the Divines. Bishop of Down and Connor and of Dromore in Ireland. Died at age 53 in Lisburn, Ireland.

Last Words: "Bury me at Dromore." He helped rebuild Dromore Cathedral after it was destroyed in a 1641 insurrection. He is buried there.

Source: *Jeremy Taylor* by Edmund Gosse (New York, 1904).

Taylor, John

(1580-1653) English pamphleteer, journalist, poet, waterman. Ferried passengers across the Thames for many years. Gave himself the title The Water Poet. Moved to Oxford during England's Civil War. Wrote royalist pamphlets. Later had a public house, the Poet's Head, in Phoenix Alley, London. Well-known in England and Scotland during his lifetime.

Last Words: "How sweet it is to rest!"

Sources: *Dictionary of Phrase and Fable* by E. Cobham Brewer (London, 1896); *Early Prose and Poetical Works of John Taylor, the Water Poet (1580-1653)* by John Taylor (London, 1888).

Taylor, Robert

(1911-1969) American actor. Screen and television star. Birth name Spangler Arlington Brugh. Starred in many leading roles. Notable movies: *Magnificent Obsession; Camille; Waterloo Bridge*. Died at age 57 of lung cancer in Santa Monica, California.

Last Words: "Tell Ursula, be happy." Spoken to Ronald Reagan who was visiting him. He was referring to his wife German-born actress Ursula Thiess. Taylor had replaced Reagan as host of the television show *Death Valley Days* in 1965, after Reagan turned to politics.

Source: *The Leading Men of MGM* by Jane Ellen Wayne (New York, 2004).

Taylor, Rowland

(1510-1555) English clergyman, martyr. Chaplain who advocated the cause of Lady Jane Grey. Resisted restoration of Roman Catholic Mass. Found guilty of treason. Executed at age 44. Third Protestant martyr to be burned at the stake during the reign of Queen Mary. He offered his boots to a bystander and gave away his clothes.

Last Words: "Merciful Father of heaven, for Jesus Christ my Saviour's sake, receive my soul into thy hands." Spoken as the fire was set. He stood without crying out or moving, with his arms folded together until one of his executioners struck him on the head.

Source: *Book of Martyrs and the Acts and Monuments of the Church* by John Fox (or Foxe). First published 1563, ed. by John Cumming (London, 1851).

Taylor, Zachary

(1784-1850) 12th President of the U.S.

American military officer. General in U.S. Army. Known as Old Rough and Ready. Defeated the Mexicans at Palo Alto and commanded Army of Rio Grande in the Mexican War. Experienced heat exhaustion at the dedication of the Washington Monument. Died at age 65 of heat stroke in the White House after 16 months in office.

Last Words: "I am about to die. I expect the summons very soon. I have tried to discharge my duties faithfully; I regret nothing, but I am sorry that I am about to leave my friends."

Source: *Old Rough and Ready: The Life and Times of Zachary Taylor* by Silas Bent McKinley and Silas Bent (New York, 1946).

Tchaikovsky, Peter Ilyich

(1840-1893) Russian musician, composer. Notable works: symphonies; concertos (piano, violin); *Romeo and Juliet* (overture); *Swan Lake; The Sleeping Beauty; Nutcracker Suite* (ballets); *Eugene Onegin* (opera). Drank contaminated water during a cholera epidemic in St. Petersburg. Became delirious. Died at age 53.

Last Words: "Proklyataya." (tr. "Accursed one.") He kept muttering this word while delirious. He used the feminine gender, suggesting he may have meant Madame von Meck (wealthy widow who was his patron and confidante for many years). His Last Words were revealed several years later to friends by his brother Modeste, who was in the room when he died.

Source: *Milton Cross's Encyclopedia of the Great Composers and Their Music* by Milton Cross and David Ewen (Garden City, NY, 1962).

Teasdale, Sara Trevor

(1884-1933) American poet. Won first Pulitzer Prize for Poetry with *Love Songs* (1918). Overdosed on sleeping pills in her apartment; found dead in her bathtub at age 48. In 1994, she was inducted into the St. Louis [Missouri] Walk of Fame.

Last Words (doubtful):

"When I am dead, and over me bright April
Shakes out her rain-drenched hair,
Tho' you should lean above me broken-hearted,
I shall not care.
I shall have peace, as leafy trees are peaceful

When rain bends down the bough,
And I shall be more silent and cold-hearted
Than you are now."
Source: Various Last Words compilations and Internet
websites.

Some sources state that Teasdale wrote her sad poem "I Shall Not Care" as a suicide note. She may have left a copy of it when she took her life; however, it was not written for that purpose. The poem was first published many years earlier. It appeared in her 1915 collection *Rivers to the Sea.*
Source: *Sara Teasdale: Woman and Poet* by William Drake (New York, 1979).

Tecumseh or Tecumtha

(1768-1813) Native American leader. Shawnee chief. Tried to organize confederation of Native American tribes to prevent European settlers from further encroaching on their land. Fought for the British during the War of 1812. Killed at about age 45 in the Battle of the Thames in Upper Canada against U.S. Cavalry.

Different Last Words:

(1) "One of my legs is shot off! But leave me one or two guns loaded; I am going to have a last shot. Be quick and go!" Spoken as he lay on the ground, fatally wounded. Account came from Andrew J. Blackbird of the Ottawa.
Source: *History of the Ottawa and Chippewa Indians of Michigan* by Andrew J. Blackbird (Ypsilanti, MI, 1887).

(2) "Be brave! Be strong! Be brave!" Spoken just before he was killed in battle.
Source: *A Sorrow in Our Heart: The Life of Tecumseh* by Allan W. Eckert (New York, 1992).

(3) "Brother warriors, we are about to enter an engagement from which I will never come out. My body will remain on the field of battle." He unbuckled his sword and handed it to a chief, saying "When my son becomes a noted warrior and able to wield a sword, give it to him."
Source: *Lives of Famous Indian Chiefs, from Cofachiqui, the Indian Princess and Powhatan; Down to and Including Chief Joseph and Geronimo* by Norman Barton Wood (Aurora, IL, 1906).

Teilhard de Chardin, Pierre

(1881-1955) French clergyman, theologian, paleontologist, philosopher. Jesuit priest. Lived in China 1927 to 1954. Notable works: *The Phenomenon of Man; Divine Milieu.* Died suddenly at age 74 in St. Patrick's Cathedral, New York City, on Easter Sunday. After Mass, he mingled with the congregation and collapsed.

Last Words: "I can't remember anything. This time I feel it's terrible."
Source: *Teilhard de Chardin* by Claude Cuenot (Baltimore, MD, 1965).

Tekakwitha or Tegakouita, Blessed Kateri, Katharine or Catherine

(1656-1680) Native American holy woman. Daughter of an Iroquois father and Algonquin mother. Known as Lily of the Mohawks. Died at age 24. Beatified in 1980 (step toward sainthood). First North American Indian to be a candidate for sainthood. Her face was scarred and disfigured by smallpox. Two Jesuits and others in her room as she lay dying witnessed her skin miraculously clear up.

Last Words (spoken): "Jesus, I love you."
Source: *New Saints and Blesseds of the Catholic Church* by Ferdinand Holböck (San Francisco, CA, 2000, citing *L'Osservatore romano,* June 30, 1980).

Last Words (written): "I am leaving you. I am going to die. Remember always what we have done together since first we met. If you change I shall accuse you before the tribunal of God. Take courage, despise the discoursings of those who have not the Faith. If they ever try to persuade you to marry, listen only to the Fathers. If you cannot serve God here, go to the Mission at Lorette. Don't give up your mortifications. I shall love you in Heaven. I shall pray for you. I shall aid you. April 17, 1680."
Source: *Catherine Tekakwitha* by Daniel Sargent (New York, 1936).

Temple, Henry John, 3rd Viscount Palmerston

(1784-1865) British nobleman, statesman, politician. Held many important positions including secretary of war, foreign secretary, home secretary and prime minister. Suffered from gout. Died at age 80 in Brocket, Hertfordshire, England.

Different Last Words:

(1) "That's article ninety-eight; now go on to the next." His thoughts were on a treaty he had been working on.

Source: *Lord Palmerston* by Herbert C.F. Bell (London, 1936).

(2) "Die, my dear doctor? That's the last thing I think of doing."

Source: *A Book About Lawyers* by John Cordy Jeaffreson (London, 1867).

Ten Boom, Cornelia Johanna Arnolda ("Corrie")

(1892-1983) Dutch resistance figure, writer, lecturer. Holocaust survivor. Protected Jews from Nazis by hiding them in her family's home in Haarlem, The Netherlands, during World War II. Arrested and sent to Ravensbrück concentration camp with her older sister Betsie who died there in 1944. The camp was liberated in 1945. Corrie told the story in *The Hiding Place,* a book that was later made into a movie. Had strokes during her final years. Died on her 91st birthday in Orange, California.

Last Words: "Ja." (tr. "Yes.") Her response when asked if she was happy. She then moved her mouth to show that she wanted to sing. Her family sang part of two Dutch hymns to her.

Source: *The Five Silent Years of Corrie Ten Boom* by Pamela Rosewell Moore (Grand Rapids, MI, 1986).

Ten Boom, Elisabeth ("Betsie")

(1885-1944) Dutch resistance figure. Citizen who hid Jews from Nazis in her home in Haarlem, The Netherlands, during World War II. Arrested and sent to Ravensbrück concentration camp with her sister Corrie. She died there in December 1944.

Last Words: "So much work to do."

Source: *The Hiding Place* by Corrie Ten Boom with John and Elizabeth Sherrill (New York, 1971). The author was her sister. The 1975 movie *The Hiding Place* was based on this book.

Tennent, William

(1705-1777) American clergyman. Pastor of Presbyterian Church in Freehold, New Jersey. During a fever, he fell into a trance that lasted three days. Relatives thought he was dead and prepared him for burial. When he recovered, he described his experience. For the rest of his life, he firmly believed he had gone to Heaven while he was unconscious. His experience attracted much attention.

Last Words: "Blessed be God, I have no wish to live, if it should be His will and pleasure to call me hence, unless it should be to see a happy issue to the severe and arduous controversy my country is engaged in; but even in this, the will of the Lord be done."

Source: *Life of the Rev. William Tennent, Formerly Pastor of the Presbyterian Church at Freehold in New Jersey—in Which is Contained, Among Other Interesting Particulars, an Account of His Being Three Days in a Trance and Apparently Lifeless* by Elias Boudinot (New York, 1848).

Tennyson, Alfred, 1st Baron Tennyson of Aldworth

(1809-1892) British poet. Poet laureate of England for 42 years. Raised to peerage in 1884 as baron, becoming the first person to achieve such rank for literary accomplishments. Notable works: "Idylls of the King"; "In Memoriam"; "Charge of the Light Brigade." Died at age 83 at Aldworth.

Last Words: "God bless you, my joy!" Whispered to his wife. Before that, he called "Hallam." These were his last conscious efforts to speak. He died at 1:30 the following morning, clasping a book of Shakespeare he had been reading.

Source: *Dear and Honoured Lady: The Correspondence between Queen Victoria and Alfred Tennyson* by Victoria, Queen of Great Britain and Alfred Tennyson, ed. by Hope Dyson and Charles Tennyson (Rutherford, NY, 1971). Charles Tennyson was Alfred's grandson.

Teresa Benedicta of the Cross, Saint

(1891-1942) German nun, holy woman, philosopher. Born Edith Stein in Orthodox Jewish family. Student of Edmund Husserl at University of Gottingen. Held a doctorate in philosophy. Converted to Roman Catholicism. Became a Carmelite nun in 1934. Arrested by the Nazis for her Jewish heritage. Killed at age 51 at Auschwitz concentration camp in Nazi-occupied Poland. Canonized in 1998.

Last Words: "Come, we are going for our people." Spoken to her sister Rosa as the Nazi SS took them away.

Source: *Constantine's Sword: The Church and the Jews—A History* by James Carroll (Boston, 2002).

Teresa of Avila, Saint

(1515-1582) Spanish writer, mystic, holy woman. Roman Catholic. Birth name Teresa de Cepeda y Ahumada. Author of works on spiritual life. Left an autobiography and many letters. Died at age 67 in Alba de Tormes, Salamanca, Spain. Canonized in 1662. One of the first two women to be named Doctor of the Church.

Different Last Words:

(1) "Oh, my Lord! My Lord and my Bridegroom, the longed-for hour has come, the hour in which I shall see Thee! Lord, now is the time to arise and go! The good time which I welcome, which is Thy will; the hour when I must leave my exile and my soul shall enjoy the fulfillment of all her desire!"

Source: *Saint Teresa of Spain* by Helen H. Colvill (New York, 1909).

(2) "Over my spirit flash and float in divine radiancy the bright and glorious visions of the world to which I go."

Source: *The Last Words (Real and Traditional) of Distinguished Men and Women Collected from Various Sources* by Frederic Rowland Marvin (New York, 1901). Marvin said "just what were her last words is very uncertain."

Terhune, Albert Payson

(1872-1942) American journalist, writer. Wrote for *New York Evening World*. Notable works: dog stories such as *Lad: a Dog; The Heart of a Dog; The Way of a Dog.* Died at age 69 at his home in Pompton Lakes, New Jersey.

Last Words: "I shall be with you. I shall surely be here. You must believe me." Spoken to his wife.

Source: *The Master of Sunnybank, a Biography of Albert Payson Terhune* by Irving Litvag (New York, 1977). Sunnybank was Terhune's New Jersey home.

Terriss, William

(1847-1897) British actor, theater manager. Birth name William Charles James Lewin. Murder victim. Member of Henry Irving's acting company. Stabbed by deranged actor Richard Prince outside the stage door of the Adelphi Theatre in London. His motive was an imagined grievance. Terriss died in the arms of his mistress, Jessie Milward. Prince was immediately apprehended.

Last Words: "I shall come back." A moment later he whispered: "Can any man be so foolish as to believe there is no afterlife?"

Source: *Haunted Theaters, Playhouse Phantoms, Opera House Horrors and Backstage Banshees* by Tom Ogden (Guilford, CT, 2009).

Terry, Dame Ellen

(1847-1928) English actress. Stage performer popular in Great Britain and North America. Last appearance as actress was 1925, the year she was made a Dame, Grand Cross of the Order of the British Empire, the first actress to be so honored. Died at age 81 at Small Hythe, Tenterden, England.

Last Words: "Up to the skies,—down to the…"

Source: *Ellen Terry and Her Secret Self* by Edward Gordon Craig (New York, 1932). The author was her son.

Tettemer, John

(1876-1949) American clergyman, writer. Roman Catholic Passionist monk. Religious name: Father Ildefonso. Opposed modernism in church. Lost his faith. Sought release from his vows. Subsequently married. Wrote autobiography, *I was a Monk*. Died at age 73 in Beverly Hills, California.

Last Words: "Good heavens, no." His response when asked if he wanted to see a priest.

Source: "Anti-Modernist Priest Completely Loses Faith" by Father James McLucas (*The Latin Mass Magazine*, Advent/Christmas 2005).

Teyte, Dame Maggie

(1888-1976) English singer. Operatic, concert and recital soprano. Member Chicago Opera Company, Boston Opera Company. Notable roles: Melissande (*Pelleas et Melisande*); Cherubino (*Marriage of Figaro*); Belinda (*Dido and Aeneas*). Retired in 1951. Made Dame Commander of the Order of the British Empire in 1958. Died at age 88 in London.

Last Words: "I have not lived like a Catholic, but I hope I shall die like one."

Source: *The Pursuit of Perfection: A Life of Maggie Teyte* by Garry O'Connor (New York, 1979).

Tezuka, Osamu

(1928-1989) Japanese manga artist, animator. Trained formally as a physician. Invented distinctive large-eye style of Japanese animation. Known as the Godfather of Anime. Created *Astro Boy* and *Kimba the White Lion*. Died at age 60 of cancer in Osaka, Honshu.

Last Words: "I'm begging you, let me work!"

Source: *Phoenix* by Osamu Tezuka (San Francisco, CA, 2003).

Thackeray, William Makepeace

(1811-1863) English novelist, illustrator, satirist. Pen name: Samuel Titmarsh. Notable works: *Vanity Fair; The Memoirs of Barry Lyndon; The History of Pendennis; The History of Henry Esmond.* Died suddenly at age 52 in London. Thackeray's last novel *Denis Duval* was left unfinished at his death.

Last Words (written): "And my heart throbbed with an exquisite bliss." They were the Last Words he revised in *Denis Duval.*

Source: *William Makepeace Thackeray. A Biography Including Hitherto Uncollected Letters and Speeches and a Bibliography of 1,300 Items* by Lewis Melville (London, 1910).

Last Words (spoken): "I didn't take enough medicine last night. I have taken some more. I shall be better presently."

Source: *An Uneasy Victorian: Thackeray the Man, 1811-1863* by Ann Monsarrat (New York, 1980).

Thadden, Elisabeth Adelheid Hildegard von

(1890-1944) Prussian-born German educator, activist. Founded private boarding school for girls that ran into opposition with Nazi government because it did not follow laws regarding non-admission or non-assistance to Jews. She joined the "Solf Circle," a group considered by the Nazis to be part of the German Resistance. After a Gestapo informant infiltrated the group, she was arrested at her post in Meaux, France, and was sent to Ravensbrück concentration camp. Sentenced to death for conspiring to commit high treason and undermining Nazi Wehrkraftzersetzung (military forces). Beheaded at Plötzensee Prison in Berlin.

Last Words: "O Herr, mach Ende mit aller unserer Not." (tr. "Oh Lord, put an end to all our suffering.") Her Last Words were taken from a verse of a Paul Gerhardt song, "Mach End."

Source: *Auf verlorenem Posten? Ein Laie erlebt den evangelischen Kirchenkampf in Hitlerdeutschland* by Reinold von Thadden (Berlin, Germany, 1948). The author was her brother.

Thalberg, Irving G.

(1899-1936) American movie producer. Production head at Metro-Goldwyn-Mayer

Notable movies: *The Good Earth; The Barretts of Wimpole Street; Marie Antoinette; Mutiny on the Bounty.* Died at age 37 of pneumonia in Santa Monica, California. Inspiration for a character in F. Scott Fitzgerald's *Last Tycoon.* The Irving G. Thalberg Memorial Award—instituted in his name—is awarded to producers whose bodies of work are of consistent high quality.

Last Words: "Don't let the children forget me." Spoken to his wife Norma Shearer, referring to his two children Irving Jr. and Katherine.

Source: "Oscar Films/The Honorees: Thalberg to Beatty: Reinventing Hollywood" by David Thomson (*New York Times,* March 12, 2000).

Thayer, William Sydney

(1864-1932) American physician, military officer, educator. Brigadier general in U.S. Army during World War I. President of the American Medical Association. Professor at Johns Hopkins Medical School. Died at age 68 of heart disease in Washington, D.C.

Last Words: "This is the end, and I am not sorry."

Source: *The Life and Convictions of William Sydney Thayer, Physician* by Edith G. Reid (New York, 1936).

Theodora, Saint

(fl. 400s) Noblewoman, holy woman. Lived in Alexandria when Zeno was emperor. Performed many miracles.

Last Words: "My sweet son, the time of my death cometh, I leave and commend thee to God; take him for thy Father and thy helper. And my sweet son, see that thou fast and pray, and serve thy brethren devoutly!" She died soon after speaking these words to the child she was falsely accused of being the father of when disguised as a monk.

Source: *The Golden Legend or Lives of the Saints.* Compiled by Jacobus de Voragine, Archbishop of Genoa, 1275, 1st ed., 1470. English ed. by William Caxton, 1483, ed. by F.S. Ellis (Edinburgh, 1900).

Theodore, Saint

(d. 287?) Italian holy man. Early Christian martyr. First saint of his name. Died during rule of Diocletian and Maximian in the city of Marine.

Last Words: "With my Christ I was, and am, and will be!" Spoken to the provost who asked whether he would be with them or

with Christ. The provost then ordered him to be burned at the stake. He died but his body remained unharmed. A sweet odor permeated the air everywhere.
Source: *The Golden Legend or Lives of the Saints.* Compiled by Jacobus de Voragine, Archbishop of Genoa, 1275, 1st ed., 1470. English ed. by William Caxton, 1483, ed. by F.S. Ellis (Edinburgh, 1900).

Theodoric the Goth, King of the Ostrogoths

(454?-526) Merovingian ruler. Conqueror of Italy. Defeated Odoacer and caused his death. Died in Ravenna at about age 72. He appears in German epic poetry as Dietrich von Bern, one of the heroes in the *Nibelungenlied*.
Last Words: "I am ill mounted. This must be the foul fiend on which I ride. Yet will I return, if God wills and Holy Mary." Spoken as he disappeared on a black horse. In German legend, the black horse, his "foul fiend," was the devil carrying the rider to a distant place where he must fight dragons until Judgment Day, then return.
Source: *Theodoric the Goth: The Barbarian Champion of Civilization* by Thomas Hodgkins (New York, 1891).

Theophrastus

(371?-287 B.C.?) Greek philosopher. Original name Tyrtanius; changed to Theophrastus by Aristotle. Friend and disciple of Aristotle. Died at about age 85. Only fragments of his writings survive.
Last Words: "Farewell, and may you be happy. Either drop my doctrine, which involves a world of labor, or stand forth its worthy champion, for you will win great glory. Life holds more disappointment than advantage. But as I can no longer discuss what we ought to do, do you go on with the inquiry into right conduct." Spoken to his disciples.
Source: *The Lives and Opinions of Eminent Philosophers* by Diogenes Laërtius, tr. by C.D. Yonge (London, 1853).

Theramenes, the Athenian

(455?-404 B.C.) Athenian statesman, military officer. General. Founding member of Thirty Tyrants. Accused of treason and condemned by Critias to drink hemlock. Executed without a trial at about age 51.
Last Words: "This to the fair Critias." Spo-

ken as he drank the poison.
Source: *A New Classical Dictionary (based on William Smith's Dictionary),* ed. by Charles Anthon (New York, 1868).

Thérèse of Lisieux, Saint

(1873-1897) French holy woman. Roman Catholic Carmelite nun. Birth name Marie-Françoise-Thérèse Martin. Known as The Little Flower of Jesus. Notable work: *The Story of a Soul* (autobiography). Died at age 24 of tuberculosis in Lisieux, France. Canonized in 1925.
Last Words: "My God, I love You!"
Source: *The Story of the Canonization of S. Thérèse of Lisieux with the Text of the Principal Documents and the Process* by S. Thérèse of Lisieux (London, 1934).

Thistlewood, Arthur

(1770-1820) British conspirator. Part of the Cato Street Conspiracy, a failed attempt to assassinate members of the British Cabinet at a London dinner party. In 1820, he and a small group of Spenceans schemed to assassinate several members of the British government at the home of the Earl of Harrowby. The group were arrested in a Cato Street loft where they had gathered. Thistlewood was convicted of treason and executed by hanging at Newgate Prison.
Different Last Words:
(1) "I now have but a few moments to live, and I hope the world will think that I have at least been sincere in my endeavours." Spoken in a low tone to a person under the scaffold just before his execution.
Source: *Old and New London: A Narrative of Its History, Its People and Its Places* by Walter Thornbury and Edward Walford (London, 1881).
(2) (doubtful): "I shall soon know the last grand secret."
Source: Various Last Words compilations and Internet websites.
Thistlewood did say this as he was about to be executed, but these were not his final words. See (1).

Thomas the Apostle, Saint

(d. 72?) Biblical figure. One of the twelve Apostles. Little is known about him except what is in the Bible. Known as Doubting Thomas, Didymus, The Twin and Apostle of India. He was doubtful about Christ's Resurrection. He had to see and touch him before he would believe. Stabbed to death with a spear in India.

Last Words: "I adore, but not this metal; I adore, but not this graven image; I adore my Master Jesus Christ in Whose name I command thee, demon of this idol, to destroy it forthwith!"

Source: *The Golden Legend or Lives of the Saints.* Compiled by Jacobus de Voragine, Archbishop of Genoa, 1275, 1st ed., 1470. English ed. by William Caxton, 1483, ed. by F.S. Ellis (Edinburgh, 1900).

Thomas, Dylan Marlais

(1914-1953) Welsh poet, writer. Notable works: "Do Not Go Gentle into That Good Night"; "A Child's Christmas in Wales." Collapsed from exhaustion and excessive drinking while on a tour in the U.S. in 1953. Became comatose. Died at age 39 in New York City.

Different Last words:

(1) "Roses plural or Rose's roses with an apostrophe?" His response to his girlfriend Liz who told him her friend had seen white mice and roses. He then lapsed into a coma and died.

Source: *Endings: Death Glorious and Otherwise, as Faced by Ten Outstanding Figures of Our Time* by Leon Prochnik (New York, 1980).

(2) (doubtful): "I've had eighteen straight whiskeys. I think that's the record," or something similar.

Source: Various Last Words compilations and Internet websites.

Thomas may have said these words while he was on his final drinking binge, but they were not his Last Words. See (1).

Thomas, George Henry

(1816-1870) American military officer. Served in the Mexican War. Union general in the U.S. Civil War. Known as the Rock of Chickamauga for his defense of the area in 1863. Helped freemen during Reconstruction. Died at age 53 in San Francisco, California.

Last Words: "I want air." He came out of his office and collapsed.

Source: *George Thomas: Virginian for the Union* by Christopher J. Einolf (Norman, OK, 2007).

Thomas, Olive

(1894-1920) American model, actress. Silent screen star. Birth name Olive R. Duffy.

Ziegfeld girl. Won "The Most Beautiful Girl in New York City" contest. She began her movie career with Fox but left to sign with Selznick. She was the first actress to be described as a "flapper." Her death in France at age 25 was controversial. Intoxicated and tired, she accidentally ingested a large amount of mercury bichloride from a flask with a label written in French. She may have thought the flask contained a sleeping preparation. She died a slow death from poisoning in a French hospital over several days.

Last Words: "Pretty weak, but I'll be all right in a little while, don't worry, darling." Spoken to Owen Moore, a former in-law who was at her bedside.

Source: *Olive Thomas: The Life and Death of a Silent Film Beauty* by Michelle Vogel (Jefferson, NC, 2007), citing her husband Jack Pickford's interview with *Los Angeles Examiner*, September 13, 1920, that detailed the events of her last days.

Thomas, Theodore

(1835-1905) German-born American musician, orchestra conductor. Formed an orchestra in New York City in the 1860s. Conductor of New York Philharmonic Society and Chicago Symphony. Died at age 69 of pneumonia in Chicago.

Last Words: "I have had a beautiful vision, a beautiful vision."

Source: *Memoirs of Theodore Thomas* by Rose Fay Thomas (New York, 1911). The author was his wife.

Thompson, Francis Joseph

(1859-1907) English poet, writer. Notable works: "The Hound of Heaven"; "The Kingdom of God" (poems); "Shelley" (essay). Became addicted to laudanum; was malnourished and suicidal. Befriended by Wilfrid and Alice Meynell, who nursed him back to health and encouraged him to write. Died at age 47 of tuberculosis and laudanum poisoning in London.

Last Words: "My withered dreams, my withered dreams." He uttered the last two lines of his poem "The Poppy [to Monica]" as he was dying.

Source: *Between Heaven and Charing Cross: The Life of Francis Thompson* by Brigid M. Boardman (New Haven, CT, 1988).

Thompson, Hunter S.

(1937-2005) American journalist, writer.

Counterculture figure. Pioneered "gonzo journalism" style of writing in which the author plays a key role in the story. Notable work: *Fear and Loathing in Las Vegas*, book that later became a movie. He was depressed and in physical pain from hip replacement surgery. Wrote goodbye note entitled "Football Season is Over." Left note for wife Anita. Committed suicide four days later at age 67.

Last Words (written): "No More Games. No More Bombs. No More Walking. No More Fun. No More Swimming. 67. That is 17 years past 50. 17 more than I needed or wanted. Boring. I am always bitchy. No Fun for anybody. 67. You are getting Greedy. Act your old age. Relax. This won't hurt."

Source: *Gonzo, the Life of Hunter S. Thompson: An Oral Biography* by Jann Wenner and Corey Seymour (New York, 2007).

Thompson, Sir John Sparrow David

(1844-1894) Canadian statesman, jurist, lawyer. Minister of justice. Prime minister of Canada. One of Bering Straits negotiators. Knighted in 1888. Died suddenly at age 49 of a heart attack while at Windsor Castle in England. Queen Victoria had just made him a member of her Privy Council.

Last Words: "I am all right, thank you." Spoken to Lord Breadalbane, who offered his arm to Thompson.

Source: *Life and Work of the Rt. Hon. Sir John Thompson: Prime Minister of Canada* by John Castell Hopkins (Toronto, ON, 1895).

Thompson, William Hale ("Big Bill")

(1867-1944) American politician, orator. Known for his flamboyant campaigning style. Served as mayor of Chicago twice: 1915 to 1923; 1927 to 1931. Ran for governor in 1936 but lost. Failed to control gangsters during his administration, but he did improve city parks, streets and playgrounds. Died at age 74 in Chicago.

Last Words: "Everything is all set, Jim.— That's right. That's right." He was referring to his business affairs.

Source: *Big Bill of Chicago* by Lloyd Wendt, Herman Kogan and Rick Kogan (Indianapolis, IN, 1953).

Thoreau, Henry David

(1817-1862) American naturalist, essayist, activist, writer. Transcendentalist. Notable works: *Walden, or Life in the Woods; A Week on the Concord and Merrimack Rivers*. His "Essay on Civil Disobedience" influenced 20th-century leaders Martin Luther King and Mohandas K. Gandhi. Died at age 44 of tuberculosis in Concord, Massachusetts.

Last Words: "Moose. Indian." His last coherent words were spoken to Transcendental poet and friend Ellery Channing the morning he died.

Source: *Henry Thoreau: Bachelor of Nature* by Léon Bazalgette, tr. Van Wyck Brooks (New York, 1924).

Thorn, Martin George

(1858-1898) American murderer. Killed Willie Guldensuppe, the ex-lover of his lover and landlady, Mrs. Augusta Nack. Thorn was executed in the electric chair at Sing Sing (Ossining Prison) in New York. Mrs. Nack was sentenced to 20 years but served only 10. The gory details of the crime received much media coverage, Thorn had sliced the body into manageable pieces and tossed them in a nearby drainage pool. People became suspicious when a farmer's white ducks turned pink.

Last Words: "I have no fear. I'm not afraid. I am positive God will forgive me." Spoken as he was strapped into the electric chair.

Source: *Bloodletters and Badmen: A Narrative Encyclopedia of American Criminals from the Pilgrims to the Present* by Jay Robert Nash (New York, 1995).

Thorndike, Edward Lee

(1874-1949) American psychologist, educator, lexicographer. Helped lay groundwork for modern educational psychology. Taught educational psychology at Columbia University. Notable works: *Animal Intelligence; The Psychology of Learning; Fundamentals of Learning*. Compiled *Thorndike-Century Junior Dictionary*. Died at age 74 in Montrose, New York.

Last Words: "Poff, You're looking at a tired old man." Spoken to a friend.

Source: *The Sane Positivist: A Biography of Edward L. Thorndike* by Geraldine M. Jonçich (Middleton, CT, 1968).

Thornton, John

(1720-1790) English merchant, philanthropist. Made much money with his investments. Gave away more than a half million dollars to Christian causes. Died at age 70 from injuries sustained in an accident.

Last Words: "Precious, precious—"

Source: *Dying Testimonies of Saved and Unsaved: Gathered from Authentic Sources* by Solomon Benjamin Shaw (Chicago, 1898).

Thrasea Paetus

(d. 66) Roman politician. Senator and Stoic who opposed Emperor Nero. When he criticized Nero, the emperor commanded the Senate to condemn him to death. When he heard the news, he cut open the veins in his arm.

Last Words: "We pour out a libation to Jupiter the Deliverer. Behold, young man, and may the gods avert the omen, but you have been born into times in which it is well to fortify the spirit with examples of courage." He called the quaestor to his side and spoke his Last Words as he bled to death.

Source: *The Annals of Imperial Rome* by Cornelius Tacitus, Book 16, tr. by Michael Grant (New York, 1973).

Thring, Edward

(1821-1887) English educator, writer. Headmaster of Uppingham School in England. Wrote textbooks. Educational trailblazer. Introduced programs in music, sports, practical activities that were unknown elsewhere.

Last Words (written): "And now to bed; sermon finished, and a blessed feeling of Sunday coming." Written in his diary.

Source: *Edward Thring Headmaster of Uppingham School, Life, Diary and Letters* by George R. Parkin (London, 1900).

Thurber, James Grover

(1894-1961) American writer, cartoonist, humorist. Frequent contributor to *New Yorker* magazine. Notable works: *The Secret Life of Walter Mitty; The Male Animal; Thurber Country; My Life and Hard Times*. Lost part of his vision in a childhood accident. Almost blind by 1950. Had brain surgery for a blood clot in 1961. After making a partial recovery, he contracted pneumonia. Died at age 66 in New York City.

Last Words: "God bless. —God damn."

Source: *Thurber: A Biography* by Burton Bernstein (New York, 1975).

Thurlow, Edward, 1st Baron

(1731-1806) English lawyer, jurist. Attorney general. Lord chancellor of England. Financial patron of Samuel Johnson and George Crabbe. Friend of William Cowper. Died at age 74 at Brighton, England.

Last Words: "I'm shot if I don't think I am dying."

Source: *Chancellor Thurlow, The Life and Times of an XVIIIth Century Lawyer* by Robert Gore-Browne (London, 1953).

Tibbles, Susette La Flesche (Inshata Theumba, "Bright Eyes")

(1854-1903) Native American writer, lecturer, translator, artist. Known as Bright Eyes, a translation of her Omaha name Inshata Theumba. Oldest daughter of Joseph La Flesche, last recognized chief of the Omaha tribe. Died at age 49 in Bancroft, Nebraska.

Last Words: "Sorry dear. Forgot you don't know our language." Spoken to a friend after she addressed her in her native Omaha language

Source: *Bright Eyes: The Story of Susette La Flesche, an Omaha Indian* by Dorothy Clarke Wilson (New York, 1974).

Tidd, Richard

(1775-1820) English bootmaker, conspirator. Member of the Cato Street Conspiracy, a failed attempt to assassinate members of the British Cabinet at a London dinner party. The conspiracy was thwarted by police. Eleven men were arrested in a Cato Street loft where they had gathered. Tidd was one of five who were found guilty of high treason and executed.

Last Words: "How are you, my hearty?" Shouted out to fellow conspirator James Ings at the last moment before his execution. Earlier, he ran up the steps of the scaffold and bowed to spectators on all sides.

Source: *Old and New London: A Narrative of Its History, Its People and Its Places* by Walter Thornbury and Edward Walford (London, 1881).

Tilden, Samuel Jones

(1814-1886) American politician, political reformer. Known as the Sage of Greystone or Sage of Gramercy Park. Conservative member of New York legislature. Helped destroy Boss Tweed ring. Governor of New

York. Candidate for U.S. President in the highly disputed election of 1876 when he won the popular vote but lost the election to Rutherford B. Hayes in the electoral college by one vote. Tilden had 184 votes; he needed 185. Declined to run again. When he died a bachelor at age 72 at Greystone, his home in Yonkers, New York, and much of his wealth were donated to the New York Public Library. His gravestone says "I still trust the people." Samuel Tilden High School in Brooklyn, the former Fort Tilden and Tilden, Nebraska, were named for him.

Last Words: "Drink."

Source: "Samuel J. Tilden Dead–Passing Away of Democracy's Great Leader" (*New York Times*, August 5, 1886).

Variation: "Water."

Source: *A Conspectus of American Biography: Being an Analytical Summary of American History and Biography, Containing also the Complete Indexes of the National Cyclopedia of American Biography* by George Derby (New York, 1906).

Tillich, Paul Johannes Oskar

(1886-1965) Prussian-born American clergyman, theologian, philosopher, educator. Left Germany in 1933 after he criticized Hitler. Emigrated to the U.S. Taught at Union Theological Seminary, Columbia and New School for Social Research. Retired, then was professor at Harvard and University of Chicago. Notable work: *Systematic Theology* (3-vol. summary of his work). Died at age 79 in Chicago.

Last Words: "All my hard work. All my work in vain. I am eating nothing at all—absolute asceticism." Spoken to a physician. He was not pleased with his hospital meals, so he canceled them.

Source: *From Time to Time* by Hannah Tillich (New York, 1973). The author was his wife.

Tillman, Patrick Daniel

(1976-2004) American athlete. Soldier, U.S. Army Ranger. Professional football player. Turned down a contract offer of $3.6 million over three years with the Arizona Cardinals to enlist in the U.S. Army. Killed by friendly fire in Afghanistan at age 27. Lincoln Law School of San Jose, California, established the Pat Tillman Scholarship in his honor. The Pat Tillman USO Center—the first USO center in Afghanistan—opened on Bagram

Air Base in 2005. Forward Operating Base Tillman, close to the Pakistan border, is named for him.

Last Words: "I am Pat f*****g Tillman, dammit! I am Pat f*****g Tillman!" Spoken as he tried to signal that American troops were shooting at American troops.

Source: "Remember His Name" by Gary Smith (*Sports Illustrated,* September 11, 2006).

Timrod, Henry

(1829-1867) American poet, military officer. Served in the Confederate Army in the U.S. Civil War. Notable poems: "Charleston"; "The Cotton-Boll"; "Carolina"; "Magnolia Cemetery." Known as Laureate of the Confederacy. Died at age 38 of tuberculosis in Columbia, South Carolina.

Last Words: "I shall soon drink of the river of eternal life."

Source: *The Last Years of Henry Timrod, 1864-1867,* ed. by Jay B. Hubbell (Durham, NC, 1941).

Tindal, Matthew

(1657-1733) English theologian, educator, writer. Deist. Fellow of All Souls' College, Oxford. Notable works: *Christianity as Old as the Creation; The Rights of the Christian Church Asserted Against the Romish and All Other Priests* (created storm of protest).

Last Words: "Oh God—if there be a God—I desire Thee to have mercy on me."

Source: *The Book of Days; A Miscellany of Popular Antiquities in Connection with the Calendar, Including Anecdote, Biography & History, Curiosities of Literature and Oddities of Human Life and Character* by Robert Chambers (London, 1832).

Titmarsh, Samuel, see Thackeray, William Makepeace.

Titus Flavius Vespasianus, Emperor of Rome

(39-81) Roman ruler. Son of Emperor Vespasian. Brother of Emperor Domitian. Coliseum was completed and Vesuvius erupted during his reign. He was a popular, peace-loving emperor described by Suetonius as the "delight and darling of mankind." Died suddenly at age 41.

Last Words: Titus complained that his life was "taken away from him though he had done nothing to deserve it. For there was no action of his that he had occasion to repent but one." He did not say what that one action was. Suetonius reported Titus's Last Words as an indirect quote.

Source: "Titus Flavius Vespasianus Augustus" in *The Lives of the Twelve Caesars* by C. Suetonius Tranquillus, tr. by Alexander Thomson, rev. by Thomas Forester (London, 1901).

Tivy, Lawrence Rider ("Tan")

(1918-2007) British military officer. Royal Air Force pilot. Lieutenant commander during World War II. Flew Swordfish torpedo bombers with the Fleet Air Arm. Survived many crashes. Was aboard HMS *Courageous*, the first carrier lost in World War II, when it was torpedoed off Ireland in 1939. He was saved after several hours in the water; 518 men were lost. He later served on the HMS *Ark Royal*, HMS *Furious*, HMS *Battler*, HMS *Attacker* and HMS *Fencer*. Successfully attacked the battleship *Strasbourg* and dropped mines on La Spezia harbor. As a Swordfish pilot, he had a crucial part in the search for the German battleship *Bismarck*. Died at age 88.

Last Words: "Say goodbye, I have had a really good innings."

Source: "Lieutenant Commander 'Tan' Tivy," *The* [Liverpool] *Daily Post*, June 4, 2007).

Tojo, Hideki

(1884-1948) Japanese politician and military leader. Prime minister during World War II. Ordered the attack on Pearl Harbor in 1941. Hanged at age 63 as a war criminal.

Last Words: "My execution is some consolation, although it certainly cannot compensate for my responsibility to the nation. But, internationally, I declare myself innocent. I gave in only to superior force.—I now walk to the gallows, happy to shoulder my responsibility."

Source: *Tojo, the Last Banzai* by Courtney Browne (New York, 1998).

Toklas, Alice Babette

(1877-1967) American writer. Life mate of Gertrude Stein. Also her secretary, cook and confidant. Met Stein when she moved to Paris at age 29. The 1933 *Autobiography of Alice B. Toklas* was written by Stein. Notable works by Toklas: *The Alice B. Toklas Cookbook; What is Remembered*. Died in Paris at age 89. The 1968 film *I Love You Alice B. Toklas!,* a satire of the hippy generation, had little to do with its namesake.

Last Word: "Yes." Her response when asked if she wanted to die.

Source: *The Biography of Alice B. Toklas* by Linda Simon (Garden City, NY, 1977).

Toland, John

(1670-1722) Irish philosopher, writer. Deist. First person to be called a "freethinker." Coined the term "Pantheism." Charged with heresy for *Life of Milton* (1698). He responded to the charge by writing *Amyntor*. Spent his last years in poor health and poor circumstances. Died at age 51 in Putney, near London.

Last Words: "I want nothing but death."

Source: *Memoirs of the Life and Writings of Mr. John Toland* by Pierre Des Maizeaux, prefixed to *The Miscellaneous Works of Mr. John Toland* (London, 1747).

Toler, John, 1st Earl of Norbury, Viscount Glandine

(1740?-1831) Irish nobleman, jurist, lawyer, statesman. Solicitor general. Attorney general, chief justice of common pleas. Stayed in office despite senility. Finally retired in 1827 when his behavior became ludicrous. Elevated to Earl of Norbury in 1827. Died at about age 91 in Dublin Ireland.

Last Words: "James, present my compliments to Lord Erne and tell him it will be a dead heat between us." Spoken to his servant about his neighbor, an English aristocrat who was far advanced in years and bedridden.

Source: *Sketches of the Irish Bar* by Richard Lalor Sheil and Robert Shelton Mackenzie (New York, 1854).

Toler, Martin, Jr.

(1955-2006) American miner, victim of the Sago Mine disaster. Foreman. One of 12 people who died in the January 2006 coal mining disaster in West Virginia. He wrote his Last Words as he awaited his impending death from carbon monoxide poisoning and asphyxiation. It took nearly four days for rescue workers to reach the bodies.

Last Words (written): "Tell all I'll see them on the other side. It wasn't bad. I just went to sleep. I love you Jr." Found scribbled "very lightly and very loosely" in block letters on the back of an insurance application he had in his pocket. His Last Words were released to the press by his brother Tom Toler. They were selected as one of *Time* magazine's "Quotes of the Year."

Source: "Miner's Scrawled Last Words Sought to Comfort Loved Ones" by Allen G. Breed (*The* [Fort Wayne] *Journal-Gazette*, January 6, 2006).

Tolstoy, Count Lev ("Leo")

(1828-1910) Russian nobleman, novelist, writer, pacifist, philosopher. One of the world's great novelists. Notable works: *War and Peace; Anna Karenina; The Cossacks; The Death of Ivan Ilyich*. Died at age 82 of pneumonia at the home of the train stationmaster in Astapovo, 200 miles from his home in Yasnaya Polyana, Russia.

Different Last Words:

(1) "The truth—I love much.—How are they?"

Source: *Family Views of Tolstoy* by Aylmer Maude and Louise Shanks Maude (London, 1926).

Variation: "Truth—I love much as they—."

Source: *Tolstoy's Major Fiction* by Edward Wasiolek (Chicago, 1974).

(2) "No, peasants do not die this way."

Source: *The Soviet Review,* Vol. 2, Part 1, 1961.

(3) "Now comes death. That's all."

Source: "Tolstoy and His Wife at Yasnaya Polyana" (*American Review of Reviews*, Vol. 42, July-December 1910). The author noted the quote was "reported by the newspapers."

(4) "I do not understand what I have to do."

Source: *Tolstoy: His Life and Work* by Derrick Leon (London, 1944).

Tone, Theobald Wolfe

(1763-1798) Irish revolutionist, independence leader, writer, lawyer. Founder of Society of United Irishmen. Leading figure in United Irishmen Independence movement. Known by many as The Father of Irish Republicans. Sentenced to death for his role in the Irish Rebellion of 1798. Died at age 35 in Dublin before sentence was carried out. A number of Gaelic Athletic Association clubs in Ireland are named for him. He is a character in Thomas Pynchon's novel *Against the Day.*

Different Last Words:

(1) "I can yet find words to thank you Sir: It is the most welcome news you could give me. What should I wish to live for?" His response to a surgeon who told him that if he attempted to move or speak he would die instantly. Tone died a short time later.

Source: *Memoirs of Theobald Wolfe Tone* by Theobald Wolfe Tone (London, 1827). The author was his son.

(2) "I find, then, I am but a bad anatomist." Spoken after a botched suicide attempt in prison for which he lingered before dying. He tried to cut his throat but severed his windpipe instead of his jugular vein.

Source: *Rebels and Informers: Stirrings of Irish Independence* by Oliver Knox (New York, 1998).

(3) "Come and take charge." Spoken to a friend.

Source: *Wolfe Tone* by Marianne Elliott (New Haven, CT, 1989).

Tonks, Henry

(1862-1937) English artist, educator, surgeon. Abandoned a medical career to work in art. One of the first English artists influenced by French Impressionism. Taught many years at Slade School. Students included Augustus John, Percy Wyndham Lewis and Stanley Spencer. Notable work: *Saturday Night in the Vale*. Died at age 74 in London.

Last Words: "You may as well say goodbye as I shall not be here in the morning."

Source: *The Life of Henry Tonks* by Joseph Hone (London, 1939).

Toole, F.X., see Boyd, Jerry.

Toombs, Robert Augustus

(1810-1885) American politician. Confederate supporter. Fought in U.S. Civil War. Opponent of Reconstruction. Tried to restore the supremacy of Georgia after the war. In later years, he suffered from blindness and alcoholism. Died at age 75 in Washington, Georgia.

Different Last Words:

(1) "I am sorry the hour is come. I hope we shall meet in a better place." Spoken to Dr. Steiner who was about to return to his home in Augusta. Toombs had been in and out of consciousness during his final days.

Source: *Robert Toombs, Statesman, Speaker, Soldier, Sage: His Career in Congress and on the Hustings— His Work in the Courts—His Work with the Army—His Life at Home* by Pleasant A. Stovall (New York, 1892).

(2) (doubtful): "Prohibitionists are men of small pints." His response when he learned some of them were holding an election in his town.

Source: Various Last Words compilations and Internet websites.

Toombs did say these words during one of his lucid moments shortly before he died, but they were not his Last Words. See (1).

Toplady, Augustus Montague

(1740-1778) English clergyman, poet, hymnist. Calvinist. Wrote popular hymn *Rock of Ages*. Died at age 37 of tuberculosis in Kensington, Middlesex, England.

Last Words: "O, what delights! Who can fathom the joys of the third heaven? What a bright sunshine has been spread around me! I have not words to express it. I know it cannot be long now till my Savior will come for me, for surely no mortal man can live after glories that God has manifested to my soul. All is light, light, light—the brightness of His own glory. O come, Lord Jesus, come; come quickly."

Source: *Dying Testimonies of Saved and Unsaved: Gathered from Authentic Sources* by Solomon Benjamin Shaw (Chicago, 1898).

Variation: "No mortal man could live after experiencing the glories which God has manifested to my soul."

Source: *Augustus M. Toplady and Contemporary Hymn-Writers* by Thomas Wright (London, 1911).

Toral, José de León

(1900-1929) Mexican seminary student, fanatic, assassin. Catholic. Murdered Mexican President-elect Alvaro Obregon. Was convinced Obregon was the anti-Christ and had to be eliminated. Shot and killed him in a restaurant in July 1928. Executed at age 28 by firing squad in Mexico City.

Last Words: "Viva!" (tr. "Long live—!") He may have been trying to give the battle cry "Viva Cristo Rex!" (tr. "Long live Christ the King!")

Source: *New York Times*, February 10, 1929.

Torres-Acosta, Saint Maria Soledad

(1826-1887) Spanish nun, social worker, holy woman. Founder of Handmaids of Mary Serving the Sick. The order is dedicated to the care of the sick in their homes. Died at age 60 in Madrid, Spain. Canonized in 1970.

Last Words: "Children, live together in peace and unity." Spoken to her Sisters.

Source: *Butler's Lives of the Saints, October* by Alban

Butler, rev. by Peter Doyle (Collegeville, MN, 1996).

Touhy, Roger ("The Terrible")

(1898-1959) American bootlegger. Served 17-year prison sentence. Shot down in front of his sister's house in Chicago by unknown gunmen soon after he was released from prison.

Last Words: "I've been expecting it. The bastards never forget." He died four hours later in a hospital.

Source: *The FBI Encyclopedia* by Michael Newton (Jefferson City, NC, 2003).

Toulouse-Lautrec, Henri de

(1864-1901) French artist, lithographer. Post-Impressionist. Full name Henri Marie Raymond de Toulouse-Lautrec Monfa. Suffered from several congenital disorders. Injured his legs when he was young. Bones did not heal properly and his legs stopped growing. Painted people and scenes of Montmartre and Moulin Rouge in Paris. Was an alcoholic. Confined to a sanatorium then to his mother's care at home. Died at age 36 at his family's estate in Chateau Malromé. His story was told in the movies *Moulin Rouge* in 1952 and 2001 and in *Lautrec* in 1998.

Last Words: "Old fool!" He was referring to his father who was trying to catch flies in his bedroom while he was dying.

Source: *The Book of Absinthe: A Cultural History* by Phil Baker (New York, 2001).

Touro, Judah

(1775-1854) American businessman. Known for his generosity and philanthropy. Wounded in War of 1812. Moved to New Orleans in 1802. Bought and endowed Jewish cemetery and helped build synagogue. When he died at age 78 in New Orleans, his estate helped to endow many Jewish congregations in the U.S. Also helped fund hospitals, orphanages and alms houses.

Last Words: "When I am dead, carry me to the spot of my birth, and bury me by the side of my mother."

Source: *The Life of Judah Touro (1775-1854)* by Leon Hünner (Philadelphia, 1946).

Toussaint L'Ouverture, Pierre François Dominique

(1743-1803) Haitian revolutionary leader.

One of the leaders of a slave insurrection that eventually led to the independence of Haiti. Rose to the rank of major general in the French Army. Proclaimed himself governor general of the entire island of Hispaniola. Captured, sent to France in 1802. Imprisoned in a dungeon in the French Alps. Died at age 60 of pneumonia, malnutrition and exposure.

Last Words (written): "Nothing can compare with the humiliation to which you subjected me today. You have taken away my watch and the money I had in my pocket. I hereby serve notice on you that these objects are my personal property and that I will call you to account for them on the day I am executed, when I shall expect you to remit them to my wife and children." Letter to his jailer.

Source: *Citizen Toussaint* by Ralph Korngold (Boston, 1944).

Traubel, Horace

(1858-1919) American writer, socialist. Follower of Eugene Debs. Close friend and one of poet Walt Whitman's literary executors. Notable work: *With Walt Whitman in Camden* (3-vol. biography of Whitman's final four years). Died at age 60 in Ontario, Canada.

Last Words: "I am tired, damned tired."

Source: *Eugene V. Debs a Man Unafraid* by McAlister Coleman (New York, 1930).

Travis, William Barret

(1809-1836) American military officer. Lieutenant colonel. Commander of The Alamo, San Antonio, Texas, when it fell in 1836. His forces were heavily outnumbered by Santa Anna's Mexican army. Travis died of a single bullet to his head early in the battle.

Last Words: "The Mexicans are upon us—give 'em hell."

Source: *Lone Star* by T.R. Fehrenbach (New York, 1980).

Treadwell, Timothy

(1957-2003) American naturalist, environmentalist, filmmaker. Birth name Timothy Dexter. Devoted himself to the study of brown bears at Katmai National Park in Alaska. Often at odds with the National Park Service and professional naturalists who argued that he was too overconfident in dealing with the bears. In 2003, Treadwell and his girlfriend Amie Huguenard were killed when a bear attacked them. During the attack, Amie was able to turn on the video camera and record (audio only) the assault as well as Treadwell's Last Words. The following day, park rangers found the remains of their campsite. Treadwell wrote a book, *Among Grizzlies: Living with Wild Bears in Alaska* that provides information about his work. Was the subject of the 2005 Werner Herzog documentary film *Grizzly Man*.

Last Words: "Get out here, I'm getting killed."

Source: *Death in the Grizzly Maze: The Timothy Treadwell Story* by Michael Lapinsky (Guilford, CT, 2005).

Tree, Sir Herbert Beerbohm

(1853-1917) British actor, theater manager. Half brother of Sir Max Beerbohm. Prominent in Victorian theater. Founded Royal Academy of Dramatic Art. Knighted in 1909. Died at age 63 in London.

Last Words: "I shall not need to study the part at all; I know it already." He was talking about a part in a play he was planning to produce.

Source: *Herbert Beerbohm Tree; Some Memories of Him and His Art Collected by Max Beerbohm,* ed. Sir Max Beerbohm (London, 1920).

Trexler, Samuel Geiss

(1877-1949) American clergyman. Lutheran church leader. Notable work: *Crusaders of the Twentieth Century; a Lutheran Story in the Empire State*. Member, vice-president and president of Board of Foreign Missions of Evangelical Lutheran Church in America.

Last Words: "I'm feeling fine. Let me see the papers." His response when asked how he was feeling.

Source: *Sword of the Spirit: A Biography of Samuel Trexler* by Edmund Devol (New York, 1954).

Tristan, Flora

(1803-1844) French writer, journalist, feminist, socialist. Birth name Flora-Celestine Thérèse Henriette Tristan Morosco. Grandmother of French artist Paul Gauguin. Notable works: *Promenades in London; Perigrinations of a Pariah* (journal about her experiences in Peru). Died at age 41 of a stroke in Bordeaux, France.

Last Words: "The sea, isn't it beautiful, so shining—but am I not in Bordeaux?"

Source: *Flora Tristan: Feminist, Socialist and Free Spirit* by Joyce Anne Schneider (New York, 1980).

Trobriand, Philippe Régis Denis de Keredern, Comte de

(1816-1897) French military officer, lawyer, poet, novelist. Emigrated to U.S. while young. General in Union Army in U.S. Civil War. With Army of the Potomac. Died at age 81 in Bayport, New York.

Last Words (written): "You will understand dear Bonnaffon, that in such condition it is out of the question for me to receive any visit, or even to designate any possible time of meeting, as by that time it is as likely that I may be underground as on it. Farewell then or 'au revoir' as the case may turn. Anyhow, I remain, Yours faithfully, R. De Trobriand." Bonnaffon was a captain in Trobriand's brigade.

Source: *The Life and Memoirs of Comte Regis de Trobriand, Major-General in the Army of the United States* by his daughter, Marie Caroline de Trobriand Post [Mrs. Charles Alfred Post] (New York, 1910).

Trollope, Anthony

(1815-1882) English novelist, short-story writer, essayist. Also wrote travel books. Notable works: *Barchester Towers; The Warden; Framley Parsonage; Doctor Thorne.* Created a family of nobles called Pallisers who appeared in several of his novels. Trollope was paralyzed by a debilitating stroke in November 1882. Died a month later at age 67 in London. Several of his stories have been serialized on radio and television.

Last Word: "No." He was unable to speak. This was the only word he could say.

Source: *The Chronicler of Barsetshire: A Life of Anthony Trollope* by R. H. Super (Ann Arbor, MI, 1990).

Trollope, Frances Milton

(1780-1863) English writer. Mother of English novelist Anthony Trollope. Spent three years in America. Wrote about her experiences in *Domestic Manners of the Americans.* Also published travel books. She supported her family with her writing. Spent her last 20 years in Florence, Italy, where she died at age 83.

Last Words: "Poor Cecilia!" Cecilia was her daughter.

Source: *Frances Trollope: Her Life and Literary Work from George III to Victoria* by Frances Eleanor Trollope (London, 1895). The author was the wife of her eldest son Thomas Adolphus Trollope.

Tromp, Maarten Harpertzoon

(1597-1653) Dutch military officer. Naval admiral. His destruction of the Spanish fleet at the Battle of the Downs ended Spanish sea power. He was mortally wounded in the naval battle at Texel between Dutch and English forces. Died at about age 56 of a musket wound to the heart in Amsterdam, Holland.

Last Words: "Take courage, children. Act so that my end will be glorious, as my life has been."

Source: *Nouvelle Biographie Générale Depuis les Temps les Plus Reculés jusqu'á Nos Jours, avec les Renseignements Bibliographiques et l'Indication des Sources à Consulter* by Jean Chrétien Ferdinand Hoefer (Paris, 1854).

Trotsky, Leon

(1879-1940) Russian revolutionary leader. Real name Lev (or Lieb) Davidovich Bronstein. Key figure in the Bolshevik seizure of power in Russia in 1917. Built up the Red Army during a subsequent civil war. Banished from Russia in 1929. Sought exile in Mexico in 1937. Attacked in his home with a pick ax. Taken to a hospital. Died at age 61 the next day. His assassin was identified as Ramón Mercader, a Spanish Communist agent.

Last Words: "Please say to our friends—I am sure—of the victory—of the Fourth International—Go forward." Dictated in English in hospital. He tried to say more; but his words were not coherent.

Source: "With Trotsky to the End" by Joseph Hansen (*Fourth International,* 1:5, October 1940).

Trujillo, Rafael

(1891-1961) Dominican Republic military officer, dictator. Full name Rafael Leónidas Trujillo Molena. General of Dominican Republic. President of the Republic. Shot and killed by members of his own armed forces while traveling in a car.

Last Words: "Ay, ay, ay, ay."

Source: *Trujillo: The Life and Times of a Caribbean Dictator* by Robert D. Crassweller (New York, 1966).

Truth, Sojourner

(1797-1883) American ex-slave, abolitionist, reformer, preacher. Women's rights advocate. Birth name Isabella Van Wagener or Baumfree. Gained freedom in 1827 with the abolition of slavery in New York. Began lecturing as an itinerant preacher in the 1840s. Changed name to Sojourner Truth in 1843. Died at around age 86 in Battle Creek, Michigan.

Last Words: "Be a follower of the Lord Jesus."

Source: *Sojourner Truth: A Life, a Symbol* by Nell Irvin Painter (New York, 1996).

Tubman, Harriet Ross

(1820?-1913) American ex-slave, abolitionist. Birth name Araminta Ross. She changed her first name to Harriet. Married John Tubman in 1840s. Became a conductor on the Underground Railroad in 1850 and helped more than 300 slaves to gain their freedom. Known as Moses of her people for leading so many out of bondage. Friend of William H. Seward, William Lloyd Garrison. Founded home for needy African Americans in Auburn, New York. Died at about age 93 of pneumonia in Auburn.

Last Words: "Swing Low Sweet Chariot." On her deathbed, she asked her family to join with her in singing for one last time the song she loved.

Source: *Harriet Tubman: Freedombound* by Janet Benge and Geoff Benge (Lynwood, WA, 2002).

Tucker, Richard

(1913-1975) American singer, cantor. Operatic tenor. Birth name Rubin Ticker. Made debut with Metropolitan Opera in 1945. Notable roles: Pinkerton, Don Jose, Radames, Rodolfo. Died at age 61 of a heart attack in Kalamazoo, Michigan, while on a concert tour.

Last Words: "What are you up to today? Tell me so I can call you after Bob and I get done rehearsing." Spoken in a telephone call to his wife. "Bob" was his close friend, baritone Robert Merrill.

Source: *Richard Tucker* by James A. Drake (New York, 1984).

Tullis, Francais ("Rusty")

(1936-2006) American mother, psychic reader, go-go dancer. Son Rocky Dennis was born with a rare craniofacial disease that caused his head to grow abnormally large, until his eventual death in 1978 at age 16. She lost her other son to AIDS. She died from injuries sustained in a motorcycle accident that occurred a month earlier. The family's story is told in the movie *Mask* (1985).

Last Words: "I can't, I can't do this anymore. I wish I could just let go."

Source: "Mother Portrayed in Film 'Mask' Dies. Francais Tullis Whose Son had Rare Disease, Had a Hard Life" (*Long Beach* [California] *Press-Telegram*, November 15, 2006).

Tupac Amaru

(1544?-1571) Inca chief. Son of Manco Capac. Last of the male line. Ordered seized by Viceroy Francisco de Toledo. Beheaded at Cuzco, Peru, before a large crowd. He raised his hand to silence the crowd then spoke these words in his native tongue.

Last Words: "Oh God, behold how mine enemies rob me of my blood."

Source: *Cuzco: A Journey to the Ancient Capital of Cuzco; With an Account of the History, Language, Literature, and Antiquities of the Incas. And Lima: A Visit to the Capital and Province of Modern Peru; With a Sketch of the Vice Regal Government, History of the Republic, and a Review of the Literature and Society of Peru. With Illustrations and Map* by Sir Clements R. Markham (London, 1856).

Turenne, Henri de La Tour d'Auvergne, Vicomte de

(1611-1675) French military leader. Marshal of France. Served in Thirty Years War. Killed in action in Baden. Napoleon considered him the greatest of all military leaders.

Last Words: "Then I will gladly come, for I particularly wish not to be killed just now." Spoken after he was warned to withdraw from the line of fire.

Source: *Marshal Turenne* by Thomas Longueville (New York, 1907).

Turgenev, Ivan

(1818-1883) Russian novelist, poet, playwright. One of Russia's most celebrated authors during his lifetime. Known for his realistic depiction of Russian life. Notable works: *A Month in the Country; Fathers and Sons; On the Eve.* Left Russia in 1862. Lived the rest of his life in Germany, England and France. Died at age 64 at Bougival, near Paris, France.

Last Words (written): "I can neither walk, nor eat, nor sleep. It tires me even to mention all this. My friend, great writer of our Russian land, heed my request. Let me know whether you receive this sheet, and permit me once more closely, closely to embrace you, your wife, and all yours. I can no more. I am tired." Letter to Tolstoy.

Source: *Turgenev: The Man, His Art, and His Age* by Avrahm Yarmolinsky (New York, 1926).

Last Words (spoken): "Come nearer—nearer. Let me feel you all near me. The moment of departing has come. Goodbye, my darlings." Spoken to his family when he emerged briefly from a coma.

Source: *Philosophy of Life and Death* by M.V. Kamath (Bombay, India, 1993).

Turgot, Anne-Robert-Jacques, Baron de Laune

(1727-1781) French statesman, economist. A founder of the science of political economics. Comptroller general of finance. Built bridges and roads. Abolished some feudal practices including corvée. Notable work: *Lettres sur les Tolerance.* Retired in 1776 to devote time to science and literature. Died at age 53 in Paris.

Last Words: "You blame me for attempting too much, but you know in my family we die of gout at fifty."

Source: *The Life and Writings of Turgot: Comptroller General of France 1774-6* by Anne Robert Jacques Turgot, ed. by W. Walker Stephens (London, 1895).

Turner, Frederick Jackson

(1861-1932) American historian, educator. Taught history at Wisconsin and Harvard. Emphasized the role of the frontier in development of the nation. Notable works: *The Frontier in American History; Rise of the New West.* His essays won a Pulitzer Prize for History in 1933. Died at age 70 of heart attack in Pasadena, California.

Last Words: "I know this is the end. Tell Max I am sorry that I haven't finished my book." Spoken to his wife.

Source: *Frederick Jackson Turner: Historian, Scholar, Teacher* by Ray Allen Billington (New York, 1973).

Turner, Joseph Mallord William

(1775-1851) English artist. Landscape and seascape painter. Renowned for his treatment of natural light. Notable works: *Norham Castle on the Tweed; Rain, Steam and Speed; Bridge of Sighs; Dido Building Carthage.* Died at age 76 in London.

Last Words: "The sun, my dear, the sun is God." Spoken as he lay dying in his bedroom in Chelsea, overlooking the Thames.

Source: *Life and Work of J.M.W. Turner R.A.* by Charles A. Swinburne (London, 1902).

Tussaud, Anne Marie Grosholtz (Madame Tussaud)

(1761-1850) French-born English businesswoman. Wax figure exhibitor. Founder of Madame Tussaud's Wax Museum in London. Died at age 88 in London.

Last Words: "I divide my property equally between you, and implore you, above all things, never to quarrel." Spoken to her two sons Joseph and François who kept the business together. London Museum is still operating today with branches throughout world.

Source: *The Romance of Madame Tussaud's* by John Theodore Tussaud (New York, 1920). The author was the great-grandson of Madame Tussaud.

Twain, Mark, see Clemens, Samuel Langhorne.

Tweed, William Marcy ("Boss Tweed")

(1823-1878) American politician, racketeer. Held many political offices. Member U.S. House of Representatives, New York state senate. He and associates plundered millions of dollars from taxpayers. Was convicted, sent to prison. Released. When sued by the state, Tweed could not post bail. He fled to Cuba, was caught, arrested, and returned to New York. Died at age 55 in jail.

Last Words: "Tilden and Fairchild, they will be satisfied now." He was referring to New York Governor Samuel Jones Tilden and New York State Attorney General Charles Fairchild who worked to destroy the Tweed Ring.

Source: *Boss Tweed, the Story of a Grim Generation* by Denis T. Lynch (New York, 1927).

Two Face (Ito Nonpa)

(d. 1865) Native American leader. Oglala chief. Two Face and Chief Black Foot brought Cheyenne captives Lucinda Eubanks and her baby safely to Fort Laramie and turned them over to the U.S. Army.

Colonel Thomas Moonlight, fort commander, accused the two chiefs of capturing and mistreating the white woman and child and had them killed by hanging.
Last Words: "Meah washita" (tr. "I am brave.")
Source: "A Cavalry Campaign Gone Wrong" by David Scott and Roy Bird (*Real West*, December 1985).

Tyler, John
(1790-1862) 10th President of the U.S. American lawyer, politician. Member U.S. House of Representatives and Senate from Virginia. Known by detractors as His Accidency. First U.S. Vice President to be elevated to the office of President on the death of his predecessor. First wife Letitia Christian died in 1842. Tyler became the first U.S. President to wed while in office when he married Julia Gardiner in 1844. Elected to Confederate House of Representatives during the Civil War but died before taking his seat. Died at age 71 in Richmond, Virginia.
Last Words: "Doctor, I am going." The doctor replied: "I hope not sir." Tyler responded: "Perhaps it is best."
Source: *John Tyler, Champion of the Old South* by Oliver Perry Chitwood (New York, 1939).

Tyler, Julia Gardiner
(1820-1889) American First Lady. Second wife of U.S. President John Tyler. Suffered a stroke. Died at age 69 in Exchange Hotel, Richmond, Virginia, in the same hotel her husband died in 27 years earlier.
Last Words: "Tea." Spoken to a medical attendant who asked her if she wanted a sip of liquor. She shook her head and whispered her Last Word before losing consciousness.
Source: *And Tyler Too: A Biography of John and Julia Gardiner Tyler* by Robert Seager (New York, 1963).

Tynan, Kenneth Peacock
(1927-1980) British theater manager, drama critic, writer. Literary manager of Britain's National Theatre. Drama critic for *The* [London] *Observer* and *New Yorker* magazine. Created controversial long-running show *Oh! Calcutta!* Died at age 53 of emphysema in Santa Monica, California.
Last Words: "Please come back soon." Spoken to his wife.

Source: *The Life of Kenneth Tynan* by Kathleen Tynan (London, 1987). The author was his wife.

Tyndale, Tindale or Tindal, William
(1494?-1536) English religious reformer, martyr. Protestant. Translated New Testament and Pentateuch into English. Came into conflict with church authorities. Tried, condemned, strangled. Body burned at the stake.
Last Words: "Lord, open the King of England's eyes."
Source: *Book of Martyrs and the Acts and Monuments of the Church* by John Fox (or Foxe). First published 1563, ed. by John Cumming (London, 1851).

Tyndall, John
(1820-1893) Irish-born British physicist. Discovered Tyndall effect: light becomes visible by the scattering of fine particles. Gave explanation for blue color of sky. Died at age 73 of an overdose of chloral hydrate when his wife gave him the wrong dosage of sleeping medicine.
Last Words: "Yes, my poor darling, you have killed your John! Let us do all we can. Tickle my throat. Get a stomach pump—Yes, I know you are all trying to rouse me." His response to his wife who told him the doctors were working to save him.
Source: *Life and Work of John Tyndall* by A.S. Eve and C.H. Creasy (London, 1945).

Tyng, Dudley Atkins
(1825-1855) American clergyman, abolitionist. Episcopal minister of the Church of the Epiphany in Philadelphia. Fatally injured in a farm accident. His arm was badly mangled when his sleeve caught in the cogwheels of a horse-powered corn sheller. Died within few hours at age 29.
Last Words: "Oh! Perfectly, perfectly." Response when asked if he was happy. Earlier, he whispered "Let us all stand up for Jesus" when asked if he knew the Lord Jesus Christ. These dying words inspired a popular hymn by George Duffield, "Stand up for Jesus."
Source: *The Child of Prayer, a Father's Memorial of D. A. Tyng* by Stephen H. Tyng (New York, 1858).

Tzu-Hsi or Cixi
(1835-1908) Chinese empress. Rose from concubine to Dowager Empress of China. Suffered a stroke. Chose her successor, her

three-year-old nephew Pu Yi. Died at age 72 in Peking (now Beijing).

Last Words: "Never again allow a woman to hold the supreme power in the State. It is against the house law of our dynasty and should be forbidden. Be careful not to allow eunuchs to meddle in government matters. The Ming dynasty was brought to ruin by eunuchs, and its fate should be a warning to my people."

Source: *The Last Empress* by Daniele Varè (Garden City, NY, 1938).

Uemura, Naomi

(1941-1984) Japanese mountain climber, adventurer. Sought to be first to climb the highest summits on each continent. First Japanese climber to reach the summit of Mount Everest. He had already stood atop the highest peaks of six continents when he tackled Mount McKinley in Alaska. He had reached the top and was on his descent in perilous weather when he lost radio contact. He was presumed dead when his snowshoes, poles and diary were found.

Last Words: "I am lost." Heard over the radio.

Sources: *The Quotable Climber* by Jonathan Waterman (Guilford, CT, 2002); "Obituaries" in *Encyclopedia Britannica Book of the Year 1985* (Chicago, 1985).

Ujimasa, Hōjō

(1538-1590) Japanese ruler, military leader. Fourth head of Hōjō clan. Daimyo of Odawara. Commanded many battles, consolidating his clan's position. After retirement his son, who assumed command, failed to hold Odawara against the forces of Toyotomi Hideyoshi. Ujimasa was forced to commit ritual suicide in the face of defeat. His Last Words were the death poem he composed for his seppuku at about age 52.

Last Words:
"Autumn wind of eve
Blow away the clouds that mass
O'er the moon's pure light.
And the mists that cloud our mind
Do thou sweep away as well.
Now we disappear
Well, what must we think of it?
From the sky we came
Now we may go back again
That is at least one point of view."

Source: *The Samurai Sourcebook* by Stephen Turnbull (London, 1998).

Umberto, King of Italy, see Humbert.

Underhill, Wilbur

(1901-1934) American bank robber. Known as the Tri-State Terror for dozens of bank robberies in Kansas, Arkansas and Oklahoma. Seriously injured in a confrontation with police in Oklahoma. Taken to a hospital where he lingered five days.

Last Words: "Tell the boys I'm coming home." Spoken when he was told he was about to die.

Source: *The Life and Death of Pretty Boy Floyd* by Jeffrey S. King (Kent, OH, 1998).

Uncle Remus, see
Harris, Joel Chandler.

Ussher, James

(1581-1656) Irish prelate, educator, theologian. Anglican Archbishop of Armagh, Church of Ireland. Vice chancellor of Trinity College, Dublin. Published chronology that dated Creation from 4004 B.C. Died at age 75 in Reigate, England.

Last Words: "But Lord, in special, forgive my sins of omission."

Source: *The Life & Death of the Most Reverend and Learned Father of Our Church Dr. James Ussher, Late Arch-Bishop of Armagh and Primate of All Ireland Published in a Sermon at His Funeral at the Abby of Westminster, April 17, 1656 and Now Reviewed With Some Other Enlargements* by Nicholas Bernard (London, 1656).

Valdés, Gabriel de la Concepcion ("Plácido")

(1809-1844) Cuban poet. Known as Plácido. One of the most popular Spanish-American poets of his era. Known for his poems about slavery. His works were translated into several languages including French, German and English. Arrested for involvement in Conspiración de la Escalera (the Ladder Conspiracy). He was tried without evidence, sentenced to death, shot and killed in Havana, Cuba, at age 35.

Last Words: "Goodbye, oh world! Here there is no mercy for me. Soldiers fire!" When the shots were fired, he was wounded and ten other men were killed. He stood up, pointed to his heart and asked his executioners: "Will no one have pity upon me? Here!

Fire here!" The firing squad shot him and he died instantly.

Source: *Cuba's Romantic Poet: The Story of Plácido* by Frederick Stimson (Chapel Hill, NC, 1974).

Valentino, Rudolph

(1895-1926) Italian-born American actor. Silent screen star. Known for romantic leading roles in silent movies such as *The Sheik* and *Blood and Sand*. Died at age 31 of complications of a perforated ulcer and blood poisoning while in New York City for opening of a movie.

Last Words: "Don't pull down the blinds! I feel fine. I want the sunlight to greet me." Spoken to a nurse who wanted to close the drapes in his hospital room.

Source: *Valentino as I Knew Him* by S. George Ullman (New York, 1926). The author was his manager.

Vallee, Hubert Prior ("Rudy")

(1901-1986) American singer, entertainer, bandleader, actor. Star of stage, screen, radio, television. Had a unique crooning style that made him a popular recording artist. Died at age 84 in North Hollywood, California, while watching the Statue of Liberty Centennial celebration on television.

Last Words: "I wish we could be there. You know how I've always loved a party." Spoken to his wife.

Source: "Rudy Vallee, RIP" (*National Review*, August 1, 1986).

Van Buren, Martin

(1782-1862) 8th President of the U.S. American lawyer, politician. Attorney general of New York. Member U.S. Senate from New York. Governor of New York; resigned to become U.S. secretary of state. Vice President of the U.S. Unsuccessful Free-Soil and Democratic candidate for U.S. President. Died at age 79 in Kinderhook, New York.

Last Words: "There is but one reliance." Spoken to his sons.

Source: *Historic Resource Study, Lindenwald: Martin Van Buren National Historic Site, New York* by John P. Platt (National Park Service, 1982); *Martin Van Buren: Romantic Age of American Politics* by John Niven (New York, 1983).

Vanderbilt, Alfred Gwynne

(1877-1915) American millionaire sportsman, victim of *Lusitania* disaster. Son of Cornelius and Alice Claypoole Gwynne Vanderbilt. Died at age 37 aboard the *Lusitania* en route from New York to Europe. Vanderbilt and his valet tried to save infant passengers by tying lifejackets to baskets to keep them afloat.

Last Words: "Come and let us save the kiddies." His comment was reported by a woman to whom he gave his lifejacket. It later became the text of a speech by the Bishop of London at a meeting of the Waifs and Strays Society.

Source: "Saving the Children" (*New York Times,* May 17, 1915).

Variation: "Find all the kiddies you can, boy." Spoken to his valet.

Source: *Fortune's Children: The Fall of the House of Vanderbilt* by Arthur T. Vanderbilt II (New York, 1989). The author was his cousin.

Vanderbilt, Cornelius ("Commodore")

(1794-1877) American steamship and railroad magnate, financier. Known as Commodore Vanderbilt. Founder of a great family fortune. Died at age 82 in New York City.

Last Words: "That's a good prayer. I shall never give up trust in Jesus. How could I let that go?" Spoken to a clergyman. Earlier, Vanderbilt gave instructions: "No flowers at my funeral; not one! No costly badges of mourning; no crape for showing off!" His instructions were obeyed.

Sources: *The Vanderbilts and the Story of Their Fortune* by William Augustus Croffut (London, 1886); *Commodore Vanderbilt: An Epic of American Achievement* by Arthur D. Howden Smith (New York, 1927).

Vanderbilt, George Washington, II

(1862-1914) American businessman. Son of William Henry Vanderbilt and Maria Louisa Kissam. Traveled extensively. Built Biltmore House near Asheville, North Carolina, between 1888 and 1895. Had booked passage on the *Titanic* but canceled. Died two years later at age 51 in Washington, D.C., after appendix surgery.

Last Words: "Edith." Spoken to his wife.

Source: *Washington Herald,* March 7, 1914.

Vanderbilt, William Henry

(1821-1885) American businessman. Son of Cornelius Vanderbilt ("Commodore"). President of New York Central Railroad.

Died at age 64 in New York.

Last Words (doubtful): "I have had no real gratification or enjoyment of any sort more than my neighbor on the next block who is worth only half a million."

Source: Various Last Word compilations and Internet websites.

He did speak these words but they were not his last ones. They were part of a longer remark he "pathetically made on one occasion," according to James Burnley. He had not been happy with his immense wealth in later years and was expressing his feelings.

Source: *Millionaires and Kings of Enterprise: The Marvelous Careers of Some Americans Who by Pluck, Foresight, and Energy Have Made Themselves Masters in the Fields of Industry and Finance* by James Burnley (London, 1901).

Vane, Sir Henry ("Sir Harry")

(1613-1662) English statesman, writer. Colonel governor of Massachusetts during the Cromwell protectorate. Brought to trial after the Restoration, charged with high treason. Found guilty, sentenced to death. Beheaded at Tower Hill.

Last Words: "Father glorify Thy servant in the sight of men, that he may glorify Thee in the discharge of his duties to Thee and to his country." After he spoke, he stretched out his arms and was beheaded.

Source: *The Dying Speeches and Behaviour of the Several State Prisoners that Have Been Executed the Last 300 Years. With Their Several Characters, From Cambden, Spotswood, Clarendon, Sprat, Burner, &C. and a Table Shewing How the Respective Sentences Were Executed, and Which of Them Were Mitigated, or Pardon'd. Being A Proper Supplement to the State-Trials* (London, 1720).

Van Gogh, Vincent Willem

(1853-1890) Dutch artist, etcher, lithographer. Post-Impressionist. Notable works: *The Potato Eaters, Portrait of Dr. Gachet, The Starry Night, Sunflowers*. Lived in Arles, Provence, France. Began painting at age 27. Sold only one painting during his lifetime. Suffered from profound depression. Shot himself. Died two days later at age 37.

Different Last Words:

(1) "Now I want to go home."

Source: *Vincent Van Gogh: A Biography* by Julius Meier-Graefe (New York, 1933).

(2) "There is no end to sorrow."

Source: *They Went That-a-Way: How the Famous, the Infamous and the Great Died* by Malcolm Forbes with Jeff Bloch (New York, 1988).

Vanini, Lucilio or Giulio Cesare

(1585-1619) Italian philosopher, clergyman, lawyer. Doctor of canon and civil law. Ordained priest. Tried for heresy, condemned as an atheist. Burned at the stake at age 34.

Last Words: "There is neither God nor devil: for if there were a God, I would pray Him to send a thunderbolt on the Council as all that is unjust and iniquitous; and if there were a devil, I would pray him to engulf it in the subterranean regions; but since there is neither one nor the other, there is nothing for me to do."

Source: *Trois Novateurs* by Ernest Lenoir (Paris, 1939).

Van Speijk or Van Speyk, Jan Carolus Josephus

(1802-1831) Dutch military officer. Naval lieutenant who became a hero for his efforts in suppressing Belgian Revolution. Joined Royal Netherlands Navy in 1820 and served in the Dutch East Indies. Successfully attacked Bangka and Java and gained nickname Terror of the Bandits. When the Belgian War of Independence broke out, he was made commander of a gunboat. He became famous for his heroic Last Words. After his boat drifted into Belgian waters, it was stormed and the Belgians demanded that he take down the Dutch flag. Versions vary, but instead of doing so, he fired a pistol (or a lit cigar) into a barrel of gunpowder while saying his Last Words just before it blew up, killing him and many others. Several ships are named in his honor.

Last words: "Dan liever de lucht in—." (tr. "Rather to blow up [into the air], then—").

Source: *'Dan liever de lucht in': Jan van Speijk en de Belgische Opstand* by Frits Rovers (Hilversum, The Netherlands, 2000).

Vanzetti, Bartolomeo

(1888-1927) Italian-born American political activist. Convicted with Nicola Sacco in a controversial trial for the murder of the paymaster and a guard at a Massachusetts shoe factory during a robbery. Many prominent people—including Dorothy Parker, Upton Sinclair, George Bernard Shaw and Jane Addams—protested the verdict, but the conviction and sentence were upheld. Sacco and Vanzetti both were executed in 1927. Maxwell Anderson's plays *Gods of the Lightning* and *Winterset,* Upton Sinclair's novel *Boston,* Edna St. Vincent Millay's poem *Justice Denied in Massachusetts* among others, were based on the case. In 1977, Governor Michael Dukakis of Massachusetts vindicated Sacco and Vanzetti by official proclamation.

Last Words: "I want to thank you, I want to thank you for everything you have done for me, warden.—I wish to tell you, all of you, that I am innocent. I have never done a crime. Maybe, oh yes, maybe sometimes I done some sin, but not a crime. I am innocent of all crime, not only of this one, but of all, of all. I am an innocent man.—I wish to forgive some people for what they are now doing to me."

Source: "Sacco and Vanzetti Put to Death Early This Morning" (*New York Times,* August 23, 1927).

Vargas, Getúlio Dornellas

(1882-1954) Brazilian statesman, politician. President of Brazil. Committed suicide at age 72, in Rio de Janeiro, a few hours after resigning amid a deepening political crisis.

Last Words (written): "To the wrath of my enemies I leave the legacy of my death. I take the sorrow of not having been able to do for the humble all that I desired." Note written sometime during his last three hours.

Source: "The Hemisphere: Goodbye to a Gaucho" (*Time* magazine, September 6, 1954).

Vaughan, Sarah Lois

(1924-1990) American musician, singer. One of the great female jazz vocalists. Known as The Divine One for her three-octave range. Nominated for two Emmy Awards; won one (1981). Won Grammy in 1982. Diagnosed with lung cancer. Made a final appearance at the Blue Note in New York City in fall 1989. Died at age 66 in Los Angeles.

Last Words: "I want to go home! Take me home." Spoken in the hospital.

Source: *The Life of Sarah Vaughan* by Leslie Gourse (New York, 1993).

Veblen, Thorstein Bunde

(1857-1929) American economist. Keen observer and critic of contemporary social and economic institutions. Expounded the theory of conspicuous consumption. Notable work: *The Theory of the Leisure Class.* Died at age 72 in Menlo Park, California.

Last Words (written): "It is also my wish, in case of death, to be cremated, if it can be conveniently done, as expeditiously and inexpensively as may be, without ritual or ceremony of any kind. That my ashes be thrown loose into the sea, or into some sizable stream running to the sea; that no tombstone, slab, epitaph, effigy, tablet, inscription or monument of any name or nature, be set up in my memory or name in any place or at any time; that no obituary, memorial, portrait, or biography of me, nor any letters written to or by me be printed or published, or in any way reproduced, copied or circulated." Note left by him.

Source: *Thorstein Veblen and His America* by Joseph Dorfman (New York, 1943).

Vedas, Brandon Carl ("Ripper")

(1981-2003) American Internet fatality. Internet Relay Chatroom (IRC) handle: "Ripper." Died at age 21 at his computer in his Phoenix, Arizona, bedroom.

Last Words: "I told u I was hardcore." Message typed to IRC watching him on his webcam minutes before he died from a drug overdose: Consumed four different prescription drugs, smoked marijuana and drank rum while some in the chartroom encouraged him to take more. Others tried frantically to locate him and save his life.

Source: "He Takes Fatal OD as Internet Pals Watch: Chatroom Vultures Egged Him to Pop More Rx Pills" by Helen Kennedy (*New York Daily News,* January 13, 2003).

Vega, Lope de

(1562-1635) Spanish playwright, poet. Full name Lope Félix de Vega y Carpio. Credited with creating Spanish national drama. Prolific playwright who wrote more than 1,500 plays and more than 400 one-act dramas. Became a monk but continued writing plays. Died at about age 73 in Madrid.

Different Last Words:

(1) (doubtful): "All right, then, I'll say it: Dante makes me sick." Spoken when he learned he was going to die.

(2) (doubtful): "True glory is in virtue. I would willingly give all the applause I have received to have performed one good action more."

Source for (1) and (2): Various Last Words compilations and Internet websites.

It is unlikely that Vega spoke the Last Words given in either (1) or (2). During his final hours, his respiration was so troubled he was unable to speak. He prayed fervently while holding a crucifix to his lips then died. Many friends were at his bedside. The description of his death was written down by one of them, his friend Juan Perez de Montalban.

Source: *The Life of Lope de Vega (1562-1635)* by Hugo Albert Rennert (Glasgow, Scotland, 1904).

Vélez, Lupe

(1908-1944) Mexican-born American actress. Screen star. Birth name Maria Guadalupe Vélez de Villalobos. Appeared in many movies but is especially remembered for a series of popular Mexican Spitfire films. Died at age 36, in Beverly Hills, California, a suicide by overdose of sleeping pills. She was divorced and pregnant.

Last Words (written): "To Harald, may God forgive you and forgive me too but I prefer to take my life away and our baby's before I bring him with shame or killing him, Lupe." On the back of the sheet, she wrote: "How could you, Harald, fake such a great love for me and my baby when all the time you didn't want us. I see no other way out for me so good-bye and good luck to you. Love, Lupe." Suicide note to actor Harald Maresch.

Source: *Strange Pilgrimages: Exile, Travel, and National Identity in Latin America, 1800-1990s* by Ingrid Elizabeth Fey and Karen Racine (Wilmington, DE, 2000).

Vercellis, Louise-Marie-Thérèse de Saint Maurice, Comtesse de

(1669-1728) French noblewoman. Married Count Hippolyte de Vercellis. Rousseau worked for her when he was a teenager. He mentioned her death in his *Confessions*.

Last Words: "Good. A woman who can fart is not dead." Spoken when she was dying, as she passed gas loudly.

Source: *Confessions*, Book II, by Jean-Jacques Rousseau, tr. by J. M. Cohen (London, 1953).

Verdi, Giuseppe Fortunino Francesco

(1813-1901) Italian musician, composer. Famed as a great operatic composer. Notable works: *Rigoletto; Il Trovatore; La Traviata; Aida; Othello; Falstaff*. Also composed sacred music. Suffered a stroke and died a few days later at age 87 at the Grand Hotel, Milan.

Last Words: "One button more or one button less." Spoken to the hotel maid when a stud fell from his hands while dressing. He had a paralytic stroke when he bent over to look for it and lost consciousness. He never regained consciousness.

Source: "Death of Giuseppe Verdi" (*History Today*, Vol. 51, No. 1, January 2001).

Verger, Louis-Jean

(1826-1857) French clergyman, assassin. Deposed. Murdered archbishop Marie Dominique Auguste Sibour in the nave of St. Etienne du Mont in Paris. Arrested, tried and executed by guillotine in Paris.

Last Words: "My brother, I charge you to make amends honorable in my name to all my superior ecclesiastics which I have offended or made sorry. Tell them that I demand pardon of them as I pardon them myself. I offer my life in expiation of my faults." Spoken to the chaplain at the scaffold just before he was executed.

Source: "The Execution of Verger. Details of the Last Hours and Execution of the Assassin of the Archbishop of Paris" (*New York Daily Times,* February 25, 1857).

Vergniaud, Pierre Victurnien

(1753-1793) French lawyer, politician, orator. Leader of Girondists. Opposed Robespierre. Guillotined at age 40 in Paris. Was the last of 21 executed together.

Last Words (written): "Potius mori quam foedari." (tr. "Rather death than crime.") Engraved on the walls of the dungeon where he had been imprisoned.

Source: "De Lamartine: Minister of Foreign Affairs of the Provisional Government of France" by Francis J. Grund (*Graham's Magazine,* Vol. XXXIII, No. 1, July 1848).

Verlaine, Paul-Marie

(1844-1896) French poet. Notable works: *Fêtes galantes; Sagesse*. Died at age 51 of pulmonary congestion at the home of an old friend Madame Eugénie Krantz in Paris.

During his final hours, he suffered from a fever and pain from a sore caused by a blister.

Last Words: "Lepelletier! François! François! Coppée! Coppée! Come, come to me." Lepelletier and Coppée were friends of Verlaine.

Source: "How Paul Verlaine Died" (*New York Times,* January 26, 1896).

Verne, Jules

(1828-1905) French novelist. Pioneered science fiction genre. Notable works: *Twenty Thousand Leagues Under the Sea; A Voyage to the Center of the Earth; Around the World in Eighty Days*. Ill with diabetes before he died at age 77 in Amiens, France. Many of his stories have been made into movies.

Last Words: "Honorine, Michel, Valentine, Suzanne are you here?" He died shortly after each of them replied to him. Michel was Verne's son. Honorine was his wife. Valentine and Suzanne were his step-daughters (Honorine's daughters by a previous marriage).

Source: *Jules Verne: The Biography of an Imagination* by George J. Waltz (New York, 1943).

Versalle, Richard

(1932-1996) American musician. Operatic singer. Tenor with Metropolitan Opera. Died at age 63 of an apparent heart attack on stage in New York during the Met premiere of *The Makropulos Case* by Leos Janacek.

Last Words: "Too bad you can only live so long." After he sang these words of the character Vitek—a law clerk who was perched on a ladder looking for files—he fell to the floor.

Source: "Richard Versalle, 63, Met Tenor, Dies After Fall in a Performance" by Lynette Holloway (*New York Times*, January 7, 1996).

Verulam, 1st Baron and Viscount St. Albans, see Bacon, Francis.

Vespasian, Emperor of Rome

(9-79) Roman ruler. Latin name Titus Flavius Vespasianus. Conquered Judaea. Coliseum construction began during his reign. Died at age 69 of fever.

Last Words: "Imperatorem stantem mori oportere." (tr. "An emperor ought to die standing.") Spoken as he struggled to get on his feet. He died in the arms of those who tried to help him.

Source: "T. Flavius Vespasianus Augustus" in *The Lives of the Twelve Caesars* by C. Suetonius Tranquillus, tr. by Alexander Thomson, rev. by Thomas Forester (London, 1901).

Vetsera, Baroness Marie Alexandrine von ("Mary")

(1871-1889) Austrian noblewoman. Mistress of Crown Prince Rudolf of Austria. Found dead with Rudolf at Mayerling, the prince's hunting lodge. She was 17, Rudolf, who was married to Princess Stephanie of Belgium, was 31. Much speculation surrounded their deaths: Murder-suicide? Double murder? Was she pregnant at the time of her death? Officially her death was ruled a suicide. All investigations and information were suppressed.

Last Words (written): "Dear Marie, Forgive me all the trouble I have caused. I thank you so much for everything you have done for me. If life becomes hard for you, and I fear it will after what we have done, follow us. It is the best thing you can do. Your Mary." Written in a letter to close friend Marie Larisch who acted as a go-between for Mary and Rudolf. The letter was found on the bedside table at Mayerling. The envelope had been opened and resealed. Larisch claims she did not receive the letter, written in German, until three weeks after Mary's death.

Source: *My Past* by Countess Marie Larisch (London, 1913).

Vianney, Saint Jean-Baptiste-Marie

(1786-1859) French clergyman, holy man. Parish priest (curé) at Ars, France. Known for his holiness and miracles. Often 300 pilgrims came to see him each day. So many people wanted to see him that a special rail line had to be built between Lyons and Ars. He slept only two hours a night so that he had time to hear confessions. Wore old clothes, ate little. Died at age 73. Canonized in 1925. Many Roman Catholic parishes have been named for him.

Last Words: "At Ars, but my body is not much." Spoken to the mayor who asked him to designate where he would be buried.

Source: *Saint John Vianney: The Curé D'Ars Today* by George William Butler (San Francisco, CA, 1988).

Vicars, Hedley Shafto Johnstone

(1826-1855) English military officer. Captain. In 1851, he became involved in religious work such as Sunday school, reading scripture and praying for the men of his company. Killed at age 28 while leading an attack at Sebastopol during the Crimean War. *Memorials* written shortly after his death were very popular and translated into several languages.

Last Words: "Cover my face; cover my face!" Spoken when he realized how serious his wound was. An artery had been severed.

Source: *Memorials of Captain Hedley Vicars: Ninety-seventh Regiment* by Catherine Marsh (New York, 1857).

Vicious, Sid

(1957-1979) English musician. Bass player with punk band the Sex Pistols. Real name Simon John Ritchie. Rock and Roll star. Stabbed and killed his girlfriend Nancy Spungen in 1978. Died of drug overdose the following year, at age 21. Subject of the movie *Sid and Nancy*.

Last Words (written): "We had a death pact. I have to keep my half of the bargain. Please bury me next to my baby. Bury me in my leather jacket, jeans and motor cycle boots. Goodbye." Suicide note.

Source: *Punk Diary: The Ultimate Trainspotter's Guide To Underground Rock, 1970-1982* by George Gimarc (San Francisco, CA, 2005).

Victor Emmanuel II, King of Italy

(1820-1878) Italian monarch. Son of King Charles Albert of Sardinia. Last King of Sardinia. First King of united Italy. Died at age 57 of fever in Rome.

Last Words: "I figli, I figli." (tr. "The children. The children.") Bystanders said he spoke in broken sentences. He murmured something about his beloved Turin and his children that they could not understand. He then fell back and died.

Source: *Life of Victor Emmanuel II, First King of Italy* by Georgina Sarah Godkin (London, 1880).

Victoria, Empress Frederick of Germany ("Vicky")

(1840-1901) English-Prussian royalty. Eldest daughter of Britain's Queen Victoria and Prince Albert. Birth name Victoria Adelaide Mary Louise. Princess Royal of Great Britain and Ireland; Crown Princess of Prussia (Germany as of 1871), Empress Frederick. Married Crown Prince Frederick William of Prussia (Emperor Frederick III). Suffered from bone cancer. Died at age 60 in Friedrichshof, Germany.

Last words: "Stop, so that I can take a last look at the garden I made in memory of a great and undying love." Spoken to her attendants.

Source: *Vicky: Princess Royal of England and German Empress* by Daphne Bennett (New York, 1971).

Victoria, Queen of the United Kingdom of Great Britain and Ireland and Empress of India

(1819-1901) British monarch. Daughter of Edward, Duke of Kent. Granddaughter of George III. Reigned for 63 years. She was in and out of consciousness for two days before she died at age 81 at Osborne House on the Isle of Wight.

Last Word: "Bertie!" Spoken to her oldest child, Albert Edward, Prince of Wales and later King Edward VII. He had been sitting and kneeling beside her bed much of the time she was dying.

Source: *The Reign of Queen Victoria* by Hector Bolitho (New York, 1934).

Vidocq, François Eugène

(1775-1857) French law officer, criminologist. Chief of specialized detective force in Paris. First great private detective. Known as the Father of Criminology. Victor Hugo based two *Les Misérables* characters on him. Poe's character Dupin in *Murders in the Rue Morgue* was inspired by him. Vidocq wrote his *Memoirs* that were best sellers and made him famous. He organized a daring robbery and was assigned to investigate it. His role was discovered and he was dismissed from the force. Died at age 82 in Paris.

Different Last Words:

(1) "You, you—my only physician." Spoken to a priest.

Source: *Vidocq: A Biography* by Philip John Stead (London, 1953).

(2) "How great is the forgiveness for such a life!"

Source: *The Last Words (Real and Traditional) of*

Distinguished Men and Women Collected from Various Sources by Frederic Rowland Marvin (New York, 1901). Marvin wrote that soon after Vidocq died, ten women showed up, each with a copy of his will, claiming his wealth was left to her. They received nothing. He left all his possessions to his landlady.

Vigny, Alfred Victor, Comte de

(1797-1863) French nobleman, military officer, poet, playwright, novelist. Served in the French Army; resigned commission in 1827 to write. Notable work: *Cinq-Mars* (historical novel). Died at age 66 of cancer in Paris.

Last Words: "Pray for me, pray to God for me."

Source: *Alfred de Vigny* by Arnold Whitridge (London, 1933).

Vijayan, M.N.

(1930-2007) Indian writer, orator, critic, social activist, educator, Marxist. Known as Vijayan Mash (Master). Taught at Madras New College, Thiruvananthapuram University College and Thalassery Brennen College. Collapsed of cardiac arrest during a televised press conference at the Thrissur Press Club. Rushed to a hospital where he died at age 77.

Last Words: "Everyone criticized the language put forward by the Padhom. Our political discussion centers on talk about language. [George Bernard] Shaw has said that only such language is listened to." He stopped abruptly and fainted.

Source: "M.N. Vijayan Passes Away" (*The Hindu,* Kerala News, October 4, 2007).

Villa, Francisco ("Pancho")

(1878-1923) Mexican military officer, revolutionary outlaw. Real name José Doroteo Arango Arámbula. Legendary bandit and general. Became a folk hero. Given a pension by the Mexican government in 1920 in exchange for laying down his guns. Assassinated in 1923 near Parral, Mexico, by his enemies. Villa has been represented in many movies by himself and by actors.

Last Words (doubtful): "Don't let it end like this. Tell them I said something." Spoken to newspaper reporters at the scene of his killing.

Source: Various Last Words compilations and Internet websites.

Villa was not talking with newspaper reporters when he was killed. He was in his automobile traveling along a street in Parral joking with Miguel Trillo and an escort when he was hit nine times by assassins' bullets. He died instantly. The details of his death are given in Friedrich Katz's comprehensive study of Villa.

Source: *The Life and Times of Pancho Villa* by Friedrich Katz (Stanford, CA, 1998).

Villars, Claude Louis Hector, Duc de

(1653-1734) French nobleman, military officer. Marshal of France. Last of Louis XIV's great generals. Given command of the army during War of Polish Succession. Died at age 81 in Turin, Italy.

Last Words: "I had always contended that that man was born luckier than I." Spoken after he heard James Fitz-James, Duke of Berwick, had just died in battle. Villars and Berwick both fought for France in the War of the Spanish Succession. Berwick was killed at the Battle of Philipsburg on June 12, 1734. Villars died five days later.

Source: *Biographie universelle*, Book XLIII by J. Fr. Michaud and Louis Gabriel Michaud (Paris, 1811-1862).

Villiers, George, 1st Duke of Buckingham

(1592-1628) English nobleman, statesman, courtier. Son of a Leicestershire country squire. Member of the English courts of James I and Charles I. Stabbed to death at age 35 in Portsmouth by a disgruntled naval officer John Felton who was angry at being passed over for promotion. Many noblemen and leaders were present but none could prevent the stroke that killed him.

Last Words: "Villain!" Spoken to Felton, who stabbed him in the heart.

Source: *The Five Hundred Best English Letters,* ed. by 1st Earl of Birkenhead (London, 1931).

Variation: "God's wounds! The villain hath killed me." Cried out as he was stabbed.

Source: *The Book of Death* by Samuel Dobree (London, 1819). He noted that some compilers reported other Last Words, but they differed little from those.

Villiers, George, 2nd Duke of Buckingham

(1628-1687) English nobleman, statesman, courtier. Son of 1st Duke of Buckingham who was murdered before he was born. Raised with the children of Charles I. Had financial problems toward the end of his life. Most of his estates were mortgaged. Died at age 59 at Kirkby Moorside, Yorkshire.

Last Words (written): "To what situation am I now reduced! Is this odious little hut a suitable lodging for a prince? Is this anxiety of mind becoming the character of a Christian? From my rank I might have expected affluence to wait upon my life: from religion and understanding peace to smile upon my end; instead of which I am afflicted with poverty and haunted by remorse; despised by my country and I fear forsaken by my God. I am forsaken by all my acquaintances, neglected by the friends of my bosom and dependents on my bounty; but no matter! I am not fit to converse with the former and have no abilities to serve the latter. Let me not however be forsaken by the good. Favour me with a visit as soon as possible. I am of opinion this is the last visit I shall ever solicit from you. My distemper is powerful. Come and pray for the departing soul of the poor, unhappy Buckingham." Letter to Dr. Barrow.

Source: *George Villiers, Second Duke of Buckingham, 1628-1687: A Study in the History of the Restoration* by Winifred, Lady Burghclere (New York, 1903).

Vincent de Paul, Saint

(1581-1660) French clergyman, holy man. Roman Catholic priest. Known for his kindness and generosity to the poor. Founded Congregation of the Priests of the Mission (Vincentians), Sisters of Charity. Society of St. Vincent de Paul named for him. Died at age 79 in Paris. Canonized in 1737.

Last Word: "Jesus."

Source: *Apostle of Charity: The Life of St. Vincent de Paul* by Theodore Maynard (New York, 1939).

Vinci, Leonardo da, see Leonardo da Vinci.

Vitellius Aulus, Emperor of Rome

(15-69) Roman ruler, military officer, statesman. Consul, proconsul. Favorite of Caligula, Claudius, Nero. Commanded legions in Germany. Proclaimed emperor by his soldiers. Put to death at age 54 in a civil war; thrown into the Tiber River.

Last Words: "Yet, I was your emperor." Spoken after he was mocked by a tribune.

The tribune then pummeled him with blows.

Source: *The Annals and the Histories* by P. Cornelius Tacitus, tr. by Alfred John Church and William Jackson Brodribb (Chicago, 1952).

Voltaire

(1694-1778) French philosopher, writer, historian. Pen name of François-Marie Arouet. Regarded as one of the greatest 18th-century authors. Known for his wit and satire. Campaigned against tyranny and racial prejudice. Wrote about moral and philosophical issues. Had a wide circle of acquaintances with whom he corresponded. Settled in Switzerland in 1754; remained there the rest of his life. Notable works: *Candide; Zadig* (novels); *Zaire* (drama); *Dictionnaire Philosophique.* Died at age 83 in Paris.

Last Words: "Adieu, mon cher Morand, je me meurs." (tr: "Farewell, my dear Morand, I am dying.") Spoken to his valet. He died a few minutes later. This account of his Last Words came from Morand.

Source: *Mémoires sur Voltaire: Et sur ses ouvrages,* Vol. 1, by Sébastian G. Longchamp, Jean-Louis Wagnière, Jacques Joseph Marie Decroix and Adrien Jean Quentin Beuchot (Paris, 1826).

Vygotsky, Lev Semenovich

(1896-1934) Russian psychologist. Noted for research and theories on development and structure of human consciousness. Founder of cultural historical psychology. Notable work: *Mind in Society.* In 1934, Stalin accused him of political error. Died at age 38 of tuberculosis at a sanitarium while preparing his defense.

Last Words: "I am ready."

Source: *Education and Technology: An Encyclopedia* by Ann Kovalchick and Kara Dawson (Santa Barbara, CA, 2003).

Waddel, Moses

(1770-1840) American clergyman, educator. Presbyterian. Founded Willington Academy in South Carolina. Teacher of John C. Calhoun. President of University of Georgia. Paralyzed for ten years before he died at age 70 in Athens, Georgia.

Last Words: "I knew him well, one of the best men I ever knew." His response while on his deathbed when someone mentioned a clergyman he knew.

Source: *A Conspectus of American Biography: Being an Analytical Summary of American History and*

Biography, Containing also the Complete Indexes of the National Cyclopedia of American Biography by George Derby (New York, 1906).

Waddell, George Edward ("Rube")

(1876-1914) American athlete. Professional baseball player. Left-handed pitcher in major leagues. Four-time 20-game winner; held six consecutive strikeout titles. Died at age 37 of tuberculosis in San Antonio, Texas. Elected to the National Baseball Hall of Fame 1946.

Last Words: "I'll be over tomorrow to show you guys how to run. I've got my weight down now." Spoken to ex-team mates who visited him in the hospital.

Source: *My Sixty-six Years in the Big Leagues; the Great Story of America's National Game* by Connie Mack (Cornelius McGillicuddy) (Philadelphia, 1950).

Wade, Benjamin Franklin

(1800-1878) American lawyer, politician, jurist. Radical Republican. Ohio state senator. Circuit judge. Member U.S. Senate from Ohio. Candidate for U.S. Vice President. Joint author of the Wade-Davis Manifesto condemning Lincoln and insisting the Senate have power over Southern Reconstruction. Died at age 77 in Jefferson, Ohio.

Last Words: "I cannot speak at all." Whispered to his wife Caroline. He died the following day.

Source: *Benjamin Franklin Wade, Radical Republican from Ohio* by Hans Louis Trefousee (New York, 1963).

Wadsworth, James Samuel

(1807-1864) American politician, military officer. General in Union Army in U.S. Civil War. Member of 147th Regiment, New York Volunteers. Saw action at Chancellorsville, Gettysburg. Killed at age 56 at the Battle of Wilderness.

Last Words: "Steady boys! Go ahead! There isn't danger enough to harm a mouse." As soon as he uttered these words, he fell from his horse mortally wounded. He was taken to a Confederate hospital where he died two days later.

Source: *Historical Sketch of the 147th Regiment* by H.H. Lyman (New York, 1900).

Wagner, Cosima Liszt von Bülow

(1837-1930) Italian-born socialite. Daughter of Franz Liszt and Countess d'Agoult. Former wife of pianist and conductor Hans von Bülow. Divorced him to marry German composer Richard Wagner. Musical director of Festspielhaus in Bayreuth, Germany, for 31 years. Her diaries (1869 to 1883) provide valuable information about Wagner during this time. Lost her eyesight in 1920. Died at age 92 in Bayreuth. Portrayed in the movie *Wagner* (1983).

Last Words: "Glorious." Then a little later she whispered "Sorrow."

Source: *Cosima Wagner, Extraordinary Daughter of Franz Liszt* by Alice Sokoloff (New York, 1969).

Wagner, Richard

(1813-1883) German musician, composer, conductor, writer. Full name Wilhelm Richard Wagner. Second wife was Cosima Von Bulow, daughter of Franz Liszt. Notable operas: *Tristan and Isolde; Der Ring des Nibelungen; Die Meistersinger*. Also wrote symphonic, choral, piano music. Died at age 69 of a heart attack in Venice, Italy.

Different Last Words:

(1) "Call my wife and the doctor."

Source: *Wagner and His Works: The Story of His Life with Critical Comments* by Henry T. Finck (New York, 1893).

(2) "I feel very bad." Wagner had planned to stroll along the Grand Canal but experienced an asthma attack as he was about to leave. He lost consciousness after speaking these words and died later that afternoon.

Sources: "Richard Wagner" (*Der Klavier-Lehrer Musik-paedagogische Zeitschrift*, Vol. 5, March 1, 1883); "Thoughts Suggested by the Death of Richard Wagner" by Dr. James I. Tucker (*Chicago Medical Journal and Examiner*, Vol. XLVI, No. 3, March 1883).

(3) "My watch!" Spoken as his watch fell from his pocket while he was having a spasm. His wife Cosima tried to help him to a sofa.

Source: *The Life of Richard Wagner* by Ernest Newman (New York, in four volumes published between 1933 and 1946).

Waiblinger, Wilhelm Friedrich

(1804-1830) German biographer, poet. While Waiblinger was a student at a seminary in Tübingen, German poet Friedrich Hölderlin lived there as a recluse. Waiblinger wrote *Friedrich Hölderlin's Life, Poetry and Madness*. Waiblinger died at age 25 in Rome, Italy.

Last Word: "Addio!" (tr. "Farewell!")

Source: *Wilhelm Waiblinger, Sein Leben und seine Werke* by Karl Frey (Aarau, Switzerland, 1904).

Wait, Marvin

(1843-1862) American politician, military officer. Son of John Turner Wait, six-term member of the U.S. House of Representatives from Connecticut. Enlisted in U.S. Civil War at age 18. 1st Lieutenant in 8th Regiment of Connecticut Volunteers, part of the group that made up Union forces at Antietam. Refused to go to the rear at Antietam despite a severely injured right arm. Instead, he seized his sword with his left hand and encouraged his men to press on until he was shot and killed.

Last Words: "Are we whipping them?" Spoken to Private Lewis D. King.

Source: *Memorial of Marvin Wait (1st Lieutenant Eighth Regiment C. V.) Killed at the Battle of Antietam, September 17th, 1862,* by Jacob Eaton (New Haven, CT, 1863).

Walker, James Alexander ("Stonewall Jim")

(1832-1901) American lawyer, farmer, politician, military officer. Brigadier general in Confederate Army in U.S. Civil War. Only commander of Stonewall Brigade who survived the war. Seriously wounded at Spotsylvania Court House. Lieutenant governor of Virginia. Member U.S. House of Representatives from Virginia. Died at age 69 in Wytheville, Virginia.

Last Words: "Help me to get up, Will. I want to stand on my feet again and die like a man and a soldier." Spoken to his daughter Willie Walker Caldwell, a successful writer.

Source: *Stonewall Jim: A Biography of General James A. Walker, CSA* by Willie Walker Caldwell (Elliston, VA, 1990).

Walker, James John ("Jimmy")

(1881-1946) American politician. Known as Beau James, Jimmy Walker. Mayor of New York. Accused of corruption. Resigned as mayor. Lived in Europe. Returned to U.S. in 1940. Died at age 65 in New York City. The movie *Beau James* (1957) was based on his life as mayor.

Last Words: "In that case, I shall abide by the wishes of a fair constituent." Spoken to the nurse who asked him to lie back when he learned she was a Democrat. He died later

that day.

Source: *Beau James: The Life and Times of Jimmy Walker* by Gene Fowler (New York, 1949).

Walker, Madam C.J.

(1867-1919) American entrepreneur, social activist, philanthropist. Birth name Sarah Breedlove. President of C.J. Walker Manufacturing Company, maker of hair products for African-American women. Became the first African-American woman millionaire. Died at age 51 of complications of hypertension in New York.

Last Words: "I want to live to help my race."

Source: *Madam C.J. Walker: Entrepreneur* by A'Lelia Perry Bundles (New York, 1991). The author was her great-great-granddaughter.

Wallace, Lewis ("Lew")

(1827-1905) American lawyer, military officer, politician, diplomat, writer. General in Union Army in U.S. Civil War. Governor of New Mexico Territory. Ambassador to Turkey. Notable work: *Ben Hur: A Tale of the Christ*, one of the most popular novels of the 19th century. Died at age 77 in Crawfordsville, Indiana.

Last Words (doubtful): "We meet in Heaven." Spoken to his wife.

Source: Various Last Words compilations and Internet sites.

These were not the Last Words of Lew Wallace. They were spoken by Union General William Hervey Lamme Wallace who was killed in the Civil War in 1862.

Source: *Life and Letters of General W.H.L. Wallace* by Isabel Wallace (Chicago, 1909). The author was his daughter.

Wallenda, Karl

(1905-1978) German-born aerialist. Founder of the Great Wallendas circus group. Planned to walk across a cable 10 stories above ground spanning two hotels in San Juan, Puerto Rico. Strong winds caused the wire to sway. He lost his balance when he was about two-thirds of the way across. He fell and landed on his back on a taxi, then hit the ground. Died at age 73 of massive internal injuries.

Last Words: "Don't worry about it. The wind is stronger on the street than up here." Spoken as he checked the wire at the tenth-floor window, about 100 feet above the sidewalk.

Source: "Sit Down, Poppy, Sit Down" (*Time* magazine, April 3, 1978). A young member of his troop called out these words, warning him to crouch for better balance.

Waller, Thomas Wright ("Fats")

(1904-1943) American musician, jazz pianist, composer, organist. Notable songs: "Ain't Misbehavin'"; "Honeysuckle Rose"; "Black and Blue"; "I've Got a Feeling I'm Falling." Died at age 39 aboard an eastbound train delayed in a snowstorm near Kansas City. Was traveling from California to New York to spend Christmas with his family. He was recovering from a bout of pneumonia. Around 2 a.m., his manager Ed Kirkeby entered their sleeping car room and commented about how cold it was.

Last Words: "You'll be okay when you get into bed." Spoken to Kirkeby. A few hours later a doctor was summoned when Waller began to tremble. He died before the doctor arrived.

Source: *Fats Waller* by Maurice Waller and Anthony Calabrese (New York, 1977). Co-author Maurice Waller was his son.

Walsh, Thomas

(1730-1759) Irish clergyman. Formerly a papist. Joined Methodists in 1749. Known as the Apostle of Ireland. Had a profound knowledge of the Scriptures. Was a Hebrew scholar. One of the most eloquent of Wesley's preachers. Part of the Great Revival. Died at age 28 of tuberculosis.

Last Words: "He is come! My beloved is mine and I am his forever!"

Source: *Dying Testimonies of Saved and Unsaved: Gathered from Authentic Sources* by Solomon Benjamin Shaw (Chicago, 1898).

Walton, Sir William Turner

(1902-1983) British musician, composer. Notable works: orchestral, choral, chamber music, ballets. Composed many film scores, including *The First of the Few, Henry V* and *Richard III.* Knighted in 1951. Notable works: *Belshazzar's Feast; Hindemith Variations; Symphony No. 1 in B Flat.* Admitted to Order of Merit 1967. Died at age 80 in Ischia, Italy, where he had made his home since 1949.

Last Words: "Don't leave me. Please don't leave me." Spoken to his wife Susana.

Source: *William Walton: Behind the Façade* by Susana Walton (Oxford, England, 1988).

Wamporas

(mid 1600s) Native American leader. Christian member of the Wampanoag tribe that commemorated the first Thanksgiving with the Pilgrims.

Last Words: "I now shall dye, but Jesus Christ calleth you that live to go to Naticke, that there you might make a church and have the ordinances of God."

Source: *Historical Sermon Preached in the John Eliot Church, South Natick, Massachusetts, November 15, 1874,* by S.D. Hosmer (South Natick, MA, 1875).

Wang, Lo-Chi

(1952-1994) Chinese airline pilot. Pilot of the ill-fated Airbus A300 flight that crashed at Nagoya, Japan, killing 271 people. The plane failed to make its initial cleared landing and the pilot decided to come in again. The crash was attributed to human failure.

Last Words: "CAL 140 going around." Spoken to the tower.

Source: "261 Die When a Flight From Taiwan Crashes in Japan" by Andrew Pollack (*New York Times*, April 27, 1994).

Ward, Mary Josephine ("Maisie")

(1889-1975) British publisher, writer. Formed Sheed & Ward, Roman Catholic publishing house, with husband Francis H. Sheed. Lectured widely on Catholic matters. Died at age 86 in New York City.

Last Words: "I still have enthusiasm. But what use is enthusiasm without energy."

Source: *Frank and Maisie: A Memoir with Parents* by Wilfrid Sheed (New York, 1985). The author was her son.

Ward, Sam

(1814-1884) American statesman, lobbyist, diplomat, writer. Pen name Carlos Lopez. Brother of Julia Ward Howe. Awarded honorary Ph.D from Tübingen University. Notable work: *Lyrical Recreations.* Inspiration for Horace Bellingham in *Dr. Claudius,* a novel by his nephew F. Marion Crawford. Died at age 70 in Pegli, Italy.

Last Words: "I think I am going to give up the ghost."

Source: *Uncle Sam Ward and His Circle (The Leisure*

Class in America) by Maud Howe Elliott (New York, 1938). The author was his niece.

Warham, William

(1450?-1532) English prelate, statesman. Lord chancellor of England. Archbishop of Canterbury. Officiated at the marriage of Henry VIII and Catherine of Aragon. Crowned Henry VIII. Friend of Erasmus. Died at around age 82 at Hackington near Canterbury. Left his books to three schools. Had few other possessions.

Last Words: "Satis viatici in cœlum." (tr. "That is enough to last till I get to heaven.") Spoken to a servant who told him he still had 30 pounds.

Source: *The General Biographical Dictionary: Containing an Historical and Critical Account of the Lives and Writings of the Most Eminent Persons in Every Nation: Particularly British and Irish; From the Earliest Accounts to the Present Time,* Vol. 31, by Alexander Chalmers (London, 1817).

Warner, Charles Dudley

(1829-1900) American writer, editor, essayist, lecturer. Contributing editor for *Harper's New Monthly Magazine.* Collaborated with Mark Twain in writing *The Gilded Age.* Died in Hartford, Connecticut, at age 71.

Last Words: "I am not well and should like to lie down. Will you call me in ten minutes? Thank you. You are very kind. In ten minutes, remember."

Source: *A Conspectus of American Biography: Being an Analytical Summary of American History and Biography, Containing also the Complete Indexes of the National Cyclopedia of American Biography* by George Derby (New York, 1906).

Warren, Earl

(1891-1974) American lawyer, jurist, statesman, politician. Governor and attorney general of California. Chief justice of the U.S. Supreme Court. Chaired Warren Commission that investigated the assassination of U.S. President John F. Kennedy. Died at age 83 in Washington, D.C. Awarded the Presidential Medal of Freedom posthumously in 1981.

Last Words: "Thank God! If you don't do it this way, it's the end of the country as we have known it!" His response to news from Justice William Brennan that the Court was forcing President Nixon to turn over the Watergate tapes to a district court. Warren was hospitalized at the time after suffering a heart attack. He died soon after speaking these words.

Source: *Super Chief: Earl Warren and His Supreme Court, a Judicial Biography* by Bernard Schwartz (New York, 1983). Schwartz also wrote *The Warren Court: A Retrospective.*

Warren, Joseph

(1741-1775) American physician, military officer. American Revolutionary War soldier. Member of Sons of Liberty, Massachusetts Committee of Correspondence. Drafted the Suffolk Reserves. President of Massachusetts Provincial Congress. Killed at age 34 at Bunker Hill (Breed's Hill) by a British soldier. Fourteen counties and six towns were named for him.

Last Words: "I am a dead man. Fight on, my brave fellows, for the salvation of your country." Cried out to his men during the battle.

Source: *Life and Times of Joseph Warren* by Richard Frothingham (Boston, 1865).

Warren, Leonard

(1911-1960) American musician, singer. Operatic baritone. Birth name Warenoff. One of the most popular performers with the Metropolitan Opera. Well-known concert, radio and recording artist. Notable roles: Rigoletto, Falstaff, Otello, Simon Boccanegra. Collapsed and died of a cerebral hemorrhage while singing the role of Don Carlo in a performance of Verdi's *La Forza del Destino* at the Met. Died at age 48.

Different Last Words:

(1) (doubtful): "Morir? Tremenda cosa." (tr. "To die? A tremendous thing." or "To die? A momentous thing.") This widespread legend is disputed by witnesses who say he was just past that aria. See (2).

Source: "La Forza del Destino; Dying Words" (*New York Times,* May 9, 1999).

(2) "Gioia, o gioia!" (tr. "Joy, oh joy.") Eyewitnesses including Met General Manager Rudolf Bing reported that Warren had completed the aria with "To Die" and had reached the point where he opened a sealed wallet, looked at the contents and sang "Gioia, o gioia!" (tr. "Joy, oh joy.") Accord-

ing to Bing, Warren did so then pitched forward and was still. He was dead within minutes.
Source: *Leonard Warren: American Baritone* by Mary Jane Phillips-Matz (New York, 2000).
Variation: "E salvo! Oh, gioia!"
Source: "La Forza del Destino; Dying Words" (*New York Times,* May 9, 1999).
(3) "Help!" Spoken to fellow performer Roald Reitan who was on stage with him and raised Warren's head slightly. Warren then went limp.
Source: "Review of Performance and Account of Leonard Warren's Death" by Raymond A. Ericson (*Musical America,* Vol. 50, No. II).

Washakie

(1815?-1900) Native American leader, warrior. Shoshoni chief. Greatly respected for his concern about his people. Sought schools, churches, hospitals and reservation for them on their land. Died at about age 85 near Fort Washakie, Wyoming. Given a full military funeral. A county, creek, lake, mount and national park in Wyoming were named for him.
Last Words: "You now have that for which we have so long and bravely fought. Keep it forever in peace and honor. Go now and rest. I shall speak to you no more." Spoken to his grieving family.
Source: "The Redskin Who Saved the White Man's Hide" by Sidney O. Reynolds (*American Heritage,* Vol. 11, No. 2, February 1960).

Washington, Booker Taliaferro

(1856-1915) American educator, social reformer, writer, former slave. Notable work: *Up From Slavery* (autobiography). Founded and headed Tuskegee Institute (now Tuskegee University) in Alabama. Died at age 59 at Tuskegee Institute.
Last Words: "Take me home. I was born in the South, I have lived and labored in the South, and I wish to die and be buried in the South."
Source: *Booker T. Washington, Educator and Interracial Interpreter* by Basil Matthews (Cambridge, MA, 1948).

Washington, George

(1732-1799) 1st President of the U.S. American military officer, politician, statesman, surveyor. Saw military action in French In-

dian War. Delegate at First and Second Continental Congresses. Elected General and Commander-in-Chief of Army of the United Colonies (1775). Hero of American Revolution. Elected President unanimously for first and second terms. Died at age 67 at Mount Vernon, his plantation in Virginia.
Last Words: "Tis well." Like many people of his era, he feared being buried alive. He told his physician to keep his body outside his vault for three days and asked him if he understood. The physician said he did. Washington then uttered these Last Words. He died a few minutes later.
Source: *Life of George Washington* by Washington Irving (New York, 1869).

Washington, Martha Dandridge Custis

(1731-1802) American First Lady. Wife of 1st President George Washington. Widow of Daniel Parke Custis, with whom she had two children who died young: Jackie in 1781 and Patsy in 1773. Martha and George Washington raised Jackie's four children. Martha died at age 70 of fever in Mount Vernon, Virginia.
Last Words: Exact words are not known. Little is known about her last hours. A communication sent by the family to an Alexandria newspaper stated she "imparted her last advice and benedictions to her weeping relations, and sent for a white gown she had previously laid aside for her last dress."
Sources: *Alexandria Gazette*, May 25, 1802; *Martha Washington* by Anne Hollingsworth Wharton (New York, 1897).

Wasserman, Jakob

(1873-1934) German writer, novelist, biographer. Notable works: *Caspar Hauser; The World's Illusion; The Dark Pilgrimage.* Known for his psychological realism. Died at age 60 in Altaussee, Austria.
Last Words: "Marta." Spoken to his wife Marta Karlweis.
Source: *Jakob Wassermann, Bild, Kampf und Werk* by Marta Karlweis (Amsterdam, The Netherlands, 1935).

Waterford, Louisa, 3rd Marchioness of

(1818-1891) Victorian painter, watercolorist. Well-known amateur artist. Birth name Louisa Anne Stuart. Born and raised in Paris. Studied art under John Ruskin. Moved to Ireland when she married 3rd Marquis of

Waterford in 1842. Her Sketchbook is in the National Portrait Gallery. Other works are at Victoria & Albert and British Museums. Many of her paintings remained within the family.

Last Words: "Oh darling Adelaide, goodness and beauty, beauty and goodness, those are ever the great things!"

Source: *The Story of Two Noble Lives Being Memorials of Charlotte, Countess Canning and Louisa Marchioness of Waterford* by Augustus J.C. Hare (London, 1893).

Waters, Ethel

(1896-1977) American musician, singer, actress. Sang jazz, pop, big band, gospel. Nominated for an Academy Award for Best Supporting Actress in 1949 for *Pinky* and an Emmy in 1962 for her performance in an episode of *Route 66* ("Goodnight Sweet Blues"). Won New York Drama Critics Award in 1950 for her role in the stage version of *Member of the Wedding.* Also appeared in the movie version. Died at age 80 of heart disease in Chatsworth, California. Posthumously made member of Gospel Music Hall of Fame and Grammy Hall of Fame.

Last Words: "Merciful father! Precious Jesus!"

Source: *Finally Home* by Juliann DeKorte (Old Tappan, NJ, 1978).

Watson, Thomas Edward

(1856-1922) American lawyer, writer, politician. Member U.S. House of Representatives and Senate from Georgia. Candidate for U.S. Vice President and President. Died at age 66 of a cerebral hemorrhage in Washington, D.C., while U.S. senator.

Last Words: "I am not afraid of death. I am not afraid to die."

Source: *The Life of Thomas E. Watson* by William Wade Brewton (Atlanta, GA, 1926).

Watt, James

(1736-1819) Scottish mechanical engineer, inventor. Perfected steam engine. Originated term "horsepower." Died at age 83 in Inverness, Scotland. Watt and kilowatt, units of power, named for him.

Last Words: "I am very sensible of the attachment you show me, and I hasten to thank you for it, as I feel that I am now come to my last illness." Spoken to friends

who had gathered around his deathbed.

Source: *The Lives of Boulton and Watt* by Samuel Smiles (Philadelphia, 1865).

Watteau, Jean-Antoine

(1684-1721) French painter. Known for landscape and genre paintings and for the use of color and movement. Notable works: *Embarkation for Cythera; Picnic in the Woods; L'Indifferent.* Suffered from tuberculosis. Health began to fail in his early 30s. Died at age 36 in Nogent-sur-Marne, France.

Last Words (doubtful): "Get rid of it. It grieves me to see it; is it possible that my Lord is so poorly served?" Spoken to a curate who had given him a shabbily made crucifix. Watteau wanted it removed immediately because he felt it was art not worthy of God.

Source: Various Last Words compilations and Internet websites.

This quote is probably fiction. In his essay "Fables of Art," Paul Barolsky wrote that the history of art is filled with an abundance of fables. He noted that stories such as that of Watteau's final words are rooted in a Renaissance fable about the sculptor Nanni Grosso. As he was dying in a hospital, he was brought a poorly made crucifix. Grosso begged to have it taken away. He detested bad art so much he insisted he would die in despair if he were not given one from the hand of Donatello.

Source: "Fables of Art" by Paul Barolsky (*Virginia Quarterly Review,* Spring 1995).

Watts, George Frederic

(1817-1904) British artist, painter, sculptor. Symbolist. Known as the Poet Painter. Academician to the Royal Academy. Painted about 300 portraits. Notable works: *Hope; King Alfred; George and the Dragon* (paintings). *Physical Energy* (sculpture; part of Cecil Rhodes Memorial in Cape Town, South Africa). Died at age 87 in Compton, Surrey, England.

Last Words: "Now I see that great book! I see that great light!"

Source: *George Frederic Watts,* Vol. 2, by Mary S. Fraser-Tytler Watts (London, 1912). The author was his wife.

Watts, Isaac

(1674-1748) English theologian, clergyman,

hymnist. Wrote about 600 hymns. Notable works: "When I Survey the Wondrous Cross"; "Am I a Soldier of the Cross"; "Joy to the World." Published books of poetry and theology. Died at age 74 in London.

Last Words: "I do." His response when asked if he experienced comfort from the words: "I will never leave thee, nor forsake thee."

Source: *Isaac Watts: His Life and Writings, His Homes and Friends* by Edwin Paxton Hood (London, 1875).

Wayne, Anthony ("Mad Anthony")

(1745-1796) American military officer, politician. Known as Mad Anthony Wayne for his daring exploits in the American Revolution. Prevented the British occupation of West Point in 1780. Fought at Fallen Timbers. Member U.S. House of Representatives from Georgia. Became ill and died at age 51 en route to Pennsylvania from Detroit. Buried at Fort Presque Isle (now Erie, Pennsylvania). His body was later moved to a family plot in southern Pennsylvania. Popular military leader. Many counties, towns and schools named for him.

Last Words: "This is the end—I am dying—I can't bear up much longer—Bury me here on the hill, by the flagpole."

Source: *A Gentleman Rebel: Mad Anthony Wayne* by John Hyde Preston (New York, 1930).

Wayne, John ("Duke")

(1907-1979) American actor. Screen star. Birth name Marion Robert Morrison. Starred in many movie classics especially western and military genres. Nominated for three Academy Awards; won in 1970 for *True Grit*. Received Congressional Gold Medal and Presidential Medal of Freedom. Died at age 72 in Los Angeles, California.

Last Words: "Of course I know who you are. You're my girl. I love you."

Source: *Duke A Love Story: An Intimate Memoir of John Wayne's Last Years* by Pat Stacy and Beverly Linet (New York, 1983).

Webb, Mary Gladys Meredith

(1881-1927) English-born novelist, essayist, poet. Wrote stories set mainly in Shropshire. Last novel was her best known: *Precious Bane*. Health began to fail. Died at age 46 in a nursing home in St. Leonard's, Sussex.

Last Words: "That will be nice." Her re-

sponse when told about tea that afternoon.

Source: *Mary Webb: Her Life and Work* by Thomas Moult (London, 1932).

Weber, Carl Maria von

(1786-1826) German musician, composer, conductor, pianist. Cousin of Mozart's wife Constanze. Notable works: *Invitation to the Dance* (piano); *Der Freischütz* (opera); also symphonic, chamber, choral, church and theater music. Suffered from tuberculosis. Was very ill while in London for concerts and rehearsals. Died there at age 39.

Last Words: "Now let me sleep." Spoken to a friend who stayed to help him get ready for bed. Weber had planned to leave London on June 6th. On June 4th he talked to his friends of his eagerness to return home. The next morning, when his friends came to his room, they found he had died during the night.

Source: *Enchanted Wanderer: The Life of Carl Maria von Weber* by Lucy Poate Stebbins and Richard Poate Stebbins (New York, 1940).

Webern, Anton Friedrich Wilhelm von

(1883-1945) Austrian musician, composer, conductor, arranger. Composed for orchestra, chorus, voice, instrument, piano, chamber music. Used twelve-tone scale. His atonal music influenced other modern composers. Music adviser for Austrian radio. Made several trips to London to conduct on the BBC. Notable works: *Im sommerwind; Six Pieces for Orchestra; Five Canons*. He was accidentally shot and killed at age 61 by an American soldier on sentry duty in the village of Mittersill, near Salzburg, during the Allied post-World War II occupation of Austria.

Last Words: "I have been shot. It is over."

Source: *Anton von Webern: A Chronicle of His Life and Work* by Hans Moldenhauer (London, 1978).

Webster, Daniel

(1782-1852) American statesman, lawyer, politician, diplomat. Member U.S. House of Representatives from New Hampshire and Massachusetts and U.S. Senate from Massachusetts. Participated in famous debates with John C. Calhoun. U.S. secretary of state twice. Negotiated Webster-Ashburton treaty with Great Britain. Unsuccessful candidate for U.S. President. Died at age 70 in

Marshfield, Massachusetts. Eight U.S. counties and seven towns, a spring and a lake have been named for him.

Last Words: "I still live!" These were his last coherent and intelligent words. He died a few hours after he spoke them. He tried to say something else but the only word his family understood was "poetry." His son then read to him one of the stanzas of Gray's "Elegy."

Source: *Life of Daniel Webster* by George Ticknor Curtis (New York, 1892).

Webster, Noah

(1758-1843) American lexicographer, educator, writer. Spent 27 years compiling the first American English dictionary: *American Dictionary of the English Language* (70,000 words). Helped Americanize the English language. Died at age 84 in New Haven, Connecticut.

Last Words: "I have struggled with many difficulties. Some I have been able to overcome, and by some I have been overcome. I have made many mistakes, but I love my country, and have labored for the youth of my country, and I trust no precept of mine has taught any dear youth to sin."

Source: *Noah Webster: Schoolmaster to America* by Harry Redcay Warfel (New York, 1936).

Weed, Stephen Hinsdale

(1831-1863) American military officer. Helped quell Kansas disturbance in 1858 and Indian skirmishes in Utah in 1860. Brigadier general in Union Army in U.S. Civil War. Fought at Chancellorsville. Wounded in action at Little Round Top, Gettysburg. Died a short time later. The area where he fell is known as Weed's Hill.

Last Words: "I would rather die here than that the rebels should gain an inch of this ground." Spoken as he fell.

Source: *Annual Report of the State Historian,* Vol. I, by the New York State Historian (Albany, NY, 1897).

Weed, Thurlow

(1797-1882) American journalist, politician. Established and edited *Albany* [New York] *Evening Journal.* Played a role in the nominations of Harrison, Clay, Taylor and Scott for U.S. President. Part of a group sent abroad by President Lincoln during the U.S.

Civil War to encourage foreign governments not to intervene on behalf of the Confederacy. Died at age 85 in New York City.

Last Words: "I want to go home!" During his final hours his mind wandered. He imagined he was having a conversation with Lincoln and General Scott about the Southern Confederacy.

Source: *Memoir of Thurlow Weed* by Thurlow W. Barnes (Boston, 1884). His grandson Thurlow Weed Barnes completed his autobiography.

Weil, Simone

(1909-1943) French philosopher, activist, writer, poet, educator. Original thinker. Worked with French resistance during World War II. Notable work: *The Need for Roots.* Died at age 34 in Ashford, Kent, England. Her death was hastened by starvation. Most of her poems and articles were published after she died.

Last Words: "When I think of my fellow citizens who are dying of hunger in France, I cannot eat." Spoken to her physician who had urged her to eat.

Source: *Simone Weil: An Intellectual Biography* by Gabriella Fiori (Athens, GA, 1989).

Weiss, Emanuel ("Mendy")

(1906-1944) American murderer. Professional hit man. Associate of Louis Lepke Buchalter, head of Murder, Inc. Electrocuted at age 37 at Ossining (Sing Sing) prison, New York, on the same day as Buchalter.

Last Words: "All I want to say is I'm innocent. I'm here on a framed-up case. Give my love to my family and everything." Spoken to newspaper reporters at his execution. He died two minutes later.

Source: *Bloodletters and Badmen: A Narrative Encyclopedia of American Criminals from the Pilgrims to the Present* by Jay Robert Nash (New York, 1995).

Weisselberg, Roland

(1933-2006) German clergyman. Retired Lutheran vicar who gained notoriety by killing himself at age 73 by self-immolation at the monastery in Erfurt, Germany, where Martin Luther took his monastic vows in 1505. Weisselberg was concerned that the Berlin Deutsche Oper planned to stage an opera with a scene showing the severed heads of Muhammad, Jesus and Buddha. He poured gasoline over his body and set fire to himself shouting his Last Words repeatedly as he died.

Last Words: "Jesus" and "Oskar." "Oskar" apparently referred to Oskar Brüsewitz, a priest who burnt himself in 1976. Weisselberg also left a farewell letter to his wife that she did not release to the public.

Source: "Priest Burns Himself to Death Over Islam" by David Crossland (*The [London] Times*, November 3, 2006).

Weizmann, Chaim

(1874-1952) Russian-born Israeli statesman, scientist, Zionist leader, educator. Worked on Balfour Declaration. President of World Zionist Organization. President of Hebrew University. First president of the State of Israel. Died at age 77 in Rehovet, Israel.

Last Words: "I'm going on a very, very long journey. Prepare everything." Spoken to his nurse.

Source: *Chaim Weizmann: A Biography* by Norman Rose (New York, 1986).

Weld, Angelina Emily Grimke

(1805-1879) American abolitionist, women's rights advocate. Sister of Sarah Moore Grimke, also an abolitionist and women's rights activist. Wrote appeals calling for the end of slavery. Notable work: *American Slavery as It Is: Testimony of a Thousand Witnesses* (compiled with her husband Theodore Weld and sister Sarah). Paralyzed by strokes during the last six years of her life. Died at age 74 in Hyde Park, Massachusetts.

Last Words: "The hire of the laborers kept back by fraud crieth: and the cries are in the ears of the Lord." She was quoting the Bible: James 5:4

Source: *The Grimke Sisters: Sarah and Angelina Grimke, the First American Women Advocates of Abolition and Women's Rights* by Catherine H. Birney (Boston, 1885). The author was a friend of the sisters.

Welles, George Orson (Orson)

(1915-1985) American actor, director, producer, writer. Star of radio, stage, television and screen. Co-founder and member of Mercury Theatre that traumatized the nation with the radio broadcast of *War of the Worlds*. Welles wrote, directed, produced and acted in *Citizen Kane,* considered one of the greatest films ever made. Won honorary

Academy Award in 1971. Winner of many other awards, including American Film Institute's Lifetime Achievement Award. Died at age 70 of a heart attack in Los Angeles.

Last Words: "This is your friend. Don't forget to tell me how your mother is." Message left on the answering machine for Henry Jaglom, after 3:00 a.m. on October 10. Welles was found dead on his apartment floor at 10:00 that morning.

Source: *What Ever Happened to Orson Welles? A Portrait of an Independent Career* by Joseph McBride (Lexington, KY, 2006).

Wellesley, Arthur,
1st Duke of Wellington

(1769-1852) British nobleman, military officer, politician, statesman. General. Known as the Iron Duke. Beethoven wrote *Wellington's Victory* (or *Battle Symphony*; opus 91) to commemorate Wellington's victory over Spain in 1813. Wellington defeated Napoleon at Waterloo in 1815, ending the Napoleonic Wars. Died at age 83 at Walmer Castle, Kent. His death was an occasion of national mourning and inspired Tennyson's ode "Death of the Duke of Wellington."

Different Last Words:

(1) "Yes, if you please." Response when offered a cup of tea.

Source: *Ballou's Dollar Monthly Magazine,* Vol. 15, January-June, 1862.

(2) "Do you know where the apothecary lives? Then send and let him know that I should like to see him. I don't feel quite well and I will lie still till he comes."

Source: *The Life of Arthur, Duke of Wellington* by G.R. Gleig (London, 1899).

Wells, Brian Douglas

(1956-2003) American pizza deliveryman. Died while delivering pizza. Time bomb explosive was strapped around his neck. He claimed that under duress he was sent on a bank robbery where he had to follow a series of steps within a limited time or the bomb would detonate. When time ran out, the bomb detonated and he was killed. The violent explosion was captured on video by an Erie, Pennsylvania, television station.

Last Words: "He pulled a key out and started a timer. I heard the thing ticking when he did it. It's gonna go off. I don't have much time. I'm not lying. Did you call my boss? Why is it nobody's trying to come get this thing off me?" Spoken frantically to the police, who were waiting for the bomb squad when the bomb detonated.

Source: "Was Pizza Deliverer a Robber or a Victim?" by Kevin Johnson (*USA TODAY*, September 17, 2003).

Wells, Herbert George ("H.G.")

(1866-1946) English novelist, journalist, sociologist, historian. Notable works: *The Invisible Man; The Time Machine; The War of the Worlds* (still widely read; all three have been made and remade into movies). Wells and Jules Verne are credited with inventing the science fiction genre. When speaking about World War I—The Great War—Wells coined the phrase "The war to end all wars" in 1914. Died at age 79 in London.

Last Words: "Go away. I'm all right." Spoken to a nurse.

Source: *H.G. Wells: A Biography* by Vincent Brome (London, 1951).

Wells, William

(1770-1812) American scout, interpreter, soldier. Known as Carrot-top (Apekonii). Taken captive by the Miamis when he was 12. Married the daughter of Miami chief Little Turtle. As an adult, he became a U.S. Army captain. Served as scout and interpreter at the Battle of Fallen Timbers. Left the army and worked as a Native American agent. Shot and killed at around age 42 by Pottawattamie in the Fort Dearborn massacre. He had tried to lead white settlers to safety dressed as a Native American.

Last Words: "Tell my wife—if you live to get there, but I think it doubtful if a single one gets there—tell her I died at my post doing the best I could. There are seven red devils over there that I have killed." Spoken after he was shot. When a group of Pottawattamie approached him, he took aim and fired at one of them. A bystander told him one of them had a gun pointed at his head. He replied "Shoot away." The Native American fired and killed him.

Source: *The Magazine of American History with Notes and Queries,* ed. by Mrs. Martha J. Lamb, Vol. XVIII, June-December 1892.

Wenceslas, King of Bohemia

(907-929) Bohemian monarch. Born near Prague. Son of Ratislav, King of Bohemia. Immortalized in the Christmas carol *Good King Wenceslas*. Died at age 22. Murdered by twin brother Boleslaus, who wanted to inherit the throne.

Last Words: "May God forgive you, brother."

Source: *Stories Behind the Great Traditions of Christmas* by Ace Collins (Grand Rapids, MI, 2003).

Wentworth, Thomas, 1st Earl of Strafford

(1593-1641) English lawyer, politician. Lord deputy of Ireland. Impeached for high treason. Beheaded at age 48 at Tower Hill, London.

Last Words: "I do as cheerfully put off my doublet at this time as ever I did when I went to bed." Spoken on the scaffold. When he was offered a blindfold, he replied: "Nay, for I will see it done."

Source: *Thomas Wentworth, First Earl of Strafford, 1593-1641* by C.V. Wedgwood (London, 1935).

Wescott, John Wesley

(1849-1927) American jurist, politician. As a Yale student he played in the first Yale-Princeton football game and rowed in the first Yale-Harvard crew—two of collegiate sport's oldest rivalries. He also helped establish modern collegiate baseball in the 1860s. Attorney general of New Jersey. Nominated Woodrow Wilson for U.S. President at the Democratic National Convention in Baltimore in 1912 and in St. Louis in 1916. He was a major proponent of the League of Nations. Died at age 78 in Haddonfield, New Jersey.

Last Words: "My darling." Spoken to his wife who was holding his hand at his deathbed.

Source: "Wescott, Sponsor of Wilson, Dead" (*New York Times,* June 12, 1927).

Wesley, Charles

(1707-1788) English hymnist, clergyman. Younger brother of John Wesley. Composed more than 6,000 hymns. Notable works: "Hark! the Herald Angels Sing"; "Jesus Lover of My Soul." Itinerant Methodist minister many years. Differed with brother on some views of Methodism, including separation from Church of England and the doctrine of perfection. Died age 80.

Last Words: "My Lord, my heart, my God!" Spoken as his family gathered around his bed.

Source: *Annotations Upon Popular Hymns* by Charles Seymour Robinson (New York, 1893).

Wesley, John

(1703-1791) English evangelist, theologian, clergyman. Ordained deacon and priest. Fellow of Lincoln College, Oxford. Missionary to Georgia. Leader of evangelical revival in England in the 18th century. Founder of Methodist Societies. Published inexpensive books on edifying subjects for Methodists. Had thousands of followers who waited patiently for hours to hear him speak. Founded orphanage and charity schools. Died at age 87 in London.

Last Word: "Farewell." He woke up in the morning, spoke this final word, then died without a groan. He was heard by Mr. Bradford, an old and faithful friend

Source: *The Life of The Rev. John Wesley, M.A., Some Time Fellow of Lincoln College, Oxford: Collected from His Private Papers and Printed Works, and Written at the Request of His Executors: To Which is Prefixed Some Accounts of His Ancestors and Relations: With the Life of the Rev. Charles Wesley, M.A. Collected from His Private Journal, and Never Before Published; The Whole Forming a History of Methodism, in Which the Principles and Economy of The Methodists Are Unfolded* by John Whitehead (London, 1793).

Wesley, Samuel (the Elder)

(1662-1735) English clergyman, poet, hymnist, writer. Rector of Epworth. Changed the spelling of the family name from Westley to Wesley. Father of John and Charles Wesley, founders of Methodism. Notable hymn: "Behold the Savior of Mankind." Most of his hymns were destroyed in a fire. Died at age 72 in Epworth.

Last Words: "Now you have done all." Spoken in the presence of his son John who had commended his father's soul to God. Samuel died without a struggle, sign or groan.

Source: *The Life and Times of the Rev. Samuel Wesley: M.A. and Father of the Revs. John and Charles Wesley, the Founders of the Methodists* by Luke Tyerman (London, 1866).

Wesley, Samuel Sebastian

(1810-1876) English musician, composer, hymnist, organist, theater conductor. Grandson of hymnist Charles Wesley. Cathedral organist. Professor of music at the Royal Academy. Wrote many anthems and hymns. Notable works: "Blessed be the God and Father"; "The Wilderness"; "O Lord, Thou art My God." Died at age 65 in Gloucester, England.

Last Words: "Let me see the sky."

Source: *A Dictionary of Music and Musicians (A.D. 1450-1880)* by John Alexander Fuller-Maitland and George Grove (New York, 1889).

Wesley, Sarah Gwynne

(1726-1822) English matron. Daughter of Welsh magistrate. Wife of Charles Wesley. Lost five children as infants. Died at age 96.

Last Words: "Open the gates! Open the gates!"

Sources: "The Value of Last Words" (*Frank Leslie's Popular Monthly*, Vol. XXXVIII, July to December 1894); *Gems Reset; or The Wesleyan Catechisms Illustrated* by Benjamin Smith (London, 1876).

Wesley, Susanna Annesley

(1669-1742) English educator, religious activist. Mother of John Wesley and 18 other children. Only eight survived to adulthood. Known as the Mother of Methodism. Operated a school in her home. Prepared textbooks for the religious training of her children.

Last Words: "Children, as soon as I am released, sing a psalm of praise to God."

Source: *The Life of The Rev. John Wesley, M.A., Some Time Fellow of Lincoln College, Oxford: Collected from His Private Papers and Printed Works, and Written at the Request of His Executors: To Which is Prefixed Some Accounts of His Ancestors and Relations: With the Life of the Rev. Charles Wesley, M.A. Collected from His Private Journal, and Never Before Published; The Whole Forming a History of Methodism, in Which the Principles and Economy of The Methodists Are Unfolded* by John Whitehead (London, 1793).

Whale, George

(1849-1925) British writer, philosopher, politician. Freethinker. Founder of Omar Khayyam Club and Samuel Pepys Society. Chairman of Rationalist Press Association. Mayor of Woolrich, England. Active in Folk-Lore Society. His Last Words were spoken as he concluded a speech while presiding at a dinner of The Rationalist Press Association. As he ended his speech, he collapsed and died at age 76.

Different Last Words:

(1) "Let us eat and drink for tomorrow we die. Do I say that? No, I say take hands and help for today we live."

Source: "Lawyer Dies as his Health is Proposed" (*New York Times*, May 5, 1925).

(2) "The light from some providential spirit or Holy Ghost is said to have guided the Church for some 1,900 years. It has not come, and when it does come I venture to suggest it will not have the dazzling effect of the light that fell on the Apostle on his way to Damascus, the light which left him dazzled for the rest of his life." He collapsed in his chair. Doctors rushed to his side and carried him from the room. He died almost immediately.

Source: *Mark These Men: A Unique Look at Selected Men of the Bible* by J. Sidlow Baxter (Grand Rapids, MI, 1992).

Whale, James

(1889-1957) English-born movie director. Notable movies: *The Man in the Iron Mask; Show Boat; The Invisible Man; Frankenstein*. Suffered series of strokes. Suicide at age 67 by drowning in a backyard pool in Hollywood. His life was the subject of the movie *Gods and Monsters* (1998).

Last Words (written): "The future is just old age and illness and pain—I must have peace and this is the only way." Suicide note. Contents were not revealed until 1987 by his life partner.

Source: *The 1950s' Most Wanted: The Top Ten Book of Rock & Roll Rebels, Cold War Crises, and All American Oddities* by Robert Rodriguez (Washington, D.C., 2006).

Whately, Richard

(1787-1863) English prelate, theologian, educator, writer, social reformer. Archbishop of Dublin. Notable work: *Historic Doubts Relative to Napoleon*. Died at age 76 in Dublin, Ireland.

Last Words: "That's right, not vile. Nothing that He made is vile." Whately was reacting to the Anglican version of the Bible the chaplain was reading, especially the use of the word "vile" in the phrase "Who shall change our vile body." The chaplain changed the wording and read it: "This body

of our humiliation."

Source: *Life and Correspondence of Richard Whately, D.D. Late Archbishop of Dublin* by E. Jane Whately (London, 1866). The author was his daughter.

Wheat, Chatham Roberdeau ("Bob")

(1826-1862) American military officer. Served in Texas War for Independence. Major in Confederate Army in U.S. Civil War. Commanded First Special Battalion, Louisiana, known as the Tiger Battalion. Shot and killed at age 36 at Gaines' Mills, Virginia.

Last Words: "Bury me on the field, boys!"

Source: *Widows by the Thousands: The Civil War Letters of Theophilus and Harriet Perry, 1862-1864* (Fayetteville, AR, 2000).

Wheaton, Lawrence ("Larry")

(1947-1982) American airline pilot, victim of airline disaster. Captain of Air Florida Flight 90 that crashed into the 14th Street Bridge over the Potomac River in Washington D.C., in 1982, one of the worst urban airway disasters in American history. Seventy-four people died. The crash was the basis for the made-for-TV movie *Flight 90: Disaster on the Potomac*.

Last Words: "I know it." Spoken to co-pilot Roger Pettit who had said: "Larry! We're going down, Larry!"

Source: *Mayday: Accident Reports and Voice Transcripts from Airline Crash Investigations* by Marion F. Sturkey (Plum Branch, SC, 2005).

Wheelock, Eleazar

(1711-1779) American clergyman, orator, educator. Congregationalist. Active in the Great Awakening. Founded Moor's Charity School. Founder and first president of Dartmouth College. Suffered from asthma in later years. Died at age 68. His son John succeeded him as president of Dartmouth.

Last Words: "Oh, my family, be faithful unto death." He died immediately after speaking these words.

Source: *Memoirs of the Rev. Eleazar Wheelock, D.D.: Founder and President of Dartmouth College and Moor's Charity School With a Summary History of the College and School* by David McClure and Elijah Parish (Newburyport, MA, 1811).

Whistler, James Abbott McNeill

(1834-1903) American-born artist who lived in London, England. Notable works: *Arrangement in Grey and Black: Portrait of the Artist's Mother* (popularly known as

Whistler's Mother); Battersea Beach; The Music Room. Died at age 69 at his home in Chelsea.

Last Words: "But why do you go so soon?" Spoken to a friend who got up to leave, fearing more than one visitor at a time would tire him. Death came a short time later.

Source: *The Life of James McNeill Whistler* by Elizabeth Robins Pennell and Joseph Pennell (London, 1908).

Whitaker, William

(1548-1595) English theologian, educator, translator. Regius professor of divinity at Cambridge. Became ill during a winter trip to London. Returned to Cambridge. Physicians let blood. A few days later, a friend found him in a cold sweat and near death. He died a short time later at age 46.

Last Words: "Life or death is welcome to me; which God pleases; for death shall be an advantage to me.— I desire not to live, but only so far as I may do God and His Church service." Spoken to a friend who was concerned about his health.

Source: "The Lives of William Whitaker, Philip De Morney, John Bruen and Richard Blackerby" in *A Christian Library Consisting of Extracts From and Abridgements of Choicest Pieces of Practical Divinity Which Have Been Published in the English Tongue*, Vol. XV (London, 1750).

White, Henry Kirke

(1785-1806) English poet, hymnist. Published a book of poems at age 18. Became famous after he died at age 21 of tuberculosis while a student at Cambridge.

Last Words (written): "Our lectures began on Friday, but I do not attend them until I am better. I have not written to my mother, nor shall I while I remain unwell. You will tell her, as a reason, that our lectures began on Friday. I know she will be uneasy if she does not hear from me, and still more so, if I tell her I am ill. I cannot write more at present than that I am your truly affectionate brother, H.K. White." Last part of his final letter to his brother.

Source: *Poems, Letters and Prose Fragments*, ed. by John Drinkwater (London, 1908).

White, Joseph Blanco
or José Maria Blanco Crespo

(1775-1841) Spanish-born British theological writer, poet. Ordained priest; abandoned the priesthood. Joined the Anglican church. Later became a Unitarian. Notable work: "Night and Death" (sonnet). Died at age 65 in Liverpool, England.

Last Words: "Now I die."

Source: *Life of the Rev. Joseph Blanco White, Written by Himself, with Portions of His Correspondence*, ed. by John Hamilton Thom (London, 1845).

White, Walter Francis

(1893-1955) American civil rights leader, writer. Part of the Harlem Renaissance. Executive secretary of NAACP. Laid groundwork for much of the desegregation that occurred in the mid-20th century. White had light skin, blond hair and blue eyes. Sinclair Lewis's novel, *Kingsblood Royal*—about a man who appears to be white but learns late in life that he is black—is based in part on White's experiences.

Last Words: "I knew that darned table was going to tip." He made this comment immediately after he left the room where he had said: "I plead the Fifth Amendment." His response to his daughter who asked whether he liked her dress. This reply is often cited as White's Last Words, probably because it carries a humorous tone, but his Last Words were about a tipping table.

Source: *A Gentle Knight: My Husband, Walter White* by Poppy Cannon (New York, 1956).

White Dog (Sun-ka Ska)

(d. 1862) Native American warrior. One of 38 Dakota warriors executed by the U.S. government at Mankato, Minnesota, for their role in the Sioux Uprising. Their mass execution, performed on a single scaffold platform, was the largest in U.S. history.

Last Words: "White Dog, I'm here! I'm here!"

Source: "Hanging of 38 Sioux" by George D. Wolfe (*True West*, December 1956).

Whitefield, George

(1714-1770) English clergyman, evangelist. Succeeded Wesley as leader of Methodists. Made evangelizing tours of Great Britain, America, Ireland. His arrival in America marked the beginning of the Great Awakening. He drew crowds in the thousands at his open-air sermons. After he delivered a sermon in Exeter, Massachusetts, he had an asthma attack. Died at age 55 the following day in Newburyport, Massachusetts.

Last Words: "I am dying." Spoken to his traveling companion as he stood at a window gasping for breath. His friend encouraged him to sit down and cover himself with a cloak. Whitefield died a short time later.

Source: *George Whitefield M.A., Field Preacher* by James Paterson Gladstone (London, 1901).

Whitgift, John

(1530?-1604) English prelate, educator. Anglican. Professor of Divinity at Cambridge. Dean of Lincoln. Bishop of Worcester. Crowned James I. Archbishop of Canterbury at the time of his death. Died at around age 74 at Lambeth, England.

Last Words: "In behalf of the Church of God."

Source: *Lives of the Archbishops of Canterbury* by W.F. Hook (London, 1875).

Whitman, Walter ("Walt")

(1819-1892) American poet, journalist, essayist. Known as the Good Gray Poet. Notable works: *Captain! My Captain!* (commemorating the death of Lincoln); *Leaves of Grass* (published in 1855 as a collection of 12 untitled poems). Stricken with paralysis in 1873. Also suffered from tuberculosis. Spent the rest of his life in Camden, New Jersey, where he died at age 72. He was nursed in his final illness by Frederick Warren Fritzinger ("Warry").

Different Last Words:

(1) "Shift, Warry." He wanted to be moved in bed.

Source: *Whitman* by Edgar Lee Masters (New York, 1937).

(2) "O, He's a dear, good fellow." Spoken about Thomas Donaldson a friend and later his biographer.

Source: *Walt Whitman the Man* by Thomas Donaldson (New York, 1897).

Whitney, William Collins

(1841-1904) American politician, businessman, statesman, financier. Founder of the prominent Whitney family. Helped overthrow the Boss Tweed Ring. Was one of the organizers of the Metropolitan Street Railway Company. Major investor in thoroughbred horse racing. U.S. secretary of the navy

during first Cleveland administration. Died at age 62 in New York City. USS *Whitney* and William C. Whitney Wilderness Area of Adirondack Park were named for him.

Last Words: "Don't get angry nurse. I love my son and daughter. It does me good to chat with them." Spoken to the nurse who had told his children he was too ill to see them.

Source: *William C. Whitney, Modern Warwick* by Mark David Hirsch (New York, 1948).

Whitrick, Kevin Neil

(1965-2007) British online suicide victim. Believed to be the first British webcam suicide. Divorced, depressed. Hanged himself while on an Internet chat site as approximately 50 people watched. He was in an "insult" chat room. Some people egged him on while others tried desperately to find his address to save him. Police arrived at the scene within minutes, but he was dead. Whitrick died at age 42 in Wellington, Telford, Shropshire, England.

Last Words: "I've had it, you think I am full of s**t, not this time."

Source: "Sad Dad Hangs Himself on Web" by Andrew Parker (*The* [UK] *Sun*, March 24, 2007).

Whittier, John Greenleaf

(1807-1892) American poet, abolitionist. Known as "The Quaker Poet." One of the five Fireside Poets. (the others: Henry Wadsworth Longfellow, James Russell Lowell, Oliver Wendell Holmes Sr., William Cullen Bryant). Notable poems: "Snow Bound"; "Barbara Frietche"; "The Barefoot Boy." Died at age 84 at Hampton Falls, New Hampshire.

Different Last Words:

(1) "I have known thee all the time." Spoken in response to question "Do you know me?" asked by his niece.

Source: *Whittier: Bard of Freedom* by Whitman Bennett (Chapel Hill, NC, 1941).

(2) "My love to the world." He died at dawn speaking these words.

Source: *Personal Recollections of John G. Whittier* by Mary B. Claflin (New York, 1893).

Whittle, Daniel Webster

(1840-1901) American evangelist, hymnist, military officer. Major in Union Army in U.S. Civil War. Wounded at the Battle of

Vicksburg. Evangelist for Dwight Moody. Wrote about 200 Gospel hymn texts. Notable lyrics: "I Know Whom I Have Believed"; "Moment by Moment"; "The Banner of the Cross." Died at age 60 in Northfield, Massachusetts.

Last Words: "It is all right. The Lord knows best; and all will result in my good. All sorrow will fade away and all pain depart as dew before the morning sun."

Source: *Memories of Eighty Years* by Fanny Crosby (Boston, 1906).

Wicksteed, Philip Henry

(1844-1927) British economist, literary critic, theologian. Member of the Fabian Society. Notable work: *The Common Sense of Political Economy*. Died at age 82 in Childrey, Berkshire, England.

Last Words: "Hurrah, hurrah!"

Source: *Philip Henry Wicksteed: His Life and Work* by C.H. Herford (London, 1931).

Wieland, Christoph Martin

(1733-1813) German poet, writer, translator. Known as the German Voltaire. Friend of Goethe, Schiller, Herder. Notable works: *Agathon; Oberon* (on which Weber based his opera); *Dschinnistan* (collection of fairy tales on which Mozart based his opera *The Magic Flute*). Died at age 79 in Weimar, Germany.

Last Words: "To be or not to be."

Source: *Wieland* by J.G. Gruber (Leipzig, Germany, 1816).

Wilberforce, William

(1759-1833) English philanthropist, abolitionist. A founder of the Antislavery Society. Member of Parliament. Died at age 73 in London.

Different Last Words:

(1) "I do not venture to speak so positively, but I hope I have." His response to his son who said to him: "You have your feet on the Rock."

Source: *Wilberforce: A Narrative* by R. Coupland (Oxford, England, 1923).

(2) "Heaven!"

(3) "I now feel so weaned from earth, my affections so much in heaven that I can leave you all without regret; yet I do not love you less, but God more."

Sources (2) and (3): *The Last Words (Real and Traditional) of Distinguished Men and Women Collected from Various Sources* by Frederic Rowland Marvin (New York, 1901).

Wild, Jonathan

(1682?-1725) English criminal, thief. Became a criminal while in debtors' prison. Hanged at Tyburn for housebreaking. Inspired characters in works by Defoe, Fielding. Prototype for Peachum in John Gay's *The Beggar's Opera* and Kurt Weill's *Threepenny Opera*.

Different Last Words:

(1) (doubtful): "There is little occasion to mention my religion, since I always thought every religion the offspring of the brain of some politician and denied the existence of that Being who is the basis and foundation of all religion and society. If I merit any pity from you, as you are men, I desire your prayers as you are Christians, the last favor that I have to ask in this world. I die in full persuasion that there is an Eternal Being and that Jesus Christ died for our sins, of Whom I humbly ask forgiveness and to Whom I commend my soul." Alleged to have been spoken on the scaffold. Wild had taken laudanum before he was executed, so he may not have been coherent enough to speak.

Source: *Jonathan Wild, Prince of Robbers* by Frederick J. Lyons (London, 1936).

(2) (doubtful): "Lord Jesus receive my soul." Frederic Rowland Marvin said there was some doubt as to the genuineness of these pious words. The quote came from Rev. Thomas Pureney, the chaplain of the prison, who was reputed to be a scoundrel.

Source: *The Last Words (Real and Traditional) of Distinguished Men and Women Collected from Various Sources* by Frederic Rowland Marvin (New York, 1901).

Wilde, Oscar Fingal O'Flahertie Wills

(1854-1900) Irish-born playwright, writer. Notable works: *The Importance of Being Earnest; Lady Windermere's Fan; The Picture of Dorian Gray; The Ballad of Reading Gaol*. Lived in exile in Paris after two years in prison. Used the name Sebastian Melmoth. Died at age 46 in a small Paris hotel.

Last Words: Unknown. Wilde is often quoted as having said: "It's the wallpaper or me—one of us has to go" or "I am dying as I have lived, beyond my means." But he did not die uttering a witty remark. In October 1900, he developed an ear abscess. He had surgery but the infection spread, causing swelling of his brain. He grew delirious during November. By the end of the month, his friends who were with him heard only a grinding sound coming from his throat. He died on November 30th without speaking.

Source: *They Went That-a-Way: How the Famous, the Infamous and the Great Died* by Malcolm Forbes with Jeff Bloch (New York, 1988).

Wilde, Sir William Robert Wills

(1815-1876) Irish surgeon, oculist, writer, editor, statistician. Father of Oscar Wilde. Author of works on archaeology, medicine, folklore. Founded and edited *Dublin Quarterly Journal of Medical Science*. Knighted in 1864 for services to statistical science, especially in connection with the Irish census. Died at age 61 in Dublin, Ireland.

Last Words: "Oh, those boys, those boys!" He was speaking about his two sons who were having a noisy party in another room.

Source: *Victorian Doctor: Being the Life of Sir William Wilde* by T.G. Wilson (New York, 1946).

Wilkes, John

(1727-1797) English radical, politician, journalist. Sheriff and lord mayor of London. Tried and imprisoned for seditious libel. Elected and expelled twice from the House of Commons. Secured greater freedom of the press in England by suing for illegal arrest and winning. Died at age 70. Wilkes-Barre, Pennsylvania, named for him and Isaac Barre for their role in championing the colonial cause in the British Parliament during the American Revolution.

Last Words: "I drink to the health of my beloved and excellent daughter." Spoken to his daughter Polly when he asked for something to drink.

Source: *Portrait of a Patriot: A Biography of John Wilkes* by Charles Chenevix Trench (Edinburgh, 1962).

Willard, Frances Elizabeth Caroline

(1839-1898) American educator, reformer, lecturer. Devoted her life to the temperance movement and women's suffrage. President of Woman's Christian Temperance Union. Dean of women at Northwestern University.

Died at age 58 of influenza in New York.

Different Last Words: "Oh, how sweet, oh, how lovely, good—good!" Her response to Temperance Union Secretary Clara Hoffman who read a telegram sent to the ailing Willard by Lady Henry Somerset.

Source: *Dying Testimonies of Saved and Unsaved: Gathered from Authentic Sources* by Solomon Benjamin Shaw (Chicago, 1898).

Variation: "How beautiful to be with God!" Whispered as she took her last breath.

Source: *Frances E. Willard: A Memorial Volume* by Anna A. Gordon (Chicago, 1898). The author had been her private secretary for many years.

William I, King of Prussia and Emperor of Germany (Kaiser Wilhelm I)

(1797-1888) German ruler. Son of Frederick William III of Prussia. Became prince regent for his brother Frederick William IV when he had a debilitating stroke that ended his ability to rule. Died at age 90 in Berlin.

Different Last Words:

(1) "That was beautiful." Response when he heard the minister say: "I trust in the Lord, my soul likewise, and I hope in His word."

Source: *Kaiser Wilhelm des Grossen: Briefe, Reden und Schriften* by Ernst Berner (Berlin, Germany, 1906).

(2) "I've always been pleased with you. You've done everything well." Spoken to his chancellor Otto von Bismarck.

Source: *The Kaisers* by Theo Aronson (Indianapolis, IN, 1971).

William II, King of Prussia and Emperor of Germany (Kaiser Wilhelm II)

(1859-1941) German ruler. Grandson of Queen Victoria of Great Britain. Full name Frederick William Victor Albert. German name Friedrich Wilhelm Viktor Albert. Known as Kaiser Wilhelm II. Prince of Prussia. Last German emperor and king of Prussia. Birth injury caused withering of his left arm. Had a reputation for his militaristic manner. Forced to abdicate as part of the Armistice that ended World War I. Died at age 82 of pneumonia in The Netherlands.

Last Words: "I am sinking." Spoken to his wife. He died a few hours later.

Source: "The Man Who Failed" (*Time* magazine, June 16, 1941).

William I, King of England (William the Conqueror)

(1027-1087) English ruler. Seriously injured

when his horse stumbled while entering the captured French town of Mantes. Infection set in. Died at age 59, five weeks later, at the Convent of St. Gervais near Rouen.

Last Words: "I commend myself to our blessed Lady, Mary the Mother of God, that she by her holy intercessions may reconcile me to her son, our Lord Jesus Christ."

Source: *William the Conqueror* by Phillips Russell (New York, 1933).

William II, King of England ("William Rufus")

(1056-1100) Son of William the Conqueror. Known as William Rufus or the Red King for his red hair and ruddy complexion. Killed in a hunting accident.

Last Words: "Shoot, Walter, shoot, as if it were the devil." Spoken to Walter Tirel (or Tyrrell), who shot and killed the king with an arrow in a hunting accident. Whether the shooting was an accident or premeditated murder is unknown.

Source: *History of the Conquest of England by the Normans; Its Causes and Its Consequences in England, Scotland, Ireland and On the Continent* by Augustin Thierry, tr. by William Hazlett (London, 1875).

William III, King of England

(1650-1702) English monarch. William II of Scotland. William III of Orange. Stadholder of the Netherlands. Posthumous child and only son of William II of Orange and Mary, daughter of Charles I of England. While riding in the park near Hampton Court in London, his horse stumbled on a mole hill. He fell, landed on his shoulder and broke his collarbone. He developed a swelling and became bedfast. Died at age 51 of pneumonia a few days later.

Last Words: "Can this last long, Bentinck?" Hans Willem Bentinck was a trusted agent of William III who brought him to England and made him Earl of Portland.

Source: *History of England from the Accession of James II,* Vol. III, by Thomas B. Macaulay (Philadelphia, 1879).

William IV, King of Great Britain and Ireland

(1765-1837) English monarch. Third son of George III. Known as the Sailor King and Silly Billy. Duke of Clarence. Succeeded to the throne at age 65. His two legitimate

children died in infancy. Was succeeded by his niece Victoria. Died at age 71 of heart failure in Windsor Castle.

Different Last Words:

(1) "Unfurl it and let me feel it. Glorious day!" "Glorious Day" was the anniversary of the Battle of Waterloo, a day William looked forward to. He asked that a banner be unfurled so that he could hold it.

Source: *Queen Victoria* by Elizabeth Longford (New York, 1964).

(2) "The Church, the Church." He died muttering these words.

Source: *The Lives of the Kings and Queens of England,* ed. by Antonia Fraser (New York, 1975).

William I, Prince of Orange ("William the Silent")

(1533-1584) Dutch ruler. Founded the Dutch Republic. First stadholder of United Provinces of the Netherlands. Known as William the Silent. Assassinated at age 51 at his home in Delft by Balthasar Gérard.

Different Last Words:

(1) "O God, have mercy upon me, and upon this poor nation." Spoken just before he was shot.

Source: *The Great Events of History: From the Beginning of the Christian Era to the Nineteenth Century* by William Francis Collier (London, 1884).

(2) "Yes." His response when asked: "Do you trust your soul to Jesus Christ?"

Source: *William the Silent* by Nina B. Baker (New York, 1947).

Williams, Alfred

(1877-1930) English poet, writer. Self-taught. Known as the Hammerman Poet. Worked as a hammerman at Great Western Railway's factory at Swindon, England. Was an expert on the Wiltshire countryside. Collected more than 800 songs from people in his area. Drew acclaim with his book *Life in a Railway Factory.* Died at age 53 of heart failure in South Marston, Wiltshire.

Last Words: "My dear! This is going to be a tragedy for us both." Spoken to his dying wife Mary. She died of cancer a few weeks later.

Source: *Alfred Williams: His Life & Work* by Leonard Clark (Oxford, England, 1945).

Williams, Charles Walter Stansby

(1886-1945) British poet, novelist, theologian, literary critic, educator. Lectured at

Oxford. Notable novels: *War in Heaven; Descent into Hell; All Hallows' Eve*. Notable criticisms: *The English Poetic Mind; Reason and Beauty in the Poetic Mind*. Died at age 58 at Oxford, England.

Last Words: "Will you say a Mass for anyone I have ever loved in any way?" Spoken to a friend who was an Anglican priest.

Source: *Charles Williams: An Exploration of His Life and Work* by Alice Mary Hadfield (Oxford, England, 1983). Hadfield's husband Charles was a colleague of Williams at Oxford.

Williams, Daniel Hale

(1856-1931) American surgeon, cardiologist. African-American physician who performed the first successful open-heart surgery. Founded Provident Hospital in Chicago, the first non-segregated hospital in the United States. Had a series of debilitating strokes. Died at age 75 in Idlewild, Michigan.

Last Words: "Take me to Idlewild." Spoken to his niece. He was referring to the town of Idlewild where his home was.

Source: *Doctor Dan* by Helen Buckler (Boston, 1954).

Williams, Edward Bennett

(1920-1988) American lawyer. Professional athletic team owner. Owned Baltimore Orioles, Washington Redskins. Represented many famous clients, including Jimmy Hoffa and Frank Sinatra. Died at age 68 of cancer in Washington, D.C. The E.B. Williams Law Library at Georgetown University was named for him.

Last Words: "Do I have to keep fighting? Can I quit?" Spoken to his physician.

Source: *The Man to See: Edward Bennett Williams* by Evan Thomas (New York, 1991).

Williams, Egbert Austin ("Bert")

(1874-1922) Bahamian-born American singer, dancer, comedian. Vaudeville performer with partner George Walker beginning in 1893. Did a solo act after Walker died in 1911. Performed with Ziegfeld Follies. Made about 80 recordings. Notable performance: "Nobody" (song). Collapsed while performing in Detroit. Died at age 47 of pneumonia in New York City.

Last Words: "Eighty percent better." Response to his physician who asked: "How do you feel?"

Source: *Introducing Bert Williams: Burnt Cork, Broadway, and the Story of America's First Black Star* by Camille F. Forbes (New York, 2008).

Williams, Eleazer

(1788?-1858) Canadian-born American clergyman. Episcopal missionary to Native Americans. Raised by Native Americans. Claimed to be the Lost Dauphin—Louis XVII, son of Louis XVI and Marie Antoinette of France. In 1841, Prince de Joinville spent time with him and decided Williams was the Dauphin. After Williams died on the St. Regis Indian Reservation at Hogansburg, New York, others came forward claiming they were the Lost Dauphin. Most likely the real Dauphin died at age 10 in Temple Prison in France, two years after his parents were killed in the French Revolution. The physician who performed an autopsy on the imprisoned child preserved his heart. In the year 2000, DNA tests on the heart and Marie Antoinette's hair confirmed that the heart came from a relative of Marie Antoinette and her family. (See also Louis XVII, King of France.)

Last Words: "Lord Jesus Christ have mercy on me, and receive my spirit."

Source: "Death of the Rev. Eleazer Williams, the Pretended Dauphin of France" (*New York Times*, September 4, 1858).

Williams, Frederick Jerome

(1972-2004) Liberian-born American deacon. Taser victim. His death at age 31 was captured on a 21-minute videotape by the Gwinnett County, Georgia, Sheriff's Department. Williams was struck with a Taser five times in 43 seconds, just four minutes after being led into the Gwinnett County police station. No charges were filed in his death. Controversial autopsy results stated he died of brain damage caused by a heart attack; there was no evidence the Taser directly caused his death.

Last Words: "I can't breathe. I can't breathe. Don't kill me, man. Don't kill me. I have a family to support. I've calmed down."

Source: Gwinnett County Sheriff's Office Video Recording, Gwinnett County, Georgia, May 25, 2004.

Variation: "Please don't kill me!"

Source: Williams family attorney Melvin Johnson reported to the *Atlanta Journal Constitution* that these were his Last Words.

Williams, Henry Horace

(1858-1940) American philosopher, theologian, philanthropist, educator. Popular professor of philosophy and theology at the University of North Carolina from 1890 to 1940. Died at age 82. Bequeathed his house, land and property to the university. Part of the land became Horace Williams Airport.

Last Words: "Horace Williams." His response when a nurse asked his name.

Source: *Horace Williams: Gadfly of Chapel Hill* by Robert Watson Winston (Chapel Hill, NC, 1942).

Williams, Hiram King ("Hank")

(1923-1953) American musician, country singer, songwriter, guitarist. Notable recordings: "Cold, Cold Heart"; "Hey Good Lookin'"; "Your Cheatin' Heart." Member of Rock and Roll Hall of Fame, Country Music Hall of Fame. Died at age 29 in his baby blue Cadillac on a road trip to Canton, Ohio. He was found dead when Charles Carr, a college student who was his chauffeur, stopped at a service station in Oak Hill, West Virginia.

Last Words: "No, I just want to get some sleep." Spoken to Carr who said he didn't know if this was the last thing he said. It's the last thing he could remember Williams telling him.

Source: *Rockin' Down the Highway: The Cars and People That Made Rock Roll* by Paul Grushkin (St. Paul, MN, 2006).

Williams, James

(1740-1780) American pioneer, military officer. Colonel in South Carolina militia. Killed in action at the Battle of King's Mountain during the American Revolution. He lived long enough to learn the British had been defeated in the battle.

Last Words: "I die contented since we have gained the victory."

Source: *James Williams, an American Patriot in the Carolina Backcountry* by William T. Graves (San Jose, CA, 2002).

Williams, John Sharp

(1854-1932) American lawyer, politician, cotton planter. Member U.S. House of Representatives and Senate from Mississippi. Died at age 78 at his plantation, Cedar Grove, near Yazoo City, Mississippi.

Last Words: "I've done things that seemed at the time worth doing. I think that if a man can get to my age and looking back, believe a majority of the things he did were worth the effort, he has nothing to regret."

Source: *John Sharp Williams* by George C. Osborn (Baton Rouge, LA, 1943).

Williams, Wendy Orlean

(1949-1998) American musician. Founder and lead singer for Punk band Plasmatics. Died at age 48 near her home in Storrs, Connecticut, from a self-inflicted gunshot wound. Left suicide notes.

Last Words (written): "The act of taking my own life is not something I am doing without a lot of thought. I don't believe that people should take their own lives without deep and thoughtful reflection over a considerable period of time. I do believe strongly, however, that the right to do so is one of the most fundamental rights that anyone in a free society should have. For me much of the world makes no sense, but my feelings about what I am doing ring loud and clear to an inner ear and a place where there is no self, only calm. Love always, Wendy." One of her suicide notes.

Source: "Wendy O., We Hardly Know You. A Final Conversation with the Plasmatics Lead Singer" by Jayne Keedle (*Hartford Advocate,* December 5, 1998).

Williamson, John Lee ("Sonny Boy")

(1914-1948) American musician, harmonica player. Played harmonic, acoustic and Chicago blues. Made many recordings. Notable ones include: "Shake That Boogie"; "Sugar Mama Blues"; "Blue Bird Blues." He was badly beaten during a mugging on a street in the South Side of Chicago, Illinois, while on his way from a bar. He slipped into a coma and died at age 34.

Last Words: "O Lord have mercy."

Source: *Nothing But the Blues: An Illustrated Documentary* by Mike Leadbitter (London, 1971).

Willie, Robert Lee

(1953-1984) American convicted murderer, rapist. Executed by electrocution in Angola State Prison, Louisiana. One of the Death Row inmates featured in the book *Dead Man Walking: An Eyewitness Account of the Death Penalty in the United States* by Sister

Helen Prejean. Willie's Last Words were addressed to Elizabeth and Vernon Harvey, the parents of Faith Hathaway, one of his victims.

Last Words: "I would just like to say, Mr. and Mrs. Harvey, that I hope you get some relief from my death. Killing people is wrong. That's why you've put me to death. It makes no difference whether it's citizens, countries, or government, killing is wrong."

Sources: *Death Watch: A Death Penalty Anthology* by Lane Nelson and Burk Foster (Upper Saddle River, NJ, 2001); *Angolite* by Louisiana State Penitentiary, Vol. 25-26 (Angola, LA, 2000).

Willkie, Wendell Lewis

(1892-1944) American lawyer, politician, business executive. Candidate for U.S. President. Died at age 52 of a heart attack while hospitalized for a throat infection in New York City.

Last Words (written): "I enjoyed our talk this morning very much. Frankly, I cannot answer your ultimate question [whom he would support] yet because I have not fully decided."

Source: *Willkie: The Events He Was Part Of, The Ideals He Fought For* by Joseph Barnes (New York, 1952).

Last Words (spoken): "Okay if you make it warm." Spoken to his nurse who asked if he would like scotch and water after he told her he couldn't talk with the cotton swab she put in his mouth.

Source: *Wendell Willkie: Fighter for Freedom* by Ellsworth Barnard (Marquette, MI, 1966).

Wills, James Robert ("Bob")

(1905-1975) American musician, songwriter, bandleader. Influenced what became known as The Bakersfield Sound. Led his band, the Texas Playboys, and appeared in numerous movies with them. Inducted into Country Music Hall of Fame, Rock and Roll Hall of Fame. Died at age 70 in Fort Worth, Texas. Received posthumous Grammy Lifetime Achievement Award in 2007.

Last Words: "Roll me down." Spoken to his wife Betty while he was watching television.

Source: *San Antonio Rose: The Life and Music of Bob Wills* by Charles Townsend (Urbana, IL, 1986).

Wilmore, Nancy Cass ("Auntie Wilmore")

(1769-1885) American supercentenarian. Reputed to be the oldest woman in the United States when she died at age 116. Born in North Carolina. Died in Wilmington, Illinois.

Last Words: "Not my will but Thine be done."

Source: "One Hundred and Sixteen. Death of the Oldest Woman in the State of Illinois" (*New York Times*, February 16, 1885).

Wilmot, John, 2nd Earl of Rochester

(1647-1680) English nobleman, poet, courtier. Known as the Wicked Earl. Led profligate life. Banished from court for lampooning Charles II. Died repentant at age 33 in Woodstock, Oxfordshire, England. He confessed the evils of his past life to Scottish bishop and historian Gilbert Burnet. The bishop helped Wilmot forsake his former life and accept religion. Charlotte Brontë patterned Edward Fairfax Rochester in *Jane Eyre* on Wilmot. The movie *The Libertine* (2004) is based on his life.

Last Words: "Has my friend [Gilbert Burnet] left me? Then I shall die shortly."

Source: *Some Passages of the Life and Death of John Earl of Rochester* by Gilbert Burnet (London, 1680). Burnet wrote the book based on interviews he had with Wilmot on his deathbed. By 1848 this biography had gone through ten editions.

Wilson, Alexander

(1766-1813) Scottish-born American poet, ornithologist, naturalist, illustrator. Moved to America in 1794. Notable work: *American Ornithology* (9 vol.). Several species of birds were named for him, including Wilson's Plover, Wilson's Phalarope, Wilson's Warbler, Wilson's Stormy Petrel.

Last Words: "Bury me where the birds will sing over my grave."

Source: *The Last Words (Real and Traditional) of Distinguished Men and Women Collected from Various Sources* by Frederic Rowland Marvin (New York, 1901). Marvin said Wilson's Last Words were not recorded. Just before he died he asked to be buried where the birds might sing over his grave.

Wilson, Edward Adrian

(1872-1912) English physician, polar explorer, naturalist, ornithologist. Participated in two polar expeditions: Discovery and Terra Nova. Was one of five men who reached the South Pole, January 17, 1912, on the Scott expedition. All five died of starvation or the cold on the return trip. Cape Wilson, Wilson Piedmont Glacier and Wilson Hills were named for him.

Last Words (written): "God knows I am sorry to be the cause of sorrow to anyone in the world, but everyone must die, and at every death there must be some sorrow. All the things I had hoped to do with you after this Expedition are as nothing now, but there are greater things for us to do in the world to come. My only regret is leaving you to struggle through your life alone, but I may be coming to you by a quicker way. I feel so happy now in having got time to write to you. One of my notes will surely reach you. Dad's little compass and Mother's little comb and looking glass are in my pocket. Your little testament and prayer book will be in my hand or in my breast pocket when the end comes. All is well." Letter to his wife while on the ill-fated South Pole expedition that was later found by a search party.

Source: *Edward Wilson of the Antarctic. Naturalist and Friend* by George Seaver (New York, 1937).

Wilson, Ellen Louise Axson

(1860-1914) American First Lady. Wife of President Woodrow Wilson. First Lady for only 17 months. Died at age 54 of Bright's disease in the White House. She is credited with convincing the President to invite influential legislators to dinner at the White House. Was major social advocate for improving condition of slums.

Last Words: "Doctor, if I go away, promise me that you will take good care of my husband." Whispered to White House attending physician Dr. Cary T. Grayson, just before she lost consciousness.

Source: "Mrs. Wilson Dies in White House–'Take Good Care of My Husband,' Her Dying Request to Dr. Grayson" (*New York Times*, August 7, 1914).

Wilson, Jackie

(1934-1984) American musician. Rock and Roll singer. Had 24 Billboard Top 40 hits during his career. Suffered a stroke and collapsed while singing on stage in Cherry Hill, New Jersey, in September 1975. Sustained brain damage from oxygen deprivation. Went into a coma. Remained on life support

the rest of his life. Died at age 49, in January 1984, in Mount Holly, New Jersey.

Last Words: "My heart is crying, crying." He was singing "Lonely Teardrops" when he collapsed.

Source: *Notable Last Facts* by William B. Brahms (Haddonfield, NJ, 2005).

Wilson, Thomas Woodrow (Woodrow)

(1856-1924) 28th President of the U.S. American politician, educator, lawyer, diplomat. Governor of New Jersey. President of Princeton University. Professor at several colleges. Coached Wesleyan football team. First wife Ellen Louise Axson died in 1914. He married Edith Bolling Galt in 1915. Attended Peace Conference in Europe in 1919 to create League of Nations and shape Treaty of Versailles. Awarded Nobel Peace Prize. Stroke in October 1919 left him paralyzed. Spent final years in seclusion. Died at age 67 in Washington, D.C.

Last Word: "Edith." Whispered to his wife when she left the room temporarily. His last coherent words were spoken the previous Friday, when he said to his physician Dr. Cary T. Grayson: "I am a broken piece of machinery. When the machinery is broken–I am ready to go."

Source: "Grayson Describes Scene at Deathbed–War President, He Says, Grew Weaker and Weaker Until He Calmly Passed Away" (*New York Times*, February 4, 1924).

Windom, William

(1827-1891) American financier, statesman, politician. Early proponent of the gold standard. Member U.S. House of Representatives, Senate from Minnesota. U.S. secretary of treasury in Garfield and Harrison administrations. Great-grandfather of actor William Windom. Died at age 63 in New York City.

Last Words: "As poison in the blood permeates arteries, veins, nerves, brain, and heart, and speedily brings paralysis or death, so does a debased or fluctuating currency permeate all arteries of trade, paralyze all kinds of business, and bring disaster to all classes of people. It is as impossible for commerce to flourish with such an instrument as it is for the human body to grow strong and vigorous with a deadly poison lurking in the blood." Spoken a moment before he died.

Source: "Windom's Dying Words" (*New York Times*, July 1, 1891).

Windsor, Duchess of
(1896-1986) American-born socialite. Full name Bessie Wallis Warfield Spencer Simpson. King Edward VIII abdicated in 1936 and married her when her divorce became final. After the duke—whom she called David—died in 1972, the increasingly senile duchess became a recluse. Died at age 89 in Paris.

Last Words: "Look at the way the sun is lighting the trees! You can see so many colors. Tell David to come in. He wouldn't want to miss this."

Source: *The Duchess of Windsor* by Charles Higham (New York, 1988).

Winne, George, Jr.
(1947-1970) American college student, war protester. Self-immolator. Protested the Vietnam War by setting himself on fire in an act of self-immolation on Revelle Plaza at the University of California, San Diego. Former member of ROTC. Was scheduled to graduate the following month with a degree in history. A memorial to him was placed in a grove of tree, east of the campus library.

Last Words: "I believe in God and the hereafter and I will see you there."

Source: "San Diego Student Who Set Self Afire in War Protest Dies" by H. Keen (*Los Angeles Times,* May 12, 1970).

Winthrop, Frederick
(1838?-1865) American military officer. Brevet brigadier general in Union Army in U.S. Civil War. First Brigade, Ayers' Division. Shot in the chest. On the way to the field hospital, he asked if the attack succeeded. Then he told the doctor he was done for. Died at age 27 at Five Forks, Virginia.

Last Words: "Straighten the line."

Source: *"Little Phil" and His Troopers: The Life of Gen. Philip H. Sheridan. Its Romance and Reality: How an Humble Lad Reached the Head of an Army* by Frank A. Burr and Richard Josiah Hinton (Providence, RI, 1888).

Winthrop, John
(1588-1649) English-born American Puritan leader. First governor of Massachusetts Bay Colony. Presided over the trial that banished Anne Hutchinson. Died at age 61 in Boston.

Last Words: "I have done too much of that work already." His response when asked to sign an order to banish a heretic.

Source: *The Rise of Religious Liberty in America: A History* by Sanford Cobb (New York, 1902).

Wirz, Henry
(1823-1865) Swiss-born American physician, military officer. Captain in Confederate Army in U.S. Civil War. Stockade commander at Andersonville prison camp. After the war, he was tried and convicted for conspiring to injure the health and destroy the lives of Federal prisoners at Andersonville. Hanged in the yard of the Old Capitol prison in Washington, D.C.

Last Words: "I go before my God—the Almighty God—He will judge between us. I am innocent, and I will die like a man." He then turned to Captain Walbridge and said: "Good-bye Captain. I thank you and the other officers of the prison, for you have all treated me well."

Source: "The Execution of Henry Wirz" (*Harper's Weekly,* Vol. IX, No. 465, November 25, 1865).

Wise, Isaac Mayer
(1819-1900) Bohemian-born American Reform Jewish rabbi. Established Union of American Hebrew Congregations, Central Conference of American Rabbis, Hebrew Union College. Died at age 80 in Cincinnati, OH.

Last Words: "Gut Shabbos!" (tr. "A good Sabbath!")

Source: *Isaac M. Wise: His Life, Work, and Thought* by James G. Heller (New York, 1965).

Wise, Stephen Samuel
(1874-1949) Hungarian-born American rabbi, social reformer. American leader of Zionist movement. President of Zionist Organization of America. President of American Jewish Congress. Founder of Free Synagogue of New York. Died at age 75 in New York City.

Last Words: "Take my hand, darlings, I am entering the Valley."

Source: *Rabbi and Minister: The Friendship of Stephen S. Wise and John Haynes Holmes* by Carl Hermann Voss (New York, 1964).

Wishart, George

(1513-1546) Scottish martyr. Convicted of heresy by a convocation of bishops led by the Archbishop of Saint Andrews, David Beaton (or Bethune). Executed at age 33 by burning at Saint Andrews, Scotland. Wishart's sympathizers sought revenge by killing Beaton two months later.

Last Words: "Come hither to me.—Lo, here is a token that I forgive thee. My heart, do thine office." Spoken as he kissed the executioner who asked for forgiveness.

Source: *Book of Martyrs and the Acts and Monuments of the Church* by John Fox (or Foxe). First published 1563, ed. by John Cumming (London, 1851).

Witt, Cornelius de,
see De Witt, Cornelius.

Witt, John de,
see De Witt, Jan, Johan or John.

Wittgenstein, Ludwig Josef Johann

(1889-1951) Austrian-born British philosopher, writer, educator. Professor at Cambridge. Brother of concert pianist Paul Wittgenstein. Notable works: *Tractatus Logico Philosophicus; Philosophical Investigations* (published posthumously). Moved into his doctor's house when he became ill. Died at age 62 of cancer in Cambridge, England.

Last Words: "Tell them I've had a wonderful life." Reported by his friend Norman Malcolm.

Source: "Wittgenstein: A Wonderful Life" by Tim Madigan (*Philosophy Now*, November/December, 2006).

Wolcot, John ("Peter Pindar")

(1738-1819) British satirist, poet, physician. Pen name Peter Pindar. Wrote witty satires on society, politics and people, especially George III. Notable works: *Lyric Odes to the Royal Academicians; Ode Upon Ode or a Peep at St. James's on New Year's Day.* Died at age 80 in London.

Last Words: "Bring me back my youth." His response when asked if anything could be done for him.

Sources: *Leben und Werke Peter Pindars* by Theodore Reitterer (Vienna, Austria, 1900); *Peter Pindar (John Wolcot)* by Robert L. Vales (New York, 1973).

Wolf, Hugo Philipp Jakob

(1860-1903) Austrian musician, composer, music critic in Vienna. Attacked Brahms; praised Wagner. Notable works include about 300 songs with piano accompaniment. Also wrote opera, incidental, orchestral, choral and chamber music. Syphilis caused mental instability. He was placed in an asylum in 1897 and released the following year. Became suicidal. Committed to a mental hospital for the remainder of his life. Gradually lost control of his mind and body. Died at age 42 in Vienna.

Last Words: "Loathsome music." His response to some of his work.

Source: *Hugo Wolf: A Biography* by Frank Walker (London, 1951).

Wolfe or Woulfe, Arthur,
Lord Kilwarden

(1739-1803) Irish jurist. Solicitor general for Ireland. Attorney general. Lord chief justice of the Kings Bench of Ireland. Made baron in 1798. Killed by a crowd during Robert Emmet's 1803 insurrection and attack on Dublin Castle. Dragged from his carriage and murdered.

Different Last Words:

(1) "Put me out of pain." Spoken as many pikes were thrust into him, nailing him to a door. This account was taken from a witness's diary and republished.

Source: *The Silence of Barbara Synge* by William John McCormack (Manchester, England, 2003).

(2) "Let no man perish in consequence of my death, but by the regular operation of the laws."

Source: *Curran and His Contemporaries* by Charles Phillips (Edinburgh, 1850).

Wolfe, Charles

(1791-1823) Irish clergyman, writer, poet. Notable work: "The Burial of Sir John Moore after Coruna" (included in The Harvard Classics.) Moore, a war hero, was killed near La Coruna, Spain, in 1809. Wolfe died at age 31 of tuberculosis.

Last Words: "Close this eye, the other is closed already; and now farewell!" Spoken to a relative who was standing near him. His friends had taken him to the seashore to die.

Source: *Remains of the Late Rev. Charles Wolfe* by Rev. John A. Russell (London, 1832).

Wolfe, James

(1727-1759) British military officer. General

who captured Quebec from the French in 1759 on the Plains of Abraham. Killed at age 32 during the battle. His victory made the subsequent British conquest of Canada possible. His last moments were depicted in the painting *The Death of General Wolfe* by Benjamin West.

Last Words: "Who run? Go one of you, my lads, with all speed to Colonel Burton, and tell him to march Webb's regiment down to the Saint Charles River, and cut off the retreat of the fugitives to the bridge. Now God be praised, I die happy." Spoken as he lay dying. When he asked "Who run?" he was responding to the shout of one of his men that the enemy was fleeing everywhere. After he spoke, he turned on his side and died.

Sources: *Life and Letters of James Wolfe* by Beckles Willson (New York, 1909); *An Historical Journal of the Campaigns in North-America* by Captain John Knox (London, 1769).

Wolfe, Thomas Clayton

(1900-1938) American novelist, short-story writer. Notable works: *Of Time and The River; Look Homeward Angel; You Can't Go Home Again.* Exploratory surgery revealed tubercular meningitis that had advanced too far for treatment. Died at age 37 a few days later in Baltimore, Maryland.

Last Words: "All right, Mabel, I'm coming." His response to his sister who had asked his name. He then lapsed into unconsciousness.

Source: *Thomas Wolfe: A Biography* by Elizabeth Nowell (Garden City, NY, 1960).

Wollstonecraft, Mary see
Godwin, Mary Wollstonecraft.

Wolsey, Thomas

(1475?-1530) English prelate, statesman. Government adviser. Cardinal who dominated the government of King Henry VIII from 1515 to 1529 and was Henry's chief adviser. Lord chancellor of England. Fell from grace when he opposed Henry's plan to divorce Catherine of Aragon. Arrested for high treason. Died on the way from York to London to stand trial. En route, his entourage stopped at the Augustinian Abbey at Leicester. Wolsey went to bed and never rose again. He told the monks he would be dead by 8 the next morning. As the clock struck eight, he expired.

Different Last Words:

(1) "Master Kingston, farewell! I can no more, but wish all things to have good success. My time draweth on fast. I may not tarry with you. And forget not, I pray you, what I have said and charged you withal, for when I am dead, ye shall peradventure, understand my words much better." Sir William Kingston was Keeper of the Tower. He was in charge of the prisoner.

Sources: *Cardinal Wolsey* by Mandell Creighton (London, 1888); *Life of Cardinal Wolsey* by George Cavendish (Chiswick, England, 1825).

(2) "I do assure you, I have often kneeled before the king, sometimes for three hours together to persuade him from his will and appetite, but could not prevail. And Master Kingston, had I but served God as diligently as I have served my king, He would not have given me over in my grey hairs. But this is the just reward that I must receive for my diligent pains and study, not regarding my service to God, but only to my prince."

Source: *Biographica Juridica: A Biographical Dictionary of the Judges of England From the Conquest to the Present Time, 1066-1870* by Edward Foss (London, 1870).

Wood, Frederick Charles

(1912?-1963) American murderer. Confessed to killing five people. Executed at Ossining (Sing Sing) prison, New York. Rebuffed attempts to have a stay of execution. He said he wanted to "ride the lightning" in the electric chair.

Last Words "Gents, this is an educational project. You are about to witness the damaging effect electricity has on wood." Spoken just before he was strapped into the chair.

Source: (*Time* magazine, March 29, 1963).

Wood, Grant

(1891-1942) American artist. Notable works: *American Gothic; Parson Weems' Fable; Spring in Town.* Taught painting at the University of Iowa. Died at age 50 of liver cancer at the university's hospital in Iowa City.

Last Word: "Nan." He spoke his sister's name. Nan Wood Graham was the model for the farmer's wife in *American Gothic.*

Source: *Artist in Iowa, a Life of Grant Wood* by Darrell Garwood (New York, 1944).

Wood, Sir Henry Joseph

(1869-1944) British musician, conductor, composer, organist. Conductor of the Promenade Concerts in London from 1895 until a few weeks before he died. Knighted in 1911. Notable works: *Fantasia on British Sea Songs* (played as the finale on the Last Night of the Prom); *Saint Dorothea* (oratorio). Died at age 75 in Hitchin, Hertfordshire, England.

Last Words: "I am not afraid to die."

Source: *Sir Henry Wood* by Reginald Pound (London, 1967).

Wooden, Timothy

(d. 1849) American settler. Perhaps the earliest white settler of Grafton, Wisconsin. His background is unknown. He claimed he grew up with the country. Known for his ability to survive without any visible means of support. Died during the 1849 cholera epidemic.

Last Words: "I ain't doin' anything else." His response to a friend who said to him: "Tim, I believe you are dying."

Source: *The Chronicles of Milwaukee: Being a Narrative History of the Town from Its Earliest Period to the Present* (Milwaukee, WI, 1860).

Woodhull, Nathaniel

(1722-1776) American military officer, politician. Member New York Provincial Congress. Revolutionary War general. Leader of Suffolk and Queens (New York) militia during the Battle of Long Island. Died at age 53 as a prisoner of war in New Utrecht, New York, of injuries sustained at Long Island. A city and a lake in New York were named for him.

Last Words: "Please supply the wants of the American prisoners from the provisions brought from my farm."

Source: *A Conspectus of American Biography: Being an Analytical Summary of American History and Biography, Containing also the Complete Indexes of the National Cyclopedia of American Biography* by George Derby (New York, 1906).

Woolf, Adeline Virginia

(1882-1941) English writer. Original surname: Stephen. Married English historian Leonard Sidney Woolf. Notable works: *Mrs. Dalloway; To the Lighthouse; Jacob's Room; A Room of One's Own*. Member of the Bloomsbury Group. Suffered from depression. Had a mental breakdown years earlier and feared it was recurring. Committed suicide at age 59 by drowning in a river.

Last Words (written): "Dearest, I feel certain I am going mad again. I feel we can't go through another of those terrible times. And I shan't recover this time. I begin to hear voices, and I can't concentrate. So I am doing what seems the best thing to do. You have given me the greatest possible happiness. You have been in every way all that anyone could be. I don't think two people could have been happier till this terrible disease came. I can't fight any longer. I know that I am spoiling your life, that without me you could work. And you will I know. You see I can't even write this properly. I can't read. What I want to say is I owe all the happiness of my life to you. You have been entirely patient with me and incredibly good. I want to say that everybody knows it. If anybody could have saved me it would have been you. Everything has gone from me but the certainty of your goodness. I can't go on spoiling your life any longer. I don't think two people could have been happier than we have been. V." Suicide note left on the mantel of the sitting room fireplace for her husband.

Sources: *Leave the Letters Till We're Dead: The Letters of Virginia Woolf*, Vol. VI, 1939-1941, ed. by Nigel Nicolson and Joanne Trautmann (London, 1980); *New York Times*, April 20, 1941.

Woollcott, Alexander Humphreys

(1887-1943) American journalist, critic, writer. Drama critic for *New York Times*. Compiled anthologies. Member of Algonquin Roundtable. Inspiration for Sheridan Whiteside, main character in *The Man Who Came to Dinner*, a play by Kaufman and Hart and later a movie. Died at age 56 in New York City while participating in *People's Platform*, radio program on the war in Europe.

Different Last Words:

(1) "Go back in there. Never mind me. Go back in there." Spoken at a radio broadcast.

Source: *Alexander Woollcott: His Life and His World* by Samuel Hopkins Adams (New York, 1945).

(2) "I am dying! Where are my tablets? Get

my glycerin tablets!"

Source: *Smart Aleck: The Wit, World, and Life of Alexander Woollcott* by Howard Teichmann (New York, 1976).

Woolman, John

(1720-1772) American abolitionist. Quaker. Traveled throughout American colonies preaching against slavery. Notable work: *Journal of John Woolman* (published posthumously). Fell ill with smallpox. Died at age 51 while visiting York, England.

Last Words (written): "I believe my being here is in the wisdom of Christ. I know not as to life or death." He was no longer able to speak.

Source: *John Woolman: American Quaker* by Janet Whitney (Boston, 1942).

Woolston, Thomas

(1670-1733) English deist, writer, freethinker. Author of *Discourses* (questioned miracles in the New Testament). His writings were determined to be blasphemous. He was tried at the Guildhall in London in 1729, found guilty, sentenced to a year in prison and given a stiff fine. Unable and unwilling to pay his fine, he remained in jail the rest of his life. Died at age 63.

Last Words: "This is a struggle which all men must go through, and which I bear not only patiently but with willingness." Spoken a few minutes before he died.

Source: *The Life of Mr. Woolston* attributed to Thomas Stackhouse (London, 1733).

Woolton, John

(1537?-1593/4) English prelate, writer. Known for his theological treatises. Notable works: *A Treatise of the Immortalitie of the Soule; Of the Conscience: A Discourse.* Bishop of Exeter. Suffered from asthma. Died at age 57 at Exeter Palace, Devon.

Last Words: "A bishop ought to die standing." He refused to die lying down.

Source: *The Christian Manual, or, Of The Life and Manners of True Christians* by John Woolton, ed. for the Parker Society (Cambridge, England, 1851).

Wordsworth, William

(1770-1850) English writer, poet. His writings reflected his interest in nature and a concern for ordinary people. Notable works: "Tintern Abbey"; "The Prelude"; "Imita-

tions of Immortality"; "Ode to Duty." Poet Laureate of England. Died at age 80 at Rydal Mount, Westmoreland, England.

Last Words: "God bless you! Is that you, Dora?" Daughter Dorothy (Dora) died three years earlier. His wife told him: "William, you are going to Dora." When a niece opened the curtains in his room, he spoke these words.

Source: *William Wordsworth: His Life, Works, and Influence* by George McLean Harper (New York, 1916).

Wotton, Sir Henry

(1568-1639) English writer, poet, educator, diplomat. Knighted in 1604. Provost of Eton. Ambassador to Venice. Friend of Earl of Essex, John Donne, Isaak Walton, John Milton. Notable works: *The Character of Some of the English Kings; The State of Christendom.* Author of the statement: "An ambassador is an honest man sent to lie abroad for his country." Became ill with fever. Died at age 71 in Eton.

Last Words: "I now see that I draw near to my harbour of death; that harbour that will secure me from all the future storms and waves of this restless world; and I praise God, I am willing to leave it, and expect a better; that world wherein dwelleth Righteousness, and I long for it."

Sources: *Walton's Lives of Dr. John Donne, Sir Henry Wotton, Mr. Richard Hooker, Mr. George Herbert, and Dr. Robert Sanderson* by Izaak Walton and Thomas Zouch (York, England, 1796); *The Life and Letters of Sir Henry Wotton* by Logan Pearsall Smith (Oxford, England, 1907).

Wright, Joseph

(1855-1930) English philologist, writer, educator. Wrote books on German, Gothic, Old English. Professor of comparative philology at Oxford. Tutor and influence on J.R.R. Tolkien. Notable work: edited *English Dialect Dictionary* (6 vol.). Died at age 75.

Last Words: "Dictionary."

Source: *The Story of Joseph Wright, Man and Scholar* by Elizabeth Mary Wright (London, 1932). The author was his wife and collaborator.

Wright, Orville

(1871-1948) American aviation pioneer. Co-inventor and builder with brother Wilbur of the first successful controllable airplane. Died at age 76 of a heart attack and complications of lung congestion in Dayton, Ohio. Last Words: "You had best let Carrie do that, Miss—she knows all my cranky little ways." Spoken to the nurse who began to prepare food for him. "Carrie" was Carrie Kaylor Grumbach who cared for his family many years.

Source: *Wilbur and Orville: A Biography of the Wright Brothers* by Fred Howard (New York, 1987).

Wright, Silas

(1795-1847) American politician, lawyer. Member of U.S. House of Representatives and Senate from New York. Member of New York State Senate. Governor of New York. Died at age 52 in Canton, New York. Last Words: He complained that a mustard plaster on his chest "was too severe to be borne." His wife removed it and went to another room to adjust it. She heard a noise, rushed to his room and found him dead.

Source: *The Life and Times of Silas Wright* by R.H. Gillet (Albany, NY, 1874).

Wu, John Baptist

(1925-2002) Chinese-born Roman Catholic prelate. Birth name Cheng-Chung. Fifth Bishop and Cardinal of Hong Kong. Died at age 77 of cancer at Queen Mary Hospital, Hong Kong. Last Words: "[May] God bless Catholics and the Church continue to develop" and "[May] Hong Kong overcome these difficult times and become more prosperous and stable." Spoken as two wishes.

Source: "Cardinal Wu's Dying Prayer for HK" (*South China Morning Post*, September 24, 2002).

Wuornos, Aileen

(1956-2002) American serial killer, prostitute. Murdered seven men in Florida. First woman to fit the FBI profile of female serial killer. Executed at age 46 by lethal injection in Florida State Prison. The movie *Monster* (2003) was based on her life. Last Words: "I'd just like to say I'm sailing with the Rock and I'll be back like Independence Day with Jesus, June 6, like the movie, big mothership and all, I'll be back."

Source: *Female Serial Killers: How and Why Women Become Monsters* by Peter Vronsky (New York, 2007).

Wyatt, Sir Thomas

(1520?-1554) English soldier. Son of poet and diplomat Thomas Wyatt. Known as Sir Thomas the Younger. Joined in an insurrection to prevent the marriage of Queen Mary and Philip of Spain in 1554. Executed for high treason. Mary's supporters hoped he would implicate Elizabeth in his conspiracy on the scaffold, but he did not. At the scaffold he made a speech accepting full responsibility for his acts and exonerating Elizabeth. Weston, his confessor, shouted out not to believe him for he had confessed otherwise before the council.

Different Last Words:

(1) "That which I said then I said, but that which I say now is true." Response to Weston.

Source: *A Chronicle at Large and Meere History of The Affayres of Englande and Kinges of the Same Deduced from the Creation of the Worlde Unto the First Habitation of Thys Island: And So By Contynuance Unto the First Yere of the Reigne of Our Most Deere and Souvreign Lady Queen Elizabeth* by Richard Grafton (London, 1569).

(2) "Then let every man beware how he taketh any thing in hand against the higher powers! Unless God be prosperable to his purpose, it will never take good effect or success, whereof you may now learn of me, and I pray God I may be the last example in this place, for that or any other life. And where it is said and noised abroad that I should accuse the lady Elizabeth and the lord Courtney, it is not so, good people, for I assure you neither they nor any other now yonder in hold was privy of my rising before I began, as I have declared no less to the queen's council, and that is most true."

Source: *The Annales, or, Generall Chronicle of England* by John Stow and Edmund Howes (London, 1615).

Wycherley, William

(1641-1716) English playwright. Restoration comic writer. Notable works: *The Plain Dealer; The Country Wife*. Credited with coining terms "nincompoop" and "happy-go-lucky." Wycherley was 74 when he married a young woman 11 days before he died. The evening before he died, he summoned her to his bedside and asked her not to deny him one last request:

Last Words: "My dear, it is only this, that you will never marry an old man again." The marriage was at the request of his cousin. Wycherley had inherited his father's estate but was forbidden to sell any of it. After he died, his cousin married his young widow and shared the inheritance.
Source: *William Wycherley*, ed. with intro and notes by W.C. Ward (London, 1896).

Wylie, Elinor Hoyt
(1885-1928) American poet, novelist. Full name Elinor Hoyt Hichborn Wylie Benet. Notable works: *Nets to Catch the Wind; Orphan Angel*. Suffered from high blood pressure. Had a mini stroke that caused slight facial paralysis. The next day a major stroke took her life. Died at age 43 in New York City.
Last Words: "Is that all it is?" She had asked for a drink of water. As her husband handed it to her, she spoke these words then fell back in a chair and died.
Source: *Elinor Wylie: The Portrait of an Unknown Lady* by Nancy Hoyt (Indianapolis, IN, 1935). The author was her sister.

Wythe, George
(1726-1806) American lawyer, jurist, politician. Represented Virginia at Continental Congress. Signer of Declaration of Independence from Virginia. Judge, Virginia High Court of Chancery. His grandnephew and namesake George Wythe Sweeney forged Wythe's signature on checks to cover mounting gambling debts. When Sweeney learned his crimes were about to be revealed, he is believed to have laced his uncle's coffee with arsenic. Wythe suffered for two weeks after ingesting the poison. He changed his will after he learned of Sweeney's forgeries. Wythe died at his home in Richmond at age 80. Sweeney was tried for murder. Lydia Broadnax, one of Wythe's black servants, witnessed Sweeney pouring a mysterious substance in the coffeepot, but Virginia law prohibited a slave from testifying against a white man. Sweeney was found not guilty. One version of this story states that Wythe left part of the family property to his slaves. Sweeney poisoned the slaves to enlarge his share. In doing so, he accidentally poisoned his grand-

uncle. Marshall-Wythe School of Law at William & Mary and a county and town in Virginia were named for Wythe.
Last Words: "Let me die righteous."
Source: *George Wythe: Teacher of Liberty* by Alonzo Thomas Dill (Williamsburg, VA, 1979).

Ximenez de Cisneros, Francisco
(1436-1517) Spanish prelate, Inquisitor general. Confessor to Queen Isabella of Castile. Archbishop of Toledo. Elevated to cardinal in 1500.
Last Words: "In Thee, O Lord, have I trusted." He spoke a prayer from the Psalms.
Source: *Grand Inquisitor: Being an Account of Cardinal Ximenez De Cisneros and His Times* by Walter Starkie (London, 1940).

Yamashita, Tomoyuki
(1885-1946) Japanese military officer. General. Known as the Tiger of Malaya. Commanded forces in Japanese Malayan campaign during World War II. Received surrender of Singapore in 1942. Took command of Japanese forces in the Philippines in 1944. Surrendered in 1945. Tried for war crimes, sentenced to death by hanging. Executed at age 60 near Los Banos, Philippines.
Last Words: "I will pray for the Japanese emperor and the emperor's family, and national prosperity. Dear father and mother I am going to your side. Please educate my children well." Spoken just before he was executed after being asked if he had any Last Words.
Source: *Old Soldiers Sometimes Lie* by Richard Hoyt (New York, 2009).

Yancey, Robert Davis ("Cap'n Bob")
(1855-1931) American lawyer, politician. Mayor of Lynchburg, Virginia. In 1940, his daughter Rebecca Yancey Williams published the book *The Vanishing Virginian* about her father. It was made into a movie in 1942.
Last Words: "I will just lie here for a few minutes—I will stay here a little while, just to please you. Don't leave me, little lady. I love to watch your bright young face. Two things in this world I have always loved—a bright young face and walking in the sunshine.
Source: *The Vanishing Virginian. With an Introduction by Douglas Southall Freeman* by Rebecca Yancey

Williams (New York, 1940). Rebecca was his daughter.

Yancey, William Lowndes

(1814-1863) American lawyer, politician, cotton planter, secessionist. Known as the Fire-Eater. Member U.S. House of Representatives from Alabama. Member of Confederate Senate. Confederate commissioner to England and France. Died at age 48 of kidney disease at his plantation near Montgomery Alabama.

Last Words: "I am dying; all is well; it is God's will—Sarah." Spoken to his wife, Sarah Caroline Earle Yancey.

Source: *The Life and Times of William Lowndes Yancey* by John W. DuBose (Birmingham, AL, 1892).

Yeats, John Butler

(1839-1922) Irish painter, playwright, novelist. Father of painter Jack Butler Yeats and poet William Butler Yeats. Moved to New York City when he was 69. Died there at age 82.

Last Words: "Remember you have promised me a sitting in the morning." Spoken to a friend.

Source: *Scenes and Portraits: Memories of Childhood and Youth* by Van Wyck Brooks (New York, 1954). Brooks formed a friendship with Yeats during the years the artist lived in New York.

Yeats, William Butler

(1865-1939) Irish poet, playwright, essayist. Leader of the Irish Renaissance. Helped establish Abbey Theatre. Awarded Nobel Prize for Literature (1923). Notable works: *The Countess Kathleen; The Land of Heart's Desire* (plays); "The Second Coming"; "The Wild Swans at Coole" (poems). Died at age 73 in Roquebrune-Cap-Martin, France.

Last Words (written): "In two or three weeks—I am now idle that I may rest after writing much verse—I will begin to write my most fundamental thoughts and the arrangement of thought which I am convinced will complete my studies. I am happy and I think full of an energy I had despaired of. It seems to me that I have found what I wanted. When I try to put all into a phrase I say 'Man can embody truth but he cannot know it.' I must embody it in the completion of my life. The abstract is not life and everywhere drags out its contradictions. You can refute Hegel but not the Saint or the

Song of Sixpence." Letter to Lady Elizabeth Pelham, January 1939.

Source: *Yeats: The Man and the Masks* by Richard Ellmann (New York, 1948).

Yellow Wolf (Hemene Mox Mox)

(1856-1935) Native American warrior, writer. Nez Perce. Nephew of Chief Joseph. Helped record history of his people. Wrote his autobiography in which he described his youth, battles, savagery of whites and his life as a fugitive. Died at age 79 at Colville Indian Reservation in Washington.

Last Words: "I am going. My old friends have come for me! They are here! Do you not see them? There stands Eshawis, and there Peopee Howisthowit and Diskoskow. They have come to take me to Ahkunkenekoo."

Source: "Yellow Wolf, Loner in the Nez Perce War" (*Frontier Times*, April 1985).

Yesenin or Esenin, Sergei

(1895-1925) Russian poet. Had several wives and lovers, including American dancer Isadora Duncan, whom he married in 1922, and Sofia Tolstaia, a granddaughter of Leo Tolstoy whom he married in 1925. Had a volatile personality. Suffered from alcoholism and erratic behavior. Spent time in a hospital for a nervous breakdown. Committed suicide by hanging himself at age 30 in a Leningrad hotel. Before his death, he wrote his last poem with his blood: "Goodbye, my friend. Goodbye!" He gave it to a friend and asked him to read it later.

Last Words (written): "In this life there's nothing new in dying, But nor, of course, is living any newer." Last lines of his farewell.

Source: *Handbook of Russian Literature* by Victor Terras (New Haven, CT, 1985).

Young, Brigham

(1801-1877) American religious leader. missionary, colonizer. Left Methodists in 1832 and joined Mormon Church. When Mormons were displaced from their settlement, he led a party of 148 to the Great Salt Lake Valley. Pioneers Day in Utah commemorates his arrival at Great Salt Lake with his followers. First governor of Territory of Utah. Died at age 76 in Salt Lake City.

Different Last Words:

(1) "I feel better."

Source: *Brigham Young* by Morris Robert Werner (New York, 1925).

(2) "Amen." Spoken as he received the Last Rites of his church.

Source: *The Last Words (Real and Traditional) of Distinguished Men and Women Collected from Various Sources* by Frederic Rowland Marvin (New York, 1901).

(3) "Joseph, Joseph, Joseph!"

Source: *The Life Story of Brigham Young: Mormon Leader, Founder of Salt Lake City, and Builder of an Empire in the Uncharted Wastes of Western America* by Susa Young Gates and Leah D. Widtsoe (New York, 1930). Susa Young Gates was his daughter.

(4) "How is the new grandson?" Young's last grandchild, Mahonri Young, was born 20 days before he died. Legend has it that these were his Last Words.

Source: "Mahonri Macintosh Young (1877-1957) SLC, Utah/New York" (sma.sns.nebo.edu/young; Springville Museum of Art, Utah). [Accessed 9/09/2009]

Young, Francis Brett

(1884-1954) English novelist, poet. Notable works: *Deep Sea; Cold Harbour; The Island; The House Under the Water*. Health began to deteriorate when he had a serious heart attack in 1944. Relocated to Cape Town, South Africa. Died there at age 59.

Last Words: "Let me go now, darling. I can't go on suffering like this." Spoken to his wife Jessie.

Source: *Francis Brett Young* by Jessica Brett Young (London, 1962). The author was his wife.

Young, Van B.

(1836-1892) American jurist, politician, lawyer. Member of Kentucky legislature. Circuit clerk. Master commissioner in chancery. Presiding judge of Kentucky Superior Court. Died at age 55 in Frankfort, Kentucky.

Last Words: "Gentlemen, it becomes my painful duty, in view of the condition of my health and the fact I can no longer serve the commonwealth as I would desire to do, to hand you my resignation, which I ask you to accept." He died soon after uttering these words.

Source: *National Cyclopaedia of American Biography Being the History of the United States as Illustrated in the Lives of the Founders, Builders, and Defenders of the Republic and of the Men and Women Who are Doing the Work and Moulding the Thought of the Present Time* (New York, 1895).

Young, Whitney Moore, Jr.

(1921-1971) American civil rights leader, educator. Dean of School of Social Work at Atlanta University. Executive director of National Urban League. Adviser to Presidents Kennedy, Johnson and Nixon. Received US. Medal of Freedom. Notable works: *To Be Equal; Beyond Racism.* Drowned at age 49 in Lagos, Nigeria, while swimming off shore with friends. Died apparently of a cerebral hemorrhage.

Last Words: "This is great." Shouted to his friends as he plunged into the water.

Source: *Four Great Americans: Tributes Delivered by President Richard Nixon* by Richard Milhous Nixon (Garden City, NY, 1972).

Younger, Robert Ewing ("Bob")

(1853-1889) American criminal, outlaw. Brother of Cole, Jim and John Younger. Member James/Younger gang. Caught robbing a bank. Convicted, sentenced to life in prison. Died at age 35 of tuberculosis in prison in Stillwater, Minnesota.

Last Words: "Don't weep for me." Whispered to his sister Retta, who visited him when he was on his deathbed in prison.

Source: *Bloodletters and Badmen: A Narrative Encyclopedia of American Criminals from the Pilgrims to the Present* by Jay Robert Nash (New York, 1995).

Ysaye, Eugène

(1858-1931) Belgian musician, violinist, composer, conductor. One of the great violin virtuosos of his era. Composed concertos, sonatas. Conductor of Cincinnati Symphony. Died at age 72 in Brussels, Belgium.

Last Words: "Splendid. —the finale just a little too fast." Spoken after his *Fourth Sonata* was played for him.

Source: *Ysaye. His Life, Work and Influence* by Antoine Ysaye and Bertram Ratcliffe (London, 1947). Antoine Ysaye was his son.

Yüan Shih-k'ai

(1859-1916) Chinese leader, monarch, statesman, military officer. President of China. Dismissed National Assembly. Attempted to reinstate the monarchy. Held the title of Emperor of China briefly in 1916. Faced strong opposition from several provinces. Abandoned monarchism in March 1916. Died three months later at age 56. Some reports circulated that he had been poisoned. Others gave the cause of his death as uremia.

Last Word: "Misled."

Source: "'Hands Off' in China Is Policy of Japan. Cabinet Meets Following Death of Yuan, But No Action Is Planned at Present" (*New York Times*, June 8, 1916).

Zaharias, Mildred Ella Didrikson ("Babe")

(1911-1956) American athlete. Most prominent female golfer of her era. Also excelled in baseball, softball, diving, bowling, basketball and more. Won gold medals in 1932 Olympics for track and field. Died at age 45 of cancer in Galveston, Texas.

Last Words: She discussed business details with her husband George: "Get this settled and get that settled and sign these papers and that paper." Finally, she said she had to conserve her energy. So she whispered. Then she stopped talking and was gone.

Source: *Babe: The Life and Legend of Babe Didrikson Zaharias* by Susan E. Cayleff (Urbana, IL, 1996).

Zahir ud-Din Muhammad, see Babar, Baber, or Babur.

Zangara, Giuseppe or Joseph

(1900-1933) Italian-born bricklayer, assassin. Attempted to assassinate U.S. President-elect Franklin Delano Roosevelt in Miami, Florida, in 1933. He missed Roosevelt but hit four spectators and Anton J. Cermak, mayor of Chicago. Cermak died from his wounds a short time later. Zangara pleaded guilty and was executed by electric chair two weeks later.

Last Words: "Goodbye. Adios to the world. Go ahead, push the button."

Source: *The Assassins* by Robert J. Donovan (New York, 1955).

Zeisberger, David

(1721-1808) Moravian missionary in America. Lived among Native Americans, especially the Munsee, from 1745 until he died at age 87 in Ohio.

Last Words: "The Savior is near! Perhaps he will soon call and take me home."

Source: *The Life and Times of David Zeisberger* by Edmund de Schweinitz (Philadelphia, 1870).

Zeitvogel, Richard

(1956?-1996) American murderer, rapist. Spent 22 of his 40 years in Missouri prisons.

Originally sent to jail for rape and armed criminal action. Executed for murder. The two murders he committed both occurred in prison. He killed his cellmate while serving a life sentence for killing another inmate.

Last Words: "Keep the faith and rock on!"

Source: *Last Suppers: Famous Final Meals from Death Row* by Ty Treadwell and Michael Vernon (Port Townsend, WA, 2001).

Zeno of Citium

(late 4th - early 3rd century B.C.) Greek philosopher. Born in Citium, Cyprus. Founded Stoic School of Philosophy. Taught in Athens more than fifty years.

Last Words: "I come, I come, why dost thou call for me?" Spoken as he struck the ground with his hand when he tripped.

Source: *The Lives and Opinions of Eminent Philosophers,* Book VII, by Diogenes Laërtius, tr. C.D. Yonge (London, 1853).

Zenzaburo, Taki

(1935?-1868) Japanese military officer. Gave the order to fire on the foreign settlement at Kobe in February 1868. Ordered by Mikado to commit hara-kiri. Ritual suicide took place in a temple. Witnesses were present from each of the foreign legations. Zenzaburo's death was the first Japanese ritual suicide witnessed by foreigners. Until then, hara-kiri had been looked upon as a traveler's myth.

Last Words: "I, and I alone, unwarrantably gave the order to fire on the foreigners at Kobe, and again as they tried to escape. For this crime I disembowel myself, and I beg you who are present to do me the honor of witnessing the act."

Source: *Tales of Old Japan* by Algernon Bertram Freeman-Mitford (Lord Redesdale) (London, 1919). Mitford wrote *Tales of Old Japan* in 1871, while he was assigned to Japan as Second Secretary to the British Legation.

Zeppelin, Count Ferdinand Adolf August Heinrich von

(1838-1917) German soldier, airship builder. Count. Fought in U.S. Civil War with Union Army in 1863. Also served in Franco-Prussian and Austro-Prussian wars. Inventor of rigid airship or dirigible. Built first airship, *Zeppelin*, in 1900. Died at age 78 in Charlottenburg, Germany of pneumonia following intestinal surgery.

Last Words: "I have perfect faith."

Source: *Zeppelin: A Biography* by Margaret Goldsmith (New York, 1931).

Zhou Enlai (Chou En-lai)

(1898-1976) Chinese leader, statesman. Lived in France, Germany and Britain from 1920 to 1924. Became Communist organizer. Commissar of Red Army during the Long March. First premier of People's Republic of China. First foreign minister. Helped arrange and implement Richard Nixon's visit to China in 1972. Died at age 77 in Beijing.

Last Words: "Little Chao, there are so many things, so many things that I have not told you, and now it is too late."

Source: *Eldest Son: Zhou Enlai and the Making of Modern China* by Han Suyin (New York, 1994).

Ziegfeld, Florenz ("Flo")

(1867-1932) American theatrical producer, impresario. Introduced the musical revue featuring fantastic sets and beautiful women with *The Follies of 1907*. Produced more than 20 *Follies*. Notable shows: *Sally* (with Marilyn Maxwell)*; Rio Rita; Show Boat; Bitter Sweet*. Died at age 65 of pleurisy in Hollywood, California. Movies about his career include *The Great Ziegfeld* (1936); *Ziegfeld Follies* (1945); and *Ziegfeld: The Man and His Women* (1978).

Last Words: "Curtain! Fast music! Lights! Ready for the last finale! Great! The show looks good. The show looks good!" He died delirious, imagining he was directing a show.

Source: *The World of Flo Ziegfeld* by Randolph Carter (New York, 1974).

Zimmermann, Johann Georg, Ritter von

(1728-1795) Swiss physician, writer. Wrote a book on solitude that was translated into many European languages. Appointed to the Court of Hanover in 1768 as physician to George III. Attended Frederick the Great during his final illness then wrote several books about him that were critical of the monarch. Died at age 66 in Hanover.

Last Words: "I am dying: Leave me alone."

Source: "The Character of Zimmermann" by Rev. E.H. Sears and Rev. Rufus Ellis (*Monthly Religious Magazine*, Vol. XXXVI, No. 4, October 1866).

Variation: "Leave me to myself. I am dying."

Source: *Vie de Zimmermann* by M. Tissot (Lausanne, Switzerland, 1797).

Zinzendorf, Count Nicolaus Ludwig von

(1700-1760) German nobleman, religious leader. Count and Lord of Zinzendorf and Pottendorf. Took interest in a persecuted Bohemian brethren sect. Reorganized them as Moravian Brethren (Renewed Church of the United Brethren.) Banished from Saxony. Spent two years in America establishing Moravian congregations in several Pennsylvania towns. Lived in England several years. When his Saxony banishment was repealed, he returned to his estate at Herrnhut, Germany, where he died at age 59.

Last Words: "Now my dear son, I am going to the Saviour, I am ready, I am quite resigned to the will of my Lord, and He is satisfied with me. If he is no longer willing to make use of me here, I am quite ready to go to Him; for there is nothing more in my way." Spoken to his son-in-law who was at his bedside.

Source: *Life of Nicholas Lewis Count Zinzendorf* by Rev. August Gottlieb Spangenberg (London, 1838). The author was Zinzendorf's assistant.

Zizka, Jan

(1360?-1424) Bohemian military officer. General, Hussite leader. Full name Zizka von Trocnow. (Zizka means one-eyed; he lost an eye as a child.) Refused to accept Holy Roman Emperor Sigismund as king of Bohemia. Fought and liberated the entire country. He entered Prague in June 1424. Died of bubonic plague later that year.

Last Words: "Make my skin into drumheads for the Bohemian cause."

Sources: *Dictionary of Phrase and Fable* by E. Cobham Brewer (Philadelphia, 1898); *Last Words: Variations on a Theme in Cultural History* by Karl Siegfried Guthke (Princeton, NJ, 1992).

Zola, Émile

(1840-1902) French, writer, novelist, political activist. Notable works: *Nana; Thérèse Raquin; Les Rougon-Macquart*. Involved in the Dreyfus case; was convinced French Jewish army officer Captain Alfred Dreyfus had been wrongly convicted of treason. In

1898, Zola wrote an open letter to a newspaper ("J'accuse") accusing the French government of anti-Semitism and of wrongfully imprisoning Dreyfus. Zola was brought to trial for libel and convicted. He spent time in exile in England then returned to France after amnesty was granted. Died at age 62 under mysterious circumstances: accidental asphyxiation by carbon monoxide caused by a stopped-up chimney. Some of his enemies were suspected, but no one was charged. Biographical movie *The Life of Emile Zola* won an Academy Award for Best Picture in 1937.

Last Words: "I feel sick. My head is splitting—No, don't you see the dog is sick too. We are both ill. It must be something we have eaten. It will pass away. Let us not bother them."

Source: *Zola and His Time: The History of His Martial Career in Letters* by Matthew Josephson (New York, 1928).

Zook, Samuel Kosciuszko

(1821-1863) American military officer. Brigadier general in Union Army in U.S. Civil War. Fatally wounded at Gettysburg. Died at age 42.

Different Last Words:

(1) "Then I am satisfied and am ready to die." His response when told the enemy was routed.

Source: *A Conspectus of American Biography: Being an Analytical Summary of American History and Biography, Containing also the Complete Indexes of the National Cyclopedia of American Biography* by George Derby (New York, 1906).

(2) "If you can't get out of the way lie down, and we will march over you."

Source: *Civil War Quotations* by Darryl Lyman (Conshohocken, PA, 1995).

Zweig, Stefan

(1881-1942) Austrian-born Jewish biographer, novelist, librettist. Wrote biographies of Marie Antoinette, Magellan, Paul Verlaine, Balzac, Dickens, Erasmus and many more. Librettist for Richard Strauss. In the 1930s, he was forbidden by the Nazis from any further collaborating with Strauss. Fled Austria. Lived in London, New York, Brazil. Despairing over the future of their native land, Zweig and his wife Lotte committed suicide in Petropolis, Brazil, during World War II.

Last Words (written): "After I saw the country of my own language fall, and my spiritual land—Europe—destroying itself, and as I reach the age of sixty, it would require immense strength to reconstruct my life, and my energy is exhausted by long years of peregrination as one without a country. Therefore, I believe it is time to end a life which was dedicated only to spiritual work, considering human liberty and my own as the greatest wealth in the world. I leave an affectionate goodbye to all my friends." Suicide letter.

Source: *Twentieth Century Authors: A Biographical Dictionary of Modern Literature,* ed. by Stanley J. Kunitz and Howard Haycraft (New York, 1942).

Zwingli, Ulrich or Huldreich

(1484-1531) Swiss clergyman, reformer. Established Reformation in Zurich. Catholic cantons of Swiss Confederation united against him and sought help from Austria. Civil war began in 1529. Armies clashed at Kappel in 1531. Zwingli, as chaplain, accompanied Zurich troops into battle and was killed at age 47. His body was dismembered and burned and the ashes were scattered.

Last Words: "They can kill the body but not the soul." A memorial marks where he fell and is inscribed with what were reported to be his Last Words.

Source: *Huldreich Zwingli: The Reformer of German Switzerland* by Samuel Macauley Jackson (New York, 1903).

Select Annotated Bibliography

Aveline, Claude, *Les Mots de la fin.* Paris: Hachette, 1957. Claude Aveline is the pseudonym of French author Evgen Avtsine. The 326-page book has 750 names. Aveline placed 150 people he considered most important in a special section with an essay on each.

Baker, Osmon Cleander, *The Last Witness; Or, The Dying Sayings of Eminent Christians and of Noted Infidels.* New York, NY: Carlton & Phillips, 1853. Baker was a bishop of the Methodist Episcopal Church. The 108-page book was published in subsequent editions.

Bartlett, John, edited by Emily Morison Beck, *Familiar Quotations A Collection of Passages, Phrases and Proverbs Traced to Their Sources in Ancient and Modern Literature.* Fifteenth and 125th Anniversary Edition. Boston. MA: Little Brown and Company, 1982. First edition was published in 1855. 1,540 pages. Index of authors. Index of subject matter. More than 22,500 quotations on many subjects. Authors appear chronologically in birth date order. Helpful for verifying a quote or Source.

Bega, *Last Words of Famous Men.* London: Williams & Norgate Ltd., 1930. Bega is the pseudonym of A. P. Codd. The 146-page book has 500 names, none belonging to the 20th century or later. The names are grouped by religious leaders, educators, statesmen, monarchs, etc. The 1930 edition was reissued in 1973 and 1977.

Birrell, Francis, and F.L. Lucas, *The Art of Dying, An Anthology.* London: Hogarth Press, 1930. 95 pages. The 272 names Birrell and Lucas chose are arranged chronologically from Jezebel (c. B.C. 843) to Mrs. Mary Emma Davidson (1930), who died saving a child from being run over by a truck in Liverpool. The year of death is given, but very little other information. The authors believed arranging entries by dates would throw some light on the changes that have occurred in human life through the centuries.

Bisbort, Alan, *Famous Last Words: Apt Observations, Pleas, Curses, Benedictions, Sour Notes, Bon Motes, and Insights from People on the Brink of Departure.* San Francisco, CA: Pomegranate Communications, Inc., 2001. About 105 names. Many are post-1955 entries. The 154-page book is divided into eight categories: Deathbed, Gallows, On the Job, etc. Last Words are not limited to the dying. And they may have been uttered by a fictional character such as Emma Bovary. The book has a Name Index and a Bibliography.

Bocock, John Paul, "The Value of Last Words." *Frank Leslie's Popular Magazine*, Vol. XXXVIII, July to December 1894. Bocock attempted to examine scientifically the likely importance, value and accuracy of reported Last Words. He noted that the Last Words of great men and women have been treasured for centuries as having more than casual value, but there seems to be good reason to believe their importance has been exaggerated. A neurologist known the world over for his research into brain lore answered at Bocock's request a number of questions intended to elicit the scientific view of the value of Last Words. Bocock gave dozens of examples and is among the first writers on Last Words to critically examine the context, origins, biases, background and likelihood of accuracy in many noted examples.

Brandreth, Gyles, *Famous Last Words and Tombstone Humor.* New York, NY: Sterling Publishing Co., Inc., 1989. Portions of this book were published in 1979 as *The Last Word.* About half of the 122-page book is devoted to "Last Words," arranged alphabetically from Abelard to Zola. A brief description follows the birth and death year. The other half of the book lists Tombstone Epitaphs. Brandreth places an emphasis on whimsical and ironic comments. The book has a Name Index.

Brewer, Ebenezer Cobham, *Dictionary of Phrase and Fable, Giving the Derivation, Source, or Origin of Common Phrases, Allusions, and Words that Have a Tale to Tell.* London: Cassell and Company, Limited; Philadelphia, PA: J.B. Lippincott, 1905. New Edition, Revised, Corrected and Enlarged. 1,440 pages. Includes a handwritten note from the 1894 Preface that mentions the first edition was published a quarter of a century earlier. Biographical information includes birth and death years, works of authors, artists and others along with years published, etc. No Sources. Few quotations.

Brownlee, William Craig, *Dying Testimony of Believers and Unbelievers.* New York, NY: American Tract Society, 1833, 28 pages. Brownlee claimed the information was collected from authentic Sources. It was intended to show that believers die with strength and happiness, while unbelievers face death with torment and terror. The book was printed at 150 Nassau Street, New York City and distributed by agents of the society in the principal cities and towns in the U.S. Le Comte said in his introduction that Brownlee drew profusely on the tract of the Puritan divine Thomas Brooks, whose *Apples of Gold for Young Men & Women, Or the Happiness of Being Good Betimes,* first published in 1657 had reached a 22nd edition in 1814.

Butler's Lives of the Saints (Alban Butler), also Herbert J. Thurston and Donald Attwater (Various editions and title versions). Initially compiled in the mid-18th century by Alban Butler, an English Roman Catholic priest and scholar. The first edition appeared between 1756 and 1759. A second revision, begun in the early 20th century by Herbert J. Thurston, S.J., was interrupted when he died. The revisions were taken over by English scholar and hagiographer Donald Attwater. This version was published in 1956. It has bibliographic accounts of more than 2,500 saints.

Chambers, Alexander, *The General Biographical Dictionary: Containing an Historical and Critical Account of the Lives and Writings of the Most Eminent Persons in Every Nation; Particularly the British and Irish; from the Earliest Accounts to the Present Time.* London: printed for J. Nichols, 1812-1817. Published in various editions and titles including *Chambers's Journal.* "Last Words of Great Men," which originally appeared in *Chambers's Journal,* was republished in *The Eclectic Magazine of Foreign Literature, Science, and Art* (Vol. LIX No. 3, May to August 1863). Last Words of nearly 50 people were given in a narrative article.

Clark, Davis W., editor, *Death-Bed Scenes or Dying With and Without Religion: Designed to Illustrate the Truth of Christianity.* New York, NY: Lane & Scott, 1852. Notable as an early work with many Last Words. Clark, a theological scholar, indicated his purpose in his title. The book is in two sections: (1) Dying Christians: Martyrs; Ministers of the Gospel; Christian Men; Christian Women; Christian Children and Youth; Dying Regrets of Wrongly Minded Professors; and (2) Dying Without Religion: The Dying Sinner; The Dying Backslider; The Dying Persecutor; The Dying Infidel; Insensibility in the Hour of Death. Some 222 people were included. Last Words (direct or indirect) were given for many of them.

Cobbin, Ingram, editor, *Dying Sayings of Eminent Christians, Especially Ministers of Various Denominations, Periods and Countries.* London: F. Westley & A.H. Davis, 1828. Names of the deceased are arranged in alphabetical order. Among the host of eminent saints listed: Bradford, Brainerd, Janeway, Fuller, Gill, Fletcher, and Ryland. A precursor to Clark with a similar theme.

Conrad, Barnaby, *Famous Last Words*. Garden City, NY: Doubleday & Company, Inc., 1961. Foreword by Clifton Fadiman. 208 pages. Names are listed alphabetically. Very similar in format to Le Comte but provides longer descriptions of people. No Sources.

Derby, George, *Conspectus of American Biography: Being an Analytical Summary of American History and Biography, Containing also the Complete Indexes of the National Cyclopaedia of American Biography*. New York, NY: J.T. White, 1906. This work was compiled after the completion of the initial edition of the *National Cyclopaedia* of *American Biography*. Derby extracted information from the thousands of biographical entries to produce a list of Last Words for more than 300 Americans.

Deslandes, André François Boureau, *Reflexion sur les grands hommes que sont morts en plaisantant*. Amsterdam: Aux dépens de la Compagnie, 1758. Published anonymously in French in Paris in 1712. Translated into English in London in 1713. Among the earliest works that treat Last Words.

de Verteuil, Joseph Donzé, *Derniers sentiments des plus illustres personages condamnés à mort*. Paris: 1775. A French work that focused on the last sentiments of condemned individuals. The author provided Last Words for many of the people he described in the book.

de Voragine, Jacobus (Archbishop of Genoa), *The Golden Legend or Lives of the Saints*. 1275, 1st English edition by William Caxton, 1483; edited by F.S. Ellis. Edinburgh: 1900. *The Golden Legend* (*Legenda Aurea* or *Legenda Sanctorum*) was initially entitled *Legenda Sanctorum (Readings of the Saints)* and was probably compiled in Latin around the year 1260. It became one of the most popular books of the late medieval period and into the Renaissance. It was one of the first books printed in the English language. The work is widely acknowledged as an embellished and fanciful hagiography, but it is nonetheless one of the few compilations of Last Words of saints who lived before the modern era. *The Golden Legend* drew upon two earlier hagiographies: Jean de Mailly's *Abbreviato in gestis miraculis sanctorum (Summary of the Deeds and Miracles of the Saints)* and Bartholomew of Trent's *Epilogum in gesta sanctorum (Afterword on the Deeds of the Saints)*.

Dobree, Samuel, compiler, *The Book of Death*. London: W. Bulmer and Co., 1819. Dobree compiled the sketches chiefly from material he found in Chambers's *Biographical Dictionary*. The book was for private circulation. Only 60 copies were printed. When a copy came up for auction on March 16, 1880, the *New York Times* reported that the title was enclosed in a wood-cut border composed of death's heads and shin-bones.

"Dying Words of Noted Persons," *Miscellaneous Notes and Queries with Answers in All Departments of Literature*. Vol. II, No. 32, February 1885. Provided 258 names over ten pages. Although it included no biographical background or other context, it did note that the collection has been the result of more than a quarter century, gathered from various Sources. Several persons were credited with different words, and some of them were noted for having uttered the words under different circumstances. The authors believed their collection was the largest ever published. The list was later reprinted in *The Encyclopedia of Death and Life in the Spirit-World* by John Reynolds Francis, Vol. I (Chicago: The Progressive Thinker Publishing House, 1895; 1906), under a section titled: "Dying Words of Distinguished Persons. The Result of More than a Quarter Century of Labor."

Egbert, Walter R., *Last Words of Famous Men and Women.* Norristown, PA: 1898. Le Comte pointed out that this book and Kaines' *Last Words of Eminent Persons* (1866) paved the way for Marvin's extensive compilation, *The Last Words (Real and Traditional) of Distinguished Men and Women* (1901).

Elder, Robert K., *Last Words of the Executed* with Foreword by Studs Terkel. Chicago: University of Chicago Press, 2010. 304 pages. An oral history of American capital punishment as heard from the gallows, the gurney and the electric chair. Names range from the famous—Nathan Hale, John Brown, Joe Hill, Ted Bundy—to the unknown.

English, Dave, *Slipping the Surly Bonds: Great Quotations on Flight.* New York, NY: McGraw-Hill, 1998. 231 pages. Unique collection of quotations written or spoken about flight. English is an airline pilot. Contents are grouped in sections such as: Air Power, Combat, Safety and Space. The Last Words are in the final section and are all sourced. Index.

English, Dave, *The Air Up There: More Great Quotations on Flight.* New York, NY: McGraw-Hill, 2003. 182 pages. Unique collection of quotations written or spoken about flight. English is an airline pilot. Contents are grouped in sections such as Ballooning, Skydiving, Piloting and Birds. The Last Words are in the final section and are all sourced. Index. The book is a sequel to *Slipping the Surly Bonds*.

Fogg, Walter, *One Thousand Sayings of History, Presented as Pictures in Prose.* New York, NY: Grosset & Dunlap, The Beacon Press, 1929. Actually the count is 1,137. Fogg included Last Words or almost Last Words for 74 people. Entries are enumerated. Each person is identified by profession, birth and death years and a brief biography. Four Indexes—Subjects, Names, Key Lines and Familiar Sayings—make it easy to navigate through the book's 919 pages.

Foote, George William and A.D. McLaren, *Infidel Death-Beds.* London: G.W. Foote and Co. Ltd., 1886. Foote attacked religious thought and preached free thinking. He was the first to give the dying free thinkers/nonbelievers a book of their own.

Forbes, Malcolm, with Jeff Bloch, *They Went That-A-Way: How the Famous and Infamous and the Great Died.* New York, NY: Simon and Schuster, 1988. Describes the deaths of 175 "famous, infamous and great people" but does not provide the Last Words for some of them. The book is not compilation of quotations. Rather, it is a study in how people "flamed out." Contents pages list names alphabetically. Index includes a person's birth and death day, month and year.

Fox(e), John, *Book of Martyrs and the Acts and Monuments of the Church.* An account of Christian martyrs throughout Western history. In chronicling their deaths, dozens of examples of Last Words are presented. Foxe began his work in 1552, He initially published in Latin and eventually in English in 1563. The last edition published in his lifetime was in 1583. He documented the deaths of Christian martyrs from the 1st to 16th centuries with an emphasis on English Protestants from the 14th to 15th centuries. Among those included: John Hus, John Wycliffe, William Tyndale, Lady Jane Grey and Martin Luther. Foxe's compilation of English martyrs, beginning with the mid 14th century, drew heavily on primary Sources including Episcopal registers, trial reports, and eyewitness testimony.

Fuld, Werner, *Lexikon der letzten Worte: letzte Botschaften berühmter Männer und Frauen von Konrad Adenauer bis Emiliano Zapata.* Munich, Germany: Piper Verlag GmbH, 2002. Names are arranged alphabetically. Index of names. Bibliography. Text is in German. 211 pages.

Green, Jonathon, compiler, *Famous Last Words.* London: Kyle Cathie Limited, 1997. First published in 1979. A later version came out in 1997 with some 2,000 names. None are sourced. The names are arranged in 18 categories such as the stature or profession of the speaker or the way he or she died. Index. Many black-and-white photographs.

Greene, Katherine and Richard, editors, *Frankly My Dear...The World's Greatest Comebacks, Snubs, Insults, One-Liners, and Last Words.* New York, NY: Fireside Book, published by Simon & Schuster, 1996. 163 pages. About a dozen Last Words are in one of the 16 sections.

Guthke, Karl S., *Last Words: Variation on a Theme in Cultural History.* Princeton, NJ: Princeton University Press, 1992. 252 pages. Guthke takes a playfully serious yet scholarly look at the history and cultural importance of Last Words, examining what they reveal about our thoughts on living and dying. The five chapters address issues such as Last Words in everyday culture; why the interest in them; whether they are authentic or fake; how they are used as entertainment; and do they have an intellectual history. All the information is well footnoted. Select Bibliography of Last Words and Index are included.

Hickman, Tom, *Death: A User's Guide.* New York, NY: Bantam Dell, Division of Random House, Inc., 2002. Index. 273 pages. Book is divided into several sections. The last one, "Not So Grim Reminders," has information on Last Words. Hickman offers some celebrated Last Words, but gives a number of reasons why you have to be suspicious about dying utterances of the famous.

Hom, Susan K., *R.I.P., Here Lie the Famous Last Words, Epitaphs, Morbid Musings & Fond Farewells of the Famous and Not-So-Famous.* New York, NY: Sterling Publishing Company, 2007. The 160-page book is grouped by: Epitaphs (cemetery wisdom); Musings (poking fun at death); and Farewells (Last Words). Index. Book is shaped like a tombstone.

Hough, Franklin B., *American Biographical Notes: Being Short Notices of Deceased Persons, Chiefly Those Not Included in Allen's or in Drake's Biographical Dictionaries Gathered From Many Sources and Arranged by Franklin B. Hough.* Albany, NY: Joel Munsell, 1875. 448 pages. Names are arranged alphabetically. Write-ups include the person's occupation, military career, college attended, age, place and cause of death. Hough was diligent about including dates. He compiled his work because he could not find needed basic biographical information about a distinguished citizen of Albany, New York.

Howie, John, *The Scots Worthies: Containing a Brief Historical Account of the Most Eminent Noblemen, Gentlemen, Ministers and Others, Who Testified or Suffered for the Cause of Reformation in Scotland: From the Beginning of the Sixteenth Century to the Year 1688.* Glasgow, Scotland: W.R. M'Phun, 1829. Mini-biographies of the great Christian reformers and Covenanters of 16th and 17th century Scotland. 672 pages.

Jacox, Francis, *At Nightfall and Midnight; Musings after Dark.* London: Hodder & Stoughton, 1873. A book about aspects of life (and death) after dark in 16 chapters and 466 pages. Final chapters focus 30 pages specifically on Last Words, including well over 50 examples. Jacox noted that "the Last Words of even the most insignificant people are held in remembrance by survivors. Those of memorable men are accounted ever memorable in world-wide literature." Jacox gave few Sources but when possible he did give quotes in the original language. He grouped his material by general categories (popes, painters, etc.) and then more specifically by individual people (Beethoven, Coke, Mirabeau,

Schiller, Talleyrand, etc.).

Kaines, Joseph, *Last Words of Eminent Persons, Comprising in the Majority of Instances, a Brief Account of Their Last Hours*. London: G. Routledge & Sons, 1866. Kaines was the first person to use "Last Words" in a book title without limiting its to a specific category. The 397-page book was the first to deal with the last hours of well-known people in professions other than religion and politics.

Kane, Joseph Nathan, *Facts About the Presidents: A Compilation of Biographical and Historical Information*. New York, NY: H.W. Wilson Co., 2009. Kane, one of the foremost reference book compilers of the 20th century, set out to systematically detail comparable facts on each President. Among the data he sought were the circumstances of their deaths and their Last Words. The first edition was published in 1959. Subsequent editions have followed.

Knapp, Andrew and William Baldwin, *The Newgate Calendar: Comprising Interesting Memoirs of the Most Notorious Characters Who Have Been Convicted of Outrages on the Laws of England Since the Commencement of the Eighteenth Century; with Occasional Anecdotes and Observations, Speeches, Confessions, and Last Exclamations of Sufferers*. Vol. I-VI. London: J. Robins & Co., 1824-1826. Began as monthly bulletin of executions produced by the keeper of Newgate Prison in London. The initial standard version was compiled in five volumes in 1774. Collections of execution accounts with details (including dozens of examples of Last Words) began to be published in the mid-18th century. Scholars have criticized the publication as being highly embellished and colored by references to social issues and contemporary events. Nevertheless, it was one of the top three or four books most often found in English homes from the mid-18th to mid-19th centuries. The 1824 edition—compiled by lawyers Andrew Knapp and William Baldwin—was later released under the title *The New Newgate Calendar*.

Latham, Edward, *Famous Sayings and Their Authors: A Collection of Historical Sayings in English, French, German, Greek, Italian, and Latin*. London: Swan Sonnenschein, 1906. Includes brief biographical background, historical context and the original language of the quotes. Although not specifically a book of final utterances, hundreds of examples are listed as Last Words. Latham cautioned the reader/researcher about the inherent doubtfulness of many sayings and pointed out three areas of concern: (1) slight or considerable inaccuracy of form; (2) inauthenticity, i.e., invention after the events to which they relate; and (3) attribution to a person other than the real author. He suggested readers be neither overly pessimistic toward historic sayings nor go to the other extreme and accept them all without question. Many persons listed have three or more sets of Last Words with no differentiation regarding their likely veracity.

Le Comte, Edward S., compiler, *Dictionary of Last Words*. New York, NY: Philosophical Library, 1955. With 1,664 quotations, the 267-page book was the largest work on the subject when it appeared in 1955 and it was the only book that documented every Source. It was also the first book on Last Words to be printed in the U.S. since Frederic Rowland Marvin's *The Last Words (Real and Traditional) of Distinguished Men and Women. Collected from Various Sources,* published in 1901. Le Comte arranged his Last Words quotes alphabetically by speakers. For the most part, he made no attempt to identify the person. When he did, he provided minimal information; for example: "bishop of London," "Puritan divine," "adventurer." Also, he gave no birth or death dates. He placed all his Sources in a special section at the back of the book. If the Source was a biography in English of the person quoted and the name appeared in the main title in some form, Le Comte did not give the title. He felt the author, city and year of publication were sufficient identification. He was right. Finding his Sources is a cinch with today's electronic search engines.

Lewin, Thomas H., *Life and Death, Being an Authentic Account of the Deaths of One Hundred Celebrated Men and Women.* London: Constable and Co., Ltd., 1910. Pro-Christian. Chronologically arranged; starts with figures from antiquity. Portraits are included.

Lockyer, Herbert, *Last Words of Saints and Sinners: 700 Final Quotes from the Famous, the Infamous, and the Inspiring Figures of History.* Grand Rapids, MI: Kregel Publications, 1969. 240 pages. Includes 700 quotes. Several Sources are named, but it is not easy to tie names to some of them. In the chapter "Farewells at Death" Lockyer said he had at his disposal a quantity of "cuttings from papers and magazines filed away through the years." In the chapter "Records of Dying Words," most of the people were Puritans, children, or unknown folks from Shropshire.

Machamer, Gene, *The Illustrated Final Farewells.* Mechanicsville, PA: Carlisle Press, 1998. 147 pages. Every name is accompanied by the person's Last Words and an illustration of the person's head drawn by biographer/illustrator/cartoonist Machamer. Birth and death years and occupation are given.

Marvin, Frederic Rowland, *The Last Words (Real and Traditional) of Distinguished Men and Women. Collected from Various Sources.* New York, NY: Fleming H. Revell Company, 1901. 336 pages (The 1902 edition has 354 pages). Marvin included 600 names arranged alphabetically. Le Comte described the book as an "impressive piece of work," but regretted that a discouraging number of Marvin's quotations could not be pinned down. The book has no Introduction or Preface. But it does have an alphabetical Index of Last Words.

Michaud, Joseph Fr. and Louis Gabriel Michaud, *Biographie universelle ancienne et moderne, ou, Histoire par ordre alphabétique: De la vie publique et privée et tous les hommes qui se sont fait remarquer par leurs écrits, leurs actions leurs talents, leurs vertue ou leurs crimes. Ouvrage entiérement neuf, redige par une Societe des gens de lettres et de savants.* Paris: Various publishers (1811-1862), including Michaud Fréres and A.T. Desplaces. Published in 85 volumes as a universal biographical dictionary, representing all times and places, but there is an emphasis on French nationals. When published, it was recognized as a triumph for the scholarly nature of its signed and often lengthy articles, prepared by some 300 contributors. Within the thousands of entries are hundreds of direct and indirect Last Words.

Moore, Virginia, *Ho for Heaven! Man's Changing Attitude Toward Dying.* New York, NY: 1946. The 200 names that appear on 299 pages are mostly duplications of Birrell-Lucas. Moore endeavored to use Last Words as building blocks for a history of the human mind from earliest times to the present.

Nash, Jay Robert, *Bloodletters and Badmen: A Narrative Encyclopedia of American Criminals from the Pilgrims to the Present.* New York, NY: M. Evans and Company Inc., 1995. More than 500 entries on 698 pages. Index and Bibliography are included. Many black-and-white illustrations. Names are arranged alphabetically. Although not a Last Words compilation, it offers many final statements of criminals.

Nelson, Lane and Burk Foster, *Death Watch: A Death Penalty Anthology.* Upper Saddle River, NJ: Prentice Hall, 2001. A section of this book appeared in *The Angolite,* November/December 2000 & January/February 2001, as "Any Last Words?" The authors discuss the mental states and choices of words of people awaiting execution. They provide 61 examples from the 16th through 20th centuries that include names, dates and locations.

Most examples, particularly later ones, provide very complete context information and detail.

O'Kill, Brian, *Exit Lines: Famous (and Not-So-Infamous) Last Words.* Harlow, Essex: Longman Group Limited, 1986. 160 pages. Has Sources for each of the 100 quotes he uses. A Bibliography with Sources for unattributed statements in the text is included and gives recommendations for further reading.

Prochnik, Leon, *Endings: Death, Glorious, and Otherwise, As Faced by Ten Outstanding Figures of Our Time.* New York, NY: 1980. 214 pages. The ten: Freud, Houdini, Robert Falcon Scott, Isadora Duncan, Mussolini, Zelda Fitzgerald, James Forrestal, Mishima, Dylan Thomas, Malcolm X. Bibliography.

Radison, Garry, *Last Words: Dying in the Old West.* Austin, TX: Eakin Press, 2002. Companion book to *Last Words of the Civil War: The Moment of Sacrifice.* 253 pages. Last Words of more than 550 Old West personalities who died between 1773 and 1954. Bibliography. References and Index are included. All the quotes are sourced. Radison reminds his readers that the validity of Last Words is an open question. Most quotations were recorded by people who were present or near enough to receive the information by accurate reporting. But he points out that readers should retain some skepticism. Last Words are sometimes remembered differently by various people who were all near the dying person. Moreover, many memoirs were written long after the event when the mind may no longer have been reliable.

Radison, Garry, *Last Words of the Civil War: The Moment of Sacrifice.* Yorkton, SK: Smoke Ridge Books, 2001. Companion book to *Last Words: Dying in the Old West.* 208 pages. Last Words of 400 Civil War participants. Index, Bibliography/Reference. B&W illustrations. Contents are grouped chronologically. All quotes are sourced.

Robinson, Ray, compiler, *Famous Last Words: Fond Farewells, Deathbed Diatribes, and Exclamations Upon Expiration.* New York, NY: Workman Publishing, 2003. A pocket book, 3 ½" x 6 ¼". 177 pages. Each quote takes up at least a full page. Robinson said in the Introduction: "I've come to appreciate the difficulty of authenticating so-called exit lines, since witnesses are often too distraught or confused to remember things accurately or simply choose to edit or improve remarks for the sake of posterity." He gave George Gipp's words to Knute Rockne as an example.

Ruffin, C. Bernard, *Last Words: A Dictionary of Deathbed Quotations.* Jefferson, NC: McFarland & Company, Inc., Publishers, 1995. 260 pages. The 2,033 enumerated names are arranged alphabetically. Each has a brief biographical sketch and birth and death years. A Key Word Index is included. On the first page of the Sources, Ruffin notes that the letter [I] indicates the words in the text are reconstructed from an indirect quotation. About one third of the Last Words have Sources. No citations are given for quotations that are found in two or more Sources.

Shaw, Solomon Benjamin, *Dying Testimonies of Saved and Unsaved: Gathered from Authentic Sources.* Chicago: S.B. Shaw, 1898. Nearly 300 testimonies in 312 pages. The focus of the book is what is said on the deathbed by Christians and non-Christians. Hundreds of direct and indirect Last Words are provided.

Slater, Scott and Alec Solomita, *Exits: Stories of Dying Moments and Parting Words.* New York, NY: E.P. Dutton, 1980. More than 175 names on 145 pages. Sources are in the Bibliography. The authors say the book is primarily an entertainment: the emphasis is on people's attitudes toward the inevitable event rather than physical details or medical analyses.

Schmidt, Willibald, *De Ultimis Morientium Verbis.* Marburg, Germany: Marpurgi Catt. Schaaf, 1914. Greek and Roman examples ranging from Homer to the New Testament and beyond. 64 pages. Thesis/dissertation in manuscript.

Stephen, Sir Leslie, George Smith and Sir Sidney Lee, *Dictionary of National Biography from the Earliest Times to 1900.* London: Oxford University Press. This work is the British answer to other national biographical collections that had been published in Europe during the preceding decades. The first volume appeared in 1885, and publication of additional volumes and revisions has continued to the present time (entries now number more than 50,000 in the 2004 online version). The volumes that appeared quarterly—in alphabetical groups until midsummer 1900, when the initial series ended with 63 volumes—are particularly important. Within the nearly 30,000 initial entries of British subjects are many Last Words.

Stevenson, Burton E., *The Macmillan Book of Proverbs, Maxims, and Famous Phrases.* New York, NY: The Macmillan Company, 1948. Although there are hundreds of general quotation books, this work was singled out by Edward Le Comte for the large number of Last Words. It includes more than 100 Last Word entries–many more than typical quotation compilations.

Strauss, Maurice Benjamin, *Familiar Medical Quotations.* Boston: Little, Brown & Co., 1968. The book ties quotations to medicine and groups them by categories. The Last Words of more than 30 people are included along with dates, context and many Sources.

Thigpen, Paul, *Last Words, Final Thoughts of Catholic Saints & Sinners.* Cincinnati, OH: St. Anthony Messenger Press, 2006. 219 pages. Index of Names with Sources. The book's intent is spiritual. Rather than reciting Last Words, Thigpen seeks through categorization and commentary to uncover certain theological and moral truths reflected in the statements.

Ward, Laura, *Famous Last Words: The Ultimate Collection of Finales and Farewells.* London: PRC Publishing Limited, 2004. 256 pages. Contents pages. The book is intended to entertain. In addition to final words, it includes fictional deathbed statements, famous last movie and book lines, and quotes from wills, epitaphs, obituaries, and inscriptions.

Index

Arsentiev, Francys, 27
Artagerses, 28
Arundel, 20th Earl of, 322
Arvers, AlexisFélix, 28
Asano, Naganori, (Takumi no Kami), 28
Ascham, Roger, 28
Ashby, Turner, 28
Ashley, Lord, 155
Askew, Anne, 29
Asplund, Carl Oscar Vilhelm Gustafsson, 29
Assad, Hafez (Al-Assad), 29
Aste, Marcello, 29
Astor, John Jacob, I, 29
Astor, John Jacob, IV, 29
Astor, Nancy Witcher Langhorne, 30
Astor, William Backhouse, 30
Astros, Paul-Thérèse-David d', 30
Atabalipa, 30
Atahualpa, 30
Atatürk, Mustafa Kemal, 30
Atcheson, George C., Jr., 31
Athanasios Diakos, 31
Athanasios the Deacon, 31
Atticus, Titus Pomponius, 31
Attlee, Clement Richard, 1st Earl Attlee and Viscount Prestwood, 31
Aubigné, Théodore Agrippa d', 31
Aubry (or Aubrey or Auberry), François (or Francis) Xavier ("F.X."), 31
Audebert, Ann, 32
Audubon, John James, 32
Augustine, Saint, 32
Augustus, Gaius Julius Caesar, 32
Aurangzeb or Aurungzebe, Emperor of Hindustan, 32
Aurelius, Quintus, 33
Aurthur, Jonathan, 33
Austen, Jane, 33
Austin, Samuel, 33
Austin, Stephen Fuller, 33
Austin, Tom, 34
Avaroa, Eduardo, 34
Averill, Jim, 34
Avery, Isaac E., 34
Azeglio, Massimo Taparelli d', 34
Babar, Baber or Babur, 34
Babcock, Maltbie Davenport, 35
Babel, Isaac Emmanuilovich, 35
Babington, Anthony, 35
Bachaumont, Louis Petit de, 35
Bachman, John, 35
Bacon, Francis, 1st Baron Verulam and Viscount St. Albans, 36
Baedeker, Frederick William, 36
Baer, Maximilian Adelbert ("Max"), 36
Baesell, Norman, 36
Bagehot, Walter, 37

Bahadur, Sam, 402
Bailey, Chauncey Wendell, Jr., 37
Bailli or Bailiff, Roche de, 37
Bailly, Jean-Sylvain, 37
Bainham, James, 37
Baker, Edward Dickinson, 37
Baker, James, 38
Baker, Josephine, 38
Baker, Lena, 38
Baker, Theodore, 38
Balboa, Vasco Núñez de, 39
Baldwin, Elias Jackson ("Lucky"), 39
Baldwin, James Arthur, 39
Ball, Lucille, 39
Balmerino, 6th Baron, 219
Balzac, Honoré de, 39
Bancroft, George, 40
Bankhead, Tallulah, 40
Bannister, John, 40
Barbellion, Wilhelm Nero Pilate, 168
Barber, Thomas Washington, 40
Barbirolli, Sir John, 40
Barbusse, Henri, 41
Barfield, Margie Velma, 41
Baring, Maurice, 41
Barker, Arthur R. ("Dock" or "Doc"), 41
Barker, Kate, 41
Barker, Ma, 41
Barkley, Alben William, 41
Barksdale, William, 42
Barnardo, Thomas John, 42
Barnato, Barney, 42
Barnave, Antoine Pierre Joseph Marie, 42
Barnes, Robert, 42
Barneveld, John, 42
Barneveldt, Jan van Olden, 42
Barnum, Phineas Taylor ("P.T."), 43
Barrie, Sir James Matthew, Baronet, 43
Barron, Clarence Walker, 43
Barrow, Isaac, 43
Barrymore, Ethel, 43
Barrymore, Georgianna Emma Drew, 44
Barrymore, John, 44
Barrymore, Maurice, 44
Barth, Karl, 44
Barthou, Jean-Louis, 45
Bartók, Béla Viktor János, 45
Barton, Clarissa Harlow ("Clara"), 45
Bartow, Francis Stebbins, 45
Basedow, Johann Bernhard, 45
Bashkirtseff, Marie, 46
Basilone, John ("Manila John"), 46
Bass, Sam, 46
Bastiat, Claude Frédéric, 46
Bastida, Gustavo Adolfo

Domínguez, 52
Battie, William, 46
Baudelaire, Charles Pierre, 46
Baum, Lyman Frank (L. Frank), 47
Baxter, Charles, 47
Baxter, John Clifford, 47
Baxter, Richard, 47
Bayard, George Dashiell, 47
Bayard, Pierre Terrail de, 47
Beaconsfield, 1st Earl of, 192
Beall, John Yates, 48
Beamer, Todd Morgan, 48
Beard, George Miller, 48
Beard, James Andrew, 49
Beardsley, Aubrey Vincent, 49
Beaton, David, 49
Beatrix, Grand Duchess of Bavaria, 49
Beauchamp, Jeroboam Orville, 49
Beaufort, Henry, 50
Beaufort, Henry, 3rd Duke of Somerset, 50
Beaumont, Joseph, 50
Beaverbrook, 1st Baron, William Maxwell Aiken XE "Aiken, William Maxwell" ("Lord Beaverbrook"), 50
Beck, Ludwig August Theodor, 50
Beck, Martha, 50, 231
Becket, Saint Thomas à, 51
Beckford, William Thomas, 51
Bécquer, Gustavo Adolfo, 52
Beddoes, Thomas Lovell, 52
Bede, Beda or Baeda, Saint ("The Venerable"), 52
Bedell, William, 52
Bee, Barnard Elliott, Jr., 53
Beebe, Roderick, 53
Beecher, Catharine Esther, 53
Beecher, Frederick H., 53
Beecher, Henry Ward, 53
Beecher, Lyman, 54
Beerbohm, Sir Henry Maximilian ("Max"), 54
Beesley, Blessed George, 54
Beethoven, Ludwig van, 54
Béhaine, Pierre Pigneau de, 55
Behan, Brendan Francis, 55
Belasco, David, 55
Belgrano, Manuel, 56
Bell, Acton, 90
Bell, Alexander Graham, 56
Bell, Currer, 90
Bell, Ellis, 91
Bell, John Any, 56
Bell, Sir Charles, 56
Bellamy, Edward, 56
Bellamy, Joseph, 57
Bellarmine, Saint Robert, 57
Bellingham, John, 57
Bellini, Vincenzo, 57
Belmont, Alva Erskine Smith Vanderbilt, 57

Belushi, John Adam, 57
Bender, Tony, 58
Benedek, Ludwig August von, 58
Benedict of Nursia, Saint, 58
Benedict XIV, Pope, 58
Benedict, Lewis, 58
Benezet, Anthony, 58
Benjamin, Judah Philip, 58
Benjamin, Park, 58
Bennett, Enoch Arnold, 59
Benson, Robert Hugh, 59
Bentham, Jeremy, 59
Benton, Thomas Hart, 59
Béranger, Pierre Jean de, 59
Berenger of Tours, 59
Bérenger, Madame De, 60
Berg, Alban Maria Johannes, 60
Berg, Morris ("Moe"), 60
Berg, Nicholas, 60
Bergman, Ingrid, 60
Berlioz, Louis Hector, 61
Bernadotte, Folke, 61
Bernard of Clairvaux, Saint, 61
Bernard, Claude, 61
Bernard, Sir Francis, 61
Bernhardt, Sarah, 62
Bernstein, Leonard, 62
Berrigan, Philip, 62
Berry, Caroline Ferdinande Louise,
    Duchesse de, 62
Berry, Charles Ferdinand, Duc de,
    62
Berry, Hiram Gregory, 63
Bérulle, Pierre de, 63
Bessarion, Johannes, 63
Bessette, Blessed Alfred, 63
Bestuzhev-Ryumin, Mikhail
    Pavlovich, 63
Bethune, David, 49
Bethune, Mary McLeod, 63
Bevan, Aneurin, 63
Béze, Théodore de or Beza,
    Theodorus, 64
Bhutto, Benazir, 64
Bhutto, Zulfikar Ali, 64
Bickerstaff, Isaac, 569
Bickersteth, Edward, 64
Biddle, Nicholas, 64
Bidwell, Daniel Davidson, 65
Bierce, Ambrose Gwinnett, 65
Biffle, Ira Oris, 65
Bilac, Olavo Brás Martins dos
    Guimarães, 65
Bilbo, Theodore Gilmore, 65
Billings, Josh, 543
Billy the Kid, 77
Bingham, Sybil Moseley, 66
Birgersdottir, Birgitta, 88
Birkenhead, 1st Earl of, 551
Birney, David Bell, 66
Biron, Armand-Louis de Gontaut,
    Duc de, 66
Bishop, Bernice Pauahi, 66

Bishop, Isabella Lucy Bird, 66
Bishop, Jesse, 66
Bisley, George, 54
Bismarck, Otto Eduard Leopold
    von, 67
Bixby, Bill, 67
Bizet, Georges, 67
Black Elk, Nicholas, 67
Black Jack, 359
Black, Hugo LaFayette, 67
Blackburn, Gideon, 67
Blackie, John Stuart, 68
Blackwell, Alexander, 68
Blaine, James Gillespie, 68
Blair, John Durburrow, 68
Blair, Samuel, 68
Blair, William, 69
Blake, Daniel, 69
Blake, William, 69
Blanc, Mel, 69
Blanchard, Sophie, 69
Blanche of Castile, 69
Blandick, Clara, 70
Blandy, Mary, 70
Blarer, Ambrosius, 70
Blasco Ibáñez, Vicente, 70
Blatchford, Samuel, 70
Blaurer, Ambrosius, 70
Blavatsky, Helena Petrovna, 70
Bledsoe, William M., 71
Blevins, Andy, 71
Blewett, Charles, 71
Bloch, Marc Leopold, 71
Blomfield, Charles James, 71
Blood, Thomas, 71
Blücher, Gebhard Leberecht von,
    Prince of Wahlstatt, 71
Blum, Léon, 72
Blum, Robert, 72
Bluntschli, Johann Kaspar, 72
Blythe, Ethel, 43
Blythe, Herbert, 44
Blythe, James, 72
Blythe, John Sidney, 44
Boas, Franz, 72
Bocarmé, Count Hippolyte, Visart
    de, 72
Bodwell, Joseph Robinson, 73
Boerhaave, Hermann, 73
Bogart, Humphrey DeForest, 73
Bogue, David, 73
Böhme, Boehme, Bohm, Boehm,
    Behme or Behmen, Jacob, 73
Boig, James, 74
Boileau-Despréaux, Nicolas, 74
Boleyn, Anne, Queen Consort of
    England, 74
Bolingbroke, Henry Saint John, 1st
    Viscount, 74
Bolívar, Simón, 75
Böll, Heinrich Theodor, 75
Bolles, Donald F., 75
Bolton, Robert, 75

Bolton, Samuel, 76
Bonaparte, Elizabeth Patterson, 76
Bonaparte, Maria Paulina, Duchess
    of Guastalla, 76
Bonaparte, Mathilde Laetitia
    Wilhelmine, 76
Bonchamps, Charles-Melchior
    Artus, Marquis de, 76
Bonhoeffer, Dietrich, 76
Boniface, Saint, 77
Bonnet, Charles, 77
Bonney, William H., 77
Bonnie Dundee, 275
Bonnot, Jules Joseph, 77
Boone, Daniel, 77
Booth, Catherine Mumford, 77
Booth, Edwin Thomas, 78
Booth, John Wilkes, 78
Booth, Junius Brutus, 78
Booth, William, 78
Boothby, Sir Robert John Graham,
    78
Borah, William Edgar, 78
Borgia, Cesare, 79
Borgia, Lucretia, 79
Borgia, Rodrigo, 14
Börne, Ludwig, 79
Borodin, Aleksandr, 79
Borromeo, Saint Charles, 80
Bosco, Saint John (Don Bosco), 80
Bossuet, Jacques Bénigne, 80
Botsaris, Marcos or Markos, 84
Bottomley, Horatio William, 80
Boufflers, Stanislas Jean, Chevalier
    de, 80
Bouhours, Dominique, 81
Bouldin, Thomas Tyler, 81
Bourbon, Louis de, 81
Bourg, Anne du, 81
Bourmont, Louis-Auguste-Victor
    de, Count de Ghaisnes, 81
Bouvier, Auguste, 81
Bow, Clara Gordon, 82
Bowditch, Henry Ingersoll, 82
Bowditch, Nathaniel, 82
Bowdre, Charlie, 82
Bowen, Joshua Robert, 82
Bowles, Samuel, 83
Boyd, Jerry ("F.X. Toole"), 83
Boyd, Kenneth Lee, 83
Boyd, William, 83
Boyer, John, 83
Boyle, Robert, 83
Bozzaris, Marco or Markos, 84
Brace, Charles Loring, 84
Braddock, Edward, 84
Bradford, Alden, 84
Bradford, Andrew, 84
Bradford, John, 84
Bradford, William, 85
Brady, Hugh, 85
Brady, James Buchanan
    ("Diamond Jim"), 85

Cameron, Julia Margaret Pattle, 114
Camoëns or Camões, Luis Vas de, 114
Camp, Henry Ward, 114
Campan, Jeanne Louise Henriette Genet, 114
Campbell, Archibald, 8th Earl of Argyll, 1st Marquis of Argyll, 114
Campbell, Archibald, 9th Earl of Argyll, 115
Campbell, Donald, 115
Campbell, George, 115
Campbell, Richard, 115
Campbell, Thomas, 115
Campbell, Timothy John ("Tim"), 115
Campbell, Willielma Maxwell, Lady Glenorchy, 116
Campion, Blessed Edmund, 116
Canaris, Wilhelm Franz, 116
Canary or Cannary, Martha Jane ("Calamity Jane"), 116
Candy Darling, 117
Candy, John Franklin, 116
Canitz, Baron Friedrich Rudolf Ludwig, 117
Canning, Charles Fox, 117
Canning, George, 117
Cano, Alonzo, 117
Canonchet, 118
Canova, Antonio, 118
Capel, Arthur, Lord Capel of Hadham, 118
Capote, Truman, 118
Captain Jack, 118
Carême, Marie-Antoine or Antonin, 118
Carew, George, 118
Carey, William, 119
Caritativo, Bart Luis, 119
Carlos, Prince of Spain (Don Carlos), 119
Carlyle, Jane Welsh Baille, 119
Carlyle, Thomas, 119
Carmichael, John, 119
Carnegie, Andrew, 119
Carnot, Marie François Sadi, 119
Caroline of Anspach, Queen of Great Britain and Ireland, 120
Carpenter, Louis, 120
Carroll, Charles, 120
Carroll, John, 120
Carroll, Lewis, 194
Carrot-top (Apekonii), 610
Carson, Christopher Houston ("Kit"), 120
Carstares or Carstairs, John, 120
Carstares or Carstairs, William, 121
Carstares, Cardinal, 121
Carter, Richard, 121

Carteret, John, 1st Earl Granville, 121
Cartwright, Thomas, 121
Caruso, Enrico, 121
Carver, George Washington, 121
Cary, Alice, 122
Cary, Phoebe, 122
Casals, Pablo, 122
Casanova or, Giacomo or Giovanni Jacopo, 122
Casaubon, Isaac, 122
Casement, Sir Roger David, 122
Caserio, Sante Geronimo, 123
Cassel, Karl Gustav, 123
Castlereagh, Robert Stewart, Viscount Castlelreagh, 123
Castlereagh, Viscount, 563
Castrillón, Manuel Fernández, 123
Castro Tartas, Isaac de, 123
Catesby, Robert, 123
Cathcart, George, 124
Catherine of Alexandria, Saint, 124
Catherine of Aragon, 124
Catherine of Siena, Saint, 124
Catlin, George, 124
Cato, Marcus Porius (the Younger), 124
Cauchy, Baron Augustin Louis, 125
Cavell, Edith Louise, 125
Cavendish, Henry, 125
Cavendish, Spencer Compton, 125
Cavour, Camillo Benso, Count di, 125
Caxton, William, 126
Cayce, Edgar, 126
Cazotte, Jacques, 126
Ceaușescu, Elena, 126
Cecil, Robert, 1st Earl of Salisbury, 126
Cecil, William, 1st Baron Burghley (or Burleigh), 127
Cecilia, Saint, 127
Cenci or Cenzi, Beatrice, 127
Cenci or Cenzi, Lucrezia, 127
Cephas, 482
Cermak, Anton Joseph, 127
Cerretti, Bonaventura, 127
Cervantes, Miguel de, 128
Cézanne, Paul, 128
Chadwick, John White, 128
Chaffee, Roger B., 128
Chaikin, Joseph, 129
Chaliapin, Feodor Ivanovich, 129
Chalmers, Thomas, 129
Chamberlain, Arthur Neville, 129
Chambers, Robert, 129
Chamfort, Sébastien Roch Nicolas, 129
Championnet, Jean Étienne Vachier, 129
Chanel, Gabrielle Bonheur ("Coco"), 130

Channing, William Ellery, 130
Chaplin, Sir Charles Spencer ("Charlie"), 130
Chapman, Annie, 130
Chapman, Gerald, 130
Chapman, Graham, 130
Chapman, John Jay, 130
Chapman, Raymond Johnson ("Ray"), 131
Chapman, Robert Hett, 131
Charlemagne, Holy Roman Emperor, 131
Charles I, Emperor of Austria-Hungary, 131
Charles I, King of England, Scotland and Ireland, 131
Charles II, King of England, Scotland and Ireland, 132
Charles II, King of Spain, Naples and Sicily, 133
Charles III, King of Spain, 134
Charles IV, King of Hungary, 131
Charles IX, King of France, 133
Charles IX, King of Sweden, 134
Charles the Affable, 132
Charles the Great, 131
Charles the Mad, 132
Charles the Well Loved, 132
Charles the Wise, 132
Charles V, Holy Roman Emperor, 131
Charles V, King of France, 132
Charles VI, King of France, 132
Charles VIII, King of France, 132
Charles X, King of France, 133
Charles XII, King of Sweden, 134
Charles, Thomas, 134
Charlotte Augusta, Princess of Wales, 134
Charlotte Sophia, Queen of Great Britain, 134
Charmion, 135
Chase, Salmon Portland, 135
Chastelard, Pierre de Boscosel de, 135
Chateaubriand, Vicomte François René de, 135
Chavez, Georges, 135
Chayefsky, Sidney Aaron ("Paddy"), 136
Chekhov, Anton Pavlovich, 136
Cheng-Chung, 627
Chénier, André Marie de, 136
Chenoweth, 136
Cherokee Bill, 270
Chesterfield, 4th Earl of, 136
Chesterton, Gilbert Keith ("G.K."), 136
Cheung, Leslie, 137
Chevalier, Maurice, 137
Chickering, Hannah Balch, 137
Childers, Robert Erskine, 137
Chin, Vincent Jen, 137

Last Words of Notable People

649

Chinese Gordon, 272
Choate, Joseph Hodges, 138
Choate, Rufus, 138
Chopin, Frèdèric François, 138
Christian III, King of Denmark and Norway, 138
Christian IV, King of Denmark and Norway, 138
Christian IX, King of Denmark, 138
Christian X, King of Denmark, 138
Christian, Fletcher, 139
Christina, Queen of Sweden, 139
Christman or Chrismond, John A., 139
Christodule, or Christodoulos, Saint, 139
Christophe, Henry, King of Haiti, 139
Chrysippus, 139
Chrysogonus, Saint, 140
Chrystostom, Saint John, 140
Chuang-Tzu or Zhuang-Tze, 140
Chubbuck, Chris, 140
Chudleigh, Baron Clifford of, 145
Chudleigh, Elizabeth, 140
Church, Frank Forrester, 140
Churchill, Charles, 141
Churchill, Jennie Jerome, 141
Churchill, John, 1st Duke of Marlborough, 141
Churchill, Randolph Frederick Edward Spencer, 141
Churchill, Sir Winston Leonard Spencer, 141
Chyträus, David, 141
Cicero, Marcus Tullius, 142
Cilley, Jonathan, 142
Clanton, Joseph Isaac ("Ike"), 142
Clanton, William Harrison ("Billy"), 142
Clare of Assisi, Saint, 142
Clare, John, 142
Clarence, Duke of, 617
Clark, George Rogers, 143
Clarke, Adam, 143
Claude, Jean, 143
Claudius, Matthias, 143
Clay, Henry, 143
Clear, Claudius, 454
Cleburne, Patrick Ronayne, 143
Clemenceau, Georges Eugene Benjamin, 144
Clemens, Olivia Langdon, 144
Clemens, Samuel Langhorne ("Mark Twain"), 144
Clement XI, Pope, 144
Clement XII, Pope, 144
Clement XIV, Pope, 144
Clément, Jacques, 144
Clemente, Roberto, 145
Clemmer, Mary, 145
Cleopatra, 145

Cleveland, Stephen Grover, 145
Clifford of Chudleigh, 1st Baron, 145
Clifford, Thomas, 145
Clift, Montgomery, 146
Clifton, John Talbot, 146
Clive, Robert, Baron Clive of Plassey, 146
Cloncurry, 2nd Lord, 374
Cloots, Jean Baptiste, Baron de, 146
Cobain, Kurt Donald, 146
Cobbe, Frances Power, 146
Cobden-Sanderson, Thomas James, 146
Cochin, Pierre-Suzanne-Augustin, 147
Cochise, 147
Cocteau, Jean Maurice Eugène Clément, 147
Cody, William Frederick ("Buffalo Bill"), 147
Coffin, Charles Carleton, 147
Coghill, George Ellett, 148
Cohan, George Michael, 148
Cohn, Harry, 148
Coke, Lord, 148
Coke, Sir Edward, 148
Colbatch, John, 148
Colbert, Auguste-François-Marie, 148
Cole, Thomas, 149
Coleridge, Samuel Taylor, 149
Coleridge-Taylor, Samuel, 149
Colette, Sidonie Gabrielle Claudine, 149
Coligny, Gaspard de Châtillon, Comte de, 149
Colley, Thomas, 150
Collingbourne, William, 150
Collins, Anthony, 150
Collins, James ("Jim"), 150
Collins, Joel, 150
Collinson, Harry, 150
Colombini, Giovanni, 151
Colquhoun, Janet Sinclair, 151
Colt, Samuel, 151
Columba, Saint, 151
Columbus, Christopher, 151
Colyngbourne, William, 150
Combe, Andrew, 151
Combe, George, 152
Comte, Isidore Auguste Marie François Xavier, 152
Condé, Henri I de Bourbon, Prince de, 81, 152
Condé, Louis I de Bourbon, Prince de, 152
Condé, Louis II de Bourbon, Prince de, 152
Conder, Josiah, 152
Confucius, 152
Connelly, Cornelia, 153

Conolly or Connolly, Arthur, 153
Conrad, Joseph, 153
Conradin, Duke of Swabia, 153
Consalvi, Ercole, 153
Constant de Rebecque, Henri-Benjamin, 153
Constantine XI, Emperor of Byzantium, 153
Conti, Princesse de, 154
Cook, Arthur Bernard, 154
Cook, James, 154
Cooke, Jay, 154
Cooke, Lord, 148
Cooke, Sam, 154
Cooke, Terence, 154
Cooke, William Winer, 155
Cookman, Alfred, 155
Coolbaugh, Michael Robert, 155
Coolidge, John Calvin, 155
Cooper, Andy, 71
Cooper, Anthony Ashley, 155
Cooper, Gary, 155
Cooper, Gladys Constance, 156
Cooper, Sir Astley Paston, 1st Baronet, 155
Copeland, John Anthony, 156
Copernicus, Nicolaus, 156
Copleston, Edward, 156
Copley, John Singleton, 156
Coppin or Copping, John, 157
Coppola, Anna Augustine ("Ann"), 157
Coppola, Frank James, 157
Corbet or Corbett, Richard, 157
Corbet, Miles, 157
Corbulo, Gnaeus Domitius, 157
Corday, Charlotte, 157
Corder, William, 158
Corey, Giles, 158
Corneille, Pierre, 158
Cornificia the Younger, 158
Cornstalk, 158
Cornwall, 1st Earl of, 259
Corot, Jean Baptiste Camille, 159
Coryat or Coryate, Thomas, 159
Cosin, John, 159
Costello, Lou, 159
Cotton, John, 159
Cotton, Joshua, 160
Courmourgi or Cumurgi, Ali, 160
Courtright, Timothy Isaiah ("Jim"), 160
Couzens, James Joseph, 160
Coveney, Joseph, 160
Cowan, Frederick W., 160
Coward, Sir Noel, 160
Cowles, Anna Roosevelt, 161
Cowper, William, 161
Cox, David, 161
Coy, Bernard, 161
Crabbe, George, 161
Craddock, Ida C., 161
Craigie, Pearl Mary Teresa

Dieneces or Dienekes, 190
Diesel, Rudolf Christian Karl, 191
Dietrich, (Marie) Marlene, 191
Digby, Sir Everard, 191
Dillon, Wentworth, 191
DiMaggio, Giuseppe Paolo, Jr. ("Joe"), 191
Diogenes, 191
Disney, Walter Elias ("Walt"), 192
Disraeli, Benjamin, 1st Earl of Beaconsfield, 192
Divine Sarah, 62
Dix, Dorothea Lynde, 192
Dixon, Henry Hall, 192
Dobbin, James Cochrane, 192
Dobbins, Oliver B., 193
Dod, John, 193
Dodd, Westley Allan, 193
Dodd, William, 193
Doddridge, Philip, 193
Dode de la Brunerie, Vicomte Guillaume, 194
Dodge, Grace Hoadley, 194
Dodgson, Charles Lutwidge ("Lewis Carroll"), 194
Dolet, Étienne, 194
Dollfuss, Engelbert, 194
Domenec, Michael, 194
Dominic, Saint, 195
Don John, 343
Donn-Byrne, Brian Oswald Patrick, 195
Donne, John, 195
Donner, Elizabeth Blue Hook, 195
Dooley, Thomas Anthony, III, 195
Doorman, Karel Willem Frederik Marie, 195
Dorman or Doorman, Isaiah, 196
Dornacker, Jane, 196
Dorney, Henry, 196
Dors or d'Ors, Diana, 196
Dos Passos, John Roderigo, 196
dos Santos, Lucia (Sister Lucia), 197
Dostie, Anthony Paul, 197
Dostler, Anton, 197
Dostoevsky, Fyodor, 197
Doughtie, Jeffery Carlton, 197
Douglas, Alexander, 10th Duke of Hamilton, 197
Douglas, George Norman, 198
Douglas, Lord Alfred Bruce, 198
Douglas, Sir Howard, 198
Douglas, Sir James, 198
Douglas, Stephen Arnold, 198
Douglass, Frederick, 199
Doumer, Paul, 199
Dowson, Ernest Christopher, 199
Doyle, Sir Arthur Conan, 199
Drake, Sir Francis, 199
Draper, Daniel James, 199
Drapier, M.B., 569
Drayton, Michael, 200

Dreiser, Theodore Herbert Albert, 200
Drelincourt, Charles, 200
Dreux, Charles D., 200
Drew, Andrew, 200
Drew, John, Jr., 201
Drew, Samuel, 201
Drexel, Saint Katharine, 201
Drucci, Vincent, 201
Druid, The, 192
Drummond, Henry, 201
Drummond, William, 201
Drusus, Marcus Livius, the Younger, 202
Du Barry, Comtesse Marie-Jeanne Bécu, 202
Du Bois, William Edward Burghardt ("W.E.B."), 202
Du Pont, Alfred Irénée, 206
Dubos, Jean-Baptiste, 202
Dubroff, Jessica Whitney, 202
Ducos, Jean-François, 203
Dudevant, Baroness, 527
Dudley, John, 1st Duke of Northumberland, 203
Duff, George, 203
Dulles, John Foster, 203
Dumas, Alexandre (père), 203
Dumas, Thomas Alexandre, 204
Dunant, Jean Henri, 204
Dunbar, Paul Laurence, 204
Duncan, Isadora, 204
Duncan, Joseph, 204
Dundee, 1st Viscount of, 274
Dunlap, James, 205
Dunn, John J., 205
Dunstan of Canterbury, Saint, 205
Dupanloup, Félix Antoine Philibert, 205
Dupetit-Thouars, Aristide Aubert, 205
Dupin, Amandine Aurore Lucie, 527
Dupleix, Marquis Joseph François, 205
Du-Plessis-Mornay, Philippe, 184
Duranti, Jean-Etienne, 206
Durham, James, 206
Durocher, Blessed Marie-Rose, 206
Durrant, William Henry ("Theo"), 206
Duse, Eleonora, 207
Duveen, Joseph, 207
Dwight, Timothy, 207
Dwyer, R. Budd ("Budd"), 207
Dwyfor, 1st Earl of, 387
Dyer, Mary Barrett, 207
Eads, James Buchanan, 208
Eagels, Jeanne, 208
Eagle of Brittany, 281
Earhart, Amelia, 208
Early, Jubal Anderson, 208

Earp, Morgan Seth, 208
Earp, Warren Baxter, 209
Earp, Wyatt Berry Stapp, 209
Eastman, George, 209
Eastman, Joseph Bartlett, 209
Eaton, Margaret O'Neale Timberlake, 210
Eaton, Theophilus, 210
Eaton, William, 210
Eddé, Raymond, 210
Eddy, Mary Morse Baker Glover, 210
Eddy, Nelson Ackerman, 211
Eddy, Prince, 12
Edelstein, Morris Michael, 211
Edgewood de Firmont, Henry Essex, 211
Edgeworth, Richard Lovell, 211
Edison, Thomas Alva, 212
Edmund or Eadmund, Saint ("The Martyr"), 212
Edward I, King of England, 212
Edward III, King of England, 212
Edward IV, King of England, 213
Edward the Confessor, 213
Edward VI, King of England, 213
Edward VII, King of United Kingdom of Great Britain and Ireland, 213
Edward VIII, King of the United Kingdom of Great Britain and Northern Ireland, 213
Edward, Duke of Kent and Strathearn, 214
Edward, Prince of Wales, 212
Edwards, Edward, 214
Edwards, Jonathan, 214
Égalité, Philippe, 463
Egbert, Henry Clay, 214
Egino or Egon, Gaugraf, 214
Egmont, Lamoral, Count of, 215
Egon, Gaugraf, 214
Eichmann, Karl Adolf, 215
Einstein, Albert, 215
Eisenhower, Dwight David, 215
El Habashy, Ahmed Mahmoud, 216
El-Batouti, Gamil, 215
Elchingen, Duke of, 452
Eldon, 1st Earl of, 538
Eligius, Saint, 219
Elijah, Biblical prophet, 216
Eliot, John, 217
Eliot, Sir Charles William, 216
Eliot, Thomas Stearns ("T.S."), 217
Elisabeth Christine, Queen of Prussia, 217
Elisabeth, Queen of Romania, 217
Elizabeth I, Queen of England, 218
Elizabeth of France, Madame, 218
Elizabeth of the Trinity, Blessed, 218

Last Words of Notable People

Franco, Francisco, 246
Francois, Marvin, 247
Frank, Anne, 247
Frank, Hans, 247
Frankfurter, Felix, 247
Franklin, Benjamin, 247
Franklin, John, 247
Franks, King of, 131
Franz Ferdinand, Archduke of
  Austria, 248
Franz Josef, Emperor of Austria,
  248
Franz, Robert, 248
Fraser, Simon (12th Baron Lovat),
  248
Frederick II, King of Prussia
  ("Frederick the Great"), 249
Frederick III, King of Prussia,
  German Emperor, 249
Frederick the Great, 249
Frederick V, King of Denmark and
  Norway, 249
Frederick VI, King of Denmark
  and Norway, 249
Frederick VIII, King of Denmark,
  249
Frederick William I, King of
  Prussia, 249
Freeman, Edward Augustus, 250
Frelinghuysen, Theodore, 250
Frémont, John Charles, 250
French, Daniel Chester, 250
French, James D., 250
Freud, Sigmund, 250
Frick, Henry Clay, 251
Frick, Wilhelm, 251
Friedell, Egon, 251
Friedrich Wilhelm Viktor Albert,
  616
Frith, John, 251
Froebel, Friedrich Wilhelm
  August, 251
Frohman, Charles, 251
Frost, Robert Lee, 251
Froude, James Anthony, 252
Fry, Elizabeth Gurney, 252
Fuller, Andrew, 252
Fuller, Arthur Buckminster, 252
Fuller, Melville Weston, 252
Fuller, Sarah Margaret, 252
Furnivall, Frederick James, 252
Fuseli, Henry or Füssli, Johan
  Heinrich, 252
Füssli, Johan Heinrich, 252
Gacy, John Wayne, 253
Gadsden, Christopher, 253
Gainsborough, Thomas, 253
Galba, Servius Sulpicius, Emperor
  of Rome, 253
Galgani, Saint Gemma, 253
Galilei, Galileo, 253
Gallaudet, Thomas Hopkins, 254
Galli-Curci, Amelita, 254

Galois, Évariste, 254
Galsworthy, John, 254
Gambetta, Léon Michel, 255
Gammage, Jonny, 255
Gandhi, Indira, 255
Gandhi, Mohandas Karamchand
  (Mahatma), 255
Garcia Lorca, Federico, 255
Garcia, Manuel ("Three-Fingered
  Jack"), 255
Gardiner, Allen Francis, 255
Gardiner, James, 256
Gardiner, Stephen, 256
Gardner, Ava Lavinia, 256
Gardner, Thomas, 256
Garfield, James Abram, 256
Garibaldi, Giuseppe, 256
Garland, Samuel, Jr., 257
Garner, John Nance, 257
Garnett or Garnet, Henry, 257
Garnett, Robert Seldon, 257
Garnock, Robert, 257
Garrett, Johnny Frank, Sr., 257
Garrett, Patrick Floyd ("Pat"), 257
Garrick, David, 258
Garrick, Violette, 258
Garrison, William Lloyd, 258
Garth, Sir Samuel, 258
Gasparin, Count Agénor de, 258
Gassendi or Gassend, Pierre, 258
Gates, Sir John, 259
Gauguin, Eugéne Henri Paul, 259
Gaunt, Elizabeth, 259
Gaveston, Piers, 259
Gaye, Marvin Pentz Jr., 259
Gazuyeva, Elza, 259
Gehrig, Henry Louis ("Lou"), 260
Gellert, Christian Fürchtegott, 260
Genghis Khan, 260
Genna, Antonio ("Tony the
  Gentleman"), 260
Genna, Michael ("Mike the
  Devil"), 260
George I, King of the Hellenes,
  261
George II, King of the Hellenes,
  261
George III, King of Great Britain
  and Ireland, 260
George IV, King of Great Britain
  and Ireland, 260
George V, King of Great Britain
  and Northern Ireland and
  Emperor of India, 261
George VI, King of Great Britain,
  Ireland, British Dominions,
  Emperor of India, 261
George, Henry, 262
Gérard, Baltazar or Balthasar, 262
Gershwin, George, 262
Gerson, Jean Charlier de, 262
Gertrude of Delft, Saint, 262
Gertrude of Helfta, Saint, 262

Gezmiş, Deniz, 263
Ghaisnes, Count de, 81
Ghiyas ud-din Khilji, 263
Giacometti, Alberto, 263
Giangir (or Giangar, Jihanger), 263
Gibbon, Edward, 263
Gibbons, James, 264
Gibbons, Jennifer, 264
Gibran, Kahlil or Khalil, 264
Gide, André Paul Guillaume, 264
Gilbert of Sempringham, Saint,
  265
Gilbert, Ann Taylor, 264
Gilbert, Sir Humphrey, 264
Gilbert, Sir William Schwenck
  ("W.S"), 264
Gilder, Richard Watson, 265
Gilfillan, George, 265
Gilman, Charlotte Perkins, 265
Gilmore, Gary Mark, 265
Ginsberg, Allen, 265
Giordano, Luca, 265
Gipp, George, 265
Girard, Catelin, 266
Girard, Stephen, 266
Gissing, George Robert, 266
Giustiniani, Saint Laurence, 266
Gladstone, William Ewart, 266
Glass, Jimmy L., 267
Glatman, Harvey Murray, 267
Glenorchy, Lady, 116
Glinka, Mikhail Ivanovich, 267
Glossbrenner, Jacob John, 267
Glover, Robert, 267
Goar of Aquitaine, Saint, 267
Godet, Frédéric Louis, 268
Godolphin, Sidney, 268
Godwin, Earl of Wessex, 268
Godwin, Frances Imlay ("Fanny"),
  268
Godwin, Mary Wollstonecraft, 268
Godwin, William, 268
Goebbels, Joseph Paul, 268
Goebbels, Madga, 269
Goebel, William, 269
Goering, Hermann Wilhelm, 269
Goethals, George Washington, 269
Goethe, Johann Wolfgang von, 269
Goffe or Goff or Gough, Thomas,
  269
Gogol, Nikolai, 270
Goldberger, Joseph, 270
Goldsborough, Fitzhugh Coyle,
  270
Goldsby, Crawford ("Cherokee
  Bill"), 270
Goldsmith, Oliver, 270
Gompers, Samuel, 270
Gonne, Maud, 270
Gooch, Arthur, 271
Gooch, Mary, 271
Good, John Mason, 271
Good, Sarah, 271

Goodman, Benjamin David ("Benny"), 271
Gordon, Adoniram Judson ("A.J."), 272
Gordon, Charles George, 272
Gordon, Elizabeth, Duchess of, 272
Gordon, John, 272
Gordon, Nathaniel, 272
Goretti, Saint Maria, 272
Gorgas, William Crawford, 273
Gorguloff, Paul, 273
Gosse, Sir Edmund William, 273
Gottschalk, Louis Moreau, 273
Gouges, Marie-Olympe de, 273
Gough, John B., 273
Gough, Thomas, 269
Gould, Glenn Herbert, 274
Gounod, Charles François, 274
Gowanlock, John, 274
Grable, Elizabeth Ruth ("Betty"), 274
Grady, Henry Woodfin, 274
Graham, Barbara Elaine Wood, 274
Graham, James, 1st Marquis, 274
Graham, John, 485
Graham, John of Claverhouse, 274
Graham, Sir James Robert George, 2nd Baronet of Netherby, 274
Grainger, George Percy Aldridge, 275
Grandier, Urbain, 275
Grant, Cary, 275
Grant, Joe, 275
Grant, Ulysses Simpson, 275
Granville, Augustus Bozzi, 275
Granville, Earl, 121
Grasso, Thomas, 276
Grattan, Henry, 276
Gray Eagle, 556
Gray, Henry Judd, 276
Gray, Robert, 276
Gray, Thomas, 276
Greble, John Trout, 276
Greeley, Horace, 276
Green, Hetty Howland Robinson, 277
Green, Joseph Henry, 277
Greene, Henry Graham, 277
Gregg, Maxey, 277
Grègoire, Henri, 277
Gregory I, Pope, Saint, 278
Gregory the Great, 278
Gregory VII, Pope, 278
Gregory XII, Pope, 278
Gregory XV, Pope, 278
Gregory XVI, Pope, 278
Grellet, Stephen, 278
Grenville, Sir Richard, 279
Grey, Jane, 279
Grey, Pearl Zane ("Zane"), 279
Gridley, Charles Vernon, 279

Grieg, Edvard Hagerup, 279
Grignan, Madame de, 541
Grimaldi, Joseph, 279
Grimston, Robert, 280
Grindscobbe, William, 280
Grisi, Giulia, 280
Griswold, Rufus Wilmot, 280
Groeneveld, Reinier, Seignior de, 280
Grossinger, Asher Selig, 280
Grotius, Hugo, 280
Groves, Anthony Norris, 281
Guastalla, Duchess of, 76
Guay, Joseph-Albert, 281
Guérin, Saint Mother Théodore, 281
Guesclin, Bertrand du, 281
Guevara, Ernesto ("Che"), 281
Guggenheim, Benjamin, 282
Guggenheim, Peggy, 282
Guiccioli, Countess Teresa, 282
Guiteau, Charles Julius, 282
Guizot, François Pierre Guillaume, 282
Gulliver, Lemuel, 569
Gunther, Mary, 282
Gurney, Joseph John, 283
Gusenberg, Frank, 283
Gussman, Charles J., 283
Gustavus Adolphus, 283
Gustavus II, King of Sweden, 283
Gustavus III, King of Sweden, 283
Guthrie, James, 283
Guzmán, Dominic de, 195
Gwenn, Edmund, 284
Gwynedd, Viscount, 387
Haakon VII, King of Norway, 284
Hackman, James, 284
Hackworth, David. H., 284
Haddo, Lord, 289
Hadley, Samuel Hopkins, 284
Hadrian, Emperor of Rome, 284
Hagey, Joseph B., 285
Haggard, Mark, 285
Hahnemann, Christian Friedrich Samuel, 285
Haig, Douglas, 1st Earl Haig, 285
Haldane, James Alexander, 285
Haldane, Robert, 285
Hale, Edward Everett, 285
Hale, John ("Johnny"), 286
Hale, Nathan, 286
Halévy, Jacques, 286
Hall, Ben, 286
Hall, John Vine, 286
Hall, Martha Wesley, 286
Hall, Patty or Pat, 287
Hall, Radclyffe, 287
Hall, Robert, 287
Halleck, Fitz-Green or Fitz-Greene, 287
Haller, Albrecht von, 287
Halliburton, Richard, 287

Halyburton, Thomas, 288
Hamerton, Philip Gilbert, 288
Hamilton, 10th Duke of, 197
Hamilton, 2nd Duke of, 289
Hamilton, Alexander, 288
Hamilton, Edith, 288
Hamilton, Louis McLane, 288
Hamilton, Patrick, 288
Hamilton-Gordon, George John James, 5th Earl of Aberdeen, 289
Hamlin, Cyrus, 289
Hamlin, Henrietta Anna Lorraine Jackson, 289
Hammerstein, Oscar, II, 289
Hammond, Henry, 289
Hamnett, Nina, 289
Hampden, John, 289
Hampton, Wade, 290
Hancock, Winfield Scott, 290
Hand, Daniel, 290
Hanna, Marcus Alonzo ("Mark"), 290
Hannibal, 290
Hansford, Thomas, 290
Hanway, Jonas, 291
Harden, Jacob, 291
Hardenberg, Georg Philipp Friedrich Freiherr von, 456
Harden-Hickey, James A., 291
Hardin, John Wesley, 291
Harding, Florence Mabel Kling DeWolfe ("Flossie"), 291
Harding, Warren Gamaliel, 291
Hardy, Oliver Norvell, 292
Hardy, Thomas, 292
Harlan, John Marshall, I, 292
Harlan, John Marshall, II, 292
Harley, John Pritt, 292
Harlow, Jean, 292
Harmison, Frank, 292
Harmsworth, Alfred Charles William, 293
Harmsworth, Harold Sidney, 293
Harpe, William Micajah ("Big"), 293
Harper, Henry Albert, 293
Harrington, Calvin Sears, 293
Harris, Henry B., 293
Harris, Jack, 294
Harris, James Thomas ("Frank"), 294
Harris, Joel Chandler, 294
Harris, Martin, 294
Harris, Robert Alton, 294
Harrison, Benjamin, 294
Harrison, Caroline Lavinia Scott, 295
Harrison, Carter H., III, 295
Harrison, Thomas, 295
Harrison, William Henry, 295
Hart, Lorenz Milton, 295
Harun al-Rashid or Haroun

Alraschid, 296
Harvey, Fred, 296
Harvey, William Henry, 296
Hašek, Jaroslav, 296
Hassler, Ferdinand Rudolph, 296
Hastings, Warren, 296
Hatfield, John, 296
Hauff, Wilhelm, 296
Hauser, Kaspar, 297
Havelock, Sir Henry, 297
Haven, Gilbert, 297
Havergal, Frances Ridley, 297
Hawker, Robert Stephen, 297
Hawthorne, Nathaniel, 297
Hawthorne, Sophia Amelia
    Peabody, 298
Hay, John Milton, 298
Haydn, Franz Joseph, 298
Haydon, Benjamin Robert, 298
Hayes, Patrick Joseph, 298
Hayes, Rutherford Birchard, 298
Hayne, Isaac, 298
Haynes, Lemuel, 299
Hayward, Susan, 299
Hayworth, Rita, 299
Hazen, Richard S., 299
Hazlitt, William, 299
Healy, James Augustine, 299
Hearn, Lafcadio, 300
Heath, Neville George Clevely,
    300
Heber, Reginald, 300
Hecker, Isaac Thomas, 300
Heckewelder, John Gottlieb
    Ernestus, 300
Hedgepath, Marion, 300
Hegel, Georg Wilhelm Friedrich,
    300
Hehaka Sapa, 67
Heilbrun, Carolyn Gold, 301
Heindel, Max, 301
Heine, Heinrich, 301
Helm, Boone, 301
Heloise, 302
Helper, Hinton Rowan, 302
Hemans, Felicia Dorothea Browne,
    302
Hemene Mox Mox, 629
Hemingway, Ernest Miller, 302
Henderson, Alexander, 302
Henderson, Ebenezer, 302
Hendricks, Thomas Andrews, 302
Henie, Sonja, 303
Henley, John, 303
Henley, William Ernest, 303
Henrietta Anne, Duchess of
    Orléans, 303
Henrietta Maria, Queen Consort of
    Charles I of England, 303
Henry Frederick, Prince of Wales,
    306
Henry II, King of England, 304
Henry III, King of France, 305

Henry IV, Holy Roman Emperor
    and King of Germany, 305
Henry IV, King of England, 304
Henry IV, King of France, 305
Henry of Bolinbroke, 304
Henry of Lancaster, 304
Henry of Navarre, 305
Henry the Lion, Duke of Saxony
    and Bavaria, 306
Henry V, King of England, 304
Henry VII, King of England, 304
Henry VIII, King of England, 304
Henry, Bayard, 305
Henry, Matthew, 305
Henry, Patrick, 305
Henry, Philip, 306
Herbert, Edward, 1st Baron Herbert
    of Cherbury, 306
Herbert, George, 306
Herbert, Sidney, Lord Herbert of
    Lea, 306
Herder, Johann Gottfried von, 306
Herrera, Leonel Torres, 307
Herrick, Myron T., 307
Herschell, William Miller, 307
Hervey, James, 307
Herzl, Theodor, 307
Hessus, Helius Eobanus, 308
Hewart, Gordon, 1st Viscount
    Hewart, 308
Hewitt, Abram Stevens, 308
Hexum, Jon-Erik, 308
Hey, Johann Wilhelm, 308
Heyburn, Weldon Brinton, 308
Heylin or Heylyn, Peter, 309
Hick, Samuel ("Sammy"), 309
Hickock, Richard Eugene ('Dick,
    309
Hickok, James Butler ("Wild
    Bill"), 309
Hicks, William Melvin ("Bill"),
    309
Higginson, Francis, 310
Hilario, Saint (Brother) Jaime, 310
Hilary, Saint, 310
Hilda or Hild of Whitby, Saint, 310
Hill, Ambrose Powell ("A.P"), 310
Hill, Benjamin Harvey, 310
Hill, Daniel Harvey, 311
Hill, Joe, 311
Hill, Paul, 311
Hill, Rowland, 311
Hill, Ureli Corelli, 311
Hillary, Richard H., 311
Hillman, Sidney, 312
Hilton, John, 312
Hiltzheimer, Jacob, 312
Himmler, Heinrich, 312
Hindenburg, Paul von, 312
Hindman, George Washington, 312
Hitchcock, Sir Alfred, 312
Hitler, Adolf, 313
Hitler, Eva Anna Braun, 313

Hoar, Ebenezer Rockwood, 313
Hobbes, John Oliver, 162
Hobbes, Thomas, 313
Hoche, Louis Lazare, 313
Hodge, Charles, 314
Hodges, Gilbert Raymond ("Gil"),
    314
Hodgeson, Benjamin H.
    ("Benny"), 314
Hodgson, Francis, 314
Hoefle or Hoeffle, Hermann, 314
Hofer, Andreas, 314
Hoffman, Abbott Howard
    ("Abbie"), 314
Hoffman, Eugene Augustus, 315
Hoffman, Louis, 447
Hoffmann, Ernst Theodor
    Amadeus ("E.T.A."), 315
Hofmannsthal, Hugo von, 315
Hogg, James, 315
Hohenzollern-Sigmaringen, Prince
    of, 231
Hokoleskwa, 158
Hokusai, Katsushika, 315
Holcroft, Thomas, 316
Holden, Oliver, 316
Holiday, Billie, 316
Holland, 1st Baron, Henry Fox, 245
Holland, Henry Scott, 316
Holliday, John Henry ("Doc"), 316
Holmes, John, 316
Holmes, Oliver Wendell, Jr., 316
Holst, Gustav, 317
Holtby, Winifred, 317
Hölty, Ludwig Heinrich Christoph,
    317
Hood, Edwin Paxton, 317
Hood, John Bell, 317
Hood, Thomas, 317
Hook, Walter Farquhar, 317
Hooker, Richard, 318
Hooker, Thomas, 318
Hooper, John, 318
Hoover, Herbert Clark, 318
Hope, James, 318
Hope, John, 318
Hope, Leslie Townes ("Bob"), 318
Hopkins, Gerard Manley, 319
Hopkins, Harry Lloyd, 319
Hopkins, John Henry, 319
Hopkins, Johns, 319
Hopkins, Samuel, 319
Hopper, Isaac Tatem, 319
Horn, Tom, 319
Horney, Karen Danielson, 320
Hotman, William, 320
Houdetot, Vicomtesse d', 320
Houdini, Harry, 320
Hough, John, 320
Houghton, John, 320
Housman, Alfred Edward or A.E.,
    320
Housman, Robert, 321

Luna, Álvaro de, 397
Lunalilo, King of the Hawaiian Islands, 397
Luther, Martin, 397
Lux, Walter H., 397
Lyon, Mary Mason, 397
Lyon, Nathaniel, 397
Lyttelton, George, 398
M'Kail, Hugh, 431
MacArthur, Douglas, 398
Macaulay, Thomas Babington,1st Baron Macaulay, 398
Maccabaeus, Judas, 398
MacDonald, George Browne, 398
MacDonald, Jeanette, 398
Macdonough, Thomas, 399
MacGregor, Robert ("Rob Roy"), 399
MacKenna, Stephen, 399
Mackenzie, Alexander, 399
Mackenzie, Sir Morell, 399
Mackintosh, Sir James, 399
Macmillan, Harold, 1st Earl of Stockton, 399
Macpherson, James ("Jamie"), 400
Madame de Pompadour, 492
Madison, Dolley Payne Todd, 400
Madison, James, 400
Maeterlinck, Count Maurice Polydore Marie Bernard, 400
Maginot, André Louis René, 400
Magruder, John Bankhead, 400
Mahan, Alfred Thayer, 401
Mahatma, 255
Mahler, Gustav, 401
Mahto-Topa, 244
Mahy, Thomas de, 228
Maier, Heinrich, 401
Main, Sylvester, 401
Maintenon, Françoise Amiable d'Aubigné, Marquise de, 401
Malcolm X, 401
Malherbe, François de, 402
Malibran, Maria Felicita, 402
Malraux, André, 402
Manchester Martyrs, 402
Mandel, Maria, 402
Mandrin, Louis, 402
Manekshaw, Sam Hormusji Framji, 402
Manet, Édouard, 403
Manila John, 46
Mankiewicz, Herman J., 403
Mankiller, Smoker, 403
Mann, Horace, 403
Manning, Henry Edward, 403
Manolete, 403
Manouchian, Missak or Michel, 404
Mansfield, 1st Earl of, 444
Mansfield, Katherine, 404
Mansfield, Richard, 404
Manzoni, Alessandro, 404

Mao Zedong or Mao Tse-Tung, 404
Marat, Jean Paul, 405
Maravich, Peter Press ("Pistol Pete"), 405
Marconi, Guglielmo, Marchese, 405
Marcus Aurelius Antonius, Emperor of Rome, 405
Margaret of Antioch, Saint, 406
Margaret of Austria, 406
Margaret of Hapsburg, 406
Margaret of Scotland, 406
Margaret or Marguerite of Angoulême, Queen of Navarre, 405
Maria Christina, Princess of the Two Sicilies, Queen of Spain, 406
Maria Theresa or Marie Thérèse, Queen of France, 406
Maria Theresa, Empress of Austria, 406
Mariam of Jesus Crucified, 407
Marianne Cope, Blessed, 407
Marie Adelaide, Princess of Sardinia, Princess of Versailles, 407
Marie Antoinette, Queen of France, 407
Marie Louise, Empress of the French, 407
Marie Thérèse Charlotte, Duchess of Angoulême, 408
Marie, Queen of Romania, 407
Marion, Francis, 408
Maris, Roger Eugene, 408
Mark Twain, 144
Mark, Saint, 408
Marlborough, 1st Duke of, 141
Marquette, Jacques ("Pere"), 408
Marryat, Frederick, 408
Marseille, Hans-Joachim ("Jochem"), 409
Marsh, John, 409
Marshal, William, 1st Earl of Pembroke and Strigul, 409
Marshall, Peter, 409
Marsiglia, Eliza H. Ballentine Charruaud, 409
Marti, José, 409
Martin of Tours, Saint, 410
Martin, Alfred Manuel ("Billy"), 410
Martin, R.A.C., 410
Martineau, Harriet, 410
Martinuzzi, Utjesenovic ("Friar George"), 410
Marto, Blessed Francisco, 410
Marto, Blessed Jacinta, 411
Marty, Christian, 411
Martyn, Henry, 411
Marvell, Andrew, Sr., 411

Marx, Julius Henry ("Groucho"), 411
Marx, Karl Heinrich, 411
Marx, Leonard ("Chico"), 412
Mary II, Queen of England, Scotland and Ireland, 413
Mary Magdalen de' Pazzi, Saint, 412
Mary of Christ Crucified, Blessed, 407
Mary of Modena, Queen Consort of England, 412
Mary Stuart, Queen of Scots, 412
Mary Tudor, Mary I, Queen of England and Ireland, 412
Mas Canosa, Jorge, 413
Masaniello, Tommaso, 413
Mason, John, 413
Massenet, Jules Emile Frédéric, 413
Masters, Edgar Lee, 413
Masterson, William Barclay ("Bat"), 414
Mata Hari, 414
Mather, Abigail Phillips, 414
Mather, Cotton, 414
Mather, Increase, 414
Mather, Richard, 415
Mathew, Theobald, 415
Mathews, Charles, 415
Mathewson, Christopher ("Christy"), 415
Mathis, June Beulah Hughes, 415
Maturin, Basil, 415
Maugham, William Somerset, 416
Maurice, John Frederick Denison, 416
Maury, Matthew Fontaine, 416
Maximilian, Emperor of Mexico, Archduke of Austria, 416
Maximilian, Saint, 416
Maxwell, C. L. ("Gunplay"), 416
Maxwell, James Clerk, 416
Mayakovsky, Vladimir Vladimirovich, 417
Mayer, Frank H., 417
Mayer, Louis B., 417
Mayhew, Jonathan, 417
Mazarin, Jules, 417
Mazzini, Giuseppe, 417
McAuley, Jeremiah ("Jerry"), 418
McCall, John ("Jack"), 418
McCandless, Christopher J., 418
McCann, William ("Reddy"), 418
McClain, James, 418
McClellan, George Brinton, 418
McCormack, John Francis, 418
McCormick, Cyrus Hall, 419
McDaniel, Hattie, 419
McGraw, John Joseph, 419
McGraw, Thomas ("Tam"), 419
McGuffey, William Holmes, 419
McIntyre, Oscar Odd ("O.O."),

Parkman, Francis, 470
Parkyakarkus, 470
Parnell, Charles Stewart, 470
Parry, Sir William Edward, 471
Parsons, Albert, 471
Parsons, Theophilus, 471
Pascal, Blaise, 471
Pascin, Jules, 471
Pasternak, Boris, 472
Pasteur, Louis, 472
Paterson, Joseph, 472
Patmore, Coventry Kersey
    Dighton, 472
Paton, John, 472
Pattison, Dorothy Wyndlow
    ("Sister Dora"), 473
Pattison, William, 473
Patton, George Smith, 473
Paul I, Emperor of Russia, 473
Paul I, King of the Hellenes, 474
Paul III, Pope, 473
Paul VI, Pope, 474
Paul, Maury Henry Biddle
    ("Cholly Knickerbocker"), 473
Paul, Saint, 474
Paulinus, Saint, 474
Pausch, Randolph Frederick
    ("Randy"), 475
Pavese, Cesare, 475
Pavlova, Anna, 475
Paxton, Elisha Franklin ("Bull"),
    475
Payne, John, 475
Payne, Lewis, 494
Payson, Edward, 476
Payton, Walter Jerry, 476
Peabody, Endicott, 476
Peabody, Everett, 476
Peabody, George, 476
Peace, Charles, 476
Peacock, Thomas Love, 476
Peale, Charles Willson, 477
Pearson, Charles Henry, 477
Peckham, Rufus Wheeler, 477
Pedro, Don, 481
Peel, Sir Robert, 477
Peerson, Anthony, 477
Péguy, Charles Pierre, 477
Pellico, Silvio, 477
Pembroke, 1st Earl of, 409
Penfield, Wilder Graves, 478
Penn, Gulielma Maria·Springett,
    478
Penn, Springett, 478
Penn, William, 478
Penrose, Boise, 478
Penruddock, John, 479
Peponila, 479
Pepys, Margaret Kite, 479
Pepys, Samuel, 479
Perceval, Spencer, 479
Percy, Walker, 479
Pericles of Athens, 480

Perkins, William, 480
Perón, Juan Domingo, 480
Perón, Maria Eva Duarte de, 480
Perpetua, Vibia, 480
Perrin, Abner Monroe, 481
Perry, Oliver Hazard, 481
Perugino, Pietro, 481
Pestel, Pavel Ivanovich, 481
Petacci, Claretta, 481
Pétain, Henri Philippe, 481
Peter I, Tsar and Emperor of
    Russia ("Peter the Great"), 482
Peter III, Emperor of Russia, 482
Peter Martyr or Peter of Verona,
    Saint, 482
Peter of Alcantara, Saint, 482
Peter the Great, 482
Peter, Prince of Portugal, 481
Peter, Saint, 482
Peters or Peter, Hugh, 482
Pettit, Roger, 483
Pheidippides, 483
Phiby, Jack, 483
Philby, Harry St. John Bridger, 483
Philby, Sinjin, 483
Philip I, King of Portugal, 484
Philip II, King of Portugal, 484
Philip II, King of Spain, 484
Philip III, King of Portugal, 484
Philip III, King of Spain, 484
Philip IV, King of Spain, 484
Philip, Saint, 483
Philippa of Hainault, Queen of
    England, 485
Phillips, David Graham, 485
Phillips, Ulrich Bonnell, 485
Phillips, Wendell, 485
Philopœmen, 485
Phocion, 486
Phoenix, River, 486
Piaf, Édith, 486
Picasso, Pablo Ruiz y, 486
Piccolo, Louis Brian, 487
Pickford, Mary, 487
Pierrepont, Elizabeth, Duchess of
    Kingston-upon Hull, 140
Pike, Albert, 487
Pike, Zebulon Montgomery, 487
Pilkington, George Lawrence, 487
Pindar, Peter, 623
Pinza, Ezio Fortunato, 487
Pio of Pietrelcina, Saint, 487
Piozzi, Hester Lynch (Mrs.
    Thrale), 487
Pirandello, Luigi, 488
Pissarro, Lucien, 488
Pitman, Sir Isaac, 488
Pitt, William, the Elder, 1st Earl of
    Chatham, 488
Pitt, William, the Younger, 488
Pius II, Pope, 489
Pius IV, Pope, 489
Pius IX, Pope and Blessed, 489

Pius V, Pope and Saint, 489
Pius VI, Pope, 489
Pius VII, Pope, 489
Pius X, Pope and Saint, 489
Pius XI, Pope, 490
Pius XII, Pope, 490
Pizarro, Francisco, 490
Placido, 592
Platt, Orville Hitchcock, 490
Plotinus, 490
Plowman, Max, 490
Plumb, Preston Bierce, 490
Plummer, Henry, 491
Poe, Edgar Allan, 491
Polk, James Knox, 491
Polk, Sarah Childress, 491
Polycarp, Saint, 491
Pompey, 492
Pompidou, Georges Jean
    Raymond, 492
Poniatowski, Józef Antoni, 492
Ponselle, Rosa, 492
Poole, William, 492
Pope, Alexander, 492
Poquelin, Jean Baptiste, 432
Porcaro, Stefano, 493
Porter, Katherine Anne, 493
Porter, Noah, 493
Porter, William Sydney, 493
Porteus, Beilby, 493
Pothinus, Saint, 493
Potter, Helen Beatrix, 493
Poundmaker, 494
Powell, Adam Clayton, Jr., 494
Powell, Lewis Thornton, 494
Power, Tyrone Edmund, Jr., 494
Pratt, Daniel Darwin, 494
Prejean, Dalton, 494
Prentiss, Elizabeth Payson, 495
Prescott, William Hickling, 495
Presley, Elvis Aaron, 495
Preston, John, 495
Prestwood, Viscount, 31
Price, Sterling, 495
Pride, Sir Thomas, 496
Priestley, Joseph, 496
Prince John, 400
Prinze, Freddie, 496
Protasius, Saint, 496
Proust, Marcel, 497
Puccini, Giacomo, 497
Pulitzer, Joseph, 497
Pulliam, Eugene Collins ("Gene"),
    497
Pusey, Edward Bouverie, 497
Pushkin, Aleksander Sergeyevich,
    497
Pushmataha, 498
Putnam, Israel ("Old Put"), 498
Pyle, Ernest Taylor ("Ernie"), 498
Quarles, Francis, 498
Quezon y Molina, Manuel Luis,
    498

Quick, John, 499
Quijano, Alfredo Rueda, 499
Quin, James, 499
Quincy, Josiah, 499
Quintus Caecilius Metellus Pius
  Scipio Nasica, 537
Quisling, Vidkun, 499
Quitman, John Anthony, 499
Rabelais, François, 500
Rachmaninoff, Sergei, 501
Racine. Jean Baptiste, 501
Radcliffe, Ann Ward, 501
Radcliffe, James, 501
Radcliffe, John, 501
Raleigh, Sir Walter, 501
Ralston, William Chapman, 502
Ramakrishna Paramahamsa, 502
Ramal, Walter, 182
Rameau, Jean-Philippe, 502
Ramée, Louise de la ("Ouida"),
  502
Ramsay, David, 502
Ramseur, Stephen Dodson
  ("Dod"), 503
Randolph, John ("John Randolph
  of Roanoke"), 503
Ranger, Charles, 444
Raphael, 503
Rapp, Johann George, 503
Rasputin, Grigori, 503
Ravachol, 503
Ravaillac, François, 504
Ravel, Maurice Joseph, 504
Ray or Wray, John, 504
Raymond, John Howard, 504
Read, Thomas Buchanan, 504
Reade, Charles, 504
Récamier, Jeanne Françoise Julie,
  505
Red Jacket, 505
Reed, John, 505
Reed, Thomas Brackett, 505
Reed, Walter, 505
Rees, Goronwy, 505
Reeves, George, 506
Reinhardt, Julia, 506
Remington, Frederic Sackrider,
  506
Renan, Joseph Ernest, 506
Renforth, James, 506
Reno, Jesse Lee, 507
Renoir, Pierre-Auguste, 507
Retzius, Anders Jahan, 507
Revel, Bernard, 507
Reynolds, John Fulton, 507
Reynolds, Sir Joshua, 508
Reynolds, Stephen, 508
Rhodes, Cecil John, 508
Ribault (or Ribaut), Jean, 508
Ribbentrop, Joachim von, 508
Rice, Henry Grantland, 508
Rice, James Clay, 509
Rice, John Holt, 509

Rich, Bernard ("Buddy"), 509
Rich, Mary, Countess of Warwick,
  509
Richard I, King of England, 509
Richard III, King of England, 509
Richelieu, Armand Jean du Plessis,
  Cardinal, Duc de, 510
Richelieu, Louis François Armand
  du Plessis, Duc de, 510
Richie, Simon John, 598
Richmond, Legh, 510
Richter, Jean Paul Friederich, 510
Richthofen, Freiherr Manfred von
  ("Red Baron"), 510
Rickey, Branch Wesley, 510
Ridley, Nicholas, 511
Riker, John Lafayette, 511
Riley, James Whitcomb, 511
Rilke, Rainer Maria, 511
Rimbaud, Jean Nicolas Arthur, 511
Ripley, Robert LeRoy, 511
Rita of Cascia, Saint, 512
Rittenhouse, David, 512
Rivarol, Antoine de, 512
Rivera, Diego, 512
Rizal, José, 512
Rizzo, Francis Lazzaro ("Frank"),
  513
Rob Roy, 399
Robert I, King of the Scots ("The
  Bruce"), 513
Robert Stewart, Viscount
  Castlereagh, 563
Robert the Bruce, 513
Robertson, Frederick William, 513
Robertson, James, 513
Robertson, Thomas William, 513
Robertson, Walford Graham, 513
Robespierre, Maximilien François
  Marie Isidore de, 514
Robinson, Edwin Arlington, 514
Robinson, Henry Crabb, 514
Robinson, William, 514
Robota, Rosa (Rojza, Rozia or
  Róza), 514
Rochambeau, Jean-Baptiste
  Donatien de Vimeur, 514
Rockefeller, John Davidson, Sr.,
  515
Rockne, Knute Kenneth, 515
Rodgers, James Charles
  ("Jimmie"), 515
Rodgers, James W., 515
Rodgers, John, 515
Rodin, François Auguste René,
  515
Rodin, Rose Beuret, 515
Rodney, 1st Baron, 516
Rodney, George Brydges, 516
Rodriguez, Blas de, 516
Rogers, John, 516
Rogers, Nathaniel Peabody, 516
Rogers, William Penn Adair

("Will"), 516
Rohan-Chabot, Louis-François-
  Auguste, Duc de, 516
Röhm, Ernst, 517
Roland de la Platière, Jean Marie,
  517
Roland de la Platière, Marie-
  Jeanne Philipon ("Madame
  Roland"), 517
Romaine, William, 517
Romanes, George John, 517
Romero y Galdames, Blessed
  Oscar Arnulfo, 517
Rommel, Erwin Johannes Eugen,
  518
Roosevelt, Anna Eleanor, 518
Roosevelt, Franklin Delano, 518
Roosevelt, Theodore, 518
Roosevelt, Theodore, Sr., 519
Root, Elihu, 519
Rosa, Salvator, 519
Roscommon, 4th Earl of, 191
Rose of Lima, Saint, 519
Rosenberg, Alfred, 519
Rosenberg, Ethel Greenglass, 519
Ross, Harold Wallace, 519
Rossetti, Christina Georgina, 520
Rossetti, Dante Gabriel, 520
Rossini, Gioacchino, 520
Rothermere, 1st Viscount, 293
Rothschild, Mayer Amschel, 520
Rothschild, Nathan Mayer, 520
Rothstein, Arnold, 520
Rousseau, Jean-Jacques, 521
Routh, Martin Joseph, 521
Rowlands, John, 559
Royer-Collard, Pierre-Paul, 521
Rubinstein, Anton Grigorevich,
  521
Rubinstein, Helena, 521
Rubinstein, Nicholas or Nikolai
  Grigorevich, 521
Rückert, Friedrich, 522
Rudolf of Hapsburg, Crown Prince
  of Austria, 522
Rumbold, Richard, 522
Runyon, Alfred Damon, 522
Ruppert, Colonel, 522
Ruppert, Jacob ("Jake"), 522
Rush, Benjamin, 523
Russell, Charles, 523
Russell, Charles Marion, 523
Russell, George William, 523
Russell, John, Viscount Amberley,
  523
Russert, Timothy John, Jr., 523
Ruth, George Herman ("Babe"),
  524
Rutherford, Samuel, 524
Ruthven, Alexander, 524
Ryan, Cornelius, 524
Ryland, John, 524
Sabatier, Raphael Bienvenu, 524

Sacco, Nicola, 525
Sadat, Mohammed Anwar Al, 525
Sagoyewatha, 505
Saint-Edme, Bourg, 525
Saint-Evremond, Charles de
    Marguetel De Saint Denis, 525
Saint-Gaudens, Augustus, 525
Saint-Pierre, Charles, Abbé de, 526
Saint-Saëns, Camille, 526
Saint-Simon, Henri de, 526
Sakharov, Andrei, 526
Sakuma, Tsutomu, 526
Saladin, 526
Salomon, Haym, 527
Saltus, Edgar Evertson, 527
Salvatoriello, 519
Salvini, Tommaso, 527
Samson, 527
San Martin, José de, 527
Sanctus of Vienne, 527
Sand, George, 527
Sandburg, Carl, 528
Sanders, George, 528
Sanderson, Frederick William, 528
Sanderson, Robert, 528
Sandoz, Jules Ami, 528
Sandri, Sandro, 528
Sanger, Margaret Higgins, 529
Sankey, Ira David, 529
Santa Anna, Antonio López de,
    529
Santayana, George, 529
Sappho, 529
Sarber, Jess L., 529
Saro-Wiwa, Kenule Beeson
    ("Ken"), 529
Saroyan, William, 530
Sarpi, Paolo or Paul, 530
Sarsfield, Patrick, Earl of Lucan,
    530
Sartre, Jean-Paul, 530
Satank, 530
Sauckel, Ernst Friedrich Christoph
    ("Fritz"), 530
Saul, King of Israel, 531
Saunders, Laurence, 531
Savage, Richard, 531
Savina, Saint, 531
Savinianus, Saint, 531
Savio, Saint Dominic, 531
Savonarola, Girolamo Maria
    Francesco Matteo, 532
Saxe, Hermann Maurice, Comte
    de, 532
Saxony and Bavaria, Duke of, 306
Scarron, Paul, 532
Schaft, Jannetje Johanna
    ("Hannie"), 532
Schell, Augustus, 532
Schiele, Egon, 533
Schiller, Johann Christophe
    Friedrich von, 533
Schimmelpenninck, Mary Anne

Galton, 533
Schlageter, Albert Leo, 533
Schlegel, Karl Wilhelm Friedrich
    von, 533
Schleiermacher, Friedrich Ernst
    Daniel, 533
Schmidt, Hans-Theodor, 534
Schmitt, Aloysius Herman, 534
Schmitz, Aron Ettore, 568
Schnorr von Carolsfeld, Ludwig,
    534
Schoenberg, Arnold, 534
Scholl, Art, 534
Scholl, Hans, 535
Scholl, Sophia Magdalena, 535
Schreiner, Olive Emilie Albertina,
    535
Schreuder, Willem, 535
Schrödinger, Erwin, 535
Schubert, Franz Peter, 536
Schultz, Dutch, 536
Schumann, Clara Josephine Wieck,
    536
Schumann, Robert Alexander, 536
Schurz, Carl, 536
Schwarzenberg, Felix, Prince of
    Austria, 536
Schweitzer, Albert, 537
Schwerin, Kurt Christoph, Graf
    von, 537
Schwind, Moritz von, 537
Scipio Nasica, 537
Scobee, Francis R. ("Dick"), 537
Scott, James, 537
Scott, John, 538
Scott, Robert Falcon, 538
Scott, Sir Walter, 538
Scott, Walter Edward ("Death
    Valley Scotty"), 538
Scott, Winfield, 538
Scriabin, Alexander, 539
Scripps, Edward Wyllis, 539
Sedgwick, John, 539
Segrave, Sir Henry O'Neal de
    Hane, 539
Selwyn, George Augustus, 539
Selznick, David Oliver, 539
Seneca, Lucius Annaeus, 539
Seraphim of Sarov, Saint, 540
Şerbănescu, Alexandru ("Alecu"),
    540
Serling, Rodman Edward ("Rod"),
    540
Serment, Louise-Anastasia, 540
Serra, Miguel José ("Junípero"),
    540
Servetus, Michael, 540
Setangya, 530
Seton, Saint Elizabeth Ann Bayley,
    540
Seume, Johann Gottfried, 541
Severus, Lucius Septimus,
    Emperor of Rome, 541

Sévigné, Françoise Marguerite de,
    541
Seward, William Henry, 541
Seymour, Edward, Duke of
    Somerset, 542
Seymour, Lady Catherine Grey,
    541
Seyss-Inquart, Artur, 542
Sforza, Galeazzo, 542
Shackleton, Sir Ernest, 542
Shaftesbury, 7th Earl of, 155
Shakespeare, William, 542
Shakur, Tupac Amaru ("2 Pac"),
    543
Sharp, Cecil James, 543
Sharp, William, 543
Shastri, Lal Bahadur, 543
Shave Head, Charles, 543
Shaw, George Bernard, 543
Shaw, Henry Wheeler ("Josh
    Billings"), 543
Shaw, Irwin, 544
Shaw, Robert Gould, 544
Shaw, Samuel, 544
Shawn, Dick, 544
Sheed, Francis Joseph (Frank), 544
Shepard, Thomas, 544
Shepherd, Ettrick, 315
Sheppard, Jack, 545
Sheridan, Philip Henry, 545
Sheridan, Richard Brinsley, 545
Sherman, John, 545
Sherman, William Tecumseh, 546
Sherwood, Mary Martha Butt, 546
Shirley, Laurence, 546
Sibelius, Johan Julius Christian
    ("Jan" or "Jean"), 546
Sickingen, Franz von, 546
Siddhartha, 100
Siddons, Sarah Kemble, 546
Sidney or Sydney, Algernon, 547
Sidney, Sir Philip, 547
Siete Iglesias, Marquis de las, 112
Sigourney, Lydia Howard Huntley,
    547
Simeon, Charles, 547
Simon, 547
Simon Peter, 482
Simpson, Bessie Wallis Warfield
    Spencer, 622
Simpson, Sir James Young, 548
Sinatra, Francis Albert ("Frank"),
    548
Sisera, 548
Sitting Bear, 530
Sitting Bull (Tatanka Yotanka),
    548
Sitwell, Dame Edith, 549
Siward (the Dane), Earl of
    Northumberland, 549
Sixtus or Zystus II, Pope, Saint,
    549
Smalridge, George, 549

Smedley, Edward, 549
Smith, Abigail Amelia Adams ("Nabby"), 549
Smith, Adam, 549
Smith, Alfred Emanuel ("Al"), 550
Smith, Bessie, 550
Smith, Donald Alexander, 1st Baron of Strathcona and Mount Royal, 550
Smith, Edward John, 550
Smith, Elliott, 551
Smith, Erastus ("Deaf, 551
Smith, Frederick Edwin, 551
Smith, Jefferson Randolph, II ("Soapy"), 551
Smith, John Eldon, 551
Smith, Joseph, 551
Smith, Logan Pearsall, 551
Smith, Michael John ("Mike"), 552
Smith, Perry Edward, 552
Smith, Sydney, 552
Smith, William, 552
Smollett, Tobias George, 552
Snow, Catherine Mandeville, 552
Snow, Edgar Parks, 553
Snow, William ("Skitch"), 553
Snyder, Adam Wilson, 553
Snyder, Ruth Brown, 553
Sobhuza II, King of Swaziland, 553
Socorro Nieves, Blessed Elias del, 553
Socrates, 554
Södermanland, Duke of, 134
Soleyman El-Haleby, 554
Somerset, 3rd Duke of, 50
Sonnier, Elmo Patrick ("Pat"), 554
Soo, Jack, 554
Sophia, Saint, 554
Sophie Charlotte, Duchess of Alencon, 554
Sophonisba, 554
Soubirous, Saint Bernadette, 555
Soucek, Karel, 555
Sousa, John Philip, 555
Southcott, Joanna, 555
Southey, Robert, 556
Spafford, Horatio Gates, 556
Speaker, Tristram ("Tris"), 556
Spellman, Francis, 556
Spencer, Herbert, 556
Spencer, Sir Stanley, 556
Spenkelink, John Arthur, 556
Spicer, John Lester ("Jack"), 557
Spies, August Vincent Theodore, 557
Spinoza, Baruch or Benedictus, 557
Spruance, Richard Ames, 557
Spurgeon, Charles Haddon, 557
Squanto, 558
St. Albans, Viscount, 36

Staaps, Frederick, 558
Staël, Madame Germaine de, 558
Stahl, Charles Sylvester ("Chick"), 558
Stallings, George Tweedy, 558
Stambulov, Stefan Nicholas, 558
Stanford, Jane Eliza Lathrop, 559
Stanhope, Philip Dormer, 136
Stanislas I, King of Poland, 559
Stanislavsky, 559
Stanley, Arthur Penrhyn, 559
Stanley, Dean, 559
Stanley, Sir Henry Morton, 559
Stanton, Charles P., 559
Stanton, Elizabeth Cady, 560
Stanton, Schuyler, 47
Starkweather, Charles, 560
Starr, Belle, 560
Stauffenberg, Graf Claus Philipp Maria Schenk von, 560
Stedman, Edmund Clarence, 560
Stein, Gertrude, 561
Steinbeck, John Ernst, 561
Steinberg, Milton, 561
Steinmetz, Charles Proteus, 561
Stengel, Charles Dillon ("Casey"), 561
Stephen, Saint, 561
Stephens, Alexander Hamilton, 562
Stephenson, Marmaduke, 562
Sterne, Laurence, 562
Steuben, Frederick William von ("Baron"), 562
Stevens, Thaddeus, 562
Stevenson, Adlai Ewing, II, 562
Stevenson, Robert Louis Balfour, 562
Stewart, Henry, Lord Darnley, 566
Stewart, James Maitland, 563
Stewart, Margaret, 406
Stewart, Robert, 2nd Marques of Londonderry, 563
Stiles, Ezra, 563
Stolberg-Stolberg, Count Friedrich Leopold von, 563
Stolypin, Pyotr Arkadyevich, 563
Stone, Harlan Fiske, 563
Stone, Lucy, 564
Stonehouse, James, 564
Story, Joseph, 564
Stowe, Harriet Beecher, 564
Strachey, Giles Lytton, 564
Strafford, 1st Earl of, 610
Straus, Oscar, 564
Straus, Rosalie Ida Blun, 564
Strauss, Johann, Jr., 564
Strauss, Richard, 565
Stravinsky, Igor, 565
Straw, Jack, 565
Streicher, Julius, 565
Stresemann, Gustav, 565
Stribling, Young, 565

Strindberg, Johan August, 566
Stroheim, Erich von, 566
Strollo, Anthony C., 58
Strong, Nathan, 566
Strozzi, Filippo, II, 566
Stuart, Henry, 566
Stuart, James Ewell Brown ("Jeb"), 566
Stuart, Jesse Hilton, 566
Suárez, Francisco, 567
Suárez, San Miguel Augustine Pro, 567
Sudbury, Simon of, 567
Suleiman I, Sultan of Turkey, 567
Suleyman, 567
Sullivan, John Lawrence, 567
Sullivan, Robert, 567
Sullivan, Sir Arthur Seymour, 567
Sumner, Charles, 567
Sun Yat-Sen, 568
Sunday, William Ashley ("Billy"), 568
Sun-ka Ska, 613
Surratt, Mary Elizabeth Eugenia Jenkins, 568
Susann, Jacqueline, 568
Sutter, John Augustus, 568
Svetschine, Madame Sophie Soymonof, 569
Svevo, Italo, 568
Swartz, Christian Frederick, 569
Swedenborg, Emanuel, 569
Sweeney, Brian D., 569
Swetchine, Madame Sophie Soymonof, 569
Swift, Gustavus Franklin, 569
Swift, Jonathan, 569
Swift, Sir Rigby Philip Watson, 570
Switzer, Carl Dean ("Alfalfa"), 570
Sylva, Carmen, 217
Symons, William Penn, 570
Synge, John Millington, 570
Tabor, Horace Austin Warner, 570
Taft, Robert Alphonso, 570
Taft, William Howard, 571
Tagore, Sir Rabindranath, 571
Tait, Archibald Campbell, 571
Talfourd, Thomas Noon, 571
Talleyrand-Perigord, Charles Maurice de, Prince of Bénévent, 571
Talleyrand-Perigord, Henri de, Comte de Chalais, 572
Talma, François Joseph, 572
Tamerlane, 572
Taney, Roger Brooke, 572
Tanner, Henry Ossawa, 572
Tarakin, Vassili, 572
Tarbell, Ida Minerva, 573
Tardieu-Malessy, Charlotte Henriette, 60

Tarsus, Saul of, 474
Tashunca-Uitco, 164
Tasso, Torquato, 573
Tatum, Art, 573
Taylor, Edward T., 573
Taylor, James Bayard, 573
Taylor, Jane, 573
Taylor, Jeremy, 573
Taylor, John, 574
Taylor, Robert, 574
Taylor, Rowland, 574
Taylor, Zachary, 574
Tchaikovsky, Peter Ilyich, 574
Teasdale, Sara Trevor, 574
Tecumseh or Tecumtha, 575
Teilhard de Chardin, Pierre, 575
Tekakwitha or Tegakouita, Blessed
    Kateri, Katharine or Catherine,
    575
Temple, Henry John, 575
Temuchin (or Temüjin), 260
Ten Boom, Cornelia Johanna
    Arnolda ("Corrie"), 576
Ten Boom, Elisabeth ("Betsie"),
    576
Tennent, William, 576
Tennyson, Alfred, 1st Baron
    Tennyson of Aldworth, 576
Tenterden, 1st Baron, 1
Teresa Benedicta of the Cross,
    Saint, 576
Teresa of Avila, Saint, 576
Terhune, Albert Payson, 577
Terriss, William, 577
Terry, Dame Ellen, 577
Tettemer, John, 577
Teyte, Dame Maggie, 577
Tezuka, Osamu, 577
Thackeray, William Makepeace,
    578
Thadden, Elisabeth Adelheid, 578
Thalberg, Irving G., 578
Thayendanegea, 87
Thayer, William Sydney, 578
Theodora, Saint, 578
Theodore, Saint, 578
Theodoric, the Goth, King of the
    Ostrogoths, 579
Theophrastus, 579
Theramenes, the Athenian, 579
Therese of Lisieux, Saint, 579
Thibault, Jacques Anatole
    François, 245
Thistlewood, Arthur, 579
Thomas the Apostle, Saint, 579
Thomas, Dylan Marlais, 580
Thomas, George Henry, 580
Thomas, Olive, 580
Thomas, Theodore, 580
Thompson, Francis Joseph, 580
Thompson, Hunter S., 580
Thompson, Sir John Sparrow
    David, 581

Thompson, William Hale ("Big
    Bill"), 581
Thoreau, Henry David, 581
Thorn, Martin George, 581
Thorndike, Edward Lee, 581
Thornton, John, 581
Thrale, Mrs., 488
Thrasea Paetus, 582
Three Fenians, 402
Thring, Edward, 582
Thurber, James Grover, 582
Thurlow, Edward, 582
Tibbles, Susette La Flesche, 582
Tidd, Richard, 582
Tilden, Samuel Jones, 582
Tillich, Paul Johannes Oskar, 583
Tillman, Patrick Daniel, 583
Timrod, Henry, 583
Timur, 572
Timur-I Lang, 572
Tindal, Matthew, 583
Tisquantum, 558
Titus Flavius Vespasianus,
    Emperor of Rome, 583
Tivy, Lawrence Rider ("Tan"), 584
Tojo, Hideki, 584
Toklas, Alice Babette, 584
Toland, John, 584
Toler, John, 1st Earl of Norbury,
    Viscount Glandine, 584
Toler, Martin, Jr., 584
Tolstoy, Count Lev ("Leo"), 585
Tone, Theobald Wolfe, 585
Tonks, Henry, 585
Toole, F.X., 83
Toombs, Robert Augustus, 585
Toplady, Augustus Montague, 586
Toral, José de León, 586
Torres-Acosta, Saint Maria
    Soledad, 586
Touhy, Roger ("The Terrible"),
    586
Toulouse-Lautrec, Henri de, 586
Touro, Judah, 586
Toussaint L'Ouverture, Pierre
    François Dominique, 586
Traubel, Horace, 587
Travis, William Barret, 587
Treadwell, Timothy, 587
Tree, Herbert Beerbohm, 587
Trexler, Samuel Geiss, 587
Tristan, Flora, 587
Trobriand, Philippe Régis Denis de
    Keredern, Comte de, 588
Trollope, Anthony, 588
Trollope, Frances Milton, 588
Tromp, Maarten Harpertzoon, 588
Trotsky, Leon, 588
Trujillo, Rafael, 588
Truth, Sojourner, 589
Tubman, Harriet Ross, 589
Tucker, Richard, 589
Tuekakas, 348

Tullis, Francais ("Rusty"), 589
Tupac Amaru, 589
Turenne, Henri de La Tour
    d'Auvergne, 589
Turgenev, Ivan, 589
Turgot, Anne-Robert-Jacques, 590
Turner, Frederick Jackson, 590
Turner, Joseph Mallord William,
    590
Tussaud, Anne Marie Grosholtz
    (Madame Tussaud), 590
Tweed, William Marcy ("Boss
    Tweed"), 590
Two Face (Ito Nonpa), 590
Tyler, John, 591
Tyler, Julia Gardiner, 591
Tynan, Kenneth Peacock, 591
Tyndale, Tindale or Tindal,
    William, 591
Tyndall, John, 591
Tyng, Dudley Atkins, 591
Tzu-Hsi or Cixi, 591
Uemura, Naomi, 592
Ujimasa, Hōjō, 592
Umberto I, King of Italy, 324
Umberto II, King of Italy, 325
Underhill, Wilbur, 592
Ussher, James, 592
Valdés, Gabriel de la Concepcion,
    ("Placido"), 592
Valentino, Rudolph, 593
Vallee, Hubert Prior ("Rudy"), 593
Van Buren, Martin, 593
Van Dyne, Edith, 47
Van Gogh, Vincent Willem, 594
Van Speyk, Jan Carolus Josephus,
    594
Vanderbilt, Alfred Gwynne, 593
Vanderbilt, Cornelius, 593
Vanderbilt, George Washington, II,
    593
Vanderbilt, William Henry, 593
Vane, Sir Henry ("Sir Harry"), 594
Vanini, Lucilio or Giulio Cesare,
    594
Vanzetti, Bartolomeo, 594
Vargas, Getúlio Dornellas, 595
Vaughan, Sarah Lois, 595
Veblen, Thorstein Bunde, 595
Vedas, Brandon Carl, 595
Vega, Lope de, 595
Velez, Lupe, 596
Vercellis, Louise-Marie-Thérèse de
    Saint Maurice, Comtesse de,
    596
Verdi, Giuseppe Fortunino
    Francesco, 596
Verger, Louis-Jean, 596
Vergniaud, Pierre Victurnien, 596
Verlaine, Paul-Marie, 596
Verne, Jules, 597
Versalle, Richard, 597
Verulam, 1st Baron, 36

Last Words of Notable People

Reference Desk Press, Inc.

Reference Desk Press, Inc., founded in 2004, is a publisher of books by librarians for librarians and researchers. RDP's corporate philosophy centers on the research experience of librarians to determine and produce unique reference sources that libraries especially need. RDP also works to support library advocacy, public support for libraries and others issues related to the changing face of librarianship.

Reference Desk Press, Inc. is committed to preserving ancient forests and natural resources. We elected to print *Last Words Of Notable People, Brahms* on 30% post consumer recycled paper, processed chlorine free. As a result, for this printing, we have saved:

23 Trees (40' tall and 6-8" diameter)
7 Million BTUs of Total Energy
2,146 Pounds of Greenhouse Gases
10,337 Gallons of Wastewater
628 Pounds of Solid Waste

Reference Desk Press, Inc. made this paper choice because our printer, Thomson-Shore, Inc., is a member of Green Press Initiative, a nonprofit program dedicated to supporting authors, publishers, and suppliers in their efforts to reduce their use of fiber obtained from endangered forests.

For more information, visit www.greenpressinitiative.org

Environmental impact estimates were made using the Environmental Defense Paper Calculator. For more information visit: www.papercalculator.org.

Colophon

Last Words of Notable People was designed and produced by Reference Desk Press, Inc., using Apple® Macintosh-based systems. The dust jacket was created with Adobe Photoshop™. The dust jacket, cover and title page fonts are Onyx® and Times New Roman®. The text pages were set in Times New Roman®, 10 point and 8 point black. The text paper is 50# Natures Natural FSC. The end paper is 80# Natures Natural. The dust jacket is 100# Gloss Enamel. Binding is Smyth sewn, cased into Arrestox B LBS L426 (Blue Ribbon) with Lustrofoil Gold Foil. Printing and binding were by Thomson-Shore, Inc.